P9-DHJ-530

RAND McNALLY

PREMIER WORLD ATLAS

Chairman, President & CEO, Rand McNally and Company
Henry J. Feinberg

Vice President and General Manager, Map & Atlas Publishing
Jayne L. Fenton

Director, Reference Business
Kendra L. Ensor

Editors
Brett R. Gover
Ann T. Natunewicz

Art Direction and Design
John C. Nelson
Jamie O'Neal

Cartography (U.S.)
V. Patrick Healy
Jon M. Leverenz
Robert K. Argersinger
Barbara Benstead-Strassheim
Kerry B. Chambers
Marzee L. Eckhoff
Winifred V. Farbman
Susan K. Hudson
Gwynn A. Lloyd
Nina Lusterman
John M. McAvoy
Robert L. Merrill
Patty A. Porter
James A. Purvis
David R. Simmons
Thomas F. Vitacco

Cartography (U.K.)
Craig Asquith

Cartography (Italy)
Giovanni Baselli
Ubaldo Uberti

Manufacturing
Terry D. Rieger

Marketing
JoEllen A. Klein

Photo Research
Feldman and Associates, Inc.

Photo Credits

(l=left, r=right, c=center, t=top, b=bottom)

Jacket/cover

Tony Stone Images: © Sally Mayman (volcano); © Art Wolfe (penguin); © John Beatty (desert); © Michael Busselle (Masai warrior); © William J Hebert (mountain and field); © Demetrio Carrasco (geishas)

Contents

© North Wind Picture Archives, iv (figures 4, 6, and 7)

Tony Stone Images: © Nicholas Parfitt, x (background); © Christopher Arnesen, x (t r); © Johnny Johnson, x (b l); © Warren Jacobs, xi (background); © Nicholas DeVore, xi (t r), xv (background); © Stephen Studd, xi (b r); © Tony Stone Images, xii (background); © Kevin Schafer, xii (m); © Joel Bennett, xiii (background and t l); © Fred Felleman, xiii (b r); © Tony Stone Images, xiv (background); © Paul Harris, xiv (t r); © Keren Su, xiv (b l); © Sylvain Grandadam, xv (t l); © Anthony Cassidy, xv (b r); © Oliver Strewe, xvi (background); © Paul Chesley, xvi (t r); © Penny Tweedie, xvi (b l); © Stuart Westmorland, xvii (background); © Chad Ehlers, xvii (t l); © Fred Bavendam, xvii (b r); © Art Wolfe, xviii (background); © Joe Cornish, xviii (b l), xix (t l); © David Hiser, xviii (t r); © David Paterson, xix (background); © David Sutherland, xix (b r); © Richard During, xx (background); © John Running, xx (t r); © Tim Davis, xx (b l); © Darrell Gulin, xxi (background); © Robert Frerck, xxi (t l)

© 1997 PhotoDisc: iii (t), vi (figure 3), viii (background), ix (background and t l), xxi (b r), xxiv (Energy)

Copyright © Corel Corp.: xxii (background, t r, and b l), xxiii (background, t l, and b r), xxiv (Land, Population, and Growth)

Satellite photo, iv (figure 1), provided by Wally Jansen, WTJ Software Series

Premier World Atlas

1999 Revised Printing

www.randmcnally.com

Published and printed in the United States of America

Rand McNally and Company.
Rand McNally premier world atlas.
p. cm.
Includes index.
ISBN 0-528-83893-8 (hardback). - - ISBN 0-528-83894-6 (paperback)
1. Atlases. I. Title. II. Title: Premier world atlas
G1021 .R45 1997 <G&M>
912- - DC21

97-11900
CIP
MAPS

Contents

INTRODUCTORY SECTION

Understanding Maps & Atlases .... iv - v
How to Use the Atlas .... vi-vii
The World & Its Seven Continents . viii - xxiv

MAPS

Index Map and Legend 1

World 2-5
World, Political 2-3
World, Physical 4-5

Europe 6-23
Europe, Political 6-7
Northern Europe 8-9
Scandinavia and the Baltic States 10-11
Northwest Europe 12-13
Mediterranean Lands 14-15
Southwest Europe 16-17
Southern Europe 18-19
Central and Eastern Europe 20-21
Eastern Europe 22-23

Asia 24-45
Asia, Political 24-25
Northern Eurasia 26-27
China, Mongolia, Korea, and Japan 28-29
Eastern China 30
Japan 31
Southeast Asia 32-33
Mainland Southeast Asia and the Philippines . . 34-35
Malaysia, Singapore, and Indonesia 36-37
Southwest Asia 38-39
India 40-41
The Middle East 42-43
Turkey and Transcaucasia 44-45

Africa 46-57
Africa, Political 46-47
Northern Africa 48-49
West Africa 50-51
Central and Southern Africa 52-53
Central Africa 54-55
Southern Africa and Madagascar 56-57

Australia and Oceania 58-63
Australia and Oceania, Political 58-59
Western Australia 60-61
Eastern Australia and New Zealand 62-63

Pacific and Indian Oceans 64-65
Atlantic Ocean 66

Antarctica 67

South America 68-74
South America, Political 68
Southern South America 69
Northern South America 70-71
Central South America 72-73
Northeast Brazil 74

North America 75-143
North America, Political 75
Mexico, Central America, and the Caribbean . . 76-77
Mexico 78-79
Central America and the Caribbean 80-81
Canada and Alaska 82-83
Canadian Province Maps 84-91
United States 92-93
U.S. State Maps 94-143

Arctic Region .... .144

INDEX

Index to the Reference Maps .... I•1-I•80

Understanding Maps & Atlases

figure 1

figure 2

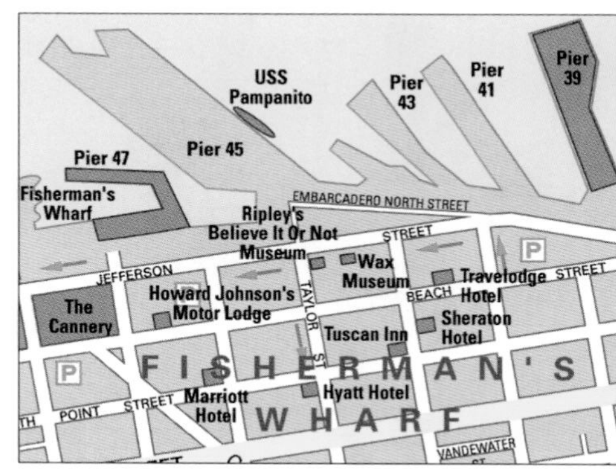

figure 3

What is a map?

A map is a representation, usually at a much-reduced size, of the location of things or places relative to one another. There are many different types of maps, including maps of the world, its regions or countries, cities, neighborhoods, and buildings. Figure 1 is a satellite image of California's San Francisco Bay area; figure 2 shows the same area represented on a road map; and figure 3 provides street-level detail of one of the city's neighborhoods.

figure 4

A set of maps bound together is called an atlas. Abraham Ortelius' *Theatrum orbis terrarum*, published in 1570, is considered to be the first modern "atlas," although it was not referred to as such for almost 20 years. In 1589, Gerardus Mercator (figure 4) coined the term when he named his collection of maps after the mythological titan Atlas, who carried the Earth on his shoulders as punishment for warring against Zeus. Since then, the definition of "atlas" has been expanded, and atlases often include additional geographic information in diagrams, tables, and text.

History of Cartography

Around 500 B.C., on a tiny clay tablet the size of a hand, the Babylonians inscribed the Earth as a flat disk (figure 5) with Babylon at the center. Geographic knowledge was also highly developed among the Egyptians, who drew maps on papyrus and carved them into temple walls. Ancient Greek philosophers and scientists debated endlessly the nature of the Earth and its place in the universe; Ptolemy, the influential geographer and astronomer, made an early attempt to map the known world (figure 6). Roman maps most often depicted boundaries, physical features, and the infrastructure of the Roman Empire. Over the following centuries, territorial expansion directly increased geographic knowledge, which in turn greatly enhanced the cartography, or map-making, of the time.

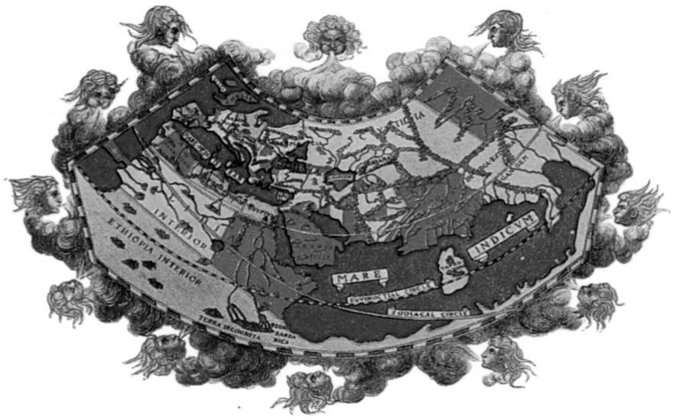

figure 5

As trade and navigation grew, maps were developed to guide merchants and explorers. The Cantino map of 1502 (figure 7) is an example of a *portolan* (sea) chart used by mariners traveling to the newly discovered Americas. Information gained from the past expeditions of John Cabot, Christopher Columbus, and Ferdinand Magellan led to great advances in the content and structure of world maps. As a result, many maps produced between 1600 and 1800, including the colored woodcut shown in figure 8, were works of art as well as geographical representations.

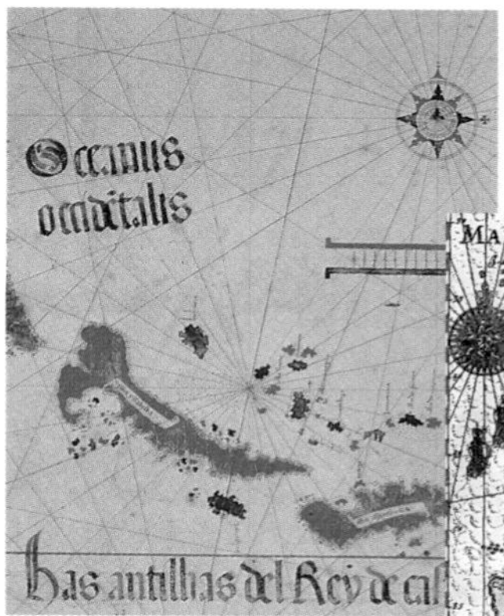

figure 6

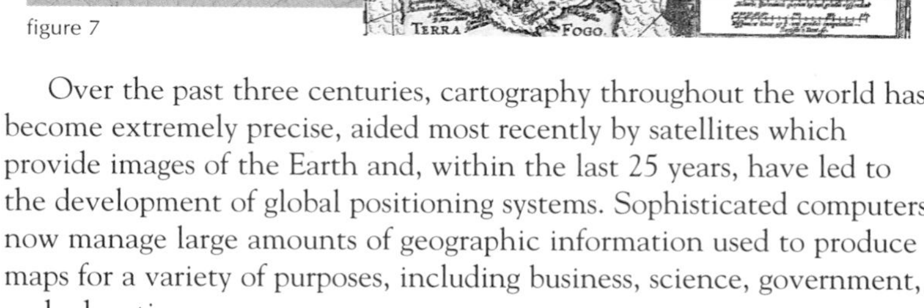

figure 8

figure 7

Over the past three centuries, cartography throughout the world has become extremely precise, aided most recently by satellites which provide images of the Earth and, within the last 25 years, have led to the development of global positioning systems. Sophisticated computers now manage large amounts of geographic information used to produce maps for a variety of purposes, including business, science, government, and education.

Latitude and Longitude

The imaginary horizontal line that circles the Earth exactly halfway between the North and South poles is called the Equator, which represents 0° latitude and lies 90° from either pole. The other lines of latitude, or parallels, measure the distance from the Equator, either north or south (figure 9). The imaginary vertical line that measures 0° longitude runs through the Greenwich Observatory in the United Kingdom, and is called the Prime Meridian. The other lines of longitude, or meridians, measure distances east and west of the Prime Meridian (figure 10), up to a maximum of 180°. Lines of latitude and longitude cross each other, forming a pattern called a grid system (figure 11). Any point on Earth can be located by its precise latitude and longitude coordinates.

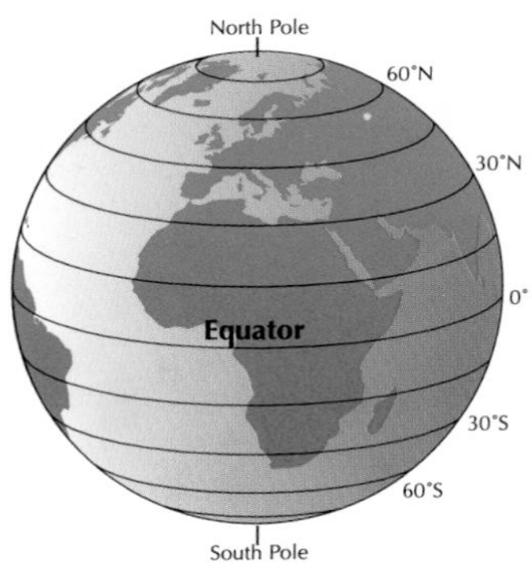

figure 9

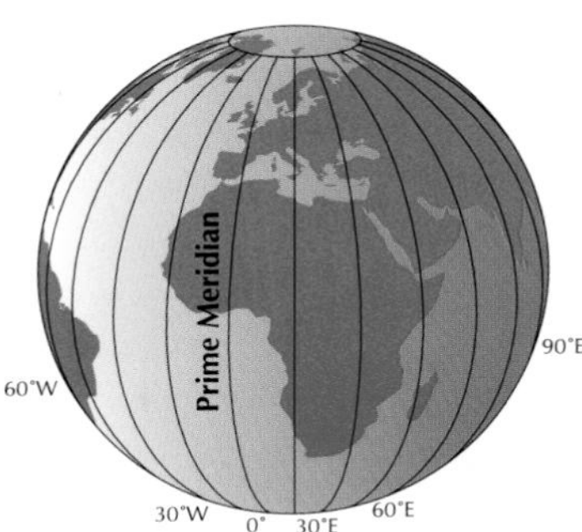

figure 10

figure 11

Map projections

Spherical representations of the Earth are called globes, while flat representations are called maps. Because globes are round and three-dimensional, they can show the continents and oceans undistorted and unbroken; therefore, they represent the Earth and its various features more correctly than do maps. Maps, however, generally feature larger scales and higher levels of detail.

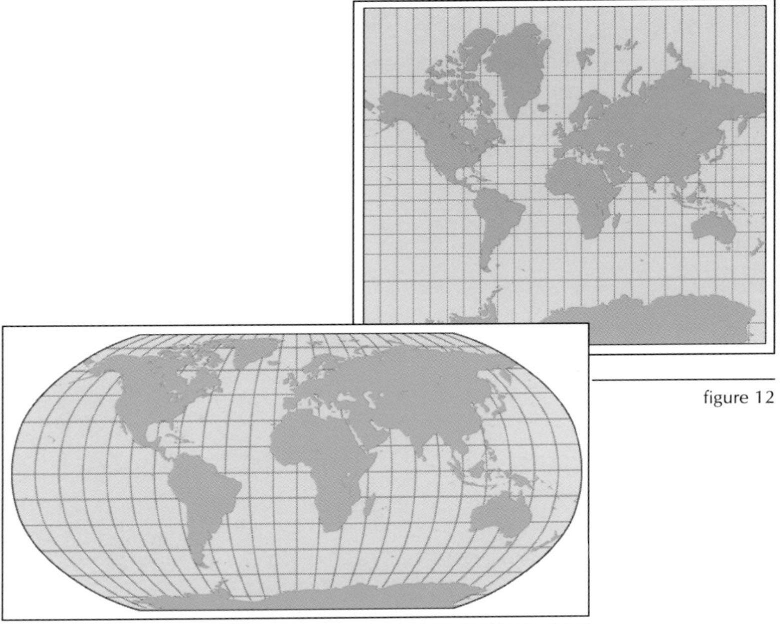

figure 12

figure 13

With the help of mathematics, cartographers are able to depict the curvature of the Earth on a two-dimensional surface. This process is called projecting a map, or creating a map projection. The size, shape, distance, area, and proportion of map features can be distorted, however, when the curves of a globe become the straight lines of a map. Distortion occurs because the Earth's spherical surface must be stretched and/or broken in places as it is flattened. Different map projections have specific properties that make them useful, and a cartographer must select the projection best-suited to the map's purpose.

The Mercator (figure 12) and the Robinson (figure 13) projections are commonly chosen for maps of the entire world. In this atlas, the Robinson is used along with four additional projections—the Lambert Azimuthal Equal Area, the Lambert Conformal Conic, the Sinusoidal, and the Azimuthal Equidisant.

Map scale

The scale of a map is the relationship between distances or areas shown on the map and the corresponding distances or areas on the Earth's surface. Large-scale maps generally show relatively small areas in greater detail than do small-scale maps, such as those of the world or the continents.

There are three different ways to express scale. Most often it is given as a fraction, such as 1:10,000,000, which means that the ratio of map distances to actual Earth distances is 1 to 10,000,000 (figure 14). Scale also can be expressed as a word phrase, such as, "One inch represents approximately 150 miles" (figure 15). Lastly, scale can be illustrated as a scale bar, labeled with miles on one side and kilometers on the other (figure 16). Any of these three scale expressions can be used to calculate distances on a map.

figure 14

One inch represents approximately 150 miles

figure 15

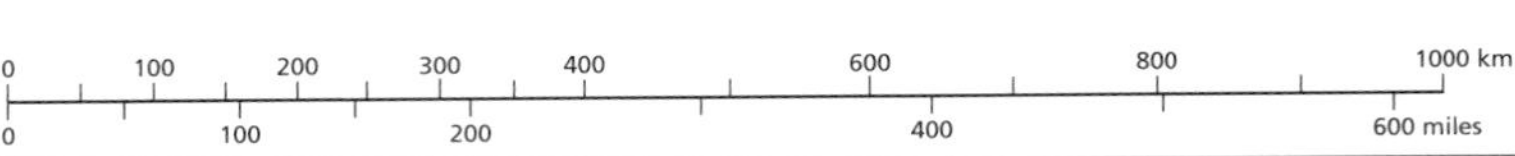

figure 16

How to Use the Atlas

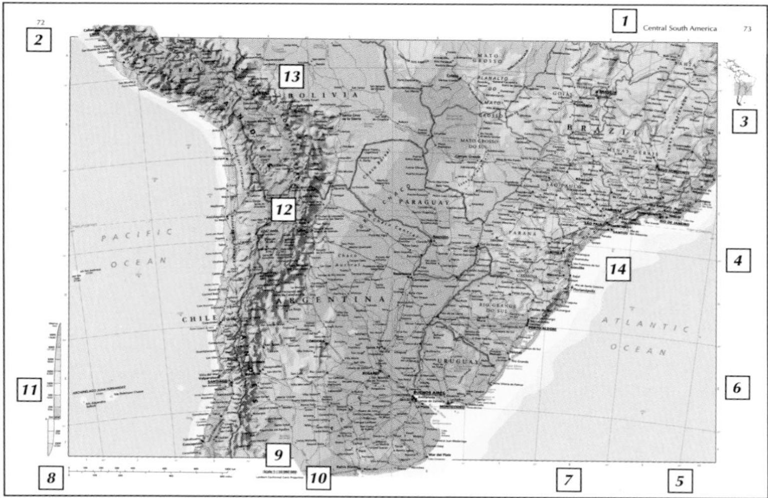

figure 1

[1] Map title
[2] Page number
[3] Locator map
[4] Latitude
[5] Longitude
[6] Index reference letter
[7] Index reference number
[8] Scale bar
[9] Scale ratio
[10] Map projection
[11] Hypsometric/bathymetric scale bar
[12] Shaded relief
[13] Hypsometric tints (to show elevation)
[14] Bathymetric tints (to show water depths)

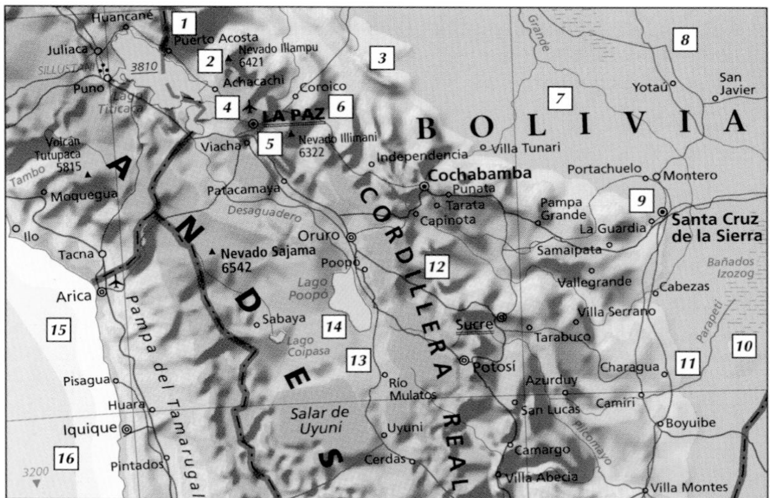

figure 2

[1] International boundary
[2] Mountain peak/elevation
[3] Hypsometric elevation tints
[4] International airport
[5] Urban area
[6] National capital
[7] Country name
[8] Road
[9] City/town
[10] Swamp
[11] River
[12] Mountain range
[13] Railroad
[14] Lake
[15] Bathymetric tints
[16] Depth of water (in meters)

What the *Premier World Atlas* includes

At the core of the *Premier World Atlas* is a collection of regional maps covering the entire world. The maps were designed to be as easy as possible to understand and use. Figure 1 is an example of a map spread contained in this atlas. The boxed numbers on this map, which correspond to items listed below it, highlight the features and information found on each map page—such as the map title, the locator map showing the area of the world depicted on the map, and the map scale.

Figure 2 is an enlarged section from the same map. As in figure 1, a few of the most common feature symbols have been highlighted. A more complete list of the map symbols used in this atlas can be found on page 1.

The atlas opens with a 17-page photographic essay devoted to the world and the continents (figure 3). Each of the seven continents is featured on two pages with photos and descriptive text. Fact blocks (figure 4) provide vital information about each continent's most notable characteristics and features.

figure 4

Europe Facts

Land area: 3.8 million square miles (9.9 million sq km)
Continental rank (in area): 6th
Estimated population: 712.1 million
Population density: 187/square mile (72/sq km)
Highest point: Gora El' Brus, Russia, 18,510 feet (5,642 m)
Lowest point: Caspian Sea, Europe-Asia, 92 feet (28 m) below sea level
Longest river: Volga, 2,194 miles (3,531 km)
Largest island: Great Britain, 88,795 square miles (229,978 sq km)
Largest lake: Caspian Sea, Europe-Asia, 143,240 square miles (370,990 sq km)
Number of countries and dependencies: 49
Largest country: Russia, Europe-Asia, 6.6 million square miles (17.1 million sq km)
Smallest country (excl. dependencies): Vatican City, 0.2 square miles (0.4 sq km)
Most populous country: Russia, Europe-Asia, 150.5 million
Largest city: Moscow, metro. area pop. 13.1 million

figure 3

Following the regional maps are individual maps of each of the United States, and the Canadian provinces (figure 5).

The last section of the *Premier World Atlas* is an 80-page index with entries for approximately 45,000 places and geographic features that appear on the maps.

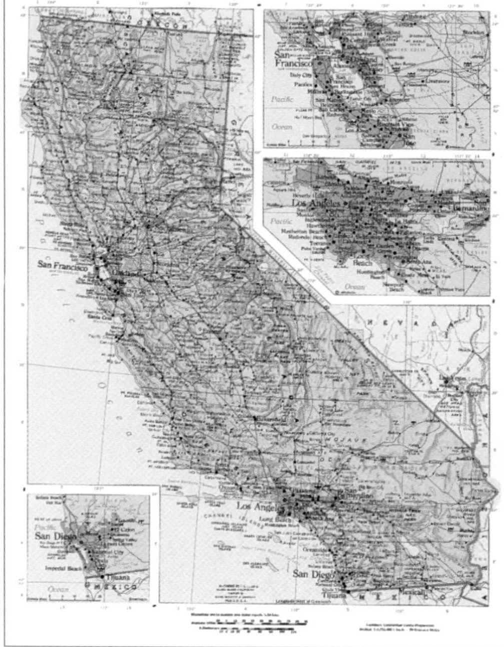

figure 5

Physical and Political Maps

The two main types of maps that appear in this atlas are physical maps and political maps. Physical maps, like the one shown in figure 6 (see next page), emphasize terrain, landforms, and elevation. Political maps, as in figure 7, emphasize countries and other political units over topography. The state and province maps found on pages 84-91 and pages 94-143 are both political and physical: they feature political coloration but also include shaded relief to depict landforms.

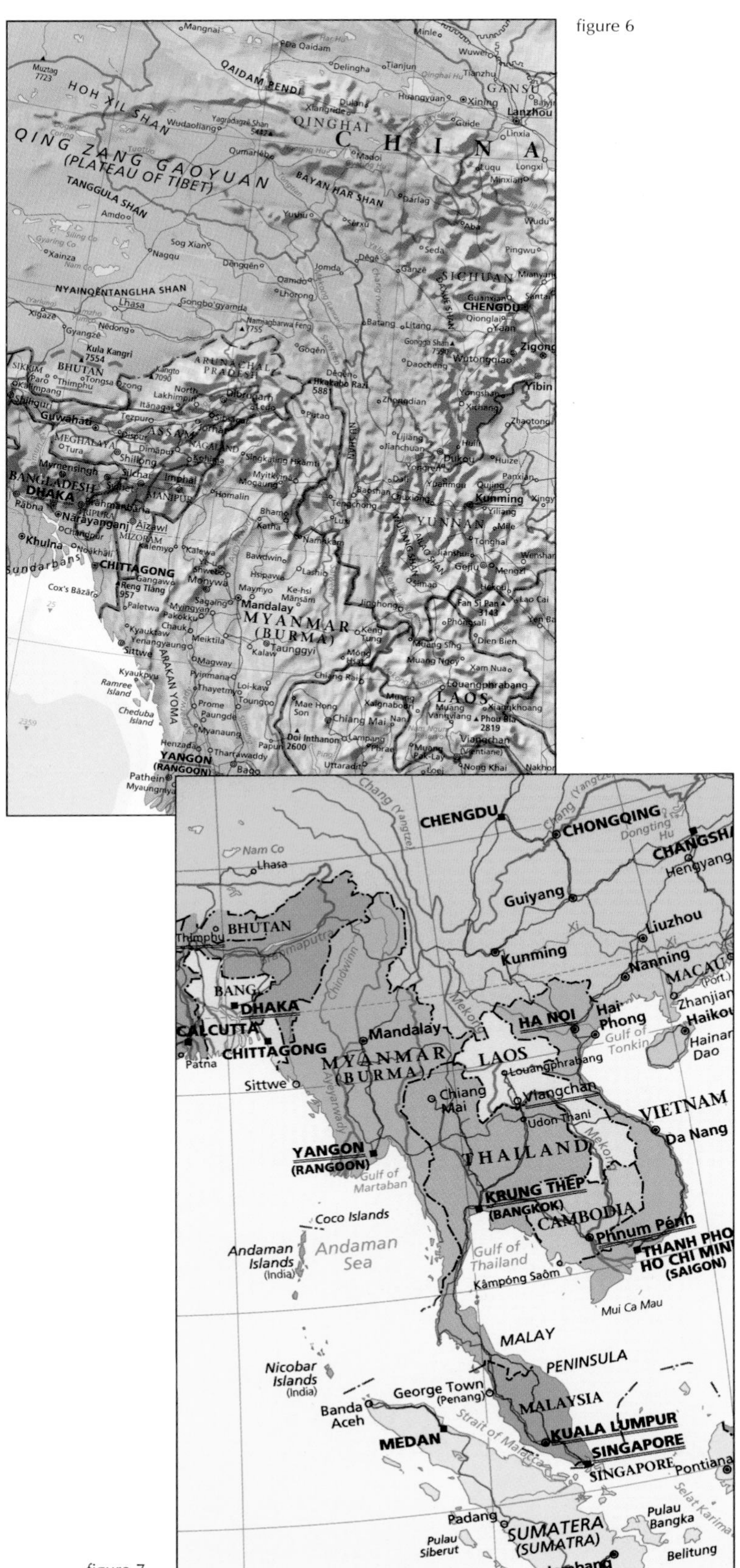

figure 6

figure 7

Measuring Distances

Using a map scale bar, it is possible to calculate the distance between any two points on a map. To find the approximate distance between Melbourne and Sydney, Australia, for example, follow these steps:

1) Lay a piece of paper on the right-hand page of the "Eastern Australia and New Zealand" map found on pages 62-63, lining up its edge with the city dots for Melbourne and Sydney. Make a mark on the paper next to each dot (figure 8).

2) Place the paper along the scale bar found below the map, and position the first mark at 0. The second mark falls about halfway between the 400-mile mark and the unlabeled 500-mile mark, indicating that the distance separating the two cities is approximately 450 miles (figure 9).

3) To confirm this measurement, make a third pencil mark (shown in red in figure 9) at the 400-mile mark. Slide the paper to the left so that the red mark lines up with 0. The white Sydney mark now falls very close to the 50-mile mark, which is unlabeled. Thus, Melbourne and Sydney are indeed approximately 450 (400 plus 50) miles apart.

figure 8

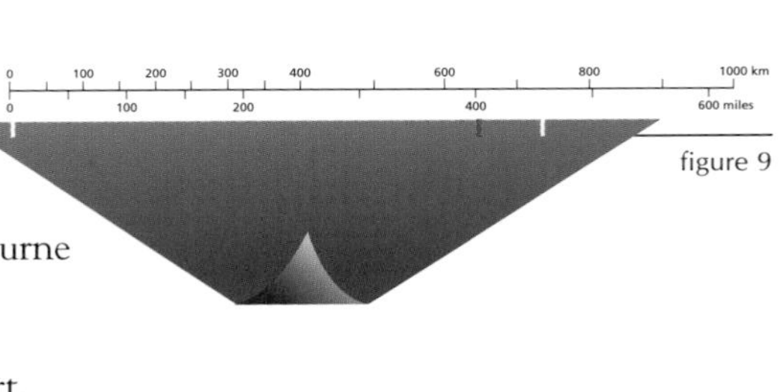

figure 9

Using the Index to Find Places

One of the most important purposes of an atlas is to help the reader locate places or features. In this atlas, each map is bordered by a letter and number grid. In the index, found in the back of the atlas on pages I•1 through I•80, every entry is assigned a map reference key, which consists of a letter and a number that correspond to a letter and a number on the grid. To locate places or features, follow the steps outlined in this example for Palembang, Indonesia:

P

Pālanpur, India	**F5**	40
Palaoa Point, C., Hi., U.S.	**C4**	104
Palapye, Bots.	**F5**	56
Palatine, Il., U.S.	**A5**	106
Palatka, Fl., U.S.	**C5**	102
Palau, ctry., Oc.	**B8**	37
Palawan, i., Phil.	**B5**	37
Pālayankottai, India	**E8**	41
Palembang, Indon.	**D2**	36
Palencia, Spain.	**G6**	17
Palermo, Italy	**D5**	18
Palestine, Ar., U.S.	**C5**	97
Palestine, Il., U.S.	**D6**	106
Palestine, Tx., U.S.	**D5**	136

figure 10

1) Look up Palembang in the index. The entry (figure 10) contains the following information: the feature name (Palembang), an abbreviation for the country (Indon.) in which Palembang is located, the map reference key (D2) that corresponds to Palembang's location on the map, and the page number (36) of the map on which Palembang can be found.

2) Turn to page 36. Look along either the left or right margin for the letter "D" —the letter code given for Palembang. The "D" denotes a narrow horizontal band, roughly 1½" wide, in which Palembang is located. Then, look along either the top or bottom margin for the number "2" —the numerical part of the code given for Palembang. The "2" denotes a narrow vertical band, also roughly 1½" wide, in which Palembang is located.

3) Using your finger, follow the "D" band and the "2" band to the area where they meet (figure 11). Palembang can be found within the darker shaded square where the bands overlap.

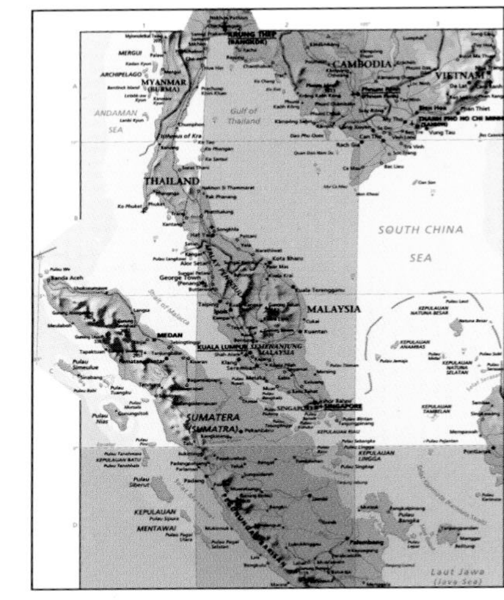

figure 11

The World & its Seven Continents

The world we humans inhabit—a world that sustains, inspires, and challenges us—is Planet Earth, a massive ball of rock spinning through the darkness of space.

On a human scale the Earth is immense, but on the incomprehensibly vast scale of the universe, it is no more significant than a grain of sand in a desert. Along with its companion planets, the Earth orbits a relatively small star we call the Sun, which is but one of 260 billion stars clustered in a great spiral-shaped galaxy known as the Milky Way, which is but one of billions of known galaxies.

Water dominates the surface of our planet; land covers only slightly more than a quarter of it. We arbitrarily call the largest pieces of land "continents": North America, South America, Africa, Antarctica, Australia, and Europe and Asia, which share a single landmass. All of the other pieces of land, from enormous Greenland to minuscule parcels of sand and rock breaking the ocean's surface, are considered islands.

Although life first appeared on the Earth perhaps 3.5 billion years ago, our own human species, Homo sapiens, has walked the planet for only 300,000 to 400,000 years—the blink of an eye in geologic time. Our distant ancestors led nomadic lives as hunters and gatherers, constantly on the move in search of prey and edible plants, fruits, and nuts. Over time they spread to every continent except Antarctica, even crossing wide seas to colonize Australia.

About 10,000 years ago, shortly after the end of the great Ice Age, a dramatic change swept through some areas of the world: humans began to cultivate crops—wheat and barley were probably the first—and to keep herds of domesticated animals, such as sheep, goats, and pigs. With the advent of agriculture came the first permanent settlements and ultimately the first civilizations.

Prior to these developments, the world's population had grown very slowly, and probably never exceeded ten million. But agriculture brought a much greater and more reliable supply of food, and the population began a climb that in modern times has reached explosive proportions. At the beginning of the first millennium A.D., perhaps 250 million people inhabited the planet. By 1850, this number had quadrupled to roughly 1.2 billion. Since then, it has nearly quintupled: today the world holds a whopping 5.8 billion people.

Nevertheless, large parts of each continent remain unpopulated or only sparsely populated. Most such areas are hostile to human life: some are too hot and dry (deserts such as the Sahara and the Gobi); some are too cold or do not have adequate growing seasons (Antarctica and the northern regions of Asia, Europe, and North America); some are too densely vegetated (the rain forests of South America and central Africa); and some are too mountainous or poor in soil (western North America and western Asia). This leaves only a small part of the Earth's surface to support all of its people.

Until the last five or so centuries, the world's peoples and civilizations were largely isolated from one another, either by great distances or by natural barriers such as mountains, deserts, and seas. As a result, a myriad of languages and cultures arose, and inhabitants of one region or continent differed greatly from those of another. Recent advances in transportation and communication have reversed this situation, and now many local languages and traditions are slowly being replaced by an emerging global culture. Suddenly, our vast world is beginning to feel very small.

World Facts

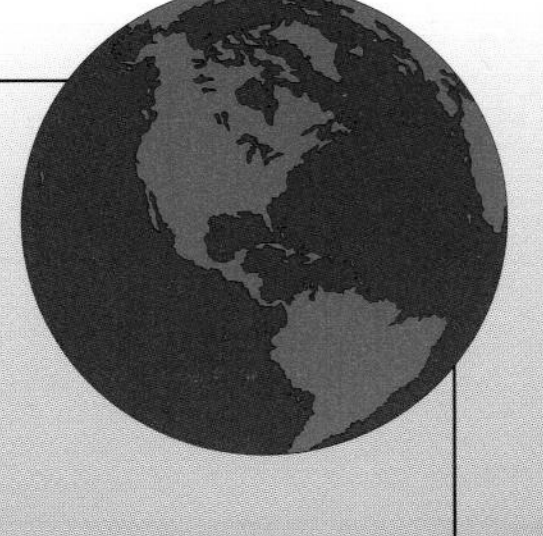

Land area: 57.9 million square miles (150.1 million sq km)
Estimated population: 5.8 billion
Population density: 99/square mile (38/sq km)
Highest point: Mt. Everest, China (Tibet)-Nepal, 29,028 feet (8,848 m)
Lowest point: Dead Sea, Israel-Jordan, 1,339 feet (408 m) below sea level
Longest river: Nile, Africa, 4,145 miles (6,671 km)
Largest island: Greenland, North America, 840,000 square miles (2.2 million sq km)
Largest lake: Caspian Sea, Asia-Europe, 143,240 square miles (371,000 sq km)
Number of countries and dependencies: 246
Largest country: Russia, Asia-Europe, 6.6 million square miles (17.1 million sq km)
Smallest country (excl. dependencies): Vatican City, Europe, 0.2 square miles (0.4 sq km)
Most populous country: China, Asia, 1.2 billion
Largest city: Tokyo, Japan, Asia, metro. area pop. 31.3 million

Africa

Africa is a land of vast spaces and infinite variety. Across its great length and breadth are found tropical rain forests, savannas teeming with wildlife, sun-scorched deserts, sprawling modern cities, and a kaleidoscope of peoples and cultures.

The Sahara, largest of the world's deserts, dominates the northern half of the continent. Reaching from the Atlantic Ocean to the Red Sea, the Sahara covers an area nearly as large as the entire continent of Europe. Few people inhabit this inhospitable landscape of shifting sand dunes, gravel-covered plains, and bare mountains, where rain seldom falls and hot, dust-laden winds blow relentlessly.

Southern Africa also contains large arid regions, most notably the Namib and Kalahari deserts. Along the equator, however, rain falls in abundance. Verdant rain forests blanket much of this region, alive with monkeys, gorillas, wild pigs, and countless species of birds and insects. Between the deserts and the rain forests lie the broad swaths of grassland known as savannas. Herds of zebras, wildebeests, giraffes, elephants, and many other animals graze on the savannas, always on the alert for lions, hyenas, and other predators. Poaching and destruction of habitat have decimated animal populations in many parts of Africa, but enormous concentrations still exist in places such as northern Botswana and the Serengeti Plain of Tanzania.

Africa's greatest rivers are the Congo, the Zambezi, the Niger, and of course the Nile, the longest river in the world. From its headwaters in Burundi, the Nile flows northward more

Left page: Acacia trees on the Serengeti Plain, Tanzania; Samburu girls, Kenya; African elephant.

Right page: Sahara near Arak, Algeria; brightly painted hut and its occupants, Lesotho; avenue of sphinxes, Luxor, Egypt.

than four thousand miles —through rugged mountains and highlands, the beautiful lake country of East Africa, and the wide marshy plain known as the Sudd—before spilling into the Mediterranean Sea.

Humans have farmed the fertile land of the Nile Delta from time immemorial, and it was here that the great civilization of the ancient Egyptians sprang up more than five thousand years ago. The marvelous archaeological legacies of this civilization include the Pyramids, the Sphinx, and the temples of Karnak and Luxor.

Among Africa's seven hundred million people there is tremendous ethnic and cultural diversity. More than eight hundred languages are spoken across the continent, and scores of distinct ethnic groups can be identified—groups such as the Tuareg and Berbers of Saharan Africa, the Masai and Kikuyu of the eastern savannas, the Fang and Bateke of the rain forests. Not surprisingly, few African countries are ethnically homogeneous.

Tremendous change has swept through Africa in the twentieth century. As recently as the 1940s, nearly the entire continent was controlled by colonial powers. In the wake of the Second World War, independence movements gathered strength, and by the end of the 1970s all of Africa's countries had shaken off their colonial shackles. For the first time in centuries, the continent was free to seek its own identity and destiny.

Africa Facts

Land area: 11.7 million square miles (30.3 million sq km)
Continental rank (in area): 2nd
Estimated population: 722.2 million
Population density: 62/square mile (24/sq km)
Highest point: Kilimanjaro, Tanzania, 19,340 feet (5,895 m)
Lowest point: Lac Assal, Djibouti, 515 feet (157 m) below sea level
Longest river: Nile, 4,145 miles (6,671 km)
Largest island: Madagascar, 226,658 square miles (587,041 sq km)
Largest lake: Lake Victoria, 26,820 square miles (69,463 sq km)
Number of countries and dependencies: 61
Largest country: Sudan, 967,500 square miles (2,505,813 sq km)
Smallest country (excl. dependencies): Seychelles, 175 square miles (453 sq km)
Most populous country: Nigeria, 102.9 million
Largest city: Cairo, metro. area pop. 13.4 million

Antarctica

The frozen continent of Antarctica lies at the very bottom of the world, buried beneath a great sheet of ice and encircled by frigid seas crowded with towering icebergs.

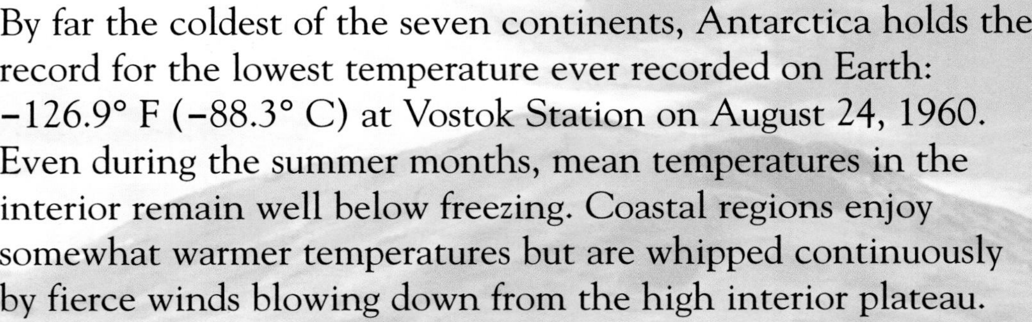

By far the coldest of the seven continents, Antarctica holds the record for the lowest temperature ever recorded on Earth: −126.9° F (−88.3° C) at Vostok Station on August 24, 1960. Even during the summer months, mean temperatures in the interior remain well below freezing. Coastal regions enjoy somewhat warmer temperatures but are whipped continuously by fierce winds blowing down from the high interior plateau.

Because of the extreme cold, most of the snow that falls over Antarctica's interior does not melt; instead, it accumulates and gradually compacts. Over the course of millions of years, this process has formed the ice sheet that now covers nearly the entire continent. Almost inconceivably massive, the sheet has an average thickness as great as the depth of the Grand Canyon; its maximum thickness is three times greater. It holds some ninety percent of all the ice on Earth, and seventy percent of the fresh water.

As the ice sheet slowly spreads outward under its own crushing weight, its edges spill into the surrounding seas, forming immense shelves that in some places extend hundreds of miles from the shore. The largest of these, the Ross Ice Shelf, covers an area as large as the entire country of France. Enormous pieces continuously break off, or "calve," from the margins of the shelves and drift northward as icebergs.

If all of Antarctica's ice were to melt, the consequences would be disastrous. Ocean levels would rise dramatically, flooding coastal regions around the world. Florida, for example, would disappear under water, as would southeast Asia's Malay Peninsula and the Low Countries of Europe. More than half of the world's people would be forced to relocate.

Antarctica's coasts, islands, and seas are as full of life as its interior is barren. Clamorous penguin rookeries, some containing tens of thousands of individuals, dot the coastline. Petrels, albatrosses, and cormorants sail the coastal skies, searching the sea for fish and crustaceans. Seven species of seal, including leopard seals, elephant seals, and crabeaters, swim the nutrient-rich Antarctic waters along with squid, octopuses, killer whales, blue whales, and more than a dozen other whale species.

To whom does Antarctica belong? This question has provoked a great deal of controversy in the twentieth century, as numerous countries have explored the continent, made territorial claims, or established research stations. The possibility of rich mineral deposits adds urgency to the question.

In 1959, twelve countries drafted and signed the Antarctic Treaty, which declares Antarctica a natural reserve to be used only for peaceful purposes, especially scientific investigation. So far, the treaty has met with great success, and today Antarctica enjoys a spirit of international cooperation unknown elsewhere in the world.

Left page: Sled and dog team; Emperor penguins.

Right page: Iceberg and ice floes; research ship anchored along sea ice; killer whale.

Antarctica Facts

Land area: 5.4 million square miles (14 million sq km)
Continental rank (in area): 5th
Estimated population: No permanent population
Highest point: Vinson Massif, 16,066 feet (4,897 m)
Lowest point: Deep Lake, 184 feet (56 m) below sea level
Longest river: Antarctica has no true rivers
Largest island: Berkner Island, 20,005 square miles (51,829 sq km)
Number of countries with territorial claims: 7
Number of countries with research stations: 18

Asia

Three out of five people on Earth live in Asia, by far the world's largest and most heavily populated continent. With its myriad of landscapes, peoples, and historical treasures, and its swelling population, Asia represents a microcosm of the entire world.

Mountain systems—some ancient, some young and still rising—are the continent's signature landform. The Himalayas, which run through Pakistan, China, India, Nepal, and Bhutan, form the loftiest range in the world. Reaching more than five miles into the heavens, Mount Everest is the world's highest mountain, but nearby Kanchenjunga, Dhawalāgiri, Annapurna, and the peak known simply as K2 are hardly less formidable.

Seemingly endless expanses of semiarid grassland, or steppes, blanket much of the vast continental interior. Just north of the Himalayas lies the remote Tibetan Plateau, nicknamed the "Rooftop of the World": its average elevation is nearly half the height of Mount Everest.

The northern third of the continent is occupied by the region known as Siberia. Its name evokes images of a bitterly cold wasteland of snow and tundra, but visitors also discover vast, pristine forests, grassy plains, and extensive marshlands.

A long belt of desert stretches from the Arabian peninsula to eastern China. Most of this arid region is virtually uninhabited, and life is harsh for the few residents. The parched landscape of the Gobi, Asia's largest desert, contains little more than tough scrub vegetation and brackish lakes.

In the far west, the Arabian peninsula is a sea of sand dunes, punctuated by an occasional oasis where tall palm trees provide the desert's only shade.

In sharp contrast to these barren landscapes, the tropical lands and islands of Southeast Asia are awash in greenery. Crops and rain forests thrive in this wet region, where seasonal monsoon rains saturate the land for months at a time.

For centuries, rivers have been a lifeline for the people of the continent. Nestled between the Tigris and Euphrates rivers is the fertile land of Mesopotamia, which supported an advanced society that flourished as early as 4000 B.C. Ruins found in the lush Indus River valley of Pakistan tell of an advanced culture dating back to around 3000 B.C. And, almost 4,000 years ago, the ancient Chinese civilization developed along the banks of the Huang (Yellow) River.

Irrigation networks are vital to Asia because rocky terrain and minimal precipitation make much of the continent ill-suited for agriculture, and all arable land must be farmed intensively. The fertile valleys and coasts of eastern and southern Asia already strain to meet the demands of Asia's soaring population.

Recent economic and technological development has allowed Japan, Singapore, Indonesia, and Korea to rise to international prominence. It is likely that this trend will continue for these and other Asian countries into the 21st century, which many observers are already referring to as "the Asian Century." It will be a time for the countries of the continent to flex their collective muscle. Since Asia represents such a large percentage of the Earth's population, what happens there might dictate what the future brings to the rest of the world.

Left page: Mount Fuji and tea fields, Japan; Kazak man with hunting eagle, Mongolia; giant panda.

Right page: Mount Everest; Dome of the Rock, Omar Mosque, Jerusalem, Israel; schoolboys in Nāgaur, India.

Asia Facts

Land area: 17.3 million square miles (44.9 million sq km)
Continental rank (in area): 1st
Estimated population: 3.5 billion
Population density: 203/square mile (78/sq km)
Highest point: Mt. Everest, China (Tibet)-Nepal, 29,028 feet (8,848 m)
Lowest point: Dead Sea, Israel-Jordan, 1,339 feet (408 m) below sea level
Longest river: Yangtze (Chang), 3,900 miles (6,300 km)
Largest island: New Guinea, 309,000 square miles (800,000 sq km)
Largest lake: Caspian Sea, Asia-Europe, 143,240 square miles (370,990 sq km)
Number of countries and dependencies: 50
Largest country: Russia, Asia-Europe, 6.6 million square miles (17.1 million sq km)
Smallest country (excl. dependencies): Maldives, 115 square miles (298 sq km)
Most populous country: China, 1.2 billion
Largest city: Tokyo, metro. area pop. 31.3 million

Australia & Oceania

The continent of Australia, along with its island neighbor New Zealand, is often classified as part of Oceania, a larger region that includes more than 25,000 islands, volcanic peaks, and coral atolls scattered across the southern Pacific Ocean.

The first European explorers to Australia came ashore near present-day Sydney and were so awed by the profusion of unfamiliar vegetation that they named the area Botany Bay. Today, eucalyptus and acacia trees, fuschias, and spear lilies thrive alongside exotic animal species such as kangaroos, wallabies, koala bears, kookaburras, and platypuses in Australia's warm climate.

Low, semiarid plateaus cover much of western Australia, taking in the Great Sandy Desert, the Gibson Desert, and the Great Victoria Desert. Here, scrubby grasses and spiky bushes break up stretches of pebble-covered land. This barren, largely uninhabited region is the Outback, whose harsh beauty and remoteness have come to epitomize "The Land Down Under" for many non-Australians.

Australia's indigenous people, called the Aborigines, arrived and settled the Outback and other parts of the continent perhaps 35,000 years prior to the Europeans. The complex Aboriginal society is based on kinship and the belief that humans, the environment, and time are intimately associated. Aborigines hold sacred numerous sites across Australia, including Uluru, or Ayers Rock, the world's largest monolith.

Among Australia's most valuable natural resources are its vast grasslands, dotted with woolly herds of grazing sheep and fenced in by the paddocks of great ranches, or stations. Australia is a major world producer and exporter of wool, veal, and mutton. Sheep herding and grazing also dominate the economy of New Zealand, where sheep outnumber humans fourteen to one.

In this century, New Zealand has aggressively developed its own resources and now ranks among the world's most economically advanced countries. Cascading rivers provide water power for burgeoning industrial development, and rich reserves of minerals, natural gas, and timber drive a strong economy. With this wealth of resources, New Zealand has become a world leader in trade, much of which passes through the superb natural harbor of Wellington, the capital city.

Left page: Dirt road through Australia's Outback; Aboriginal man, northern Australia; koala bear, Australia.

Right page: Rock Islands, Palau; Mount Cook, New Zealand's highest peak; school of sweetips.

New Zealand has two main islands, both of which are mountainous and ruggedly beautiful. On South Island, icy glaciers cut through the Southern Alps, and dazzling fjords such as Milford Sound indent the southwestern coast. The smaller North Island, home to three-quarters of the country's population, is dominated by a central volcanic plateau over which tower three impressive peaks: Ruapehu, Ngauruhoe, and Tongariro.

Papua New Guinea, on the eastern half of the island of New Guinea, is an uneven mixture of lush rain forests, swamplands, and steep volcanic mountains. Along with many of the smaller islands of Oceania, it lies on the southwestern section of the Ring of Fire—a band of active volcanoes that encircles the Pacific Ocean.

Every year, thousands of winter-weary tourists escape to Oceania's tropical island paradises, such as Tahiti, Fiji, and Guam. Here, they revel in the endless stretches of sandy beaches, secluded coves, and absolute isolation, half a world away from their homes.

Australia & Oceania Facts

Land area: 3.3 million square miles (8.5 million sq km)
Continental rank (in area): 7th
Estimated population: 29.0 million
Population density: 8.8/square mile (3.4/sq km)
Highest point: Mt. Wilhelm, Papua New Guinea, 14,793 feet (4,509 m)
Lowest point: Lake Eyre, South Australia, 52 feet (16 m) below sea level
Longest river: Murray-Darling, 2,330 miles (3,750 km)
Largest island: New Guinea, Oceania-Asia, 309,000 square miles (800,000 sq km)
Largest lake: Lake Eyre, 3,700 square miles (9,500 sq km)
Number of countries and dependencies: 33
Largest country: Australia, 3 million square miles (7.7 million sq km)
Smallest country (excl. dependencies): Nauru, 8.1 square miles (21 sq km)
Most populous country: Australia, 18.4 million
Largest city: Sydney, metro. area pop. 3.5 million

Europe

Human settlements and civilizations have flourished in Europe for more than four thousand years, benefiting from the generally mild climate and the abundance of arable land, navigable rivers, and natural resources. The continent today ranks with East Asia and South Asia as one of the three greatest population centers in the world.

The northern half of Europe bears dramatic evidence of past ice ages. During the Pleistocene epoch, immense sheets and rivers of ice plowed across the region, rounding the mountains of Scandinavia and Scotland, scouring river valleys to create Norway's deep fjords, and depositing a thick layer of sand, gravel, and boulder-filled clay across the landscape. This glacial deposition played a major part in the formation of the Great European Plain, which stretches in an arc from western France to the Urals. The western part of the plain is Europe's most intensively farmed region as well as its most densely populated, home to such great cities as Paris, Amsterdam, Berlin, Stockholm, Warsaw, and Moscow.

Uplands and mountain systems dominate the southern half of the continent. The Pyrenees, Alps, and Carpathians together form a nearly unbroken band of mountains stretching from the Atlantic to central Romania. Until the advent of modern transportation, this formidable natural barrier impeded overland travel between the Mediterranean region and the rest of Europe, especially when winter snows fell on the mountain passes. As a result, a distinct Mediterranean culture evolved, and it remains strong today.

Thanks to a warm ocean current called the North Atlantic Drift, northwestern Europe enjoys a climate far milder than those of lands at similar latitudes in North America and Asia. The current warms and moistens offshore air masses, which then flow across the British Isles, the Low Countries, France, Denmark, Germany, and surrounding lands. As this maritime air moves into eastern Europe, its effects become weaker and weaker, and climates become increasingly extreme. Mountain systems block the air masses from the Mediterranean region, which has a hotter, drier climate.

Europe has been home to many great civilizations, including those of the Minoans, Mycenaeans, Greeks, and Romans. With the collapse of the Roman Empire, Europe plunged into a period of relative decline and darkness, but emerged roughly one thousand years later into the light of the Renaissance, a glorious rebirth that pervaded nearly every field of human endeavor but especially art and science.

Left page: Ibexes on mountainside above lake, Interlaken, Switzerland; farmer picking grapes, Italy; Big Ben, London.

Right page: Highlands of Scotland; Cibeles Fountain, Madrid; St. Basil's Cathedral, Moscow.

The Renaissance also marked the beginning of an era of exploration and expansion. Great powers such as England, Spain, Portugal, and France explored, conquered, and colonized lands all over the world—Africa, the Americas, Australia, India, and other parts of Asia. As gold, silver, and other riches poured into Europe, emigrants poured out, spreading European ideas, languages, and cultures to nearly every part of the globe. The Industrial and Agricultural revolutions further increased the continent's wealth and dominance. Through the first part of the 20th century, Europe held sway over the world as no continent had ever done before or is likely to do in the future.

Europe Facts

Land area: 3.8 million square miles (9.9 million sq km)
Continental rank (in area): 6th
Estimated population: 712.9 million
Population density: 188/square mile (72/sq km)
Highest point: Gora El'brus, Russia, 18,510 feet (5,642 m)
Lowest point: Caspian Sea, Europe-Asia, 92 feet (28 m) below sea level
Longest river: Volga, 2,194 miles (3,531 km)
Largest island: Great Britain, 88,795 square miles (229,978 sq km)
Largest lake: Caspian Sea, Europe-Asia, 143,240 square miles (370,990 sq km)
Number of countries and dependencies: 49
Largest country: Russia, Europe-Asia, 6.6 million square miles (17.1 million sq km)
Smallest country (excl. dependencies): Vatican City, 0.2 square miles (0.4 sq km)
Most populous country: Russia, Europe-Asia, 150.5 million
Largest city: Moscow, metro. area pop. 13.1 million

North America

Almost 30,000 years ago, the first North Americans arrived on the continent after crossing the Bering land bridge from Asia. Before them lay a rich land of dense forests, virgin streams and lakes, and prairies where great herds of bison roamed.

These same treasures beckoned the first European settlers to North America in the early 16th century. For nearly 500 years, emigrants from all corners of the globe have been pouring onto the continent in search of a better life. Many have realized their dreams, and along the way North America has become the world's wealthiest and most influential continent.

Among its richest resources are vast tracts of arable land. The farmland of the Great Plains is so productive that this region has been called "the Breadbasket of the World." The United States and Canada are world leaders in food production, harvesting so much wheat, corn, barley, soybeans, oats, sugar, and fruit each year that thousands of surplus tons can be exported.

Sweeping mountain systems frame the plains in the east and west. Eastern North America is traversed by the ancient, well-weathered Appalachian Mountains, which stretch from Newfoundland south through Georgia. The soaring Rockies extend from western Canada into New Mexico, showcasing some of

the continent's most dramatic landscapes. Mexico's greatest mountain ranges, the Sierra Madres, collide to form a spiny, volcanic backbone that continues into Central America.

Fed by hundreds of tributaries, the Mississippi-Missouri river system—North America's longest—cuts a path through the center of the continent. The mighty river both embraces and disregards those who settle along its banks, providing fertile farmland and access to a vital transport corridor, but also periodically flooding adjacent farms and towns.

Canada, the United States, and Mexico comprise almost 90% of North America. The United States and Canada have diversified, service-oriented economies, and increasingly urban populations. Mexico, although poorer than its northern neighbors, has in recent decades become a key manufacturing center and a popular tourist destination.

Brilliant tropical vegetation and exotic wildlife abound in the seven countries of Central America, which occupy a slender isthmus connecting Mexico and South America. Unlike the rest of North America, Central America has a population that is both dispersed and predominantly rural.

Many people in Mexico and Central America are of mixed Spanish and Indian ancestry, a rich heritage defined by a proud culture. This blending is less evident in remote areas, where Indian villages have remained virtually unchanged for centuries. In the cities, however, a strong Indian influence intermingles with architectural remnants of the colonial era and dramatic evidence of modern development.

To the east lie the balmy islands of the Caribbean Sea, including Cuba, Hispaniola, the West Indies, Jamaica, and Puerto Rico. Each boasts a colorful culture that reflects the diverse mix of peoples—Europeans, Africans, and Indians—who found themselves thrown together during the colonial past.

Left page: Jasper National Park, Canadian Rockies, Alberta; Tarahumara man, Mexico; red-eyed tree frog, Central America.

Right page: farmhouse and fields near Moscow, Idaho; El Tajin, a Mayan temple in Veracruz, Mexico; spikes of wheat.

North America Facts

Land area: 9.5 million square miles (24.7 million sq km)
Continental rank (in area): 3rd
Estimated population: 459.6 million
Population density: 48/square mile (19/sq km)
Highest point: Mt. McKinley, Alaska, U.S., 20,320 feet (6,194 m)
Lowest point: Death Valley, California, U.S., 282 feet (84 m) below sea level
Longest river: Mississippi-Missouri, 3,740 miles (6,019 km)
Largest island: Greenland, 840,000 square miles (2,175,600 sq km)
Largest lake: Lake Superior, Canada-U.S., 31,700 square miles (82,100 sq km)
Number of countries and dependencies: 38
Largest country: Canada, 3.8 million square miles (10 million sq km)
Smallest country (excl. dependencies): St. Kitts and Nevis, 104 square miles (269 sq km)
Most populous country: United States, 265.1 million
Largest city: Mexico City, metro. area pop. 18.4 million

South America

South America is a land of untamed beauty and tremendous diversity—in its landscapes, plant and animal life, and people.

Large parts of the continent remain as wild and pristine as they were when the first humans arrived more than eleven millennia ago. Human movement and settlement have been hindered by the rugged Andes mountains and the nearly impenetrable Amazonian rain forest.

The Andes, which curve along the continent's western edge from Venezuela in the north to Tierra del Fuego in the south, form the longest mountain system in the world. The loftiest Andean peaks reach greater heights than any others in the Western Hemisphere.

High in the Andes, clear, cold streams wander among moss-covered boulders, merge with one another, and eventually tumble out of the mountains as the Marañon and Ucayali rivers. These are the principal tributaries of the world's mightiest river, the Amazon. Crossing nearly the entire breadth of the continent, the Amazon carries one-fifth of all of the world's flowing water.

The rain forest that covers much of the Amazon's vast drainage basin holds an astonishing abundance and variety of life. Still largely unexplored, the rain forest is a torrid, watery realm of slow-moving rivers and sloughs, of colorful birds, insects, and flowers, and of trees growing so densely that little sunlight

reaches the forest floor. Most of Amazonia's animals and insects live high up in the forest canopy and rarely descend to the ground.

Archaeologists believe that the first humans to reach South America were groups of hunters and gatherers migrating southward from North America some 11,000 to 14,000 years ago. Thousands of years later, the descendants of these first arrivals built several great civilizations on the continent, including the magnificent Inca Empire, which reached its maximum extent during the period AD 1100—1350. The city of Cusco, in present-day Peru, served as the Incas' capital, and today tourists are drawn to the many splendid ruins in and around the city.

Left page: Incan ruins, Machupicchu, Peru; Quechua woman and child, Peru; great blue heron, Galapagos Islands.

Right page: Iguassu Falls, Argentina-Brazil; colonial buildings, Bahia, Brazil; bird of paradise flower, Amazonia.

The arrival of Europeans in the early 1500s, and their subsequent conquest and colonization of the continent, were disastrous to the indigenous peoples: it is estimated that three-quarters of the population died as a result of European diseases, warfare, and forced labor.

Although the colonial period came to an end in the 1800s, its architectural legacy endures in cathedrals, plazas, houses, and government buildings found in cities throughout the continent.

Nine out of ten South Americans live within 150 miles of the coast; much of the interior is only sparsely settled. For this reason, South America is sometimes spoken of as "the hollow continent." In recent decades, millions of people have abandoned their small farms and villages in search of a better life in the city.

This trend has greatly swollen the populations of many of the largest cities, including São Paulo, Rio de Janeiro, Buenos Aires, and Caracas. As a new millennium begins, the crowding and frenzy of such cities stand in sharp contrast to remote interior villages, where the people live just as they have for centuries and time seems to stand still.

South America Facts

Land area: 6.9 million square miles (17.8 million sq km)
Continental rank (in area): 4th
Estimated population: 319.5 million
Population density: 46/square mile (18/sq km)
Highest point: Cerro Aconcagua, Argentina, 22,831 feet (6,959 m)
Lowest point: Salinas Chicas, Argentina, 138 feet (42m) below sea level
Longest river: Amazon, 4,000 miles (6,400 km)
Largest island: Tierra del Fuego, 18,600 square miles (48,200 sq km)
Largest lake: Lake Titicaca, Bolivia-Peru, 3,200 square miles (8,300 sq km)
Number of countries and dependencies: 15
Largest country: Brazil, 3.3 million square miles (8.5 million sq km)
Smallest country (excl. dependencies): Suriname, 63,251 square miles (163,820 sq km)
Most populous country: Brazil, 161.7 million
Largest city: São Paulo, metro. area pop. 16.7 million

Land

The Earth has a total surface area of 197 million square miles (510.2 million sq km). Water, including oceans, seas, lakes, and rivers, covers nearly three-quarters of this area; land only one-quarter. The largest landmass is Eurasia, shared by the continents of Europe and Asia. Eurasia represents 36.5% of the Earth's total land area (but only 10.7% of the total surface area). The largest continent is Asia, which accounts for 30% of the total land area. Africa ranks second, with 20% of the total land area.

The smallest continent by far is Australia, which holds only 5.1% of the world's land. When it is grouped with New Zealand and the other islands of Oceania, the figure rises only slightly, to 5.7%.

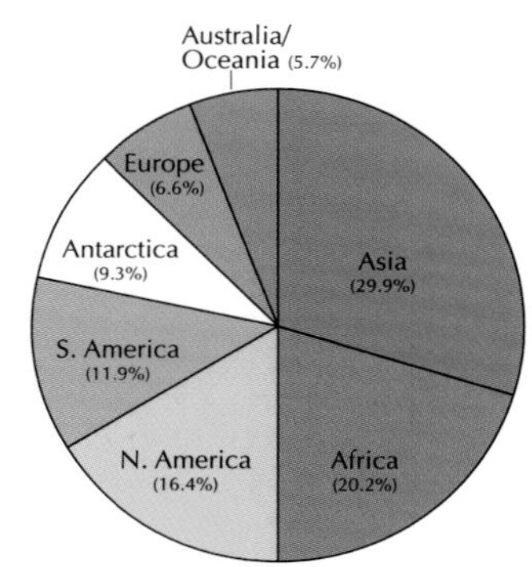

Percentage of world land area

Energy

A large percentage of the world's energy is used for manufacturing. This fact helps explain the great variances among the continents in the consumption of energy. Highly developed North America, with only 8% of the world's population, consumes nearly 30% of the world's energy, and more than five times as much as Africa and South America combined.

For two continents, energy consumption exceeds production: North America produces roughly nine-tenths of the energy it consumes, and Europe only three-fifths. In contrast, Africa consumes less than two-fifths of the energy it produces.

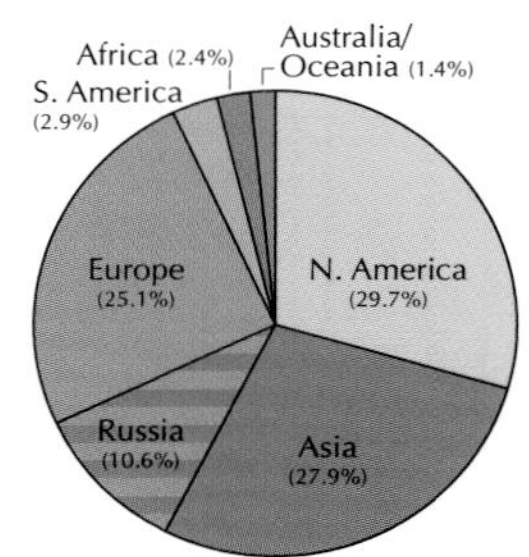

Percentage of world energy consumption

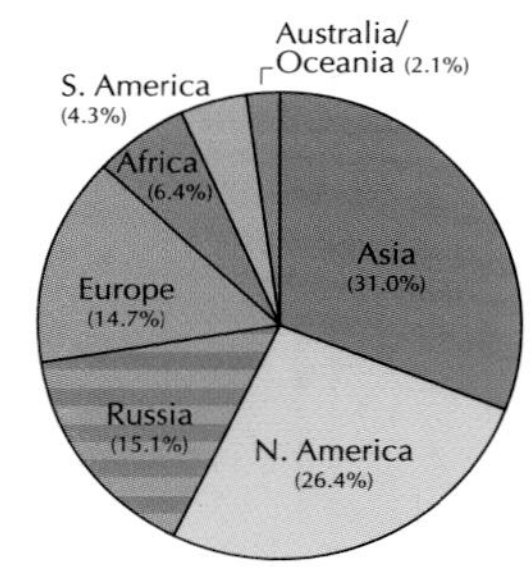

Percentage of world energy production

Population

Asia is the world's most populous continent, and has been for at least two millennia. Its current population of 3.5 billion represents an astonishing 60% of the world's people, nearly five times as much as any other continent. It is home to the world's two most populous countries: China, with nearly 1.2 billion people, and India, with 900 million. Four other Asian countries rank among the ten most populous in the world: Indonesia (4th), Pakistan (7th), Japan (8th), and Bangladesh (9th).

Europe and Africa each contain roughly 700 million people. Europe, however, has only one-third the land area of Africa, so its population density is three times greater. Antarctica has no permanent population and therefore does not appear on the graph.

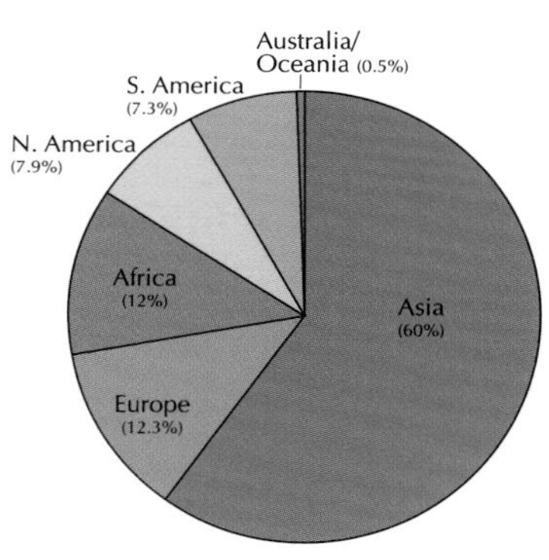

Percentage of world population

population Growth

The world's population is growing at a rapid pace: at present, the annual rate of natural increase (births minus deaths) is 1.5%. Today, the world holds 5.8 billion people; some experts predict that by the year 2050 this number will have increased by two-thirds, to 9.8 billion.

The largest part of the growth is taking place in Asia, which already is home to three-fifths of the world's people. Of every hundred people added to the Earth's population each year, 65 are Asian. Africa is also gaining a larger share of the world total: the continent's current population represents 12% of the world total, but its growth accounts for more than 19% of the annual world increase.

Europe, on the other hand, is seeing its share of the world population erode. Although Europe is the second most populous continent, its annual growth represents less than 2% of the world total.

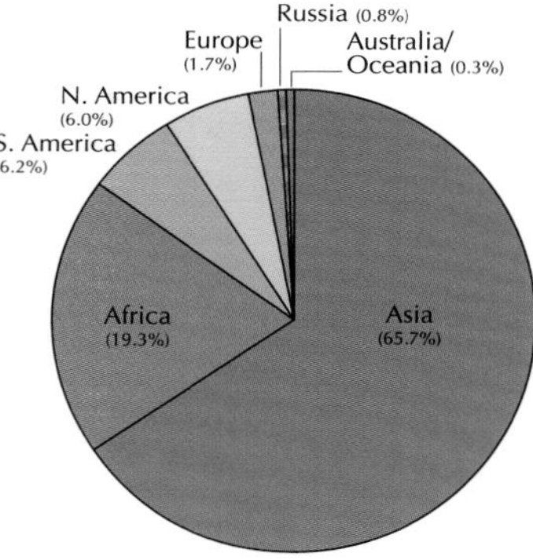

Percentage of world population growth

Legend

World and Regional Maps

Hydrographic Features

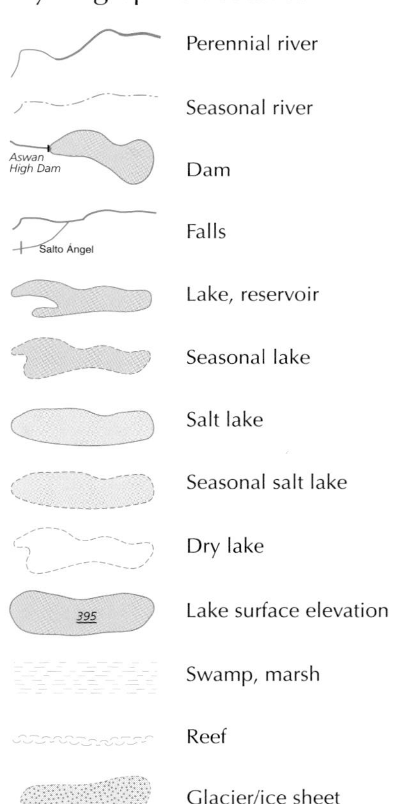

Perennial river
Seasonal river
Dam
Falls
Lake, reservoir
Seasonal lake
Salt lake
Seasonal salt lake
Dry lake
Lake surface elevation
Swamp, marsh
Reef
Glacier/ice sheet

Topographic Features

Elevations and depths are given in meters.

764 Depth of water
2278 Elevation above sea level
1700 Elevation below sea level
Mountain pass
Huo Shan 1774 Mountain peak/elevation

The highest elevation on each continent is underlined.
The highest elevation in each country is shown in boldface.

Transportation Features

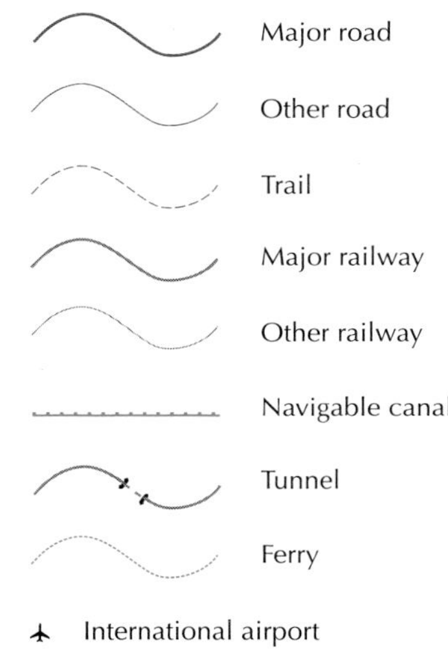

Major road
Other road
Trail
Major railway
Other railway
Navigable canal
Tunnel
Ferry
International airport
Other airport

Political Features

International Boundaries (First-order political unit)

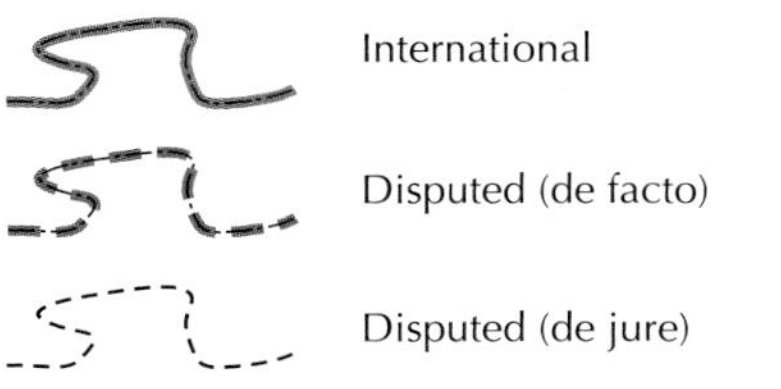

International
Disputed (de facto)
Disputed (de jure)
Indefinite/undefined
Demarcation line

Internal Boundaries

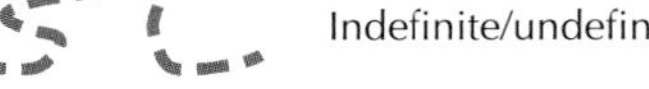

State/province

NORMANDIE Cultural/historic region
(Denmark) Administering country

Cities and Towns

The size of symbol and type indicates the relative importance of the locality.

LONDON
CHICAGO
Milwaukee
Tacna
Iquitos
Old Crow
Mettawa
Urban area

Capitals

MEXICO CITY / Bonn — Country, dependency
RIO DE JANEIRO / Perth — State, province
MANCHESTER / Chester — County

Cultural Features

National park
Point of interest
Wall
Ruins

State and Province Maps

Pages 84-91 and Pages 94-143

Capital
County seat
Military installation
Point of interest
Mountain peak
International boundary
State/province boundary
County boundary
Road
Railroad
Urban area

0 1000 2000 4000 6000 8000 10000 km

0 1000 2000 4000 6000 miles

Scale 1 : 90 000 000

Robinson Projection

ARCTIC OCEAN
PACIFIC OCEAN
INDIAN OCEAN
SOUTHERN OCEAN
RUSSIA
KAZAKSTAN
MONGOLIA
CHINA
INDIA
IRAN
TURKEY
SAUDI ARABIA
EGYPT
LIBYA
SUDAN
ETHIOPIA
CHAD
NIGER
ANGOLA
NAMIBIA
SOUTH AFRICA
MADAGASCAR
JAPAN
PHILIPPINES
MALAYSIA
INDONESIA
AUSTRALIA
NEW ZEALAND
MICRONESIA
MELANESIA
ENDERBY LAND
WILKES LAND
BEIJING
SHANGHAI
MOSKVA (MOSCOW)
TÔKYÔ
MANILA
JAKARTA
DELHI
CALCUTTA
MUMBAI
SYDNEY
MELBOURNE
Tropic of Cancer
Equator
Tropic of Capricorn
Arctic Circle
Antarctic Circle
of Greenwich

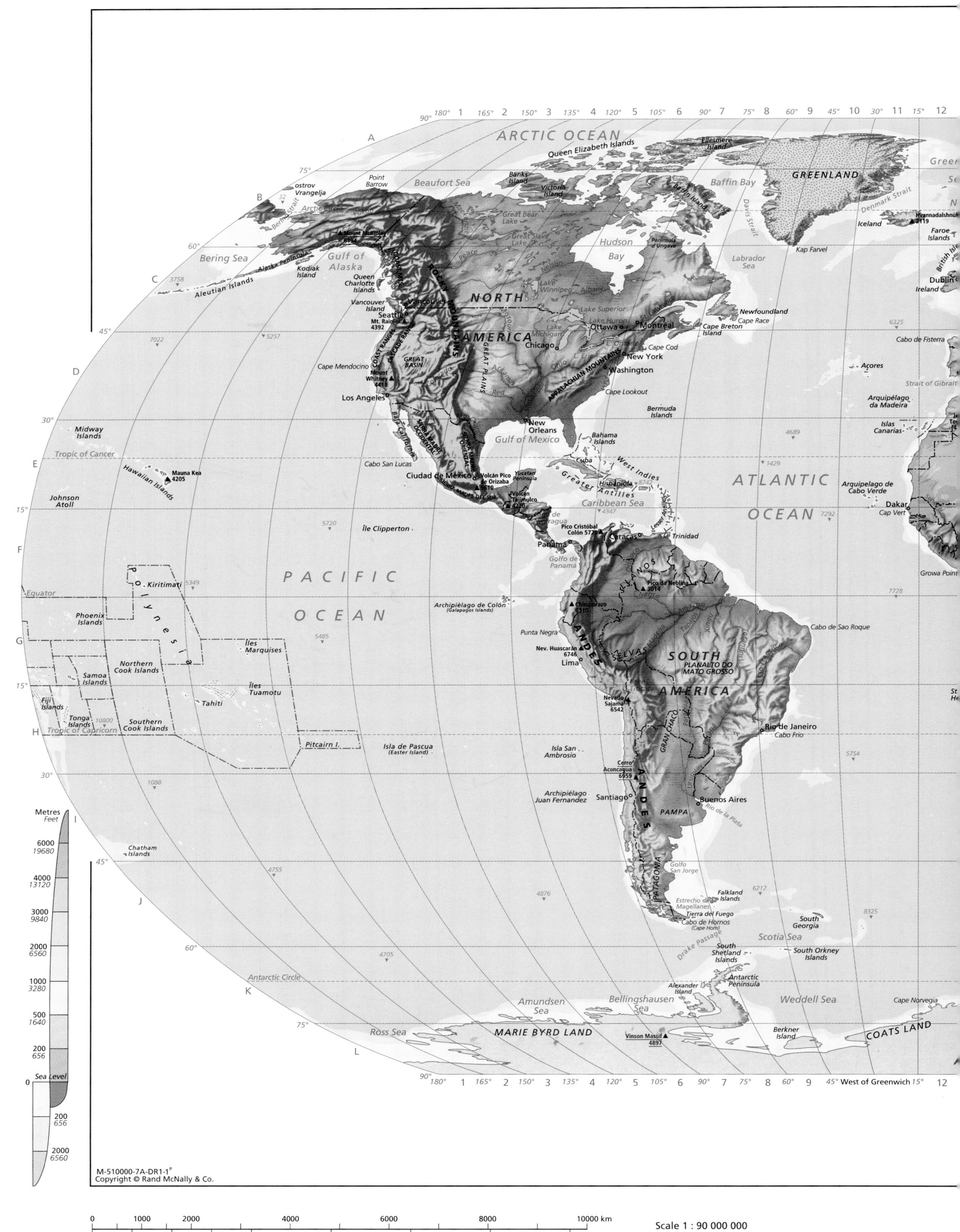

ARCTIC OCEAN
Queen Elizabeth Islands
Ellesmere Island
GREENLAND
Banks Island
Victoria Island
Beaufort Sea
Baffin Bay
Baffin Island
Davis Strait
Denmark Strait
Iceland
Hvannadalshnúkur 2119
Faroe Islands
Point Barrow
ostrov Vrangelja
Bering Strait
Arctic Circle
Mount McKinley 6194
Great Bear Lake
Great Slave Lake
Hudson Bay
Peninsula d'Ungava
Labrador Sea
Kap Farvel
Bering Sea
Alaska Peninsula
Gulf of Alaska
Kodiak Island
Aleutian Islands
Queen Charlotte Islands
Vancouver Island
Vancouver
Seattle
Mt. Rainier 4392
ROCKY MOUNTAINS
NORTH AMERICA
Lake Winnipeg
Lake Superior
Lake Huron
Lake Michigan
Ottawa
Montréal
Newfoundland
Cape Race
Cape Breton Island
Cape Cod
New York
Washington
Chicago
Dublin
Ireland
British Isles
Cabo de Fisterra
Açores
Strait of Gibraltar
Arquipélago da Madeira
Islas Canarias
Cape Mendocino
GREAT BASIN
Mount Whitney 4418
Los Angeles
GREAT PLAINS
APPALACHIAN MOUNTAINS
Cape Lookout
Bermuda Islands
New Orleans
Gulf of Mexico
Bahama Islands
Cuba
West Indies
Hispaniola
Greater Antilles
Caribbean Sea
Lesser Antilles
Trinidad
Midway Islands
Tropic of Cancer
Hawaiian Islands
Mauna Kea 4205
Johnson Atoll
Baja California
SIERRA MADRE OCCIDENTAL
SIERRA MADRE ORIENTAL
Cabo San Lucas
Ciudad de México
Volcán Pico de Orizaba 5610
Yucatan Peninsula
Volcán Tajumulco 4220
ATLANTIC OCEAN
Arquipelago de Cabo Verde
Dakar
Cap Vert
Île Clipperton
Pico Cristóbal Colón 5775
Caracas
Panamá
Golfo de Panamá
LLANOS
Pico da Neblina 3014
PACIFIC OCEAN
Kiritimati
Polynesia
Equator
Phoenix Islands
Archipiélago de Colón (Galapagos Islands)
Chimborazo 6310
Growa Point
Cabo de Sao Roque
Punta Negra
ANDES
Nev. Huascarán 6746
Lima
SELVAS
SOUTH AMERICA
PLANALTO DO MATO GROSSO
Îles Marquises
Northern Cook Islands
Samoa Islands
Îles Tuamotu
Tahiti
Fiji Islands
Tonga Islands
Southern Cook Islands
Tropic of Capricorn
Nevado Sajama 6542
GRAN CHACO
Rio de Janeiro
Cabo Frio
Pitcairn I.
Isla de Pascua (Easter Island)
Isla San Ambrosio
Cerro Aconcagua 6959
Archipiélago Juan Fernandez
Santiago
Buenos Aires
Rio de la Plata
PAMPA
Chatham Islands
PATAGONIA
Golfo San Jorge
Falkland Islands
Estrecho de Magellanes
Tierra del Fuego
Cabo de Hornos (Cape Horn)
South Georgia
Scotia Sea
Drake Passage
South Shetland Islands
South Orkney Islands
Antarctic Circle
Antarctic Peninsula
Alexander Island
Amundsen Sea
Bellingshausen Sea
Weddell Sea
Cape Norvegia
Ross Sea
MARIE BYRD LAND
Vinson Massif 4897
Berkner Island
COATS LAND
West of Greenwich
Metres
Feet
6000 19680
4000 13120
3000 9840
2000 6560
1000 3280
500 1640
200 656
Sea Level
200 656
2000 6560
M-510000-7A-DR1-1
Copyright © Rand McNally & Co.
0 1000 2000 4000 6000 8000 10000 km
0 1000 2000 4000 6000 miles
Scale 1 : 90 000 000
Robinson Projection

ARCTIC OCEAN
Barents Sea
Karskoe more
more Laptevyh
Vostočno-Sibirskoe more
Zemlja Franca-Iosefa
Severnaja Zemlja
Novosibirskie ostrova
Novaja Zemlja
Nordkapp
ZAPADNO-SIBIRSKAJA RAVNINA
URAL'SKIE GORY
Ekaterinburg
Moskva
SIBIR' (SIBERIA)
ASIA
Sea of Okhotsk
Bering Sea
ALTAI
Ulaanbaatar
GOBI
Beijing
Sea of Japan
Hokkaidō
Honshū
Tōkyō
Black Sea
Istanbul
Mediterranean Sea
Cyprus
El-Qahira
Tehran
TIEN SHAN
KUNLUN SHAN
HINDU KUSH
Qing Zang Gaoyuan
HIMALAYAS
Delhi
Shanghai
East China Sea
Yellow Sea
PACIFIC OCEAN
Tropic of Cancer
Taiwan
ARABIAN PENINSULA
AFRICA
Arabian Sea
Mumbai
Bay of Bengal
Krung Thep
INDOCHINA
South China Sea
Manila
Philippine Sea
Micronesia
Caroline Islands
Equator
Sri Lanka
Maldive Islands
Sumatera
BORNEO
Greater Sunda Islands
Jakarta
NEW GUINEA
Melanesia
Coral Sea
INDIAN OCEAN
MADAGASCAR
Mauritius
Reunion
AUSTRALIA
GREAT VICTORIA DESERT
GREAT DIVIDING RANGE
Sydney
Melbourne
Tasmania
Tasman Sea
Tropic of Capricorn
Cape Town
Cape of Good Hope
Île Amsterdam
Îles Kerguélen
Heard Island
SOUTHERN OCEAN
Macquarie Island
Antarctic Circle
ENDERBY LAND
WILKES LAND
VICTORIA LAND
Ross Sea
MAUD LAND

GREENLAND SEA
ICELAND
Reykjavík
Akureyri
Ísafjörður
Seydisfjördur
Hvannadalshnúkur 2119
Arctic Circle
NORWEGIAN SEA
ATLANTIC OCEAN
FAROE ISLANDS (Den.)
Tórshavn
SHETLAND ISLANDS (U.K.)
ORKNEY ISLANDS
Rockall (U.K.)
HEBRIDES
NORWAY
VESTERÅLEN
LOFOTEN
Bodø
Mo i Rana
Namsos
Trondheim
Kristiansund
Ålesund
Molde
Galdhøpiggen 2469
JOTUNHEIMEN
Bergen
Haugesund
Stavanger
OSLO
Drammen
Skien
Kristiansand
Lindesnes
Skagerrak
Kattegat
Göteborg
DENMARK
Ålborg
Århus
Esbjerg
Odense
Flensburg
KØBENHAVN (COPENHAGEN)
Malmö
Helsingborg
Halmstad
Bornholm (Den.)
NORTH SEA
UNITED KINGDOM
Inverness
Aberdeen
Dundee
GLASGOW
EDINBURGH
Londonderry
Belfast
Carlisle
NEWCASTLE UPON TYNE
Middlesbrough
LEEDS
LIVERPOOL
MANCHESTER
Sheffield
Leicester
Nottingham
BIRMINGHAM
Norwich
Ipswich
Oxford
Swansea
Cardiff
Bristol
LONDON
Dover
Southampton
Plymouth
Brighton
Land's End
ISLES OF SCILLY
IRELAND
Sligo
Galway
DUBLIN
Limerick
Cork
Waterford
Mizen Head
Irish Sea
CELTIC SEA
English Channel
Strait of Dover
CHANNEL ISLANDS (U.K.)
NETHERLANDS
Groningen
AMSTERDAM
's-Gravenhage
ROTTERDAM
Utrecht
ANTWERPEN
BRUXELLES
BELGIUM
LUXEMBOURG
Luxembourg
GERMANY
HAMBURG
Bremen
Bremerhaven
Kiel
Lübeck
Hannover
BERLIN
Münster
ESSEN
Dortmund
DÜSSELDORF
KÖLN
Bonn
Magdeburg
Leipzig
Dresden
Chemnitz
Erfurt
Wiesbaden
FRANKFURT AM MAIN
MANNHEIM
Würzburg
Nürnberg
Saarbrücken
STUTTGART
Regensburg
Augsburg
MÜNCHEN
Szczecin
Bydgoszcz
Poznań
Wrocław
PRAHA
CZECH REPUBLIC
Plzeň
Brno
Linz
WIEN (VIENNA)
AUSTRIA
Salzburg
Innsbruck
Graz
Klagenfurt
Győr
SWITZERLAND
Bern
Zürich
Basel
Lausanne
Genève
LIECH.
Vaduz
FRANCE
PARIS
LILLE
Amiens
Le Havre
Rouen
Cherbourg
Caen
Brest
Saint-Malo
Rennes
Le Mans
Angers
Nantes
Orléans
Tours
Reims
Metz
Nancy
Strasbourg
Mulhouse
Dijon
Besançon
Poitiers
La Rochelle
Limoges
Bourges
Clermont-Ferrand
LYON
Saint-Étienne
Grenoble
Bordeaux
Toulouse
Montpellier
Nîmes
Avignon
MARSEILLE
Toulon
Nice
Perpignan
MONACO
Mont Blanc 4807
ALPS
Bay of Biscay
PYRENEES
ANDORRA
Andorra la Vella
SPAIN
MADRID
A Coruña
Gijón
Oviedo
Santander
Bilbao
Donostia
Vigo
Ourense
León
Burgos
Valladolid
Salamanca
Segovia
Zaragoza
Pamplona
Lleida
BARCELONA
Tarragona
Castelló de la Plana
VALÈNCIA
Toledo
Badajoz
Albacete
Córdoba
Sevilla
Granada
Jaén
Murcia
Elx
Alacant
Cartagena
Cádiz
Málaga
Huelva
Mulhacén 3482
ILLES BALEARS (BALEARIC ISLANDS)
Mallorca
Palma de Mallorca
Menorca
Eivissa
PORTUGAL
LISBOA
Porto
Braga
Coimbra
Setúbal
Évora
Faro
Cabo de São Vicente
Cabo de Finisterra
GIBRALTAR (U.K.)
Strait of Gibraltar
ITALY
TORINO
MILANO
Brescia
Verona
Padova
Venezia (Venice)
GENOVA
Parma
Bologna
La Spezia
Pisa
Firenze
Livorno
SAN MARINO
Perugia
Ancona
Pescara
VATICAN CITY
ROMA (ROME)
NAPOLI
Salerno
Foggia
Bari
Brindisi
Taranto
Cosenza
Catanzaro
Reggio di Calabria
Messina
Palermo
Catania
Siracusa
Agrigento
Trapani
SICILIA (SICILY)
Monte Etna 3323
CORSE (CORSICA) (Fr.)
Bastia
Ajaccio
SARDEGNA (SARDINIA) (It.)
Sassari
Olbia
Nuoro
Cagliari
LIGURIAN SEA
TYRRHENIAN SEA
ADRIATIC SEA
APENNINO
SLOVENIA
Ljubljana
Trieste
CROATIA
Zagreb
Rijeka
Zadar
Split
BOSNIA HERZEGOVINA
Dubrovnik
MALTA
Valletta
MEDITERRANEAN SEA
MOROCCO
CASABLANCA
Rabat
Salé
Tanger
Tétouan
Larache
El-Jadida
Safi
Essaouira
Meknès
Fès
Oujda
Khouribga
Marrakech
Agadir
Jebel Toubkal 4165
Beni-Mellal
Er-Rachidia
ATLAS MOUNTAINS
Ceuta (Sp.)
Melilla (Sp.)
Al Hoceima
ALGERIA
EL DJAZAÏR (ALGIERS)
Wahran
Mestghanem
Sidi bel Abbès
Ech Cheliff
Tizi-Ouzou
Bejaïa
Skikda
Annaba
Qacentina
Setif
Batna
Tebessa
Beskra
Laghouat
TUNISIA
Tunis
Bizerte
Kairouan
Sousse
Sfax
Gafsa
Isola di Pantelleria (It.)
Isole Pelagie (It.)
West of Greenwich
East of Greenwich
D-550000-2A-DR1-1
Copyright © Rand McNally & Co.
Scale 1 : 15 000 000
Equidistant Conic Projection
1600 km
1000 miles

BARENTS SEA
OSTROV KOLGUEV
Poluostrov Kanin
Murmansk
KOL'SKIJ POLUOSTROV
BELOE MORE
Arhangel'sk
Severodvinsk
FINLAND
HELSINKI
Gulf of Finland
SANKT-PETERBURG (ST. PETERSBURG)
Ladožskoe ozero
Onežskoe ozero
Petrozavodsk
Tallinn
ESTONIA
Lake Peipus
RIGA
LATVIA
LITHUANIA
Vilnius
MINSK
BELARUS
Smolensk
MOSKVA (MOSCOW)
Tver'
Jaroslavl'
Vologda
Rybinskoe vodohranilišče
Nižnij Novgorod (Gor'kij)
Kazan'
Kirov
Perm'
Iževsk
Ufa
Samara
Saratov
Volgograd
Astrahan'
RUSSIA
URAL'SKIE GORY (URAL MOUNTAINS)
ZAPADNO-SIBIRSKAJA RAVNINA
Ekaterinburg
Čeljabinsk
Tjumen'
Surgut
Orenburg
Magnitogorsk
Orsk
KAZAKSTAN
Aral Sea
UZBEKISTAN
TURKMENISTAN
CASPIAN DEPRESSION (PRIKASPIJSKAJA NIZMENNOST')
CASPIAN SEA
KYÏV (KIEV)
UKRAINE
Kharkiv
Dnipropetrovs'k
Donets'k
Odesa
Rostov-na-Donu
Sea of Azov
KRYMS'KYI PIVOSTRIV
Sevastopol'
Simferopol'
MOLDOVA
Chişinău
CARPATHIAN MOUNTAINS
ROMANIA
BUCUREŞTI
BULGARIA
SOFIJA
BLACK SEA
CAUCASUS
GEORGIA
Tbilisi
ARMENIA
Yerevan
AZERBAIJAN
Baki
Groznyj
Mahačkala
TURKEY
ANKARA
İstanbul
İzmir
ANATOLIA
TOROS DAĞLARI
KURDISTAN
MESOPOTAMIA
SYRIA
IRAQ
BAGHDAD
IRAN
TEHRĀN
RESHTEH-YE KŪHHĀ-YE ALBORZ
KŪHHĀ-YE ZĀGROS
Eşfahān
GREECE
ATHINAI (ATHENS)
AEGEAN SEA
KRITI (CRETE)
NORTH CYPRUS
CYPRUS
Nicosia
LEBANON
Arctic Circle

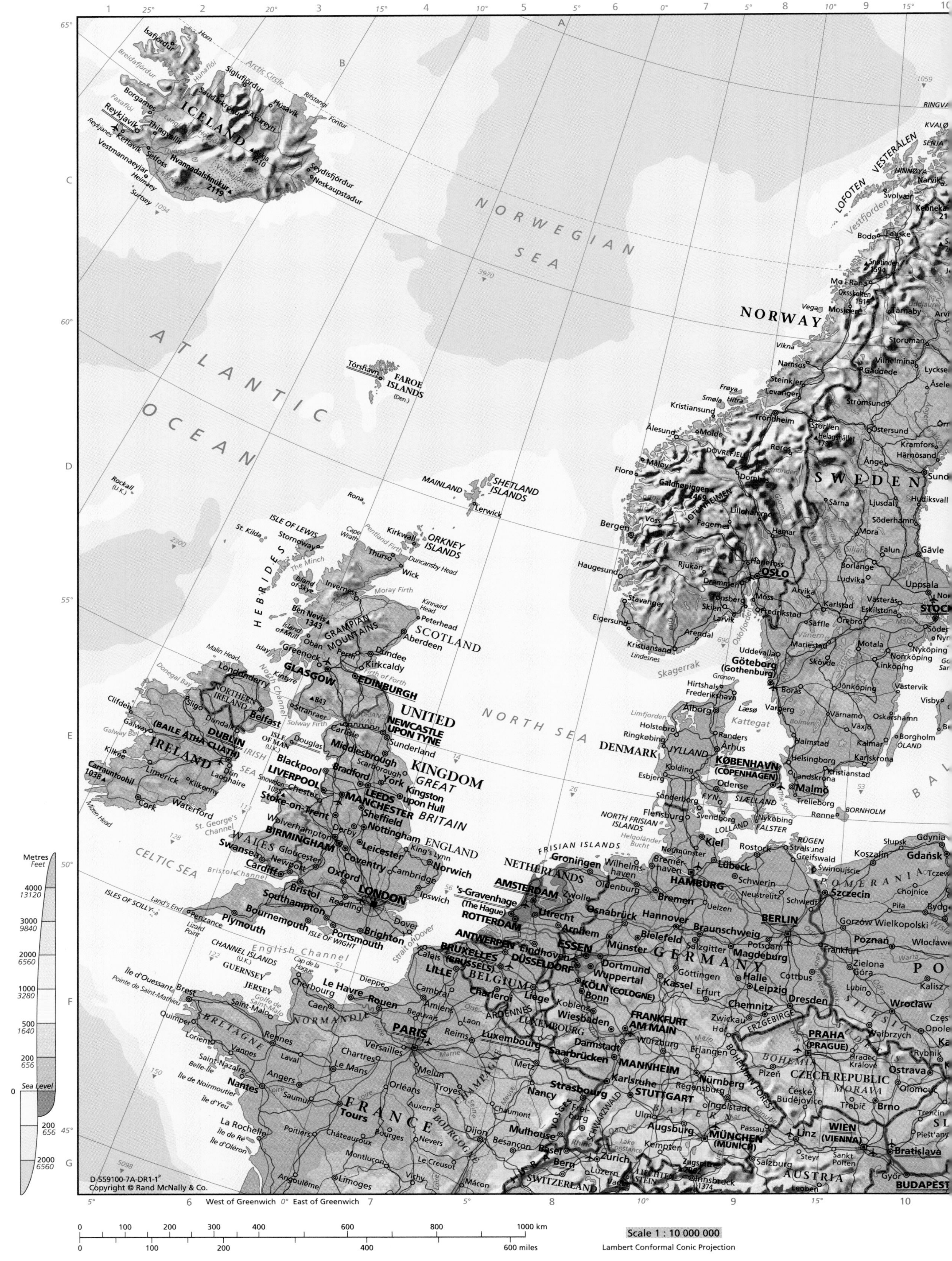

0 100 200 300 400 600 800 1000 km
0 100 200 400 600 miles

Scale 1 : 10 000 000

Lambert Conformal Conic Projection

BARENTS SEA
BELOE MORE
FINLAND
ESTONIA
LATVIA
LITHUANIA
BELARUS
UKRAINE
RUSSIA
MOLDOVA
ROMANIA
KAZAKSTAN
MOSKVA (MOSCOW)
SANKT-PETERBURG (SAINT PETERSBURG)
HELSINKI
Tallinn
RIGA
Vilnius
MINSK
KYÏV (KIEV)
KOL'SKIJ POLUOSTROV
KARELIJA
KOMI
TIMANSKIJ KRJAŽ
SEVERNYE UVALY
URAL'SKIE GORY (URAL MOUNTAINS)
ZAPADNO-SIBIRSKAJA RAVNINA
VALDAJSKAJA VOZVYŠENNOST'
SREDNERUSSKAJA VOZVYŠENNOST'
PRIVOLŽSKAJA VOZVYŠENNOST'
PRIPET MARSHES
DONSKAJA GRJADA
Caspian Depression (Prikaspijskaja nizmennost')
CASPIAN SEA
Sea of Azov
KALMYKIJA
TATARIJA
UDMURTIJA
MORDOVIJA
DAGESTAN
Arkhangel'sk
Murmansk
Petrozavodsk
Vologda
Jaroslavl'
NIŽNIJ NOVGOROD (GOR'KIJ)
KAZAN'
SAMARA (KUIBYŠEV)
SARATOV
VOLGOGRAD
ROSTOV-NA-DONU
Voronež
KHARKIV
DNIPROPETROVS'K
DONETS'K
Kirov
Syktyvkar
PERM'
Ufa

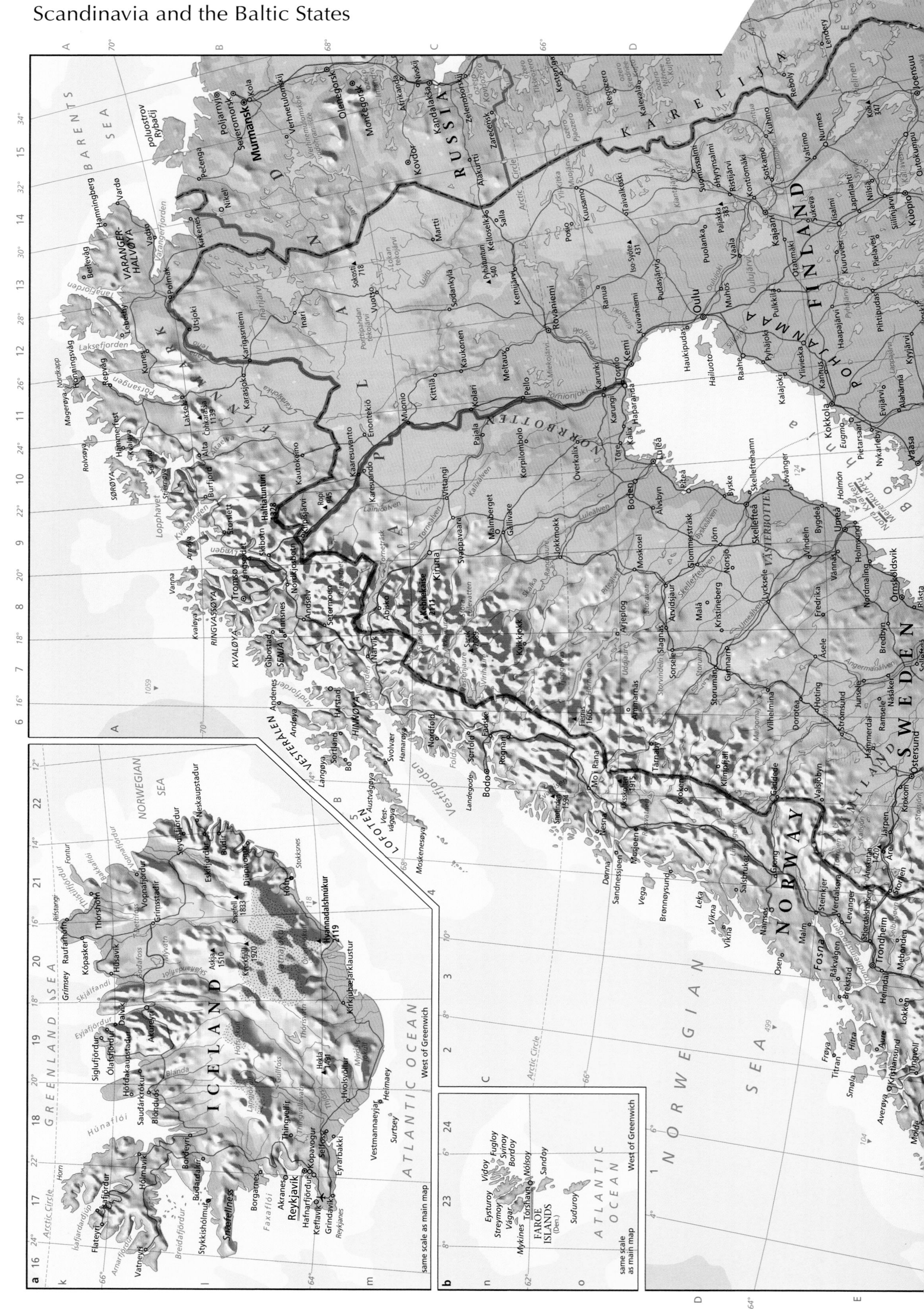
BARENTS SEA
RUSSIA
KARELIJA
FINLAND
POHJANMAA
NORRBOTTEN
VÄSTERBOTTEN
SWEDEN
NORWAY
NORWEGIAN SEA
LOFOTEN
VESTERÅLEN
Murmansk
Oulu
Trondheim
Bodø
Tromsø
Hammerfest
Kiruna
Luleå
Kemi
Tornio
Haparanda
Rovaniemi
Umeå
Östersund
Arctic Circle
ICELAND
GREENLAND SEA
NORWEGIAN SEA
ATLANTIC OCEAN
Reykjavík
Akureyri
Vatnajökull
Hvannadalshnúkur 2119
same scale as main map
West of Greenwich
FAROE ISLANDS (Den.)
Tórshavn
ATLANTIC OCEAN

Scale 1 : 5 000 000

Lambert Conformal Conic Projection

0 50 100 150 200 300 400 500 km

0 50 100 200 300 miles

East of Greenwich

Metres	Feet
2000	6560
1000	3280
500	1640
200	656
Sea Level	0
200	656
2000	6560

SHETLAND ISLANDS (U.K.)
Unst
Fetlar
Yell
Whalsay
St. Magnus Bay
MAINLAND
Lerwick
Bressay
Foula
To Tórshavn
ATLANTIC OCEAN
Fair Isle
NORTH SEA
Westray
Rousay
Sanday
Stronsay
MAINLAND
Kirkwall
ORKNEY ISLANDS
Hoy
South Ronaldsay
Pentland firth
Thurso
Duncansby Head
John o' Groats
West of Greenwich
To Lerwick
To Bressay
ORKNEY ISLANDS
Pentland Firth
Flannan Islands
St. Kilda
OUTER HEBRIDES
Butt of Lewis
Stornoway
ISLE OF LEWIS
Cape Wrath
Durness
The Minch
Ben More Assynt 998
Lochinver
Helmsdale
Brora
Dornoch
Wick
North Uist
Benbecula
South Uist
Lochboisdale
Barra
The Little Minch
Ullapool
Portree
ISLAND OF SKYE
Kyle of Lochalsh
Dingwall
Moray Firth
Nairn
Elgin
Portsoy
Kinnaird Head
Fraserburgh
Peterhead
Inverness
SCOTLAND
Loch Ness
Ben Macdui 1309
Aberdeen
Sea of the Hebrides
Rum
Mallaig
Eigg
Coll
Fort William
Ben Nevis 1343
NORTHWEST HIGHLANDS
GRAMPIAN MOUNTAINS
Stonehaven
Montrose
INNER HEBRIDES
Tiree
ISLAND OF MULL
Tobermory
Oban
Inveraray
Firth of Lorn
Dundee
Arbroath
Perth
St. Andrews
Glenrothes
Fife Ness
Colonsay
Kirkcaldy
Dunfermline
Firth of Forth
JURA
ISLAY
Greenock
Port Ellen
Kintyre
GLASGOW
EDINBURGH
GREAT
Motherwell
Kilmarnock
Galashiels
Berwick-upon-Tweed
Alnwick
ISLAND OF ARRAN
Firth of Clyde
Campbeltown
Ayr
Moffat
SOUTHERN UPLANDS
Rathlin Island
Malin Head
GIANT'S CAUSEWAY
North Channel
Girvan
Merrick 843
Dumfries
Stranraer
Gatehouse of Fleet
Solway Firth
HADRIAN'S WALL
UNITED
NEWCASTLE UPON TYNE
Sunderland
Hartlepool
Aran Island
Errigal Mountain 752
Buncrana
Coleraine
Londonderry
Ballymena
Larne
Strabane
Rocky Point
Donegal
NORTHERN IRELAND
ULSTER
Lough Neagh
Omagh
Donegal Bay
Erris Head
Ballina
Belfast
Bangor
Sligo
Portadown
Achill Head
Lough Conn
Castlebar
Clew Bay
Carrick on Shannon
Newry
Downpatrick
Carlisle
Penrith
Lake District
Scafell Pikes 978
Whitehaven
Durham
Middlesbrough
Darlington
ISLE OF MAN (U.K.)
Douglas
Kendal
Barrow-in-Furness
Scarborough
KINGDOM
Bridlington
Ripon
York
CONNAUGHT
Mweelrea 817
Clifden
Roscommon
Longford
Dundalk
Ballieborough
Dundalk Bay
Drogheda
Morecambe Bay
Lancaster
Blackpool
LEEDS
Galway
Lough Corrib
Lough Ree
Athlone
Royal Canal
IRISH SEA
Preston
Bradford
Kingston upon Hull
Galway Bay
ARAN ISLANDS
IRELAND
Grand Canal
DUBLIN (BAILE ÁTHA CLIATH)
Huddersfield
CLIFFS OF MOHER
Ennistimon
Kildare
Port Laoise
Dun Laoghaire
ANGLESEY
LIVERPOOL
Bolton
MANCHESTER
BRITAIN
Grimsby
Loop Head
Kilkee
Lough Derg
LEINSTER
WICKLOW MOUNTAINS 924
Holyhead
Bangor
Snowdon 1085
Sheffield
ENGLAND
Limerick
Caernarfon
Wrexham
Chester
Stoke-on-Trent
Lincoln
Wicklow
Mouth of the Shannon
Shannon
Carlow
Newcastle West
Kilkenny
Arklow
Pwllheli
Mansfield
Nottingham
Skegness
MUNSTER
Tralee
Braich y Pwll
Stafford
Derby
Boston
The Wash
Cromer
Dingle Bay
Clonmel
Enniscorthy
Cardigan Bay
Telford
Killarney
Mallow
Wexford
Shrewsbury
Leicester
King's Lynn
Norwich
Cahirciveen
Carrauntoohil 1038
Blackwater
Waterford
Aberystwyth
Wolverhampton
Walsall
BIRMINGHAM
Peterborough
Great Yarmouth
Kenmare
Rosslare
Dungarvan
New Quay
Coventry
Lowestoft
Bantry
Cork
Carnsore Point
St. George's Channel
Cardigan
Builth Wells
Dudley
Northampton
Ely
Bury Saint Edmunds
Bantry Bay
Youghal
Fishguard
CAMBRIAN MOUNTAINS
Hereford
Worcester
Banbury
Bedford
Skull
Kinsale
Old Head of Kinsale
St. David's Head
Llandovery
WALES
Cambridge
Ipswich
Mizen Head
Carmarthen
Milford Haven
Pembroke
Merthyr Tydfil
Gloucester
Cheltenham
Milton Keynes
Colchester
Harwich
Swansea
Port Talbot
Newport
Oxford
Luton
Harlow
Clacton-on-Sea
CELTIC SEA
Cardiff
Bristol
Swindon
LONDON
Chelmsford
Bristol Channel
Slough
Southend-on-Sea
Lundy
Weston-super-Mare
Bath
Reading
Basingstoke
Guildford
Canterbury
Ramsgate
Barnstaple
Bridgwater
STONEHENGE
Bude
Taunton
Winchester
Reigate
Crawley
Folkestone
Dover
Strait of Dover
Oostende
Southampton
Worthing
Brighton
Hastings
Calais
Exeter
Bournemouth
Newquay
CORNWALL
Plymouth
Dorchester
Lyme Bay
Poole
Weymouth
Portsmouth
Eastbourne
Saint-Omer
Redruth
Saint Austell
Torquay
Bill of Portland
ISLE OF WIGHT
Boulogne-sur-Mer
COLLINES DE L'ARTOIS
LILLE
Penzance
Land's End
Falmouth
Start Point
Berck
Lens
Arras
ISLES OF SCILLY
Lizard Point
English Channel
Abbeville
Albert
Dieppe
Amiens
Alderney
Cap de la Hague
Pointe de Barfleur
Fécamp
Cherbourg
Baie de la Seine
Bolbec
Yvetot
Neufchâtel-en-Bray
GUERNSEY (U.K.)
St. Peter Port
CHANNEL ISLANDS
Sark
Le Havre
Rouen
Beauvais
Compiègne
ATLANTIC
Carentan
Bayeux
St. Helier
JERSEY (U.K.)
Caen
Lisieux
Creil
Coutances
Saint-Lô
Sillon de Talbert
NORMANDIE
ÎLE-DE-FRANCE
Golfe de Saint-Malo
Évreux
Saint-Denis
Saint-Pol-de-Léon
Lannion
Vire
Versailles
PARIS
Île d'Ouessant
Landerneau
Morlaix
Granville
Argentan
Brest
Guingamp
Saint-Malo
LE MONT-SAINT-MICHEL
Dreux
Pointe de Saint-Mathieu
Saint-Brieuc
Dinan
COLLINES DU PERCHE
Rambouillet
Corbeil-Essonnes
Iroise
Douarnenez
Loudéac
Fougères
Alençon
Melun
OCEAN
Pointe du Raz
Châteaulin
BRETAGNE
Rennes
Vitré
Mayenne
Nogent-le-Rotrou
Chartres
Étampes
Quimper
MAINE
Concarneau
Quimperlé
Mauron
Laval
Châteaudun
Pointe de Penmarc'h
Hennebont
Sablé-sur-Sarthe
Le Mans
Montargis
Lorient
Vannes
Châteaubriant
Vendôme
Île de Groix
Carnac
Redon
Orléans
Quiberon
Muzillac
Segré
La Flèche
Le Palais
Blain
Angers
Blois
Belle-Île
Saint-Nazaire
Tours
FRANCE
La Baule-Escoublac
Loire
Romorantin-Lanthenay
Salbris
ANJOU
Nantes
Saumur
Cholet
TOURAINE
Vierzon
Noirmoutier
Île de Noirmoutier
Rezé
Machecoul
Thouars
Ligueil
Bourges
Saint-Jean-de-Monts
Châtellerault
Châteauroux
Issoudun
Bressuire
Île d'Yeu
To Santander, Barakaldo
West of Greenwich 0° East of Greenwich
Metres Feet
3000 9840
2000 6560
1000 3280
500 1640
200 656
Sea Level
0
200 656
2000 6560
D-559594-7A-DR1-1
Copyright © Rand McNally & Co.
0 50 100 150 200 300 400 500 km
0 50 100 200 300 miles
Scale 1 : 5 000 000
Lambert Conformal Conic Projection

NORWAY
SWEDEN
DENMARK
GERMANY
POLAND
CZECH REPUBLIC
AUSTRIA
SWITZERLAND
NETHERLANDS
SLOVAKIA
HUNGARY
SLOVENIA
CROATIA
ITALY
LIECHTENSTEIN
BALTIC SEA
Skagerrak
Kattegat
Deutsche Bucht
FRISIAN ISLANDS
OSTFRIESISCHE INSELN
WADDENEILANDEN
NORTH FRISIAN ISLANDS
JYLLAND
FYN
SJÆLLAND
BORNHOLM (Den.)
GOTLAND
ÖLAND
RÜGEN
USEDOM
SKÅNE
SMÅLAND
HALLAND
BLEKINGE
VÄSTERGÖTLAND
ÖSTERGÖTLAND
VORPOMMERN
MECKLENBURG
POMERANIA
SILESIA
SAXONY
BOHEMIA
MORAVA
SUDETES
HARZ
THÜRINGER WALD
ORE MOUNTAINS
BOHEMIAN FOREST
SCHWARZWALD (BLACK FOREST)
VOSGES
ARDENNES
EIFEL
HUNSRÜCK
FRANKEN
SCHWABEN
CARPATHIAN MTS.
HOHE TAUERN
NIEDERE TAUERN
CARNIC ALPS
RHAETIAN ALPS
KØBENHAVN (COPENHAGEN)
BERLIN
PRAHA (PRAGUE)
WIEN (VIENNA)
Bratislava
Luxembourg
Bern
Göteborg (Gothenburg)
HAMBURG
MÜNCHEN (MUNICH)
FRANKFURT AM MAIN
KÖLN (COLOGNE)
DÜSSELDORF
ESSEN
STUTTGART
MANNHEIM
Bremen
Hannover
Leipzig
Dresden
Szczecin
Poznań
Wrocław
Gdańsk
Gdynia
Malmö
Kiel
Lübeck
Rostock
Nürnberg
Bonn

ATLANTIC OCEAN
UNITED KINGDOM
LONDON
Southampton
Bournemouth
Plymouth
Brighton
Portsmouth
Dover
ISLES OF SCILLY
Land's End
Penzance
Lizard Point
ISLE OF WIGHT
English Channel
Strait of Dover
CHANNEL ISLANDS
GUERNSEY
JERSEY
NETHERLANDS
Arnhem
ANTWERPEN
BRUXELLES (BRUSSEL)
Eindhoven
ESSEN
DÜSSELDORF
Dortmund
Wuppertal
KÖLN (COLOGNE)
Münster
Bielefeld
Salzgitter
Magdeburg
Halle
Leipzig
Göttingen
Kassel
Erfurt
Chemnitz
Zwickau
Hof
LILLE
BELGIUM
Charleroi
Liège
Calais
Cambrai
Amiens
Bonn
Koblenz
Wiesbaden
FRANKFURT AM MAIN
GERMANY
ARDENNES
LUX.
Luxembourg
Saarbrücken
Darmstadt
MANNHEIM
Würzburg
Erlangen
Nürnberg
Karlsruhe
Regensburg
Ingolstadt
STUTTGART
Ulm
Augsburg
BAYERN
MÜNCHEN (MUNICH)
Passau
SCHWARZWALD
Freiburg
Kempten
Zugspitze 2962
Innsbruck
Cherbourg
Cap de la Hague
Le Havre
Dieppe
Rouen
Caen
Beauvais
Laon
Golfe de Saint-Malo
Saint-Malo
NORMANDIE
Brest
Île d'Ouessant
Pointe de Saint-Mathieu
Quimper
BRETAGNE
Rennes
Lorient
Vannes
Laval
PARIS
Versailles
Reims
Metz
Nancy
Strasbourg
VOSGES
Chartres
Le Mans
Melun
Troyes
CHAMPAGNE
Angers
Saint-Nazaire
Belle-Île
Nantes
Île de Noirmoutier
Orléans
Auxerre
Chaumont
Mulhouse
Basel
Saumur
Tours
Bourges
Dijon
Besançon
Zürich
Bern
Luzern
Île d'Yeu
BOURGOGNE
Châteauroux
Nevers
Poitiers
La Rochelle
Île de Ré
Île d'Oléron
FRANCE
Montluçon
Le Creusot
Mâcon
Lausanne
SWITZERLAND
Lake Geneva
Genève
LIECHTENSTEIN
Vaduz
Limoges
Angoulême
Clermont-Ferrand
Vichy
Bay of Biscay
Bordeaux
Arcachon
Périgueux
Brive-la-Gaillarde
Saint-Étienne
LYON
Mont Blanc 4807
Chambéry
Aosta
Dufourspitze 4637
Novara
Bergamo
Brescia
Verona
Venezia (Venice)
Trento
Bolzano
Udine
Belluno
Trieste
DOLOMITI
MASSIF CENTRAL
Aurillac
Valence
Grenoble
Barre des Écrins 4102
TORINO
MILANO
Pavia
Padova
Piacenza
Parma
Ferrara
Bologna
Mont-de-Marsan
Agen
Montauban
CÉVENNES
1753
3841
Cuneo
GENOVA
La Spezia
Módena
Ravenna
Rimini
Bayonne
Pau
Toulouse
Lourdes
Carcassonne
Montpellier
Nîmes
Avignon
Alès
PROVENCE
Aix-en-Provence
Savona
Imperia
San Remo
MONACO
Nice
Cannes
LIGURIAN SEA
Pisa
Livorno
Prato
Firenze (Florence)
Siena
Forlì
SAN MARINO
Arezzo
Perugia
LANGUEDOC
Narbonne
MARSEILLE
Toulon
Golfe du Lion
Perpignan
Cap de Creus
PYRENEES
ANDORRA
Pico de Aneto 3404
Andorra la Vella
CATALUNYA
Girona
Mataró
Sabadell
BARCELONA
Tarragona
Lleida
Huesca
A Coruña
Cabo Ortegal
Santiago de Compostela
Cabo de Fisterra
Gijón
Oviedo
Lugo
Santander
Bilbao
Donostia
Gasteiz
Pamplona
Logroño
GALICIA
CORDILLERA CANTÁBRICA
León
Vigo
Ourense
Ponferrada
Burgos
Palencia
Braga
Bragança
Porto
Douro
Zamora
Valladolid
Soria
Zaragoza
SISTEMA IBÉRICO
Aveiro
Coimbra
Guarda
Salamanca
Segovia
Ávila
SERRA DA ESTRELA
Estrela 1993
PORTUGAL
Castelo Branco
Plasencia
SISTEMA CENTRAL
Guadalajara
Alcalá de Henares
MADRID
Getafe
Santarém
Tagus
Toledo
Teruel
Cuenca
Tortosa
LISBOA (LISBON)
Cáceres
Mérida
Badajoz
SPAIN
Setúbal
Évora
Guadiana
Ciudad Real
Castelló de la Plana
Golf de València
VALÈNCIA
Puertollano
LA MANCHA
Albacete
Beja
SIERRA MORENA
Córdoba
Linares
MALLORCA
MENORCA
Palma de Mallorca
Artà
Maó
EIVISSA
Eivissa
Formentera
ILLES BALEARS (BALEARIC ISLANDS) (Sp.)
Cap de la Nau
Portimão
Cabo de São Vicente
Faro
ALGARVE
Huelva
Sevilla
Guadalquivir
Golfo de Cádiz
ANDALUCÍA
Jaén
Elx
Alacant
Murcia
CORDILLERA PENIBÉTICA
Cádiz
Jerez de la Frontera
Granada
Mulhacén 3482
SIERRA NEVADA
Lorca
Cartagena
Cabo de Palos
Algeciras
GIBRALTAR (U.K.)
Málaga
Almería
Strait of Gibraltar
Tanger
Ceuta (Sp.)
Tétouan
Larache
Al-Hoceima
Isla de Alborán (Sp.)
Mestghanem
Wahran (Oran)
Melilla (Sp.)
Kénitra
Salé
Rabat
Ouezzane
Taounate
Taza
Meknès
Fès
Taourirt
Berkane
Oujda
Jerada
Guercif
Berguent
Tilimsen
Sidi bel Abbès
Saïda
Mouaskar
Ech Cheliff
EL DJAZAÏR (ALGIERS)
El Boulaïda
Tizi-Ouzou
Bouïra
Bejaïa
Skikda
Cap de Fer
Annaba
Bizerte
La Galite
TUNIS
Carthage
Nabeul
Hammamet
Golfe de Tunis
Cap Bon
Béja
Guelma
Qacentina
Sétif
ATLAS TELLIEN
ATLAS MOUNTAINS
Tihert
Batna
Chott el Hodna
Bou Saâda
Aïn el Beïda
Khenchla
Tbessa
El Kef
Kairouan
Sousse
Monastir
Mokníne
Golfe de Hammamet
Jebel Chambi 1544
Kasserine
MOROCCO
MOYEN ATLAS
Khenifra
Oued-Zem
Chott ech Chergui
HAUTS PLATEAUX
Aflou
El Djelfa
Beskra
Awled Djellal
Oued Djedi
Chott Melrhir
Chott Merouane
TUNISIA
Sfax
Gafsa
Tozeur
Nefta
ÎLES KERKENNA
Golfe de Gabès
Gabès
Île de Jerba
Chott Jerid
Douz
Médenine
Azilal
HAUT ATLAS
Jbel Irhil M'Goun 4071
Er-Rachidia
Bouârfa
Figuig
El Beyyadh
ATLAS SAHARIEN
Djebel Aissa 2235
Laghouat
Djamâa
El Wad
Touggourt
El Grara
Berriyyane
Ghardaïa
Béchar
Erfoud
Zagora
HAMMADA DU GUIR
Abadla
ALGERIA
Wargla
Hassi Messaoud
GRAND ERG OCCIDENTAL
Béni Abbas
El Menia
El Agreb
GRAND ERG ORIENTAL
Tabelbala
Kerzaz
Timimoun
Charouine
Oued Mia
Oued Saoura
Sba
Adrar
PLATEAU DU TADEMAÏT
In Belbel
Titaf
Foggaret ez Zoua
In Salah
Aoulef
Reggane
Chenachane
Hassi Bel Guebbour
PLATEAU DU TINGHERT
Ohanet
Bordj Omar Idriss
I-n-Amenas
Tiguentourine
Ghadāmis
Dirj
Sināwin
Nālūt
Jādū
Mizdah
Yafran
Gharyān
Al-'Azīzīyah
Az-Zāwiyah
Zuwārah
Ţarābulus (Tripoli)
JEFFARA
AL-JIFARAH
JABAL NAFŪSAH
Remada
Al-Qaryah ash-Sharqīyah
AL-HAMĀDAH AL-HAMRĀ'
HAMĀDAT TINGHERT
Emgayet
CORSE (CORSICA) (Fr.)
Cap Corse
Bastia
Monte Cinto 2706
Ajaccio
Porto-Vecchio
Strait of Bonifacio
Isola d'Elba
Grosseto
ITALY
Terni
L'Aquila
Viterbo
Civitavecchia
ROMA (ROME)
VATICAN CITY
Latina
Sassari
Olbia
Alghero
SARDEGNA (SARDINIA) (It.)
Nuoro
Punta La Marmora 1834
Oristano
Iglesias
Cagliari
Capo Teulada
TYRRHENIAN SEA
MEDITERRANEAN
Isola di Ustica
Trapani
Palermo
ISOLE EGADI
Caltanissetta
Agrigento
Isola di Pantelleria (It.)
ISOLE PELAGIE (It.)
Metres Feet
4000 13120
3000 9840
2000 6560
1000 3280
500 1640
200 656
Sea Level
0
200 656
2000 6560
D-556400-7A-DR1-1
Copyright © Rand McNally & Co.
West of Greenwich 0° East of Greenwich
0 100 200 300 400 600 800 1000 km
0 100 200 400 600 miles
Scale 1 : 10 000 000
Lambert Conformal Conic Projection

POLAND
WARSZAWA (WARSAW)
Łódź
Kraków
Wrocław
Lublin
BELARUS
KYÏV (KIEV)
UKRAINE
KHARKIV
Donets'k
DNIPROPETROVS'K
Zaporizhzhia
Mariupol'
ROSTOV-NA-DONU
RUSSIA
Sea of Azov
SLOVAKIA
Bratislava
BUDAPEST
HUNGARY
CARPATHIAN MOUNTAINS
MOLDOVA
Chişinău
ODESA
Kherson
Mykolaïv
ROMANIA
Cluj-Napoca
Iaşi
Braşov
Galaţi
Ploieşti
BUCUREŞTI (BUCHAREST)
Constanţa
BEOGRAD (BELGRADE)
Craiova
BLACK SEA
Simferopol'
Sevastopol'
CAUCASUS
GEORGIA
Batumi
BOSNIA AND HERZEGOVINA
Sarajevo
YUGOSLAVIA
SOFIJA (SOFIA)
BULGARIA
Varna
Burgas
Plovdiv
Skopje
MACEDONIA
ALBANIA
Tiranë
GREECE
Thessaloníki (Salonika)
ATHÍNAI (ATHENS)
AEGEAN SEA
İSTANBUL
İzmit
Bursa
ANKARA
TURKEY
Samsun
Trabzon
İZMİR
Konya
Kayseri
Adana
Antalya
Gaziantep
Malatya
TOROS DAĞLARI
IONIAN SEA
KRÍTI (CRETE)
Iráklion
Ródhos (Rhodes)
NORTH CYPRUS
CYPRUS
Nicosia
SYRIA
Halab (Aleppo)
Ḥimṣ
LEBANON
Bayrūt (Beirut)
DIMASHQ (DAMASCUS)
ISRAEL
TEL AVIV-YAFO
Yerushalayim (Jerusalem)
'Ammān
JORDAN
Hefa (Haifa)
Ghazzah
MEDITERRANEAN SEA
Khalīj Surt
Banghāzī
Tubruq
BARQAH (CYRENAICA)
LIBYA
EGYPT
EL-ISKANDARÎYA (ALEXANDRIA)
EL-QÂHIRA (CAIRO)
EL-GÎZA
Bûr Sa'îd (Port Said)
El-Suweis (Suez)
SINAI
WESTERN DESERT
EASTERN DESERT
AS-SAHRĀ' AL-LĪBĪYAH (LIBYAN DESERT)
SAUDI ARABIA
RED SEA

UNITED KINGDOM
IRELAND
FRANCE
GERMANY
BELGIUM
NETHERLANDS
LUXEMBOURG
SWITZERLAND
ENGLAND
WALES
NORTH SEA
CELTIC SEA
ATLANTIC OCEAN
English Channel
St. George's Channel
Bristol Channel
Strait of Dover
Bay
LONDON
PARIS
AMSTERDAM
BRUXELLES (BRUSSEL)
Luxembourg
Bern
ROTTERDAM
's-Gravenhage (The Hague)
ANTWERPEN (ANTWERP)
DÜSSELDORF
KÖLN (COLOGNE)
ESSEN
LILLE
LYON
Saint-Étienne
Bordeaux
Nantes
Rennes
Brest
Le Havre
Rouen
Strasbourg
Grenoble
Genève
TORINO
Cork
Limerick
Waterford
Cardiff
Swansea
Bristol
Plymouth
Southampton
Portsmouth
Bournemouth
Brighton
BIRMINGHAM
Leicester
Nottingham
Stoke-on-Trent
Norwich
Oxford
Cambridge
CHANNEL ISLANDS
ISLE OF WIGHT
ISLES OF SCILLY
BRETAGNE
NORMANDIE
MASSIF CENTRAL

PORTUGAL
SPAIN
MOROCCO
MEDITERRANEAN SEA
ILLES BALEARS (BALEARIC ISLANDS)
MADRID
LISBOA (LISBON)
BARCELONA
L'Hospitalet de Llobregat
MARSEILLE
EL DJAZAÏR (ALGIERS)
Wahran (Oran)
VALÈNCIA
Zaragoza
Sevilla (Seville)
Córdoba
Granada
Málaga
Murcia
Cartagena
Alacant
Valladolid
Bilbao
Porto
Tanger
GIBRALTAR (U.K.)
MALLORCA
MENORCA
EIVISSA
Formentera
PYRENEES
CORDILLERA CANTÁBRICA
SISTEMA CENTRAL
SISTEMA IBÉRICO
SIERRA MORENA
SIERRA NEVADA
ATLAS MOUNTAINS
Golfe du Lion
Golfo de Cádiz
Costa del Sol
Strait of Gibraltar
Scale 1 : 5 000 000
Lambert Conformal Conic Projection
West of Greenwich 0° East of Greenwich
D-559900-7A-DR1-1°
Copyright © Rand McNally & Co.

SWITZERLAND
AUSTRIA
SLOVENIA
CROATIA
BOSNIA AND HERZEGOVINA
FRANCE
ITALY
TUNISIA
ALGERIA
MALTA
SAN MARINO
VATICAN CITY
MONACO
LIECHTEN-STEIN
ALPS
BERNER ALPEN
RHAETIAN ALPS
HOHE TAUERN
NIEDERE TAUERN
CARNIC ALPS
DOLOMITI
MARITIME ALPS
DINARIC ALPS
APPENNINO LIGURE
APPENNINO TOSCO-EMILIANO
APPENNINO UMBRO-MARCHIGIANO
APPENNINO ABRUZZESE
APPENNINO LUCANO
APPENNINO CALABRESE
APENNINES
NEBRODI
MEDJERDA MOUNTAINS
LIGURIAN SEA
TYRRHENIAN SEA
ADRIATIC SEA
IONIAN SEA
MEDITERRANEAN SEA
Gulf of Venice
Golfo di Genova
Strait of Bonifacio
Strait of Sicily
Malta Channel
Golfo di Taranto
Golfo di Manfredonia
Golfo di Napoli
Golfo di Salerno
Golfo di Gaeta
Golfo di Cagliari
Golfo di Oristano
Golfo dell'Asinara
Golfo di Squillace
Golfo di Sant'Eufemia
Golfo di Policastro
Golfo di Castellammare
Golfe de Tunis
Golfe de Hammamet
Riviera di Ponente
Riviera di Levante
CORSE (CORSICA) (Fr.)
SARDEGNA (SARDINIA) (It.)
SICILIA (SICILY)
ISOLE EOLIE O LIPARI
ISOLE EGADI
ISOLE PONZIANE
ISOLE PELAGIE (It.)
Isola d'Elba
Isola di Capri
Isola d'Ischia
Isola di Pantelleria (It.)
Isola di Lampedusa
Isola di Linosa
Isola di Ustica
Isole Tremiti
Bern
Zürich
Genève (Geneva)
Lausanne
Innsbruck
Graz
Klagenfurt
Ljubljana
Zagreb
Trieste
Rijeka
Split
Dubrovnik
Mostar
TORINO (TURIN)
MILANO (MILAN)
GENOVA
Venézia (Venice)
Bologna
Firenze (Florence)
ROMA (ROME)
NAPOLI (NAPLES)
Bari
Palermo
Messina
Catania
Reggio di Calabria
Cagliari
Sassari
Ajaccio
Bastia
Nice
Cannes
Valletta
TUNIS
Bizerte
Sousse
Kairouan
Annaba
Scale 1 : 5 000 000
Lambert Conformal Conic Projection
East of Greenwich
Metres / Feet
Sea Level
D-556000-7A-DR1-1
Copyright © Rand McNally & Co.

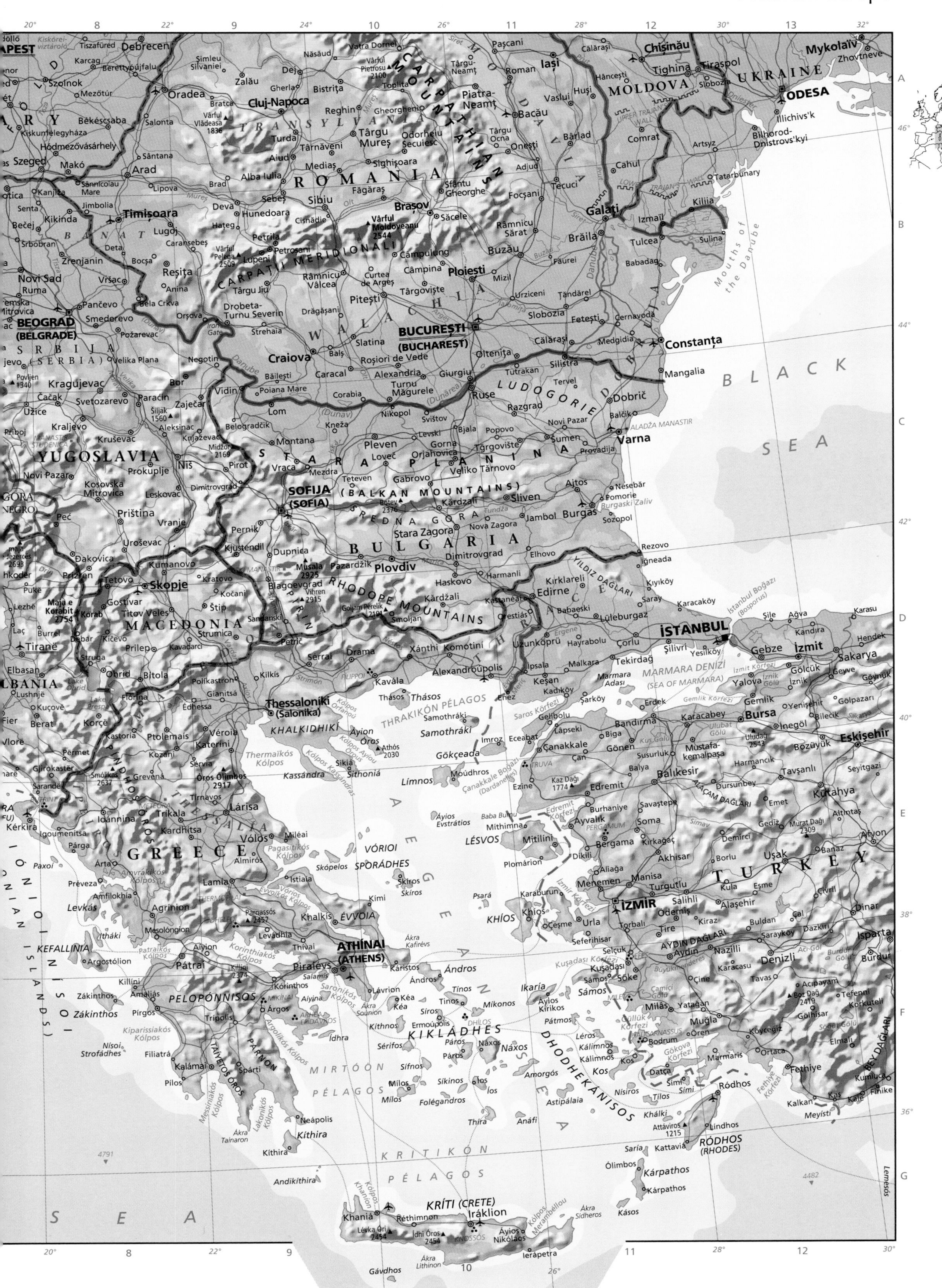

DENMARK
BALTIC SEA
RUSSIA
LITHUANIA
Kaliningrad
Vilnius
Kaunas
Gulf of Gdansk
Gdańsk
POMERANIA
MAZURY
GERMANY
BERLIN
BRANDENBURG
MECKLENBURG
VORPOMMERN
SACHSEN
POLAND
WARSZAWA
(WARSAW)
Łódź
Poznań
Wrocław
Kraków
Katowice
KUJAWY
SILESIA
SUDETES
ORE MOUNTAINS
CZECH REPUBLIC
PRAHA
(PRAGUE)
BOHEMIA
MORAVA
BOHEMIAN FOREST
Brno
Ostrava
BESKIDS
CARPATHIAN MOUNTAINS
SLOVAKIA
Bratislava
WIEN
(VIENNA)
AUSTRIA
ALPS
NIEDERE TAUERN
Graz
Linz
Salzburg
HUNGARY
BUDAPEST
ALFÖLD
Debrecen
Szeged
SLOVENIA
Ljubljana
CROATIA
Zagreb
SLAVONIJA
ISTRA
Rijeka
Trieste
BOSNIA AND HERZEGOVINA
Sarajevo
DINARIC ALPS
DALMACIJA
ADRIATIC SEA
YUGOSLAVIA
SRBIJA
(SERBIA)
BEOGRAD
(BELGRADE)
VOJVODINA
BANAT
ROMANIA
TRANSYLVANIA
CARPAŢII MERIDIONALI
WALACHIA
Cluj-Napoca
Timişoara
BUCUREŞ
(BUCHARE
BULGAR
GALICIA
Lublin
Hrodna
Brest
L'viv
Metres
Feet
2000
6560
1000
3280
500
1640
200
656
0
Sea Level
200
656
2000
6560
East of Greenwich
Scale 1 : 5 000 000
Lambert Conformal Conic Projection
0 50 100 150 200 300 400 500 km
0 50 100 200 300 miles
D-559592-7A-DR1-1
Copyright © Rand McNally & Co.

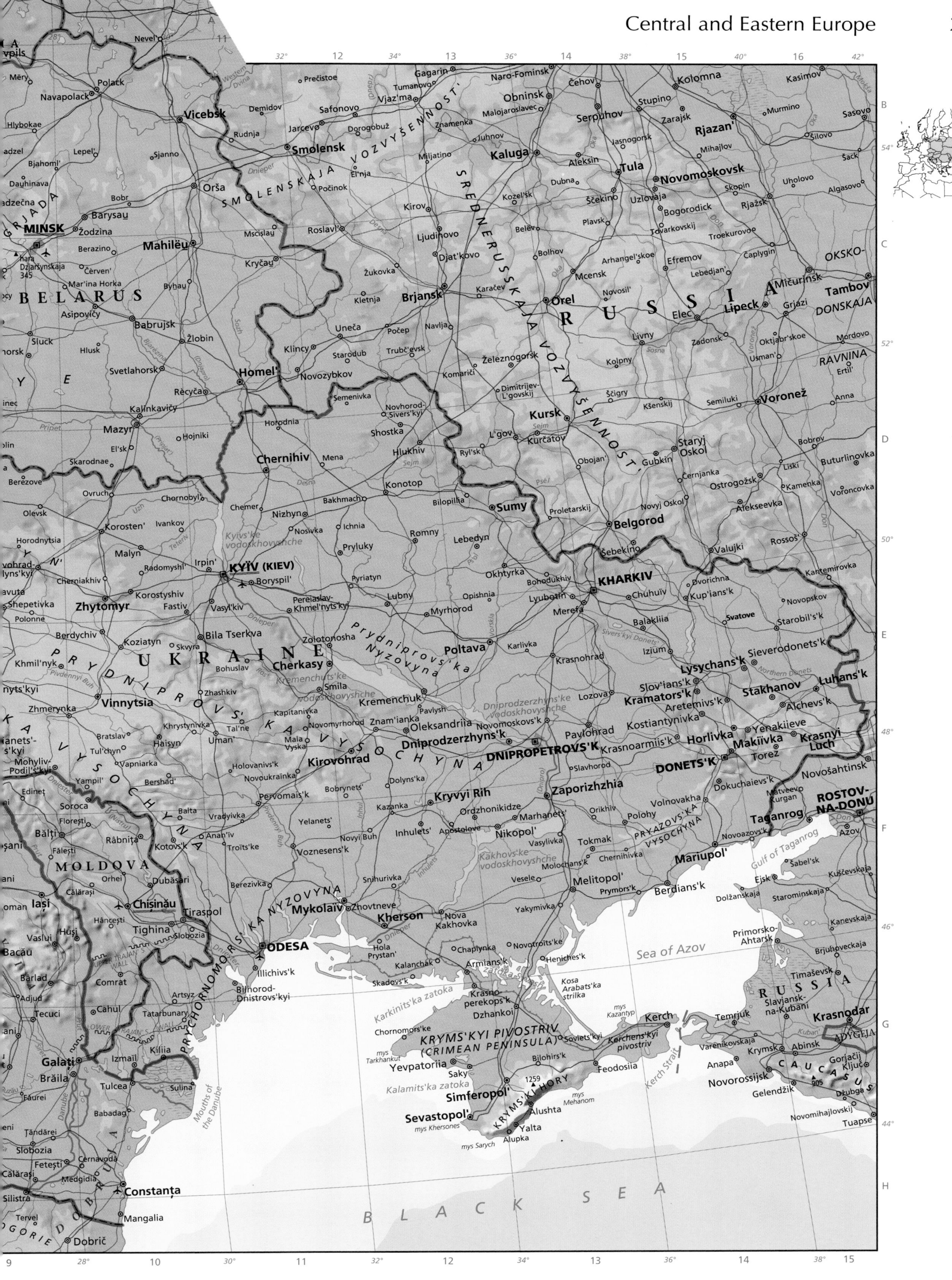
BELARUS
RUSSIA
UKRAINE
MOLDOVA
MINSK
KYÏV (KIEV)
KHARKIV
DNIPROPETROVS'K
DONETS'K
ODESA
ROSTOV-NA-DONU
Smolensk
Vicebsk
Mahilëu
Homel'
Brjansk
Orel
Kursk
Belgorod
Voronež
Tula
Kaluga
Rjazan'
Lipeck
Tambov
Chernihiv
Sumy
Poltava
Zhytomyr
Vinnytsia
Cherkasy
Kirovohrad
Kremenchuk
Zaporizhzhia
Kryvyi Rih
Mykolaïv
Kherson
Chișinău
Tiraspol
Simferopol'
Sevastopol'
Kerch
Mariupol'
Taganrog
Luhans'k
Krasnodar
Novorossijsk
Constanța
Galați
Brăila
Iași
Sea of Azov
BLACK SEA
Gulf of Taganrog
KRYMS'KYI PIVOSTRIV (CRIMEAN PENINSULA)
SREDNERUSSKAJA VOZVYŠENNOST'
SMOLENSKAJA VOZVYŠENNOST'
PRYDNIPROVS'KA NYZOVYNA
PRYDNIPROVS'KA VYSOCHYNA
PRYCHORNOMORS'KA NYZOVYNA
PRYAZOVS'KA VYSOCHYNA
OKSKO-DONSKAJA RAVNINA
CAUCASUS
DOBRUJA
Dnieper
Desna
Don
Pripet
Mouths of the Danube
Kerch Strait
Kyïvs'ke vodoskhovyshche
Kremenchuts'ke vodoskhovyshche
Kakhovs'ke vodoskhovyshche
Dniprodzerzhyns'ke vodoskhovyshche

Metres
Feet
4000
13120
3000
9840
2000
6560
1000
3280
500
1640
200
656
0
Sea Level
200
656
2000
6560
B A R E N T S
S E A
PEČORSKOE MORE
B E L O E M O R E
OSTROV KOLGUEV
POLUOSTROV KANIN
KOL'SKIJ POLUOSTROV
SOLOVECKIE OSTROVA
Gulf of Finland
Gulf of Riga
Gulf of Bothnia
BALTIC SEA
NORWAY
SWEDEN
FINLAND
ESTONIA
LATVIA
LITHUANIA
BELARUS
RUSSIA
R U S S I A
KARELIJA
KOMI
UDMURTIJA
TATARIJA
MARIJ EL
ČUVAŠIJA
MORDOVIJA
BAŠKIRIJA
URAL'SKIE GORY
(URAL MOUNTAINS)
ZAPADNO-SIBIRSKAJA RAVNINA
TIMANSKIJ KRJAŽ
Bol'šezemel'skaja Tundra
SEVERNYE UVALY
VALDAJSKAJA VOZVYŠENNOST'
SALPAUSSELKÄ
MOSKVA
(MOSCOW)
SANKT-PETERBURG
(SAINT PETERSBURG)
HELSINKI
STOCKHOLM
TALLINN
RIGA
VILNIUS
MINSK
WARSZAWA
(WARSAW)
Kaliningrad
Arhangel'sk
Murmansk
NIŽNIJ NOVGOROD
(GOR'KIJ)
KAZAN'
PERM'
EKATERINBURG
ČELJABINSK
UFA
Vorkuta
Syktyvkar
Kirov
Vologda
Jaroslavl'
Tver'
Smolensk
Brjansk
Kaluga
Tula
Rjazan'
Vladimir
Ivanovo
Kostroma
Čeboksary
Iževsk
Uljanovsk
Toljatti
Saransk
Magnitogorsk
Sterlitamak
Tjumen'

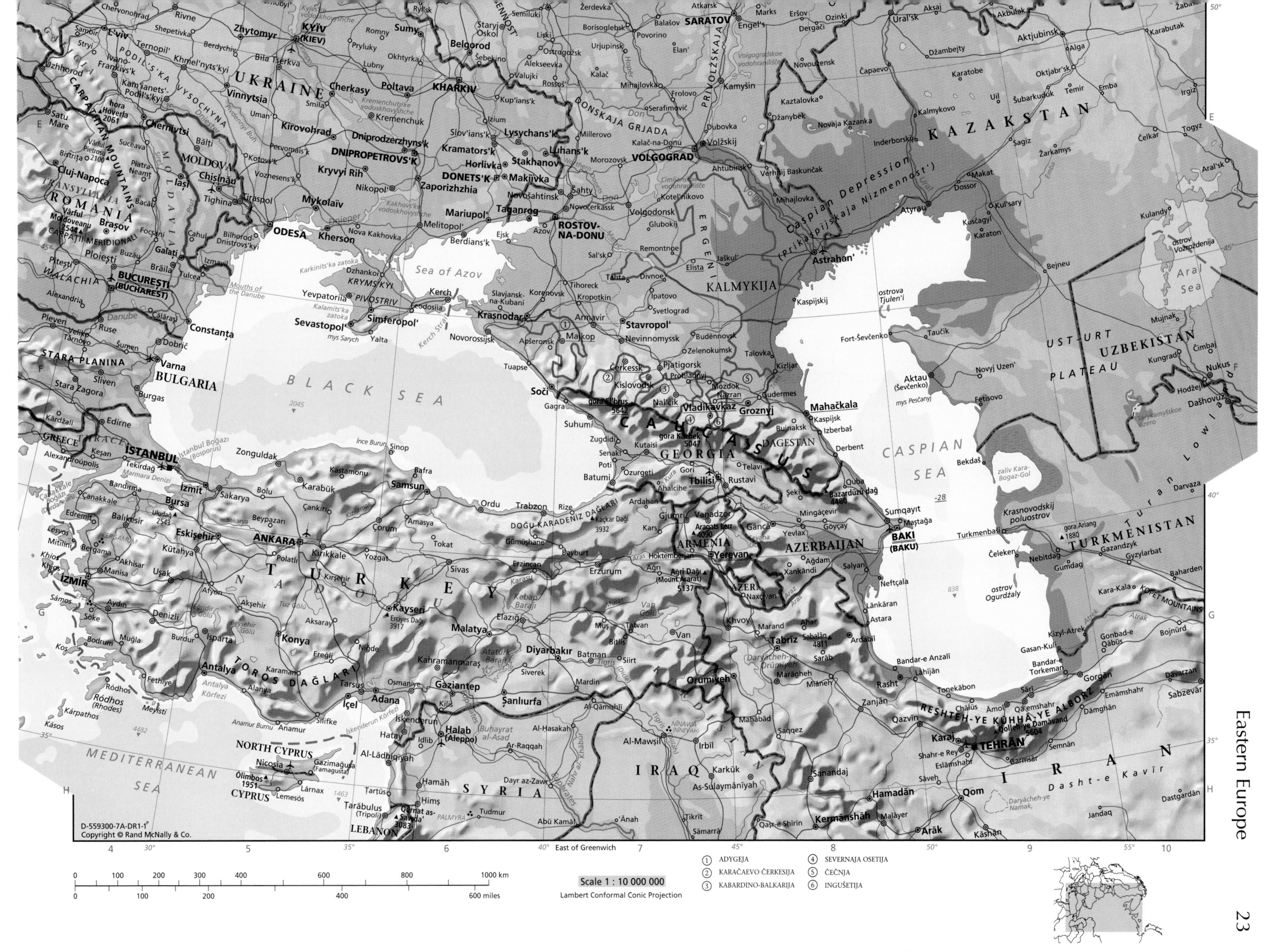
UKRAINE
ROMANIA
MOLDOVA
BULGARIA
GREECE
TURKEY
GEORGIA
ARMENIA
AZERBAIJAN
KAZAKSTAN
UZBEKISTAN
TURKMENISTAN
IRAN
IRAQ
SYRIA
LEBANON
CYPRUS
NORTH CYPRUS
KALMYKIJA
DAGESTAN
BLACK SEA
CASPIAN SEA
Sea of Azov
Aral Sea
MEDITERRANEAN SEA
CAUCASUS
CARPATHIAN MOUNTAINS
STARA PLANINA
TOROS DAĞLARI
UST-URT PLATEAU
Caspian Depression (Prikaspijskaja Nizmennost')
VOLGOGRAD
ROSTOV-NA-DONU
KHARKIV
KYÏV (KIEV)
ODESA
BUCUREŞTI (BUCHAREST)
İSTANBUL
ANKARA
Tbilisi
Yerevan
BAKI (BAKU)
TEHRĀN
SARATOV
Astrachan'
Simferopol'
Sevastopol'
Krasnodar
Stavropol'
Mahačkala
Groznyj
Chişinău
Varna
Burgas
Constanţa
İzmir
Bursa
Konya
Adana
Trabzon
Samsun
Erzurum
Tabrīz
Rasht
Qom
Hamadān
Aktau (Ševčenko)
Atyrau
Ural'sk
Aktjubinsk
Nukus
Halab (Aleppo)
Nicosia
D-559300-7A-DR1-1
Copyright © Rand McNally & Co.
East of Greenwich
0 100 200 300 400 600 800 1000 km
0 100 200 400 600 miles
Scale 1 : 10 000 000
Lambert Conformal Conic Projection
1 ADYGEJA
2 KARAČAEVO ČERKESIJA
3 KABARDINO-BALKARIJA
4 SEVERNAJA OSETIJA
5 ČEČNJA
6 INGUŠETIJA

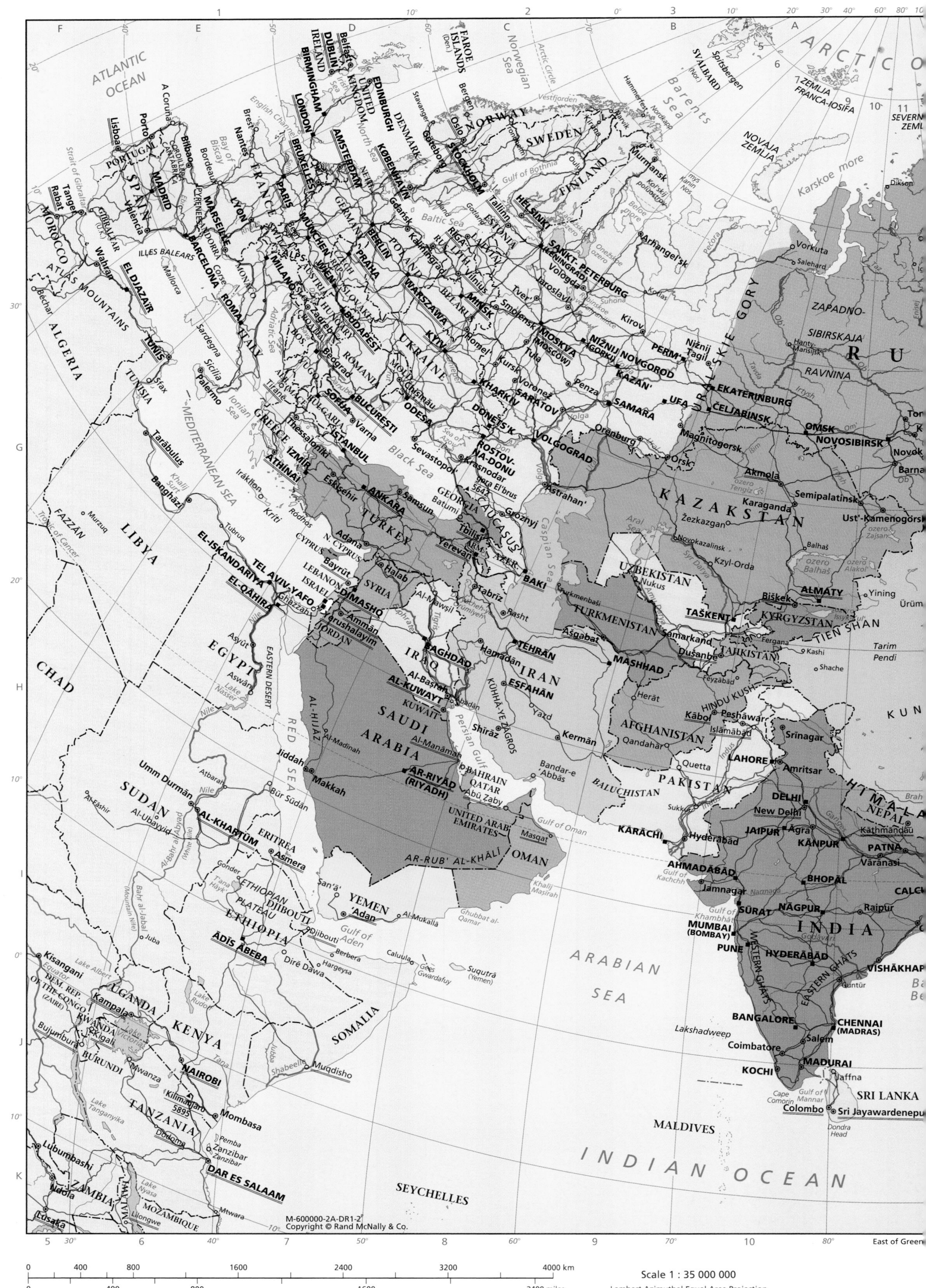
ATLANTIC OCEAN
ARCTIC OCEAN
Norwegian Sea
Barents Sea
North Sea
Bay of Biscay
English Channel
Baltic Sea
Gulf of Bothnia
Karskoe more
MEDITERRANEAN SEA
Adriatic Sea
Ionian Sea
Black Sea
Sea of Azov
Caspian Sea
Aral Sea
RED SEA
Persian Gulf
Gulf of Oman
Gulf of Aden
ARABIAN SEA
INDIAN OCEAN
Arctic Circle
Tropic of Cancer
Equator
FAROE ISLANDS (Den.)
SVALBARD (Nor.)
ZEMLJA FRANCA-IOSIFA
NOVAJA ZEMLJA
IRELAND
DUBLIN
UNITED KINGDOM
EDINBURGH
BIRMINGHAM
LONDON
NORWAY
Oslo
Bergen
SWEDEN
STOCKHOLM
FINLAND
HELSINKI
DENMARK
KØBENHAVN
AMSTERDAM
BRUXELLES
FRANCE
PARIS
LYON
MARSEILLE
PORTUGAL
Lisboa
Porto
SPAIN
MADRID
BARCELONA
Valencia
ANDORRA
GIBRALTAR (U.K.)
MOROCCO
Rabat
Tanger
ALGERIA
EL DJAZAÏR
ATLAS MOUNTAINS
TUNISIA
TUNIS
ITALY
ROMA
MILANO
Sardegna
Sicilia
Palermo
GERMANY
BERLIN
MÜNCHEN
PRAHA
WIEN
AUSTRIA
SWITZERLAND
POLAND
WARSZAWA
Gdańsk
HUNGARY
BUDAPEST
SLOVAKIA
Zagreb
Beograd
ROMANIA
BUCUREŞTI
BULGARIA
SOFIJA
Tiranë
GREECE
ATHÍNAI
Thessaloníki
Kriti
ESTONIA
Tallinn
LATVIA
RIGA
LITHUANIA
Vilnius
Kaliningrad
BELARUS
MINSK
UKRAINE
KYIV
ODESA
KHARKIV
MOLDOVA
Chişinău
SANKT-PETERBURG
MOSKVA (MOSCOW)
NIŽNIJ NOVGOROD
KAZAN'
SAMARA
SARATOV
VOLGOGRAD
ROSTOV-NA-DONU
Astrahan'
Arhangel'sk
Murmansk
PERM'
EKATERINBURG
ČELJABINSK
UFA
OMSK
NOVOSIBIRSK
URAL'SKIE GORY
ZAPADNO-SIBIRSKAJA RAVNINA
Vorkuta
Salehard
TURKEY
ANKARA
ISTANBUL
İZMİR
CYPRUS
N. CYPRUS
GEORGIA
Tbilisi
ARMENIA
Yerevan
AZERBAIJAN
BAKI
CAUCASUS
SYRIA
DIMASHQ
Halab
LEBANON
Bayrūt
ISRAEL
TEL AVIV-YAFO
Yerushalayim
JORDAN
'Ammān
IRAQ
BAGHDĀD
IRAN
TEHRĀN
ESFAHĀN
MASHHAD
Tabrīz
Shīrāz
KUWAIT
AL-KUWAYT
SAUDI ARABIA
AR-RIYĀD (RIYADH)
Jiddah
Makkah
BAHRAIN
QATAR
UNITED ARAB EMIRATES
Abū Zaby
OMAN
Masqat
YEMEN
Şan'ā'
'Adan
AR-RUB' AL-KHĀLĪ
KAZAKSTAN
ALMATY
Akmola
UZBEKISTAN
TAŠKENT
TURKMENISTAN
Ašgabat
TAJIKISTAN
Dušanbe
KYRGYZSTAN
Biškek
TIEN SHAN
AFGHANISTAN
Kābol
HINDU KUSH
PAKISTAN
Islāmābād
LAHORE
KARĀCHI
BALUCHISTAN
INDIA
DELHI
New Delhi
MUMBAI (BOMBAY)
HYDERĀBĀD
BANGALORE
CHENNAI (MADRAS)
KĀNPUR
JAIPUR
AHMADĀBĀD
NĀGPUR
PUNE
KOCHI
MADURAI
WESTERN GHATS
EASTERN GHATS
NEPAL
Kāthmāndau
SRI LANKA
Colombo
MALDIVES
Lakshadweep
LIBYA
Tarābulus
Banghāzī
EGYPT
EL-QĀHIRA
EL-ISKANDARIYA
Aswān
Lake Nasser
EASTERN DESERT
SUDAN
AL-KHARTŪM
Umm Durmān
CHAD
ERITREA
Asmera
ETHIOPIA
ĀDĪS ĀBEBA
DJIBOUTI
Djibouti
SOMALIA
Muqdisho
KENYA
NAIROBI
Mombasa
UGANDA
Kampala
RWANDA
Kigali
BURUNDI
Bujumbura
TANZANIA
Dodoma
DAR ES SALAAM
Kilimanjaro 5895
Zanzibar
DEM. REP. OF THE CONGO (ZAIRE)
Kisangani
Lubumbashi
ZAMBIA
Lusaka
MALAWI
MOZAMBIQUE
SEYCHELLES
Lake Victoria
Lake Tanganyika
Lake Nyasa
M-600000-2A-DR1-2
Copyright © Rand McNally & Co.
East of Greenwich
0 400 800 1600 2400 3200 4000 km
0 400 800 1600 2400 miles
Scale 1 : 35 000 000
Lambert Azimuthal Equal Area Projection

NOVOSIBIRSKIE OSTROVA
Vostočno-Sibirskoe more
proliv Longa
Arctic Circle
Uel'kal'
Anadyr'
mys Navarin
Markovo
Ambarčik
Srednekolymsk
Bering Sea
Kavača
mys Oljutorskij
ostrov Karaginskij
POLUOSTROV KAMČATKA
Attu Island
Cape Wrangell
ALEUTIAN ISLANDS (U.S.)
Tiksi
Kazače
HREBET ČERSKOGO
zaliv Šelihova
Jamsk
Palana
SREDINNYJ HREBET
Petropavlovsk-Kamčatskij
Verhojansk
VERHOJANSKIJ HREBET
Magadan
Ohotsk
Sea of Okhotsk
mys Lopatka
Žigansk
Lena
Jakutsk
Ajan
mys Elizavety
Oha
Aleksandrovsk-Sahalinskij
OSTROV SAHALIN (SAKHALIN)
mys Terpenija
KURIL'SKIE OSTROVA (KURIL ISLANDS)
Južno-Sahalinsk
Tatarskij proliv
Tommot
Aldan
Lensk
STANOVOJ HREBET
SIBIR' SIBERIA
Skovorodino
Komsomol'sk-na-Amure
Habarovsk
SIHOTE-ALIN'
Asahikawa
HOKKAIDŌ
Ozero Bajkal
Irkutsk
Ulan-Ude
Čita
Hailar
Qiqihar
Jiamusi
Vladivostok
Sapporo
Hakodate
Aomori
Sendai
PACIFIC OCEAN
HARBIN
Jilin
Sea of Japan
HONSHŪ
Niigata
TŌKYŌ
YOKOHAMA
Ulaanbaatar
Kerulen
CHANGCHUN
FUSHUN
NORTH KOREA
SHENYANG
Dandong
P'YONGYANG
Kanazawa
NAGOYA
KYŌTO
ŌSAKA
JAPAN
MONGOLIA
Zhangjiakou
BEIJING
DALIAN
SŎUL (SEOUL)
SOUTH KOREA
Taegu
PUSAN
HIROSHIMA
Shikoku
FUKUOKA
KYŪSHŪ
GOBI
Hohhot
TIANJIN
Bo Hai
JINAN
Yellow Sea
Mokp'o
Korea Strait
Cheju-do
Kagoshima
TAIYUAN
Shijiazhuang
Qingdao
Yinchuan
Xuzhou
Farallon de Pajaros
NORTHERN MARIANA ISLANDS (U.S.)
Lanzhou
Zhengzhou
SHANGHAI
East China Sea
Amami-ō-shima
NANSEI-SHOTO (RYUKYU ISLANDS)
Okinawa-jima
Naha
XI'AN
NANJING
Ningbo
CHINA
WUHAN
Hangzhou
Wenzhou
Agrihan
Anatahan
Saipan
Rota
Agana
GUAM (U.S.)
CHENGDU
CHONGQING
Nanchang
CHANGSHA
Fuzhou
T'AIPEI
TAIWAN
Hengyang
Guiyang
Xiamen
Tainan
KAOHSIUNG
Philippine Sea
FEDERATED STATES OF MICRONESIA
Kunming
Liuzhou
GUANGZHOU
XIANGGANG (HONG KONG)
Luzon Strait
Nanning
MACAU (Port.)
Zhanjiang
HA NOI
Hai Phong
Gulf of Tonkin
Haikou
Hainan Dao
Baguio
PHILIPPINES
Quezon City
Mandalay
MYANMAR (BURMA)
LAOS
Louangphrabang
South China Sea
LUZON
Naga
Samar
Chiang Mai
Viangchan
VIETNAM
MANILA
Mindoro
Masbate
Sibuyan Sea
Cebu
Koror
PALAU
New Ireland
Udon Thani
Da Nang
Panay
Iloilo
Negros
MINDANAO
Kavieng
Rabaul
YANGON (RANGOON)
THAILAND
Gulf of Martaban
KRUNG THEP (BANGKOK)
Palawan
Sulu Sea
Davao
Cape San Agustin
Bismarck Sea
Coco Islands
CAMBODIA
Phnum Penh
THANH PHO HO CHI MINH (SAIGON)
Zamboanga
Moro Gulf
Tinaca Point
Wewak
Madang
New Britain
Andaman Sea
Gulf of Thailand
Kâmpóng Saôm
Balabac Strait
Gunong Kinabalu 4101
Celebes Sea
Morotai
HALMAHERA
Biak
Jayapura
Lae
Mui Ca Mau
Manado
PAPUA NEW GUINEA
Port Moresby
MALAY PENINSULA
Bandar Seri Begawan
BRUNEI
Puncak Jaya 5030
NEW GUINEA
Gulf of Papua
George Town (Penang)
MALAYSIA
Laut Maluku
Laut Seram
Teluk Tomini
Banda Aceh
Kuching
BORNEO
Pulau Taliabu
Seram (Ceram)
Pulau Yos Sudarso
Torres Strait
Cape York
MEDAN
KUALA LUMPUR
Strait of Malacca
SINGAPORE
Pontianak
Kapuas
(KALIMANTAN)
SULAWESI (CELEBES)
Teluk Tolo
Buru
Arafura Sea
Selat Makasar
Balikpapan
Pulau Buton
Cape Wessel
Cape Arnhem
CAPE YORK PENINSULA
Coral Sea
Padang
Selat Karimata
Pulau Bangka
Banjarmasin
Teluk Bone
Laut Banda
Gulf of Carpentaria
SUMATERA (SUMATRA)
Pulau Siberut
Belitung
Tanjung Puting
Tanjung Selatan
Ujungpandang
INDONESIA
Cairns
Palembang
Laut Jawa
Dili
Timor
Melville Island
Laut Bali
Laut Flores
Flores
Laut Sawu
Kupang
Timor Sea
AUSTRALIA
Tanjungkarang-Telukbetung
Selat Sunda
JAKARTA
BANDUNG
JAWA (JAVA)
Madura
SURABAYA
Sumbawa
Bali
Lombok
Sumba
Darwin
Tropic of Cancer
Equator

M-700000-7A-DR1-2

0 200 400 600 800 1200 1600 km

0 200 400 800 miles

Scale 1 : 20 000 000

Lambert Conformal Conic Projection

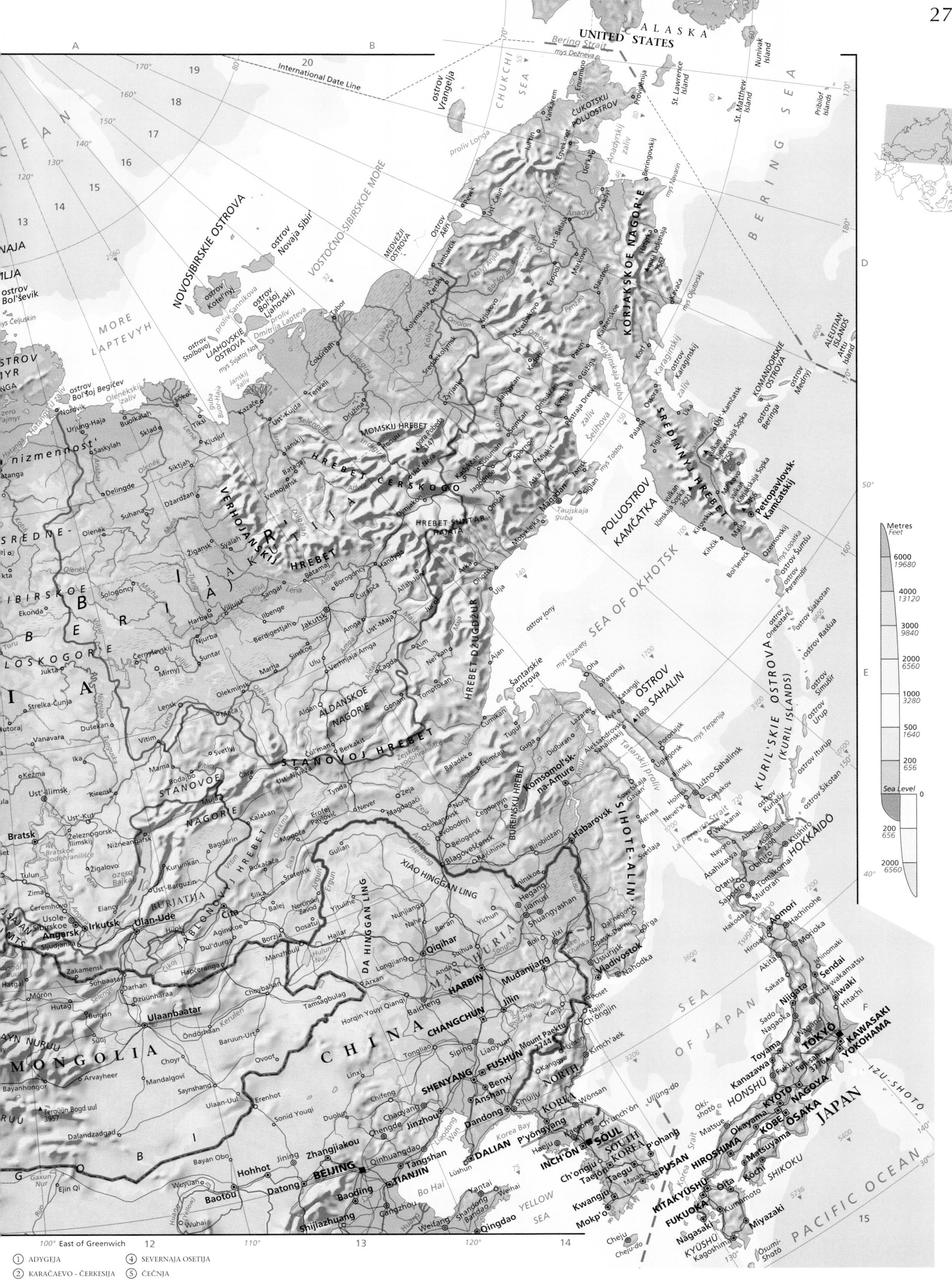
UNITED STATES
ALASKA
Bering Strait
mys Dežneva
International Date Line
CHUKCHI SEA
ostrov Vrangelja
ČUKOTSKIJ POLUOSTROV
St. Lawrence Island
St. Matthew Island
Nunivak Island
Pribilof Islands
BERING SEA
Anadyrskij zaliv
Anadyr
KORJAKSKOE NAGOR'E
NOVOSIBIRSKIE OSTROVA
ostrov Novaja Sibir'
ostrov Kotel'nyj
ostrov Bol'šoj Ljahovskij
LJAHOVSKIE OSTROVA
VOSTOČNO-SIBIRSKOE MORE
MEDVEŽ'I OSTROVA
MORE LAPTEVYH
ostrov Bol'ševik
ostrov Bol'šoj Begičev
ALEUTIAN ISLANDS
Attu Island
KOMANDORSKIE OSTROVA
ostrov Beringa
ostrov Mednyj
ostrov Karaginskij
Karaginskij zaliv
SREDINNYJ HREBET
Ključevskaja Sopka 4750
Petropavlovsk-Kamčatskij
POLUOSTROV KAMČATKA
zaliv Šelihova
Penžinskaja guba
MOMSKIJ HREBET
gora Pobeda 3147
HREBET ČERSKOGO
VERHOJANSKIJ HREBET
HREBET SUNTAR-HAJATA
Magadan
Tauiskaja guba
SEA OF OKHOTSK
ostrov Iony
HREBET DŽUGDŽUR
Šantarskie ostrova
OSTROV SAHALIN
Južno-Sahalinsk
Tatarskij proliv
La Pérouse Strait
KURIL'SKIE OSTROVA (KURIL ISLANDS)
ostrov Iturup
ostrov Kunašir
HOKKAIDŌ
Sapporo
Jakutsk
Lena
ALDANSKOE NAGOR'E
STANOVOJ HREBET
STANOVOE NAGOR'E
JABLONOVYJ HREBET
BURJATIJA
ozero Bajkal
Irkutsk
Ulan-Ude
Čita
Bratsk
Angarsk
Komsomol'sk-na-Amure
BUREINSKIJ HREBET
SIHOTE-ALIN'
Habarovsk
Blagoveščensk
Vladivostok
XIAO HINGGAN LING
DA HINGGAN LING
MANCHURIA
Qiqihar
HARBIN
Mudanjiang
CHANGCHUN
Jilin
SHENYANG
FUSHUN
Mount Paektu 2744
NORTH KOREA
P'yŏngyang
SOUL
SOUTH KOREA
INCH'ON
PUSAN
Korea Bay
DALIAN
Dandong
Bo Hai
YELLOW SEA
BEIJING
TIANJIN
Datong
Baotou
Hohhot
Qingdao
Shijiazhuang
MONGOLIA
Ulaanbaatar
CHINA
SEA OF JAPAN
JAPAN
HONSHŪ
TOKYO
KAWASAKI
YOKOHAMA
NAGOYA
KYOTO
OSAKA
KOBE
HIROSHIMA
SHIKOKU
KYŪSHŪ
FUKUOKA
KITAKYŪSHŪ
Nagasaki
Kagoshima
Sendai
Aomori
Niigata
IZU-SHOTŌ
PACIFIC OCEAN
Metres / Feet
6000 19680
4000 13120
3000 9840
2000 6560
1000 3280
500 1640
200 656
Sea Level 0
200 656
2000 6560
100° East of Greenwich
110°
120°
130°
140°
① ADYGEJA
② KARAČAEVO - ČERKESIJA
③ KABARDINO-BALKARIJA
④ SEVERNAJA OSETIJA
⑤ ČEČNJA
⑥ INGUŠETIJA

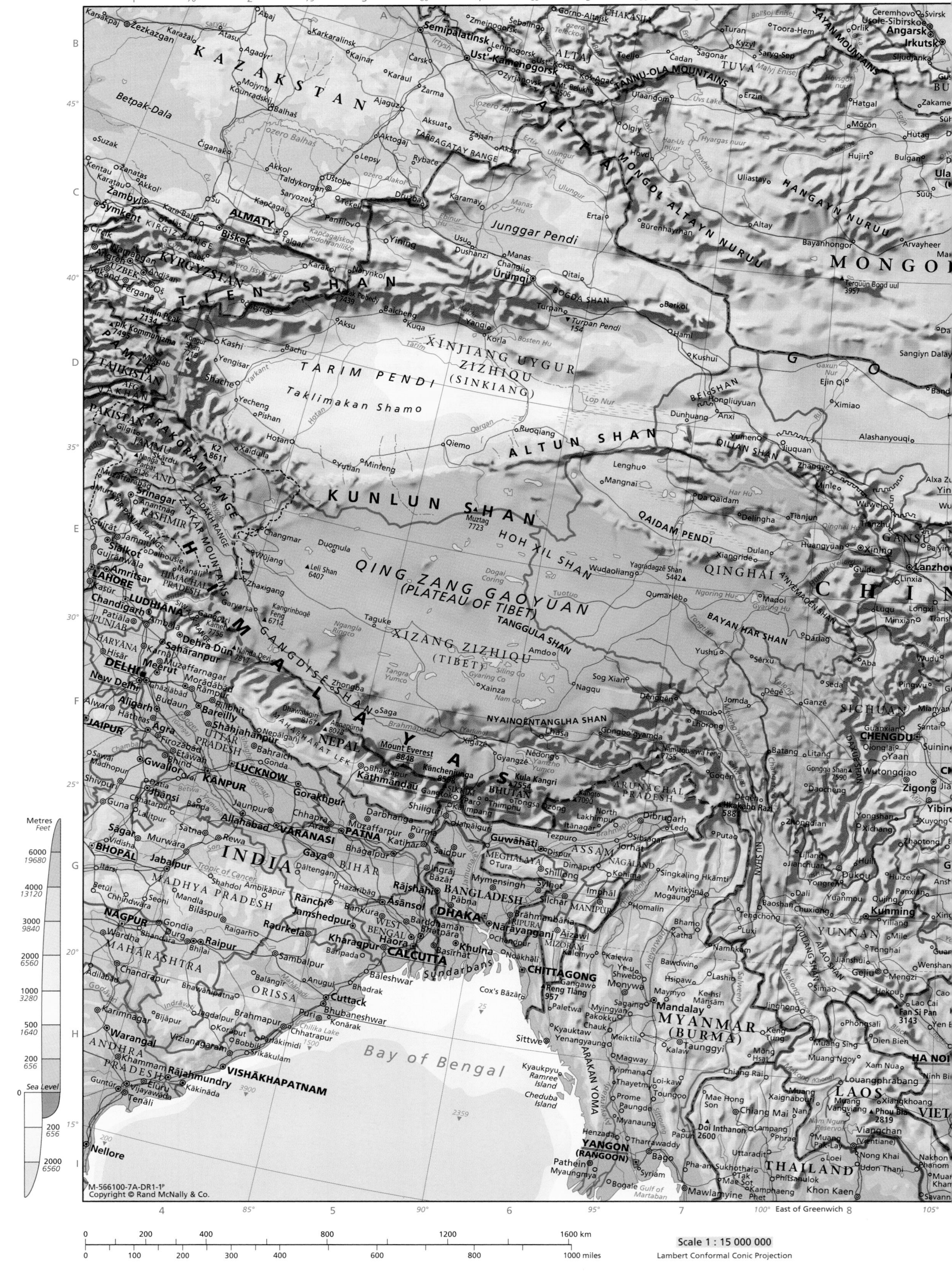

KAZAKSTAN
KYRGYZSTAN
TAJIKISTAN
PAKISTAN
JAMMU AND KASHMIR
INDIA
NEPAL
BHUTAN
BANGLADESH
MYANMAR (BURMA)
THAILAND
LAOS
MONGOLIA
CHINA
TIEN SHAN
ALTAI
MONGOL ALTAYN NURUU
HANGAYN NURUU
TANNU-OLA MOUNTAINS
SAYAN MOUNTAINS
TARBAGATAY RANGE
Junggar Pendi
TARIM PENDI
Taklimakan Shamo
XINJIANG UYGUR ZIZHIQU (SINKIANG)
ALTUN SHAN
KUNLUN SHAN
QILIAN SHAN
QAIDAM PENDI
QINGHAI
HOH XIL SHAN
QING ZANG GAOYUAN (PLATEAU OF TIBET)
XIZANG ZIZHIQU (TIBET)
TANGGULA SHAN
BAYAN HAR SHAN
GANGDISE SHAN
NYAINQENTANGHLA SHAN
HIMALAYAS
KARAKORAM RANGE
PAMIR
SICHUAN
YUNNAN
GANSU
ASSAM
Bay of Bengal
Betpak-Dala
ALMATY
Bishkek
Ürümqi
Kashi
Lhasa
Kathmandu
Mount Everest 8848
K2 8611
Kanchenjunga 8598
Muztag 7723
DELHI
New Delhi
LAHORE
LUCKNOW
KANPUR
PATNA
VARANASI
CALCUTTA
DHAKA
CHITTAGONG
Mandalay
YANGON (RANGOON)
CHENGDU
Kunming
Lanzhou
Semipalatinsk
Ust'-Kamenogorsk
Irkutsk
Angarsk
NAGPUR
BHOPAL
JAIPUR
VISHĀKHAPATNAM
Nellore
Metres / Feet
6000 / 19680
4000 / 13120
3000 / 9840
2000 / 6560
1000 / 3280
500 / 1640
200 / 656
0 Sea Level
200 / 656
2000 / 6560
M-566100-7A-DR1-1°
Copyright © Rand McNally & Co.
East of Greenwich
0 200 400 800 1200 1600 km
0 100 200 300 400 600 800 1000 miles
Scale 1 : 15 000 000
Lambert Conformal Conic Projection

RUSSIA
SIBIR'
MANCHURIA
HEILONGJIANG
JILIN
LIAONING
NEI MONGGOL ZIZHIQU
(INNER MONGOLIA)
DA HINGGAN LING
XIAO HINGGAN LING
SIKHOTE-ALIN'
HEBEI
SHANXI
SHANDONG
HENAN
JIANGSU
ANHUI
HUBEI
ZHEJIANG
JIANGXI
HUNAN
FUJIAN
GUANGDONG
NORTH KOREA
SOUTH KOREA
JAPAN
HOKKAIDŌ
HONSHŪ
SHIKOKU
KYŪSHŪ
TAIWAN
PHILIPPINES
LUZON
SEA OF JAPAN
(EAST SEA)
YELLOW SEA
EAST CHINA SEA
SOUTH CHINA SEA
PHILIPPINE SEA
PACIFIC OCEAN
Sea of Okhotsk
OSTROV SAHALIN
KURIL'SKIE OSTROVA
(KURIL ISLANDS)
NANSEI-SHOTŌ (RYUKYU ISLANDS)
IZU-SHOTŌ
ŌSUMI-SHOTŌ
BATAN ISLANDS
BABUYAN ISLANDS
HAINAN DAO
Luzon Strait
Bashi Channel
Taiwan Strait
Korea Strait
La Perouse Strait
Tropic of Cancer
BEIJING
TIANJIN
SHENYANG
HARBIN
CHANGCHUN
DALIAN
SHANGHAI
NANJING
WUHAN
CHANGSHA
GUANGZHOU
XIANGGANG
(HONG KONG)
T'AIPEI
KAOHSIUNG
P'YŎNGYANG
SŎUL
(SEOUL)
INCH'ŎN
PUSAN
TŌKYŌ
YOKOHAMA
KAWASAKI
NAGOYA
ŌSAKA
KYŌTO
KŌBE
HIROSHIMA
KITAKYŪSHŪ
FUKUOKA
SAPPORO
Vladivostok
Habarovsk
Komsomol'sk-na-Amure
Blagoveščensk
Čita
Hohhot
Datong
Taiyuan
Shijiazhuang
Jinan
Qingdao
Zhengzhou
Kaifeng
Luoyang
Xuzhou
Hefei
Hangzhou
Ningbo
Nanchang
Fuzhou
Xiamen
Shantou
Haikou
Macau
Mount Paektu
2744
Fuji-san
3776
Yü Shan
3997
Halla-san
1950
Cheju-do
Okinawa-jima
Naha
Miyako-jima
Iriomote-jima
Tungsha Tao
(Pratas Island)
(Claimed by China and Taiwan)
Xisha Qundao
(Paracel Islands)
Okino-Tori-shima
(Japan)

MONGOLIA
GOBI
NEI MONGGOL ZIZHIQU (INNER MONGOLIA)
NINGXIA HUIZU ZIZHIQU
GANSU
QINGHAI
SHAANXI
SHANXI
HEBEI
LIAONING
SHANDONG
HENAN
JIANGSU
ANHUI
HUBEI
SICHUAN
ZHEJIANG
JIANGXI
HUNAN
GUIZHOU
FUJIAN
YUNNAN
GUANGXI ZHUANGZU ZIZHIQU
GUANGDONG
CHINA
TAIWAN
LAOS
VIETNAM
THAI.
PHILIPPINES
HAINAN
YELLOW SEA
Bo Hai
SOUTH CHINA SEA
Gulf of Tonkin
Taiwan Strait
Bashi Channel
Luzon Strait
BEIJING (PEKING)
TIANJIN (TIENTSIN)
SHENYANG
DALIAN
Hohhot
Baotou
Datong
Shijiazhuang
TAIYUAN
Jinan
Qingdao
Zhengzhou
Luoyang
XI'AN
Lanzhou
Xining
Yinchuan
CHENGDU
CHONGQING
WUHAN
NANJING (NANKING)
SHANGHAI
Hangzhou
Hefei
Nanchang
CHANGSHA
Guiyang
Kunming
Nanning
GUANGZHOU (CANTON)
SHENZHEN
XIANGGANG (HONG KONG)
MACAU (Port.)
Fuzhou
Xiamen
T'AIPEI
KAOHSIUNG
Haikou
HA NOI
Hai Phong
Metres / Feet
4000 / 13120
3000 / 9840
2000 / 6560
1000 / 3280
500 / 1640
200 / 656
0 Sea Level
200 / 656
2000 / 6560
M-560898-7A-DR1-1
Copyright © Rand McNally & Co.
East of Greenwich
0 100 200 300 400 600 800 1000 km
0 100 200 400 600 miles
Scale 1 : 10 000 000
Lambert Conformal Conic Projection

RUSSIA
CHINA
MANCHURIA
HEILONGJIANG
JILIN
XIAO HINGGAN LING
ZHANGGUANGCAI LING
SIHOTE-ALIN'
NORTH KOREA
SOUTH KOREA
JAPAN
SEA OF JAPAN
(EAST SEA)
SEA OF OKHOTSK
PACIFIC OCEAN
OSTROV SAHALIN (SAKHALIN)
KURIL'SKIE OSTROVA (KURIL ISLANDS)
Formerly part of Japan, Malaja Kuril'skaja, Šikotan, Kunašir, and Iturup, occupied by Russia since 1945, are claimed by Japan pending a final peace treaty.
La Perouse Strait
Tatarskij proliv
HOKKAIDŌ
HONSHŪ
SHIKOKU
KYŪSHŪ
ŌU-SAMMYAKU
CHŪGOKU-SANCHI
IZU-SHOTŌ
NANSEI-SHOTŌ (RYUKYU ISLANDS)
Oshima-hantō
Noto-hantō
Sado
Oki-shotō
Ullŭng-do (S. Korea)
TŌKYŌ
YOKOHAMA
KAWASAKI
NAGOYA
KYŌTO
ŌSAKA
KŌBE
HIROSHIMA
KITAKYŪSHŪ
FUKUOKA
Sapporo
Sendai
Vladivostok
Harbin
Mudanjiang
Ostrov Iturup (Etorofu-tō)
Ostrov Kunašir (Kunashiri-tō)
Fuji-san 3776
a same scale as main map
EAST CHINA SEA (DONG HAI)
NANSEI-SHOTŌ (RYUKYU ISLANDS)
AMAMI-SHOTŌ
OKINAWA-SHOTŌ
Okinawa
Naha
Nago
Metres
Feet
3000 9840
2000 6560
1000 3280
500 1640
200 656
Sea Level 0
200 656
2000 6560
W-561500-7A-DR1-2
Copyright © Rand McNally & Co.
East of Greenwich
Scale 1 : 8 000 000
Lambert Conformal Conic Projection
0 100 200 300 400 600 800 km
0 50 100 150 200 300 400 500 miles

CHINA
MYANMAR (BURMA)
LAOS
THAILAND
CAMBODIA
VIETNAM
INDIA
TAIWAN
MALAYSIA
BRUNEI
INDONESIA
INDOCHINA
YUNNAN
GUANGXI ZHUANGZU ZIZHIQU
GUANGDONG
HUNAN
JIANGXI
FUJIAN
MANIPUR
Kunming
Nanning
Guangzhou
GUANGZHOU
XIANGGANG (HONG KONG)
MACAU (Port.)
Shenzhen
Xinjiulong
Jiulong
Shantou
Xiamen
Zhangzhou
Quanzhou
Liuzhou
Guilin
Wuzhou
Zhanjiang
Maoming
Haikou
HAINAN
HAINAN DAO
Qiongzhong
Sanya
Baoting
Gulf of Tonkin
Mandalay
Monywa
Sagaing
Taunggyi
YANGON (RANGOON)
Pathein
Mawlamyine
Gulf of Martaban
Henzada
Prome
Toungoo
Pyinmana
Myitkyina
Bhamo
Lashio
Imphal
Aizawl
Silchar
Tropic of Cancer
HA NOI
Hai Phong
Nam Dinh
Thanh Hoa
Vinh
Hue
Da Nang
Quy Nhon
Nha Trang
Da Lat
Buon Ma Thuot
Phan Thiet
Phan Rang
Bien Hoa
THANH PHO HO CHI MINH (SAIGON)
Can Tho
Rach Gia
Ca Mau
Vientiane
Louangphrabang
Savannakhet
Pakxe
Phou Bia 2819
Fan Si Pan 3143
KRUNG THEP (BANGKOK)
Chiang Mai
Nakhon Ratchasima
Nakhon Sawan
Udon Thani
Khon Kaen
Ubon Ratchathani
Hat Yai
Songkhla
Phuket
Surat Thani
Nakhon Si Thammarat
Doi Inthanon 2600
Phnum Pénh (Phnom Penh)
Bătdâmbâng
Kâmpóng Saôm
Phnum Aôral 1813
Gulf of Thailand
Isthmus of Kra
PHANOM DONGRAK RANGE
BILAUKTAUNG RANGE
MALAY PENINSULA
Strait of Malacca
KUALA LUMPUR
George Town (Penang)
Ipoh
Kuala Terengganu
Kota Bharu
Kuantan
Melaka
Johor Bahru
SINGAPORE
Gunung Tahan 2187
Kota Kinabalu
Gunung Kinabalu 4101
Sandakan
Bandar Seri Begawan
SABAH
SARAWAK
Kuching
Sibu
Miri
BORNEO (KALIMANTAN)
Pontianak
Banjarmasin
Balikpapan
Samarinda
Palangkaraya
Medan
Banda Aceh
Padang
Pekanbaru
Palembang
Jambi
Bengkulu
Tanjungkarang-Telukbetung
SUMATERA (SUMATRA)
PEGUNUNGAN BARISAN
Gunung Kerinci 3800
JAKARTA
BANDUNG
SEMARANG
SURABAYA
Yogyakarta
Surakarta
Malang
Bogor
Cirebon
Madura
JAWA (JAVA)
Bali
Lombok
SUMBAWA
SUMBA
NUSA TENGGARA (LESSER SUNDA ISLANDS)
Laut Jawa
GREATER SUNDA ISLANDS
Ujungpandang
SULAWESI (CELEBES)
MANILA
MINDORO
PALAWAN
Puerto Princesa
Sulu
SULU ARCHIPELAGO
SOUTH CHINA SEA
Xisha Qundao (Paracel Islands)
Spratly Islands
Kepulauan Natuna Besar
Kepulauan Anambas
Kepulauan Riau
Bangka
Belitung
ANDAMAN AND NICOBAR ISLANDS (India)
North Andaman
Middle Andaman
South Andaman
Little Andaman
Port Blair
Car Nicobar Island
Great Nicobar
Andaman Sea
Ten Degree Channel
Mergui Archipelago
INDIAN OCEAN
CHRISTMAS ISLAND (Austl.)
Equator
Metres
Feet
Sea Level
M-600098-7A-DR1-2
Copyright © Rand McNally & Co.
East of Greenwich
Scale 1 : 15 000 000
Sinusoidal Projection
1600 km
1000 miles

PHILIPPINE SEA
PACIFIC OCEAN
NORTHERN MARIANA ISLANDS (U.S)
MARIANA ISLANDS
Farallon de Pajaros
Maug Islands
Asuncion Island
Agrihan
Pagan
Alamagan
Guguan
Sarigan
Anatahan
Farallon de Medinilla
Saipan
Tinian
Rota
Agana
GUAM (U.S)
Tropic of Cancer
FEDERATED STATES OF MICRONESIA
Yap
Fais
Eauripik
Pulap
Palau Islands
Koror
Babelthuap
Beliliou
Ngeaur
Sonsorol Islands
PALAU
Caroline Islands
Equator
PHILIPPINES
MINDANAO
Davao
Cagayan de Oro
HALMAHERA
Morotai
MALUKU (MOLUCCAS)
Laut Banda
Laut Seram
Ambon
Manokwari
Biak
Sorong
Jayapura
PEGUNUNGAN VAN REES
PEGUNUNGAN MAOKE
Puncak Jaya 5030
Puncak Trikora 4750
NEW GUINEA
PAPUA NEW GUINEA
Mount Wilhelm 4509
Mount Hagen
Goroka
Lae
Madang
Wewak
Vanimo
Port Moresby
Daru
Merauke
OWEN STANLEY RANGE
BISMARCK ARCHIPELAGO
Bismarck Sea
NEW IRELAND
NEW BRITAIN
Rabaul
ADMIRALTY ISLANDS
Manus Island
Solomon Sea
Gulf of Papua
Torres Strait
ARAFURA SEA
Timor Sea
TIMOR
Dili
KEPULAUAN ARU
KEPULAUAN TANIMBAR
AUSTRALIA
CAPE YORK PENINSULA
Arnhem Land
Darwin
Thursday Island
Melville Island
Bathurst Island

BHUTAN
INDIA
BANGLADESH
DHAKA
CALCUTTA
CHITTAGONG
MYANMAR (BURMA)
YANGON (RANGOON)
Mandalay
THAILAND
KRUNG THEP (BANGKOK)
LAOS
Viangchan (Vientiane)
CAMBODIA
Phnum Penh (Phnom Penh)
HA NOI
MALAYSIA
INDONESIA
SICHUAN
YUNNAN
Kunming
GUIZHOU
Guiyang
ARUNACHAL PRADESH
ASSAM
NAGALAND
MANIPUR
MIZORAM
TRIPURA
MEGHALAYA
WEST BENGAL
BIHAR
SIKKIM
Bay of Bengal
Andaman Sea
Gulf of Thailand
Gulf of Martaban
INDIAN OCEAN
Strait of Malacca
Isthmus of Kra
MALAY PENINSULA
ANDAMAN ISLANDS
NICOBAR ISLANDS
ANDAMAN AND NICOBAR ISLANDS (India)
MERGUI ARCHIPELAGO
SUMATERA (SUMATRA)
SEMENANJUNG MALAYSIA
ARAKAN YOMA
PEGU YOMA
CHIN HILLS
NAGA HILLS
MANGIN RANGE
KUMON RANGE
DAWNA RA.
BILAUKTAUNG RANGE
TAUNGNYO RANGE
PHANOM DONGRAK RANGE
WULIANG SHAN
AILAO SHAN
YUN LING
NU SHAN
INDOCHINA
Mouths of the Ganges
Tropic of Cancer
Ten Degree Channel
Preparis North Channel
Preparis South Channel
Coco Channel
Duncan Passage
Sombrero Channel
Great Channel
Port Blair
Chiang Mai
Mawlamyine
Pathein
Sittwe
Lashio
Taunggyi
Nakhon Ratchasima
Khon Kaen
Louangphrabang
George Town (Penang)
Kuala Terengganu
Ipoh
Hat Yai
Songkhla
Phuket
Banda Aceh
Metres
Feet
6000 19680
4000 13120
3000 9840
2000 6560
1000 3280
500 1640
200 656
Sea Level
0
200 656
2000 6560
M-569891-7A-DR1-1
Copyright © Rand McNally & Co.
East of Greenwich
0 100 200 300 400 600 800 1000 km
0 100 200 300 400 600 miles
Scale 1 : 10 000 000
Lambert Conformal Conic Projection

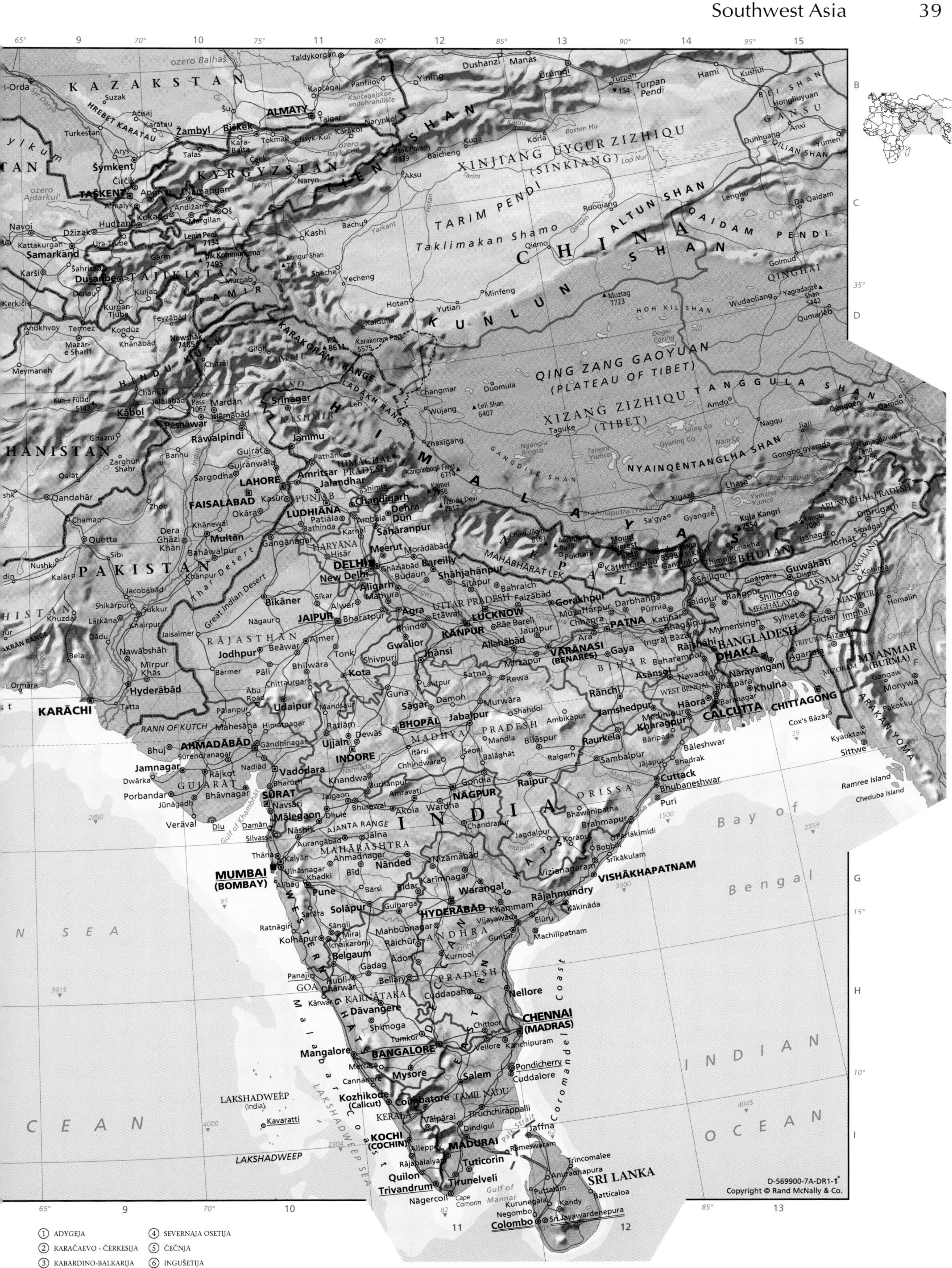
KAZAKSTAN
ALMATY
Biškek
KYRGYZSTAN
TAŠKENT
Samarkand
Dušanbe
TAJIKISTAN
PAMIR
TIEN SHAN
XINJIANG UYGUR ZIZHIQU
(SINKIANG)
TARIM PENDI
Taklimakan Shamo
ALTUN SHAN
QAIDAM PENDI
CHINA
KUNLUN SHAN
QINGHAI
QING ZANG GAOYUAN
(PLATEAU OF TIBET)
XIZANG ZIZHIQU
(TIBET)
TANGGULA SHAN
NYAINQÊNTANGLHA SHAN
HINDU KUSH
KARAKORAM RANGE
Kābol
Peshāwar
Islāmābād
Rāwalpindi
LAHORE
FAISALABAD
Multān
Quetta
PAKISTAN
KARĀCHI
Hyderābād
Thar Desert
Great Indian Desert
HIMALAYA
NEPAL
Kāthmāndau
Mount Everest
BHUTAN
Thimphu
DELHI
New Delhi
JAIPUR
LUCKNOW
KANPUR
VĀRĀNASI
(BENARES)
PATNA
BANGLADESH
DHAKA
CALCUTTA
CHITTAGONG
MYANMAR
(BURMA)
AHMADĀBĀD
SURAT
MUMBAI
(BOMBAY)
INDORE
BHOPĀL
NAGPUR
Pune
HYDERĀBĀD
INDIA
VISHĀKHAPATNAM
BANGALORE
CHENNAI
(MADRAS)
Mysore
Salem
Coimbatore
Kozhikode
(Calicut)
KOCHI
(COCHIN)
MADURAI
Trivandrum
SRI LANKA
Colombo
Sri Jayawardenepura
Bay of Bengal
INDIAN OCEAN
LAKSHADWEEP
(India)
Kavaratti
LAKSHADWEEP SEA
Gulf of Mannar
Coromandel Coast
Malabar Coast
WESTERN GHATS
EASTERN GHATS
D-569900-7A-DR1-1
Copyright © Rand McNally & Co.
1 ADYGEJA
2 KARAČAEVO - ČERKESIJA
3 KABARDINO-BALKARIJA
4 SEVERNAJA OSETIJA
5 ČEČNJA
6 INGUŠETIJA

KAZAKSTAN
KYRGYZSTAN
UZBEKISTAN
TAJIKISTAN
AFGHANISTAN
PAKISTAN
CHINA
BHUTAN
ALMATY
Biškek
TAŠKENT
Dušanbe
Kābol
Peshāwar
Rawalpindi
Islāmābād
LAHORE
FAISALABAD
Multān
Srīnagar
DELHI
New Delhi
LUCKNOW
KĀNPUR
PATNA
Kāthmāndau
Lhasa
Thimphu
TARIM PENDI
Taklimakan Shamo
XINJIANG UYGUR ZIZHIQU
(SINKIANG)
XIZANG ZIZHIQU
(TIBET)
QING ZANG GAOYUAN
(PLATEAU OF TIBET)
QAIDAM PENDI
QINGHAI
GANSU
KUNLUN SHAN
ALTUN SHAN
HOH XIL SHAN
TANGGULA SHAN
GANGDISÊ SHAN
NYAINQÊNTANGLHA SHAN
QILIAN SHAN
TIEN SHAN
PAMIR
HINDU KUSH
KARAKORAM RANGE
LADAKH RANGE
ZASKAR MOUNTAINS
HIMALAYAS
K2 (Qogir Feng) 8611
Mount Everest 8848
Kānchenjunga 8598
Nanga Parbat 8126
Great Indian Desert
RĀJASTHĀN
UTTAR PRADESH
PUNJAB
HARYĀNA
HIMACHAL PRADESH
BIHĀR
ASSAM
MEGHĀLAYA
NAGALAND
MANIPUR
ARUNĀCHAL PRADESH
SIKKIM
Indus
Ganges (Ganga)
Brahmaputra
70°
75°
80°
85°
90°
95°
40°
35°
30°
25°

A Area occupied by Pakistan and claimed by India.
B Area claimed and occupied by India; status disputed by Pakistan.
C Area occupied by China and claimed by India.
D Area occupied by India and claimed by China.
Scale 1 : 10 000 000
Lambert Conformal Conic Projection
East of Greenwich
D-566200-7A-DR1-1
Copyright © Rand McNally & Co.
Metres
Feet
Sea Level
ARABIAN SEA
Bay of Bengal
INDIAN OCEAN
ANDAMAN SEA
MYANMAR (BURMA)
SRI LANKA
MALDIVES
LAKSHADWEEP
ANDAMAN AND NICOBAR ISLANDS (India)
NICOBAR ISLANDS
ANDAMAN ISLANDS
MUMBAI (BOMBAY)
CHENNAI (MADRAS)
CALCUTTA
HYDERĀBĀD
BANGALORE
KOCHI (COCHIN)
VISHĀKHAPATNAM
NĀGPUR
CHITTAGONG
Colombo
Malabar Coast
Coromandel Coast
WESTERN GHĀTS
EASTERN GHĀTS
Mouths of the Ganges
Ten Degree Channel
Nine Degree Channel
Eight Degree Channel
Gulf of Mannar
Palk Strait
Preparis North Channel
Preparis South Channel
Great Channel
Duncan Passage
Gulf of Khambhāt

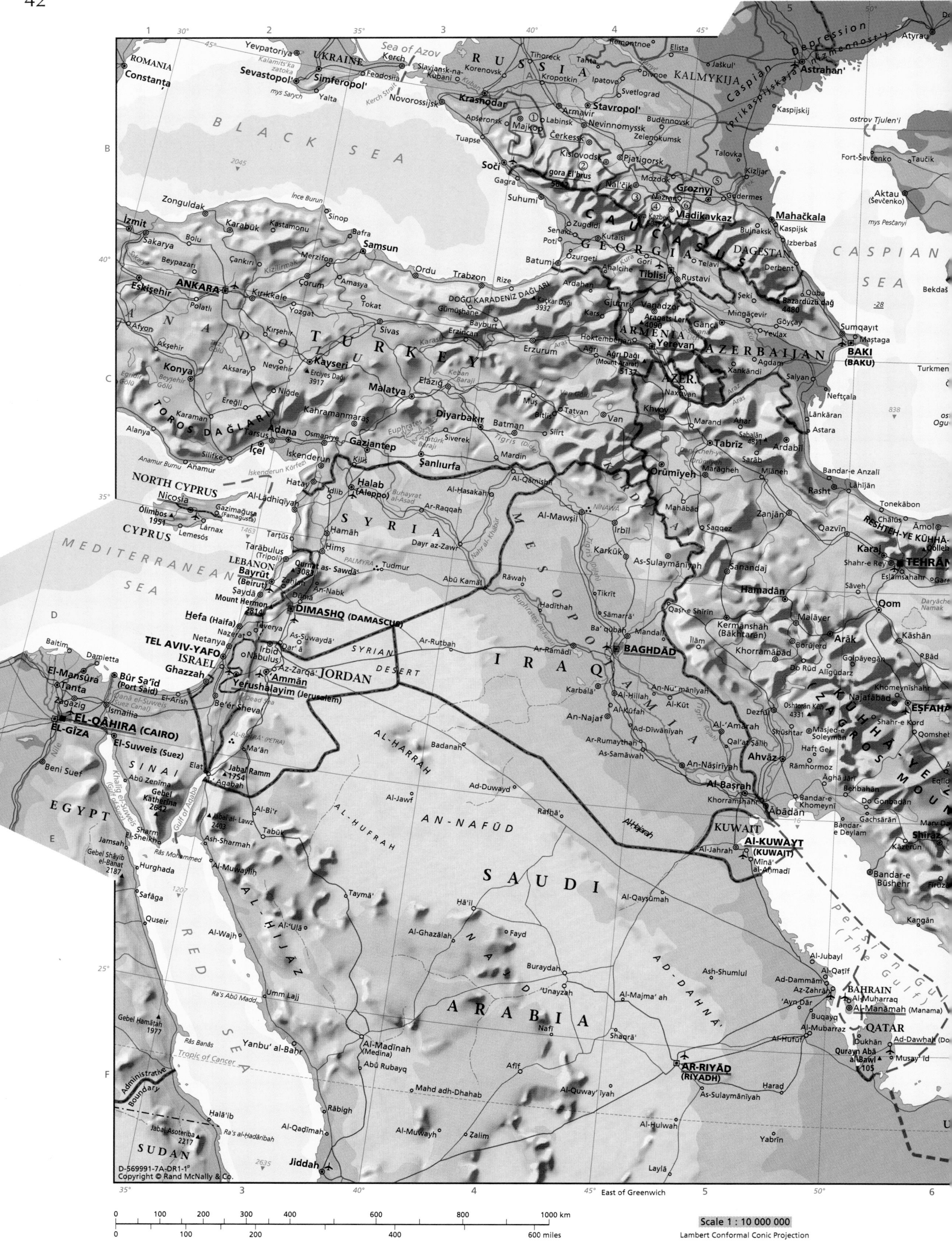
ROMANIA
Constanța
UKRAINE
Yevpatoriya
Sevastopol'
Simferopol'
Yalta
Kerch
Feodosiya
Sea of Azov
RUSSIA
Krasnodar
Novorossijsk
Stavropol'
Armavir
Majkop
Nevinnomyssk
Čerkessk
Kislovodsk
Pjatigorsk
Budënnovsk
Tihoreck
Elista
KALMYKIJA
Caspian Depression
Astrahan'
Atyrau
Kaspijskij
ostrov Tjulen'i
Fort-Ševčenko
Aktau (Ševčenko)
Tuapse
Soči
Gagra
Suhumi
gora El'brus 5642
Nal'čik
Mozdok
Groznyj
Nazran'
Vladikavkaz
Gudermes
Kizljar
Mahačkala
Kaspijsk
Izberbaš
Bujnaksk
DAGESTAN
Derbent
CASPIAN SEA
BLACK SEA
CAUCASUS
GEORGIA
Zugdidi
Kutaisi
Poti
Senaki
Batumi
Ozurgeti
Gori
Tbilisi
Rustavi
Telavi
Ahalcihe
Ardahan
Kars
Gjumri
Vanadzor
Aragats Lerr 4090
ARMENIA
Yerevan
Hoktemberjan
Ağrı Dağı (Mount Ararat) 5137
AZERBAIJAN
Gäncä
Mingäçevir
Göyçay
Yevlax
Şeki
Quba
Bazardüzü dağ 4480
Sumqayıt
BAKI (BAKU)
Maştaga
Xankändi
Agdam
AZER.
Naxçıvan
Salyan
Neftçala
Länkäran
Astara
Turkmen
Zonguldak
İnce Burun
Sinop
Bafra
Samsun
İzmit
Karabük
Kastamonu
Sakarya
Bolu
Beypazarı
Çankırı
Merzifon
Amasya
Çorum
Ordu
Trabzon
Rize
Eskişehir
ANKARA
Kırıkkale
Polatlı
Yozgat
Tokat
DOĞU KARADENİZ DAĞLARI
Kaçkar Dağı 3932
Gümüşhane
Bayburt
Afyon
Akşehir
Kırşehir
Sivas
Erzincan
Erzurum
Ağrı
TURKEY
ANADOLU
Konya
Aksaray
Nevşehir
Kayseri
Erciyes Dağı 3917
Malatya
Elazığ
Muş
Bitlis
Tatvan
Van
Van Gölü
Niğde
Ereğli
Karaman
TOROS DAĞLARI
Kahramanmaraş
Diyarbakır
Batman
Siirt
Alanya
Tarsus
Adana
Osmaniye
Gaziantep
Şanlıurfa
Siverek
Mardin
Silifke
İçel
İskenderun
Anamur Burnu
Anamur
Hatay
Kilis
NORTH CYPRUS
Nicosia
Gazimağusa (Famagusta)
Ólimbos 1951
Lárnax
Lemesós
CYPRUS
MEDITERRANEAN SEA
Al-Lādhiqīyah
Idlib
Halab (Aleppo)
Buhayrat al-Asad
Ar-Raqqah
Al-Ḥasakah
Al-Qāmishlī
SYRIA
Ṭarṭūs
Ḥamāh
Ḥimṣ
Ṭarābulus (Tripoli)
LEBANON
Qurnat as-Sawdā' 3083
Bayrūt (Beirut)
Ṣaydā
Mount Hermon 2814
Zaḥlah
An-Nabk
Dūmā
DIMASHQ (DAMASCUS)
PALMYRA
Tudmur
Dayr az-Zawr
Abū Kamāl
Al-Mawṣil
NĪNAWĀ
Irbīl
Karkūk
As-Sulaymānīyah
MESOPOTAMIA
Rāwah
Tikrīt
Sāmarrā'
Ḥadīthah
Ba'qūbah
Mandalī
Ar-Ramādī
BAGHDĀD
IRAQ
Karbalā'
Al-Ḥillah
Al-Kūfah
An-Najaf
Ad-Dīwānīyah
An-Nu'mānīyah
Al-Kūt
Al-'Amārah
Qal'at Ṣāliḥ
Ar-Rumaythah
As-Samāwah
An-Nāṣirīyah
Al-Baṣrah
Khorramshahr
Ābādān
KUWAIT
Al-KUWAYT (KUWAIT)
Al-Jahrah
Mīnā' al-Aḥmadī
Hefa (Haifa)
Netanya
Nazerat
Teverya
TEL AVIV-YAFO
ISRAEL
Nābulus
Irbid
Dar'ā
As-Suwaydā'
Az-Zarqā'
'Ammān
JORDAN
Yerushalayim (Jerusalem)
Ghazzah
Be'ér Sheva'
Dead Sea
Ar-Ruṭbah
SYRIAN DESERT
Ma'ān
AL-BATRĀ' (PETRA)
Jabal Ramm 1754
Elat
'Aqabah
Baltim
Damietta
El-Mansûra
Tanta
Bûr Sa'îd (Port Said)
Zagazig
Ismailia
El-'Arîsh
EL-QÂHIRA (CAIRO)
EL-GÎZA
El-Suweis (Suez)
Nile
Beni Suef
SINAI
Abû Zenîma
Gebel Katherina 2642
EGYPT
Sharm el-Sheikh
Gulf of Aqaba
Jamsah
Gebel Shâyib el-Banat 2187
Hurghada
Safâga
Quseir
Al-Jawf
Badanah
Ad-Duwayd
Rafḥā'
Al-Bi'r
AL-HARRAH
AL-HUFRAH
AN-NAFŪD
Tabūk
Jabal al-Lawz 2403
Ash-Sharmah
Al-Muwayliḥ
Taymā'
SAUDI ARABIA
AL-ḤIJĀZ
Al-'Ulā
Al-Wajh
Ḥā'il
Al-Ghazālah
Fayd
NAJD
Al-Qayṣūmah
Buraydah
'Unayzah
Al-Majma'ah
AD-DAHNĀ'
Ash-Shumlul
Al-Jubayl
Al-Qaṭīf
Ad-Dammām
Az-Zahrān
'Ayn Dār
Buqayq
BAHRAIN
Al-Muḥarraq
Al-Manāmah (Manama)
QATAR
Ad-Dawḥah
Dukhān
Musay'īd
Qurayn Abā al-Bawl 105
Al-Hufūf
Al-Mubarraz
Shaqrā'
Nafī
Umm Lajj
Ra's Abū Madd
RED SEA
Gebel Ḥamāṭah 1977
Râs Banâs
Yanbu' al-Baḥr
Tropic of Cancer
Al-Madīnah (Medina)
Abū Rubayq
Afīf
AR-RIYĀḌ (RIYADH)
As-Sulaymānīyah
Ḥaraḍ
Al-Quway'īyah
Mahd adh-Dhahab
Rābigh
Al-Qaḍīmah
Al-Muwayh
Ẓalim
Al-Hulwah
Yabrīn
Laylā
Jiddah
Halā'ib
Jabal Asoteriba 2217
SUDAN
Administrative Boundary
Ra's al-Ḥadāribah
Persian Gulf (The Gulf)
Tabrīz
Ahar
Sabalān 4811
Ardabīl
Marand
Khvoy
Orūmīyeh
Marāgheh
Sarāb
Mīāneh
Bandar-e Anzalī
Rasht
Lāhījān
Tonekābon
Chālūs
Āmol
Mahābād
Saqqez
Zanjān
Qazvīn
RESHTEH-YE KŪHHĀ-YE ALBORZ
Karaj
Shahr-e Rey
TEHRĀN
Eslāmshahr
Sāveh
Qom
Daryācheh-ye Namak
Sanandaj
Hamadān
Malāyer
Arāk
Kāshān
Qaṣr-e Shīrīn
Kermānshāh (Bākhtarān)
Īlām
Borūjerd
Khorramābād
Golpāyegān
Dō Rūd
Alīgūdarz
Khomeynīshahr
Najafābād
EṢFAHĀN
Shahr-e Kord
Oshtorān Kūh 4331
Dezfūl
Shūshtar
Masjed-e Soleymān
Haft Gel
Ahvāz
Rāmhormoz
Āghā Jārī
Behbahān
Do Gonbadān
Gachsārān
Bandar-e Khomeynī
Bandar-e Deylam
Shīrāz
Kāzerūn
Bandar-e Būshehr
Kangān
ZAGROS MOUNTAINS
D-569991-7A-DR1-1
Copyright © Rand McNally & Co.
East of Greenwich
0 100 200 300 400 600 800 1000 km
0 100 200 400 600 miles
Scale 1 : 10 000 000
Lambert Conformal Conic Projection

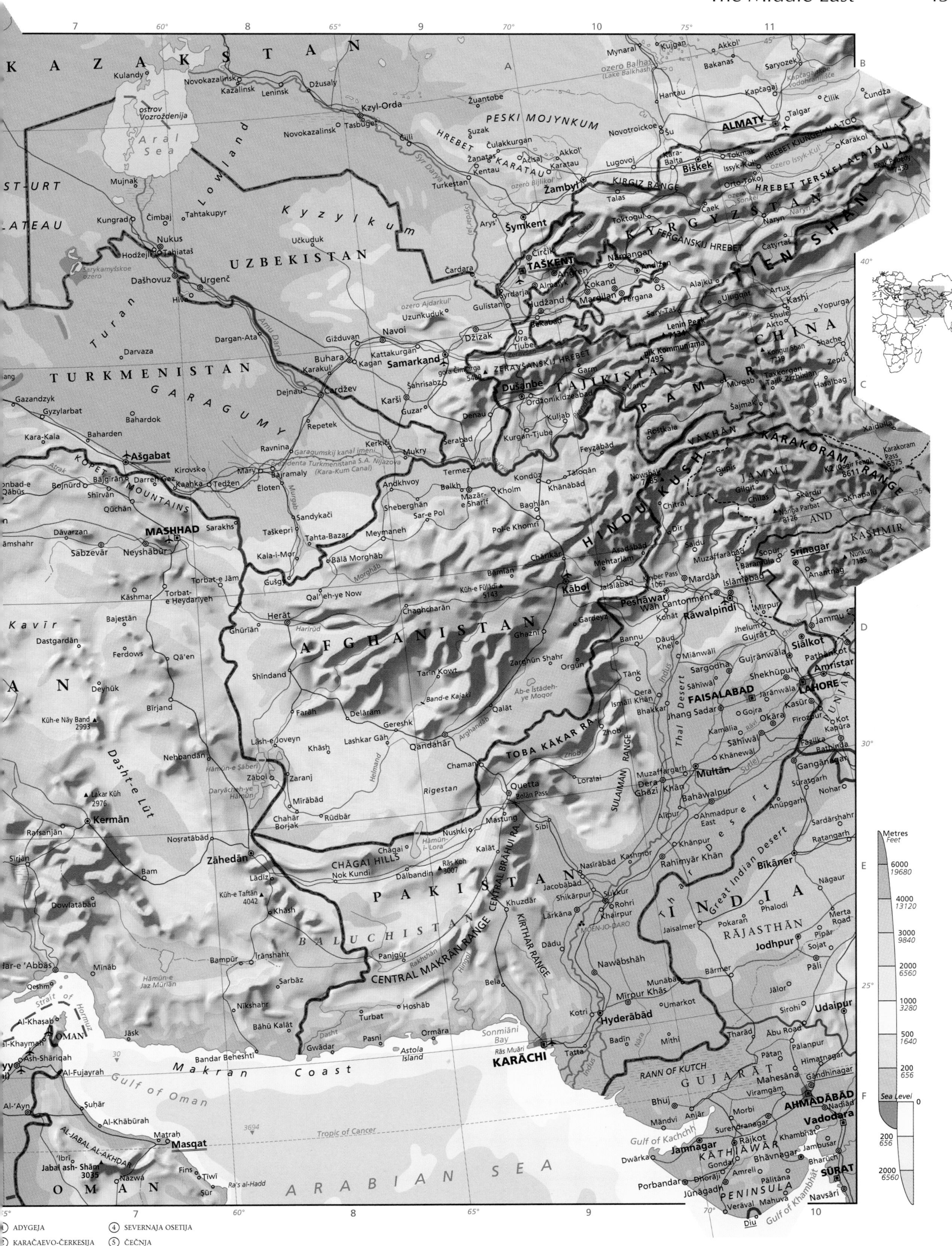
KAZAKSTAN
UZBEKISTAN
TURKMENISTAN
KYRGYZSTAN
TAJIKISTAN
AFGHANISTAN
PAKISTAN
INDIA
CHINA
OMAN
JAMMU AND KASHMIR
Aral Sea
ostrov Vozroždenija
Turan Lowland
Kyzylkum
GARAGUMY
PESKI MOJYNKUM
TIEN SHAN
PAMIR
HINDU KUSH
KARAKORAM RANGE
TOBA KĀKAR RA.
SULAIMĀN RANGE
KĪRTHAR RANGE
CENTRAL MAKRĀN RANGE
CENTRAL BRĀHUI RA.
CHĀGAI HILLS
BALUCHISTAN
KOPET MOUNTAINS
Thar Desert
Great Indian Desert
RĀJASTHĀN
GUJARĀT
RANN OF KUTCH
KĀTHIĀWĀR PENINSULA
Makran Coast
Gulf of Oman
ARABIAN SEA
Gulf of Kachchh
Gulf of Khambhāt
Strait of Hormuz
Tropic of Cancer
Dasht-e Lūt
Kavīr
Rigestan
ALMATY
Biškek
TAŠKENT
Dušanbe
Kābol
Islāmābād
Ašgabat
MASHHAD
KARĀCHI
LAHORE
FAISALABAD
AHMADĀBĀD
Masqat
Samarkand
Buhara
Herāt
Qandahār
Quetta
Peshāwar
Rāwalpindi
Multān
Hyderābād
Srinagar
Kermān
Zāhedān
Nukus
Kzyl-Orda
Šymkent
Žambyl
Kashi
Jodhpur
Vadodara
SŪRAT
Udaipur
Bīkāner
Jamnagar
Rājkot
Metres
Feet
6000 19680
4000 13120
3000 9840
2000 6560
1000 3280
500 1640
200 656
Sea Level 0
200 656
2000 6560
ADYGEJA
KARAČAEVO-ČERKESIJA
KABARDINO-BALKARIJA
SEVERNAJA OSETIJA
ČEČNJA
INGUŠETIJA

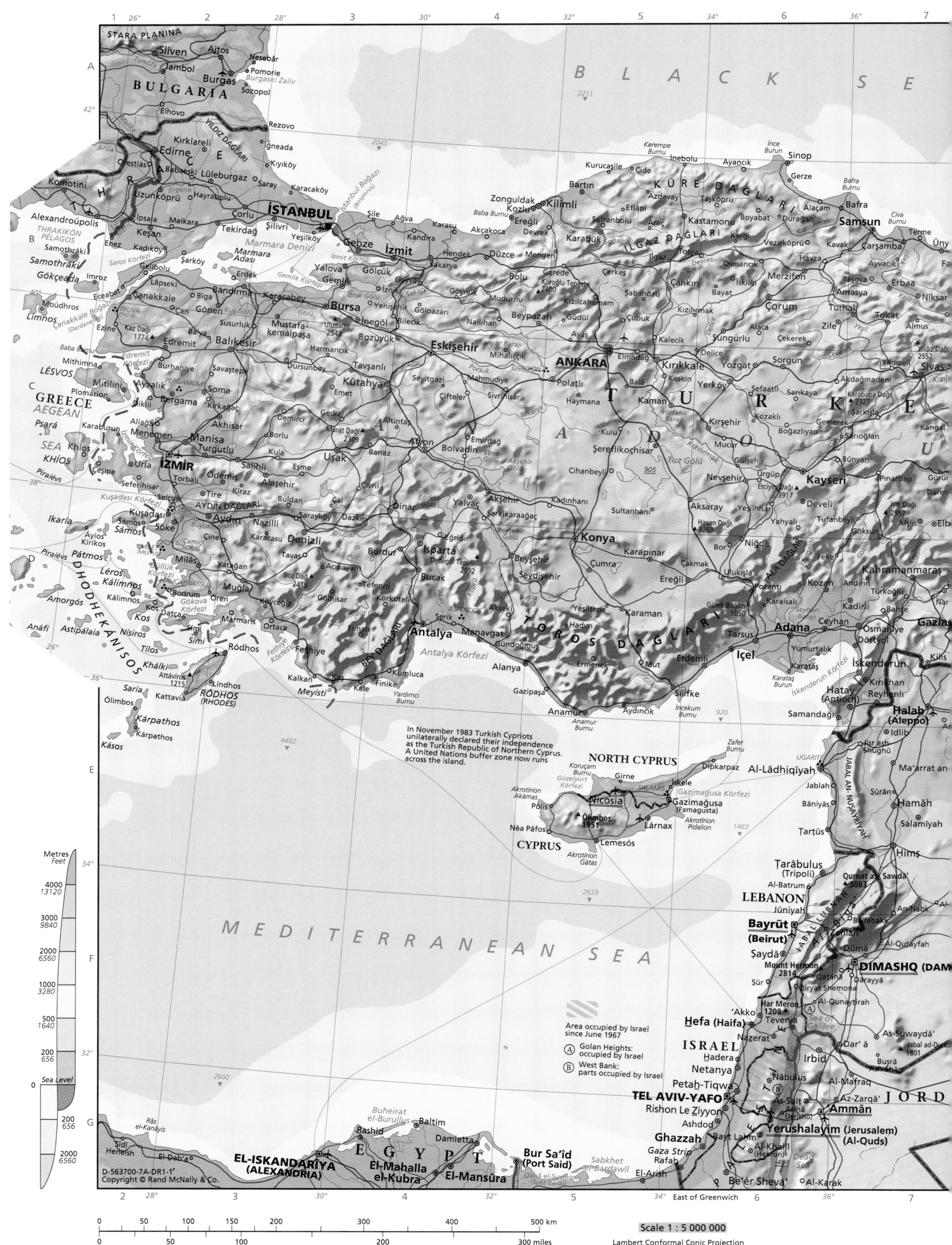
BLACK SEA
MEDITERRANEAN SEA
AEGEAN SEA
BULGARIA
GREECE
TURKEY
ANATOLIA
THRACE
NORTH CYPRUS
CYPRUS
LEBANON
ISRAEL
EGYPT
DHODHEKANISOS
İSTANBUL
ANKARA
İZMİR
Bursa
Eskişehir
Konya
Kayseri
Adana
Antalya
Samsun
Nicosia
Bayrūt (Beirut)
DIMASHQ
TEL AVIV-YAFO
Yerushalayim (Jerusalem) (Al-Quds)
'Ammān
Halab (Aleppo)
EL-ISKANDARĪYA (ALEXANDRIA)
Bur Sa'îd (Port Said)
KÜRE DAĞLARI
ILGAZ DAĞLARI
TOROS DAĞLARI
In November 1983 Turkish Cypriots unilaterally declared their independence as the Turkish Republic of Northern Cyprus. A United Nations buffer zone now runs across the island.
Area occupied by Israel since June 1967
A Golan Heights: occupied by Israel
B West Bank: parts occupied by Israel
Metres Feet
4000 13120
3000 9840
2000 6560
1000 3280
500 1640
200 656
0 Sea Level
200 656
2000 6560
East of Greenwich
D-563700-7A-DR1-1°
Copyright © Rand McNally & Co.
Scale 1 : 5 000 000
Lambert Conformal Conic Projection
0 50 100 150 200 300 400 500 km
0 50 100 200 300 miles

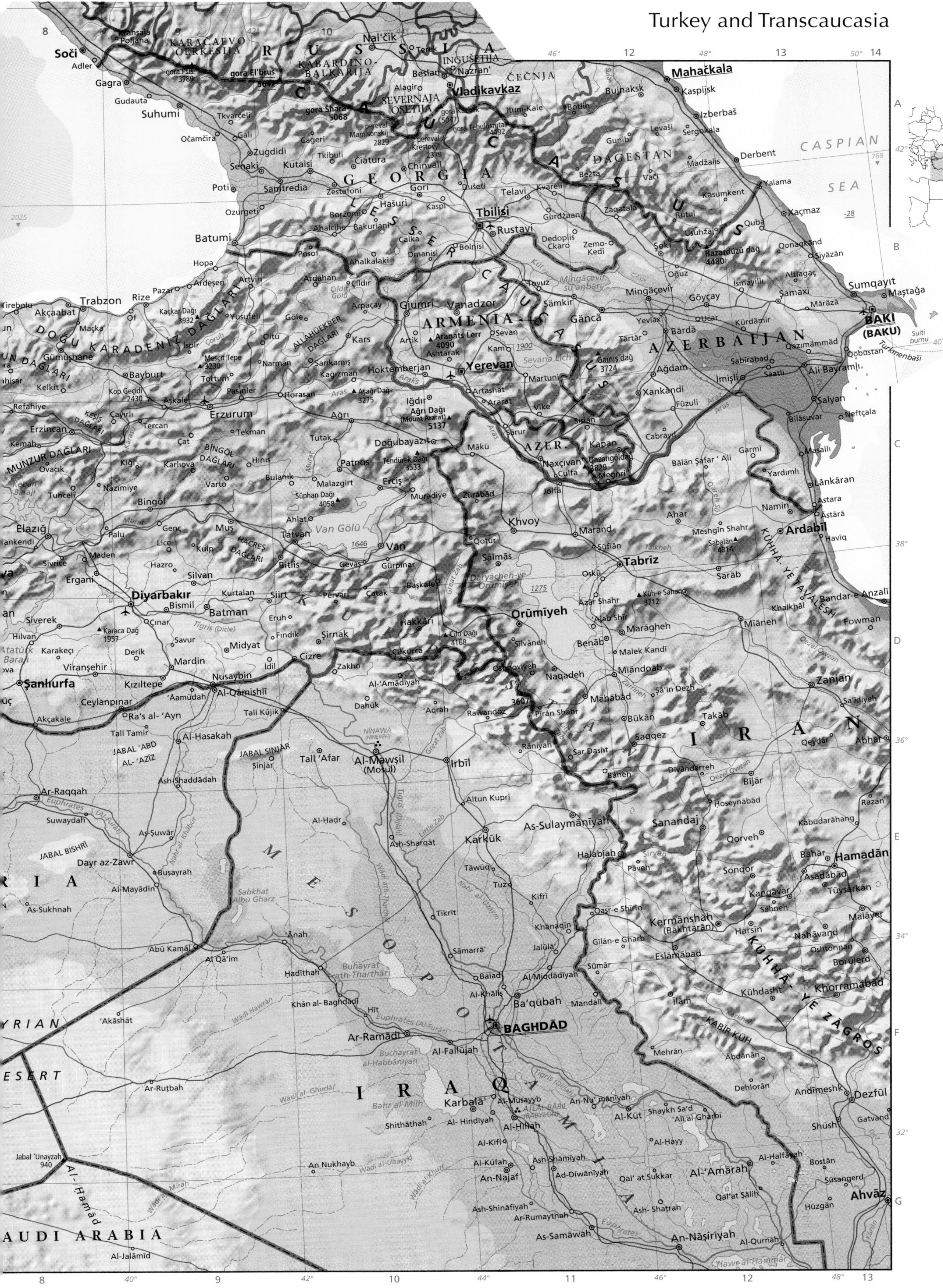
R U S S I A
Soči
Adler
Gagra
Gudauta
Suhumi
Tkvarčeli
Očamčira
Gali
Zugdidi
Senaki
Poti
Samtredia
Kutaisi
Tkibuli
Čiatura
Zestafoni
Ozurgeti
Batumi
Nal'čik
Beslan
Nazran'
INGUŠETIJA
ČEČNJA
KARAČAEVO ČERKESIJA
KABARDINO-BALKARIJA
SEVERNAJA OSETIJA
Vladikavkaz
Alagir
gora El'brus 5642
gora Šhara 5068
C A U C A S U S
Mahačkala
Kaspijsk
Bujnaksk
Izberbaš
Sergokala
Derbent
DAGESTAN
Gunib
Levaši
Madžalis
Vači
Bežta
Botlih
Itum-Kale
CASPIAN SEA
Yalama
Kasumkent
Xaçmaz
Rutul
Usuhčaj
Quba
Bazardüzü dağ 4480
Qonaqkənd
Siyəzən
Sumqayıt
Maştağa
BAKI (BAKU)
Ələt
Qobustan
Türkmenbaşi
G E O R G I A
Gori
Chinvali
Dušeti
Kaspi
Telavi
Kvareli
Gurdžaani
Tbilisi
Rustavi
Borzomi
Bakuriani
Ahalcihe
Hašuri
Calka
Bolnisi
Dmanisi
Ahalkalaki
Dedoplis Ckaro
Zemo-Kedi
Zaqatala
Şəki
Mingəçevir
Ismayıllı
Altıağac
Şamaxı
Göyçay
Oğuz
Kür
Mingəçevir su anbarı
Gəncə
Şəmkir
Tovuz
A Z E R B A I J A N
Yevlax
Bərdə
Tərtər
Ağdam
Xankəndi
Füzuli
Kürdəmir
Əli Bayramlı
İmişli
Sabirabad
Saatlı
Salyan
Neftçala
Biləsuvar
Cəbrayıl
Masallı
Lənkəran
Astara
Yardımlı
A R M E N I A
Gjumri
Vanadzor
Aragats Lerr 4090
Ashtarak
Artik
Sevan
Sevana Lich
Yerevan
Hoktemberjan
Artashat
Ararat
Martuni
Vike
Sisian
Kapan
Meghri
Gamış dağ 3724
AZER.
Naxçıvan
Culfa
Şərur
Qazangödağ 3829
L E S S E R C A U C A S U S
Hopa
Artvin
Ardeşen
Pazar
Rize
Trabzon
Akçaabat
Tirebolu
Of
Maçka
Gümüşhane
Bayburt
Kelkit
Ispir
Yusufeli
Kaçkar Dağı 3932
DOĞU KARADENİZ DAĞLARI
Ardahan
Çıldır
Göle
Oltu
Kars
Arpaçay
Sarıkamış
Kağızman
Narman
Tortum
Mescit Tepe 3230
Pasinler
Horasan
Aşkale
Erzurum
Kop Geçidi 2430
Erzincan
Refahiye
Tercan
Çayırlı
Tekman
Çat
Hınıs
Karlıova
Kiğı
Kemah
MUNZUR DAĞLARI
BİNGÖL DAĞLARI
Ovacık
Tunceli
Nazımiye
Bingöl
Varto
Bulanık
Malazgirt
Patnos
Erciş
Muradiye
Ağrı
Tutak
Doğubayazıt
Iğdır
Ağrı Dağı (Mount Ararat) 5137
Tendürek Dağı 3533
Süphan Dağı 4058
Ahlat
Tatvan
Van Gölü
Van
Muş
Genç
Lice
Kulp
Palu
Elazığ
Maden
Sivrice
Hazro
Ergani
Silvan
Bitlis
Gevaş
Gürpınar
Başkale
Çatak
Pervari
Diyarbakır
Bismil
Kurtalan
Siirt
Batman
Eruh
Şirnak
Hakkâri
Cilo Dağı 4168
Çukurca
Siverek
Hilvan
Karakeçi
Çınar
Savur
Midyat
Mardin
Derik
Viranşehir
Şanlıurfa
Kızıltepe
Nusaybin
İdil
Cizre
Ceylanpınar
Akçakale
Al-Qāmishlī
'Āmūdah
Ra's al-'Ayn
Tall Tamir
Al-Ḥasakah
JABAL 'ABD AL-'AZĪZ
JABAL SINJĀR
Sinjār
Tall 'Afar
Tall Kūjik
Zākhō
Dahūk
Al-'Amādīyah
'Aqrah
Rawāndūz
Al-Mawṣil (Mosul)
NĪNAWĀ (NINEVEH)
Irbīl
Altun Kupri
Kirkūk
As-Sulaymānīyah
Ḥalabjah
Ash-Shaddādah
Ar-Raqqah
Suwaydah
As-Ṣuwār
Dayr az-Zawr
Buṣayrah
Al-Mayādīn
As-Sukhnah
Abū Kamāl
Al-Qā'im
JABAL BISHRĪ
S Y R I A
SYRIAN DESERT
M E S O P O T A M I A
'Ānah
Ḥadīthah
Buḥayrat ath-Tharthār
Tikrīt
Sāmarrā'
Balad
Al-Khāliṣ
Ba'qūbah
Al-Miqdādīyah
Khān al-Baghdādī
Hīt
Ar-Ramādī
Al-Fallūjah
BAGHDĀD
Buḥayrat al-Ḥabbānīyah
'Akāshāt
Ar-Ruṭbah
I R A Q
Karbalā'
Al-Musayyib
Al-Hindīyah
Al-Ḥillah
ATLĀL BĀBIL (BABYLON)
Al-Kifl
Al-Kūfah
An-Najaf
Ash-Shāmīyah
Ad-Dīwānīyah
Shithāthah
An Nukhayb
Bahr al-Milh
Jabal 'Unayzah 940
Al-Ḥamād
S A U D I A R A B I A
Al-Jalāmīd
Ash-Shināfīyah
Ar-Rumaythah
As-Samāwah
An-Nāṣirīyah
Al-Qurnah
Al-Kūt
An-Nu'mānīyah
Shaykh Sa'd
'Alī al-Gharbī
Al-Ḥayy
Qal'at Sukkar
Al-'Amārah
Qal'at Ṣāliḥ
Ash-Shaṭrah
Hawr al-Ḥammār
I R A N
Khvoy
Marand
Jolfā
Ahar
Meshgīn Shahr
Ardabīl
Namīn
Āstārā
Sabalān 4814
Tabrīz
Sarāb
Sūfiān
Salmās
Qoṭūr
Oskū
Daryācheh-ye Orūmīyeh
Kūh-e Sahand 3712
Āzar Shahr
Orūmīyeh
Marāgheh
Malek Kandī
Mīāneh
Miyāndoāb
Naqadeh
Oshnovīyeh
Mahābād
Būkān
Saqqez
Sar Dasht
Pīrān Shahr
Bāneh
Zanjān
Abhar
Qeydār
Bījār
Dīvāndarreh
Sanandaj
Qorveh
Hamadān
Asadābād
Kangāvar
Tūysarkān
Malāyer
Nahāvand
Kermānshāh (Bākhtarān)
Harsīn
Eslāmābād
Gīlān-e Gharb
Qaṣr-e Shīrīn
Pāveh
Mandalī
Īlām
Mehrān
Dehlorān
Kūhdasht
Khorramābād
Borūjerd
Andīmeshk
Dezfūl
Shūsh
Gotvand
Bostān
Sūsangerd
Ahvāz
Hūzgān
KŪHHĀ-YE ZĀGROS
KABĪR KŪH
KŪHHĀ-YE TAVĀLESH
Bandar-e Anzalī
Fowman
Khalkhāl
Rasht
Euphrates
Tigris
Great Zab
Little Zab
Wādī ath-Tharthār
Wādī Ḥawrān
Aras
Kür
8
9
10
11
12
13
14
40°
42°
44°
46°
48°
50°
32°
34°
36°
38°
A
B
C
D
E
F
G

ATLANTIC OCEAN
NORWEGIAN SEA
GREENLAND SEA
BARENTS SEA
KARSKOE MORE
NORTH SEA
BALTIC SEA
BLACK SEA
CASPIAN SEA
Aral Sea
MEDITERRANEAN SEA
Tyrrhenian Sea
Ionian Sea
Aegean Sea
Adriatic Sea
Labrador Sea
Hudson Bay
Hudson Strait
Davis Strait
Denmark Strait
Strait of Gibraltar
Bay of Biscay
English Channel
Persian Gulf
Gulf of Oman
Gulf of Bothnia
CANADA
BAFFIN ISLAND
GREENLAND (Denmark)
ICELAND
Reykjavík
FAROE ISLANDS (Den.)
SHETLAND ISLANDS (U.K.)
ORKNEY ISLANDS
SPITSBERGEN
SVALBARD (Nor.)
Bjørnøya (Nor.)
Jan Mayen (Nor.)
ZEMLJA FRANCA-IOSIFA
NOVAJA ZEMLJA
SEVERNAJA ZEMLJA
UNITED KINGDOM
IRELAND
DUBLIN
LONDON
EDINBURGH
Belfast
Manchester
Cardiff
Cork
NORWAY
Oslo
Bergen
Trondheim
SWEDEN
STOCKHOLM
FINLAND
HELSINKI
DENMARK
KØBENHAVN
NETH.
AMSTERDAM
BELGIUM
BRUXELLES
LUX.
FRANCE
PARIS
MARSEILLE
Bordeaux
Nantes
Brest
Nice
Corse (Fr.)
ANDORRA
SPAIN
MADRID
BARCELONA
VALÈNCIA
Bilbao
A Coruña
ILLES BALEARS
Mallorca
PORTUGAL
LISBOA
Porto
GIBRALTAR (U.K.)
GERMANY
BERLIN
HAMBURG
FRANKFURT
MÜNCHEN
Bonn
SWITZ.
Bern
AUSTRIA
WIEN
CZECH REP.
PRAHA
SLOVAKIA
HUNGARY
BUDAPEST
POLAND
WARSZAWA
Gdańsk
Kraków
ITALY
ROMA
MILANO
NAPOLI
Venezia
Palermo
Sicilia
Sardegna (It.)
MALTA
SLO.
CROATIA
Zagreb
BOS.
Sarajevo
YUGO.
Beograd
MACE.
Skopje
ALB.
Tiranë
GREECE
ATHINAI
Thessaloníki
Kríti
Iráklion
BULGARIA
SOFIJA
ROMANIA
BUCUREŞTI
MOLDOVA
Chişinău
UKRAINE
KYIV
KHARKIV
ODESA
DNIPROPETROVS'K
DONETS'K
L'viv
Sevastopol'
BELARUS
MINSK
Homel'
LITHUANIA
Vilnius
LATVIA
RIGA
ESTONIA
Tallinn
RUSSIA
R U S S I A
MOSKVA
SANKT-PETERBURG
NIŽNIJ NOVGOROD
KAZAN'
SAMARA
SARATOV
VOLGOGRAD
ROSTOV-NA-DONU
PERM'
UFA
EKATERINBURG
ČELJABINSK
OMSK
NOVOSIBIRSK
Arhangel'sk
Murmansk
Vologda
Jaroslavl'
Tula
Voronež
Penza
Kirov
Kotlas
Novgorod
Tver'
Smolensk
Brjansk
Krasnodar
Astrahan'
Orenburg
Orsk
Magnitogorsk
Tomsk
Kemerovo
Novokuzneck
Barnaul
Krasnojarsk
Vorkuta
Salehard
Noril'sk
Jakutsk
URAL'SKIE GORY
ZAPADNO-SIBIRSKAJA RAVNINA
SREDNESIBIRSKOE PLOSKOGORE
CAUCASUS
GEORGIA
Tbilisi
ARMENIA
Yerevan
AZERBAIJAN
BAKI
KAZAKSTAN
ALMATY
Akmola
Karaganda
Semipalatinsk
Atyrau
Aral'sk
UZBEKISTAN
TAŠKENT
Samarkand
Nukus
TURKMENISTAN
Ašgabat
KYRGYZSTAN
Biškek
TAJIKISTAN
Dušanbe
AFGHANISTAN
Kābol
Herāt
Qandahār
PAKISTAN
KARĀCHI
Peshāwar
Quetta
IRAN
TEHRĀN
ESFAHĀN
MASHHAD
Tabrīz
Kermān
Shīrāz
Hamadān
Bandar-e 'Abbās
TURKEY
ANKARA
İSTANBUL
İZMIR
Adana
Samsun
Eskişehir
İskenderun
Diyarbakir
CYPRUS
SYRIA
DIMASHQ
Halab
LEBANON
Bayrūt
ISRAEL
Yerushalayim
JORDAN
'Ammān
IRAQ
BAGHDĀD
Al-Basrah
Al-Mawşil
KUWAIT
AL-KUWAYT
SAUDI ARABIA
AR-RIYĀD
Makkah
Jiddah
Al-Madīnah
BAHRAIN
Al-Manāmah
QATAR
UNITED ARAB EMIRATES
Abū Zaby
OMAN
Masqaţ
EGYPT
EL-QÂHIRA
EL-ISKANDARÎYA
Aswân
Asyûţ
LIBYA
Ţarābulus
Banghāzī
TUNISIA
TUNIS
Sfax
ALGERIA
EL DJAZAÏR
Wahran
Annaba
MOROCCO
Rabat
CASABLANCA
Fès
Tanger
Marrakech
Oujda
ATLAS MOUNTAINS
WESTERN SAHARA
El Aaiún
MAURITANIA
ARQUIPÉLAGO DA MADEIRA (Port.)
Funchal
ISLAS CANARIAS (Spain)
AÇORES (Port.)
Ponta Delgada
SAHARA
Tropic of Cancer
Arctic Circle

GUINEA
Conakry
Freetown
SIERRA LEONE
Monrovia
LIBERIA
COTE D'IVOIRE
Bouaké
Yamoussoukro
ABIDJAN
GHANA
Kumasi
ACCRA
TOGO
Lomé
BENIN
Porto-Novo
NIGERIA
Abuja
Kano
Kaduna
Ogbomosho
Ibadan
LAGOS
Enugu
Port-Harcourt
CAMEROON
Douala
Yaoundé
Gulf of Guinea
SAO TOME AND PRINCIPE
São Tomé
EQUAT. GUINEA
Malabo
Libreville
GABON
CONGO
Brazzaville
Pointe-Noire
KINSHASA
Matadi
CENTRAL AFRICAN REPUBLIC
Bangui
DEM. REP. OF THE CONGO (ZAIRE)
Kisangani
Mbandaka
Kananga
Lubumbashi
Likasi
RWANDA
Kigali
BURUNDI
Bujumbura
UGANDA
Kampala
KENYA
Nairobi
Mombasa
ETHIOPIA
ADIS ABEBA
Dire Dawa
DJIBOUTI
Djibouti
SOMALIA
Muqdisho
TANZANIA
Dodoma
DAR ES SALAAM
Zanzibar
Kilimanjaro 5895
ANGOLA
LUANDA
Lobito
Huambo
Namibe
ZAMBIA
Ndola
Lusaka
MALAWI
Lilongwe
Blantyre
MOZAMBIQUE
Beira
MAPUTO
ZIMBABWE
Harare
Bulawayo
NAMIBIA
Windhoek
Walvis Bay
Lüderitz
BOTSWANA
Gaborone
KALAHARI DESERT
SOUTH AFRICA
PRETORIA
JOHANNESBURG
Bloemfontein
DURBAN
East London
Port Elizabeth
CAPE TOWN (KAAPSTAD)
Cape of Good Hope
LESOTHO
Maseru
SWAZILAND
Mbabane
MADAGASCAR
ANTANANARIVO
Toamasina
Toliara
Tolañaro
COMOROS
Moroni
MAYOTTE (Fr.)
SEYCHELLES
Victoria
MAURITIUS
Port Louis
RÉUNION (Fr.)
Saint-Denis
MASCARENE ISLANDS
Rodrigues
Mozambique Channel
INDIAN OCEAN
ATLANTIC OCEAN
Ascension (St. Hel.)
ST. HELENA (U.K.)
TRISTAN DA CUNHA GROUP (St. Hel.)
Gough Island (St. Hel.)
PRINCE EDWARD ISLANDS (S. Afr.)
ARCHIPEL CROZET (Fr.)
Equator
Tropic of Capricorn
West of Greenwich 0° East of Greenwich
Scale 1 : 35 000 000
Lambert Azimuthal Equal Area
0 400 800 1600 2400 3200 4000 km
0 400 800 1600 2400 miles
M-800000-2A-DR1-2
Copyright © Rand McNally & Co.

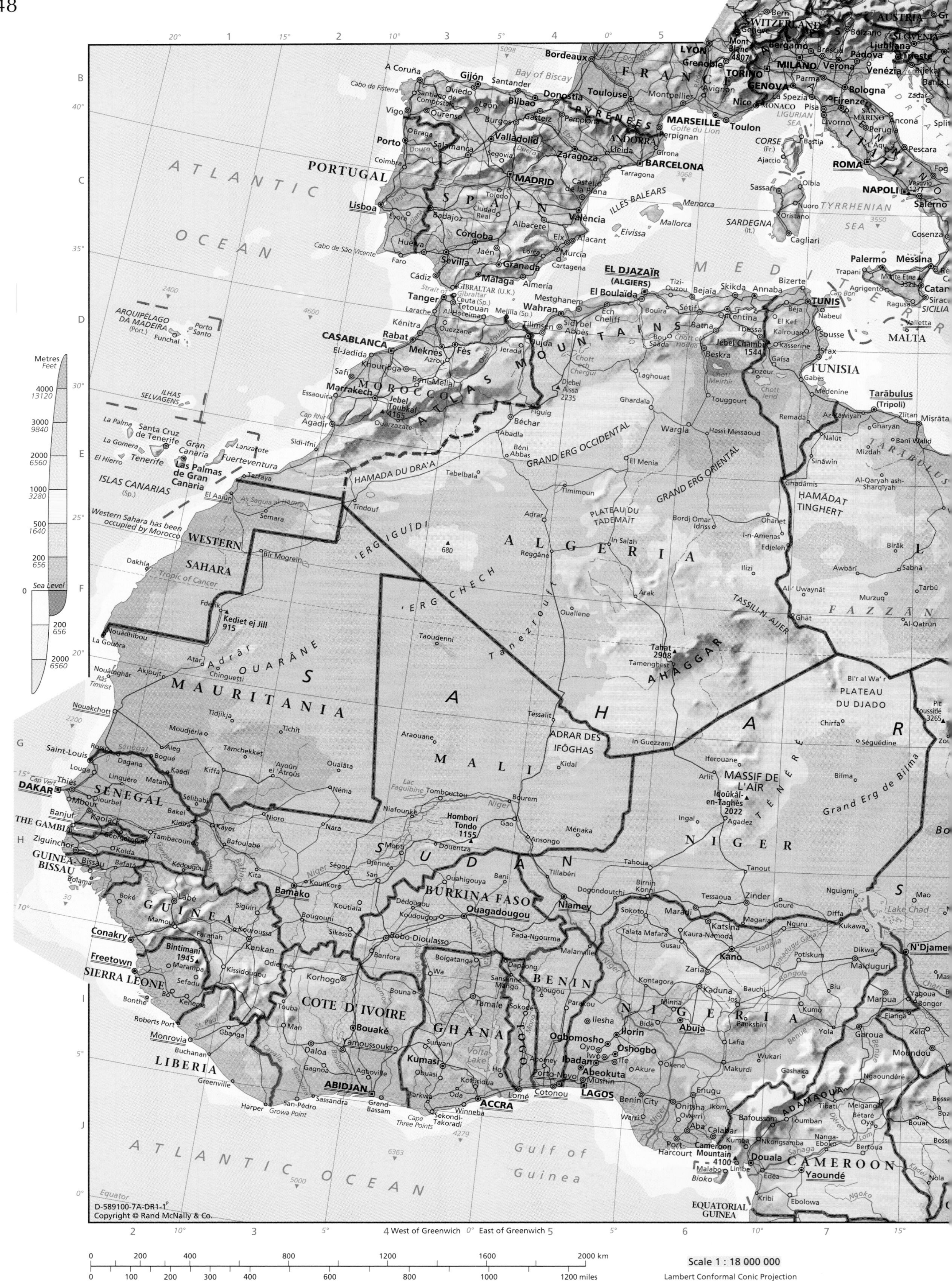
ATLANTIC OCEAN
Bay of Biscay
PORTUGAL
SPAIN
FRANCE
ANDORRA
SWITZERLAND
AUSTRIA
SLOVENIA
ITALY
TYRRHENIAN SEA
MEDITERRANEAN SEA
MALTA
TUNISIA
EL DJAZAÏR (ALGIERS)
ALGERIA
MOROCCO
ATLAS MOUNTAINS
WESTERN SAHARA
Western Sahara has been occupied by Morocco
ISLAS CANARIAS (Sp.)
ARQUIPÉLAGO DA MADEIRA (Port.)
ILHAS SELVAGENS
MAURITANIA
MALI
SAHARA
NIGER
SENEGAL
THE GAMBIA
GUINEA-BISSAU
GUINEA
SIERRA LEONE
LIBERIA
COTE D'IVOIRE
BURKINA FASO
GHANA
TOGO
BENIN
NIGERIA
CAMEROON
EQUATORIAL GUINEA
SUDAN
GRAND ERG OCCIDENTAL
GRAND ERG ORIENTAL
AHAGGAR
MASSIF DE L'AÏR
Gulf of Guinea
Equator
Tropic of Cancer
Metres
Feet
Sea Level
D-589100-7A-DR1-1
Copyright © Rand McNally & Co.
West of Greenwich
East of Greenwich
2000 km
1200 miles
Scale 1 : 18 000 000
Lambert Conformal Conic Projection

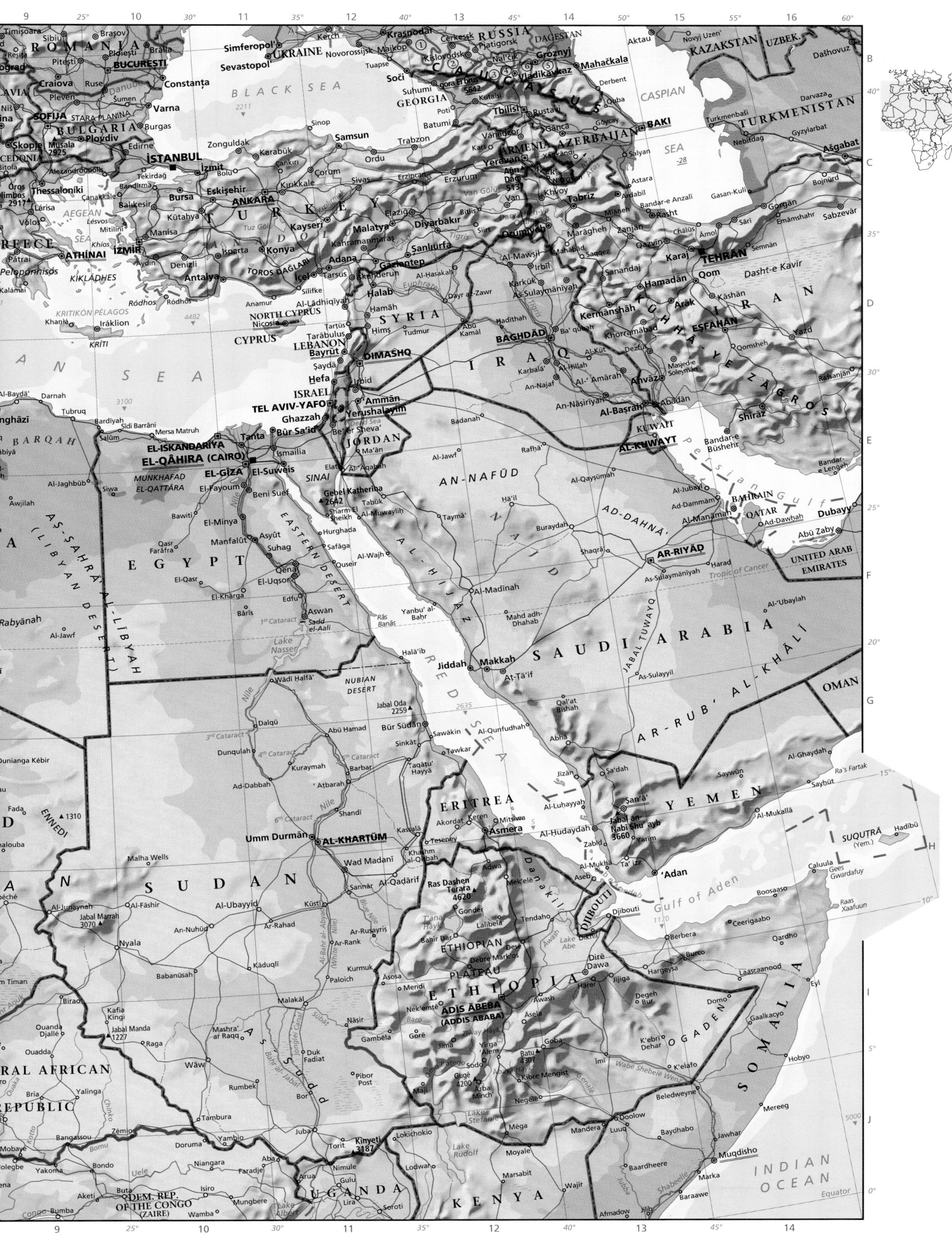

YGEJA
RAČAEVO - ČERKESIJA
BARDINO-BALKARIJA
(4) SEVERNAJA OSETIJA
(5) ČEČNJA
(6) INGUŠETIJA

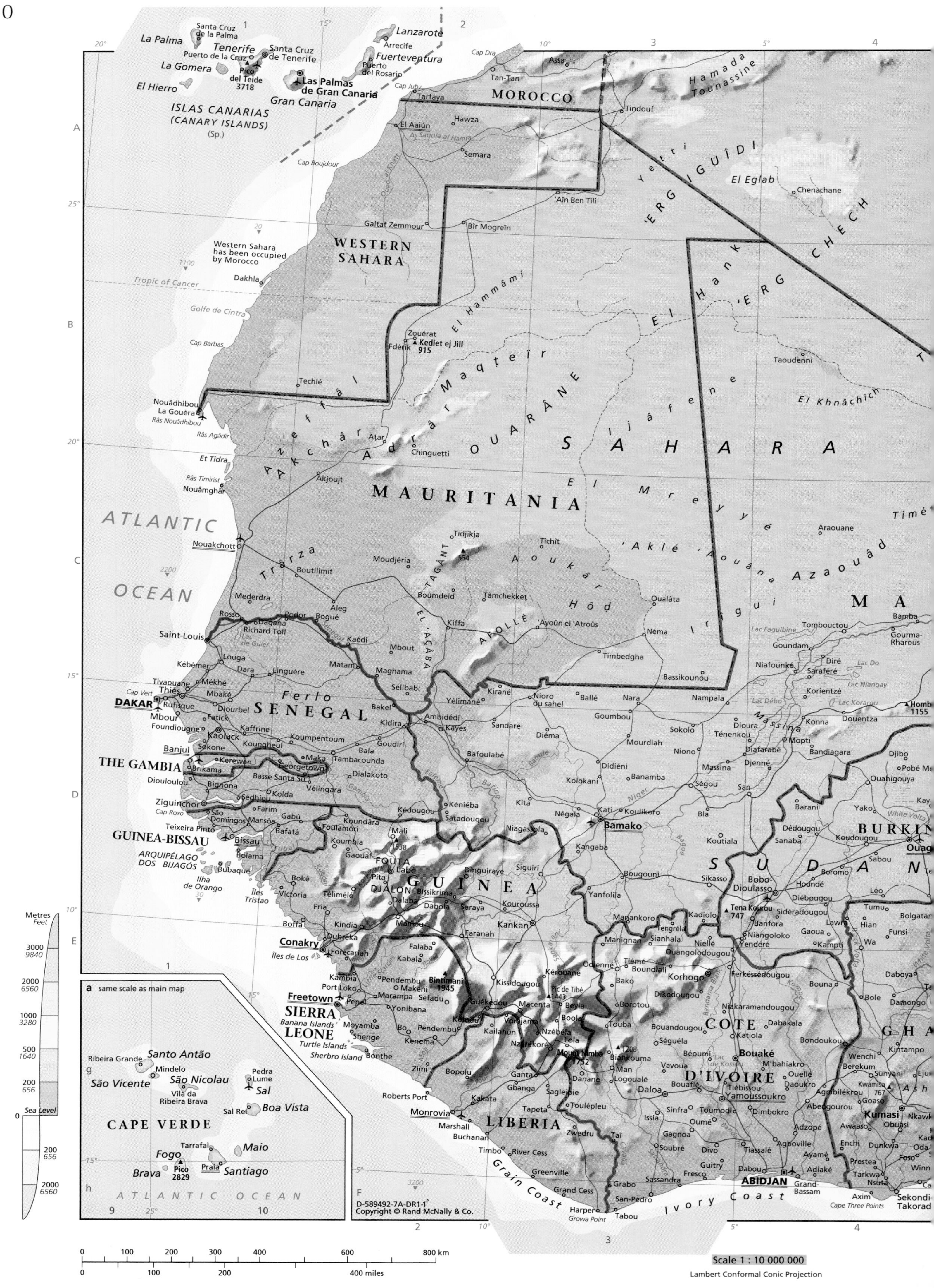
ISLAS CANARIAS
(CANARY ISLANDS)
(Sp.)
La Palma
Santa Cruz de la Palma
Tenerife
Puerto de la Cruz
Santa Cruz de Tenerife
La Gomera
Pico del Teide 3718
El Hierro
Las Palmas de Gran Canaria
Gran Canaria
Lanzarote
Arrecife
Fuerteventura
Puerto del Rosario
Cap Dra
Cap Juby
Tarfaya
Tan-Tan
Assa
MOROCCO
Tindouf
Hamada Tounassine
El Aaiún
Hawza
As Saquia al Hamra
Semara
Cap Boujdour
Oued al Khatt
'Aïn Ben Tili
Yetti
'ERG IGUÎDI
El Eglab
Chenachane
Galtat Zemmour
Bîr Mogreïn
WESTERN SAHARA
Western Sahara has been occupied by Morocco
Dakhla
Tropic of Cancer
Golfe de Cintra
Cap Barbas
El Hammâmi
Zouérat
Fdérik
Kediet ej Jill 915
El Hank
'ERG CHECH
Taoudenni
Techlé
Nouâdhibou
La Gouèra
Râs Nouâdhibou
Râs Agâdir
Maqteïr
Azeffâl
Adrar
Akchâr
Atar
Chinguetti
OUARÂNE
Ijâfene
El Khnâchîch
SAHARA
Et Tîdra
Râs Timirist
Nouâmghâr
Akjoujt
MAURITANIA
El Mreyyé
ATLANTIC OCEAN
Nouakchott
Tidjikja
Tichît
'Aklé 'Aouâna
Araouane
Azaouâd
Trârza
Boutilimit
Moudjéria
TAGANT
554
Aoukâr
Mederdra
Boûmdeïd
Tâmchekket
Hôd
Oualâta
Rosso
Dagana
Podor
Bogué
Aleg
Richard Toll
Saint-Louis
Lac de Guier
Kaédi
Kiffa
AFOLLÉ
'Ayoûn el 'Atroûs
Néma
Irîgui
Lac Faguibine
Tombouctou
Bamba
Gourma-Rharous
Goundam
Kébémer
Louga
Dara
Linguère
Matam
Mbout
Maghama
EL 'AÇÂBA
Timbedgha
Bassikounou
Niafounké
Diré
Saraféré
Lac Do
Lac Niangay
Korientzé
Tivaouane
Mékhé
Cap Vert
Thiès
Mbaké
Ferlo
Sélibabi
DAKAR
Rufisque
Diourbel
SENEGAL
Bakel
Yélimané
Kiranè
Nioro du sahel
Ballé
Nara
Nampala
Lac Débo
Lac Korarou
Hombori 1155
Mbour
Fatick
Foundiougne
Kaolack
Kaffrine
Koumpentoum
Kidira
Ambidédi
Kayes
Sandaré
Diéma
Goumbou
Sokolo
Diouara
Ténenkou
Massina
Konna
Douentza
Mopti
Bandiagara
Diafarabé
Djenné
Mourdiah
Niono
Banjul
Sokone
Koungheul
Goudiri
Bala
Bafoulabé
Kerewan
THE GAMBIA
Brikama
Maka
Georgetown
Tambacounda
Dialakoto
Basse Santa Su
Vélingara
Bafing
Didiéni
Banamba
Kolokani
Ségou
Macina
San
Dioulouloù
Bignona
Kolda
Sédhiou
Ziguinchor
Farim
Cap Roxo
São Domingos
Mansôa
Gabú
Koundâra
Kédougou
Kéniéba
Satadougou
Kita
Kati
Koulikoro
Négala
Niger
Bla
Barani
Yako
Kaya
Teixeira Pinto
Bafatá
Foulamôri
Bissau
GUINEA-BISSAU
Bolama
ARQUIPÉLAGO DOS BIJAGÓS
Bubaque
Ilha de Orango
Mali 1538
Koumbia
Gaoual
FOUTA DJALON
Labé
Pita
Dalaba
Niagassola
Bamako
Kangaba
Siguiri
Dinguiraye
GUINEA
Bougouni
Koutiala
Sikasso
Bobo-Dioulasso
Dédougou
Koudougou
Sanaba
BURKINA
Ouagadougou
Sabou
Boromo
Houndé
Léo
SUDAN
Boké
Îles Tristao
Victoria
Télimélé
Bissikrima
Dabola
Kouroussa
Saraya
Yanfolila
Diébougou
Tena Kourou 747
Banfora
Sidéradougou
Boffa
Fria
Kindia
Mamou
Kankan
Faranah
Mankoro
Tengrela
Kadiolo
Niangoloko
Yendéré
Gaoua
Kampti
Tumu
Bolgatanga
Hian
Funsi
Wa
Dubréka
Conakry
Forécariah
Îles de Los
Falaba
Kabala
Manigna
Sianhala
Niellé
Ouangolodougou
Kambia
Port Loko
Pendembu
Makeni
Bintimani 1945
Kissidougou
Odienné
Tiémé
Boundiali
Kérouané
Korhogo
Ferkéssédougou
Bouna
Daboya
Freetown
Pepel
Marampa
Sefadu
Yonibana
Guékédou
Macenta
Pic de Tibé 1443
Beyla
Bako
Borotou
Dikodougou
Nikaramandougou
Bole
Damongo
SIERRA LEONE
Banana Islands
Moyamba
Shenge
Turtle Islands
Sherbro Island
Bonthe
Bo
Kenema
Pendembu
Kailahun
Koindu
Voinjama
Nzérékoré
Nzébéla
Boola
Touba
Lola
Mount Nimba 1752
Biankouma
1208
Bouandougou
Séguéla
COTE D'IVOIRE
Dabakala
Katiola
Bondoukou
Kintampo
GHANA
Zimi
Bopolu
Gbanga
Ganta
Danané
Man
Logouale
Béoumi
Lac de Kossou
Vavoua
Bouaké
M'bahiakro
Ouellé
Daoukro
Wenchi
Berekum
Sunyani
Kwamisa 767
Ejura
Roberts Port
Monrovia
Kakata
Saglepie
Daloa
Bouaflé
Tiébissou
Yamoussoukro
Agnibilékrou
Goaso
Kumasi
Marshall
Buchanan
LIBERIA
Tapeta
Toulépleu
Issia
Sinfra
Toumodi
Dimbokro
Abengourou
Awaso
Obuasi
Timbo
River Cess
Zwedru
Taï
Gagnoa
Oumé
Soubré
Divo
Tiassalé
Agboville
Adzopé
Akoupé
Ayamé
Enchi
Dunkwa
Greenville
Guitry
Fresco
Dabou
ABIDJAN
Grand-Bassam
Adiaké
Prestea
Tarkwa
Nsuta
Grain Coast
Grand Cess
Sassandra
Grabo
San-Pédro
Harper
Growa Point
Tabou
Ivory Coast
Axim
Cape Three Points
Sekondi-Takoradi
a same scale as main map
Ribeira Grande
Santo Antão
Mindelo
São Vicente
São Nicolau
Vila da Ribeira Brava
Pedra Lume
Sal
Sal Rei
Boa Vista
CAPE VERDE
Tarrafal
Fogo
Maio
Brava
Pico 2829
Praia
Santiago
ATLANTIC OCEAN
Metres Feet
3000 9840
2000 6560
1000 3280
500 1640
200 656
Sea Level
200 656
2000 6560
D-589492-7A-DR1-1
Copyright © Rand McNally & Co.
0 100 200 300 400 600 800 km
0 100 200 400 miles
Scale 1 : 10 000 000
Lambert Conformal Conic Projection

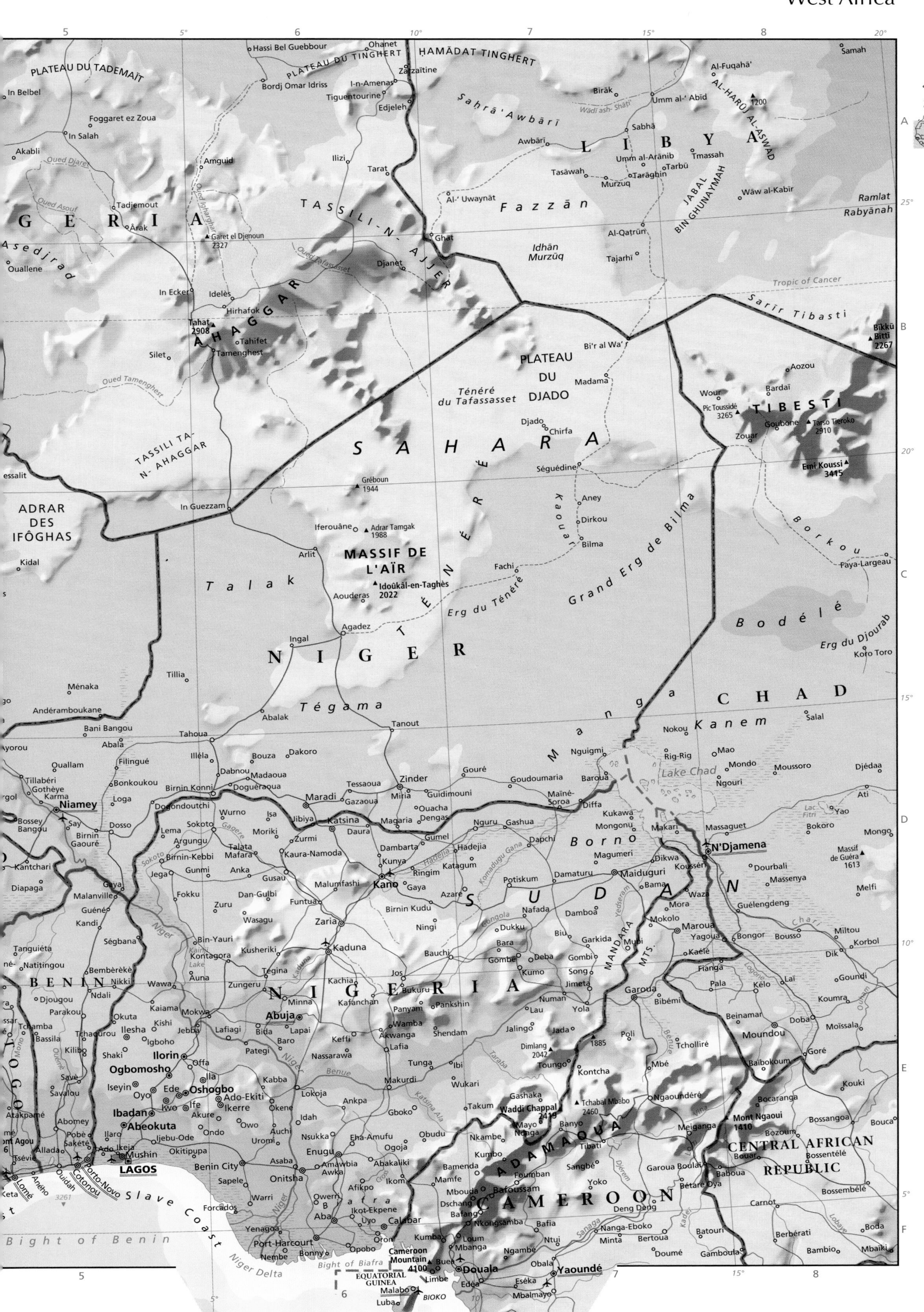

PLATEAU DU TADEMAÏT
PLATEAU DU TINGHERT
ḤAMĀDAT TINGHERT
Ṣaḥrā' Awbārī
AL-HARŪJ AL-ASWAD
L I B Y A
Fazzān
Idhān Murzūq
JABAL BIN GHUNAYMAH
Ramlat Rabyānah
TASSILI-N-AJJER
AHAGGAR
TASSILI TA-N-AHAGGAR
ADRAR DES IFÔGHAS
G E R I A
Asedjrad
Tropic of Cancer
Sarīr Tibasti
PLATEAU DU DJADO
Ténéré du Tafassasset
TIBESTI
S A H A R A
TÉNÉRÉ
MASSIF DE L'AÏR
Talak
Grand Erg de Bilma
Erg du Ténéré
Kaouar
Borkou
Bodélé
Erg du Djourab
N I G E R
Tégama
Manga
C H A D
Kanem
Lake Chad
Borno
S U D A N
N I G E R I A
MANDARA MTS.
ADAMAOUA
CAMEROON
CENTRAL AFRICAN REPUBLIC
BENIN
TOGO
EQUATORIAL GUINEA
BIOKO
Bight of Benin
Slave Coast
Niger Delta
Bight of Biafra
Tahat 2908
Bikkū Bitti 2267
Emi Koussi 3415
Pic Toussidé 3265
Tarso Tieroko 2910
Gréboun 1944
Adrar Tamgak 1988
Idoûkâl-en-Taghès 2022
Garet el Djenoun 2327
Massif de Guéra 1613
Dimlang 2042
Tchabal Mbabo 2460
Waddi Chappal 2419
Mont Ngaoui 1410
Cameroon Mountain 4100
Tamenghest
In Salah
In Guezzam
Djanet
Ghat
Sabhā
Murzuq
Agadez
Arlit
Zinder
Maradi
Tahoua
Niamey
N'Djamena
Faya-Largeau
Kano
Kaduna
Zaria
Maiduguri
Abuja
Ilorin
Ogbomosho
Oshogbo
Ibadan
Abeokuta
LAGOS
Porto-Novo
Cotonou
Lomé
Benin City
Onitsha
Enugu
Port-Harcourt
Calabar
Douala
Yaoundé
Malabo
Garoua
Ngaoundéré
Bafoussam
Moundou
Sarh
Tibati
Bertoua

NIGERIA
CAMEROON
CENTRAL AFRICAN REPUBLIC
SUDAN
UGANDA
EQUATORIAL GUINEA
SAO TOME AND PRINCIPE
GABON
CONGO
DEM. REP. OF THE CONGO (ZAIRE)
RWANDA
BURUNDI
TANZANIA
ANGOLA
ZAMBIA
MALAWI
MOZAM
ZIMBABWE
BOTSWANA
NAMIBIA
SOUTH AFRICA
LESOTHO
SWAZILAND
ATLANTIC
OCEAN
KALAHARI DESERT
NAMIB DESERT
KAOKO VELD
GREAT KARROO
DRAKENSBERG
RIFT VALLEY
MONTS MITUMBA
Lake Victoria
Lake Tanganyika
Lake Kariba
Okavango Delta
Tropic of Capricorn
Equator
Yaoundé
Douala
Libreville
Brazzaville
KINSHASA
Bangui
Kampala
Kigali
LUANDA
Lusaka
Harare
Windhoek
Gaborone
PRETORIA
JOHANNESBURG
MAPUTO
Maseru
Bloemfontein
DURBAN
CAPE TOWN (KAAPSTAD)
Port Elizabeth
East London (Oos-Londen)
Cape of Good Hope
Kaap Agulhas
Metres Feet
4000 13120
3000 9840
2000 6560
1000 3280
500 1640
200 656
Sea Level
0
200 656
2000 6560
East of Greenwich
0 200 400 800 1200 1600 2000 km
0 100 200 300 400 600 800 1000 1200 miles
Scale 1 : 18 000 000
Lambert Conformal Conic Projection
D-589200-7A-DR1-1

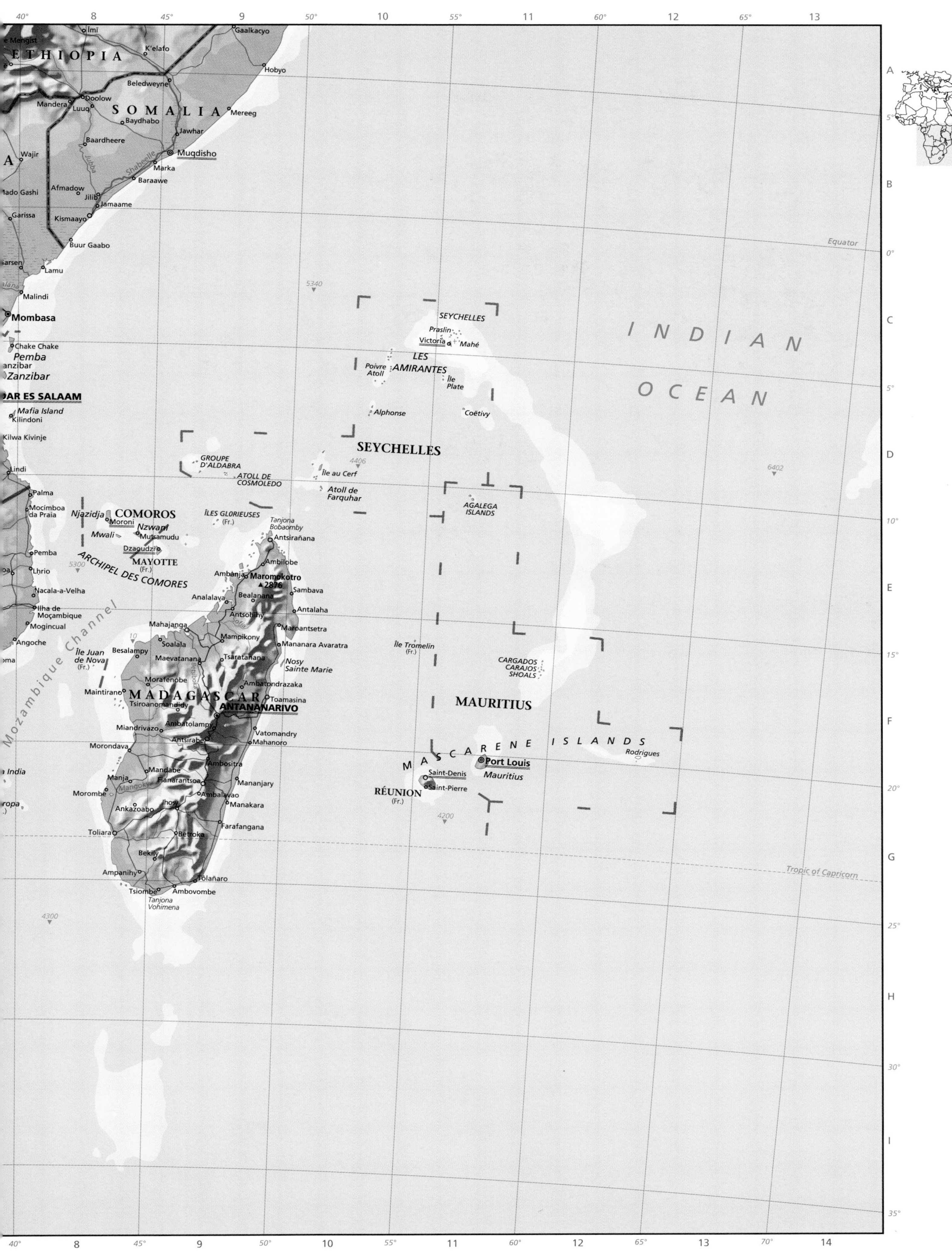
ETHIOPIA
SOMALIA
Muqdisho
Mogadishu
Gaalkacyo
Hobyo
Beledweyne
Mereeg
Jawhar
Baydhabo
Baardheere
Marka
Baraawe
Kismaayo
Jamaame
Buur Gaabo
Lamu
Malindi
Mombasa
Chake Chake
Pemba
Zanzibar
Mafia Island
Kilindoni
Kilwa Kivinje
Lindi
Palma
Mocimboa da Praia
Pemba
Lhrio
Nacala-a-Velha
Ilha de Moçambique
Mogincual
Angoche
Mozambique Channel
COMOROS
Moroni
Njazidja
Mwali
Nzwani
Mutsamudu
Dzaoudzi
MAYOTTE (Fr.)
ARCHIPEL DES COMORES
GROUPE D'ALDABRA
ATOLL DE COSMOLEDO
ÎLES GLORIEUSES (Fr.)
Tanjona Bobaomby
Antsiraňana
Ambilobe
Ambanja
Maromokotro
2876
Sambava
Antalaha
Analalava
Bealanana
Antsohihy
Mahajanga
Soalala
Maroantsetra
Mampikony
Mananara Avaratra
Besalampy
Maevatanana
Tsaratanana
Nosy Sainte Marie
Île Juan de Nova (Fr.)
Morafenobe
Ambatondrazaka
Maintirano
MADAGASCAR
Toamasina
Tsiroanomandidy
ANTANANARIVO
Miandrivazo
Ambatolampy
Vatomandry
Mahanoro
Antsirabe
Morondava
Ambositra
Mandabe
Manja
Fianarantsoa
Mananjary
Morombe
Ambalavao
Manakara
Ankazoabo
Ihosy
Farafangana
Toliara
Betroka
Bekily
Ampanihy
Tolañaro
Tsiombe
Ambovombe
Tanjona Vohimena
SEYCHELLES
Praslin
Victoria
Mahé
LES AMIRANTES
Poivre Atoll
Île Plate
Alphonse
Coëtivy
Île au Cerf
Atoll de Farquhar
AGALEGA ISLANDS
Île Tromelin (Fr.)
CARGADOS CARAJOS SHOALS
MAURITIUS
MASCARENE ISLANDS
Rodrigues
Port Louis
Mauritius
Saint-Denis
Saint-Pierre
RÉUNION (Fr.)
INDIAN OCEAN
Equator
Tropic of Capricorn
5340
4406
6402
5300
4200
4300

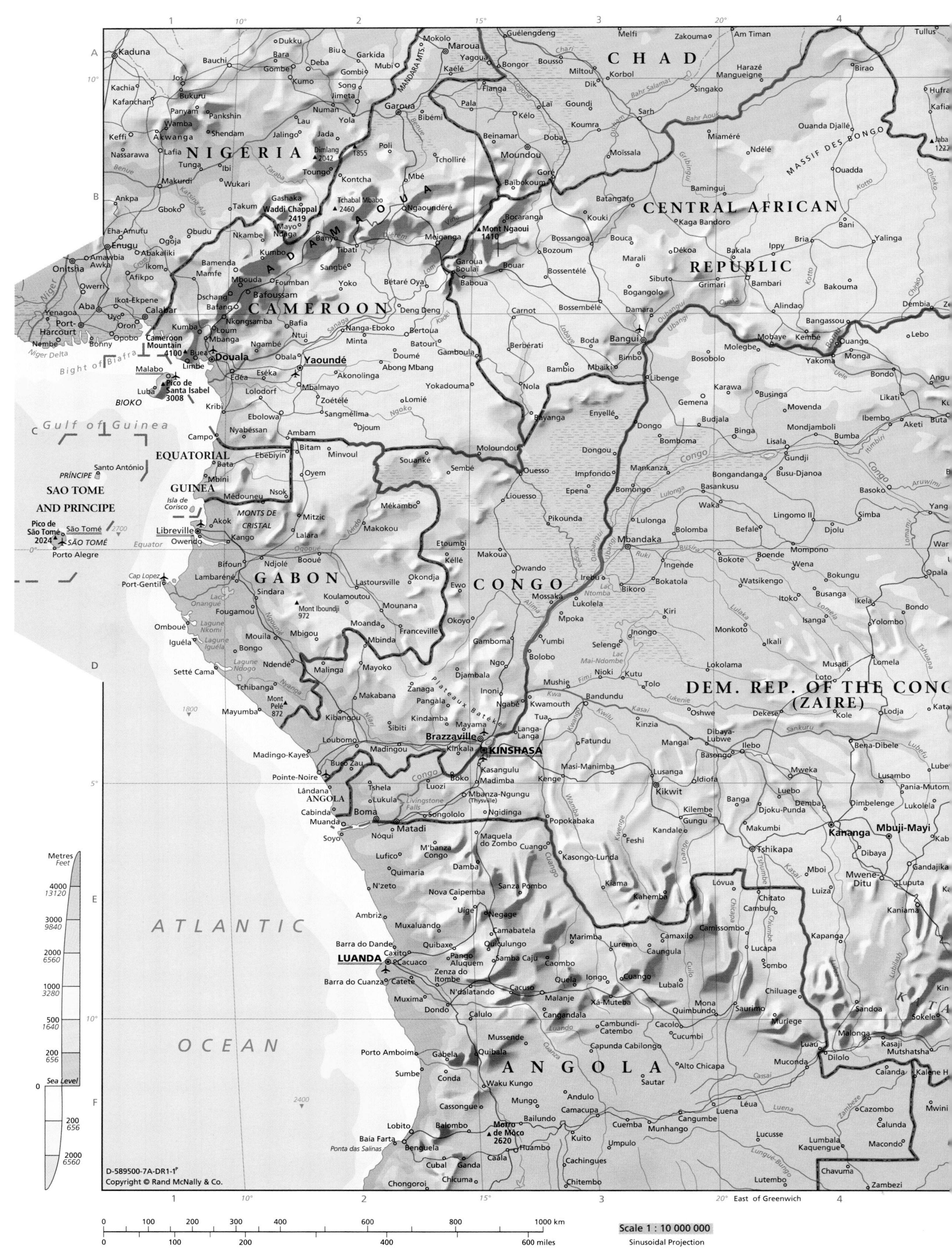
CHAD
NIGERIA
CAMEROON
CENTRAL AFRICAN REPUBLIC
EQUATORIAL GUINEA
SAO TOME AND PRINCIPE
GABON
CONGO
DEM. REP. OF THE CONGO (ZAIRE)
ANGOLA
ATLANTIC OCEAN
Gulf of Guinea
Bight of Biafra
ADAMAOUA
MASSIF DES BONGO
Plateaux Batéké
Yaoundé
Libreville
Malabo
São Tomé
Bangui
Brazzaville
KINSHASA
LUANDA
Douala
Cameroon Mountain 4100
Pico de Santa Isabel 3008
Pico de São Tomé 2024
Mont Ngaoui 1410
Morro de Môco 2620
Equator
East of Greenwich
Metres
Feet
4000
13120
3000
9840
2000
6560
1000
3280
500
1640
200
656
Sea Level
0
200
656
2000
6560
D-589500-7A-DR1-1
Copyright © Rand McNally & Co.
Scale 1 : 10 000 000
Sinusoidal Projection
0 100 200 300 400 600 800 1000 km
0 100 200 400 600 miles

SUDAN
ETHIOPIAN PLATEAU
ETHIOPIA
SOMALIA
UGANDA
KENYA
RWANDA
BURUNDI
TANZANIA
MALAWI
MOZAMBIQUE
ZAMBIA
COMOROS
ARCHIPEL DES COMORES
INDIAN
OCEAN
RIFT VALLEY
MONTS MITUMBA
MONTS MULUMBE
MUCHINGA MOUNTAINS
KIPENGERE RANGE
AHMAR MOUNTAINS
As Sudd
Ogaden
Chalbi Desert
Serengeti Plain
Masai Steppe
Lake Victoria
Lake Rudolf (Lake Turkana)
Lake Nyasa (Lake Malawi)
Lake Stefanie
Lake Albert
Lake Edward
Lake Kyoga
Lake Rukwa
Lake Mweru
Lake Bangweulu
Lake Natron
Lake Eyasi
Lake Manyara
ĀDĪS ĀBEBA (ADDIS ABABA)
NAIROBI
Kampala
Kigali
Bujumbura
Dodoma
DAR ES SALAAM
Muqdisho
Moroni
Mombasa
Zanzibar
Pemba
Mafia Island
Kilimanjaro 5895
Kirinyaga (Mount Kenya) 5199
Margherita Peak 5109
Volcan Karisimbi 4507
Equator
Gulf of Aden
A
B
C
D
E
F
5
6
7
8
30°
35°
40°
0°
5°
10°

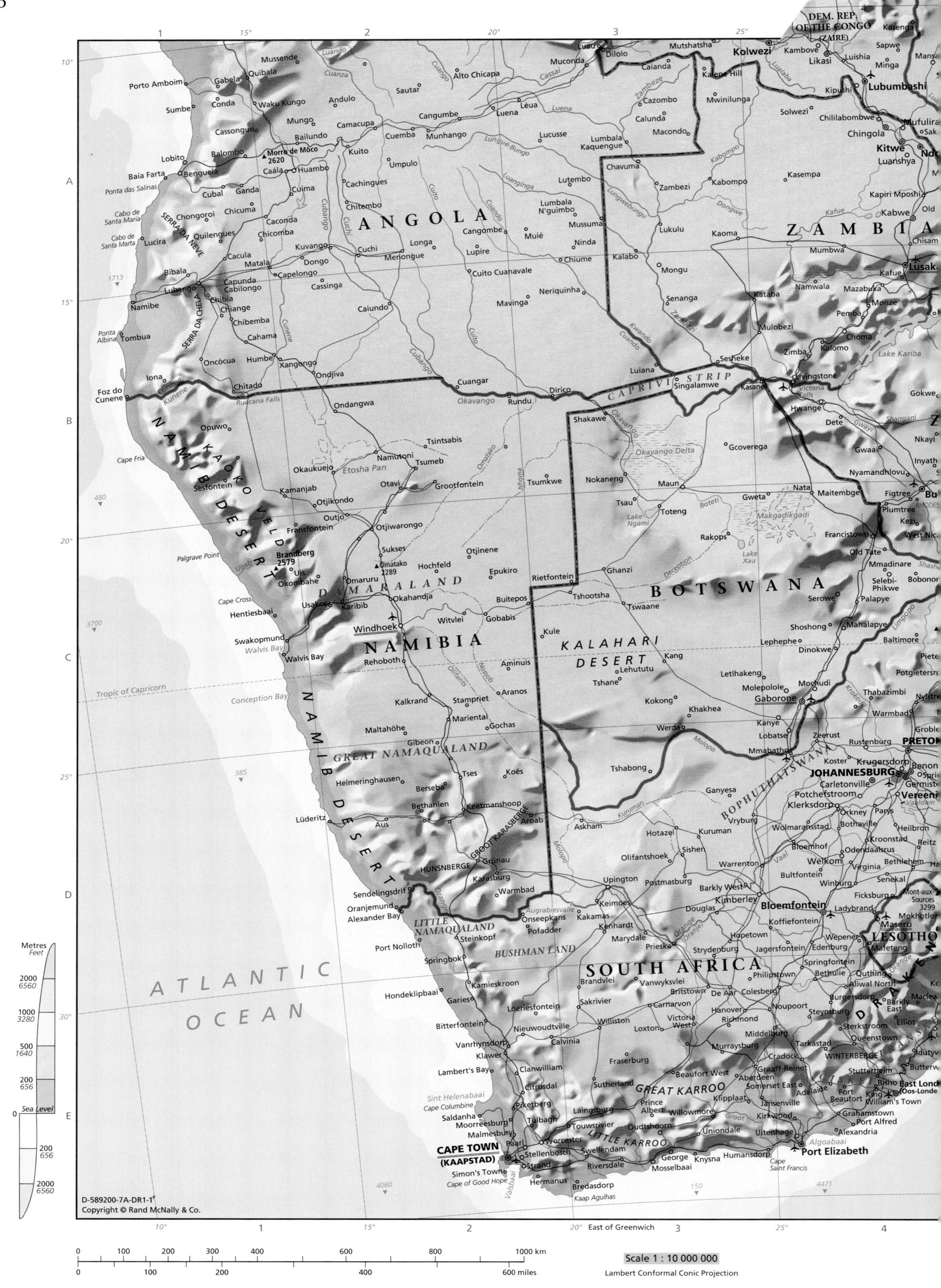
ANGOLA
ZAMBIA
NAMIBIA
BOTSWANA
SOUTH AFRICA
LESOTHO
DEM. REP. OF THE CONGO (ZAIRE)
ATLANTIC OCEAN
KALAHARI DESERT
NAMIB DESERT
KAOKO VELD
DAMARALAND
GREAT NAMAQUALAND
LITTLE NAMAQUALAND
BUSHMAN LAND
GREAT KARROO
LITTLE KARROO
CAPRIVI STRIP
BOPHUTHATSWANA
SERRA DA NEVE
SERRA DA CHELA
GROOT KARASBERGE
HUNSNBERGE
WINTERBERGE
Tropic of Capricorn
Etosha Pan
Okavango Delta
Makgadikgadi
Lake Ngami
Lake Xau
Lake Kariba
Victoria Falls
Ruacana Falls
Walvis Bay
Conception Bay
Palgrave Point
Cape Cross
Cape Fria
Ponta das Salinas
Cabo de Santa Maria
Cabo de Santa Marta
Ponta Albina
Sint Helenabaai
Cape Columbine
Cape of Good Hope
Kaap Agulhas
Cape Saint Francis
Algoabaai
Morro de Môco 2620
Brandberg 2579
Omatako 2289
Mont-aux-Sources 3299
Cunene
Kunene
Cuanza
Cubango
Okavango
Cuando
Kwando
Zambeze
Zambezi
Luena
Cuito
Kafue
Limpopo
Molopo
Kuruman
Orange
Oranje
Vaal
Nossob
Olifants
Ugab
Boteti
Deception
Kabompo
Lungwebungu
Luangwa
Shangani
Gwayi
CAPE TOWN (KAAPSTAD)
Windhoek
Gaborone
Lusaka
Maseru
JOHANNESBURG
Bloemfontein
Port Elizabeth
Lubumbashi
Kolwezi
Luanda
Benguela
Lobito
Huambo
Lubango
Namibe
Tombua
Menongue
Kuito
Saurimo
Cuito Cuanavale
Swakopmund
Lüderitz
Keetmanshoop
Rehoboth
Rundu
Tsumeb
Grootfontein
Otjiwarongo
Okahandja
Gobabis
Mariental
Oranjemund
Alexander Bay
Port Nolloth
Springbok
Upington
Kimberley
Mafikeng
Francistown
Maun
Ghanzi
Serowe
Selebi-Phikwe
Palapye
Livingstone
Kasane
Kitwe
Ndola
Chingola
Mufulira
Kabwe
Mongu
Senanga
Lambert's Bay
Saldanha
Stellenbosch
Paarl
Worcester
Oudtshoorn
George
Mosselbaai
Knysna
Beaufort West
Graaff-Reinet
Grahamstown
Port Alfred
East London (Oos-Londen)
King William's Town
Queenstown
Aliwal North
Colesberg
De Aar
Klerksdorp
Potchefstroom
Vereeniging
Welkom
Kroonstad
Krugersdorp
Rustenburg
Zeerust
D-589200-7A-DR1-1
Copyright © Rand McNally & Co.
Metres
Feet
2000
6560
1000
3280
500
1640
200
656
Sea Level
0
East of Greenwich
10°
15°
20°
25°
30°
A
B
C
D
E
1
2
3
4
0 100 200 300 400 600 800 1000 km
0 100 200 400 600 miles
Scale 1 : 10 000 000
Lambert Conformal Conic Projection

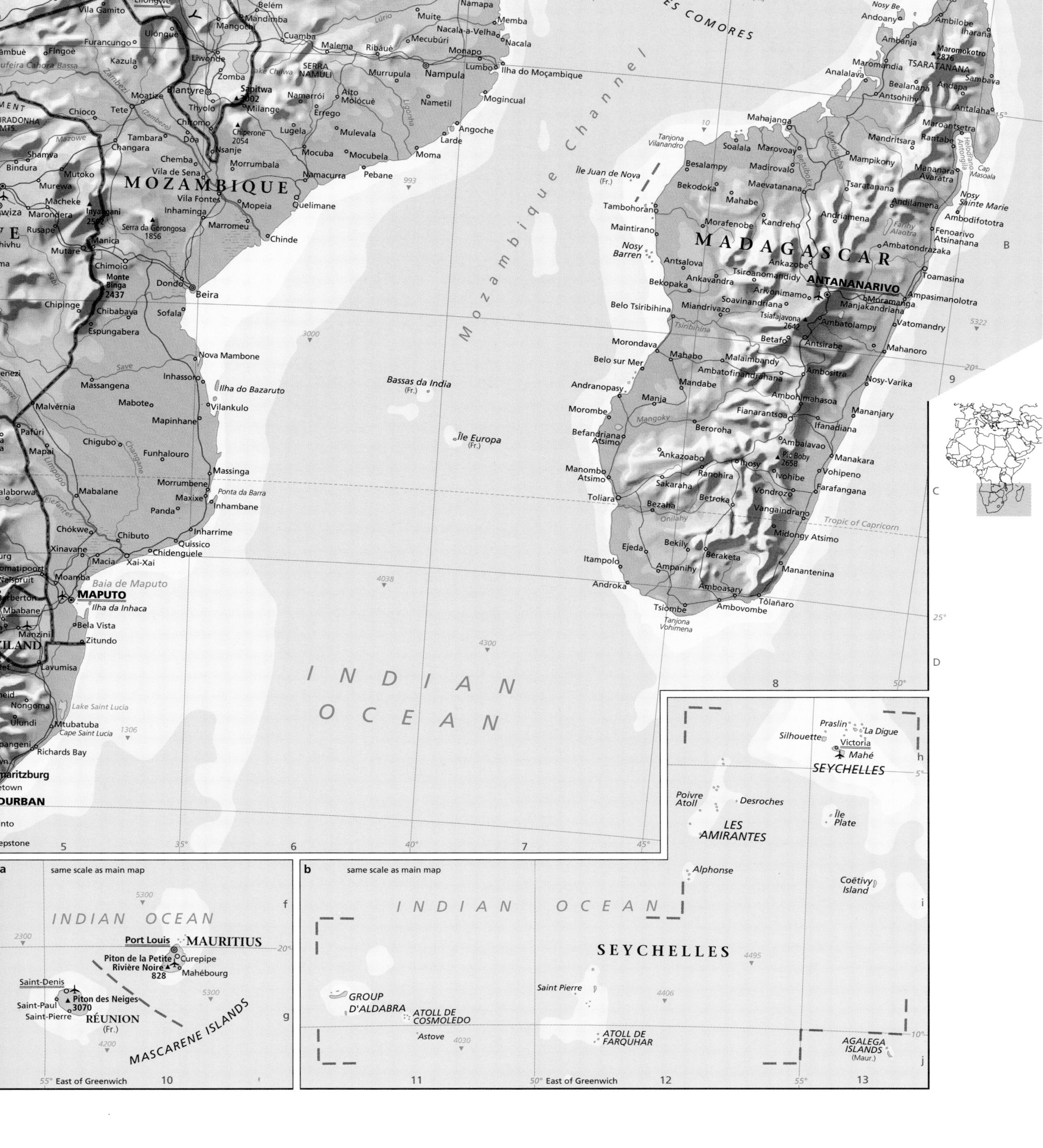
TANZANIA
MOZAMBIQUE
MALAWI
MADAGASCAR
COMOROS
MAYOTTE
Mozambique Channel
ARCHIPEL DES COMORES
INDIAN OCEAN
MAPUTO
ANTANANARIVO
Moroni
Mamoudzou
Lilongwe
Beira
Nampula
Quelimane
Toliara
Toamasina
Mahajanga
Antsiranana
Fianarantsoa
Tropic of Capricorn
Bassas da India
Île Europa
Île Juan de Nova
MAURITIUS
Port Louis
RÉUNION
Saint-Denis
MASCARENE ISLANDS
SEYCHELLES
Victoria
Mahé
LES AMIRANTES
GROUP D'ALDABRA
ATOLL DE COSMOLEDO
ATOLL DE FARQUHAR
AGALEGA ISLANDS
same scale as main map
East of Greenwich

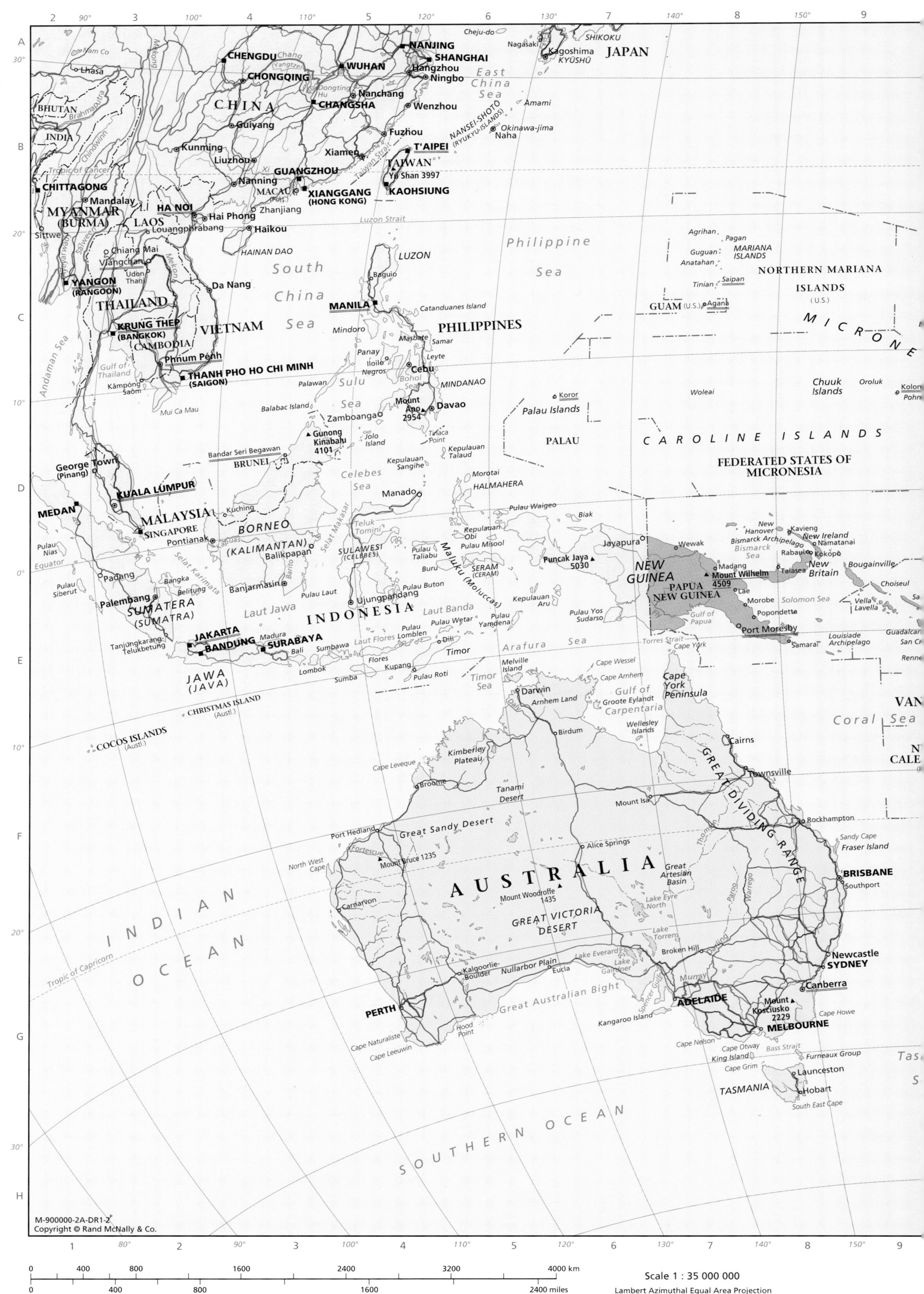

0 400 800 1600 2400 3200 4000 km

0 400 800 1600 2400 miles

Scale 1 : 35 000 000

Lambert Azimuthal Equal Area Projection

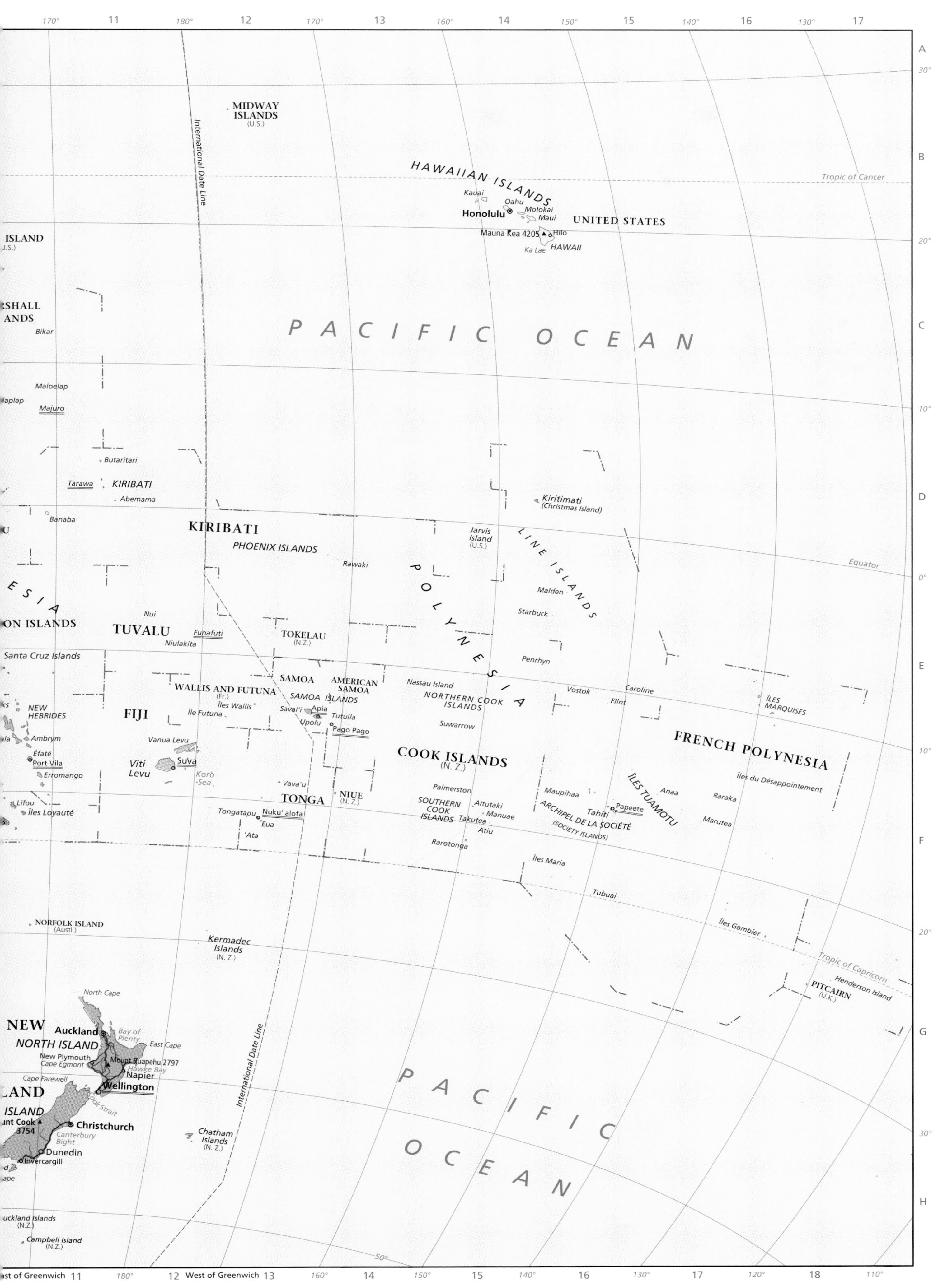
MIDWAY ISLANDS (U.S.)
International Date Line
HAWAIIAN ISLANDS
Kauai
Oahu
Molokai
Maui
Honolulu
UNITED STATES
Mauna Kea 4205
Hilo
Ka Lae
HAWAII
Tropic of Cancer
PACIFIC OCEAN
Bikar
Maloelap
Majuro
Butaritari
Tarawa
KIRIBATI
Abemama
Banaba
Kiritimati (Christmas Island)
KIRIBATI
PHOENIX ISLANDS
Jarvis Island (U.S.)
LINE ISLANDS
Rawaki
POLYNESIA
Equator
Malden
Starbuck
Nui
TUVALU
Funafuti
Niulakita
TOKELAU (N.Z.)
Penrhyn
Santa Cruz Islands
SAMOA
AMERICAN SAMOA
Nassau Island
Vostok
Caroline
ÎLES MARQUISES
WALLIS AND FUTUNA (Fr.)
Îles Wallis
SAMOA ISLANDS
NORTHERN COOK ISLANDS
Flint
NEW HEBRIDES
FIJI
Île Futuna
Savai'i
Apia
Upolu
Tutuila
Pago Pago
Suwarrow
FRENCH POLYNESIA
Ambrym
Vanua Levu
Éfaté
Port Vila
Viti Levu
Suva
COOK ISLANDS (N. Z.)
Erromango
Koro Sea
Vava'u
Îles du Désappointement
TONGA
NIUE (N. Z.)
Palmerston
ÎLES TUAMOTU
Anaa
Raraka
Lifou
Îles Loyauté
Tongatapu
Nuku'alofa
'Eua
'Ata
SOUTHERN COOK ISLANDS
Aitutaki
Manuae
Takutea
Atiu
Maupihaa
Tahiti
Papeete
ARCHIPEL DE LA SOCIÉTÉ (SOCIETY ISLANDS)
Marutea
Rarotonga
Îles Maria
Tubuai
Îles Gambier
NORFOLK ISLAND (Austl.)
Kermadec Islands (N. Z.)
Tropic of Capricorn
Henderson Island
PITCAIRN (U.K.)
North Cape
NEW ZEALAND
NORTH ISLAND
Auckland
Bay of Plenty
East Cape
New Plymouth
Cape Egmont
Mount Ruapehu 2797
Hawke Bay
Napier
Cape Farewell
Wellington
Cook Strait
SOUTH ISLAND
Mount Cook 3754
Christchurch
Canterbury Bight
Dunedin
Invercargill
Chatham Islands (N. Z.)
PACIFIC OCEAN
Auckland Islands (N.Z.)
Campbell Island (N.Z.)
East of Greenwich
West of Greenwich

INDONESIA
Pangkajene
Marek
Maros
Sinjai
SULAWESI (CELEBES)
Ujungpandang
Gunung Lompobatang 2871
Bantaeng
Bulukumba
Takalar
Jeneponto
Selat Selayar
Pising
Sikeli
Pulau Kabaena
Raha
Lawele
Pulau Buton
Baubau
Pasarwajo
Pulau Wangiwangi
KEPULAUAN TUKANGBESI
Pulau Binongko
Pulau Doangdoangan-Besar
Pulau Masalembu Besar
Benteng
Pulau Selayar
Barangbarang
Ujung
Pulau Tanahjampea
Pulau Kalao
Pulau Kalaotoa
Laut Banda
Pulau Nila
KEPULAUAN KAI
Tual
Banda Elat
Komfane
Pulau Wokam
Dobo
Pulau Kobroor
Rebi
Rabal
Pulau Trangan
Doka
Sia
Tafermaar
KEPULAUAN ARU
NEW GUINEA
Kokenau
MADURA
Sumenep
Pamekasan
Pulau Kangean
Pabean
Pulau Sepanjang
Laut Bali
Laut Flores
Probolinggo
Bondowoso
Jember
Banyuwangi
JAWA (JAVA)
Denpasar
BALI
Nusa Penida
Singaraja
Gunung Agung 3142
Selat Lombok
Mataram
Selong
Praya
LOMBOK
Selat Alas
Pulau Moyo
Gunung Tambora 2850
Sumbawa Besar
Raba
Dompu
Taliwang
Plampang
SUMBAWA
Selat Sumba
Selat Sape
Pulau Komodo
Pulau Rinca
Reo
Labuhanbajo
Ruteng
FLORES
Ende
Maumere
Larantuka
Pulau Lomblen
Pulau Pantar
Selat Alor
Pulau Alor
Kalabahi
Selat Ombai
Pulau Wetar
Lioppa
Ilwaki
Selat Wetar
Pulau Atauro
Pulau Romang
Pulau Kisar
KEPULAUAN LETI
Pulau Damar
KEPULAUAN BABAR
Tepa
Pulau Babar
Pulau Masela
Pulau Yamdena
Larat
KEPULAUAN TANIMBAR
Saumlaki
Adaut
Eliase
Pulau Selaru
Dili
Lautem
Tutuala
Aileu
Manatuto
Maubara
Atambua
Tata Mailau 2315
TIMOR
Gunung Mutis 2427
Kefamenanu
Soe
Barate
Kupang
Baa
Pulau Roti
Sedah
Nembrala
Tanjung Sasar
Memboro
Waingapu
Tanjung Karoso
Waikabubak
Payeti
Melolo
SUMBA
Baing
Laut Sawu
Seba
Pulau Sawu
Nusa Tenggara (Lesser Sunda Islands)
ARAFURA SEA
TIMOR SEA
Ashmore Islands
Cartier Islands
Scott Reef
INDIAN OCEAN
Cape Van Diemen
Bathurst Island
Melville Island
Dundas Strait
Cobourg Peninsula
Cape Croker
Croker Island
Goulburn Islands
WESSEL ISLANDS
Cape Wessel
Elcho Island
Buckingham Bay
Nhulunbuy
Cape Arnhem
Van Diemen Gulf
Clarence Strait
Beagle Gulf
Charles Point
Darwin
Humpty Doo
Oenpelli
Maningrida
Jabiru
Arnhem Bay
FREDERICK HILLS
Rum Jungle
Batchelor
Adelaide River
Anson Bay
Tipperary
Pine Creek
Arnhem Land
Blue Mud Bay
Warwick Channel
Groote Eylandt
Cape Londonderry
Joseph Bonaparte Gulf
Admiralty Gulf
Kalumburu
Katherine
Cape Beatrice
Limmen Bight
Maria Island
Gulf of Carpentaria
Sir Edward Pellew Group
Vanderlin Island
York Sound
Adèle Island
Wyndham
Kununurra
Willeroo
Mataranka
Roper Valley
Larrimah
Birdum
Auvergne
Buccaneer Archipelago
Collier Bay
Cape Leveque
Gibb River
Karunjie
Lake Argyle
Kildurk
Victoria River Downs
Waterloo
Montejinni
Top Springs
Daly Waters
Dunmarra
Borroloola
Beagle Bay
Kimberley Plateau
King Sound
Dampier Land
Derby
Yeeda
KING LEOPOLD RANGES
Mount Ord 947
Mount Lush 781
Mount Wells 983
Kimberley Downs
Ord River
Mount Napier 487
Camfield
Wave Hill
McArthur River
Newcastle Waters
Broome
Roebuck Bay
Thangoo
Liveringa
Fitzroy Crossing
Turner
Inverway
Lake Woods
Barkly Tableland
Eva Downs
Cape Latouche Treville
Lagrange Bay
Noonkanbah
Halls Creek
Hooker Creek
NORTHERN TERRITORY
Banka Banka
Lagrange
EDGAR RANGES
Christmas Creek
Gordon Downs
Rockhampton Downs
Anna Plains
Billiluna
Tanami
Frewena
Alexandria
Eighty Mile Beach
Mandora
Wallal Downs
Mount Samuel 433
Tennant Creek
Wonarah
Ranken Store
Great Sandy Desert
Lake Gregory
Tanami Desert
The Granites
The Granites 436
Camooweal
Port Hedland
Goldsworthy
Shay Gap
Wauchope
Soudan
Avon Downs
Dampier
Wickham
Roebourne
Karratha
Warrawagine
Lake White
Barrow Island
Marble Bar
Lake Waukarlycarly
Percival Lakes
Lake Hazlett
Willowra
Murray Downs
Lake Nash
Millstream
Yarraloola
Onslow
Pannawonica
Nullagine
AUSTRALIA
Mount Singleton
Barrow Creek
Stirling
Urandangi

WESTERN AUSTRALIA
SOUTH AUSTRALIA
Gibson Desert
Simpson Desert
GREAT VICTORIA DESERT
Nullarbor Plain
HAMPTON TABLELAND
DARLING RANGE
PERTH
ADELAIDE
Kalgoorlie-Boulder
Coolgardie
Geraldton
Albany
Esperance
Norseman
Port Augusta
Coober Pedy
Uluru (Ayers Rock) 863
KANGAROO ISLAND
EYRE PENINSULA
YORKE PENINSULA
Spencer Gulf
GAWLER RANGES
ARCHIPELAGO OF THE RECHERCHE
Great Australian Bight
SOUTHERN OCEAN
Metres
Feet
Sea Level
M-590294-7A-DR1-1
Copyright © Rand McNally & Co.
East of Greenwich
Scale 1 : 10 000 000
Lambert Conformal Conic Projection
1000 km
600 miles

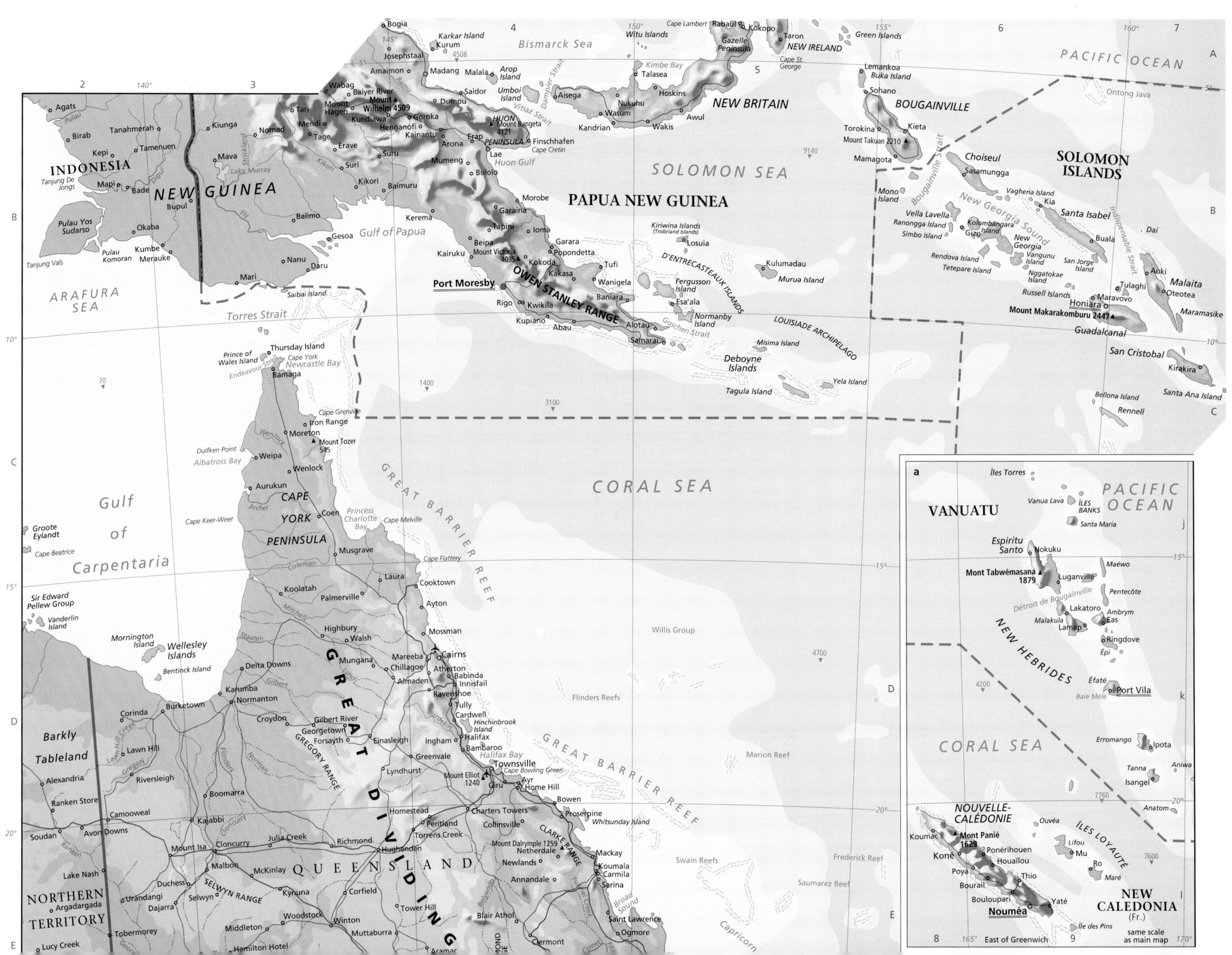

PACIFIC OCEAN
Bismarck Sea
NEW BRITAIN
NEW IRELAND
BOUGAINVILLE
SOLOMON ISLANDS
SOLOMON SEA
PAPUA NEW GUINEA
INDONESIA
NEW GUINEA
ARAFURA SEA
Torres Strait
Gulf of Papua
OWEN STANLEY RANGE
Port Moresby
Honiara
Guadalcanal
D'ENTRECASTEAUX ISLANDS
LOUISIADE ARCHIPELAGO
CORAL SEA
Gulf of Carpentaria
CAPE YORK PENINSULA
GREAT BARRIER REEF
GREAT DIVIDING RANGE
QUEENSLAND
NORTHERN TERRITORY
Barkly Tableland
Cairns
Townsville
Mackay
a
VANUATU
PACIFIC OCEAN
NEW HEBRIDES
Port Vila
CORAL SEA
NOUVELLE-CALÉDONIE
NEW CALEDONIA (Fr.)
Nouméa
ÎLES LOYAUTÉ
same scale as main map
East of Greenwich

AUSTRALIA
SOUTH AUSTRALIA
NEW SOUTH WALES
VICTORIA
TASMANIA
A.C.T.
NEW ZEALAND
NORTH ISLAND
SOUTH ISLAND
FIJI
TASMAN SEA
SOUTHERN OCEAN
PACIFIC OCEAN
Bass Strait
Cook Strait
Foveaux Strait
Great Artesian Basin
GREAT DIVIDING RANGE
GREY RANGE
NORTH FLINDERS RANGE
GAWLER RANGES
LIVERPOOL RANGE
SNOWY MTS.
SOUTHERN ALPS
Simpson Desert
Sturt Stony Desert
Darling Downs
Lake Eyre North
Kangaroo Island
King Island
Flinders Island
FURNEAUX GROUP
Spencer Gulf
Encounter Bay
Bay of Plenty
Hawke Bay
Canterbury Bight
BRISBANE
SYDNEY
MELBOURNE
ADELAIDE
Canberra
Hobart
Newcastle
Wollongong
Geelong
Southport (Gold Coast)
Launceston
Auckland
Wellington
Christchurch
Dunedin
Hamilton
Suva
Mount Kosciusko 2229
Mount Cook 3754
Mount Ruapehu 2797
Tomanivi 1323
Scale 1 : 10 000 000
Lambert Conformal Conic Projection
A.C.T.= AUSTRALIAN CAPITAL TERRITORY
same scale as main map
East of Greenwich
Metres
Feet
Sea Level
M-590293-7A-DR1-1°
Copyright © Rand McNally & Co.

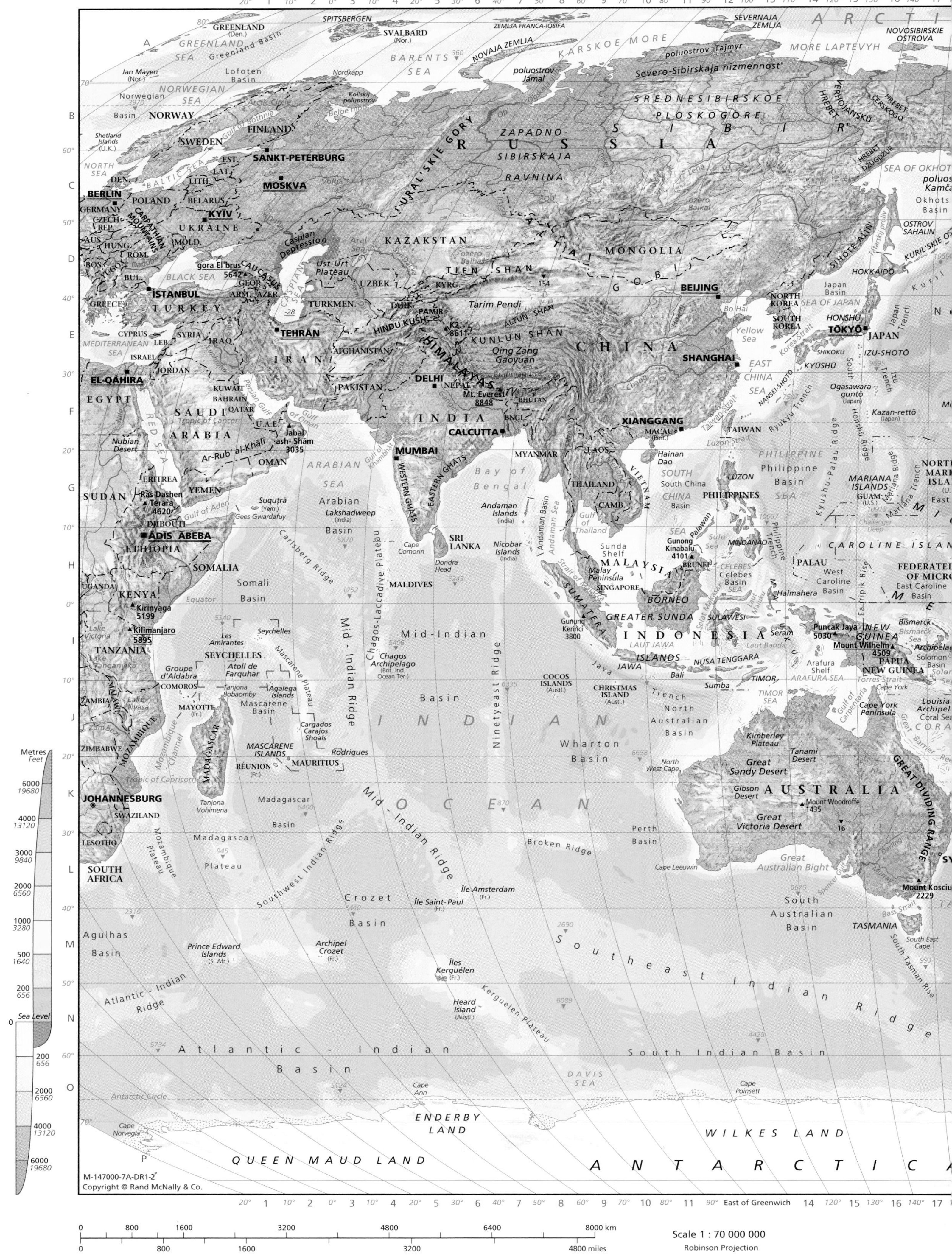

GREENLAND (Den.)
SPITSBERGEN
SVALBARD (Nor.)
SEVERNAJA ZEMLJA
NOVOSIBIRSKIE OSTROVA
ZEMLJA FRANCA-IOSIFA
GREENLAND SEA
Greenland Basin
BARENTS SEA
NOVAJA ZEMLJA
KARSKOE MORE
poluostrov Tajmyr
MORE LAPTEVYH
Jan Mayen (Nor.)
Lofoten Basin
Nordkapp
poluostrov Jamal
Severo-Sibirskaja nizmennost'
NORWEGIAN SEA
Norwegian Basin
Arctic Circle
Kol'skij poluostrov
SREDNESIBIRSKOE PLOSKOGORE
NORWAY
FINLAND
Gulf of Bothnia
URAL'SKIE GORY
ZAPADNO-SIBIRSKAJA RAVNINA
R U S S I A
HREBET ČERSKOGO
VERHOJANSKIJ HREBET
HREBET DŽUGDŽUR
Shetland Islands (U.K.)
SWEDEN
SANKT-PETERBURG
EST.
LAT.
NORTH SEA
BALTIC SEA
DEN.
LITH.
MOSKVA
SEA OF OKHOTSK
Okhotsk Basin
BERLIN
GERMANY
POLAND
BELARUS
KYÏV
ozero Bajkal
CZECH REP.
CARPATHIAN MOUNTAINS
UKRAINE
AUS.
HUNG.
MOLD.
Caspian Depression
Aral Sea
KAZAKSTAN
ALTAI
MONGOLIA
SIHOTE-ALIN'
OSTROV SAHALIN
ROM.
BOS.
YUGOS.
BUL.
gora El'brus 5642
CAUCASUS
BLACK SEA
Ust-Urt Plateau
TIEN SHAN
GOBI
HOKKAIDO
Japan Basin
ISTANBUL
GEOR.
ARM.
AZER.
CASPIAN SEA
UZBEK.
KYRG.
BEIJING
NORTH KOREA
SEA OF JAPAN
GREECE
TURKEY
TURKMEN.
TAJIK.
PAMIR
Tarim Pendi
Bo Hai
SOUTH KOREA
HONSHU
TŌKYŌ
JAPAN
CYPRUS
MEDITERRANEAN SEA
LEB.
SYRIA
IRAQ
TEHRĀN
HINDU KUSH
K2 8611
KUNLUN SHAN
ALTUN SHAN
Yellow Sea
ISRAEL
JORDAN
IRAN
AFGHANISTAN
HIMALAYAS
Qing Zang Gaoyuan
CHINA
SHANGHAI
SHIKOKU
KYŪSHŪ
IZU-SHOTO
EL-QÂHIRA
EGYPT
KUWAIT
BAHRAIN
QATAR
Persian Gulf
PAKISTAN
DELHI
NEPAL
Mt. Everest 8848
BHUTAN
EAST CHINA SEA
Ogasawara-guntō (Japan)
Kazan-rettō (Japan)
SAUDI ARABIA
Tropic of Cancer
U.A.E.
Gulf of Oman
Jabal ash-Sham 3035
INDIA
CALCUTTA
BNGL.
XIANGGANG
MACAU
TAIWAN
Nubian Desert
RED SEA
Ar-Rub' al-Khālī
OMAN
MUMBAI
MYANMAR
LAOS
Hainan Dao
Luzon Strait
PHILIPPINE SEA
Philippine Basin
NORTHERN MARIANA ISLANDS
ARABIAN SEA
WESTERN GHATS
EASTERN GHATS
Bay of Bengal
THAILAND
VIETNAM
LUZON
SOUTH CHINA SEA
South China Basin
PHILIPPINES
MARIANA ISLANDS
GUAM (U.S.)
SUDAN
ERITREA
YEMEN
Ras Dashen Terara 4620
Gulf of Aden
DJIBOUTI
Suqutrā (Yem.)
Gees Gwardafuy
Arabian Basin
Lakshadweep (India)
Andaman Islands (India)
CAMB.
Gulf of Thailand
Palawan
Sulu Sea
ĀDIS ĀBEBA
ETHIOPIA
SOMALIA
Carlsberg Ridge
Cape Comorin
SRI LANKA
Nicobar Islands (India)
Sunda Shelf
Gunong Kinabalu 4101
BRUNEI
MINDANAO
CAROLINE ISLANDS
PALAU
FEDERATED STATES OF MICRONESIA
UGANDA
KENYA
Somali Basin
Equator
Dondra Head
MALDIVES
MALAYSIA
Malay Peninsula
SINGAPORE
CELEBES SEA
Celebes Basin
West Caroline Basin
East Caroline Basin
Halmahera
Kirinyaga 5199
Lake Victoria
Kilimanjaro 5895
TANZANIA
Les Amirantes
Seychelles
SEYCHELLES
Atoll de Farquhar
Mid - Indian Ridge
Chagos-Laccadive Plateau
Mid-Indian
Chagos Archipelago (Brit. Ind. Ocean Ter.)
SUMATERA
Gunung Kerinci 3800
GREATER SUNDA ISLANDS
BORNEO
SULAWESI
INDONESIA
Seram
Puncak Jaya 5030
NEW GUINEA
Mount Wilhelm 4509
PAPUA NEW GUINEA
Bismarck Sea
Solomon Basin
Groupe d'Aldabra
COMOROS
Tanjona Bobaomby
Agalega Islands
Mascarene Plateau
Mascarene Basin
COCOS ISLANDS (Austl.)
CHRISTMAS ISLAND (Austl.)
Java Trench
LAUT JAWA
JAWA
Bali
NUSA TENGGARA
Sumba
TIMOR
ARAFURA SEA
Torres Strait
Cape York
ZAMBIA
Lake Nyasa
MALAWI
MAYOTTE (Fr.)
MOZAMBIQUE
Mozambique Channel
MADAGASCAR
Cargados Carajos Shoals
INDIAN OCEAN
Basin
Ninetyeast Ridge
North Australian Basin
TIMOR SEA
Gulf of Carpentaria
Cape York Peninsula
Coral Sea
ZIMBABWE
MASCARENE ISLANDS
RÉUNION (Fr.)
MAURITIUS
Rodrigues
Wharton Basin
North West Cape
Kimberley Plateau
Tanami Desert
Great Sandy Desert
GREAT DIVIDING RANGE
Tropic of Capricorn
JOHANNESBURG
SWAZILAND
Tanjona Vohimena
Madagascar Basin
Mid - Indian Ridge
Gibson Desert
AUSTRALIA
Mount Woodroffe 1435
Great Victoria Desert
LESOTHO
Mozambique Plateau
Madagascar Plateau
Southwest Indian Ridge
Broken Ridge
Perth Basin
SOUTH AFRICA
Cape Leeuwin
Great Australian Bight
Mount Kosciusko 2229
Crozet Basin
Île Amsterdam (Fr.)
Île Saint-Paul (Fr.)
South Australian Basin
Bass Strait
TASMANIA
South East Cape
Agulhas Basin
Prince Edward Islands (S. Afr.)
Archipel Crozet (Fr.)
Southeast Indian Ridge
South Tasman Rise
Îles Kerguélen (Fr.)
Atlantic - Indian Ridge
Heard Island (Austl.)
Kerguelen Plateau
Atlantic - Indian Basin
South Indian Basin
DAVIS SEA
Cape Ann
Cape Poinsett
Antarctic Circle
ENDERBY LAND
WILKES LAND
Cape Norvegia
QUEEN MAUD LAND
ANTARCTICA
East of Greenwich
Metres Feet
6000 19680
4000 13120
3000 9840
2000 6560
1000 3280
500 1640
200 656
Sea Level
0
200 656
2000 6560
4000 13120
6000 19680
M-147000-7A-DR1-2
0 800 1600 3200 4800 6400 8000 km
0 800 1600 3200 4800 miles
Scale 1 : 70 000 000
Robinson Projection

OCEAN
Canada Basin
Prince Patrick Island
QUEEN ELIZABETH ISLANDS
Axel Heiberg Island
ELLESMERE ISLAND
Melville Island
North Magnetic Pole (1975)
Devon Island
Banks Island
Prince of Wales Island
Somerset Island
VICTORIA ISLAND
Amundsen Gulf
Baffin Bay
Baffin Basin
BAFFIN ISLAND
GREENLAND (Den.)
Gunnbjørn Fjeld 3700
Davis Strait
Arctic Circle
ostrov Vrangelja
CHUKCHI SEA
Bering Strait
Point Barrow
BEAUFORT SEA
BROOKS RANGE
ALASKA (U.S.)
Anadyrskij zaliv
Mount McKinley 6194
ALASKA RANGE
Mount Logan 5959
Mackenzie
MACKENZIE MOUNTAINS
Great Bear Lake
Great Slave Lake
Foxe Basin
Southampton Island
Hudson Strait
Hudson Bay
Péninsule d'Ungava
Irminger Basin
Kap Farvel
LABRADOR SEA
Labrador Basin
LABRADOR
BERING SEA
Aleutian Basin
Alaska Peninsula
Kodiak Island
Gulf of Alaska
COAST MTS.
ROCKY MOUNTAINS
Lake Athabasca
Belcher Islands
Nelson
ALEUTIAN ISLANDS
Aleutian Trench
International Date Line
QUEEN CHARLOTTE ISLANDS
Mount Waddington 3994
CANADA
Lake Winnipeg
VANCOUVER ISLAND
CASCADE RANGE
COAST RANGES
GREAT PLAINS
Lake Superior
Lake Huron
Lake Michigan
Ottawa
Montréal
Lake Ontario
Lake Erie
CHICAGO
NEWFOUNDLAND
Cape Cod
NEW YORK
Washington
APPALACHIAN MOUNTAINS
Mississippi
Missouri
Ohio
Arkansas
Great Salt Lake
Great Basin 86
Mendocino Fracture Zone
Cape Mendocino
Mount Whitney 4418
LOS ANGELES
UNITED STATES
North ATLANTIC
Cape Lookout
American Basin
BERMUDA (U.K.)
Blake Plateau
PACIFIC OCEAN
Murray Fracture Zone
Musicians Seamounts
Red
Rio Grande
HOUSTON
MIDWAY ISLANDS (U.S.)
Hawaiian Ridge
HAWAIIAN ISLANDS (U.S.)
Oahu
Hawaii
Isla Guadalupe (Mex.)
Baja California
Golfo de California
SIERRA MADRE OCCIDENTAL
SIERRA MADRE ORIENTAL
Gulf of Mexico
Mexico Basin
Straits of Florida
BAHAMAS
Tropic of Cancer
OCEAN
Molokai Fracture Zone
Cabo San Lucas
MEXICO
CIUDAD DE MÉXICO
Volcán Pico de Orizaba 5610
SIERRA MADRE DEL SUR
Yucatan Peninsula
CUBA
WEST INDIES
GREATER ANTILLES
HAITI
DOM. REP.
JAMAICA
BELIZE
GUAT.
HONDURAS
EL SALV.
NICARAGUA
CARIBBEAN SEA
Johnston Atoll (U.S.)
Clarion Fracture Zone
Islas Revillagigedo (Mex.)
Middle America Trench
Île Clipperton (Fr.)
Guatemala Basin
Lago de Nicaragua
COSTA RICA
PANAMA
VEN.
Christmas Ridge
Central Pacific Basin
Ratak Chain
POLYNESIA
Clipperton Fracture Zone
Isla del Coco (C.R.)
Cocos Ridge
Panama Basin
COLOMBIA
BOGOTÁ
KIRIBATI
Howland Island (U.S.)
Baker Island (U.S.)
Kiritimati
LINE ISLANDS
Jarvis Island (U.S.)
PHOENIX ISLANDS
Equator
Archipiélago de Colón (Galapagos Islands) (Ec.)
ECUADOR
Chimborazo 6310
Punta Pariñas
TUVALU
TOKELAU (N.Z.)
KIRIBATI
Îles Marquises
PERU
BRAZIL
Nevado Huascarán 6746
Lima
ANDES
Northern Cook Islands
FRENCH POLYNESIA
WALLIS AND FUTUNA (Fr.)
SAMOA
AMERICAN SAMOA
North Fiji Basin
FIJI
Suva
COOK ISLANDS (N.Z.)
Archipel de la Société
ÎLES TUAMOTU
Tuamotu Ridge
Tahiti
East Pacific Rise
Peru Basin
Peru-Chile Trench
NEW HEBRIDES
TONGA
Tonga Ridge
Tonga Trench
Southern Cook Islands
NIUE (N.Z.)
Austral Seamounts
Îles Gambier
PITCAIRN (U.K.)
Nazca Ridge
New Hebrides Trench
South Fiji Basin
Lau Ridge
ÎLES AUSTRALES
Pitcairn Island
Isla Sala y Gómez (Chile)
Sala y Gomez Ridge
Tropic of Capricorn
NORFOLK ISLAND (Austl.)
Kermadec Islands (N.Z.)
Kermadec Ridge
Kermadec Trench
Isla de Pascua (Easter Island) (Chile)
Cerro Aconcagua 6959
Southwest PACIFIC OCEAN
Archipiélago Juan Fernández (Chile)
SANTIAGO
North Cape
Louisville Ridge
CHILE
PAMPA
NORTH ISLAND
Chile Rise
NEW ZEALAND
Cook Strait
Chatham Rise
Chatham Islands (N.Z.)
Pacific Basin
Isla Grande de Chiloé
ARGENTINA
Mount Cook 3754
Bounty Trough
Bounty Islands (N.Z.)
PATAGONIA
Golfo San Jorge
Argentine Basin
Campbell Plateau
Antipodes Islands (N.Z.)
ATLANTIC OCEAN
FALKLAND ISLANDS (U.K.)
Strait of Magellan
TIERRA DEL FUEGO
Cabo de Hornos (Cape Horn)
Drake Passage
SCOTIA SEA
Pacific - Antarctic Ridge
Southeast Pacific Basin
South Shetland Islands (U.K.)
South Orkney Islands (U.K.)
Scott Island
Antarctic Circle
AMUNDSEN SEA
BELLINGSHAUSEN SEA
Alexander Island
ANTARCTIC PENINSULA
Atlantic - Indian Basin
Cape Adare
Thurston Island
ROSS SEA
WEDDELL SEA
Roosevelt Island
Vinson Massif 4897
BERKNER ISLAND
Ronne Ice Shelf
Ross Ice Shelf
MARIE BYRD LAND
West of Greenwich

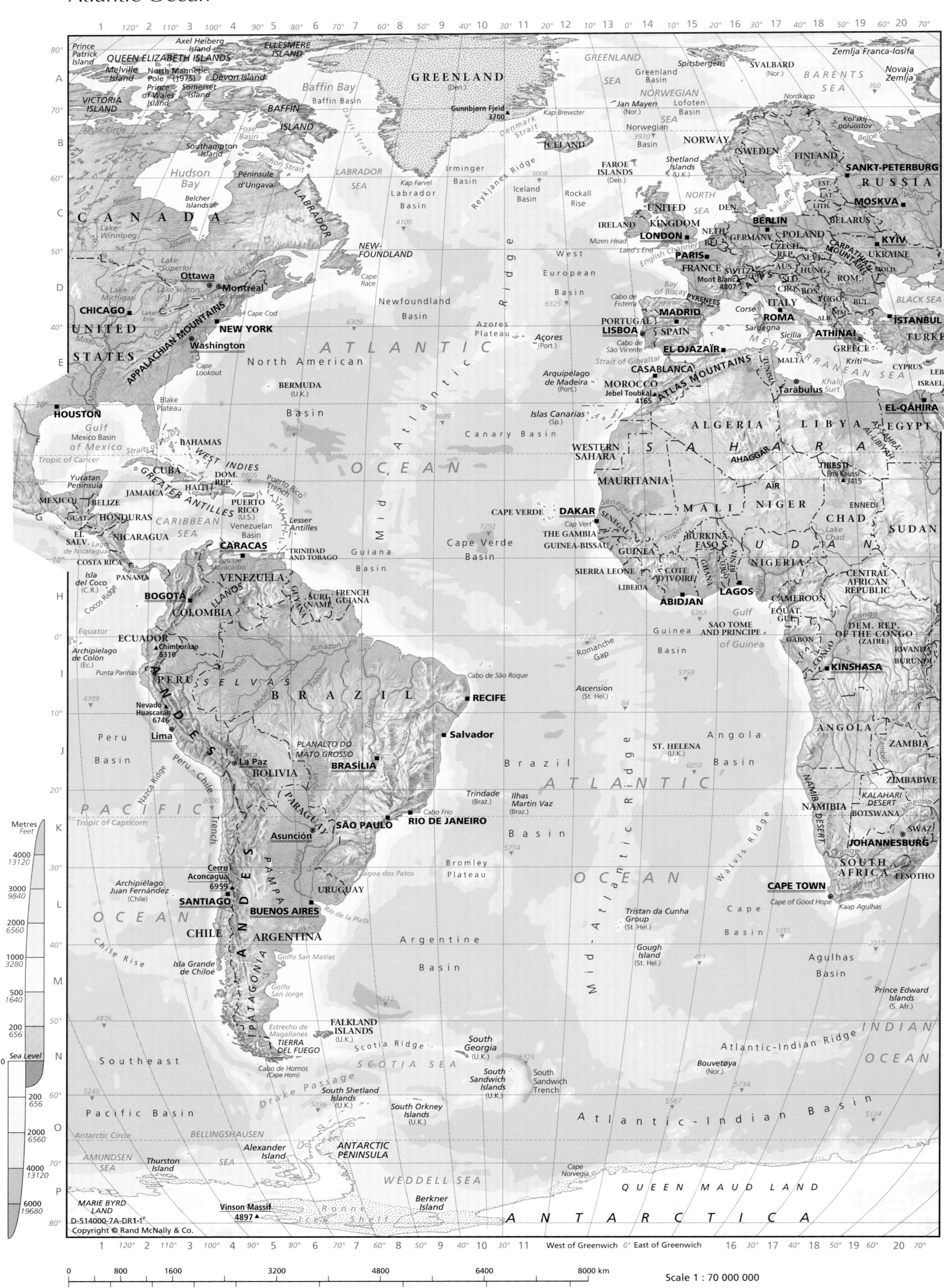

QUEEN ELIZABETH ISLANDS
Prince Patrick Island
Axel Heiberg Island
ELLESMERE ISLAND
Melville Island
North Magnetic Pole (1975)
Devon Island
Prince of Wales Island
Somerset Island
VICTORIA ISLAND
Baffin Bay
Baffin Basin
GREENLAND (Den.)
Gunnbjørn Fjeld 3700
BAFFIN ISLAND
Davis Strait
Arctic Circle
Foxe Basin
Southampton Island
Hudson Strait
Hudson Bay
Péninsule d'Ungava
LABRADOR SEA
LABRADOR
Belcher Islands
Nelson
C A N A D A
Lake Winnipeg
Albany
Lake Superior
Ottawa
Montréal
Lake Michigan
Lake Huron
Lake Erie
Lake Ontario
CHICAGO
Cape Cod
NEW YORK
Washington
UNITED STATES
Missouri
Ohio
APPALACHIAN MOUNTAINS
Mississippi
Cape Lookout
HOUSTON
Gulf of Mexico
Mexico Basin
Straits of Florida
Tropic of Cancer
Blake Plateau
BAHAMAS
WEST INDIES
CUBA
Yucatan Peninsula
HAITI
DOM. REP.
Puerto Rico Trench
JAMAICA
GREATER ANTILLES
PUERTO RICO (U.S.)
MEXICO
BELIZE
GUAT.
HONDURAS
CARIBBEAN SEA
Venezuelan Basin
Lesser Antilles
EL SALV.
NICARAGUA
Lago de Nicaragua
COSTA RICA
PANAMA
CARACAS
TRINIDAD AND TOBAGO
Lago de Maracaibo
VENEZUELA
GUYANA
SURINAME
FRENCH GUIANA
Isla del Coco (C.R.)
Cocos Ridge
BOGOTÁ
COLOMBIA
LLANOS
Equator
ECUADOR
Archipiélago de Colón (Ec.)
Chimborazo 6310
Negro
Amazon
Punta Pariñas
PERU
SELVAS
BRAZIL
Tapajós
Xingu
Tocantins
Madeira
Cabo de São Roque
RECIFE
Nevado Huascarán 6746
ANDES
Lima
Salvador
Peru Basin
PLANALTO DO MATO GROSSO
São Francisco
La Paz
Lago Titicaca
BRASÍLIA
BOLIVIA
Peru-Chile Trench
Nazca Ridge
PARAGUAY
Paraná
Cabo Frio
RIO DE JANEIRO
SÃO PAULO
PACIFIC OCEAN
Tropic of Capricorn
Asunción
Uruguai
Cerro Aconcagua 6959
Archipiélago Juan Fernández (Chile)
SANTIAGO
PAMPA
Lagoa dos Patos
URUGUAY
BUENOS AIRES
Rio de la Plata
CHILE
ARGENTINA
Chile Rise
Isla Grande de Chiloé
Golfo San Matías
Golfo San Jorge
PATAGONIA
Estrecho de Magallanes
FALKLAND ISLANDS (U.K.)
TIERRA DEL FUEGO
Scotia Ridge
South Georgia (U.K.)
SCOTIA SEA
Cabo de Hornos (Cape Horn)
Drake Passage
South Shetland Islands (U.K.)
South Orkney Islands (U.K.)
South Sandwich Islands (U.K.)
South Sandwich Trench
Southeast Pacific Basin
BELLINGSHAUSEN SEA
Antarctic Circle
AMUNDSEN SEA
Thurston Island
Alexander Island
ANTARCTIC PENINSULA
WEDDELL SEA
MARIE BYRD LAND
Vinson Massif 4897
Ronne Ice Shelf
Berkner Island
Cape Norvegia
QUEEN MAUD LAND
ANTARCTICA
Denmark Strait
Kap Brewster
GREENLAND SEA
Greenland Basin
Spitsbergen
SVALBARD (Nor.)
Zemlja Franca-Iosifa
Novaja Zemlja
BARENTS SEA
Nordkapp
NORWEGIAN SEA
Jan Mayen (Nor.)
Lofoten Basin
Norwegian Basin
Kol'skij poluostrov
Beloe more
ICELAND
NORWAY
SWEDEN
FINLAND
Gulf of Bothnia
Kap Farvel
Labrador Basin
Irminger Basin
Reykjanes Ridge
Iceland Basin
FAROE ISLANDS (Den.)
Shetland Islands (U.K.)
Rockall Rise
SANKT-PETERBURG
RUSSIA
EST.
LAT.
LITH.
MOSKVA
Volga
NORTH SEA
DEN.
Baltic Sea
UNITED KINGDOM
IRELAND
BERLIN
BELARUS
Mizen Head
LONDON
NETH.
BEL.
GERMANY
POLAND
KYIV
Land's End
English Channel
PARIS
CZECH REP.
SLVK.
UKRAINE
CARPATHIAN MOUNTAINS
NEW-FOUNDLAND
Cape Race
West European Basin
FRANCE
SWITZ.
AUS.
HUNG.
MOLD.
ROM.
Mont Blanc 4807
ALPS
SLO.
CRO.
BOS.
YUGO.
BUL.
Danube
Bay of Biscay
PYRENEES
BLACK SEA
Cabo de Fisterra
Newfoundland Basin
Mid-Atlantic Ridge
Corse
ITALY
ROMA
ALB.
ISTANBUL
PORTUGAL
LISBOA
MADRID
SPAIN
Sardegna
Sicilia
ATHINAI
GREECE
TURKEY
Azores Plateau
Açores (Port.)
Cabo de São Vicente
EL DJAZAÏR
MEDITERRANEAN SEA
ATLANTIC OCEAN
North American Basin
Strait of Gibraltar
MALTA
Kriti
CYPRUS
CASABLANCA
TUNISIA
ATLAS MOUNTAINS
Arquipélago de Madeira (Port.)
MOROCCO
Jebel Toubkal 4165
Tarābulus
Khalij Surt
ISRAEL
BERMUDA (U.K.)
Islas Canarias (Sp.)
EL-QÂHIRA
EGYPT
Canary Basin
ALGERIA
LIBYA
WESTERN SAHARA
SAHARA
AHAGGAR
TIBESTI
Emi Koussi 3415
MAURITANIA
AÏR
MALI
NIGER
ENNEDI
CAPE VERDE
DAKAR
Cap Vert
SENEGAL
CHAD
Lake Chad
SUDAN
Cape Verde Basin
THE GAMBIA
GUINEA-BISSAU
GUINEA
BURKINA FASO
Guiana Basin
SIERRA LEONE
LIBERIA
COTE D'IVOIRE
GHANA
TOGO
BENIN
NIGERIA
LAGOS
CENTRAL AFRICAN REPUBLIC
ABIDJAN
CAMEROON
EQUAT. GUI.
Gulf of Guinea
SAO TOME AND PRINCIPE
Guinea Basin
Romanche Gap
GABON
CONGO
DEM. REP. OF THE CONGO (ZAIRE)
RWANDA
BURUNDI
KINSHASA
Lake Tanganyika
Ascension (St. Hel.)
ANGOLA
ZAMBIA
Angola Basin
ST. HELENA (U.K.)
Brazil Basin
Trindade (Braz.)
Ilhas Martin Vaz (Braz.)
NAMIBIA
NAMIB DESERT
ZIMBABWE
KALAHARI DESERT
BOTSWANA
Limpopo
Walvis Ridge
SWAZ.
JOHANNESBURG
Bromley Plateau
Orange
SOUTH AFRICA
LESOTHO
CAPE TOWN
Cape of Good Hope
Kaap Agulhas
Tristan da Cunha Group (St. Hel.)
Cape Basin
Argentine Basin
Gough Island (St. Hel.)
Agulhas Basin
Prince Edward Islands (S. Afr.)
Atlantic-Indian Ridge
INDIAN OCEAN
Bouvetøya (Nor.)
Atlantic-Indian Basin
West of Greenwich
East of Greenwich
Metres
Feet
4000 13120
3000 9840
2000 6560
1000 3280
500 1640
200 656
Sea Level
200 656
2000 6560
4000 13120
6000 19680
D-514000-7A-DR1-1
0 800 1600 3200 4800 6400 8000 km
0 800 1600 3200 4800 miles
Scale 1 : 70 000 000
Robinson Projection

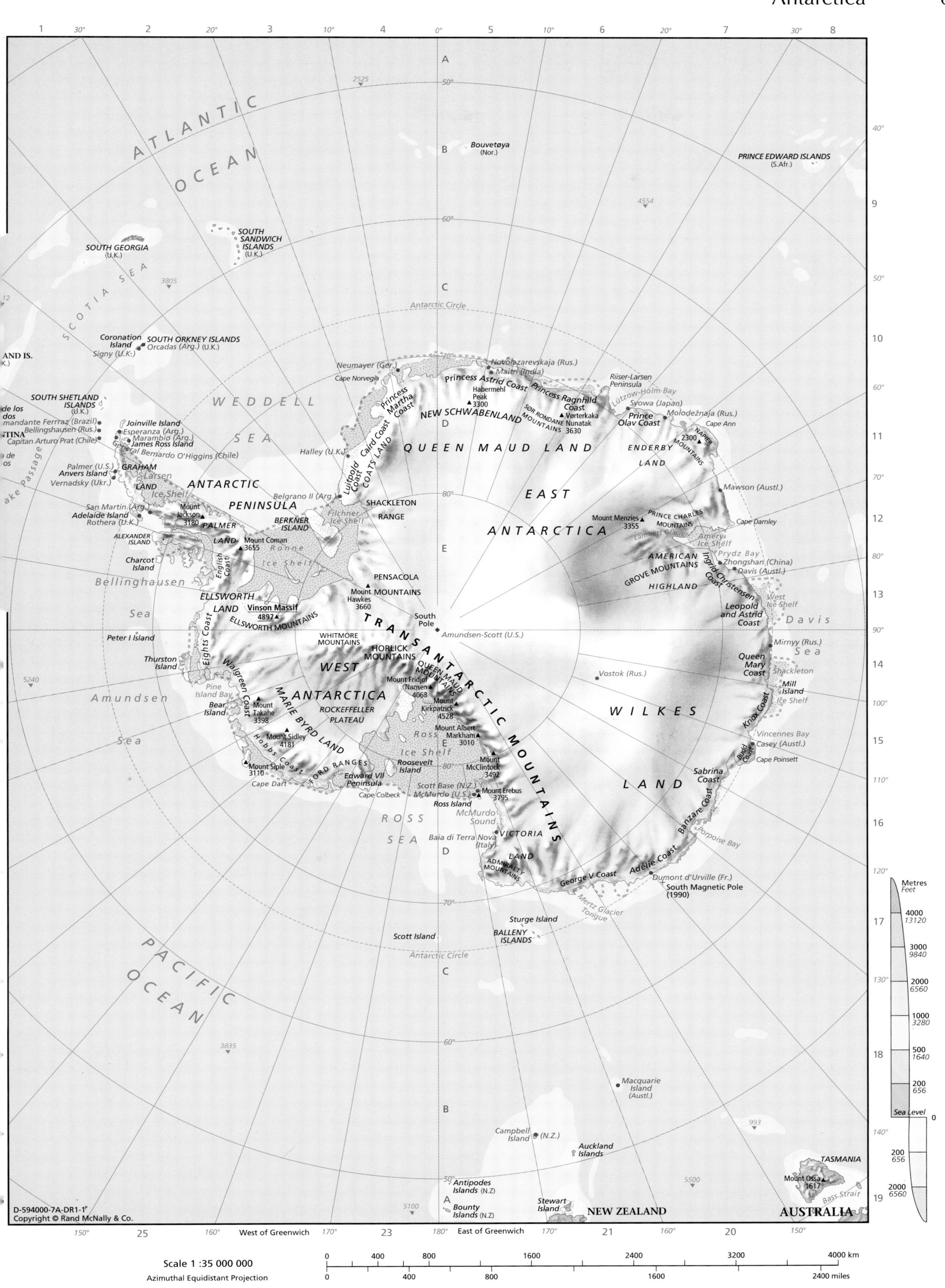

Scale 1:35 000 000

Azimuthal Equidistant Projection

0 400 800 1600 2400 3200 4000 km

0 400 800 1600 2400 miles

0 400 800 1600 2400 3200 4000 km
0 400 800 1600 2400 miles

Scale 1 : 35 000 000
Lambert Azimuthal Equal Area Projection

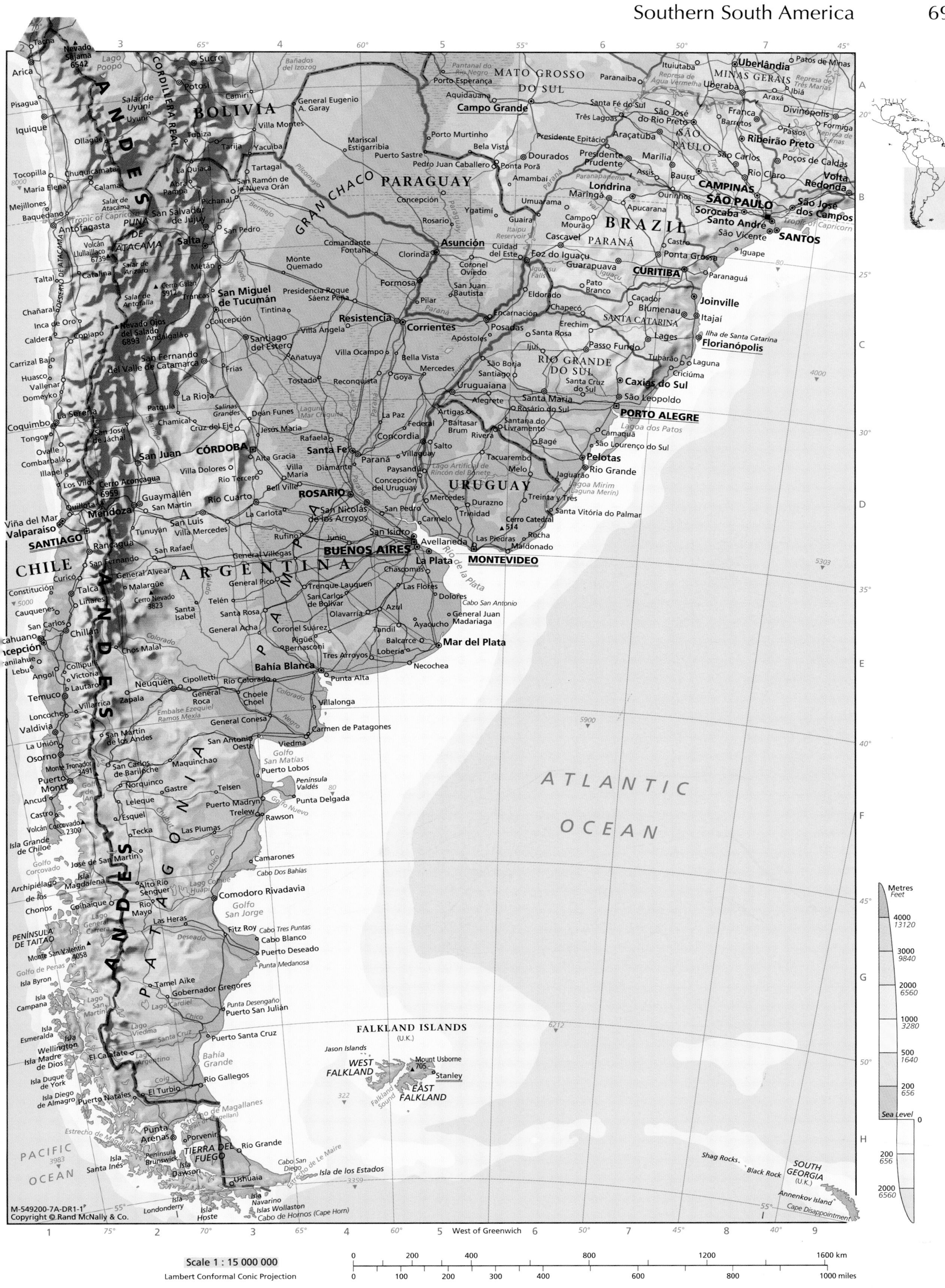
BOLIVIA
PARAGUAY
BRAZIL
URUGUAY
ARGENTINA
CHILE
ANDES
CORDILLERA REAL
GRAN CHACO
PAMPA
PATAGONIA
MATO GROSSO DO SUL
MINAS GERAIS
SÃO PAULO
PARANÁ
SANTA CATARINA
RIO GRANDE DO SUL
PUNA DE ATACAMA
DESIERTO DE ATACAMA
TIERRA DEL FUEGO
ATLANTIC OCEAN
PACIFIC OCEAN
FALKLAND ISLANDS (U.K.)
WEST FALKLAND
EAST FALKLAND
Stanley
Mount Usborne 705
Jason Islands
Falkland Sound
SOUTH GEORGIA (U.K.)
Shag Rocks
Black Rock
Annenkov Island
Cape Disappointment
Sucre
Potosí
Uyuni
Salar de Uyuni
Tupiza
Tarija
Villa Montes
Yacuiba
Camiri
Arica
Tacna
Iquique
Pisagua
Tocopilla
María Elena
Mejillones
Antofagasta
Calama
Chuquicamata
Taltal
Chañaral
Caldera
Copiapó
Vallenar
La Serena
Coquimbo
Ovalle
Illapel
Los Vilos
Viña del Mar
Valparaíso
SANTIAGO
Rancagua
San Fernando
Curicó
Talca
Linares
Constitución
Cauquenes
Chillán
Concepción
Los Angeles
Angol
Victoria
Temuco
Valdivia
Osorno
Puerto Montt
Castro
Isla Grande de Chiloé
Coihaique
Puerto Natales
Punta Arenas
Porvenir
Ushuaia
Río Grande
Cabo de Hornos (Cape Horn)
Isla de los Estados
Estrecho de Magallanes
Estrecho de Le Maire
Nevado Sajama 6542
Cerro Aconcagua 6959
Nevado Ojos del Salado 6893
Cerro Galán 5912
Llullaillaco 6739
Cerro Nevado 3823
Monte Tronador 3491
Monte San Valentín 4058
Volcán Corcovado 2300
Tropic of Capricorn
La Quiaca
San Salvador de Jujuy
Salta
San Miguel de Tucumán
Santiago del Estero
San Fernando del Valle de Catamarca
La Rioja
San Juan
Mendoza
San Luis
San Rafael
CÓRDOBA
Río Cuarto
Villa María
ROSARIO
Santa Fe
Paraná
Resistencia
Corrientes
Formosa
Posadas
Goya
Reconquista
Concordia
BUENOS AIRES
La Plata
Mar del Plata
Tandil
Olavarría
Azul
Santa Rosa
General Pico
Bahía Blanca
Neuquén
Cipolletti
Viedma
Carmen de Patagones
San Carlos de Bariloche
Esquel
Puerto Madryn
Trelew
Rawson
Península Valdés
Golfo San Matías
Golfo San Jorge
Comodoro Rivadavia
Puerto Deseado
Puerto San Julián
Puerto Santa Cruz
Río Gallegos
El Calafate
MONTEVIDEO
Salto
Paysandú
Rivera
Tacuarembó
Melo
Durazno
Maldonado
Rocha
Colonia
Asunción
Concepción
Encarnación
Ciudad del Este
Pedro Juan Caballero
Campo Grande
Ponta Porã
Dourados
Uberlândia
Uberaba
Ribeirão Preto
Londrina
Maringá
Campinas
SÃO PAULO
SANTOS
Sorocaba
Santo André
São José dos Campos
CURITIBA
Ponta Grossa
Foz do Iguaçu
Cascavel
Guarapuava
Joinville
Blumenau
Itajaí
Florianópolis
Passo Fundo
Caxias do Sul
PORTO ALEGRE
Santa Maria
Uruguaiana
Pelotas
Rio Grande
Lagoa dos Patos
Lagoa Mirim
Río de la Plata
Metres Feet
4000 13120
3000 9840
2000 6560
1000 3280
500 1640
200 656
Sea Level 0
West of Greenwich
M-549200-7A-DR1-1P
Copyright © Rand McNally & Co.
Scale 1 : 15 000 000
Lambert Conformal Conic Projection
0 200 400 800 1200 1600 km
0 100 200 300 400 600 800 1000 miles

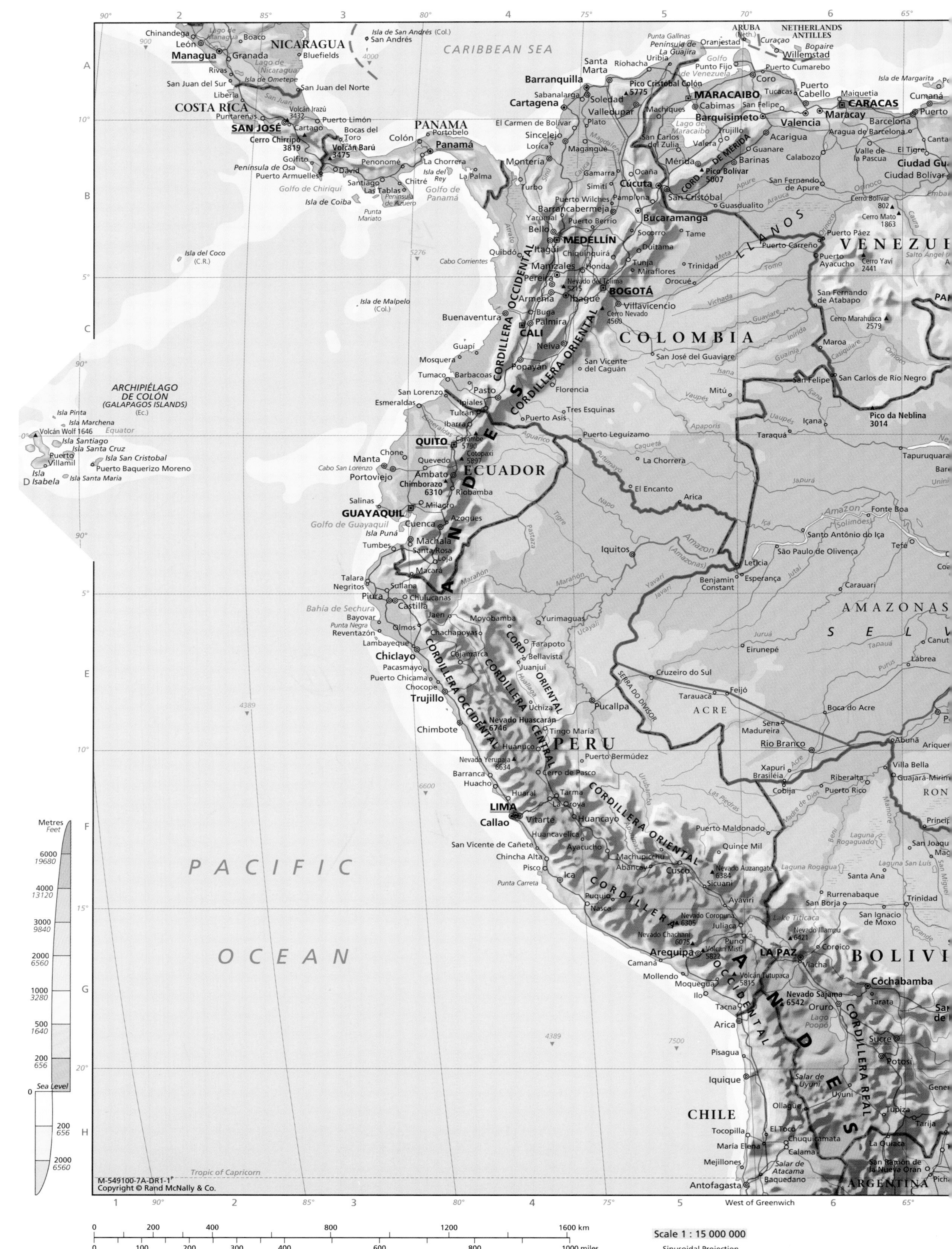
CARIBBEAN SEA
NICARAGUA
Managua
Chinandega
León
Boaco
Granada
Bluefields
Lago de Nicaragua
Rivas
Isla de Ometepe
San Juan del Sur
Liberia
San Juan del Norte
COSTA RICA
Puntarenas
SAN JOSÉ
Volcán Irazú 3432
Cartago
Puerto Limón
Cerro Chirripó 3819
Bocas del Toro
Volcán Barú 3475
Golfito
Península de Osa
Puerto Armuelles
David
Golfo de Chiriquí
Isla de Coiba
PANAMA
Colón
Portobelo
Panamá
La Chorrera
Penonomé
Santiago
Chitré
Las Tablas
Península de Azuero
Isla del Rey
La Palma
Golfo de Panamá
Punta Mariato
Isla de San Andrés (Col.)
San Andrés
Isla del Coco (C.R.)
Isla de Malpelo (Col.)
Cabo Corrientes
ARCHIPIÉLAGO DE COLÓN (GALAPAGOS ISLANDS) (Ec.)
Isla Pinta
Isla Marchena
Volcán Wolf 1646
Equator
Isla Santiago
Isla Santa Cruz
Puerto Villamil
Isla San Cristobal
Puerto Baquerizo Moreno
Isla Isabela
Isla Santa María
ARUBA (Neth.)
NETHERLANDS ANTILLES
Oranjestad
Curaçao
Bonaire
Willemstad
Punta Gallinas
Península de La Guajira
Uribia
Riohacha
Santa Marta
Barranquilla
Cartagena
Sabanalarga
Soledad
Valledupar
Pico Cristóbal Colón 5775
Golfo de Venezuela
Punto Fijo
Coro
Punta Cumarebo
MARACAIBO
Cabimas
Lago de Maracaibo
Machiques
San Felipe
Tucacas
Puerto Cabello
Barquisimeto
Valencia
Maracay
Maiquetia
CARACAS
Isla de Margarita
Cumaná
Barcelona
Aragua de Barcelona
Acarigua
Guanare
Barinas
Calabozo
Valle de la Pascua
El Tigre
Ciudad Bolívar
San Fernando de Apure
Trujillo
Valera
San Carlos del Zulia
Mérida
CORD. DE MÉRIDA
Pico Bolívar 5007
El Carmen de Bolívar
Sincelejo
Lorica
Magangué
Plato
Montería
Gamarra
Ocaña
Turbo
Simití
Cúcuta
Pamplona
San Cristóbal
Guasdualito
Puerto Wilches
Barrancabermeja
Yarumal
Puerto Berrío
Bucaramanga
Bello
MEDELLÍN
Socorro
Tame
LLANOS
Puerto Páez
Cerro Bolívar 802
Cerro Mato 1863
Itagüí
Quibdó
Chiquinquirá
Duitama
Tunja
Puerto Carreño
Puerto Ayacucho
Cerro Yavi 2441
VENEZUELA
Manizales
Honda
Miraflores
Trinidad
Pereira
Nevado del Tolima 5215
Orocué
Armenia
Ibagué
BOGOTÁ
Villavicencio
Cerro Nevado 4560
San Fernando de Atabapo
Cerro Marahuaca 2579
Buga
Palmira
Buenaventura
CALI
CORDILLERA OCCIDENTAL
CORDILLERA ORIENTAL
Neiva
COLOMBIA
San José del Guaviare
Maroa
Guapí
Mosquera
Tumaco
Barbacoas
Popayán
San Vicente del Caguán
San Felipe
San Carlos de Río Negro
Pico da Neblina 3014
Pasto
Florencia
San Lorenzo
Esmeraldas
Ipiales
Mitú
Tulcán
Tres Esquinas
Ibarra
Puerto Asís
Içana
Taraquá
QUITO
Cayambe 5790
Puerto Leguízamo
Cotopaxi 5897
Chone
Manta
Quevedo
La Chorrera
ECUADOR
Cabo San Lorenzo
Ambato
Portoviejo
Chimborazo 6310
Riobamba
El Encanto
Salinas
GUAYAQUIL
Milagro
Arica
Golfo de Guayaquil
Azogues
Cuenca
Isla Puná
Machala
Tumbes
Santa Rosa
Loja
Macará
Iquitos
Fonte Boa
Santo Antônio do Iça
São Paulo de Olivença
Tefé
Leticia
Esperança
Benjamin Constant
Amazon (Solimões)
Talara
Negritos
Sullana
Piura
Chulucanas
Castilla
Bahía de Sechura
Bayovar
Punta Negra
Reventazón
Olmos
Jaén
Moyobamba
Yurimaguas
Chachapoyas
Lambayeque
Chiclayo
Pacasmayo
Cajamarca
Tarapoto
Bellavista
Juanjuí
CORD. ORIENTAL
CORDILLERA CENTRAL
CORDILLERA OCCIDENTAL
Puerto Chicama
Chocope
Trujillo
Uchiza
Pucallpa
Chimbote
Nevado Huascarán 6746
Tingo María
Huánuco
PERU
Nevado Yerupajá 6634
Puerto Bermúdez
Barranca
Cerro de Pasco
Huacho
Huaral
Tarma
LIMA
Callao
La Oroya
Vitarte
Huancayo
Huancavelica
San Vicente de Cañete
Ayacucho
Chincha Alta
Pisco
Machupicchu
Abancay
Cusco
Nevado Auzangate 6384
Sicuani
Punta Carreta
Ica
Puquio
Nasca
Ayaviri
Nevado Coropuna 6305
Juliaca
Nevado Chachani 6075
Volcán Misti 5822
Puno
Lake Titicaca
Arequipa
Camaná
Mollendo
Moquegua
Ilo
Volcán Tutupaca 5815
Tacna
Arica
Pisagua
Iquique
CHILE
Tocopilla
María Elena
Mejillones
Antofagasta
Baquedano
Salar de Atacama
Calama
Chuquicamata
El Toco
Ollagüe
Uyuni
Salar de Uyuni
Potosí
Sucre
Tupiza
Tarija
La Quiaca
San Ramón de la Nueva Orán
ARGENTINA
LA PAZ
Viacha
Coroico
Nevado Illampu 6421
Cochabamba
Nevado Sajama 6542
Oruro
Lago Poopó
Tarata
BOLIVIA
CORDILLERA REAL
ANDES
Rurrenabaque
San Borja
San Ignacio de Moxo
Trinidad
Santa Ana
Riberalta
Puerto Rico
Cobija
Xapuri
Brasiléia
Villa Bella
Guajará-Mirim
Abunã
Rio Branco
Sena Madureira
Cruzeiro do Sul
Feijó
Tarauacá
ACRE
SERRA DO DIVISOR
Boca do Acre
Eirunepé
Carauari
AMAZONAS
SELVAS
Lábrea
Tapuruquara
Puerto Maldonado
Quince Mil
Laguna Rogaguado
Laguna Rogagua
PACIFIC OCEAN
Tropic of Capricorn
Metres Feet
6000 19680
4000 13120
3000 9840
2000 6560
1000 3280
500 1640
200 656
Sea Level
200 656
2000 6560
M-549100-7A-DR1-1
Copyright © Rand McNally & Co.
West of Greenwich
0 200 400 800 1200 1600 km
0 100 200 300 400 600 800 1000 miles
Scale 1 : 15 000 000
Sinusoidal Projection

ATLANTIC OCEAN
BRAZIL
GUYANA
SURINAME
FRENCH GUIANA
Georgetown
Paramaribo
Cayenne
Macapá
BELÉM
São Luís
Teresina
FORTALEZA
Natal
João Pessoa
RECIFE
Maceió
Aracaju
SALVADOR
BRASÍLIA
GOIÂNIA
Cuiabá
Campo Grande
BELO HORIZONTE
Vitória
RIO DE JANEIRO
SÃO PAULO
PARÁ
AMAPÁ
MARANHÃO
PIAUÍ
CEARÁ
PERNAMBUCO
PARAÍBA
ALAGOAS
SERGIPE
BAHIA
TOCANTINS
GOIÁS
MATO GROSSO
MATO GROSSO DO SUL
MINAS GERAIS
ESPÍRITO SANTO
SÃO PAULO
PARANÁ
Equator
Tropic of Capricorn

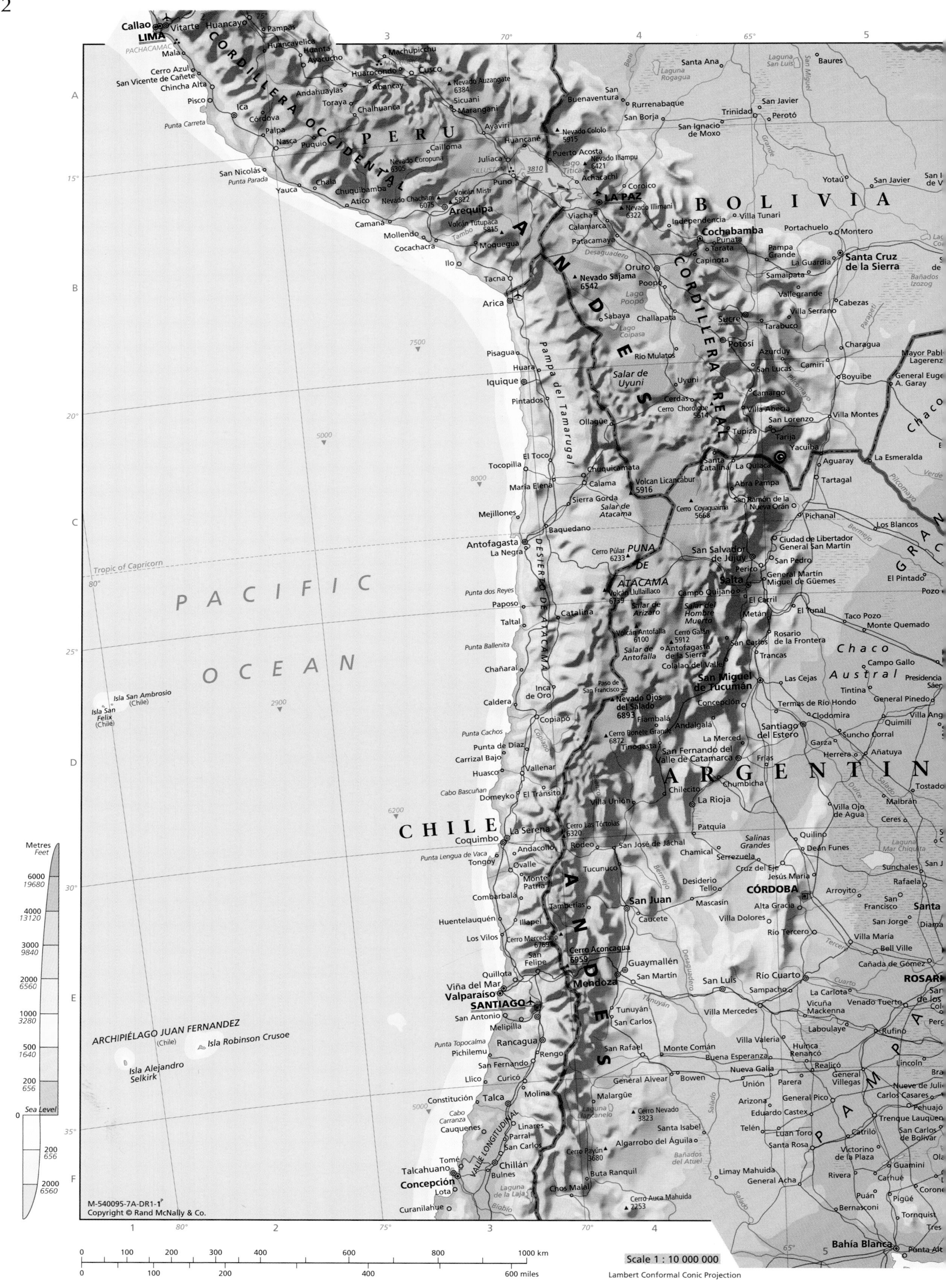

PACIFIC
OCEAN
PERU
BOLIVIA
CHILE
ARGENTINA
ANDES
CORDILLERA OCCIDENTAL
CORDILLERA REAL
Pampa del Tamarugal
DESIERTO DE ATACAMA
PUNA DE ATACAMA
Chaco Austral
Tropic of Capricorn
Callao
LIMA
Vitarte
Huancayo
Pampas
PACHACAMAC
Mala
Huancavelica
Huanta
Ayacucho
Machupicchu
Huarocondo
Cusco
Cerro Azul
San Vicente de Cañete
Chincha Alta
Andahuaylas
Abancay
Nevado Auzangate 6384
Sicuani
Marangani
Pisco
Ica
Toraya
Chalhuanca
Córdova
Palpa
Nasca
Puquio
Punta Carreta
Ayaviri
Caylloma
Huancané
Nevado Coropuna 6305
Juliaca
San Nicolás
Punta Parada
Yauca
Chala
Chuquibamba
Atico
Nevado Chachani 6075
Volcán Misti 5822
Arequipa
Puno
Camaná
Volcán Tutupaca 5815
Mollendo
Cocachacra
Moquegua
Ilo
Tacna
Arica
Nevado Cololo 5915
Puerto Acosta
Nevado Illampu 6421
Lago Titicaca
Achacachi
Coroico
LA PAZ
Nevado Illimani 6322
Viacha
Calamarca
Patacamaya
Desaguadero
Oruro
Nevado Sajama 6542
Poopó
Lago Poopó
Sabaya
Challapata
Lago Coipasa
Río Mulatos
Salar de Uyuni
Uyuni
Cerdas
Cerro Chorolque 5614
Ollagüe
Santa Ana
Laguna Rogagua
Laguna San Luis
Baures
San Buenaventura
Rurrenabaque
San Borja
Trinidad
San Javier
Perotó
San Ignacio de Moxo
Yotaú
San Javier
Independencia
Villa Tunari
Cochabamba
Punata
Tarata
Capinota
Portachuelo
Montero
Pampa Grande
La Guardia
Santa Cruz de la Sierra
Samaipata
Vallegrande
Bañados Izozog
Cabezas
Villa Serrano
Sucre
Tarabuco
Potosí
Charagua
Azurduy
Camiri
San Lucas
Boyuibe
Camargo
Villa Abecia
Villa Montes
San Lorenzo
Tarija
Tupiza
Yacuiba
Mayor Pablo Lagerenza
General Eugenio A. Garay
Chaco
Pisagua
Huara
Iquique
Pintados
Tocopilla
El Toco
Chuquicamata
Calama
María Elena
Volcán Licancabur 5916
Sierra Gorda
Salar de Atacama
Mejillones
Baquedano
Antofagasta
La Negra
Cerro Púlar 6233
Volcán Llullaillaco 6739
Salar de Arizaro
Punta dos Reyes
Paposo
Catalina
Taltal
Volcán Antofalla 6100
Salar de Antofalla
Cerro Galán 5912
Antofagasta de la Sierra
Salar del Hombre Muerto
Punta Ballenita
Chañaral
Paso de San Francisco
Inca de Oro
Caldera
Nevado Ojos del Salado 6893
Copiapó
Fiambalá
Cerro Bonete Grande 6872
Tinogasta
Punta Cachos
Punta de Díaz
Carrizal Bajo
Huasco
Vallenar
Cabo Bascuñán
Domeyko
El Tránsito
Villa Unión
Cerro Las Tórtolas 6320
La Serena
Coquimbo
Punta Lengua de Vaca
Tongoy
Andacollo
Ovalle
Rodeo
Monte Patria
Combarbalá
Tucunuco
Tamberías
Huentelauquén
Illapel
Los Vilos
Cerro Mercedario 6769
San Felipe
Cerro Aconcagua 6959
Quillota
Viña del Mar
Valparaíso
SANTIAGO
San Antonio
Melipilla
Mendoza
Rancagua
Punta Topocalma
Pichilemu
Rengo
San Fernando
Llico
Curicó
Molina
Constitución
Talca
Cabo Carranza
Cauquenes
Linares
Parral
San Carlos
Tomé
Talcahuano
Concepción
Lota
Chillán
Bulnes
Curanilahue
VALLE LONGITUDINAL
La Quiaca
Santa Catalina
Abra Pampa
Aguaray
Tartagal
La Esmeralda
Pilcomayo
Cerro Coyaguaima 5668
San Ramón de la Nueva Orán
Pichanal
Los Blancos
Ciudad de Libertador General San Martín
San Salvador de Jujuy
Perico
San Pedro
Salta
General Martín Miguel de Güemes
El Pintado
Pozo
Campo Quijano
El Carril
Metán
El Tunal
Taco Pozo
Monte Quemado
Rosario de la Frontera
Trancas
San Carlos
Colalao del Valle
San Miguel de Tucumán
Campo Gallo
Tintina
Presidencia Roque Sáenz Peña
Las Cejas
Concepción
Termas de Río Hondo
General Pinedo
Clodomira
Andalgalá
Santiago del Estero
Quimilí
Villa Ángela
La Merced
Suncho Corral
San Fernando del Valle de Catamarca
Frías
Garza
Herrera
Añatuya
Chumbicha
Chilecito
La Rioja
Tostado
Malbrán
Villa Ojo de Agua
Ceres
Patquía
Salinas Grandes
Quilino
Chamical
Serrezuela
Deán Funes
Laguna Mar Chiquita
San José de Jáchal
Cruz del Eje
Jesús María
Sunchales
Rafaela
Desiderio Tello
CÓRDOBA
Arroyito
San Francisco
San Juan
Mascasín
Alta Gracia
Caucete
Villa Dolores
San Jorge
Río Tercero
Villa María
Bell Ville
Guaymallén
San Martín
San Luis
Río Cuarto
Cañada de Gómez
ROSARIO
Sampacho
La Carlota
Vicuña Mackenna
Venado Tuerto
Tunuyán
San Carlos
Villa Mercedes
Laboulaye
Rufino
San Rafael
Monte Comán
Villa Valeria
Huinca Renancó
Buena Esperanza
Realicó
Nueva Galia
General Alvear
Bowen
General Villegas
Lincoln
Malargüe
Unión
Parera
Nueve de Julio
Carlos Casares
Arizona
General Pico
Eduardo Castex
Pehuajó
Cerro Nevado 3823
Laguna Llancanelo
Santa Isabel
Trenque Lauquen
Telén
Luan Toro
Catriló
San Carlos de Bolívar
Algarrobo del Águila
Santa Rosa
Victorino de la Plaza
Cerro Payún 3680
Bañados del Atuel
Guamini
Buta Ranquil
Limay Mahuida
Rivera
Carhué
General Acha
Chos Malal
Puán
Pigüé
Laguna de la Laja
Cerro Auca Mahuida 2253
Bernasconi
Tornquist
Bahía Blanca
Punta Alta
PAMPA
GRAN CHACO
Isla San Ambrosio (Chile)
Isla San Félix (Chile)
ARCHIPIÉLAGO JUAN FERNANDEZ (Chile)
Isla Robinson Crusoe
Isla Alejandro Selkirk
7500
5000
8000
2900
6200
5000
Metres
Feet
6000
19680
4000
13120
3000
9840
2000
6560
1000
3280
500
1640
200
656
Sea Level
0
200
656
2000
6560
A
B
C
D
E
F
1
2
3
4
5
15°
20°
25°
30°
35°
80°
75°
70°
65°
0
100
200
300
400
600
800
1000 km
0
100
200
400
600 miles
Scale 1 : 10 000 000
Lambert Conformal Conic Projection
M-540095-7A-DR1-1

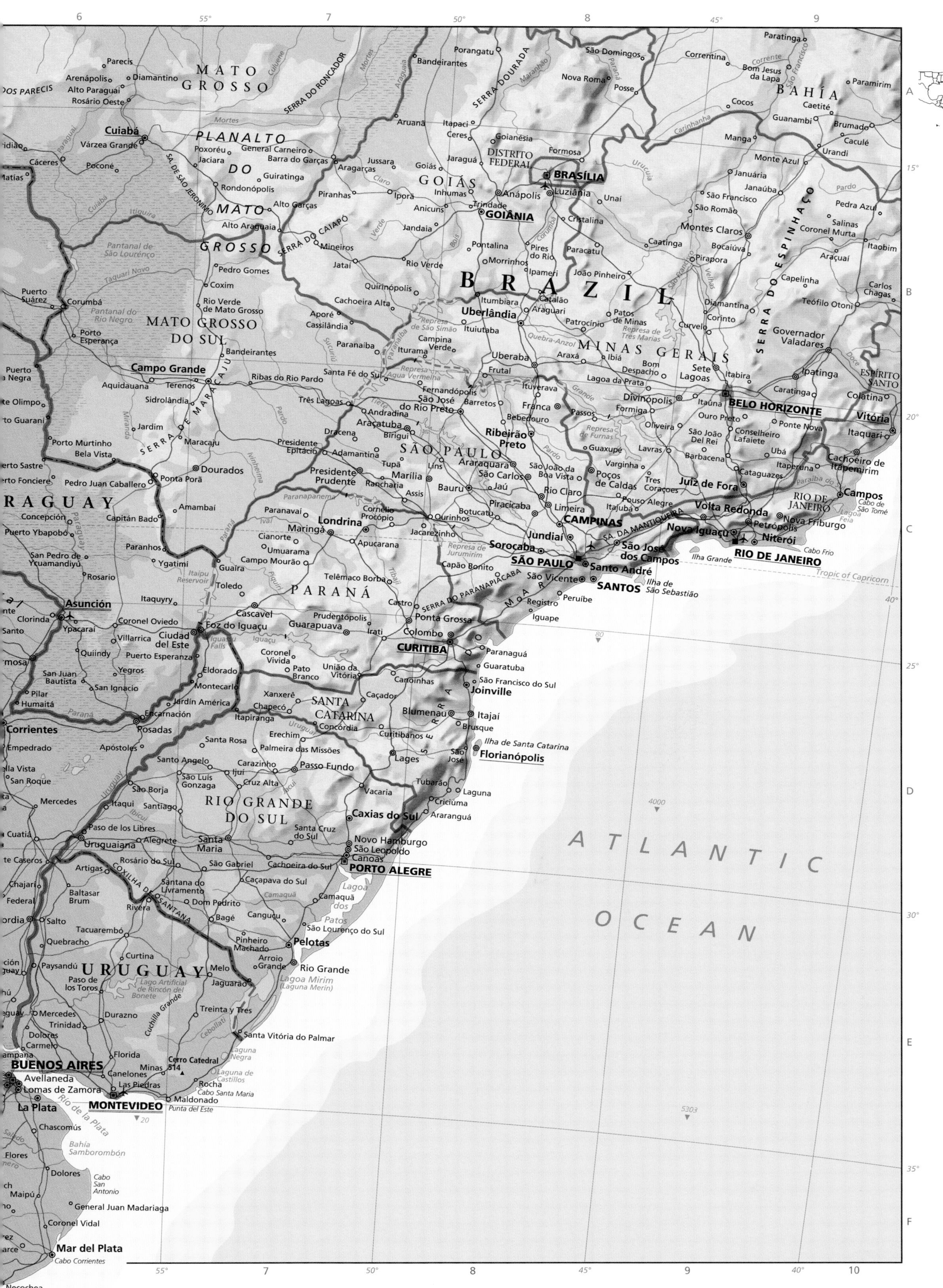
MATO GROSSO
PLANALTO DO MATO GROSSO
MATO GROSSO DO SUL
GOIÁS
DISTRITO FEDERAL
BRASÍLIA
BAHÍA
BRAZIL
MINAS GERAIS
SÃO PAULO
PARANÁ
SANTA CATARINA
RIO GRANDE DO SUL
RIO DE JANEIRO
ESPÍRITO SANTO
PARAGUAY
URUGUAY
Asunción
BUENOS AIRES
MONTEVIDEO
BELO HORIZONTE
RIO DE JANEIRO
SÃO PAULO
CURITIBA
PORTO ALEGRE
GOIÂNIA
CAMPINAS
SANTOS
Cuiabá
Campo Grande
Florianópolis
Tropic of Capricorn
ATLANTIC OCEAN

ATLANTIC OCEAN
BRAZIL
PARÁ
MARANHÃO
PIAUÍ
CEARÁ
RIO GRANDE DO NORTE
PARAÍBA
PERNAMBUCO
ALAGOAS
SERGIPE
BAHIA
TOCANTINS
GOIÁS
DISTRITO FEDERAL
MINAS GERAIS
ESPÍRITO SANTO
RIO DE JANEIRO
SÃO PAULO
PARANÁ
MATO GROSSO
MATO GROSSO DO SUL
AMAPÁ
Equator
Tropic of Capricorn
BELÉM
São Luís
Teresina
FORTALEZA
Natal
João Pessoa
Recife
Maceió
Aracaju
SALVADOR
BRASÍLIA
GOIÂNIA
BELO HORIZONTE
Vitória
RIO DE JANEIRO
SÃO PAULO
Macapá
Imperatriz
Marabá
Petrolina
Juazeiro do Norte
Campina Grande
Feira de Santana
Vitória da Conquista
Ilhéus
Montes Claros
Uberlândia
Juiz de Fora
Campinas
Santos
Londrina
Ilha de Marajó
Ilha do Bananal
SERRA DOS CARAJÁS
SERRA DO RONCADOR
SERRA DO ESTRONDO
SERRA DOURADA
CHAPADA DAS MANGABEIRAS
SERRA DA URUÇUÍ
SERRA DE IBIAPABA
SERRA GRANDE
SERRA DO ESPINHAÇO
SERRA DA MANTIQUEIRA
SERRA DO MAR
Represa de Sobradinho
Represa de Tucuruí
Represa Boa Esperança
Represa de Três Marias
Tocantins
Araguaia
São Francisco
Parnaíba
Amazon
Cabo de São Roque
Cabo Frio
Cabo de São Tomé
Ilha Grande
Ilha de São Sebastião
West of Greenwich
Metres
Feet
Sea Level
M-540393-7A-DR1-1
Copyright © Rand McNally & Co.
Scale 1 : 10 000 000
Lambert Conformal Conic Projection
0 100 200 300 400 600 800 1000 km
0 100 200 400 600 miles

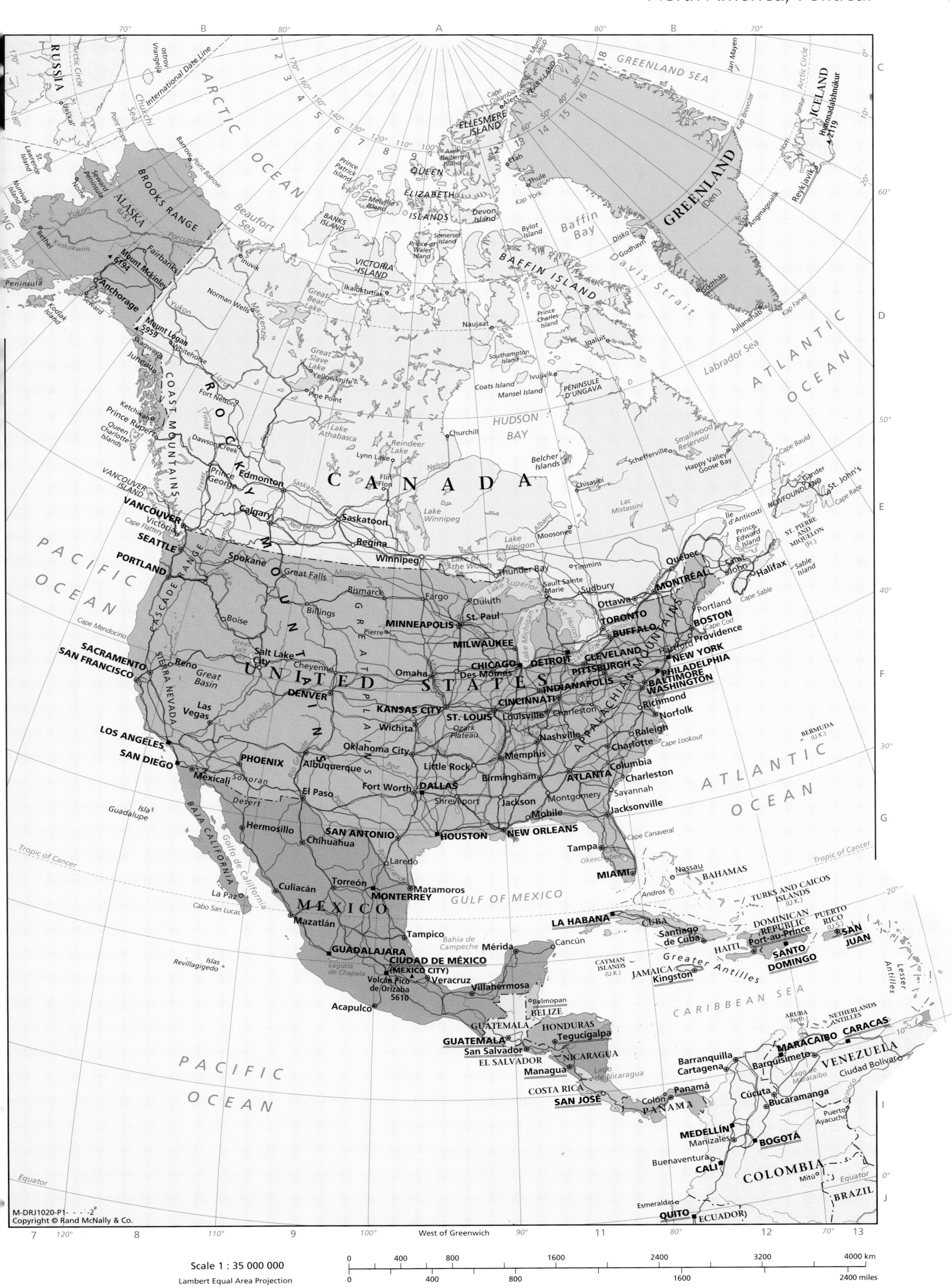

Scale 1 : 35 000 000

Lambert Equal Area Projection

M-DRJ1020-P1- - - -2

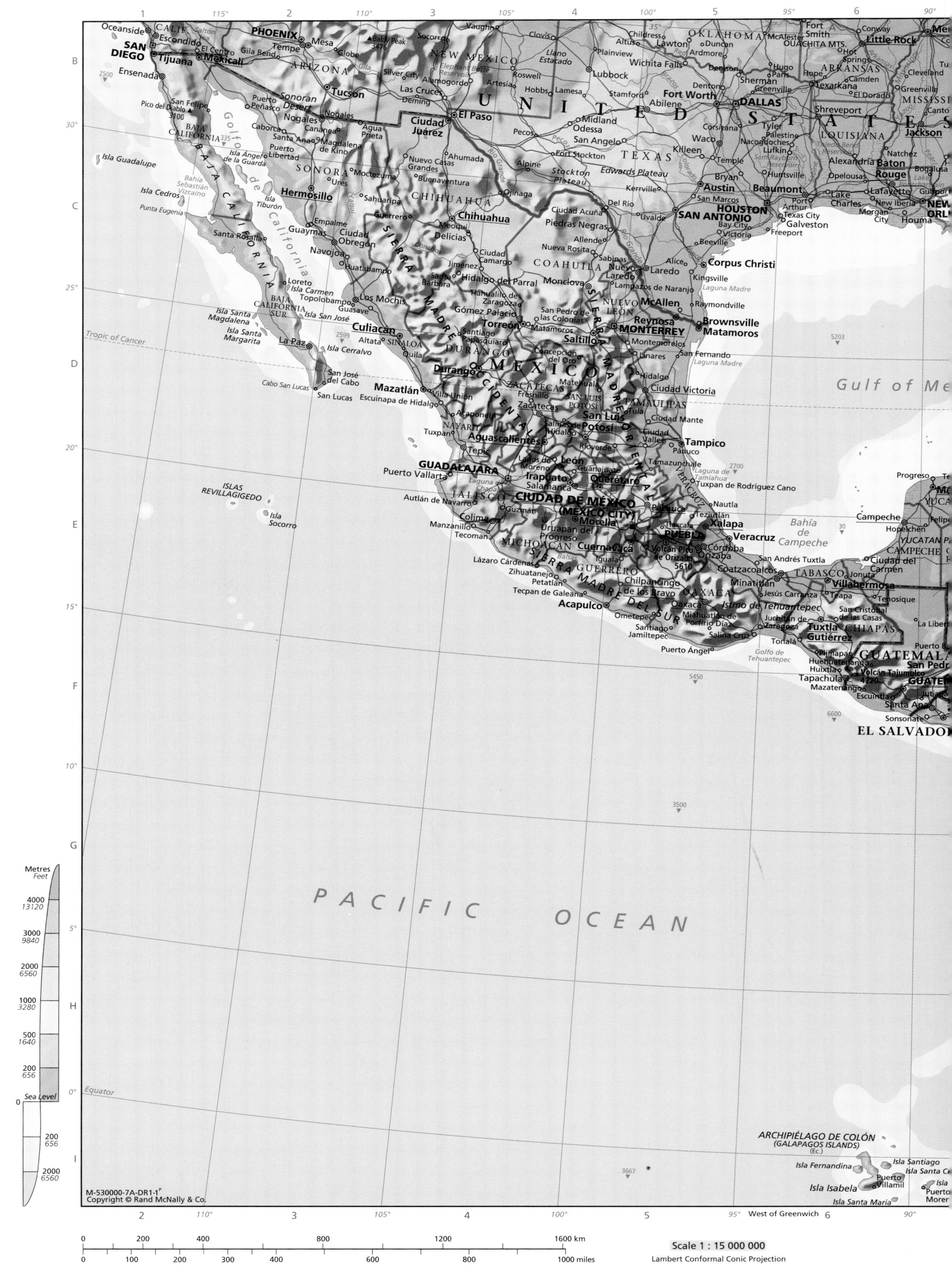

0 200 400 800 1200 1600 km

0 100 200 300 400 600 800 1000 miles

Scale 1 : 15 000 000

Lambert Conformal Conic Projection

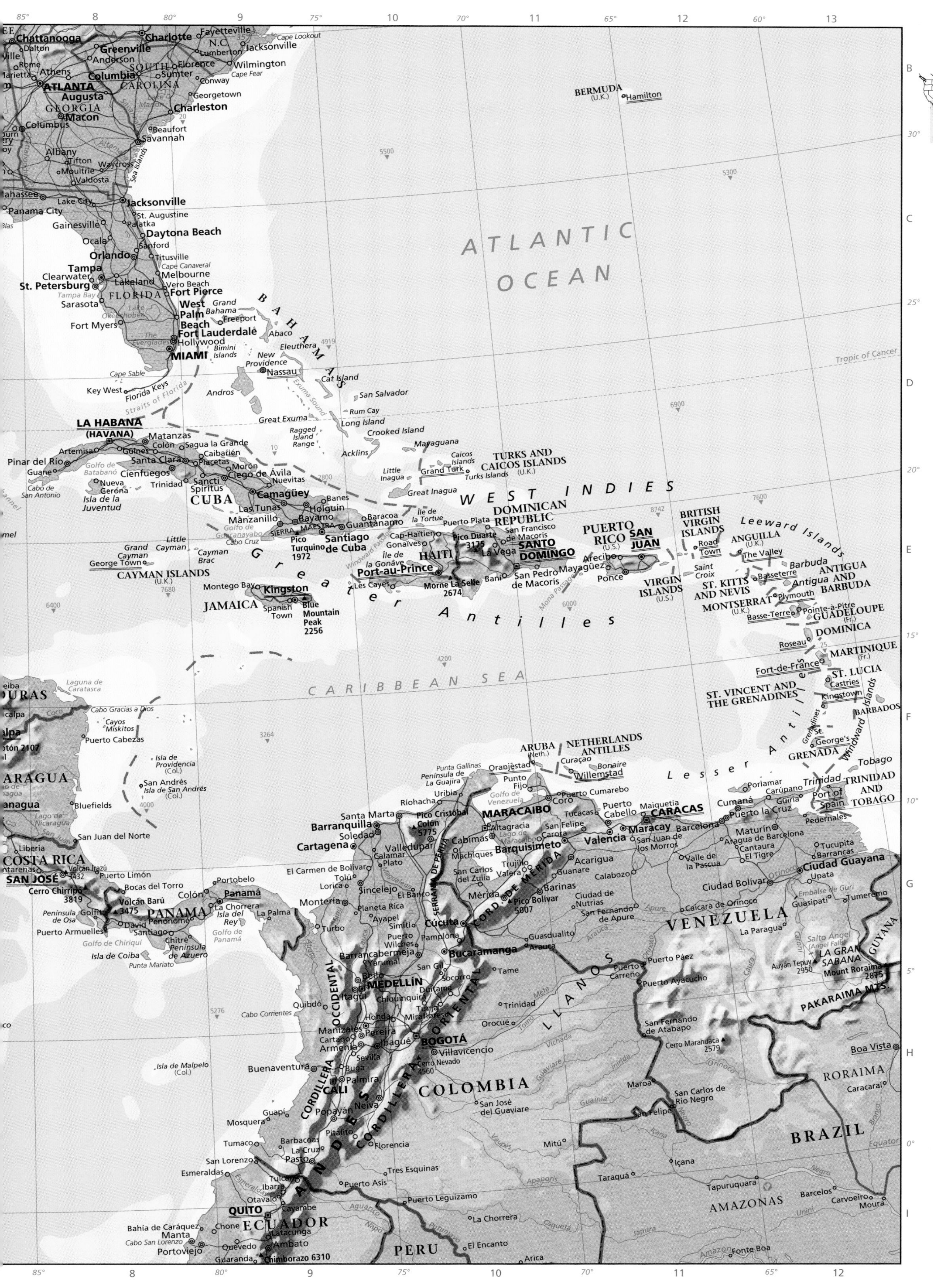
ATLANTIC OCEAN
CARIBBEAN SEA
WEST INDIES
Greater Antilles
Lesser Antilles
Leeward Islands
Windward Islands
BAHAMAS
BERMUDA (U.K.)
Hamilton
Tropic of Cancer
CUBA
LA HABANA (HAVANA)
JAMAICA
Kingston
CAYMAN ISLANDS (U.K.)
HAITI
Port-au-Prince
DOMINICAN REPUBLIC
SANTO DOMINGO
PUERTO RICO (U.S.)
SAN JUAN
TURKS AND CAICOS ISLANDS (U.K.)
BRITISH VIRGIN ISLANDS
VIRGIN ISLANDS (U.S.)
ANGUILLA (U.K.)
ST. KITTS AND NEVIS
ANTIGUA AND BARBUDA
MONTSERRAT (U.K.)
GUADELOUPE (Fr.)
DOMINICA
MARTINIQUE (Fr.)
ST. LUCIA
ST. VINCENT AND THE GRENADINES
BARBADOS
GRENADA
TRINIDAD AND TOBAGO
ARUBA (Neth.)
NETHERLANDS ANTILLES
VENEZUELA
CARACAS
COLOMBIA
BOGOTÁ
ECUADOR
QUITO
PERU
BRAZIL
GUYANA
PANAMA
Panamá
COSTA RICA
SAN JOSÉ
FLORIDA
GEORGIA
SOUTH CAROLINA
ATLANTA
MIAMI
ANDES
LLANOS
Equator

SAN DIEGO
El Cajon
Chula Vista
Tijuana
CALIFORNIA
El Centro
Mexicali
Yuma
San Luis Río Colorado
Gila Bend
Casa Grande
ARIZONA
Tucson
Green Valley
Nogales
Bisbee
Douglas
Agua Prieta
San Carlos
Clifton
Mount Graham 3267
Whitewater Baldy 3321
Truth or Consequences
Silver City
Lordsburg
Deming
Willcox
Chiricahua Peak 2986
Alamogordo
NEW MEXICO
Las Cruces
El Paso
Ciudad Juárez
Dell City
Guadalupe Peak 2667
Roswell
Artesia
Hobbs
Carlsbad
Pecos
Van Horn
Fort Stockton
Alpine
Marfa
Presidio
Ojinaga
Descanso
El Sauzal
Ensenada
Santo Tomás
Punta Colnett
Pico del Diablo 3100
San Felipe
Puerto Peñasco
Sonoyta
Cabo San Quintín
BAJA CALIFORNIA
Rosario de Arriba
Golfo de California
Enchilayas
Caborca
Magdalena de Kino
Santa Ana
Cananea
Nacozari de García
Benjamín Hill
Puerto Libertad
SONORA
Moctezuma
Carbo
Ures
Hermosillo
Bahía Kino
Isla Tiburón
Isla Ángel de la Guarda
Isla Guadalupe
Isla Cedros
Bahía Sebastián Vizcaíno
Guerrero Negro
Punta Eugenia
Punta San Roque
San Ignacio
Santa Rosalía
Mulegé
Guaymas
Empalme
Ortiz
Vícam
Esperanza
Ciudad Obregón
Navojoa
Huatabampo
Sahuaripa
Nuevo Casas Grandes
Ascensión
Samalayuca
Ahumada
El Sueco
Buenaventura
Las Varas
Madera
Temosachic
CHIHUAHUA
Chihuahua
Guerrero
Cerro El Nopal 3060
Cuauhtémoc
Delicias
Meoqui
Aldama
Maclovio Herrera
Ciudad Camargo
Jiménez (Ciudad Jiménez)
Hidalgo del Parral
Valle de Olivos
San Francisco del Oro
Santa Bárbara
Bolsón de Mapimí
Ceballos
Creel
SIERRA MADRE OCCIDENTAL
BAJA CALIFORNIA SUR
SIERRA DE LA GIGANTA
Loreto
Isla Carmen
Ligui
Los Mochis
Topolobampo
General Juan José Ríos
Guasave
SINALOA
Guamúchil
Morelos
El Tecuán
Cerro las Iglesias 3110
Cerro Ocotes 3150
Indé
Tlahualilo de Zaragoza
Bermejillo
Gómez Palacio
Torreón
Tepehuanes
Topia
Santiago Papasquiaro
Nazas
Cuencamé de Ceniceros
DURANGO
Cerro La Bandera 3230
Otinapa
Durango
Miguel Auza
El Salto
Sombrerete
Escollos Alijos
Isla Santa Magdalena
Cabo San Lázaro
Ciudad Constitución
Isla Santa Margarita
Isla San José
Isla del Espíritu Santo
Isla Cerralvo
La Paz
Tropic of Cancer
Las Casitas 2164
Punta Arena
Santiago
San José del Cabo
Cabo San Lucas
San Lucas
Pericos
Culiacán
Altata
Costa Rica
Quila
Higuera de Abuya
Mazatlán
Villa Unión
Rosario
Escuinapa de Hidalgo
Acaponeta
Tecuala
Tuxpan
Ruiz
NAYARIT
Santiago Ixcuintla
Tepic
ISLAS TRES MARÍAS
Compostela
Las Varas
Ahuacatlán
Punta de Mita
Puerto Vallarta
Cabo Corrientes
Zapopan
Ameca
JALISCO
Sayula
Autlán de Navarro
Colima
COLIMA
Tecomán
Manzanillo
Jerez de García Salinas
ZACATECAS
Aguascalientes
ISLAS REVILLAGIGEDO (Mex.)
Isla San Benedicto
Isla Roca Partida
Isla Socorro
Isla Clarión
PACIFIC OCEAN
Lázaro Cárdenas
Metres
Feet
4000 13120
3000 9840
2000 6560
1000 3280
500 1640
200 656
Sea Level
0
200 656
2000 6560
W-532000-7A-DR1-2
Copyright © Rand McNally & Co.
West of Greenwich
0 100 200 300 400 600 800 km
0 50 100 150 200 300 400 500 miles
Scale 1 : 8 000 000
Lambert Conformal Conic Projection

Gulf of Mexico
Bahía de Campeche
Caribbean Sea
UNITED STATES
TEXAS
LOUISIANA
MISSISSIPPI
ALABAMA
FLORIDA
ARKANSAS
DALLAS
HOUSTON
SAN ANTONIO
NEW ORLEANS
Corpus Christi
Brownsville
Matamoros
Tampico
Veracruz
Xalapa
CIUDAD DE MÉXICO (MEXICO CITY)
PUEBLA
Oaxaca
Acapulco
Villahermosa
Campeche
Mérida
Cancún
YUCATAN PENINSULA
QUINTANA ROO
CAMPECHE
TABASCO
CHIAPAS
BELIZE
GUATEMALA
HONDURAS
EL SALVADOR
SIERRA MADRE DEL SUR
SIERRA MADRE DE CHIAPAS
Mexican State Abbreviations
AGS = AGUASCALIENTES
TLAX = TLAXCALA
D.F. = DISTRITO FEDERAL

0 100 200 300 400 600 800 km
0 50 100 150 200 300 400 500 miles

Scale 1 : 8 000 000

Lambert Conformal Conic Projection

ATLANTIC OCEAN
BAHAMAS
TURKS AND CAICOS ISLANDS
HISPANIOLA
HAITI
DOMINICAN REPUBLIC
SANTO DOMINGO
Port-au-Prince
PUERTO RICO (U.S.)
SAN JUAN
BRITISH VIRGIN ISLANDS
VIRGIN ISLANDS (U.S.)
LESSER ANTILLES
ANGUILLA (U.K.)
ANTIGUA AND BARBUDA
ST. KITTS AND NEVIS
MONTSERRAT (U.K.)
GUADELOUPE (Fr.)
DOMINICA
MARTINIQUE (Fr.)
ST. LUCIA
ST. VINCENT AND THE GRENADINES
BARBADOS
GRENADA
TRINIDAD AND TOBAGO
ARUBA (Neth.)
NETHERLANDS ANTILLES
LEEWARD ISLANDS
WINDWARD ISLANDS
CARIBBEAN SEA
VENEZUELA
CARACAS
COLOMBIA
BOGOTÁ
GUYANA
BRAZIL
LLANOS

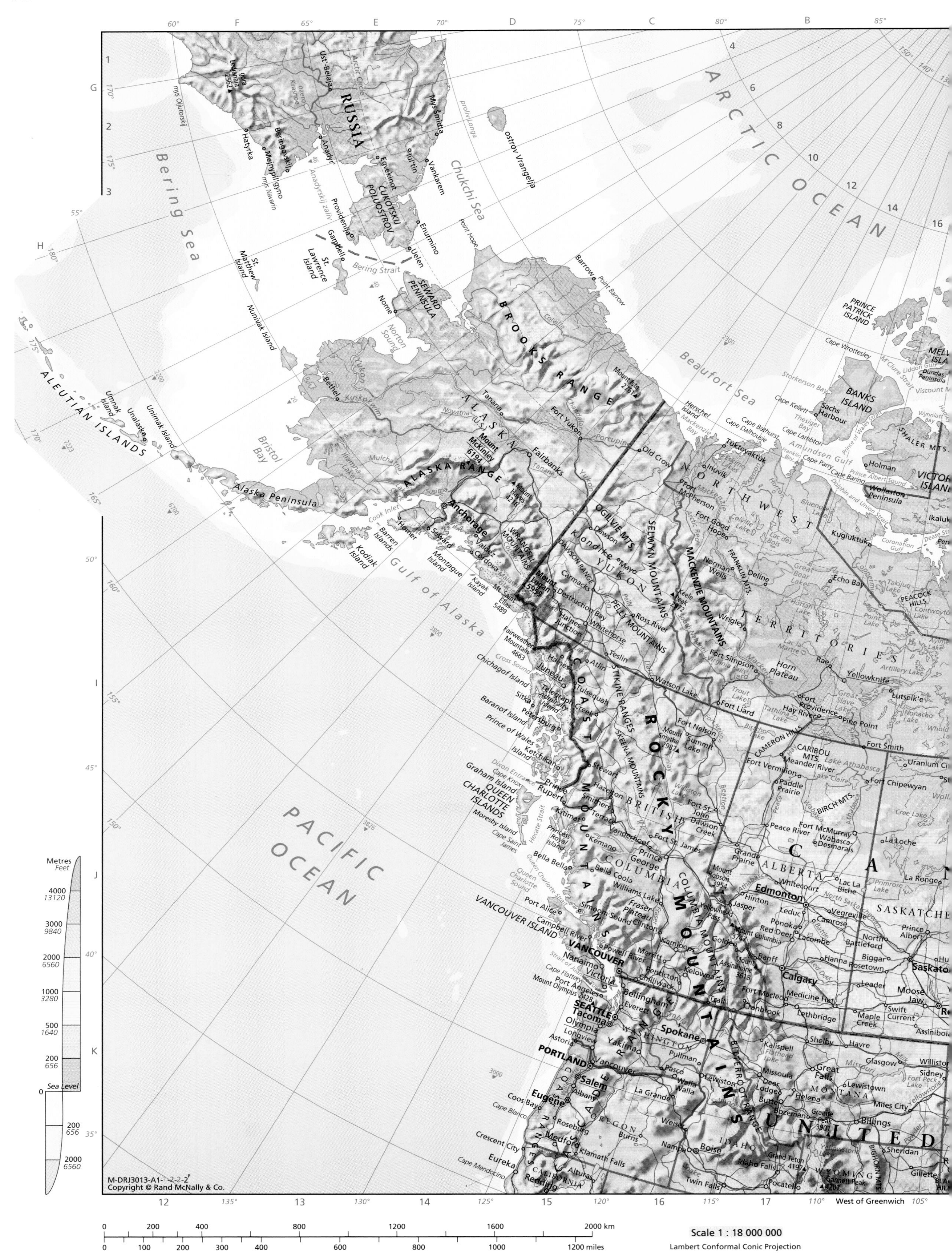
RUSSIA
ARCTIC OCEAN
Chukchi Sea
Bering Sea
Bering Strait
SEWARD PENINSULA
BROOKS RANGE
ALASKA RANGE
ALEUTIAN ISLANDS
Alaska Peninsula
Bristol Bay
Gulf of Alaska
Beaufort Sea
NORTHWEST TERRITORIES
YUKON
BRITISH COLUMBIA
ALBERTA
SASKATCHE
ROCKY MOUNTAINS
COAST MOUNTAINS
MACKENZIE MOUNTAINS
PACIFIC OCEAN
VANCOUVER ISLAND
QUEEN CHARLOTTE ISLANDS
Anchorage
Fairbanks
Juneau
Whitehorse
Yellowknife
Edmonton
Calgary
VANCOUVER
Victoria
SEATTLE
Spokane
PORTLAND
Salem
Eugene
Boise
WASHINGTON
OREGON
IDAHO
MONTANA
WYOMING
CALIFORNIA
UNITED
Metres
Feet
4000 13120
3000 9840
2000 6560
1000 3280
500 1640
200 656
Sea Level
200 656
2000 6560
West of Greenwich
M-DRJ3013-A1-
Copyright © Rand McNally & Co.
0 200 400 800 1200 1600 2000 km
0 100 200 300 400 600 800 1000 1200 miles
Scale 1 : 18 000 000
Lambert Conformal Conic Projection

GREENLAND (Den.)
ICELAND
FAROE ISLANDS (Den.)
Tórshavn
Reykjavík
Akureyri
Hvannadalshnúkur 2119
ELLESMERE ISLAND
AXEL HEIBERG ISLAND
DEVON ISLAND
BAFFIN ISLAND
SOMERSET ISLAND
BOOTHIA PENINSULA
MELVILLE PENINSULA
FOXE PENINSULA
SOUTHAMPTON ISLAND
PÉNINSULE D'UNGAVA
META INCOGNITA PENINSULA
Lincoln Sea
Greenland Sea
Denmark Strait
Baffin Bay
Davis Strait
Labrador Sea
Foxe Basin
Hudson Strait
Hudson Bay
James Bay
Ungava Bay
Gulf of St. Lawrence
Gulf of Maine
ATLANTIC OCEAN
Arctic Circle
All islands within Hudson Bay, James Bay, and Ungava Bay lie within Nunavut.
Thule (Qaanaaq)
Upernavik
Godthåb (Nuuk)
Gunnbjørn Field 3700
Mont Forel 3360
Angmagssalik
Iqaluit
Iglulik
Naujaat
Arviat
Churchill
York Factory
Labrador
NEWFOUNDLAND
Happy Valley-Goose Bay
St. John's
Gander
Corner Brook
ÎLE D'ANTICOSTI
QUÉBEC
ONTARIO
MANITOBA
NUNAVUT
CANADA
Chibougamau
Sept-Îles
Gaspé
Québec
MONTRÉAL
Ottawa
TORONTO
Sudbury
Thunder Bay
Winnipeg
Charlottetown
PRINCE EDWARD ISLAND
NOVA SCOTIA
NEW BRUNSWICK
Halifax
Sydney
Fredericton
Saint John
SAINT PIERRE AND MIQUELON (Fr.)
Sable Island
APPALACHIAN MOUNTAINS
LONG RANGE MOUNTAINS
MONTS OTISH
LES LAURENTIDES
MAINE
Augusta
Bangor
Portland
BOSTON
Providence
Albany
Syracuse
Rochester
Buffalo
NEW YORK
Newark
Trenton
PHILADELPHIA
Hartford
New Haven
Detroit
Windsor
London
Hamilton
Kitchener
Lansing
Flint
Grand Rapids
Milwaukee
Madison
Rockford
CHICAGO
Gary
MINNEAPOLIS
St. Paul
Duluth
Superior
Green Bay
Appleton
Marquette
Sault Sainte Marie
Lake Superior
Lake Michigan
Lake Huron
Lake Erie
Lake Ontario
Lake of the Woods
Lake Winnipeg
20
21
23
24
25
26
27
G
H
I
J
K
95°
80°
75°
70°
65°
60°
55°
50°
45°
40°
35°

Note: Map colors do not reflect elevation.

Statute Miles 10 0 10 20 30 40 50 60 70

Kilometers 10 0 10 20 40 60 80 100

Oblique Cylindrical Projection

Statute Miles 10 0 10 20 30 40 50 60 70 80 90 100

Kilometers 10 0 10 20 40 60 80 100 120 140

Oblique Cylindrical Projection

Note: Map colors do not reflect elevation.

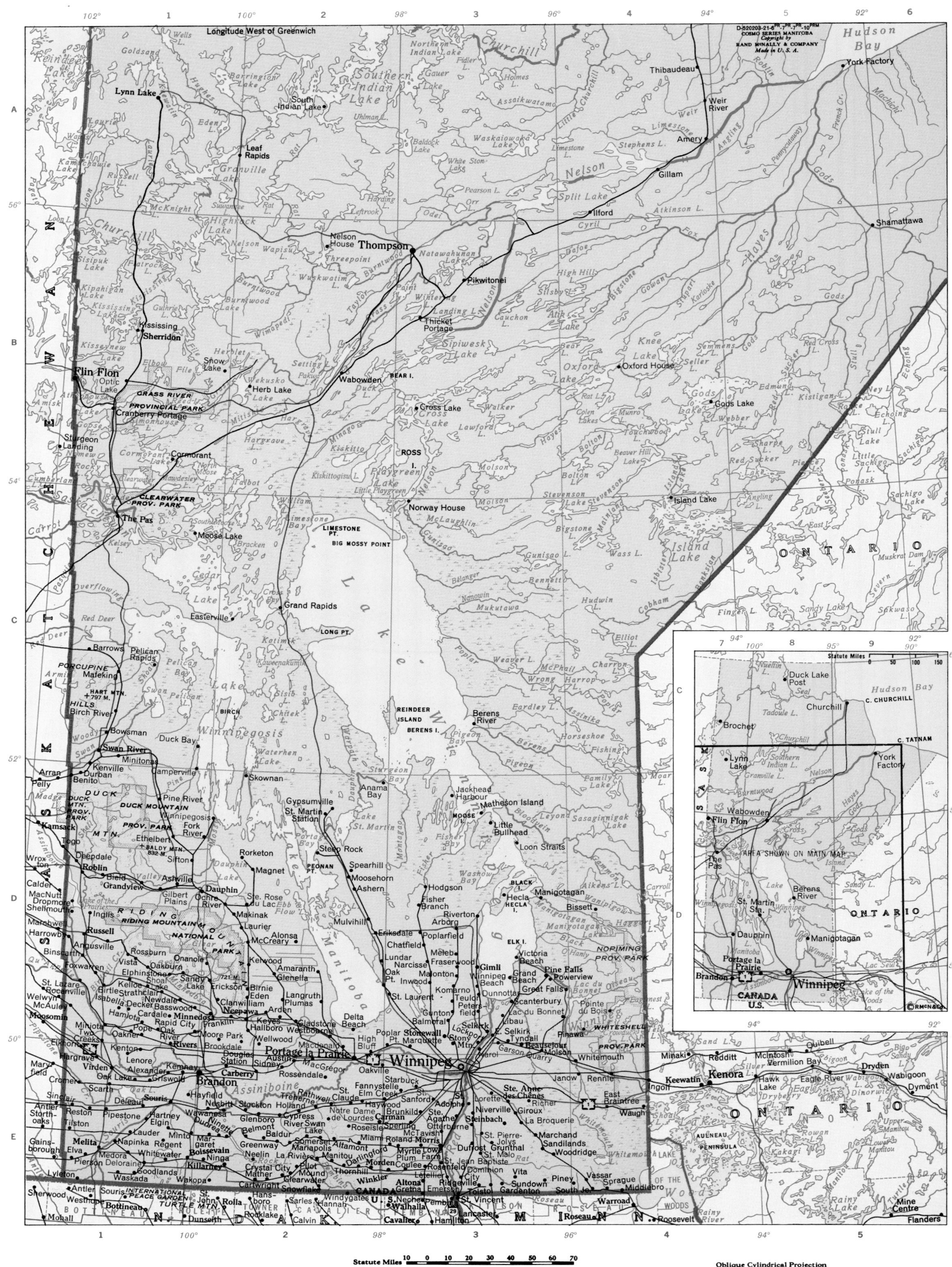

Note: Map colors do not reflect elevation.

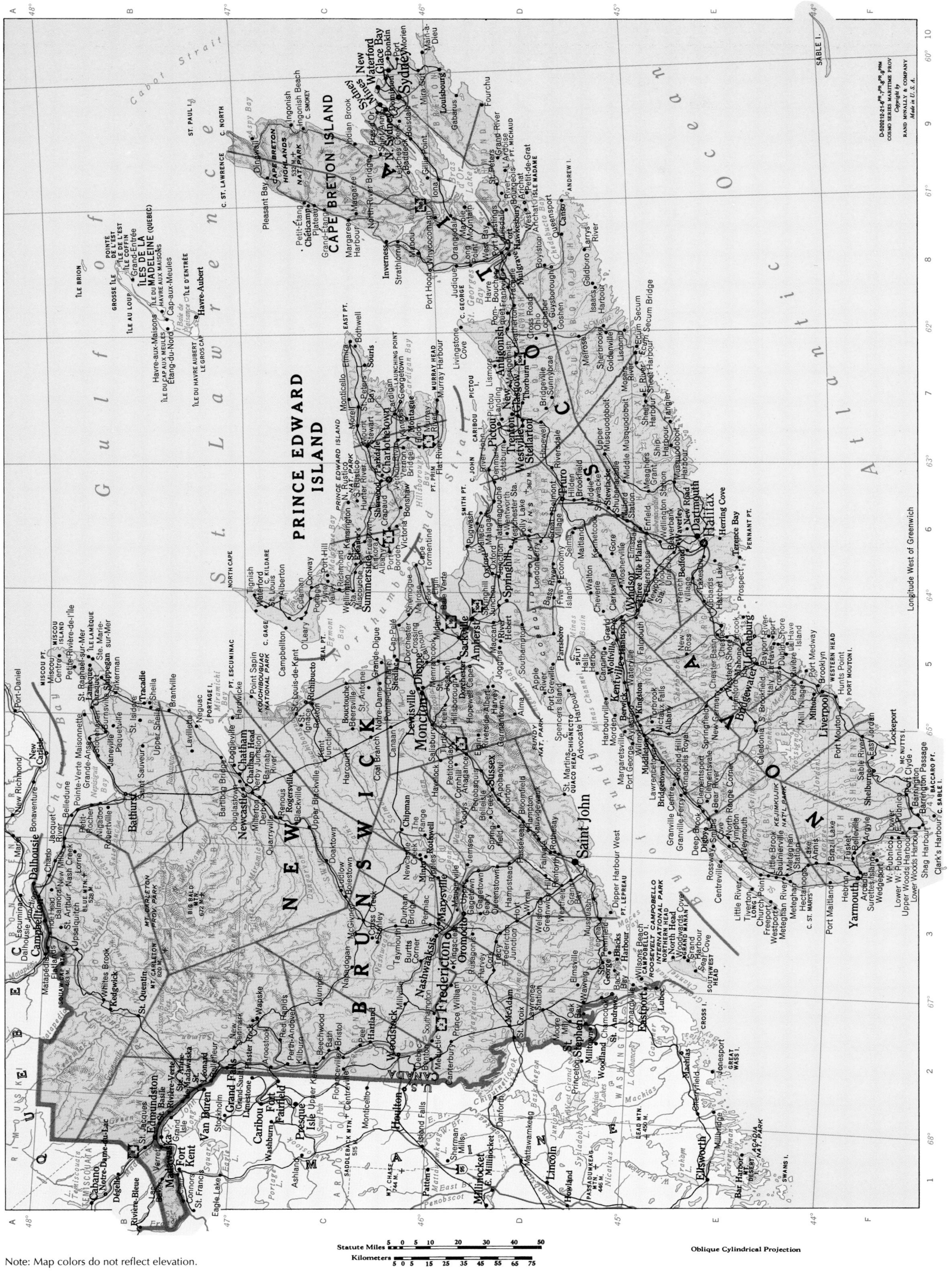

Note: Map colors do not reflect elevation.

Statute Miles 5 0 5 10 20 30 40 50 60
Kilometers 5 0 5 10 20 30 40 50 60 70 80

Lambert Conformal Conic Projection

Note: Map colors do not reflect elevation.

Statute Miles 5 0 5 10 20 30 40 50

Kilometers 5 0 5 15 25 35 45 55 65 75

Oblique Cylindrical Projection

Note: Map colors do not reflect elevation.

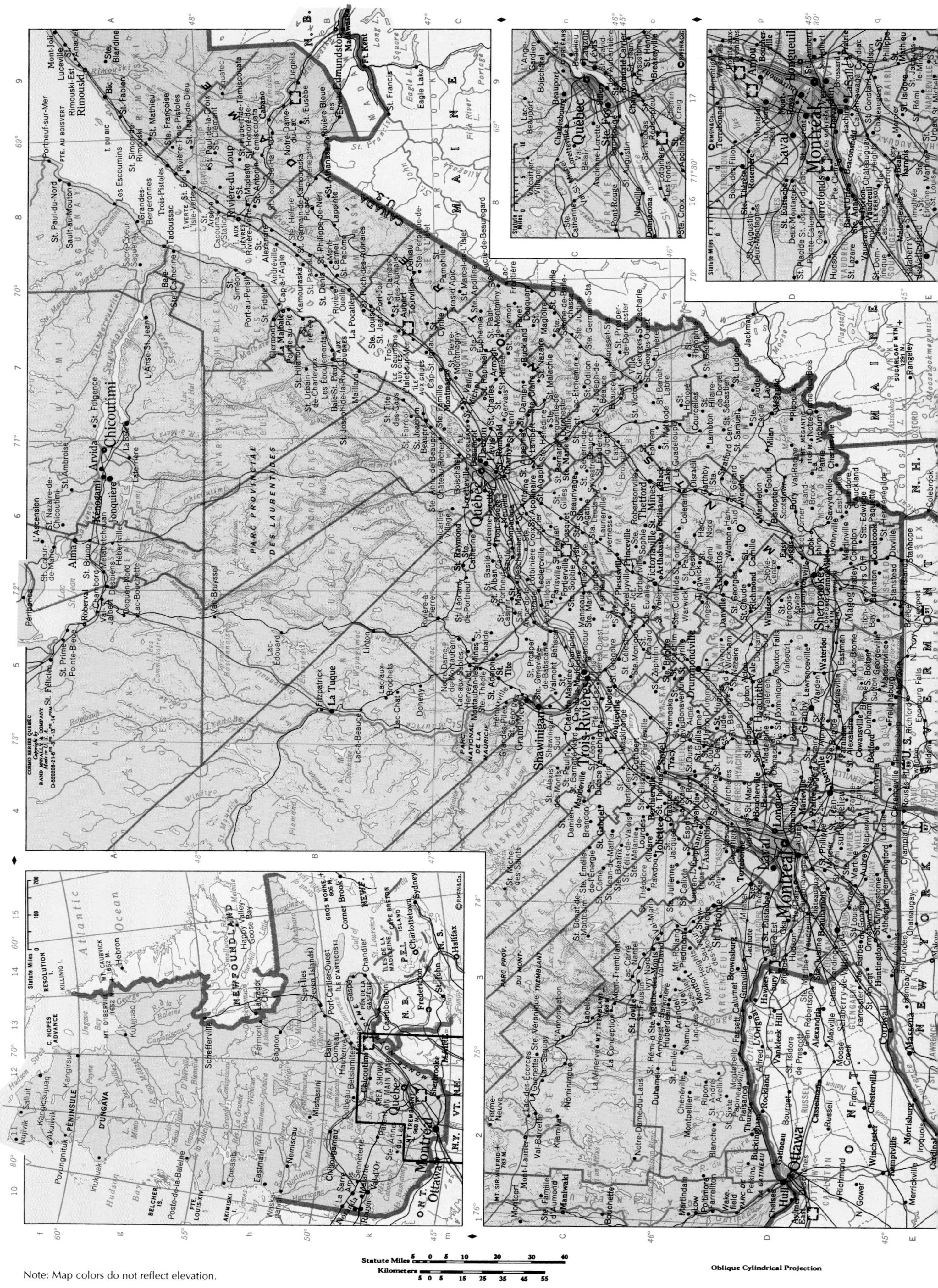

Note: Map colors do not reflect elevation.

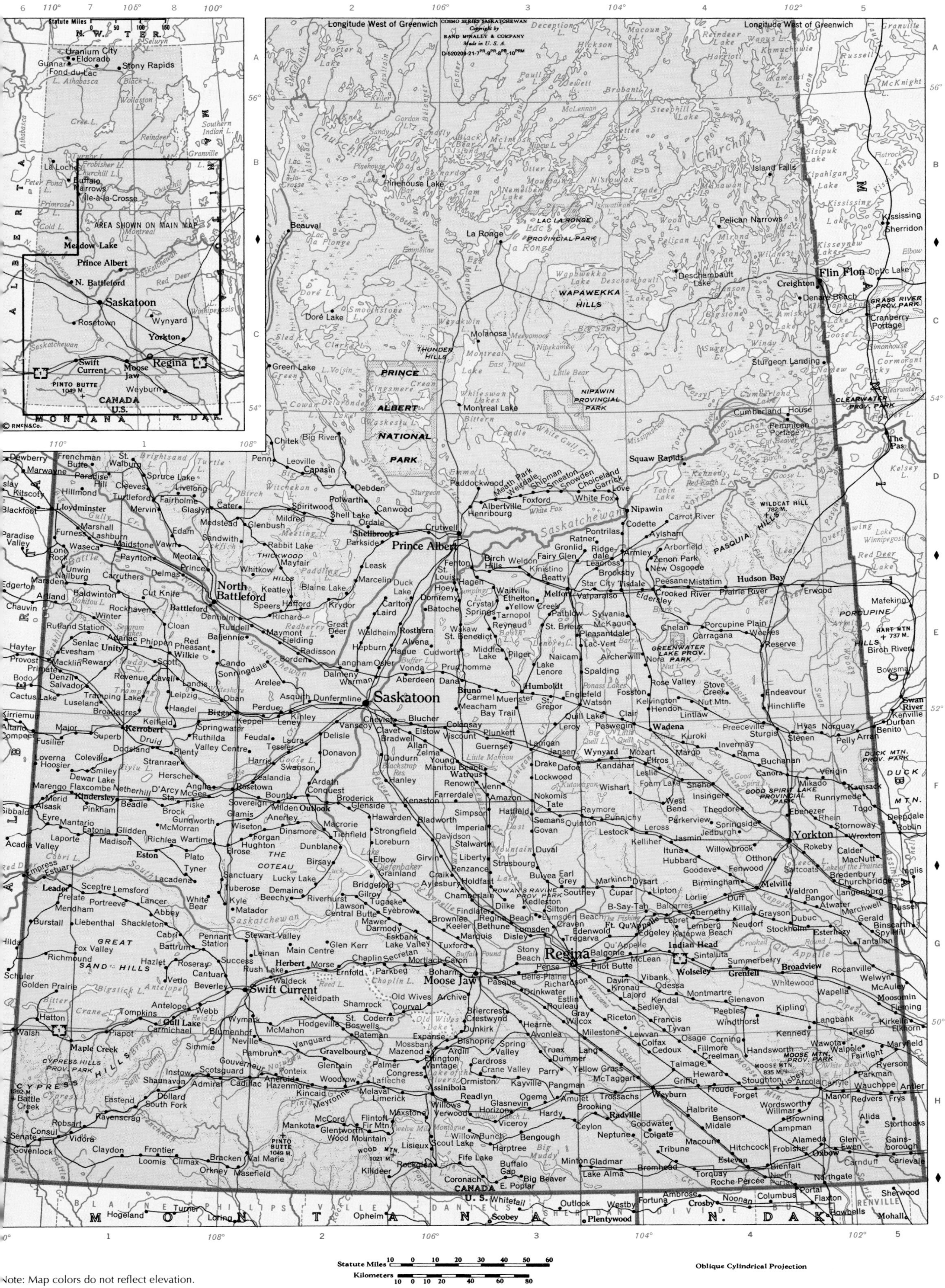
Longitude West of Greenwich
COSMO SERIES SASKATCHEWAN
Copyright by RAND McNALLY & COMPANY
Made in U. S. A.
AREA SHOWN ON MAIN MAP
N. W. TER.
ALBERTA
MANITOBA
MONTANA
N. DAK.
CANADA
U.S.
Uranium City
Eldorado
Stony Rapids
Gunnar
Fond-du-Lac
L. Athabasca
Meadow Lake
Prince Albert
N. Battleford
Saskatoon
Rosetown
Wynyard
Yorkton
Swift Current
Moose Jaw
Regina
Weyburn
PINTO BUTTE 1049 M.
Beauval
La Ronge
LAC LA RONGE PROVINCIAL PARK
Pinehouse Lake
Island Falls
Pelican Narrows
Flin Flon
Creighton
Denare Beach
Sherridon
Kississing
Deschambault Lake
WAPAWEKKA HILLS
Sturgeon Landing
Cumberland House
The Pas
Squaw Rapids
Nipawin
PRINCE ALBERT NATIONAL PARK
NIPAWIN PROVINCIAL PARK
Montreal Lake
Molanosa
Green Lake
Doré Lake
Big River
Lloydminster
North Battleford
Prince Albert
Melfort
Tisdale
Hudson Bay
Humboldt
Wynyard
Wadena
Kindersley
Rosetown
Outlook
Yorkton
Melville
Indian Head
Regina
Moose Jaw
Swift Current
Weyburn
Estevan
Radville
Assiniboia
Maple Creek
Shaunavon
Gull Lake
Kerrobert
Unity
Biggar
Leader
Eston
Wolseley
Grenfell
Broadview
Esterhazy
Kamsack
Canora
Kelvington
Lanigan
Watrous
Davidson
Craik
Fort Qu'Appelle
Lumsden
Carlyle
Oxbow
Carnduff
Bienfait
Coronach
Rockglen
CYPRESS HILLS PROV. PARK
GREENWATER LAKE PROV. PARK
DUCK MTN. PROV. PARK
GOOD SPIRIT LAKE PROVINCIAL PARK
MOOSE MTN. PROV. PARK
GRASS RIVER PROV. PARK
CLEARWATER PROV. PARK
ROWAN'S RAVINE PROV. PARK
WOOD MTN. 1021 M.
PINTO BUTTE 1049 M.
WILDCAT HILL 782 M.
HART MTN. 737 M.
MOOSE MTN. 835 M.
PORCUPINE HILLS
PASQUIA HILLS
THICKWOOD HILLS
THUNDER HILLS
THE COTEAU
GREAT SAND HILLS
CYPRESS HILLS
Lake Diefenbaker
Saskatchewan
Churchill
Qu'Appelle
MONTANA
N. DAK.
Statute Miles 10 0 10 20 30 40 50 60
Kilometers 10 0 10 20 40 60 80
Oblique Cylindrical Projection
Note: Map colors do not reflect elevation.

VANCOUVER ISLAND
BRITISH COLUMBIA
ALBERTA
SASKATCHEWAN
C A N
Calgary
Saskatoon
Regina
Edmonton
VANCOUVER
Victoria
SEATTLE
Tacoma
Olympia
Spokane
WASHINGTON
PORTLAND
Salem
Eugene
OREGON
Boise
IDAHO
MONTANA
Helena
Great Falls
Billings
ROCKY MOUNTAINS
WYOMING
Cheyenne
Casper
Salt Lake City
UTAH
GREAT BASIN
NEVADA
Reno
Las Vegas
SACRAMENTO
SAN FRANCISCO
OAKLAND
San Jose
Fresno
Bakersfield
CALIFORNIA
LOS ANGELES
Long Beach
Anaheim
Santa Ana
SAN DIEGO
Tijuana
Mexicali
SIERRA NEVADA
COAST RANGES
CASCADE RANGE
PHOENIX
Tucson
ARIZONA
Flagstaff
DENVER
Colorado Springs
COLORADO
Albuquerque
Santa Fe
NEW MEXICO
El Paso
Ciudad Juárez
UNITED
TEXAS
Amarillo
Lubbock
NORTH DAKOTA
SOUTH DAKOTA
NEBRASKA
Rapid City
Bismarck
PACIFIC OCEAN
BAJA CALIFORNIA
Golfo de California
Sonoran Desert
SONORA
Hermosillo
CHIHUAHUA
Chihuahua
SIERRA MADRE OCCIDENTAL
SIERRA MADRE ORIENTAL
M E X I C O
COAHUILA
MONTERREY
Saltillo
Torreón
Culiacán
La Paz
DURANGO
SINALOA
Tropic of Cancer
HAWAIIAN ISLANDS
Kauai
Oahu
Honolulu
Molokai
Lanai
Maui
Hawaii
HAWAII
Mauna Kea 4205
Mauna Loa 4169
West of Greenwich
same scale as main map

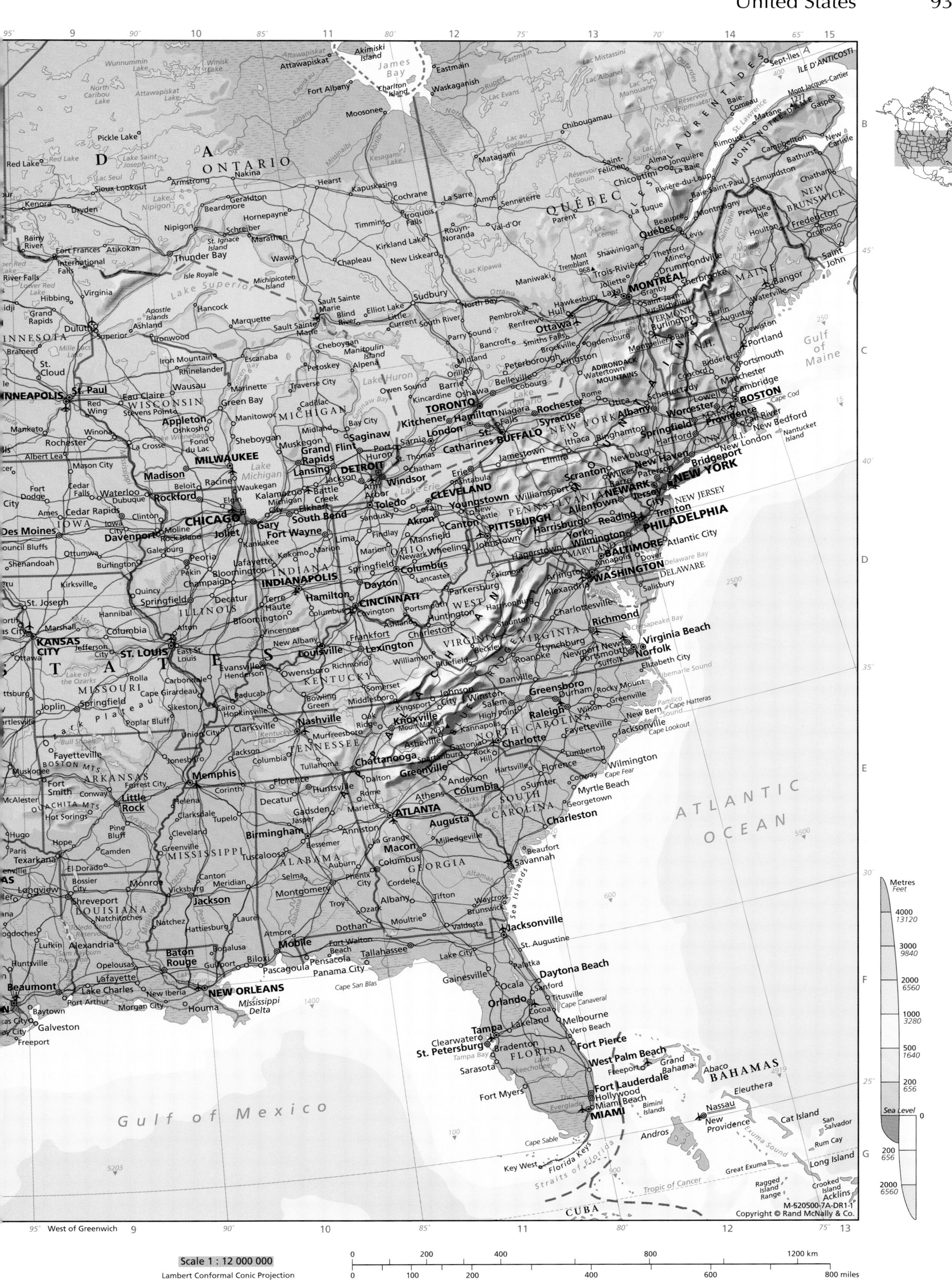
ONTARIO
QUÉBEC
James Bay
Lake Superior
Lake Michigan
Lake Huron
Lake Erie
Lake Ontario
MICHIGAN
WISCONSIN
MINNESOTA
IOWA
ILLINOIS
INDIANA
OHIO
PENNSYLVANIA
NEW YORK
VERMONT
N.H.
MAINE
MASS.
CONN.
R.I.
NEW JERSEY
DELAWARE
MARYLAND
WEST VIRGINIA
VIRGINIA
KENTUCKY
TENNESSEE
NORTH CAROLINA
SOUTH CAROLINA
GEORGIA
FLORIDA
ALABAMA
MISSISSIPPI
LOUISIANA
ARKANSAS
MISSOURI
NEW BRUNSWICK
BAHAMAS
CUBA
ATLANTIC OCEAN
Gulf of Mexico
Gulf of Maine
Straits of Florida
Tropic of Cancer
Mississippi Delta
TORONTO
MONTRÉAL
Ottawa
Québec
MINNEAPOLIS
St. Paul
MILWAUKEE
CHICAGO
DETROIT
CLEVELAND
PITTSBURGH
BUFFALO
NEW YORK
BOSTON
PHILADELPHIA
BALTIMORE
WASHINGTON
INDIANAPOLIS
CINCINNATI
Columbus
ST. LOUIS
KANSAS CITY
Louisville
Nashville
Memphis
Charlotte
Richmond
Norfolk
Virginia Beach
ATLANTA
Birmingham
Jacksonville
Orlando
Tampa
St. Petersburg
MIAMI
NEW ORLEANS
Baton Rouge
Mobile
Jackson
Little Rock
Des Moines
Madison
Thunder Bay
Sudbury
Nassau
Metres
Feet
4000
13120
3000
9840
2000
6560
1000
3280
500
1640
200
656
Sea Level
0
200
656
2000
6560
95° West of Greenwich
M-520500-7A-DR1-1
Copyright © Rand McNally & Co.
Scale 1 : 12 000 000
Lambert Conformal Conic Projection
0 200 400 800 1200 km
0 100 200 400 600 800 miles

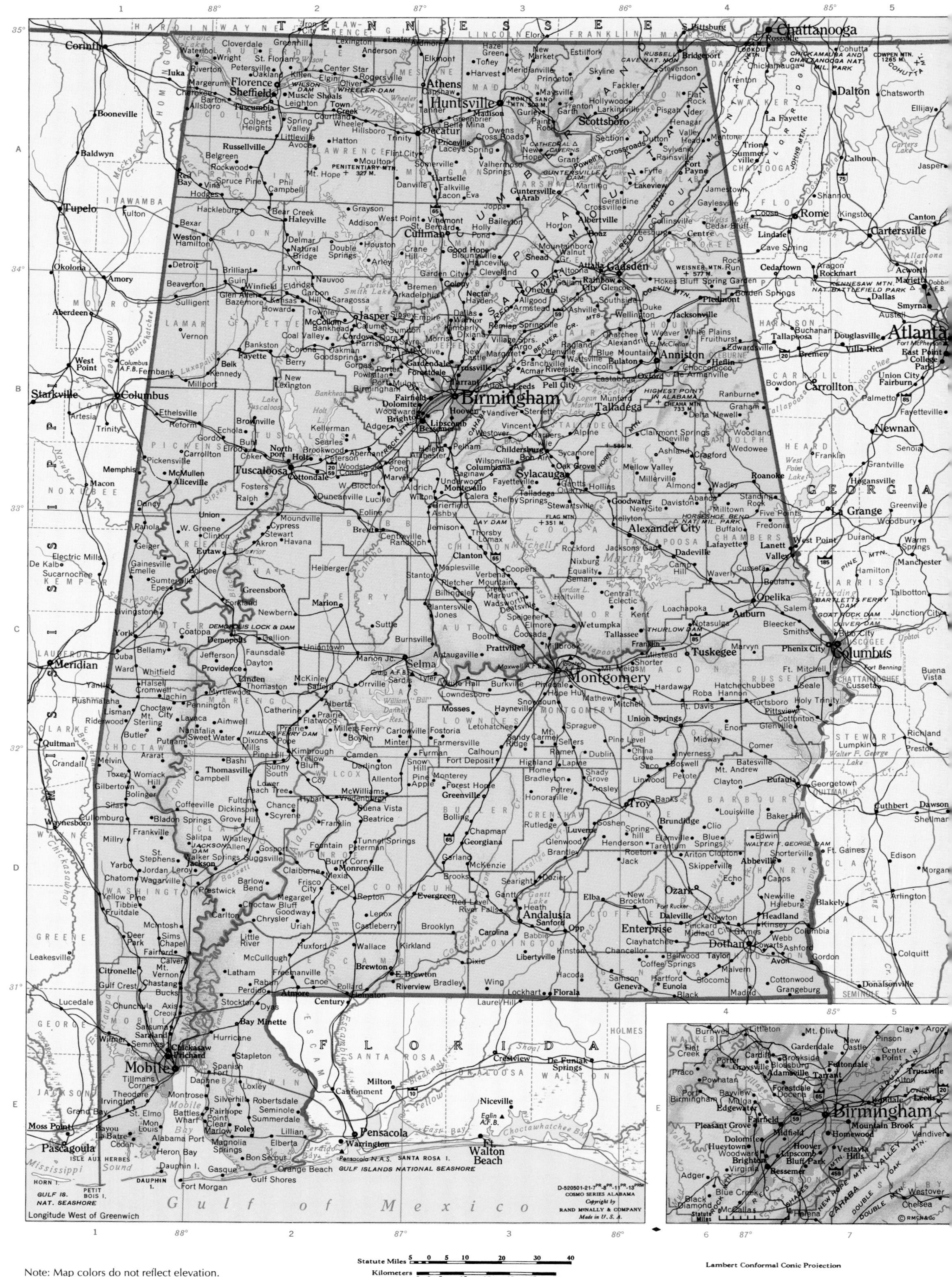

Note: Map colors do not reflect elevation.

Note: Map colors do not reflect elevation.

UTAH
GLEN CANYON NAT. RECR. AREA
Hurricane
St. George
Kanab
Fredonia
Colorado City
Littlefield
Page
Navajo Mountain
Mexican Hat
Aneth
Teec Nos Pos
Las Vegas
Henderson
Boulder City
LAKE MEAD NATIONAL RECREATION AREA
Hoover Dam
Overton
Moapa
Jacob Lake
Marble Canyon
Kaibito
Kayenta
Shonto
Tonalea
Tuba City
Moenkopi
Moenave
North Rim
Grand Canyon
GRAND CANYON NATIONAL PARK
HAVASUPAI INDIAN RES.
HUALAPAI IND. RES.
Peach Springs
Cameron
NAVAJO INDIAN RES.
HOPI INDIAN RESERVATION
Hotevilla
Second Mesa
Shongopovi
Polacca
Keams Canyon
Jeddito
Pinon
Chinle
Many Farms
Lukachukai
Round Rock
Rock Pt.
Salina
Nazlini
Steamboat Canyon
Ganado
Kin-li-chee
St. Michaels
Window Rock
Ft. Defiance
Sawmill
Greasewood
Klagetoh
Wide Ruins
Dilkon
Indian Wells
Sanders
Chambers
Navajo
Houck
Lupton
Gallup
Truxton
Nelson
Hackberry
Valentine
Chloride
Davis Dam
Kingman
Bullhead City
Oatman
Mohave Valley
Needles
Topock
Yucca
Wikieup
Seligman
Ash Fork
Williams
Flagstaff
Mountainaire
Leupp
Winslow
Joseph City
Holbrook
Woodruff
Zuni
Drake
Paulden
Chino Valley
Clarkdale
Jerome
Cottonwood
Cornville
Sedona
Rimrock
Camp Verde
Happy Jack
Long Valley
Prescott
Dewey
Humboldt
Mayer
Skull Valley
Iron Springs
Bagdad
Hillside
Kirkland
Date
Yarnell
Congress
Wagoner
Crown King
Bumble Bee
Black Canyon City
Pine
Payson
Young
Heber
Overgaard
Clay Springs
Pinedale
Show Low
Snowflake
Taylor
Concho
St. Johns
Vernon
Pinetop-Lakeside
McNary
Springerville
Eagar
Cibecue
Cedar Creek
Whiteriver
Nutrioso
Alpine
Ft. Apache
FORT APACHE INDIAN RESERVATION
Lake Havasu City
Parker
Vidal
Rice
Midland
Blythe
Ripley
Palo Verde
Ehrenberg
Quartzsite
Bouse
Wenden
Salome
Aguila
Wickenburg
Morristown
Wittmann
Waddell
Peoria
Glendale
Phoenix
Scottsdale
Tempe
Mesa
Chandler
Gilbert
Buckhorn
Avondale
Goodyear
Buckeye
Arlington
Palo Verde
Hassayampa
Tonopah
Cave Creek
New River
Sunflower
Roosevelt
Tonto Basin
Tortilla Flat
Miami
Claypool
Globe
San Carlos
SAN CARLOS INDIAN RES.
Superior
Florence
Kearny
Hayden
Winkelman
Christmas
Coolidge
Valley Farms
Randolph
Casa Grande
Eloy
Arizola
Picacho
Red Rock
Stanfield
Maricopa
Mobile
Gila Bend
Theba
Sentinel
Aztec
Dateland
Tacna
Wellton
Mohawk
Roll
Yuma
Somerton
Gadsden
San Luis
San Luis Río Colorado
Ajo
Why
Lukeville
Hickiwan
Sells
Ventana
Anegam
Gu Achi
Tucson
S. Tucson
Marana
Rillito
Casas Adobes
Catalina
Vail
Sahuarita
Green Valley
Amado
Tubac
Carmen
Arivaca
Sasabe
Nogales
Patagonia
Sonoita
Elgin
Huachuca City
Sierra Vista
Benson
Pomerene
St. David
Tombstone
Bisbee
Douglas
Agua Prieta
Naco
Pirtleville
McNeal
Elfrida
Willcox
Bowie
San Simon
Cochise
Dragoon
Safford
Thatcher
Pima
Solomon
San Jose
Duncan
Franklin
Clifton
Morenci
Bylas
Ft. Thomas
Eden
Klondyke
Mammoth
San Manuel
Oracle
Bonita
SONORA
Cananea
Fronteras
Caborca
Altar
Santa Ana
Magdalena
Nacozari
Arizpe
Cumpas
Oputo
MEXICO
U.S.
CALIFORNIA
NEVADA
NEW MEXICO
COLORADO
D-520503-21-7PR-9PR-11PR-13PRM
COSMO SERIES ARIZONA
Copyright by RAND McNALLY & COMPANY
Made in U. S. A.
Longitude West of Greenwich
Statute Miles
Kilometers
Lambert Conformal Conic Projection
Note: Map colors do not reflect elevation.

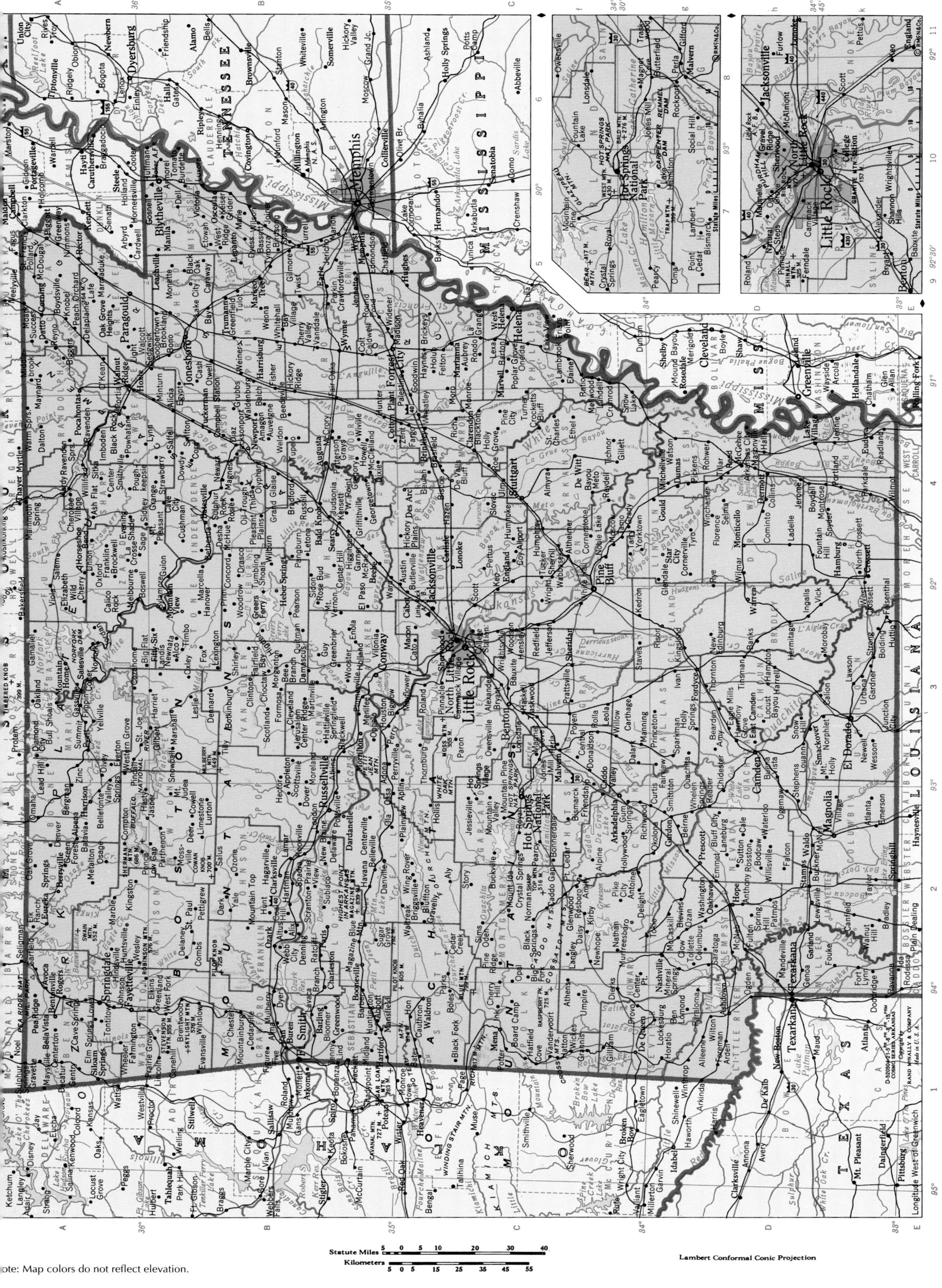

ote: Map colors do not reflect elevation.

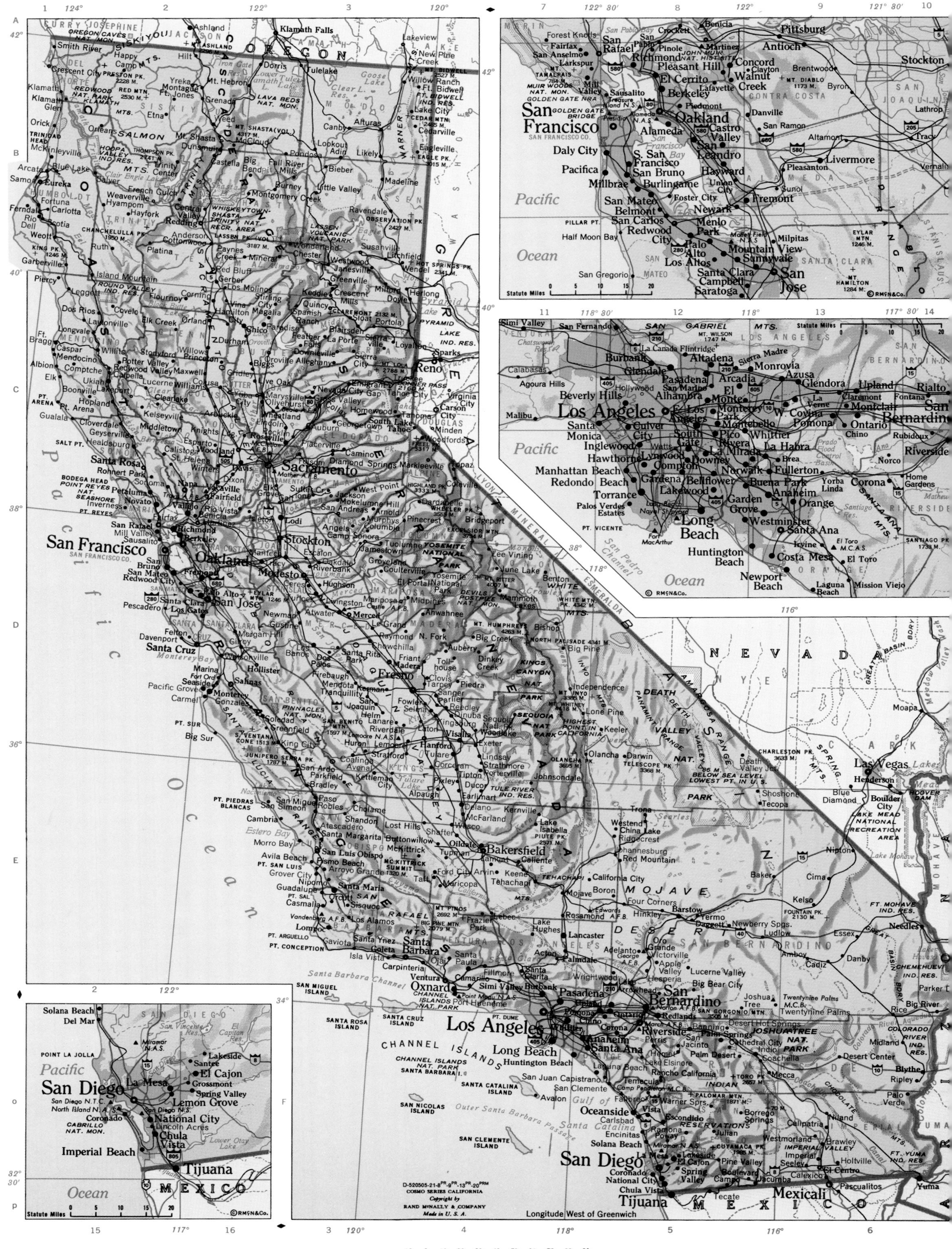

Statute Miles 10 0 10 20 30 40 50 60 70 80 90

Kilometers 10 0 10 20 40 60 80 100 120

Lambert Conformal Conic Projection

Note: Map colors do not reflect elevation.

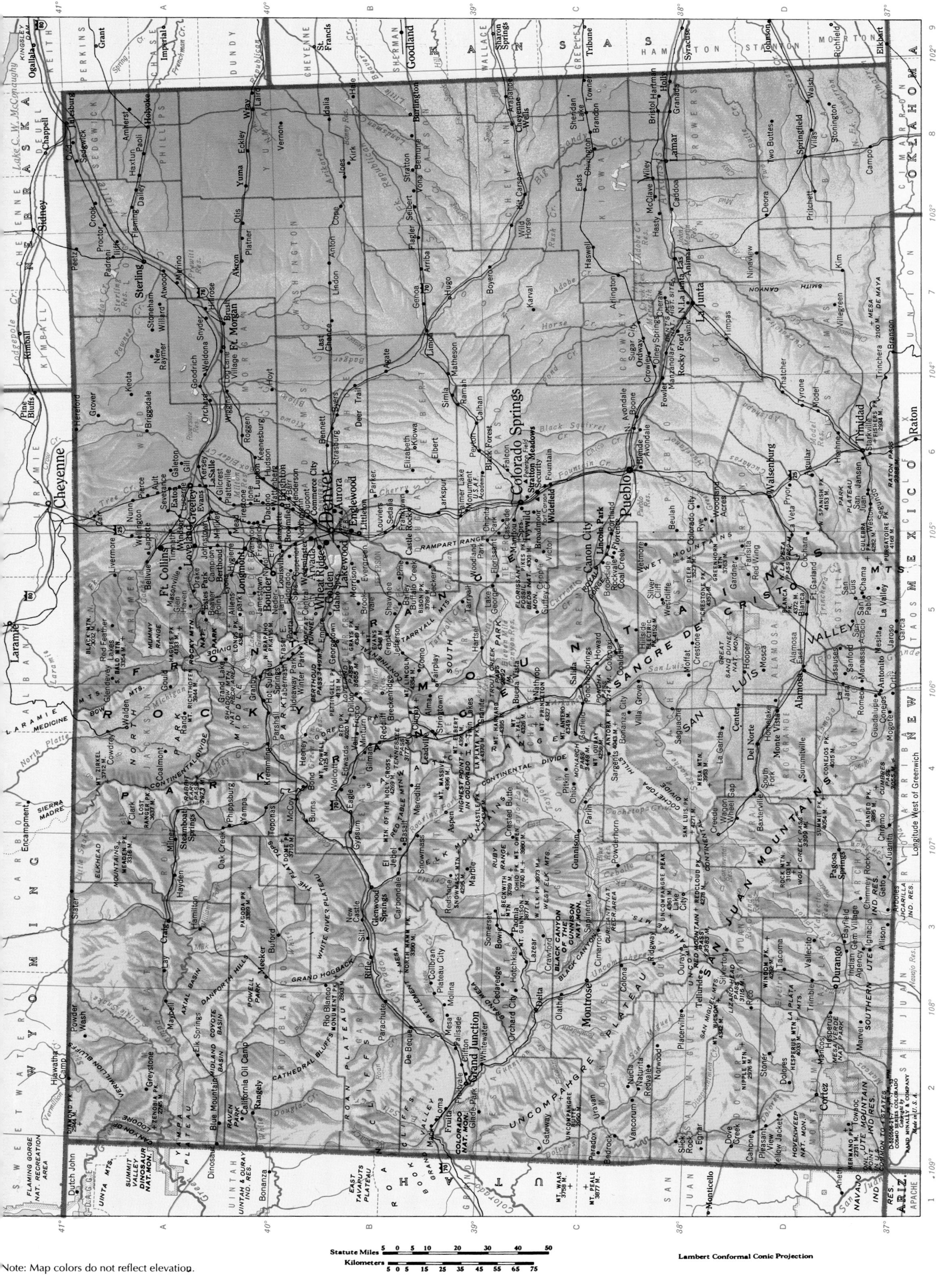

Statute Miles 5 0 5 10 20 30 40 50

Kilometers 5 0 5 15 25 35 45 55 65 75

Lambert Conformal Conic Projection

Note: Map colors do not reflect elevation.

Note: Map colors do not reflect elevation.

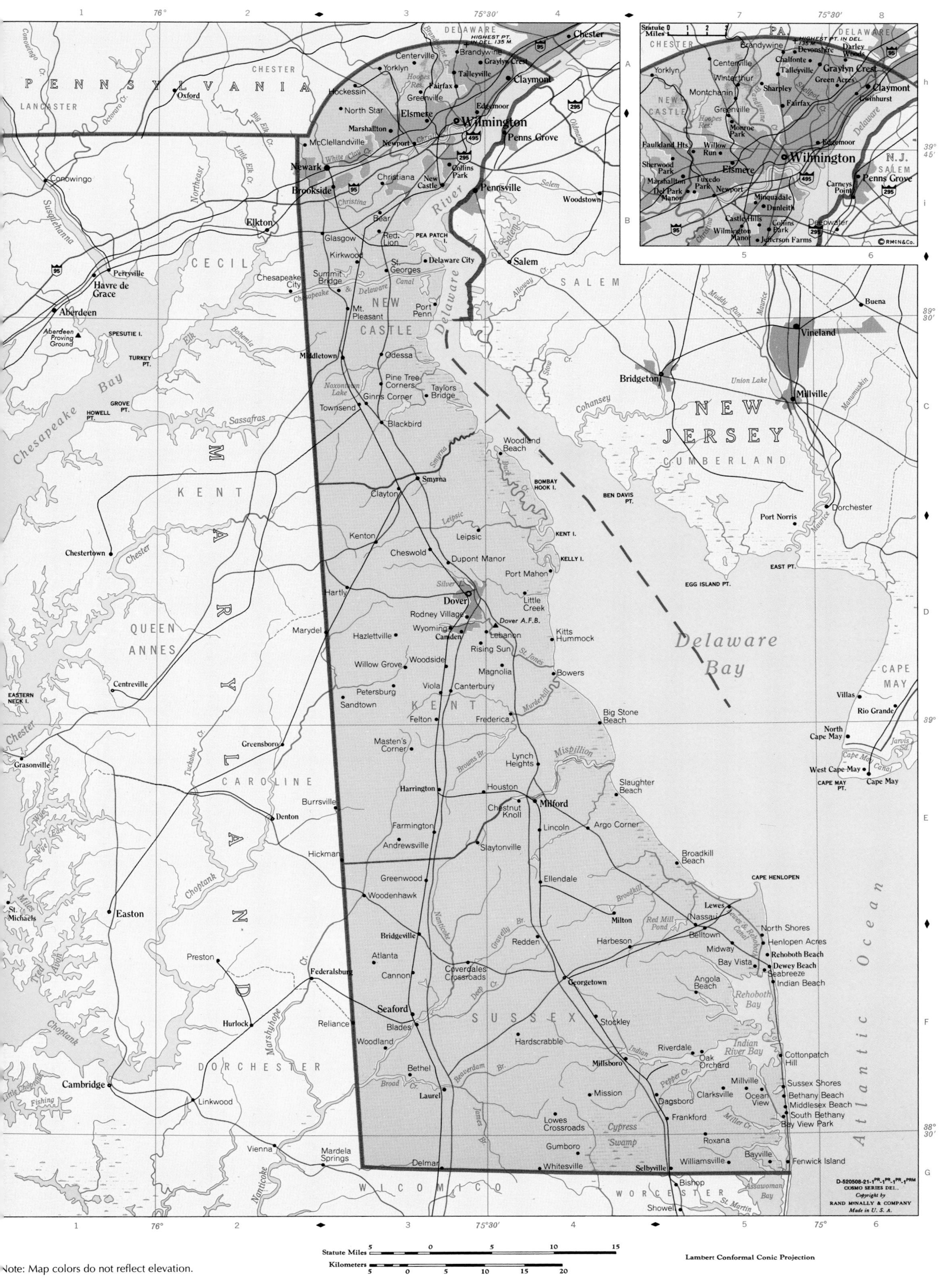

Note: Map colors do not reflect elevation.

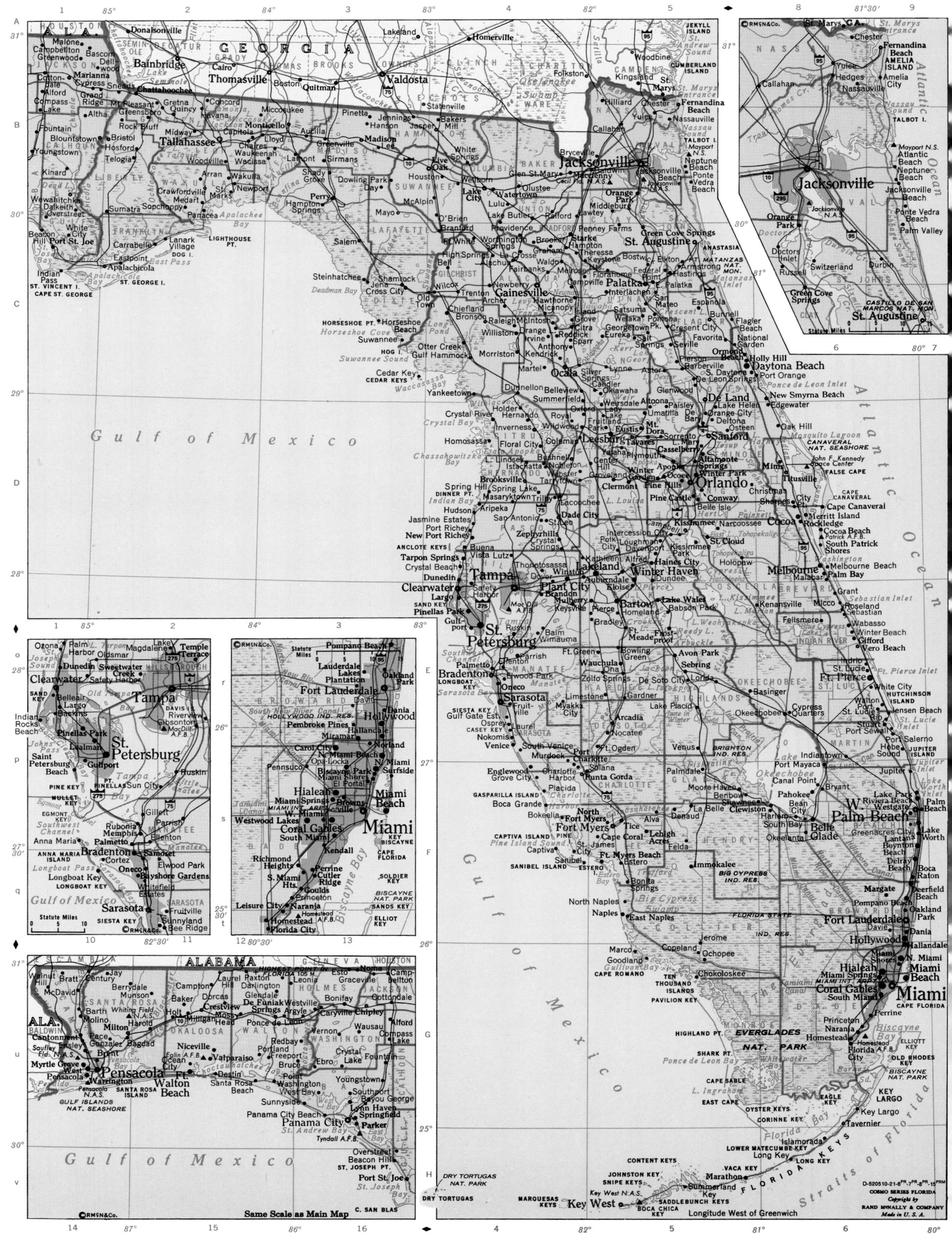

Note: Map colors do not reflect elevation.

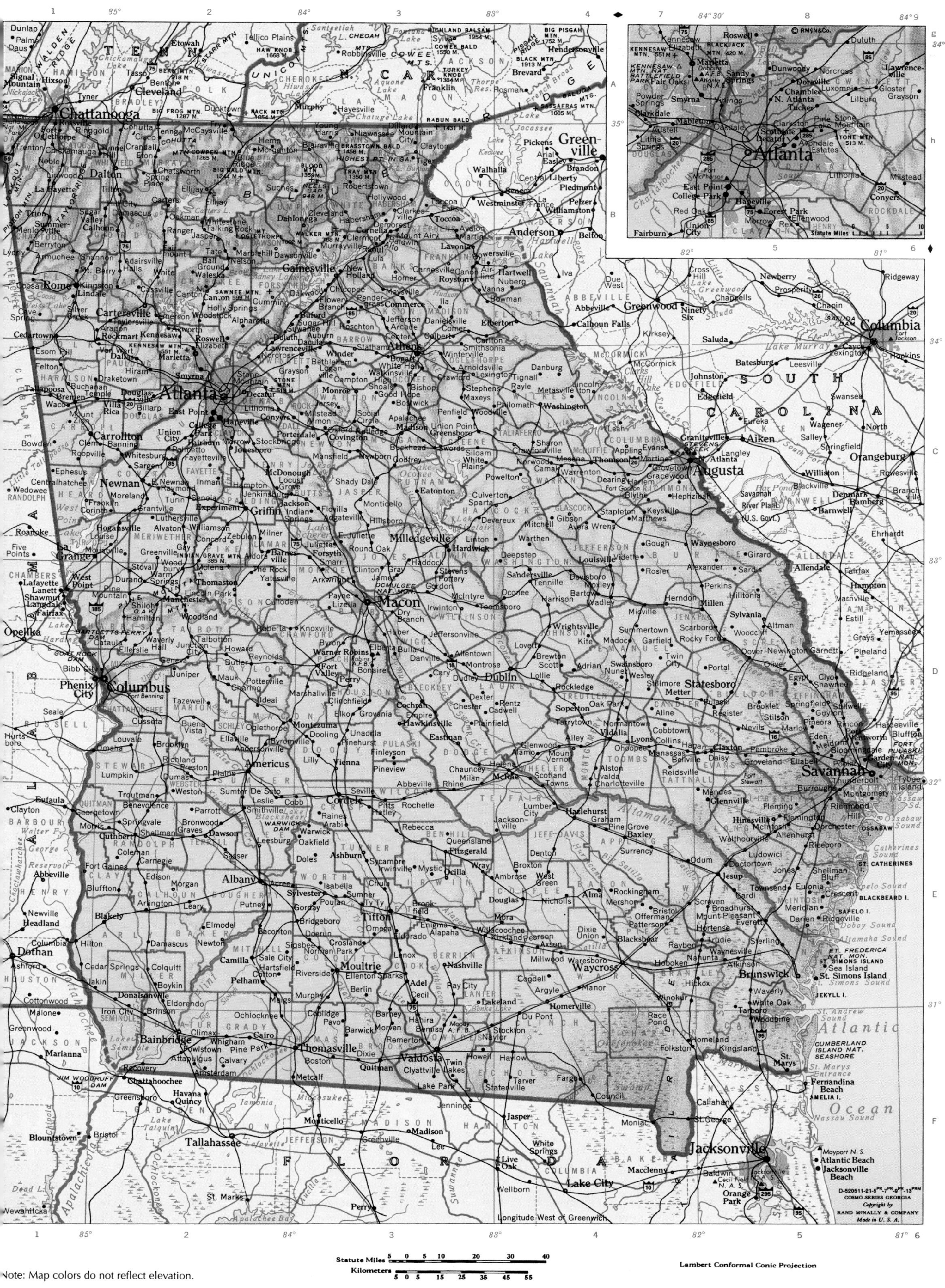

Statute Miles 5 0 5 10 20 30 40

Kilometers 5 0 5 15 25 35 45 55

Lambert Conformal Conic Projection

Note: Map colors do not reflect elevation.

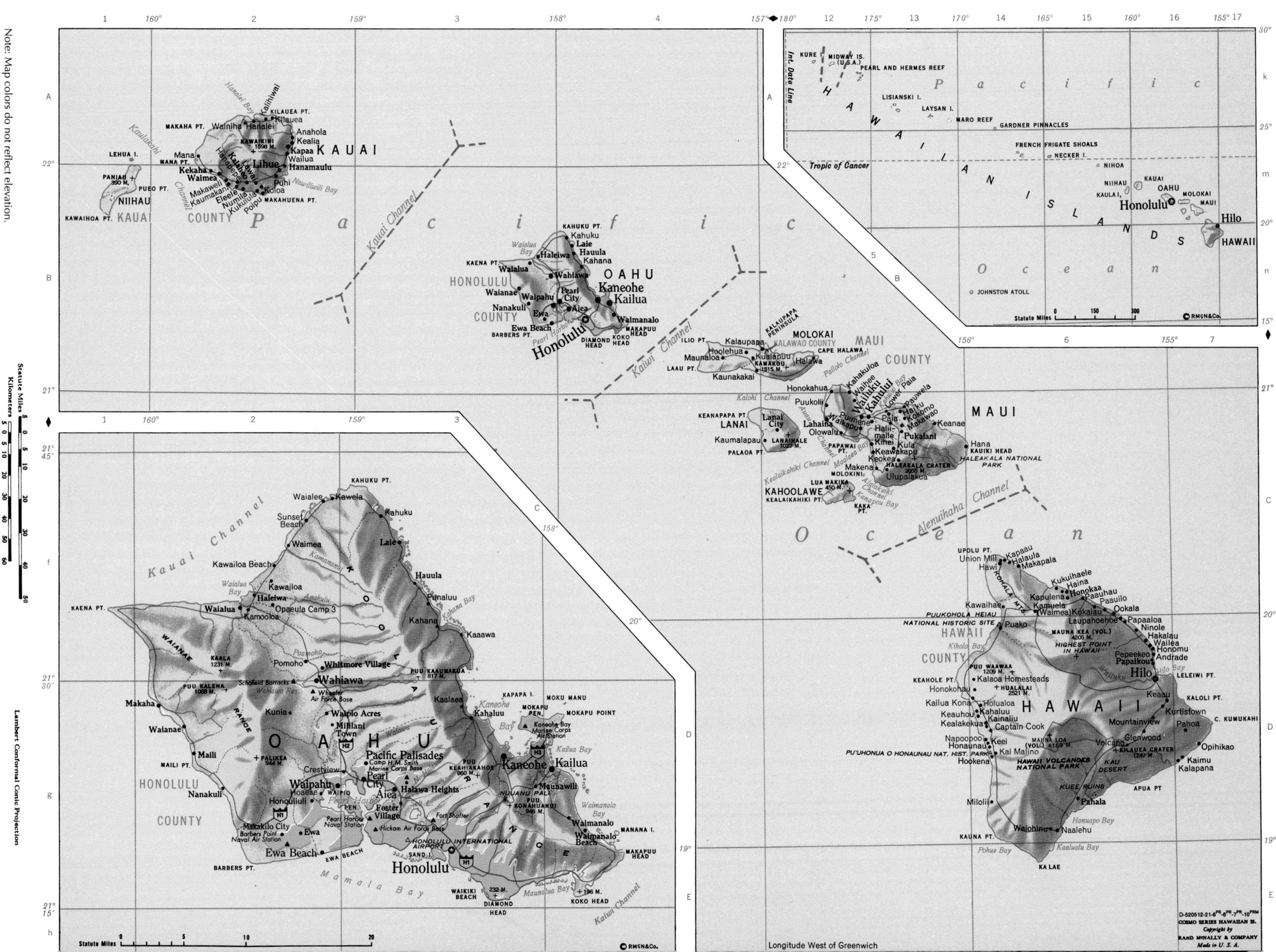

Note: Map colors do not reflect elevation.

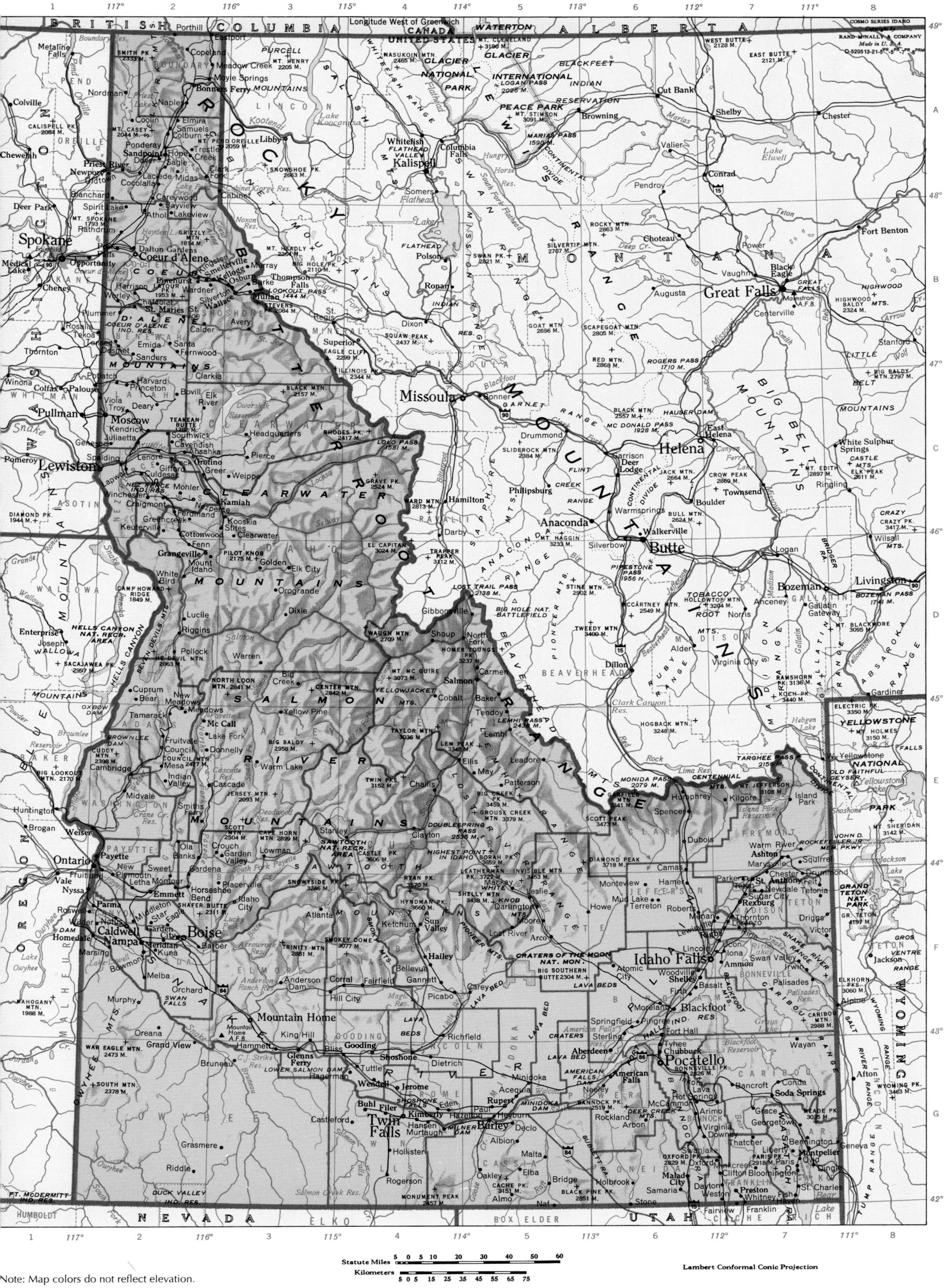

Note: Map colors do not reflect elevation.

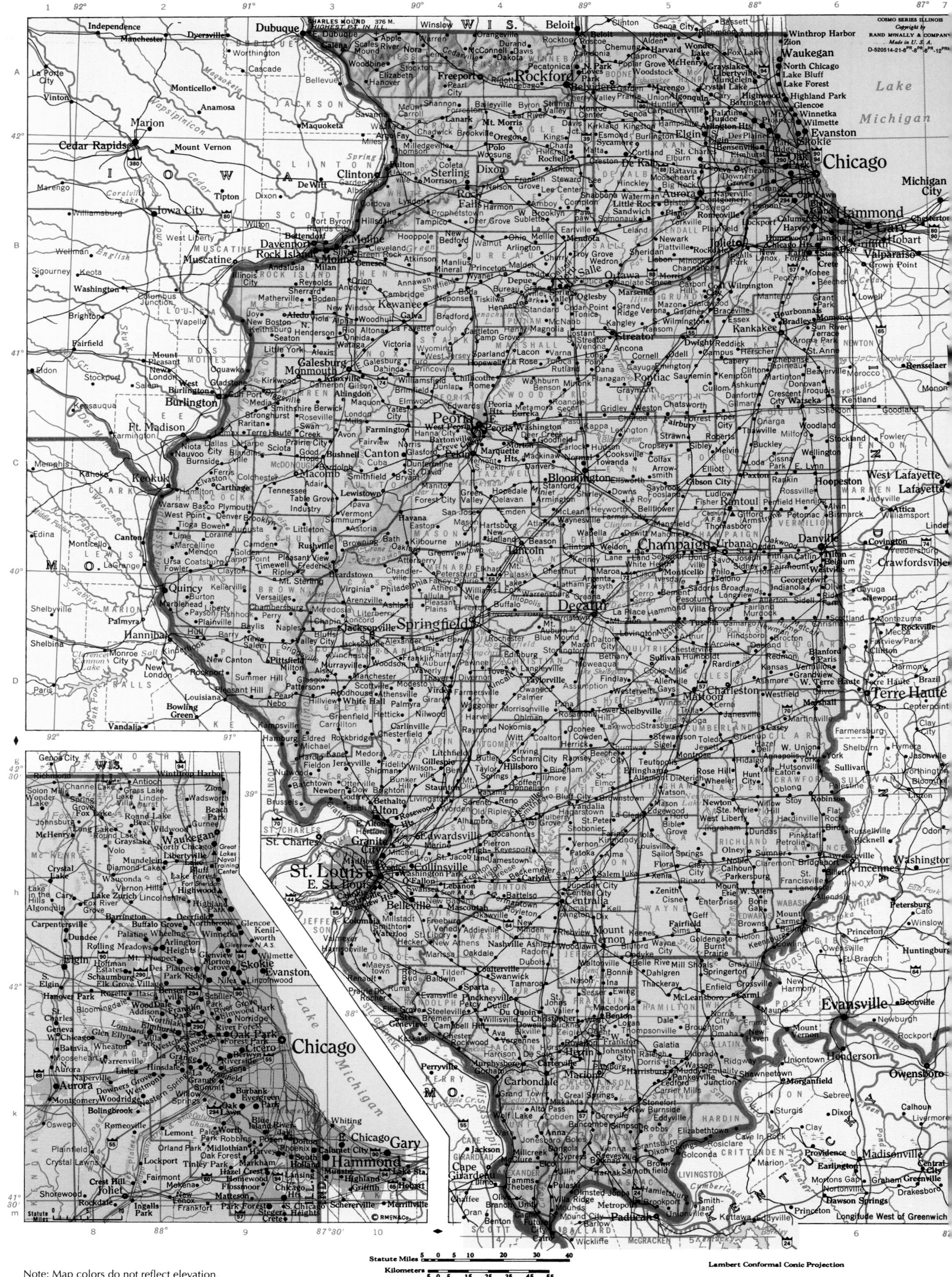

Note: Map colors do not reflect elevation.

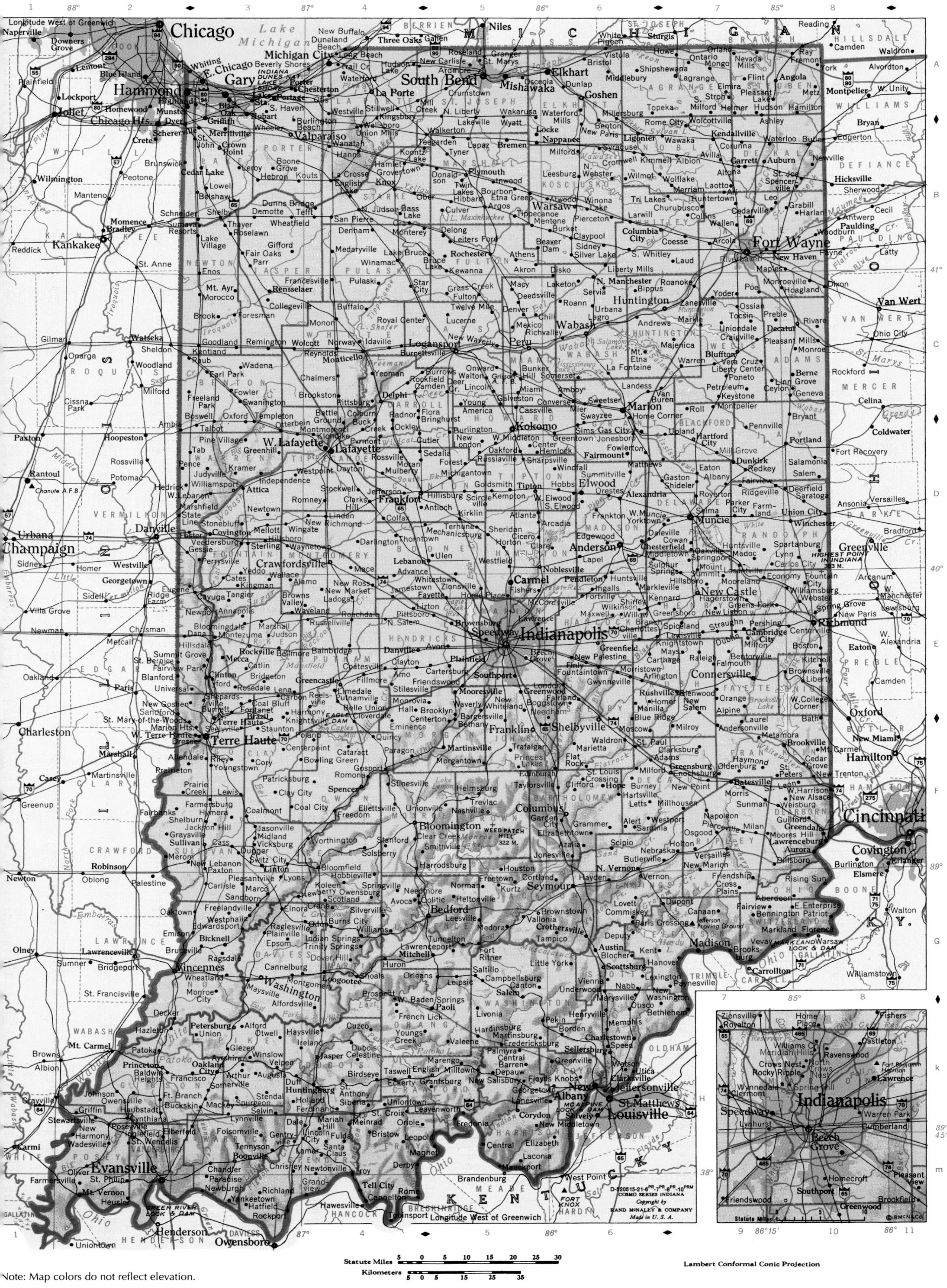

Note: Map colors do not reflect elevation.

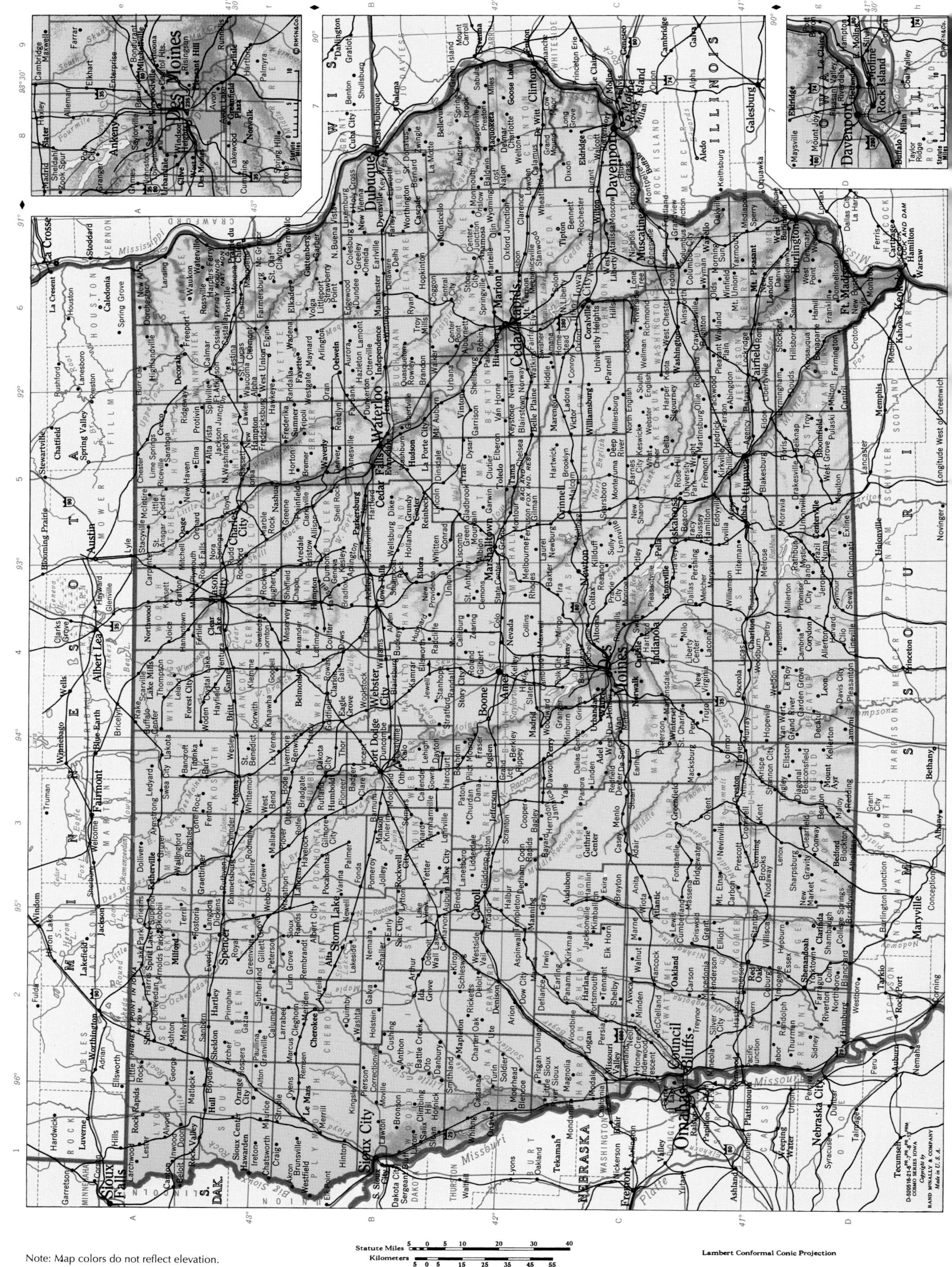

Note: Map colors do not reflect elevation.

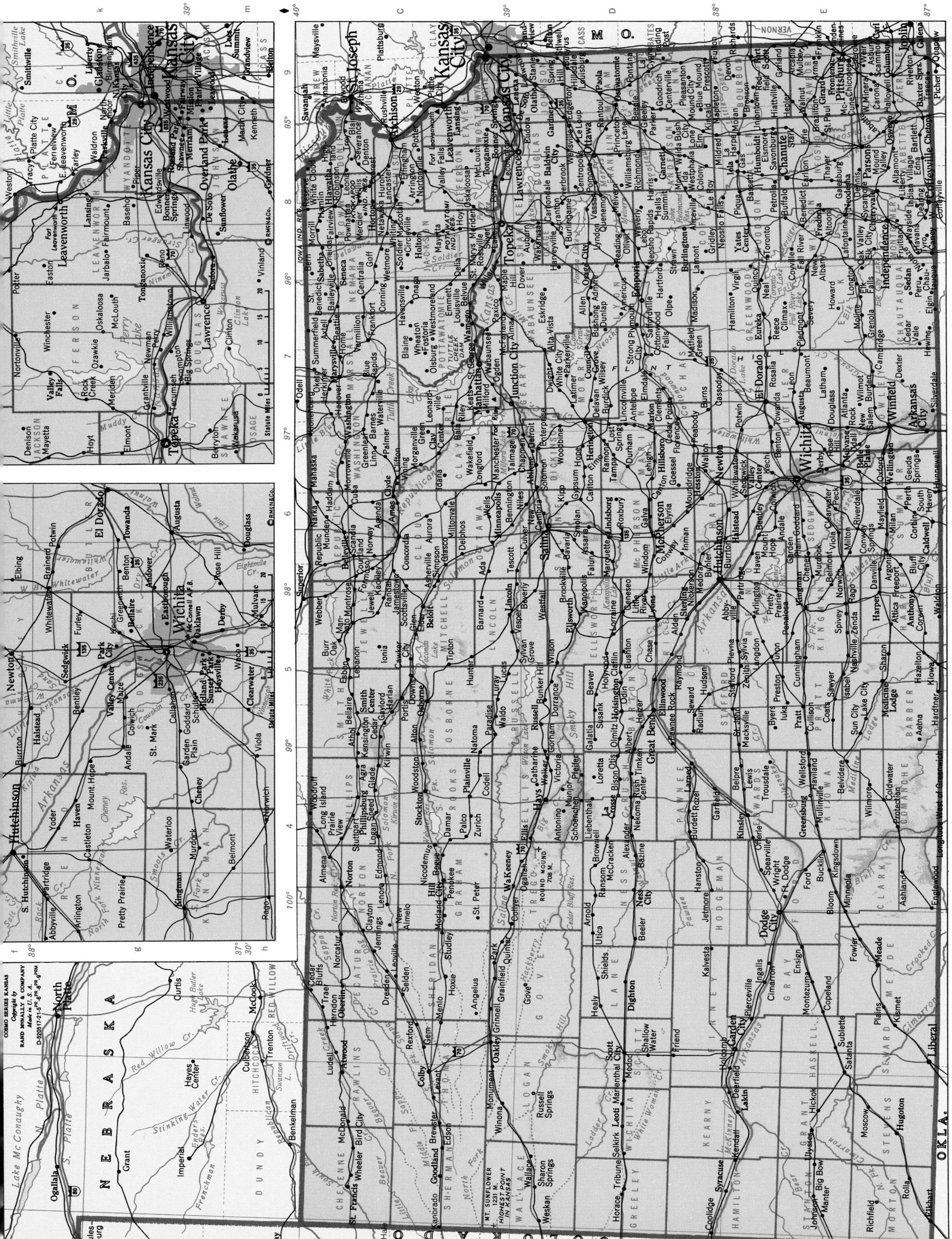

Statute Miles 5 0 5 15 25 35 45

Kilometers 5 0 5 15 25 35 45 55 65

Lambert Conformal Conic Projection

Note: Map colors do not reflect elevation.

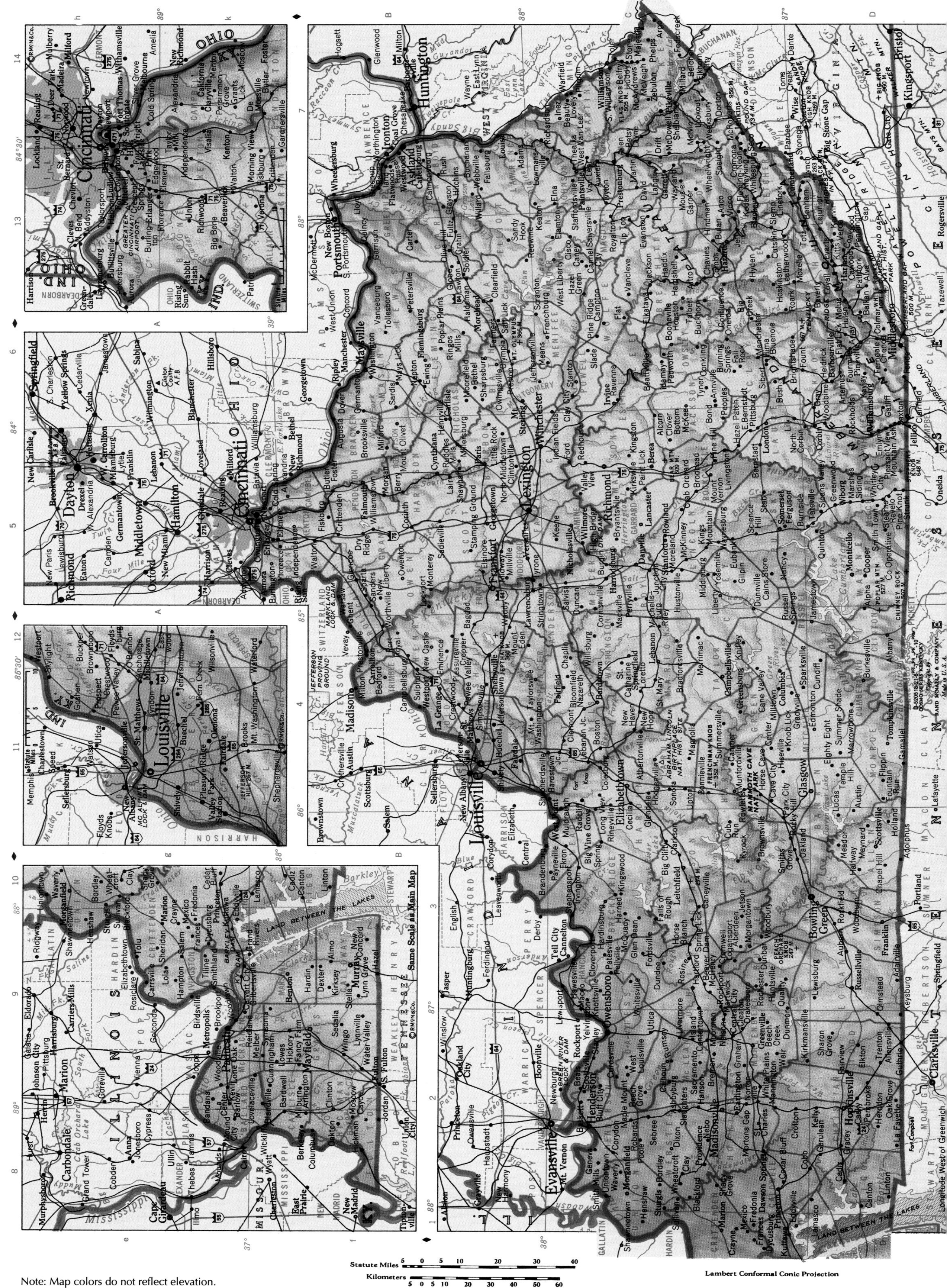

Note: Map colors do not reflect elevation.

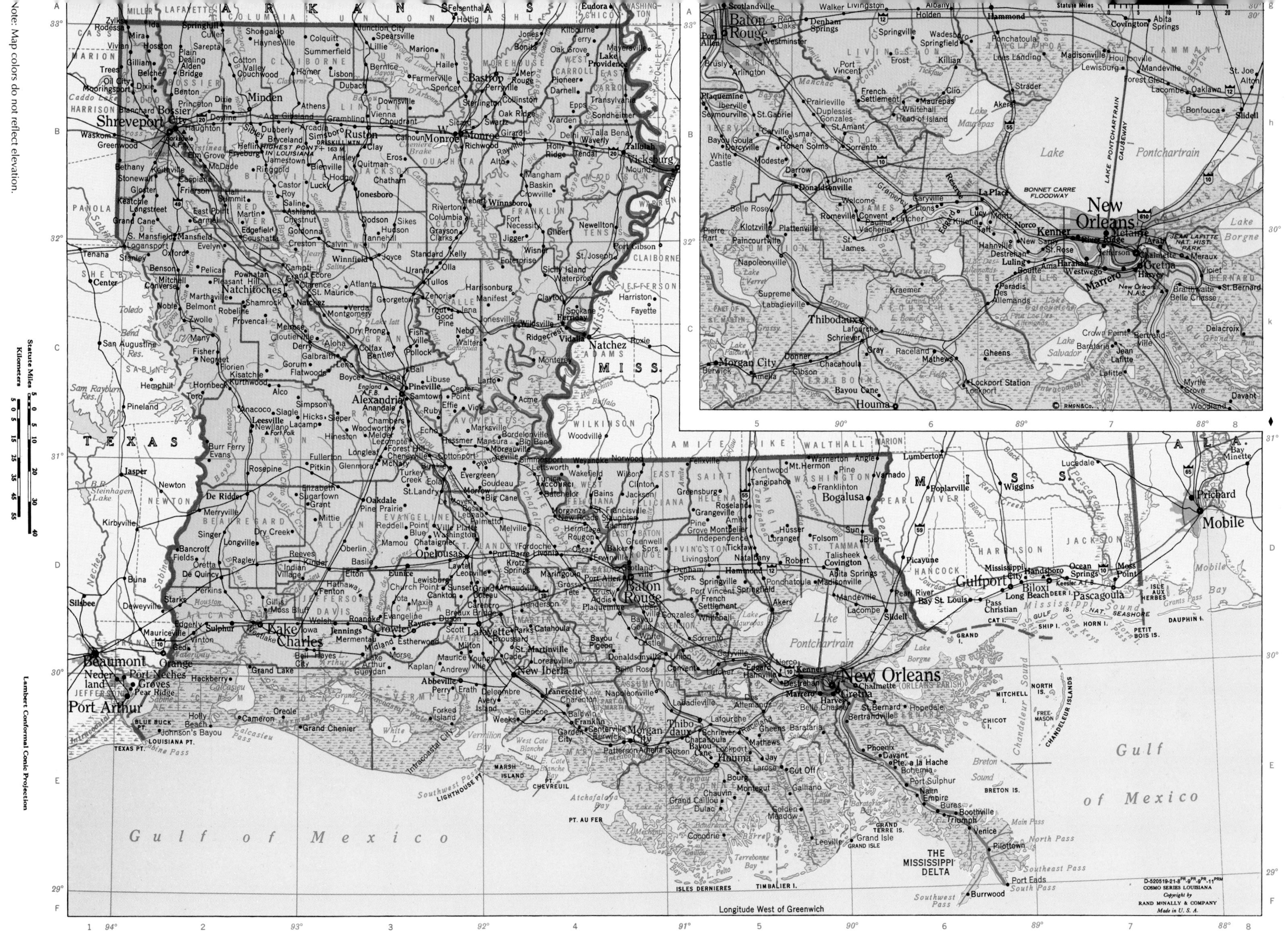

Statute Miles 5 0 5 10 20 30 40

Kilometers 5 0 5 15 25 35 45 55

Lambert Conformal Conic Projection

Note: Map colors do not reflect elevation.

Note: Map colors do not reflect elevation.

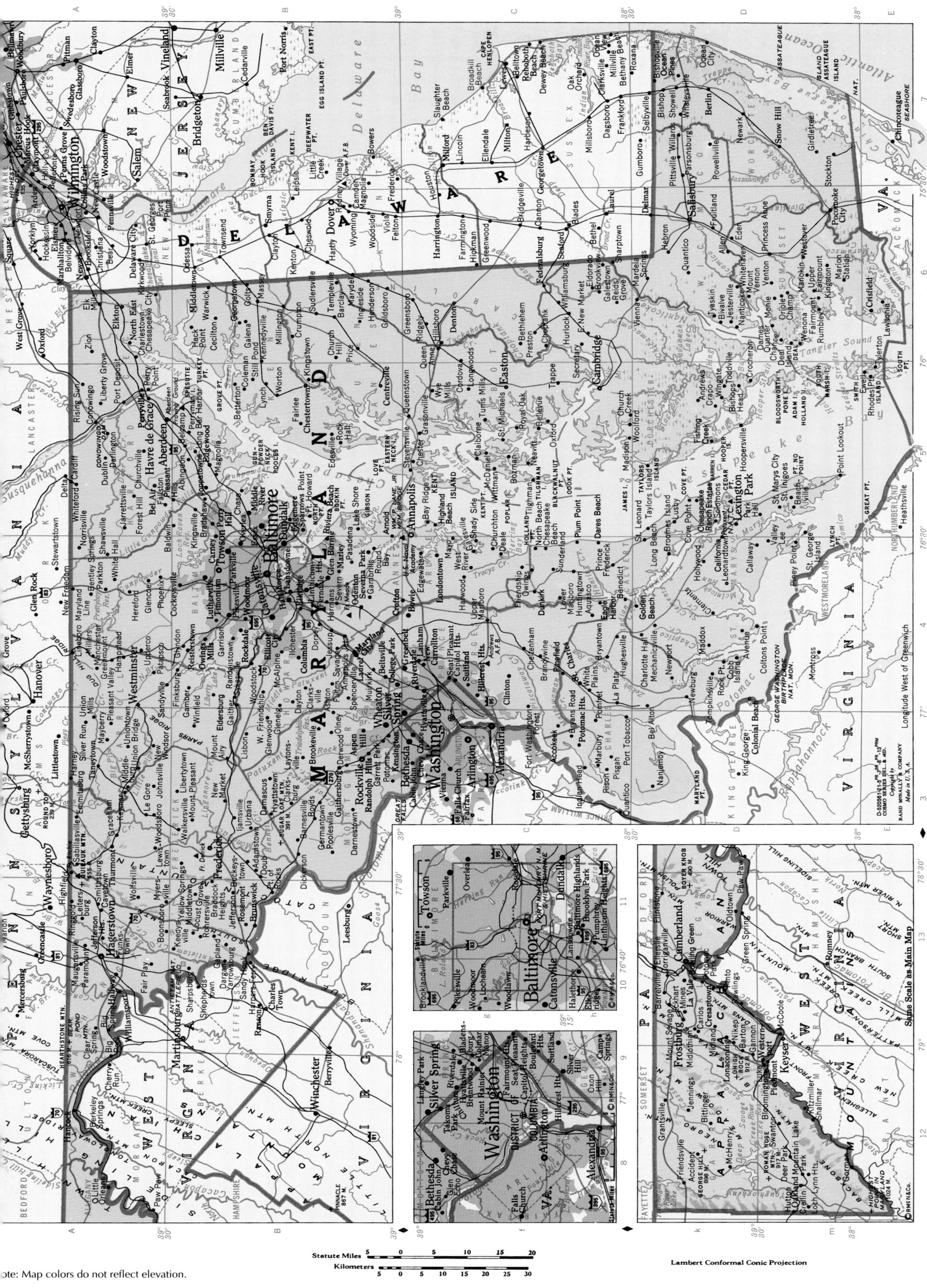

Statute Miles 5 0 5 10 15 20

Kilometers 5 0 5 10 15 20 25 30

Lambert Conformal Conic Projection

ote: Map colors do not reflect elevation.

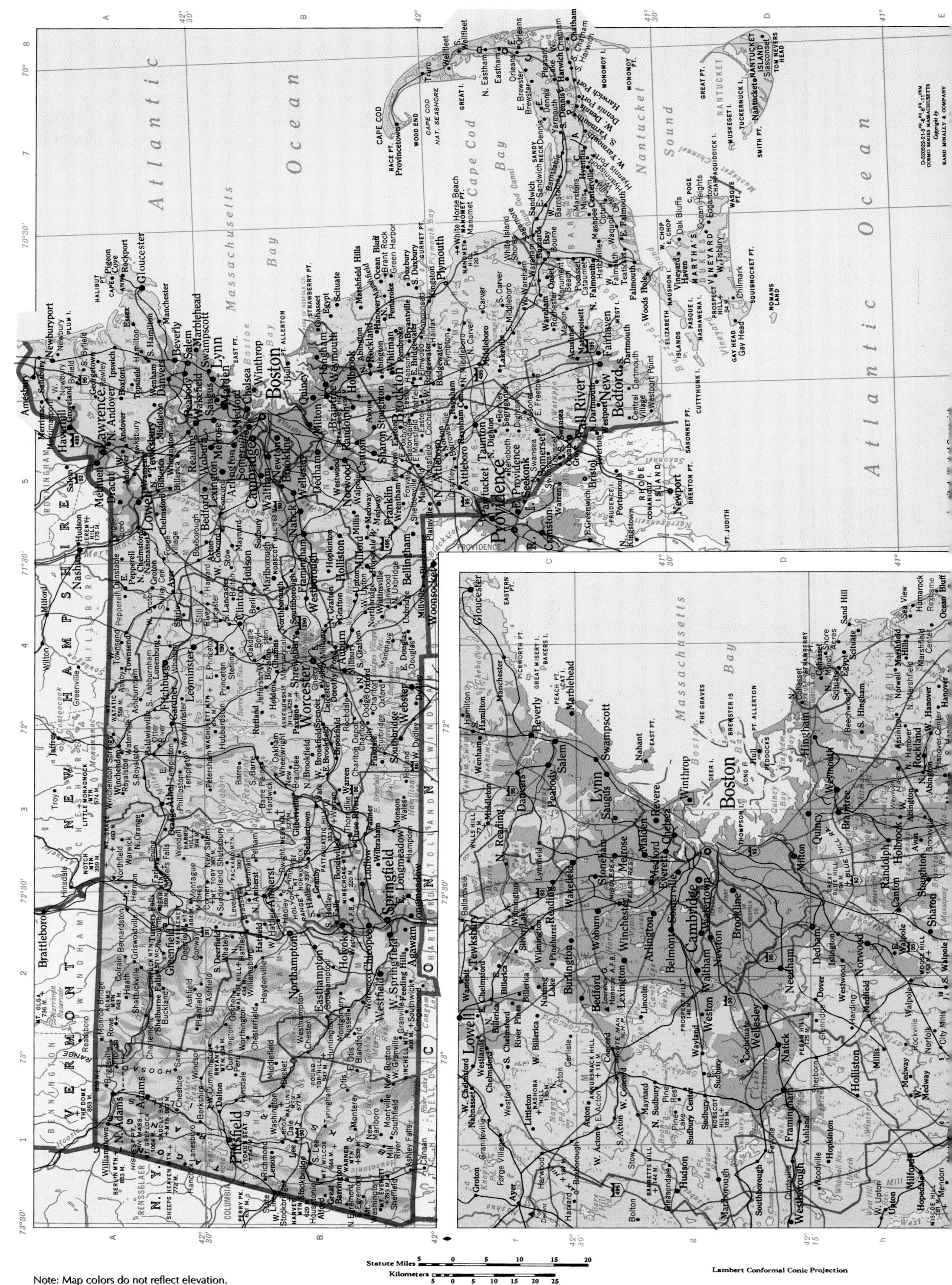

Note: Map colors do not reflect elevation.

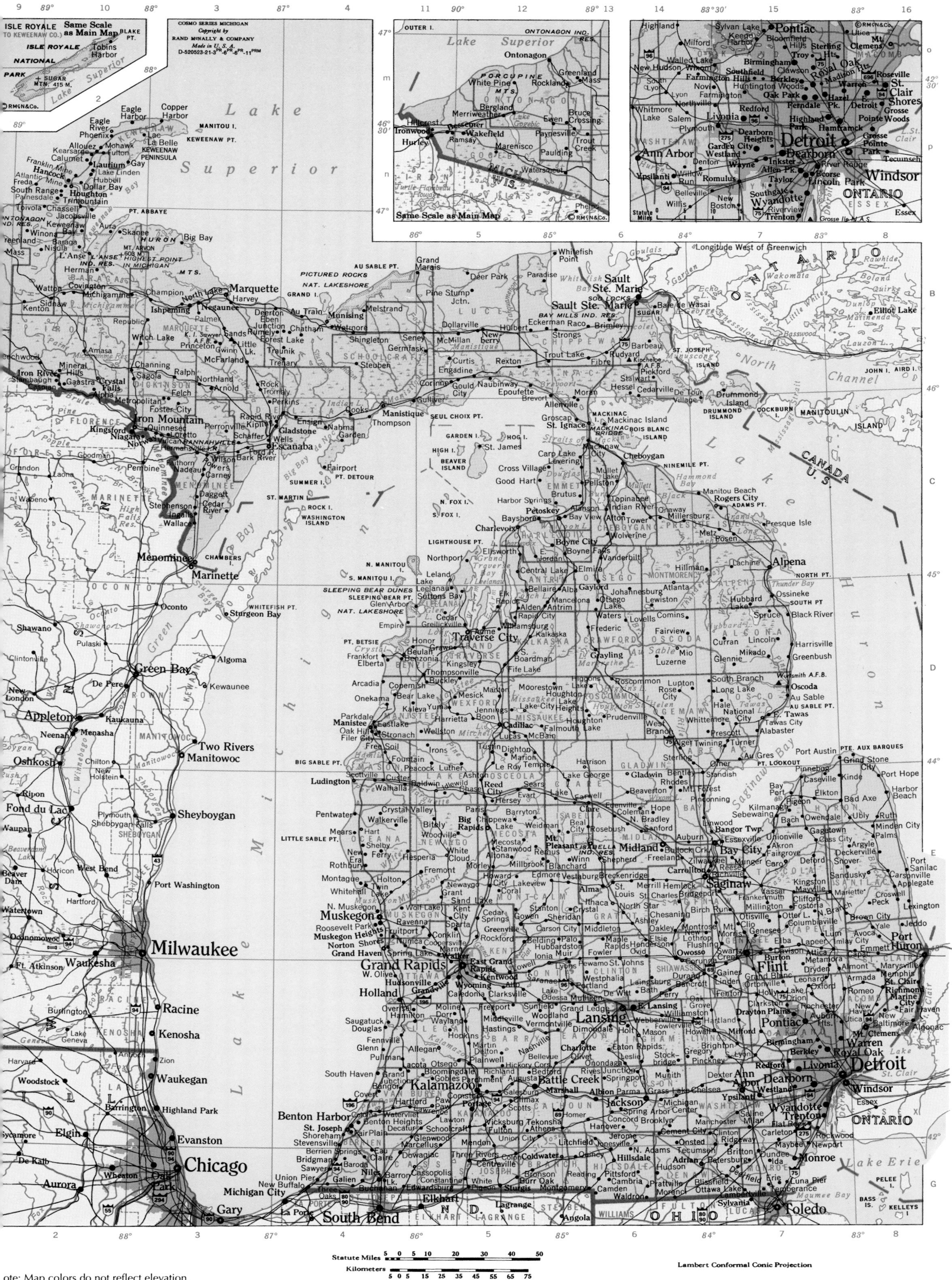

Note: Map colors do not reflect elevation.

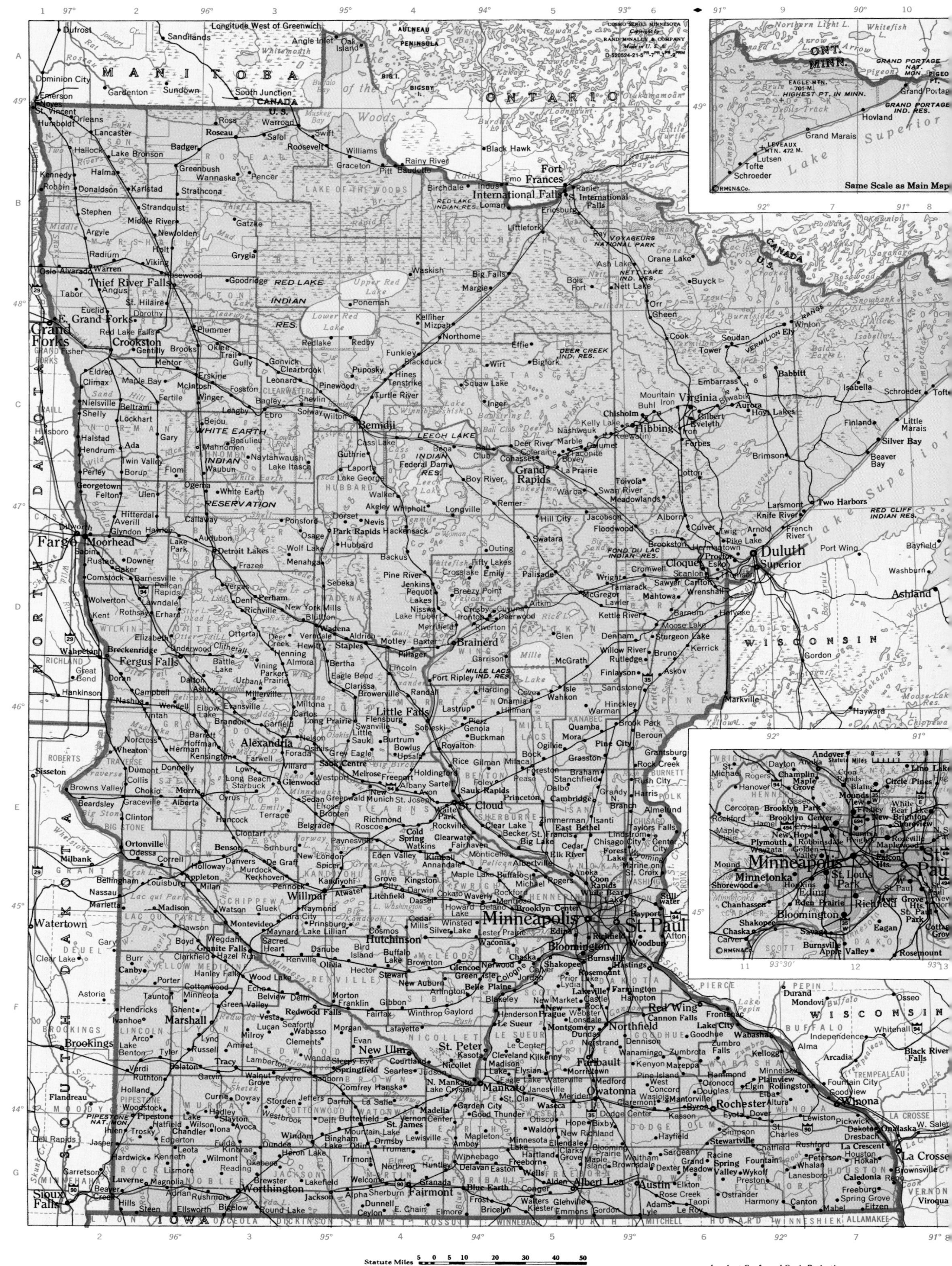

Note: Map colors do not reflect elevation.

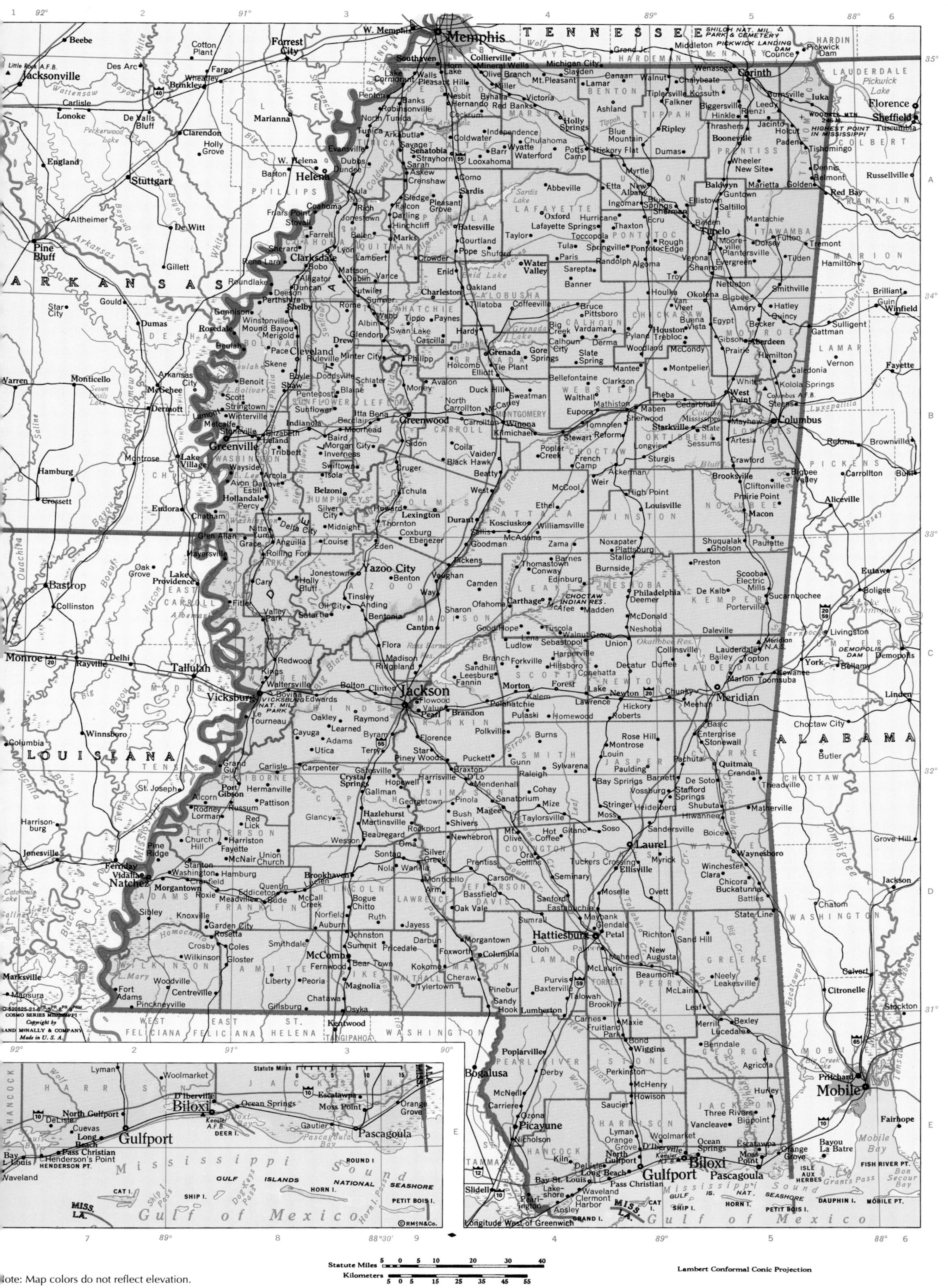

Note: Map colors do not reflect elevation.

Statute Miles 5 0 5 10 20 30 40

Kilometers 5 0 5 15 25 35 45 55

Lambert Conformal Conic Projection

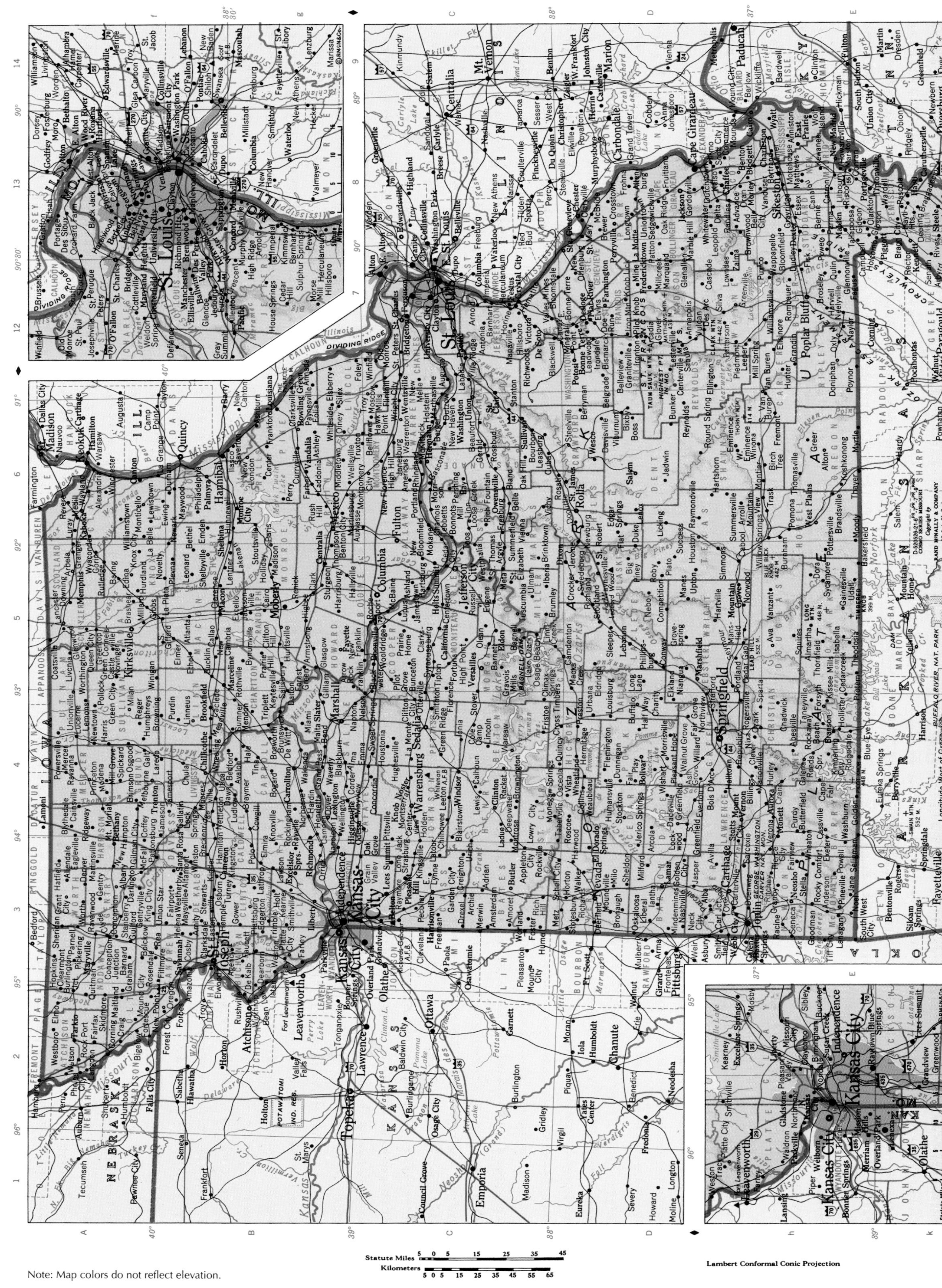

Statute Miles 5 0 5 15 25 35 45

Kilometers 5 0 5 15 25 35 45 55 65

Lambert Conformal Conic Projection

Note: Map colors do not reflect elevation.

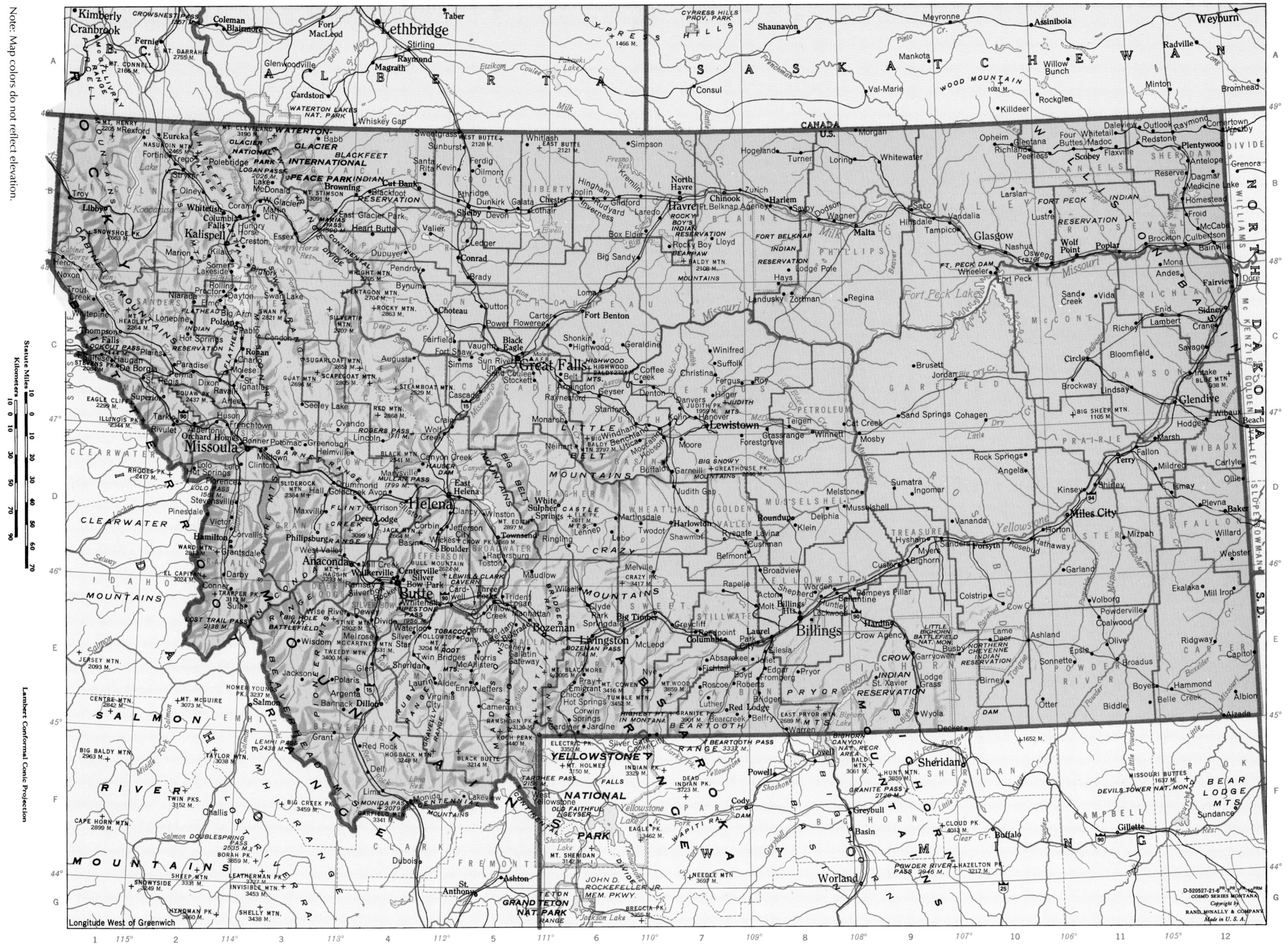

Note: Map colors do not reflect elevation.

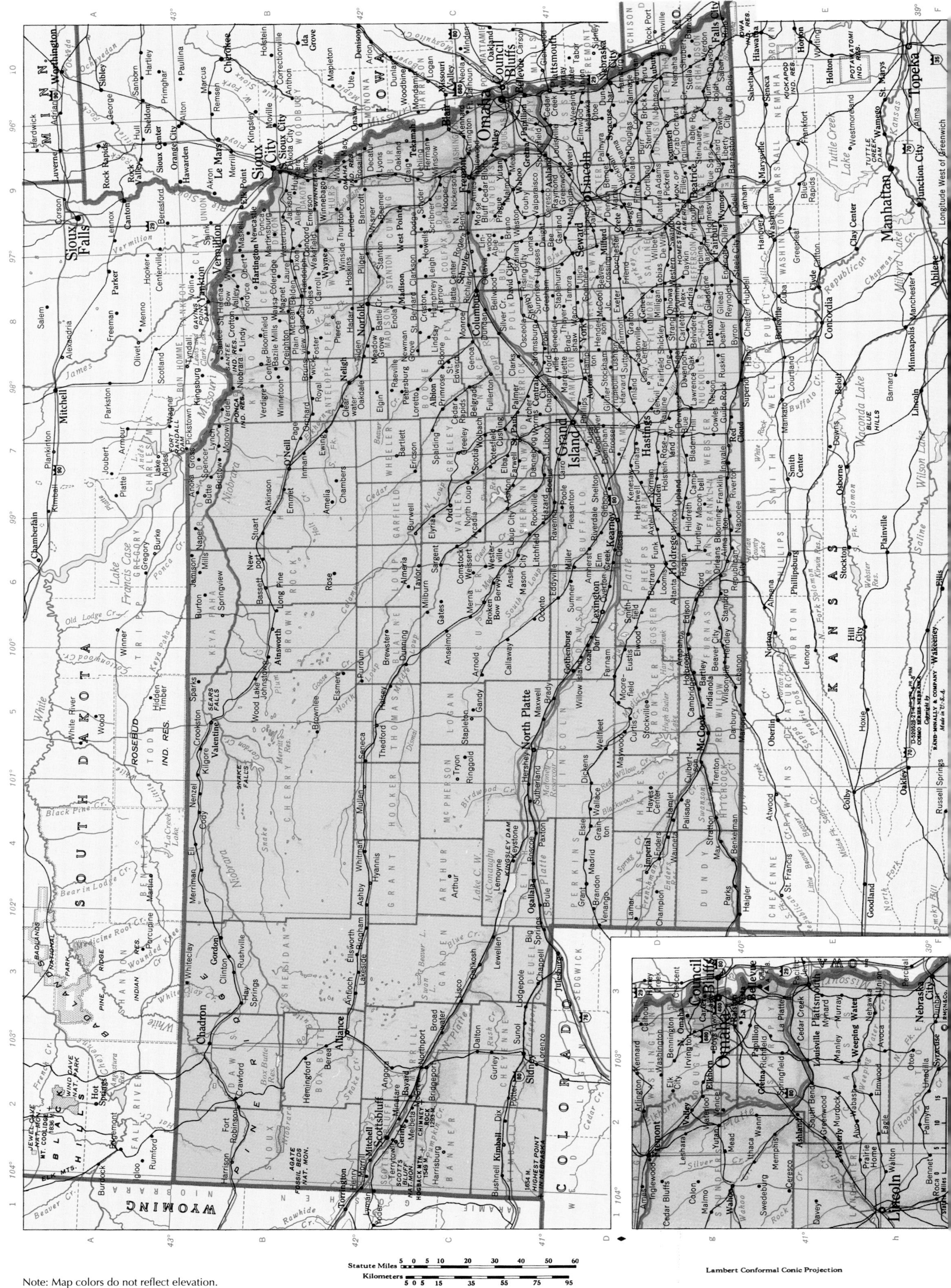

Statute Miles 5 0 5 10 20 30 40 50 60

Kilometers 5 0 5 15 35 55 75 95

Lambert Conformal Conic Projection

Note: Map colors do not reflect elevation.

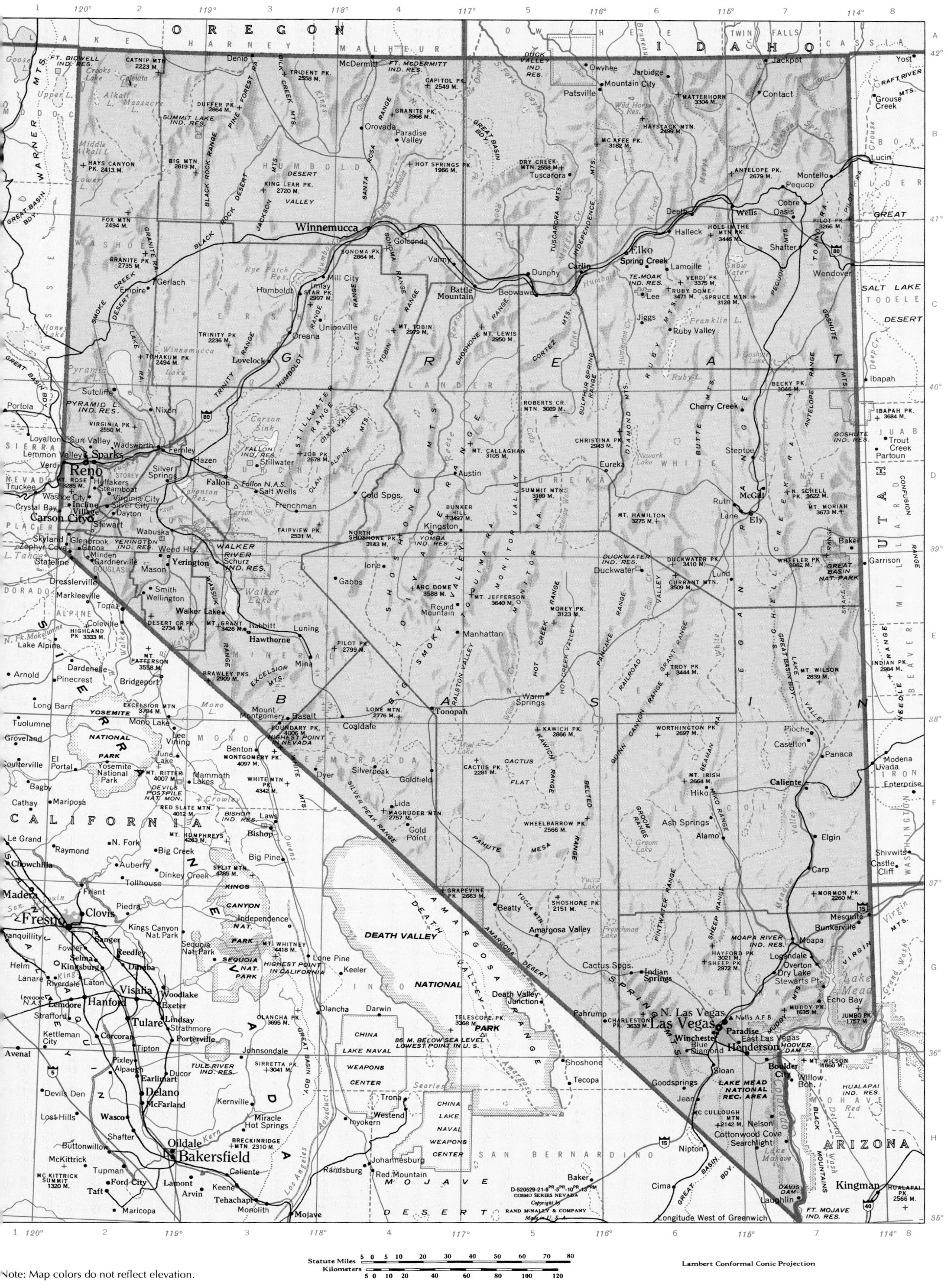

Note: Map colors do not reflect elevation.

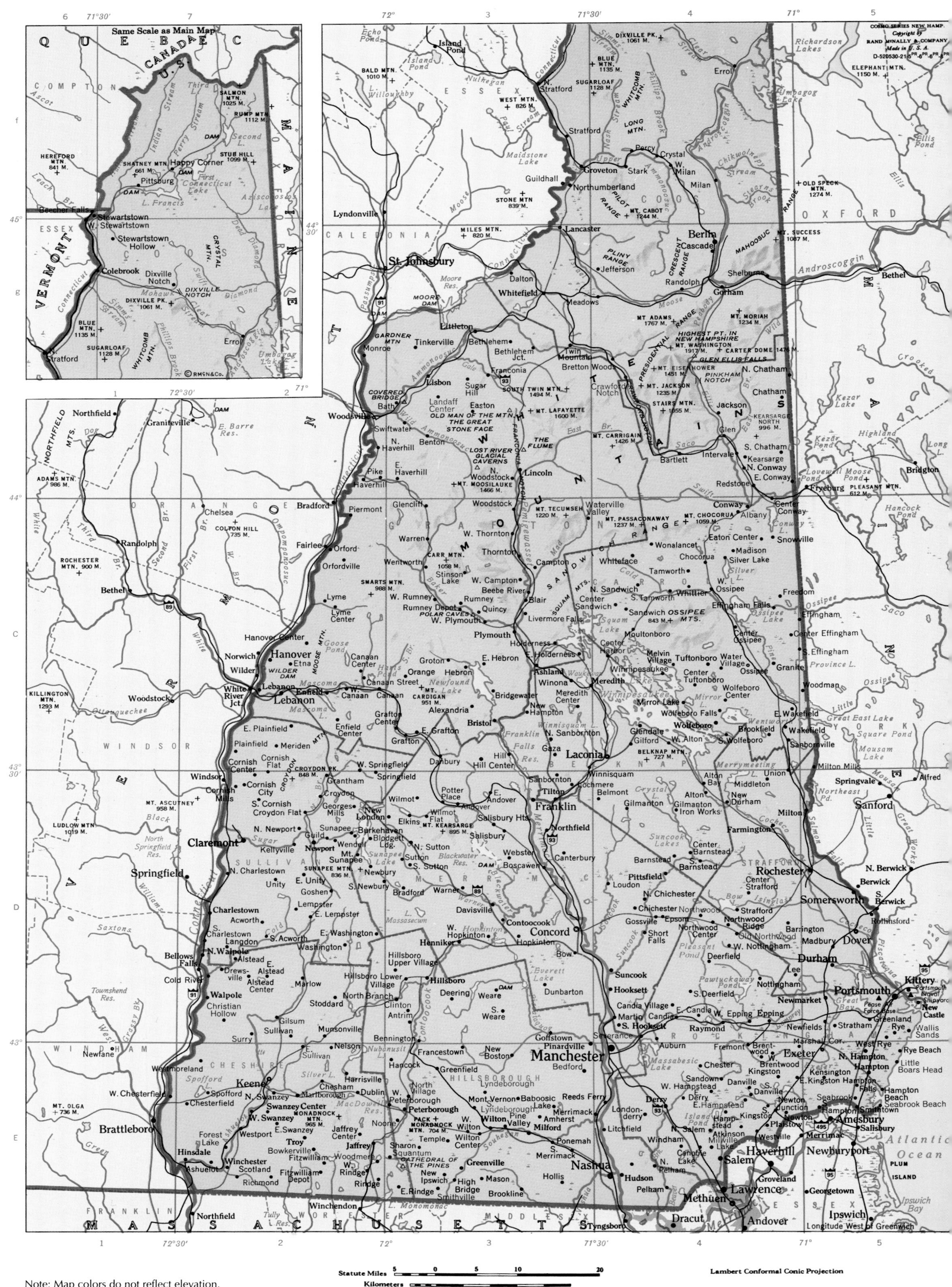

Same Scale as Main Map
QUEBEC
CANADA
U.S.
MAINE
VERMONT
COMPTON
ESSEX
COOS
CALEDONIA
ORANGE
GRAFTON
WINDSOR
SULLIVAN
MERRIMACK
BELKNAP
CARROLL
STRAFFORD
ROCKINGHAM
HILLSBOROUGH
CHESHIRE
WINDHAM
OXFORD
YORK
FRANKLIN
WORCESTER
MIDDLESEX
ESSEX
MASSACHUSETTS
WHITE MOUNTAINS
PRESIDENTIAL RANGE
HIGHEST PT. IN NEW HAMPSHIRE MT. WASHINGTON 1917 M.
Pittsburg
Colebrook
Dixville Notch
Errol
Berlin
Gorham
Lancaster
Littleton
Franconia
Lincoln
Conway
Plymouth
Hanover
Lebanon
Laconia
Wolfeboro
Franklin
Claremont
Concord
Rochester
Dover
Durham
Portsmouth
Keene
Peterborough
Manchester
Nashua
Salem
Exeter
Hampton
St. Johnsbury
Brattleboro
Haverhill
Lawrence
Sanford
Atlantic Ocean
COSMO SERIES NEW HAMP.
Copyright by RAND McNALLY & COMPANY
Made in U. S. A.
Statute Miles 5 0 5 10 20
Kilometers 5 0 5 10 15 20 25
Lambert Conformal Conic Projection
Note: Map colors do not reflect elevation.

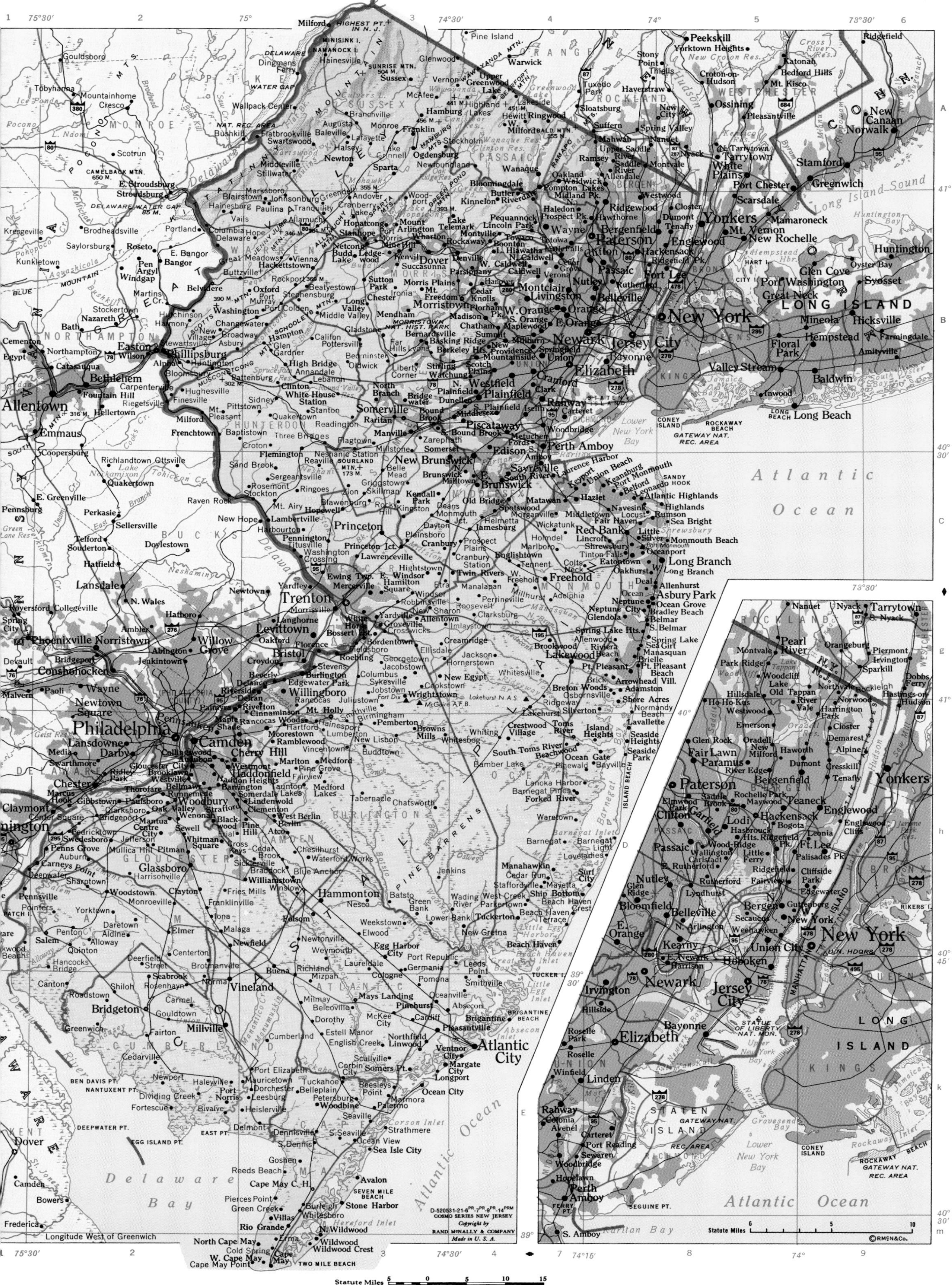

Note: Map colors do not reflect elevation.

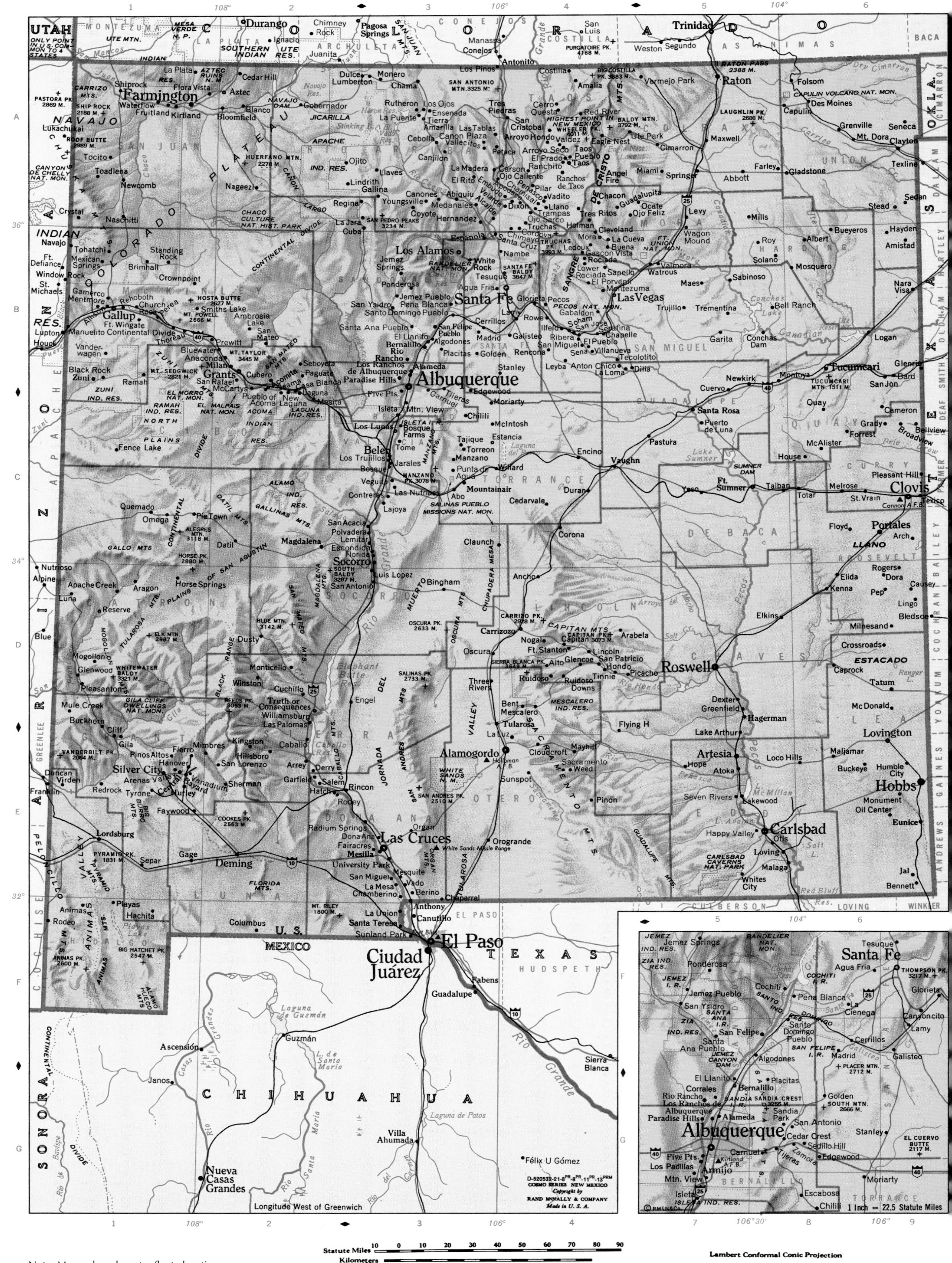

Note: Map colors do not reflect elevation.

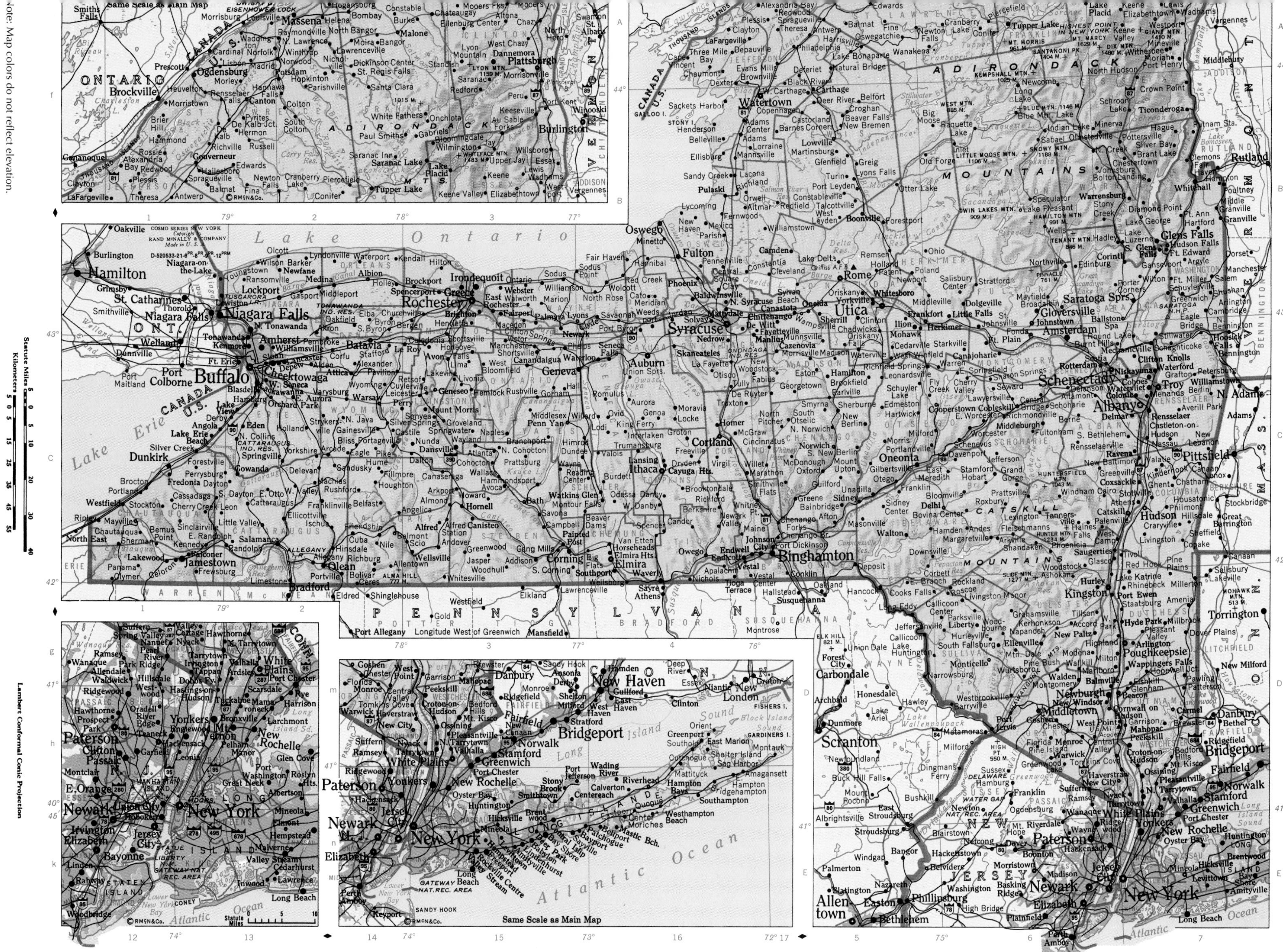
Statute Miles 5 0 5 10 20 30 40
Kilometers 5 0 5 15 25 35 45 55
Lambert Conformal Conic Projection
Lake Ontario
Lake Erie
Atlantic Ocean
Same Scale as Main Map
Note: Map colors do not reflect elevation.

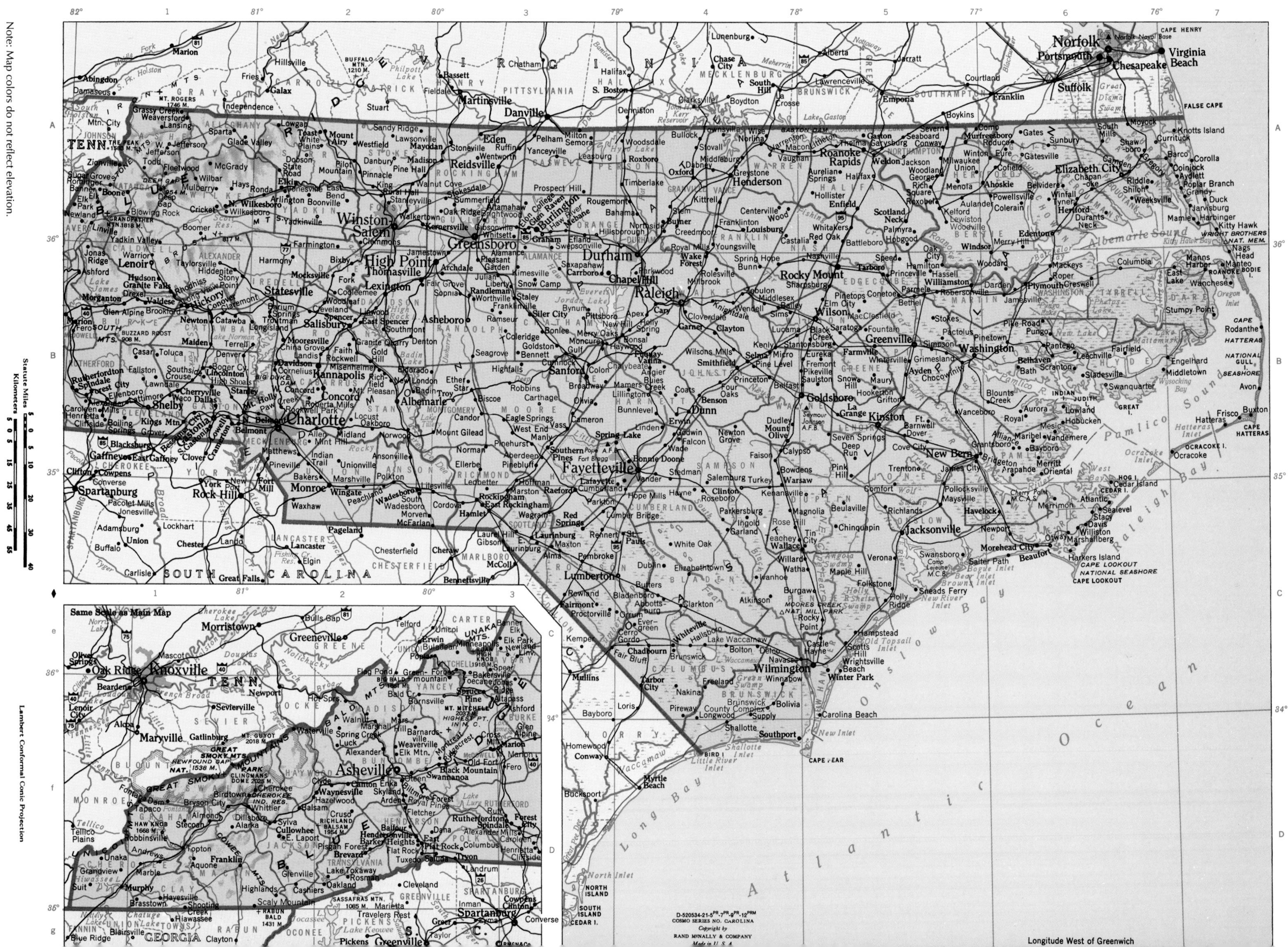

Note: Map colors do not reflect elevation.

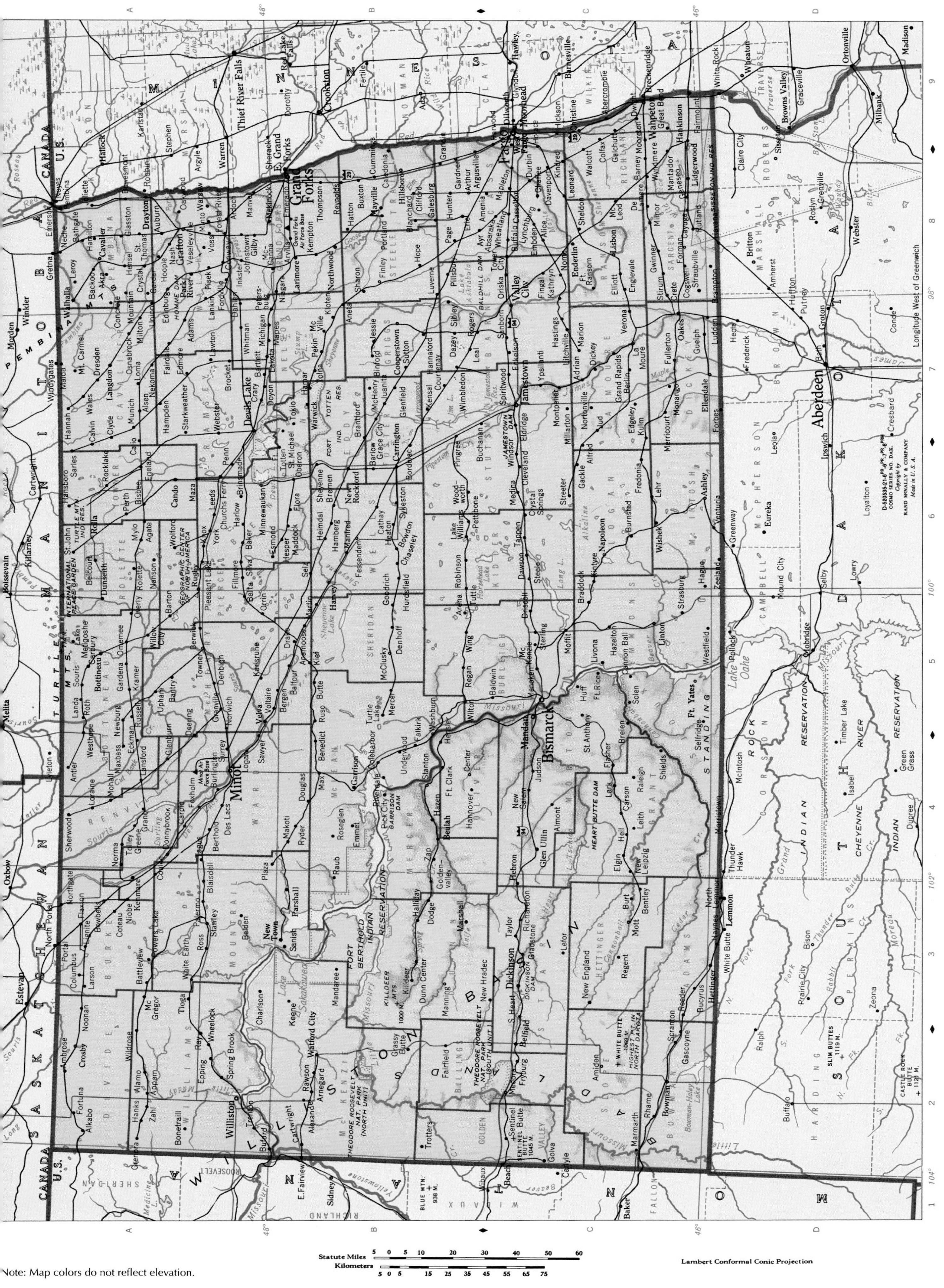

Note: Map colors do not reflect elevation.

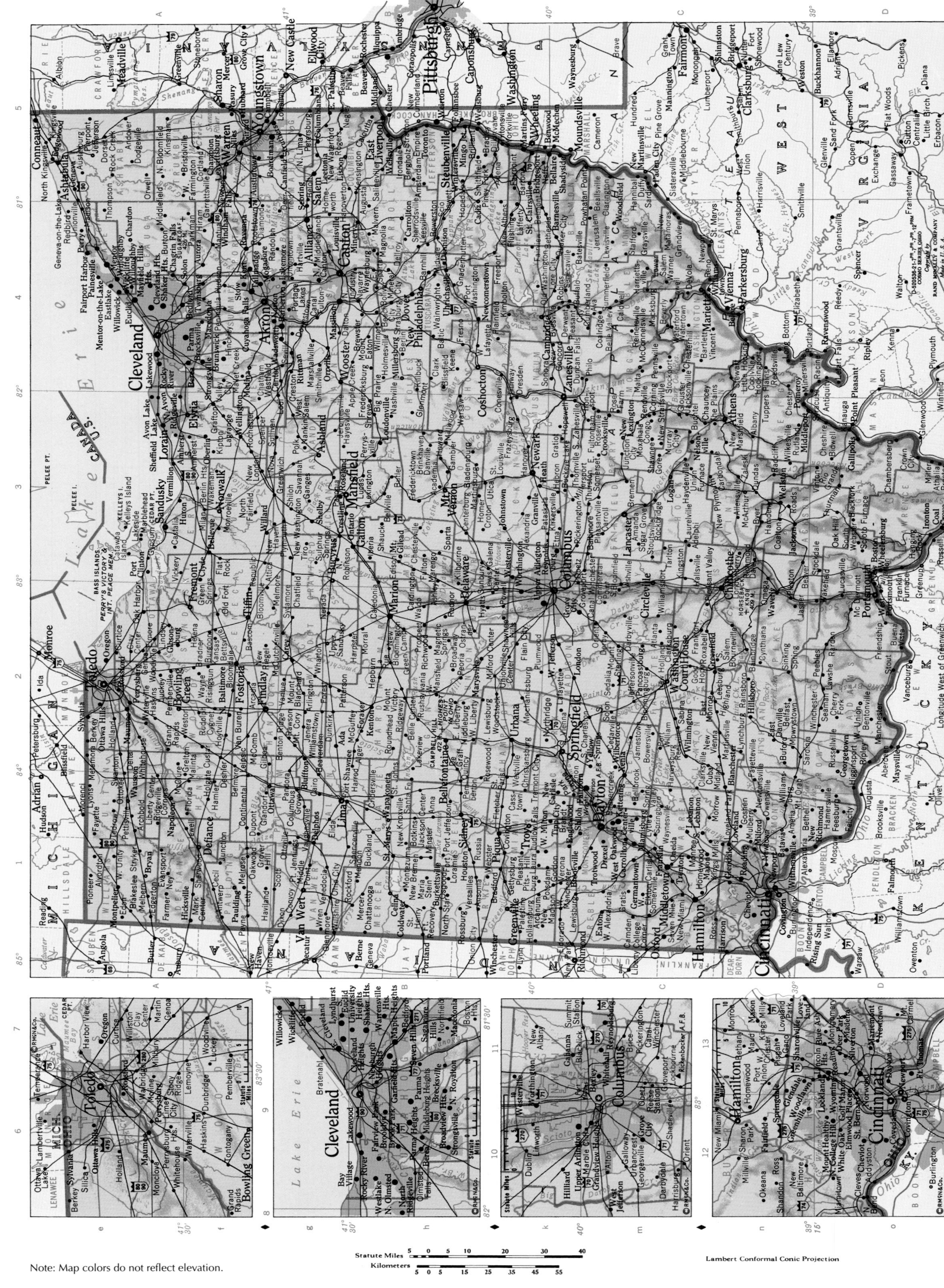

Note: Map colors do not reflect elevation.

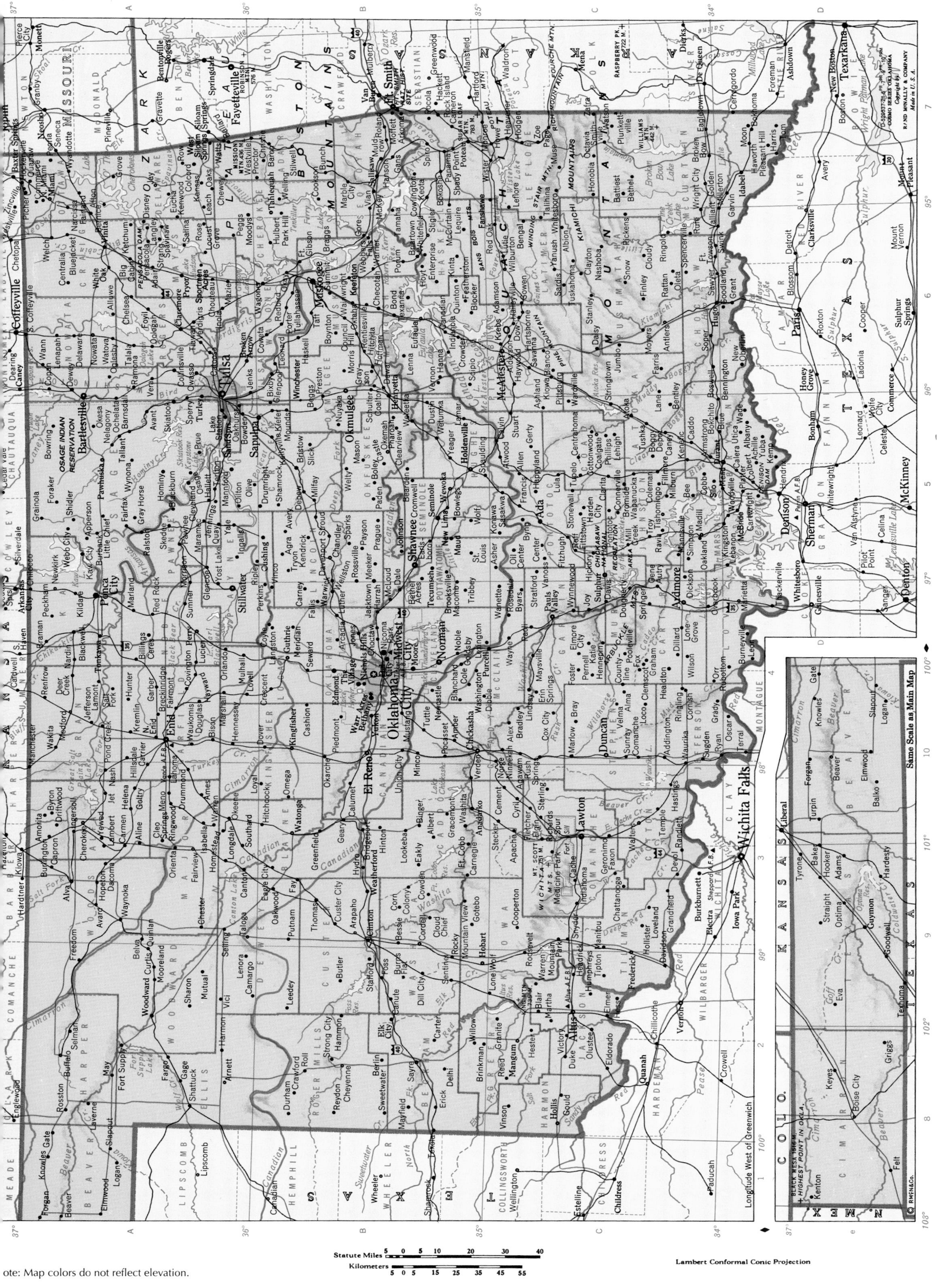
Statute Miles 5 0 5 10 20 30 40
Kilometers 5 0 5 15 25 35 45 55
Lambert Conformal Conic Projection
Same Scale as Main Map
Longitude West of Greenwich
ote: Map colors do not reflect elevation.

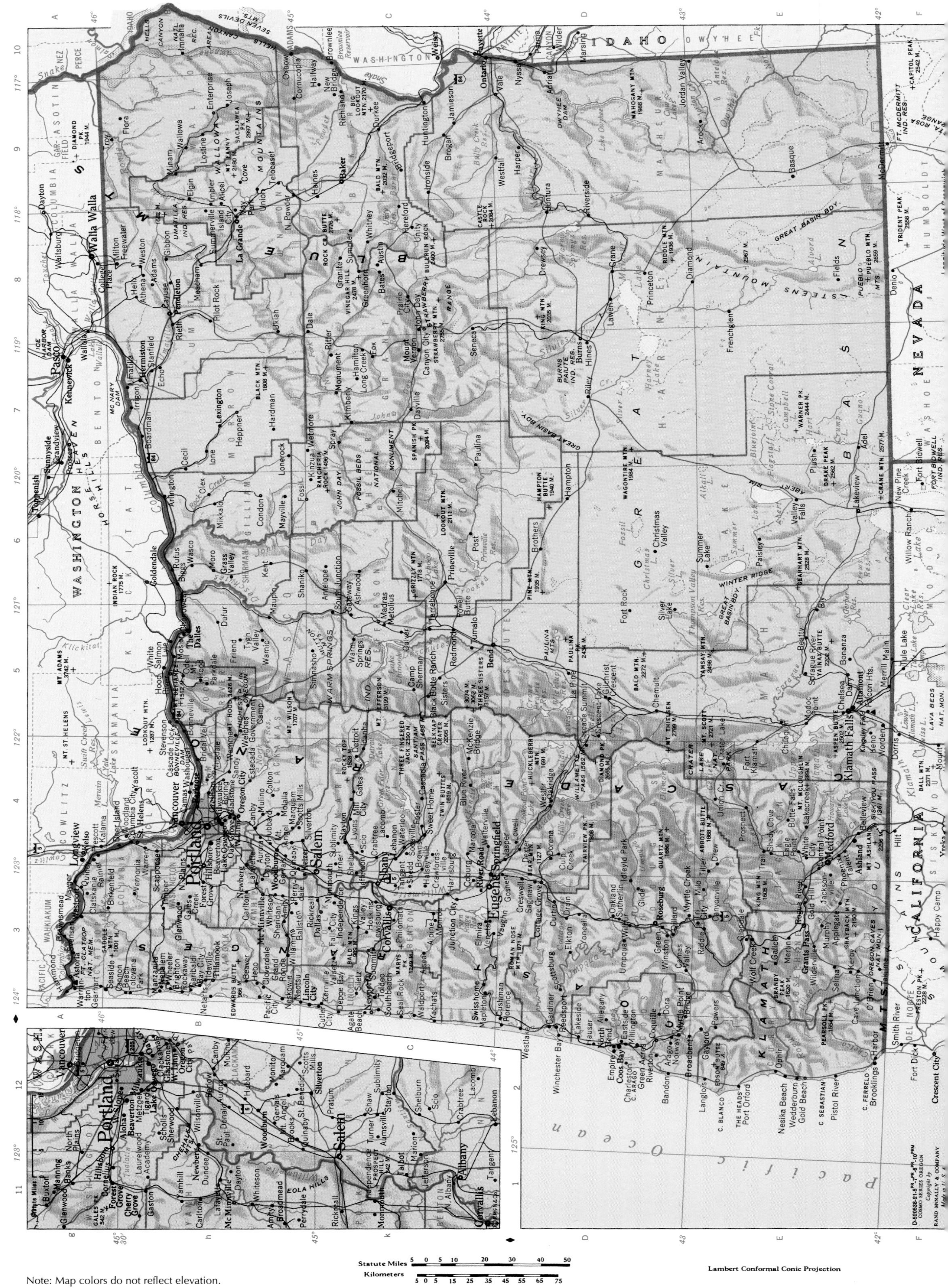

Statute Miles 5 0 5 10 20 30 40 50

Kilometers 5 0 5 15 25 35 45 55 65 75

Note: Map colors do not reflect elevation.

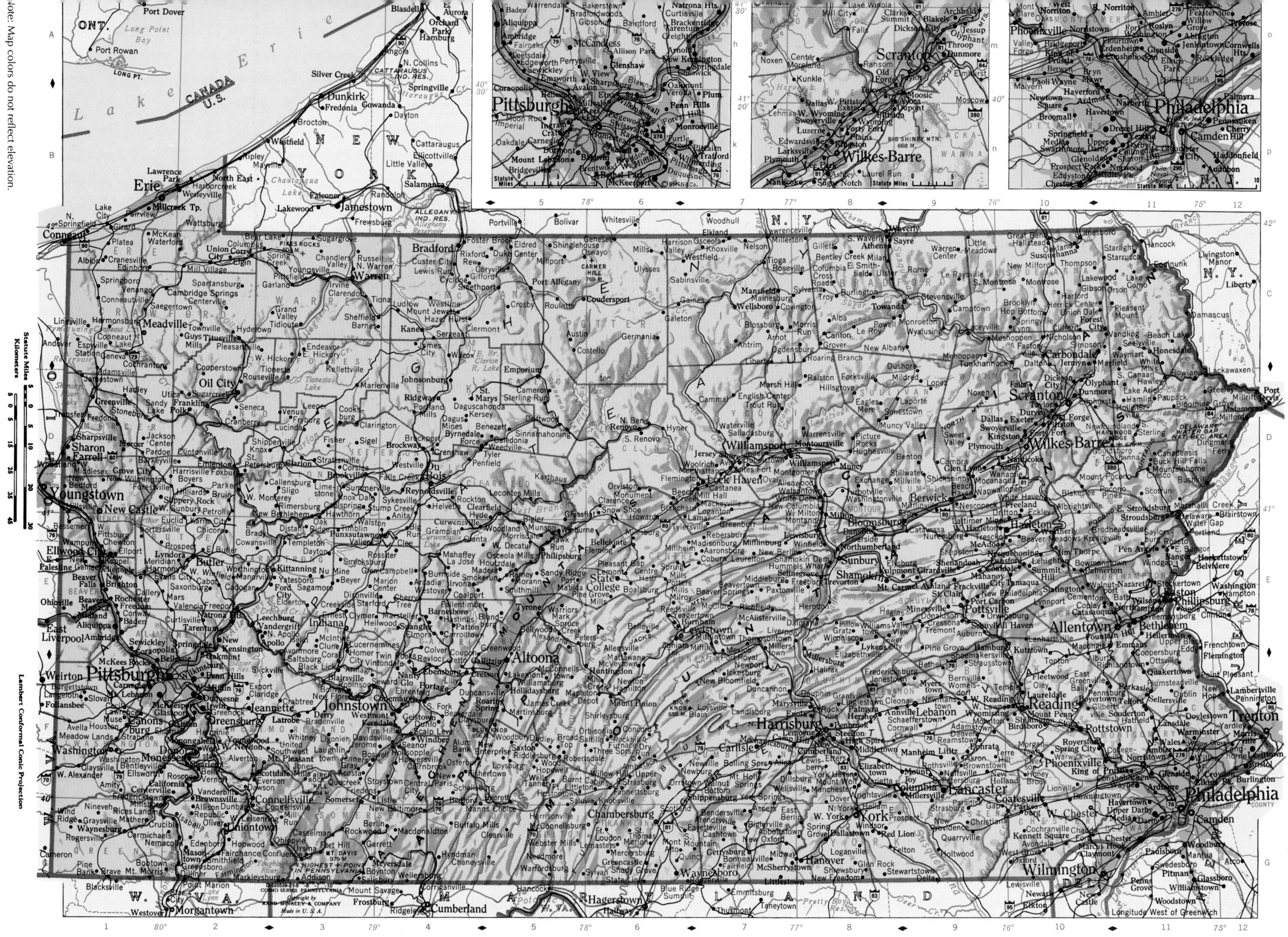
Pittsburgh
Philadelphia
Scranton
Wilkes-Barre
Harrisburg
Erie
Allentown
Statute Miles
Kilometers
Lambert Conformal Conic Projection
Note: Map colors do not reflect elevation.

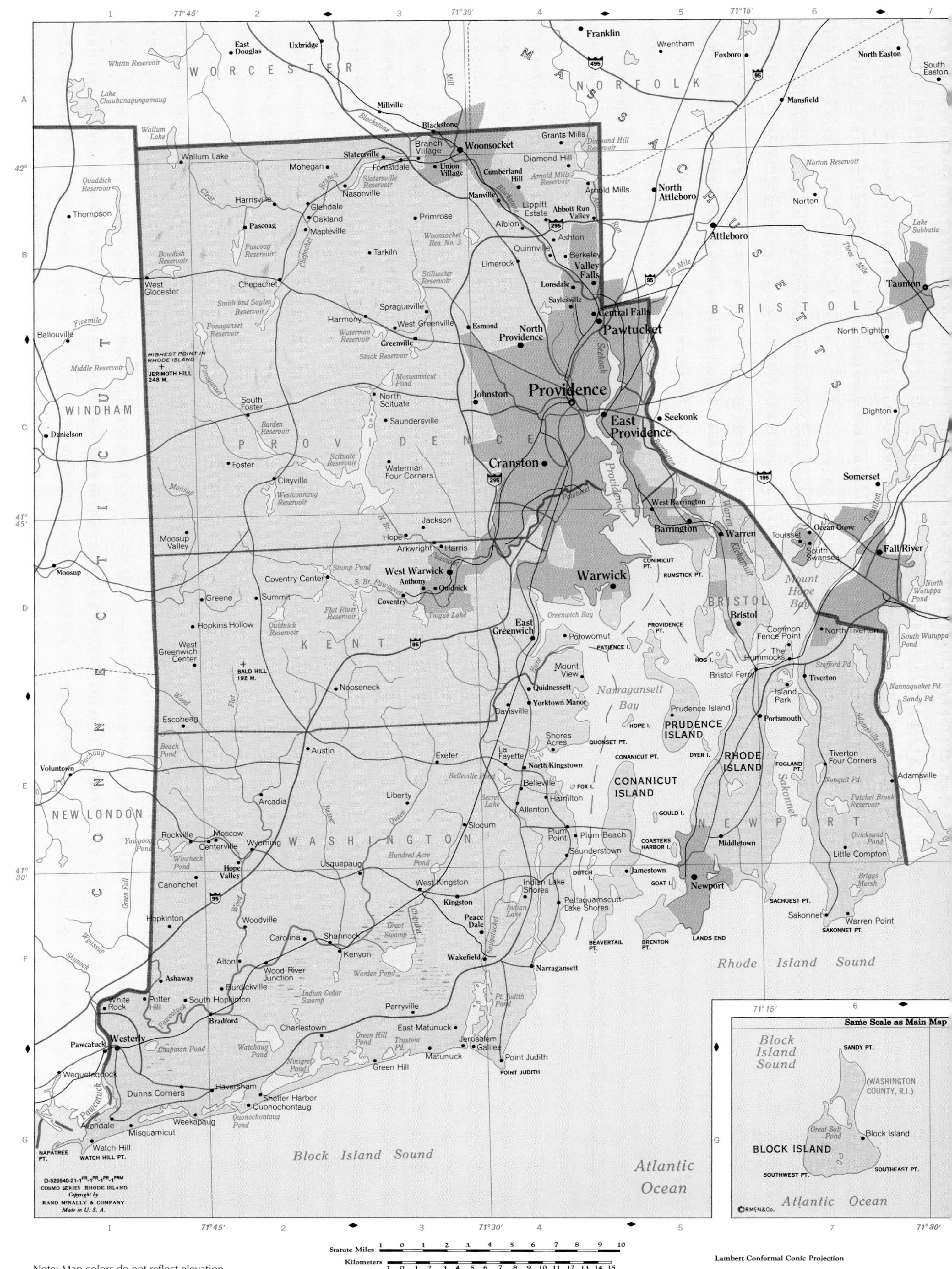

Note: Map colors do not reflect elevation.

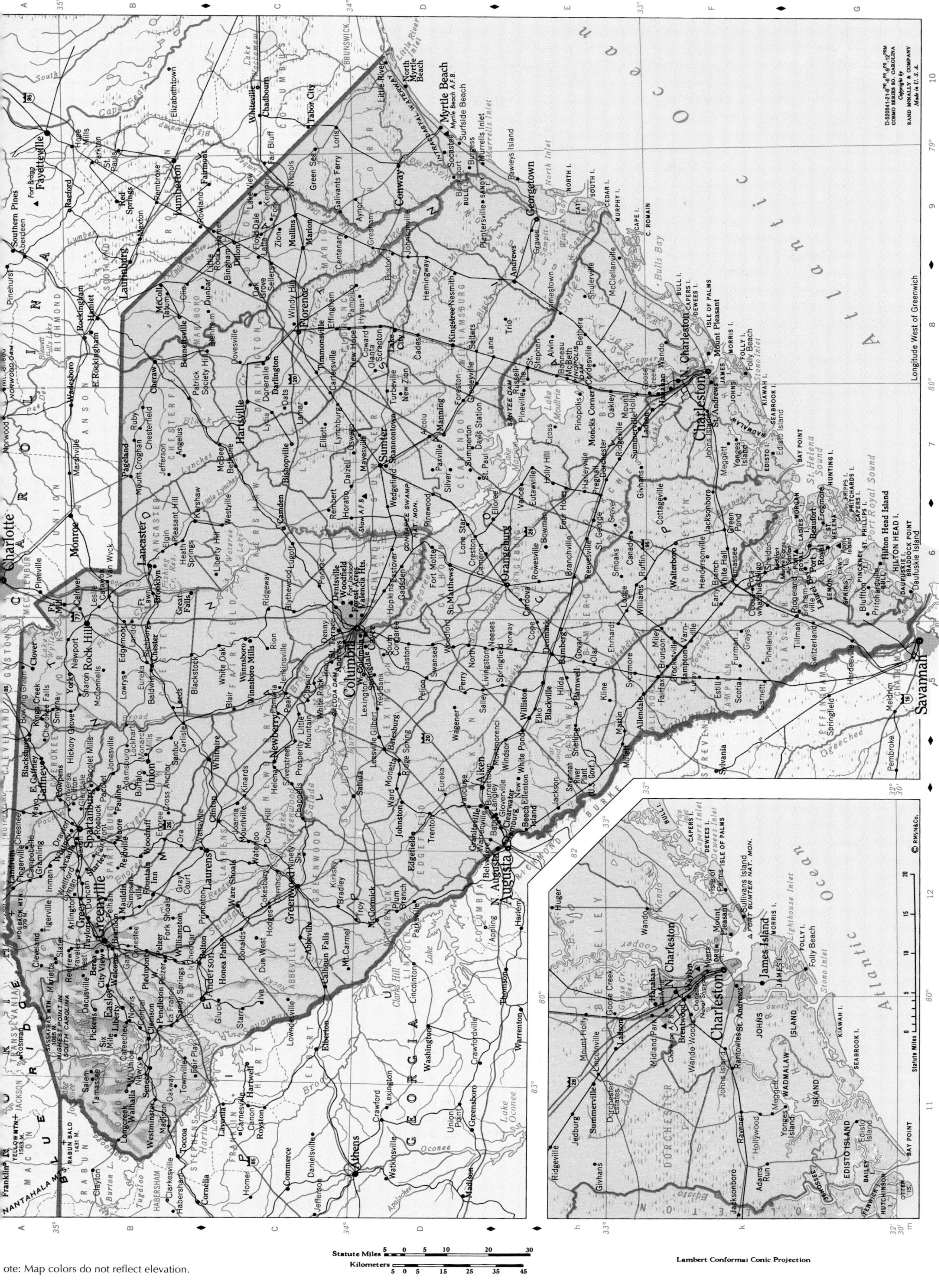

Statute Miles 5 0 5 10 20 30
Kilometers 5 0 5 15 25 35 45

ote: Map colors do not reflect elevation.

Lambert Conformal Conic Projection

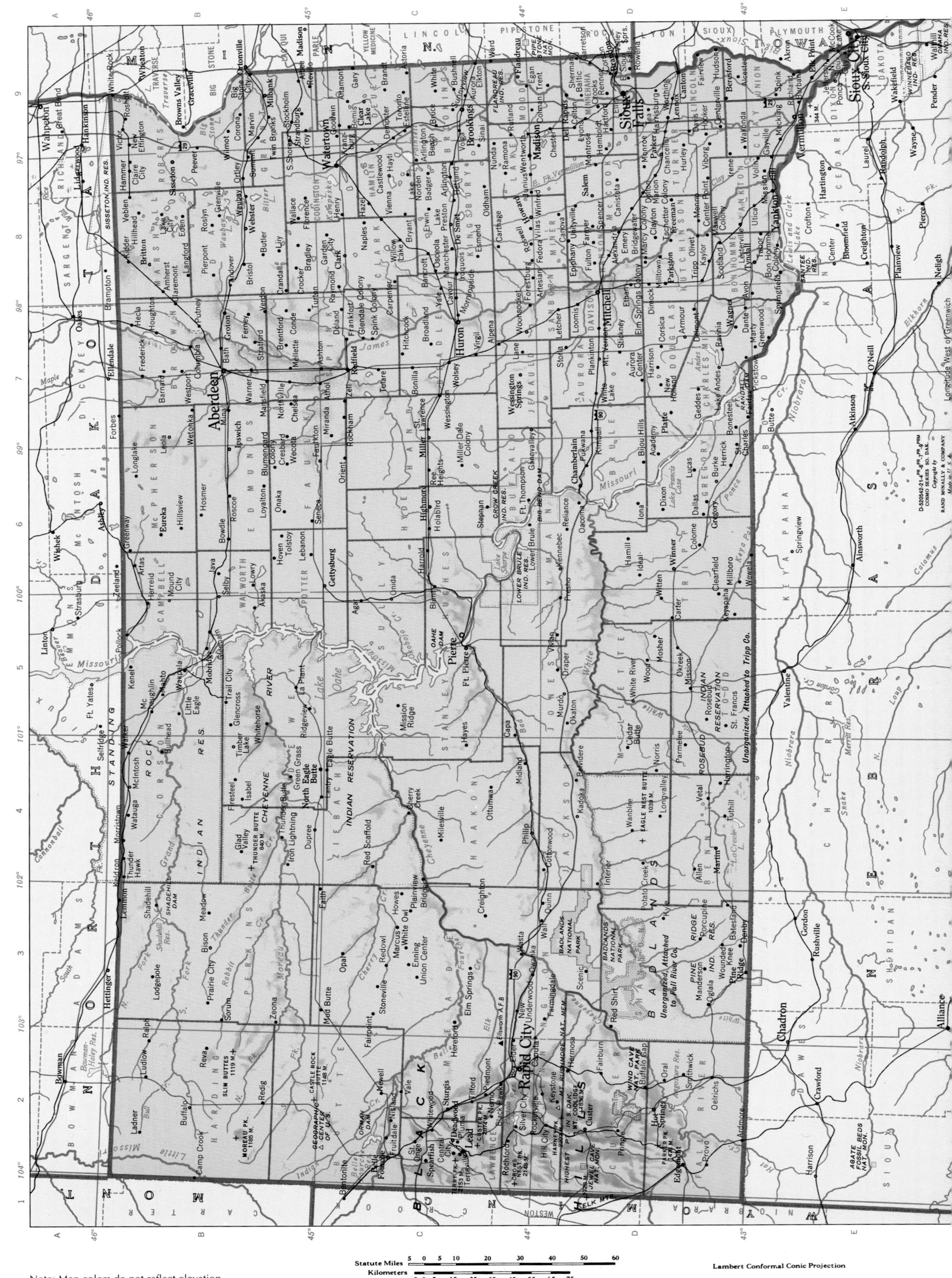

Note: Map colors do not reflect elevation.

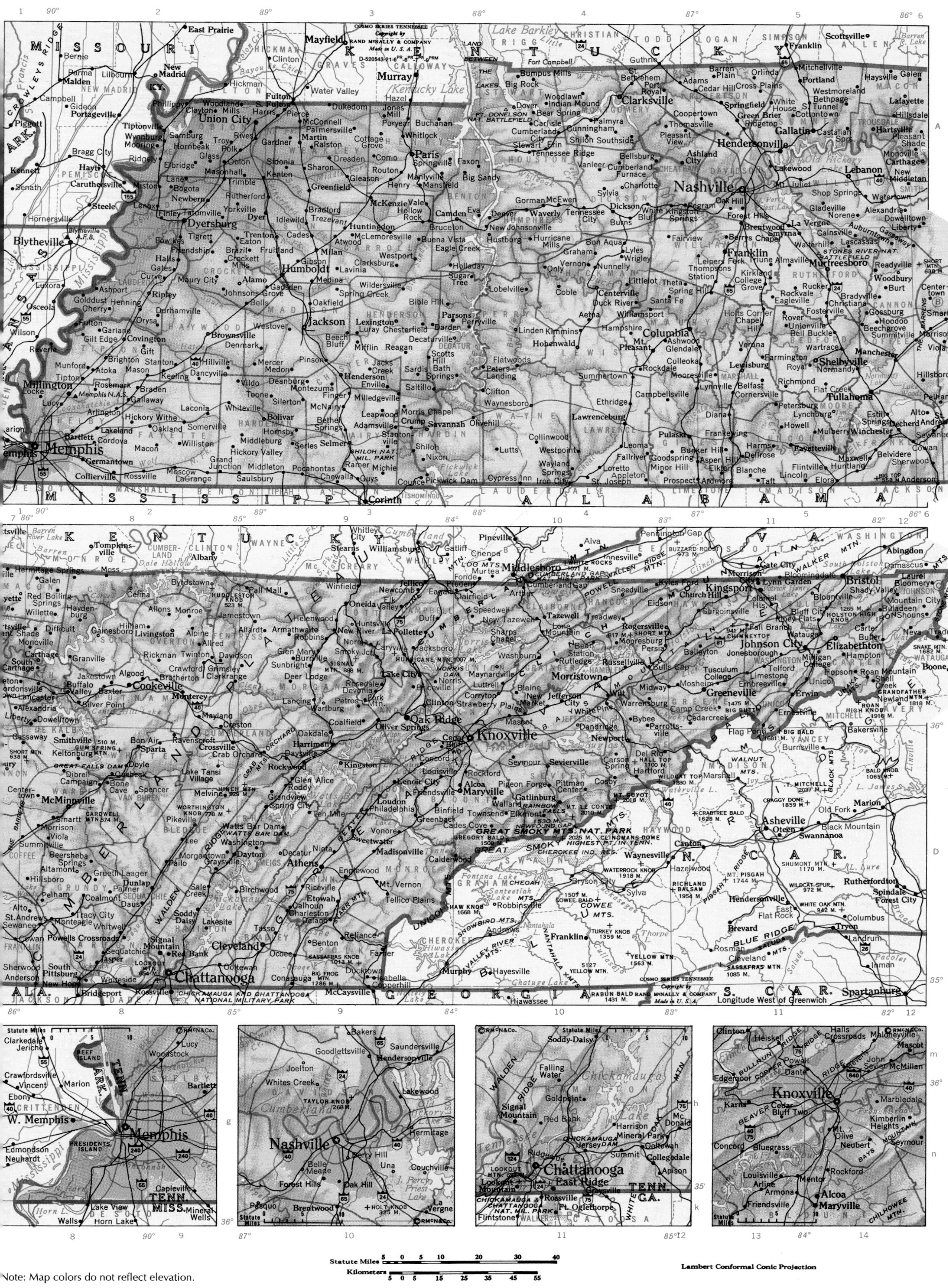

Note: Map colors do not reflect elevation.

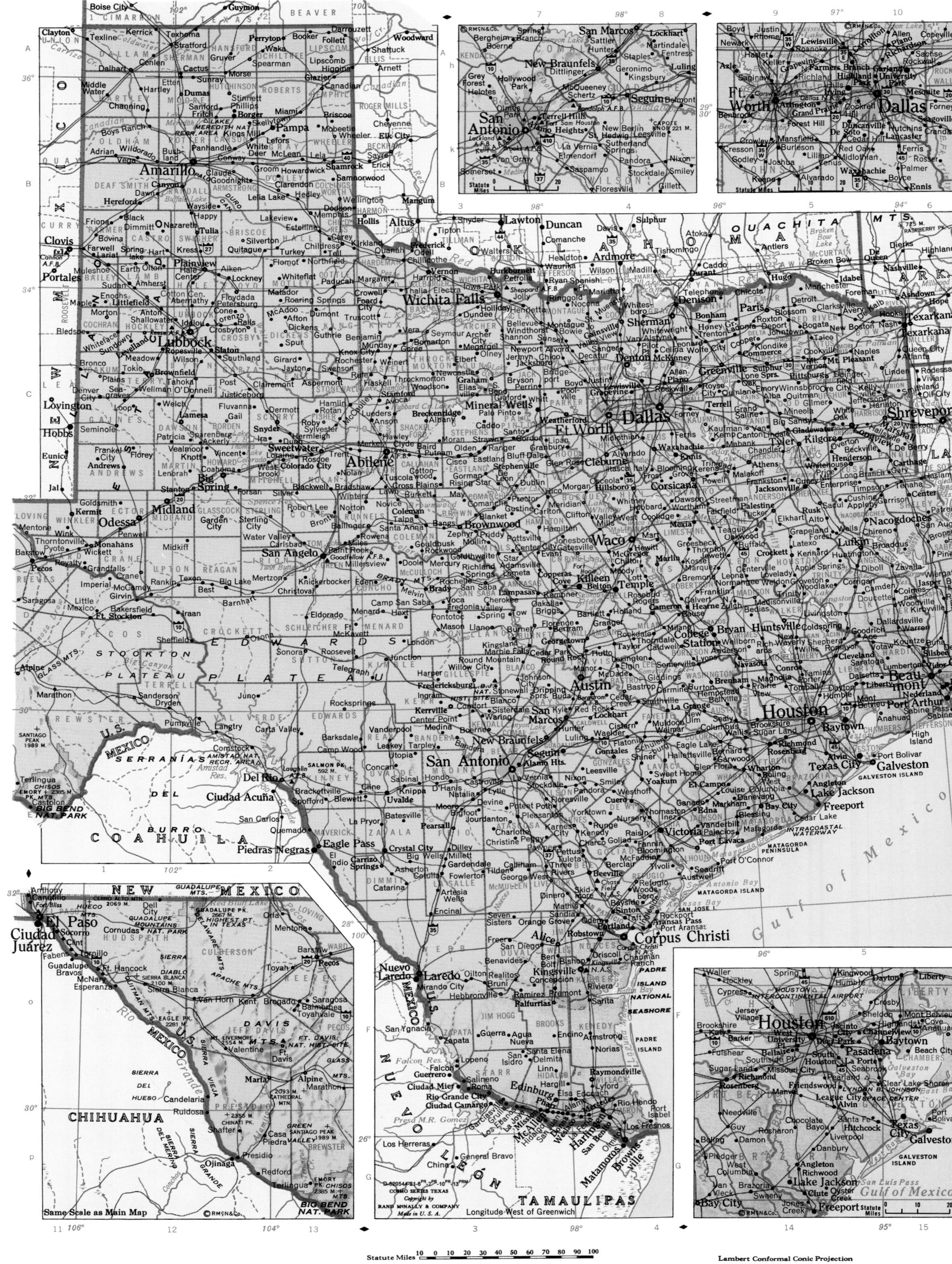

Note: Map colors do not reflect elevation.

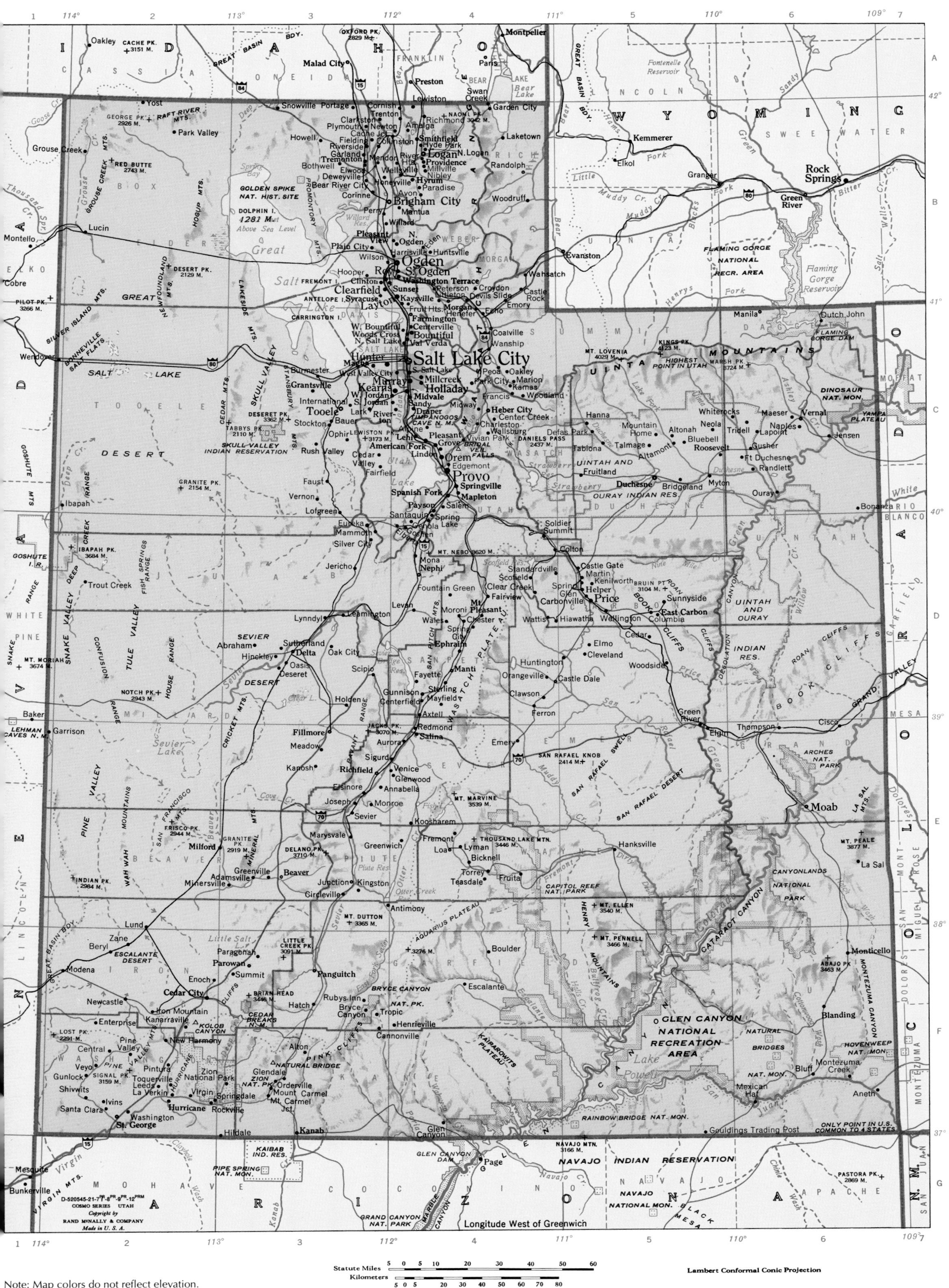

Note: Map colors do not reflect elevation.

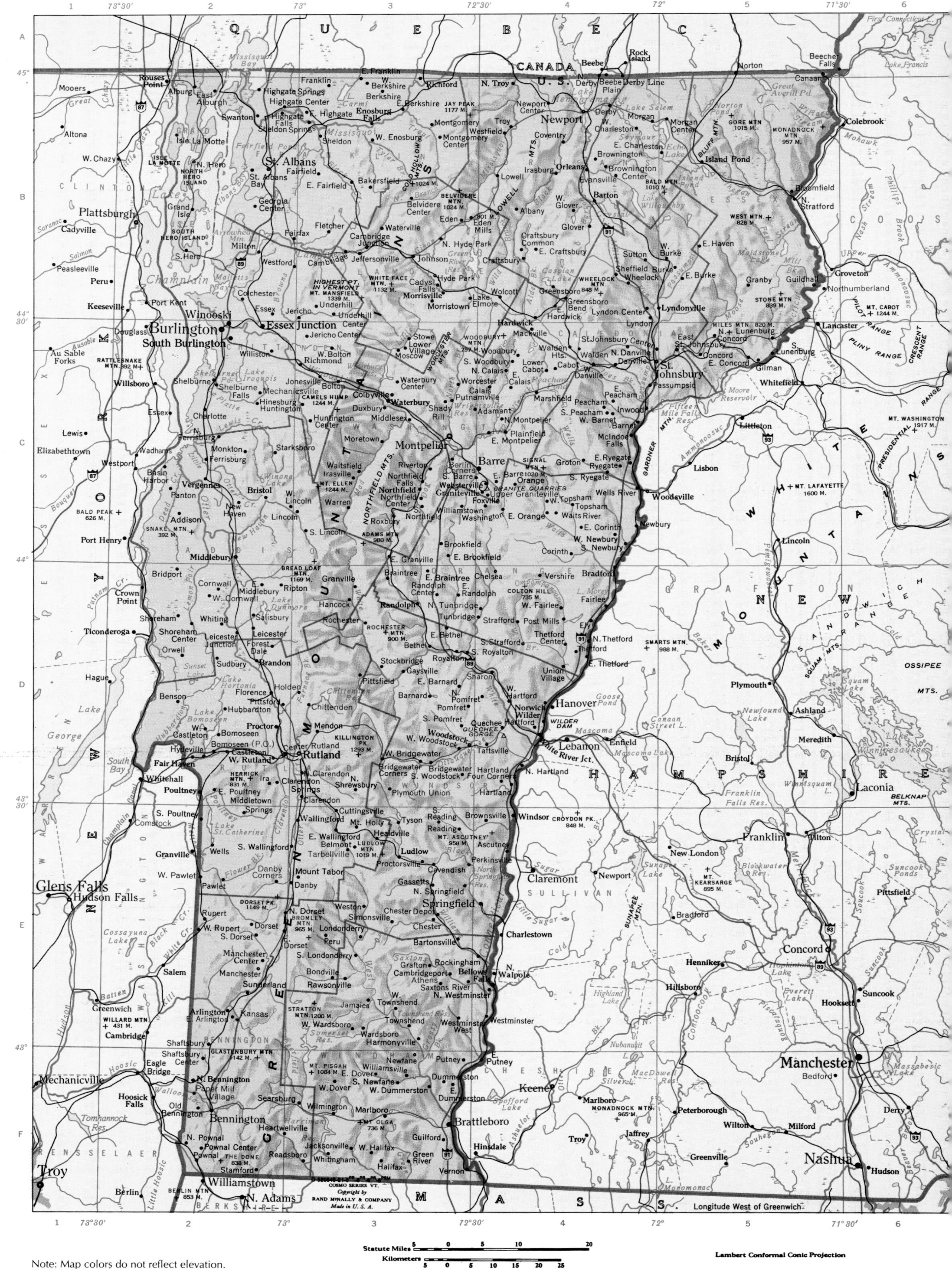

Note: Map colors do not reflect elevation.

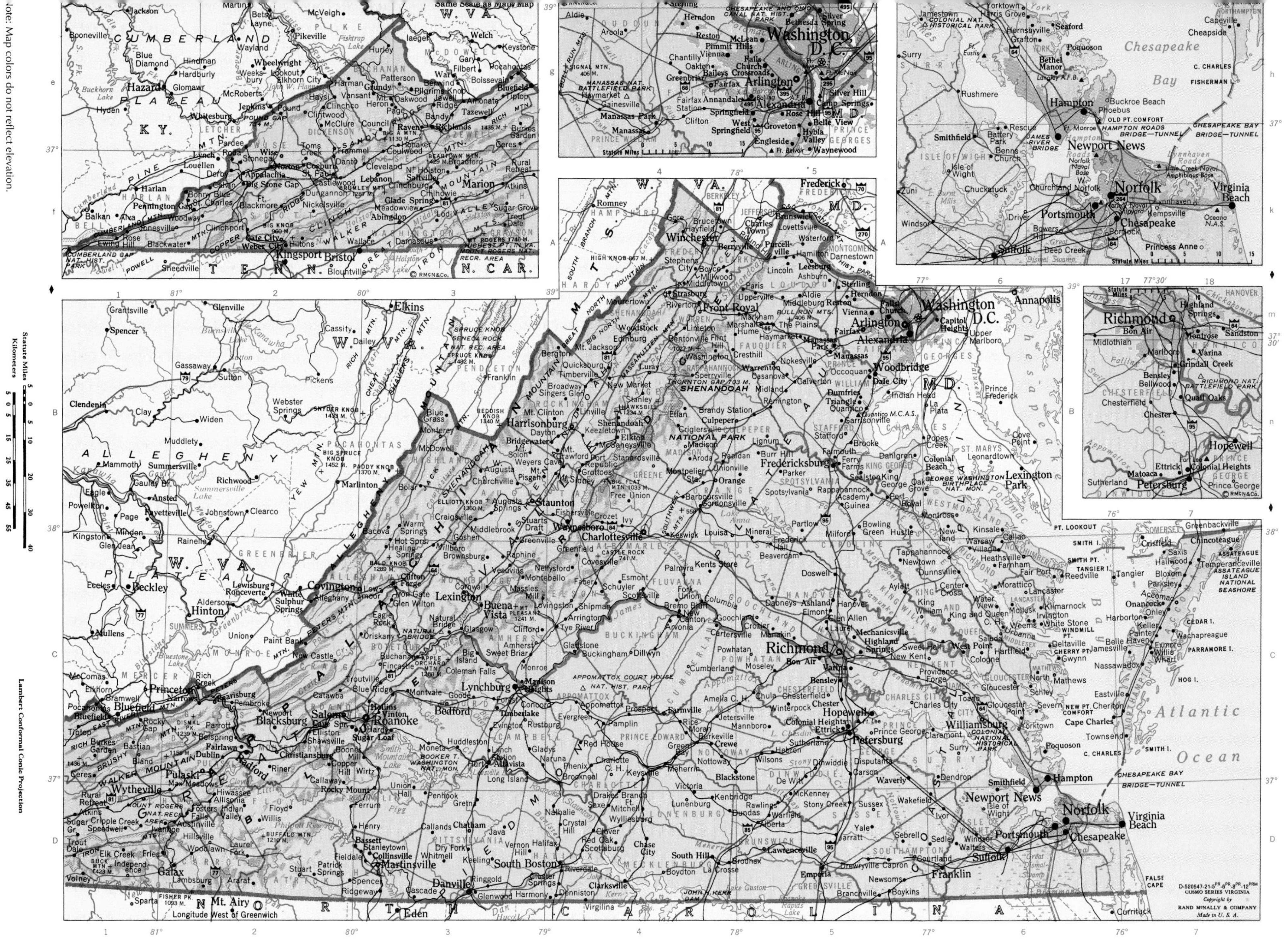

Statute Miles 5 0 5 10 20 30 40

Kilometers 5 0 5 15 25 35 45 55

Lambert Conformal Conic Projection

Note: Map colors do not reflect elevation.

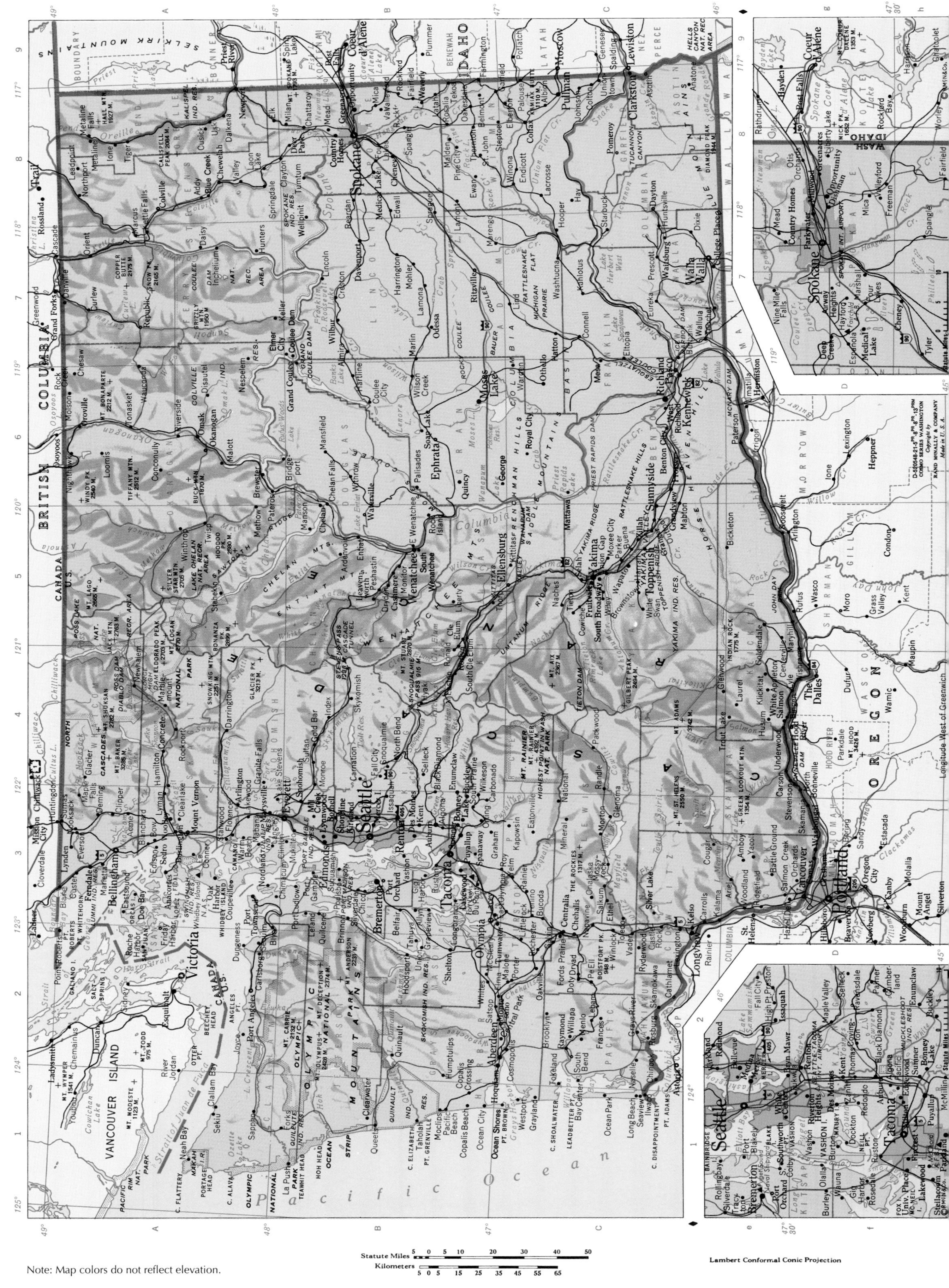

Note: Map colors do not reflect elevation.

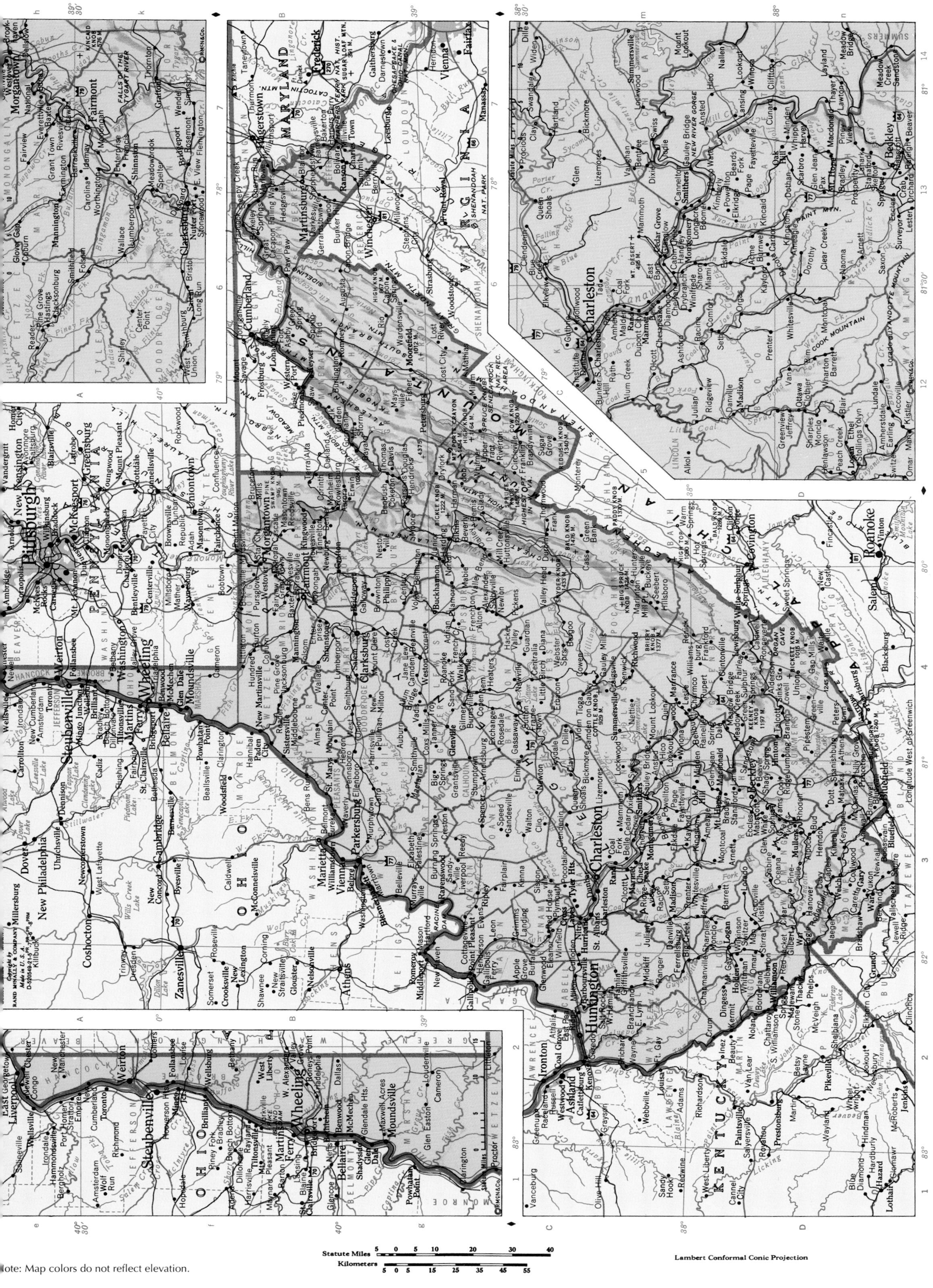

Note: Map colors do not reflect elevation.

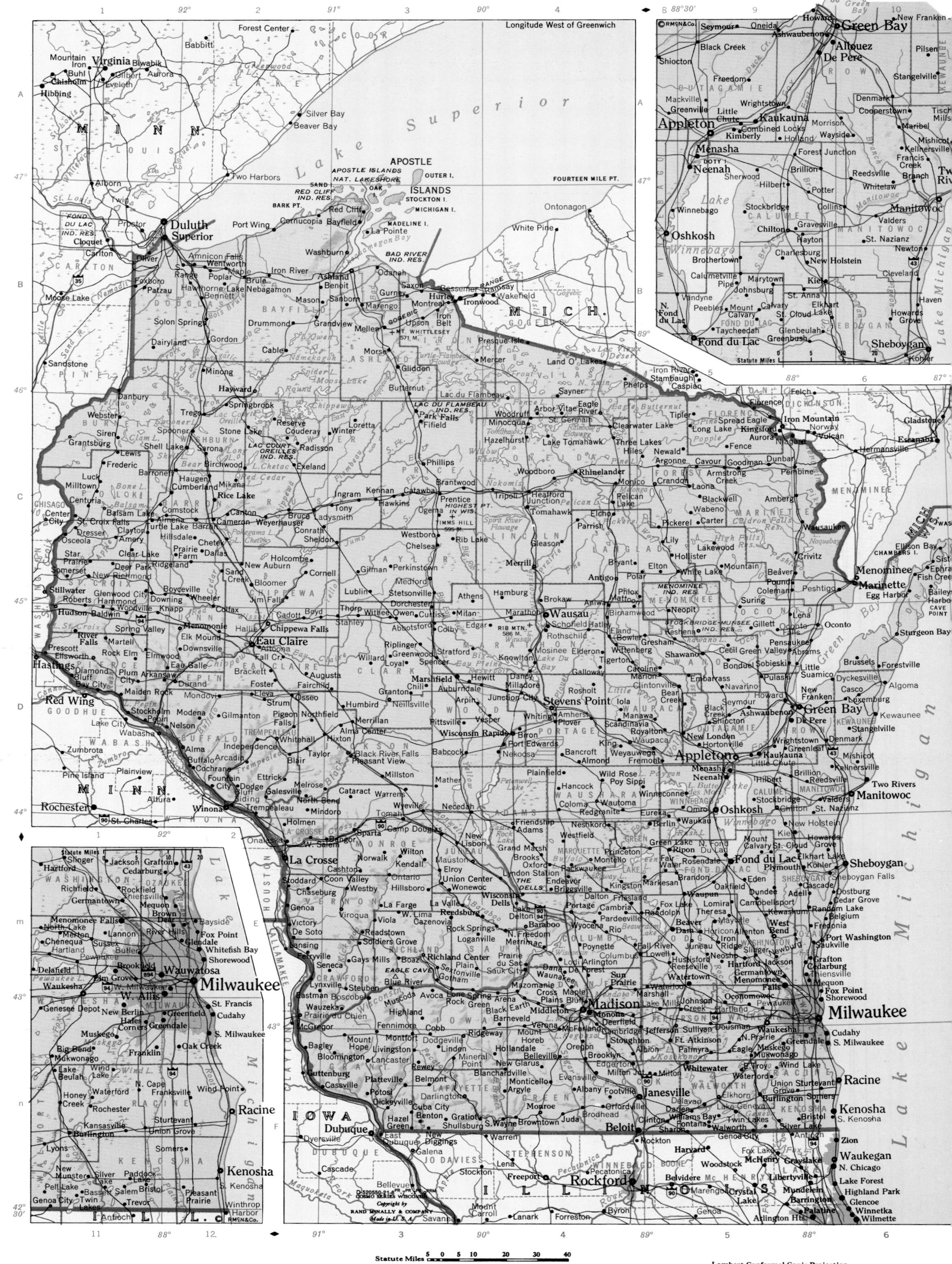

Note: Map colors do not reflect elevation.

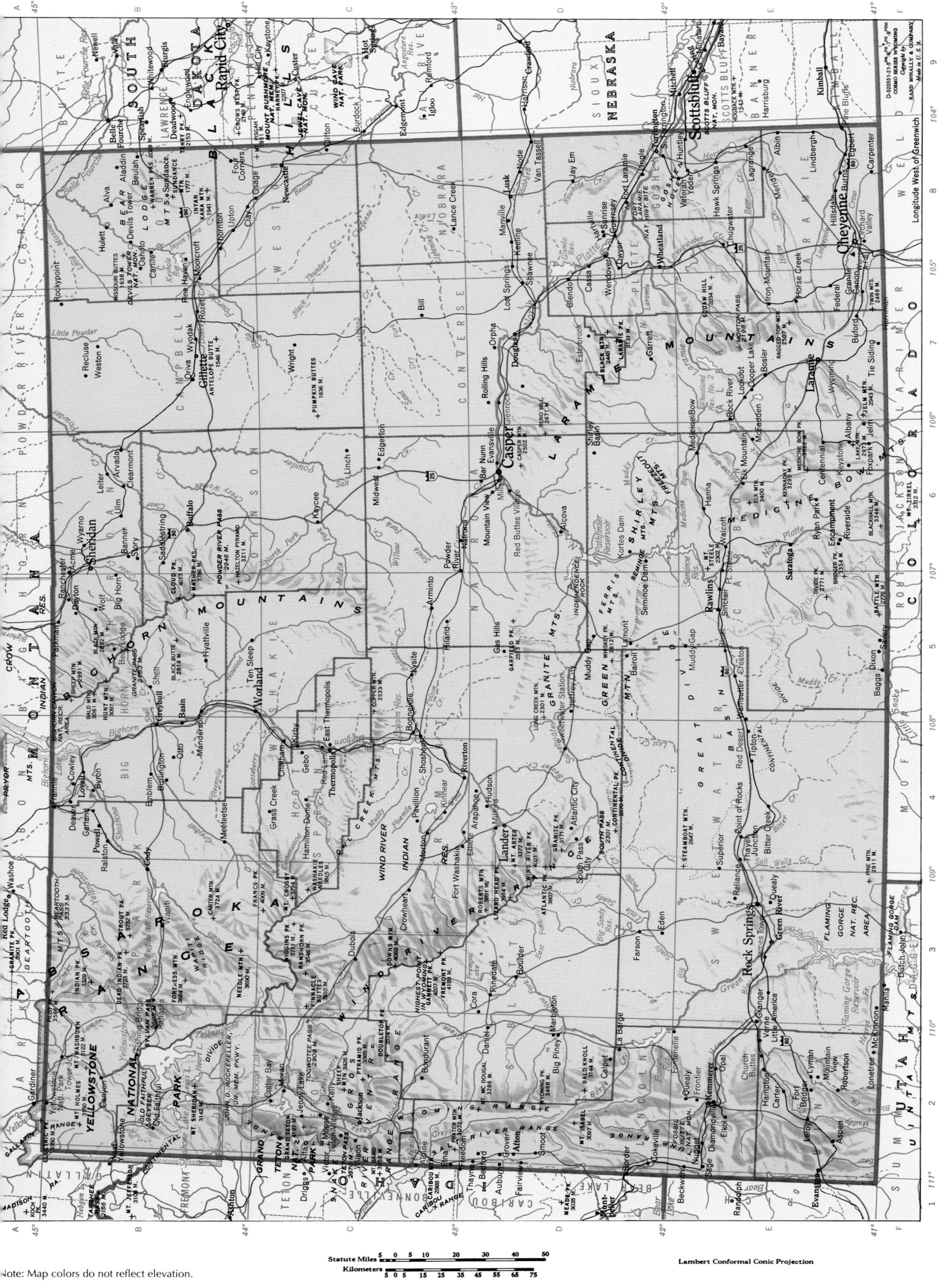

Statute Miles 5 0 5 10 20 30 40 50
Kilometers 5 0 5 15 25 35 45 55 65 75

Lambert Conformal Conic Projection

Note: Map colors do not reflect elevation.

0 400 800 1600 2400 3200 4000 km
0 400 800 1600 2400 miles

Scale 1 : 35 000 000
Azimuthal Equidistant Projection

Index to World Reference Maps

Introduction to the Index

This index includes in a single alphabetical list approximately 45,000 names of features that appear on the reference maps. Each name is followed by the name of the country or continent in which it is located, a map reference key, and a page reference.

Names The names of cities appear in the index in regular type. The names of all other features appear in *italics,* followed by descriptive terms (hill, mtn., state) to indicate their nature.

Abbreviations of names on the maps have been standardized as much as possible. Names that are abbreviated on the maps are generally spelled out in full in the index.

Country names and names of features that extend beyond the boundaries of one country are followed by the name of the continent in which each is located. Country designations follow the names of all other places in the index. The locations of places in the United States, Canada, and the United Kingdom are further defined by abbreviations that indicate the state, province, or political division in which each is located.

All abbreviations used in the index are defined in the List of Abbreviations below.

Alphabetization Names are alphabetized in the order of the letters of the English alphabet. Spanish *ll* and *ch,* for example, are not treated as distinct letters. Furthermore, diacritical marks are disregarded in alphabetization—German or Scandinavian *ä* or *ö* are treated as *a* or *o.*

The names of physical features may appear inverted, since they are always alphabetized under the proper, not the generic, part of the name, thus: "Gibraltar, Strait of". Otherwise every entry, whether consisting of one word or more, is alphabetized as a single continuous entity. "Lakeland", for example, appears after "La Crosse" and before "La Salle". Names beginning with articles (Le Havre, Den Helder, Al-Manāmah) are not inverted. Names beginning "St.", "Ste." and "Sainte" are alphabetized as though spelled "Saint".

In the case of identical names, towns are listed first, then political divisions, then physical features. Entries that are completely identical are listed alphabetically by country name.

Map Reference Keys and Page References The map reference keys and page references are found in the last two columns of each entry.

Each map reference key consists of a letter and number. The letters appear along the sides of the maps. Lowercase letters indicate reference to inset maps. Numbers appear across the tops and bottoms of the maps.

Map reference keys for point features, such as cities and mountain peaks, indicate the locations of the symbols. For other features, such as countries, mountain ranges, or rivers, locations are given for the names.

The page number generally refers to the main map for the country in which the feature is located. Page references to two-page maps always refer to the left-hand page.

List of Abbreviations

Ab., Can.	Alberta, Can.
Afg.	Afghanistan
Afr.	Africa
Ak., U.S.	Alaska, U.S.
Al., U.S.	Alabama, U.S.
Alb.	Albania
Alg.	Algeria
Am. Sam.	American Samoa
And.	Andorra
anch.	anchorage
Ang.	Angola
Anguilla	Anguilla
Ant.	Antarctica
Antig.	Antigua and Barbuda
Ar., U.S.	Arkansas, U.S.
Arg.	Argentina
Arm.	Armenia
Aruba	Aruba
Asia	Asia
Aus.	Austria
Austl.	Australia
Az., U.S.	Arizona, U.S.
Azer.	Azerbaijan
b.	bay, gulf, inlet, lagoon
Bah.	Bahamas
Bahr.	Bahrain
Barb.	Barbados
B.C., Can.	British Columbia, Can.
Bdi.	Burundi
Bel.	Belgium
Belize	Belize
Bela.	Belarus
Benin	Benin
Ber.	Bermuda
Bhu.	Bhutan
B.I.O.T.	British Indian Ocean Territory
Bngl.	Bangladesh
Bol.	Bolivia
Bos.	Bosnia and Herzegovina
Bots.	Botswana
Braz.	Brazil
Br. Vir. Is.	British Virgin Islands
Bru.	Brunei
Bul.	Bulgaria
Burkina	Burkina Faso
c.	cape, point
Ca., U.S.	California, U.S.
Camb.	Cambodia
Cam.	Cameroon
Can.	Canada
C.A.R.	Central African Republic
Cay. Is.	Cayman Islands
Chad	Chad
Chile	Chile
China	China
Christ. I.	Christmas Island
C. Iv.	Cote d'Ivoire
clf.	cliff, escarpment
Co., U.S.	Colorado, U.S.
co.	county, parish
Cocos Is.	Cocos (Keeling) Islands
Col.	Colombia
Com.	Comoros
Congo	Congo
cont.	continent
Cook Is.	Cook Islands
C.R.	Costa Rica
crat.	crater
Cro.	Croatia
Ct., U.S.	Connecticut, U.S.
ctry.	independent country
Cuba	Cuba
C.V.	Cape Verde
Cyp.	Cyprus
Czech Rep.	Czech Republic
D.C., U.S.	District of Columbia, U.S.
De., U.S.	Delaware, U.S.
Den.	Denmark
dep.	dependency, colony
depr.	depression
dept.	department, district
des.	desert
Dji.	Djibouti
Dom.	Dominica
Dom. Rep.	Dominican Republic
D.R.C.	Democratic Republic of the Congo
Ec.	Ecuador
Egypt	Egypt
El Sal.	El Salvador
Eng., U.K.	England, U.K.
Eq. Gui.	Equatorial Guinea
Erit.	Eritrea
Est.	Estonia
est.	estuary
Eth.	Ethiopia
Eur.	Europe
Falk. Is.	Falkland Islands
Far. Is.	Faroe Islands
Fiji	Fiji
Fin.	Finland
Fl., U.S.	Florida, U.S.
for.	forest, moor
Fr.	France
Fr. Gu.	French Guiana
Fr. Poly.	French Polynesia
Ga., U.S.	Georgia, U.S.
Gabon	Gabon
Gam.	Gambia
Gaza Str.	Gaza Strip
Geor.	Georgia
Ger.	Germany
Ghana	Ghana
Gib.	Gibraltar
Golan Hts.	Golan Heights
Grc.	Greece
Gren.	Grenada
Grnld.	Greenland
Guad.	Guadeloupe
Guam	Guam
Guat.	Guatemala
Guernsey	Guernsey
Gui.	Guinea
Gui.-B.	Guinea-Bissau
Guy.	Guyana
Haiti	Haiti
Hi., U.S.	Hawaii, U.S.
hist.	historic site, ruins
hist. reg.	historic region
Hond.	Honduras
Hung.	Hungary
i.	island
Ia., U.S.	Iowa, U.S.
Ice.	Iceland
ice	ice feature, glacier
Id., U.S.	Idaho, U.S.
Il., U.S.	Illinois, U.S.
In., U.S.	Indiana, U.S.
India	India
Indon.	Indonesia
I. of Man	Isle of Man
Iran	Iran
Iraq	Iraq
Ire.	Ireland
Isr.	Israel
is.	islands
Italy	Italy
Jam.	Jamaica
Japan	Japan
Jersey	Jersey
Jer.	Jericho Area
Jord.	Jordan
Kaz.	Kazakstan
Kenya	Kenya
Kir.	Kiribati
Ks., U.S.	Kansas, U.S.
Kuw.	Kuwait
Ky., U.S.	Kentucky, U.S.
Kyrg.	Kyrgyzstan
l.	lake, pond
La., U.S.	Louisiana, U.S.
Laos	Laos
Lat.	Latvia
Leb.	Lebanon
Leso.	Lesotho
Lib.	Liberia
Libya	Libya
Liech.	Liechtenstein
Lith.	Lithuania
Lux.	Luxembourg
Ma., U.S.	Massachusetts, U.S.
Macau	Macau
Mac.	Macedonia
Madag.	Madagascar
Malay.	Malaysia
Mald.	Maldives
Mali	Mali
Malta	Malta
Marsh. Is.	Marshall Islands
Mart.	Martinique
Maur.	Mauritania
May.	Mayotte
Mb., Can.	Manitoba, Can.
Md., U.S.	Maryland, U.S.
Me., U.S.	Maine, U.S.
Mex.	Mexico
Mi., U.S.	Michigan, U.S.
Micron.	Micronesia, Federated States of
Mid. Is.	Midway Islands
mil.	military installation
Mn., U.S.	Minnesota, U.S.
Mo., U.S.	Missouri, U.S.
Mol.	Moldova
Mon.	Monaco
Mong.	Mongolia
Monts.	Montserrat
Mor.	Morocco
Moz.	Mozambique
Mrts.	Mauritius
Ms., U.S.	Mississippi, U.S.
Mt., U.S.	Montana, U.S.
mth.	river mouth or channel
mtn.	mountain
mts.	mountains
Mwi.	Malawi
Myan.	Myanmar
N.A.	North America
Nauru	Nauru
N.B., Can.	New Brunswick, Can.
N.C., U.S.	North Carolina, U.S.
N. Cal.	New Caledonia
N. Cyp.	Cyprus, North
N.D., U.S.	North Dakota, U.S.
Ne., U.S.	Nebraska, U.S.
Nepal	Nepal
Neth.	Netherlands
Neth. Ant.	Netherlands Antilles
Nf., Can.	Newfoundland, Can.
N.H., U.S.	New Hampshire, U.S.
Nic.	Nicaragua
Nig.	Nigeria
Niger	Niger
N. Ire., U.K.	Northern Ireland, U.K.
Niue	Niue
N.J., U.S.	New Jersey, U.S.
N. Kor.	Korea, North
N.M., U.S.	New Mexico, U.S.
N. Mar. Is.	Northern Mariana Islands
Nmb.	Namibia
Nor.	Norway
Norf. I.	Norfolk Island
N.S., Can.	Nova Scotia, Can.
N.T., Can.	Northwest Territories, Can.
Nu., Can.	Nunavut, Can.
Nv., U.S.	Nevada, U.S.
N.Y., U.S.	New York, U.S.
N.Z.	New Zealand
Oc.	Oceania
Oh., U.S.	Ohio, U.S.
Ok., U.S.	Oklahoma, U.S.
Oman	Oman
On., Can.	Ontario, Can.
Or., U.S.	Oregon, U.S.
Pa., U.S.	Pennsylvania, U.S.
Pak.	Pakistan
Palau	Palau
Pan.	Panama
Pap. N. Gui.	Papua New Guinea
Para.	Paraguay
P.E., Can.	Prince Edward Island, Can.
pen.	peninsula
Peru	Peru
Phil.	Philippines
Pit.	Pitcairn
pl.	plain, flat
plat.	plateau, highland
Pol.	Poland
Port.	Portugal
P.Q., Can.	Quebec, Can.
P.R.	Puerto Rico
prov.	province, region
Qatar	Qatar
Reu.	Reunion
reg.	physical region
res.	reservoir
rf.	reef, shoal
R.I., U.S.	Rhode Island, U.S.
Rom.	Romania
Russia	Russia
Rw.	Rwanda
S.A.	South America
S. Afr.	South Africa
Samoa	Samoa
Sau. Ar.	Saudi Arabia
S.C., U.S.	South Carolina, U.S.
sci.	scientific station
Scot., U.K.	Scotland, U.K.
S.D., U.S.	South Dakota, U.S.
Sen.	Senegal
Sey.	Seychelles
S. Geor.	South Georgia and the South Sandwich Islands
Sing.	Singapore
Sk., Can.	Saskatchewan, Can.
S. Kor.	Korea, South
S.L.	Sierra Leone
Slvk.	Slovakia
Slvn.	Slovenia
S. Mar.	San Marino
Sol. Is.	Solomon Islands
Som.	Somalia
Spain	Spain
Sp. N. Afr.	Spanish North Africa
Sri L.	Sri Lanka
state	state, republic, canton
St. Hel.	St. Helena
St. K./N.	St. Kitts and Nevis
St. Luc.	St. Lucia
stm.	stream (river, creek)
St. P./M.	St. Pierre and Miquelon
strt.	strait
S. Tom./P.	Sao Tome and Principe
St. Vin.	St. Vincent and the Grenadines
Sudan	Sudan
Sur.	Suriname
Swaz.	Swaziland
sw.	swamp, marsh
Swe.	Sweden
Switz.	Switzerland
Syria	Syria
Tai.	Taiwan
Taj.	Tajikistan
Tan.	Tanzania
T./C. Is.	Turks and Caicos Islands
ter.	territory
Thai.	Thailand
Tn., U.S.	Tennessee, U.S.
Togo	Togo
Tok.	Tokelau
Tonga	Tonga
Trin.	Trinidad and Tobago
Tun.	Tunisia
Tur.	Turkey
Turk.	Turkmenistan
Tuvalu	Tuvalu
Tx., U.S.	Texas, U.S.
U.A.E.	United Arab Emirates
Ug.	Uganda
U.K.	United Kingdom
Ukr.	Ukraine
Ur.	Uruguay
U.S.	United States
Ut., U.S.	Utah, U.S.
Uzb.	Uzbekistan
Va., U.S.	Virginia, U.S.
val.	valley, watercourse
Vanuatu	Vanuatu
Vat.	Vatican City
Ven.	Venezuela
Viet.	Vietnam
V.I.U.S.	Virgin Islands (U.S.)
vol.	volcano
Vt., U.S.	Vermont, U.S.
Wa., U.S.	Washington, U.S.
Wake I.	Wake Island
Wales, U.K.	Wales, U.K.
Wal./F.	Wallis and Futuna
W.B.	West Bank
Wi., U.S.	Wisconsin, U.S.
W. Sah.	Western Sahara
wtfl.	waterfall
W.V., U.S.	West Virginia, U.S.
Wy., U.S.	Wyoming, U.S.
Yemen	Yemen
Yk., Can.	Yukon Territory, Can.
Yugo.	Yugoslavia
Zam.	Zambia
Zimb.	Zimbabwe

Name — Map Ref. — Page

A

Aachen, Ger. **E10** 12
Aali, Sadd el-, Egypt **F11** 48
Äänekoski, Fin. **E11** 10
Aba, China **E8** 28
Aba, Nig. **E6** 50
Abaco, i., Bah. **C9** 76
Ābādān, Iran **D5** 42
Ābādeh, Iran **D6** 42
Abadla, Alg. **D4** 48
Abaeté, Braz. **E2** 74
Abaetetuba, Braz. **B2** 74
Abag Qi, China **C10** 28
Abaj, Kaz. **B2** 28
Abajo Peak, mtn., Ut., U.S. **F6** 137
Abakaliki, Nig. **E6** 50
Abakan, Russia **D11** 26
Abala, Niger **D5** 50
Abancay, Peru **F5** 70
Abashiri, Japan **B4** 31
Abau, Pap. N. Gui. **I12** 32
Ābay see Blue Nile, stm., Afr. **H11** 48
Ābaya Hāyk', l., Eth. **B7** 54
Abaza, Russia **D11** 26
Abbaye, Point, c., Mi., U.S. **B2** 115
Abbeville, Fr. **B7** 16
Abbeville, Al., U.S. **D4** 94
Abbeville, Ga., U.S. **E3** 103
Abbeville, La., U.S. **E3** 111
Abbeville, S.C., U.S. **C3** 133
Abbeville, co., S.C., U.S. **C2** 133
Abbotsford, Wi., U.S. **D3** 142
Abbott Butte, mtn., Or., U.S. **E4** 130
Abbott Run, stm., U.S. **B4** 132
Abbott Run Valley, R.I., U.S. **B4** 132
Ābdānān, Iran **F12** 44
Abdulino, Russia **D9** 22
Abe, Lake, l., Afr. **H13** 48
Abéché, Chad **H9** 48
Abengourou, C. Iv. **E4** 50
Åbenrå, Den. **I3** 10
Abeokuta, Nig. **E5** 50
Aberdeen, Scot., U.K. **B5** 12
Aberdeen, Id., U.S. **G6** 105
Aberdeen, Md., U.S. **A5** 113
Aberdeen, Ms., U.S. **B5** 117
Aberdeen, N.C., U.S. **B3** 126
Aberdeen, Oh., U.S. **D2** 128
Aberdeen, S.D., U.S. **B7** 134
Aberdeen, Wa., U.S. **C2** 140
Aberdeen Lake, l., Nu., Can. **E20** 82
Abernathy, Tx., U.S. **C2** 136
Abert, Lake, l., Or., U.S. **E6** 130
Abert Rim, clf, Or., U.S. **E6** 130
Aberystwyth, Wales, U.K. **D4** 12
Abez', Russia **A11** 22
Abhā, Sau. Ar. **G4** 38
Abhar, Iran **D13** 44
Abidjan, C. Iv. **E4** 50
Abilene, Ks., U.S. **D6** 109
Abilene, Tx., U.S. **C3** 136
Abingdon, Il., U.S. **C3** 106
Abingdon, Md., U.S. **B5** 113
Abingdon, Va., U.S. **f10** 139
Abington, Ma., U.S. **B6** 114
Abington [Township], Pa., U.S. **o21** 131
Abinsk, Russia **G15** 20
Abisko, Swe. **B8** 10
Abita Springs, La., U.S. **D5** 111
Abitibi, stm., On., Can. **H23** 82
Åbo see Turku, Fin. **F10** 10
Abomey, Benin **E5** 50
Abongabong, Gunung, mtn., Indon. **C1** 36
Abong Mbang, Cam. **C2** 54
Abou-Deïa, Chad **H8** 48
Abraham Lake, res., Ab., Can. **C2** 84
Abraham Lincoln Birthplace National Historic Site, hist., Ky., U.S. **C4** 110
Abra Pampa, Arg. **C4** 72
Absaroka Range, mts., U.S. **F7** 143
Absarokee, Mt., U.S. **E7** 119
Absecon, N.J., U.S. **E4** 123
Absecon Inlet, b., N.J., U.S. **E4** 123
Abu Dhabi see Abū Ẓaby, U.A.E. **F6** 42
Abū Ḥamad, Sudan **G11** 48
Abuja, Nig. **E6** 50
Abū Kamāl, Syria **E9** 44
Abū Madd, Ra's, c., Sau. Ar. **F3** 42
Abū Maṭāriq, Sudan **A5** 54
Abunã, Braz. **E6** 70
Ābu Road, India **E2** 40
Abū Ẓaby (Abu Dhabi), U.A.E. **F6** 42
Abu Zenîma, Egypt **F10** 14
Abyad, Al-Baḥr al- (White Nile), stm., Sudan **H11** 48
Abyei, Sudan **B5** 54
Academia, Oh., U.S. **B3** 128
Acadia, co., La., U.S. **D3** 111
Acadia National Park, Me., U.S. **D4** 112
Açailândia, Braz. **B2** 74
Acámbaro, Mex. **C4** 78
Acaponeta, Mex. **C3** 78
Acapulco, Mex. **D5** 78
Acarai Mountains, mts., S.A. **C8** 70
Acaraú, Braz. **B3** 74
Acarigua, Ven. **B6** 70
Acayucan, Mex. **D6** 78
Accomack, co., Va., U.S. **C7** 139
Accoville, W.V., U.S. **D3** 141
Accra, Ghana **E4** 50
Achacachi, Bol. **B4** 72
Achalpur, India **E3** 40
Acheng, China **B13** 28
Acı Göl, l., Tur. **D3** 44
Ačinsk, Russia **D11** 26
Acireale, Italy **F5** 18
Ačisaj, Kaz. **B9** 42
Ackerman, Ms., U.S. **B4** 117
Ackley, Ia., U.S. **B4** 108
Acklins, i., Bah. **D10** 76
Acoma Indian Reservation, N.M., U.S. **C2** 124
Aconcagua, Cerro, mtn., Arg. **E4** 72
Acopiara, Braz. **C4** 74
Açores, is., Port. **F7** 46
A Coruña, Spain **F2** 16
Acre, state, Braz. **E5** 70
Acton, Ma., U.S. **B5** 114
Acton Vale, P.Q., Can. **D5** 90
Acushnet, Ma., U.S. **C6** 114
Acworth, Ga., U.S. **B2** 103
Ada, Ghana **E5** 50
Ada, Mn., U.S. **C2** 116
Ada, Oh., U.S. **B2** 128
Ada, Ok., U.S. **C5** 129
Ada, co., Id., U.S. **F2** 105
Ada, Mount, mtn., Ak., U.S. **m22** 95
Adair, Ia., U.S. **C3** 108
Adair, Ok., U.S. **A6** 129
Adair, co., Ia., U.S. **C3** 108
Adair, co., Ky., U.S. **C4** 110
Adair, co., Mo., U.S. **A5** 118
Adair, co., Ok., U.S. **B7** 129
Adairsville, Ga., U.S. **B2** 103
Adairville, Ky., U.S. **D3** 110
Adak Island, i., Ak., U.S. **E4** 95
Adak Naval Station, mil., Ak., U.S. **E4** 95
Adam, Oman **F7** 38
Adamantina, Braz. **F1** 74
Adamaoua, prov., Cam. **E7** 50
Adamaoua, mts., Afr. **B2** 54
Adamawa see Adamaoua, mts., Afr. **B2** 54
Adam Island, i., Md., U.S. **D5** 113
Adams, Ma., U.S. **A1** 114
Adams, Mn., U.S. **G6** 116
Adams, N.Y., U.S. **B4** 125
Adams, Wi., U.S. **E4** 142
Adams, co., Co., U.S. **B6** 99
Adams, co., Ia., U.S. **C3** 108
Adams, co., Id., U.S. **E2** 105
Adams, co., Il., U.S. **D2** 106
Adams, co., In., U.S. **C8** 107
Adams, co., Ms., U.S. **D2** 117
Adams, co., N.D., U.S. **C3** 127
Adams, co., Ne., U.S. **D7** 120
Adams, co., Oh., U.S. **D2** 128
Adams, co., Pa., U.S. **G7** 131
Adams, co., Wa., U.S. **B7** 140
Adams, co., Wi., U.S. **D4** 142
Adams, Mount, mtn., N.H., U.S. **B4** 122
Adams, Mount, mtn., Wa., U.S. **C4** 140
Adams Point, c., Mi., U.S. **C7** 115
Adams Run, S.C., U.S. **k11** 133
Adamstown, Pa., U.S. **F9** 131
Adamsville, Al., U.S. **f7** 94
Adamsville, R.I., U.S. **E6** 132
Adamsville, Tn., U.S. **B3** 135
Adamsville Brook, stm., R.I., U.S. **E6** 132
'Adan (Aden), Yemen **H5** 38
Adana, Tur. **D6** 44
Adare, Cape, c., Ant. **D22** 67
Adda, stm., Italy **B2** 18
Ad-Dabbah, Sudan **G11** 48
Ad-Dahnā', des., Sau. Ar. **E5** 38
Ad-Dāmir, Sudan **G2** 38
Ad-Dammām, Sau. Ar. **E5** 38
Ad-Dawḥah (Doha), Qatar **E6** 42
Aḍ-Ḍiffah (Libyan Plateau), plat., Afr. **E9** 14
Addis, La., U.S. **D4** 111
Addis Ababa see Ādīs Ābeba, Eth. **B7** 54
Addison, Al., U.S. **A2** 94
Addison, Ct., U.S. **C5** 100
Addison, Il., U.S. **k8** 106
Addison, N.Y., U.S. **C3** 125
Addison, co., Vt., U.S. **C2** 138
Ad-Dīwānīyah, Iraq **D5** 42
Addyston, Oh., U.S. **o12** 128
Adel, Ga., U.S. **E3** 103
Adel, Ia., U.S. **C3** 108
Adelaide, Austl. **G2** 62
Adelaide, S. Afr. **E4** 56
Adelaide Island, i., Ant. **C33** 67
Adelaide River, Austl. **C5** 60
Adelanto, Ca., U.S. **E5** 98
Adèle Island, i., Austl. **D3** 60
Adelie Coast, Ant. **C19** 67
Aden see 'Adan, Yemen **H5** 38
Aden, Gulf of, b. **H5** 38
Adi, Pulau, i., Indon. **D8** 36
Adiaké, C. Iv. **E4** 50
Adige, stm., Italy **B3** 18
Ādīgrat, Eth. **H3** 38
Ādilābād, India **F3** 40
Adimi, Russia **B15** 28
Adirondack Mountains, mts., N.Y., U.S. **A6** 125
Ādīs Ābeba (Addis Ababa), Eth. **B7** 54
Adıyaman, Tur. **D8** 44
Adjuntas, Presa de las see Vicente Guerrero, Presa, res., Mex. **C5** 78
Adler, Russia **A8** 44
Admiralty Bay, b., Ak., U.S. **A9** 95
Admiralty Gulf, b., Austl. **C4** 60
Admiralty Inlet, b., Nu., Can. **D22** 82
Admiralty Island, i., Ak., U.S. **m22** 95
Admiralty Islands, is., Pap. N. Gui. **G12** 32
Admiralty Mountains, mts., Ant. **D21** 67
Ado, Nig. **E5** 50
Adobe Creek Reservoir, res., Co., U.S. **C7** 99
Ado-Ekiti, Nig. **E6** 50
Ādoni, India **F3** 40
Adour, stm., Fr. **F6** 16
Adra, Spain **I5** 16
Adrar, Alg. **E4** 48
Adrâr, reg., Maur. **B2** 50
Adrian, Ga., U.S. **D4** 103
Adrian, Mi., U.S. **G6** 115
Adrian, Mn., U.S. **G3** 116
Adrian, Mo., U.S. **C3** 118
Adrianople see Edirne, Tur. **B2** 44
Adriatic Sea, Eur. **C5** 18
Adusa, D.R.C. **C5** 54
Advance, Mo., U.S. **D8** 118
Ādwa, Eth. **H12** 48
Adygeja, state, Russia **E5** 26
Adzopé, C. Iv. **E4** 50
Aegean Sea **E10** 18
Aën, ostrov, i., Russia **C18** 26
A Estrada, Spain **F2** 16
Afadjoto, mtn., Ghana **E5** 50
Afars and Issas see Djibouti, ctry., Afr. **H13** 48
Afghanistan, ctry., Asia **D8** 42
Afgooye, Som. **C9** 54
Afikpo, Nig. **E6** 50
Aflou, Alg. **E4** 14
Afmadow, Som. **J13** 48
Afognak Island, i., Ak., U.S. **D9** 95
Africa **E14** 4
Afşin, Tur. **C7** 44
Afton, Ia., U.S. **C3** 108
Afton, Mn., U.S. **F6** 116
Afton, Ok., U.S. **A7** 129
Afton, Wy., U.S. **D2** 143
Afyon, Tur. **C4** 44
Agadez, Niger **C6** 50
Agadir, Mor. **D2** 48
Agadyr', Kaz. **E9** 26
Agalak, Sudan **A6** 54
Agalega Islands, is., Mrts. **E11** 52
Agana, Guam **D11** 32
Agartala, India **E6** 40
Agate Fossil Beds National Monument, Ne., U.S. **B2** 120
Agattu Island, i., Ak., U.S. **E2** 95
Agawam, Ma., U.S. **B2** 114
Agboville, C. Iv. **E4** 50
Ağdam, Azer. **C12** 44
Agde, Fr. **F8** 16
Agen, Fr. **E7** 16
Agency, Ia., U.S. **D5** 108
Agency, Mo., U.S. **B3** 118
Āghā Jārī, Iran **D5** 42
Aginskoe, Russia **D13** 26
Agnew, Austl. **F3** 60
Agnibilékrou, C. Iv. **E4** 50
Agou, Mont, mtn., Togo **E5** 50
Agoura Hills, Ca., U.S. **m11** 98
Āgra, India **D3** 40
Ağrı, Tur. **C10** 44
Ağrı Dağı, mtn., Tur. **C11** 44
Agrigento, Italy **F4** 18
Agrihan, i., N. Mar. Is. **C12** 32
Agrínion, Grc. **E8** 18
Agrópoli, Italy **D5** 18
Água Branca, Braz. **C3** 74
Aguachica, Col. **D5** 80
Aguadas, Col. **D4** 80
Aguadulce, Pan. **D3** 80
Agua Fria, N.M., U.S. **B3** 124
Agua Fria, stm., Az., U.S. **D3** 96
Aguán, stm., Hond. **B2** 80
Agua Prieta, Mex. **A3** 78
A Guardia, Spain **G2** 16
Aguarico, stm., S.A. **D4** 70
Aguascalientes, Mex. **C4** 78
Aguascalientes, state, Mex. **C4** 78
Águas Formosas, Braz. **E3** 74
Água Vermelha, Represa de, res., Braz. **G9** 70
Aguelhok, Mali **C5** 50
Aguila, Az., U.S. **D2** 96
Águilas, Spain **I6** 16
Agulhas, Kaap, c., S. Afr. **E3** 56
Agulhas Basin **M15** 66
Agustín Codazzi, Col. **C5** 80
Ahaggar, mts., Alg. **F6** 48
Ahaggar, Tassili ta-n-, plat., Alg. **B5** 50
Ahalcihe, Geor. **B10** 44
Ahalkalaki, Geor. **B10** 44
Ahar, Iran **C5** 42
Ahklun Mountains, mts., Ak., U.S. **D7** 95
Ahlat, Tur. **C10** 44
Ahmadābād, India **E2** 40
Ahmadnagar, India **F2** 40
Ahmadpur East, Pak. **E10** 42
Ahmar Mountains, mts., Eth. **B8** 54
Ahoskie, N.C., U.S. **A6** 126
Ahtanum Creek, stm., Wa., U.S. **C5** 140
Ahtubinsk, Russia **E6** 26
Ahuacatlán, Mex. **C4** 78
Ahumada, Mex. **A3** 78
Ahvāz, Iran **D5** 42
Ahvenanmaa see Åland, is., Fin. **G9** 10
Aialik, Cape, c., Ak., U.S. **D10** 95
Aiea, Hi., U.S. **B4** 104
Aiken, S.C., U.S. **D4** 133
Aiken, co., S.C., U.S. **D4** 133
Ailao Shan, mts., China **G8** 28
Aileron, Austl. **E5** 60
Ailinglaplap, atoll, Marsh. Is. **D10** 58
Ailsa Craig, On., Can. **D3** 89
Aim, Russia **D15** 26
Aimorés, Braz. **E3** 74
Aïn el Beïda, Alg. **D5** 14
Ainslie Lake, l., N.S., Can. **C8** 87
Ainsworth, Ne., U.S. **B6** 120
Aïn Témouchent, Alg. **J6** 16
Aïn Wessara, Alg. **J8** 16
Aïr, Massif de l', mts., Niger **C6** 50
Airdrie, Ab., Can. **D3** 84
Aïssa, Djebel, mtn., Alg. **D4** 48
Aitape, Pap. N. Gui. **G11** 32
Aitkin, Mn., U.S. **D5** 116
Aitkin, co., Mn., U.S. **D5** 116
Aitutaki, atoll, Cook Is. **F14** 58
Aiud, Rom. **F7** 20
Aix, Mount, mtn., Wa., U.S. **C4** 140
Aix-en-Provence, Fr. **F9** 16
Aix-les-Bains, Fr. **E9** 16
Aíyina, i., Grc. **F9** 18
Aíyion, Grc. **E9** 18
Āīzawl, India **E6** 40
Aizu-wakamatsu, Japan **D16** 28
'Ajab Shīr, Iran **D11** 44
Ajaccio, Fr. **D2** 18
Ajaguz, Kaz. **E9** 26
Ajan, Russia **D15** 26
Ajanta, India **E3** 40
Ajanta Range, mts., India **E3** 40
Ajax, On., Can. **D6** 89
Ajdābiyā, Libya **D9** 48
Ajdarkul', ozero, l., Uzb. **B9** 42
Ajdyrlinskij, Russia **D10** 22
Ajjer, Tassili-n-, plat., Alg. **E6** 48
Ajmer, India **D2** 40
Ajo, Az., U.S. **E3** 96
Āk'ak'ī Besek'a, Eth. **B7** 54
'Akāshāt, Iraq **F8** 44
Akbou, Alg. **I9** 16
Akbulak, Russia **D10** 22
Akçaabat, Tur. **B8** 44
Akçadağ, Tur. **C7** 44
Akçakale, Tur. **D8** 44
Akçakoca, Tur. **B4** 44
Akchâr, reg., Maur. **C1** 50
Ak-Chin Indian Reservation, Az., U.S. **E3** 96
Akdağmadeni, Tur. **C6** 44
Aketi, D.R.C. **C4** 54
Akhḍar, Al-Jabal al-, mts., Oman **F7** 42
Akhisar, Tur. **C2** 44
Akiachak, Ak., U.S. **C7** 95
Akita, Japan **D16** 28
Akjoujt, Maur. **C2** 50
Akkajaure, l., Swe. **C7** 10
Akkol', Kaz. **E9** 26
Akkol', Kaz. **B10** 42
'Aklé ('Aouâna), reg., Afr. **C3** 50
Akmola, Kaz. **D9** 26
Akok, Gabon **C1** 54
Akola, India **E3** 40
Akonolinga, Cam. **C2** 54
Akordat, Erit. **G12** 48
Akranes, Ice. **l17** 10a
Akron, Co., U.S. **A7** 99
Akron, Ia., U.S. **B1** 108
Akron, In., U.S. **B5** 107
Akron, N.Y., U.S. **B2** 125
Akron, Oh., U.S. **A4** 128
Akron, Pa., U.S. **F9** 131
Aksaj, Kaz. **D9** 22
Aksaray, Tur. **C6** 44
Aksarka, Russia **A12** 22
Akşehir, Tur. **C4** 44
Akşehir Gölü, l., Tur. **C4** 44
Akseki, Tur. **D4** 44
Aksu, China **C4** 28
Aksuat, Kaz. **E10** 26
Āksum, Eth. **H3** 38
Aktau, Kaz. **E7** 26
Aktjubinsk, Kaz. **D7** 26
Akto, China **B3** 40
Aktogaj, Kaz. **E9** 26
Akune, Japan **D1** 31
Akure, Nig. **E6** 50
Akureyri, Ice. **l19** 10a
Akwanga, Nig. **E6** 50
Akžar, Kaz. **B4** 28
Alabama, state, U.S. **C3** 94
Alabama, stm., Al., U.S. **D2** 94
Alabaster, Al., U.S. **B3** 94
Alaca, Tur. **B6** 44
Alaçam, Tur. **B6** 44
Alacant, Spain **H6** 16
Alachua, Fl., U.S. **C4** 102
Alachua, co., Fl., U.S. **C4** 102
Aladža manastir, Bul. **C12** 18
Alagir, Russia **A11** 44
Alagoas, state, Braz. **C4** 74
Alagoinhas, Braz. **D4** 74
Alagón, Spain **G6** 16
Alahärmä, Fin. **E10** 10
Alajuela, C.R. **C3** 80
Alakanuk, Ak., U.S. **C7** 95
Alakol', ozero, l., Kaz. **E10** 26
Alalakeiki Channel, strt., Hi., U.S. **C5** 104
Al-'Amādīyah, Iraq **D10** 44
Alamagan, i., N. Mar. Is. **C12** 32
Alamance, co., N.C., U.S. **B3** 126
Al-'Amārah, Iraq **D5** 42
Alameda, Ca., U.S. **h8** 98
Alameda, N.M., U.S. **B3** 124
Alameda, co., Ca., U.S. **D3** 98
Alameda Naval Air Station, mil., Ca., U.S. **h8** 98
Alamito Creek, stm., Tx., U.S. **p12** 136
Alamo, Ga., U.S. **D4** 103
Alamo, Nv., U.S. **F6** 121
Alamo, Tn., U.S. **B2** 135
Alamo, Tx., U.S. **F3** 136
Alamogordo, N.M., U.S. **E4** 124
Alamo Heights, Tx., U.S. **E3** 136
Alamo Hueco Mountains, mts., N.M., U.S. **F1** 124
Alamo Indian Reservation, N.M., U.S. **C2** 124
Alamo Lake, res., Az., U.S. **C2** 96
Alamosa, Co., U.S. **D5** 99
Alamosa, co., Co., U.S. **D5** 99
Alamosa, stm., Co., U.S. **D4** 99
Alamosa Creek, stm., N.M., U.S. **D2** 124
Alamosa East, Co., U.S. **D5** 99
Åland, is., Fin. **G9** 10
Ålands hav, Eur. **F8** 10
Alandur, India **G4** 40
Alanya, Tur. **D4** 44
Alapaevsk, Russia **C11** 22
Alapaha, Ga., U.S. **E3** 103
Alapaha, stm., U.S. **E3** 103
Al-'Aqabah, Jord. **E3** 42
Alas, Selat, strt., Indon. **E5** 36
Alaşehir, Tur. **C3** 44
Alashanyouqi, China **C8** 28
Alaska, state, U.S. **C9** 95
Alaska, Gulf of, b., Ak., U.S. **D10** 95
Alaska Peninsula, pen., Ak., U.S. **D8** 95
Alaska Range, mts., Ak., U.S. **C9** 95
Alatna, stm., Ak., U.S. **B9** 95
Alatyr', Russia **D8** 22
Alava, Cape, c., Wa., U.S. **A1** 140
Alavus, Fin. **E10** 10
Al-'Ayn, U.A.E. **F7** 42
Al-'Azīzīyah, Libya **E6** 14
Alba, Italy **B2** 18
Al-Bāb, Syria **D7** 44
Albacete, Spain **H6** 16
Alba Iulia, Rom. **F7** 20
Albania, ctry., Eur. **D7** 18
Albano Laziale, Italy **D4** 18
Albany, Austl. **G2** 60
Albany, Ga., U.S. **E2** 103
Albany, Il., U.S. **B3** 106
Albany, In., U.S. **D7** 107
Albany, Ky., U.S. **D4** 110
Albany, La., U.S. **g10** 111
Albany, Mn., U.S. **E4** 116
Albany, Mo., U.S. **A3** 118
Albany, N.Y., U.S. **C7** 125
Albany, Or., U.S. **C3** 130
Albany, Tx., U.S. **C3** 136
Albany, Wi., U.S. **F4** 142
Albany, co., N.Y., U.S. **C6** 125
Albany, co., Wy., U.S. **E7** 143
Albany, stm., On., Can. **o18** 89
Al-Baṣrah, Iraq **D5** 42
Al-Batrā' (Petra), hist., Jord. **D3** 42
Al-Batrūn, Leb. **E6** 44
Al-Bayḍā', Libya **D9** 48
Albemarle, N.C., U.S. **B2** 126
Albemarle, co., Va., U.S. **C4** 139
Albemarle Island see Isabela, Isla, i., Ec. **D1** 70
Albemarle Lake, l., Ms., U.S. **C2** 117
Albemarle Sound, strt., N.C., U.S. **A6** 126
Albert, Fr. **B8** 16
Albert, Lake, l., Afr. **C6** 54
Alberta, prov., Can. **C4** 84
Alberta, Mount, mtn., Ab., Can. **C2** 84
Albert City, Ia., U.S. **B3** 108
Albert Lea, Mn., U.S. **G5** 116
Albert Markham, Mount, mtn., Ant. **E22** 67
Albert Nile, stm., Ug. **C6** 54
Alberton, P.E., Can. **C5** 87
Albertson, N.Y., U.S. **k13** 125
Albertville see Kalemie, D.R.C. **E5** 54
Albertville, Fr. **E10** 16
Albertville, Al., U.S. **A3** 94
Albertville, Mn., U.S. **E5** 116
Albi, Fr. **F8** 16
Albia, Ia., U.S. **C5** 108
Albion, Il., U.S. **E5** 106
Albion, In., U.S. **B7** 107
Albion, Mi., U.S. **F6** 115
Albion, Ne., U.S. **C7** 120
Albion, N.Y., U.S. **B2** 125
Albion, Pa., U.S. **C1** 131
Albion, R.I., U.S. **B4** 132
Albion, Wa., U.S. **C8** 140
Al-Biqā', val., Leb. **F6** 44
Alborán, Isla de, i., Spain **J5** 16
Ålborg, Den. **H3** 10
Alborz, Reshteh-ye Kūhhā-ye, mts., Iran **C6** 42
Albox, Spain **I5** 16

Name | Map Ref. | Page

Ālbū Gharz, Sabkhat, pl., Asia **E9** 44
Albuquerque, N.M., U.S. **B3** 124
Alburquerque, Spain **H3** 16
Alburtis, Pa., U.S. **F10** 131
Albury, Austl. **H4** 62
Alcalá de Henares, Spain **G5** 16
Alcalde, N.M., U.S. **A3** 124
Alcamo, Italy **F4** 18
Alcañiz, Spain **G6** 16
Alcántara Uno, Embalse de, res., Spain **H3** 16
Alcantarilla, Spain **I6** 16
Alcázar de San Juan, Spain **H5** 16
Alcazarquivir see Er-Rachidia, Mor. **E3** 14
Alcester, S.D., U.S. **D9** 134
Alchevs'k, Ukr. **E15** 20
Alcoa, Tn., U.S. **D10** 135
Alcobaça, Braz. **G12** 70
Alcobendas, Spain **G5** 16
Alcoi, Spain **H6** 16
Alcolu, S.C., U.S. **D7** 133
Alcona, co., Mi., U.S. **D7** 115
Alcorn, co., Ms., U.S. **A5** 117
Aldabra, Groupe d', i., Sey. **i11** 57b
Aldama, Mex. **B3** 78
Aldan, Russia **D14** 26
Aldan, stm., Russia **C15** 26
Aldan Plateau see Aldanskoe nagor'e, plat., Russia **D14** 26
Aldanskoe nagor'e, plat., Russia **D14** 26
Alden, Ia., U.S. **B4** 108
Alden, Mn., U.S. **G5** 116
Alden, N.Y., U.S. **C2** 125
Alder Brook, stm., Vt., U.S. **B4** 138
Alderney, i., Guernsey **F5** 12
Alderson, W.V., U.S. **D4** 141
Aldrich, Al., U.S. **B3** 94
Aledo, Il., U.S. **B3** 106
Aleg, Maur. **C2** 50
Alegres Mountain, mtn., N.M., U.S. **C2** 124
Alegrete, Braz. **D6** 72
Alejandro Selkirk, Isla, i., Chile **E1** 72
Alejsk, Russia **D10** 26
Aleksandrov, Russia **C6** 22
Aleksandrovsk-Sahalinskij, Russia **D16** 26
Alekseevka, Russia **D15** 20
Aleksin, Russia **B14** 20
Aleksinac, Yugo. **C8** 18
Alençon, Fr. **C7** 16
Alenquer, Braz. **D9** 70
Alenuihaha Channel, strt., Hi., U.S. **C5** 104
Aleppo see Ḥalab, Syria **D7** 44
Alert Bay, B.C., Can. **D4** 85
Alès, Fr. **E9** 16
Alessándria, Italy **B2** 18
Ålesund, Nor. **E2** 10
Aleutian Basin **B4** 144
Aleutian Islands, is., Ak., U.S. **E3** 95
Aleutian Range, mts., Ak., U.S. **D9** 95
Aleutian Trench **B4** 144
Aleutka, Russia **B18** 28
Alex, Ok., U.S. **C4** 129
Alexander, co., Il., U.S. **F4** 106
Alexander, co., N.C., U.S. **B1** 126
Alexander, Lake, l., Mn., U.S. **D4** 116
Alexander Archipelago, is., Ak., U.S. **D12** 95
Alexander Bay, S. Afr. **D2** 56
Alexander City, Al., U.S. **C4** 94
Alexander Island, i., Ant. **C33** 67
Alexandra, N.Z. **q12** 63c
Alexandretta see İskenderun, Tur. **D7** 44
Alexandria, On., Can. **B10** 89
Alexandria see El-Iskandarîya, Egypt **E9** 48
Alexandria, Rom. **H8** 20
Alexandria, S. Afr. **E4** 56
Alexandria, In., U.S. **D6** 107
Alexandria, Ky., U.S. **B5** 110
Alexandria, La., U.S. **C3** 111
Alexandria, Mn., U.S. **E3** 116
Alexandria, Tn., U.S. **A5** 135
Alexandria, Va., U.S. **B5** 139
Alexandroúpolis, Grc. **D10** 18
Alexis, Il., U.S. **B3** 106
Alfalfa, co., Ok., U.S. **A3** 129
Al-Fallūjah, Iraq **F10** 44
Al-Fāshir, Sudan **H10** 48
Alföld, pl., Hung. **F6** 20
Alfred, On., Can. **B10** 89
Alfred, N.Y., U.S. **C3** 125
Al-Fujayrah, U.A.E. **E7** 42
Al-Furāt see Euphrates, stm., Asia **D4** 42
Alga, Kaz. **E10** 22
Algarrobo del Águila, Arg. **F4** 72
Algarve, hist. reg., Port. **I2** 16
Algeciras, Spain **I4** 16
Alger, Oh., U.S. **B2** 128
Alger, co., Mi., U.S. **B4** 115
Algeria, ctry., Afr. **E5** 48
Al-Ghaydah, Yemen **G6** 38
Al-Ghazālah, Sau. Ar. **E4** 42
Alghero, Italy **D2** 18
Algiers see El Djazaïr, Alg. **C5** 48
Algoabaai, b., S. Afr. **E4** 56
Algoma, Wi., U.S. **D6** 142
Algona, Ia., U.S. **A3** 108
Algona, Wa., U.S. **B3** 140
Algonac, Mi., U.S. **F8** 115
Algonquin, Il., U.S. **A5** 106
Algonquin Provincial Park, On., Can. **B6** 89
Algood, Tn., U.S. **C8** 135
Al-Ḥajarah, reg., Asia **E5** 42
Al-Ḥalfāyah, Iraq **G12** 44
Al-Ḥamād, pl., Sau. Ar. **G8** 44
Alhambra, Ca., U.S. **m12** 98
Al-Ḥarrah, Sau. Ar. **D3** 42
Al-Harūj al-Aswad, hills, Libya **A8** 50
Al-Ḥasakah, Syria **D9** 44
Al-Ḥawrah, Yemen **H5** 38
Al-Ḥayy, Iraq **F12** 44
Al-Ḥijāz, reg., Sau. Ar. **E3** 38
Al-Ḥillah, Iraq **D4** 42
Al-Hoceima, Mor. **C4** 48
Al-Ḥudaydah, Yemen **H4** 38
Al-Ḥufrah, reg., Sau. Ar. **E3** 42
Al-Hufūf, Sau. Ar. **E5** 38
Al-Ḥulwah, Sau. Ar. **F5** 38
Aliağo, Tur. **C2** 44
'Alī al-Gharbī, Iraq **F12** 44
Alībāg, India **F2** 40
Äli Bayramlı, Azer. **C13** 44
Alicante see Alacant, Spain **H6** 16
Alice, Tx., U.S. **F3** 136
Alice Lake, l., Mn., U.S. **C7** 116
Alice Springs, Austl. **E5** 60
Aliceville, Al., U.S. **B1** 94
Alīgarh, India **D3** 40
Alīgūdarz, Iran **D5** 42
Alingsås, Swe. **H5** 10
Alīpur, Pak. **E10** 42
Aliquippa, Pa., U.S. **E1** 131
Aliwal North, S. Afr. **E4** 56
Alix, Ab., Can. **C4** 84
Al-Jaghbūb, Libya **E9** 48
Al-Jahrah, Kuw. **E5** 42
Al-Jalāmīd, Sau. Ar. **G9** 44
Al-Jawārah, Oman **G7** 38
Al-Jawf, Libya **F9** 48
Al-Jawf, Sau. Ar. **E3** 38
Al-Jubayl, Sau. Ar. **E5** 38
Al-Junaynah, Sudan **H9** 48
Aljustrel, Port. **I2** 16
Alkali Lake, l., Nv., U.S. **B2** 121
Alkali Lake, l., Or., U.S. **E6** 130
Alkaline Lake, l., N.D., U.S. **C6** 127
Al-Karak, Jord. **G6** 44
Al-Khābūrah, Oman **F7** 38
Al-Khalīl (Hebron), W.B. **G6** 44
Al-Kharṭūm, Sudan **G11** 48
Al-Khaṣab, Oman **E7** 42
Al-Khums, Libya **E6** 14
Al-Kifl, Iraq **F11** 44
Alkmaar, Neth. **D9** 12
Al-Kūfah, Iraq **D4** 42
Al-Kūt, Iraq **D5** 42
Al-Kuwayt (Kuwait), Kuw. **E5** 42
Al-Lādhiqīyah, Syria **E6** 44
Allagash, stm., Me., U.S. **B3** 112
Allagash Lake, l., Me., U.S. **B3** 112
Allahābād, India **D4** 40
Allah-Jun', Russia **C15** 26
Allamakee, co., Ia., U.S. **A6** 108
Allan, Sk., Can. **F2** 91
Allanmyo, Myan. **C3** 34
Allardt, Tn., U.S. **C9** 135
Allatoona Lake, res., Ga., U.S. **B2** 103
Alldays, S. Afr. **C4** 56
Allegan, Mi., U.S. **F5** 115
Allegan, co., Mi., U.S. **F5** 115
Allegany, N.Y., U.S. **C2** 125
Allegany, co., Md., U.S. **k13** 113
Allegany, co., N.Y., U.S. **C2** 125
Allegany Indian Reservation, N.Y., U.S. **C2** 125
Alleghany, co., N.C., U.S. **A1** 126
Alleghany, co., Va., U.S. **C2** 139
Allegheny, co., Pa., U.S. **E2** 131
Allegheny, stm., U.S. **E2** 131
Allegheny Reservoir, res., U.S. **B4** 131
Allemands, Lac Des, l., La., U.S. **E5** 111
Allen, Ok., U.S. **C5** 129
Allen, co., In., U.S. **B7** 107
Allen, co., Ks., U.S. **E8** 109
Allen, co., Ky., U.S. **D3** 110
Allen, co., La., U.S. **D3** 111
Allen, co., Oh., U.S. **B1** 128
Allen, Mount, mtn., Ak., U.S. **C11** 95
Allendale, N.J., U.S. **A4** 123
Allendale, S.C., U.S. **E5** 133
Allendale, co., S.C., U.S. **F5** 133
Allende, Mex. **B4** 78
Allen Park, Mi., U.S. **p15** 115
Allenton, R.I., U.S. **E4** 132
Allenton, Wi., U.S. **E5** 142
Allentown, Pa., U.S. **E11** 131
Alleppey, India **H3** 40
Allerton, Point, c., Ma., U.S. **B6** 114
Alliance, Ne., U.S. **B3** 120
Alliance, Oh., U.S. **B4** 128
Allier, stm., Fr. **D8** 16
Alligator, stm., N.C., U.S. **B6** 126
Alligator Lake, l., Me., U.S. **D4** 112
Allison, Ia., U.S. **B5** 108
Allison, Pa., U.S. **G2** 131
Allison Park, Pa., U.S. **h14** 131
Alliston [Beeton Tecumseth and Tottenham], On., Can. **C5** 89
Al-Līth, Sau. Ar. **F4** 38
Allouez, Wi., U.S. **h9** 142
Alloway Creek, stm., N.J., U.S. **D2** 123
Al-Luḥayyah, Yemen **G4** 38
Allumette Lake, l., Can. **B7** 89
Allyn, Wa., U.S. **B3** 140
Alma, P.Q., Can. **A6** 90
Alma, Ar., U.S. **B1** 97
Alma, Ga., U.S. **E4** 103
Alma, Ks., U.S. **C7** 109
Alma, Mi., U.S. **E6** 115
Alma, Ne., U.S. **D6** 120
Alma, Wi., U.S. **D2** 142
Alma-Ata see Almaty, Kaz. **E9** 26
Almada, Port. **H2** 16
Almadén, Spain **H4** 16
Al-Madīnah (Medina), Sau. Ar. **F3** 38
Al-Mafraq, Jord. **F7** 44
Almalyk, Uzb. **E8** 26
Al-Manāmah (Manama), Bahr. **E6** 42
Almanor, Lake, l., Ca., U.S. **B3** 98
Almansa, Spain **H6** 16
Al-Marj, Libya **D9** 48
Almaty, Kaz. **E9** 26
Al-Mawṣil, Iraq **C4** 42
Al-Mayādīn, Syria **E9** 44
Almelo, Neth. **D10** 12
Almenara, Braz. **E3** 74
Almendralejo, Spain **H3** 16
Almería, Spain **I5** 16
Almería, Golfo de, b., Spain **I5** 16
Al'metevsk, Russia **D7** 26
Al-Mijlad, Sudan **A5** 54
Al-Miqdādīyah, Iraq **F11** 44
Almirante, Pan. **D3** 80
Almont, Mi., U.S. **F7** 115
Almonte, On., Can. **B8** 89
Almonte, Spain **I3** 16
Al-Mubarraz, Sau. Ar. **F5** 38
Al-Mubarraz, Sau. Ar. **E5** 42
Al-Muḥarraq, Bahr. **E6** 42
Al-Mukallā, Yemen **H5** 38
Al-Mukhā, Yemen **H4** 38
Al-Muwayliḥ, Sau. Ar. **E3** 38
Alnön, i., Swe. **E7** 10
Alnwick, Eng., U.K. **C6** 12
Aloha, Or., U.S. **h12** 130
Alor, Pulau, i., Indon. **E6** 36
Alor Setar, Malay. **B2** 36
Alpena, Mi., U.S. **C7** 115
Alpena, co., Mi., U.S. **D7** 115
Alpha Cordillera **E33** 144
Alpharetta, Ga., U.S. **B2** 103
Alphonse, i., Sey. **i12** 57b
Alpine, Az., U.S. **D6** 96
Alpine, Tx., U.S. **D1** 136
Alpine, Ut., U.S. **C4** 137
Alpine, co., Ca., U.S. **C4** 98
Alps, mts., Eur. **B5** 14
Al-Qaḍārif, Sudan **H12** 48
Al-Qā'im, Iraq **E9** 44
Al-Qāmishlī, Syria **D9** 44
Al-Qaryah ash-Sharqīyah, Libya **D7** 48
Al-Qaryatayn, Syria **E7** 44
Al-Qaṭīf, Sau. Ar. **E6** 38
Al-Qaṭrūn, Libya **F7** 48
Al-Qayṣūmah, Sau. Ar. **E5** 38
Al-Quds see Jerusalem, Isr. **G6** 44
Al-Qunayṭirah, Syria **F6** 44
Al-Qunfudhah, Sau. Ar. **G4** 38
Al-Qurnah, Iraq **G12** 44
Al-Quṭayfah, Syria **F7** 44
Als, i., Den. **I3** 10
Alsace, hist. reg., Fr. **C10** 16
Alsasua, Spain **F5** 16
Alta, Nor. **B10** 10
Alta, Ia., U.S. **B2** 108
Altadena, Ca., U.S. **m12** 98
Alta Gracia, Arg. **E5** 72
Altagracia, Ven. **C5** 80
Altai, mts., Asia **B5** 28
Altaj, state, Russia **A5** 28
Altamaha, stm., Ga., U.S. **E4** 103
Altamira, Braz. **D9** 70
Altamont, Il., U.S. **D5** 106
Altamont, Ks., U.S. **E8** 109
Altamont, Or., U.S. **E5** 130
Altamont, Tn., U.S. **D8** 135
Altamonte Springs, Fl., U.S. **D5** 102
Altamura, Italy **D6** 18
Altata, Mex. **C3** 78
Altavista, Va., U.S. **C3** 139
Altay, Mong. **B7** 28
Altay Mountains see Altai, mts., Asia **B5** 28
Altevatnet, l., Nor. **B8** 10
Altheimer, Ar., U.S. **C4** 97
Alto, Ga., U.S. **B3** 103
Alto, N.M., U.S. **D4** 124
Alto Araguaia, Braz. **G9** 70
Alto Garças, Braz. **B7** 72
Alton, Ia., U.S. **B2** 108
Alton, Il., U.S. **E3** 106
Alton, Mo., U.S. **E6** 118
Alton, N.H., U.S. **D4** 122
Altona, Mb., Can. **E3** 86
Alton Bay, N.H., U.S. **D4** 122
Altoona, Al., U.S. **A3** 94
Altoona, Fl., U.S. **D5** 102
Altoona, Ia., U.S. **C4** 108
Altoona, Pa., U.S. **E5** 131
Altoona, Wi., U.S. **D2** 142
Alto Paraguai, Braz. **A6** 72
Alto Parnaíba, Braz. **E10** 70
Alto Río Senguer, Arg. **G2** 69
Altun Shan, mts., China **D5** 28
Alturas, Ca., U.S. **B3** 98
Altus, Ok., U.S. **C2** 129
Altus Air Force Base, mil., Ok., U.S. **C2** 129
Altus Reservoir, res., Ok., U.S. **C2** 129
Al-'Ubaylah, Sau. Ar. **F6** 38
Al-Ubayyiḍ, Sudan **H10** 48
Alucra, Tur. **B8** 44
Alum Bank, Pa., U.S. **F4** 131
Alum Creek, stm., Oh., U.S. **k11** 128
Alupka, Ukr. **G13** 20
Al-'Uqaylah, Libya **E7** 14
Alushta, Ukr. **G13** 20
Al-'Uwaynāt, Libya **E7** 48
Alva, Fl., U.S. **F5** 102
Alva, Ok., U.S. **A3** 129
Alvarado, Mex. **D5** 78
Alvarado, Tx., U.S. **C4** 136
Álvaro Obregón, Presa, res., Mex. **B3** 78
Älvdalen, Swe. **F6** 10
Alvin, Tx., U.S. **E5** 136
Alvinston, On., Can. **E3** 89
Älvkarleby, Swe. **F7** 10
Alvord Lake, l., Or., U.S. **E8** 130
Al-Wajh, Sau. Ar. **E3** 38
Alwar, India **D3** 40
Alxa Zuoqi, China **D9** 28
Alzira, Spain **H6** 16
Ama, La., U.S. **k11** 111
Amacuro, stm., S.A. **D7** 80
Amadeus, Lake, l., Austl. **E5** 60
Amador, co., Ca., U.S. **C3** 98
Amagansett, N.Y., U.S. **n16** 125
Amahai, Indon. **D7** 36
Amakusa-nada, Japan **D1** 31
Amakusa Sea see Amakusa-nada, Japan **D1** 31
Åmål, Swe. **G5** 10
Amalfi, Col. **D4** 80
Amalfi, Italy **D5** 18
Amaliás, Grc. **F8** 18
Amambaí, Braz. **H8** 70
Amami-Ō-shima, i., Japan **E1** 31
Amami-shotō, is., Japan **g6** 31a
Amana, Ia., U.S. **C6** 108
Amapá, Braz. **C9** 70
Amapá, state, Braz. **C9** 70
Amarante, Braz. **E11** 70
Amarapura, Myan. **B3** 34
Amargosa, stm., U.S. **D5** 98
Amargosa Desert, des., U.S. **G5** 121
Amargosa Range, mts., U.S. **G5** 121
Amargosa Valley, Nv., U.S. **G5** 121
Amarillo, Tx., U.S. **B2** 136
Amarkantak, India **E4** 40
Amasya, Tur. **B6** 44
Amatignak Island, i., Ak., U.S. **E4** 95
Amawbia Awka, Nig. **E6** 50
Amazon (Solimões) (Amazonas), stm., S.A. **D9** 70
Amazonas see Amazon, stm., S.A. **D9** 70
Ambāla, India **C3** 40
Ambalavao, Madag. **C8** 56
Ambanja, Madag. **A8** 56
Ambarčik, Russia **C18** 26
Ambato, Ec. **D4** 70
Ambatofinandrahana, Madag. **C8** 56
Ambatolampy, Madag. **B8** 56
Ambatondrazaka, Madag. **B8** 56
Amberg, Ger. **F12** 12
Ambikāpur, India **E4** 40
Ambilobe, Madag. **A8** 56
Ambler, Pa., U.S. **F11** 131
Amboasary, Madag. **C8** 56
Ambodifototra, Madag. **B8** 56
Ambon, Indon. **D7** 36
Ambon, Pulau, i., Indon. **D7** 36
Ambositra, Madag. **C8** 56
Ambovombe, Madag. **D8** 56
Amboy, Il., U.S. **B4** 106
Ambridge, Pa., U.S. **E1** 131
Ambriz, Ang. **E2** 54
Ambrym, i., Vanuatu **k9** 62a
Ambunti, Pap. N. Gui. **G11** 32
Āmbūr, India **G3** 40
Amchitka Island, i., Ak., U.S. **E3** 95
Amchitka Pass, strt., Ak., U.S. **E4** 95
Amderma, Russia **C8** 26
Amdo, China **E6** 28
Ameca, Mex. **C4** 78
Amelia, La., U.S. **E4** 111
Amelia, Oh., U.S. **C1** 128
Amelia, co., Va., U.S. **C4** 139
Amelia Court House, Va., U.S. **C5** 139
Amelia Island, i., Fl., U.S. **k9** 102
American, stm., Ca., U.S. **C3** 98
American Falls, Id., U.S. **G6** 105
American Falls Dam, Id., U.S. **G6** 105
American Falls Reservoir, res., Id., U.S. **F5** 105
American Fork, Ut., U.S. **C4** 137
American Highland, plat., Ant. **D12** 67
American Samoa, dep., Oc. **F12** 58
Americus, Ga., U.S. **D2** 103
Americus, Ks., U.S. **D7** 109
Amersfoort, Neth. **D9** 12
Amery, Wi., U.S. **C1** 142
Amery Ice Shelf, Ant. **C12** 67
Ames, Ia., U.S. **B4** 108
Amesbury, Ma., U.S. **A6** 114
Amfilokhía, Grc. **E8** 18
Amga, Russia **C15** 26
Amga, stm., Russia **C14** 26
Amgun', stm., Russia **D15** 26
Amherst, Ma., U.S. **B2** 114
Amherst, N.H., U.S. **E3** 122
Amherst, N.Y., U.S. **C2** 125
Amherst, Oh., U.S. **A3** 128
Amherst, Va., U.S. **C3** 139
Amherst, Wi., U.S. **D4** 142
Amherst, co., Va., U.S. **C3** 139
Amherstburg, On., Can. **E1** 89
Amherstdale, W.V., U.S. **n12** 141
Amiens, Fr. **C8** 16
Aminuis, Nmb. **C2** 56
Amirantes, Les, is., Sey. **i12** 57b
Amisk Lake, l., Sk., Can. **C4** 91
Amistad, Presa de la (Amistad Reservoir), res., N.A. **B4** 78
Amistad National Recreation Area, Tx., U.S. **E2** 136
Amistad Reservoir (Amistad, Presa de la), res., N.A. **B4** 78
Amite, La., U.S. **D5** 111
Amite, co., Ms., U.S. **D3** 117
Amite, stm., La., U.S. **D5** 111
Amity, Or., U.S. **B3** 130
Amityville, N.Y., U.S. **E7** 125
Amlia Island, i., Ak., U.S. **E5** 95
'Ammān, Jord. **D3** 42
Ammon, Id., U.S. **F7** 105
Ammonoosuc, stm., N.H., U.S. **B3** 122
Āmol, Iran **C6** 42
Amorgós, i., Grc. **F10** 18
Amory, Ms., U.S. **B5** 117
Amos, P.Q., Can. **k11** 90
Åmot, Nor. **G2** 10
Amoy see Xiamen, China **G11** 28
Ampanihy, Madag. **C7** 56
Ampasimanolotra, Madag. **B8** 56
Amposta, Spain **G7** 16
Amrāvati, India **E3** 40
Amreli, India **E2** 40
Amritsar, India **C2** 40
Amroha, India **D3** 40
Amsterdam, Neth. **D9** 12
Amsterdam, N.Y., U.S. **C6** 125
Amstetten, Aus. **F14** 12
Am Timan, Chad **A4** 54
Amu Darya, stm., Asia **B8** 42
Amukta Pass, strt., Ak., U.S. **E5** 95
Amundsen Gulf, b., Can. **D15** 82
Amundsen Sea, Ant. **C30** 67
Amuntai, Indon. **D5** 36
Amur (Heilong), stm., Asia **D16** 26
Amvrakikós Kólpos, b., Grc. **E8** 18
Anaa, atoll, Fr. Poly. **F15** 58
Anaco, Ven. **D7** 80
Anacoco, La., U.S. **C2** 111
Anaconda, Mt., U.S. **D4** 119
Anaconda Range, mts., Mt., U.S. **E3** 119
Anacortes, Wa., U.S. **A3** 140
Anacostia, stm., U.S. **C4** 113
Anacostia, Northwest Branch, stm., Md., U.S. **B3** 113
Anadarko, Ok., U.S. **B3** 129
Anadolu, hist. reg., Tur. **C6** 44
Anadyr', Russia **C19** 26
Anadyr', stm., Russia **C19** 26
Anadyr, Gulf of see Anadyrskij zaliv, b., Russia **C20** 26
Anadyrskij zaliv, b., Russia **C20** 26
'Ānah, Iraq **E9** 44
Anaheim, Ca., U.S. **F5** 98
Anahola, Hi., U.S. **A2** 104
Anahuac, Tx., U.S. **E5** 136
Anakāpalle, India **F4** 40
Analalava, Madag. **A8** 56
Ana María, Golfo de, b., Cuba **A4** 80
Anambas, Kepulauan, is., Indon. **C3** 36
Anamosa, Ia., U.S. **B6** 108
Anamur, Tur. **D5** 44
Anan, Japan **D2** 31
Anan'ïv, Ukr. **F11** 20
Anantapur, India **G3** 40
Anantnāg, India **C3** 40
Anapa, Russia **G14** 20
Anápolis, Braz. **E2** 74
Anastasia Island, i., Fl., U.S. **C5** 102
Anatahan, i., N. Mar. Is. **C12** 32

Name — Map Ref. — Page

Anatolia see Anadolu, hist. reg., Tur. C6 44
Anatom, i., Vanuatu I9 62a
Añatuya, Arg. D5 72
Anbei, China A7 40
Ancaster, On., Can. D4 89
Ancha, Sierra, mts., Az., U.S. D4 96
Anchorage, Ak., U.S. C10 95
Anchorage, Ky., U.S. g11 110
Anchor Point, Ak., U.S. D9 95
Anchor Point, c., Ak., U.S. h15 95
Ancienne-Lorette, P.Q., Can. C6 90
Anclote Keys, is., Fl., U.S. D4 102
Ancona, Italy C4 18
Ancud, Chile F2 69
Anda, China B13 28
Andacollo, Chile E3 72
Andalgalá, Arg. D4 72
Åndalsnes, Nor. E2 10
Andalucía, hist. reg., Spain I4 16
Andalusia, Al., U.S. D3 94
Andalusia, Il., U.S. B3 106
Andaman and Nicobar Islands, ter., India G6 40
Andaman Basin H12 64
Andaman Islands, is., India G6 40
Andaman Sea, Asia E3 34
Andamooka, Austl. G2 62
Andapa, Madag. A8 56
Andéramboukane, Mali C5 50
Anderson, Ak., U.S. C10 95
Anderson, Ca., U.S. B2 98
Anderson, In., U.S. D6 107
Anderson, Mo., U.S. E3 118
Anderson, S.C., U.S. B2 133
Anderson, co., Ks., U.S. D8 109
Anderson, co., Ky., U.S. C4 110
Anderson, co., S.C., U.S. B2 133
Anderson, co., Tn., U.S. C9 135
Anderson, co., Tx., U.S. D5 136
Anderson, stm., N.T., Can. E14 82
Anderson, stm., In., U.S. H4 107
Anderson, Mount, mtn., Wa., U.S. B2 140
Anderson Ranch Reservoir, res., Id., U.S. F3 105
Andes, mts., S.A. B4 72
Andes, Lake, l., S.D., U.S. D7 134
Andfjorden, strt., Nor. B7 10
Andhra Pradesh, prov., India F3 40
Andīmeshk, Iran F13 44
Andirlang, China B4 40
Andižan, Uzb. E9 26
Andkhvoy, Afg. C9 42
Andoany, Madag. A8 56
Andong, S. Kor. D13 28
Andorra, ctry., Eur. F7 16
Andorra-la-Vella, And. F7 16
Andover, Ks., U.S. g12 109
Andover, Ma., U.S. A5 114
Andover, Mn., U.S. m12 116
Andover, Oh., U.S. A5 128
Andover Lake, res., Ct., U.S. C6 100
Andøya, i., Nor. B6 10
Andradina, Braz. F1 74
Andreanof Islands, is., Ak., U.S. E4 95
Andrew, co., Mo., U.S. B3 118
Andrew Island, i., N.S., Can. D9 87
Andrews, In., U.S. C6 107
Andrews, N.C., U.S. f9 126
Andrews, S.C., U.S. E8 133
Andrews, Tx., U.S. C1 136
Andrews, co., Tx., U.S. C1 136
Andrews Air Force Base, mil., Md., U.S. C4 113
Andria, Italy D6 18
Andriamena, Madag. B8 56
Androka, Madag. D7 56
Andropov see Rybinsk, Russia D5 26
Andros, i., Bah. D9 76
Ándros, i., Grc. F10 18
Androscoggin, co., Me., U.S. D2 112
Androscoggin, stm., Me., U.S. D2 112
Androscoggin Lake, l., Me., U.S. D2 112
Āndrott Island, i., India G2 40
Andudu, D.R.C. C5 54
Andújar, Spain H4 16
Andulo, Ang. F3 54
Anegada, i., Br. Vir. Is. B7 80
Anegada Passage, strt., N.A. B7 80
Aného, Togo E5 50
Aneto, mtn., Spain F7 16
Aney, Niger C7 50
Ang'angxi, China B12 28
Angara, stm., Russia D11 26
Angarsk, Russia D12 26
Ånge, Swe. E6 10
Ángel, Salto (Angel Falls), wtfl., Ven. B7 70
Ángel de la Guarda, Isla, i., Mex. B2 78
Angeles, Phil. C8 34
Angeles Point, c., Wa., U.S. A2 140
Angel Falls see Ángel, Salto, wtfl, Ven. B7 70
Ängelholm, Swe. H5 10
Angelina, co., Tx., U.S. D5 136
Angels Camp, Ca., U.S. C3 98
Ångermanälven, stm., Swe. E7 10
Angers, Fr. D6 16
Angier, N.C., U.S. B4 126
Angkor Wat, hist., Camb. D4 34
Anglesey, i., Wales, U.K. D4 12
Angleton, Tx., U.S. E5 136
Angmagssalik, Grnld. E32 82
Ango, D.R.C. C5 54
Angoche, Moz. B6 56
Angol, Chile E2 69
Angola, In., U.S. A8 107
Angola, N.Y., U.S. C1 125
Angola, ctry., Afr. F3 54
Angola Basin J14 66
Angola Swamp, sw., N.C., U.S. C5 126
Angoon, Ak., U.S. D13 95
Angora see Ankara, Tur. C5 44
Angoram, Pap. N. Gui. G11 32
Angostura see Ciudad Bolívar, Ven. B7 70
Angostura, Presa de la, res., Mex. D6 78
Angostura Reservoir, res., S.D., U.S. D2 134
Angoulême, Fr. E7 16
Angren, Uzb. E9 26
Angu, D.R.C. C4 54
Anguilla, Ms., U.S. C3 117
Anguilla, dep., N.A. E12 76
Anguille, Cape, c., Nf., Can. E2 88
Anguo, China B4 30
Anholt, i., Den. H4 10
Anhua, China D3 30
Anhui, state, China E11 28
Aniak, Ak., U.S. C8 95
Anil, Braz. B3 74
Animas, stm., U.S. D3 99
Animas Mountains, mts., N.M., U.S. F1 124
Animas Peak, mtn., N.M., U.S. F2 124
Animas Valley, val., N.M., U.S. F1 124
Anina, Rom. G6 20
Anita, Ia., U.S. C3 108
Aniva, zaliv, b., Russia B16 28
Aniwa, i., Vanuatu I9 62a
Anjār, India E2 40
Anjou, P.Q., Can. p19 90
Anjou, hist. reg., Fr. D6 16
Anjouan see Nzwani, i., Com. A7 56
Anjudin, Russia B10 22
Ankang, China E9 28
Ankara, Tur. C5 44
Ankavandra, Madag. B8 56
Ankazoabo, Madag. C7 56
Ankazobe, Madag. B8 56
Ankeny, Ia., U.S. C4 108
Anking see Anqing, China E11 28
Ankoro, D.R.C. E5 54
Anlong, China D2 30
Anlu, China E10 28
Ann, Cape, c., Ma., U.S. A6 114
Anna, Russia D16 20
Anna, Il., U.S. F4 106
Anna, Oh., U.S. B1 128
Anna, Lake, res., Va., U.S. B5 139
Annaba, Alg. C6 48
An-Nabk, Syria E7 44
An-Nafūd, des., Sau. Ar. E4 38
An-Najaf, Iraq D4 42
An-Najaf, state, Iraq G11 44
Anna Maria, Fl., U.S. p10 102
Anna Maria Island, i., Fl., U.S. q10 102
Annandale, Mn., U.S. E4 116
Annandale, Va., U.S. g12 139
Anna Plains, Austl. D3 60
Annapolis, Md., U.S. C5 113
Annapolis, stm., N.S., Can. E4 87
Annapolis Junction, Md., U.S. B4 113
Annapolis Royal, N.S., Can. E4 87
Annapūrṇa, mtn., Nepal D4 40
Ann Arbor, Mi., U.S. F7 115
An-Nāṣirīyah, Iraq D5 42
Annawan, Il., U.S. B4 106
Anne Arundel, co., Md., U.S. B4 113
Annecy, Fr. E10 16
Annenkov Island, i., S. Geor. H9 69
Annette, Ak., U.S. n24 95
An Nhon, Viet. D5 34
Anning, China E1 30
Anniston, Al., U.S. B4 94
Annobón, i., Eq. Gui. C1 52
An-Nuhūd, Sudan H10 48
An Nukhayb, Iraq F10 44
An-Nu'mānīyah, Iraq D5 42
Annville, Pa., U.S. F8 131
Anoka, Mn., U.S. E5 116
Anoka, co., Mn., U.S. E5 116
Anori, Braz. D7 70
Anqing, China E11 28
Ansai, China B2 30
Ansbach, Ger. F12 12
Anshan, China C12 28
Anshun, China F9 28
Anson, Me., U.S. D3 112
Anson, Tx., U.S. C3 136
Anson, co., N.C., U.S. B2 126
Ansongo, Mali C5 50
Ansonia, Ct., U.S. D3 100
Ansonia, Oh., U.S. B1 128
Ansted, W.V., U.S. C3 141
Antalaha, Madag. A9 56
Antalya, Tur. D4 44
Antalya, Gulf of see Antalya Körfezi, b., Tur. D4 44
Antalya Körfezi, b., Tur. D4 44
Antananarivo, Madag. B8 56
Antarctica L13 4
Antarctic Peninsula, pen., Ant. D35 67
Antelope, co., Ne., U.S. B7 120
Antelope Creek, stm., Wy., U.S. C7 143
Antelope Island, i., Ut., U.S. B3 137
Antelope Peak, mtn., Nv., U.S. B7 121
Antelope Range, mts., Nv., U.S. D7 121
Antelope Reservoir, res., Or., U.S. E9 130
Antelope Wash, val., Nv., U.S. D5 121
Antequera, Spain I4 16
Antero, Mount, mtn., Co., U.S. C4 99
Antero Reservoir, res., Co., U.S. C5 99
Anthon, Ia., U.S. B2 108
Anthony, Fl., U.S. C4 102
Anthony, Ks., U.S. E5 109
Anthony, N.M., U.S. F3 124
Anthony, R.I., U.S. D3 132
Anthony, Tx., U.S. o11 136
Anthony Creek, stm., W.V., U.S. D4 141
Antibes, Fr. F10 16
Anticosti, Île d', i., P.Q., Can. k14 90
Antietam National Battlefield, hist., Md., U.S. B2 113
Antigo, Wi., U.S. C4 142
Antigua, i., Antig. B7 80
Antigua and Barbuda, ctry., N.A. E12 76
Antioch see Hatay, Tur. D7 44
Antioch, Ca., U.S. h9 98
Antioch, Il., U.S. A5 106
Antioquia, Col. D4 80
Antipodes Islands, is., N.Z. N20 64
Antlers, Ok., U.S. C6 129
Antofagasta, Chile B2 69
Antofalla, Salar de, pl., Arg. D4 72
Anton, Tx., U.S. C1 136
Antongila, Helodrano, b., Madag. B8 56
Antônio Bezerra, Braz. B4 74
Antonito, Co., U.S. D5 99
Antora Peak, mtn., Co., U.S. C4 99
Antrim, N.H., U.S. D3 122
Antrim, co., Mi., U.S. C5 115
Antsalova, Madag. B7 56
Antsirabe, Madag. B8 56
Antsirañana, Madag. A8 56
Antsohihy, Madag. A8 56
Antwerp see Antwerpen, Bel. E9 12
Antwerp, Oh., U.S. A1 128
Antwerpen (Antwerp), Bel. E9 12
Anugul, India E5 40
Anūpgarh, India D2 40
Anuradhapura, Sri L. H4 40
Anxi, China C7 28
Anxiang, China D3 30
Anyang, China D10 28
A'nyêmaqên Shan, mts., China D7 28
Anyue, China C2 30
Anžero-Sudžensk, Russia D10 26
Anzio, Italy D4 18
Aoga-shima, i., Japan E15 28
Aoji-ri, N. Kor. B2 31
Aomori, Japan C16 28
Aoral, Mount see Aôral, Phnum, mtn., Camb. D4 34
Aôral, Phnum, mtn., Camb. D4 34
Aosta, Italy B1 18
'Aouâna ('Aklé), reg., Afr. C3 50
Aouderas, Niger C6 50
Aouk, Bahr, stm., Afr. I9 48
Aoukâr, reg., Maur. C3 50
Aozou, Chad B8 50
Apache, Ok., U.S. C3 129
Apache, co., Az., U.S. B6 96
Apache Junction, Az., U.S. m9 96
Apache Peak, mtn., Az., U.S. F5 96
Apalachee Bay, b., Fl., U.S. B2 102
Apalachicola, Fl., U.S. C2 102
Apalachicola, stm., Fl., U.S. B1 102
Apalachicola Bay, b., Fl., U.S. C2 102
Apaporis, stm., S.A. C5 70
Aparri, Phil. C8 34
Apartadó, Col. D4 80
Apatity, Russia C5 26
Apatzingán de la Constitución, Mex. D4 78
Apeldoorn, Neth. D9 12
Apennines see Appennino, mts., Italy C4 18
Apex, N.C., U.S. B4 126
Apia, Samoa F12 58
Apiacás, Serra dos, plat., Braz. E8 70
Apishapa, stm., Co., U.S. D6 99
Aplington, Ia., U.S. B5 108
Apo, Mount, mtn., Phil. E9 34
Apollo, Pa., U.S. E2 131
Apopka, Fl., U.S. D5 102
Apopka, Lake, l., Fl., U.S. D5 102
Apostle Islands, is., Wi., U.S. A3 142
Apostle Islands National Lakeshore, Wi., U.S. A3 142
Apóstoles, Arg. D6 72
Apostolove, Ukr. F12 20
Appalachia, Va., U.S. f9 139
Appalachian Mountains, mts., N.A. D11 92
Appanoose, co., Ia., U.S. D5 108
Appennino, mts., Italy C4 18
Appennino Ligure, mts., Italy B2 18
Apple, stm., Wi., U.S. C1 142
Apple Creek, Oh., U.S. B4 128
Applegate, Or., U.S. E3 130
Applegate, stm., Or., U.S. E3 130
Appleton, Mn., U.S. E2 116
Appleton, Wi., U.S. D5 142
Appleton City, Mo., U.S. C3 118
Apple Valley, Ca., U.S. E5 98
Apple Valley, Mn., U.S. n12 116
Appling, co., Ga., U.S. E4 103
Appomattox, Va., U.S. C4 139
Appomattox, co., Va., U.S. C4 139
Appomattox, stm., Va., U.S. C4 139
Appomattox Court House National Historical Park, Va., U.S. C4 139
Apšeronsk, Russia B3 42
Apua Point, c., Hi., U.S. D6 104
Apucarana, Braz. F1 74
Apure, stm., Ven. B6 70
Apurímac, stm., Peru F5 70
Aqaba, Gulf of, b. E2 42
'Aqrah, Iraq D10 44
Aquarius Mountains, mts., Az., U.S. C2 96
Aquidauana, Braz. H8 70
Ara, India D4 40
Arab, Al., U.S. A3 94
'Arab, Baḥr al-, stm., Sudan A4 54
Arabi, La., U.S. k11 111
Arabian Basin G9 64
Arabian Desert see Eastern Desert, des., Egypt E11 48
Arabian Gulf see Persian Gulf, b., Asia E6 42
Arabian Sea G8 38
Aracaju, Braz. D4 74
Aracati, Braz. B4 74
Araçatuba, Braz. F1 74
Aracruz, Braz. E3 74
Araçuaí, Braz. E3 74
Arad, Rom. F6 20
Arafura Sea E7 58
Arafura Shelf I16 64
Aragac, gora see Aragats Lerr, mtn., Arm. B11 44
Aragarças, Braz. G9 70
Aragats Lerr, mtn., Arm. B11 44
Arago, Cape, c., Or., U.S. D2 130
Aragon, Ga., U.S. B1 103
Aragón, hist. reg., Spain G6 16
Araguacema, Braz. E10 70
Aragua de Barcelona, Ven. B7 70
Araguaia, stm., Braz. E10 70
Araguaína, Braz. C2 74
Araguari, Braz. E2 74
Araguatins, Braz. C2 74
Arāk, Alg. E5 48
Arāk, Iran D5 42
Arakan Yoma, mts., Myan. B2 34
Arakkonam, India G3 40
Araks (Aras) (Araz), stm., Asia B10 44
Aral see Aral'sk, Kaz. E8 26
Aral Sea, Asia B7 42
Aral'sk, Kaz. E8 26
Aranda de Duero, Spain G5 16
Aranjuez, Spain G5 16
Aranos, Nmb. C2 56
Aransas, co., Tx., U.S. E4 136
Aransas Bay, b., Tx., U.S. E4 136
Aransas Pass, Tx., U.S. F4 136
Aranyaprathet, Thai. D4 34
Araouane, Mali C4 50
Arapaho, Ok., U.S. B3 129
Arapahoe, Ne., U.S. D6 120
Arapahoe, co., Co., U.S. B6 99
Arapiraca, Braz. C4 74
Arapkir, Tur. C8 44
Arapongas, Braz. F1 74
Araranguá, Braz. D8 72
Araraquara, Braz. F2 74
Ararat, Arm. C11 44
Ararat, Austl. H3 62
Ararat, Mount see Ağrı Dağı, mtn., Tur. C11 44
Aras (Araks) (Araz), stm., Asia C12 44
Arauca, Col. D5 80
Arauquita, Col. D5 80
Araxá, Braz. E2 74
Araz (Araks) (Aras), stm., Asia C12 44
Ārba Minch', Eth. B7 54
Arboga, Swe. G6 10
Arborg, Mb., Can. D3 86
Arbroath, Scot., U.K. B5 12
Arbuckle, Lake, l., Fl., U.S. E5 102
Arbuckle Mountains, mts., Ok., U.S. C4 129
Arbuckles, Lake of the, res., Ok., U.S. C5 129
Arcachon, Fr. E6 16
Arcade, Ga., U.S. B3 103
Arcade, N.Y., U.S. C2 125
Arcadia, Ca., U.S. m12 98
Arcadia, Fl., U.S. E5 102
Arcadia, In., U.S. D5 107
Arcadia, La., U.S. B3 111
Arcadia, Mo., U.S. D7 118
Arcadia, S.C., U.S. B4 133
Arcadia, Wi., U.S. D2 142
Arcanum, Oh., U.S. C1 128
Arcata, Ca., U.S. B1 98
Arc Dome, mtn., Nv., U.S. E4 121
Archangel see Arhangel'sk, Russia C6 26
Archbald, Pa., U.S. m18 131
Archbold, Oh., U.S. A1 128
Archdale, N.C., U.S. B3 126
Archer, Fl., U.S. C4 102
Archer, co., Tx., U.S. C3 136
Archer City, Tx., U.S. C3 136
Arches National Park, Ut., U.S. E6 137
Archie, Mo., U.S. C3 118
Archuleta, co., Co., U.S. D3 99
Arco, Id., U.S. F5 105
Arcola, Il., U.S. D5 106
Arcoverde, Braz. C4 74
Arctic Ocean E36 144
Ardabīl, Iran C5 42
Ardahan, Tur. B10 44
Ardakān, Iran D6 42
Årdalstangen, Nor. F2 10
Ardennes, reg., Eur. B9 16
Ardeşen, Tur. B9 44
Ardmore, Al., U.S. A3 94
Ardmore, In., U.S. A5 107
Ardmore, Ok., U.S. C4 129
Ardmore, Tn., U.S. B5 135
Ardsley, N.Y., U.S. g13 125
Arecibo, P.R. B6 80
Areia Branca, Braz. B4 74
Arena, Point, c., Ca., U.S. C2 98
Arena, Punta, c., Mex. C3 78
Arenac, co., Mi., U.S. D7 115
Arenápolis, Braz. A6 72
Arenas, Cayo, i., Mex. C6 78
Arendal, Nor. G3 10
Arequipa, Peru G5 70
Arévalo, Spain G4 16
Arezzo, Italy C3 18
Argenta, Il., U.S. D5 106
Argentan, Fr. C6 16
Argentina, ctry., S.A. E3 69
Argentino, Lago, l., Arg. H2 69
Argentnie Basin L9 66
Argeş, stm., Rom. G8 20
Arghandāb, stm., Afg. D9 42
Argolikós Kólpos, b., Grc. F9 18
Argonne, reg., Fr. C9 16
Árgos, Grc. F9 18
Argos, In., U.S. B5 107
Argostólion, Grc. E8 18
Argun' (Ergun), stm., Asia A12 28
Argungu, Nig. D5 50
Argyle, Mn., U.S. B2 116
Argyle, Wi., U.S. F4 142
Arhangel'sk, Russia C6 26
Arhangel'skoe, Russia C14 20
Arhéa Epídavros, hist., Grc. F9 18
Århus, Den. H4 10
Arica, Chile A2 69
Arica, Col. D5 70
Arichat, N.S., Can. D8 87
Arid, Cape, c., Austl. G3 60
Arīḥā (Jericho), Gaza Str. G6 44
Arikaree, stm., U.S. B8 99
Arima, Trin. C7 80
Arinos, stm., Braz. F8 70
Ariquemes, Braz. E7 70
Aristazabal Island, i., B.C., Can. C3 85
Ariton, Al., U.S. D4 94
Arivonimamo, Madag. B8 56
Arizaro, Salar de, pl., Arg. D4 72
Arizona, Arg. F4 72
Arizona, state, U.S. C4 96
Arizona Sunsites, Az., U.S. F6 96
Arjay, Ky., U.S. D6 110
Arjeplog, Swe. C7 10
Arjona, Col. C4 80
Arka, Russia C16 26
Arkabutla Lake, res., Ms., U.S. A4 117
Arkadelphia, Ar., U.S. C2 97
Arkalyk, Kaz. D8 26
Arkansas, co., Ar., U.S. C4 97
Arkansas, state, U.S. C3 97
Arkansas, stm., U.S. E9 92
Arkansas City, Ks., U.S. E6 109
Arkoma, Ok., U.S. B7 129
Arktičeskogo Instituta, ostrova, is., Russia B10 26
Arles, Fr. F9 16
Arlington, Ga., U.S. E2 103
Arlington, Ma., U.S. B5 114

Name	Map Ref.	Page
Arlington, Mn., U.S.	F4	116
Arlington, N.C., U.S.	A2	126
Arlington, Ne., U.S.	C9	120
Arlington, N.Y., U.S.	D7	125
Arlington, Oh., U.S.	B2	128
Arlington, S.C., U.S.	B3	133
Arlington, S.D., U.S.	C8	134
Arlington, Tn., U.S.	B2	135
Arlington, Tx., U.S.	n9	136
Arlington, Va., U.S.	B5	139
Arlington, Vt., U.S.	E2	138
Arlington, Wa., U.S.	A3	140
Arlington, co., Va., U.S.	g12	139
Arlington, Lake, res., Tx., U.S.	n9	136
Arlington Heights, Il., U.S.	A5	106
Arlit, Niger	C6	50
Arlon, Bel.	F9	12
Arma, Ks., U.S.	E9	109
Armada, Mi., U.S.	F8	115
Armadale, Austl.	G2	60
Armagh, P.Q., Can.	C7	90
Armagnac, hist. reg., Fr.	F7	16
Armavir, Russia	B4	42
Armenia, Col.	C4	70
Armenia, ctry., Asia	B11	44
Armians'k, Ukr.	F12	20
Armidale, Austl.	G5	62
Armijo, N.M., U.S.	k7	124
Armour, S.D., U.S.	D7	134
Armstrong, B.C., Can.	D8	85
Armstrong, Ia., U.S.	A3	108
Armstrong, co., Pa., U.S.	E2	131
Armstrong, co., Tx., U.S.	B2	136
Armstrong Creek, stm., W.V., U.S.	m13	141
Arnaudville, La., U.S.	D4	111
Arnett, W.V., U.S.	D3	141
Arnhem, Neth.	E10	12
Arnhem, Cape, c., Austl.	C6	60
Arnhem Bay, b., Austl.	C6	60
Arnhem Land, reg., Austl.	C5	60
Arno, stm., Italy	C3	18
Arnold, Mn., U.S.	D6	116
Arnold, Mo., U.S.	C7	118
Arnold, Ne., U.S.	C5	120
Arnold, Pa., U.S.	h14	131
Arnold Mills, R.I., U.S.	B4	132
Arnold Mills Reservoir, res., R.I., U.S.	B4	132
Arnold's Cove, Nf., Can.	E4	88
Arnolds Park, Ia., U.S.	A2	108
Arnøya, Nor.	A9	10
Arnprior, On., Can.	B8	89
Aroab, Nmb.	D2	56
Aroostook, co., Me., U.S.	B4	112
Ar-Rahad, Sudan	H11	48
Arraias, Braz.	F10	70
Ar-Ramādī, Iraq	D4	42
Arran, Island of, i., Scot., U.K.	C4	12
Ar-Rank, Sudan	H11	48
Ar-Raqqah, Syria	E8	44
Arras, Fr.	B8	16
Arrecife, Spain	A2	50
Arriaga, Mex.	D6	78
Ar-Riyāḍ (Riyadh), Sau. Ar.	F5	38
Arroio Grande, Braz.	E7	72
Arrowhead Mountain Lake, res., Vt., U.S.	B2	138
Arrowrock Reservoir, res., Id., U.S.	F3	105
Arrowwood Lake, res., N.D., U.S.	B7	127
Arroyito, Arg.	E5	72
Arroyo Grande, Ca., U.S.	E3	98
Ar-Rubʿ al-Khālī, des., Asia	G6	38
Ar-Rumaythah, Iraq	D4	42
Ar-Ruṣayriṣ, Sudan	H11	48
Ar-Ruṭbah, Iraq	D4	42
Arsenev, Russia	C14	28
Árta, Grc.	E8	18
Artà, Spain	H8	16
Artašat (Artashat), Arm.	C11	44
Artashat (Artašat), Arm.	C11	44
Art'em, Russia	C14	28
Artemisa, Cuba	A3	80
Artemivs'k, Ukr.	E14	20
Artëmovsk, Russia	D11	26
Artemus, Ky., U.S.	D6	110
Arter, Mount, mtn., Wy., U.S.	D4	143
Artesia, N.M., U.S.	E5	124
Arthabaska, P.Q., Can.	C6	90
Arthur, On., Can.	D4	89
Arthur, Il., U.S.	D5	106
Arthur, co., Ne., U.S.	C4	120
Arthur, Lake, l., La., U.S.	D3	111
Arthur, Lake, res., Pa., U.S.	E1	131
Arthur Kill, stm., N.J., U.S.	k8	123
Artigas, Ur.	E6	72
Artik, Arm.	B10	44
Artsyz, Ukr.	F10	20
Artvin, Tur.	B9	44
Aru, Kepulauan, is., Indon.	H10	32
Aru, Tanjung, c., Indon.	D5	36
Arua, Ug.	C6	54
Aruanã, Braz.	G9	70
Aruba, dep., N.A.	C6	80
Arunāchal Pradesh, prov., India	D6	40
Aruppukkottai, India	H3	40
Arusha, Tan.	D7	54
Aruwimi, stm., D.R.C.	C4	54
Arvada, Co., U.S.	B5	99
Arvayheer, Mong.	B8	28
Arvidsjaur, Swe.	D8	10
Arvika, Swe.	G5	10
Arvin, Ca., U.S.	E4	98
Arvon, Mount, mtn., Mi., U.S.	B2	115
Arvonia, Va., U.S.	C4	139
Arxan, China	B11	28
Arys', Kaz.	E8	26
Arzamas, Russia	C7	22
Arzew, Golfe d', b., Alg.	J6	16
Aša, Russia	D10	22
Asaba, Nig.	E6	50
Asad, Buḥayrat al-, res., Syria	D8	44
Asad, Lake see Asad, Buḥayrat al-, res., Syria	D8	44
Asadābād, Afg.	C10	42
Asadābād, Iran	E13	44
Asahi-dake, vol., Japan	B4	31
Asahikawa, Japan	C16	28
Āsānsol, India	E5	40
Asbest, Russia	C11	22
Asbestos, P.Q., Can.	D6	90
Asbury Park, N.J., U.S.	C4	123
Ascensión, Mex.	A3	78
Ascension, co., La., U.S.	D5	111
Ascension, i., St. Hel.	J8	46
Ascoli Piceno, Italy	C4	18
Aseb, Erit.	H13	48
Åseda, Swe.	H6	10
Āsela, Eth.	B7	54
Åsele, Swe.	D7	10
Ašgabat, Turk.	F7	26
Ashanti, prov., Ghana	E4	50
Ashaway, R.I., U.S.	F1	132
Ashburn, Ga., U.S.	E3	103
Ashburton, N.Z.	p13	63c
Ashburton, stm., Austl.	E2	60
Ashcroft, B.C., Can.	D7	85
Ashdod, Isr.	G6	44
Ashdown, Ar., U.S.	D1	97
Ashe, co., N.C., U.S.	A1	126
Asheboro, N.C., U.S.	B3	126
Ashepoo, stm., S.C., U.S.	F6	133
Ashern, Mb., Can.	D2	86
Asherton, Tx., U.S.	E3	136
Asheville, N.C., U.S.	f10	126
Ash Flat, Ar., U.S.	A4	97
Ashford, Al., U.S.	D4	94
Ashford, W.V., U.S.	m12	141
Ash Grove, Mo., U.S.	D4	118
Ashikaga, Japan	C3	31
Ashkhabad see Ašgabat, Turk.	F7	26
Ashland, Al., U.S.	B4	94
Ashland, Il., U.S.	D3	106
Ashland, Ks., U.S.	E4	109
Ashland, Ky., U.S.	B7	110
Ashland, Ma., U.S.	g10	114
Ashland, Me., U.S.	B4	112
Ashland, Mo., U.S.	C5	118
Ashland, Ne., U.S.	C9	120
Ashland, N.H., U.S.	C3	122
Ashland, Oh., U.S.	B3	128
Ashland, Or., U.S.	E4	130
Ashland, Pa., U.S.	E9	131
Ashland, Va., U.S.	C5	139
Ashland, Wi., U.S.	B3	142
Ashland, co., Oh., U.S.	B3	128
Ashland, co., Wi., U.S.	B3	142
Ashland, Mount, mtn., Or., U.S.	E4	130
Ashland City, Tn., U.S.	A4	135
Ashland Reservoir, res., Ma., U.S.	h10	114
Ashley, In., U.S.	A7	107
Ashley, N.D., U.S.	C6	127
Ashley, Oh., U.S.	B3	128
Ashley, Pa., U.S.	n17	131
Ashley, co., Ar., U.S.	D4	97
Ashley, stm., S.C., U.S.	F7	133
Ashley Creek, stm., Ut., U.S.	C6	137
Ashmore, Il., U.S.	D5	106
Ashmore Islands, is., Austl.	C3	60
Ashokan Reservoir, res., N.Y., U.S.	D6	125
Ash-Shaddādah, Syria	D9	44
Ash-Shāmīyah, Iraq	F11	44
Ash-Shāriqah, U.A.E.	E7	42
Ash-Sharqāṭ, Iraq	E10	44
Ash-Shaṭrah, Iraq	G12	44
Ash-Shiḥr, Yemen	H5	38
Ash-Shināfīyah, Iraq	G11	44
Ashtabula, Oh., U.S.	A5	128
Ashtabula, co., Oh., U.S.	A5	128
Ashtabula, Lake, res., N.D., U.S.	B8	127
Ashtarak, Arm.	B11	44
Ashton, Id., U.S.	E7	105
Ashton, Il., U.S.	B4	106
Ashton, Md., U.S.	B3	113
Ashton, R.I., U.S.	B4	132
Ashuanipi Lake, l., Nf., Can.	h8	88
Ashuelot, stm., N.H., U.S.	E2	122
Ashville, Al., U.S.	B3	94
Ashville, Oh., U.S.	C3	128
Ashwaubenon, Wi., U.S.	D5	142
Asi, stm., Asia	D7	44
Asia	C19	4
Asilah, Mor.	J3	16
Asinara, Golfo dell', b., Italy	D2	18
Asinara, Isola, i., Italy	D2	18
Asino, Russia	D10	26
Asipovičy, Bela.	C10	20
'Asīr, reg., Sau. Ar.	G4	38
Aşkale, Tur.	C9	44
Askersund, Swe.	G6	10
Askham, S. Afr.	D3	56
Asmara see Asmera, Erit.	G12	48
Asmera, Erit.	G12	48
Āsosa, Eth.	A6	54
Asotin, Wa., U.S.	C8	140
Asotin, co., Wa., U.S.	C8	140
Asotin Creek, stm., Wa., U.S.	C8	140
Aspen, Co., U.S.	B4	99
Aspen Butte, mtn., Or., U.S.	E4	130
Aspendos, hist., Tur.	D4	44
Aspermont, Tx., U.S.	C2	136
Aspinwall, Pa., U.S.	k14	131
Aspy Bay, b., N.S., Can.	C9	87
Assa, Mor.	A3	50
Assabet, stm., Ma., U.S.	g9	114
As-Safīrah, Syria	D7	44
As-Salṭ, Jord.	F6	44
Assam, prov., India	D6	40
As-Samāwah, Iraq	D5	42
Assateague Island, i., U.S.	D7	113
Assateague Island National Seashore, U.S.	D7	113
Assawoman Bay, b., Md., U.S.	D7	113
Assiniboine, stm., Can.	E2	86
Assiniboine, Mount, mtn., Can.	D3	84
Assis, Braz.	F1	74
Assu, Braz.	C4	74
As-Sudd, reg., Sudan	I11	48
As-Sulaymānīyah, Iraq	C5	42
As-Sulaymānīyah, Sau. Ar.	F5	38
As-Sulayyil, Sau. Ar.	F5	38
As-Sumayḥ, Sudan	B5	54
Assumption, Il., U.S.	D4	106
Assumption, co., La., U.S.	E4	111
As-Suwaydā', Syria	F7	44
Astara, Azer.	C13	44
Āstārā, Iran	C13	44
Asti, Italy	B2	18
Astipálaia, i., Grc.	F11	18
Astorga, Spain	F3	16
Astoria, Il., U.S.	C3	106
Astoria, Or., U.S.	A3	130
Astove, i., Sey.	j11	57b
Astrahan', Russia	E6	26
Asunción, Para.	D6	72
Asuncion Island, i., N. Mar. Is.	C12	32
Aswān, Egypt	F11	48
Aswan High Dam see Aali, Sadd el-, Egypt	F11	48
Asyūt, Egypt	E11	48
'Ata, i., Tonga	G12	58
Atacama, Desierto de, des., Chile	C2	69
Atacama, Puna de, plat., S.A.	C4	72
Atacama, Salar de, pl., Chile	B3	69
Atakpamé, Togo	E5	50
Atambua, Indon.	E6	36
Aṭar, Maur.	B2	50
Atascadero, Ca., U.S.	E3	98
Atascosa, co., Tx., U.S.	E3	136
Atasu, Kaz.	E9	26
Atatürk Barajı, res., Tur.	D8	44
Atauro, Pulau, i., Indon.	E7	36
'Aṭbarah, Sudan	G11	48
Atbasar, Kaz.	D8	26
Atchafalaya, stm., La., U.S.	D4	111
Atchafalaya Bay, b., La., U.S.	E4	111
Atchison, Ks., U.S.	C8	109
Atchison, co., Ks., U.S.	C8	109
Atchison, co., Mo., U.S.	A2	118
Athabasca, Ab., Can.	B4	84
Athabasca, stm., Ab., Can.	G17	82
Athabasca, Lake, l., Can.	G17	82
Athena, Or., U.S.	B8	130
Athens, On., Can.	C9	89
Athens see Athínai, Grc.	E9	18
Athens, Al., U.S.	A3	94
Athens, Ga., U.S.	C3	103
Athens, Il., U.S.	D4	106
Athens, Mi., U.S.	F5	115
Athens, N.Y., U.S.	C7	125
Athens, Oh., U.S.	C3	128
Athens, Pa., U.S.	C8	131
Athens, Tn., U.S.	D9	135
Athens, Tx., U.S.	C5	136
Athens, W.V., U.S.	D3	141
Athens, Wi., U.S.	C3	142
Athens, co., Oh., U.S.	C3	128
Atherton, Austl.	D4	62
Athi, stm., Kenya	D7	54
Athínai (Athens), Grc.	E9	18
Athol, Ma., U.S.	A3	114
Áthos, mtn., Grc.	D10	18
Ati, Chad	D8	50
Atiak, Ug.	C6	54
Atik Lake, l., Mb., Can.	B4	86
Atikonak Lake, l., Nf., Can.	h8	88
Atiu, i., Cook Is.	G14	58
Atka, Russia	C17	26
Atka Island, i., Ak., U.S.	E5	95
Atkarsk, Russia	D8	22
Atkins, Ar., U.S.	B3	97
Atkins, Va., U.S.	D1	139
Atkinson, Il., U.S.	B3	106
Atkinson, Ne., U.S.	B7	120
Atkinson, N.H., U.S.	E4	122
Atkinson, co., Ga., U.S.	E4	103
Atlanta, Ga., U.S.	C2	103
Atlanta, Il., U.S.	C4	106
Atlanta, In., U.S.	D5	107
Atlanta, Mi., U.S.	C6	115
Atlanta, Tx., U.S.	C5	136
Atlantic, Ia., U.S.	C2	108
Atlantic, N.C., U.S.	C6	126
Atlantic, co., N.J., U.S.	E3	123
Atlantic Beach, Fl., U.S.	m9	102
Atlantic City, N.J., U.S.	E4	123
Atlantic Highlands, N.J., U.S.	C4	123
Atlantic-Indian Basin	O12	66
Atlantic-Indian Ridge	N14	66
Atlantic Ocean	E9	66
Atlantic Peak, mtn., Wy., U.S.	D3	143
Atlas Mountains, mts., Afr.	D4	48
Atlas Saharien, mts., Alg.	E3	14
Atlas Tellien, mts., Alg.	D4	14
Atlin Lake, l., Can.	G13	82
Atmore, Al., U.S.	D2	94
Atna Peak, mtn., B.C., Can.	C3	85
Atoka, Ok., U.S.	C5	129
Atoka, Tn., U.S.	B2	135
Atoka, co., Ok., U.S.	C5	129
Atoka Reservoir, res., Ok., U.S.	C5	129
Atrak (Atrek), stm., Asia	C7	42
Atrato, stm., Col.	B4	70
Atrek (Atrak), stm., Asia	C6	42
Aṭ-Ṭā'if, Sau. Ar.	F4	38
Attalla, co., Ms., U.S.	B4	117
Attalla, Al., U.S.	A3	94
Attapu, Laos	D5	34
Attawapiskat, stm., On., Can.	n18	89
Attica, In., U.S.	D3	107
Attica, Ks., U.S.	E5	109
Attica, N.Y., U.S.	C2	125
Attica, Oh., U.S.	A3	128
Attleboro, Ma., U.S.	C5	114
Attu Island, i., Ak., U.S.	E2	95
Atuel, Bañados del, sw., Arg.	F4	72
Åtvidaberg, Swe.	G7	10
Atwater, Ca., U.S.	D3	98
Atwater, Mn., U.S.	E4	116
Atwood, On., Can.	D3	89
Atwood, Il., U.S.	D5	106
Atwood, Ks., U.S.	C2	109
Atwood, Tn., U.S.	B3	135
Atwood Lake, res., Oh., U.S.	B4	128
Atyrau, Kaz.	E7	26
Auau Channel, strt., Hi., U.S.	C5	104
Aubagne, Fr.	F9	16
Auberry, Ca., U.S.	D4	98
Auburn, Al., U.S.	C4	94
Auburn, Ca., U.S.	C3	98
Auburn, Ga., U.S.	B3	103
Auburn, Il., U.S.	D4	106
Auburn, In., U.S.	B7	107
Auburn, Ks., U.S.	D8	109
Auburn, Ky., U.S.	D3	110
Auburn, Ma., U.S.	B4	114
Auburn, Me., U.S.	D2	112
Auburn, Mi., U.S.	E6	115
Auburn, Ne., U.S.	D10	120
Auburn, N.Y., U.S.	C4	125
Auburn, Wa., U.S.	B3	140
Auburndale, Fl., U.S.	D5	102
Auburn Heights, Mi., U.S.	F7	115
Aubusson, Fr.	E8	16
Auch, Fr.	F7	16
Auchi, Nig.	E6	50
Aucilla, stm., Fl., U.S.	B3	102
Auckland, N.Z.	o13	63c
Auckland Islands, is., N.Z.	J10	58
Audrain, co., Mo., U.S.	B6	118
Audubon, Ia., U.S.	C3	108
Audubon, N.J., U.S.	D2	123
Audubon, co., Ia., U.S.	C2	108
Augathella, Austl.	F4	62
Auglaize, co., Oh., U.S.	B1	128
Auglaize, stm., Oh., U.S.	A1	128
Augrabiesvalle, wtfl, S. Afr.	D3	56
Au Gres, Mi., U.S.	D7	115
Augsburg, Ger.	F12	12
Augusta, Austl.	G1	60
Augusta, Italy	F5	18
Augusta, Ar., U.S.	B4	97
Augusta, Ga., U.S.	C5	103
Augusta, Ks., U.S.	E7	109
Augusta, Ky., U.S.	B6	110
Augusta, Me., U.S.	D3	112
Augusta, Mi., U.S.	F5	115
Augusta, Wi., U.S.	D2	142
Augusta, co., Va., U.S.	B3	139
Augustów, Pol.	C7	20
Augustus, Mount, mtn., Austl.	E2	60
Aulander, N.C., U.S.	A5	126
Aulneau Peninsula, pen., On., Can.	E4	86
Ault, Co., U.S.	A6	99
Aumsville, Or., U.S.	k12	130
Aurangābād, India	F3	40
Aurangābād, India	E4	40
Aure, Nor.	E3	10
Aurelia, Ia., U.S.	B2	108
Aurich, Ger.	D10	12
Aurillac, Fr.	E8	16
Aurora, On., Can.	C5	89
Aurora, Co., U.S.	B6	99
Aurora, Il., U.S.	B5	106
Aurora, In., U.S.	F8	107
Aurora, Mn., U.S.	C6	116
Aurora, Mo., U.S.	E4	118
Aurora, Ne., U.S.	D7	120
Aurora, Oh., U.S.	A4	128
Aurora, S.D., U.S.	C9	134
Aurora, Ut., U.S.	E4	137
Aurora, co., S.D., U.S.	D7	134
Aus, Nmb.	D2	56
Au Sable, Mi., U.S.	D7	115
Au Sable, stm., Mi., U.S.	D6	115
Ausable, stm., N.Y., U.S.	f11	125
Au Sable Forks, N.Y., U.S.	f11	125
Au Sable Point, c., Mi., U.S.	D7	115
Au Sable Point, c., Mi., U.S.	B4	115
Austell, Ga., U.S.	h7	103
Austin, In., U.S.	G6	107
Austin, Mn., U.S.	G6	116
Austin, Nv., U.S.	D4	121
Austin, Tx., U.S.	D4	136
Austin, co., Tx., U.S.	E4	136
Austintown, Oh., U.S.	A5	128
Austinville, Va., U.S.	D2	139
Australia, ctry., Oc.	G7	58
Australia, i., Austl.	H21	4
Australian Capital Territory, ter., Austl.	H4	62
Austral Seamounts	K23	64
Austria, ctry., Eur.	G14	12
Autauga, co., Al., U.S.	C3	94
Autaugaville, Al., U.S.	C3	94
Autlán de Navarro, Mex.	D4	78
Auvergne, hist. reg., Fr.	E8	16
Auxerre, Fr.	D8	16
Auxier, Ky., U.S.	C7	110
Auxvasse, Mo., U.S.	B6	118
Auyán Tepuy, mtn., Ven.	B7	70
Auzangate, Nevado, mtn., Peru	F5	70
Ava, Mo., U.S.	E5	118
Avallon, Fr.	D8	16
Avalon, Ca., U.S.	F4	98
Avalon, Pa., U.S.	h13	131
Avalon, Lake, res., N.M., U.S.	E5	124
Avalon Peninsula, pen., Nf., Can.	E5	88
Avaré, Braz.	F2	74
Aveiro, Port.	G2	16
Avella, Pa., U.S.	F1	131
Avellaneda, Arg.	E6	72
Avellino, Italy	D5	18
Avenal, Ca., U.S.	E3	98
Avery, co., N.C., U.S.	e11	126
Aves, Islas de, is., Ven.	C6	80
Avesta, Swe.	F7	10
Avezzano, Italy	C4	18
Avignon, Fr.	F9	16
Ávila, Spain	G4	16
Avilés, Spain	F4	16
Avilla, In., U.S.	B7	107
Avis, Pa., U.S.	D7	131
Aviston, Il., U.S.	E4	106
Avoca, Ia., U.S.	C2	108
Avoca, Pa., U.S.	m18	131
Avola, Italy	F5	18
Avon, Ct., U.S.	B4	100
Avon, Il., U.S.	C3	106
Avon, Ma., U.S.	B5	114
Avon, Mn., U.S.	E4	116
Avon, N.Y., U.S.	C3	125
Avon, Oh., U.S.	A3	128
Avondale, Az., U.S.	D3	96
Avondale, Co., U.S.	C6	99
Avondale, Pa., U.S.	G10	131
Avondale Estates, Ga., U.S.	h8	103
Avon Lake, Ia., U.S.	e8	108
Avon Lake, Oh., U.S.	A3	128
Avonmore, Pa., U.S.	E3	131
Avon Park, Fl., U.S.	E5	102
Avoyelles, co., La., U.S.	C3	111
Awaaso, Ghana	E4	50
Āwarē, Eth.	B8	54
Āwasa, Eth.	B7	54
Āwash, Eth.	B8	54
Āwash, stm., Eth.	H13	48
Awbārī, Libya	E7	48
Awbārī, Ṣaḥrā', reg., Libya	A7	50
Awjilah, Libya	E9	48
Awled Djellal, Alg.	E5	14
Awlef, Alg.	F4	14
Axim, Ghana	F4	50
Axiós (Vardar), stm., Eur.	D9	18
Axis, Al., U.S.	E1	94
Axtell, Ne., U.S.	D6	120
Ayacucho, Arg.	F6	72
Ayacucho, Peru	F5	70
Ayamé, C. Iv.	E4	50
Ayancık, Tur.	B6	44
Ayapel, Col.	D4	80
Ayaviri, Peru	F5	70
Ayden, N.C., U.S.	B5	126
Aydın, Tur.	D2	44
Ayer, Ma., U.S.	A4	114
Ayers Cliff, P.Q., Can.	D5	90
Ayeyarwady, stm., Myan.	C3	34
Áyios Nikólaos, Grc.	G10	18
Ayíou Órous, Kólpos, b., Grc.	D10	18
Aylesford, N.S., Can.	D5	87

Name — Map Ref. — Page

Aylmer, Mount, mtn., Ab., Can. D3 84
Aylmer East, P.Q., Can. D2 90
Aylmer West, On., Can. E4 89
'Ayn Dār, Sau. Ar. E5 42
Ayorou, Niger D5 50
'Ayoûn el 'Atroûs, Maur. C3 50
Ayr, Austl. D4 62
Ayr, Scot., U.K. C4 12
Ayvalık, Tur. C2 44
Āzamgarh, India D4 40
Azaouâd, reg., Mali C4 50
Azare, Nig. D7 50
Āzar Shahr, Iran D11 44
Azdavay, Tur. B5 44
Azeffâl, dunes, Afr. B2 50
Azerbaijan, ctry., Asia B12 44
Azilal, Mor. E2 14
Aziscohos Lake, l., Me., U.S. C1 112
Azle, Tx., U.S. n9 136
Azogues, Ec. D4 70
Azores see Açores, is., Port. F7 46
Azores Plateau D10 66
Azov, Russia F15 20
Azov, Sea of, Eur. F14 20
Azraq, Al-Baḥr al- see Blue Nile, stm., Afr. H11 48
Azrou, Mor. D3 48
Aztec, N.M., U.S. A2 124
Aztec Peak, mtn., Az., U.S. D5 96
Aztec Ruins National Monument, N.M., U.S. A1 124
Azua, Dom. Rep. B5 80
Azuaga, Spain H4 16
Azuero, Península de, pen., Pan. D3 80
Azul, Arg. F6 72
Azurduy, Bol. B5 72
Azusa, Ca., U.S. m13 98
Az-Ẓahrān, Sau. Ar. E5 42
Az-Zarqā', Jord. D3 42
Az-Zāwiyah, Libya D7 48

B

Baa, Indon. F6 36
Baardheere, Som. J13 48
Babadag, Rom. G10 20
Babaeski, Tur. B2 44
Babaevo, Russia C6 22
Babanūsah, Sudan H10 48
Babar, Kepulauan, is., Indon. E7 36
Babb Creek, stm., Pa., U.S. C7 131
Babbitt, Mn., U.S. C7 116
Babbitt, Nv., U.S. E3 121
Bab el Mandeb see Mandeb, Bab el, strt. H4 38
Babelthuap, i., Palau E9 32
Bābil, Aṭlāl (Babylon), hist., Iraq F11 44
Babine, stm., B.C., Can. B4 85
Babine Lake, l., B.C., Can. B5 85
Babine Range, mts., B.C., Can. B4 85
Babo, Indon. D8 36
Baboquivari Mountains, mts., Az., U.S. F4 96
Baboquivari Peak, mtn., Az., U.S. F4 96
Babruisk, Bela. C10 20
Babuškin, Russia A9 28
Babuyan Channel, strt., Phil. C8 34
Babuyan Island, i., Phil. C8 34
Babuyan Islands, is., Phil. C8 34
Babylon, N.Y., U.S. n15 125
Babylon see Bābil, Aṭlāl, hist., Iraq F11 44
Baca, co., Co., U.S. D8 99
Bacabal, Braz. B3 74
Bacan, Pulau, i., Indon. D7 36
Bacău, Rom. F9 20
Bachu, China D3 28
Back, stm., S.C., U.S. h12 133
Bačka Palanka, Yugo. B7 18
Backbone Mountain, mtn., U.S. m12 113
Bac Lieu, Viet. E5 34
Bac Ninh, Viet. B5 34
Bacolod, Phil. D8 34
Bacon, co., Ga., U.S. E4 103
Baconton, Ga., U.S. E2 103
Bacoor, Phil. D8 34
Bād, Iran D6 42
Bad, stm., S.D., U.S. C5 134
Bad, stm., Wi., U.S. B3 142
Badagara, India G3 40
Badajoz, Spain H3 16
Badalona, Spain G8 16
Bādāmi, India F3 40
Badanah, Sau. Ar. D4 38
Bad Axe, Mi., U.S. E8 115
Baddeck, N.S., Can. C9 87
Baden, Aus. G14 12
Baden, On., Can. D4 89
Baden, Pa., U.S. E1 131
Baden-Baden, Ger. F11 12
Badger, Nf., Can. D3 88
Bad Hersfeld, Ger. E11 12
Badīn, Pak. F9 42
Badin, N.C., U.S. B2 126
Badin Lake, res., N.C., U.S. B2 126
Bad Kreuznach, Ger. F10 12
Badlands, hills, S.D., U.S. D3 134
Badlands, reg., U.S. C2 127
Badlands National Park, S.D., U.S. D3 134
Bad Reichenhall, Ger. G13 12
Bad River Indian Reservation, Wi., U.S. B3 142
Bad Tölz, Ger. G12 12
Badulla, Sri L. H4 40
Badwater Creek, stm., Wy., U.S. C5 143
Bafang, Cam. B2 54
Bafatá, Gui.-B. D2 50
Baffin Basin C29 144
Baffin Bay, b., N.A. D26 82
Baffin Bay, b., Tx., U.S. E4 136
Baffin Bugt see Baffin Bay, b., N.A. D26 82
Baffin Island, i., Nu., Can. D24 82
Bafia, Cam. C2 54
Bafing, stm., Afr. D2 50
Bafoulabé, Mali D2 50
Bafoussam, Cam. B2 54
Bafra, Tur. B6 44
Bafwasende, D.R.C. C5 54
Bagaces, C.R. C2 80
Bagamoyo, Tan. E7 54
Baganga, Phil. E9 34
Bagansiapiapi, Indon. C2 36
Bagdad see Baghdād, Iraq D4 42
Bagdad, Az., U.S. C2 96
Bagdad, Fl., U.S. u14 102
Bagdarin, Russia D13 26
Bagé, Braz. E7 72
Baggs, Wy., U.S. E5 143
Baghdād, Iraq D4 42
Bagheria, Italy E4 18
Baghlān, Afg. C9 42
Bagley, Mn., U.S. C3 116
Bagnères-de-Bigorre, Fr. F7 16
Bago, Myan. C3 34
Baguio, Phil. C8 34
Bahamas, ctry., N.A. C9 76
Bahār, Iran E13 44
Baharampur, India E5 40
Baharden, Turk. C7 42
Bahardok, Turk. C7 42
Bahāwalpur, Pak. E10 42
Bahçe, Tur. D7 44
Bahia, state, Braz. D3 74
Bahía, Islas de la, is., Hond. B2 80
Bahía Blanca, Arg. F5 72
Bahir Dar, Eth. H12 48
Bahraich, India D4 40
Bahrain, ctry., Asia E6 42
Bahta, Russia C10 26
Bāhū Kalāt, Iran E8 42
Baía Farta, Ang. F2 54
Baia Mare, Rom. F7 20
Baicheng, China B12 28
Baicheng, China C4 28
Baidoa see Baydhabo, Som. J13 48
Baie-Comeau, P.Q., Can. k13 90
Baie-d'Urfé, P.Q., Can. q19 90
Baie-Saint-Paul, P.Q., Can. B7 90
Baie Verte, Nf., Can. D3 88
Baihe, China C3 30
Baikal, Lake see Bajkal, ozero, l., Russia D12 26
Baile Átha Cliath see Dublin, Ire. D3 12
Băilești, Rom. G7 20
Bailey, co., Tx., U.S. B1 136
Bailey Island, Me., U.S. g8 112
Bailey Island, i., S.C., U.S. k11 133
Baileys Crossroads, Va., U.S. g12 139
Bailundo, Ang. F3 54
Bainbridge, Ga., U.S. F2 103
Bainbridge, In., U.S. E4 107
Bainbridge, Oh., U.S. C2 128
Bainbridge Island, i., Wa., U.S. e10 140
Baing, Indon. F6 36
Baird, Tx., U.S. C3 136
Bairdford, Pa., U.S. h14 131
Baird Inlet, b., Ak., U.S. C7 95
Baird Mountains, mts., Ak., U.S. B7 95
Bairin Zuoqi, China C11 28
Bairnsdale, Austl. H4 62
Bais, Phil. E8 34
Baishuijiang, China C2 30
Baitou Shan see Paektu, Mount, mtn., Asia C13 28
Baiyin, China D8 28
Baja, Hung. F5 20
Baja California, state, Mex. A1 78
Baja California, pen., Mex. B2 78
Baja California Norte see Baja California, state, Mex. A1 78
Baja California Sur, state, Mex. B2 78
Bajestān, Iran D7 42
Bajkal, ozero, l., Russia D12 26
Bajkit, Russia C11 26
Bajkonur, Kaz. E8 26
Bajmak, Russia D10 22
Bajo Boquete, Pan. D3 80
Bajramaly, Turk. C8 42
Bakala, C.A.R. B4 54
Bakanas, Kaz. B11 42
Bakel, Sen. D2 50
Baker, La., U.S. D4 111
Baker, Mt., U.S. D12 119
Baker, Or., U.S. C9 130
Baker, co., Fl., U.S. B4 102
Baker, co., Ga., U.S. E2 103
Baker, co., Or., U.S. C9 130
Baker, stm., N.H., U.S. C3 122
Baker, Mount, mtn., Wa., U.S. A4 140
Baker Air Force Base, mil., Ar., U.S. B6 97
Baker Butte, mtn., Az., U.S. C4 96
Baker Island, i., Oc. H21 64
Baker Island, i., Ak., U.S. n22 95
Baker Lake, l., Austl. F4 60
Baker Lake, l., Me., U.S. B3 112
Baker Lake, res., Wa., U.S. A4 140
Bakersfield, Ca., U.S. E4 98
Bakers Island, i., Ma., U.S. f12 114
Bakerstown, Pa., U.S. h14 131
Bakhmach, Ukr. D12 20
Bakı (Baku), Azer. B13 44
Bako, Eth. B7 54
Bakouma, C.A.R. B4 54
Baku see Bakı, Azer. B13 44
Bala, Sen. D2 50
Balabac Island, i., Phil. E7 34
Balabac Strait, strt., Asia E7 34
Ba'labakk, Leb. F7 44
Baladĕk, Russia D15 26
Bālāghāt, India E4 40
Balaguer, Spain G7 16
Balakliia, Ukr. E14 20
Balakovo, Russia D6 26
Balama, Moz. A6 56
Balambangan, Pulau, i., Malay. B5 36
Bālā Morghāb, Afg. C8 42
Balāngīr, India E4 40
Balašov, Russia D6 26
Balassagyarmat, Hung. F5 20
Balaton, Mn., U.S. F3 116
Balaton, l., Hung. F4 20
Balbina, Represa, res., Braz. D8 70
Balcad, Som. C9 54
Balcarce, Arg. F6 72
Balcarres, Sk., Can. G4 91
Balclutha, N.Z. p12 63c
Bald Eagle Lake, l., Mn., U.S. C7 116
Bald Eagle Lake, l., Mn., U.S. m12 116
Baldhill Dam, N.D., U.S. B7 127
Bald Knob, Ar., U.S. B4 97
Bald Knoll, mtn., Wy., U.S. D2 143
Bald Mountain, mtn., Or., U.S. C9 130
Bald Mountain, mtn., Or., U.S. D5 130
Bald Mountain, mtn., Wy., U.S. B5 143
Bald Mountains, mts., N.C., U.S. f10 126
Baldwin, Fl., U.S. B5 102
Baldwin, Ga., U.S. B3 103
Baldwin, La., U.S. E4 111
Baldwin, Mi., U.S. E5 115
Baldwin, Pa., U.S. k14 131
Baldwin, S.C., U.S. B5 133
Baldwin, Wi., U.S. D1 142
Baldwin, co., Al., U.S. E2 94
Baldwin, co., Ga., U.S. C3 103
Baldwin City, Ks., U.S. D8 109
Baldwinsville, N.Y., U.S. B4 125
Baldwinville, Ma., U.S. A3 114
Baldwyn, Ms., U.S. A5 117
Baldy Mountain, mtn., B.C., Can. D7 85
Baldy Mountain, mtn., Mb., Can. D1 86
Baldy Mountain, mtn., Mt., U.S. B7 119
Baldy Mountain, mtn., N.M., U.S. A4 124
Baldy Peak, mtn., Az., U.S. D6 96
Balearic Islands see Balears, Illes, is., Spain H7 16
Balears, Illes (Balearic Islands), is., Spain H7 16
Baleia, Ponta da, c., Braz. E4 74
Baleine, Rivière à la, stm., P.Q., Can. g13 90
Balej, Russia D13 26
Baler, Phil. C8 34
Bāleshwar, India E5 40
Balezino, Russia C9 22
Balfate, Hond. B2 80
Balfour, N.C., U.S. f10 126
Balhaš, Kaz. E9 26
Balhaš, ozero, l., Kaz. E9 26
Bali, i., Indon. E5 36
Bali, Laut (Bali Sea), Indon. E5 36
Balıkesir, Tur. C2 44
Balikpapan, Indon. D5 36
Balimo, Pap. N. Gui. H11 32
Balintang Channel, strt., Phil. C8 34
Bali Sea see Bali, Laut, Indon. E5 36
Balkan Mountains see Stara Planina, mts., Eur. C9 18
Balkaria see Kabardino-Balkarija, state, Russia E6 26
Balkh, Afg. C9 42
Balkhash, Lake see Balhaš, ozero, l., Kaz. E9 26
Ball, La., U.S. C3 111
Balladonia, Austl. G3 60
Ballālpur, India F3 40
Ballarat, Austl. H3 62
Ballard, co., Ky., U.S. e8 110
Ball Club Lake, l., Mn., U.S. C5 116
Balleny Islands, is., Ant. C21 67
Ball Ground, Ga., U.S. B2 103
Ballina, Austl. F5 62
Ballina, Ire. C2 12
Ballinger, Tx., U.S. D3 136
Ball Mountain Lake, res., Vt., U.S. E3 138
Ballston Spa, N.Y., U.S. B7 125
Ballwin, Mo., U.S. f12 118
Bally, Pa., U.S. F10 131
Ballymena, N. Ire., U.K. C3 12
Balmoral, N.B., Can. B3 87
Balmoral Castle, hist., Scot., U.K. B5 12
Balmville, N.Y., U.S. D6 125
Balombo, Ang. F2 54
Balqash Köli see Balhaš, ozero, l., Kaz. E9 26
Balş, Rom. G8 20
Balsam Lake, Wi., U.S. C1 142
Balsam Lake, l., Wi., U.S. C1 142
Balsas, Braz. E10 70
Balsas, stm., Mex. D4 78
Balta, Ukr. F10 20
Baltasar Brum, Ur. E6 72
Bălți, Mol. F9 20
Baltic, Ct., U.S. C7 100
Baltic, S.D., U.S. D9 134
Baltic Sea, Eur. I7 10
Baltijsk, Russia B5 20
Baltim, Egypt E10 14
Baltimore, Md., U.S. B4 113
Baltimore, Oh., U.S. C3 128
Baltimore, co., Md., U.S. B4 113
Baltimore Highlands, Md., U.S. h11 113
Baluchistan, hist. reg., Asia E8 42
Bālurghāt, India D5 40
Balygyčan, Russia C17 26
Bam, Iran E7 42
Bama, Nig. D7 50
Bamako, Mali D3 50
Bamba, Mali C4 50
Bambari, C.A.R. B4 54
Bamberg, Ger. F12 12
Bamberg, S.C., U.S. E5 133
Bamberg, co., S.C., U.S. E5 133
Bambesi, Eth. B6 54
Bamenda, Cam. B2 54
Bāmīān, Afg. D9 42
Bamingui, C.A.R. B4 54
Bampūr, Iran E8 42
Banaba, i., Kir. E10 58
Banalia, D.R.C. C5 54
Banamba, Mali D3 50
Bananal, Ilha do, i., Braz. D1 74
Banana River, b., Fl., U.S. D6 102
Bananga, India H6 40
Banâs, Râs, c., Egypt F12 48
Banat, hist. reg., Eur. G6 20
Banaz, Tur. C3 44
Banbury, Eng., U.K. D6 12
Bancroft, On., Can. B7 89
Bancroft, Ia., U.S. A3 108
Bancroft see Chililabombwe, Zam. A4 56
Bānda, India D4 40
Banda, Kepulauan, is., Indon. D7 36
Banda, Laut (Banda Sea), Indon. E7 36
Banda Aceh, Indon. B1 36
Bandama, stm., C. Iv. E4 50
Bandar Beheshtī, Iran E8 42
Bandar-e 'Abbās, Iran E7 42
Bandar-e Anzalī, Iran C5 42
Bandar-e Būshehr, Iran E6 42
Bandar-e Deylam, Iran E6 42
Bandar-e Khomeynī, Iran D5 42
Bandar-e Lengeh, Iran E6 42
Bandar-e Torkeman, Iran C6 42
Bandar Seri Begawan, Bru. C4 36
Banda Sea see Banda, Laut, Indon. E7 36
Banded Peak, mtn., Co., U.S. D4 99
Bandeira, Pico da, mtn., Braz. F3 74
Bandeirantes, Braz. B7 72
Bandelier National Monument, N.M., U.S. B3 124
Bandera, co., Tx., U.S. E3 136
Bandiagara, Mali D4 50
Bandiantaolehai, China C8 28
Bandırma, Tur. B2 44
Bandon, Or., U.S. D2 130
Ban Don, Ao, b., Thai. E3 34
Bandundu, D.R.C. D3 54
Bandung, Indon. E3 36
Bāneh, Iran E11 44
Banes, Cuba A4 80
Banff National Park, Ab., Can. D2 84
Banfora, Burkina D4 50
Bangalore, India G3 40
Bangassou, C.A.R. C4 54
Banggai, Indon. D6 36
Banggai, Kepulauan, is., Indon. G7 32
Banggi, Pulau, i., Malay. B5 36
Banghāzī, Libya D9 48
Bangka, Pulau, i., Indon. D3 36
Bangka, Selat, strt., Indon. D3 36
Bangkalan, Indon. E4 36
Bangkinang, Indon. C2 36
Bangko, Indon. D2 36
Bangkok see Krung Thep, Thai. D4 34
Bangladesh, ctry., Asia B2 34
Bang Mun Nak, Thai. C4 34
Ban Gnômmarat Kèo, Laos C5 34
Bangor, N. Ire., U.K. C4 12
Bangor, Wales, U.K. D4 12
Bangor, Me., U.S. D4 112
Bangor, Mi., U.S. F4 115
Bangor, Pa., U.S. E11 131
Bangor, Wi., U.S. E3 142
Bangor Township, Mi., U.S. E7 115
Bangs, Tx., U.S. D3 136
Bangs, Mount, mtn., Az., U.S. A2 96
Bangui, C.A.R. C3 54
Bangweulu, Lake, l., Zam. A4 56
Ban Houayxay, Laos B4 34
Bani, Burkina D4 50
Baní, Dom. Rep. B5 80
Baniara, Pap. N. Gui. B4 62
Banister, stm., Va., U.S. D4 139
Banī Walīd, Libya D7 48
Bāniyās, Syria E6 44
Banja Luka, Bos. B6 18
Banjarmasin, Indon. D4 36
Banjul, Gam. D1 50
Banka Banka, Austl. D5 60
Bankhead Lake, res., Al., U.S. B2 94
Banks, co., Ga., U.S. B3 103
Banks, Îles, is., Vanuatu j9 62a
Banks Island, i., B.C., Can. C2 85
Banks Lake, res., Wa., U.S. B6 140
Banks Strait, strt., Austl. I4 62
Bānkura, India E5 40
Ban Nalè, Laos C4 34
Banner, co., Ne., U.S. C2 120
Banner Elk, N.C., U.S. A1 126
Banning, Ca., U.S. F5 98
Bannock, co., Id., U.S. G6 105
Bannock Peak, mtn., Id., U.S. F6 105
Bannock Range, mts., Id., U.S. G6 105
Bannu, Pak. D10 42
Ban Pong, Thai. D3 34
Ban Signo, Laos C5 34
Banská Bystrica, Slvk. E5 20
Bānswāra, India E2 40
Bantaeng, Indon. E6 36
Bantam, stm., Ct., U.S. B3 100
Bantam Lake, l., Ct., U.S. C3 100
Banyo, Cam. B2 54
Banyuwangi, Indon. E4 36
Banzare Coast, Ant. C17 67
Baode, China D10 28
Baodi, China B4 30
Baoding, China D11 28
Bao Ha, Viet. B4 34
Baoji, China E9 28
Baojing, China D2 30
Bao Lac, Viet. D5 34
Baoqing, China A2 31
Baoshan, China F7 28
Baoting, China H9 28
Baotou, China C9 28
Baoying, China E11 28
Ba'qūbah, Iraq D4 42
Baquedano, Chile B2 69
Bara, Nig. D7 50
Baraawe, Som. J13 48
Baraboo, Wi., U.S. E4 142
Baraboo, stm., Wi., U.S. E3 142
Baracoa, Cuba A5 80
Baraga, Mi., U.S. B2 115
Baraga, co., Mi., U.S. B2 115
Barahona, Dom. Rep. B5 80
Barakaldo, Spain F5 16
Baram, stm., Malay. C4 36
Bāramūla, India C2 40
Baranagar, India E5 40
Baranavičy, Bela. C9 20
Barani, Burkina D4 50
Baranof Island, i., Ak., U.S. m22 95
Barataria, La., U.S. E5 111
Barataria Bay, b., La., U.S. E6 111
Barauni, India D5 40
Barbacena, Braz. F3 74
Barbacoas, Col. C4 70
Barbados, ctry., N.A. F12 76
Barbar, Sudan G11 48
Barbas, Cap, c., W. Sah. B1 50
Barbastro, Spain F7 16
Barber, co., Ks., U.S. E5 109
Barbers Point, c., Hi., U.S. B3 104
Barbers Point Naval Air Station, mil., Hi., U.S. g9 104
Barberton, S. Afr. D5 56
Barberton, Oh., U.S. A4 128
Barbour, co., Al., U.S. D4 94
Barbour, co., W.V., U.S. B4 141
Barboursville, W.V., U.S. C2 141
Barbourville, Ky., U.S. D6 110
Barbuda, i., Antig. B7 80
Barcaldine, Austl. E4 62
Barcelona, Spain G8 16
Barcelona, Ven. B6 70
Barcelos, Braz. D7 70

Name **Map Ref.** **Page**

Barcroft, Lake, res., Va., U.S. **g12** 139
Bārdā, Azer. **B12** 44
Bardaï, Chad **B8** 50
Bardawīl, Sabkhet el-, b., Egypt **G5** 44
Bardejov, Slvk. **E6** 20
Barden Reservoir, res., R.I., U.S. **C2** 132
Bardīyah, Libya **D10** 48
Bardstown, Ky., U.S. **C4** 110
Bardwell, Ky., U.S. **f9** 110
Bardwell Lake, res., Tx., U.S. **C4** 136
Bareilly, India **D3** 40
Barents Sea, Eur. **B6** 26
Barents Trough **D20** 144
Bargersville, In., U.S. **E5** 107
Bar Harbor, Me., U.S. **D4** 112
Bari, Italy **D6** 18
Barika, Alg. **J9** 16
Barillas, Guat. **B1** 80
Barīm, i., Yemen **H4** 38
Barinas, Ven. **B6** 70
Bāripada, India **E5** 40
Bârîs, Egypt **F11** 48
Barisāl, Bngl. **E6** 40
Barisan, Pegunungan, mts., Indon. **D2** 36
Barkam, China **C1** 30
Barker Heights, N.C., U.S. **f10** 126
Barkhamsted Reservoir, res., Ct., U.S. **B3** 100
Barkley, Lake, res., U.S. **f10** 110
Barkley Sound, strt., B.C., Can. **E5** 85
Barkly East, S. Afr. **E4** 56
Barkly Tableland, plat., Austl. **D6** 60
Barkol, China **C6** 28
Bark Point, c., Wi., U.S. **B2** 142
Barksdale Air Force Base, mil., La., U.S. **B2** 111
Bârlad, Rom. **F9** 20
Barlee, Lake, l., Austl. **F2** 60
Barletta, Italy **D6** 18
Barling, Ar., U.S. **B1** 97
Barlow, Ky., U.S. **e8** 110
Bārmer, India **D2** 40
Barmera, Austl. **G3** 62
Barnaul, Russia **D10** 26
Barnegat Bay, b., N.J., U.S. **D4** 123
Barnegat Inlet, b., N.J., U.S. **D4** 123
Barnes, co., N.D., U.S. **B7** 127
Barnesboro, Pa., U.S. **E4** 131
Barnes Sound, strt., Fl., U.S. **G6** 102
Barnesville, Ga., U.S. **C2** 103
Barnesville, Mn., U.S. **D2** 116
Barnesville, Oh., U.S. **C4** 128
Barnhart, Mo., U.S. **C7** 118
Barnsdall, Ok., U.S. **A5** 129
Barnstable, Ma., U.S. **C7** 114
Barnstable, co., Ma., U.S. **C7** 114
Barnstaple, Eng., U.K. **E4** 12
Barnwell, S.C., U.S. **E5** 133
Barnwell, co., S.C., U.S. **E5** 133
Baro, Nig. **E6** 50
Barpeta, India **D6** 40
Barqah (Cyrenaica), hist. reg., Libya **E8** 14
Barques, Pointe aux, c., Mi., U.S. **D8** 115
Barquisimeto, Ven. **A6** 70
Barra, Braz. **D3** 74
Barra, i., Scot., U.K. **B3** 12
Barra, Ponta da, c., Moz. **C6** 56
Barrackville, W.V., U.S. **B4** 141
Barra do Corda, Braz. **C2** 74
Barra do Cuanza, Ang. **E2** 54
Barra do Dande, Ang. **E2** 54
Barra do Garças, Braz. **B7** 72
Barra Mansa, Braz. **F3** 74
Barranca, Peru **F4** 70
Barrancabermeja, Col. **B5** 70
Barrancas, Ven. **D7** 80
Barranquilla, Col. **A5** 70
Barras, Braz. **B3** 74
Barre, Vt., U.S. **C4** 138
Barre, Lake, l., La., U.S. **E5** 111
Barre Falls Reservoir, res., Ma., U.S. **B4** 114
Barreiras, Braz. **D3** 74
Barreiro, Port. **H2** 16
Barreiros, Braz. **C4** 74
Barren, co., Ky., U.S. **D4** 110
Barren, stm., Ky., U.S. **C3** 110
Barren, Nosy, is., Madag. **B7** 56
Barren Island, i., Md., U.S. **D5** 113
Barren Islands, is., Ak., U.S. **h15** 95
Barren River Lake, res., Ky., U.S. **D3** 110
Barretos, Braz. **F2** 74
Barrett, W.V., U.S. **D3** 141
Barrhead, Ab., Can. **B3** 84
Barrie, On., Can. **C5** 89
Barrie Island, i., On., Can. **B2** 89
Barrière, B.C., Can. **D7** 85
Barrier Range, mts., Austl. **G3** 62
Barrington, Il., U.S. **A5** 106
Barrington, N.J., U.S. **D2** 123
Barrington, R.I., U.S. **D5** 132
Barrington, stm., R.I., U.S. **C5** 132
Barron, Wi., U.S. **C2** 142
Barron, co., Wi., U.S. **C2** 142
Barron Lake, Mi., U.S. **G4** 115
Barrow, Ak., U.S. **A8** 95
Barrow, co., Ga., U.S. **B3** 103
Barrow, Point, c., Ak., U.S. **A8** 95
Barrow Creek, Austl. **E5** 60
Barrow-in-Furness, Eng., U.K. **C5** 12
Barrow Island, i., Austl. **E2** 60
Barry, Il., U.S. **D2** 106
Barry, co., Mi., U.S. **F5** 115
Barry, co., Mo., U.S. **E4** 118
Barrys Bay, On., Can. **B7** 89
Bārsi, India **F3** 40
Barstow, Ca., U.S. **E5** 98
Bartholomew, co., In., U.S. **F6** 107
Bartholomew, Bayou, stm., U.S. **D4** 97
Bartica, Guy. **B8** 70
Bartın, Tur. **B5** 44
Bartlesville, Ok., U.S. **A6** 129
Bartlett, N.H., U.S. **B4** 122
Bartlett, Tn., U.S. **B2** 135
Bartlett, Tx., U.S. **D4** 136
Bartlett Reservoir, res., Az., U.S. **D4** 96
Bartletts Ferry Dam, U.S. **C4** 94
Barton, Oh., U.S. **B5** 128
Barton, Vt., U.S. **B4** 138
Barton, co., Ks., U.S. **D5** 109
Barton, co., Mo., U.S. **D3** 118
Barton, stm., Vt., U.S. **B4** 138
Bartonville, Il., U.S. **C4** 106
Bartoszyce, Pol. **B6** 20
Bartow, Fl., U.S. **E5** 102
Bartow, co., Ga., U.S. **B2** 103
Barú, Volcán, vol., Pan. **D3** 80
Barun Su, China **A3** 30
Baruun-Urt, Mong. **B10** 28
Barysaŭ, Bela. **B10** 20
Basalt, Co., U.S. **B3** 99
Basankusu, D.R.C. **C3** 54
Bascuñán, Cabo, c., Chile **D3** 72
Basehor, Ks., U.S. **k16** 109
Basel, Switz. **G10** 12
Bashan Lake, l., Ct., U.S. **D6** 100
Bashaw, Ab., Can. **C4** 84
Bashi Channel, strt., Asia **B8** 34
Basilan Island, i., Phil. **E8** 34
Basile, La., U.S. **D3** 111
Basin, Wy., U.S. **B4** 143
Basingstoke, Eng., U.K. **E6** 12
Basīrhāt, India **E5** 40
Baskahegan Lake, l., Me., U.S. **C5** 112
Başkale, Tur. **C10** 44
Basking Ridge, N.J., U.S. **B3** 123
Baškirija, state, Russia **D7** 26
Basoko, D.R.C. **C4** 54
Basra see Al-Başrah, Iraq **D5** 42
Bassano, Ab., Can. **D4** 84
Bassar, Togo **E5** 50
Bassein see Pathein, Myan. **C2** 34
Basse Santa Su, Gam. **D2** 50
Basse-Terre, Guad. **B7** 80
Basseterre, St. K./N. **B7** 80
Basse-Terre, i., Guad. **B7** 80
Bassett, Ne., U.S. **B6** 120
Bassett, Va., U.S. **D3** 139
Bassett Peak, mtn., Az., U.S. **E5** 96
Bassikounou, Maur. **C3** 50
Bass Islands, is., Oh., U.S. **A3** 128
Bass Lake, In., U.S. **B4** 107
Bass Strait, strt., Austl. **H4** 62
Basswood Lake, l., Mn., U.S. **B7** 116
Båstad, Swe. **H5** 10
Bastia, Fr. **C2** 18
Bastrop, La., U.S. **B4** 111
Bastrop, Tx., U.S. **D4** 136
Bastrop, co., Tx., U.S. **D4** 136
Basu, Pulau, i., Indon. **D2** 36
Basutoland see Lesotho, ctry., Afr. **D4** 56
Bata, Eq. Gui. **C1** 54
Batabanó, Golfo de, b., Cuba **A3** 80
Batac, Phil. **C8** 34
Batagaj, Russia **C15** 26
Batala, India **C3** 40
Batamaj, Russia **C14** 26
Batang, China **E7** 28
Batang, Indon. **E3** 36
Batangafo, C.A.R. **B3** 54
Batangas, Phil. **D8** 34
Batan Islands, is., Phil. **B8** 34
Batanta, Pulau, i., Indon. **D8** 36
Batavia see Jakarta, Indon. **E3** 36
Batavia, Il., U.S. **B5** 106
Batavia, N.Y., U.S. **C2** 125
Batavia, Oh., U.S. **C1** 128
Batchelor, Austl. **C5** 60
Batchelor Bay, b., N.C., U.S. **B6** 126
Bătdâmbâng, Camb. **D4** 34
Batemans Bay, Austl. **H5** 62
Bates, co., Mo., U.S. **C3** 118
Batesburg, S.C., U.S. **D4** 133
Batesville, Ar., U.S. **B4** 97
Batesville, In., U.S. **F7** 107
Batesville, Ms., U.S. **A4** 117
Bath, N.B., Can. **C2** 87
Bath, On., Can. **C8** 89
Bath, Eng., U.K. **E5** 12
Bath, Me., U.S. **E3** 112
Bath, N.Y., U.S. **C3** 125
Bath, Pa., U.S. **E11** 131
Bath, S.C., U.S. **D4** 133
Bath, co., Ky., U.S. **B6** 110
Bath, co., Va., U.S. **B3** 139
Bathinda, India **C3** 40
Bathurst, Austl. **G4** 62
Bathurst, N.B., Can. **B4** 87
Bathurst see Banjul, Gam. **D1** 50
Bathurst Island, i., Austl. **C5** 60
Batiscan, stm., P.Q., Can. **B5** 90
Batman, Tur. **D9** 44
Batna, Alg. **C6** 48
Baton Rouge, La., U.S. **D4** 111
Batouri, Cam. **C2** 54
Batsto, stm., N.J., U.S. **D3** 123
Batten Kill, stm., U.S. **E2** 138
Batticaloa, Sri L. **H4** 40
Battle, stm., Can. **H17** 82
Battle Creek, Ia., U.S. **B2** 108
Battle Creek, Mi., U.S. **F5** 115
Battle Creek, Ne., U.S. **C8** 120
Battle Ground, In., U.S. **C4** 107
Battle Ground, Wa., U.S. **D3** 140
Battle Lake, Mn., U.S. **D3** 116
Battle Mountain, Nv., U.S. **C5** 121
Battle Mountain, mtn., Wy., U.S. **E5** 143
Batu, mtn., Eth. **B7** 54
Batu, Kepulauan, is., Indon. **D1** 36
Batumi, Geor. **B9** 44
Batu Pahat, Malay. **C2** 36
Baturaja, Indon. **D2** 36
Baturité, Braz. **B4** 74
Baubau, Indon. **E6** 36
Bauchi, Nig. **D6** 50
Baudette, Mn., U.S. **B4** 116
Bauld, Cape, c., Nf., Can. **C4** 88
Baures, Bol. **A5** 72
Bauru, Braz. **F2** 74
Bauska, Lat. **H11** 10
Bautzen, Ger. **E14** 12
Bavispe, stm., Mex. **A3** 78
Bawdwin, Myan. **B3** 34
Bawean, Pulau, i., Indon. **E4** 36
Bawiti, Egypt **E10** 48
Baxley, Ga., U.S. **E4** 103
Baxter, Ia., U.S. **C4** 108
Baxter, Mn., U.S. **D4** 116
Baxter, Tn., U.S. **C8** 135
Baxter, co., Ar., U.S. **A3** 97
Baxter Springs, Ks., U.S. **E9** 109
Bay, Ar., U.S. **B5** 97
Bay, co., Fl., U.S. **u16** 102
Bay, co., Mi., U.S. **E6** 115
Bayamo, Cuba **A4** 80
Bayamón, P.R. **B6** 80
Bayan Har Shan, mts., China **E7** 28
Bayanhongor, Mong. **B8** 28
Bayano, Lago, res., Pan. **D4** 80
Bayan Obo, China **C10** 28
Bayard, Ne., U.S. **C2** 120
Bayard, N.M., U.S. **E1** 124
Bayboro, N.C., U.S. **B6** 126
Bay Bulls, Nf., Can. **E5** 88
Bayburt, Tur. **B9** 44
Bay City, Mi., U.S. **E7** 115
Bay City, Or., U.S. **B3** 130
Bay City, Tx., U.S. **E5** 136
Bay de Verde, Nf., Can. **D5** 88
Baydhabo, Som. **J13** 48
Bayeux, Fr. **C6** 16
Bayfield, On., Can. **D3** 89
Bayfield, Co., U.S. **D3** 99
Bayfield, Wi., U.S. **B3** 142
Bayfield, co., Wi., U.S. **B2** 142
Baylor, co., Tx., U.S. **C3** 136
Bay Mills Indian Reservation, Mi., U.S. **B6** 115
Bay Minette, Al., U.S. **E2** 94
Bayombong, Phil. **C8** 34
Bayonne, Fr. **F6** 16
Bayonne, N.J., U.S. **B4** 123
Bayou Bodcau Reservoir, res., La., U.S. **B2** 111
Bayou D'Arbonne Lake, res., La., U.S. **B3** 111
Bayou George, Fl., U.S. **u16** 102
Bayou Goula, La., U.S. **D4** 111
Bayou La Batre, Al., U.S. **E1** 94
Bayovar, Peru **E3** 70
Bay Point, c., S.C., U.S. **G7** 133
Bayport, Mn., U.S. **E6** 116
Bayport, N.Y., U.S. **n15** 125
Bayreuth, Ger. **F12** 12
Bay Ridge, Md., U.S. **C5** 113
Bay Roberts, Nf., Can. **E5** 88
Bayrūt (Beirut), Leb. **F6** 44
Bays, Lake of, l., On., Can. **B5** 89
Bay Saint Louis, Ms., U.S. **E4** 117
Bay Shore, N.Y., U.S. **E7** 125
Bayshore Gardens, Fl., U.S. **q10** 102
Bayside, Wi., U.S. **m12** 142
Bay Springs, Ms., U.S. **D4** 117
Bayt Laḩm, W.B. **G6** 44
Baytown, Tx., U.S. **E5** 136
Bayview, Al., U.S. **f7** 94
Bay Village, Oh., U.S. **h9** 128
Baza, Spain **I5** 16
Bazardjuzju, gora see Bazardüzü dağ, mtn., Azer. **B12** 44
Bazardüzü dağ, mtn., Azer. **B12** 44
Bazaruto, Ilha do, i., Moz. **C6** 56
Bazhong, China **C2** 30
Be, Nosy, i., Madag. **A8** 56
Beach, Il., U.S. **h9** 106
Beach, N.D., U.S. **C1** 127
Beachburg, On., Can. **B8** 89
Beach City, Oh., U.S. **B4** 128
Beach Haven Inlet, b., N.J., U.S. **D4** 123
Beach Pond, res., U.S. **C8** 100
Beachville, On., Can. **D4** 89
Beachwood, N.J., U.S. **D4** 123
Beacon, Austl. **G2** 60
Beacon, N.Y., U.S. **D7** 125
Beacon Falls, Ct., U.S. **D3** 100
Beaconsfield, P.Q., Can. **q19** 90
Beadle, co., S.D., U.S. **C7** 134
Beagle Gulf, b., Austl. **C4** 60
Bealanana, Madag. **A8** 56
Beale, Cape, c., B.C., Can. **E5** 85
Beale Air Force Base, mil., Ca., U.S. **C3** 98
Bear, De., U.S. **B3** 101
Bear, stm., U.S. **B3** 137
Bear Creek, Al., U.S. **A2** 94
Bear Creek, stm., Or., U.S. **E4** 130
Bear Creek, stm., Wy., U.S. **E8** 143
Bear Creek, stm., U.S. **E2** 109
Bearden, Ar., U.S. **D3** 97
Beardstown, Il., U.S. **C3** 106
Bear Inlet, b., N.C., U.S. **C5** 126
Bear Island see Bjørnøya, i., Nor. **B3** 26
Bear Lake, co., Id., U.S. **G7** 105
Bear Lake, l., Wi., U.S. **C2** 142
Bear Lake, l., U.S. **C5** 92
Bear Lake, l., U.S. **A4** 137
Bear Lodge Mountains, mts., Wy., U.S. **B8** 143
Bear Mountain, mtn., Or., U.S. **D4** 130
Bearpaw Mountains, mts., Mt., U.S. **B7** 119
Bear River, N.S., Can. **E4** 87
Bear River City, Ut., U.S. **B3** 137
Beartooth Pass, Wy., U.S. **B3** 143
Beartooth Range, mts., U.S. **E7** 119
Bear Town, Ms., U.S. **D3** 117
Beās, stm., India **C3** 40
Beata, Isla, i., Dom. Rep. **B5** 80
Beatrice, Ne., U.S. **D9** 120
Beatrice, Cape, c., Austl. **C2** 62
Beatty, Nv., U.S. **G5** 121
Beattyville, Ky., U.S. **C6** 110
Beaufort, N.C., U.S. **C6** 126
Beaufort, S.C., U.S. **G6** 133
Beaufort, co., N.C., U.S. **B5** 126
Beaufort, co., S.C., U.S. **G6** 133
Beaufort Marine Corps Air Station, mil., S.C., U.S. **F6** 133
Beaufort Sea, N.A. **D12** 82
Beaufort West, S. Afr. **E3** 56
Beauharnois, P.Q., Can. **D4** 90
Beau Lake, l., Me., U.S. **A3** 112
Beaumont, Ab., Can. **C4** 84
Beaumont, Ms., U.S. **D5** 117
Beaumont, Tx., U.S. **D5** 136
Beaune, Fr. **D9** 16
Beauport, P.Q., Can. **n17** 90
Beaupré, P.Q., Can. **B7** 90
Beauregard, co., La., U.S. **D2** 111
Beausejour, Mb., Can. **D3** 86
Beauvais, Fr. **C8** 16
Beauval, Sk., Can. **B2** 91
Beaver, Ok., U.S. **A1** 129
Beaver, Pa., U.S. **E1** 131
Beaver, Ut., U.S. **E3** 137
Beaver, W.V., U.S. **D3** 141
Beaver, co., Ok., U.S. **e10** 129
Beaver, co., Pa., U.S. **E1** 131
Beaver, co., Ut., U.S. **E2** 137
Beaver, stm., Can. **B2** 91
Beaver, stm., N.Y., U.S. **B6** 125
Beaver, stm., R.I., U.S. **E2** 132
Beaver, stm., Ut., U.S. **E2** 137
Beaver, stm., U.S. **A2** 129
Beaverbank, N.S., Can. **E6** 87
Beaver Brook, stm., U.S. **E4** 122
Beaver City, Ne., U.S. **D6** 120
Beavercreek, Oh., U.S. **C1** 128
Beaver Creek, stm., N.D., U.S. **C1** 127
Beaver Creek, stm., N.D., U.S. **C5** 127
Beaver Creek, stm., Ok., U.S. **C3** 129
Beaver Creek, stm., Tn., U.S. **m13** 135
Beaver Creek, stm., Wy., U.S. **D4** 143
Beaver Creek, stm., U.S. **E4** 120
Beaver Creek, stm., U.S. **C8** 143
Beaverdale, Pa., U.S. **F4** 131
Beaver Dam, Ky., U.S. **C3** 110
Beaver Dam, Wi., U.S. **E5** 142
Beaverdam Branch, stm., De., U.S. **F3** 101
Beaverdam Lake, res., Wi., U.S. **E5** 142
Beaver Falls, Pa., U.S. **E1** 131
Beaverhead, co., Mt., U.S. **E3** 119
Beaverhead, stm., Mt., U.S. **E4** 119
Beaverhead Mountains, mts., U.S. **D5** 105
Beaverhill Lake, l., Ab., Can. **C4** 84
Beaver Island, i., Mi., U.S. **C5** 115
Beaver Lake, res., Ar., U.S. **A2** 97
Beaverlodge, Ab., Can. **B1** 84
Beaver Meadows, Pa., U.S. **E10** 131
Beaver Run Reservoir, res., Pa., U.S. **F2** 131
Beavertail Point, c., R.I., U.S. **F4** 132
Beaverton, Mi., U.S. **E6** 115
Beaverton, Or., U.S. **B4** 130
Beāwar, India **D2** 40
Bebedouro, Braz. **C8** 72
Bécancour, P.Q., Can. **C5** 90
Bečej, Yugo. **B8** 18
Béchar, Alg. **D4** 48
Becharof Lake, l., Ak., U.S. **D8** 95
Bechuanaland see Botswana, ctry., Afr. **C3** 56
Beckemeyer, Il., U.S. **E4** 106
Becker, Mn., U.S. **E5** 116
Becker, co., Mn., U.S. **D3** 116
Beckham, co., Ok., U.S. **B2** 129
Beckley, W.V., U.S. **D3** 141
Becky Peak, mtn., Nv., U.S. **D7** 121
Bedelē, Eth. **B7** 54
Bedford, P.Q., Can. **D5** 90
Bedford, Eng., U.K. **D6** 12
Bedford, Ia., U.S. **D3** 108
Bedford, In., U.S. **G5** 107
Bedford, Ky., U.S. **B4** 110
Bedford, Ma., U.S. **B5** 114
Bedford, N.H., U.S. **E3** 122
Bedford, Oh., U.S. **A4** 128
Bedford, Pa., U.S. **F4** 131
Bedford, Va., U.S. **C3** 139
Bedford, co., Pa., U.S. **G4** 131
Bedford, co., Tn., U.S. **B5** 135
Bedford, co., Va., U.S. **C3** 139
Bedford Hills, N.Y., U.S. **D7** 125
Bee, co., Tx., U.S. **E4** 136
Beebe, P.Q., Can. **D5** 90
Beebe, Ar., U.S. **B4** 97
Beecher, Il., U.S. **B6** 106
Beech Fork, stm., Ky., U.S. **C4** 110
Beech Grove, In., U.S. **E5** 107
Beech Island, S.C., U.S. **E4** 133
Beemer, Ne., U.S. **C9** 120
Bee Ridge, Fl., U.S. **q11** 102
Beersheba see Be'ér Sheva', Isr. **D2** 42
Be'ér Sheva', Isr. **D2** 42
Beeton (part of Alliston Beeton Tecumseth and Tottenham), On., Can. **C5** 89
Beeville, Tx., U.S. **E4** 136
Befale, D.R.C. **C4** 54
Befandriana Atsimo, Madag. **C7** 56
Bega, Austl. **H4** 62
Beggs, Ok., U.S. **B5** 129
Behbahān, Iran **D6** 42
Behm Canal, strt., Ak., U.S. **n24** 95
Bei'an, China **B13** 28
Beigi, Eth. **B6** 54
Beihai, China **G9** 28
Beijing, China **D11** 28
Beiliu, China **E3** 30
Beipiao, China **C12** 28
Beira, Moz. **B5** 56
Beirut see Bayrūt, Leb. **F6** 44
Bei Shan, mts., China **C7** 28
Beitbridge, Zimb. **C5** 56
Beizhen, China **A5** 30
Beizhen, China **B4** 30
Beja, Port. **I3** 16
Béja, Tun. **C6** 48
Bejaïa, Alg. **C6** 48
Bejaïa, Golfe de, b., Alg. **I9** 16
Béjar, Spain **G4** 16
Bejneu, Kaz. **E7** 26
Bekaa Valley see Al-Biqā', val., Leb. **F6** 44
Bekabad, Uzb. **B9** 42
Bekasi, Indon. **E3** 36
Bekdaš, Turk. **B6** 42
Békéscsaba, Hung. **F6** 20
Bekily, Madag. **C8** 56
Bekodoka, Madag. **B8** 56
Bela, India **D4** 40
Bela, Pak. **E9** 42
Bela Crkva, Yugo. **B8** 18
Bel Air, Md., U.S. **A5** 113
Bel Alton, Md., U.S. **D4** 113
Belarus, ctry., Eur. **C9** 20
Belau see Palau, ctry., Oc. **F10** 32
Bela Vista, Braz. **H8** 70
Bela Vista, Moz. **D5** 56
Belcamp, Md., U.S. **B5** 113
Bełchatów, Pol. **D5** 20
Belchertown, Ma., U.S. **B3** 114
Belcourt, N.D., U.S. **A6** 127
Belden, Ms., U.S. **A5** 117
Belding, Mi., U.S. **E5** 115
Beledweyne, Som. **J13** 48
Belém, Braz. **B2** 74
Belém, Moz. **A6** 56
Belém de São Francisco, Braz. **C4** 74
Belen, N.M., U.S. **C3** 124
Belëv, Russia **C14** 20
Belfair, Wa., U.S. **B3** 140
Belfast, S. Afr. **D5** 56
Belfast, N. Ire., U.K. **C4** 12
Belfast, Me., U.S. **D3** 112
Belfield, N.D., U.S. **C2** 127
Belford, N.J., U.S. **C4** 123
Belfort, Fr. **D10** 16
Belfry, Ky., U.S. **C7** 110
Belgaum, India **F2** 40
Belgium, Wi., U.S. **E6** 142

Name	Map Ref.	Page
Belgium, ctry., Eur.	B9	16
Belgorod, Russia	D5	26
Belgrade, Mn., U.S.	E3	116
Belgrade, Mt., U.S.	E5	119
Belgrade see Beograd, Yugo.	B8	18
Belhaven, N.C., U.S.	B6	126
Beliliou, i., Palau	E9	32
Belington, W.V., U.S.	B5	141
Belitung, i., Indon.	D3	36
Belize, ctry., N.A.	B2	80
Belize City, Belize	B2	80
Belknap, co., N.H., U.S.	C3	122
Belknap Crater, crat., Or., U.S.	C5	130
Bell, co., Ky., U.S.	D6	110
Bell, co., Tx., U.S.	D4	136
Bella Coola, stm., B.C., Can.	C4	85
Bellaire, Ks., U.S.	g12	109
Bellaire, Mi., U.S.	D5	115
Bellaire, Oh., U.S.	C5	128
Bellaire, Tx., U.S.	r14	136
Bellamy, Al., U.S.	C1	94
Bellary, India	F3	40
Bella Vista, Arg.	D6	72
Bellavista, Peru	E4	70
Bella Vista, Ar., U.S.	A1	97
Bellbrook, Oh., U.S.	C1	128
Belle, Mo., U.S.	C6	118
Belle, W.V., U.S.	C3	141
Belle, stm., La., U.S.	k9	111
Belleair, Fl., U.S.	p10	102
Belle Bay, b., Nf., Can.	E4	88
Belle Chasse, La., U.S.	E5	111
Bellefontaine, Oh., U.S.	B2	128
Bellefonte, Pa., U.S.	E6	131
Belle Fourche, S.D., U.S.	C2	134
Belle Fourche, stm., U.S.	C3	134
Belle Fourche Reservoir, res., S.D., U.S.	C2	134
Belle Glade, Fl., U.S.	F6	102
Belle-Île, i., Fr.	D5	16
Belle Isle, Fl., U.S.	D5	102
Belle Isle, i., Nf., Can.	C4	88
Belle Isle, Strait of, strt., Nf., Can.	C3	88
Belle Meade, Tn., U.S.	g10	135
Belle Plaine, Ia., U.S.	C5	108
Belle Plaine, Ks., U.S.	E6	109
Belle Plaine, Mn., U.S.	F5	116
Belle River, On., Can.	E2	89
Belle Rose, La., U.S.	D4	111
Belle Vernon, Pa., U.S.	F2	131
Belleview, Fl., U.S.	C4	102
Belle View, Va., U.S.	g12	139
Belleville, On., Can.	C7	89
Belleville, Il., U.S.	E4	106
Belleville, Ks., U.S.	C6	109
Belleville, Mi., U.S.	p15	115
Belleville, N.J., U.S.	B4	123
Belleville, Pa., U.S.	E6	131
Belleville, Wi., U.S.	F4	142
Belleville Pond, l., R.I., U.S.	E4	132
Bellevue, Ia., U.S.	B7	108
Bellevue, Id., U.S.	F4	105
Bellevue, Ky., U.S.	h13	110
Bellevue, Mi., U.S.	F5	115
Bellevue, Ne., U.S.	C10	120
Bellevue, Oh., U.S.	A3	128
Bellevue, Pa., U.S.	F1	131
Bellevue, Wa., U.S.	e11	140
Bellflower, Ca., U.S.	n12	98
Bellingham, Ma., U.S.	B5	114
Bellingham, Wa., U.S.	A3	140
Bellingshausen Sea, Ant.	C32	67
Bellinzona, Switz.	A2	18
Bell Island, i., Nf., Can.	C4	88
Bellmawr, N.J., U.S.	D2	123
Bello, Col.	B4	70
Bellows Falls, Vt., U.S.	E4	138
Bellport, N.Y., U.S.	n16	125
Bells, Tn., U.S.	B2	135
Bells Creek, stm., W.V., U.S.	m13	141
Belluno, Italy	A4	18
Bell Ville, Arg.	E5	72
Bellville, Oh., U.S.	B3	128
Bellville, Tx., U.S.	E4	136
Bellwood, Il., U.S.	k9	106
Bellwood, Pa., U.S.	E5	131
Bellwood, Va., U.S.	n18	139
Belmar, N.J., U.S.	C4	123
Belmond, Ia., U.S.	B4	108
Belmont, On., Can.	E3	89
Belmont, Ca., U.S.	h8	98
Belmont, Ma., U.S.	g11	114
Belmont, Ms., U.S.	A5	117
Belmont, N.C., U.S.	B1	126
Belmont, N.H., U.S.	D4	122
Belmont, W.V., U.S.	B3	141
Belmont, Wi., U.S.	F3	142
Belmont, co., Oh., U.S.	C4	128
Belmonte, Braz.	G12	70
Belmopan, Belize	B2	80
Bel-Nor, Mo., U.S.	f13	118
Beloe, ozero, l., Russia	C5	26
Beloeil, P.Q., Can.	D4	90
Beloe more, Russia	C5	26
Belogorsk, Russia	D14	26
Belo Horizonte, Braz.	E3	74
Beloit, Ks., U.S.	C5	109
Beloit, Oh., U.S.	B5	128
Beloit, Wi., U.S.	F4	142
Belomorsk, Russia	C5	26
Beloreck, Russia	D10	22
Belorussia see Belarus, ctry., Eur.	C9	20
Belo Tsiribihina, Madag.	B7	56
Belpre, Oh., U.S.	C4	128
Belt, Mt., U.S.	C6	119
Belted Range, mts., Nv., U.S.	F5	121
Belton, Mo., U.S.	C3	118
Belton, S.C., U.S.	B3	133
Belton, Tx., U.S.	D4	136
Belton Lake, res., Tx., U.S.	D4	136
Beltrami, co., Mn., U.S.	B3	116
Beltsville, Md., U.S.	B4	113
Beluha, gora, mtn., Asia	B5	28
Belūr, India	G3	40
Belvedere, S.C., U.S.	D4	133
Belvidere, Il., U.S.	A5	106
Belvidere, N.J., U.S.	B2	123
Belyj, ostrov, i., Russia	B8	26
Belyj Jar, Russia	D10	26
Belzoni, Ms., U.S.	B3	117
Bembèrèkè, Benin	D5	50
Bement, Il., U.S.	D5	106
Bemidji, Mn., U.S.	C4	116
Bemidji, Lake, l., Mn., U.S.	C4	116
Benāb, Iran	D11	44
Bena-Dibele, D.R.C.	D4	54
Benalla, Austl.	H4	62
Benares see Vārānasi, India	D4	40
Benavente, Spain	F4	16
Benavides, Tx., U.S.	F3	136
Benbecula, i., Scot., U.K.	B3	12
Benbrook Lake, res., Tx., U.S.	n9	136
Bencubbin, Austl.	G2	60
Bend, Or., U.S.	C5	130
Ben Davis Point, c., N.J., U.S.	E2	123
Bendeleben, Mount, mtn., Ak., U.S.	B7	95
Bendigo, Austl.	H3	62
Benedict, Md., U.S.	C4	113
Benedito Leite, Braz.	E11	70
Benevento, Italy	D5	18
Benewah, co., Id., U.S.	B2	105
Bengal, Bay of, b., Asia	F5	40
Bengbu, China	E11	28
Benghazi see Banghāzī, Libya	D9	48
Bengkalis, Pulau, i., Indon.	C2	36
Bengkulu, Indon.	D2	36
Bengtsfors, Swe.	G5	10
Benguela, Ang.	F2	54
Bengweulu Swamps, sw., Zam.	A5	56
Benham, Ky., U.S.	D7	110
Ben Hill, co., Ga., U.S.	E3	103
Beni, D.R.C.	C5	54
Beni, stm., Bol.	F6	70
Béni Abbas, Alg.	D4	48
Benicia, Ca., U.S.	C2	98
Benidorm, Spain	H6	16
Beni-Mellal, Mor.	D3	48
Benin, ctry., Afr.	D5	50
Benin, Bight of, b., Afr.	E5	50
Benin City, Nig.	E6	50
Beni Saf, Alg.	J6	16
Beni Suef, Egypt	E11	48
Benito Juárez, Arg.	F6	72
Benjamin Constant, Braz.	D5	70
Benkelman, Ne., U.S.	D4	120
Benld, Il., U.S.	D4	106
Bennett, Co., U.S.	B6	99
Bennett, co., S.D., U.S.	D4	134
Bennettsville, S.C., U.S.	B8	133
Bennington, Ne., U.S.	g12	120
Bennington, N.H., U.S.	D3	122
Bennington, Vt., U.S.	F2	138
Bennington, co., Vt., U.S.	E2	138
Benoit, Ms., U.S.	B2	117
Benoni, S. Afr.	D4	56
Bénoué see Benue, stm., Afr.	E6	50
Bensenville, Il., U.S.	B6	106
Bensheim, Ger.	F11	12
Bensley, Va., U.S.	C5	139
Benson, Az., U.S.	F5	96
Benson, Mn., U.S.	E3	116
Benson, N.C., U.S.	B4	126
Benson, co., N.D., U.S.	A6	127
Bent, co., Co., U.S.	D7	99
Benteng, Indon.	E6	36
Bentinck Island, i., Austl.	D2	62
Bentinck Island, i., Myan.	D3	34
Bentley, Ab., Can.	C3	84
Bentleyville, Pa., U.S.	F1	131
Benton, Ar., U.S.	C3	97
Benton, Il., U.S.	E5	106
Benton, Ks., U.S.	E6	109
Benton, Ky., U.S.	f9	110
Benton, La., U.S.	B2	111
Benton, Pa., U.S.	D9	131
Benton, Tn., U.S.	B7	135
Benton, Wi., U.S.	F3	142
Benton, co., Ar., U.S.	A1	97
Benton, co., Ia., U.S.	B5	108
Benton, co., In., U.S.	C3	107
Benton, co., Mn., U.S.	E4	116
Benton, co., Mo., U.S.	C4	118
Benton, co., Ms., U.S.	A4	117
Benton, co., Or., U.S.	C3	130
Benton, co., Tn., U.S.	A3	135
Benton, co., Wa., U.S.	C6	140
Benton City, Wa., U.S.	C6	140
Benton Harbor, Mi., U.S.	F4	115
Benton Heights, Mi., U.S.	F4	115
Bentonville, Ar., U.S.	A1	97
Ben Tre, Viet.	D5	34
Bent's Old Fort National Historic Site, hist., Co., U.S.	C7	99
Bentung, Malay.	C2	36
Benue, stm., Afr.	E6	50
Benwood, W.V., U.S.	f8	141
Benxi, China	C12	28
Benzie, co., Mi., U.S.	D4	115
Beograd (Belgrade), Yugo.	B8	18
Béoumi, C. Iv.	E3	50
Beowawe, Nv., U.S.	C5	121
Beppu, Japan	D2	31
Beraketa, Madag.	C8	56
Berat, Alb.	D7	18
Berau, Teluk, b., Indon.	D8	36
Berazino, Bela.	C10	20
Berbera, Som.	H14	48
Berbérati, C.A.R.	C3	54
Berck, Fr.	B7	16
Berdians'k, Ukr.	F14	20
Berdigestjah, Russia	C14	26
Berdychiv, Ukr.	E10	20
Berea, Ky., U.S.	C5	110
Berea, Oh., U.S.	A4	128
Berea, S.C., U.S.	B3	133
Berehove, Ukr.	E7	20
Berekum, Ghana	E4	50
Berens, stm., Can.	C3	86
Beresford, S.D., U.S.	D9	134
Berettyóújfalu, Hung.	F6	20
Berezhany, Ukr.	E8	20
Berezivka, Ukr.	F11	20
Berezniki, Russia	D7	26
Berëzovo, Russia	C8	26
Berg, Swe.	F7	10
Bergama, Tur.	C2	44
Bergamo, Italy	B2	18
Bergen, Ger.	D12	12
Bergen, Nor.	F1	10
Bergen, co., N.J., U.S.	A4	123
Bergenfield, N.J., U.S.	B4	123
Bergerac, Fr.	E7	16
Bergland, Mi., U.S.	m12	115
Berguent, Mor.	E3	14
Berhala, Selat, strt., Indon.	D2	36
Beringa, ostrov, i., Russia	D18	26
Beringov proliv see Bering Strait, strt.	F6	82
Beringovskij, Russia	C19	26
Bering Sea	G3	82
Bering Strait, strt.	F6	82
Berkakit, Russia	D14	26
Berkane, Mor.	E3	14
Berkeley, Ca., U.S.	D2	98
Berkeley, Mo., U.S.	f13	118
Berkeley, R.I., U.S.	B4	132
Berkeley, co., S.C., U.S.	E8	133
Berkeley, co., W.V., U.S.	B6	141
Berkeley Heights, N.J., U.S.	B4	123
Berkeley Springs, W.V., U.S.	B6	141
Berkley, Mi., U.S.	F7	115
Berks, co., Pa., U.S.	F9	131
Berkshire, co., Ma., U.S.	B1	114
Berkshire Hills, hills, Ma., U.S.	B1	114
Berlevåg, Nor.	A13	10
Berlin, Ger.	D13	12
Berlin, Ct., U.S.	C5	100
Berlin, Md., U.S.	D7	113
Berlin, N.H., U.S.	B4	122
Berlin, N.J., U.S.	D3	123
Berlin, Pa., U.S.	G4	131
Berlin, Wi., U.S.	E5	142
Berlin Lake, res., Oh., U.S.	A4	128
Bermejo, stm., S.A.	C5	72
Bermuda, dep., N.A.	B12	76
Bern, Switz.	A1	18
Bernalillo, N.M., U.S.	B3	124
Bernalillo, co., N.M., U.S.	C3	124
Bernardsville, N.J., U.S.	B3	123
Bernasconi, Arg.	F5	72
Berne see Bern, Switz.	A1	18
Berne, In., U.S.	C8	107
Berner Alpen, mts., Switz.	A1	18
Bernese Alps see Berner Alpen, mts., Switz.	A1	18
Bernice, La., U.S.	B3	111
Bernie, Mo., U.S.	E8	118
Bernier Island, i., Austl.	E1	60
Bernina, Piz, mtn., Eur.	A2	18
Beroroha, Madag.	C8	56
Berrien, co., Ga., U.S.	E3	103
Berrien, co., Mi., U.S.	F4	115
Berrien Springs, Mi., U.S.	G4	115
Berry, Al., U.S.	B2	94
Berry, hist. reg., Fr.	D7	16
Berryessa, Lake, res., Ca., U.S.	C2	98
Berry Hill, Tn., U.S.	g10	135
Berryville, Ar., U.S.	A2	97
Berryville, Va., U.S.	A5	139
Berseba, Nmb.	D2	56
Bershad', Ukr.	E10	20
Berthierville, P.Q., Can.	C4	90
Berthoud, Co., U.S.	A5	99
Berthoud Pass, Co., U.S.	B5	99
Bertie, co., N.C., U.S.	A5	126
Bertoua, Cam.	C2	54
Bertrand, Mo., U.S.	E8	118
Bertrand, Ne., U.S.	D6	120
Berwick, Ia., U.S.	e8	108
Berwick, La., U.S.	E4	111
Berwick, Me., U.S.	E2	112
Berwick, Pa., U.S.	D9	131
Berwick-upon-Tweed, Eng., U.K.	C6	12
Berwyn, Ab., Can.	A2	84
Berwyn, Il., U.S.	k9	106
Berwyn, Pa., U.S.	o20	131
Besalampy, Madag.	B7	56
Besançon, Fr.	D9	16
Beskids, mts., Eur.	E5	20
Beskra, Alg.	D6	48
Beslan, Russia	A11	44
Besni, Tur.	D7	44
Bessemer, Al., U.S.	B3	94
Bessemer, Mi., U.S.	n11	115
Bessemer, Pa., U.S.	E1	131
Bessemer City, N.C., U.S.	B1	126
Bétaré Oya, Cam.	B2	54
Betatakin Ruin, hist., Az., U.S.	A5	96
Bethalto, Il., U.S.	E3	106
Bethanien, Nmb.	D2	56
Bethany, Ct., U.S.	D4	100
Bethany, Il., U.S.	D5	106
Bethany, Mo., U.S.	A3	118
Bethany, Ok., U.S.	B4	129
Bethany, W.V., U.S.	A4	141
Bethany Beach, De., U.S.	F5	101
Bethel, Ak., U.S.	C7	95
Bethel, Ct., U.S.	D2	100
Bethel, Me., U.S.	D2	112
Bethel, N.C., U.S.	B5	126
Bethel, Oh., U.S.	D1	128
Bethel, Vt., U.S.	D3	138
Bethel Park, Pa., U.S.	k14	131
Bethel Springs, Tn., U.S.	B3	135
Bethesda, Md., U.S.	C3	113
Bethesda, Oh., U.S.	B4	128
Bethlehem, S. Afr.	D4	56
Bethlehem, Ct., U.S.	C3	100
Bethlehem, N.H., U.S.	B3	122
Bethlehem, Pa., U.S.	E11	131
Bethlehem see Bayt Laḥm, W.B.	G6	44
Bethulie, S. Afr.	E4	56
Betong, Malay.	C4	36
Betong, Thai.	E4	34
Betoota, Austl.	F3	62
Betpak-Dala, des., Kaz.	E8	26
Betroka, Madag.	C8	56
Betsiboka, stm., Madag.	B8	56
Betsie, Point, c., Mi., U.S.	D4	115
Betsy Layne, Ky., U.S.	C7	110
Bettendorf, Ia., U.S.	C7	108
Bettiah, India	D4	40
Betūl, India	E3	40
Betwa, stm., India	D3	40
Betzdorf, Ger.	E10	12
Beulah, Co., U.S.	C6	99
Beulah, N.D., U.S.	B4	127
Beulah, Lake, l., Ms., U.S.	B3	117
Beulaville, N.C., U.S.	C5	126
Beuthen see Bytom, Pol.	D5	20
B. Everett Jordan Lake, res., N.C., U.S.	B3	126
Beverley Head, c., Nf., Can.	D2	88
Beverly, Ma., U.S.	A6	114
Beverly, N.J., U.S.	C3	123
Beverly, Oh., U.S.	C4	128
Beverly, W.V., U.S.	C5	141
Beverly Hills, Ca., U.S.	m12	98
Beverly Shores, In., U.S.	A4	107
Bexar, co., Tx., U.S.	E3	136
Bexley, Oh., U.S.	m11	128
Beyla, Gui.	E3	50
Beypazarı, Tur.	B4	44
Beyşehir, Tur.	D4	44
Beyşehir Gölü, l., Tur.	D4	44
Bežeck, Russia	C6	22
Béziers, Fr.	F8	16
Bhadohi, India	D4	40
Bhadrāchalam, India	F4	40
Bhadrak, India	E5	40
Bhadra Reservoir, res., India	G3	40
Bhadrāvati, India	G3	40
Bhāgalpur, India	D5	40
Bhāgīrathi see Ganges, stm., India	D5	40
Bhakkar, Pak.	D10	42
Bhaktapur, Nepal	D5	40
Bhamo, Myan.	B3	34
Bhandāra, India	E3	40
Bharatpur, India	D3	40
Bharūch, India	E2	40
Bhātpāra, India	E5	40
Bhāvnagar, India	E2	40
Bhawānipatna, India	F4	40
Bhilai, India	E4	40
Bhīlwāra, India	D2	40
Bhīma, stm., India	F3	40
Bhind, India	D3	40
Bhiwāni, India	D3	40
Bhongīr, India	F3	40
Bhopāl, India	E3	40
Bhubaneshwar, India	E5	40
Bhuj, India	E1	40
Bhusāwal, India	E3	40
Bhutan, ctry., Asia	D6	40
Bia, Mount see Bia, Phou, mtn., Laos	C4	34
Bia, Phou, mtn., Laos	C4	34
Biafra, Bight of, Afr.	C1	54
Biak, i., Indon.	G10	32
Biała Podlaska, Pol.	D7	20
Białogard, Pol.	B4	20
Białystok, Pol.	C7	20
Bianco, Monte (Blanc, Mont), mtn., Eur.	B1	18
Biankouma, C. Iv.	E3	50
Biaora, India	E3	40
Biaro, Pulau, i., Indon.	C7	36
Biarritz, Fr.	F6	16
Bibala, Ang.	A1	56
Bibb, co., Al., U.S.	C2	94
Bibb, co., Ga., U.S.	D3	103
Bibémi, Cam.	B2	54
Biberach an der Riss, Ger.	F11	12
Bic, P.Q., Can.	A9	90
Bic, Île du, i., P.Q., Can.	A9	90
Biche, Lac la, l., Ab., Can.	B4	84
Bicknell, In., U.S.	G3	107
Bīd, India	F3	40
Bida, Nig.	E6	50
Bīdar, India	F3	40
Biddeford, Me., U.S.	E2	112
Bidwell, Mount, mtn., Ca., U.S.	B3	98
Biel, Switz.	A1	18
Bielefeld, Ger.	E11	12
Biella, Italy	B2	18
Bielsko-Biała, Pol.	E5	20
Bielsk Podlaski, Pol.	C7	20
Bien Hoa, Viet.	D5	34
Bienville, co., La., U.S.	B2	111
Bienville, Lac, l., P.Q., Can.	g12	90
Big, stm., Mo., U.S.	c7	118
Biga, Tur.	B2	44
Big Bald, mtn., Ga., U.S.	B2	103
Big Bald Mountain, mtn., N.B., Can.	B3	87
Big Baldy, mtn., Id., U.S.	E3	105
Big Baldy Mountain, mtn., Mt., U.S.	D6	119
Big Bay De Noc, b., Mi., U.S.	C4	115
Big Bear City, Ca., U.S.	E5	98
Big Belt Mountains, mts., Mt., U.S.	D5	119
Big Bend, Wi., U.S.	n11	142
Big Bend Dam, S.D., U.S.	C6	134
Big Bend National Park, Tx., U.S.	E1	136
Big Birch Lake, l., Mn., U.S.	E4	116
Big Black, stm., Me., U.S.	B3	112
Big Black, stm., Ms., U.S.	C3	117
Big Blue, stm., In., U.S.	E6	107
Big Burro Mountains, mts., N.M., U.S.	E1	124
Big Cabin Creek, stm., Ok., U.S.	A6	129
Big Coal, stm., W.V., U.S.	C3	141
Big Costilla Peak, mtn., N.M., U.S.	A4	124
Big Creek, stm., Tn., U.S.	e8	135
Big Creek Lake, res., Al., U.S.	E1	94
Big Creek Peak, mtn., Id., U.S.	E5	105
Big Cypress Indian Reservation, Fl., U.S.	F5	102
Big Cypress Swamp, sw., Fl., U.S.	F5	102
Big Darby Creek, stm., Oh., U.S.	C2	128
Big Delta, Ak., U.S.	C10	95
Big Duke Dam, N.C., U.S.	B2	126
Big Eau Pleine, stm., Wi., U.S.	D3	142
Big Eau Pleine Reservoir, res., Wi., U.S.	D4	142
Big Escambia Creek, stm., U.S.	D2	94
Big Flats, N.Y., U.S.	C4	125
Bigfork, Mt., U.S.	B2	119
Big Fork, stm., Mn., U.S.	B5	116
Biggs, Ca., U.S.	C3	98
Big Hatchet Peak, mtn., N.M., U.S.	F1	124
Big Hole, stm., Mt., U.S.	E4	119
Big Hole National Battlefield, hist., Mt., U.S.	E3	119
Big Horn, co., Mt., U.S.	E9	119
Big Horn, co., Wy., U.S.	B4	143
Bighorn Canyon National Recreation Area, U.S.	F8	119
Bighorn Lake, res., U.S.	E8	119
Big Horn Mountains, mts., Az., U.S.	D2	96
Bighorn Mountains, mts., U.S.	C6	92
Bighorn Mountains, mts., U.S.	B5	143
Bight, Head of, b., Austl.	G5	60
Big Kandiyohi Lake, l., Mn., U.S.	F4	116
Big Lake, Mn., U.S.	E5	116
Big Lake, Tx., U.S.	D2	136
Big Lake, l., Me., U.S.	C5	112
Biglerville, Pa., U.S.	G7	131
Big Lookout Mountain, mtn., Or., U.S.	C9	130
Big Lost, stm., Id., U.S.	F5	105
Big Mossy Point, c., Mb., Can.	C2	86
Big Mountain, mtn., Nv., U.S.	B2	121
Big Muddy, stm., Il., U.S.	F4	106
Big Nemaha, stm., Ne., U.S.	D10	120
Bignona, Sen.	D1	50

Name — Map Ref. — Page

Big Otter, stm., Va., U.S. **C3** 139
Big Pine Lake, l., Mn., U.S. **D3** 116
Big Pine Mountain, mtn., Ca., U.S. **E4** 98
Big Piney, Wy., U.S. **D2** 143
Big Piney, stm., Mo., U.S. **D5** 118
Bigpoint, Ms., U.S. **E5** 117
Big Rapids, Mi., U.S. **E5** 115
Big Rib, stm., Wi., U.S. **C3** 142
Big River, Sk., Can. **D2** 91
Big Sable Point, c., Mi., U.S. **D4** 115
Big Sandy, Mt., U.S. **B6** 119
Big Sandy, Tx., U.S. **C5** 136
Big Sandy, stm., Az., U.S. **C2** 96
Big Sandy, stm., Tn., U.S. **B3** 135
Big Sandy, stm., Wy., U.S. **D3** 143
Big Sandy, stm., U.S. **C2** 141
Big Sandy Creek, stm., W.V., U.S. **C3** 141
Big Sandy Lake, l., Mn., U.S. **D5** 116
Big Sandy Reservoir, res., Wy., U.S. **D3** 143
Big Sheep Mountain, mtn., Mt., U.S. **C11** 119
Big Sioux, stm., U.S. **E9** 134
Big Smoky Valley, val., Nv., U.S. **E4** 121
Big Snowy Mountains, mts., Mt., U.S. **D7** 119
Big Southern Butte, mtn., Id., U.S. **F5** 105
Big South Fork, stm., Ky., U.S. **k13** 110
Big Spring, Tx., U.S. **C2** 136
Big Stone, co., Mn., U.S. **E2** 116
Big Stone City, S.D., U.S. **B9** 134
Big Stone Gap, Va., U.S. **f9** 139
Big Stone Lake, l., U.S. **E2** 116
Big Sunflower, stm., Ms., U.S. **B3** 117
Big Thompson, stm., Co., U.S. **A5** 99
Big Timber, Mt., U.S. **E7** 119
Big Trout Lake, l., On., Can. **n17** 89
Big Walnut Creek, stm., Oh., U.S. **m11** 128
Big Wood, stm., Id., U.S. **F4** 105
Bihać, Bos. **B5** 18
Bīhar, India **D5** 40
Bihār, prov., India **E5** 40
Biharamulo, Tan. **D6** 54
Bijagós, Arquipélago dos, is., Gui.-B. **D1** 50
Bijāpur, India **F3** 40
Bījār, Iran **E12** 44
Bijeljina, Bos. **B7** 18
Bijie, China **F9** 28
Bijsk, Russia **D10** 26
Bīkāner, India **D2** 40
Bikar, atoll, Marsh. Is. **C10** 58
Bikeqi, China **C10** 28
Bikin, Russia **B14** 28
Bikini, atoll, Marsh. Is. **C10** 58
Bīkkū Bīttī, mtn., Libya **F8** 48
Bikoro, D.R.C. **D3** 54
Bilāspur, India **C3** 40
Bilāspur, India **E4** 40
Biläsuvar, Azer. **C13** 44
Bila Tserkva, Ukr. **E11** 20
Bilauktaung Range, mts., Asia **D3** 34
Bilbao, Spain **F5** 16
Bilecik, Tur. **B4** 44
Biłgoraj, Pol. **D7** 20
Bilhorod-Dnistrovs'kyi, Ukr. **F11** 20
Bili, D.R.C. **C5** 54
Bilk Creek Mountains, mts., Nv., U.S. **B3** 121
Billerica, Ma., U.S. **A5** 114
Billings, Mo., U.S. **D4** 118
Billings, Mt., U.S. **E8** 119
Billings, co., N.D., U.S. **B2** 127
Billings Heights, Mt., U.S. **E8** 119
Bill Williams, stm., Az., U.S. **C1** 96
Bill Williams Mountain, mtn., Az., U.S. **B3** 96
Bilma, Niger **C7** 50
Bilohirs'k, Ukr. **G13** 20
Bilopillia, Ukr. **D13** 20
Biloxi, Ms., U.S. **E5** 117
Biloxi, stm., Ms., U.S. **E4** 117
Biloxi Bay, b., Ms., U.S. **f8** 117
Biltmore Forest, N.C., U.S. **f10** 126
Bimbo, C.A.R. **C3** 54
Bimini Islands, is., Bah. **C9** 76
Bīna-Etāwa, India **E3** 40
Bindura, Zimb. **B5** 56
Binga, D.R.C. **C4** 54
Binga, Monte, mtn., Afr. **B5** 56
Bingamon Creek, stm., W.V., U.S. **k10** 141
Bingara, Austl. **F5** 62
Bingen, Wa., U.S. **D4** 140
Binger, Ok., U.S. **B3** 129
Bingham, Me., U.S. **C3** 112
Bingham, co., Id., U.S. **F6** 105
Binghamton, N.Y., U.S. **C5** 125
Bingöl, Tur. **C9** 44
Binhai, China **E12** 28
Binh Son, Viet. **C5** 34
Binjai, Indon. **C1** 36
Binongko, Pulau, i., Indon. **E6** 36
Bintan, Pulau, i., Indon. **C2** 36
Bintimani, mtn., S.L. **E2** 50
Bintuhan, Indon. **D2** 36
Bintulu, Malay. **C4** 36
Bintuni, Indon. **D8** 36
Binxian, China **B4** 30
Binyang, China **B5** 34
Bin-Yauri, Nig. **D5** 50
Binzert see Bizerte, Tun. **C6** 48
Biobío, stm., Chile **F3** 72
Bioko, i., Eq. Gui. **C1** 54
Birāk, Libya **E7** 48
Bi'r al Wa'r, Libya **F7** 48
Birao, C.A.R. **A4** 54
Birch, stm., W.V., U.S. **C4** 141
Birch Island, i., Mb., Can. **C2** 86
Birch Lake, l., Mn., U.S. **C7** 116
Birch River, Mb., Can. **C1** 86
Birch Run, Mi., U.S. **E7** 115
Birchy Bay, Nf., Can. **D4** 88
Bird Creek, stm., Ok., U.S. **A6** 129
Bird Island, Mn., U.S. **F4** 116
Bird Island, i., N.C., U.S. **D4** 126
Birdsboro, Pa., U.S. **F10** 131
Birdum, Austl. **D5** 60
Birecik, Tur. **D8** 44
Birigui, Braz. **F1** 74
Bīrjand, Iran **D7** 42
Birmingham, Eng., U.K. **D6** 12
Birmingham, Al., U.S. **B3** 94
Birmingham, Mi., U.S. **F7** 115
Birmitrapur, India **E4** 40
Bîr Mogreïn, Maur. **A2** 50
Birnin-Kebbi, Nig. **D5** 50
Birnin Konni, Niger **D6** 50
Birnin Kudu, Nig. **D6** 50
Birobidžan, Russia **E15** 26
Biron, Wi., U.S. **D4** 142
Birsk, Russia **C10** 22
Birtle, Mb., Can. **D1** 86
Biržai, Lith. **H11** 10
Bisbee, Az., U.S. **F6** 96
Biscay, Bay of (Gascogne, Golfe de), b., Eur. **E5** 16
Biscayne, Key, i., Fl., U.S. **s13** 102
Biscayne Bay, b., Fl., U.S. **G6** 102
Biscayne National Monument, Fl., U.S. **G6** 102
Biscayne Park, Fl., U.S. **s13** 102
Biscoe, N.C., U.S. **B3** 126
Bishkek see Biškek, Kyrg. **E9** 26
Bishop, Ca., U.S. **D4** 98
Bishop, Tx., U.S. **F4** 136
Bishop's Falls, Nf., Can. **D4** 88
Bishopville, S.C., U.S. **C7** 133
Biškek, Kyrg. **E9** 26
Bislig, Phil. **E9** 34
Bismarck, Il., U.S. **C6** 106
Bismarck, Mo., U.S. **D7** 118
Bismarck, N.D., U.S. **C5** 127
Bismarck Archipelago, is., Pap. N. Gui. **G12** 32
Bismarck Range, mts., Pap. N. Gui. **H11** 32
Bismarck Sea, Pap. N. Gui. **G12** 32
Bismil, Tur. **D9** 44
Bison Peak, mtn., Co., U.S. **B5** 99
Bissau, Gui.-B. **D1** 50
Bissikrima, Gui. **D2** 50
Bistineau, Lake, res., La., U.S. **B2** 111
Bistrița, Rom. **F8** 20
Bitam, Gabon **C2** 54
Bitlis, Tur. **C10** 44
Bitola, Mac. **D8** 18
Bitou, Burkina **D4** 50
Bitter Creek, stm., Wy., U.S. **E4** 143
Bitterfontein, S. Afr. **E2** 56
Bitter Lake, l., S.D., U.S. **B8** 134
Bitterroot, stm., Mt., U.S. **D2** 119
Bitterroot Range, mts., U.S. **B4** 92
Bitterroot Range, mts., U.S. **B3** 105
Bitung, Indon. **C7** 36
Biu, Nig. **D7** 50
Biwabik, Mn., U.S. **C6** 116
Biwa-ko, l., Japan **C3** 31
Bixby, Ok., U.S. **B6** 129
Biyang, China **C3** 30
Bizerte, Tun. **C6** 48
Bjala, Bul. **C10** 18
Bjarèzina, stm., Bela. **C10** 20
Bjelovar, Cro. **B6** 18
Bjørnøya, i., Nor. **B3** 26
Bla, Mali **D3** 50
Black, stm., Asia **B4** 34
Black, stm., Ar., U.S. **B4** 97
Black, stm., Az., U.S. **D5** 96
Black, stm., La., U.S. **C4** 111
Black, stm., Mi., U.S. **E8** 115
Black, stm., N.C., U.S. **C4** 126
Black, stm., N.Y., U.S. **B4** 125
Black, stm., S.C., U.S. **D8** 133
Black, stm., Vt., U.S. **E3** 138
Black, stm., Wi., U.S. **D3** 142
Blackall, Austl. **E4** 62
Black Bear Creek, stm., Ok., U.S. **A4** 129
Blackbeard Island, i., Ga., U.S. **E5** 103
Blackburn, Mount, mtn., Ak., U.S. **C11** 95
Black Butte, mtn., Mt., U.S. **F5** 119
Black Butte Lake, res., Ca., U.S. **C2** 98
Black Canyon, val., Co., U.S. **C3** 99
Black Canyon City, Az., U.S. **C3** 96
Black Canyon of the Gunnison National Monument, Co., U.S. **C3** 99
Black Creek, B.C., Can. **E5** 85
Black Creek, Wi., U.S. **D5** 142
Black Creek, stm., S.C., U.S. **B7** 133
Black Creek, stm., U.S. **B1** 124
Black Diamond, Ab., Can. **D3** 84
Black Diamond, Wa., U.S. **B4** 140
Blackduck, Mn., U.S. **C4** 116
Black Eagle, Mt., U.S. **C5** 119
Black Earth, Wi., U.S. **E4** 142
Blackfalds, Ab., Can. **C4** 84
Blackfeet Indian Reservation, Mt., U.S. **B4** 119
Blackfoot, Id., U.S. **F6** 105
Blackfoot, stm., Mt., U.S. **C3** 119
Blackfoot Mountains, mts., Id., U.S. **F7** 105
Blackfoot Reservoir, res., Id., U.S. **G7** 105
Blackford, co., In., U.S. **D7** 107
Black Forest, Co., U.S. **C6** 99
Black Forest see Schwarzwald, mts., Ger. **F11** 12
Blackhall Mountain, mtn., Wy., U.S. **E6** 143
Black Hawk, S.D., U.S. **C2** 134
Black Hawk, co., Ia., U.S. **B5** 108
Black Hills, mts., U.S. **C2** 134
Blackjack Mountain, mtn., Ga., U.S. **h8** 103
Black Lake, P.Q., Can. **C6** 90
Black Lake, l., Mi., U.S. **C6** 115
Black Lake, l., N.Y., U.S. **f9** 125
Black Lick, Pa., U.S. **F3** 131
Black Mesa, mtn., Ok., U.S. **e8** 129
Black Mingo Creek, stm., S.C., U.S. **D9** 133
Blackmore, Mount, mtn., Mt., U.S. **E6** 119
Black Mountain, N.C., U.S. **f10** 126
Black Mountain, mtn., Az., U.S. **E4** 96
Black Mountain, mtn., Co., U.S. **A5** 99
Black Mountain, mtn., Id., U.S. **C3** 105
Black Mountain, mtn., Mt., U.S. **D4** 119
Black Mountain, mtn., Or., U.S. **B7** 130
Black Mountain, mtn., Wy., U.S. **B5** 143
Black Mountain, mtn., Wy., U.S. **D7** 143
Black Mountain, mtn., U.S. **D7** 110
Black Mountains, mts., Az., U.S. **B1** 96
Black Peak, mtn., Az., U.S. **C1** 96
Black Pine Peak, mtn., Id., U.S. **G5** 105
Blackpool, Eng., U.K. **D5** 12
Black Range, mts., N.M., U.S. **D2** 124
Black River Falls, Wi., U.S. **D3** 142
Black Rock, Ar., U.S. **A4** 97
Black Rock, N.M., U.S. **B1** 124
Black Rock, rock, S. Geor. **H8** 69
Black Rock Desert, des., Nv., U.S. **B3** 121
Black Rock Range, mts., Nv., U.S. **B3** 121
Blacksburg, S.C., U.S. **A4** 133
Blacksburg, Va., U.S. **C2** 139
Black Sea **F5** 22
Blacks Fork, stm., U.S. **E3** 143
Blacks Harbour, N.B., Can. **D3** 87
Blackshear, Ga., U.S. **E4** 103
Blackstone, Ma., U.S. **B4** 114
Blackstone, Va., U.S. **C5** 139
Blackstone, stm., R.I., U.S. **B4** 132
Black Thunder Creek, stm., Wy., U.S. **C8** 143
Blackville, N.B., Can. **C4** 87
Blackville, S.C., U.S. **E5** 133
Black Volta, stm., Afr. **D4** 50
Blackwalnut Point, c., Md., U.S. **C5** 113
Black Warrior, stm., Al., U.S. **C2** 94
Blackwater, stm., Ire. **D2** 12
Blackwater, stm., Fl., U.S. **u15** 102
Blackwater, stm., Md., U.S. **D5** 113
Blackwater, stm., N.H., U.S. **D3** 122
Blackwater, stm., Va., U.S. **D6** 139
Blackwater Reservoir, res., N.H., U.S. **D3** 122
Blackwell, Ok., U.S. **A4** 129
Blackwood, N.J., U.S. **D2** 123
Bladen, co., N.C., U.S. **C4** 126
Bladenboro, N.C., U.S. **C4** 126
Bladensburg, Md., U.S. **f9** 113
Blades, De., U.S. **F3** 101
Blagoevgrad, Bul. **D9** 18
Blagoveščensk, Russia **D14** 26
Blaine, Me., U.S. **B5** 112
Blaine, Mn., U.S. **m12** 116
Blaine, Tn., U.S. **C10** 135
Blaine, Wa., U.S. **A3** 140
Blaine, co., Id., U.S. **F4** 105
Blaine, co., Mt., U.S. **B7** 119
Blaine, co., Ne., U.S. **C6** 120
Blaine, co., Ok., U.S. **B3** 129
Blaine Lake, Sk., Can. **E2** 91
Blair, Ne., U.S. **C9** 120
Blair, Ok., U.S. **C2** 129
Blair, W.V., U.S. **n12** 141
Blair, Wi., U.S. **D2** 142
Blair, co., Pa., U.S. **E5** 131
Blairstown, Ia., U.S. **C5** 108
Blairsville, Pa., U.S. **F3** 131
Blake Island, i., Wa., U.S. **e11** 140
Blakely, Ga., U.S. **E2** 103
Blakely, Pa., U.S. **m18** 131
Blake Plateau **E6** 66
Blake Point, c., Mi., U.S. **h10** 115
Blanc, Cap see Nouâdhibou, Râs, c., Afr. **B1** 50
Blanc, Mont (Bianco, Monte), mtn., Eur. **B1** 18
Blanca Peak, mtn., Co., U.S. **D5** 99
Blanchard, La., U.S. **B2** 111
Blanchard, Ok., U.S. **B4** 129
Blanchard, stm., Oh., U.S. **A1** 128
Blanchardville, Wi., U.S. **F4** 142
Blanchester, Oh., U.S. **C2** 128
Blanco, Tx., U.S. **D3** 136
Blanco, co., Tx., U.S. **D3** 136
Blanco, Cape, c., Or., U.S. **E2** 130
Bland, Mo., U.S. **C6** 118
Bland, co., Va., U.S. **C1** 139
Blanding, Ut., U.S. **F6** 137
Blandinsville, Il., U.S. **C3** 106
Blanquilla, Isla, i., Ven. **C7** 80
Blantyre, Mwi. **B5** 56
Blasdell, N.Y., U.S. **C2** 125
Blawnox, Pa., U.S. **k14** 131
Bleckley, co., Ga., U.S. **D3** 103
Bledsoe, co., Tn., U.S. **D8** 135
Blekinge, hist. reg., Swe. **H6** 10
Blende, Co., U.S. **C6** 99
Blenheim, On., Can. **E3** 89
Blenheim, N.Z. **p13** 63c
Blennerhassett, W.V., U.S. **B3** 141
Blind, stm., La., U.S. **h10** 111
Blind River, On., Can. **A2** 89
Blissfield, Mi., U.S. **G7** 115
Blitar, Indon. **E4** 36
Block Island, R.I., U.S. **h7** 132
Block Island, i., R.I., U.S. **h7** 132
Block Island Sound, strt., U.S. **G2** 132
Bloemfontein, S. Afr. **D4** 56
Bloemhof, S. Afr. **D4** 56
Blois, Fr. **D7** 16
Blommestein Meer see Brokopondo Stuwmeer, res., Sur. **C8** 70
Blönduós, Ice. **l18** 10a
Blood Mountain, mtn., Ga., U.S. **B3** 103
Bloodsworth Island, i., Md., U.S. **D5** 113
Bloodvein, stm., Can. **D3** 86
Bloomer, Wi., U.S. **C2** 142
Bloomfield, On., Can. **D7** 89
Bloomfield, Ct., U.S. **B5** 100
Bloomfield, Ia., U.S. **D5** 108
Bloomfield, In., U.S. **F4** 107
Bloomfield, Ky., U.S. **C4** 110
Bloomfield, Mo., U.S. **E8** 118
Bloomfield, Ne., U.S. **B8** 120
Bloomfield, N.J., U.S. **h8** 123
Bloomfield, N.M., U.S. **A2** 124
Bloomfield Hills, Mi., U.S. **o15** 115
Bloomingdale, Ga., U.S. **D5** 103
Bloomingdale, Il., U.S. **k8** 106
Bloomingdale, N.J., U.S. **A4** 123
Bloomingdale, Tn., U.S. **C11** 135
Blooming Prairie, Mn., U.S. **G5** 116
Bloomington, Il., U.S. **C4** 106
Bloomington, In., U.S. **F4** 107
Bloomington, Mn., U.S. **F5** 116
Bloomington, Tx., U.S. **E4** 136
Bloomington, Wi., U.S. **F3** 142
Bloomington, Lake, res., Il., U.S. **C5** 106
Bloomsburg, Pa., U.S. **E9** 131
Bloomville, Oh., U.S. **A2** 128
Blossburg, Pa., U.S. **C7** 131
Blossom, Tx., U.S. **C5** 136
Blount, co., Al., U.S. **B3** 94
Blount, co., Tn., U.S. **D10** 135
Blountstown, Fl., U.S. **B1** 102
Blountsville, Al., U.S. **A3** 94
Blountville, Tn., U.S. **C11** 135
Blowing Rock, N.C., U.S. **A1** 126
Blue, stm., Co., U.S. **B4** 99
Blue, stm., In., U.S. **H5** 107
Blue, stm., Mo., U.S. **k10** 118
Blue, stm., Ok., U.S. **C5** 129
Blue Ash, Oh., U.S. **o13** 128
Blue Buck Point, c., La., U.S. **E2** 111
Blue Creek, W.V., U.S. **m13** 141
Blue Creek, stm., W.V., U.S. **m13** 141
Blue Cypress Lake, l., Fl., U.S. **E6** 102
Blue Diamond, Nv., U.S. **G6** 121
Blue Earth, Mn., U.S. **G4** 116
Blue Earth, co., Mn., U.S. **G4** 116
Blue Earth, stm., Mn., U.S. **G4** 116
Bluefield, Va., U.S. **C1** 139
Bluefield, W.V., U.S. **D3** 141
Bluefields, Nic. **C3** 80
Blue Grass, Ia., U.S. **C7** 108
Blue Hill, Me., U.S. **D4** 112
Blue Hill, Ne., U.S. **D7** 120
Blue Hill Range, hills, Ma., U.S. **h11** 114
Blue Hills, Ct., U.S. **B5** 100
Blue Island, Il., U.S. **B6** 106
Bluejoint Lake, l., Or., U.S. **E7** 130
Blue Lake, Ca., U.S. **B2** 98
Blue Mesa Reservoir, res., Co., U.S. **C3** 99
Blue Mound, Il., U.S. **D4** 106
Blue Mountain, Ms., U.S. **A4** 117
Blue Mountain, mtn., Mt., U.S. **C12** 119
Blue Mountain, mtn., N.M., U.S. **D2** 124
Blue Mountain, mtn., Pa., U.S. **F6** 131
Blue Mountain Lake, res., Ar., U.S. **B2** 97
Blue Mountain Peak, mtn., Jam. **B4** 80
Blue Mountains, mts., U.S. **B4** 92
Blue Nile, stm., Afr. **H11** 48
Blue Point, Me., U.S. **g7** 112
Blue Rapids, Ks., U.S. **C7** 109
Blue Ridge, Va., U.S. **C3** 139
Blue Ridge, mts., U.S. **D11** 92
Blue Ridge Summit, Pa., U.S. **G7** 131
Blue Springs, Mo., U.S. **h11** 118
Bluestone, stm., W.V., U.S. **D3** 141
Bluestone Lake, res., U.S. **D4** 141
Bluewell, W.V., U.S. **D3** 141
Bluff, N.Z. **q12** 63c
Bluff City, Tn., U.S. **C11** 135
Bluff Creek, stm., Ok., U.S. **A4** 129
Bluff Lake, res., Ms., U.S. **B5** 117
Bluff Park, Al., U.S. **g7** 94
Bluffs, Il., U.S. **D3** 106
Bluffton, In., U.S. **C7** 107
Bluffton, Oh., U.S. **B2** 128
Bluffton, S.C., U.S. **G6** 133
Blumenau, Braz. **D8** 72
Bly, Or., U.S. **E5** 130
Blying Sound, strt., Ak., U.S. **h17** 95
Blyth, On., Can. **D3** 89
Blythe, Ca., U.S. **F6** 98
Blytheville, Ar., U.S. **B6** 97
Bo, S.L. **E2** 50
Boaco, Nic. **C2** 80
Boa Esperança, Represa, res., Braz. **E11** 70
Boalsburg, Pa., U.S. **E6** 131
Boardman, Oh., U.S. **A5** 128
Boardman, Or., U.S. **B7** 130
Boa Vista, Braz. **C7** 70
Boa Vista, i., C.V. **g10** 50a
Boaz, Al., U.S. **A3** 94
Bobai, China **E2** 30
Bobaomby, Tanjona, c., Madag. **A8** 56
Bobbili, India **F4** 40
Bobcaygeon, On., Can. **C6** 89
Bobo-Dioulasso, Burkina **D4** 50
Bobonong, Bots. **C4** 56
Bobrov, Russia **D16** 20
Bobrynets', Ukr. **E12** 20
Bobtown, Pa., U.S. **G2** 131
Boby, mtn., Madag. **C8** 56
Boca Chica Key, i., Fl., U.S. **H5** 102
Boca Ciega Bay, b., Fl., U.S. **p10** 102
Boca do Acre, Braz. **E6** 70
Boca Grande, Fl., U.S. **F4** 102
Bocaiúva, Braz. **E3** 74
Bocaranga, C.A.R. **B3** 54
Boca Raton, Fl., U.S. **F6** 102
Bocas del Toro, Pan. **D3** 80
Bochnia, Pol. **E6** 20
Bochum, Ger. **E10** 12
Boconó, Ven. **D5** 80
Bocșa, Rom. **G6** 20
Bodajbo, Russia **D13** 26
Bodega Head, c., Ca., U.S. **C2** 98
Bodélé, reg., Chad **C8** 50
Boden, Swe. **D9** 10
Bodhan, India **F3** 40
Bodie Island, i., N.C., U.S. **B7** 126
Bodkin Point, c., Md., U.S. **B5** 113
Bodø, Nor. **C6** 10
Bodrum, Tur. **D2** 44
Boende, D.R.C. **D4** 54
Boerne, Tx., U.S. **E3** 136
Boeuf, stm., La., U.S. **C4** 111
Boeuf, Lake, l., La., U.S. **k10** 111
Boffa, Gui. **D2** 50
Bogale, Myan. **C3** 34
Bogalusa, La., U.S. **D6** 111
Bogangolo, C.A.R. **B3** 54
Bogart, Ga., U.S. **C3** 103
Bogata, Tx., U.S. **C5** 136
Boğazlıyan, Tur. **C6** 44
Bogda Shan, mts., China **C5** 28
Boger City, N.C., U.S. **B1** 126
Bogo, Phil. **D8** 34
Bogor, Indon. **E3** 36
Bogorodick, Russia **C15** 20
Bogotá, Col. **C5** 70
Bogota, N.J., U.S. **h8** 123
Bogué, Maur. **C2** 50
Bogue Chitto, Ms., U.S. **D3** 117
Bogue Chitto, stm., U.S. **D5** 111
Bogue Inlet, b., N.C., U.S. **C5** 126
Bogue Phalia, stm., Ms., U.S. **B3** 117
Bo Hai, b., China **D11** 28

Name — Map Ref. — Page

Bohai Haixia, strt., China **D12** 28
Bohemia, hist. reg., Czech Rep. **E3** 20
Bohodukhiv, Ukr. **D13** 20
Bohol, i., Phil. **E8** 34
Bohol Sea, Phil. **E8** 34
Bohuslav, Ukr. **E11** 20
Boiling Springs, N.C., U.S. **B1** 126
Boiling Springs, Pa., U.S. **F7** 131
Bois Blanc Island, i., Mi., U.S. **C6** 115
Bois Brule, stm., Wi., U.S. **B2** 142
Boischâtel, P.Q., Can. **C6** 90
Bois-des-Filion, P.Q., Can. **p19** 90
Bois de Sioux, stm., Mn., U.S. **E2** 116
Boise, Id., U.S. **F2** 105
Boise, co., Id., U.S. **F3** 105
Boise City, Ok., U.S. **e8** 129
Boissevain, Mb., Can. **E1** 86
Boissevain, Va., U.S. **e10** 139
Boistfort Peak, mtn., Wa., U.S. **C2** 140
Bojeador, Cape, c., Phil. **C8** 34
Bojnūrd, Iran **C7** 42
Boké, Gui. **D2** 50
Boknafjorden, strt., Nor. **G1** 10
Boko, Congo **D2** 54
Bokoro, Chad **D8** 50
Bokungu, D.R.C. **D4** 54
Bolama, Gui.-B. **D1** 50
Bolbec, Fr. **C7** 16
Bole, Ghana **E4** 50
Bolesławiec, Pol. **D3** 20
Boley, Ok., U.S. **B5** 129
Bolgatanga, Ghana **D4** 50
Bolhov, Russia **C14** 20
Boli, China **B14** 28
Bolingbrook, Il., U.S. **k8** 106
Bolivar, Mo., U.S. **D4** 118
Bolivar, Oh., U.S. **B4** 128
Bolivar, Tn., U.S. **B3** 135
Bolivar, W.V., U.S. **B7** 141
Bolivar, co., Ms., U.S. **B3** 117
Bolívar, Cerro, mtn., Ven. **B6** 70
Bolivar, Lake, l., Ms., U.S. **B3** 117
Bolívar, Pico, mtn., Ven. **B5** 70
Bolivia, ctry., S.A. **G7** 70
Bollinger, co., Mo., U.S. **D7** 118
Bollnäs, Swe. **F7** 10
Bolnisi, Geor. **B11** 44
Bolobo, D.R.C. **D3** 54
Bologna, Italy **B3** 18
Bologoe, Russia **C5** 22
Bolomba, D.R.C. **C3** 54
Bol'šaja Murta, Russia **D11** 26
Bolsena, Lago di, l., Italy **C3** 18
Bol'šereck, Russia **D17** 26
Bol'ševik, ostrov, i., Russia **B12** 26
Bol'šezemel'skaja Tundra, reg., Russia **A9** 22
Bol'šoj Begičev, ostrov, i., Russia **B13** 26
Bol'šoj Enisej, stm., Russia **A7** 28
Bol'šoj Kamen', Russia **B2** 31
Bol'šoj Ljahovskij, ostrov, i., Russia **B16** 26
Bolton, Eng., U.K. **D5** 12
Bolton, Ms., U.S. **C3** 117
Bolton Lakes, l., Ct., U.S. **B6** 100
Bolton Landing, N.Y., U.S. **B7** 125
Bolu, Tur. **B4** 44
Bolvadin, Tur. **C4** 44
Bolzano, Italy **A3** 18
Boma, D.R.C. **E2** 54
Bombay see Mumbai, India **F2** 40
Bombay Hook Island, i., De., U.S. **C4** 101
Bomberai, Semenanjung, pen., Indon. **D8** 36
Bom Despacho, Braz. **B8** 72
Bomdila, India **D6** 40
Bom Jesus da Lapa, Braz. **D3** 74
Bomongo, D.R.C. **C3** 54
Bomoseen, Lake, l., Vt., U.S. **D2** 138
Bomu, stm., Afr. **C4** 54
Bon, Cap, c., Tun. **C7** 48
Bon Accord, Ab., Can. **C4** 84
Bon Air, Va., U.S. **C5** 139
Bonaire, Ga., U.S. **D3** 103
Bonaire, i., Neth. Ant. **C6** 80
Bonanza Peak, mtn., Wa., U.S. **A5** 140
Bonaparte, Mount, mtn., Wa., U.S. **A6** 140
Bonasila Dome, mtn., Ak., U.S. **C7** 95
Bonaventure, P.Q., Can. **A4** 87
Bonavista, Nf., Can. **D5** 88
Bonavista, Cape, c., Nf., Can. **D5** 88
Bonavista Bay, b., Nf., Can. **D5** 88
Bond, co., Il., U.S. **E4** 106
Bondo, D.R.C. **C4** 54
Bondo, D.R.C. **D4** 54
Bondoukou, C. Iv. **E4** 50
Bondsville, Ma., U.S. **B3** 114
Bonduel, Wi., U.S. **D5** 142
Bondurant, Ia., U.S. **C4** 108
Bône see Annaba, Alg. **C6** 48
Bone, Gulf of see Bone, Teluk, b., Indon. **D6** 36
Bone, Teluk, b., Indon. **D6** 36
Bone Lake, l., Wi., U.S. **C1** 142
Bongandanga, D.R.C. **C4** 54
Bongka, Indon. **D6** 36
Bongo, Massif des, mts., C.A.R. **B4** 54
Bongor, Chad **D8** 50
Bonham, Tx., U.S. **C4** 136
Bon Homme, co., S.D., U.S. **D8** 134
Bonifacio, Strait of, strt., Eur. **D2** 18
Bonifay, Fl., U.S. **u16** 102
Bonin Islands see Ogasawara-guntō, is., Japan **F16** 64
Bonita Springs, Fl., U.S. **F5** 102
Bonkoukou, Niger **D5** 50
Bonn, Ger. **E10** 12
Bonneauville, Pa., U.S. **G7** 131
Bonne Bay, b., Nf., Can. **D3** 88
Bonner, co., Id., U.S. **A2** 105
Bonners Ferry, Id., U.S. **A2** 105
Bonner Springs, Ks., U.S. **C9** 109
Bonnet Carre Floodway, La., U.S. **h11** 111
Bonne Terre, Mo., U.S. **D7** 118
Bonneville, co., Id., U.S. **F7** 105
Bonneville Dam, U.S. **B4** 130
Bonneville Peak, mtn., Id., U.S. **F6** 105
Bonneville Salt Flats, pl., Ut., U.S. **C2** 137
Bonney Lake, Wa., U.S. **B3** 140
Bonnie Doone, N.C., U.S. **B4** 126
Bonnie Rock, Austl. **G2** 60
Bonny, Nig. **F6** 50
Bonny Reservoir, res., Co., U.S. **B8** 99
Bonnyville, Ab., Can. **B5** 84
Bono, Ar., U.S. **B5** 97
Bon Secour, Al., U.S. **E2** 94
Bonthe, S.L. **E2** 50
Bontoc, Phil. **C8** 34
Booker, Tx., U.S. **A2** 136
Booker T. Washington National Monument, Va., U.S. **C3** 139
Boola, Gui. **E3** 50
Boolaloo, Austl. **E2** 60
Boomer, W.V., U.S. **C3** 141
Boone, Ia., U.S. **B4** 108
Boone, N.C., U.S. **A1** 126
Boone, co., Ar., U.S. **A2** 97
Boone, co., Ia., U.S. **B3** 108
Boone, co., Il., U.S. **A5** 106
Boone, co., In., U.S. **D4** 107
Boone, co., Ky., U.S. **B5** 110
Boone, co., Mo., U.S. **B5** 118
Boone, co., Ne., U.S. **C7** 120
Boone, co., W.V., U.S. **C3** 141
Boone, stm., Ia., U.S. **B4** 108
Boone Lake, res., Tn., U.S. **C11** 135
Booneville, Ar., U.S. **B2** 97
Booneville, Ms., U.S. **A5** 117
Boonsboro, Md., U.S. **A2** 113
Boonton, N.J., U.S. **B4** 123
Boonville, In., U.S. **H3** 107
Boonville, Mo., U.S. **C5** 118
Boonville, N.C., U.S. **A2** 126
Boonville, N.Y., U.S. **B5** 125
Boosaaso, Som. **H14** 48
Boothbay Harbor, Me., U.S. **E3** 112
Boothia, Gulf of, b., Nu., Can. **D21** 82
Booths Creek, stm., W.V., U.S. **h11** 141
Boothville, La., U.S. **E6** 111
Booué, Gabon **D2** 54
Bophuthatswana, hist. reg., S. Afr. **D4** 56
Bopolu, Lib. **E2** 50
Bor, Sudan **I11** 48
Bor, Tur. **D6** 44
Bor, Yugo. **B9** 18
Borah Peak, mtn., Id., U.S. **E5** 105
Borås, Swe. **H5** 10
Borba, Braz. **D8** 70
Bordeaux, Fr. **E6** 16
Borden, co., Tx., U.S. **C2** 136
Bordentown, N.J., U.S. **C3** 123
Bordj Bou Arreridj, Alg. **J9** 16
Bordj Omar Idriss, Alg. **E6** 48
Borðoy, i., Far. Is. **n23** 10b
Borgarnes, Ice. **l17** 10a
Borger, Tx., U.S. **B2** 136
Borgholm, Swe. **H7** 10
Borgne, Lake, b., La., U.S. **D6** 111
Borisoglebsk, Russia **D7** 22
Borken, Ger. **E10** 12
Borkou, reg., Chad **C8** 50
Borlänge, Swe. **F6** 10
Borneo (Kalimantan), i., Asia **D4** 36
Bornholm, i., Den. **I6** 10
Borno, prov., Nig. **D7** 50
Borogoncy, Russia **C15** 26
Boromo, Burkina **D4** 50
Boron, Ca., U.S. **E5** 98
Borongan, Phil. **D9** 34
Boroviči, Russia **D5** 26
Borrego Springs, Ca., U.S. **F5** 98
Borroloola, Austl. **D6** 60
Borşa, Rom. **F8** 20
Borūjerd, Iran **D5** 42
Boryslav, Ukr. **E7** 20
Boryspil', Ukr. **D11** 20
Borzja, Russia **D13** 26
Boržomi, Geor. **B10** 44
Bosanski Novi, Bos. **B6** 18
Boscobel, Wi., U.S. **E3** 142
Bose, China **G9** 28
Boshan, China **D11** 28
Bosna, stm., Bos. **B6** 18
Bosnia and Herzegovina, ctry., Eur. **B6** 18
Bosnik, Indon. **G10** 32
Bosobolo, D.R.C. **C3** 54
Bosporus see İstanbul Boğazı, strt., Tur. **B3** 44
Bosque, co., Tx., U.S. **D4** 136
Bossangoa, C.A.R. **B3** 54
Bossembélé, C.A.R. **B3** 54
Bossentélé, C.A.R. **B3** 54
Bossier, co., La., U.S. **B2** 111
Bossier City, La., U.S. **B2** 111
Bostān, Iran **G13** 44
Bosten Hu, l., China **C5** 28
Boston, Eng., U.K. **D6** 12
Boston, Ga., U.S. **F3** 103
Boston, Ma., U.S. **B5** 114
Boston Bay, b., Ma., U.S. **B6** 114
Boston Mountains, mts., Ar., U.S. **B2** 97
Boswell, In., U.S. **C3** 107
Boswell, Ok., U.S. **C6** 129
Boswell, Pa., U.S. **F3** 131
Botetourt, co., Va., U.S. **C3** 139
Bothell, Wa., U.S. **B3** 140
Bothnia, Gulf of, b., Eur. **F8** 10
Bothwell, On., Can. **E3** 89
Botkins, Oh., U.S. **B1** 128
Botlih, Russia **A12** 44
Botoşani, Rom. **F9** 20
Bo Trach, Viet. **C5** 34
Botswana, ctry., Afr. **C3** 56
Bottineau, N.D., U.S. **A5** 127
Bottineau, co., N.D., U.S. **A4** 127
Botucatu, Braz. **F2** 74
Botwood, Nf., Can. **D4** 88
Bouaflé, C. Iv. **E3** 50
Bouaké, C. Iv. **E3** 50
Bouar, C.A.R. **B3** 54
Bouarfa, Mor. **E3** 14
Bouca, C.A.R. **B3** 54
Boucherville, P.Q., Can. **D4** 90
Bouctouche, N.B., Can. **C5** 87
Boudreaux, Lake, l., La., U.S. **E5** 111
Bougainville, i., Pap. N. Gui. **B6** 62
Bougainville, Détroit de, strt., Vanuatu **k9** 62a
Bougie see Bejaïa, Alg. **C6** 48
Bougouni, Mali **D3** 50
Bouïra, Alg. **C5** 48
Boujdour, Cap, c., W. Sah. **A2** 50
Boulder, Co., U.S. **A5** 99
Boulder, Mt., U.S. **D4** 119
Boulder, co., Co., U.S. **A5** 99
Boulder City, Nv., U.S. **H7** 121
Boulevard Heights, Md., U.S. **f9** 113
Boulia, Austl. **E2** 62
Boulogne-sur-Mer, Fr. **B7** 16
Boulsa, Burkina **D4** 50
Bouna, C. Iv. **E4** 50
Boundary, co., Id., U.S. **A2** 105
Boundary Bay, b., Wa., U.S. **A3** 140
Boundary Peak, mtn., Nv., U.S. **F3** 121
Bound Brook, N.J., U.S. **B3** 123
Boundiali, C. Iv. **E3** 50
Bountiful, Ut., U.S. **C4** 137
Bounty Islands, is., N.Z. **M21** 64
Bounty Trough **M20** 64
Bourail, N. Cal. **I9** 62a
Bourbeuse, stm., Mo., U.S. **C6** 118
Bourbon, In., U.S. **B5** 107
Bourbon, Mo., U.S. **C6** 118
Bourbon, co., Ks., U.S. **E9** 109
Bourbon, co., Ky., U.S. **B5** 110
Bourbonnais, Il., U.S. **B6** 106
Bourem, Mali **C4** 50
Bourg, La., U.S. **E5** 111
Bourg-en-Bresse, Fr. **D9** 16
Bourges, Fr. **D8** 16
Bourgogne, hist. reg., Fr. **D9** 16
Bourke, Austl. **G4** 62
Bournemouth, Eng., U.K. **E5** 12
Bou Saâda, Alg. **C5** 48
Bouse, Az., U.S. **D2** 96
Bousso, Chad **D8** 50
Boutilimit, Maur. **C2** 50
Boutte, La., U.S. **k11** 111
Bouvetøya, i., Ant. **B5** 67
Bouza, Niger **D6** 50
Bovey, Mn., U.S. **C5** 116
Bovina, Tx., U.S. **B1** 136
Bow, N.H., U.S. **D3** 122
Bow, stm., Ab., Can. **D4** 84
Bowden, Ab., Can. **D4** 84
Bowdish Reservoir, res., R.I., U.S. **B1** 132
Bowdon, Ga., U.S. **C1** 103
Bowen, Arg. **F4** 72
Bowen, Austl. **D4** 62
Bowie, Az., U.S. **E6** 96
Bowie, Md., U.S. **C4** 113
Bowie, Tx., U.S. **C4** 136
Bowie, co., Tx., U.S. **C5** 136
Bow Island, Ab., Can. **E5** 84
Bow Lake, l., N.H., U.S. **D4** 122
Bowling Green, Fl., U.S. **E5** 102
Bowling Green, Ky., U.S. **D3** 110
Bowling Green, Mo., U.S. **B6** 118
Bowling Green, Oh., U.S. **A2** 128
Bowling Green, S.C., U.S. **A5** 133
Bowling Green, Va., U.S. **B5** 139
Bowling Green, Cape, c., Austl. **D4** 62
Bowman, Ga., U.S. **B3** 103
Bowman, N.D., U.S. **C2** 127
Bowman, S.C., U.S. **E6** 133
Bowman, co., N.D., U.S. **C2** 127
Bowman Creek, stm., Pa., U.S. **m16** 131
Bowman-Haley Lake, res., N.D., U.S. **C2** 127
Bowral, Austl. **G5** 62
Bowron, stm., B.C., Can. **C7** 85
Bowstring Lake, l., Mn., U.S. **C5** 116
Box Butte, co., Ne., U.S. **B2** 120
Box Butte Reservoir, res., Ne., U.S. **B2** 120
Box Elder, S.D., U.S. **C2** 134
Box Elder, co., Ut., U.S. **B2** 137
Boxford, Ma., U.S. **A6** 114
Boxing, China **B4** 30
Boyabat, Tur. **B6** 44
Boyang, China **D4** 30
Boyce, La., U.S. **C3** 111
Boyceville, Wi., U.S. **C1** 142
Boyd, Tx., U.S. **C4** 136
Boyd, co., Ky., U.S. **B7** 110
Boyd, co., Ne., U.S. **B7** 120
Boyden, Ia., U.S. **A2** 108
Boyd Lake, l., Me., U.S. **C4** 112
Boyer, stm., Ia., U.S. **C2** 108
Boyertown, Pa., U.S. **F10** 131
Boykins, Va., U.S. **D5** 139
Boyle, Ab., Can. **B4** 84
Boyle, Ms., U.S. **B3** 117
Boyle, co., Ky., U.S. **C5** 110
Boyne City, Mi., U.S. **C6** 115
Boynton Beach, Fl., U.S. **F6** 102
Boyoma Falls see Stanley Falls, wtfl, D.R.C. **C5** 54
Boysen Reservoir, res., Wy., U.S. **C4** 143
Boys Town, Ne., U.S. **g12** 120
Bozeman, Mt., U.S. **E5** 119
Bozeman Pass, Mt., U.S. **E6** 119
Bozhen, China **D11** 28
Bozhou, China **C4** 30
Bozoum, C.A.R. **B3** 54
Bozova, Tur. **D8** 44
Bozüyük, Tur. **C3** 44
Bra, Italy **B1** 18
Bracebridge, On., Can. **B5** 89
Bräcke, Swe. **E6** 10
Bracken, co., Ky., U.S. **B5** 110
Brackenridge, Pa., U.S. **h15** 131
Brackettville, Tx., U.S. **E2** 136
Brad, Rom. **F7** 20
Braddock, Pa., U.S. **k14** 131
Braddock Heights, Md., U.S. **B2** 113
Braddock Point, c., S.C., U.S. **G6** 133
Bradenton, Fl., U.S. **E4** 102
Bradenville, Pa., U.S. **F3** 131
Bradford, Eng., U.K. **D5** 12
Bradford, Ar., U.S. **B4** 97
Bradford, Oh., U.S. **B1** 128
Bradford, Pa., U.S. **C4** 131
Bradford, R.I., U.S. **F2** 132
Bradford, Tn., U.S. **A3** 135
Bradford, Vt., U.S. **D4** 138
Bradford, co., Fl., U.S. **C4** 102
Bradford, co., Pa., U.S. **C8** 131
Bradford [West Gwillimbury], On., Can. **C5** 89
Bradfordwoods, Pa., U.S. **h13** 131
Bradley, Il., U.S. **B6** 106
Bradley, Me., U.S. **D4** 112
Bradley, W.V., U.S. **D3** 141
Bradley, co., Ar., U.S. **D3** 97
Bradley, co., Tn., U.S. **D9** 135
Bradley Beach, N.J., U.S. **C4** 123
Bradner, Oh., U.S. **A2** 128
Bradshaw, Md., U.S. **B5** 113
Bradshaw Mountains, mts., Az., U.S. **C3** 96
Brady, Tx., U.S. **D3** 136
Braga, Port. **G2** 16
Bragado, Arg. **F5** 72
Bragança, Braz. **B2** 74
Bragança, Port. **G3** 16
Braham, Mn., U.S. **E5** 116
Brāhmanbāria, Bngl. **E6** 40
Brahmapur, India **F4** 40
Brahmaputra (Yarlung), stm., Asia **D6** 40
Braidwood, Il., U.S. **B5** 106
Brăila, Rom. **G9** 20
Brainerd, Mn., U.S. **D4** 116
Braintree, Ma., U.S. **B5** 114
Brampton, On., Can. **D5** 89
Bramwell, W.V., U.S. **D3** 141
Branch, co., Mi., U.S. **G5** 115
Branch, stm., R.I., U.S. **B3** 132
Branch, stm., Wi., U.S. **h10** 142
Branch Lake, l., Me., U.S. **D4** 112
Branch Village, R.I., U.S. **B3** 132
Branchville, S.C., U.S. **E6** 133
Branco, stm., Braz. **C7** 70
Brandberg, mtn., Nmb. **C1** 56
Brandenburg, Ger. **D13** 12
Brandenburg, Ky., U.S. **C3** 110
Brandon, Mb., Can. **E2** 86
Brandon, Fl., U.S. **E4** 102
Brandon, Ms., U.S. **C4** 117
Brandon, S.C., U.S. **B3** 133
Brandon, S.D., U.S. **D9** 134
Brandon, Vt., U.S. **D2** 138
Brandon, Wi., U.S. **E5** 142
Brandvlei, S. Afr. **E3** 56
Brandy Peak, mtn., Or., U.S. **E3** 130
Brandywine, Md., U.S. **C4** 113
Brandywine Creek, stm., U.S. **A3** 101
Branford, Ct., U.S. **D4** 100
Branford Hills, Ct., U.S. **D4** 100
Branson, Mo., U.S. **E4** 118
Brantford, On., Can. **D4** 89
Brantley, Al., U.S. **D3** 94
Brantley, co., Ga., U.S. **E4** 103
Brant Rock, Ma., U.S. **B6** 114
Brantville, N.B., Can. **B5** 87
Bras d'Or Lake, l., N.S., Can. **D9** 87
Brasil, ctry., S.A. **D2** 74
Brasiléia, Braz. **F6** 70
Brasília, Braz. **E2** 74
Braşov, Rom. **G8** 20
Brasstown Bald, mtn., Ga., U.S. **B3** 103
Brassua Lake, res., Me., U.S. **C3** 112
Bratenahl, Oh., U.S. **g9** 128
Bratislava, Slvk. **E4** 20
Bratsk, Russia **D12** 26
Bratskoe vodohranilišče, res., Russia **D12** 26
Bratsk Reservoir see Bratskoe vodohranilišče, res., Russia **D12** 26
Brattleboro, Vt., U.S. **F3** 138
Braunau am Inn, Aus. **F13** 12
Braunschweig, Ger. **D12** 12
Brava, i., C.V. **h10** 50a
Bravo (Rio Grande), stm., N.A. **B5** 78
Brawley, Ca., U.S. **F6** 98
Brawley Peaks, mts., Nv., U.S. **E3** 121
Braxton, co., W.V., U.S. **C4** 141
Bray, Ok., U.S. **C4** 129
Braymer, Mo., U.S. **B4** 118
Brazeau, stm., Ab., Can. **C2** 84
Brazil, In., U.S. **E3** 107
Brazil, ctry., S.A. **D5** 68
Brazil Basin **J11** 66
Brazoria, Tx., U.S. **r14** 136
Brazoria, co., Tx., U.S. **E5** 136
Brazos, co., Tx., U.S. **D4** 136
Brazos, stm., Tx., U.S. **D4** 136
Brazzaville, Congo **D3** 54
Brčko, Bos. **B7** 18
Brea, Ca., U.S. **n13** 98
Breakenridge, Mount, mtn., B.C., Can. **E7** 85
Breathitt, co., Ky., U.S. **C6** 110
Breaux Bridge, La., U.S. **D4** 111
Breckenridge, Co., U.S. **B4** 99
Breckenridge, Mi., U.S. **E6** 115
Breckenridge, Mn., U.S. **D2** 116
Breckenridge, Tx., U.S. **C3** 136
Breckinridge, co., Ky., U.S. **C3** 110
Brecksville, Oh., U.S. **A4** 128
Břeclav, Czech Rep. **E4** 20
Breda, Neth. **E9** 12
Bredasdorp, S. Afr. **E3** 56
Bredy, Russia **D11** 22
Breese, Il., U.S. **E4** 106
Breiðafjörður, b., Ice. **l17** 10a
Brejo, Braz. **D11** 70
Bremen, Ger. **D11** 12
Bremen, Ga., U.S. **C1** 103
Bremen, In., U.S. **B5** 107
Bremen, Oh., U.S. **C3** 128
Bremer, co., Ia., U.S. **B5** 108
Bremer Bay, Austl. **G2** 60
Bremerhaven, Ger. **D11** 12
Bremerton, Wa., U.S. **B3** 140
Bremond, Tx., U.S. **D4** 136
Brenham, Tx., U.S. **D4** 136
Brenner Pass, Eur. **A3** 18
Brent, Al., U.S. **C2** 94
Brent, Fl., U.S. **u14** 102
Brenton Point, c., R.I., U.S. **F5** 132
Brentwood, Ca., U.S. **h9** 98
Brentwood, Md., U.S. **f9** 113
Brentwood, Mo., U.S. **f13** 118
Brentwood, N.Y., U.S. **E7** 125
Brentwood, Pa., U.S. **k14** 131
Brentwood, S.C., U.S. **k11** 133
Brentwood, Tn., U.S. **A5** 135
Brescia, Italy **B3** 18
Breslau see Wrocław, Pol. **D4** 20
Bressuire, Fr. **D6** 16
Brèst, Bela. **C7** 20
Brest, Fr. **C4** 16
Bretagne, hist. reg., Fr. **C5** 16
Breton, Pertuis, strt., Fr. **D6** 16
Breton Islands, is., La., U.S. **E6** 111
Breton Sound, strt., La., U.S. **E6** 111
Breueh, Pulau, i., Indon. **E1** 32
Brevard, N.C., U.S. **f10** 126
Brevard, co., Fl., U.S. **E6** 102
Breves, Braz. **B1** 74
Brevoort Lake, l., Mi., U.S. **B6** 115
Brewer, Me., U.S. **D4** 112
Brewster, Ma., U.S. **C7** 114

Name	Map Ref.	Page
Brewster, N.Y., U.S.	D7	125
Brewster, Oh., U.S.	B4	128
Brewster, Wa., U.S.	A6	140
Brewster, co., Tx., U.S.	E1	136
Brewster, Kap, c., Grnld.	D35	82
Brewster Islands, is., Ma., U.S.	g12	114
Brewton, Al., U.S.	D2	94
Brezhnev see Naberežnye Čelny, Russia	D7	26
Bria, C.A.R.	B4	54
Brian Boru Peak, mtn., B.C., Can.	B4	85
Brian Head, mtn., Ut., U.S.	F3	137
Briceville, Tn., U.S.	C9	135
Brick [Township], N.J., U.S.	C4	123
Bridal Veil Falls, wtfl, Ut., U.S.	C4	137
Bridgehampton, N.Y., U.S.	n16	125
Bridgeport, Al., U.S.	A4	94
Bridgeport, Ct., U.S.	E3	100
Bridgeport, Il., U.S.	E6	106
Bridgeport, Mi., U.S.	E7	115
Bridgeport, Ne., U.S.	C2	120
Bridgeport, Oh., U.S.	B5	128
Bridgeport, Pa., U.S.	o20	131
Bridgeport, Tx., U.S.	C4	136
Bridgeport, W.V., U.S.	B4	141
Bridgeport, Wa., U.S.	B6	140
Bridger, Mt., U.S.	E8	119
Bridger Peak, mtn., Wy., U.S.	E5	143
Bridger Range, mts., Mt., U.S.	E6	119
Bridgeton, Mo., U.S.	C7	118
Bridgeton, N.J., U.S.	E2	123
Bridgetown, Austl.	G2	60
Bridgetown, Barb.	C7	80
Bridgetown, N.S., Can.	E4	87
Bridgeville, De., U.S.	F3	101
Bridgeville, Pa., U.S.	k13	131
Bridgewater, Ma., U.S.	C6	114
Bridgewater, N.J., U.S.	B3	123
Bridgewater, Va., U.S.	B4	139
Bridgman, Mi., U.S.	G4	115
Bridgton, Me., U.S.	D2	112
Bridgwater, Eng., U.K.	E5	12
Bridlington, Eng., U.K.	C6	12
Brielle, N.J., U.S.	C4	123
Brigantine, N.J., U.S.	E4	123
Brigantine Beach, N.J., U.S.	E4	123
Brigden, On., Can.	E2	89
Briggs Marsh, sw., R.I., U.S.	F6	132
Brigham City, Ut., U.S.	B3	137
Bright, Austl.	H4	62
Brighton, On., Can.	C7	89
Brighton, Eng., U.K.	E6	12
Brighton, Al., U.S.	B3	94
Brighton, Co., U.S.	B6	99
Brighton, Ia., U.S.	C6	108
Brighton, Il., U.S.	D3	106
Brighton, Mi., U.S.	F7	115
Brighton, N.Y., U.S.	B3	125
Brighton, Tn., U.S.	B2	135
Brighton Indian Reservation, Fl., U.S.	E5	102
Brikama, Gam.	D1	50
Brilliant, Al., U.S.	A2	94
Brilliant, Oh., U.S.	B5	128
Brillion, Wi., U.S.	D5	142
Brimfield, Il., U.S.	C4	106
Brindisi, Italy	D6	18
Brinkley, Ar., U.S.	C4	97
Brinnon, Wa., U.S.	B3	140
Brisbane, Austl.	F5	62
Briscoe, co., Tx., U.S.	B2	136
Bristol, N.B., Can.	C2	87
Bristol, Eng., U.K.	E5	12
Bristol, Ct., U.S.	C4	100
Bristol, In., U.S.	A6	107
Bristol, N.H., U.S.	C3	122
Bristol, R.I., U.S.	D5	132
Bristol, Tn., U.S.	C11	135
Bristol, Va., U.S.	f9	139
Bristol, Vt., U.S.	C2	138
Bristol, co., Ma., U.S.	C5	114
Bristol, co., R.I., U.S.	D5	132
Bristol Bay, b., Ak., U.S.	D7	95
Bristol Channel, strt., U.K.	E5	12
Bristol [Township], Pa., U.S.	F12	131
Bristow, Ok., U.S.	B5	129
British Columbia, prov., Can.	C6	85
British Guiana see Guyana, ctry., S.A.	B8	70
British Honduras see Belize, ctry., N.A.	B2	80
British Indian Ocean Territory, dep., Afr.	I10	64
British Isles, is., Eur.	C12	4
British Virgin Islands, dep., N.A.	E12	76
Britstown, S. Afr.	E3	56
Britt, Ia., U.S.	A4	108
Brittany see Bretagne, hist. reg., Fr.	C5	16
Britton, S.D., U.S.	B8	134
Brive-la-Gaillarde, Fr.	E7	16
Brjansk, Russia	D5	26
Brjuhoveckaja, Russia	G15	20
Brno, Czech Rep.	E4	20
Broad, stm., S.C., U.S.	C5	133
Broad Brook, Ct., U.S.	B5	100
Broadkill, stm., De., U.S.	E4	101
Broadkill Beach, De., U.S.	E5	101
Broad Run, stm., Va., U.S.	g11	139
Broad Sound, b., Austl.	E4	62
Broadus, Mt., U.S.	E11	119
Broadview Heights, Oh., U.S.	h9	128
Broadwater, co., Mt., U.S.	D5	119
Broadway, N.C., U.S.	B3	126
Broadway, Va., U.S.	B4	139
Brockman, Mount, mtn., Austl.	E2	60
Brockport, N.Y., U.S.	B3	125
Brockton, Ma., U.S.	B5	114
Brockton Reservoir, res., Ma., U.S.	h11	114
Brockville, On., Can.	C9	89
Brockway, Pa., U.S.	D4	131
Brodhead, Ky., U.S.	C5	110
Brodhead, Wi., U.S.	F4	142
Brodheadsville, Pa., U.S.	E11	131
Brodnica, Pol.	C5	20
Brody, Ukr.	D8	20
Broken Arrow, Ok., U.S.	A6	129
Broken Bow, Ne., U.S.	C6	120
Broken Bow, Ok., U.S.	C7	129
Broken Bow Lake, res., Ok., U.S.	C7	129
Broken Hill, Austl.	G3	62
Broken Hill see Kabwe, Zam.	A4	56
Broken Ridge	L12	64
Brokopondo, Sur.	C8	70
Brokopondo Stuwmeer, res., Sur.	C8	70
Brome, Lac, l., P.Q., Can.	D5	90
Bromley Plateau	K10	66
Bromptonville, P.Q., Can.	D6	90
Bronson, Mi., U.S.	G5	115
Bronx, co., N.Y., U.S.	E7	125
Bronxville, N.Y., U.S.	h13	125
Brook, In., U.S.	C3	107
Brooke, co., W.V., U.S.	A4	141
Brookfield, N.S., Can.	D6	87
Brookfield, Ct., U.S.	D2	100
Brookfield, Il., U.S.	k9	106
Brookfield, Mo., U.S.	B4	118
Brookfield, Wi., U.S.	m11	142
Brookfield Center, Ct., U.S.	D2	100
Brookhaven, Ms., U.S.	D3	117
Brookhaven, W.V., U.S.	h11	141
Brookings, Or., U.S.	E2	130
Brookings, S.D., U.S.	C9	134
Brookings, co., S.D., U.S.	C9	134
Brookland, Ar., U.S.	B5	97
Brooklandville, Md., U.S.	g10	113
Brooklet, Ga., U.S.	D5	103
Brookline, Ma., U.S.	B5	114
Brooklyn, N.S., Can.	E5	87
Brooklyn, Ct., U.S.	B8	100
Brooklyn, Ia., U.S.	C5	108
Brooklyn, In., U.S.	E5	107
Brooklyn, Mi., U.S.	F6	115
Brooklyn, Ms., U.S.	D4	117
Brooklyn, Oh., U.S.	h9	128
Brooklyn, S.C., U.S.	B6	133
Brooklyn, Wi., U.S.	F4	142
Brooklyn Center, Mn., U.S.	E5	116
Brooklyn Park, Md., U.S.	h11	113
Brooklyn Park, Mn., U.S.	m12	116
Brookneal, Va., U.S.	C4	139
Brook Park, Oh., U.S.	h9	128
Brookport, Il., U.S.	F5	106
Brooks, Ab., Can.	D5	84
Brooks, Ky., U.S.	g11	110
Brooks, co., Ga., U.S.	F3	103
Brooks, co., Tx., U.S.	F3	136
Brooks Air Force Base, mil., Tx., U.S.	k7	136
Brookshire, Tx., U.S.	E5	136
Brookside, Al., U.S.	f7	94
Brookside, De., U.S.	B3	101
Brooks Range, mts., Ak., U.S.	B9	95
Brookston, In., U.S.	C4	107
Brooksville, Fl., U.S.	D4	102
Brooksville, Ky., U.S.	B5	110
Brooksville, Ms., U.S.	B5	117
Brookville, In., U.S.	F8	107
Brookville, Oh., U.S.	C1	128
Brookville, Pa., U.S.	D3	131
Brookville Lake, res., In., U.S.	E7	107
Brookwood, Al., U.S.	B2	94
Brookwood, N.J., U.S.	C4	123
Broomall, Pa., U.S.	p20	131
Broome, Austl.	D3	60
Broome, co., N.Y., U.S.	C5	125
Broomfield, Co., U.S.	B5	99
Brossard, P.Q., Can.	q20	90
Broussard, La., U.S.	D4	111
Broward, co., Fl., U.S.	F6	102
Browerville, Mn., U.S.	D4	116
Brown, co., Il., U.S.	D3	106
Brown, co., In., U.S.	F5	107
Brown, co., Ks., U.S.	C8	109
Brown, co., Mn., U.S.	F4	116
Brown, co., Ne., U.S.	B6	120
Brown, co., Oh., U.S.	D2	128
Brown, co., S.D., U.S.	B7	134
Brown, co., Tx., U.S.	D3	136
Brown, co., Wi., U.S.	D6	142
Brown, Point, c., Wa., U.S.	C1	140
Brown City, Mi., U.S.	E8	115
Brown Deer, Wi., U.S.	m12	142
Brownfield, Tx., U.S.	C1	136
Browning, Mt., U.S.	B3	119
Brownlee Dam, U.S.	E2	105
Brownlee Reservoir, res., U.S.	C10	130
Browns, stm., Vt., U.S.	B2	138
Browns Branch, stm., De., U.S.	E3	101
Brownsburg, P.Q., Can.	D3	90
Brownsburg, In., U.S.	E5	107
Brownsdale, Mn., U.S.	G6	116
Browns Inlet, b., N.C., U.S.	C5	126
Browns Mills, N.J., U.S.	D3	123
Browns Peak, mtn., Az., U.S.	D4	96
Brownstown, In., U.S.	G5	107
Browns Valley, Mn., U.S.	E2	116
Brownsville, Fl., U.S.	s13	102
Brownsville, Ky., U.S.	C3	110
Brownsville, Or., U.S.	C4	130
Brownsville, Pa., U.S.	F2	131
Brownsville, Tn., U.S.	B2	135
Brownsville, Tx., U.S.	G4	136
Brownton, Mn., U.S.	F4	116
Brownville Junction, Me., U.S.	C3	112
Brownwood, Tx., U.S.	D3	136
Brownwood, Lake, res., Tx., U.S.	D3	136
Broxton, Ga., U.S.	E4	103
Bruce, Ms., U.S.	B4	117
Bruce, Wi., U.S.	C2	142
Bruce, Mount, mtn., Austl.	E2	60
Bruce National Park, On., Can.	B3	89
Bruce Peninsula, pen., On., Can.	B3	89
Bruce Rock, Austl.	G2	60
Bruceton, Tn., U.S.	A3	135
Bruderheim, Ab., Can.	C4	84
Brugge, Bel.	E8	12
Bruin Point, mtn., Ut., U.S.	D5	137
Brule, co., S.D., U.S.	D6	134
Brule, stm., U.S.	C5	142
Brule Lake, l., Mn., U.S.	k9	116
Brumado, Braz.	D3	74
Brundidge, Al., U.S.	D4	94
Bruneau, stm., U.S.	G3	105
Brunei see Bandar Seri Begawan, Bru.	C4	36
Brunei, ctry., Asia	F6	34
Bruno, Sk., Can.	E3	91
Brunswick see Braunschweig, Ger.	D12	12
Brunswick, Ga., U.S.	E5	103
Brunswick, Md., U.S.	B2	113
Brunswick, Me., U.S.	E3	112
Brunswick, Mo., U.S.	B4	118
Brunswick, Oh., U.S.	A4	128
Brunswick, co., N.C., U.S.	C4	126
Brunswick, co., Va., U.S.	D5	139
Brunswick, Península, pen., Chile	H2	69
Brunswick Naval Air Station, mil., Me., U.S.	E3	112
Brush, Co., U.S.	A7	99
Brushy Mountains, mts., N.C., U.S.	B1	126
Brusly, La., U.S.	D4	111
Brusque, Braz.	D8	72
Brussels see Bruxelles, Bel.	E9	12
Brussels, On., Can.	D3	89
Bruxelles (Brussels), Bel.	E9	12
Bryan, Oh., U.S.	A1	128
Bryan, Tx., U.S.	D4	136
Bryan, co., Ga., U.S.	D5	103
Bryan, co., Ok., U.S.	D5	129
Bryans Road, Md., U.S.	C3	113
Bryant, Ar., U.S.	C3	97
Bryantville, Ma., U.S.	B6	114
Bryce Canyon National Park, Ut., U.S.	F3	137
Bryn Mawr, Wa., U.S.	e11	140
Bryson City, N.C., U.S.	f9	126
Brzeg, Pol.	D4	20
Bua Yai, Thai.	C4	34
Bu'ayrat al-Hasun, Libya	E7	14
Bubaque, Gui.-B.	D1	50
Bucak, Tur.	D4	44
Bucaramanga, Col.	B5	70
Buccaneer Archipelago, is., Austl.	D3	60
Buchanan, Lib.	E2	50
Buchanan, Ga., U.S.	C1	103
Buchanan, Mi., U.S.	G4	115
Buchanan, Va., U.S.	C3	139
Buchanan, co., Ia., U.S.	B6	108
Buchanan, co., Mo., U.S.	B3	118
Buchanan, co., Va., U.S.	e9	139
Buchans, Nf., Can.	D3	88
Bucharest see București, Rom.	G9	20
Buckatunna, Ms., U.S.	D5	117
Buckeye, Az., U.S.	D3	96
Buckeye Lake, Oh., U.S.	C3	128
Buckhannon, W.V., U.S.	C4	141
Buck Hill Falls, Pa., U.S.	D11	131
Buckhorn Lake, res., Ky., U.S.	C6	110
Buckingham, P.Q., Can.	D2	90
Buckingham, co., Va., U.S.	C4	139
Buckley, Wa., U.S.	B3	140
Bucklin, Ks., U.S.	E4	109
Bucklin, Mo., U.S.	B5	118
Buck Mountain, mtn., Wa., U.S.	A6	140
Buckner, Mo., U.S.	h11	118
Bucks, co., Pa., U.S.	F11	131
Buckskin Mountains, mts., Az., U.S.	C2	96
Bucksport, Me., U.S.	D4	112
Bucksport, S.C., U.S.	D9	133
Buco Zau, Ang.	D2	54
București (Bucharest), Rom.	G9	20
Bucyrus, Oh., U.S.	B3	128
Buda, Tx., U.S.	D4	136
Budapest, Hung.	F5	20
Budaun, India	D3	40
Budd Lake, l., N.J., U.S.	B3	123
Bude, Ms., U.S.	D3	117
Budënnovsk, Russia	B4	42
Búðir, Ice.	l21	10a
Budjala, D.R.C.	C3	54
Buea, Cam.	C1	54
Buechel, Ky., U.S.	B4	110
Buena, N.J., U.S.	D3	123
Buena, Wa., U.S.	C5	140
Buena Esperanza, Arg.	E4	72
Buena Park, Ca., U.S.	n12	98
Buenaventura, Col.	C4	70
Buenaventura, Mex.	B3	78
Buena Vista, Co., U.S.	C4	99
Buena Vista, Fl., U.S.	D4	102
Buena Vista, Ga., U.S.	D2	103
Buena Vista, Va., U.S.	C3	139
Buena Vista, co., Ia., U.S.	B2	108
Buenos Aires, Arg.	E6	72
Buffalo, Ia., U.S.	C7	108
Buffalo, Mn., U.S.	E5	116
Buffalo, Mo., U.S.	D4	118
Buffalo, N.Y., U.S.	C2	125
Buffalo, Ok., U.S.	A2	129
Buffalo, S.C., U.S.	B4	133
Buffalo, Tx., U.S.	D5	136
Buffalo, W.V., U.S.	C3	141
Buffalo, Wi., U.S.	D2	142
Buffalo, Wy., U.S.	B6	143
Buffalo, co., Ne., U.S.	D6	120
Buffalo, co., S.D., U.S.	C6	134
Buffalo, co., Wi., U.S.	D2	142
Buffalo, stm., Ar., U.S.	B3	97
Buffalo, stm., Mn., U.S.	D2	116
Buffalo, stm., Tn., U.S.	B4	135
Buffalo, stm., Wi., U.S.	D2	142
Buffalo Bill Reservoir, res., Wy., U.S.	B3	143
Buffalo Center, Ia., U.S.	A4	108
Buffalo Creek, stm., W.V., U.S.	h10	141
Buffalo Creek, stm., W.V., U.S.	n12	141
Buffalo Creek, stm., U.S.	f8	141
Buffalo Grove, Il., U.S.	h9	106
Buffalo Lake, Mn., U.S.	F4	116
Buffalo Lake, l., Ab., Can.	C4	84
Buffalo Lake, res., Tx., U.S.	B1	136
Buffalo Lake, res., Wi., U.S.	E4	142
Buffumville Lake, res., Ma., U.S.	B4	114
Buford, Ga., U.S.	B2	103
Bug, stm., Eur.	C6	20
Buga, Col.	C4	70
Bugsuk Island, i., Phil.	E7	34
Bugt, China	B12	28
Bugul'ma, Russia	D9	22
Buguruslan, Russia	D9	22
Buhara, Uzb.	F8	26
Buhl, Id., U.S.	G4	105
Buhl, Mn., U.S.	C6	116
Buhler, Ks., U.S.	D6	109
Buies Creek, N.C., U.S.	B4	126
Buitepos, Nmb.	C2	56
Buj, Russia	C7	22
Bujnaksk, Russia	A12	44
Bujumbura, Bdi.	D5	54
Bukačača, Russia	D13	26
Bukama, D.R.C.	E5	54
Būkān, Iran	D12	44
Bukavu, D.R.C.	D5	54
Bukeya, D.R.C.	F5	54
Bukittinggi, Indon.	D2	36
Bukoba, Tan.	D6	54
Bula, Indon.	D8	36
Bulan, Phil.	D8	34
Bulan, Ky., U.S.	C6	110
Bulancak, Tur.	B8	44
Bulandshahr, India	D3	40
Bulanık, Tur.	C10	44
Bulawayo, Zimb.	C4	56
Buldan, Tur.	C3	44
Bulgan, Mong.	B8	28
Bulgaria, ctry., Eur.	C10	18
Bulkley, stm., B.C., Can.	B4	85
Bullaxaar, Som.	A8	54
Bull Creek, stm., S.D., U.S.	B2	134
Bullfinch, Austl.	G2	60
Bullfrog Creek, stm., Ut., U.S.	F5	137
Bullhead City, Az., U.S.	B1	96
Bull Island, i., S.C., U.S.	D9	133
Bull Island, i., S.C., U.S.	F8	133
Bull Island, i., S.C., U.S.	G6	133
Bullitt, co., Ky., U.S.	C4	110
Bull Mountain, mtn., Mt., U.S.	D4	119
Bulloch, co., Ga., U.S.	D5	103
Bullock, co., Al., U.S.	C4	94
Bullock Creek, Mi., U.S.	E6	115
Bull Run, stm., Va., U.S.	g11	139
Bullrun Rock, mtn., Or., U.S.	C8	130
Bulls Bay, b., S.C., U.S.	F8	133
Bulls Gap, Tn., U.S.	C10	135
Bull Shoals, Ar., U.S.	A3	97
Bull Shoals Lake, res., U.S.	D9	92
Bull Shoals Lake, res., U.S.	A3	97
Bully Creek Reservoir, res., Or., U.S.	C9	130
Bultfontein, S. Afr.	D4	56
Bumba, D.R.C.	C4	54
Bumping, stm., Wa., U.S.	C4	140
Buna, Tx., U.S.	D6	136
Bunbury, Austl.	G2	60
Buncombe, co., N.C., U.S.	f10	126
Bundaberg, Austl.	E5	62
Būndi, India	D3	40
Bungoma, Kenya	C6	54
Bungo-suidō, strt., Japan	E14	28
Bunia, D.R.C.	C6	54
Bunker Hill, Il., U.S.	D4	106
Bunker Hill, In., U.S.	C5	107
Bunker Hill, W.V., U.S.	m12	141
Bunker Hill, W.V., U.S.	B6	141
Bunker Hill, mtn., Nv., U.S.	D4	121
Bunkerville, Nv., U.S.	G7	121
Bunkie, La., U.S.	D3	111
Bunnell, Fl., U.S.	C5	102
Buntok, Indon.	D4	36
Bünyan, Tur.	C6	44
Buolkalah, Russia	B13	26
Buon Ma Thuot, Viet.	D5	34
Buor-Haja, guba, b., Russia	B15	26
Buqayq, Sau. Ar.	E5	42
Bura, Kenya	D7	54
Burang, China	C4	40
Buras, La., U.S.	E6	111
Buraydah, Sau. Ar.	E4	38
Burbank, Ca., U.S.	E4	98
Burbank, Il., U.S.	k9	106
Burbank, Wa., U.S.	C7	140
Burco, Som.	I14	48
Burdickville, R.I., U.S.	F2	132
Burdur, Tur.	D4	44
Burdur Gölü, l., Tur.	D4	44
Bureau, co., Il., U.S.	B4	106
Bureinskij hrebet, mts., Russia	D15	26
Bürenhayrhan, Mong.	B6	28
Burfjord, Nor.	B10	10
Burgas, Bul.	C11	18
Burgaski Zaliv, b., Bul.	C11	18
Burgaw, N.C., U.S.	C5	126
Burgeo, Nf., Can.	E3	88
Burgersdorp, S. Afr.	E4	56
Burgettstown, Pa., U.S.	F1	131
Burgin, Ky., U.S.	C5	110
Burgo de Osma, Spain	G5	16
Burgos, Spain	F5	16
Burgundy see Bourgogne, hist. reg., Fr.	D9	16
Burhaniye, Tur.	C2	44
Burhānpur, India	E3	40
Burias Island, i., Phil.	D8	34
Burin, Nf., Can.	E4	88
Burin Peninsula, pen., Nf., Can.	E4	88
Buri Ram, Thai.	C4	34
Burjatija, state, Russia	D13	26
Burkburnett, Tx., U.S.	B3	136
Burke, S.D., U.S.	D6	134
Burke, co., Ga., U.S.	C4	103
Burke, co., N.C., U.S.	B1	126
Burke, co., N.D., U.S.	A3	127
Burke Channel, strt., B.C., Can.	C4	85
Burkesville, Ky., U.S.	D4	110
Burketown, Austl.	D2	62
Burkina Faso, ctry., Afr.	D4	50
Burk's Falls, On., Can.	B5	89
Burleigh, co., N.D., U.S.	C5	127
Burleson, Tx., U.S.	n9	136
Burleson, co., Tx., U.S.	D4	136
Burley, Id., U.S.	G5	105
Burlingame, Ca., U.S.	h8	98
Burlingame, Ks., U.S.	D8	109
Burlington, On., Can.	D5	89
Burlington, Co., U.S.	B8	99
Burlington, Ia., U.S.	D6	108
Burlington, Ks., U.S.	D8	109
Burlington, Ky., U.S.	A5	110
Burlington, Ma., U.S.	f11	114
Burlington, N.C., U.S.	A3	126
Burlington, N.D., U.S.	A4	127
Burlington, N.J., U.S.	C3	123
Burlington, Vt., U.S.	C2	138
Burlington, Wa., U.S.	A3	140
Burlington, Wi., U.S.	F5	142
Burlington, co., N.J., U.S.	D3	123
Burlington Beach, In., U.S.	B3	107
Burlington Junction, Mo., U.S.	A2	118
Burlit, Russia	A2	31
Burma see Myanmar, ctry., Asia	B3	34
Burnaby, B.C., Can.	E6	85
Burnet, Tx., U.S.	D3	136
Burnet, co., Tx., U.S.	D3	136
Burnett, co., Wi., U.S.	C1	142
Burney, Ca., U.S.	B3	98
Burnham, Pa., U.S.	E6	131
Burnie, Austl.	I4	62
Burns, Or., U.S.	D7	130
Burns, Tn., U.S.	A4	135
Burns, Wy., U.S.	E8	143
Burns Flat, Ok., U.S.	B2	129
Burnside, Ky., U.S.	D5	110
Burns Lake, B.C., Can.	B5	85

Name — Map Ref. — Page

Burns Paiute Indian Reservation, Or., U.S. D7 130
Burnsville, Mn., U.S. F5 116
Burnsville, Ms., U.S. A5 117
Burnsville, N.C., U.S. f10 126
Burnsville Lake, res., W.V., U.S. C4 141
Burnt Islands, Nf., Can. E2 88
Burnt Mills, Lake, l., Va., U.S. k14 139
Burntside Lake, l., Mn., U.S. C6 116
Burntwood, stm., Mb., Can. B2 86
Burra, Austl. G2 62
Burrel, Alb. D8 18
Burr Oak, Mi., U.S. G5 115
Burr Oak Reservoir, res., Oh., U.S. C3 128
Burrton, Ks., U.S. D6 109
Bursa, Tur. B3 44
Bûr Sa'îd, Egypt D11 48
Būr Sūdān, Sudan G12 48
Burt, co., Ne., U.S. C9 120
Burt Lake, l., Mi., U.S. C6 115
Burton, Mi., U.S. F7 115
Burton, Oh., U.S. A4 128
Burtts Corner, N.B., Can. C3 87
Buru, i., Indon. D7 36
Burullus, Buheirat el-, l., Egypt G4 44
Burundi, ctry., Afr. D5 54
Burwell, Ne., U.S. C6 120
Bury Saint Edmunds, Eng., U.K. D7 12
Busanga, D.R.C. D4 54
Bushman Land, hist. reg., S. Afr. D2 56
Bushnell, Fl., U.S. D4 102
Bushnell, Il., U.S. C3 106
Bush River, b., Md., U.S. B5 113
Busia, Ug. C6 54
Businga, D.R.C. C4 54
Busira, stm., D.R.C. D3 54
Busko-Zdrój, Pol. D6 20
Buṣrá ash-Shām, Syria F7 44
Busselton, Austl. G2 60
Busuanga Island, i., Phil. D8 34
Busu-Djanoa, D.R.C. C4 54
Buta, D.R.C. C4 54
Butare, Rw. D5 54
Butaritari, atoll, Kir. D11 58
Bute Inlet, b., B.C., Can. D5 85
Butembo, D.R.C. C5 54
Butere, Kenya C6 54
Buthidaung, Myan. B2 34
Butiaba, Ug. C6 54
Butler, Al., U.S. C1 94
Butler, Ga., U.S. D2 103
Butler, In., U.S. B8 107
Butler, Ky., U.S. B5 110
Butler, Mo., U.S. C3 118
Butler, N.J., U.S. B4 123
Butler, Oh., U.S. B3 128
Butler, Pa., U.S. E2 131
Butler, Wi., U.S. m11 142
Butler, co., Al., U.S. D3 94
Butler, co., Ia., U.S. B5 108
Butler, co., Ks., U.S. E7 109
Butler, co., Ky., U.S. C3 110
Butler, co., Mo., U.S. E7 118
Butler, co., Ne., U.S. C8 120
Butler, co., Oh., U.S. C1 128
Butler, co., Pa., U.S. E2 131
Butner, N.C., U.S. A4 126
Buton, Pulau, i., Indon. D6 36
Butrint, hist., Alb. E8 18
Buttahatchee, stm., U.S. B5 117
Butte, Mt., U.S. E4 119
Butte, co., Ca., U.S. C3 98
Butte, co., Id., U.S. F5 105
Butte, co., S.D., U.S. C2 134
Butte des Morts, Lake, l., Wi., U.S. D5 142
Butte Mountains, mts., Nv., U.S. D6 121
Butternut Lake, l., Wi., U.S. C5 142
Butterworth, Malay. B2 36
Buttonwillow, Ca., U.S. E4 98
Butts, co., Ga., U.S. C3 103
Butuan, Phil. E9 34
Buturlinovka, Russia D16 20
Buulobarde, Som. C9 54
Buur Gaabo, Som. D8 54
Buxton, N.C., U.S. B7 126
Büyük Ağrı Dağı see Ağrı Dağı, mtn., Tur. C11 44
Büyükmenderes, stm., Tur. D2 44
Buzuluk, Russia D9 22
Buzzards Bay, Ma., U.S. C6 114
Buzzards Bay, b., Ma., U.S. C6 114
Bwendi, D.R.C. C5 54
Bydgoszcz, Pol. C5 20
Byelorussia see Belarus, ctry., Eur. C9 20
Byers, Co., U.S. B6 99
Byesville, Oh., U.S. C4 128
Byhalia, Ms., U.S. A4 117
Byḫau, Bela. C11 20
Bylas, Az., U.S. D5 96
Byng, Ok., U.S. C5 129
Byrdstown, Tn., U.S. C8 135
Byro, Austl. F2 60
Byron, Ga., U.S. D3 103
Byron, Il., U.S. A4 106
Byron, Mn., U.S. F6 116
Byron, Wy., U.S. B4 143
Byron, Cape, c., Austl. F5 62
Byron Bay, Austl. F5 62
Byrranga, gory, mts., Russia B12 26
Bytom, Pol. D5 20
Bytów, Pol. B4 20
Byzantium see İstanbul, Tur. B3 44

C

Caála, Ang. F3 54
Caatinga, Braz. B8 72
Cabadbaran, Phil. E9 34
Cabaiguán, Cuba A4 80
Caballo Mountains, mts., N.M., U.S. E2 124
Caballo Reservoir, res., N.M., U.S. E2 124
Cabanatuan, Phil. C8 34
Cabano, P.Q., Can. B9 90
Cabarrus, co., N.C., U.S. B2 126
Cabbage Swamp, sw., Fl., U.S. m9 102
Cabedelo, Braz. C5 74
Cabell, co., W.V., U.S. C2 141
Cabeza del Buey, Spain H4 16
Cabimas, Ven. A5 70
Cabin Creek, W.V., U.S. m13 141
Cabin Creek, stm., W.V., U.S. m13 141
Cabinda, Ang. E2 54
Cabinet Gorge Reservoir, res., U.S. B1 119
Cabinet Mountains, mts., Mt., U.S. B1 119
Cabin John, Md., U.S. C3 113
Cabo, Braz. C4 74
Cabo Blanco, Arg. G3 69
Cabonga, Réservoir, res., P.Q., Can. I24 82
Cabool, Mo., U.S. D5 118
Caborca, Mex. C2 78
Cabot, Ar., U.S. C3 97
Cabot, Mount, mtn., N.H., U.S. A4 122
Cabot Head, c., On., Can. B3 89
Cabrayıl, Azer. C12 44
Cabri, Sk., Can. G1 91
Cabrillo National Monument, Ca., U.S. o15 98
Caçador, Braz. D7 72
Čačak, Yugo. C8 18
Caçapava do Sul, Braz. E7 72
Cacapon, stm., W.V., U.S. B6 141
Cáceres, Braz. G8 70
Cáceres, Spain H3 16
Cache, Ok., U.S. C3 129
Cache, co., Ut., U.S. B4 137
Cache, stm., Ar., U.S. C4 97
Cache, stm., Il., U.S. F4 106
Cache Bay, On., Can. A5 89
Cache Creek, B.C., Can. D7 85
Cache la Poudre, stm., Co., U.S. A5 99
Cache Mountain, mtn., Ak., U.S. B10 95
Cache Peak, mtn., Id., U.S. G5 105
Cachimbo, Serra do, mts., Braz. E8 70
Cachingues, Ang. F3 54
Cachoeira do Sul, Braz. E7 72
Cachoeiro de Itapemirim, Braz. F3 74
Cacolo, Ang. F3 54
Caconda, Ang. A2 56
Cactus Flat, pl., Nv., U.S. F5 121
Cactus Peak, mtn., Nv., U.S. F5 121
Cacuaco, Ang. E2 54
Caculé, Braz. A9 72
Čadan, Russia D11 26
Caddo, Ok., U.S. C5 129
Caddo, co., La., U.S. B2 111
Caddo, co., Ok., U.S. B3 129
Caddo, stm., Ar., U.S. C2 97
Caddo Creek, stm., Ok., U.S. C4 129
Caddo Lake, res., U.S. B2 111
Cadillac, Mi., U.S. D5 115
Cadillac Mountain, mtn., Me., U.S. D4 112
Cadiz, Phil. D8 34
Cádiz, Spain I3 16
Cadiz, Ky., U.S. D2 110
Cadiz, Oh., U.S. B4 128
Cádiz, Golfo de, b., Eur. I3 16
Cadiz, Gulf of see Cádiz, Golfo de, b., Eur. I3 16
Cadott, Wi., U.S. D2 142
Čaek, Kyrg. A2 40
Caen, Fr. C6 16
Caernarfon, Wales, U.K. D4 12
Caesar Creek Lake, res., Oh., U.S. C2 128
Caetité, Braz. D3 74
Cagayan de Oro, Phil. E8 34
Cagayan Islands, is., Phil. E8 34
Cagayan Sulu Island, i., Phil. E7 34
Čagda, Russia D15 26
Cagles Mill Lake, res., In., U.S. F4 107
Cagliari, Italy E2 18
Cagliari, Golfo di, b., Italy E2 18
Caguas, P.R. B6 80
Cahaba, stm., Al., U.S. C2 94
Cahama, Ang. B1 56
Cahokia, Il., U.S. E3 106
Cahora Bassa, Albufeira, res., Moz. B5 56
Cahors, Fr. E7 16
Cahul, Mol. G10 20
Caiapó, Serra do, mts., Braz. B7 72
Caibarién, Cuba A4 80
Caicara de Orinoco, Ven. D6 80
Caicó, Braz. C4 74
Caicos Islands, is., T./C. Is. A5 80
Caicos Passage, strt., N.A. A5 80
Cailloma, Peru B3 72
Caillou Bay, b., La., U.S. E5 111
Caillou Lake, l., La., U.S. E5 111
Caimanera, Cuba B4 80
Cairnbrook, Pa., U.S. F4 131
Cairns, Austl. D4 62
Cairo see El-Qâhira, Egypt D11 48
Cairo, Ga., U.S. F2 103
Cairo, Il., U.S. F4 106
Cairo, Ne., U.S. D7 120
Caiundo, Ang. B2 56
Cajamarca, Peru E4 70
Cajazeiras, Braz. C4 74
Calabar, Nig. F6 50
Calabozo, Ven. B6 70
Calagua Islands, is., Phil. D8 34
Calahorra, Spain F6 16
Calais, Fr. B7 16
Calais, Me., U.S. C5 112
Calama, Chile B3 69
Calamian Group, is., Phil. D7 34
Calamus, stm., Ne., U.S. B6 120
Calapan, Phil. D8 34
Călăraşi, Mol. F10 20
Călăraşi, Rom. G9 20
Calatayud, Spain G6 16
Calaveras, co., Ca., U.S. C3 98
Calayan Island, i., Phil. C8 34
Calbayog, Phil. D8 34
Calcasieu, co., La., U.S. D2 111
Calcasieu, stm., La., U.S. D2 111
Calcasieu Lake, l., La., U.S. E2 111
Calcasieu Pass, strt., La., U.S. E2 111
Calçoene, Braz. C9 70
Calcutta, India E5 40
Calcutta, Oh., U.S. B5 128
Calcutta Lake, l., Nv., U.S. B2 121
Caldas da Rainha, Port. H2 16
Caldera, Chile C2 69
Calderwood, Tn., U.S. D10 135
Caldron Falls Reservoir, res., Wi., U.S. C5 142
Caldwell, Id., U.S. F2 105
Caldwell, Ks., U.S. E6 109
Caldwell, N.J., U.S. B4 123
Caldwell, Oh., U.S. C4 128
Caldwell, Tx., U.S. D4 136
Caldwell, co., Ky., U.S. C2 110
Caldwell, co., La., U.S. B3 111
Caldwell, co., Mo., U.S. B3 118
Caldwell, co., N.C., U.S. B1 126
Caldwell, co., Tx., U.S. E4 136
Caledon, On., Can. D5 89
Caledonia, Mi., U.S. F5 115
Caledonia, Mn., U.S. G7 116
Caledonia, Ms., U.S. B5 117
Caledonia, N.Y., U.S. C3 125
Caledonia, co., Vt., U.S. C4 138
Calera, Al., U.S. B3 94
Calera, Ok., U.S. D5 129
Calexico, Ca., U.S. F6 98
Calgary, Ab., Can. D3 84
Calhoun, Ga., U.S. B2 103
Calhoun, Ky., U.S. C2 110
Calhoun, co., Al., U.S. B4 94
Calhoun, co., Ar., U.S. D3 97
Calhoun, co., Fl., U.S. B1 102
Calhoun, co., Ga., U.S. E2 103
Calhoun, co., Ia., U.S. B3 108
Calhoun, co., Il., U.S. D3 106
Calhoun, co., Mi., U.S. F5 115
Calhoun, co., Ms., U.S. B4 117
Calhoun, co., S.C., U.S. D6 133
Calhoun, co., Tx., U.S. E4 136
Calhoun, co., W.V., U.S. C3 141
Calhoun City, Ms., U.S. B4 117
Calhoun Falls, S.C., U.S. C2 133
Cali, Col. C4 70
Calico Rock, Ar., U.S. A3 97
Calicut see Kozhikode, India G3 40
Caliente, Nv., U.S. F7 121
California, Mo., U.S. C5 118
California, Pa., U.S. F2 131
California, state, U.S. D4 98
California, Golfo de, b., Mex. B2 78
California, Gulf of see California, Golfo de, b., Mex. B2 78
California Aqueduct, Ca., U.S. E4 98
Calipatria, Ca., U.S. F6 98
Calispell Peak, mtn., Wa., U.S. A8 140
Calistoga, Ca., U.S. C2 98
Callaghan, Mount, mtn., Nv., U.S. D5 121
Callahan, co., Tx., U.S. C3 136
Callao, Peru F4 70
Callaway, co., Mo., U.S. C6 118
Calling Lake, l., Ab., Can. B4 84
Calloway, co., Ky., U.S. f9 110
Calmar, Ab., Can. C4 84
Calmar, Ia., U.S. A6 108
Caloosahatchee, stm., Fl., U.S. F5 102
Caltanissetta, Italy F4 18
Calulo, Ang. E2 54
Calumet, P.Q., Can. D3 90
Calumet, Mi., U.S. A2 115
Calumet, co., Wi., U.S. D5 142
Calumet, Lake, l., Il., U.S. k9 106
Calumet City, Il., U.S. B6 106
Calunda, Ang. F4 54
Caluula, Som. H15 48
Calvert, Tx., U.S. D4 136
Calvert, co., Md., U.S. C4 113
Calvert City, Ky., U.S. e9 110
Calverton Park, Mo., U.S. f13 118
Calvillo, Mex. C4 78
Calvinia, S. Afr. E2 56
Camabatela, Ang. E3 54
Camaçari, Braz. D4 74
Camacupa, Ang. F3 54
Camagüey, Cuba A4 80
Camaná, Peru G5 70
Camanche, Ia., U.S. C7 108
Camano Island, i., Wa., U.S. A3 140
Camaquã, Braz. E7 72
Camará, Braz. D7 70
Camargo, Bol. C4 72
Camargue, reg., Fr. F9 16
Camarones, Arg. F3 69
Camas, Spain I3 16
Camas, Wa., U.S. D3 140
Camas, co., Id., U.S. F4 105
Ca Mau, Viet. E5 34
Ca Mau, Mui, c., Viet. E4 34
Cambodia, ctry., Asia D4 34
Cambrai, Fr. B8 16
Cambria, Ca., U.S. E3 98
Cambria, Wi., U.S. E4 142
Cambria, co., Pa., U.S. E4 131
Cambridge, On., Can. D4 89
Cambridge, Eng., U.K. D7 12
Cambridge, Ia., U.S. C4 108
Cambridge, Il., U.S. B3 106
Cambridge, Ma., U.S. B5 114
Cambridge, Md., U.S. C5 113
Cambridge, Mn., U.S. E5 116
Cambridge, Ne., U.S. D5 120
Cambridge, N.Y., U.S. B7 125
Cambridge, Oh., U.S. B4 128
Cambridge, Wi., U.S. F4 142
Cambridge City, In., U.S. E7 107
Cambridge Reservoir, res., Ma., U.S. g10 114
Cambridge Springs, Pa., U.S. C1 131
Cambulo, Ang. E4 54
Cambundi-Catembo, Ang. F3 54
Camden, Al., U.S. D2 94
Camden, Ar., U.S. D3 97
Camden, De., U.S. D3 101
Camden, In., U.S. C4 107
Camden, Me., U.S. D3 112
Camden, N.J., U.S. D2 123
Camden, N.Y., U.S. B5 125
Camden, Oh., U.S. C1 128
Camden, S.C., U.S. C6 133
Camden, Tn., U.S. A3 135
Camden, co., Ga., U.S. F5 103
Camden, co., Mo., U.S. C5 118
Camden, co., N.C., U.S. A6 126
Camden, co., N.J., U.S. D3 123
Camdenton, Mo., U.S. D5 118
Camelback Mountain, mtn., Az., U.S. k9 96
Cameron, Az., U.S. B4 96
Cameron, La., U.S. E2 111
Cameron, Mo., U.S. B3 118
Cameron, Tx., U.S. D4 136
Cameron, W.V., U.S. B4 141
Cameron, Wi., U.S. C2 142
Cameron, co., La., U.S. E2 111
Cameron, co., Pa., U.S. D5 131
Cameron, co., Tx., U.S. F4 136
Cameron Hills, hills, Can. G16 82
Cameroon, ctry., Afr. J7 48
Cameroon Mountain, vol., Cam. C1 54
Cametá, Braz. B2 74
Çamiçi Gölü, l., Tur. D2 44
Camiguin Island, i., Phil. C8 34
Camiguin Island, i., Phil. E8 34
Camilla, Ga., U.S. E2 103
Camino, Ca., U.S. C3 98
Camiranga, Braz. D10 70
Camiri, Bol. C5 72
Camissombo, Ang. E4 54
Cammack Village, Ar., U.S. C3 97
Camocim, Braz. B3 74
Camooweal, Austl. D2 62
Camorta Island, i., India H6 40
Camotes Sea, Phil. D8 34
Camp, co., Tx., U.S. C5 136
Campana, Arg. E6 72
Campbell, Ca., U.S. k8 98
Campbell, Fl., U.S. D5 102
Campbell, Mo., U.S. E7 118
Campbell, Oh., U.S. A5 128
Campbell, co., Ky., U.S. B5 110
Campbell, co., S.D., U.S. B5 134
Campbell, co., Tn., U.S. C9 135
Campbell, co., Va., U.S. C3 139
Campbell, co., Wy., U.S. B7 143
Campbellford, On., Can. C7 89
Campbell Hill, hill, Oh., U.S. B2 128
Campbell Island, i., N.Z. J10 58
Campbell Lake, l., Or., U.S. E7 130
Campbell Plateau M20 64
Campbellsburg, In., U.S. G5 107
Campbellsburg, Ky., U.S. B4 110
Campbells Creek, stm., W.V., U.S. m13 141
Campbellsport, Wi., U.S. E5 142
Campbellsville, Ky., U.S. C4 110
Campbellton, N.B., Can. A3 87
Campbellton, Nf., Can. D4 88
Campbelltown, Austl. G5 62
Campbeltown, Scot., U.K. C4 12
Campeche, Mex. D6 78
Campeche, state, Mex. D6 78
Campeche, Bahía de, b., Mex. D6 78
Campeche, Gulf of see Campeche, Bahía de, b., Mex. D6 78
Camperdown, Austl. H3 62
Camperville, Mb., Can. D1 86
Cam Pha, Viet. B5 34
Camp Hill, Al., U.S. C4 94
Camp Hill, Pa., U.S. F8 131
Camp H. M. Smith Marine Corps Base, mil., Hi., U.S. g10 104
Camp Howard Ridge, mtn., Id., U.S. D2 105
Câmpina, Rom. G8 20
Campina Grande, Braz. C4 74
Campinas, Braz. F2 74
Campina Verde, Braz. E2 74
Camp Lejeune Marine Corps Base, mil., N.C., U.S. C5 126
Campo, Cam. C1 54
Campobasso, Italy D5 18
Campobello Island, i., N.B., Can. E3 87
Campo de la Cruz, Col. C5 80
Campo Formoso, Braz. D3 74
Campo Gallo, Arg. D5 72
Campo Grande, Braz. H9 70
Campo Maior, Braz. B3 74
Campo Mourão, Braz. F1 74
Campos, Braz. F3 74
Campos Sales, Braz. C3 74
Camp Pendleton Marine Corps Base, mil., Ca., U.S. F5 98
Camp Point, Il., U.S. C2 106
Camp Springs, Md., U.S. f9 113
Campti, La., U.S. C2 111
Campton, N.H., U.S. C3 122
Câmpulung, Rom. G8 20
Câmpulung Moldovenesc, Rom. F8 20
Camp Verde, Az., U.S. C4 96
Camp Verde Indian Reservation, Az., U.S. C4 96
Cam Ranh, Viet. D5 34
Camrose, Ab., Can. C4 84
Çan, Tur. B2 44
Canaan, Ct., U.S. A2 100
Canaan, N.H., U.S. C2 122
Canaan, stm., N.B., Can. C4 87
Canada, ctry., N.A. G17 82
Canada Basin D1 144
Canada Bay, b., Nf., Can. C3 88
Cañada de Gómez, Arg. E5 72
Canada Falls Lake, res., Me., U.S. C2 112
Canadensis, Pa., U.S. D11 131
Canadian, Tx., U.S. B2 136
Canadian, co., Ok., U.S. B3 129
Canadian, stm., U.S. D7 92
Canaima, Ven. D7 80
Canajoharie, N.Y., U.S. C6 125
Çanakkale, Tur. B2 44
Çanakkale Boğazı (Dardanelles), strt., Tur. C1 44
Canal Flats, B.C., Can. D10 85
Canal Fulton, Oh., U.S. B4 128
Canal Winchester, Oh., U.S. C3 128
Canandaigua, N.Y., U.S. C3 125
Canandaigua Lake, l., N.Y., U.S. C3 125
Cananea, Mex. A2 78
Canarias, Islas (Canary Islands), is., Spain A1 50
Canary Basin F10 66
Canary Islands see Canarias, Islas, is., Spain A1 50
Cañasgordas, Col. D4 80
Canastota, N.Y., U.S. B5 125
Canaveral, Cape, c., Fl., U.S. D6 102
Canaveral National Seashore, Fl., U.S. D6 102
Canavieiras, Braz. E4 74
Canberra, Austl. H4 62
Canby, Mn., U.S. F2 116
Canby, Or., U.S. B4 130
Cancún, Mex. C7 78
Candeias, Braz. D4 74
Candia see Iráklion, Grc. G10 18
Candiac, P.Q., Can. q19 90
Candle Lake, l., Sk., Can. D3 91
Candler, co., Ga., U.S. D4 103
Candlewood, Lake, l., Ct., U.S. D1 100

Name	Map Ref.	Page
Candlewood Isle, Ct., U.S.	D2	100
Candlewood Shores, Ct., U.S.	D2	100
Cando, N.D., U.S.	A6	127
Candor, N.C., U.S.	B3	126
Cane, stm., La., U.S.	C2	111
Canelones, Ur.	E6	72
Caney, Ks., U.S.	E8	109
Caney, stm., Ok., U.S.	A5	129
Caney Creek, stm., Tx., U.S.	r14	136
Caney Fork, stm., Tn., U.S.	C8	135
Canfield, Oh., U.S.	A5	128
Cangas de Narcea, Spain	F3	16
Cangkuang, Tanjung, c., Indon.	E3	36
Cangombe, Ang.	A2	56
Canguçu, Braz.	E7	72
Cangumbe, Ang.	F3	54
Cangyuan, China	B3	34
Cangzhou, China	D11	28
Caniapiscau, stm., P.Q., Can.	g13	90
Canicattì, Italy	F4	18
Canindé, Braz.	B4	74
Canistear Reservoir, res., N.J., U.S.	A4	123
Canisteo, N.Y., U.S.	C3	125
Canisteo, stm., N.Y., U.S.	C3	125
Canistota, S.D., U.S.	D8	134
Çankırı, Tur.	B5	44
Canmore, Ab., Can.	D3	84
Cannanore, India	G3	40
Cannelton, In., U.S.	I4	107
Cannes, Fr.	F10	16
Canning, N.S., Can.	D5	87
Cannon, co., Tn., U.S.	B5	135
Cannon, stm., Mn., U.S.	F5	116
Cannon Air Force Base, mil., N.M., U.S.	C6	124
Cannonball, stm., N.D., U.S.	C5	127
Cannon Beach, Or., U.S.	B3	130
Cannondale, Ct., U.S.	E2	100
Cannon Falls, Mn., U.S.	F6	116
Cannonsburg, Ky., U.S.	B7	110
Cannonsville Reservoir, res., N.Y., U.S.	C5	125
Canoas, Braz.	D7	72
Canoinhas, Braz.	D7	72
Canon, Ga., U.S.	B3	103
Canon City, Co., U.S.	C5	99
Canonsburg, Pa., U.S.	F1	131
Cantabrian Mountains see Cantábrica, Cordillera, mts., Spain	F4	16
Cantábrica, Cordillera, mts., Spain	F4	16
Cantaura, Ven.	B7	70
Canterbury, Eng., U.K.	E7	12
Canterbury, De., U.S.	D3	101
Canterbury Bight, b., N.Z.	p13	63c
Can Tho, Viet.	E5	34
Canton see Guangzhou, China	E3	30
Canton, Ct., U.S.	B4	100
Canton, Ga., U.S.	B2	103
Canton, Il., U.S.	C3	106
Canton, Ks., U.S.	D6	109
Canton, Ma., U.S.	B5	114
Canton, Mo., U.S.	A6	118
Canton, Ms., U.S.	C3	117
Canton, N.C., U.S.	f10	126
Canton, N.Y., U.S.	f9	125
Canton, Oh., U.S.	B4	128
Canton, Ok., U.S.	A3	129
Canton, Pa., U.S.	C8	131
Canton, S.D., U.S.	D9	134
Canton, Tx., U.S.	C5	136
Canton Lake, res., Ok., U.S.	A3	129
Cantonment, Fl., U.S.	u14	102
Canutama, Braz.	E7	70
Canutillo, Tx., U.S.	o11	136
Čany, ozero, l., Russia	D9	26
Canyon, Tx., U.S.	B2	136
Canyon, co., Id., U.S.	F2	105
Canyon City, Or., U.S.	C8	130
Canyon de Chelly National Monument, Az., U.S.	A6	96
Canyon Ferry Lake, res., Mt., U.S.	D5	119
Canyon Lake, Tx., U.S.	E3	136
Canyon Lake, res., Tx., U.S.	E3	136
Canyonlands National Park, Ut., U.S.	E6	137
Canyonville, Or., U.S.	E3	130
Cao Bang, Viet.	B5	34
Caoxian, China	C4	30
Capac, Mi., U.S.	F8	115
Čapaevo, Kaz.	D9	22
Cap-à-l'Aigle, P.Q., Can.	B7	90
Capanema, Braz.	B2	74
Capão Bonito, Braz.	F2	74
Cap-aux-Meules, P.Q., Can.	B8	87
Cap-de-la-Madeleine, P.Q., Can.	C5	90
Cape Barren Island, i., Austl.	I4	62
Cape Basin	L14	66
Cape Breton Highlands National Park, N.S., Can.	C9	87
Cape Breton Island, i., N.S., Can.	C9	87
Cape Broyle, Nf., Can.	E5	88
Cape Canaveral, Fl., U.S.	D6	102
Cape Charles, Va., U.S.	C6	139
Cape Coast, Ghana	E4	50
Cape Cod Bay, b., Ma., U.S.	C7	114
Cape Cod Canal, Ma., U.S.	C6	114
Cape Cod National Seashore, Ma., U.S.	C7	114
Cape Coral, Fl., U.S.	F5	102
Cape Elizabeth, Me., U.S.	E2	112
Cape Fear, stm., N.C., U.S.	C4	126
Cape Girardeau, Mo., U.S.	D8	118
Cape Girardeau, co., Mo., U.S.	D8	118
Cape Hatteras National Seashore, N.C., U.S.	B7	126
Cape Horn Mountain, mtn., Id., U.S.	E3	105
Cape Island, i., S.C., U.S.	E9	133
Capelinha, Braz.	E3	74
Capelongo, Ang.	A2	56
Cape Lookout National Seashore, N.C., U.S.	C6	126
Cape May, N.J., U.S.	F3	123
Cape May, co., N.J., U.S.	E3	123
Cape May Court House, N.J., U.S.	E3	123
Capers Inlet, b., S.C., U.S.	k12	133
Capers Island, i., S.C., U.S.	F8	133
Capers Island, i., S.C., U.S.	G6	133
Cape Sable Island, i., N.S., Can.	F4	87
Cape Town (Kaapstad), S. Afr.	E2	56
Cape Verde Basin	G10	66
Cape Verde, ctry., Afr.	g9	50a
Cape York Peninsula, pen., Austl.	C3	62
Cap-Haïtien, Haiti	B5	80
Capinota, Bol.	B4	72
Capitan, N.M., U.S.	D4	124
Capitan Mountains, mts., N.M., U.S.	D4	124
Capitan Peak, mtn., N.M., U.S.	D4	124
Capitol Heights, Ia., U.S.	e8	108
Capitol Heights, Md., U.S.	C4	113
Capitol Peak, mtn., Nv., U.S.	B4	121
Capitol Reef National Park, Ut., U.S.	E4	137
Čaplygin, Russia	C15	20
Cap-Pelé, N.B., Can.	C5	87
Capreol, On., Can.	p19	89
Capri, Isola di, i., Italy	D5	18
Capricorn Channel, strt., Austl.	E5	62
Capricorn Group, is., Austl.	E5	62
Caprivi Strip, hist. reg., Nmb.	B3	56
Cap-Rouge, P.Q., Can.	n17	90
Cap-Saint-Ignace, P.Q., Can.	B7	90
Captain Cook, Hi., U.S.	D6	104
Captiva, Fl., U.S.	F4	102
Captiva Island, i., Fl., U.S.	F4	102
Capulin Volcano National Monument, N.M., U.S.	A6	124
Capunda Cabilongo, Ang.	F2	54
Caquetá (Japurá), stm., S.A.	D5	70
Čara, Russia	D13	26
Caracal, Rom.	G8	20
Caracaraí, Braz.	C7	70
Caracas, Ven.	A6	70
Carajás, Braz.	E9	70
Carajás, Serra dos, hills, Braz.	E9	70
Carangola, Braz.	F3	74
Caransebeş, Rom.	G7	20
Caraquet, N.B., Can.	B5	87
Caratasca, Laguna de, b., Hond.	B3	80
Caratinga, Braz.	E3	74
Carauari, Braz.	D6	70
Caravaca de la Cruz, Spain	H6	16
Caravelas, Braz.	G12	70
Caraway, Ar., U.S.	B5	97
Carazinho, Braz.	D7	72
Carberry, Mb., Can.	E2	86
Carbon, co., Mt., U.S.	E7	119
Carbon, co., Pa., U.S.	E10	131
Carbon, co., Ut., U.S.	D5	137
Carbon, co., Wy., U.S.	E5	143
Carbondale, Co., U.S.	B3	99
Carbondale, Il., U.S.	F4	106
Carbondale, Ks., U.S.	D8	109
Carbondale, Pa., U.S.	C10	131
Carbonear, Nf., Can.	E5	88
Carbon Hill, Al., U.S.	B2	94
Carbonia, Italy	E2	18
Carcassonne, Fr.	F8	16
Čardara, Kaz.	B9	42
Cárdenas, Cuba	A3	80
Cárdenas, Mex.	D6	78
Cardiff, Wales, U.K.	E5	12
Cardigan, Wales, U.K.	D4	12
Cardigan Bay, b., P.E., Can.	C7	87
Cardigan Bay, b., Wales, U.K.	D4	12
Cardinal, On., Can.	C9	89
Cardington, Oh., U.S.	B3	128
Cardston, Ab., Can.	E4	84
Cardwell, Mo., U.S.	E7	118
Čardžev, Turk.	F8	26
Carei, Rom.	F7	20
Careiro, Braz.	D8	70
Carelia see Karelia, hist. reg., Eur.	C12	6
Carencro, La., U.S.	D3	111
Carentan, Fr.	C6	16
Caretta, W.V., U.S.	D3	141
Carey, Id., U.S.	F5	105
Carey, Oh., U.S.	B2	128
Carey Downs, Austl.	F2	60
Cargados Carajos Shoals, is., Mrts.	F11	52
Caribbean Sea	C4	80
Cariboo Mountains, mts., B.C., Can.	C7	85
Caribou, Me., U.S.	B5	112
Caribou, co., Id., U.S.	G7	105
Caribou Island, i., N.S., Can.	D7	87
Caribou Lake, l., Me., U.S.	C3	112
Caribou Mountain, mtn., Id., U.S.	F7	105
Caribou Mountains, mts., Ab., Can.	f7	84
Caribou Range, mts., Id., U.S.	F7	105
Caripito, Ven.	C7	80
Carl Blackwell, Lake, res., Ok., U.S.	A4	129
Carlet, Spain	H6	16
Carleton, Mi., U.S.	F7	115
Carleton, Mount, mtn., N.B., Can.	B3	87
Carleton Place, On., Can.	B8	89
Carletonville, S. Afr.	D4	56
Carlin, Nv., U.S.	C5	121
Carlinville, Il., U.S.	D4	106
Carlisle, Eng., U.K.	C5	12
Carlisle, Ar., U.S.	C4	97
Carlisle, Ia., U.S.	C4	108
Carlisle, In., U.S.	G3	107
Carlisle, Ky., U.S.	B5	110
Carlisle, Oh., U.S.	C1	128
Carlisle, Pa., U.S.	F7	131
Carlisle, co., Ky., U.S.	f8	110
Carl Junction, Mo., U.S.	D3	118
Carlos Casares, Arg.	F5	72
Carlos Chagas, Braz.	E3	74
Carlow, Ire.	D3	12
Carlsbad see Karlovy Vary, Czech Rep.	D2	20
Carlsbad, Ca., U.S.	F5	98
Carlsbad, N.M., U.S.	E5	124
Carlsbad Caverns National Park, N.M., U.S.	E5	124
Carlsberg Ridge	H8	64
Carlstadt, N.J., U.S.	h8	123
Carlton, Mn., U.S.	D6	116
Carlton, Or., U.S.	B3	130
Carlton, co., Mn., U.S.	D6	116
Carlyle, Il., U.S.	E4	106
Carlyle Lake, res., Il., U.S.	E4	106
Carman, Mb., Can.	E2	86
Carmanville, Nf., Can.	D4	88
Carmarthen, Wales, U.K.	E4	12
Carmel, Ca., U.S.	D3	98
Carmel, In., U.S.	E5	107
Carmel, N.Y., U.S.	D7	125
Carmelo, Ur.	E6	72
Carmen, Isla, i., Mex.	B2	78
Carmen, Isla del, i., Mex.	D6	78
Carmen de Patagones, Arg.	F4	69
Carmi, Il., U.S.	E5	106
Carmi, Lake, l., Vt., U.S.	B3	138
Carnamah, Austl.	F2	60
Carnarvon, Austl.	E1	60
Carnarvon, S. Afr.	E3	56
Carnation, Wa., U.S.	B4	140
Carnegie, Ok., U.S.	B3	129
Carnegie, Pa., U.S.	F1	131
Carnegie, Lake, l., Austl.	F3	60
Carneys Point, N.J., U.S.	D2	123
Carnic Alps, mts., Eur.	A4	18
Car Nicobar Island, i., India	H6	40
Carnot, C.A.R.	C3	54
Caro, Mi., U.S.	E7	115
Carol City, Fl., U.S.	s13	102
Caroleen, N.C., U.S.	B1	126
Carolina, Braz.	C2	74
Carolina, R.I., U.S.	F2	132
Carolina, W.V., U.S.	k10	141
Carolina Beach, N.C., U.S.	C5	126
Caroline, co., Md., U.S.	C6	113
Caroline, co., Va., U.S.	C5	139
Caroline, atoll, Kir.	E15	58
Caroline Islands, is., Oc.	D8	58
Caroní, stm., Ven.	C7	70
Carora, Ven.	C5	80
Carpathian Mountains, mts., Eur.	E6	20
Carpații Meridionali, mts., Rom.	G7	20
Carpentaria, Gulf of, b., Austl.	F7	58
Carpenter Dam, Ar., U.S.	g7	97
Carpentersville, Il., U.S.	A5	106
Carpentras, Fr.	E9	16
Carpina, Braz.	C4	74
Carpinteria, Ca., U.S.	E4	98
Carrabelle, Fl., U.S.	C2	102
Carranza, Cabo, c., Chile	F3	72
Carrara, Italy	B3	18
Carrauntoohil, mtn., Ire.	D2	12
Carrboro, N.C., U.S.	B3	126
Carreta, Punta, c., Peru	F4	70
Carrick on Shannon, Ire.	C3	12
Carrie, Mount, mtn., Wa., U.S.	B2	140
Carriere, Ms., U.S.	E4	117
Carrier Mills, Il., U.S.	F5	106
Carrington, N.D., U.S.	B6	127
Carrington Island, i., Ut., U.S.	C3	137
Carrizal Bajo, Chile	C2	69
Carrizo Creek, stm., U.S.	A1	136
Carrizo Mountain, mtn., N.M., U.S.	D4	124
Carrizo Mountains, mts., U.S.	A6	96
Carrizozo, N.M., U.S.	D4	124
Carroll, Ia., U.S.	B3	108
Carroll, co., Ar., U.S.	A2	97
Carroll, co., Ga., U.S.	C1	103
Carroll, co., Ia., U.S.	B3	108
Carroll, co., Il., U.S.	A4	106
Carroll, co., In., U.S.	C4	107
Carroll, co., Ky., U.S.	B4	110
Carroll, co., Md., U.S.	A3	113
Carroll, co., Mo., U.S.	B4	118
Carroll, co., Ms., U.S.	B4	117
Carroll, co., N.H., U.S.	C4	122
Carroll, co., Oh., U.S.	B4	128
Carroll, co., Tn., U.S.	B3	135
Carroll, co., Va., U.S.	D2	139
Carrollton, Al., U.S.	B1	94
Carrollton, Ga., U.S.	C1	103
Carrollton, Il., U.S.	D3	106
Carrollton, Ky., U.S.	B4	110
Carrollton, Mi., U.S.	E7	115
Carrollton, Mo., U.S.	B4	118
Carrollton, Oh., U.S.	B4	128
Carrolltown, Pa., U.S.	E4	131
Carrot, stm., Can.	D4	91
Carry Falls Reservoir, res., N.Y., U.S.	f10	125
Çarşamba, Tur.	B7	44
Čarsk, Kaz.	B4	28
Carson, Ia., U.S.	C2	108
Carson, Wa., U.S.	D4	140
Carson, co., Tx., U.S.	B2	136
Carson, stm., Nv., U.S.	D2	121
Carson City, Mi., U.S.	E6	115
Carson City, Nv., U.S.	D2	121
Carson Lake, l., Nv., U.S.	D3	121
Carson Sink, l., Nv., U.S.	D3	121
Carson Spring, Tn., U.S.	D10	135
Carstairs, Ab., Can.	D3	84
Cartagena, Col.	A4	70
Cartagena, Spain	I6	16
Cartago, C.R.	D3	80
Carter, co., Ky., U.S.	B6	110
Carter, co., Mo., U.S.	E7	118
Carter, co., Mt., U.S.	E12	119
Carter, co., Ok., U.S.	C4	129
Carter, co., Tn., U.S.	C11	135
Carteret, N.J., U.S.	B4	123
Carteret, co., N.C., U.S.	C6	126
Carter Lake, Ia., U.S.	C2	108
Carter Mountain, mtn., Wy., U.S.	B3	143
Carters Lake, res., Ga., U.S.	B2	103
Cartersville, Ga., U.S.	B2	103
Carterville, Il., U.S.	F4	106
Carterville, Mo., U.S.	D3	118
Carthage, Tun.	F3	18
Carthage, Il., U.S.	C2	106
Carthage, In., U.S.	E6	107
Carthage, Mo., U.S.	D3	118
Carthage, Ms., U.S.	C4	117
Carthage, N.C., U.S.	B3	126
Carthage, N.Y., U.S.	B5	125
Carthage, Tn., U.S.	C8	135
Carthage, Tx., U.S.	C5	136
Carthage, hist., Tun.	F3	18
Cartier Islands, is., Austl.	C3	60
Cartwright, Nf., Can.	B3	88
Cartwright, Ok., U.S.	D5	129
Caruaru, Braz.	C4	74
Carúpano, Ven.	A7	70
Carutapera, Braz.	D10	70
Caruthersville, Mo., U.S.	E8	118
Carver, Ma., U.S.	C6	114
Carver, Mn., U.S.	F5	116
Carver, co., Mn., U.S.	F5	116
Carville, La., U.S.	h9	111
Carvoeiro, Braz.	D7	70
Cary, Il., U.S.	A5	106
Cary, N.C., U.S.	B4	126
Caryville, Tn., U.S.	C9	135
Casablanca, Mor.	D3	48
Casa Grande, Az., U.S.	E4	96
Casa Grande National Monument, Az., U.S.	E4	96
Casale Monferrato, Italy	B2	18
Casa Nova, Braz.	C3	74
Casas Adobes, Az., U.S.	E5	96
Cascade, Co., U.S.	C6	99
Cascade, Ia., U.S.	B6	108
Cascade, Id., U.S.	E2	105
Cascade, Mt., U.S.	C5	119
Cascade, co., Mt., U.S.	C5	119
Cascade Locks, Or., U.S.	B5	130
Cascade Range, mts., N.A.	C3	92
Cascade Reservoir, res., Id., U.S.	E3	105
Cascade Tunnel, Wa., U.S.	B4	140
Cascais, Port.	H2	16
Cascavel, Braz.	D7	72
Casco Bay, b., Me., U.S.	E3	112
Caserta, Italy	D5	18
Caseville, Mi., U.S.	E7	115
Casey, Il., U.S.	D6	106
Casey, co., Ky., U.S.	C5	110
Casey, Mount, mtn., Id., U.S.	A2	105
Casey Key, i., Fl., U.S.	E4	102
Cashion, Az., U.S.	m8	96
Cashmere, Wa., U.S.	B5	140
Cashton, Wi., U.S.	E3	142
Casino, Austl.	F5	62
Casper, Wy., U.S.	D6	143
Casper Mountain, mtn., Wy., U.S.	D6	143
Caspian, Mi., U.S.	B2	115
Caspian Depression (Prikaspijskaja nizmennost'), pl.	E8	22
Caspian Lake, l., Vt., U.S.	B4	138
Caspian Sea	F9	22
Cass, co., Ia., U.S.	C3	108
Cass, co., Il., U.S.	D3	106
Cass, co., In., U.S.	C5	107
Cass, co., Mi., U.S.	G4	115
Cass, co., Mn., U.S.	D4	116
Cass, co., Mo., U.S.	C3	118
Cass, co., N.D., U.S.	C8	127
Cass, co., Ne., U.S.	D9	120
Cass, co., Tx., U.S.	C5	136
Cass, stm., Mi., U.S.	E7	115
Cassai (Kasai), stm., Afr.	F4	54
Cass City, Mi., U.S.	E7	115
Casselberry, Fl., U.S.	D5	102
Casselman, On., Can.	B9	89
Casselman, stm., U.S.	k12	113
Casselton, N.D., U.S.	C8	127
Cassia, co., Id., U.S.	G5	105
Cassiar, B.C., Can.	m17	85
Cassilândia, Braz.	E1	74
Cassinga, Ang.	B2	56
Cassino, Italy	D4	18
Cass Lake, Mn., U.S.	C4	116
Cass Lake, l., Mn., U.S.	C4	116
Cassongue, Ang.	F2	54
Cassopolis, Mi., U.S.	G4	115
Cassumba, Ilha, i., Braz.	E4	74
Cassville, Ga., U.S.	B2	103
Cassville, Mo., U.S.	E4	118
Cassville, Wi., U.S.	F3	142
Castalia, Oh., U.S.	A3	128
Castanea, Pa., U.S.	D7	131
Castanhal, Braz.	B2	74
Castellammare, Golfo di, b., Italy	E4	18
Castelló de la Plana, Spain	H6	16
Castelo Branco, Port.	H3	16
Castelsarrasin, Fr.	F7	16
Castelvetrano, Italy	F4	18
Castilla, Peru	E3	70
Castilla la Nueva, hist. reg., Spain	H4	16
Castilla la Vieja, hist. reg., Spain	G5	16
Castillo de San Marcos National Monument, Fl., U.S.	n9	102
Castine, Me., U.S.	D4	112
Castlebar, Ire.	D2	12
Castleberry, Al., U.S.	D2	94
Castle Dale, Ut., U.S.	D4	137
Castle Dome Mountains, mts., Az., U.S.	D1	96
Castle Dome Peak, mtn., Az., U.S.	D1	96
Castlegar, B.C., Can.	E9	85
Castle Hayne, N.C., U.S.	C5	126
Castle Hills, De., U.S.	i7	101
Castlemaine, Austl.	H3	62
Castle Mountains, mts., Mt., U.S.	D6	119
Castle Peak, mtn., Co., U.S.	B4	99
Castle Peak, mtn., Id., U.S.	E4	105
Castle Point, Mo., U.S.	f13	118
Castle Rock, Co., U.S.	B6	99
Castle Rock, Wa., U.S.	C3	140
Castle Rock, mtn., Or., U.S.	C8	130
Castle Rock Lake, res., Wi., U.S.	E4	142
Castleton, Vt., U.S.	D2	138
Castlewood, Va., U.S.	f9	139
Castor, Ab., Can.	C5	84
Castor, stm., Mo., U.S.	D7	118
Castres, Fr.	F8	16
Castries, St. Luc.	C7	80
Castro, Braz.	C7	72
Castro, Chile	F2	69
Castro, co., Tx., U.S.	B1	136
Castro Valley, Ca., U.S.	h8	98
Castrovillari, Italy	E6	18
Castroville, Tx., U.S.	E3	136
Castuera, Spain	H4	16
Caswell, co., N.C., U.S.	A3	126
Cataguazes, Braz.	C9	72
Catahoula, co., La., U.S.	C4	111
Catahoula Lake, l., La., U.S.	C3	111
Catalão, Braz.	E2	74
Catalina, Nf., Can.	D5	88
Catalina, Chile	C3	69
Catalunya, hist. reg., Spain	F7	16
Catanduanes Island, i., Phil.	D8	34
Catania, Italy	F5	18
Catanzaro, Italy	E6	18
Cataouatche, Lake, l., La., U.S.	k11	111
Catarino Rodríguez, Mex.	C4	78
Catarman, Phil.	D8	34
Catasauqua, Pa., U.S.	E11	131
Cataumet, Ma., U.S.	C6	114
Catawba, co., N.C., U.S.	B1	126
Catawba, stm., S.C., U.S.	B6	133
Catawba, South Fork, stm., N.C., U.S.	B1	126

Name	Map Ref.	Page
Catawissa, Pa., U.S.	**E9**	131
Catbalogan, Phil.	**D8**	34
Catete, Ang.	**E2**	54
Cathance, Lake, l., Me., U.S.	**D5**	112
Cathedral City, Ca., U.S.	**F5**	98
Cathedral of the Pines, N.H., U.S.	**E3**	122
Catherine, Lake, res., Ar., U.S.	**C3**	97
Cat Island, i., Bah.	**D9**	76
Cat Island, i., Ma., U.S.	**f12**	114
Cat Island, i., Ms., U.S.	**E4**	117
Cat Island, i., S.C., U.S.	**E9**	133
Catlettsburg, Ky., U.S.	**B7**	110
Catlin, Il., U.S.	**C6**	106
Catnip Mountain, mtn., Nv., U.S.	**B2**	121
Catoche, Cabo, c., Mex.	**C7**	78
Catonsville, Md., U.S.	**B4**	113
Catoosa, Ok., U.S.	**A6**	129
Catoosa, co., Ga., U.S.	**B1**	103
Catriló, Arg.	**F5**	72
Catron, co., N.M., U.S.	**D1**	124
Catskill, N.Y., U.S.	**C7**	125
Catskill Mountains, mts., N.Y., U.S.	**C6**	125
Catt, Mount, mtn., B.C., Can.	**B3**	85
Cattaraugus, co., N.Y., U.S.	**C2**	125
Cattaraugus Creek, stm., N.Y., U.S.	**C2**	125
Cattaraugus Indian Reservation, N.Y., U.S.	**C2**	125
Čatyrtaš, Kyrg.	**A3**	40
Caubvick, Mount (Iberville, Mont d'), mtn., Can.	**f9**	88
Cauca, stm., Col.	**B5**	70
Caucasia, Col.	**D4**	80
Caucasus, mts.	**A10**	44
Caucete, Arg.	**E4**	72
Caucomgomoc Lake, l., Me., U.S.	**B3**	112
Caungula, Ang.	**E3**	54
Cauquenes, Chile	**E2**	69
Caura, stm., Ven.	**B7**	70
Cavalier, N.D., U.S.	**A8**	127
Cavalier, co., N.D., U.S.	**A7**	127
Cave City, Ar., U.S.	**B4**	97
Cave City, Ky., U.S.	**C4**	110
Cave Creek, Az., U.S.	**D4**	96
Cave Junction, Or., U.S.	**E3**	130
Cave Point, c., Wi., U.S.	**D6**	142
Cave Run Lake, res., Ky., U.S.	**B6**	110
Cave Spring, Ga., U.S.	**B1**	103
Cave Spring, Va., U.S.	**C2**	139
Cavetown, Md., U.S.	**A2**	113
Caviana de Fora, Ilha, i., Braz.	**A2**	74
Cavite, Phil.	**D8**	34
Cawood, Ky., U.S.	**D6**	110
Cawston, B.C., Can.	**E8**	85
Caxias, Braz.	**B3**	74
Caxias do Sul, Braz.	**D7**	72
Caxito, Ang.	**E2**	54
Cayambe, vol., Ec.	**C4**	70
Cayce, S.C., U.S.	**D5**	133
Cayenne, Fr. Gu.	**C9**	70
Cayman Brac, i., Cay. Is.	**B4**	80
Cayman Islands, dep., N.A.	**E8**	76
Cayuga, In., U.S.	**E3**	107
Cayuga, co., N.Y., U.S.	**C4**	125
Cayuga Heights, N.Y., U.S.	**C4**	125
Cayuga Lake, l., N.Y., U.S.	**C4**	125
Cazenovia, N.Y., U.S.	**C5**	125
Cazombo, Ang.	**F4**	54
Ceará, state, Braz.	**C4**	74
Ceará-Mirim, Braz.	**C4**	74
Ceballos, Mex.	**B4**	78
Čeboksary, Russia	**D6**	26
Cebu, Phil.	**D8**	34
Cebu, i., Phil.	**D8**	34
Cecil, co., Md., U.S.	**A6**	113
Cecil Field Naval Air Station, mil., Fl., U.S.	**B5**	102
Cecilia, Ky., U.S.	**C4**	110
Cecina, Italy	**C3**	18
Čečnja, state, Russia	**E6**	26
Cedar, co., Ia., U.S.	**C6**	108
Cedar, co., Mo., U.S.	**D4**	118
Cedar, co., Ne., U.S.	**B8**	120
Cedar, stm., Ne., U.S.	**B7**	120
Cedar, stm., Wa., U.S.	**B4**	140
Cedar, stm., U.S.	**C6**	108
Cedar Bluff, Al., U.S.	**A4**	94
Cedar Bluff Reservoir, res., Ks., U.S.	**D4**	109
Cedar Bluff Two, Tn., U.S.	**D9**	135
Cedar Breaks National Monument, Ut., U.S.	**F3**	137
Cedarburg, Wi., U.S.	**E6**	142
Cedar City, Ut., U.S.	**F2**	137
Cedar Creek, stm., N.D., U.S.	**C3**	127
Cedar Creek, stm., N.J., U.S.	**D4**	123
Cedar Creek, stm., Oh., U.S.	**e7**	128
Cedar Creek Lake, res., Tx., U.S.	**C4**	136
Cedar Crest, N.M., U.S.	**k8**	124
Cedaredge, Co., U.S.	**C3**	99
Cedar Falls, Ia., U.S.	**B5**	108
Cedar Grove, N.J., U.S.	**B4**	123
Cedar Grove, W.V., U.S.	**C3**	141
Cedar Grove, Wi., U.S.	**E6**	142
Cedar Hill, Mo., U.S.	**g12**	118
Cedar Hill, Tx., U.S.	**n10**	136
Cedarhurst, N.Y., U.S.	**k13**	125
Cedar Island, i., N.C., U.S.	**C6**	126
Cedar Island, i., S.C., U.S.	**E9**	133
Cedar Island, i., Va., U.S.	**C7**	139
Cedar Key, Fl., U.S.	**C3**	102
Cedar Keys, is., Fl., U.S.	**C3**	102
Cedar Lake, In., U.S.	**B3**	107
Cedar Lake, res., Mb., Can.	**C1**	86
Cedar Lake, res., Il., U.S.	**F4**	106
Cedar Mountain, mtn., Ca., U.S.	**B3**	98
Cedar Point, c., Md., U.S.	**D5**	113
Cedar Point, c., Oh., U.S.	**A3**	128
Cedar Point, c., Oh., U.S.	**e7**	128
Cedar Rapids, Ia., U.S.	**C6**	108
Cedar Springs, Mi., U.S.	**E5**	115
Cedartown, Ga., U.S.	**B1**	103
Cedar Vale, Ks., U.S.	**E7**	109
Cedarville, Oh., U.S.	**C2**	128
Cedros, Isla, i., Mex.	**B1**	78
Ceduna, Austl.	**G5**	60
Ceerigaabo, Som.	**H14**	48
Cefalonia see Kefallinía, i., Grc.	**E8**	18
Cefalù, Italy	**F5**	18
Čegdomyn, Russia	**D15**	26
Cegléd, Hung.	**F5**	20
Čehov, Russia	**B14**	20
Čehov, Russia	**A4**	31
Çekerek, Tur.	**B6**	44
Çekerek, stm., Tur.	**C6**	44
Celaya, Mex.	**C4**	78
Celebes see Sulawesi, i., Indon.	**D6**	36
Celebes Basin	**H15**	64
Celebes Sea, Asia	**C6**	36
Čeleken, Turk.	**C6**	42
Celina, Oh., U.S.	**B1**	128
Celina, Tn., U.S.	**C8**	135
Celina, Tx., U.S.	**C4**	136
Čeljabinsk, Russia	**D8**	26
Celje, Slvn.	**A5**	18
Čeljuskin, mys, c., Russia	**B12**	26
Čelkar, Kaz.	**E7**	26
Celle, Ger.	**D11**	12
Celtic Sea, Eur.	**B3**	16
Cement, Ok., U.S.	**C3**	129
Cementon, Pa., U.S.	**E10**	131
Cenderawasih, Teluk, b., Indon.	**G10**	32
Cenderawasih Bay see Cenderawasih, Teluk, b., Indon.	**G10**	32
Centennial Mountains, mts., Id., U.S.	**E7**	105
Center, Co., U.S.	**D4**	99
Center, N.D., U.S.	**B4**	127
Center, Tx., U.S.	**D5**	136
Centerbrook, Ct., U.S.	**D6**	100
Centerburg, Oh., U.S.	**B3**	128
Centereach, N.Y., U.S.	**n15**	125
Centerfield, Ut., U.S.	**D4**	137
Center Hill Lake, res., Tn., U.S.	**C8**	135
Center Moriches, N.Y., U.S.	**n16**	125
Center Mountain, mtn., Id., U.S.	**D3**	105
Center Point, Al., U.S.	**f7**	94
Center Point, Ia., U.S.	**B6**	108
Centerville, Ia., U.S.	**D5**	108
Centerville, In., U.S.	**E8**	107
Centerville, La., U.S.	**E4**	111
Centerville, Ma., U.S.	**C7**	114
Centerville, Oh., U.S.	**C1**	128
Centerville, Pa., U.S.	**F2**	131
Centerville, S.D., U.S.	**D9**	134
Centerville, Tn., U.S.	**B4**	135
Centerville, Ut., U.S.	**C4**	137
Central, Phil.	**D8**	34
Central, N.M., U.S.	**E1**	124
Central, S.C., U.S.	**B2**	133
Central, Cordillera, mts., Col.	**E4**	80
Central, Cordillera, mts., Peru	**E4**	70
Central, Massif, mts., Fr.	**E8**	16
Central, Sistema, mts., Spain	**G4**	16
Central African Republic, ctry., Afr.	**B3**	54
Central City, Co., U.S.	**B5**	99
Central City, Ia., U.S.	**B6**	108
Central City, Il., U.S.	**E4**	106
Central City, Ky., U.S.	**C2**	110
Central City, Ne., U.S.	**C7**	120
Central City, Pa., U.S.	**F4**	131
Central Falls, R.I., U.S.	**B4**	132
Central Heights, Az., U.S.	**D5**	96
Centralia, Il., U.S.	**E4**	106
Centralia, Mo., U.S.	**B5**	118
Centralia, Wa., U.S.	**C3**	140
Central Islip, N.Y., U.S.	**n15**	125
Central Lake, Mi., U.S.	**C5**	115
Central Makrān Range, mts., Pak.	**E8**	42
Central Pacific Basin	**G21**	64
Central Park, Wa., U.S.	**C2**	140
Central Point, Or., U.S.	**E4**	130
Central Siberian Uplands see Srednesibirskoe ploskogor'e, plat., Russia	**C12**	26
Central Square, N.Y., U.S.	**B4**	125
Central Valley, Ca., U.S.	**B2**	98
Central Valley, N.Y., U.S.	**D6**	125
Central Village, Ct., U.S.	**C8**	100
Centre, Al., U.S.	**A4**	94
Centre, co., Pa., U.S.	**E6**	131
Centre Hall, Pa., U.S.	**E6**	131
Centreville, Al., U.S.	**C2**	94
Centreville, Il., U.S.	**E3**	106
Centreville, Md., U.S.	**B5**	113
Centreville, Mi., U.S.	**G5**	115
Centreville, Ms., U.S.	**D2**	117
Centuria, Wi., U.S.	**C1**	142
Century, Fl., U.S.	**u14**	102
Ceos see Kéa, i., Grc.	**F10**	18
Ceram see Seram, i., Indon.	**D7**	36
Ceram Sea see Seram, Laut, Indon.	**D7**	36
Cerbat Mountains, mts., Az., U.S.	**B1**	96
Cerdas, Bol.	**C4**	72
Ceredo, W.V., U.S.	**C2**	141
Čeremhovo, Russia	**D12**	26
Čerepovec, Russia	**D5**	26
Ceres, Arg.	**D5**	72
Ceres, Braz.	**E2**	74
Ceres, Ca., U.S.	**D3**	98
Ceresco, Ne., U.S.	**C9**	120
Cerignola, Italy	**D5**	18
Čerkessk, Russia	**E6**	26
Čerlak, Russia	**D9**	26
Čermoz, Russia	**C10**	22
Černavodă, Rom.	**G10**	20
Černjahovsk, Russia	**B6**	20
Černjanka, Russia	**D14**	20
Černobyl', Ukr.	**D11**	20
Černuška, Russia	**C10**	22
Černyševskij, Russia	**C13**	26
Cerralvo, Isla, i., Mex.	**C3**	78
Cerritos, Mex.	**C4**	78
Cerro Azul, Peru	**A2**	72
Cerro de Pasco, Peru	**F4**	70
Cerro Gordo, Il., U.S.	**D5**	106
Cerro Gordo, co., Ia., U.S.	**A4**	108
Čerskij, Russia	**C18**	26
Čerskogo, hrebet, mts., Russia	**C15**	26
Červen', Bela.	**C10**	20
Cervino see Matterhorn, mtn., Eur.	**A1**	18
Cesena, Italy	**B4**	18
Cēsis, Lat.	**H11**	10
České Budějovice, Czech Rep.	**E3**	20
Çeşme, Tur.	**C2**	44
Češskaja guba, b., Russia	**A8**	22
Cessnock, Austl.	**G5**	62
Cetinje, Yugo.	**C7**	18
Ceuta, Sp. N. Afr.	**J4**	16
Cévennes, reg., Fr.	**E8**	16
Ceyhan, Tur.	**D6**	44
Ceyhan, stm., Tur.	**D6**	44
Ceylanpınar, Tur.	**D9**	44
Ceylon see Sri Lanka, ctry., Asia	**H4**	40
Cha-am, Thai.	**D3**	34
Chachani, Nevado, vol., Peru	**G5**	70
Chachapoyas, Peru	**E4**	70
Chachoengsao, Thai.	**D4**	34
Chaco, stm., N.M., U.S.	**A1**	124
Chaco Austral, reg., Arg.	**D5**	72
Chaco Boreal, reg., Para.	**C5**	72
Chaco Central, reg., Arg.	**C5**	72
Chaco Culture National Historic Park, N.M., U.S.	**A2**	124
Chacon, Cape, c., Ak., U.S.	**n24**	95
Chad, ctry., Chad	**G8**	48
Chad, Lake, l., Afr.	**D7**	50
Chadbourn, N.C., U.S.	**C4**	126
Chadds Ford, Pa., U.S.	**G10**	131
Chadron, Ne., U.S.	**B3**	120
Chadwicks, N.Y., U.S.	**B5**	125
Chaffee, Mo., U.S.	**D8**	118
Chaffee, co., Co., U.S.	**C4**	99
Chaffin, Ma., U.S.	**B4**	114
Chaghcharān, Afg.	**D9**	42
Chagos Archipelago, is., B.I.O.T.	**I10**	64
Chagos-Laccadive Plateau	**I10**	64
Chagrin Falls, Oh., U.S.	**A4**	128
Chaguaramas, Ven.	**D6**	80
Chahār Borjak, Afg.	**D8**	42
Chai Nat, Thai.	**C4**	34
Chaiyaphum, Thai.	**C4**	34
Chajarí, Arg.	**E6**	72
Chakachamna Lake, l., Ak., U.S.	**g15**	95
Chakari, Zimb.	**B4**	56
Chakasija, state, Russia	**A5**	28
Chala, Peru	**B3**	72
Chalatenango, El Sal.	**C2**	80
Chalbi Desert, des., Kenya	**C7**	54
Chalcidice see Khalkidhikí, hist. reg., Grc.	**D9**	18
Chalcis see Khalkís, Grc.	**E9**	18
Chaleur Bay, b., Can.	**B4**	87
Chalfonte, De., U.S.	**h7**	101
Chalk River, On., Can.	**A7**	89
Challapata, Bol.	**B4**	72
Challenger Deep	**G17**	64
Challis, Id., U.S.	**E4**	105
Chalmette, La., U.S.	**E6**	111
Châlons-en-Champagne, Fr.	**C9**	16
Chalon-sur-Saône, Fr.	**D9**	16
Chālūs, Iran	**C6**	42
Chama, N.M., U.S.	**A3**	124
Chama, Rio, stm., N.M., U.S.	**A3**	124
Chaman, Pak.	**D9**	42
Chambal, stm., India	**D3**	40
Chamberlain, S.D., U.S.	**D6**	134
Chamberlain Lake, l., Me., U.S.	**B3**	112
Chamberlin, Mount, mtn., Ak., U.S.	**B10**	95
Chambers, co., Al., U.S.	**C4**	94
Chambers, co., Tx., U.S.	**E5**	136
Chambersburg, Pa., U.S.	**G6**	131
Chambers Island, i., Wi., U.S.	**C6**	142
Chambéry, Fr.	**E9**	16
Chambi, Jebel, mtn., Tun.	**C6**	48
Chamblee, Ga., U.S.	**h8**	103
Chambly, P.Q., Can.	**D4**	90
Chamical, Arg.	**E4**	72
Chamisal, N.M., U.S.	**A4**	124
Chāmpa, India	**E4**	40
Champagne, hist. reg., Fr.	**C9**	16
Champaign, Il., U.S.	**C5**	106
Champaign, co., Il., U.S.	**C5**	106
Champaign, co., Oh., U.S.	**B2**	128
Champasak, Laos	**D5**	34
Champion, Oh., U.S.	**A5**	128
Champlain, Lake, l., N.A.	**C13**	92
Champlin, Mn., U.S.	**m12**	116
Champotón, Mex.	**D6**	78
Chañaral, Chile	**C2**	69
Chance, Md., U.S.	**D6**	113
Chanchelulla Peak, mtn., Ca., U.S.	**B2**	98
Chandalar, stm., Ak., U.S.	**B10**	95
Chandeleur Islands, is., La., U.S.	**E7**	111
Chandeleur Sound, strt., La., U.S.	**E6**	111
Chandīgarh, India	**C3**	40
Chandler, P.Q., Can.	**k14**	90
Chandler, Az., U.S.	**D4**	96
Chandler, In., U.S.	**H3**	107
Chandler, Ok., U.S.	**B5**	129
Chandler, Tx., U.S.	**C5**	136
Chandler Heights, Az., U.S.	**m9**	96
Chāndpur, Bngl.	**E6**	40
Chandrapur, India	**F3**	40
Chang (Yangtze), stm., China	**E9**	28
Chang, Ko, i., Thai.	**D4**	34
Changane, stm., Moz.	**C5**	56
Changara, Moz.	**B5**	56
Chang Cheng (Great Wall), China	**B2**	30
Changchun, China	**C13**	28
Changde, China	**F10**	28
Changhua, Tai.	**E5**	30
Changji, China	**C5**	28
Changjiang, China	**H9**	28
Changli, China	**B4**	30
Changmar, China	**E3**	28
Changning, China	**B3**	34
Changsha, China	**F10**	28
Changshu, China	**C5**	30
Changting, China	**F11**	28
Changwu, China	**B2**	30
Changzhi, China	**D10**	28
Changzhou, China	**E12**	28
Chanhassen, Mn., U.S.	**n11**	116
Channahon, Il., U.S.	**B5**	106
Channel Islands, is., Eur.	**C5**	16
Channel Islands National Park, Ca., U.S.	**F4**	98
Channel Lake, Il., U.S.	**H8**	106
Channel-Port-aux-Basques, Nf., Can.	**E2**	88
Channelview, Tx., U.S.	**r14**	136
Chanthaburi, Thai.	**D4**	34
Chantilly, Va., U.S.	**g12**	139
Chanute, Ks., U.S.	**E8**	109
Chao'an, China	**G11**	28
Chao Hu, l., China	**E11**	28
Chaoxian, China	**C4**	30
Chaoyang, China	**C12**	28
Chaoyang, China	**E4**	30
Chapadinha, Braz.	**B3**	74
Chapala, Laguna de, l., Mex.	**C4**	78
Chaparral, Col.	**E4**	80
Chapecó, Braz.	**D7**	72
Chapel Hill, N.C., U.S.	**B3**	126
Chapel Hill, Tn., U.S.	**B5**	135
Chaplin, stm., Ky., U.S.	**C4**	110
Chaplin Lake, l., Sk., Can.	**G2**	91
Chaplynka, Ukr.	**F12**	20
Chapman, Ks., U.S.	**D6**	109
Chapman Pond, l., R.I., U.S.	**F1**	132
Chapmanville, W.V., U.S.	**D2**	141
Chappaquiddick Island, i., Ma., U.S.	**D7**	114
Chappell, Ne., U.S.	**C3**	120
Charagua, Bol.	**B5**	72
Charcas, Mex.	**C4**	78
Chardon, Oh., U.S.	**A4**	128
Charenton, La., U.S.	**E4**	111
Chari, stm., Afr.	**H8**	48
Chārīkār, Afg.	**C9**	42
Chariton, Ia., U.S.	**C4**	108
Chariton, co., Mo., U.S.	**B4**	118
Chariton, stm., U.S.	**A5**	118
Charity, Guy.	**B8**	70
Charleroi, Bel.	**E9**	12
Charleroi, Pa., U.S.	**F2**	131
Charles, co., Md., U.S.	**C3**	113
Charles, stm., Ma., U.S.	**B5**	114
Charles, Cape, c., Va., U.S.	**C6**	139
Charles A. Goodwin Dam, Ct., U.S.	**B3**	100
Charlesbourg, P.Q., Can.	**n17**	90
Charles City, Ia., U.S.	**A5**	108
Charles City, co., Va., U.S.	**C5**	139
Charles Mill Lake, res., Oh., U.S.	**B3**	128
Charles Mix, co., S.D., U.S.	**D7**	134
Charles Mound, hill, Il., U.S.	**A3**	106
Charleston, Ar., U.S.	**B1**	97
Charleston, Il., U.S.	**D5**	106
Charleston, Mo., U.S.	**E8**	118
Charleston, Ms., U.S.	**A3**	117
Charleston, Or., U.S.	**D2**	130
Charleston, S.C., U.S.	**F8**	133
Charleston, Tn., U.S.	**D9**	135
Charleston, W.V., U.S.	**C3**	141
Charleston, co., S.C., U.S.	**F8**	133
Charleston Air Force Base, mil., S.C., U.S.	**k11**	133
Charleston Naval Shipyard, mil., S.C., U.S.	**k12**	133
Charleston Peak, mtn., Nv., U.S.	**G6**	121
Charlestown, In., U.S.	**H6**	107
Charlestown, N.H., U.S.	**D2**	122
Charlestown, R.I., U.S.	**F2**	132
Charles Town, W.V., U.S.	**B7**	141
Charleville, Austl.	**F4**	62
Charleville-Mézières, Fr.	**C9**	16
Charlevoix, Mi., U.S.	**C5**	115
Charlevoix, co., Mi., U.S.	**C5**	115
Charlevoix, Lake, l., Mi., U.S.	**C5**	115
Charlo, N.B., Can.	**B3**	87
Charlotte, Mi., U.S.	**F6**	115
Charlotte, N.C., U.S.	**B2**	126
Charlotte, Tn., U.S.	**A4**	135
Charlotte, Tx., U.S.	**E3**	136
Charlotte, co., Fl., U.S.	**F5**	102
Charlotte, co., Va., U.S.	**C4**	139
Charlotte Amalie, V.I.U.S.	**B6**	80
Charlotte Hall, Md., U.S.	**D4**	113
Charlotte Harbor, Fl., U.S.	**F4**	102
Charlotte Harbor, b., Fl., U.S.	**F4**	102
Charlottesville, Va., U.S.	**B4**	139
Charlottetown, P.E., Can.	**C6**	87
Charlton, co., Ga., U.S.	**F4**	103
Charmco, W.V., U.S.	**C4**	141
Charny, P.Q., Can.	**C6**	90
Charters Towers, Austl.	**E4**	62
Chartres, Fr.	**C7**	16
Chascomús, Arg.	**F6**	72
Chase, B.C., Can.	**D8**	85
Chase, Md., U.S.	**B5**	113
Chase, co., Ks., U.S.	**D7**	109
Chase, co., Ne., U.S.	**D4**	120
Chase City, Va., U.S.	**D4**	139
Chaska, Mn., U.S.	**F5**	116
Chassahowitzka Bay, b., Fl., U.S.	**D4**	102
Chassell, Mi., U.S.	**B2**	115
Châteaubriant, Fr.	**D6**	16
Châteaudun, Fr.	**C7**	16
Châteauguay, P.Q., Can.	**D4**	90
Château-Richer, P.Q., Can.	**C6**	90
Châteauroux, Fr.	**D7**	16
Châtellerault, Fr.	**D7**	16
Chatfield, Mn., U.S.	**G6**	116
Chatham, N.B., Can.	**B4**	87
Chatham, On., Can.	**E2**	89
Chatham, Il., U.S.	**D4**	106
Chatham, La., U.S.	**B3**	111
Chatham, Ma., U.S.	**C8**	114
Chatham, N.J., U.S.	**B4**	123
Chatham, N.Y., U.S.	**C7**	125
Chatham, Va., U.S.	**D3**	139
Chatham, co., Ga., U.S.	**E5**	103
Chatham, co., N.C., U.S.	**B3**	126
Chatham Islands, is., N.Z.	**I12**	58
Chatham Rise	**M21**	64
Chatham Strait, strt., Ak., U.S.	**m22**	95
Châtillon-sur-Seine, Fr.	**D9**	16
Chatom, Al., U.S.	**D1**	94
Chatsworth, Ga., U.S.	**B2**	103
Chatsworth, Il., U.S.	**C5**	106
Chatsworth Reservoir, res., Ca., U.S.	**m11**	98
Chattahoochee, Fl., U.S.	**B2**	102
Chattahoochee, co., Ga., U.S.	**D2**	103
Chattahoochee, stm., U.S.	**E1**	103
Chattanooga, Tn., U.S.	**D8**	135
Chattaroy, W.V., U.S.	**D2**	141
Chattooga, co., Ga., U.S.	**B1**	103
Chattooga, stm., U.S.	**B1**	133
Chatuge Lake, res., U.S.	**g9**	126
Chaudière, stm., P.Q., Can.	**C7**	90
Chauk, Myan.	**B2**	34
Chaumont, Fr.	**C9**	16
Chauncey, Oh., U.S.	**C3**	128
Chauny, Fr.	**C8**	16
Chautauqua, co., Ks., U.S.	**E7**	109
Chautauqua, co., N.Y., U.S.	**C1**	125
Chautauqua Lake, l., N.Y., U.S.	**C1**	125
Chauvin, La., U.S.	**E5**	111
Chaves, Port.	**G3**	16

Name	Map Ref.	Page
Chaves, co., N.M., U.S.	D5	124
Cheaha Mountain, mtn., Al., U.S.	B4	94
Cheat, Shavers Fork, stm., W.V., U.S.	B5	141
Cheatham, co., Tn., U.S.	A4	135
Cheb, Czech Rep.	D2	20
Chebanse, Il., U.S.	C6	106
Cheboygan, Mi., U.S.	C6	115
Cheboygan, co., Mi., U.S.	C6	115
Chech, 'Erg, des., Afr.	B4	50
Chechaouen, Mor.	J4	16
Chechnya see Čečnja, state, Russia	E6	26
Checotah, Ok., U.S.	B6	129
Chedabucto Bay, b., N.S., Can.	D8	87
Cheduba Island, i., Myan.	C2	34
Cheektowaga, N.Y., U.S.	C2	125
Cheeseman Lake, res., Co., U.S.	B5	99
Chehalem Mountains, mts., Or., U.S.	h12	130
Chehalis, Wa., U.S.	C3	140
Chehalis, stm., Wa., U.S.	C2	140
Cheju, S. Kor.	E13	28
Cheju-do, i., S. Kor.	E13	28
Chekhov see Čehov, Russia	B14	20
Chekhov see Čehov, Russia	A4	31
Chelan, Wa., U.S.	B5	140
Chelan, co., Wa., U.S.	B4	140
Chelan, Lake, l., Wa., U.S.	A5	140
Chelan Mountains, mts., Wa., U.S.	A5	140
Chelif, Oued, stm., Alg.	D4	14
Chełm, Pol.	D7	20
Chełmno, Pol.	C5	20
Chelmsford, Eng., U.K.	E7	12
Chelmsford, Ma., U.S.	A5	114
Chelsea, P.Q., Can.	D2	90
Chelsea, Al., U.S.	g7	94
Chelsea, Ma., U.S.	B5	114
Chelsea, Mi., U.S.	F6	115
Chelsea, Ok., U.S.	A6	129
Cheltenham, Eng., U.K.	E5	12
Cheltenham, Md., U.S.	C4	113
Chelyabinsk see Čeljabinsk, Russia	D8	26
Chelyan, W.V., U.S.	C3	141
Chemba, Moz.	B5	56
Chemehuevi Indian Reservation, Ca., U.S.	E6	98
Chemnitz, Ger.	E13	12
Chemquasabamticook Lake (Ross Lake), l., Me., U.S.	B3	112
Chemung, co., N.Y., U.S.	C4	125
Chemung, stm., Pa., U.S.	C8	131
Chemung Lake, l., On., Can.	C6	89
Chenāb, stm., Asia	C2	40
Chenango, co., N.Y., U.S.	C5	125
Chenango, stm., N.Y., U.S.	C5	125
Chenango Bridge, N.Y., U.S.	C5	125
Chenes, River Aux, b., La., U.S.	k12	111
Chénéville, P.Q., Can.	D2	90
Cheney, Ks., U.S.	E6	109
Cheney, Wa., U.S.	B8	140
Cheney Reservoir, res., Ks., U.S.	E6	109
Cheneyville, La., U.S.	C3	111
Chengde, China	C11	28
Chengdu, China	E8	28
Chengmai, China	F2	30
Chengshan Jiao, c., China	D12	28
Chengxian, China	C2	30
Chennai (Madras), India	G4	40
Chenoa, Il., U.S.	C5	106
Chenoweth, Or., U.S.	B5	130
Chenxi, China	D3	30
Chenzhou, China	F10	28
Chepachet, R.I., U.S.	B2	132
Chepachet, stm., R.I., U.S.	B2	132
Chequamegon Bay, b., Wi., U.S.	B3	142
Cher, stm., Fr.	D7	16
Cheraw, S.C., U.S.	B8	133
Cherbaniani Reef, rf., India	G2	40
Cherbourg, Fr.	C6	16
Cherchell, Alg.	I8	16
Chergui, Chott ech, l., Alg.	D5	48
Cherkasy, Ukr.	E11	20
Cherkessia see Karačaevo-Čerkesija, state, Russia	E6	26
Cherniakhiv, Ukr.	D10	20
Chernihiv, Ukr.	D11	20
Chernivtsi, Ukr.	E8	20
Chernobyl see Černobyl', Ukr.	D11	20
Cherokee, Al., U.S.	A2	94
Cherokee, Ia., U.S.	B2	108
Cherokee, Ks., U.S.	E9	109
Cherokee, Ok., U.S.	A3	129
Cherokee, co., Al., U.S.	A4	94
Cherokee, co., Ga., U.S.	B2	103
Cherokee, co., Ia., U.S.	B2	108
Cherokee, co., Ks., U.S.	E9	109
Cherokee, co., N.C., U.S.	f8	126
Cherokee, co., Ok., U.S.	B6	129
Cherokee, co., S.C., U.S.	A4	133
Cherokee, co., Tx., U.S.	D5	136
Cherokee Indian Reservation, N.C., U.S.	f9	126
Cherokee Lake, res., Tn., U.S.	C10	135
Cherokees, Lake O' The, res., Ok., U.S.	A7	129
Cherokee Village, Ar., U.S.	A4	97
Cherry, co., Ne., U.S.	B4	120
Cherry Creek, stm., S.D., U.S.	C3	134
Cherry Hill, N.J., U.S.	D2	123
Cherry Point, c., Va., U.S.	C6	139
Cherry Point Marine Corps Air Station, mil., N.C., U.S.	C6	126
Cherryvale, Ks., U.S.	E8	109
Cherry Valley, Ar., U.S.	B5	97
Cherry Valley, Il., U.S.	A5	106
Cherryville, N.C., U.S.	B1	126
Cherskiy Mountains see Čerskogo, hrebet, mts., Russia	C15	26
Chervonohrad, Ukr.	D8	20
Chesaning, Mi., U.S.	E6	115
Chesapeake, Oh., U.S.	D3	128
Chesapeake, Va., U.S.	D6	139
Chesapeake, W.V., U.S.	C3	141
Chesapeake and Delaware Canal, U.S.	B3	101
Chesapeake Bay, b., U.S.	D12	92
Chesapeake Bay Bridge-Tunnel, Va., U.S.	D7	139
Chesapeake Beach, Md., U.S.	C4	113
Chesapeake City, Md., U.S.	A6	113
Chesdin, Lake, res., Va., U.S.	C5	139
Chesha Bay see Češskaja guba, b., Russia	A8	22
Cheshire, Ct., U.S.	D4	100
Cheshire, co., N.H., U.S.	E2	122
Cheshire Reservoir, res., Ma., U.S.	A1	114
Chesley, On., Can.	C3	89
Chesnee, S.C., U.S.	A4	133
Chester, Eng., U.K.	D5	12
Chester, Ca., U.S.	B3	98
Chester, Ct., U.S.	D6	100
Chester, Ga., U.S.	D3	103
Chester, Il., U.S.	F4	106
Chester, Md., U.S.	C5	113
Chester, Mt., U.S.	B6	119
Chester, N.H., U.S.	E4	122
Chester, N.Y., U.S.	D6	125
Chester, Pa., U.S.	G11	131
Chester, S.C., U.S.	B5	133
Chester, Va., U.S.	C5	139
Chester, Vt., U.S.	E3	138
Chester, W.V., U.S.	A4	141
Chester, co., Pa., U.S.	G10	131
Chester, co., S.C., U.S.	B5	133
Chester, co., Tn., U.S.	B3	135
Chester, stm., Md., U.S.	B5	113
Chester Basin, N.S., Can.	E5	87
Chester Depot, Vt., U.S.	E3	138
Chesterfield, In., U.S.	D6	107
Chesterfield, S.C., U.S.	B7	133
Chesterfield, co., S.C., U.S.	B7	133
Chesterfield, co., Va., U.S.	C5	139
Chesterton, In., U.S.	A3	107
Chestertown, Md., U.S.	B5	113
Chesterville, On., Can.	B9	89
Chesuncook Lake, l., Me., U.S.	C3	112
Cheswick, Pa., U.S.	h14	131
Cheswold, De., U.S.	D3	101
Cheta see Heta, stm., Russia	B11	26
Chetac, Lake, l., Wi., U.S.	C2	142
Chetco, stm., Or., U.S.	E2	130
Chetek, Wi., U.S.	C2	142
Chetek, Lake, l., Wi., U.S.	C2	142
Chetopa, Ks., U.S.	E8	109
Chetumal, Mex.	D7	78
Chetumal, Bahia, b., N.A.	B2	80
Chetwynd, B.C., Can.	B7	85
Chevak, Ak., U.S.	C6	95
Cheviot, Oh., U.S.	C1	128
Chevreuil, Point, c., La., U.S.	E4	111
Chevy Chase, Md., U.S.	C3	113
Chewack, stm., Wa., U.S.	A5	140
Chewelah, Wa., U.S.	A8	140
Cheyenne, Ok., U.S.	B2	129
Cheyenne, Wy., U.S.	E8	143
Cheyenne, co., Co., U.S.	C8	99
Cheyenne, co., Ks., U.S.	C2	109
Cheyenne, co., Ne., U.S.	C2	120
Cheyenne, stm., U.S.	C7	92
Cheyenne, stm., U.S.	C4	134
Cheyenne, Dry Fork, stm., Wy., U.S.	C7	143
Cheyenne River Indian Reservation, S.D., U.S.	B4	134
Cheyenne Wells, Co., U.S.	C8	99
Chhapra, India	D4	40
Chhatarpur, India	E3	40
Chhatrapur, India	F5	40
Chhindwāra, India	E3	40
Chi, stm., Thai.	C4	34
Chiai, Tai.	E5	30
Chiange, Ang.	B1	56
Chiang Kham, Thai.	C4	34
Chiang Khan, Thai.	C4	34
Chiang Mai, Thai.	C3	34
Chiang Rai, Thai.	C3	34
Chiapas, state, Mex.	D6	78
Chiba, Japan	C4	31
Chiblow Lake, l., On., Can.	A1	89
Chibougamau, P.Q., Can.	k12	90
Chibuto, Moz.	C5	56
Chicago, Il., U.S.	B6	106
Chicago Heights, Il., U.S.	B6	106
Chicago Sanitary and Ship Canal, Il., U.S.	k8	106
Chicamacomico, stm., Md., U.S.	D6	113
Chicapa, stm., Afr.	E4	54
Chichagof Island, i., Ak., U.S.	m22	95
Chichén Itzá, hist., Mex.	C7	78
Chickahominy, stm., Va., U.S.	C5	139
Chickamauga, Ga., U.S.	B1	103
Chickamauga and Chattanooga National Military Park, U.S.	k11	135
Chickamauga Dam, Tn., U.S.	h11	135
Chickamauga Lake, res., Tn., U.S.	D8	135
Chickasaw, Al., U.S.	E1	94
Chickasaw, co., Ia., U.S.	A5	108
Chickasaw, co., Ms., U.S.	B5	117
Chickasawhay, stm., Ms., U.S.	D5	117
Chickasaw National Recreation Area, Ok., U.S.	C5	129
Chickasha, Ok., U.S.	B4	129
Chickasha, Lake, res., Ok., U.S.	B3	129
Chickwolnepy Stream, stm., N.H., U.S.	A4	122
Chiclayo, Peru	E4	70
Chico, Ca., U.S.	C3	98
Chico, stm., Arg.	F3	69
Chicomba, Ang.	A1	56
Chicopee, Ga., U.S.	B3	103
Chicopee, Ma., U.S.	B2	114
Chicora, Pa., U.S.	E2	131
Chicot, Lake, l., Ar., U.S.	D4	97
Chicot Island, i., La., U.S.	E6	111
Chicoutimi, P.Q., Can.	A6	90
Chicoutimi, stm., P.Q., Can.	A6	90
Chidambaram, India	G3	40
Chiefland, Fl., U.S.	C4	102
Chieti, Italy	C5	18
Chifeng, China	C11	28
Chignecto, Cape, c., N.S., Can.	D5	87
Chignecto Bay, b., Can.	D5	87
Chigubo, Moz.	C5	56
Chihli, Gulf of see Bo Hai, b., China	D11	28
Chihuahua, Mex.	B3	78
Chihuahua, state, Mex.	B3	78
Chihuahuan Desert, des., N.A.	A3	78
Chikaskia, stm., U.S.	A4	129
Chik Ballāpur, India	G3	40
Chikmagalūr, India	G3	40
Chilās, Pak.	C10	42
Childersburg, Al., U.S.	B3	94
Childress, Tx., U.S.	B2	136
Childress, co., Tx., U.S.	B2	136
Chile, ctry., S.A.	D2	69
Chilecito, Arg.	D4	72
Chile Rise	L29	64
Chilhowie, Va., U.S.	f10	139
Chililabombwe, Zam.	A4	56
Chilko, stm., B.C., Can.	D6	85
Chilko Lake, l., B.C., Can.	D5	85
Chillán, Chile	E2	69
Chillicothe, Il., U.S.	C4	106
Chillicothe, Mo., U.S.	B4	118
Chillicothe, Oh., U.S.	C3	128
Chilliwack, B.C., Can.	E7	85
Chillum, Md., U.S.	f9	113
Chiloé, Isla Grande de, i., Chile	F2	69
Chiloquin, Or., U.S.	E5	130
Chilpancingo de los Bravo, Mex.	D5	78
Chilton, Wi., U.S.	D5	142
Chilton, co., Al., U.S.	C3	94
Chiluage, Ang.	E4	54
Chilung, Tai.	D5	30
Chimacum, Wa., U.S.	A3	140
Chimayo, N.M., U.S.	A4	124
Chimborazo, vol., Ec.	D4	70
Chimbote, Peru	E4	70
Chimney Rock, mtn., Ne., U.S.	C2	120
Chimoio, Moz.	B5	56
China, ctry., Asia	D8	28
China Grove, N.C., U.S.	B2	126
China Lake, l., Me., U.S.	D3	112
Chinandega, Nic.	C2	80
Chincha Alta, Peru	F4	70
Chinchilla, Austl.	F5	62
Chincoteague, Va., U.S.	C7	139
Chincoteague Bay, b., U.S.	D7	113
Chinde, Moz.	B6	56
Chindwinn, stm., Myan.	A3	34
Chingola, Zam.	A4	56
Chinguetti, Maur.	B2	50
Chin Hills, hills, Myan.	B2	34
Chinhoyi, Zimb.	B5	56
Chinitna Point, c., Ak., U.S.	h15	95
Chinju, S. Kor.	D13	28
Chinle, Az., U.S.	A6	96
Chino, Ca., U.S.	F5	98
Chinook, Mt., U.S.	B7	119
Chinook, Wa., U.S.	C2	140
Chinook, Lake, res., Or., U.S.	C5	130
Chino Valley, Az., U.S.	C3	96
Chinsali, Zam.	A5	56
Chinvali, Geor.	A10	44
Chioco, Moz.	B5	56
Chioggia, Italy	B4	18
Chios see Khíos, Grc.	E11	18
Chipata, Zam.	A5	56
Chipita Park, Co., U.S.	C6	99
Chipley, Fl., U.S.	u16	102
Chipman, N.B., Can.	C4	87
Chipola, stm., Fl., U.S.	B1	102
Chippewa, co., Mi., U.S.	B6	115
Chippewa, co., Mn., U.S.	E3	116
Chippewa, co., Wi., U.S.	C2	142
Chippewa, stm., Mn., U.S.	E3	116
Chippewa, stm., Wi., U.S.	D2	142
Chippewa, Lake, l., Wi., U.S.	C2	142
Chippewa Falls, Wi., U.S.	D2	142
Chipuxet, stm., R.I., U.S.	F3	132
Chiquimula, Guat.	C2	80
Chiquinquirá, Col.	B5	70
Chīrāla, India	F4	40
Chirfa, Niger	B7	50
Chiricahua Mountains, mts., Az., U.S.	E6	96
Chiricahua National Monument, Az., U.S.	F6	96
Chiricahua Peak, mtn., Az., U.S.	F6	96
Chirikof Island, i., Ak., U.S.	D8	95
Chiriquí, Golfo de, b., Pan.	D3	80
Chiriquí, Laguna de, b., Pan.	D3	80
Chiromo, Mwi.	B6	56
Chirripó, Cerro, mtn., C.R.	D3	80
Chisago, co., Mn., U.S.	E6	116
Chisago City, Mn., U.S.	E6	116
Ch'ishan, Tai.	E5	30
Chisholm, Me., U.S.	D2	112
Chisholm, Mn., U.S.	C6	116
Chishui, stm., China	D2	30
Chişinău, Mol.	F10	20
Chisos Mountains, mts., Tx., U.S.	E1	136
Chita see Čita, Russia	D13	26
Chitado, Ang.	B1	56
Chitato, Ang.	E4	54
Chitembo, Ang.	F3	54
Chitina, stm., Ak., U.S.	g19	95
Chitose, Japan	B4	31
Chitradurga, India	G3	40
Chitrāl, Pak.	C10	42
Chitré, Pan.	D3	80
Chittagong, Bngl.	E6	40
Chittaurgarh, India	E2	40
Chittenango, N.Y., U.S.	B5	125
Chittenden, co., Vt., U.S.	C2	138
Chittenden Reservoir, res., Vt., U.S.	D3	138
Chittoor, India	G3	40
Chitungwiza, Zimb.	B5	56
Chiumbe (Tshumbe), stm., Afr.	E4	54
Chiume, Ang.	B3	56
Chivacoa, Ven.	C6	80
Chivilcoy, Arg.	E5	72
Chôâm Khsant, Camb.	D4	34
Chocolate Mountains, mts., U.S.	F6	98
Chocope, Peru	E4	70
Choctaw, Ok., U.S.	B4	129
Choctaw, co., Al., U.S.	C1	94
Choctaw, co., Ms., U.S.	B4	117
Choctaw, co., Ok., U.S.	C6	129
Choctawhatchee Bay, b., Fl., U.S.	u15	102
Choctaw Indian Reservation, Ms., U.S.	C4	117
Choele Choel, Arg.	E3	69
Chojnice, Pol.	C4	20
Chókwe, Moz.	C5	56
Cholet, Fr.	D6	16
Choluteca, Hond.	C2	80
Choluteca, stm., Hond.	C2	80
Choma, Zam.	B4	56
Chomutov, Czech Rep.	D2	20
Chon Buri, Thai.	D4	34
Chone, Ec.	D3	70
Chong'an, China	D4	30
Ch'ŏngjin, N. Kor.	C13	28
Ch'ŏngju, S. Kor.	D13	28
Chongqing, China	F9	28
Chongxin, China	B2	30
Chongzuo, China	G9	28
Chŏnju, S. Kor.	D13	28
Chonos, Archipiélago de los, is., Chile	G2	69
Choptank, stm., Md., U.S.	C6	113
Chornomors'ke, Ukr.	G12	20
Chortkiv, Ukr.	E8	20
Chōshi, Japan	C4	31
Chos Malal, Arg.	F3	72
Choteau, Mt., U.S.	C4	119
Chouteau, Ok., U.S.	A6	129
Chouteau, co., Mt., U.S.	C6	119
Chowan, co., N.C., U.S.	A6	126
Chowan, stm., N.C., U.S.	A6	126
Chowchilla, Ca., U.S.	D3	98
Choybalsan, Mong.	B10	28
Choyr, Mong.	B9	28
Chrisman, Il., U.S.	D6	106
Christchurch, N.Z.	p13	63c
Christian, co., Il., U.S.	D4	106
Christian, co., Ky., U.S.	D2	110
Christian, co., Mo., U.S.	E4	118
Christiana, De., U.S.	B3	101
Christiana, Pa., U.S.	G9	131
Christiansburg, Va., U.S.	C2	139
Christian Sound, strt., Ak., U.S.	n22	95
Christina, stm., Ab., Can.	A5	84
Christina, stm., De., U.S.	B3	101
Christina, Lake, l., Mn., U.S.	D3	116
Christina Peak, mtn., Nv., U.S.	D6	121
Christmas, Fl., U.S.	D5	102
Christmas Island, dep., Oc.	I4	32
Christmas Island, i., Christ. I.	F4	58
Christmas Island see Kiritimati, atoll, Kir.	D14	58
Christmas Lake, l., Or., U.S.	D6	130
Christmas Ridge	G22	64
Christopher, Il., U.S.	F4	106
Chubbuck, Id., U.S.	G6	105
Chubut, stm., Arg.	F3	69
Chugach Islands, is., Ak., U.S.	h16	95
Chugach Mountains, mts., Ak., U.S.	g18	95
Chugwater, Wy., U.S.	E8	143
Chugwater Creek, stm., Wy., U.S.	E8	143
Chuhuïv, Ukr.	E14	20
Chukchi Sea	E5	82
Chukotsk Peninsula see Čukotskij poluostrov, pen., Russia	C20	26
Chula Vista, Ca., U.S.	F5	98
Chulucanas, Peru	E3	70
Chumbicha, Arg.	D4	72
Chumphon, Thai.	D3	34
Chum Saeng, Thai.	C4	34
Chunchula, Al., U.S.	E1	94
Chungking see Chongqing, China	F9	28
Chuntuquí, Guat.	B1	80
Chupadera Mesa, mtn., N.M., U.S.	D3	124
Chuquibamba, Peru	B3	72
Chuquicamata, Chile	B3	69
Chur, Switz.	A2	18
Church Hill, Tn., U.S.	C11	135
Churchill, Mb., Can.	f9	86
Churchill, co., Nv., U.S.	D3	121
Churchill, stm., Can.	G21	82
Churchill, stm., Nf., Can.	h9	88
Churchill, Cape, c., Mb., Can.	f9	86
Churchill, Mount, mtn., B.C., Can.	E6	85
Churchill Falls, wtfl, Nf., Can.	h8	88
Churchill Lake, l., Sk., Can.	m7	91
Churchill Lake, l., Me., U.S.	B3	112
Church Point, La., U.S.	D3	111
Church Rock, N.M., U.S.	B1	124
Churchton, Md., U.S.	C4	113
Churchville, N.Y., U.S.	B3	125
Chūru, India	D2	40
Churubusco, In., U.S.	B7	107
Chuska Mountains, mts., Az., U.S.	A6	96
Chuuk Islands, is., Micron.	D9	58
Chuvashia see Čuvašija, state, Russia	D6	26
Chuxian, China	C4	30
Chuxiong, China	F8	28
Cianjur, Indon.	E3	36
Cianorte, Braz.	C7	72
Ċiatura, Geor.	A10	44
Cibecue, Az., U.S.	C5	96
Cibola, co., N.M., U.S.	C1	124
Cibolo Creek, stm., Tx., U.S.	h7	136
Cicero, Il., U.S.	B6	106
Cicero, In., U.S.	D5	107
Cide, Tur.	B5	44
Ciechanów, Pol.	C6	20
Ciego de Ávila, Cuba	A4	80
Cienfuegos, Cuba	A3	80
Cieza, Spain	H6	16
Çifteler, Tur.	C4	44
Čiganak, Kaz.	E9	26
Çihanbeyli, Tur.	C5	44
Çiili, Kaz.	B9	42
Čikoj, stm., Asia	D12	26
Cilacap, Indon.	E3	36
Çıldır Gölü, l., Tur.	B10	44
Čilik, Kaz.	B11	42
Cimarron, Ks., U.S.	E3	109
Cimarron, N.M., U.S.	A5	124
Cimarron, co., Ok., U.S.	e8	129
Cimarron, stm., U.S.	D8	92
Čimbaj, Uzb.	B7	42
Cimljanskoe vodohranilišče, res., Russia	E7	22
Cina, Tanjung, c., Indon.	E2	36
Çınar, Tur.	D9	44
Cincinnati, Oh., U.S.	C1	128
Çine, Tur.	D3	44
Cinnaminson, N.J., U.S.	D3	123
Cintalapa, Mex.	D6	78
Cinto, Monte, mtn., Fr.	C2	18

Name / Map Ref. / Page

Cintra, Golfe de, b., W. Sah. B1 50
Cipolletti, Arg. E3 69
Čirčik, Uzb. E8 26
Circle, Ak., U.S. B11 95
Circle, Mt., U.S. C11 119
Circle Pines, Mn., U.S. m12 116
Circleville, Oh., U.S. C3 128
Cirebon, Indon. E3 36
Cirò Marina, Italy E6 18
Cisco, Tx., U.S. C3 136
Ciskei, hist. reg., S. Afr. E4 56
Cisnădie, Rom. G8 20
Cispus, stm., Wa., U.S. C4 140
Cissna Park, Il., U.S. C6 106
Čistopol', Russia C9 22
Čita, Russia D13 26
Citlaltépetl, Volcán see Pico de Orizaba, Volcán, vol., Mex. D5 78
Citra, Fl., U.S. C4 102
Citronelle, Al., U.S. D1 94
Citrus, co., Fl., U.S. D4 102
City of Refuge National Historical Park, Hi., U.S. D5 104
City View, S.C., U.S. B3 133
Ciudad Acuña, Mex. B4 78
Ciudad Anáhuac, Mex. B4 78
Ciudad Bolívar, Ven. B7 70
Ciudad Camargo, Mex. B5 78
Ciudad Camargo, Mex. B3 78
Ciudad Constitución, Mex. C2 78
Ciudad del Carmen, Mex. D6 78
Ciudad del Este, Para. D7 72
Ciudad de Libertador General San Martín, Arg. C5 72
Ciudad de México (Mexico City), Mex. D5 78
Ciudad de Nutrias, Ven. D6 80
Ciudad Guayana, Ven. B7 70
Ciudad Juárez, Mex. A3 78
Ciudad Madero, Mex. C5 78
Ciudad Mante, Mex. C5 78
Ciudad Miguel Alemán, Mex. B5 78
Ciudad Netzahualcóyotl, Mex. D5 78
Ciudad Obregón, Mex. B3 78
Ciudad Ojeda, Ven. C5 80
Ciudad Real, Spain H5 16
Ciudad Rodrigo, Spain G3 16
Ciudad Valles, Mex. C5 78
Ciudad Victoria, Mex. C5 78
Ciutadella, Spain G8 16
Civitanova Marche, Italy C4 18
Civitavecchia, Italy C3 18
Çivril, Tur. C3 44
Cizre, Tur. D10 44
C.J. Strike Reservoir, res., Id., U.S. G3 105
Clackamas, Or., U.S. h12 130
Clackamas, co., Or., U.S. B4 130
Clacton-on-Sea, Eng., U.K. E7 12
Claflin, Ks., U.S. D5 109
Claiborne, co., La., U.S. B2 111
Claiborne, co., Ms., U.S. D3 117
Claiborne, co., Tn., U.S. C10 135
Claiborne, Lake, res., La., U.S. B3 111
Clair, N.B., Can. B1 87
Claire, Lake, l., Ab., Can. f8 84
Clair Engle Lake, res., Ca., U.S. B2 98
Clairton, Pa., U.S. F2 131
Clallam, co., Wa., U.S. B1 140
Clallam Bay, Wa., U.S. A1 140
Clam Lake, l., Wi., U.S. C1 142
Clan Alpine Mountains, mts., Nv., U.S. D4 121
Clanton, Al., U.S. C3 94
Clanwilliam, S. Afr. E2 56
Clara City, Mn., U.S. F3 116
Clara Peak, mtn., Az., U.S. C2 96
Clare, Mi., U.S. E6 115
Clare, co., Mi., U.S. E6 115
Claremont, Ca., U.S. m13 98
Claremont, N.C., U.S. B1 126
Claremont, N.H., U.S. D2 122
Claremont, mtn., Ca., U.S. C3 98
Claremore, Ok., U.S. A6 129
Clarence, Ia., U.S. C6 108
Clarence, Mo., U.S. B5 118
Clarence Strait, strt., Austl. C5 60
Clarence Strait, strt., Ak., U.S. n23 95
Clarendon, Ar., U.S. C4 97
Clarendon, Tx., U.S. B2 136
Clarendon, co., S.C., U.S. D7 133
Clarendon, stm., Vt., U.S. E2 138
Clarendon Hills, Il., U.S. k9 106
Clarenville, Nf., Can. D4 88
Claresholm, Ab., Can. D4 84
Claridge, Pa., U.S. F2 131
Clarinda, Ia., U.S. D2 108
Clarion, Ia., U.S. B4 108
Clarion, Pa., U.S. D3 131
Clarion, co., Pa., U.S. D3 131
Clarion, stm., Pa., U.S. D3 131
Clarión, Isla, i., Mex. D2 78
Clarion Fracture Zone G25 64
Clarissa, Mn., U.S. D4 116
Clark, N.J., U.S. B4 123
Clark, S.D., U.S. C8 134
Clark, co., Ar., U.S. C2 97
Clark, co., Id., U.S. E6 105
Clark, co., Il., U.S. D6 106
Clark, co., In., U.S. H6 107
Clark, co., Ks., U.S. E4 109
Clark, co., Ky., U.S. C5 110
Clark, co., Mo., U.S. A6 118
Clark, co., Nv., U.S. G6 121
Clark, co., Oh., U.S. C2 128
Clark, co., S.D., U.S. C8 134
Clark, co., Wa., U.S. D3 140
Clark, co., Wi., U.S. D3 142
Clark, Lake, l., Ak., U.S. C9 95
Clark, Point, c., On., Can. C3 89
Clarkdale, Az., U.S. C3 96
Clarkdale, Ga., U.S. h7 103
Clarke, co., Al., U.S. D2 94
Clarke, co., Ga., U.S. C3 103
Clarke, co., Ia., U.S. D4 108
Clarke, co., Ms., U.S. C5 117
Clarke, co., Va., U.S. A4 139
Clarke Island, i., Austl. I4 62
Clarkesville, Ga., U.S. B3 103
Clarkfield, Mn., U.S. F3 116
Clark Fork, stm., U.S. C1 119
Clarks, La., U.S. B3 111
Clarks, stm., Ky., U.S. f9 110
Clarksburg, Md., U.S. B3 113
Clarksburg, W.V., U.S. B4 141
Clarksdale, Ms., U.S. A3 117
Clarks Grove, Mn., U.S. G5 116
Clark's Harbour, N.S., Can. F4 87
Clarks Hill, In., U.S. D4 107
Clarks Hill Lake, res., U.S. E11 92
Clarkson, Ky., U.S. C3 110
Clarkson, Ne., U.S. C8 120
Clarks Summit, Pa., U.S. m18 131
Clarkston, Ga., U.S. h8 103
Clarkston, Mi., U.S. F7 115
Clarkston, Ut., U.S. B3 137
Clarkston, Wa., U.S. C8 140
Clarksville, Ar., U.S. B2 97
Clarksville, De., U.S. F5 101
Clarksville, Ia., U.S. B5 108
Clarksville, In., U.S. H6 107
Clarksville, Tn., U.S. A4 135
Clarksville, Tx., U.S. C5 136
Clarksville, Va., U.S. D4 139
Clarkton, Mo., U.S. E8 118
Clarkton, N.C., U.S. C4 126
Clatskanie, Or., U.S. A3 130
Clatsop, co., Or., U.S. A3 130
Claude, Tx., U.S. B2 136
Clawson, Mi., U.S. o15 115
Claxton, Ga., U.S. D5 103
Clay, Ky., U.S. C2 110
Clay, co., Al., U.S. B4 94
Clay, co., Ar., U.S. A5 97
Clay, co., Fl., U.S. B5 102
Clay, co., Ga., U.S. E2 103
Clay, co., Ia., U.S. A2 108
Clay, co., Il., U.S. E5 106
Clay, co., In., U.S. F3 107
Clay, co., Ks., U.S. C6 109
Clay, co., Ky., U.S. C6 110
Clay, co., Mn., U.S. D2 116
Clay, co., Mo., U.S. B3 118
Clay, co., Ms., U.S. B5 117
Clay, co., N.C., U.S. f9 126
Clay, co., Ne., U.S. D7 120
Clay, co., S.D., U.S. E8 134
Clay, co., Tn., U.S. C8 135
Clay, co., Tx., U.S. C3 136
Clay, co., W.V., U.S. C3 141
Clay Center, Ks., U.S. C6 109
Clay Center, Ne., U.S. D7 120
Clay City, Il., U.S. E5 106
Clay City, In., U.S. F3 107
Clay City, Ky., U.S. C6 110
Clay Creek, stm., S.D., U.S. D8 134
Claymont, De., U.S. A4 101
Clayoquot Sound, strt., B.C., Can. E4 85
Claypool, Az., U.S. D5 96
Claysburg, Pa., U.S. F5 131
Claysville, Pa., U.S. F1 131
Clayton, Al., U.S. D4 94
Clayton, De., U.S. C3 101
Clayton, Ga., U.S. B3 103
Clayton, In., U.S. E4 107
Clayton, La., U.S. C4 111
Clayton, Mo., U.S. f13 118
Clayton, N.C., U.S. B4 126
Clayton, N.J., U.S. D2 123
Clayton, N.M., U.S. A6 124
Clayton, N.Y., U.S. A4 125
Clayton, Ok., U.S. C6 129
Clayton, co., Ga., U.S. C2 103
Clayton, co., Ia., U.S. B6 108
Claytor Lake, res., Va., U.S. C2 139
Clear, stm., R.I., U.S. B2 132
Clear Boggy Creek, stm., Ok., U.S. C5 129
Clear Creek, co., Co., U.S. B5 99
Clear Creek, stm., Tn., U.S. C9 135
Clear Creek, stm., Wy., U.S. B6 143
Cleare, Cape, c., Ak., U.S. D10 95
Clearfield, Ky., U.S. B6 110
Clearfield, Pa., U.S. D5 131
Clearfield, Ut., U.S. B3 137
Clearfield, co., Pa., U.S. D5 131
Clear Fork, stm., W.V., U.S. n13 141
Clear Fork, stm., W.V., U.S. D3 141
Clearlake, Ca., U.S. C2 98
Clear Lake, Ia., U.S. A4 108
Clear Lake, S.D., U.S. C9 134
Clearlake, Wa., U.S. A3 140
Clear Lake, Wi., U.S. C1 142
Clear Lake, l., Ia., U.S. A4 108
Clear Lake, l., Ut., U.S. D3 137
Clear Lake, res., Ca., U.S. C2 98
Clear Lake Reservoir, res., Ca., U.S. B3 98
Clear Lake Shores, Tx., U.S. r15 136
Clear Stream, stm., N.H., U.S. g7 122
Clearwater, B.C., Can. D7 85
Clearwater, Fl., U.S. E4 102
Clearwater, Ks., U.S. E6 109
Clearwater, S.C., U.S. E4 133
Clearwater, co., Id., U.S. C3 105
Clearwater, co., Mn., U.S. C3 116
Clearwater, stm., Can. A5 84
Clearwater, stm., Id., U.S. C2 105
Clearwater, stm., Mn., U.S. C3 116
Clearwater Lake, res., Mo., U.S. D7 118
Clearwater Mountains, mts., Id., U.S. C2 105
Cleburne, Tx., U.S. C4 136
Cleburne, co., Al., U.S. B4 94
Cleburne, co., Ar., U.S. B3 97
Cle Elum, Wa., U.S. B5 140
Cle Elum, stm., Wa., U.S. B4 140
Cle Elum Lake, res., Wa., U.S. B4 140
Clementon, N.J., U.S. D3 123
Clemmons, N.C., U.S. A2 126
Clemson, S.C., U.S. B2 133
Clendenin, W.V., U.S. C3 141
Clendening Lake, res., Oh., U.S. B4 128
Cleona, Pa., U.S. F9 131
Clermont, Austl. E4 62
Clermont, P.Q., Can. B7 90
Clermont, Fl., U.S. D5 102
Clermont, co., Oh., U.S. C1 128
Clermont-Ferrand, Fr. E8 16
Cleveland, Al., U.S. A3 94
Cleveland, Ga., U.S. B3 103
Cleveland, Mn., U.S. F5 116
Cleveland, Ms., U.S. B3 117
Cleveland, N.C., U.S. B2 126
Cleveland, Oh., U.S. A4 128
Cleveland, Ok., U.S. A5 129
Cleveland, Tn., U.S. D9 135
Cleveland, Tx., U.S. D5 136
Cleveland, Wi., U.S. k10 142
Cleveland, co., Ar., U.S. D3 97
Cleveland, co., N.C., U.S. B1 126
Cleveland, co., Ok., U.S. B4 129
Cleveland, Mount, mtn., Mt., U.S. B3 119
Cleveland Heights, Oh., U.S. A4 128
Cleves, Oh., U.S. o12 128
Clew Bay, b., Ire. D2 12
Clewiston, Fl., U.S. F6 102
Cliff Island, i., Me., U.S. g7 112
Clifford, On., Can. D4 89
Cliffside, N.C., U.S. B1 126
Cliffside Park, N.J., U.S. h9 123
Clifton, Az., U.S. D6 96
Clifton, Co., U.S. B2 99
Clifton, Il., U.S. C6 106
Clifton, N.J., U.S. B4 123
Clifton, S.C., U.S. B4 133
Clifton, Tn., U.S. B4 135
Clifton, Tx., U.S. D4 136
Clifton Forge, Va., U.S. C3 139
Clifton Knolls, N.Y., U.S. C7 125
Clifton Springs, N.Y., U.S. C3 125
Clinch, co., Ga., U.S. F4 103
Clinch, stm., U.S. D9 135
Clinchco, Va., U.S. e9 139
Clinch Mountain, mtn., U.S. C10 135
Clingmans Dome, mtn., U.S. D10 135
Clinton, B.C., Can. D7 85
Clinton, On., Can. D3 89
Clinton, Ar., U.S. B3 97
Clinton, Ct., U.S. D5 100
Clinton, Ia., U.S. C7 108
Clinton, Il., U.S. C5 106
Clinton, In., U.S. E3 107
Clinton, Ky., U.S. f9 110
Clinton, La., U.S. D4 111
Clinton, Ma., U.S. B4 114
Clinton, Md., U.S. C4 113
Clinton, Me., U.S. D3 112
Clinton, Mi., U.S. F7 115
Clinton, Mo., U.S. C4 118
Clinton, Ms., U.S. C3 117
Clinton, N.C., U.S. C4 126
Clinton, N.Y., U.S. B5 125
Clinton, Ok., U.S. B3 129
Clinton, S.C., U.S. C4 133
Clinton, Tn., U.S. C9 135
Clinton, Ut., U.S. B3 137
Clinton, Wa., U.S. B3 140
Clinton, Wi., U.S. F5 142
Clinton, co., Ia., U.S. C7 108
Clinton, co., Il., U.S. E4 106
Clinton, co., In., U.S. D4 107
Clinton, co., Ky., U.S. D4 110
Clinton, co., Mi., U.S. F6 115
Clinton, co., Mo., U.S. B3 118
Clinton, co., N.Y., U.S. f11 125
Clinton, co., Oh., U.S. C2 128
Clinton, co., Pa., U.S. D6 131
Clinton, Lake, res., Il., U.S. C5 106
Clinton Lake, res., Ks., U.S. m15 109
Clinton Reservoir, res., N.J., U.S. A4 123
Clintonville, Wi., U.S. D5 142
Clintwood, Va., U.S. e9 139
Clio, Al., U.S. D4 94
Clio, Mi., U.S. E7 115
Clio, S.C., U.S. B8 133
Clipperton, Île, atoll, Oc. G28 64
Clipperton Fracture Zone H25 64
Clive, Ia., U.S. e8 108
Clodomira, Arg. D5 72
Cloncurry, Austl. E3 62
Clonmel, Ire. D3 12
Cloquet, Mn., U.S. D6 116
Cloquet, stm., Mn., U.S. C6 116
Clorinda, Arg. D6 72
Closter, N.J., U.S. B5 123
Clothier, W.V., U.S. n12 141
Cloud, co., Ks., U.S. C6 109
Cloudcroft, N.M., U.S. E4 124
Cloud Peak, mtn., Wy., U.S. B5 143
Clover, S.C., U.S. A5 133
Cloverdale, Al., U.S. A2 94
Cloverdale, Ca., U.S. C2 98
Cloverdale, In., U.S. E4 107
Cloverport, Ky., U.S. C3 110
Clovis, Ca., U.S. D4 98
Clovis, N.M., U.S. C6 124
Cluj-Napoca, Rom. F7 20
Clute, Tx., U.S. r14 136
Clyde, Ks., U.S. C6 109
Clyde, N.C., U.S. f10 126
Clyde, N.Y., U.S. B4 125
Clyde, Oh., U.S. A3 128
Clyde, Tx., U.S. C3 136
Clyde, Firth of, b., Scot., U.K. C4 12
Clymer, Pa., U.S. E3 131
Cnossus see Knossós, hist., Grc. G10 18
Coachella, Ca., U.S. F5 98
Coachella Canal, Ca., U.S. F6 98
Coahoma, Tx., U.S. C2 136
Coahoma, co., Ms., U.S. A3 117
Coahuila, state, Mex. B4 78
Coal, co., Ok., U.S. C5 129
Coal, stm., W.V., U.S. C3 141
Coal Branch, N.B., Can. C4 87
Coal City, Il., U.S. B5 106
Coal Creek, stm., Ok., U.S. B6 129
Coaldale, Ab., Can. E4 84
Coal Fork, W.V., U.S. C3 141
Coal Fork, stm., W.V., U.S. m13 141
Coalgate, Ok., U.S. C5 129
Coal Grove, Oh., U.S. D3 128
Coal Hill, Ar., U.S. B2 97
Coalhurst, Ab., Can. E4 84
Coalinga, Ca., U.S. D3 98
Coalmont, Tn., U.S. D8 135
Coalville, Ut., U.S. C4 137
Coalwood, W.V., U.S. D3 141
Coaraci, Braz. D4 74
Coari, Braz. D7 70
Coasters Harbor Island, i., R.I., U.S. E5 132
Coast Mountains, mts., N.A. G13 82
Coast Ranges, mts., U.S. C3 92
Coatesville, Pa., U.S. G10 131
Coaticook, P.Q., Can. D6 90
Coats, N.C., U.S. B4 126
Coats Land, reg., Ant. D2 67
Coatzacoalcos, Mex. D6 78
Cobalt, On., Can. p19 89
Cobán, Guat. B1 80
Cobar, Austl. G4 62
Cobb, co., Ga., U.S. C2 103
Cobb, stm., Mn., U.S. G5 116
Cobble Mountain Reservoir, res., Ma., U.S. B2 114
Cobbosseecontee Lake, l., Me., U.S. D3 112
Cobden, On., Can. B8 89
Cobden, Il., U.S. F4 106
Cobequid Mountains, mts., N.S., Can. D5 87
Cobham, stm., Can. C4 86
Cobija, Bol. F6 70
Cobleskill, N.Y., U.S. C6 125
Cobourg, On., Can. D6 89
Cobourg Peninsula, pen., Austl. C5 60
Cóbuè, Moz. A5 56
Cobun Creek, stm., W.V., U.S. h11 141
Coburg, Ger. E12 12
Coburg, Or., U.S. C3 130
Cocachacra, Peru B3 72
Cochabamba, Bol. B4 72
Cocheco, stm., N.H., U.S. D5 122
Cochin see Kochi, India H3 40
Cochise, co., Az., U.S. F5 96
Cochise Head, mtn., Az., U.S. E6 96
Cochiti Indian Reservation, N.M., U.S. h8 124
Cochiti Reservoir, res., N.M., U.S. B3 124
Cochituate, Ma., U.S. g10 114
Cochituate, Lake, l., Ma., U.S. g10 114
Cochran, Ga., U.S. D3 103
Cochran, co., Tx., U.S. C1 136
Cochrane, Ab., Can. D3 84
Cochrane, On., Can. o19 89
Cochranton, Pa., U.S. C1 131
Cocke, co., Tn., U.S. D10 135
Cockeysville, Md., U.S. B4 113
Cockrell Hill, Tx., U.S. n10 136
Coco, stm., N.A. F8 76
Coco, Cayo, i., Cuba A4 80
Coco, Isla del, i., C.R. D2 80
Cocoa, Fl., U.S. D6 102
Cocoa Beach, Fl., U.S. D6 102
Coco Channel, strt., Asia D2 34
Coco Islands, is., Myan. D2 34
Coconino, co., Az., U.S. B3 96
Cocopah Indian Reservation, Az., U.S. E1 96
Cocos Islands, dep., Oc. F3 58
Cocos Ridge H5 66
Cod, Cape, c., Ma., U.S. C7 114
Codajás, Braz. D7 70
Coden, Al., U.S. E1 94
Codington, co., S.D., U.S. C8 134
Codó, Braz. B3 74
Cody, Wy., U.S. B3 143
Coeburn, Va., U.S. f9 139
Coen, Austl. C3 62
Coeroeni (Corentyne), stm., S.A. C8 70
Coëtivy, i., Sey. i13 57b
Coeur d'Alene, Id., U.S. B2 105
Coeur d'Alene, stm., Id., U.S. B2 105
Coeur d'Alene Indian Reservation, Id., U.S. B2 105
Coeur d'Alene Lake, res., Id., U.S. B2 105
Coeur d'Alene Mountains, mts., Id., U.S. B2 105
Coffee, co., Al., U.S. D3 94
Coffee, co., Ga., U.S. E4 103
Coffee, co., Tn., U.S. B5 135
Coffeeville, Ms., U.S. B4 117
Coffey, co., Ks., U.S. D8 109
Coffeyville, Ks., U.S. E8 109
Coffs Harbour, Austl. G5 62
Coggon, Ia., U.S. B6 108
Cognac, Fr. E6 16
Cohansey, stm., N.J., U.S. E2 123
Cohasset, Ma., U.S. B6 114
Cohasset, Mn., U.S. C5 116
Cohocton, stm., N.Y., U.S. C3 125
Cohoes, N.Y., U.S. C7 125
Cohoon, Lake, res., Va., U.S. k14 139
Cohutta Mountain, mtn., Ga., U.S. B2 103
Coiba, Isla de, i., Pan. D3 80
Coihaique, Chile G2 69
Coimbatore, India G3 40
Coimbra, Port. G2 16
Coipasa, Lago, l., Bol. B4 72
Cojutepeque, El Sal. C2 80
Cokato, Mn., U.S. E4 116
Coke, co., Tx., U.S. D2 136
Cokeville, Wy., U.S. D2 143
Čokurdah, Russia B16 26
Colac, Austl. H3 62
Colatina, Braz. E3 74
Colbeck, Cape, c., Ant. D25 67
Colbert, Ok., U.S. D5 129
Colbert, co., Al., U.S. A2 94
Colborne, On., Can. C7 89
Colby, Ks., U.S. C2 109
Colby, Wi., U.S. D3 142
Colchester, Eng., U.K. E7 12
Colchester, Ct., U.S. C6 100
Colchester, Il., U.S. C3 106
Colcord, Ok., U.S. A7 129
Cold, stm., N.H., U.S. D2 122
Cold, stm., N.H., U.S. C4 122
Cold Bay, Ak., U.S. E7 95
Cold Lake, Ab., Can. B5 84
Cold Spring, Ky., U.S. A5 110
Cold Spring, Mn., U.S. E4 116
Coldwater, On., Can. C5 89
Coldwater, Ks., U.S. E4 109
Coldwater, Mi., U.S. G5 115
Coldwater, Ms., U.S. A4 117
Coldwater, Oh., U.S. B1 128
Coldwater, stm., Ms., U.S. A3 117
Coldwater Creek, stm., U.S. e9 129
Cole, co., Mo., U.S. C5 118
Colebrook, N.H., U.S. g7 122
Colebrook River Lake, res., Ct., U.S. A3 100
Cole Camp, Mo., U.S. C4 118
Coleen, stm., Ak., U.S. B11 95
Coleman, Mi., U.S. E6 115
Coleman, Tx., U.S. D3 136
Coleman, Wi., U.S. C5 142
Coleman, co., Tx., U.S. D3 136
Coleraine, N. Ire., U.K. C3 12
Coleraine, Mn., U.S. C5 116
Coles, co., Il., U.S. D5 106
Colesberg, S. Afr. E4 56
Colfax, Ca., U.S. C3 98
Colfax, Ia., U.S. C4 108
Colfax, Il., U.S. C5 106
Colfax, In., U.S. D4 107
Colfax, La., U.S. C3 111
Colfax, Wa., U.S. C8 140
Colfax, Wi., U.S. D2 142
Colfax, co., Ne., U.S. C8 120
Colfax, co., N.M., U.S. A5 124
Colhué Huapi, Lago, l., Arg. G3 69
Colima, Mex. D4 78

Name — Map Ref. — Page

Colima, state, Mex. **D4** 78
Colinas, Braz. **C3** 74
Coll, i., Scot., U.K. **B3** 12
College, Ak., U.S. **B10** 95
Collegedale, Tn., U.S. **h11** 135
College Park, Ga., U.S. **C2** 103
College Park, Md., U.S. **C4** 113
College Place, Wa., U.S. **C7** 140
College Station, Ar., U.S. **C3** 97
College Station, Tx., U.S. **D4** 136
Collegeville, In., U.S. **C3** 107
Collegeville, Pa., U.S. **F11** 131
Colleton, co., S.C., U.S. **F6** 133
Collie, Austl. **G2** 60
Collier, co., Fl., U.S. **F5** 102
Colliers, W.V., U.S. **f8** 141
Collierville, Tn., U.S. **B2** 135
Collin, co., Tx., U.S. **C4** 136
Collingdale, Pa., U.S. **p20** 131
Collingswood, N.J., U.S. **D2** 123
Collingsworth, co., Tx., U.S. **B2** 136
Collingwood, On., Can. **C4** 89
Collins, Ms., U.S. **D4** 117
Collins Park, De., U.S. **B3** 101
Collinsville, Al., U.S. **A4** 94
Collinsville, Ct., U.S. **B4** 100
Collinsville, Il., U.S. **E4** 106
Collinsville, Ms., U.S. **C5** 117
Collinsville, Ok., U.S. **A6** 129
Collinwood, Tn., U.S. **B4** 135
Collipulli, Chile **E2** 69
Colmar, Fr. **C10** 16
Colmar Manor, Md., U.S. **f9** 113
Colo, Ia., U.S. **B4** 108
Cologne see Köln, Ger. **E10** 12
Coloma, Mi., U.S. **F4** 115
Colombia, ctry., S.A. **C5** 70
Colombo, Braz. **D8** 72
Colombo, Sri L. **H3** 40
Colón, Arg. **E5** 72
Colón, Cuba **A3** 80
Colón, Pan. **D3** 80
Colon, Mi., U.S. **G5** 115
Colón, Archipiélago de (Galapagos Islands), is., Ec. **C2** 70
Colonial Beach, Va., U.S. **B6** 139
Colonial Heights, Tn., U.S. **C11** 135
Colonial Heights, Va., U.S. **C5** 139
Colonial National Historical Park, Va., U.S. **C6** 139
Colonie, N.Y., U.S. **C7** 125
Colorado, co., Tx., U.S. **E4** 136
Colorado, state, U.S. **B5** 99
Colorado, stm., Arg. **E4** 69
Colorado, stm., N.A. **E5** 92
Colorado, stm., Tx., U.S. **D3** 136
Colorado City, Az., U.S. **A3** 96
Colorado City, Co., U.S. **D6** 99
Colorado City, Tx., U.S. **C2** 136
Colorado City, Lake, res., Tx., U.S. **C2** 136
Colorado National Monument, Co., U.S. **B2** 99
Colorado River Aqueduct, Ca., U.S. **F6** 98
Colorado River Indian Reservation, U.S. **D1** 96
Colorado Springs, Co., U.S. **C6** 99
Colquitt, Ga., U.S. **E2** 103
Colquitt, co., Ga., U.S. **E3** 103
Colstrip, Mt., U.S. **E10** 119
Colton, S.D., U.S. **D9** 134
Coltons Point, Md., U.S. **D4** 113
Columbia, Al., U.S. **D4** 94
Columbia, Il., U.S. **E3** 106
Columbia, Ky., U.S. **C4** 110
Columbia, Md., U.S. **B4** 113
Columbia, Mo., U.S. **C5** 118
Columbia, Ms., U.S. **D4** 117
Columbia, N.C., U.S. **B6** 126
Columbia, Pa., U.S. **F9** 131
Columbia, S.C., U.S. **C5** 133
Columbia, Tn., U.S. **B4** 135
Columbia, co., Ar., U.S. **D2** 97
Columbia, co., Fl., U.S. **B4** 102
Columbia, co., Ga., U.S. **C4** 103
Columbia, co., N.Y., U.S. **C7** 125
Columbia, co., Or., U.S. **B3** 130
Columbia, co., Pa., U.S. **D9** 131
Columbia, co., Wa., U.S. **C7** 140
Columbia, co., Wi., U.S. **E4** 142
Columbia, stm., N.A. **B3** 92
Columbia, Mount, mtn., Can. **C2** 84
Columbia City, In., U.S. **B7** 107
Columbia City, Or., U.S. **B4** 130
Columbia Falls, Mt., U.S. **B2** 119
Columbia Heights, Mn., U.S. **m12** 116
Columbia Lake, res., Ct., U.S. **C6** 100
Columbia Mountains, mts., B.C., Can. **C7** 85
Columbia Mountains, mts., N.A. **H15** 82
Columbiana, Al., U.S. **B3** 94
Columbiana, Oh., U.S. **B5** 128
Columbiana, co., Oh., U.S. **B5** 128
Columbiaville, Mi., U.S. **E7** 115
Columbus, Ga., U.S. **D2** 103
Columbus, In., U.S. **F6** 107
Columbus, Ks., U.S. **E9** 109
Columbus, Ms., U.S. **B5** 117
Columbus, Mt., U.S. **E7** 119
Columbus, N.C., U.S. **f10** 126
Columbus, Ne., U.S. **C8** 120
Columbus, N.M., U.S. **F2** 124
Columbus, Oh., U.S. **C2** 128
Columbus, Tx., U.S. **E4** 136
Columbus, Wi., U.S. **E4** 142
Columbus, co., N.C., U.S. **C4** 126
Columbus Air Force Base, mil., Ms., U.S. **B5** 117
Columbus Grove, Oh., U.S. **B1** 128
Columbus Junction, Ia., U.S. **C6** 108
Columbus Lake, res., Ms., U.S. **B5** 117
Colusa, Ca., U.S. **C2** 98
Colusa, co., Ca., U.S. **C2** 98
Colver, Pa., U.S. **E4** 131
Colville, Wa., U.S. **A8** 140
Colville, stm., Ak., U.S. **B9** 95
Colville, stm., Wa., U.S. **A8** 140
Colville Indian Reservation, Wa., U.S. **A6** 140
Colvos Passage, strt., Wa., U.S. **f10** 140
Colwich, Ks., U.S. **E6** 109
Colwood, B.C., Can. **h12** 85
Comacchio, Italy **B4** 18
Comacchio, Valli di, l., Italy **B4** 18
Comal, co., Tx., U.S. **E3** 136
Comalcalco, Mex. **D6** 78
Coman, Mount, mtn., Ant. **D34** 67
Comanche, Ok., U.S. **C4** 129
Comanche, Tx., U.S. **D3** 136
Comanche, co., Ks., U.S. **E4** 109
Comanche, co., Ok., U.S. **C3** 129
Comanche, co., Tx., U.S. **D3** 136
Comandante Fontana, Arg. **D6** 72
Comayagua, Hond. **C2** 80
Combahee, stm., S.C., U.S. **F6** 133
Combarbalá, Chile **D2** 69
Comber, On., Can. **E2** 89
Combermere Bay, b., Myan. **C2** 34
Combined Locks, Wi., U.S. **h9** 142
Combs, Ky., U.S. **C6** 110
Comer, Ga., U.S. **B3** 103
Comfort, Tx., U.S. **E3** 136
Comilla, Bngl. **E6** 40
Comitán, Mex. **D6** 78
Comite, stm., La., U.S. **D4** 111
Commerce, Ga., U.S. **B3** 103
Commerce, Ok., U.S. **A7** 129
Commerce, Tx., U.S. **C5** 136
Commerce City, Co., U.S. **B6** 99
Committee Bay, b., Nu., Can. **E22** 82
Common Fence Point, R.I., U.S. **D6** 132
Communism Peak see Kommunizma, pik, mtn., Taj. **F9** 26
Como, Italy **B2** 18
Como, Ms., U.S. **A4** 117
Como, Lago di, l., Italy **B2** 18
Comodoro Rivadavia, Arg. **G3** 69
Comores, Archipel des, is., Afr. **A7** 56
Comorin, Cape, c., India **H3** 40
Comoros, ctry., Afr. **A7** 56
Comox, B.C., Can. **E5** 85
Compiègne, Fr. **C8** 16
Compostela, Mex. **C4** 78
Compton, P.Q., Can. **D6** 90
Compton, Ca., U.S. **n12** 98
Comrat, Mol. **F10** 20
Comstock, Mi., U.S. **F5** 115
Conakry, Gui. **E2** 50
Conanicut Island, i., R.I., U.S. **E5** 132
Conanicut Point, c., R.I., U.S. **E5** 132
Concarneau, Fr. **D5** 16
Conceição da Barra, Braz. **E4** 74
Conceição do Araguaia, Braz. **C2** 74
Concepción, Arg. **D4** 72
Concepción, Chile **E2** 69
Concepción, Para. **C6** 72
Concepción del Oro, Mex. **C4** 78
Concepción del Uruguay, Arg. **E6** 72
Conception, Point, c., Ca., U.S. **E3** 98
Conception Bay, b., Nf., Can. **E5** 88
Conception Bay South, Nf., Can. **E5** 88
Conchas Lake, res., N.M., U.S. **B5** 124
Concho, co., Tx., U.S. **D3** 136
Concho, stm., Tx., U.S. **D2** 136
Conchos, stm., Mex. **B3** 78
Concord, Ca., U.S. **h8** 98
Concord, Ma., U.S. **B5** 114
Concord, Mi., U.S. **F6** 115
Concord, Mo., U.S. **g13** 118
Concord, N.C., U.S. **B2** 126
Concord, N.H., U.S. **D3** 122
Concord, stm., Ma., U.S. **A5** 114
Concordia, Arg. **E6** 72
Concórdia, Braz. **D7** 72
Concordia, Ks., U.S. **C6** 109
Concordia, Mo., U.S. **C4** 118
Concordia, co., La., U.S. **C4** 111
Concrete, Wa., U.S. **A4** 140
Conda, Ang. **F2** 54
Condobolin, Austl. **G4** 62
Condon, Or., U.S. **B6** 130
Condoto, Col. **D4** 80
Conecuh, co., Al., U.S. **D2** 94
Conecuh, stm., U.S. **D3** 94
Conejos, co., Co., U.S. **D4** 99
Conejos, stm., Co., U.S. **D4** 99
Conejos Peak, mtn., Co., U.S. **D4** 99
Conemaugh, Pa., U.S. **F4** 131
Conemaugh River Lake, res., Pa., U.S. **F3** 131
Congamond Lakes, l., U.S. **A4** 100
Congaree, stm., S.C., U.S. **D6** 133
Congaree Swamp National Monument, S.C., U.S. **D6** 133
Congo, ctry., Afr. **D3** 54
Congo (Zaïre), stm., Afr. **D2** 54
Congo, Democratic Republic of the, ctry., Afr. **D4** 54
Congress, Az., U.S. **C3** 96
Conimicut Point, c., R.I., U.S. **D5** 132
Conklin, N.Y., U.S. **C5** 125
Connaught, hist. reg., Ire. **D2** 12
Conneaut, Oh., U.S. **A5** 128
Conneaut Creek, stm., Oh., U.S. **A5** 128
Conneaut Lake, l., Pa., U.S. **C1** 131
Connecticut, state, U.S. **C5** 100
Connecticut, stm., U.S. **C5** 100
Connell, Wa., U.S. **C7** 140
Connellsville, Pa., U.S. **F2** 131
Connersville, In., U.S. **E7** 107
Conover, N.C., U.S. **B1** 126
Conowingo, Md., U.S. **A5** 113
Conrad, Ia., U.S. **B5** 108
Conrad, Mt., U.S. **B5** 119
Conroe, Tx., U.S. **D5** 136
Conselheiro Lafaiete, Braz. **F3** 74
Conselheiro Pena, Braz. **E3** 74
Conshohocken, Pa., U.S. **F11** 131
Consolación del Sur, Cuba **A3** 80
Con Son, is., Viet. **E5** 34
Consort, Ab., Can. **C5** 84
Constance see Konstanz, Ger. **G11** 12
Constance, Lake, l., Eur. **A2** 18
Constanța, Rom. **G10** 20
Constantina, Spain **I4** 16
Constantine see Qacentina, Alg. **C6** 48
Constantine, Mi., U.S. **G5** 115
Constantine, Cape, c., Ak., U.S. **D8** 95
Constantinople see İstanbul, Tur. **B3** 44
Constitución, Chile **E2** 69
Contas, stm., Braz. **D3** 74
Content Keys, is., Fl., U.S. **H5** 102
Continental, Oh., U.S. **A1** 128
Continental Peak, mtn., Wy., U.S. **D4** 143
Continental Reservoir, res., Co., U.S. **D3** 99
Contoocook, N.H., U.S. **D3** 122
Contoocook, stm., N.H., U.S. **D3** 122
Contra Costa, co., Ca., U.S. **D3** 98
Contrecoeur, P.Q., Can. **D4** 90
Converse, In., U.S. **C6** 107
Converse, S.C., U.S. **B4** 133
Converse, co., Wy., U.S. **C7** 143
Convoy, Oh., U.S. **B1** 128
Conway, Ar., U.S. **B3** 97
Conway, Fl., U.S. **D5** 102
Conway, Mo., U.S. **D5** 118
Conway, N.C., U.S. **A5** 126
Conway, N.H., U.S. **C4** 122
Conway, Pa., U.S. **E1** 131
Conway, S.C., U.S. **D9** 133
Conway, co., Ar., U.S. **B3** 97
Conway, Lake, res., Ar., U.S. **B3** 97
Conway Lake, l., N.H., U.S. **C4** 122
Conway Springs, Ks., U.S. **E6** 109
Conyers, Ga., U.S. **C2** 103
Coober Pedy, Austl. **F5** 60
Cook, Mn., U.S. **C6** 116
Cook, co., Ga., U.S. **E3** 103
Cook, co., Il., U.S. **B6** 106
Cook, co., Mn., U.S. **k9** 116
Cook, Cape, c., B.C., Can. **D4** 85
Cook, Mount, mtn., N.Z. **p12** 63c
Cooke, co., Tx., U.S. **C4** 136
Cookes Peak, mtn., N.M., U.S. **E2** 124
Cookeville, Tn., U.S. **C8** 135
Cook Inlet, b., Ak., U.S. **D9** 95
Cook Islands, dep., Oc. **F13** 58
Cook Point, c., Md., U.S. **C5** 113
Cookshire, P.Q., Can. **D6** 90
Cookson, Ok., U.S. **B7** 129
Cook Strait, strt., N.Z. **p13** 63c
Cooktown, Austl. **D4** 62
Cooleemee, N.C., U.S. **B2** 126
Coolgardie, Austl. **G3** 60
Coolidge, Az., U.S. **E4** 96
Coolidge, Ga., U.S. **E3** 103
Cooma, Austl. **H4** 62
Coonabarabran, Austl. **G4** 62
Coonamble, Austl. **G4** 62
Coonoor, India **G3** 40
Coon Rapids, Ia., U.S. **C3** 108
Coon Rapids, Mn., U.S. **E5** 116
Coon Valley, Wi., U.S. **E2** 142
Cooper, Tx., U.S. **C5** 136
Cooper, co., Mo., U.S. **C5** 118
Cooper, stm., S.C., U.S. **F8** 133
Cooper Creek, stm., Austl. **F2** 62
Cooper Mountain, mtn., Ak., U.S. **g17** 95
Coopersburg, Pa., U.S. **F11** 131
Cooperstown, N.D., U.S. **B7** 127
Cooperstown, N.Y., U.S. **C6** 125
Coopersville, Mi., U.S. **E5** 115
Coorow, Austl. **F2** 60
Coos, co., N.H., U.S. **A4** 122
Coos, co., Or., U.S. **D2** 130
Coos, stm., Or., U.S. **D2** 130
Coosa, co., Al., U.S. **C3** 94
Coosa, stm., U.S. **C3** 94
Coosada, Al., U.S. **C3** 94
Coosawhatchie, stm., S.C., U.S. **F5** 133
Coos Bay, Or., U.S. **D2** 130
Cootamundra, Austl. **G4** 62
Copalis Beach, Wa., U.S. **B1** 140
Copan, Ok., U.S. **A6** 129
Copan Reservoir, res., Ok., U.S. **A6** 129
Copenhagen see København, Den. **I5** 10
Copiah, co., Ms., U.S. **D3** 117
Copiapó, Chile **C2** 69
Coplay, Pa., U.S. **E10** 131
Copper, stm., Ak., U.S. **C11** 95
Copperas Cove, Tx., U.S. **D4** 136
Copper Butte, mtn., Wa., U.S. **A7** 140
Copper Mountain, mtn., Wy., U.S. **C5** 143
Copper Mountains, mts., Az., U.S. **E2** 96
Coquille, Or., U.S. **D2** 130
Coquimbo, Chile **C2** 69
Corabia, Rom. **H8** 20
Coral Gables, Fl., U.S. **G6** 102
Coral Sea, Oc. **F9** 58
Coral Sea Basin **J18** 64
Coralville, Ia., U.S. **C6** 108
Coralville Lake, res., Ia., U.S. **C5** 108
Coraopolis, Pa., U.S. **E1** 131
Corbeil-Essonnes, Fr. **C8** 16
Corbin, Ky., U.S. **D5** 110
Corcoran, Ca., U.S. **D4** 98
Corcoran, Mn., U.S. **m11** 116
Corcovado, Golfo, b., Chile **F2** 69
Corcovado, Volcán, vol., Chile **F2** 69
Cordele, Ga., U.S. **E3** 103
Cordell, Ok., U.S. **B3** 129
Cordell Hull Lake, res., Tn., U.S. **C8** 135
Córdoba, Arg. **E5** 72
Córdoba, Mex. **D5** 78
Córdoba, Spain **I4** 16
Córdova, Peru **A2** 72
Cordova see Córdoba, Spain **I4** 16
Cordova, Ak., U.S. **C10** 95
Cordova, Al., U.S. **B2** 94
Cordova, N.C., U.S. **C3** 126
Cordova, N.M., U.S. **A4** 124
Cordova Peak, mtn., Ak., U.S. **C10** 95
Corentyne (Coeroeni), stm., S.A. **C8** 70
Corfu see Kérkira, Grc. **E7** 18
Corfu see Kérkira, i., Grc. **E7** 18
Coria, Spain **H3** 16
Corinna, Me., U.S. **D3** 112
Corinne, Ut., U.S. **B3** 137
Corinne Key, i., Fl., U.S. **G6** 102
Corinth see Kórinthos, Grc. **F9** 18
Corinth, Ms., U.S. **A5** 117
Corinth, N.Y., U.S. **B7** 125
Corinth, Gulf of see Korinthiakós Kólpos, b., Grc. **E9** 18
Corinto, Braz. **E3** 74
Corisco, Isla de, i., Eq. Gui. **C1** 54
Cork, Ire. **E2** 12
Çorlu, Tur. **B2** 44
Cormorant Lake, l., Mb., Can. **B1** 86
Cornelia, Ga., U.S. **B3** 103
Cornélio Procópio, Braz. **F1** 74
Cornelius, N.C., U.S. **B2** 126
Cornelius, Or., U.S. **g11** 130
Cornell, Wi., U.S. **C2** 142
Corner Brook, Nf., Can. **D3** 88
Cornersville, Tn., U.S. **B5** 135
Cornfield Point, c., Ct., U.S. **D6** 100
Cornie Bayou, stm., U.S. **D3** 97
Corning, Ar., U.S. **A5** 97
Corning, Ca., U.S. **C2** 98
Corning, Ia., U.S. **D3** 108
Corning, N.Y., U.S. **C3** 125
Cornish, Me., U.S. **E2** 112
Corno Grande, mtn., Italy **C4** 18
Cornville, Az., U.S. **C4** 96
Cornwall, On., Can. **B10** 89
Cornwall, Pa., U.S. **F9** 131
Cornwall, hist. reg., Eng., U.K. **E4** 12
Cornwall on Hudson, N.Y., U.S. **D6** 125
Coro, Ven. **A6** 70
Coroatá, Braz. **B3** 74
Corocoro Island, i., S.A. **D7** 80
Čoroh, stm., Asia **B9** 44
Coroico, Bol. **B4** 72
Coromandel Coast, India **G4** 40
Corona, Ca., U.S. **F5** 98
Coronado, Ca., U.S. **F5** 98
Coronado, Bahía de, b., C.R. **D3** 80
Coronado National Memorial, Az., U.S. **F5** 96
Coronation, Ab., Can. **C5** 84
Coronation Gulf, b., Nu., Can. **E17** 82
Coronation Island, i., Ant. **B36** 67
Coronation Island, i., Ak., U.S. **n22** 95
Coronel Murta, Braz. **B9** 72
Coronel Oviedo, Para. **D6** 72
Coronel Suárez, Arg. **F5** 72
Coronel Vivida, Braz. **D7** 72
Coropuna, Nevado, vol., Peru **G5** 70
Corozal, Belize **B2** 80
Corozal, Col. **D4** 80
Corpus Christi, Tx., U.S. **F4** 136
Corpus Christi Naval Air Station, mil., Tx., U.S. **F4** 136
Correctionville, Ia., U.S. **B2** 108
Correntina, Braz. **A9** 72
Corrib, Lough, l., Ire. **D2** 12
Corrientes, Arg. **D6** 72
Corrientes, Cabo, c., Col. **B4** 70
Corrientes, Cabo, c., Mex. **C3** 78
Corrigan, Tx., U.S. **D5** 136
Corriganville, Md., U.S. **k13** 113
Corrigin, Austl. **G2** 60
Corriverton, Guy. **B8** 70
Corry, Pa., U.S. **C2** 131
Corse (Corsica), i., Fr. **C2** 18
Corse, Cap, c., Fr. **C2** 18
Corsica, S.D., U.S. **D7** 134
Corsica see Corse, i., Fr. **C2** 18
Corsicana, Tx., U.S. **C4** 136
Corson, co., S.D., U.S. **B4** 134
Corson Inlet, b., N.J., U.S. **E3** 123
Cort Adelaer, Kap, c., Grnld. **F31** 82
Corte, Fr. **C2** 18
Cortés, Mar de see California, Golfo de, b., Mex. **B2** 78
Cortez, Co., U.S. **D2** 99
Cortez, Fl., U.S. **q10** 102
Cortez, Sea of see California, Golfo de, b., Mex. **B2** 78
Cortez Mountains, mts., Nv., U.S. **C5** 121
Cortland, Il., U.S. **B5** 106
Cortland, N.Y., U.S. **C4** 125
Cortland, Oh., U.S. **A5** 128
Cortland, co., N.Y., U.S. **C4** 125
Çorum, Tur. **B6** 44
Corumbá, Braz. **G8** 70
Corunna see A Coruña, Spain **F2** 16
Corunna, Mi., U.S. **F6** 115
Coruripe, Braz. **D4** 74
Corvallis, Or., U.S. **C3** 130
Corydon, Ia., U.S. **D4** 108
Corydon, In., U.S. **H5** 107
Corydon, Ky., U.S. **C2** 110
Coryell, co., Tx., U.S. **D4** 136
Cos see Kos, i., Grc. **F11** 18
Cosenza, Italy **E6** 18
Coshocton, Oh., U.S. **B4** 128
Coshocton, co., Oh., U.S. **B4** 128
Cosmoledo, Atoll de, i., Sey. **i11** 57b
Cosmopolis, Wa., U.S. **C2** 140
Cosmos, Mn., U.S. **F4** 116
Cosne-sur-Loire, Fr. **D8** 16
Cossatot, stm., Ar., U.S. **C1** 97
Costa Mesa, Ca., U.S. **n13** 98
Costa Rica, Mex. **C3** 78
Costa Rica, ctry., N.A. **F8** 76
Costilla, co., Co., U.S. **D5** 99
Coswig, Ger. **E13** 12
Cotabato, Phil. **E8** 34
Coteau-Landing, P.Q., Can. **D3** 90
Cote d'Ivoire, ctry., Afr. **E3** 50
Cotonou, Benin **E5** 50
Cotopaxi, vol., Ec. **D4** 70
Cottage Grove, Mn., U.S. **n13** 116
Cottage Grove, Or., U.S. **D3** 130
Cottage Grove Reservoir, res., Or., U.S. **D3** 130
Cottam, On., Can. **E2** 89
Cottbus, Ger. **E14** 12
Cotter, Ar., U.S. **A3** 97
Cottle, co., Tx., U.S. **B2** 136
Cottleville, Mo., U.S. **f12** 118
Cotton, co., Ok., U.S. **C3** 129
Cottondale, Al., U.S. **B2** 94
Cotton Plant, Ar., U.S. **B4** 97
Cottonport, La., U.S. **C3** 111
Cotton Valley, La., U.S. **B2** 111
Cottonwood, Al., U.S. **D4** 94
Cottonwood, Az., U.S. **C3** 96
Cottonwood, Ca., U.S. **B2** 98
Cottonwood, Id., U.S. **C2** 105
Cottonwood, Mn., U.S. **F3** 116
Cottonwood, co., Mn., U.S. **F3** 116
Cottonwood, stm., Ks., U.S. **D7** 109

Name — Map Ref. — Page

Cottonwood, stm., Mn., U.S. **F3** 116
Cottonwood Creek, stm., Wy., U.S. **C4** 143
Cottonwood Falls, Ks., U.S. **D7** 109
Cotuit, Ma., U.S. **C7** 114
Cotulla, Tx., U.S. **E3** 136
Coudersport, Pa., U.S. **C5** 131
Cougar Reservoir, res., Or., U.S. **C4** 130
Coulee Creek, stm., Wa., U.S. **g13** 140
Coulee Dam, Wa., U.S. **B7** 140
Coulee Dam National Recreation Area, Wa., U.S. **A7** 140
Coulterville, Il., U.S. **E4** 106
Counce, Tn., U.S. **B3** 135
Council, Id., U.S. **E2** 105
Council Bluffs, Ia., U.S. **C2** 108
Council Grove, Ks., U.S. **D7** 109
Council Grove Lake, res., Ks., U.S. **D7** 109
Council Mountain, mtn., Id., U.S. **E2** 105
Country Homes, Wa., U.S. **B8** 140
Coupeville, Wa., U.S. **A3** 140
Courland Lagoon, b., Eur. **B6** 20
Courtenay, B.C., Can. **E5** 85
Courte Oreilles, Lac, l., Wi., U.S. **C2** 142
Courtland, On., Can. **E4** 89
Courtland, Al., U.S. **A2** 94
Courtland, Va., U.S. **D5** 139
Coushatta, La., U.S. **B2** 111
Cove Creek, stm., Ut., U.S. **E3** 137
Covedale, Oh., U.S. **o12** 128
Coventry, Eng., U.K. **D6** 12
Coventry, Ct., U.S. **B6** 100
Coventry, R.I., U.S. **D3** 132
Cove Point, c., Md., U.S. **D5** 113
Covilhã, Port. **G3** 16
Covina, Ca., U.S. **m13** 98
Covington, Ga., U.S. **C3** 103
Covington, In., U.S. **D3** 107
Covington, Ky., U.S. **A5** 110
Covington, La., U.S. **D5** 111
Covington, Oh., U.S. **B1** 128
Covington, Tn., U.S. **B2** 135
Covington, Va., U.S. **C3** 139
Covington, co., Al., U.S. **D3** 94
Covington, co., Ms., U.S. **D4** 117
Cowan, Tn., U.S. **B5** 135
Cowansville, P.Q., Can. **D5** 90
Cowarts, Al., U.S. **D4** 94
Cow Creek, stm., Wa., U.S. **C7** 140
Cowee Mountains, mts., N.C., U.S. **f9** 126
Cowell, Austl. **G2** 62
Cowen, Mount, mtn., Mt., U.S. **E6** 119
Coweta, Ok., U.S. **B6** 129
Coweta, co., Ga., U.S. **C2** 103
Cow Head, Nf., Can. **D3** 88
Cowichan Bay, B.C., Can. **g12** 85
Cow Lakes, l., Or., U.S. **D9** 130
Cowley, Wy., U.S. **B4** 143
Cowley, co., Ks., U.S. **E7** 109
Cowlington, Ok., U.S. **B7** 129
Cowlitz, co., Wa., U.S. **C2** 140
Cowlitz, stm., Wa., U.S. **C3** 140
Cowpasture, stm., Va., U.S. **B3** 139
Cowpen Mountain, mtn., Ga., U.S. **B2** 103
Cowpens, S.C., U.S. **A4** 133
Cowra, Austl. **G4** 62
Coxim, Braz. **G9** 70
Coxsackie, N.Y., U.S. **C7** 125
Cox's Bāzār, Bngl. **E6** 40
Cox's Cove, Nf., Can. **D2** 88
Coyuca de Catalán, Mex. **D4** 78
Cozad, Ne., U.S. **D6** 120
Cozumel, Mex. **C7** 78
Cozumel, Isla, i., Mex. **C7** 78
Crab Creek, stm., Wa., U.S. **B7** 140
Crab Creek, stm., Wa., U.S. **C6** 140
Crab Orchard, Ky., U.S. **C5** 110
Crab Orchard, Tn., U.S. **D9** 135
Crab Orchard, W.V., U.S. **n13** 141
Crab Orchard Lake, res., Il., U.S. **F4** 106
Crabtree, Pa., U.S. **F3** 131
Crabtree Mills, P.Q., Can. **D4** 90
Cracow see Kraków, Pol. **D5** 20
Cradock, S. Afr. **E4** 56
Crafton, Pa., U.S. **k13** 131
Craig, Ak., U.S. **D13** 95
Craig, Co., U.S. **A3** 99
Craig, co., Ok., U.S. **A6** 129
Craig, co., Va., U.S. **C2** 139
Craig Air Force Base, mil., Al., U.S. **C3** 94
Craig Creek, stm., Va., U.S. **C2** 139
Craighead, co., Ar., U.S. **B5** 97
Craigsville, Va., U.S. **B3** 139
Craigsville, W.V., U.S. **C4** 141
Craiova, Rom. **G7** 20
Cramerton, N.C., U.S. **B1** 126
Cranberry Lake, l., N.Y., U.S. **A6** 125
Cranberry Portage, Mb., Can. **B1** 86
Cranbrook, Austl. **G2** 60
Cranbrook, B.C., Can. **E10** 85
Crandall, Tx., U.S. **n10** 136
Crandon, Wi., U.S. **C5** 142
Crane, Mo., U.S. **E4** 118
Crane, Tx., U.S. **D1** 136
Crane, co., Tx., U.S. **D1** 136
Crane Creek, stm., Oh., U.S. **e7** 128
Crane Creek Reservoir, res., Id., U.S. **E2** 105
Crane Lake, l., Il., U.S. **C3** 106
Crane Lake, l., Mn., U.S. **B6** 116
Crane Mountain, mtn., Or., U.S. **E6** 130
Crane Prairie Reservoir, res., Or., U.S. **D5** 130
Cranford, N.J., U.S. **B4** 123
Cranston, R.I., U.S. **C4** 132
Crater Lake, l., Or., U.S. **E4** 130
Crater Lake National Park, Or., U.S. **E4** 130
Craters of the Moon National Monument, Id., U.S. **F5** 105
Crateús, Braz. **C3** 74
Crato, Braz. **C4** 74
Craven, co., N.C., U.S. **B5** 126
Crawford, Ga., U.S. **C3** 103
Crawford, Ms., U.S. **B5** 117
Crawford, Ne., U.S. **B2** 120
Crawford, co., Ar., U.S. **B1** 97
Crawford, co., Ga., U.S. **D3** 103
Crawford, co., Ia., U.S. **B2** 108
Crawford, co., Il., U.S. **D6** 106
Crawford, co., In., U.S. **H4** 107
Crawford, co., Ks., U.S. **E9** 109
Crawford, co., Mi., U.S. **D6** 115
Crawford, co., Mo., U.S. **D6** 118
Crawford, co., Oh., U.S. **B3** 128
Crawford, co., Pa., U.S. **C1** 131
Crawford, co., Wi., U.S. **E3** 142
Crawford Lake, l., Me., U.S. **C5** 112
Crawford Notch State Park, N.H., U.S. **B4** 122
Crawfordsville, Ar., U.S. **B5** 97
Crawfordsville, In., U.S. **D4** 107
Crawfordville, Fl., U.S. **B2** 102
Crawley, Eng., U.K. **E6** 12
Crazy Mountains, mts., Mt., U.S. **D6** 119
Crazy Peak, mtn., Mt., U.S. **D6** 119
Crazy Woman Creek, stm., Wy., U.S. **B6** 143
Creal Springs, Il., U.S. **F5** 106
Creedmoor, N.C., U.S. **A4** 126
Creek, co., Ok., U.S. **B5** 129
Cree Lake, l., Sk., Can. **m7** 91
Creemore, On., Can. **C4** 89
Creighton, Ne., U.S. **B8** 120
Creighton, Pa., U.S. **h14** 131
Creil, Fr. **C8** 16
Crema, Italy **B2** 18
Cremona, Italy **B3** 18
Crenshaw, Ms., U.S. **A3** 117
Crenshaw, co., Al., U.S. **D3** 94
Creola, Al., U.S. **E1** 94
Cres, Otok, i., Cro. **B5** 18
Cresaptown, Md., U.S. **k13** 113
Crescent, Ok., U.S. **B4** 129
Crescent, Or., U.S. **D5** 130
Crescent, Lake, l., Wa., U.S. **A2** 140
Crescent City, Ca., U.S. **B1** 98
Crescent City, Fl., U.S. **C5** 102
Crescent Lake, l., Fl., U.S. **C5** 102
Crescent Lake, l., Or., U.S. **D5** 130
Crescent Springs, Ky., U.S. **h13** 110
Cresco, Ia., U.S. **A5** 108
Cresskill, N.J., U.S. **h9** 123
Cresson, Pa., U.S. **F4** 131
Cressona, Pa., U.S. **E9** 131
Crested Butte, Co., U.S. **C4** 99
Crest Hill, Il., U.S. **k8** 106
Crestline, Oh., U.S. **B3** 128
Creston, B.C., Can. **E9** 85
Creston, Ia., U.S. **C3** 108
Creston, Oh., U.S. **B4** 128
Crestone Peak, mtn., Co., U.S. **D5** 99
Crestview, Fl., U.S. **u15** 102
Crestview, Hi., U.S. **g10** 104
Crestwood, Ky., U.S. **B4** 110
Crestwood Village, N.J., U.S. **D4** 123
Creswell, Or., U.S. **D3** 130
Crete, Il., U.S. **B6** 106
Crete, Ne., U.S. **D9** 120
Crete see Kríti, i., Grc. **G10** 18
Crete, Sea of see Kritikón Pélagos, Grc. **G10** 18
Creve Coeur, Il., U.S. **C4** 106
Crewe, Va., U.S. **C4** 139
Criciúma, Braz. **D8** 72
Cricket, N.C., U.S. **A1** 126
Cridersville, Oh., U.S. **B1** 128
Crimean Mountains see Kryms'ki hory, mts., Ukr. **G13** 20
Crimean Peninsula see Kryms'kyi pivostriv, pen., Ukr. **G12** 20
Crisfield, Md., U.S. **E6** 113
Crisp, co., Ga., U.S. **E3** 103
Cristalândia, Braz. **F10** 70
Cristalina, Braz. **E2** 74
Cristóbal Colón, Pico, mtn., Col. **A5** 70
Crittenden, Ky., U.S. **B5** 110
Crittenden, co., Ar., U.S. **B5** 97
Crittenden, co., Ky., U.S. **e9** 110
Crivitz, Wi., U.S. **C6** 142
Crna Gora (Montenegro), prov., Yugo. **C7** 18
Croatia, ctry., Eur. **B5** 18
Crocker, Mo., U.S. **D5** 118
Crockett, Ca., U.S. **g8** 98
Crockett, Tx., U.S. **D5** 136
Crockett, co., Tn., U.S. **B2** 135
Crockett, co., Tx., U.S. **D2** 136
Crofton, Ky., U.S. **C2** 110
Crofton, Md., U.S. **B4** 113
Crofton, Ne., U.S. **B8** 120
Croix, Lac la, l., Mn., U.S. **B6** 116
Croker, Cape, c., Austl. **C5** 60
Croker, Cape, c., On., Can. **C4** 89
Croker Island, i., Austl. **C5** 60
Cromona, Ky., U.S. **C7** 110
Cromwell, Ct., U.S. **C5** 100
Crook, co., Or., U.S. **C6** 130
Crook, co., Wy., U.S. **B8** 143
Crooked, stm., Or., U.S. **C6** 130
Crooked Creek, stm., Pa., U.S. **C7** 131
Crooked Creek, stm., U.S. **E3** 109
Crooked Creek Lake, res., Pa., U.S. **E3** 131
Crooked Island, i., Bah. **D10** 76
Crooked Island Passage, strt., Bah. **A5** 80
Crooked Lake, l., Fl., U.S. **E5** 102
Crooked Lake, l., Mn., U.S. **B7** 116
Crooks, S.D., U.S. **D9** 134
Crooks Lake, l., Nv., U.S. **B2** 121
Crookston, Mn., U.S. **C2** 116
Crooksville, Oh., U.S. **C3** 128
Crosby, Mn., U.S. **D5** 116
Crosby, N.D., U.S. **A2** 127
Crosby, Tx., U.S. **r14** 136
Crosby, co., Tx., U.S. **C2** 136
Crosby, Mount, mtn., Wy., U.S. **C3** 143
Crosbyton, Tx., U.S. **C2** 136
Cross, co., Ar., U.S. **B5** 97
Cross Bay, b., Mb., Can. **C2** 86
Cross City, Fl., U.S. **C3** 102
Cross Creek, stm., W.V., U.S. **f8** 141
Crossett, Ar., U.S. **D4** 97
Crossfield, Ab., Can. **D3** 84
Cross Island, i., Me., U.S. **D5** 112
Cross Lake, Mb., Can. **B3** 86
Crosslake, Mn., U.S. **D4** 116
Cross Lake, l., Me., U.S. **A4** 112
Cross Lake, res., La., U.S. **B2** 111
Cross Lanes, W.V., U.S. **C3** 141
Crossman Peak, mtn., Az., U.S. **C1** 96
Cross Plains, Tn., U.S. **A5** 135
Cross Plains, Tx., U.S. **C3** 136
Cross Plains, Wi., U.S. **E4** 142
Cross Sound, strt., Ak., U.S. **k21** 95
Crossville, Al., U.S. **A4** 94
Crossville, Il., U.S. **E5** 106
Crossville, Tn., U.S. **D8** 135
Croswell, Mi., U.S. **E8** 115
Crothersville, In., U.S. **G6** 107
Crotone, Italy **E6** 18
Croton-on-Hudson, N.Y., U.S. **D7** 125
Crouse, N.C., U.S. **B1** 126
Crow, stm., Mn., U.S. **F4** 116
Crow Agency, Mt., U.S. **E9** 119
Crow Creek, stm., U.S. **A6** 99
Crow Creek Indian Reservation, S.D., U.S. **C6** 134
Crowder, Ms., U.S. **A3** 117
Crowell, Tx., U.S. **C3** 136
Crow Indian Reservation, Mt., U.S. **E9** 119
Crowley, La., U.S. **D3** 111
Crowley, Tx., U.S. **n9** 136
Crowley, co., Co., U.S. **C7** 99
Crowley, Lake, res., Ca., U.S. **D4** 98
Crowleys Ridge, mtn., U.S. **B5** 97
Crown Point, In., U.S. **B3** 107
Crown Point, La., U.S. **k11** 111
Crownpoint, N.M., U.S. **B1** 124
Crow Peak, mtn., Mt., U.S. **D5** 119
Crowsnest Pass, Ab., Can. **E3** 84
Crowsnest Pass, Can. **E3** 84
Crow Wing, co., Mn., U.S. **D4** 116
Crow Wing, stm., Mn., U.S. **D4** 116
Crozet, Va., U.S. **B4** 139
Crozet, Archipel, is., Afr. **N15** 46
Crozet Basin **L9** 64
Cruces, Cuba **A3** 80
Crump Lake, l., Or., U.S. **E7** 130
Cruz, Cabo, c., Cuba **B4** 80
Cruz Alta, Braz. **D7** 72
Cruz del Eje, Arg. **E5** 72
Cruzeiro, Braz. **F2** 74
Cruzeiro do Sul, Braz. **E5** 70
Crystal, Mn., U.S. **m12** 116
Crystal, stm., Co., U.S. **B3** 99
Crystal Bay, Nv., U.S. **D1** 121
Crystal Bay, b., Fl., U.S. **D4** 102
Crystal Beach, Fl., U.S. **D4** 102
Crystal City, Mb., Can. **E2** 86
Crystal City, Mo., U.S. **C7** 118
Crystal City, Tx., U.S. **E3** 136
Crystal Falls, Mi., U.S. **B2** 115
Crystal Lake, Ct., U.S. **B6** 100
Crystal Lake, Fl., U.S. **u16** 102
Crystal Lake, Il., U.S. **A5** 106
Crystal Lake, l., Ct., U.S. **B6** 100
Crystal Lake, l., Mi., U.S. **D4** 115
Crystal Lake, l., N.H., U.S. **D4** 122
Crystal Lake, l., Vt., U.S. **B4** 138
Crystal Lawns, Il., U.S. **k8** 106
Crystal Pond, res., Ct., U.S. **B7** 100
Crystal River, Fl., U.S. **D4** 102
Crystal Springs, Ms., U.S. **D3** 117
Ču, stm., Asia **B10** 42
Cúa, Ven. **C6** 80
Cuamba, Moz. **A6** 56
Cuando (Kwando), stm., Afr. **B3** 56
Cuangar, Ang. **B2** 56
Cuango, Ang. **E3** 54
Cuango, Ang. **E3** 54
Cuango (Kwango), stm., Afr. **E3** 54
Cuanza, stm., Ang. **E3** 52
Cuauhtémoc, Mex. **B3** 78
Cuba, Il., U.S. **C3** 106
Cuba, Mo., U.S. **C6** 118
Cuba, N.M., U.S. **A3** 124
Cuba, N.Y., U.S. **C2** 125
Cuba, ctry., N.A. **D9** 76
Cuba City, Wi., U.S. **F3** 142
Cubal, Ang. **F2** 54
Cubango (Okavango), stm., Afr. **B2** 56
Cubero, N.M., U.S. **B2** 124
Çubuk, Tur. **B5** 44
Cucharas, stm., Co., U.S. **D6** 99
Cúcuta, Col. **B5** 70
Cudahy, Wi., U.S. **F6** 142
Cuddalore, India **G3** 40
Cuddapah, India **G3** 40
Cuddy Mountain, mtn., Id., U.S. **E2** 105
Cue, Austl. **F2** 60
Cuenca, Ec. **D4** 70
Cuenca, Spain **G5** 16
Cuencamé de Ceniceros, Mex. **C4** 78
Cuernavaca, Mex. **D5** 78
Cuero, Tx., U.S. **E4** 136
Cuiabá, Braz. **G8** 70
Cuilo (Kwilu), stm., Afr. **E3** 54
Cuima, Ang. **A2** 56
Cuíto, stm., Ang. **B2** 56
Cuito Cuanavale, Ang. **B2** 56
Cuitzeo, Lago de, l., Mex. **D4** 78
Cuivre, West Fork, stm., Mo., U.S. **B6** 118
Cukai, Malay. **C2** 36
Čukotskij poluostrov, pen., Russia **C20** 26
Čulakkurgan, Kaz. **B9** 42
Culberson, co., Tx., U.S. **o12** 136
Culbertson, Mt., U.S. **B12** 119
Culbertson, Ne., U.S. **D5** 120
Culebra Peak, mtn., Co., U.S. **D5** 99
Culfa, Azer. **C11** 44
Culiacán, Mex. **C3** 78
Cullen, La., U.S. **B2** 111
Cullera, Spain **H6** 16
Cullman, Al., U.S. **A3** 94
Cullman, co., Al., U.S. **A3** 94
Culloden, W.V., U.S. **C2** 141
Cullowhee, N.C., U.S. **f9** 126
Čul'man, Russia **D14** 26
Culpeper, Va., U.S. **B4** 139
Culpeper, co., Va., U.S. **B5** 139
Culver, In., U.S. **B5** 107
Culver City, Ca., U.S. **m12** 98
Culvers Lake, l., N.J., U.S. **A3** 123
Čulym, Russia **D10** 26
Čulym, stm., Russia **D10** 26
Cumaná, Ven. **A7** 70
Cumberland, B.C., Can. **E5** 85
Cumberland, Ky., U.S. **D7** 110
Cumberland, Md., U.S. **k13** 113
Cumberland, Wi., U.S. **C2** 142
Cumberland, co., Il., U.S. **D5** 106
Cumberland, co., Ky., U.S. **D4** 110
Cumberland, co., Me., U.S. **E2** 112
Cumberland, co., N.C., U.S. **C4** 126
Cumberland, co., N.J., U.S. **E2** 123
Cumberland, co., Pa., U.S. **F7** 131
Cumberland, co., Tn., U.S. **D8** 135
Cumberland, co., Va., U.S. **C4** 139
Cumberland, stm., U.S. **D4** 110
Cumberland, Lake, res., Ky., U.S. **D5** 110
Cumberland Center, Me., U.S. **g7** 112
Cumberland Foreside, Me., U.S. **E2** 112
Cumberland Gap, U.S. **D6** 110
Cumberland Gap National Historical Park, U.S. **D6** 110
Cumberland Hill, R.I., U.S. **B4** 132
Cumberland Island National Seashore, Ga., U.S. **F5** 103
Cumberland Lake, l., Sk., Can. **C4** 91
Cumbres Pass, Co., U.S. **D4** 99
Čumikan, Russia **D15** 26
Cuming, co., Ne., U.S. **C9** 120
Cumming, Ga., U.S. **B2** 103
Çumra, Tur. **D5** 44
Cunani, Braz. **C9** 70
Čundža, Kaz. **B11** 42
Cunene (Kunene), stm., Afr. **B1** 56
Cuneo, Italy **B1** 18
Čunja, stm., Russia **C11** 26
Cunnamulla, Austl. **F4** 62
Cunningham, Ky., U.S. **f9** 110
Cupar, Sk., Can. **G3** 91
Curaçao, i., Neth. Ant. **C6** 80
Curanilahue, Chile **E2** 69
Čurapča, Russia **C15** 26
Curecanti National Recreation Area, Co., U.S. **C3** 99
Curepipe, Mrts. **g10** 57a
Curicó, Chile **D2** 69
Curitiba, Braz. **D8** 72
Curitibanos, Braz. **D7** 72
Curlew Creek, stm., Wa., U.S. **A7** 140
Curlew Lake, l., Wa., U.S. **A7** 140
Currais Novos, Braz. **C4** 74
Currant Mountain, mtn., Nv., U.S. **E6** 121
Current, stm., U.S. **A5** 97
Currituck, co., N.C., U.S. **A6** 126
Curry, co., N.M., U.S. **C6** 124
Curry, co., Or., U.S. **E2** 130
Curtea de Argeș, Rom. **G8** 20
Curtin Springs, Austl. **F5** 60
Curtis, Ne., U.S. **D5** 120
Curtis Island, i., Austl. **E5** 62
Curtisville, Pa., U.S. **E2** 131
Cururupu, Braz. **B3** 74
Curuzú Cuatiá, Arg. **D6** 72
Curvelo, Braz. **E3** 74
Curwensville, Pa., U.S. **E4** 131
Curwensville Lake, res., Pa., U.S. **E4** 131
Curwood, Mount, mtn., Mi., U.S. **B2** 115
Cusco, Peru **F5** 70
Cushing, Ok., U.S. **B5** 129
Cushman, Lake, res., Wa., U.S. **B2** 140
Čusovoj, Russia **C10** 22
Cusseta, Ga., U.S. **D2** 103
Custer, S.D., U.S. **D2** 134
Custer, co., Co., U.S. **C5** 99
Custer, co., Id., U.S. **E4** 105
Custer, co., Mt., U.S. **D11** 119
Custer, co., Ne., U.S. **C6** 120
Custer, co., Ok., U.S. **B2** 129
Custer, co., S.D., U.S. **D2** 134
Custer Battlefield National Monument, Mt., U.S. **E9** 119
Cut, Nuhu, i., Indon. **E8** 36
Cut Bank, Mt., U.S. **B4** 119
Cut Bank Creek, stm., N.D., U.S. **A4** 127
Cutchogue, N.Y., U.S. **m16** 125
Cuthbert, Ga., U.S. **E2** 103
Cutler Ridge, Fl., U.S. **s13** 102
Cut Off, La., U.S. **E5** 111
Cuttack, India **E5** 40
Cuttyhunk Island, i., Ma., U.S. **D6** 114
Čuvašija, state, Russia **D6** 26
Cuvier, Cape, c., Austl. **E1** 60
Cuxhaven, Ger. **D11** 12
Cuyahoga, co., Oh., U.S. **A4** 128
Cuyahoga, stm., Oh., U.S. **A4** 128
Cuyahoga Falls, Oh., U.S. **A4** 128
Cuyama, stm., Ca., U.S. **E4** 98
Cuyamaca Peak, mtn., Ca., U.S. **F5** 98
Cuyo Islands, is., Phil. **D8** 34
Cuyuni, stm., S.A. **D7** 80
C.W. McConaughy, Lake, res., Ne., U.S. **C4** 120
Cyclades see Kikládhes, is., Grc. **F10** 18
Cynthiana, In., U.S. **H2** 107
Cynthiana, Ky., U.S. **B5** 110
Cypress Creek, stm., Tx., U.S. **r14** 136
Cypress Hills Provincial Park, Sk., Can. **H1** 91
Cypress Lake, l., Fl., U.S. **D5** 102
Cypress Quarters, Fl., U.S. **E6** 102
Cypress Swamp, sw., U.S. **F4** 101
Cyprus, ctry., Asia **E5** 44
Cyprus, North see North Cyprus, ctry., Asia **E5** 44
Cyrenaica see Barqah, hist. reg., Libya **E8** 14
Cyril, Ok., U.S. **C3** 129
Cythera see Kíthira, i., Grc. **F9** 18
Cythnos see Kíthnos, i., Grc. **F10** 18
Czech Republic, ctry., Eur. **E3** 20
Częstochowa, Pol. **D5** 20

D

Dabajuro, Ven. **C5** 80
Dabeiba, Col. **D4** 80
Dabhoi, India **E2** 40
Dabie Shan, mts., China **E11** 28
Dabola, Gui. **D2** 50
Dabou, C. Iv. **E4** 50
Daboya, Ghana **E4** 50
Dacca see Dhaka, Bngl. **E6** 40
Dac Glei, Viet. **C5** 34
Dachau, Ger. **F12** 12
Dacono, Co., U.S. **A6** 99
Dacula, Ga., U.S. **C3** 103
Dade, co., Fl., U.S. **G6** 102
Dade, co., Ga., U.S. **B1** 103

Name | Map Ref. | Page

Dade, co., Mo., U.S. D4 118
Dade City, Fl., U.S. D4 102
Dadeville, Al., U.S. C4 94
Dādra and Nagar Haveli, prov., India E2 40
Dādu, Pak. E9 42
Daet, Phil. D8 34
Dafang, China D2 30
Dafeng, China C5 30
Daga Medo, Eth. B8 54
Dagana, Sen. C1 50
Dagestan, state, Russia E6 26
Dagestan see Altaj, state, Russia A5 28
Daggett, co., Ut., U.S. C6 137
Dagsboro, De., U.S. F5 101
Dagu, China B4 30
Daguan, China D1 30
Dagupan, Phil. C8 34
Da Hinggan Ling, mts., China B12 28
Dahlak Archipelago, is., Erit. G4 38
Dahlonega, Ga., U.S. B3 103
Dāhod, India E2 40
Dahomey see Benin, ctry., Afr. D5 50
Dahra, Libya E8 48
Dahūk, Iraq D10 44
Dailing, China A1 31
Daingerfield, Tx., U.S. C5 136
Dairen see Dalian, China D12 28
Dakar, Sen. D1 50
Dakhla, W. Sah. B1 50
Dākoānk, India H6 40
Dakoro, Niger D6 50
Dakota, co., Mn., U.S. F5 116
Dakota, co., Ne., U.S. B9 120
Dakota City, Ia., U.S. B3 108
Dakota City, Ne., U.S. B9 120
Đakovica, Yugo. C8 18
Đakovo, Cro. B7 18
Dalaba, Gui. D2 50
Dalälven, stm., Swe. F7 10
Dalandzadgad, Mong. C8 28
Dalarna, hist. reg., Swe. F6 10
Da Lat, Viet. D5 34
Dālbandin, Pak. E8 42
Dalby, Austl. F5 62
Dale, In., U.S. H4 107
Dale, co., Al., U.S. D4 94
Dale City, Va., U.S. B5 139
Dale Hollow Lake, res., U.S. C8 135
Daleville, Al., U.S. D4 94
Daleville, In., U.S. D6 107
Dalhart, Tx., U.S. A1 136
Dalhousie, N.B., Can. A3 87
Dalhousie, India C3 40
Dali, China F8 28
Dali, China C2 30
Dalian, China D12 28
Dall, Mount, mtn., Ak., U.S. f15 95
Dallam, co., Tx., U.S. A1 136
Dallas, Ga., U.S. C2 103
Dallas (part of Melcher), Ia., U.S. C4 108
Dallas, N.C., U.S. B1 126
Dallas, Or., U.S. C3 130
Dallas, Pa., U.S. D10 131
Dallas, Tx., U.S. C4 136
Dallas, co., Al., U.S. C2 94
Dallas, co., Ar., U.S. D3 97
Dallas, co., Ia., U.S. C3 108
Dallas, co., Mo., U.S. D4 118
Dallas, co., Tx., U.S. C4 136
Dallas Center, Ia., U.S. C4 108
Dallas City, Il., U.S. C2 106
Dallas Naval Air Station, mil., Tx., U.S. n9 136
Dallastown, Pa., U.S. G8 131
Dalli Rājhara, India E4 40
Dall Island, i., Ak., U.S. n23 95
Dalmacija, hist. reg., Eur. C6 18
Dalmatia see Dalmacija, hist. reg., Eur. C6 18
Dal'negorsk, Russia E15 26
Dal'nerečensk, Russia B14 28
Daloa, C. Iv. E3 50
Dalqū, Sudan F11 48
Dāltenganj, India E4 40
Dalton, Ga., U.S. B2 103
Dalton, Ma., U.S. B1 114
Dalton, Oh., U.S. B4 128
Dalton, Pa., U.S. C10 131
Dalton Gardens, Id., U.S. B2 105
Dalupiri Island, i., Phil. C8 34
Dalvík, Ice. l19 10a
Dalwallinu, Austl. G2 60
Daly, stm., Austl. C5 60
Daly City, Ca., U.S. h8 98
Daly Waters, Austl. D5 60
Damān, India E2 40
Damanhûr, Egypt E10 14
Damar, Pulau, i., Indon. E7 36
Damaraland, hist. reg., Nmb. C2 56
Damariscotta, Me., U.S. D3 112
Damariscotta Lake, l., Me., U.S. D3 112
Damascus see Dimashq, Syria F7 44
Damascus, Md., U.S. B3 113
Damascus, Va., U.S. f10 139
Damaturu, Nig. D7 50
Damāvand, Qolleh-ye, vol., Iran C6 42
Damba, Ang. E3 54
Dambarta, Nig. D6 50
Dāmghān, Iran C6 42
Damietta, Egypt E10 14
Damoh, India E3 40
Damongo, Ghana E4 50
Dampier, Austl. E2 60
Dampier, Selat, strt., Indon. D8 36
Dan, stm., U.S. D3 139
Dana, In., U.S. E3 107
Danakil, reg., Afr. H13 48
Danané, C. Iv. E3 50
Da Nang, Viet. C5 34
Danbury, Ct., U.S. D2 100
Danbury, Tx., U.S. r14 136
Dandeli, India F2 40
Dandong, China C12 28
Dandridge, Tn., U.S. C10 135
Dane, co., Wi., U.S. E4 142
Danfeng, China C3 30
Dangchang, China C1 30
Dangriga, Belize B2 80
Dangshan, China C4 30
Dania, Fl., U.S. F6 102
Daniels, co., Mt., U.S. B11 119
Danielson, Ct., U.S. B8 100
Daniels Pass, Ut., U.S. C4 137
Danilov, Russia C7 22
Danlí, Hond. C2 80
Dannemora, N.Y., U.S. f11 125
Dannevirke, N.Z. p14 63c
Dansville, N.Y., U.S. C3 125
Dante, Va., U.S. f9 139
Danube, stm., Eur. C9 14
Danube, Mouths of the, mth., Eur. G10 20
Danvers, Il., U.S. C4 106
Danvers, Ma., U.S. A6 114
Danville, P.Q., Can. D5 90
Danville, Ar., U.S. B2 97
Danville, Ca., U.S. h9 98
Danville, Ia., U.S. D6 108
Danville, Il., U.S. C6 106
Danville, In., U.S. E4 107
Danville, Ky., U.S. C5 110
Danville, Oh., U.S. B3 128
Danville, Pa., U.S. E8 131
Danville, Va., U.S. D3 139
Danxian, China F2 30
Danzig see Gdańsk, Pol. B5 20
Daocheng, China F8 28
Daoukro, C. Iv. E4 50
Daoxian, China D3 30
Dapaong, Togo D5 50
Dapchi, Nig. D7 50
Daphne, Al., U.S. E2 94
Da Qaidam, China D7 28
Dar'ā, Syria F7 44
Dārāb, Iran E6 42
Darabani, Rom. E9 20
Dārayyā, Syria F7 44
Darbhanga, India D5 40
Darby, Mt., U.S. D2 119
Darby, Pa., U.S. G11 131
Dardanelle, Ar., U.S. B2 97
Dardanelle Lake, res., Ar., U.S. B2 97
Dardanelles see Çanakkale Boğazı, strt., Tur. C1 44
Dare, co., N.C., U.S. B7 126
Darende, Tur. C7 44
Dar es Salaam, Tan. E7 54
Dargan-Ata, Turk. B8 42
Dargaville, N.Z. o13 63c
Darhan, Mong. B9 28
Darien, Ct., U.S. E2 100
Darien, Ga., U.S. E5 103
Darien, Wi., U.S. F5 142
Dārjiling, India D5 40
Darke, co., Oh., U.S. B1 128
Darlag, China E7 28
Darley Woods, De., U.S. h8 101
Darling, stm., Austl. G3 62
Darling, Lake, res., N.D., U.S. A4 127
Darling Range, mts., Austl. G2 60
Darlington, Eng., U.K. C6 12
Darlington, In., U.S. D4 107
Darlington, Md., U.S. A5 113
Darlington, S.C., U.S. C8 133
Darlington, Wi., U.S. F3 142
Darlington, co., S.C., U.S. C8 133
Darłowo, Pol. B4 20
Darmstadt, Ger. F11 12
Darnah, Libya D9 48
Darnley, Cape, c., Ant. C12 67
Darrah, Mount, mtn., Can. E3 84
Darreh Gaz, Iran C7 42
Darrington, Wa., U.S. A4 140
Dart, Cape, c., Ant. D27 67
Daru, Pap. N. Gui. H11 32
Darvaza, Turk. E7 26
Darwin, Austl. C5 60
Dašhovuz, Turk. E7 26
Dassel, Mn., U.S. E4 116
Dastgardān, Iran D7 42
Date, Japan B4 31
Datia, India D3 40
Datil Mountains, mts., N.M., U.S. C2 124
Datong, China C10 28
Datong, China B1 30
Datu, Tanjung, c., Asia C3 36
Daufuskie Island, i., S.C., U.S. G6 133
Daung Kyun, i., Myan. D3 34
Dauphin, Mb., Can. D1 86
Dauphin, co., Pa., U.S. F8 131
Dauphin, stm., Mb., Can. D2 86
Dauphin Island, Al., U.S. E1 94
Dauphin Island, i., Al., U.S. E1 94
Dauphin Lake, l., Mb., Can. D2 86
Dāvangere, India G3 40
Davao, Phil. E9 34
Davao Gulf, b., Phil. E9 34
Dāvarzan, Iran C7 42
Daveluyville, P.Q., Can. C5 90
Davenport, Fl., U.S. D5 102
Davenport, Ia., U.S. C7 108
Davenport, Ok., U.S. B5 129
Davenport, Wa., U.S. B7 140
David, Pan. D3 80
David City, Ne., U.S. C8 120
Davidson, N.C., U.S. B2 126
Davidson, co., N.C., U.S. B2 126
Davidson, co., Tn., U.S. A5 135
Davidsville, Pa., U.S. F4 131
Davie, Fl., U.S. F6 102
Davie, co., N.C., U.S. B2 126
Daviess, co., In., U.S. G3 107
Daviess, co., Ky., U.S. C2 110
Daviess, co., Mo., U.S. B3 118
Davis, Ca., U.S. C3 98
Davis, Ok., U.S. C4 129
Davis, W.V., U.S. B5 141
Davis, co., Ia., U.S. D5 108
Davis, co., Ut., U.S. C3 137
Davis, Mount, mtn., Pa., U.S. G3 131
Davis Creek, stm., W.V., U.S. m12 141
Davis Dam, U.S. H7 121
Davis Islands, is., Fl., U.S. p11 102
Davis Lake, l., Or., U.S. E5 130
Davis-Monthan Air Force Base, mil., Az., U.S. E5 96
Davison, Mi., U.S. E7 115
Davison, co., S.D., U.S. D7 134
Davis Sea, Ant. C13 67
Davisstræde see Davis Strait, strt., N.A. E28 82
Davis Strait, strt., N.A. E28 82
Davisville, R.I., U.S. E4 132
Dawa, stm., Afr. C7 54
Dawei, Myan. D3 34
Dawes, co., Ne., U.S. B2 120
Dawna Range, mts., Myan. C3 34
Daws Island, i., S.C., U.S. G6 133
Dawson, Ga., U.S. E2 103
Dawson, Mn., U.S. F2 116
Dawson, co., Ga., U.S. B2 103
Dawson, co., Mt., U.S. C11 119
Dawson, co., Ne., U.S. D6 120
Dawson, co., Tx., U.S. C1 136
Dawson, Isla, i., Chile H2 69
Dawson, Mount, mtn., B.C., Can. D9 85
Dawson Creek, B.C., Can. B7 85
Dawson Springs, Ky., U.S. C2 110
Dax, Fr. F6 16
Daxian, China E9 28
Daxing, China B4 30
Daxue Shan, mts., China E8 28
Day, co., S.D., U.S. B8 134
Dayao, China A4 34
Dayong, China D3 30
Dayr az-Zawr, Syria E9 44
Daysland, Ab., Can. C4 84
Dayton, Ia., U.S. B3 108
Dayton, In., U.S. D4 107
Dayton, Ky., U.S. h14 110
Dayton, Md., U.S. B4 113
Dayton, Mn., U.S. m12 116
Dayton, Nv., U.S. D2 121
Dayton, Oh., U.S. C1 128
Dayton, Or., U.S. B3 130
Dayton, Tn., U.S. D8 135
Dayton, Tx., U.S. D5 136
Dayton, Va., U.S. B4 139
Dayton, Wa., U.S. C8 140
Dayton, Wy., U.S. B5 143
Daytona Beach, Fl., U.S. C5 102
Dayu, China F10 28
Da Yunhe (Grand Canal), China D11 28
Dayville, Ct., U.S. B8 100
Dazhu, China C2 30
De Aar, S. Afr. E3 56
Dead, North Branch, stm., Me., U.S. C2 112
Dead, South Branch, stm., Me., U.S. C2 112
Dead Creek, stm., Vt., U.S. C2 138
Dead Diamond, stm., N.H., U.S. g7 122
Dead Indian Peak, mtn., Wy., U.S. B3 143
Dead Lake, l., Mn., U.S. D3 116
Dead Lakes, l., Fl., U.S. B1 102
Deadman Bay, b., Fl., U.S. C3 102
Deadman Creek, stm., Wa., U.S. g14 140
Dead Sea, l., Asia G6 44
Deadwood, S.D., U.S. C2 134
Deadwood Reservoir, res., Id., U.S. E3 105
Deaf Smith, co., Tx., U.S. B1 136
Deakin, Austl. G4 60
Deale, Md., U.S. C4 113
Deal Island, Md., U.S. D6 113
Deal Island, i., Md., U.S. D6 113
De'an, China D4 30
Dean, stm., B.C., Can. C4 85
Dean Channel, strt., B.C., Can. C4 85
Deán Funes, Arg. E5 72
Dearborn, Mi., U.S. F7 115
Dearborn, co., In., U.S. F7 107
Dearborn Heights, Mi., U.S. p15 115
Death Valley, val., Ca., U.S. D5 98
Death Valley National Park, U.S. D5 98
Deba, Nig. D7 50
De Baca, co., N.M., U.S. C5 124
Debao, China E2 30
De Bary, Fl., U.S. D5 102
Debauch Mountain, mtn., Ak., U.S. C8 95
Dęblin, Pol. D6 20
Debre Birhan, Eth. B7 54
Debrecen, Hung. F6 20
Debre Mark'os, Eth. A7 54
Debre Tabor, Eth. H3 38
Debre Zeyit, Eth. B7 54
De Cade, Lake, l., La., U.S. E5 111
Decatur, Al., U.S. A3 94
Decatur, Ar., U.S. A1 97
Decatur, Ga., U.S. C2 103
Decatur, Il., U.S. D5 106
Decatur, In., U.S. C8 107
Decatur, Mi., U.S. F5 115
Decatur, Ms., U.S. C4 117
Decatur, Ne., U.S. B9 120
Decatur, Tn., U.S. D9 135
Decatur, Tx., U.S. C4 136
Decatur, co., Ga., U.S. F2 103
Decatur, co., Ia., U.S. D4 108
Decatur, co., In., U.S. F6 107
Decatur, co., Ks., U.S. C3 109
Decatur, co., Tn., U.S. B3 135
Decatur, Lake, res., Il., U.S. D5 106
Decaturville, Tn., U.S. B3 135
Decazeville, Fr. E8 16
Deccan, plat., India G3 40
Deception, Mount, mtn., Wa., U.S. B2 140
Decherd, Tn., U.S. B5 135
Děčín, Czech Rep. D3 20
Decize, Fr. D8 16
Deckerville, Mi., U.S. E8 115
Decorah, Ia., U.S. A6 108
Dedham, Ma., U.S. B5 114
Dedoplis Ckaro, Geor. B12 44
Dédougou, Burkina D4 50
Deep, stm., N.C., U.S. B3 126
Deep Creek, stm., Ut., U.S. F3 137
Deep Creek, stm., Ut., U.S. B3 137
Deep Creek, stm., Ut., U.S. C2 137
Deep Creek, stm., Wa., U.S. g13 140
Deep Creek Lake, res., Md., U.S. K12 113
Deep Creek Mountains, mts., Id., U.S. G6 105
Deep Fork, stm., Ok., U.S. B5 129
Deep Inlet, b., Nf., Can. g10 88
Deep Red Creek, stm., Ok., U.S. C3 129
Deep River, On., Can. A7 89
Deep River, Ct., U.S. D6 100
Deer Creek, stm., Oh., U.S. C2 128
Deer Creek Indian Reservation, Mn., U.S. C5 116
Deerfield, Il., U.S. h9 106
Deerfield, Ks., U.S. E2 109
Deerfield, Ma., U.S. A2 114
Deerfield, Mi., U.S. G7 115
Deerfield, Wi., U.S. E4 142
Deerfield, stm., U.S. A2 114
Deerfield Beach, Fl., U.S. F6 102
Deer Island, pen., Ma., U.S. g12 114
Deer Island, i., Ms., U.S. f8 117
Deer Isle, i., Me., U.S. D4 112
Deer Lake, Nf., Can. D3 88
Deer Lake, l., Nf., Can. D3 88
Deer Lake, l., Mn., U.S. C5 116
Deer Lodge, Mt., U.S. D4 119
Deer Lodge, co., Mt., U.S. E3 119
Deer Park, N.Y., U.S. n15 125
Deer Park, Oh., U.S. o13 128
Deer Park, Wa., U.S. B8 140
Deer Peak, mtn., Co., U.S. C5 99
Deer River, Mn., U.S. C5 116
Defiance, Oh., U.S. A1 128
Defiance, co., Oh., U.S. A1 128
Defiance, Mount, mtn., Or., U.S. B5 130
De Forest, Wi., U.S. E4 142
De Funiak Springs, Fl., U.S. u15 102
Dêgê, China E7 28
Degeh Bur, Eth. B8 54
Dégelis, P.Q., Can. B9 90
Degerfors, Swe. G6 10
De Graff, Oh., U.S. B2 128
De Gray Lake, res., Ar., U.S. C2 97
Dehiwala-Mount Lavinia, Sri L. H3 40
Dehlorān, Iran F12 44
Dehra Dūn, India C3 40
Dehui, China C13 28
Dej, Rom. F7 20
Dejnau, Turk. C8 42
De Kalb, Il., U.S. B5 106
De Kalb, Ms., U.S. C5 117
De Kalb, Tx., U.S. C5 136
De Kalb, co., Al., U.S. A4 94
De Kalb, co., Ga., U.S. C2 103
De Kalb, co., Il., U.S. B5 106
De Kalb, co., In., U.S. B7 107
De Kalb, co., Mo., U.S. B3 118
De Kalb, co., Tn., U.S. D8 135
Dekese, D.R.C. D4 54
Delafield, Wi., U.S. m11 142
Delanco, N.J., U.S. C3 123
De Land, Fl., U.S. C5 102
Delano, Ca., U.S. E4 98
Delano, Mn., U.S. E5 116
Delano Peak, mtn., Ut., U.S. E3 137
Delārām, Afg. D8 42
Delaronde Lake, l., Sk., Can. C2 91
Delavan, Il., U.S. C4 106
Delavan, Wi., U.S. F5 142
Delaware, Oh., U.S. B2 128
Delaware, co., Ia., U.S. B6 108
Delaware, co., In., U.S. D7 107
Delaware, co., N.Y., U.S. C5 125
Delaware, co., Oh., U.S. B2 128
Delaware, co., Ok., U.S. A7 129
Delaware, co., Pa., U.S. G11 131
Delaware, state, U.S. D3 101
Delaware, stm., Ks., U.S. C8 109
Delaware, stm., U.S. G11 131
Delaware, East Branch, stm., N.Y., U.S. C5 125
Delaware Bay, b., U.S. D13 92
Delaware City, De., U.S. B3 101
Delaware Lake, res., Oh., U.S. B3 128
Delaware Water Gap, N.J., U.S. B2 123
Delaware Water Gap National Recreation Area, U.S. B2 123
Delbarton, W.V., U.S. D2 141
Delcambre, La., U.S. E4 111
Del City, Ok., U.S. B4 129
De Leon, Tx., U.S. C3 136
De Leon Springs, Fl., U.S. C5 102
Delfzijl, Neth. D10 12
Delgado, Cabo, c., Moz. A7 56
Delhi, India D3 40
Delhi, La., U.S. B4 111
Delhi, N.Y., U.S. C6 125
Delice, stm., Tur. B6 44
Delicias, Mex. B3 78
Delingde, Russia B13 26
Delingha, China D7 28
De Lisle, Ms., U.S. E4 117
Dellenbaugh, Mount, mtn., Az., U.S. A2 96
Dell Rapids, S.D., U.S. D9 134
Dellys, Alg. I8 16
Del Mar, Ca., U.S. o15 98
Delmar, De., U.S. G3 101
Delmar, Md., U.S. D6 113
Delmar, N.Y., U.S. C7 125
Delmenhorst, Ger. D11 12
Del Norte, Co., U.S. D4 99
Del Norte, co., Ca., U.S. B2 98
Deloraine, Mb., Can. E1 86
Delos see Dhílos, hist., Grc. F10 18
Del Park Manor, De., U.S. i7 101
Delphi, In., U.S. C4 107
Delphi see Dhelfoí, hist., Grc. E9 18
Delphos, Oh., U.S. B1 128
Delran, N.J., U.S. C3 123
Delray Beach, Fl., U.S. F6 102
Del Rio, Tx., U.S. E2 136
Delson, P.Q., Can. q19 90
Delta, Co., U.S. C2 99
Delta, Oh., U.S. A2 128
Delta, Ut., U.S. D3 137
Delta, co., Co., U.S. C3 99
Delta, co., Mi., U.S. C3 115
Delta, co., Tx., U.S. C5 136
Delta, reg., Ms., U.S. B3 117
Delta Junction, Ak., U.S. C10 95
Delta Peak, mtn., B.C., Can. A3 85
Delta Reservoir, res., N.Y., U.S. B5 125
Deltaville, Va., U.S. C6 139
Deltona, Fl., U.S. D5 102
Del Verme Falls, wtfl, Eth. B8 54
Demarest, N.J., U.S. h9 123
Demba, D.R.C. E4 54
Dembia, C.A.R. B4 54
Dembī Dolo, Eth. B6 54
Demidov, Russia B11 20
Deming, N.M., U.S. E2 124
Demirci, Tur. C3 44
Demjanskoe, Russia D8 26
Demmin, Ger. D13 12
Democratic Republic of the Congo see Congo, Democratic Republic of the, ctry., Afr. D4 52
Demopolis, Al., U.S. C2 94
Demorest, Ga., U.S. B3 103
Demotte, In., U.S. B3 107
Dempo, Gunung, vol., Indon. D2 36
Demta, Indon. G11 32
Denakil see Danakil, reg., Afr. H13 48
Denali National Park, Ak., U.S. C9 95
Denan, Eth. B8 54
Denare Beach, Sk., Can. C4 91

Name — Map Ref. — Page

Denau, Uzb. F8 26
Dengas, Niger D6 50
Dengkou, China A2 30
Dêngqên, China E7 28
Dengxian, China C3 30
Denham, Austl. F1 60
Denham, Mount, mtn., Jam. B4 80
Denham Springs, La., U.S. D5 111
Den Helder, Neth. D9 12
Dénia, Spain H7 16
Deniliquin, Austl. H4 62
Denison, Ia., U.S. B2 108
Denison, Tx., U.S. C4 136
Denison Dam, U.S. D5 129
Denizli, Tur. D3 44
Denmark, Austl. G2 60
Denmark, S.C., U.S. E5 133
Denmark, Wi., U.S. D6 142
Denmark, ctry., Eur. I4 10
Denmark Strait, strt. E34 82
Dennehotso, Az., U.S. A6 96
Dennis, Ma., U.S. C7 114
Dennison, Oh., U.S. B4 128
Dennis Port, Ma., U.S. C7 114
Denny Terrace, S.C., U.S. C5 133
Denpasar, Indon. E5 36
Dent, co., Mo., U.S. D6 118
Denton, Md., U.S. C6 113
Denton, N.C., U.S. B2 126
Denton, Tx., U.S. C4 136
Denton, co., Tx., U.S. C4 136
D'Entrecasteaux, Point, c., Austl. G2 60
D'Entrecasteaux Islands, is., Pap. N. Gui. H13 32
Dentsville, S.C., U.S. C6 133
Denver, Co., U.S. B6 99
Denver, Ia., U.S. B5 108
Denver, Pa., U.S. F9 131
Denver, co., Co., U.S. B6 99
Denver City, Tx., U.S. C1 136
Denville, N.J., U.S. B4 123
Deoghar, India E5 40
Deolāli, India F2 40
De Pere, Wi., U.S. D5 142
Depew, N.Y., U.S. C2 125
Depoe Bay, Or., U.S. C2 130
Deposit, N.Y., U.S. C5 125
Depue, Il., U.S. B4 106
Dêqên, China F7 28
Deqing, China E3 30
De Queen, Ar., U.S. C1 97
De Queen Reservoir, res., Ar., U.S. C1 97
De Quincy, La., U.S. D2 111
Dera Ghāzi Khān, Pak. E10 42
Dera Ismāīl Khān, Pak. D10 42
Derbent, Russia E6 26
Derby, Austl. D3 60
Derby, Eng., U.K. D6 12
Derby, Ct., U.S. D3 100
Derby, Ks., U.S. E6 109
Derby, Vt., U.S. B4 138
Derby Line, Vt., U.S. A4 138
Derg, Lough, l., Ire. D2 12
Dergači, Russia D8 22
De Ridder, La., U.S. D2 111
Derik, Tur. D9 44
Derma, Ms., U.S. B4 117
Dermott, Ar., U.S. D4 97
Dernieres, Isles, is., La., U.S. E5 111
Derry see Londonderry, N. Ire., U.K. C3 12
Derry, N.H., U.S. E4 122
Derry, Pa., U.S. F3 131
Derventa, Bos. B6 18
Derwood, Md., U.S. B3 113
Des Allemands, La., U.S. E5 111
Désappointement, Îles du, is., Fr. Poly. F15 58
Des Arc, Ar., U.S. C4 97
Desbiens, P.Q., Can. A6 90
Descanso, Mex. A1 78
Deschaillons [-sur-Saint-Laurent], P.Q., Can. C5 90
Deschambault, P.Q., Can. C6 90
Deschambault Lake, l., Sk., Can. C4 91
Deschutes, co., Or., U.S. D5 130
Deschutes, stm., Or., U.S. B6 130
Desē, Eth. H12 48
Deseado, stm., Arg. G3 69
Desengaño, Punta, c., Arg. G3 69
Deseret Peak, mtn., Ut., U.S. C3 137
Deseronto, On., Can. C7 89
Desert Creek Peak, mtn., Nv., U.S. E2 121
Desert Hot Springs, Ca., U.S. F5 98
Desert Peak, mtn., Ut., U.S. B2 137
Desert Valley, val., Nv., U.S. B3 121
Desha, Ar., U.S. B4 97
Desha, co., Ar., U.S. D4 97
Deshler, Ne., U.S. D8 120
Deshler, Oh., U.S. A2 128
Des Lacs, stm., N.D., U.S. A4 127
Desloge, Mo., U.S. D7 118
De Smet, S.D., U.S. C8 134
Des Moines, Ia., U.S. C4 108
Des Moines, Wa., U.S. B3 140
Des Moines, co., Ia., U.S. D6 108
Des Moines, stm., U.S. D5 108
Desna, stm., Eur. D11 20
De Soto, Ia., U.S. C3 108
De Soto, Il., U.S. F4 106
De Soto, Ks., U.S. D9 109
De Soto, Mo., U.S. C7 118
De Soto, co., Fl., U.S. E5 102
De Soto, co., La., U.S. B2 111
De Soto, co., Ms., U.S. A3 117
Despard, W.V., U.S. k10 141
Des Peres, Mo., U.S. f13 118
Des Plaines, Il., U.S. A6 106
Des Plaines, stm., U.S. k8 106
Desroches, i., Sey. i12 57b
Dessau, Ger. E13 12
Destin, Fl., U.S. u15 102
Destrehan, La., U.S. E5 111
Detour, Point, c., Mi., U.S. C4 115
Detroit, Mi., U.S. F7 115
Detroit Lake, res., Or., U.S. C4 130
Detroit Lakes, Mn., U.S. D3 116
Dettifoss, wtfl, Ice. I20 10a
Deuel, co., Ne., U.S. C3 120
Deuel, co., S.D., U.S. C9 134
Deutsche Bucht, b., Ger. C10 12
Deux-Montagnes, P.Q., Can. p19 90
Deux Montagnes, Lac des, l., P.Q., Can. q19 90
Deva, Rom. G7 20
De Valls Bluff, Ar., U.S. C4 97
Develi, Tur. C6 44
Deventer, Neth. D10 12
DeView, Bayou, stm., Ar., U.S. B4 97
Devils Island see Diable, Île du, i., Fr. Gu. B9 70
Devils Lake, N.D., U.S. A7 127
Devils Lake, l., N.D., U.S. A6 127
Devils Paw, mtn., Ak., U.S. k23 95
Devils Postpile National Monument, Ca., U.S. D4 98
Devils Tower National Monument, Wy., U.S. B8 143
Devil Track Lake, l., Mn., U.S. k9 116
Devine, Tx., U.S. E3 136
DeVola, Oh., U.S. C4 128
Devon, Ab., Can. C4 84
Devonport, Austl. I4 62
Devonshire, De., U.S. h7 101
Devrek, Tur. B4 44
Dewar, Ok., U.S. B6 129
Dewās, India E3 40
Dewees Inlet, b., S.C., U.S. k12 133
Dewees Island, i., S.C., U.S. F8 133
Dewey, Az., U.S. C3 96
Dewey, Ok., U.S. A6 129
Dewey, co., Ok., U.S. B2 129
Dewey, co., S.D., U.S. B4 134
Dewey Beach, De., U.S. F5 101
Dewey Lake, res., Ky., U.S. C7 110
Deweyville, Tx., U.S. D6 136
De Witt, Ar., U.S. C4 97
De Witt, Ia., U.S. C7 108
De Witt, Mi., U.S. F6 115
De Witt, N.Y., U.S. B4 125
De Witt, co., Il., U.S. C4 106
De Witt, co., Tx., U.S. E4 136
Dexing, China D4 30
Dexter, Ia., U.S. C3 108
Dexter, Me., U.S. C3 112
Dexter, Mi., U.S. F7 115
Dexter, Mo., U.S. E8 118
Dexter, N.M., U.S. D5 124
Dexter, Lake, l., Fl., U.S. C5 102
Dezfūl, Iran D5 42
Dezhou, China D11 28
Dežneva, mys, c., Russia C21 26
Dhahran see Az-Zahrān, Sau. Ar. E5 42
Dhaka, Bngl. E6 40
Dhamtari, India E4 40
Dhanbād, India E5 40
Dhār, India E3 40
Dharān, Nepal D5 40
Dharmapuri, India G3 40
Dhawalāgiri, mtn., Nepal D4 40
Dhelfoí, hist., Grc. E9 18
Dhenkānāl, India E5 40
Dhílos, hist., Grc. F10 18
Dhodhekánisos, is., Grc. F11 18
Dhone, India F3 40
Dhoomadheere, Som. C8 54
Dhorāji, India E2 40
Dhuburi, India D5 40
Dhule, India E2 40
Diable, Île du, i., Fr. Gu. B9 70
Diablo, Canyon, val., Az., U.S. C4 96
Diablo, Mount, mtn., Ca., U.S. h9 98
Diablo, Pico del, mtn., Mex. A1 78
Diablo Dam, Wa., U.S. A4 140
Diablo Lake, res., Wa., U.S. A4 140
Diablo Range, mts., Ca., U.S. D3 98
Diablotins, Morne, vol., Dom. B7 80
Diaca, Moz. A6 56
Dialakoto, Sen. D2 50
Diamante, Arg. C4 72
Diamantina, Braz. E3 74
Diamantina, stm., Austl. E3 62
Diamantino, Braz. F8 70
Diamond Harbour, India E5 40
Diamond Head, crat., Hi., U.S. B4 104
Diamond Hill, R.I., U.S. B4 132
Diamond Hill Reservoir, res., R.I., U.S. A4 132
Diamond Lake, Il., U.S. h9 106
Diamond Lake, l., Or., U.S. D4 130
Diamond Mountains, mts., Nv., U.S. D6 121
Diamond Peak, mtn., Co., U.S. A2 99
Diamond Peak, mtn., Id., U.S. E5 105
Diamond Peak, mtn., Or., U.S. D4 130
Diamond Peak, mtn., Wa., U.S. C8 140
Diamondville, Wy., U.S. E2 143
Dianbai, China E3 30
Dianjiang, China C2 30
Dianópolis, Braz. F10 70
Diapaga, Burkina D5 50
Diaz, Ar., U.S. B4 97
Dibaya, D.R.C. E4 54
D'Iberville, Ms., U.S. E5 117
Diboll, Tx., U.S. D5 136
Dibrugarh, India D6 40
Dickens, co., Tx., U.S. C2 136
Dickenson, co., Va., U.S. e9 139
Dickerson, Md., U.S. B3 113
Dickey, co., N.D., U.S. C7 127
Dickeyville, Wi., U.S. F3 142
Dickinson, N.D., U.S. C3 127
Dickinson, co., Ia., U.S. A2 108
Dickinson, co., Ks., U.S. D6 109
Dickinson, co., Mi., U.S. B3 115
Dickinson Dam, N.D., U.S. C3 127
Dickson, Ok., U.S. C5 129
Dickson, Tn., U.S. A4 135
Dickson, co., Tn., U.S. A4 135
Dickson City, Pa., U.S. D10 131
Dicle see Tigris, stm., Asia D5 42
Didao, China A2 31
Didbiran, Russia D15 26
Didsbury, Ab., Can. D3 84
Dīdwāna, India D2 40
Diefenbaker, Lake, res., Sk., Can. F2 91
Diego de Almagro, Isla, i., Chile H1 69
Diégo-Suarez see Antsirañana, Madag. A8 56
Diéma, Mali D3 50
Dien Bien, Viet. B4 34
Diepholz, Ger. D11 12
Dieppe, N.B., Can. C5 87
Dieppe, Fr. C7 16
Dierks, Ar., U.S. C1 97
Di'er Songhua see Songhua, stm., China B14 28
Dif, Kenya C8 54
Diffa, Niger D7 50
Dighton, Ks., U.S. D3 109
Digne, Fr. E10 16
Digos, Phil. E9 34
Digul, stm., Indon. H10 32
Diinsor, Som. C8 54
Dijlah see Tigris, stm., Asia D5 42
Dijon, Fr. D9 16
Dike, Ia., U.S. B5 108
Dikhil, Dji. H13 48
Dikili, Tur. C2 44
Dikson, Russia B10 26
Dikwa, Nig. D7 50
Dīla, Eth. B7 54
Dili, Indon. E7 36
Dillard, Or., U.S. D3 130
Dill City, Ok., U.S. B2 129
Dilley, Tx., U.S. E3 136
Dillingham, Ak., U.S. D8 95
Dillon, Mt., U.S. E4 119
Dillon, S.C., U.S. C9 133
Dillon, co., S.C., U.S. C9 133
Dillon Lake, res., Oh., U.S. B3 128
Dillon Reservoir, res., Co., U.S. B4 99
Dillonvale, Oh., U.S. B5 128
Dillsboro, In., U.S. F7 107
Dillsburg, Pa., U.S. F7 131
Dilolo, D.R.C. F4 54
Dilworth, Mn., U.S. D2 116
Dimāpur, India D6 40
Dimashq (Damascus), Syria F7 44
Dimbokro, C. Iv. E4 50
Dimitrovgrad, Bul. C10 18
Dimitrovgrad, Russia D6 26
Dimlang, mtn., Nig. E7 50
Dimmit, co., Tx., U.S. E3 136
Dimmitt, Tx., U.S. B1 136
Dimondale, Mi., U.S. F6 115
Dinagat Island, i., Phil. D9 34
Dinājpur, Bngl. D5 40
Dinan, Fr. C5 16
Dinar, Tur. C4 44
Dinaric Alps, mts., Eur. G4 20
Dindigul, India G3 40
Dinghai, China E12 28
Dingle Bay, b., Ire. D1 12
Dingmans Ferry, Pa., U.S. D12 131
Dingolfing, Ger. F13 12
Dingtao, China B4 30
Dinguiraye, Gui. D2 50
Dingxiang, China B3 30
Dingxing, China B4 30
Dinner Point, c., Fl., U.S. D4 102
Dinokwe, Bots. C4 56
Dinosaur National Monument, U.S. C6 137
Dinuba, Ca., U.S. D4 98
Dinwiddie, co., Va., U.S. C5 139
Dioura, Mali D3 50
Diourbel, Sen. D1 50
Dipolog, Phil. E8 34
Dīr, Pak. C10 42
Diré, Mali C4 50
Dirē Dawa, Eth. B8 54
Dirico, Ang. B3 56
Dirj, Libya E6 14
Dirk Hartog Island, i., Austl. F1 60
Dirkou, Niger C7 50
Dirty Devil, stm., Ut., U.S. E5 137
Disappointment, Cape, c., S. Geor. H9 69
Disappointment, Cape, c., Wa., U.S. C1 140
Disappointment, Lake, l., Austl. E3 60
Dishman, Wa., U.S. g14 140
Disko, i., Grnld. E28 82
Dismal, stm., Ne., U.S. C5 120
Dispur, India D6 40
Disraëli, P.Q., Can. D6 90
District of Columbia, dept., U.S. f8 113
Distrito Federal, state, Braz. E2 74
Distrito Federal, state, Mex. D5 78
Diu, India E2 40
Dīvāndarreh, Iran E12 44
Divernon, Il., U.S. D4 106
Divide, co., N.D., U.S. A2 127
Divide Peak, mtn., Wy., U.S. E5 143
Divinópolis, Braz. F3 74
Divisor, Serra do, plat., S.A. E5 70
Divnoe, Russia A4 42
Divo, C. Iv. E3 50
Divriği, Tur. C8 44
Dix, stm., Ky., U.S. C5 110
Dixfield, Me., U.S. D2 112
Dixie, co., Fl., U.S. C3 102
Dixie Valley, val., Nv., U.S. D4 121
Dixon, Ca., U.S. C3 98
Dixon, Il., U.S. B4 106
Dixon, Mo., U.S. D5 118
Dixon, N.M., U.S. A4 124
Dixon, co., Ne., U.S. B9 120
Dixon Entrance, strt., N.A. H13 82
Dixonville, Pa., U.S. E3 131
Diyarbakır, Tur. D9 44
Djado, Plateau du, plat., Niger B7 50
Djamâa, Alg. E5 14
Djambala, Congo D2 54
Djanet, Alg. B6 50
Djat'kovo, Russia C13 20
Djemila, hist., Alg. I9 16
Djenné, Mali D4 50
Djibo, Burkina D4 50
Djibouti, Dji. H13 48
Djibouti, ctry., Afr. H13 48
Djoku-Punda, D.R.C. E4 54
Djougou, Benin E5 50
Djoum, Cam. C2 54
Djugu, D.R.C. C6 54
Djurtjuli, Russia C9 22
Dmitrija Lapteva, proliv, strt., Russia B16 26
Dmitrijev-L'govskij, Russia C13 20
Dnepropetrovsk see Dnipropetrovs'k, Ukr. E13 20
Dnestr see Dniester, stm., Eur. F11 20
Dnieper (Dnepr) (Dnipro), stm., Eur. F12 20
Dniester (Nistru) (Dnister), stm., Eur. F11 20
Dniprodzerzhyns'k, Ukr. E13 20
Dniprodzerzhyns'ke vodoskhovyshche, res., Ukr. E13 20
Dnipropetrovs'k, Ukr. E13 20
Dnister see Dniester, stm., Eur. F11 20
Dno, Russia C5 22
Dôa, Moz. B5 56
Doaktown, N.B., Can. C3 87
Doba, Chad E8 50
Dobbs Ferry, N.Y., U.S. g13 125
Dobele, Lat. H10 10
Doberai, Jazirah, pen., Indon. D8 36
Dobo, Indon. H9 32
Doboj, Bos. B7 18
Dobrič, Bul. C11 18
Dobrjanka, Russia C10 22
Dobruja, hist. reg., Eur. H9 20
Dobson, N.C., U.S. A2 126
Doce, stm., Braz. E3 74
Docena, Al., U.S. f7 94
Doctors Lake, l., Fl., U.S. m8 102
Doddridge, co., W.V., U.S. B4 141
Dodecanese see Dhodhekánisos, is., Grc. F11 18
Dodge, Ne., U.S. C9 120
Dodge, co., Ga., U.S. D3 103
Dodge, co., Mn., U.S. G6 116
Dodge, co., Ne., U.S. C9 120
Dodge, co., Wi., U.S. E5 142
Dodge Center, Mn., U.S. F6 116
Dodge City, Ks., U.S. E3 109
Dodgeville, Wi., U.S. F3 142
Dodoma, Tan. E7 54
Doerun, Ga., U.S. E3 103
Doe Run, Mo., U.S. D7 118
Dog, stm., Vt., U.S. C3 138
Dogai Coring, l., China E5 28
Dog Island, i., Fl., U.S. C2 102
Dog Keys Pass, strt., Ms., U.S. g8 117
Dog Lake, l., Mb., Can. D2 86
Do Gonbadān, Iran D6 42
Dogondoutchi, Niger D5 50
Doğubayazıt, Tur. C11 44
Doğu Karadeniz Dağları, mts., Tur. B8 44
Doha see Ad-Dawḥah, Qatar E6 42
Dokka, Nor. F4 10
Dokuchaievs'k, Ukr. F14 20
Dolbeau, P.Q., Can. k12 90
Dole, Fr. D9 16
Dolgeville, N.Y., U.S. B6 125
Dolinsk, Russia B16 28
Dollar Bay, Mi., U.S. A2 115
Dolomite, Al., U.S. B3 94
Dolomites see Dolomiti, mts., Italy A3 18
Dolomiti, mts., Italy A3 18
Dolores, Arg. E6 72
Dolores, Co., U.S. D2 99
Dolores, Ur. F6 72
Dolores, co., Co., U.S. D2 99
Dolores, stm., U.S. E7 137
Dolphin Island, i., Ut., U.S. B3 137
Dolton, Il., U.S. k9 106
Dolyns'ka, Ukr. E12 20
Dombås, Nor. E3 10
Dome Mountain, mtn., Az., U.S. k9 96
Dome Peak, mtn., Co., U.S. B3 99
Domeyko, Chile C2 69
Dominica, ctry., N.A. E12 76
Dominican Republic, ctry., N.A. H12 75
Dominique, Canal de la see Martinique Passage, strt., N.A. B7 80
Domo, Eth. I14 48
Dom Pedrito, Braz. E7 72
Don, stm., Russia E6 26
Dona Ana, N.M., U.S. E3 124
Dona Ana, co., N.M., U.S. E2 124
Donaldsonville, La., U.S. D4 111
Donalsonville, Ga., U.S. E2 103
Donau see Danube, stm., Eur. C9 14
Donauwörth, Ger. F12 12
Don Benito, Spain H4 16
Dondo, Ang. E2 54
Dondo, Moz. B5 56
Dondra Head, c., Sri L. H4 40
Donegal, Ire. C2 12
Donegal Bay, b., Ire. C2 12
Doneraile, S.C., U.S. C8 133
Donets'k, Ukr. F14 20
Dong, stm., China B7 34
Dong'an, China D3 30
Dongara, Austl. F1 60
Dongchuan, China D1 30
Dongfang, China H9 28
Donggala, Indon. D5 36
Donghai Dao, i., China G10 28
Dong Hoi, Viet. C5 34
Dongjingcheng, China B1 31
Dongo, Ang. A2 56
Dongping, China B4 30
Dongsheng, China B3 30
Dongtai, China C5 30
Dongting Hu, l., China F10 28
Dongzhi, China C4 30
Doniphan, Mo., U.S. E7 118
Doniphan, Ne., U.S. D7 120
Doniphan, co., Ks., U.S. C8 109
Donkey Creek, stm., Wy., U.S. B7 143
Donkin, N.S., Can. C10 87
Donley, co., Tx., U.S. B2 136
Dønna, Nor. C5 10
Donna, Tx., U.S. F3 136
Donnacona, P.Q., Can. C6 90
Donnellson, Ia., U.S. D6 108
Donner Pass, Ca., U.S. C3 98
Donnybrook, Austl. G2 60
Donora, Pa., U.S. F2 131
Donostia (San Sebastián), Spain F6 16
Donskaja grjada, hills, Eur. E7 22
Don Upland see Donskaja grjada, hills, Eur. E7 22
Doolow, Som. J13 48
Dooly, co., Ga., U.S. D3 103
Doonerak, Mount, mtn., Ak., U.S. B9 95
Door, co., Wi., U.S. D6 142
Dora, Al., U.S. B2 94
Doraville, Ga., U.S. h8 103
Dorcheat, Bayou, stm., U.S. B2 111
Dorchester, N.B., Can. D5 87
Dorchester, Eng., U.K. E5 12
Dorchester, Ne., U.S. D8 120
Dorchester, co., Md., U.S. D5 113
Dorchester, co., S.C., U.S. E7 133
Dordogne, stm., Fr. E7 16
Dordrecht, Neth. E9 12
Doré Lake, l., Sk., Can. C2 91

Name — Map Ref. — Page

Dorena Lake, res., Or., U.S. **D3** 130
Dori, Burkina **D4** 50
Dorion-Vaudreuil, P.Q., Can. **q18** 90
Dormont, Pa., U.S. **k13** 131
Dornbirn, Aus. **G11** 12
Dorogobuž, Russia **B12** 20
Dorohoi, Rom. **F9** 20
Dorothy Pond, Ma., U.S. **B4** 114
Dorr, Mi., U.S. **F5** 115
Dorre Island, i., Austl. **F1** 60
Dorset, Vt., U.S. **E2** 138
Dorsey, Md., U.S. **B4** 113
Dortmund, Ger. **E10** 12
Dorton, Ky., U.S. **C7** 110
Dörtyol, Tur. **D7** 44
Do Rūd, Iran **D5** 42
Doruma, D.R.C. **C5** 54
Dorval, P.Q., Can. **q19** 90
Dosatuj, Russia **D13** 26
Dos Bahías, Cabo, c., Arg. **G3** 69
Dosso, Niger **D5** 50
Dossor, Kaz. **E9** 22
Dothan, Al., U.S. **D4** 94
Douala, Cam. **C1** 54
Douarnenez, Fr. **C4** 16
Double Beach, Ct., U.S. **D4** 100
Double Island Point, c., Austl. **F5** 62
Doublespring Pass, Id., U.S. **E5** 105
Double Springs, Al., U.S. **A2** 94
Doubletop Peak, mtn., Wy., U.S. **C2** 143
Doubs, stm., Eur. **D9** 16
Douentza, Mali **C4** 50
Dougherty, co., Ga., U.S. **E2** 103
Douglas, I. of Man **C4** 12
Douglas, S. Afr. **D3** 56
Douglas, Az., U.S. **F6** 96
Douglas, Ga., U.S. **E4** 103
Douglas, Mi., U.S. **F4** 115
Douglas, Wy., U.S. **D7** 143
Douglas, co., Co., U.S. **B6** 99
Douglas, co., Ga., U.S. **C2** 103
Douglas, co., Il., U.S. **D5** 106
Douglas, co., Ks., U.S. **D8** 109
Douglas, co., Mn., U.S. **E3** 116
Douglas, co., Mo., U.S. **E5** 118
Douglas, co., Ne., U.S. **C9** 120
Douglas, co., Nv., U.S. **E2** 121
Douglas, co., Or., U.S. **D3** 130
Douglas, co., S.D., U.S. **D7** 134
Douglas, co., Wa., U.S. **B6** 140
Douglas, co., Wi., U.S. **B2** 142
Douglas, Mount, mtn., Ak., U.S. **D9** 95
Douglas Channel, strt., B.C., Can. **C3** 85
Douglas Lake, l., Mi., U.S. **C6** 115
Douglas Lake, res., Tn., U.S. **D10** 135
Douglass, Ks., U.S. **E7** 109
Douglastown, N.B., Can. **B4** 87
Douglasville, Ga., U.S. **C2** 103
Dourados, Braz. **H9** 70
Dourbali, Chad **D8** 50
Douro (Duero), stm., Eur. **G2** 16
Dousman, Wi., U.S. **E5** 142
Dove Creek, Co., U.S. **D2** 99
Dover, Eng., U.K. **E7** 12
Dover, Ar., U.S. **B2** 97
Dover, De., U.S. **D3** 101
Dover, Fl., U.S. **D4** 102
Dover, Ma., U.S. **h10** 114
Dover, N.H., U.S. **D5** 122
Dover, N.J., U.S. **B3** 123
Dover, Oh., U.S. **B4** 128
Dover, Pa., U.S. **F8** 131
Dover, Tn., U.S. **A4** 135
Dover, Strait of, strt., Eur. **B7** 16
Dover Air Force Base, mil., De., U.S. **D4** 101
Dover-Foxcroft, Me., U.S. **C3** 112
Dover Plains, N.Y., U.S. **D7** 125
Dowagiac, Mi., U.S. **G4** 115
Dowlatābād, Iran **E7** 42
Downers Grove, Il., U.S. **B5** 106
Downey, Ca., U.S. **n12** 98
Downey, Id., U.S. **G6** 105
Downingtown, Pa., U.S. **F10** 131
Downpatrick, N. Ire., U.K. **C4** 12
Downs, Ks., U.S. **C5** 109
Downs Mountain, mtn., Wy., U.S. **C3** 143
Downton, Mount, mtn., B.C., Can. **C5** 85
Dows, Ia., U.S. **B4** 108
Doylestown, Oh., U.S. **B4** 128
Doylestown, Pa., U.S. **F11** 131
Doyline, La., U.S. **B2** 111
Dra'a, Hamada du, des., Alg. **E3** 48
Dracena, Braz. **F1** 74
Dracut, Ma., U.S. **A5** 114
Drăgăşani, Rom. **G8** 20
Dragør, Den. **I5** 10
Drain, Or., U.S. **D3** 130
Drakensberg, mts., Afr. **D4** 56
Drake Passage, strt. **B33** 67
Drake Peak, mtn., Or., U.S. **E6** 130
Dráma, Grc. **D10** 18
Drammen, Nor. **G4** 10
Draper, Ut., U.S. **C4** 137
Drau (Dráva), stm., Eur. **F2** 20
Dráva (Drau), stm., Eur. **G4** 20
Drayton, On., Can. **D4** 89
Drayton, N.D., U.S. **A8** 127
Drayton, S.C., U.S. **B4** 133
Drayton Plains, Mi., U.S. **F7** 115
Drayton Valley, Ab., Can. **C3** 84
Dresden, On., Can. **E2** 89
Dresden, Ger. **E13** 12
Dresden, Oh., U.S. **B3** 128
Dresden, Tn., U.S. **A3** 135
Dresslerville, Nv., U.S. **E2** 121
Dreux, Fr. **C7** 16
Drew, Ms., U.S. **B3** 117
Drew, co., Ar., U.S. **D4** 97
Drews Reservoir, res., Or., U.S. **E6** 130
Drexel, Mo., U.S. **C3** 118
Drexel, N.C., U.S. **B1** 126
Drexel, Oh., U.S. **C1** 128
Drift, Ky., U.S. **C7** 110
Driggs, Id., U.S. **F7** 105
Drinit, Gjiri i, b., Alb. **D7** 18
Driskill Mountain, hill, La., U.S. **B3** 111
Drobeta-Turnu Severin, Rom. **G7** 20
Drogheda, Ire. **D3** 12
Drohobych, Ukr. **E7** 20
Drumheller, Ab., Can. **D4** 84
Drum Island, i., S.C., U.S. **k12** 133
Drummond, Lake, l., Va., U.S. **D6** 139
Drummond Island, i., Mi., U.S. **C7** 115
Drummondville, P.Q., Can. **D5** 90
Drumright, Ok., U.S. **B5** 129
Druskininkai, Lith. **I11** 10
Družba, Kaz. **B4** 28
Družina, Russia **C16** 26
Drybranch, W.V., U.S. **m13** 141
Dry Cimarron, stm., U.S. **A6** 124
Dry Creek Mountain, mtn., Nv., U.S. **B5** 121
Dryden, On., Can. **o16** 89
Dryden, N.Y., U.S. **C4** 125
Dry Fork, stm., Mo., U.S. **D6** 118
Dry Fork, stm., W.V., U.S. **D3** 141
Dry Fork, stm., W.V., U.S. **B5** 141
Dry Ridge, Ky., U.S. **B5** 110
Dry Tortugas, is., Fl., U.S. **H5** 102
Dschang, Cam. **B1** 54
Duarte, Pico, mtn., Dom. Rep. **B5** 80
Dubach, La., U.S. **B3** 111
Dubai see Dubayy, U.A.E. **E7** 42
Dubăsari, Mol. **F10** 20
Du Bay, Lake, res., Wi., U.S. **D4** 142
Dubayy (Dubai), U.A.E. **E7** 42
Dubbo, Austl. **G4** 62
Dublin (Baile Átha Cliath), Ire. **D3** 12
Dublin, Ga., U.S. **D4** 103
Dublin, In., U.S. **E7** 107
Dublin, N.H., U.S. **E2** 122
Dublin, Oh., U.S. **k10** 128
Dublin, Pa., U.S. **F11** 131
Dublin, Tx., U.S. **C3** 136
Dublin, Va., U.S. **C2** 139
Dubno, Ukr. **D8** 20
Dubois, In., U.S. **H4** 107
Du Bois, Pa., U.S. **D4** 131
Dubois, Wy., U.S. **C3** 143
Dubois, co., In., U.S. **H4** 107
Duboistown, Pa., U.S. **D7** 131
Dubovka, Russia **E7** 22
Dubréka, Gui. **E2** 50
Dubrovnik, Cro. **C7** 18
Dubrovytsia, Ukr. **D9** 20
Dubuque, Ia., U.S. **B7** 108
Dubuque, co., Ia., U.S. **B7** 108
Duchesne, Ut., U.S. **C5** 137
Duchesne, co., Ut., U.S. **C5** 137
Duchesne, stm., Ut., U.S. **C5** 137
Duck, stm., Tn., U.S. **B4** 135
Duck Bay, Mb., Can. **C1** 86
Duck Creek, stm., Oh., U.S. **C4** 128
Duck Creek, stm., Wi., U.S. **h9** 142
Duck Lake, Sk., Can. **E2** 91
Duck Lake, l., Me., U.S. **C4** 112
Duck Mountain Provincial Park, Sk., Can. **F5** 91
Duck Valley Indian Reservation, U.S. **B5** 121
Duckwater Indian Reservation, Nv., U.S. **E6** 121
Duckwater Peak, mtn., Nv., U.S. **E6** 121
Du Couedic, Cape, c., Austl. **H2** 62
Dudinka, Russia **C10** 26
Dudley, Eng., U.K. **D5** 12
Dudley, Ma., U.S. **B4** 114
Duenweg, Mo., U.S. **D3** 118
Duero (Douro), stm., Eur. **G4** 16
Due West, S.C., U.S. **C3** 133
Duffer Peak, mtn., Nv., U.S. **B3** 121
Dufourspitze, mtn., Eur. **B1** 18
Dugdemona, stm., La., U.S. **B3** 111
Dugger, In., U.S. **F3** 107
Dugi Otok, i., Cro. **C5** 18
Duifken Point, c., Austl. **C3** 62
Duisburg, Ger. **E10** 12
Duitama, Col. **B5** 70
Duke Island, i., Ak., U.S. **n24** 95
Dukes, co., Ma., U.S. **D6** 114
Duk Fadiat, Sudan **I11** 48
Dukhān, Qatar **E6** 42
Dukku, Nig. **D7** 50
Dukou, China **F8** 28
Dulan, China **D7** 28
Dulce, N.M., U.S. **A2** 124
Dulce, stm., Arg. **E5** 72
Dul'durga, Russia **D13** 26
Duluth, Ga., U.S. **B2** 103
Duluth, Mn., U.S. **D6** 116
Dūmā, Syria **F7** 44
Dumaguete, Phil. **E8** 34
Dumai, Indon. **C2** 36
Dumaran Island, i., Phil. **D7** 34
Dumas, Ar., U.S. **D4** 97
Dumas, Tx., U.S. **B2** 136
Dumfries, Scot., U.K. **C5** 12
Dumfries, Va., U.S. **B5** 139
Dumont, Ia., U.S. **B5** 108
Dumont, N.J., U.S. **B5** 123
Dumraon, India **D4** 40
Duna see Danube, stm., Eur. **C9** 14
Dunai see Danube, stm., Eur. **C9** 14
Dunaïvtsi, Ukr. **E9** 20
Dunaj see Danube, stm., Eur. **C9** 14
Dunărea see Danube, stm., Eur. **C9** 14
Dunaújváros, Hung. **F5** 20
Dunav see Danube, stm., Eur. **C9** 14
Dunay see Danube, stm., Eur. **C9** 14
Dunbar, Pa., U.S. **G2** 131
Dunbar, W.V., U.S. **C3** 141
Duncan, B.C., Can. **E6** 85
Duncan, Az., U.S. **E6** 96
Duncan, Ok., U.S. **C4** 129
Duncan, S.C., U.S. **B3** 133
Duncan Falls, Oh., U.S. **C4** 128
Duncan Lake, res., B.C., Can. **D9** 85
Duncannon, Pa., U.S. **F7** 131
Duncan Passage, strt., India **G6** 40
Duncansville, Pa., U.S. **F5** 131
Duncanville, Tx., U.S. **n10** 136
Dundalk, On., Can. **C4** 89
Dundalk, Ire. **C3** 12
Dundalk, Md., U.S. **B4** 113
Dundalk Bay, b., Ire. **D3** 12
Dundas, On., Can. **D5** 89
Dundee, S. Afr. **D5** 56
Dundee, Scot., U.K. **B5** 12
Dundee, Fl., U.S. **D5** 102
Dundee, Il., U.S. **A5** 106
Dundee, Mi., U.S. **G7** 115
Dundee, N.Y., U.S. **C4** 125
Dundee, Or., U.S. **h11** 130
Dundy, co., Ne., U.S. **D4** 120
Dunedin, N.Z. **q13** 63c
Dunedin, Fl., U.S. **D4** 102
Dunellen, N.J., U.S. **B4** 123
Dunfermline, Scot., U.K. **B5** 12
Dūngarpur, India **E2** 40
Dungarvan, Ire. **D3** 12
Dungeness, stm., Wa., U.S. **A2** 140
Dungu, D.R.C. **C5** 54
Dunham, P.Q., Can. **D5** 90
Dunhuang, China **C6** 28
Dunkard Creek, stm., U.S. **B4** 141
Dunkerque, Fr. **B8** 16
Dunkerton, Ia., U.S. **B5** 108
Dunkirk see Dunkerque, Fr. **B8** 16
Dunkirk, In., U.S. **D7** 107
Dunkirk, N.Y., U.S. **C1** 125
Dunkirk, Oh., U.S. **B2** 128
Dunklin, co., Mo., U.S. **E7** 118
Dunkwa, Ghana **E4** 50
Dún Laoghaire, Ire. **D3** 12
Dunlap, Ia., U.S. **C2** 108
Dunlap, Il., U.S. **C4** 106
Dunlap, In., U.S. **A6** 107
Dunlap, Tn., U.S. **D8** 135
Dunleary see Dún Laoghaire, Ire. **D3** 12
Dunleith, De., U.S. **i7** 101
Dunloup Creek, stm., W.V., U.S. **n13** 141
Dunmore, Pa., U.S. **D10** 131
Dunmore, Lake, l., Vt., U.S. **D2** 138
Dunn, N.C., U.S. **B4** 126
Dunn, co., N.D., U.S. **B3** 127
Dunn, co., Wi., U.S. **D2** 142
Dunnellon, Fl., U.S. **C4** 102
Dunnville, On., Can. **E5** 89
Dunqulah, Sudan **G11** 48
Dunseith, N.D., U.S. **A5** 127
Dunsmuir, Ca., U.S. **B2** 98
Dunville, Nf., Can. **E5** 88
Dunwoody, Ga., U.S. **h8** 103
Duolun, China **C11** 28
Duomula, China **E4** 28
Du Page, co., Il., U.S. **B5** 106
Du Page, stm., Il., U.S. **k8** 106
Duplin, co., N.C., U.S. **C5** 126
Dupnica, Bul. **C9** 18
Dupont, Co., U.S. **B6** 99
Dupont, Pa., U.S. **n18** 131
Dupont City, W.V., U.S. **m12** 141
Dupont Manor, De., U.S. **D3** 101
Duque de York, Isla, i., Chile **H1** 69
Duquesne, Pa., U.S. **F2** 131
Du Quoin, Il., U.S. **E4** 106
Durand, Il., U.S. **A4** 106
Durand, Mi., U.S. **F6** 115
Durand, Wi., U.S. **D2** 142
Durango, Mex. **E8** 78
Durango, Co., U.S. **D3** 99
Durango, state, Mex. **E8** 78
Durant, Ia., U.S. **C7** 108
Durant, Ms., U.S. **B4** 117
Durant, Ok., U.S. **D5** 129
Durazno, Ur. **E6** 72
Durban, S. Afr. **D5** 56
Durg, India **E4** 40
Durgāpur, India **E5** 40
Durham, On., Can. **C4** 89
Durham, Eng., U.K. **C6** 12
Durham, Ca., U.S. **C3** 98
Durham, Ct., U.S. **D5** 100
Durham, N.C., U.S. **B4** 126
Durham, N.H., U.S. **D5** 122
Durham, co., N.C., U.S. **A4** 126
Durmitor, mtn., Yugo. **C7** 18
Durrell, Nf., Can. **D4** 88
Durrës, Alb. **D7** 18
Dursunbey, Tur. **C3** 44
D'Urville Island, i., N.Z. **p13** 63c
Duryea, Pa., U.S. **D10** 131
Dušanbe, Taj. **F8** 26
Dušekan, Russia **C12** 26
Dushan, China **F9** 28
Dushanbe see Dušanbe, Taj. **F8** 26
Dushanzi, China **C4** 28
Duson, La., U.S. **D3** 111
Düsseldorf, Ger. **E10** 12
Dutchess, co., N.Y., U.S. **D7** 125
Dutch Island, i., R.I., U.S. **F4** 132
Dutton, On., Can. **E3** 89
Dutton, Mount, mtn., Ut., U.S. **E3** 137
Duval, co., Fl., U.S. **B5** 102
Duval, co., Tx., U.S. **F3** 136
Duxbury, Ma., U.S. **B6** 114
Duyun, China **F9** 28
Düzce, Tur. **B4** 44
Dvina Bay see Dvinskaja guba, b., Russia **A6** 22
Dvinskaja guba, b., Russia **A6** 22
Dwārka, India **E1** 40
Dwight, Il., U.S. **B5** 106
Dwight D. Eisenhower Lock, N.Y., U.S. **f9** 125
Dworshak Reservoir, res., Id., U.S. **C3** 105
Dyer, In., U.S. **A2** 107
Dyer, Tn., U.S. **A3** 135
Dyer, co., Tn., U.S. **A2** 135
Dyer Island, i., R.I., U.S. **E5** 132
Dyersburg, Tn., U.S. **A2** 135
Dyersville, Ia., U.S. **B6** 108
Dyess Air Force Base, mil., Tx., U.S. **C3** 136
Dysart, Ia., U.S. **B5** 108
Džalinda, Russia **A12** 28
Džambejty, Kaz. **D9** 22
Džanybek, Kaz. **E8** 22
Džardžan, Russia **C14** 26
Dzaudzhikau see Vladikavkaz, Russia **E6** 26
Dzerzhinsk see Dzjaržynsk, Bela. **C9** 20
Dzerzhinsk see Dzeržinsk, Russia **C7** 22
Dzeržinsk, Russia **C7** 22
Džetygara, Kaz. **D8** 26
Dzhambul see Žambyl, Kaz. **E9** 26
Dzhankoi, Ukr. **G13** 20
Dzierżoniów, Pol. **D4** 20
Džizak, Uzb. **E8** 26
Dzjaržynsk, Bela. **C9** 20
Džubga, Russia **G15** 20
Džugdžur, hrebet, mts., Russia **D15** 26
Dzungarian Basin see Junggar Pendi, China **B5** 28
Džusaly, Kaz. **A8** 42
Dzüünharaa, Mong. **B9** 28
Dzuunmod, Mong. **B9** 28

E

Eads, Co., U.S. **C8** 99
Eagan, Mn., U.S. **n12** 116
Eagar, Az., U.S. **C6** 96
Eagle, Co., U.S. **B4** 99
Eagle, Id., U.S. **F2** 105
Eagle, Ne., U.S. **h12** 120
Eagle, Wi., U.S. **F5** 142
Eagle, co., Co., U.S. **B4** 99
Eagle, stm., Nf., Can. **B2** 88
Eagle Creek Reservoir, res., In., U.S. **E5** 107
Eagle Grove, Ia., U.S. **B4** 108
Eagle Key, i., Fl., U.S. **G6** 102
Eagle Lake, Me., U.S. **A4** 112
Eagle Lake, Mn., U.S. **F5** 116
Eagle Lake, Tx., U.S. **E4** 136
Eagle Lake, l., Ca., U.S. **B3** 98
Eagle Lake, l., Me., U.S. **B3** 112
Eagle Lake, l., Me., U.S. **A4** 112
Eagle Lake, l., Ms., U.S. **C3** 117
Eagle Lake, l., Wi., U.S. **C4** 142
Eagle Mountain, mtn., Mn., U.S. **k9** 116
Eagle Mountain Lake, res., Tx., U.S. **m9** 136
Eagle Nest Lake, l., N.M., U.S. **A4** 124
Eagle Pass, Tx., U.S. **E2** 136
Eagle Peak, mtn., Ca., U.S. **B3** 98
Eagle Point, Or., U.S. **E4** 130
Eagle River, Wi., U.S. **C4** 142
Eagletail Mountains, mts., Az., U.S. **D2** 96
Eagletail Peak, mtn., Az., U.S. **D2** 96
Eagletown, Ok., U.S. **C7** 129
Earle, Ar., U.S. **B5** 97
Earlham, Ia., U.S. **C3** 108
Earlimart, Ca., U.S. **E4** 98
Earlington, Ky., U.S. **C2** 110
Earlville, Ia., U.S. **B6** 108
Earlville, Il., U.S. **B5** 106
Early, Ia., U.S. **B2** 108
Early, co., Ga., U.S. **E2** 103
Earth, Tx., U.S. **B1** 136
Easley, S.C., U.S. **B2** 133
East, stm., Ct., U.S. **D5** 100
East, stm., N.Y., U.S. **k13** 125
East, stm., Wi., U.S. **h9** 142
East Alton, Il., U.S. **E3** 106
East Angus, P.Q., Can. **D6** 90
East Arlington, Vt., U.S. **E2** 138
East Aurora, N.Y., U.S. **C2** 125
East Bangor, Pa., U.S. **E11** 131
East Bank, W.V., U.S. **m13** 141
East Barre, Vt., U.S. **C4** 138
East Baton Rouge, co., La., U.S. **D4** 111
East Bay, b., Fl., U.S. **u16** 102
East Bay, b., Tx., U.S. **R15** 136
East Beckwith Mountain, mtn., Co., U.S. **C3** 99
East Berlin, Ct., U.S. **C5** 100
East Berlin, Pa., U.S. **G8** 131
East Bernard, Tx., U.S. **E4** 136
East Bernstadt, Ky., U.S. **C5** 110
East Bethel, Mn., U.S. **E5** 116
East Billerica, Ma., U.S. **f11** 114
Eastborough, Ks., U.S. **g12** 109
Eastbourne, Eng., U.K. **E7** 12
East Brady, Pa., U.S. **E2** 131
East Branch Clarion River Lake, res., Pa., U.S. **C4** 131
East Brewton, Al., U.S. **D2** 94
East Bridgewater, Ma., U.S. **B6** 114
East Brimfield Lake, res., Ma., U.S. **B3** 114
East Brooklyn, Ct., U.S. **B8** 100
East Broughton, P.Q., Can. **C6** 90
East Brunswick, N.J., U.S. **C4** 123
East Butte, mtn., Mt., U.S. **B5** 119
East Cache Creek, stm., Ok., U.S. **C3** 129
East Caicos, i., T./C. Is. **A5** 80
East Cape, c., N.Z. **o14** 63c
East Cape, c., Fl., U.S. **G5** 102
East Carbon, Ut., U.S. **D5** 137
East Caroline Basin **H17** 64
East Carroll, co., La., U.S. **B4** 111
East Chicago, In., U.S. **A3** 107
East China Sea, Asia **F12** 28
East Chop, c., Ma., U.S. **D6** 114
East Cleveland, Oh., U.S. **g9** 128
East Cote Blanche Bay, b., La., U.S. **E4** 111
East Dennis, Ma., U.S. **C7** 114
East Derry, N.H., U.S. **E4** 122
East Detroit, Mi., U.S. **p16** 115
East Douglas, Ma., U.S. **B4** 114
East Dubuque, Il., U.S. **A3** 106
Eastend, Sk., Can. **H1** 91
Easter Island see Pascua, Isla de, i., Chile **K28** 64
Eastern Bay, b., Md., U.S. **C5** 113
Eastern Desert, des., Egypt **E11** 48
Eastern Ghāts, mts., India **G3** 40
Eastern Neck Island, i., Md., U.S. **B5** 113
Eastern Point, c., Ma., U.S. **f13** 114
Eastern Sayans see Vostočnyj Sajan, mts., Russia **D11** 26
Easterville, Mb., Can. **C2** 86
East Falkland, i., Falk. Is. **H5** 69
East Falmouth, Ma., U.S. **C6** 114
East Feliciana, co., La., U.S. **D4** 111
East Flat Rock, N.C., U.S. **f10** 126
East Fork, stm., Wy., U.S. **D3** 143
East Fork Lake, res., Oh., U.S. **C1** 128
East Frisian Islands see Ostfriesische Inseln, is., Ger. **D10** 12
East Gaffney, S.C., U.S. **A4** 133
East Galesburg, Il., U.S. **C3** 106
East Granby, Ct., U.S. **B5** 100
East Grand Forks, Mn., U.S. **C2** 116
East Grand Rapids, Mi., U.S. **F5** 115
East Greenville, Pa., U.S. **F10** 131
East Greenwich, R.I., U.S. **D4** 132
East Gwillimbury, On., Can. **C5** 89
East Hampstead, N.H., U.S. **E4** 122
East Hampton, Ct., U.S. **C5** 100
Easthampton, Ma., U.S. **B2** 114
East Hartford, Ct., U.S. **B5** 100
East Hartland, Ct., U.S. **B4** 100
East Haven, Ct., U.S. **D4** 100
East Helena, Mt., U.S. **D5** 119
East Jordan, Mi., U.S. **C5** 115
Eastlake, Oh., U.S. **A4** 128

Name — Map Ref. — Page

East Lake Tohopekaliga, l., Fl., U.S. **D5** 102
Eastland, Tx., U.S. **C3** 136
Eastland, co., Tx., U.S. **C3** 136
East Lansing, Mi., U.S. **F6** 115
East Las Vegas, Nv., U.S. **G6** 121
East Liverpool, Oh., U.S. **B5** 128
East London (Oos-Londen), S. Afr. **E4** 56
East Longmeadow, Ma., U.S. **B2** 114
East Los Angeles, Ca., U.S. **m12** 98
East Lyme, Ct., U.S. **D7** 100
East Lynn Lake, res., W.V., U.S. **C2** 141
Eastmain-Opinaca, Réservoir, res., P.Q., Can. **h11** 90
Eastman, P.Q., Can. **D5** 90
Eastman, Ga., U.S. **D3** 103
East Mariana Basin **G18** 64
East Matunuck, R.I., U.S. **F3** 132
East Middlebury, Vt., U.S. **D2** 138
East Millinocket, Me., U.S. **C4** 112
East Moline, Il., U.S. **B3** 106
East Montpelier, Vt., U.S. **C4** 138
East Naples, Fl., U.S. **F5** 102
East Newnan, Ga., U.S. **C2** 103
East Nishnabotna, stm., Ia., U.S. **C2** 108
East Norriton, Pa., U.S. **o20** 131
East Olympia, Wa., U.S. **C3** 140
Easton, Md., U.S. **C5** 113
Easton, Pa., U.S. **E11** 131
Easton Reservoir, res., Ct., U.S. **E2** 100
East Orange, N.J., U.S. **B4** 123
East Orleans, Ma., U.S. **C8** 114
Eastover, S.C., U.S. **D6** 133
East Pacific Rise **M27** 64
East Pakistan see Bangladesh, ctry., Asia **B2** 34
East Palatka, Fl., U.S. **C5** 102
East Palestine, Oh., U.S. **B5** 128
East Pass, strt., Fl., U.S. **C2** 102
East Pea Ridge, W.V., U.S. **C2** 141
East Peoria, Il., U.S. **C4** 106
East Pepperell, Ma., U.S. **A4** 114
East Petersburg, Pa., U.S. **F9** 131
East Pittsburgh, Pa., U.S. **k14** 131
Eastpoint, Fl., U.S. **C2** 102
East Point, Ga., U.S. **C2** 103
East Point, c., P.E., Can. **C8** 87
East Point, c., Ma., U.S. **B6** 114
East Point, c., N.J., U.S. **E2** 123
Eastport, Nf., Can. **D5** 88
Eastport, Me., U.S. **D6** 112
East Prairie, Mo., U.S. **E8** 118
East Providence, R.I., U.S. **C4** 132
East Pryor Mountain, mtn., Mt., U.S. **E8** 119
East Quogue, N.Y., U.S. **n16** 125
East Range, mts., Nv., U.S. **C4** 121
East Ridge, Tn., U.S. **h11** 135
East River, Ct., U.S. **D5** 100
East Rochester, N.Y., U.S. **B3** 125
East Rockingham, N.C., U.S. **C3** 126
East Rutherford, N.J., U.S. **h8** 123
East Saint Louis, Il., U.S. **E3** 106
East Sea see Japan, Sea of, Asia **C14** 28
East Selkirk, Mb., Can. **D3** 86
East Siberian Sea see Vostočno-Sibirskoe more, Russia **B17** 26
Eastsound, Wa., U.S. **A3** 140
East Spencer, N.C., U.S. **B2** 126
East Stroudsburg, Pa., U.S. **D11** 131
East Tawas, Mi., U.S. **D7** 115
East Troy, Wi., U.S. **F5** 142
East Vestal, N.Y., U.S. **C4** 125
East View, W.V., U.S. **k10** 141
East Walker, stm., U.S. **E2** 121
East Walpole, Ma., U.S. **h11** 114
East Wareham, Ma., U.S. **C6** 114
East Washington, Pa., U.S. **F1** 131
East Wenatchee, Wa., U.S. **B5** 140
East Windsor, N.J., U.S. **C3** 123
East York, On., Can. **D5** 89
Eaton, Co., U.S. **A6** 99
Eaton, In., U.S. **D7** 107
Eaton, Oh., U.S. **C1** 128
Eaton, co., Mi., U.S. **F6** 115
Eaton Rapids, Mi., U.S. **F6** 115
Eatonton, Ga., U.S. **C3** 103
Eatontown, N.J., U.S. **C4** 123
Eatonville, Wa., U.S. **C3** 140
Eau Claire, Wi., U.S. **D2** 142
Eau Claire, co., Wi., U.S. **D2** 142
Eau Claire, stm., Wi., U.S. **D2** 142
Eau Claire, Lac à l', l., P.Q., Can. **g11** 90
Eauripik Rise **H17** 64
Ebano, Mex. **C5** 78
Ebebiyín, Eq. Gui. **C2** 54
Ebensburg, Pa., U.S. **F4** 131
Eber Gölü, l., Tur. **C4** 44
Eberswalde-Finow, Ger. **D13** 12
Ebetsu, Japan **B4** 31
Ebinur Hu, l., China **B4** 28
Ebolowa, Cam. **C2** 54
Ebre see Ebro, stm., Spain **G7** 16
Ebre, Delta de l', Spain **G7** 16
Ebro, stm., Spain **G7** 16
Eccles, W.V., U.S. **n13** 141
Ech Cheliff, Alg. **C5** 48
Echeng, China **C3** 30
Echo Bay, Nv., U.S. **G7** 121
Echo Lake, l., Me., U.S. **D3** 112
Echo Lake, l., Vt., U.S. **B5** 138
Echols, co., Ga., U.S. **F4** 103
Echuca, Austl. **H3** 62
Écija, Spain **I4** 16
Eckerö, i., Fin. **F8** 10
Eckhart Mines, Md., U.S. **k13** 113
Eckville, Ab., Can. **C3** 84
Eclectic, Al., U.S. **C3** 94
Econfina, stm., Fl., U.S. **B3** 102
Écorces, Rivière aux, stm., P.Q., Can. **A6** 90
Ecorse, Mi., U.S. **p15** 115
Ecru, Ms., U.S. **A4** 117
Ector, co., Tx., U.S. **D1** 136
Ecuador, ctry., S.A. **D4** 70
Edcouch, Tx., U.S. **F4** 136
Eddy, co., N.D., U.S. **B7** 127
Eddy, co., N.M., U.S. **E5** 124
Eddystone, Pa., U.S. **p20** 131
Eddyville, Ia., U.S. **C5** 108
Eddyville, Ky., U.S. **e9** 110
Ede, Nig. **E5** 50
Edéa, Cam. **C2** 54
Eden, Ga., U.S. **D5** 103
Eden, Md., U.S. **D6** 113
Eden, N.C., U.S. **A3** 126
Eden, N.Y., U.S. **C2** 125
Eden, Tx., U.S. **D3** 136
Edenburg, S. Afr. **D4** 56
Eden Prairie, Mn., U.S. **n12** 116
Edenton, N.C., U.S. **A6** 126
Eden Valley, Mn., U.S. **E4** 116
Edfu, Egypt **F11** 48
Edgar, Ne., U.S. **D8** 120
Edgar, Wi., U.S. **D4** 142
Edgar, co., Il., U.S. **D6** 106
Edgard, La., U.S. **D5** 111
Edgartown, Ma., U.S. **D6** 114
Edgecombe, co., N.C., U.S. **B5** 126
Edgecumbe, Cape, c., Ak., U.S. **m21** 95
Edgefield, S.C., U.S. **D4** 133
Edgefield, co., S.C., U.S. **D4** 133
Edgeley, N.D., U.S. **C7** 127
Edgemere, Md., U.S. **B5** 113
Edgemont, S.D., U.S. **D2** 134
Edgemoor, De., U.S. **A3** 101
Edgeøya, i., Nor. **B4** 26
Edgerton, Ks., U.S. **D8** 109
Edgerton, Mn., U.S. **G2** 116
Edgerton, Oh., U.S. **A1** 128
Edgerton, Wi., U.S. **F4** 142
Edgerton, Wy., U.S. **C6** 143
Edgewater, Al., U.S. **f7** 94
Edgewater, Fl., U.S. **D6** 102
Edgewater, Md., U.S. **C4** 113
Edgewater, N.J., U.S. **h9** 123
Edgewater Park, N.J., U.S. **C3** 123
Edgewood, Ia., U.S. **B6** 108
Edgewood, In., U.S. **D6** 107
Edgewood, Ky., U.S. **h13** 110
Edgewood, Md., U.S. **B5** 113
Edgewood, N.M., U.S. **B3** 124
Edgewood, Oh., U.S. **A5** 128
Edgewood, Pa., U.S. **k14** 131
Edgewood, Wa., U.S. **f11** 140
Edgeworth, Pa., U.S. **h13** 131
Édhessa, Grc. **D9** 18
Edina, Mn., U.S. **F5** 116
Edina, Mo., U.S. **A5** 118
Edinboro, Pa., U.S. **C1** 131
Edinburg, Il., U.S. **D4** 106
Edinburg, Tx., U.S. **F3** 136
Edinburg, Va., U.S. **B4** 139
Edinburgh, Scot., U.K. **C5** 12
Edinburgh, In., U.S. **F6** 107
Edineț, Mol. **E9** 20
Edirne, Tur. **B2** 44
Edison, Ga., U.S. **E2** 103
Edison, N.J., U.S. **B4** 123
Edisto, stm., S.C., U.S. **E6** 133
Edisto Island, i., S.C., U.S. **F7** 133
Edith, Mount, mtn., Mt., U.S. **D5** 119
Edjeleh, Alg. **E6** 48
Edmond, Ok., U.S. **B4** 129
Edmonds, Wa., U.S. **B3** 140
Edmonson, co., Ky., U.S. **C3** 110
Edmonton, Ab., Can. **C4** 84
Edmonton, Ky., U.S. **D4** 110
Edmore, Mi., U.S. **E5** 115
Edmunds, co., S.D., U.S. **B6** 134
Edmundston, N.B., Can. **B1** 87
Edna, Tx., U.S. **E4** 136
Edon, Oh., U.S. **A1** 128
Édouard, Lac, l., P.Q., Can. **B5** 90
Edremit, Tur. **C2** 44
Edremit Körfezi, b., Tur. **C2** 44
Edson, Ab., Can. **C2** 84
Edson Butte, mtn., Or., U.S. **E2** 130
Eduardo Castex, Arg. **F5** 72
Edward, Lake, l., Afr. **D5** 54
Edwards, Ms., U.S. **C3** 117
Edwards, co., Il., U.S. **E5** 106
Edwards, co., Ks., U.S. **E4** 109
Edwards, co., Tx., U.S. **E2** 136
Edwards Air Force Base, mil., Ca., U.S. **E5** 98
Edwardsburg, Mi., U.S. **G4** 115
Edwards Butte, mtn., Or., U.S. **B3** 130
Edwardsville, Il., U.S. **E4** 106
Edwardsville, Ks., U.S. **k16** 109
Edwardsville, Pa., U.S. **n17** 131
Edward VII Peninsula, pen., Ant. **D25** 67
Eel, stm., Ca., U.S. **B2** 98
Eel, stm., In., U.S. **C6** 107
Eel, stm., In., U.S. **F3** 107
Éfaté, i., Vanuatu **k9** 62a
Efes (Ephesus), hist., Tur. **D2** 44
Effigy Mounds National Monument, Ia., U.S. **A6** 108
Effingham, Il., U.S. **D5** 106
Effingham, co., Ga., U.S. **D5** 103
Effingham, co., Il., U.S. **D5** 106
Efland, N.C., U.S. **A3** 126
Efremov, Russia **C15** 20
Egadi, Isole, is., Italy **E4** 18
Egan Range, mts., Nv., U.S. **E7** 121
Eganville, On., Can. **B7** 89
Egedesminde, Grnld. **E29** 82
Eger, Hung. **F6** 20
Eggenfelden, Ger. **F13** 12
Egg Harbor City, N.J., U.S. **D3** 123
Egg Island Point, c., N.J., U.S. **E2** 123
Egijn, stm., Mong. **A8** 28
Eglin Air Force Base, mil., Fl., U.S. **u15** 102
Egmont, Cape, c., N.Z. **o13** 63c
Egmont, Mount see Taranaki, Mount, vol., N.Z. **o13** 63c
Egmont Bay, b., P.E., Can. **C5** 87
Egmont Channel, strt., Fl., U.S. **p10** 102
Egmont Key, i., Fl., U.S. **p10** 102
Eğridir, Tur. **D4** 44
Eğridir Gölü, l., Tur. **C4** 44
Egvekinot, Russia **C20** 26
Egypt, ctry., Afr. **E10** 48
Egypt, Lake of, res., Il., U.S. **F5** 106
Eha-Amufu, Nig. **E6** 50
Ehrenberg, Az., U.S. **D1** 96
Eibar, Spain **F5** 16
Eielson Air Force Base, mil., Ak., U.S. **C10** 95
Eigersund, Nor. **G2** 10
Eight Degree Channel, strt., Asia **H2** 40
Eights Coast, Ant. **D31** 67
Eighty Mile Beach, Austl. **D3** 60
Eindhoven, Neth. **E9** 12
Eirunepé, Braz. **E6** 70
Eisenach, Ger. **E12** 12
Eisenerz, Aus. **G14** 12
Eisenhower, Mount, mtn., N.H., U.S. **B4** 122
Eisenhüttenstadt, Ger. **D14** 12
Eisenstadt, Aus. **G15** 12
Eivissa, Spain **H7** 16
Eivissa (Ibiza), i., Spain **H7** 16
Ejin Qi, China **C8** 28
Ejsk, Russia **F15** 20
Ejura, Ghana **E4** 50
Ekaterinburg, Russia **D8** 26
Ekibastuz, Kaz. **D9** 26
Ekimčan, Russia **D15** 26
Ekonda, Russia **C12** 26
Ela, Myan. **C3** 34
El Aaiún, W. Sah. **A2** 50
Elaine, Ar., U.S. **C5** 97
El-Alamein, Egypt **E9** 14
Elan', Russia **D7** 22
Elancy, Russia **D12** 26
El-Arish, Egypt **E10** 14
Elat, Isr. **E2** 42
Elat, Gulf of see Aqaba, Gulf of, b. **E2** 42
Elath see Elat, Isr. **E2** 42
Elazığ, Tur. **C8** 44
Elba, Al., U.S. **D3** 94
Elba, Isola d', i., Italy **C3** 18
El Banco, Col. **D5** 80
Elbasan, Alb. **D7** 18
Elbe see Labe, stm., Eur. **E14** 12
Elberfeld, In., U.S. **H3** 107
Elbert, co., Co., U.S. **B6** 99
Elbert, co., Ga., U.S. **B4** 103
Elbert, Mount, mtn., Co., U.S. **B4** 99
Elberta, Ga., U.S. **D3** 103
Elberton, Ga., U.S. **B4** 103
El Beyyadh, Alg. **E4** 14
Elbistan, Tur. **C7** 44
Elbląg, Pol. **B5** 20
El Boulaïda, Alg. **C5** 48
Elbow, stm., Ab., Can. **D3** 84
Elbow Lake, Mn., U.S. **E3** 116
El'brus, gora, mtn., Russia **E6** 26
Elbrus, Mount see El'brus, gora, mtn., Russia **E6** 26
Elburn, Il., U.S. **B5** 106
Elburz Mountains see Alborz, Reshteh-ye Kūhhā-ye, mts., Iran **C6** 42
El Cajon, Ca., U.S. **F5** 98
El Calafate, Arg. **H2** 69
El Callao, Ven. **D7** 80
El Campo, Tx., U.S. **E4** 136
El Capitan, mtn., Mt., U.S. **D2** 119
El Capitan Reservoir, res., Ca., U.S. **o16** 98
El Carmen de Bolívar, Col. **B4** 70
El Centro, Ca., U.S. **F6** 98
El Cerrito, Ca., U.S. **h8** 98
Elcho Island, i., Austl. **C6** 60
El Cuervo Butte, mtn., N.M., U.S. **k9** 124
Elda, Spain **H6** 16
El-Dab'a, Egypt **G3** 44
El Djazaïr (Algiers), Alg. **C5** 48
El Djelfa, Alg. **E4** 14
Eldon, Ia., U.S. **D5** 108
Eldon, Mo., U.S. **C5** 118
Eldora, Ia., U.S. **B4** 108
Eldorado, Arg. **D7** 72
El Dorado, Ar., U.S. **D3** 97
Eldorado, Il., U.S. **F5** 106
El Dorado, Ks., U.S. **E7** 109
Eldorado, Tx., U.S. **D2** 136
El Dorado, Ven. **D7** 80
El Dorado, co., Ca., U.S. **C3** 98
Eldorado Peak, mtn., Wa., U.S. **A4** 140
Eldorado Springs, Co., U.S. **B5** 99
El Dorado Springs, Mo., U.S. **D3** 118
Eldoret, Kenya **C7** 54
Eldridge, Ia., U.S. **C7** 108
Eleanor, W.V., U.S. **C3** 141
Elec, Russia **D5** 26
Electra, Tx., U.S. **C3** 136
Electra Lake, res., Co., U.S. **D3** 99
Electric Peak, mtn., Co., U.S. **C5** 99
Electric Peak, mtn., Mt., U.S. **E6** 119
Elefantes (Olifants), stm., Afr. **C5** 56
El Encanto, Col. **D5** 70
Elephant Butte Reservoir, res., N.M., U.S. **D2** 124
Eleuthera, i., Bah. **C9** 76
Eleven Mile Canyon Reservoir, res., Co., U.S. **C5** 99
Eleven Point, stm., U.S. **A4** 97
El-Fayoum, Egypt **E11** 48
Elgin, Scot., U.K. **B5** 12
Elgin, Ia., U.S. **B6** 108
Elgin, Il., U.S. **A5** 106
Elgin, Mn., U.S. **F6** 116
Elgin, N.D., U.S. **C4** 127
Elgin, Ne., U.S. **C7** 120
Elgin, Ok., U.S. **C3** 129
Elgin, Or., U.S. **B9** 130
Elgin, S.C., U.S. **B6** 133
Elgin, Tx., U.S. **D4** 136
El-Gîza, Egypt **E11** 48
Elgon, Mount, mtn., Afr. **C6** 54
El Grara, Alg. **E4** 14
El Ḥammâmi, reg., Maur. **B2** 50
El Ḥank, clf, Afr. **B3** 50
El Hierro, i., Spain **A1** 50
Elhovo, Bul. **C11** 18
Eliase, Indon. **E8** 36
Elida, Oh., U.S. **B1** 128
El-Iskandarîya, Egypt **D10** 48
Elista, Russia **E6** 26
Elizabeth, Austl. **G2** 62
Elizabeth, Co., U.S. **B6** 99
Elizabeth, N.J., U.S. **B4** 123
Elizabeth, W.V., U.S. **B3** 141
Elizabeth, Cape, c., Wa., U.S. **B1** 140
Elizabeth City, N.C., U.S. **A6** 126
Elizabeth Islands, is., Ma., U.S. **D6** 114
Elizabethton, Tn., U.S. **C11** 135
Elizabethtown, Ky., U.S. **C4** 110
Elizabethtown, N.C., U.S. **C4** 126
Elizabethtown, Pa., U.S. **F8** 131
Elizabethville, Pa., U.S. **E8** 131
Elizavety, mys, c., Russia **D16** 26
El-Jadida, Mor. **D3** 48
El Jebel, Co., U.S. **B3** 99
Ełk, Pol. **C7** 20
Elk, co., Ks., U.S. **E7** 109
Elk, co., Pa., U.S. **D4** 131
Elk, stm., Co., U.S. **A4** 99
Elk, stm., Ks., U.S. **E7** 109
Elk, stm., W.V., U.S. **C3** 141
Elk, stm., Wi., U.S. **C3** 142
Elk, stm., U.S. **A2** 94
Elkader, Ia., U.S. **B6** 108
Elk City, Id., U.S. **D3** 105
Elk City, Ok., U.S. **B2** 129
Elk City Lake, res., Ks., U.S. **E7** 109
Elk Creek, stm., Ok., U.S. **B2** 129
Elk Creek, stm., S.D., U.S. **C3** 134
El Kef, Tun. **C6** 48
Ēl Kerē, Eth. **B8** 54
Elkford, B.C., Can. **D10** 85
Elk Grove, Ca., U.S. **C3** 98
Elk Grove Village, Il., U.S. **h9** 106
El-Khârga, Egypt **E11** 48
Elkhart, In., U.S. **A6** 107
Elkhart, Ks., U.S. **E2** 109
Elkhart, Tx., U.S. **D5** 136
Elkhart, co., In., U.S. **A6** 107
Elkhart, stm., In., U.S. **B6** 107
Elkhart Lake, Wi., U.S. **E5** 142
Elkhead Mountains, mts., Co., U.S. **A3** 99
Elkhorn, Mb., Can. **E1** 86
Elk Horn, Ia., U.S. **C2** 108
Elkhorn, Ne., U.S. **g12** 120
Elkhorn, Wi., U.S. **F5** 142
Elkhorn, stm., Ne., U.S. **B7** 120
Elkhorn City, Ky., U.S. **C7** 110
Elkhorn Peaks, mts., Id., U.S. **F7** 105
Elkin, N.C., U.S. **A2** 126
Elkins, Ar., U.S. **A1** 97
Elkins, W.V., U.S. **C5** 141
Elkland, Pa., U.S. **C7** 131
Elk Mills, Md., U.S. **A6** 113
Elk Mound, Wi., U.S. **D2** 142
Elk Mountain, Wy., U.S. **E6** 143
Elk Mountain, mtn., N.M., U.S. **D1** 124
Elk Mountain, mtn., Wy., U.S. **E6** 143
Elk Mountains, mts., Co., U.S. **B3** 99
Elk Mountains, mts., U.S. **D1** 134
Elko, Nv., U.S. **C6** 121
Elko, co., Nv., U.S. **B6** 121
Elk Peak, mtn., Mt., U.S. **D6** 119
Elk Point, Ab., Can. **C5** 84
Elk Point, S.D., U.S. **E9** 134
Elk Rapids, Mi., U.S. **D5** 115
Elkridge, Md., U.S. **B4** 113
Elk River, Mn., U.S. **E5** 116
Elkton, Ky., U.S. **D2** 110
Elkton, Md., U.S. **A6** 113
Elkton, Mi., U.S. **E7** 115
Elkton, S.D., U.S. **C9** 134
Elkton, Va., U.S. **B4** 139
Elkview, W.V., U.S. **m13** 141
Elkville, Il., U.S. **F4** 106
Ellaville, Ga., U.S. **D2** 103
Ellen, Mount, mtn., Ut., U.S. **E5** 137
Ellendale, De., U.S. **E4** 101
Ellendale, N.D., U.S. **C7** 127
Ellensburg, Wa., U.S. **C5** 140
Ellenton, Fl., U.S. **E4** 102
Ellenville, N.Y., U.S. **D6** 125
Ellerbe, N.C., U.S. **B3** 126
Ellerslie, Md., U.S. **k13** 113
Ellesmere Island, i., Nu., Can. **B24** 82
Ellettsville, In., U.S. **F4** 107
Ellice Islands see Tuvalu, ctry., Oc. **E11** 58
Ellicott City, Md., U.S. **B4** 113
Ellijay, Ga., U.S. **B2** 103
Ellington, Ct., U.S. **B6** 100
Ellington, Mo., U.S. **D7** 118
Ellinwood, Ks., U.S. **D5** 109
Elliot, S. Afr. **E4** 56
Elliot Lake, On., Can. **A2** 89
Elliott, Ms., U.S. **B4** 117
Elliott, co., Ky., U.S. **B6** 110
Elliott Bay, b., Wa., U.S. **e11** 140
Elliott Key, i., Fl., U.S. **G6** 102
Ellis, Ks., U.S. **D4** 109
Ellis, co., Ks., U.S. **D4** 109
Ellis, co., Ok., U.S. **A2** 129
Ellis, co., Tx., U.S. **C4** 136
Ellis, stm., N.H., U.S. **B4** 122
Elliston, Va., U.S. **C2** 139
Ellisville, Mo., U.S. **f12** 118
Ellisville, Ms., U.S. **D4** 117
Ellore see Elūru, India **F4** 40
Elloree, S.C., U.S. **D6** 133
Ellport, Pa., U.S. **E1** 131
Ellsworth, Ks., U.S. **D5** 109
Ellsworth, Me., U.S. **D4** 112
Ellsworth, Pa., U.S. **F1** 131
Ellsworth, Wi., U.S. **D1** 142
Ellsworth, co., Ks., U.S. **D5** 109
Ellsworth Air Force Base, mil., S.D., U.S. **C2** 134
Ellsworth Land, reg., Ant. **D32** 67
Ellsworth Mountains, mts., Ant. **D32** 67
Ellwood City, Pa., U.S. **E1** 131
Elm, stm., N.D., U.S. **B8** 127
Elma, Ia., U.S. **A5** 108
Elma, Wa., U.S. **C2** 140
Elmadağ, Tur. **C5** 44
El-Mahalla el-Kubra, Egypt **G4** 44
Elmalı, Tur. **D3** 44
El-Mansûra, Egypt **E10** 14
Elm City, N.C., U.S. **B5** 126
Elm Creek, Ne., U.S. **D6** 120
Elmendorf Air Force Base, mil., Ak., U.S. **C10** 95
El Menia, Alg. **D5** 48
Elm Grove, Wi., U.S. **m11** 142
Elmhurst, Il., U.S. **B6** 106
Elmhurst, Pa., U.S. **D10** 131
El-Minya, Egypt **E11** 48
Elmira, N.Y., U.S. **C4** 125
El Mirage, Az., U.S. **k8** 96
Elmira Heights, N.Y., U.S. **C4** 125
El Mohammadia, Alg. **J7** 16
Elmont, N.Y., U.S. **k13** 125
Elmora, Pa., U.S. **E4** 131
Elmore, Mn., U.S. **G4** 116
Elmore, Oh., U.S. **A2** 128
Elmore, co., Al., U.S. **C3** 94
Elmore, co., Id., U.S. **F3** 105
El Morro National Monument, N.M., U.S. **B1** 124
El Mreyyé, reg., Maur. **C3** 50
Elmsdale, N.S., Can. **E6** 87
Elmshorn, Ger. **D11** 12
Elm Springs, Ar., U.S. **A1** 97
Elmvale, On., Can. **C5** 89
Elmwood, Il., U.S. **C3** 106
Elmwood, Wi., U.S. **D1** 142
Elmwood Park, Il., U.S. **k9** 106

Name | Map Ref. | Page

Elmwood Park, N.J., U.S. **h8** 123
Elmwood Place, Oh., U.S. **o13** 128
Elnora, In., U.S. **G3** 107
Eloise, Fl., U.S. **E5** 102
Elon College, N.C., U.S. **A3** 126
Elora, On., Can. **D4** 89
Elorza, Ven. **D6** 80
Ěloten, Turk. **C8** 42
Eloy, Az., U.S. **E4** 96
El Paso, Il., U.S. **C4** 106
El Paso, Tx., U.S. **o11** 136
El Paso, co., Co., U.S. **C6** 99
El Paso, co., Tx., U.S. **o11** 136
El Pital, Cerro, mtn., N.A. **C2** 80
El Portal, Fl., U.S. **s13** 102
El Prado, N.M., U.S. **A4** 124
El Progreso, Hond. **B2** 80
El Puerto de Santa María, Spain **I3** 16
El-Qâhira (Cairo), Egypt **D10** 48
El-Qasr, Egypt **E10** 48
El Reno, Ok., U.S. **B4** 129
Elrose, Sk., Can. **F1** 91
Elroy, Wi., U.S. **E3** 142
Elsa, Tx., U.S. **F3** 136
Elsah, Il., U.S. **E3** 106
El Salto, Mex. **C3** 78
El Salvador, ctry., N.A. **C2** 80
El Sauzal, Mex. **A1** 78
Elsberry, Mo., U.S. **B7** 118
Elsie, Mi., U.S. **E6** 115
Elsinore, Ut., U.S. **E3** 137
El'sk, Bela. **D10** 20
Elsmere, De., U.S. **B3** 101
Elsmere, Ky., U.S. **B5** 110
El Sueco, Mex. **B3** 78
El-Suweis, Egypt **E11** 48
Eltham, N.Z. **o13** 63c
El Tigre, Ven. **B7** 70
El Toco, Chile **C4** 72
Elton, La., U.S. **D3** 111
El Toro Marine Corps Air Station, mil., Ca., U.S. **n13** 98
El Turbio, Arg. **H2** 69
El-Uqsor, Egypt **E11** 48
Elūru, India **F4** 40
El Vado Reservoir, res., N.M., U.S. **A3** 124
Elvas, Port. **H3** 16
Elvins, Mo., U.S. **D7** 118
El Wad, Alg. **E5** 14
El Wak, Kenya **C8** 54
Elwell, Lake, res., Mt., U.S. **B5** 119
Elwha, stm., Wa., U.S. **A2** 140
Elwood, In., U.S. **D6** 107
Elwood, Ks., U.S. **C9** 109
Elwood, Ne., U.S. **D6** 120
Elx, Spain **H6** 16
Ely, Eng., U.K. **D7** 12
Ely, Mn., U.S. **C7** 116
Ely, Nv., U.S. **D7** 121
Elyria, Oh., U.S. **A3** 128
Elysburg, Pa., U.S. **E8** 131
Emāmshahr, Iran **C7** 42
Emanuel, co., Ga., U.S. **D4** 103
Emba, Kaz. **E10** 22
Emba, stm., Kaz. **E7** 26
Embarras, stm., Il., U.S. **E6** 106
Embarrass, stm., Wi., U.S. **D5** 142
Embro, On., Can. **D4** 89
Embu, Kenya **D7** 54
Emden, Ger. **D10** 12
Emerald, Austl. **E4** 62
Emerson, Mb., Can. **E3** 86
Emerson, Ga., U.S. **B2** 103
Emerson, Ne., U.S. **B9** 120
Emerson, N.J., U.S. **h8** 123
Emery, co., Ut., U.S. **E5** 137
Emet, Tur. **C3** 44
Emiliano Zapata, Mex. **D6** 78
Emily, Mn., U.S. **D5** 116
Emily, Lake, l., Mn., U.S. **E3** 116
Eminence, Ky., U.S. **B4** 110
Emirdağ, Tur. **C4** 44
Emmaus, Pa., U.S. **E11** 131
Emmen, Neth. **D10** 12
Emmet, co., Ia., U.S. **A3** 108
Emmet, co., Mi., U.S. **C6** 115
Emmetsburg, Ia., U.S. **A3** 108
Emmett, Id., U.S. **F2** 105
Emmitsburg, Md., U.S. **A3** 113
Emmonak, Ak., U.S. **C7** 95
Emmons, co., N.D., U.S. **C5** 127
Emory Peak, mtn., Tx., U.S. **E1** 136
Empalme, Mex. **B2** 78
Empangeni, S. Afr. **D5** 56
Empedrado, Arg. **D6** 72
Emperor Seamounts **D19** 64
Empire, La., U.S. **E6** 111
Empire, Nv., U.S. **C2** 121
Empoli, Italy **C3** 18
Emporia, Ks., U.S. **D7** 109
Emporia, Va., U.S. **D5** 139
Emporium, Pa., U.S. **D5** 131
Empty Quarter see Ar-Rub' al-Khālī, des., Asia **G6** 38
Emsworth, Pa., U.S. **h13** 131
Encampment, Wy., U.S. **E6** 143
Encarnación, Para. **D6** 72
Enchilayas, Mex. **A2** 78
Encinitas, Ca., U.S. **F5** 98
Encontrados, Ven. **D5** 80
Encounter Bay, b., Austl. **H2** 62
Ende, Indon. **E6** 36
Enderby, B.C., Can. **D8** 85
Enderby Land, reg., Ant. **D9** 67
Enderlin, N.D., U.S. **C8** 127
Enders Reservoir, res., Ne., U.S. **D4** 120
Endicott, N.Y., U.S. **C4** 125
Endicott Mountains, mts., Ak., U.S. **B9** 95
Endless Lake, l., Me., U.S. **C4** 112
Endwell, N.Y., U.S. **C4** 125
Enewetak, atoll, Marsh. Is. **C10** 58
Enfield (Thompsonville), Ct., U.S. **B5** 100
Enfield, N.C., U.S. **A5** 126
Enfield, N.H., U.S. **C2** 122
Engel's, Russia **D6** 26
Enggano, Pulau, i., Indon. **E2** 36
England, Ar., U.S. **C4** 97
England, prov., U.K. **D6** 12
Englee, Nf., Can. **C3** 88
Engleside, Va., U.S. **g12** 139
Englewood, Co., U.S. **B6** 99
Englewood, Fl., U.S. **F4** 102
Englewood, N.J., U.S. **B5** 123
Englewood, Oh., U.S. **C1** 128
Englewood, Tn., U.S. **D9** 135
Englewood Cliffs, N.J., U.S. **h9** 123
English, In., U.S. **H5** 107
English Bāzār see Ingrāj Bāzār, India **E5** 40
English Channel, strt., Eur. **C5** 16
English Coast, Ant. **D33** 67
Enid, Ok., U.S. **A4** 129
Enid Lake, res., Ms., U.S. **A4** 117
Enigma, Ga., U.S. **E3** 103
Enisej (Yenisey), stm., Russia **C10** 26
eNjesuthi, mtn., Afr. **D4** 56
Enka, N.C., U.S. **f10** 126
Enköping, Swe. **G7** 10
Enna, Italy **F5** 18
Ennedi, plat., Chad **G9** 48
Ennis, Mt., U.S. **E5** 119
Ennis, Tx., U.S. **C4** 136
Enoch, Ut., U.S. **F2** 137
Enola, Pa., U.S. **F8** 131
Enontekiö, Fin. **B10** 10
Enoree, S.C., U.S. **B4** 133
Enoree, stm., S.C., U.S. **B3** 133
Enosburg Falls, Vt., U.S. **B3** 138
Enriquillo, Lago, l., Dom. Rep. **B5** 80
Enschede, Neth. **D10** 12
Ensenada, Mex. **A1** 78
Enshi, China **E9** 28
Enshu Bay see Enshū-nada, Japan **D3** 31
Enshū-nada, Japan **D3** 31
Ensley, Fl., U.S. **u14** 102
Entebbe, Ug. **C6** 54
Enterprise, Al., U.S. **D4** 94
Enterprise, Ks., U.S. **D6** 109
Enterprise, Or., U.S. **B9** 130
Enterprise, Ut., U.S. **F2** 137
Enterprise, W.V., U.S. **B4** 141
Entiat, stm., Wa., U.S. **B5** 140
Entiat, Lake, l., Wa., U.S. **B5** 140
Entiat Mountains, mts., Wa., U.S. **B5** 140
Entroncamento, Port. **H2** 16
Enugu, Nig. **E6** 50
Enumclaw, Wa., U.S. **B4** 140
Enurmino, Russia **C20** 26
Enyamba, D.R.C. **D5** 54
Eola Hills, hills, Or., U.S. **h11** 130
Epena, Congo **C3** 54
Épernay, Fr. **C8** 16
Ephesus see Efes, hist., Tur. **D2** 44
Ephraim, Ut., U.S. **D4** 137
Ephrata, Pa., U.S. **F9** 131
Ephrata, Wa., U.S. **B6** 140
Épi, i., Vanuatu **I9** 62a
Épinal, Fr. **C10** 16
Epirus see Ípeiros, hist. reg., Grc. **E8** 18
Epping, N.H., U.S. **D4** 122
Epukiro, Nmb. **C2** 56
Epworth, Ia., U.S. **B7** 108
Eqlīd, Iran **D6** 42
Equatorial Guinea, ctry., Afr. **C1** 54
Erath, La., U.S. **E3** 111
Erath, co., Tx., U.S. **C3** 136
Erbaa, Tur. **B7** 44
Erciş, Tur. **C10** 44
Erciyes Dağı, vol., Tur. **C6** 44
Érd, Hung. **F5** 20
Erdek, Tur. **B2** 44
Erdemli, Tur. **D6** 44
Erdene see Ulaan-Uul, Mong. **C10** 28
Erebus, Mount, mtn., Ant. **D21** 67
Erechim, Braz. **D7** 72
Ereğli, Tur. **D5** 44
Ereğli, Tur. **B4** 44
Erenhot, China **C10** 28
Erfoud, Mor. **E3** 14
Erfurt, Ger. **E12** 12
Ergani, Tur. **C8** 44
Ergel, Mong. **C9** 28
Ergene, stm., Tur. **B2** 44
Ergeni, hills, Russia **E6** 26
Ergun see Argun', stm., Asia **D14** 26
Erick, Ok., U.S. **B2** 129
Erickson, Mb., Can. **D2** 86
Erie, Co., U.S. **A5** 99
Erie, Il., U.S. **B3** 106
Erie, Ks., U.S. **E8** 109
Erie, Mi., U.S. **G7** 115
Erie, Pa., U.S. **B1** 131
Erie, co., N.Y., U.S. **C2** 125
Erie, co., Oh., U.S. **A3** 128
Erie, co., Pa., U.S. **C1** 131
Erie, Lake, l., N.A. **C11** 92
Erie Canal, N.Y., U.S. **B5** 125
Erimo-misaki, c., Japan **C16** 28
Erin, On., Can. **D4** 89
Erin, Tn., U.S. **A4** 135
Eritrea, ctry., Afr. **G12** 48
Erlangen, Ger. **F12** 12
Erlanger, Ky., U.S. **A5** 110
Erling, Lake, res., Ar., U.S. **D2** 97
Ermelo, S. Afr. **D4** 56
Ermenek, Tur. **D5** 44
Ermolaevo, Russia **D10** 22
Ermoúpolis, Grc. **F10** 18
Erne, Lower Lough, l., N. Ire., U.K. **C3** 12
Erne, Upper Lough, l., Eur. **C3** 12
Erode, India **G3** 40
Erofej Pavlovič, Russia **D14** 26
Eropol, Russia **C18** 26
Er-Rachidia, Mor. **E3** 14
Errego, Moz. **B6** 56
Erromango, i., Vanuatu **I9** 62a
Eršov, Russia **D8** 22
Ertai, China **B6** 28
Ertil', Russia **D16** 20
Ertis see Irtysh, stm., Asia **D8** 26
Ertix see Irtysh, stm., Asia **D8** 26
Erwin, N.C., U.S. **B4** 126
Erwin, Tn., U.S. **C11** 135
Eryuan, China **A3** 34
Erzgebirge, mts., Eur. **E9** 8
Erzin, Russia **D11** 26
Erzincan, Tur. **C8** 44
Erzurum, Tur. **C9** 44
Esa'ala, Pap. N. Gui. **H13** 32
Esbjerg, Den. **I3** 10
Escalante, Ut., U.S. **F4** 137
Escalante, stm., Ut., U.S. **F4** 137
Escalon, Ca., U.S. **D3** 98
Escambia, co., Al., U.S. **D2** 94
Escambia, co., Fl., U.S. **u14** 102
Escambia, stm., Fl., U.S. **u14** 102
Escanaba, Mi., U.S. **C3** 115
Escanaba, stm., Mi., U.S. **B3** 115
Escárcega, Mex. **D6** 78
Escarpada Point, c., Phil. **C8** 34
Escatawpa, Ms., U.S. **E5** 117
Escatawpa, stm., U.S. **D5** 117
Escondido, Ca., U.S. **F5** 98
Escondido, stm., Nic. **C3** 80
Escoumins, Rivière des, stm., P.Q., Can. **A8** 90
Escuinapa de Hidalgo, Mex. **C3** 78
Escuintla, Guat. **C1** 80
Escuminac, Point, c., N.B., Can. **B5** 87
Eséka, Cam. **C2** 54
Eşfahān, Iran **D6** 42
Esil', Kaz. **D8** 26
Ěškar-Ola, Russia **D6** 26
Eskilstuna, Swe. **G7** 10
Eskimo Lakes, l., N.T., Can. **E13** 82
Eskişehir, Tur. **C4** 44
Esla, stm., Spain **G4** 16
Eslāmābād, Iran **E12** 44
Eslāmshahr, Iran **C6** 42
Eşme, Tur. **C3** 44
Esmeralda, co., Nv., U.S. **F4** 121
Esmeraldas, Ec. **C4** 70
Esmond, R.I., U.S. **B4** 132
Espanola, On., Can. **A3** 89
Espanola, N.M., U.S. **B3** 124
Esparto, Ca., U.S. **C2** 98
Esperança, Braz. **B3** 70
Esperance, Austl. **G3** 60
Esperance Bay, b., Austl. **G3** 60
Esperanza, Arg. **E5** 72
Esperanza, Mex. **B3** 78
Espinhaço, Serra do, mts., Braz. **E3** 74
Espinho, Port. **G2** 16
Espírito Santo, state, Braz. **E3** 74
Espiritu Santo, i., Vanuatu **j9** 62a
Espíritu Santo, Isla del, i., Mex. **C2** 78
Esplanada, Braz. **D4** 74
Espoo, Fin. **F11** 10
Espungabera, Moz. **C5** 56
Espy, Pa., U.S. **D9** 131
Esquel, Arg. **F2** 69
Esquimalt, B.C., Can. **E6** 85
Esquina, Arg. **D6** 72
Essaouira, Mor. **D3** 48
Essej, Russia **C12** 26
Essen, Ger. **E10** 12
Essendon, Mount, mtn., Austl. **E3** 60
Essequibo, stm., Guy. **C8** 70
Essex, On., Can. **E2** 89
Essex, Ct., U.S. **D6** 100
Essex, Ia., U.S. **D2** 108
Essex, Ma., U.S. **A6** 114
Essex, Md., U.S. **B5** 113
Essex, Vt., U.S. **B2** 138
Essex, co., Ma., U.S. **A5** 114
Essex, co., N.J., U.S. **B4** 123
Essex, co., N.Y., U.S. **B7** 125
Essex, co., Va., U.S. **C6** 139
Essex, co., Vt., U.S. **B5** 138
Essex Junction, Vt., U.S. **C2** 138
Essexville, Mi., U.S. **E7** 115
Esslingen am Neckar, Ger. **F11** 12
Estacada, Or., U.S. **B4** 130
Estacado, Llano, pl., U.S. **C1** 136
Estados, Isla de los, i., Arg. **H4** 69
Eşṭahbān, Iran **E6** 42
Estância, Braz. **D4** 74
Estancia, N.M., U.S. **C3** 124
Estcourt, S. Afr. **D4** 56
Estelí, Nic. **C2** 80
Estella, Spain **F5** 16
Estelline, S.D., U.S. **C9** 134
Estepona, Spain **I4** 16
Estero Bay, b., Ca., U.S. **E3** 98
Estero Bay, b., Fl., U.S. **F5** 102
Estero Island, i., Fl., U.S. **F5** 102
Estes Park, Co., U.S. **A5** 99
Estherville, Ia., U.S. **A3** 108
Estherwood, La., U.S. **D3** 111
Estill, S.C., U.S. **F5** 133
Estill, co., Ky., U.S. **C6** 110
Estill Springs, Tn., U.S. **B5** 135
Estonia, ctry., Eur. **G11** 10
Estremadura, hist. reg., Port. **H2** 16
Esztergom, Hung. **F5** 20
Etah, Grnld. **C25** 82
Étampes, Fr. **C8** 16
Étang-du-Nord, P.Q., Can. **B8** 87
Etāwah, India **D3** 40
Ethel, W.V., U.S. **n12** 141
Ethel Creek, Austl. **E3** 60
Ethiopia, ctry., Afr. **I12** 48
Etna, Pa., U.S. **k14** 131
Etna, Monte, vol., Italy **F5** 18
Etobicoke, On., Can. **D5** 89
Etolin Island, i., Ak., U.S. **m23** 95
Etolin Strait, strt., Ak., U.S. **C6** 95
Etosha Pan, pl., Nmb. **B2** 56
Etowah, Tn., U.S. **D9** 135
Etowah, co., Al., U.S. **A3** 94
Etowah, stm., Ga., U.S. **B2** 103
Et Tîdra, i., Maur. **C1** 50
Ettrick, Va., U.S. **C5** 139
Eua, i., Tonga **G12** 58
Euboea see Évvoia, i., Grc. **E9** 18
Euboea, Gulf of see Vórios Evvoïkós Kólpos, b., Grc. **E9** 18
Eucla, Austl. **G4** 60
Euclid, Oh., U.S. **A4** 128
Eudora, Ar., U.S. **D4** 97
Eudora, Ks., U.S. **D8** 109
Eufaula, Al., U.S. **D4** 94
Eufaula, Ok., U.S. **B6** 129
Eufaula Lake, res., Ok., U.S. **B6** 129
Eugene, Or., U.S. **C3** 130
Eugenia, Punta, c., Mex. **B1** 78
Eugmo, i., Fin. **E10** 10
Eunice, La., U.S. **D3** 111
Eunice, N.M., U.S. **E6** 124
Euphrates (Al-Furāt), stm., Asia **D4** 42
Eupora, Ms., U.S. **B4** 117
Eureka, Ca., U.S. **B1** 98
Eureka, Il., U.S. **C4** 106
Eureka, Ks., U.S. **E7** 109
Eureka, Mo., U.S. **f12** 118
Eureka, Mt., U.S. **B1** 119
Eureka, Nv., U.S. **D6** 121
Eureka, S.C., U.S. **B5** 133
Eureka, S.D., U.S. **B6** 134
Eureka, co., Nv., U.S. **D5** 121
Eureka Springs, Ar., U.S. **A2** 97
Euroa, Austl. **H4** 62
Europe **C13** 4
Eustis, Fl., U.S. **D5** 102
Eutaw, Al., U.S. **C2** 94
Eutsuk Lake, l., B.C., Can. **C4** 85
Evangeline, co., La., U.S. **D3** 111
Evans, Co., U.S. **A6** 99
Evans, Ga., U.S. **C4** 103
Evans, W.V., U.S. **C3** 141
Evans, co., Ga., U.S. **D5** 103
Evans, Mount, mtn., Co., U.S. **B5** 99
Evansburg, Ab., Can. **C3** 84
Evans City, Pa., U.S. **E1** 131
Evansdale, Ia., U.S. **B5** 108
Evanston, Il., U.S. **A6** 106
Evanston, Wy., U.S. **E2** 143
Evansville, Il., U.S. **E4** 106
Evansville, In., U.S. **I2** 107
Evansville, Wi., U.S. **F4** 142
Evansville, Wy., U.S. **D6** 143
Eva Perón see La Plata, Arg. **F6** 72
Evart, Mi., U.S. **E5** 115
Evarts, Ky., U.S. **D6** 110
Eveleth, Mn., U.S. **C6** 116
Evensk, Russia **C17** 26
Everest, Mount, mtn., Asia **D5** 40
Everett, Ma., U.S. **g11** 114
Everett, Pa., U.S. **F5** 131
Everett, Wa., U.S. **B3** 140
Everett Lake, res., N.H., U.S. **D3** 122
Everglades National Park, Fl., U.S. **G5** 102
Evergreen, Al., U.S. **D3** 94
Evergreen, Co., U.S. **B5** 99
Evergreen Park, Il., U.S. **k9** 106
Everly, Ia., U.S. **A2** 108
Everson, Wa., U.S. **A3** 140
Evje, Nor. **G2** 10
Évora, Port. **H3** 16
Évreux, Fr. **C7** 16
Évros (Marica) (Meriç), stm., Eur. **D11** 18
E.V. Spence Reservoir, res., Tx., U.S. **D2** 136
Évvoia, i., Grc. **E9** 18
Ewa, Hi., U.S. **B3** 104
Ewa Beach, Hi., U.S. **B3** 104
Ewa Beach, Hi., U.S. **g9** 104
Ewing Township, N.J., U.S. **C3** 123
Ewo, Congo **D2** 54
Excelsior Mountain, mtn., Ca., U.S. **C4** 98
Excelsior Mountains, mts., Nv., U.S. **E3** 121
Excelsior Springs, Mo., U.S. **B3** 118
Exeter, On., Can. **D3** 89
Exeter, Eng., U.K. **E5** 12
Exeter, Ca., U.S. **D4** 98
Exeter, Ne., U.S. **D8** 120
Exeter, N.H., U.S. **E5** 122
Exeter, Pa., U.S. **D10** 131
Exeter, stm., N.H., U.S. **E5** 122
Exira, Ia., U.S. **C3** 108
Exmore, Va., U.S. **C7** 139
Exmouth, Austl. **E1** 60
Exmouth Gulf, b., Austl. **E1** 60
Experiment, Ga., U.S. **C2** 103
Exploits, stm., Nf., Can. **D3** 88
Exploits, Bay of, b., Nf., Can. **D4** 88
Export, Pa., U.S. **F2** 131
Extremadura, hist. reg., Spain **H3** 16
Exuma Cays, is., Bah. **A4** 80
Exuma Sound, strt., Bah. **D9** 76
Eyasi, Lake, l., Tan. **D7** 54
Eyl, Som. **I14** 48
Eylar Mountain, mtn., Ca., U.S. **D3** 98
Eyota, Mn., U.S. **G6** 116
Eyre, Austl. **G4** 60
Eyre North, Lake, l., Austl. **F2** 62
Eyre Peninsula, pen., Austl. **G6** 60
Ezequiel Ramos Mexía, Embalse, res., Arg. **E3** 69
Ezine, Tur. **C2** 44

F

Fabens, Tx., U.S. **o11** 136
Fabius, stm., Mo., U.S. **A6** 118
Fabriano, Italy **C4** 18
Fachi, Niger **C7** 50
Factoryville, Pa., U.S. **C10** 131
Fada, Chad **G9** 48
Fada-Ngourma, Burkina **D5** 50
Faenza, Italy **B3** 18
Faeroe Islands see Faroe Islands, is., Far. Is. **B12** 4
Făgăraş, Rom. **G8** 20
Fagernes, Nor. **F3** 10
Fagersta, Swe. **G6** 10
Fairacres, N.M., U.S. **E3** 124
Fairbank, Ia., U.S. **B5** 108
Fairbanks, Ak., U.S. **C10** 95
Fair Bluff, N.C., U.S. **C3** 126
Fairborn, Oh., U.S. **C1** 128
Fairburn, Ga., U.S. **C2** 103
Fairbury, Il., U.S. **C5** 106
Fairbury, Ne., U.S. **D8** 120
Fairchance, Pa., U.S. **G2** 131
Fairchild Air Force Base, mil., Wa., U.S. **g13** 140
Fairdale, Ky., U.S. **B4** 110
Fairfax, Ca., U.S. **C2** 98
Fairfax, De., U.S. **A3** 101
Fairfax, Ia., U.S. **C6** 108
Fairfax, Mn., U.S. **F4** 116
Fairfax, Mo., U.S. **A2** 118
Fairfax, Ok., U.S. **A5** 129
Fairfax, S.C., U.S. **F5** 133
Fairfax, Va., U.S. **B5** 139
Fairfax, co., Va., U.S. **B5** 139
Fairfield, Al., U.S. **B3** 94
Fairfield, Ca., U.S. **C2** 98
Fairfield, Ct., U.S. **E2** 100
Fairfield, Ia., U.S. **C6** 108
Fairfield, Il., U.S. **E5** 106
Fairfield, Me., U.S. **D3** 112
Fairfield, Mt., U.S. **C5** 119
Fairfield, Oh., U.S. **n12** 128
Fairfield, Tx., U.S. **D4** 136
Fairfield, co., Ct., U.S. **D2** 100
Fairfield, co., Oh., U.S. **C3** 128
Fairfield, co., S.C., U.S. **C5** 133
Fairfield Bay, Ar., U.S. **B3** 97
Fairfield Pond, l., Vt., U.S. **B3** 138
Fair Grove, Mo., U.S. **D4** 118
Fair Grove, N.C., U.S. **B2** 126
Fairhaven, Ma., U.S. **C6** 114
Fair Haven, Mi., U.S. **F8** 115
Fair Haven, N.J., U.S. **C4** 123
Fair Haven, Vt., U.S. **D2** 138
Fairhope, Al., U.S. **E2** 94
Fair Isle, i., Scot., U.K. **i19** 12a
Fairland, In., U.S. **E6** 107
Fairland, Ok., U.S. **A7** 129
Fair Lawn, N.J., U.S. **h8** 123
Fairlawn, Va., U.S. **C2** 139
Fairlea, W.V., U.S. **D4** 141
Fairmont, Il., U.S. **C6** 106
Fairmont, Mn., U.S. **G4** 116
Fairmont, N.C., U.S. **C3** 126
Fairmont, Ne., U.S. **D8** 120
Fairmont, W.V., U.S. **B4** 141

Name	Map Ref.	Page
Fairmount, Ga., U.S.	**B2**	103
Fairmount, In., U.S.	**D6**	107
Fairmount Heights, Md., U.S.	**f9**	113
Fair Oaks, Ga., U.S.	**h7**	103
Fairoaks, Pa., U.S.	**h13**	131
Fair Plain, Mi., U.S.	**F4**	115
Fairport, N.Y., U.S.	**B3**	125
Fairport Harbor, Oh., U.S.	**A4**	128
Fairvale, N.B., Can.	**D4**	87
Fairview, Ab., Can.	**A1**	84
Fairview, Mt., U.S.	**C12**	119
Fairview, N.J., U.S.	**h8**	123
Fairview, Ok., U.S.	**A3**	129
Fairview, Pa., U.S.	**B1**	131
Fairview, Tn., U.S.	**B4**	135
Fairview, Ut., U.S.	**D4**	137
Fairview Heights, Il., U.S.	**E3**	106
Fairview Park, In., U.S.	**E3**	107
Fairview Park, Oh., U.S.	**g9**	128
Fairview Peak, mtn., Nv., U.S.	**D3**	121
Fairview Peak, mtn., Or., U.S.	**D4**	130
Fairway, Ks., U.S.	**k16**	109
Fairweather Mountain, mtn., N.A.	**G12**	82
Fais, i., Micron.	**E11**	32
Faisalabad, Pak.	**D10**	42
Faison, N.C., U.S.	**B4**	126
Faizābād, India	**D4**	40
Fakfak, Indon.	**D8**	36
Fakse Bugt, b., Den.	**I5**	10
Faku, China	**C12**	28
Falaba, S.L.	**E2**	50
Falam, Myan.	**B2**	34
Falconer, N.Y., U.S.	**C1**	125
Falcon Heights, Mn., U.S.	**n12**	116
Falcon Heights, Or., U.S.	**E5**	130
Fălești, Mol.	**F9**	20
Falfurrias, Tx., U.S.	**F3**	136
Falher, Ab., Can.	**B2**	84
Falkenberg, Swe.	**H5**	10
Falkland Islands, dep., S.A.	**H4**	69
Falkland Islands, is., Falk. Is.	**J9**	4
Falkland Sound, strt., Falk. Is.	**H4**	69
Falköping, Swe.	**G5**	10
Falkville, Al., U.S.	**A3**	94
Fall, stm., Ks., U.S.	**E7**	109
Fall Branch, Tn., U.S.	**C11**	135
Fallbrook, Ca., U.S.	**F5**	98
Fall City, Wa., U.S.	**B4**	140
Fall Creek, Wi., U.S.	**D2**	142
Falling Creek, stm., Va., U.S.	**n17**	139
Falling Rock Creek, stm., W.V., U.S.	**m13**	141
Fall Mountain Lake, Ct., U.S.	**C4**	100
Fallon, Nv., U.S.	**D3**	121
Fallon, co., Mt., U.S.	**D12**	119
Fallon Indian Reservation, Nv., U.S.	**D3**	121
Fallon Naval Air Station, mil., Nv., U.S.	**D3**	121
Fall River, Ma., U.S.	**C5**	114
Fall River, Wi., U.S.	**E4**	142
Fall River, co., S.D., U.S.	**D2**	134
Fall River Lake, res., Ks., U.S.	**E7**	109
Falls, co., Tx., U.S.	**D4**	136
Falls Church, Va., U.S.	**g12**	139
Falls City, Ne., U.S.	**D10**	120
Falls City, Or., U.S.	**C3**	130
Falls Creek, Pa., U.S.	**D4**	131
Fallston, Md., U.S.	**A5**	113
Falmouth, N.S., Can.	**E5**	87
Falmouth, Eng., U.K.	**E4**	12
Falmouth, Ky., U.S.	**B5**	110
Falmouth, Ma., U.S.	**C6**	114
Falmouth, Me., U.S.	**E2**	112
Falmouth, Va., U.S.	**B5**	139
False Bay see Valsbaai, b., S. Afr.	**E2**	56
False Cape, c., Fl., U.S.	**D6**	102
False Cape, c., Va., U.S.	**D7**	139
Falster, i., Den.	**I5**	10
Fălticeni, Rom.	**F9**	20
Falun, Swe.	**F6**	10
Fanchang, China	**C4**	30
Fancy Farm, Ky., U.S.	**f9**	110
Fangak, Sudan	**B6**	54
Fangcheng, China	**E2**	30
Fangcheng, China	**C3**	30
Fangxian, China	**C3**	30
Fangzheng, China	**A1**	31
Fannin, co., Ga., U.S.	**B2**	103
Fannin, co., Tx., U.S.	**C4**	136
Fanny, Mount, mtn., Or., U.S.	**B9**	130
Fano, Italy	**C4**	18
Fan Si Pan, mtn., Viet.	**B4**	34
Faradje, D.R.C.	**C5**	54
Faradofay see Tôlañaro, Madag.	**D8**	56
Farafangana, Madag.	**C8**	56
Farāh, Afg.	**D8**	42
Farallon de Medinilla, i., N. Mar. Is.	**C12**	32
Farallon de Pajaros, i., N. Mar. Is.	**B12**	32
Faranah, Gui.	**D2**	50
Farasān, Jazā'ir, is., Sau. Ar.	**G4**	38
Farewell, Cape, c., N.Z.	**p13**	63c
Fargo, Ga., U.S.	**F4**	103
Fargo, N.D., U.S.	**C9**	127
Faribault, Mn., U.S.	**F5**	116
Faribault, co., Mn., U.S.	**G4**	116
Farīdābād, India	**D3**	40
Farley, Ia., U.S.	**B6**	108
Farmer City, Il., U.S.	**C5**	106
Farmers Branch, Tx., U.S.	**n10**	136
Farmersburg, In., U.S.	**F3**	107
Farmerville, La., U.S.	**B3**	111
Farmingdale, Me., U.S.	**D3**	112
Farmington, Ar., U.S.	**A1**	97
Farmington, Ct., U.S.	**C4**	100
Farmington, Ia., U.S.	**D6**	108
Farmington, Il., U.S.	**C3**	106
Farmington, Me., U.S.	**D2**	112
Farmington, Mi., U.S.	**p15**	115
Farmington, Mn., U.S.	**F5**	116
Farmington, Mo., U.S.	**D7**	118
Farmington, N.H., U.S.	**D4**	122
Farmington, N.M., U.S.	**A1**	124
Farmington, Ut., U.S.	**C4**	137
Farmington, stm., Ct., U.S.	**B4**	100
Farmington Hills, Mi., U.S.	**o15**	115
Farmland, In., U.S.	**D7**	107
Farmville, N.C., U.S.	**B5**	126
Farmville, Va., U.S.	**C4**	139
Farnham, P.Q., Can.	**D5**	90
Faro, Braz.	**D8**	70
Faro, Port.	**I3**	16
Faroe Islands, dep., Eur.	**o23**	10b
Faroe Islands, is., Far. Is.	**B12**	4
Fårön, i., Swe.	**H8**	10
Fårösund, Swe.	**H8**	10
Farquhar, Atoll de, is., Sey.	**j12**	57b
Farrell, Pa., U.S.	**D1**	131
Farrukhābād, India	**D3**	40
Fartak, Ra's, c., Yemen	**G6**	38
Farvel, Kap, c., Grnld.	**G31**	82
Farwell, Mi., U.S.	**E6**	115
Farwell, Tx., U.S.	**B1**	136
Fasā, Iran	**E6**	42
Fastiv, Ukr.	**D10**	20
Fatick, Sen.	**D1**	50
Fatsa, Tur.	**B7**	44
Faulk, co., S.D., U.S.	**B6**	134
Faulkland Heights, De., U.S.	**i7**	101
Faulkner, co., Ar., U.S.	**B3**	97
Faulkton, S.D., U.S.	**B6**	134
Fauquier, co., Va., U.S.	**B5**	139
Fauske, Nor.	**C6**	10
Fawnie Nose, mtn., B.C., Can.	**C5**	85
Faxaflói, b., Ice.	**l17**	10a
Faya-Largeau, Chad	**C8**	50
Fayd, Sau. Ar.	**E4**	42
Fayette, Al., U.S.	**B2**	94
Fayette, Ia., U.S.	**B6**	108
Fayette, Mo., U.S.	**B5**	118
Fayette, Ms., U.S.	**D2**	117
Fayette, Oh., U.S.	**A1**	128
Fayette, co., Al., U.S.	**B3**	94
Fayette, co., Ga., U.S.	**C2**	103
Fayette, co., Ia., U.S.	**B6**	108
Fayette, co., Il., U.S.	**D5**	106
Fayette, co., In., U.S.	**E7**	107
Fayette, co., Ky., U.S.	**B5**	110
Fayette, co., Oh., U.S.	**C2**	128
Fayette, co., Pa., U.S.	**G2**	131
Fayette, co., Tn., U.S.	**B2**	135
Fayette, co., Tx., U.S.	**E4**	136
Fayette, co., W.V., U.S.	**C3**	141
Fayetteville, Ar., U.S.	**A1**	97
Fayetteville, Ga., U.S.	**C2**	103
Fayetteville, N.C., U.S.	**B4**	126
Fayetteville, Pa., U.S.	**G6**	131
Fayetteville, Tn., U.S.	**B5**	135
Fayetteville, W.V., U.S.	**C3**	141
Fāzilka, India	**C2**	40
Fazzān, hist. reg., Libya	**A7**	50
Fdérik, Maur.	**B2**	50
Fear, Cape, c., N.C., U.S.	**D5**	126
Feather, stm., Ca., U.S.	**C3**	98
Fécamp, Fr.	**C7**	16
Federal, Arg.	**E6**	72
Federalsburg, Md., U.S.	**C6**	113
Federated States of Micronesia see Micronesia, Federated States of, ctry., Oc.	**D8**	58
Feeding Hills, Ma., U.S.	**B2**	114
Fehmarn, i., Ger.	**C12**	12
Feijó, Braz.	**E5**	70
Feira de Santana, Braz.	**D4**	74
Felipe Carrillo Puerto, Mex.	**D7**	78
Fellsmere, Fl., U.S.	**E6**	102
Felton, Ca., U.S.	**D2**	98
Felton, De., U.S.	**D3**	101
Femunden, l., Nor.	**E4**	10
Fence, stm., Mi., U.S.	**B2**	115
Fence Lake, l., Wi., U.S.	**C4**	142
Fenelon Falls, On., Can.	**C6**	89
Fengcheng, China	**F11**	28
Fengdu, China	**F9**	28
Fengfeng, China	**B3**	30
Fenghuang, China	**D2**	30
Fengning, China	**A4**	30
Fengqing, China	**B3**	34
Fengqiu, China	**B3**	30
Fengrun, China	**B4**	30
Fengtai, China	**C4**	30
Fengzhen, China	**A3**	30
Fenimore Pass, strt., Ak., U.S.	**E4**	95
Fennimore, Wi., U.S.	**F3**	142
Fennville, Mi., U.S.	**F4**	115
Fenoarivo Atsinanana, Madag.	**B8**	56
Fenton, Mi., U.S.	**F7**	115
Fentress, co., Tn., U.S.	**C9**	135
Fenwick Island, i., S.C., U.S.	**k11**	133
Fenyang, China	**D10**	28
Fenyi, China	**D3**	30
Feodosiia, Ukr.	**G13**	20
Fer, Point au, c., La., U.S.	**E4**	111
Ferdinand, In., U.S.	**H4**	107
Ferdows, Iran	**D7**	42
Fergana, Uzb.	**E9**	26
Fergana Mountains see Ferganskij hrebet, mts., Kyrg.	**A2**	40
Ferganskij hrebet, mts., Kyrg.	**A2**	40
Fergus, On., Can.	**D4**	89
Fergus, co., Mt., U.S.	**C7**	119
Fergus Falls, Mn., U.S.	**D2**	116
Ferguson, Ky., U.S.	**C5**	110
Ferguson, Mo., U.S.	**C7**	118
Ferkéssédougou, C. Iv.	**E3**	50
Ferlo, reg., Sen.	**C2**	50
Ferme-Neuve, P.Q., Can.	**C2**	90
Fermo, Italy	**C4**	18
Fermont, P.Q., Can.	**h13**	90
Fernandina Beach, Fl., U.S.	**B5**	102
Fernandópolis, Braz.	**F1**	74
Fernando Póo see Bioko, i., Eq. Gui.	**C1**	54
Fernán-Núñez, Spain	**I4**	16
Fern Creek, Ky., U.S.	**g11**	110
Ferndale, Ca., U.S.	**B1**	98
Ferndale, Md., U.S.	**B4**	113
Ferndale, Mi., U.S.	**P15**	115
Ferndale, Pa., U.S.	**F4**	131
Ferndale, Wa., U.S.	**A3**	140
Fernie, B.C., Can.	**E10**	85
Fernley, Nv., U.S.	**D2**	121
Fern Ridge Lake, res., Or., U.S.	**C3**	130
Fernwood, Id., U.S.	**B2**	105
Fernwood, Ms., U.S.	**D3**	117
Feroe Islands see Faroe Islands, dep., Far. Is.	**C5**	8
Ferrara, Italy	**B3**	18
Ferrelo, Cape, c., Or., U.S.	**E2**	130
Ferriday, La., U.S.	**C4**	111
Ferris, Tx., U.S.	**C4**	136
Ferris Mountains, mts., Wy., U.S.	**D5**	143
Ferro see El Hierro, i., Spain	**A1**	50
Ferrol, Spain	**F2**	16
Ferron, Ut., U.S.	**D4**	137
Ferrum, Va., U.S.	**D2**	139
Ferry, co., Wa., U.S.	**A7**	140
Ferry Farms, Va., U.S.	**B5**	139
Ferryland, Nf., Can.	**E5**	88
Ferry Point, c., N.J., U.S.	**k7**	123
Fertile, Mn., U.S.	**C2**	116
Fès, Mor.	**D4**	48
Feshi, D.R.C.	**E3**	54
Fessenden, N.D., U.S.	**B6**	127
Festus, Mo., U.S.	**C7**	118
Fetești, Rom.	**G9**	20
Fethiye, Tur.	**D3**	44
Fetisovo, Kaz.	**B6**	42
Feuilles, Rivière aux, stm., P.Q., Can.	**g12**	90
Feyzābād, Afg.	**C10**	42
Fianarantsoa, Madag.	**C8**	56
Fianga, Chad	**E8**	50
Fichē, Eth.	**B7**	54
Ficksburg, S. Afr.	**D4**	56
Fidalgo Island, i., Wa., U.S.	**A3**	140
Fieldale, Va., U.S.	**D3**	139
Fields, Lake, l., Fl., U.S.	**B3**	102
Fields, Lake, l., La., U.S.	**k10**	111
Fier, Alb.	**D7**	18
Fifteenmile Creek, stm., Wy., U.S.	**B4**	143
Fifteen Mile Falls Reservoir, res., U.S.	**C5**	138
Fifth Cataract, wtfl, Sudan	**G11**	48
Figtree, Zimb.	**C4**	56
Figueira da Foz, Port.	**G2**	16
Figueres, Spain	**F8**	16
Figuig, Mor.	**D4**	48
Fiji, ctry., Oc.	**m10**	63b
Filchner Ice Shelf, Ant.	**D1**	67
Filer, Id., U.S.	**G4**	105
Filingué, Niger	**D5**	50
Filippoi, hist., Grc.	**D10**	18
Fillmore, Ca., U.S.	**E4**	98
Fillmore, Ut., U.S.	**E3**	137
Fillmore, co., Mn., U.S.	**G6**	116
Fillmore, co., Ne., U.S.	**D8**	120
Fimi, stm., D.R.C.	**D3**	54
Findlay, Il., U.S.	**D5**	106
Findlay, Oh., U.S.	**A2**	128
Fingoè, Moz.	**B5**	56
Finike, Tur.	**D4**	44
Finke, Austl.	**F5**	60
Finland, ctry., Eur.	**E12**	10
Finland, Gulf of, b., Eur.	**G10**	10
Finley, Austl.	**H4**	62
Finley, Tn., U.S.	**A2**	135
Finney, co., Ks., U.S.	**D3**	109
Finnmark, prov., Nor.	**B11**	10
Finn Mountain, mtn., Ak., U.S.	**C8**	95
Fins, Oman	**F7**	42
Finspång, Swe.	**G6**	10
Fircrest, Wa., U.S.	**f10**	140
Firebaugh, Ca., U.S.	**D3**	98
Firenze (Florence), Italy	**C3**	18
Firestone, Co., U.S.	**A6**	99
Fīrozābād, India	**D3**	40
Fīrozpur, India	**C2**	40
First Cataract, wtfl, Egypt	**F11**	48
First Connecticut Lake, l., N.H., U.S.	**f7**	122
Fīrūzābād, Iran	**E6**	42
Fish, stm., Al., U.S.	**E2**	94
Fish, stm., Me., U.S.	**A4**	112
Fish Creek, stm., W.V., U.S.	**g8**	141
Fisher, Il., U.S.	**C5**	106
Fisher, co., Tx., U.S.	**C2**	136
Fisher Bay, b., Mb., Can.	**D3**	86
Fishermans Island, i., Va., U.S.	**h15**	139
Fishers, In., U.S.	**E5**	107
Fishers Island, i., N.Y., U.S.	**m16**	125
Fishers Peak, mtn., Co., U.S.	**D6**	99
Fishersville, Va., U.S.	**B4**	139
Fishing Bay, b., Md., U.S.	**D5**	113
Fishing Creek, Md., U.S.	**D5**	113
Fishing Creek, stm., N.C., U.S.	**A5**	126
Fishing Creek, stm., S.C., U.S.	**B5**	133
Fishing Creek, stm., W.V., U.S.	**B4**	141
Fishing Creek Reservoir, res., S.C., U.S.	**B6**	133
Fishkill, N.Y., U.S.	**D7**	125
Fish Lake, l., Ut., U.S.	**E4**	137
Fish River Lake, l., Me., U.S.	**B4**	112
Fishtrap Lake, res., Ky., U.S.	**C7**	110
Fiskdale, Ma., U.S.	**B3**	114
Fisterra, Cabo de, c., Spain	**F2**	16
Fitchburg, Ma., U.S.	**A4**	114
Fitri, Lac, l., Chad	**D8**	50
Fitzgerald, Ga., U.S.	**E3**	103
Fitz Roy, Arg.	**G3**	69
Fitzroy, stm., Austl.	**D3**	60
Fitzroy Crossing, Austl.	**D4**	60
Fitzwilliam, N.H., U.S.	**E2**	122
Fitzwilliam Island, i., On., Can.	**B3**	89
Fiume see Rijeka, Cro.	**B5**	18
Five Island Lake, l., Ia., U.S.	**A3**	108
Fivemile Creek, stm., Wy., U.S.	**C4**	143
Five Points, N.M., U.S.	**B3**	124
Fizi, D.R.C.	**D5**	54
Flagler, co., Fl., U.S.	**C5**	102
Flagler Beach, Fl., U.S.	**C5**	102
Flagstaff, Az., U.S.	**B4**	96
Flagstaff Lake, l., Or., U.S.	**E7**	130
Flambeau, stm., Wi., U.S.	**C3**	142
Flaming Gorge Dam, Ut., U.S.	**C6**	137
Flaming Gorge National Recreation Area, U.S.	**E3**	143
Flaming Gorge Reservoir, res., U.S.	**C6**	92
Flaming Gorge Reservoir, res., U.S.	**E3**	143
Flanagan, Il., U.S.	**C5**	106
Flandreau, S.D., U.S.	**C9**	134
Flandreau Indian Reservation, S.D., U.S.	**C9**	134
Flat, stm., Mi., U.S.	**E5**	115
Flat, stm., N.C., U.S.	**A4**	126
Flat, stm., R.I., U.S.	**E2**	132
Flat Brook, stm., N.J., U.S.	**A3**	123
Flathead, co., Mt., U.S.	**B2**	119
Flathead, South Fork, stm., Mt., U.S.	**C3**	119
Flathead Indian Reservation, Mt., U.S.	**C2**	119
Flathead Lake, l., Mt., U.S.	**C2**	119
Flathead Valley, val., Mt., U.S.	**C2**	119
Flat Lake, l., La., U.S.	**k9**	111
Flat Lick, Ky., U.S.	**D6**	110
Flatonia, Tx., U.S.	**E4**	136
Flat River, Mo., U.S.	**D7**	118
Flat River Reservoir, res., R.I., U.S.	**D3**	132
Flat Rock, Mi., U.S.	**F7**	115
Flat Rock, N.C., U.S.	**f10**	126
Flatrock, stm., In., U.S.	**F6**	107
Flattery, Cape, c., Austl.	**C4**	62
Flattery, Cape, c., Wa., U.S.	**A1**	140
Flatwoods, Ky., U.S.	**B7**	110
Fleetwood, Pa., U.S.	**F10**	131
Fleming, co., Ky., U.S.	**B6**	110
Fleming-Neon, Ky., U.S.	**C7**	110
Flemingsburg, Ky., U.S.	**B6**	110
Flemington, N.J., U.S.	**B3**	123
Flemington, Pa., U.S.	**D7**	131
Flen, Swe.	**G7**	10
Flensburg, Ger.	**C11**	12
Fletcher, N.C., U.S.	**f10**	126
Fletcher, Ok., U.S.	**C3**	129
Flinders, stm., Austl.	**D3**	62
Flinders Bay, b., Austl.	**G2**	60
Flinders Island, i., Austl.	**H4**	62
Flinders Reefs, rf., Austl.	**D4**	62
Flin Flon, Mb., Can.	**B1**	86
Flint, Mi., U.S.	**E7**	115
Flint, i., Kir.	**F14**	58
Flint, stm., Ga., U.S.	**E2**	103
Flint City, Al., U.S.	**A3**	94
Flint Creek Range, mts., Mt., U.S.	**D3**	119
Flint Run, stm., W.V., U.S.	**k9**	141
Flippin, Ar., U.S.	**A3**	97
Flisa, Nor.	**F5**	10
Flomaton, Al., U.S.	**D2**	94
Flora, Il., U.S.	**E5**	106
Flora, In., U.S.	**C4**	107
Flora, Ms., U.S.	**C3**	117
Florala, Al., U.S.	**D3**	94
Floral City, Fl., U.S.	**D4**	102
Florence see Firenze, Italy	**C3**	18
Florence, Al., U.S.	**A2**	94
Florence, Az., U.S.	**D4**	96
Florence, Co., U.S.	**C5**	99
Florence, Ks., U.S.	**D7**	109
Florence, Ky., U.S.	**A5**	110
Florence, Ms., U.S.	**C3**	117
Florence, N.J., U.S.	**C3**	123
Florence, Or., U.S.	**D2**	130
Florence, S.C., U.S.	**C8**	133
Florence, co., S.C., U.S.	**C8**	133
Florence, co., Wi., U.S.	**C5**	142
Florenceville, N.B., Can.	**C2**	87
Florencia, Col.	**C4**	70
Flores, i., Indon.	**E6**	36
Flores, Laut (Flores Sea), Indon.	**E6**	36
Flores Sea see Flores, Laut, Indon.	**E6**	36
Floreşti, Mol.	**F10**	20
Floresville, Tx., U.S.	**E3**	136
Florham Park, N.J., U.S.	**B4**	123
Floriano, Braz.	**C3**	74
Florianópolis, Braz.	**D8**	72
Florida, Cuba	**A4**	80
Florida, N.Y., U.S.	**D6**	125
Florida, Ur.	**E6**	72
Florida, state, U.S.	**E5**	102
Florida, Cape, c., Fl., U.S.	**G6**	102
Florida, Straits of, strt., N.A.	**G11**	92
Florida Bay, b., Fl., U.S.	**H6**	102
Floridablanca, Col.	**D5**	80
Florida City, Fl., U.S.	**G6**	102
Florida Keys, is., Fl., U.S.	**H6**	102
Florida Mountains, mts., N.M., U.S.	**E2**	124
Florida State Indian Reservation, Fl., U.S.	**F5**	102
Florien, La., U.S.	**C2**	111
Flórina, Grc.	**D8**	18
Florissant, Mo., U.S.	**f13**	118
Florissant Fossil Beds National Monument, Co., U.S.	**C5**	99
Florø, Nor.	**F1**	10
Flossmoor, Il., U.S.	**k9**	106
Flovilla, Ga., U.S.	**C3**	103
Flower Brook, stm., Vt., U.S.	**E2**	138
Flowery Branch, Ga., U.S.	**B3**	103
Flowood, Ms., U.S.	**C3**	117
Floyd, co., Ga., U.S.	**B1**	103
Floyd, co., Ia., U.S.	**A5**	108
Floyd, co., In., U.S.	**H6**	107
Floyd, co., Ky., U.S.	**C7**	110
Floyd, co., Tx., U.S.	**B2**	136
Floyd, co., Va., U.S.	**D2**	139
Floyd, stm., Ia., U.S.	**B1**	108
Floydada, Tx., U.S.	**C2**	136
Floyds Fork, stm., Ky., U.S.	**B4**	110
Floyds Knobs, In., U.S.	**H6**	107
Flushing see Vlissingen, Neth.	**E8**	12
Flushing, Mi., U.S.	**E7**	115
Flushing, Oh., U.S.	**B4**	128
Fluvanna, co., Va., U.S.	**C4**	139
Foard, co., Tx., U.S.	**B3**	136
Foča, Bos.	**C7**	18
Focşani, Rom.	**G9**	20
Foggia, Italy	**D5**	18
Fogland Point, c., R.I., U.S.	**E6**	132
Fogo, Nf., Can.	**D4**	88
Fogo, i., C.V.	**g10**	50a
Fogo, Cape, c., Nf., Can.	**D5**	88
Fogo Island, i., Nf., Can.	**D4**	88
Foix, Fr.	**F7**	16
Fokku, Nig.	**D5**	50
Folda, b., Nor.	**C6**	10
Foley, Al., U.S.	**E2**	94
Foley, Mn., U.S.	**E5**	116
Foligno, Italy	**C4**	18
Folkestone, Eng., U.K.	**E7**	12
Folkston, Ga., U.S.	**F4**	103
Follansbee, W.V., U.S.	**A4**	141
Folly Beach, S.C., U.S.	**F8**	133
Folly Island, i., S.C., U.S.	**F8**	133
Folsom, Ca., U.S.	**C3**	98
Fomboni, Com.	**A7**	56
Fonda, Ia., U.S.	**B3**	108
Fond du Lac, Wi., U.S.	**E5**	142
Fond du Lac, co., Wi., U.S.	**E5**	142
Fond du Lac Indian Reservation, Mn., U.S.	**D6**	116
Fonseca, Golfo de, b., N.A.	**C2**	80
Fontainebleau, Fr.	**C8**	16
Fontana, Ca., U.S.	**m14**	98
Fontana, Wi., U.S.	**F5**	142
Fontana Lake, res., N.C., U.S.	**f9**	126
Fontanelle, Ia., U.S.	**C3**	108
Fonte Boa, Braz.	**D6**	70
Fontenay-le-Comte, Fr.	**D6**	16
Fontenelle Reservoir, res., Wy., U.S.	**D2**	143
Fontur, c., Ice.	**k21**	10a
Foochow see Fuzhou, China	**F11**	28
Footville, Wi., U.S.	**F4**	142

Name | Map Ref. | Page

Foraker, Mount, mtn., Ak., U.S. f16 95
Forbes, Austl. G4 62
Forbes, Mount, mtn., Ab., Can. D2 84
Forcados, Nig. E6 50
Forchheim, Ger. F12 12
Ford, co., Il., U.S. C5 106
Ford, co., Ks., U.S. E4 109
Ford, stm., Mi., U.S. C3 115
Ford City, Ca., U.S. E4 98
Ford City, Pa., U.S. E2 131
Fordoche, La., U.S. D4 111
Fords Prairie, Wa., U.S. C2 140
Fordyce, Ar., U.S. D3 97
Forécariah, Gui. E2 50
Forel, Mont, mtn., Grnld. E32 82
Foreman, Ar., U.S. D1 97
Forest, On., Can. D2 89
Forest, Ms., U.S. C4 117
Forest, Oh., U.S. B2 128
Forest, co., Pa., U.S. C3 131
Forest, co., Wi., U.S. C5 142
Forest, stm., N.D., U.S. A8 127
Forest Acres, S.C., U.S. C6 133
Forestburg, Ab., Can. C4 84
Forest City, Ia., U.S. A4 108
Forest City, N.C., U.S. B1 126
Forest City, Pa., U.S. C11 131
Forestdale, R.I., U.S. B3 132
Forest Dale, Vt., U.S. D2 138
Forest Glen, La., U.S. h12 111
Forest Grove, Or., U.S. B3 130
Forest Hill, Md., U.S. A5 113
Forest Hills, Pa., U.S. k14 131
Forest Knolls, Ca., U.S. g7 98
Forest Lake, Mn., U.S. E6 116
Forest Park, Ga., U.S. h8 103
Forest Park, Il., U.S. k9 106
Forillon, Parc National de, P.Q., Can. k14 90
Fork Creek, stm., W.V., U.S. m12 141
Forked Deer, stm., Tn., U.S. B2 135
Forkland, Al., U.S. C2 94
Forks, Wa., U.S. B1 140
Forlì, Italy B4 18
Formentera, i., Spain H7 16
Formia, Italy D4 18
Formiga, Braz. F2 74
Formosa, Arg. D6 72
Formosa, Braz. E2 74
Formosa see Taiwan, ctry., Asia B8 34
Formosa, Serra, plat., Braz. F9 70
Formosa Strait see Taiwan Strait, strt., Asia E4 30
Forney, Tx., U.S. C4 136
Forrest, Austl. G4 60
Forrest, Il., U.S. C5 106
Forrest, co., Ms., U.S. D4 117
Forrest City, Ar., U.S. B5 97
Forrester Island, i., Ak., U.S. n23 95
Forreston, Il., U.S. A4 106
Forsayth, Austl. D3 62
Forst, Ger. E14 12
Forsyth, Ga., U.S. C3 103
Forsyth, Il., U.S. D5 106
Forsyth, Mo., U.S. E4 118
Forsyth, Mt., U.S. D10 119
Forsyth, co., Ga., U.S. B2 103
Forsyth, co., N.C., U.S. A2 126
Fortaleza, Braz. B4 74
Fort Apache Indian Reservation, Az., U.S. D5 96
Fort-Archambault see Sarh, Chad B3 54
Fort Ashby, W.V., U.S. B6 141
Fort Atkinson, Wi., U.S. F5 142
Fort Beaufort, S. Afr. E4 56
Fort Belknap Indian Reservation, Mt., U.S. B8 119
Fort Belvoir, mil., Va., U.S. g12 139
Fort Bend, co., Tx., U.S. E5 136
Fort Benjamin Harrison, mil., In., U.S. k10 107
Fort Benning, mil., Ga., U.S. D2 103
Fort Benton, Mt., U.S. C6 119
Fort Berthold Indian Reservation, N.D., U.S. B3 127
Fort Bidwell Indian Reservation, Ca., U.S. B3 98
Fort Bliss, mil., Tx., U.S. o11 136
Fort Bragg, Ca., U.S. C2 98
Fort Bragg, mil., N.C., U.S. B3 126
Fort Branch, In., U.S. H2 107
Fort Calhoun, Ne., U.S. C9 120
Fort Campbell, mil., U.S. A4 135
Fort Carson, mil., Co., U.S. C6 99
Fort Chipewyan, Ab., Can. f8 84
Fort Clatsop National Memorial, hist., Or., U.S. A3 130
Fort Cobb, Ok., U.S. B3 129
Fort Cobb Reservoir, res., Ok., U.S. B3 129
Fort Collins, Co., U.S. A5 99
Fort Coulonge, P.Q., Can. B8 89
Fort-Dauphin see Tôlañaro, Madag. D8 56
Fort Davis, Tx., U.S. o13 136
Fort Davis National Historic Site, hist., Tx., U.S. o13 136
Fort Defiance, Az., U.S. B6 96
Fort-de-France, Mart. C7 80
Fort Deposit, Al., U.S. D3 94
Fort Detrick, mil., Md., U.S. B3 113
Fort Dix, mil., N.J., U.S. C3 123
Fort Dodge, Ia., U.S. B3 108
Fort Donelson National Battlefield, Tn., U.S. A4 135
Fort Edward, N.Y., U.S. B7 125
Fort Erie, On., Can. E6 89
Fort Eustis, mil., Va., U.S. h14 139
Fort Fairfield, Me., U.S. B5 112
Fort Frances, On., Can. o16 89
Fort Gaines, Ga., U.S. E1 103
Fort Gay, W.V., U.S. C2 141
Fort Gibson, Ok., U.S. B6 129
Fort Gibson Lake, res., Ok., U.S. A6 129
Fort Gordon, mil., Ga., U.S. C4 103
Fort Greely, mil., Ak., U.S. C10 95
Forth, Firth of, b., Scot., U.K. B5 12
Fort Hall, Id., U.S. F6 105
Fort Hall Indian Reservation, Id., U.S. F6 105
Fort Hood, mil., Tx., U.S. D4 136
Fort Howard, Md., U.S. B5 113
Fort Huachuca, mil., Az., U.S. F5 96
Fort Jackson, mil., S.C., U.S. C6 133
Fort Jefferson National Monument, Fl., U.S. H4 102
Fort Kent, Me., U.S. A4 112
Fort Knox, mil., Ky., U.S. B4 110
Fort-Lamy see N'Djamena, Chad D8 50
Fort Laramie, Wy., U.S. D8 143
Fort Laramie National Historic Site, hist., Wy., U.S. D8 143
Fort Lauderdale, Fl., U.S. F6 102
Fort Lawn, S.C., U.S. B6 133
Fort Leavenworth, mil., Ks., U.S. C9 109
Fort Lee, N.J., U.S. B5 123
Fort Lee, mil., Va., U.S. C5 139
Fort Leonard Wood, mil., Mo., U.S. D5 118
Fort Lewis, mil., Wa., U.S. B3 140
Fort Loramie, Oh., U.S. B1 128
Fort Loudon, Pa., U.S. G6 131
Fort Loudoun Lake, res., Tn., U.S. D9 135
Fort Lupton, Co., U.S. A6 99
Fort MacArthur, mil., Ca., U.S. n12 98
Fort Macleod, Ab., Can. E4 84
Fort Madison, Ia., U.S. D6 108
Fort Matanzas National Monument, Fl., U.S. C5 102
Fort McClellan, mil., Al., U.S. B4 94
Fort McDermitt Indian Reservation, U.S. B4 121
Fort McDowell Indian Reservation, Az., U.S. D4 96
Fort McHenry National Monument And Historic Shrine, Md., U.S. g11 113
Fort McMurray, Ab., Can. A5 84
Fort Meade, Fl., U.S. E5 102
Fort Meade, mil., Md., U.S. B4 113
Fort Meadow Reservoir, res., Ma., U.S. g9 114
Fort Mill, S.C., U.S. A6 133
Fort Mitchell, Al., U.S. C4 94
Fort Mitchell, Ky., U.S. h13 110
Fort Mojave Indian Reservation, U.S. C1 96
Fort Monmouth, mil., N.J., U.S. C4 123
Fort Monroe, mil., Va., U.S. h15 139
Fort Morgan, Co., U.S. A7 99
Fort Myer, mil., Va., U.S. g12 139
Fort Myers, Fl., U.S. F5 102
Fort Myers Beach, Fl., U.S. F5 102
Fort Nelson, B.C., Can. m18 85
Fort Oglethorpe, Ga., U.S. B1 103
Fort Payne, Al., U.S. A4 94
Fort Peck Indian Reservation, Mt., U.S. B11 119
Fort Peck Lake, res., Mt., U.S. C9 119
Fort Pierce, Fl., U.S. E6 102
Fort Pierce Inlet, b., Fl., U.S. E6 102
Fort Pierre, S.D., U.S. C5 134
Fort Plain, N.Y., U.S. C6 125
Fort Polk, mil., La., U.S. C2 111
Fort Portal, Ug. A6 54
Fort Randall Dam, S.D., U.S. D7 134
Fort Recovery, Oh., U.S. B1 128
Fortress Mountain, mtn., Wy., U.S. B3 143
Fort Richardson, mil., Ak., U.S. C10 95
Fort Riley, mil., Ks., U.S. C7 109
Fort Ritchie, mil., Md., U.S. A3 113
Fort Rucker, mil., Al., U.S. D4 94
Fort Saint James, B.C., Can. B5 85
Fort Saint John, B.C., Can. A7 85
Fort Sam Houston, mil., Tx., U.S. k7 136
Fort Saskatchewan, Ab., Can. C4 84
Fort Scott, Ks., U.S. E9 109
Fort-Ševčenko, Kaz. E7 26
Fort Shafter, mil., Hi., U.S. g10 104
Fort Shawnee, Oh., U.S. B1 128
Fort Sill, mil., Ok., U.S. C3 129
Fort Smith, Ar., U.S. B1 97
Fort Stewart, mil., Ga., U.S. D5 103
Fort Stockton, Tx., U.S. D1 136
Fort Sumner, N.M., U.S. C5 124
Fort Sumter National Monument, S.C., U.S. k12 133
Fort Supply Lake, res., Ok., U.S. A2 129
Fort Thomas, Ky., U.S. h14 110
Fort Totten, N.D., U.S. B7 127
Fort Totten Indian Reservation, N.D., U.S. B7 127
Fortuna, Ca., U.S. B1 98
Fortune, Nf., Can. E4 88
Fortune Bay, b., Nf., Can. E4 88
Fort Union National Monument, N.M., U.S. B5 124
Fort Valley, Ga., U.S. D3 103
Fort Vermilion, Ab., Can. f7 84
Fortville, In., U.S. E6 107
Fort Wainwright, mil., Ak., U.S. C10 95
Fort Walton Beach, Fl., U.S. u15 102
Fort Washington Forest, Md., U.S. C4 113
Fort Wayne, In., U.S. B7 107
Fort William, Scot., U.K. B4 12
Fort Wingate, N.M., U.S. B1 124
Fort Worth, Tx., U.S. C4 136
Fort Wright, Ky., U.S. h13 110
Forty Fort, Pa., U.S. D10 131
Fort Yukon, Ak., U.S. B10 95
Fort Yuma Indian Reservation, Ca., U.S. F6 98
Foshan, China G10 28
Foso, Ghana E4 50
Fossano, Italy B1 18
Fossil Butte National Monument, Wy., U.S. E2 143
Fossil Lake, l., Or., U.S. D6 130
Foss Reservoir, res., Ok., U.S. B2 129
Fosston, Mn., U.S. C3 116
Foster, Or., U.S. C4 130
Foster, co., N.D., U.S. B6 127
Foster Village, Hi., U.S. g10 104
Fostoria, Oh., U.S. A2 128
Fougamou, Gabon D2 54
Fougères, Fr. C6 16
Fouke, Ar., U.S. D2 97
Foulamôri, Gui. D2 50
Foumban, Cam. B2 54
Foundiougne, Sen. D1 50
Fountain, Co., U.S. C6 99
Fountain, co., In., U.S. D3 107
Fountain City, In., U.S. E8 107
Fountain City, Wi., U.S. D2 142
Fountain Hill, Pa., U.S. E11 131
Fountain Inn, S.C., U.S. B3 133
Fountain Peak, mtn., Ca., U.S. E6 98
Fourche LaFave, stm., Ar., U.S. C2 97
Fourche Maline, stm., Ok., U.S. C6 129
Four Mountains, Islands of, is., Ak., U.S. E6 95
Four Oaks, N.C., U.S. B4 126
Fourth Cataract, wtfl, Sudan G11 48
Fouta Djalon, reg., Gui. D2 50
Foveaux Strait, strt., N.Z. q12 63c
Fowler, Ca., U.S. D4 98
Fowler, Co., U.S. C6 99
Fowler, In., U.S. C3 107
Fowler, Mi., U.S. E6 115
Fowlerville, Mi., U.S. F6 115
Fowman, Iran D13 44
Fox, stm., Mb., Can. B4 86
Fox, stm., Mi., U.S. B4 115
Fox, stm., Wi., U.S. D5 142
Fox, stm., U.S. B5 106
Fox, stm., U.S. A6 118
Foxboro, On., Can. C7 89
Foxboro, Ma., U.S. B5 114
Fox Creek, Ab., Can. B2 84
Foxe Basin, b., Nu., Can. E24 82
Fox Island, i., R.I., U.S. E4 132
Fox Island, i., Wa., U.S. f10 140
Fox Islands, is., Ak., U.S. E6 95
Fox Lake, Il., U.S. A5 106
Fox Lake, Wi., U.S. E5 142
Fox Lake, l., Il., U.S. h8 106
Fox Mountain, mtn., Nv., U.S. B2 121
Fox Point, Wi., U.S. E6 142
Fox River Grove, Il., U.S. h8 106
Foxworth, Ms., U.S. D4 117
Foz do Cunene, Ang. B1 56
Foz do Iguaçu, Braz. D7 72
Frackville, Pa., U.S. E9 131
Fraga, Spain G7 16
Fram Basin E22 144
Framingham, Ma., U.S. B5 114
Franca, Braz. F2 74
Franca-Iosifa, Zemlja, is., Russia B7 26
France, ctry., Eur. D8 16
Francesville, In., U.S. C4 107
Franceville, Gabon D2 54
Francis, Lake, l., N.H., U.S. f7 122
Francis Case, Lake, res., S.D., U.S. D6 134
Francistown, Bots. C4 56
Franconia, N.H., U.S. B3 122
Franconia Notch, N.H., U.S. B3 122
Francs Peak, mtn., Wy., U.S. C3 143
Franken, hist. reg., Ger. E11 12
Frankenmuth, Mi., U.S. E7 115
Frankford, On., Can. C7 89
Frankford, De., U.S. F5 101
Frankfort, Il., U.S. m9 106
Frankfort, In., U.S. D4 107
Frankfort, Ks., U.S. C7 109
Frankfort, Ky., U.S. B5 110
Frankfort, Mi., U.S. D4 115
Frankfort, N.Y., U.S. B5 125
Frankfort, Oh., U.S. C2 128
Frankfurt, Ger. D14 12
Frankfurt am Main, Ger. E11 12
Franklin, Ga., U.S. C1 103
Franklin, In., U.S. F5 107
Franklin, Ky., U.S. D3 110
Franklin, La., U.S. E4 111
Franklin, Ma., U.S. B5 114
Franklin, N.C., U.S. f9 126
Franklin, Ne., U.S. D7 120
Franklin, N.H., U.S. D3 122
Franklin, N.J., U.S. A3 123
Franklin, Oh., U.S. C1 128
Franklin, Pa., U.S. D2 131
Franklin, Tn., U.S. B5 135
Franklin, Tx., U.S. D4 136
Franklin, Va., U.S. D6 139
Franklin, W.V., U.S. C5 141
Franklin, Wi., U.S. n11 142
Franklin, co., Al., U.S. A2 94
Franklin, co., Ar., U.S. B2 97
Franklin, co., Fl., U.S. C2 102
Franklin, co., Ga., U.S. B3 103
Franklin, co., Ia., U.S. B4 108
Franklin, co., Id., U.S. G7 105
Franklin, co., Il., U.S. E4 106
Franklin, co., In., U.S. F7 107
Franklin, co., Ks., U.S. D8 109
Franklin, co., Ky., U.S. B5 110
Franklin, co., La., U.S. B4 111
Franklin, co., Ma., U.S. A2 114
Franklin, co., Me., U.S. C2 112
Franklin, co., Mo., U.S. C6 118
Franklin, co., Ms., U.S. D3 117
Franklin, co., N.C., U.S. A4 126
Franklin, co., Ne., U.S. D7 120
Franklin, co., N.Y., U.S. f10 125
Franklin, co., Oh., U.S. B2 128
Franklin, co., Pa., U.S. G6 131
Franklin, co., Tn., U.S. B5 135
Franklin, co., Tx., U.S. C5 136
Franklin, co., Va., U.S. D3 139
Franklin, co., Vt., U.S. B2 138
Franklin, co., Wa., U.S. C6 140
Franklin, Point, c., Ak., U.S. A8 95
Franklin D. Roosevelt Lake, res., Wa., U.S. B7 140
Franklin Falls Reservoir, res., N.H., U.S. C3 122
Franklin Grove, Il., U.S. B4 106
Franklin Lake, l., Nv., U.S. C6 121
Franklin Park, Il., U.S. k9 106
Franklinton, La., U.S. D5 111
Franklinton, N.C., U.S. A4 126
Franklinville, N.Y., U.S. C2 125
Frankston, Tx., U.S. C5 136
Frankton, In., U.S. D6 107
Fransfontein, Nmb. C2 56
Franz Josef Land see Franca-Iosifa, Zemlja, is., Russia B7 26
Fraser, stm., B.C., Can. E7 85
Fraser, stm., Nf., Can. g9 88
Fraser, Mount, mtn., Can. C8 85
Fraserburg, S. Afr. E3 56
Fraserburgh, Scot., U.K. B5 12
Fraser Island, i., Austl. F5 62
Fraser Lake, B.C., Can. B5 85
Fraser Plateau, plat., B.C., Can. D6 85
Frazee, Mn., U.S. D3 116
Frazeysburg, Oh., U.S. B3 128
Frazier Park, Ca., U.S. E4 98
Frederic, Wi., U.S. C1 142
Frederica, De., U.S. D4 101
Fredericia, Den. I3 10
Frederick, Co., U.S. A6 99
Frederick, Md., U.S. B3 113
Frederick, Ok., U.S. C2 129
Frederick, co., Md., U.S. B3 113
Frederick, co., Va., U.S. A4 139
Fredericksburg, Ia., U.S. B5 108
Fredericksburg, Tx., U.S. D3 136
Fredericksburg, Va., U.S. B5 139
Frederick Sound, strt., Ak., U.S. m23 95
Fredericktown, Mo., U.S. D7 118
Fredericktown, Oh., U.S. B3 128
Fredericktown, Pa., U.S. F1 131
Fredericton, N.B., Can. D3 87
Fredericton Junction, N.B., Can. D3 87
Frederikshåb, Grnld. F29 82
Frederikshavn, Den. H4 10
Fredonia, Az., U.S. A3 96
Fredonia, Ks., U.S. E8 109
Fredonia, N.Y., U.S. C1 125
Fredonia, Wi., U.S. E6 142
Fredrikstad, Nor. G4 10
Freeborn, co., Mn., U.S. G5 116
Freeburg, Il., U.S. E4 106
Freedom, Pa., U.S. E1 131
Freedom, Wy., U.S. D2 143
Freehold, N.J., U.S. C4 123
Freeland, Mi., U.S. E6 115
Freeland, Pa., U.S. D10 131
Freelandville, In., U.S. G3 107
Freel Peak, mtn., Ca., U.S. C4 98
Freels, Cape, c., Nf., Can. E5 88
Freels, Cape, c., Nf., Can. D5 88
Freeman, S.D., U.S. D8 134
Freeman, Lake, l., In., U.S. C4 107
Freemansburg, Pa., U.S. E11 131
Freemason Island, i., La., U.S. E7 111
Freeport, Bah. C9 76
Freeport, Il., U.S. A4 106
Freeport, Me., U.S. E2 112
Freeport, N.Y., U.S. n15 125
Freeport, Pa., U.S. E2 131
Freeport, Tx., U.S. E5 136
Freer, Tx., U.S. F3 136
Freestone, co., Tx., U.S. D4 136
Freetown, S.L. E2 50
Freetown, In., U.S. G5 107
Freezeout Mountains, mts., Wy., U.S. D6 143
Fregenal de la Sierra, Spain H3 16
Freiburg, Ger. G10 12
Freising, Ger. F12 12
Freistadt, Aus. F14 12
Fréjus, Fr. F10 16
Fremantle, Austl. G2 60
Fremont, Ca., U.S. D2 98
Fremont, Ia., U.S. C5 108
Fremont, In., U.S. A8 107
Fremont, Mi., U.S. E5 115
Fremont, N.C., U.S. B5 126
Fremont, Ne., U.S. C9 120
Fremont, Oh., U.S. A2 128
Fremont, co., Co., U.S. C5 99
Fremont, co., Ia., U.S. D2 108
Fremont, co., Id., U.S. E7 105
Fremont, co., Wy., U.S. C4 143
Fremont, stm., Ut., U.S. E4 137
Fremont Island, i., Ut., U.S. B3 137
Fremont Lake, l., Wy., U.S. D3 143
Fremont Peak, mtn., Wy., U.S. C3 143
French Broad, stm., U.S. D10 135
Frenchburg, Ky., U.S. C6 110
French Creek, stm., Pa., U.S. C2 131
French Frigate Shoals, rf., Hi., U.S. m14 104
French Guiana, dep., S.A. C9 70
French Lick, In., U.S. G4 107
Frenchman Bay, b., Me., U.S. D4 112
Frenchman Creek, stm., U.S. D4 120
Frenchman Hills, hills, Wa., U.S. C6 140
Frenchman Lake, l., Nv., U.S. G6 121
French Polynesia, dep., Oc. F15 58
French Settlement, La., U.S. D5 111
French Somaliland see Djibouti, ctry., Afr. H13 48
Frenda, Alg. J7 16
Freshfield, Mount, mtn., Can. D2 84
Fresnillo, Mex. C4 78
Fresno, Ca., U.S. D4 98
Fresno, co., Ca., U.S. D4 98
Fresno Reservoir, res., Mt., U.S. B6 119
Frewsburg, N.Y., U.S. C1 125
Freycinet Peninsula, pen., Austl. I4 62
Fria, Gui. D2 50
Fria, Cape, c., Nmb. B1 56
Friars Point, Ms., U.S. A3 117
Frías, Arg. D4 72
Fribourg, Switz. A1 18
Friday Harbor, Wa., U.S. A2 140
Fridley, Mn., U.S. m12 116
Fridtjof Nansen, Mount, mtn., Ant. E25 67
Friedrichshafen, Ger. G11 12
Friend, Ne., U.S. D8 120
Friendsville, Tn., U.S. D9 135
Fries, Va., U.S. D2 139
Frio, co., Tx., U.S. E3 136
Frio, stm., Tx., U.S. E3 136
Frio, Cabo, c., Braz. F3 74
Friona, Tx., U.S. B1 136
Fripps Island, i., S.C., U.S. G7 133
Frisco, Co., U.S. B4 99
Frisco City, Al., U.S. D2 94
Frisco Peak, mtn., Ut., U.S. E2 137
Frisian Islands, is., Eur. D9 12
Frissell, Mount, mtn., U.S. A2 100
Fritch, Tx., U.S. B2 136
Friza, proliv, strt., Russia B17 28
Frobisher Bay, b., Nu., Can. F26 82
Frobisher Lake, l., Sk., Can. m7 91
Frolovo, Russia E7 22
Frome, Lake, l., Austl. G3 62
Frontenac, Ks., U.S. E9 109
Frontera, Mex. D6 78
Frontera, Mex. B4 78
Frontier, co., Ne., U.S. D5 120
Front Range, mts., Co., U.S. A5 99
Front Royal, Va., U.S. B4 139
Frosinone, Italy D4 18

Name — Map Ref. — Page

Frostburg, Md., U.S. **k13** 113
Frostproof, Fl., U.S. **E5** 102
Frøya, i., Nor. **E3** 10
Fruita, Co., U.S. **B2** 99
Fruit Heights, Ut., U.S. **B4** 137
Fruitland, Id., U.S. **F2** 105
Fruitland, Md., U.S. **D6** 113
Fruitland, N.M., U.S. **A1** 124
Fruitland Park, Fl., U.S. **D5** 102
Fruitport, Mi., U.S. **E4** 115
Fruitvale, B.C., Can. **E9** 85
Fruitvale, Co., U.S. **B2** 99
Fruitvale, Wa., U.S. **C5** 140
Fruitville, Fl., U.S. **E4** 102
Frunze see Biškek, Kyrg. **E9** 26
Frutal, Braz. **E2** 74
Fryeburg, Me., U.S. **D2** 112
Fu'an, China **D4** 30
Fuding, China **D5** 30
Fuerte, stm., Mex. **B3** 78
Fuerte Olimpo, Para. **C6** 72
Fuerteventura, i., Spain **A2** 50
Fuga Island, i., Phil. **C8** 34
Fuji, Japan **C3** 31
Fuji, Mount see Fuji-san, vol., Japan **D15** 28
Fujian, state, China **F11** 28
Fujin, China **B14** 28
Fuji-san, vol., Japan **D15** 28
Fujiyama see Fuji-san, vol., Japan **D15** 28
Fukui, Japan **D15** 28
Fukuoka, Japan **E14** 28
Fukushima, Japan **C4** 31
Fukuyama, Japan **D2** 31
Fūlādī, Kūh-e, mtn., Afg. **D9** 42
Fulaga Passage, i., Fiji **m11** 63b
Fulda, Ger. **E11** 12
Fulda, Mn., U.S. **G3** 116
Fuling, China **D2** 30
Fullerton, Ca., U.S. **n13** 98
Fullerton, Ne., U.S. **C8** 120
Fulton, Il., U.S. **B3** 106
Fulton, Ky., U.S. **f9** 110
Fulton, Md., U.S. **B4** 113
Fulton, Mo., U.S. **C6** 118
Fulton, Ms., U.S. **A5** 117
Fulton, N.Y., U.S. **B4** 125
Fulton, co., Ar., U.S. **A4** 97
Fulton, co., Ga., U.S. **C2** 103
Fulton, co., Il., U.S. **C3** 106
Fulton, co., In., U.S. **B5** 107
Fulton, co., Ky., U.S. **f8** 110
Fulton, co., N.Y., U.S. **B6** 125
Fulton, co., Oh., U.S. **A1** 128
Fulton, co., Pa., U.S. **G5** 131
Fultondale, Al., U.S. **f7** 94
Funafuti, i., Tuvalu **E11** 58
Funchal, Port. **D1** 48
Fundy, Bay of, b., Can. **D4** 87
Fundy National Park, N.B., Can. **D4** 87
Funhalouro, Moz. **C5** 56
Funing, China **B4** 30
Funing, China **C4** 30
Funkstown, Md., U.S. **A2** 113
Funsi, Ghana **D4** 50
Funtua, Nig. **D6** 50
Fuping, China **C2** 30
Fuqing, China **D4** 30
Fuquay-Varina, N.C., U.S. **B4** 126
Furnace Brook, stm., Vt., U.S. **D3** 138
Furnas, co., Ne., U.S. **D6** 120
Furnas, Represa de, res., Braz. **F2** 74
Furneaux Group, is., Austl. **I4** 62
Fürstenwalde, Ger. **D14** 12
Furudal, Swe. **F6** 10
Fushun, China **C12** 28
Fusui, China **G9** 28
Futuna, Île, i., Wal./F. **F12** 58
Fuxin, China **A5** 30
Fuyang, China **E11** 28
Fuyu, China **B12** 28
Fuyuan, China **D1** 30
Fuzhou, China **F11** 28
Fuzhou, China **F11** 28
Füzuli, Azer. **C12** 44
Fyffe, Al., U.S. **A4** 94
Fyn, i., Den. **I4** 10

G

Gaalkacyo, Som. **I14** 48
Gabbs, Nv., U.S. **E4** 121
Gabela, Ang. **F2** 54
Gaberones see Gaborone, Bots. **C4** 56
Gabès, Tun. **D7** 48
Gabon, ctry., Afr. **D2** 54
Gaborone, Bots. **C4** 56
Gabriola, B.C., Can. **f12** 85
Gabrovo, Bul. **C10** 18
Gabú, Gui.-B. **D2** 50
Gachsārān, Iran **D6** 42
Gadag, India **F3** 40
Gäddede, Swe. **D6** 10
Gadsden, Al., U.S. **A3** 94
Gadsden, co., Fl., U.S. **B2** 102
Gadwāl, India **F3** 40
Gaeta, Italy **D4** 18
Gaeta, Golfo di, b., Italy **D4** 18
Gaffney, S.C., U.S. **A4** 133
Gafsa, Tun. **D6** 48
Gag, Pulau, i., Indon. **D7** 36
Gagarin, Russia **B13** 20
Gage, co., Ne., U.S. **D9** 120
Gagetown, N.B., Can. **D3** 87
Gagnoa, C. Iv. **E3** 50
Gagra, Geor. **A9** 44
Gahanna, Oh., U.S. **k11** 128
Gaillard, Lake, l., Ct., U.S. **D5** 100
Gaines, co., Tx., U.S. **C1** 136
Gainesboro, Tn., U.S. **C8** 135
Gaines Creek, stm., Ok., U.S. **C6** 129
Gainesville, Fl., U.S. **C4** 102
Gainesville, Ga., U.S. **B3** 103
Gainesville, Mo., U.S. **E5** 118
Gainesville, Tx., U.S. **C4** 136
Gainesville, Va., U.S. **g11** 139
Gairdner, Lake, l., Austl. **G2** 62
Gaithersburg, Md., U.S. **B3** 113
Gaixian, China **C12** 28
Gaizina Kalns, hill, Lat. **H11** 10
Gajny, Russia **B9** 22
Galán, Cerro, mtn., Arg. **D4** 72
Galapagos Islands see Colón, Archipiélago de, is., Ec. **C2** 70
Galashiels, Scot., U.K. **C5** 12
Galați, Rom. **G9** 20
Galatia, Il., U.S. **F5** 106
Galax, Va., U.S. **D2** 139
Galdhøpiggen, mtn., Nor. **F3** 10
Galela, Indon. **C7** 36
Galena, Ak., U.S. **C8** 95
Galena, Il., U.S. **A3** 106
Galena, Ks., U.S. **E9** 109
Galesburg, Il., U.S. **C3** 106
Galesburg, Mi., U.S. **F5** 115
Gales Ferry, Ct., U.S. **D7** 100
Galesville, Md., U.S. **C4** 113
Galesville, Wi., U.S. **D2** 142
Galeton, Pa., U.S. **C6** 131
Gali, Geor. **A9** 44
Galič, Russia **C7** 22
Galicia, hist. reg., Eur. **E7** 20
Galilee, Sea of, l., Isr. **F6** 44
Galion, Oh., U.S. **B3** 128
Galisteo Creek, stm., N.M., U.S. **k8** 124
Galiuro Mountains, mts., Az., U.S. **E5** 96
Gallant, Al., U.S. **B3** 94
Gallatin, Mo., U.S. **B4** 118
Gallatin, Tn., U.S. **A5** 135
Gallatin, co., Il., U.S. **F5** 106
Gallatin, co., Ky., U.S. **B5** 110
Gallatin, co., Mt., U.S. **E5** 119
Gallatin, stm., Mt., U.S. **E5** 119
Gallatin Range, mts., Mt., U.S. **E5** 119
Gallaway, Tn., U.S. **B2** 135
Galle, Sri L. **H4** 40
Gallia, co., Oh., U.S. **D3** 128
Galliano, La., U.S. **E5** 111
Gallinas, Punta, c., Col. **A5** 70
Gallinas Mountains, mts., N.M., U.S. **C2** 124
Gallipoli, Italy **D6** 18
Gallipoli see Gelibolu, Tur. **B2** 44
Gallipolis, Oh., U.S. **D3** 128
Gallitzin, Pa., U.S. **F4** 131
Gällivare, Swe. **C9** 10
Gallo Mountains, mts., N.M., U.S. **C1** 124
Galloo Island, i., N.Y., U.S. **B4** 125
Gallup, N.M., U.S. **B1** 124
Galt, Ca., U.S. **C3** 98
Galtat Zemmour, W. Sah. **A2** 50
Galva, Il., U.S. **B3** 106
Galva, Ks., U.S. **D6** 109
Galveston, In., U.S. **C5** 107
Galveston, Tx., U.S. **E5** 136
Galveston, co., Tx., U.S. **E5** 136
Galveston Bay, b., Tx., U.S. **E5** 136
Galveston Island, i., Tx., U.S. **E5** 136
Galway, Ire. **D2** 12
Galway Bay, b., Ire. **D2** 12
Gamarra, Col. **B5** 70
Gambēla, Eth. **B6** 54
Gambell, Ak., U.S. **C5** 95
Gambia, stm., Afr. **D2** 50
Gambia, The, ctry., Afr. **D1** 50
Gambier, Oh., U.S. **B3** 128
Gambier, Îles, is., Fr. Poly. **G16** 58
Gambo, Nf., Can. **D4** 88
Gamboma, Congo **D3** 54
Gamboula, C.A.R. **C3** 54
Gambrills, Md., U.S. **B4** 113
Gan, stm., China **D4** 30
Ganado, Az., U.S. **B6** 96
Ganado, Tx., U.S. **E4** 136
Gananoque, On., Can. **C8** 89
Gäncä, Azer. **B12** 44
Gand see Gent, Bel. **E8** 12
Ganda, Ang. **F2** 54
Gandajika, D.R.C. **E4** 54
Gandak, stm., Asia **D4** 40
Gander, Nf., Can. **D4** 88
Gander, stm., Nf., Can. **D4** 88
Gander Lake, l., Nf., Can. **D4** 88
Gandesa, Spain **G7** 16
Gāndhinagar, India **E2** 40
Gandhi Reservoir see Gāndhi Sāgar, res., India **E3** 40
Gāndhi Sāgar, res., India **E3** 40
Gandia, Spain **H6** 16
Gandu, Braz. **D4** 74
Ganga see Ganges, stm., Asia **D5** 40
Gangānagar, India **D2** 40
Gangaw, Myan. **B2** 34
Gangdisê Shan, mts., China **E4** 28
Ganges, B.C., Can. **g12** 85
Ganges (Ganga), stm., Asia **D5** 40
Ganges, Mouths of the, mth., Asia **B1** 34
Gang Mills, N.Y., U.S. **C3** 125
Gangotri, India **C3** 40
Gangtok, India **D5** 40
Gangu, China **E9** 28
Gannett Peak, mtn., Wy., U.S. **C3** 143
Ganquan, China **B2** 30
Gansu, state, China **D8** 28
Gantt, S.C., U.S. **B3** 133
Gantt Lake, res., Al., U.S. **D3** 94
Ganzê, China **E8** 28
Ganzhou, China **F10** 28
Gao, Mali **C4** 50
Gao'an, China **D4** 30
Gaolan, China **B1** 30
Gaomi, China **B4** 30
Gaoping, China **B3** 30
Gaoua, Burkina **D4** 50
Gaoual, Gui. **D2** 50
Gaoxian, China **D1** 30
Gaoyi, China **B3** 30
Gaoyou, China **C4** 30
Gaoyou Hu, l., China **C4** 30
Gaozhou, China **E3** 30
Gap, Fr. **E10** 16
Gap, Pa., U.S. **G9** 131
Gapan, Phil. **C8** 34
Garagumskij kanal imeni Prezidenta Turkmenistana S.A. Nijazova (Kara-Kum Canal), Turk. **C8** 42
Garagumy, des., Turk. **F7** 26
Garanhuns, Braz. **C4** 74
Garber, Ok., U.S. **A4** 129
Garberville, Ca., U.S. **B2** 98
Garda, Lago di, l., Italy **B3** 18
Garden, co., Ne., U.S. **C3** 120
Gardena, Ca., U.S. **n12** 98
Garden City, Ga., U.S. **D5** 103
Garden City, Id., U.S. **F2** 105
Garden City, Ks., U.S. **E3** 109
Garden City, Mi., U.S. **p15** 115
Garden City, Mo., U.S. **C3** 118
Gardendale, Al., U.S. **B3** 94
Garden Grove, Ca., U.S. **n13** 98
Garden Island, i., Mi., U.S. **C5** 115
Garden Plain, Ks., U.S. **E6** 109
Gardeyz, Afg. **D9** 42
Gardiner, Me., U.S. **D3** 112
Gardiner, Mt., U.S. **E6** 119
Gardiner, Or., U.S. **D2** 130
Gardiners Island, i., N.Y., U.S. **m16** 125
Gardner, Il., U.S. **B5** 106
Gardner, Ks., U.S. **D9** 109
Gardner, Ma., U.S. **A4** 114
Gardner Canal, strt., B.C., Can. **C3** 85
Gardner Lake, l., Ct., U.S. **C6** 100
Gardner Lake, l., Me., U.S. **D5** 112
Gardner Pinnacles, Hi., U.S. **k14** 104
Gardnerville, Nv., U.S. **E2** 121
Garfield, N.J., U.S. **h8** 123
Garfield, co., Co., U.S. **B2** 99
Garfield, co., Mt., U.S. **C9** 119
Garfield, co., Ne., U.S. **C6** 120
Garfield, co., Ok., U.S. **A4** 129
Garfield, co., Ut., U.S. **F4** 137
Garfield, co., Wa., U.S. **C8** 140
Garfield Heights, Oh., U.S. **h9** 128
Garfield Mountain, mtn., Mt., U.S. **F4** 119
Garfield Peak, mtn., Wy., U.S. **D5** 143
Garibaldi, Or., U.S. **B3** 130
Garibaldi, Mount, mtn., B.C., Can. **E6** 85
Garies, S. Afr. **E2** 56
Garissa, Kenya **D7** 54
Garland, N.C., U.S. **C4** 126
Garland, Tx., U.S. **n10** 136
Garland, Ut., U.S. **B3** 137
Garland, co., Ar., U.S. **C2** 97
Garm, Taj. **C10** 42
Garmī, Iran **C13** 44
Garmisch-Partenkirchen, Ger. **G12** 12
Garmsār, Iran **C6** 42
Garnavillo, Ia., U.S. **B6** 108
Garner, Ia., U.S. **A4** 108
Garner, N.C., U.S. **B4** 126
Garnet Range, mts., Mt., U.S. **D3** 119
Garnett, Ks., U.S. **D8** 109
Garnish, Nf., Can. **E4** 88
Garonne, stm., Eur. **E6** 16
Garoua, Cam. **B2** 54
Garoua Boulaï, Cam. **B2** 54
Garrard, co., Ky., U.S. **C5** 110
Garretson, S.D., U.S. **D9** 134
Garrett, In., U.S. **B7** 107
Garrett, co., Md., U.S. **k12** 113
Garrett Park, Md., U.S. **B3** 113
Garrettsville, Oh., U.S. **A4** 128
Garrison, Ky., U.S. **B6** 110
Garrison, Md., U.S. **B4** 113
Garrison, N.D., U.S. **B4** 127
Garrison Dam, N.D., U.S. **B4** 127
Garsen, Kenya **D8** 54
Garut, Indon. **E3** 36
Garvin, co., Ok., U.S. **C4** 129
Garwolin, Pol. **D6** 20
Gary, In., U.S. **A3** 107
Gary, W.V., U.S. **D3** 141
Garyarsa, China **E4** 28
Garysburg, N.C., U.S. **A5** 126
Garyville, La., U.S. **D5** 111
Garza, co., Tx., U.S. **C2** 136
Garza-Little Elm Reservoir, res., Tx., U.S. **C4** 136
Gasan-Kuli, Turk. **C6** 42
Gas City, In., U.S. **D6** 107
Gascogne, hist. reg., Fr. **F7** 16
Gasconade, co., Mo., U.S. **C6** 118
Gasconade, stm., Mo., U.S. **C6** 118
Gascony see Gascogne, hist. reg., Fr. **F7** 16
Gascoyne, stm., Austl. **E1** 60
Gascoyne Junction, Austl. **F2** 60
Gashaka, Nig. **E7** 50
Gashua, Nig. **D7** 50
Gasparilla Island, i., Fl., U.S. **F4** 102
Gaspé, P.Q., Can. **k14** 90
Gaspésie, Péninsule de la, pen., P.Q., Can. **k13** 90
Gassaway, W.V., U.S. **C4** 141
Gassville, Ar., U.S. **A3** 97
Gasteiz, Spain **F5** 16
Gaston, In., U.S. **D7** 107
Gaston, N.C., U.S. **A5** 126
Gaston, S.C., U.S. **D5** 133
Gaston, co., N.C., U.S. **B1** 126
Gaston, Lake, res., U.S. **A5** 126
Gaston Dam, N.C., U.S. **A5** 126
Gastonia, N.C., U.S. **B1** 126
Gastre, Arg. **F3** 69
Gatčina, Russia **C5** 22
Gate City, Va., U.S. **f9** 139
Gates, Tn., U.S. **B2** 135
Gates, co., N.C., U.S. **A6** 126
Gates of the Arctic National Park, Ak., U.S. **B9** 95
Gatesville, Tx., U.S. **D4** 136
Gatineau, P.Q., Can. **D2** 90
Gatineau, stm., P.Q., Can. **D2** 90
Gatineau, Parc de la, P.Q., Can. **D2** 90
Gatlinburg, Tn., U.S. **D10** 135
Gatton, Austl. **F5** 62
Gauley, stm., W.V., U.S. **C3** 141
Gauley Bridge, W.V., U.S. **C3** 141
Gaustatoppen, mtn., Nor. **G3** 10
Gautier, Ms., U.S. **f8** 117
Gávdhos, i., Grc. **G10** 18
Gavins Point Dam, U.S. **B8** 120
Gävle, Swe. **F7** 10
Gawler Ranges, mts., Austl. **G2** 62
Gaya, India **E5** 40
Gaya, Nig. **D6** 50
Gaya, Niger **D5** 50
Gay Head, c., Ma., U.S. **D6** 114
Gaylord, Mi., U.S. **C6** 115
Gaylord, Mn., U.S. **F4** 116
Gayndah, Austl. **F5** 62
Gaza see Ghazzah, Gaza Str. **G6** 44
Gazandzyk, Turk. **C7** 42
Gazaoua, Niger **D6** 50
Gaza Strip, Asia **G6** 44
Gaziantep, Tur. **D7** 44
Gazimağusa (Famagusta), N. Cyp. **E5** 44
Gazimağusa Körfezi, b., N. Cyp. **E6** 44
Gazipaşa, Tur. **D5** 44
Gbanga, Lib. **E3** 50
Gboko, Nig. **E6** 50
Gdańsk, Pol. **B5** 20
Gdov, Russia **G12** 10
Gdynia, Pol. **B5** 20
Gearhart, Or., U.S. **A3** 130
Gearhart Mountain, mtn., Or., U.S. **E6** 130
Geary, N.B., Can. **D3** 87
Geary, Ok., U.S. **B3** 129
Geary, co., Ks., U.S. **D7** 109
Geauga, co., Oh., U.S. **A4** 128
Gebe, Pulau, i., Indon. **D7** 36
Gebze, Tur. **B3** 44
Gediz, Tur. **C3** 44
Geelong, Austl. **H3** 62
Geesthacht, Ger. **D12** 12
Geilo, Nor. **F3** 10
Geistown, Pa., U.S. **F4** 131
Geist Reservoir, res., In., U.S. **E6** 107
Geita, Tan. **D6** 54
Gejiu, China **G8** 28
Gela, Italy **F5** 18
Gelasa, Selat, strt., Indon. **D3** 36
Gelendžik, Russia **G15** 20
Gelibolu, Tur. **B2** 44
Gelsenkirchen, Ger. **E10** 12
Gem, co., Id., U.S. **E2** 105
Gemena, D.R.C. **C3** 54
Gemlik, Tur. **B3** 44
Gemlik Körfezi, b., Tur. **B3** 44
Genalē (Jubba), stm., Afr. **B8** 54
Genç, Tur. **C9** 44
General Acha, Arg. **F5** 72
General Alvear, Arg. **F4** 72
General Carneiro, Braz. **B7** 72
General Carrera, Lago, l., S.A. **G2** 69
General Conesa, Arg. **F4** 69
General Eugenio A. Garay, Para. **C5** 72
General Juan José Ríos, Mex. **B3** 78
General Juan Madariaga, Arg. **F6** 72
General La Madrid, Arg. **F5** 72
General Pico, Arg. **F5** 72
General Pinedo, Arg. **D5** 72
General Roca, Arg. **E3** 69
General Villegas, Arg. **F5** 72
Genesee, Id., U.S. **C2** 105
Genesee, Mi., U.S. **E7** 115
Genesee, co., Mi., U.S. **E7** 115
Genesee, co., N.Y., U.S. **B2** 125
Genesee, stm., N.Y., U.S. **C2** 125
Geneseo, Il., U.S. **B3** 106
Geneseo, N.Y., U.S. **C3** 125
Geneva see Genève, Switz. **A1** 18
Geneva, Al., U.S. **D4** 94
Geneva, Il., U.S. **B5** 106
Geneva, In., U.S. **C8** 107
Geneva, Ne., U.S. **D8** 120
Geneva, N.Y., U.S. **C4** 125
Geneva, Oh., U.S. **A5** 128
Geneva, co., Al., U.S. **D4** 94
Geneva, Lake, l., Eur. **A1** 18
Geneva, Lake, l., Wi., U.S. **F5** 142
Geneva-on-the-Lake, Oh., U.S. **A5** 128
Genève (Geneva), Switz. **A1** 18
Gengma, China **B3** 34
Genoa see Genova, Italy **B2** 18
Genoa, Il., U.S. **A5** 106
Genoa, Ne., U.S. **C8** 120
Genoa, Nv., U.S. **D2** 121
Genoa, Oh., U.S. **A2** 128
Genoa, Gulf of see Genova, Golfo di, b., Italy **B2** 18
Genoa City, Wi., U.S. **F5** 142
Genola, Ut., U.S. **D4** 137
Genova, Italy **B2** 18
Genova, Golfo di, b., Italy **B2** 18
Gent, Bel. **E8** 12
Gentry, Ar., U.S. **A1** 97
Gentry, co., Mo., U.S. **A3** 118
Geographe Bay, b., Austl. **G2** 60
George, S. Afr. **E3** 56
George, Ia., U.S. **A2** 108
George, co., Ms., U.S. **E5** 117
George, stm., P.Q., Can. **g13** 90
George, Cape, c., N.S., Can. **D8** 87
George, Lake, l., Fl., U.S. **C5** 102
George, Lake, l., N.Y., U.S. **B7** 125
George B. Stevenson Reservoir, res., Pa., U.S. **D6** 131
George Peak, mtn., Ut., U.S. **B2** 137
George Town, Austl. **I4** 62
Georgetown, Austl. **D3** 62
Georgetown, P.E., Can. **C7** 87
George Town, Cay. Is. **B3** 80
Georgetown, Gam. **D2** 50
Georgetown, Guy. **B8** 70
George Town (Penang), Malay. **B2** 36
Georgetown, Ca., U.S. **C3** 98
Georgetown, Co., U.S. **B5** 99
Georgetown, Ct., U.S. **D2** 100
Georgetown, De., U.S. **F4** 101
Georgetown, Ga., U.S. **E1** 103
Georgetown, Il., U.S. **D6** 106
Georgetown, In., U.S. **H6** 107
Georgetown, Ky., U.S. **B5** 110
Georgetown, Ma., U.S. **A6** 114
Georgetown, Oh., U.S. **D2** 128
Georgetown, S.C., U.S. **E9** 133
Georgetown, Tx., U.S. **D4** 136
Georgetown, co., S.C., U.S. **E9** 133
George V Coast, Ant. **C20** 67
George Washington Birthplace National Monument, Va., U.S. **B6** 139
George Washington Carver National Monument, Mo., U.S. **E3** 118
George West, Tx., U.S. **E3** 136
Georgia, ctry., Asia **A10** 44
Georgia, state, U.S. **D3** 103
Georgiana, Al., U.S. **D3** 94
Georgian Bay, b., On., Can. **B3** 89
Georgina, stm., Austl. **E2** 62
Gera, Ger. **E13** 12
Gerald, Mo., U.S. **C6** 118
Geraldine, Al., U.S. **A4** 94
Geraldton, Austl. **F1** 60
Geraldton, On., Can. **o18** 89
Gerber Reservoir, res., Or., U.S. **E5** 130
Gerdine, Mount, mtn., Ak., U.S. **C9** 95
Gerede, Tur. **B5** 44
Gereshk, Afg. **D8** 42
Gering, Ne., U.S. **C2** 120
Gerlach, Nv., U.S. **C2** 121
Gerlachovský štít, mtn., Slvk. **E6** 20

Name — Map Ref. — Page

Germantown, Il., U.S. E4 106
Germantown, Md., U.S. B3 113
Germantown, Oh., U.S. C1 128
Germantown, Tn., U.S. B2 135
Germantown, Wi., U.S. E5 142
Germany, ctry., Eur. E12 12
Germiston, S. Afr. D4 56
Gerona see Girona, Spain G8 16
Geronimo, Ok., U.S. C3 129
Gervais, Or., U.S. B4 130
Gêrzê, China C4 40
Geser, Indon. D8 36
Getafe, Spain G5 16
Gettysburg, Pa., U.S. G7 131
Gettysburg, S.D., U.S. C6 134
Geyve, Tur. B4 44
Ghadāmis, Libya E6 48
Ghāghara, stm., Asia D4 40
Ghana, ctry., Afr. E4 50
Ghanzi, Bots. C3 56
Ghardaïa, Alg. D5 48
Gharyān, Libya D7 48
Ghāt, Libya F7 48
Għawdex, i., Malta F5 18
Ghazāl, Baḩr al-, stm., Sudan B5 54
Ghāziābād, India D3 40
Ghāzīpur, India D4 40
Ghaznī, Afg. D9 42
Ghazzah, Gaza Str. G6 44
Gheen, Mn., U.S. C6 116
Gheorgheni, Rom. F8 20
Gherla, Rom. F7 20
Ghilizane, Alg. J7 16
Ghūrīān, Afg. D8 42
Gianitsá, Grc. D9 18
Giant's Causeway, N. Ire., U.K. C3 12
Giants Neck, Ct., U.S. D7 100
Gibara, Cuba A4 80
Gibbon, Mn., U.S. F4 116
Gibbon, Ne., U.S. D7 120
Gibbons, Ab., Can. C4 84
Gibb River, Austl. D4 60
Gibbstown, N.J., U.S. D2 123
Gibeon, Nmb. D2 56
Gibraltar, dep., Eur. I4 16
Gibraltar, Strait of, strt. J4 16
Gibsland, La., U.S. B2 111
Gibson, Ga., U.S. C4 103
Gibson, co., In., U.S. H2 107
Gibson, co., Tn., U.S. A3 135
Gibsonburg, Oh., U.S. A2 128
Gibson City, Il., U.S. C5 106
Gibson Desert, des., Austl. E3 60
Gibsonia, Pa., U.S. h14 131
Gibson Island, i., Md., U.S. B5 113
Gibsons, B.C., Can. E6 85
Gibsonton, Fl., U.S. p11 102
Gibsonville, N.C., U.S. A3 126
Giddings, Tx., U.S. D4 136
Gideon, Mo., U.S. E8 118
Gien, Fr. D8 16
Giessen, Ger. E11 12
Gifford, Fl., U.S. E6 102
Gifford, Il., U.S. C5 106
Gifford Creek, Austl. E2 60
Gifu, Japan D15 28
Gig Harbor, Wa., U.S. B3 140
Giglio, Isola del, i., Italy C3 18
Gihon, stm., Vt., U.S. B3 138
Gijón, Spain F4 16
Gila, co., Az., U.S. D5 96
Gila, stm., U.S. E5 92
Gila Bend, Az., U.S. E3 96
Gila Bend Indian Reservation, Az., U.S. D3 96
Gila Bend Mountains, mts., Az., U.S. D2 96
Gila Cliff Dwellings National Monument, N.M., U.S. D1 124
Gila Mountains, mts., Az., U.S. D6 96
Gila Peak, mtn., Az., U.S. D6 96
Gila River Indian Reservation, Az., U.S. D4 96
Gilbert, Az., U.S. D4 96
Gilbert, Ia., U.S. B4 108
Gilbert, La., U.S. B4 111
Gilbert, Mn., U.S. C6 116
Gilbert Islands see Kiribati, is., Kir. D11 58
Gilbert Peak, mtn., Wa., U.S. C4 140
Gilbert Plains, Mb., Can. D1 86
Gilbertsville, Ky., U.S. f9 110
Gilbertsville, Pa., U.S. F10 131
Gilbertville, Ia., U.S. B5 108
Gilbués, Braz. E10 70
Gilchrist, Or., U.S. D5 130
Gilchrist, co., Fl., U.S. C4 102
Gilcrest, Co., U.S. A6 99
Giles, co., Tn., U.S. B4 135
Giles, co., Va., U.S. C2 139
Gilford Island, i., B.C., Can. D4 85
Gilgandra, Austl. G4 62
Gilgil, Kenya D7 54
Gilgit, Pak. C10 42
Gillam, Mb., Can. A4 86
Gillespie, Il., U.S. D4 106
Gillespie, co., Tx., U.S. D3 136
Gillespie Dam, Az., U.S. D3 96
Gillett, Ar., U.S. C4 97
Gillett, Wi., U.S. D5 142
Gillette, Wy., U.S. B7 143
Gilliam, co., Or., U.S. B6 130
Gilman, Il., U.S. C5 106
Gilman, Vt., U.S. C5 138
Gilmanton, N.H., U.S. D4 122
Gilmer, Tx., U.S. C5 136
Gilmer, co., Ga., U.S. B2 103
Gilmer, co., W.V., U.S. C4 141
Gilpin, co., Co., U.S. B5 99
Gilroy, Ca., U.S. D3 98
Gīmbī, Eth. B7 54
Gimie, Mount, vol., St. Luc. C7 80
Gimli, Mb., Can. D3 86
Gingoog, Phil. E9 34
Gīnīr, Eth. B8 54
Giralia, Austl. E1 60
Girard, Il., U.S. D4 106
Girard, Ks., U.S. E9 109
Girard, Oh., U.S. A5 128
Girard, Pa., U.S. B1 131
Girardot, Col. E5 80
Girardville, Pa., U.S. E9 131
Giresun, Tur. B8 44
Girona, Spain G8 16
Gironde, est., Fr. E6 16
Girvan, Scot., U.K. C4 12
Gisborne, N.Z. o14 63c
Gitarama, Rw. D5 54
Gitega, Bdi. D5 54
Giurgiu, Rom. H8 20
Giyon, Eth. B7 54
Giza see El-Gîza, Egypt E11 48
Giza, Pyramids of, Egypt F10 14
Gižduvan, Uzb. B8 42
Gižiga, Russia C18 26
Giżycko, Pol. B6 20
Gjirokastër, Alb. D8 18
Gjøvik, Nor. F4 10
Gjumri, Arm. B10 44
Glacier, co., Mt., U.S. B3 119
Glacier Bay, b., Ak., U.S. k21 95
Glacier Bay National Park, Ak., U.S. D12 95
Glacier National Park, B.C., Can. D9 85
Glacier National Park, Mt., U.S. B2 119
Glacier Peak, mtn., Wa., U.S. A4 140
Gladbrook, Ia., U.S. B5 108
Glade Creek, stm., W.V., U.S. n13 141
Glade Creek, stm., W.V., U.S. n14 141
Glade Creek, stm., Wa., U.S. C6 140
Glades, co., Fl., U.S. F5 102
Glade Spring, Va., U.S. f10 139
Gladewater, Tx., U.S. C5 136
Gladstone, Austl. E5 62
Gladstone, Mb., Can. D2 86
Gladstone, Mi., U.S. C4 115
Gladstone, Mo., U.S. h10 118
Gladstone, Or., U.S. B4 130
Gladwin, Mi., U.S. E6 115
Gladwin, co., Mi., U.S. D6 115
Glåma, stm., Nor. F4 10
Glascock, co., Ga., U.S. C4 103
Glasford, Il., U.S. C4 106
Glasgow, Scot., U.K. C4 12
Glasgow, Ky., U.S. C4 110
Glasgow, Mo., U.S. B5 118
Glasgow, Mt., U.S. B10 119
Glasgow, Va., U.S. C3 139
Glasgow, W.V., U.S. m13 141
Glassboro, N.J., U.S. D2 123
Glasscock, co., Tx., U.S. D2 136
Glassport, Pa., U.S. F2 131
Glastonbury, Ct., U.S. C5 100
Glazier Lake, l., Me., U.S. A3 112
Glazov, Russia D7 26
Gleason, Tn., U.S. A3 135
Glen Allan, Ms., U.S. B2 117
Glen Allen, Va., U.S. C5 139
Glenboro, Mb., Can. E2 86
Glenbrook, Nv., U.S. D2 121
Glen Burnie, Md., U.S. B4 113
Glen Canyon Dam, Az., U.S. A4 96
Glen Canyon National Recreation Area, U.S. F5 137
Glencoe, On., Can. E3 89
Glencoe, Al., U.S. B4 94
Glencoe, Il., U.S. A6 106
Glencoe, Mn., U.S. F4 116
Glen Cove, N.Y., U.S. h13 125
Glendale, Az., U.S. D3 96
Glendale, Ca., U.S. m12 98
Glendale, Ms., U.S. D4 117
Glendale, Oh., U.S. C1 128
Glendale, Or., U.S. E3 130
Glendale, R.I., U.S. B2 132
Glendale, S.C., U.S. B4 133
Glen Dale, W.V., U.S. B4 141
Glendale, Wi., U.S. m12 142
Glendale Heights, W.V., U.S. g8 141
Glendive, Mt., U.S. C12 119
Glendo, Wy., U.S. D7 143
Glendora, Ca., U.S. m13 98
Glendo Reservoir, res., Wy., U.S. D8 143
Glenelg, Md., U.S. B4 113
Glen Ellis Falls, wtfl, N.H., U.S. B4 122
Glen Ellyn, Il., U.S. k8 106
Glenham, N.Y., U.S. D7 125
Glen Innes, Austl. F5 62
Glen Jean, W.V., U.S. D3 141
Glen Lake, l., Mi., U.S. D5 115
Glen Lyon, Pa., U.S. D9 131
Glenmora, La., U.S. D3 111
Glenn, co., Ca., U.S. C2 98
Glennallen, Ak., U.S. f19 95
Glenns Ferry, Id., U.S. G3 105
Glennville, Ga., U.S. E5 103
Glenolden, Pa., U.S. p20 131
Glenpool, Ok., U.S. B5 129
Glen Raven, N.C., U.S. A3 126
Glen Ridge, N.J., U.S. h8 123
Glen Rock, N.J., U.S. h8 123
Glen Rock, Pa., U.S. G8 131
Glenrock, Wy., U.S. D7 143
Glen Rose, Tx., U.S. C4 136
Glenrothes, Scot., U.K. B5 12
Glenroy, Austl. E1 60
Glens Falls, N.Y., U.S. B7 125
Glen Ullin, N.D., U.S. C4 127
Glenview, Il., U.S. h9 106
Glenville, Mn., U.S. G5 116
Glenville, W.V., U.S. C4 141
Glenwood, Nf., Can. D4 88
Glenwood, Ar., U.S. C2 97
Glenwood, Ga., U.S. D4 103
Glenwood, Ia., U.S. C2 108
Glenwood, Mn., U.S. E3 116
Glenwood, Va., U.S. D3 139
Glenwood City, Wi., U.S. C1 142
Glenwood Springs, Co., U.S. B3 99
Glidden, Ia., U.S. B3 108
Glide, Or., U.S. D3 130
Glittertinden, mtn., Nor. F3 10
Gliwice, Pol. D5 20
Globe, Az., U.S. D5 96
Głogów, Pol. D4 20
Gloster, Ms., U.S. D2 117
Gloucester, On., Can. h12 89
Gloucester, Eng., U.K. E5 12
Gloucester, Ma., U.S. A6 114
Gloucester, Va., U.S. C6 139
Gloucester, co., N.J., U.S. D2 123
Gloucester, co., Va., U.S. C6 139
Gloucester City, N.J., U.S. D2 123
Gloucester Point, Va., U.S. C6 139
Glouster, Oh., U.S. C3 128
Glover Island, i., Nf., Can. D3 88
Gloversville, N.Y., U.S. B6 125
Glovertown, Nf., Can. D4 88
Gloverville, S.C., U.S. E4 133
Glubokij, Russia E7 22
Głuchołazy, Pol. D4 20
Gluck, S.C., U.S. C2 133
Glyndon, Md., U.S. B4 113
Glyndon, Mn., U.S. D2 116
Glynn, co., Ga., U.S. E5 103
Gmünd, Aus. F14 12
Gmunden, Aus. G13 12
Gnadenhutten, Oh., U.S. B4 128
Gnarp, Swe. E11 10
Gniezno, Pol. C4 20
Gnowangerup, Austl. G2 60
Goa, prov., India F2 40
Goālpāra, India D6 40
Goat Island, i., R.I., U.S. F5 132
Goat Mountain, mtn., Mt., U.S. C3 119
Goat Rock Dam, U.S. C4 94
Goba, Eth. B7 54
Gobabis, Nmb. C2 56
Gobernador Gregores, Arg. G2 69
Gobi, des., Asia C7 28
Gobles, Mi., U.S. F5 115
Gobō, Japan D3 31
Goðafoss, wtfl, Ice. I20 10a
Godāvari, stm., India F3 40
Goddard, Ks., U.S. E6 109
Goderich, On., Can. D3 89
Godfrey, Il., U.S. E3 106
Godhavn, Grnld. E29 82
Godhra, India E2 40
Gödöllő, Hung. F5 20
Gods, stm., Mb., Can. A5 86
Gods Lake, l., Mb., Can. B4 86
Godthåb (Nuuk), Grnld. F29 82
Goff Creek, stm., Ok., U.S. e9 129
Goffstown, N.H., U.S. D3 122
Gogebic, co., Mi., U.S. n12 115
Gogebic, Lake, l., Mi., U.S. m12 115
Goiana, Braz. C5 74
Goianésia, Braz. E2 74
Goiânia, Braz. E2 74
Goiás, Braz. E1 74
Goiás, state, Braz. F10 70
Gojra, Pak. D10 42
Gök, stm., Tur. B6 44
Gökçeada, i., Tur. B1 44
Gökova Körfezi, b., Tur. D2 44
Göksun, Tur. C7 44
Gokwe, Zimb. B4 56
Golāghāt, India D6 40
Golconda, Il., U.S. F5 106
Golconda, Nv., U.S. C4 121
Gölcük, Tur. B3 44
Gold Bar, Wa., U.S. B4 140
Gold Beach, Or., U.S. E2 130
Gold Coast see Southport, Austl. F5 62
Golden, B.C., Can. D9 85
Golden, Co., U.S. B5 99
Golden City, Mo., U.S. D3 118
Goldendale, Wa., U.S. D5 140
Golden Gate Bridge, Ca., U.S. h7 98
Golden Gate National Recreation Area, Ca., U.S. h7 98
Golden Hinde, mtn., B.C., Can. E5 85
Golden Meadow, La., U.S. E5 111
Golden Spike National Historic Site, hist., Ut., U.S. B3 137
Golden Valley, Mn., U.S. n12 116
Golden Valley, co., Mt., U.S. D7 119
Golden Valley, co., N.D., U.S. B2 127
Goldfield, Ia., U.S. B4 108
Goldfield, Nv., U.S. F4 121
Gold Hill, Or., U.S. E3 130
Goldsboro, N.C., U.S. B5 126
Goldsby, Ok., U.S. B4 129
Goldsworthy, Austl. E2 60
Goldthwaite, Tx., U.S. D3 136
Goleniów, Pol. C3 20
Goleta, Ca., U.S. E4 98
Golfito, C.R. D3 80
Golf Manor, Oh., U.S. o13 128
Gölhisar, Tur. D3 44
Goliad, Tx., U.S. E4 136
Goliad, co., Tx., U.S. E4 136
Gölköy, Tur. B7 44
Golmud, China B6 40
Golpāyegān, Iran D6 42
Goma, D.R.C. D5 54
Gomati, stm., India D4 40
Gombe, Nig. D7 50
Gombi, Nig. D7 50
Gomel see Homel', Bela. C11 20
Gómez Palacio, Mex. B4 78
Gonaïves, Haiti B5 80
Gonam, Russia D15 26
Gonâve, Golfe de la, b., Haiti B5 80
Gonâve, Île de la, i., Haiti B5 80
Gonbad-e Qābūs, Iran C7 42
Gonda, India D4 40
Gondal, India E2 40
Gonder, Eth. H12 48
Gondia, India E4 40
Gönen, Tur. B2 44
Gongbo'gyamda, China E6 28
Gongcheng, China E3 30
Gongga Shan, mtn., China F8 28
Gongxian, China C3 30
Gongzhuling, China C12 28
Gonzales, Ca., U.S. D3 98
Gonzales, La., U.S. D5 111
Gonzales, Tx., U.S. E4 136
Gonzales, co., Tx., U.S. E4 136
González, Mex. C5 78
Gonzalez, Fl., U.S. u14 102
Goochland, co., Va., U.S. C5 139
Goode, Mount, mtn., Ak., U.S. g18 95
Goodfellow Air Force Base, mil., Tx., U.S. D2 136
Good Hope, Cape of, c., S. Afr. E2 56
Good Hope Mountain, mtn., B.C., Can. D5 85
Goodhue, co., Mn., U.S. F6 116
Gooding, Id., U.S. G4 105
Gooding, co., Id., U.S. F4 105
Goodland, In., U.S. C3 107
Goodland, Ks., U.S. C2 109
Goodlettsville, Tn., U.S. g10 135
Goodman, Mo., U.S. E3 118
Goodman, Ms., U.S. C4 117
Good Pine, La., U.S. C3 111
Goodsprings, Nv., U.S. H6 121
Goodview, Mn., U.S. F7 116
Goodwater, Al., U.S. B3 94
Goodwell, Ok., U.S. e9 129
Goodyear, Az., U.S. D3 96
Goondiwindi, Austl. F5 62
Goose, stm., N.D., U.S. B8 127
Goose Bay, b., Nf., Can. B1 88
Gooseberry Creek, stm., Wy., U.S. B4 143
Goose Creek, S.C., U.S. F7 133
Goose Creek, stm., Va., U.S. C3 139
Goose Creek, stm., U.S. G5 105
Goose Creek Reservoir, res., S.C., U.S. k11 133
Goose Lake, l., U.S. C3 92
Goose Lake, l., U.S. B3 98
Goose Pond, l., N.H., U.S. C2 122
Goqên, China F7 28
Gorakhpur, India D4 40
Gorda, Punta, c., Cuba A3 80
Gordion, hist., Tur. C4 44
Gordo, Al., U.S. B2 94
Gordon, Ga., U.S. D3 103
Gordon, Ne., U.S. B3 120
Gordon, co., Ga., U.S. B2 103
Gordon Downs, Austl. D4 60
Gordonsville, Tn., U.S. C8 135
Gordonsville, Va., U.S. B4 139
Goré, Chad E8 50
Gorē, Eth. B7 54
Gore, N.Z. q12 63c
Gore, Ok., U.S. B6 129
Gore Bay, On., Can. B2 89
Gore Point, c., Ak., U.S. h16 95
Gore Range, mts., Co., U.S. B4 99
Goreville, Il., U.S. F5 106
Gorgān, Iran C6 42
Gorge High Dam, Wa., U.S. A4 140
Gorham, Me., U.S. E2 112
Gorham, N.H., U.S. B4 122
Gori, Geor. A11 44
Gorizia, Italy B4 18
Gorjačij Ključ, Russia G15 20
Gor'kij see Nižnij Novgorod, Russia D6 26
Gorkiy Reservoir see Gor'kovskoe vodohranilišče, res., Russia C7 22
Gor'kovskoe vodohranilišče, res., Russia C7 22
Görlitz, Ger. E14 12
Gorlovka see Horlivka, Ukr. E15 20
Gorman, Tx., U.S. C3 136
Gorna Orjahovica, Bul. C10 18
Gornjackij, Russia A11 22
Gorno-Altajsk, Russia D10 26
Gornozavodsk, Russia B16 28
Gorodec, Russia C7 22
Goroka, Pap. N. Gui. H12 32
Gorong, Pulau, i., Indon. D8 36
Gorontalo, Indon. C6 36
Gorzów Wielkopolski, Pol. C3 20
Gosford, Austl. G5 62
Goshen, In., U.S. A6 107
Goshen, N.Y., U.S. D6 125
Goshen, Oh., U.S. C1 128
Goshen, co., Wy., U.S. D8 143
Goshute Indian Reservation, U.S. D7 121
Goshute Lake, l., Nv., U.S. C7 121
Goshute Mountains, mts., Nv., U.S. C7 121
Goslar, Ger. E12 12
Gosnells, Austl. G2 60
Gosper, co., Ne., U.S. D6 120
Gosport, In., U.S. F4 107
Gossinga, Sudan B5 54
Gostivar, Mac. D8 18
Gostyń, Pol. D4 20
Gostynin, Pol. C5 20
Göteborg (Gothenburg), Swe. H4 10
Gothenburg see Göteborg, Swe. H4 10
Gothenburg, Ne., U.S. D5 120
Gotland, i., Swe. H8 10
Gotō-rettō, is., Japan E13 28
Gotska Sandön, i., Swe. G8 10
Göttingen, Ger. E11 12
Goubone, Chad B8 50
Goudoumaria, Niger D7 50
Gough Island, i., St. Hel. N9 46
Gouin, Réservoir, res., P.Q., Can. I25 82
Goulburn, Austl. G4 62
Goulburn Islands, is., Austl. C5 60
Gould, Ar., U.S. D4 97
Goulding, Fl., U.S. u14 102
Gould Island, i., R.I., U.S. E5 132
Goulds, Fl., U.S. s13 102
Goundam, Mali C4 50
Goundi, Chad E8 50
Gouré, Niger D7 50
Gouverneur, N.Y., U.S. f9 125
Gove, co., Ks., U.S. D3 109
Governador Valadares, Braz. E3 74
Govind Ballabh Pant Reservoir see Govind Ballabh Pant Sāgar, res., India E4 40
Govind Ballabh Pant Sāgar, res., India E4 40
Gowanda, N.Y., U.S. C2 125
Gower, Mo., U.S. B3 118
Gowrie, Ia., U.S. B3 108
Goya, Arg. D6 72
Göyçay, Azer. B12 44
Gozo see Għawdex, i., Malta F5 18
Graaff-Reinet, S. Afr. E3 56
Grabill, In., U.S. B8 107
Grabo, C. Iv. F3 50
Grace, Id., U.S. G7 105
Graceville, Fl., U.S. u16 102
Graceville, Mn., U.S. E2 116
Gracewood, Ga., U.S. C4 103
Gracias a Dios, Cabo, c., N.A. F8 76
Gradaús, Braz. E9 70
Grady, co., Ga., U.S. F2 103
Grady, co., Ok., U.S. C4 129
Graettinger, Ia., U.S. A3 108
Grafton, Austl. F5 62
Grafton, Il., U.S. E3 106
Grafton, Ma., U.S. B4 114
Grafton, N.D., U.S. A8 127
Grafton, Oh., U.S. A3 128
Grafton, Va., U.S. h15 139
Grafton, W.V., U.S. B4 141
Grafton, Wi., U.S. E6 142
Grafton, co., N.H., U.S. C3 122
Graham, N.C., U.S. A3 126
Graham, Tx., U.S. C3 136
Graham, co., Az., U.S. E5 96
Graham, co., Ks., U.S. C4 109
Graham, co., N.C., U.S. f9 126

Name — Map Ref. — Page

Graham, Lake, res., Tx., U.S. C3 136
Graham, Mount, mtn., Az., U.S. E6 96
Graham Island, i., B.C., Can. C1 85
Graham Lake, l., Me., U.S. D4 112
Graham Land, reg., Ant. C34 67
Grahamstown, S. Afr. E4 56
Grahn, Ky., U.S. B6 110
Grainger, co., Tn., U.S. C10 135
Grain Valley, Mo., U.S. B3 118
Grajaú, Braz. C2 74
Grajewo, Pol. C7 20
Grambling, La., U.S. B3 111
Gramercy, La., U.S. h10 111
Granada, Col. E5 80
Granada, Nic. C2 80
Granada, Spain I5 16
Granbury, Tx., U.S. C4 136
Granby, P.Q., Can. D5 90
Granby, Co., U.S. A5 99
Granby, Ct., U.S. B4 100
Granby, Mo., U.S. E3 118
Granby, Lake, res., Co., U.S. A5 99
Gran Canaria, i., Spain A1 50
Gran Chaco, reg., S.A. C5 72
Grand, co., Co., U.S. A4 99
Grand, co., Ut., U.S. E6 137
Grand, stm., On., Can. D4 89
Grand, stm., Mi., U.S. E5 115
Grand, stm., Mo., U.S. A3 118
Grand, stm., Oh., U.S. A4 128
Grand, stm., S.D., U.S. B4 134
Grand Bahama, i., Bah. C9 76
Grand Bank, Nf., Can. E4 88
Grand-Bassam, C. Iv. E4 50
Grand Bay, N.B., Can. D3 87
Grand Bay, Al., U.S. E1 94
Grand Bend, On., Can. D3 89
Grand Blanc, Mi., U.S. F7 115
Grand Caillou, La., U.S. E5 111
Grand Canal see Da Yunhe, China D11 28
Grand Canyon, Az., U.S. A3 96
Grand Canyon, val., Az., U.S. A3 96
Grand Canyon National Park, Az., U.S. B3 96
Grand Cayman, i., Cay. Is. B3 80
Grand Centre, Ab., Can. B5 84
Grand Cess, Lib. F3 50
Grand Coteau, La., U.S. D3 111
Grand Coulee, Wa., U.S. B6 140
Grand Coulee Dam, Wa., U.S. B6 140
Grande, stm., Bol. G7 70
Grande, stm., Braz. F1 74
Grande, stm., Ven. D7 80
Grande, Bahía, b., Arg. H3 69
Grande, Boca, mth., Ven. D7 80
Grande, Ilha, i., Braz. F3 74
Grande, Rio see Rio Grande, stm., N.A. B5 78
Grande-Anse, N.B., Can. B4 87
Grande Cache, Ab., Can. C1 84
Grande Comore see Njazidja, i., Com. A7 56
Grande de Matagalpa, stm., Nic. C3 80
Grande de Santiago, stm., Mex. C4 78
Grande do Gurupá, Ilha, i., Braz. B1 74
Grand-Entrée, P.Q., Can. B8 87
Grande Prairie, Ab., Can. B1 84
Grand Erg de Bilma, des., Niger C7 50
Grand Erg Occidental, des., Alg. D5 48
Grand Erg Oriental, des., Alg. D6 48
Grande rivière de la Baleine, stm., P.Q., Can. g11 90
Grande Ronde, stm., U.S. C8 140
Grandes, Salinas, pl., Arg. E4 72
Grandes-Bergeronnes, P.Q., Can. A8 90
Grande-Terre, i., Guad. B7 80
Grand Falls (Grand-Sault), N.B., Can. B2 87
Grand Falls, wtfl, Me., U.S. C5 112
Grand Falls [-Windsor], Nf., Can. D4 88
Grandfather Mountain, mtn., N.C., U.S. A1 126
Grandfield, Ok., U.S. C3 129
Grand Forks, B.C., Can. E8 85
Grand Forks, N.D., U.S. B8 127
Grand Forks, co., N.D., U.S. B8 127
Grand Forks Air Force Base, mil., N.D., U.S. B8 127
Grand Harbour, N.B., Can. E3 87
Grand Haven, Mi., U.S. E4 115
Grand Island, Ne., U.S. D7 120
Grand Island, i., La., U.S. D6 111
Grand Island, i., Mi., U.S. B4 115
Grand Isle, La., U.S. E6 111
Grand Isle, co., Vt., U.S. B2 138
Grand Isle, i., La., U.S. E6 111
Grand Junction, Co., U.S. B2 99
Grand Junction, Ia., U.S. B3 108
Grand Lake, l., N.B., Can. D3 87
Grand Lake, l., Nf., Can. D3 88
Grand Lake, l., La., U.S. E6 111
Grand Lake, l., La., U.S. E3 111
Grand Lake, l., Mi., U.S. C7 115
Grand Lake, l., Oh., U.S. B1 128
Grand Lake Matagamon, l., Me., U.S. B4 112
Grand Lake Seboeis, l., Me., U.S. B4 112
Grand Ledge, Mi., U.S. F6 115
Grand Manan Island, i., N.B., Can. E3 87
Grand Marais, Mn., U.S. k9 116
Grand Meadow, Mn., U.S. G6 116
Grand-Mère, P.Q., Can. C5 90
Grand Mound, Ia., U.S. C7 108
Grand Portage Indian Reservation, Mn., U.S. k10 116
Grand Portage National Monument, Mn., U.S. h10 116
Grand Prairie, Tx., U.S. n10 136
Grand Rapids, Mi., U.S. F5 115
Grand Rapids, Mn., U.S. C5 116
Grand Rapids, Oh., U.S. f6 128
Grand Saline, Tx., U.S. C5 136
Grand Terre Islands, is., La., U.S. E6 111
Grand Teton, mtn., Wy., U.S. C2 143
Grand Teton National Park, Wy., U.S. C2 143
Grand Tower, Il., U.S. F4 106
Grand Traverse, co., Mi., U.S. D5 115
Grand Traverse Bay, b., Mi., U.S. C5 115
Grand Turk, T./C. Is. A5 80
Grand Valley, On., Can. D4 89
Grandview, Mb., Can. D1 86
Grandview, In., U.S. I4 107
Grandview, Mo., U.S. C3 118
Grandview, Wa., U.S. C6 140
Grandview Heights, Oh., U.S. m10 128
Grandville, Mi., U.S. F5 115
Grandy, N.C., U.S. A7 126
Granger, Ia., U.S. C4 108
Granger, In., U.S. A5 107
Granger, Tx., U.S. D4 136
Granger, Wa., U.S. C5 140
Grängesberg, Swe. F6 10
Grangeville, Id., U.S. D2 105
Gran Guardia, Arg. D6 72
Granisle, B.C., Can. B4 85
Granite, Ok., U.S. C2 129
Granite, co., Mt., U.S. D3 119
Granite City, Il., U.S. E3 106
Granite Falls, Mn., U.S. F3 116
Granite Falls, N.C., U.S. B1 126
Granite Falls, Wa., U.S. A4 140
Granite Lake, res., Nf., Can. D3 88
Granite Mountain, mtn., Ak., U.S. B7 95
Granite Mountains, mts., Az., U.S. E2 96
Granite Mountains, mts., Wy., U.S. D5 143
Granite Pass, Wy., U.S. B5 143
Granite Peak, mtn., Mt., U.S. E7 119
Granite Peak, mtn., Nv., U.S. C2 121
Granite Peak, mtn., Nv., U.S. B4 121
Granite Peak, mtn., Ut., U.S. E3 137
Granite Peak, mtn., Ut., U.S. C2 137
Granite Peak, mtn., Wy., U.S. D4 143
Granite Quarry, N.C., U.S. B2 126
Granite Range, mts., Nv., U.S. C2 121
Graniteville, S.C., U.S. D4 133
Graniteville, Vt., U.S. C4 138
Granja, Braz. B3 74
Grant, Al., U.S. A3 94
Grant, Mi., U.S. E5 115
Grant, Ne., U.S. D4 120
Grant, co., Ar., U.S. C3 97
Grant, co., In., U.S. D6 107
Grant, co., Ks., U.S. E2 109
Grant, co., Ky., U.S. B5 110
Grant, co., La., U.S. C3 111
Grant, co., Mn., U.S. E2 116
Grant, co., N.D., U.S. C4 127
Grant, co., Ne., U.S. C4 120
Grant, co., N.M., U.S. E1 124
Grant, co., Ok., U.S. A4 129
Grant, co., Or., U.S. C7 130
Grant, co., S.D., U.S. B8 134
Grant, co., W.V., U.S. B5 141
Grant, co., Wa., U.S. B6 140
Grant, co., Wi., U.S. F3 142
Grant, Mount, mtn., Nv., U.S. E3 121
Grant City, Mo., U.S. A3 118
Grant Park, Il., U.S. B6 106
Grant Range, mts., Nv., U.S. E6 121
Grants, N.M., U.S. B2 124
Grantsburg, Wi., U.S. C1 142
Grants Pass, Or., U.S. E3 130
Grantsville, Ut., U.S. C3 137
Grantsville, W.V., U.S. C3 141
Grant Town, W.V., U.S. B4 141
Grantville, Ga., U.S. C2 103
Granville, Fr. C6 16
Granville, Il., U.S. B4 106
Granville, N.Y., U.S. B7 125
Granville, Oh., U.S. B3 128
Granville, W.V., U.S. h11 141
Granville, co., N.C., U.S. A4 126
Granville Lake, l., Mb., Can. A1 86
Grapeland, Tx., U.S. D5 136
Grapeview, Wa., U.S. B3 140
Grapevine, Tx., U.S. C4 136
Grapevine Lake, res., Tx., U.S. n9 136
Grapevine Peak, mtn., Nv., U.S. G4 121
Gräsö, i., Swe. F8 10
Grasonville, Md., U.S. C5 113
Grass, stm., Mb., Can. B2 86
Grass, stm., N.Y., U.S. f9 125
Grasse, Fr. F10 16
Grass Lake, Il., U.S. h8 106
Grass Lake, Mi., U.S. F6 115
Grass Lake, l., Il., U.S. h8 106
Grass Valley, Ca., U.S. C3 98
Grassy Brook, stm., Vt., U.S. E3 138
Grassy Lake, l., La., U.S. k9 111
Grates Point, c., Nf., Can. D5 88
Gratiot, co., Mi., U.S. E6 115
Gratis, Oh., U.S. C1 128
Grave Creek, stm., W.V., U.S. g8 141
Gravelly Branch, stm., De., U.S. F4 101
Gravelly Range, mts., Mt., U.S. E4 119
Gravenhage, 's- see 's-Gravenhage, Neth. D8 12
Gravenhurst, On., Can. C5 89
Grave Peak, mtn., Id., U.S. C4 105
Graves, co., Ky., U.S. f9 110
Gravette, Ar., U.S. A1 97
Gray, Fr. D9 16
Gray, Ga., U.S. C3 103
Gray, Ky., U.S. D5 110
Gray, La., U.S. k10 111
Gray, Me., U.S. g7 112
Gray, co., Ks., U.S. E3 109
Gray, co., Tx., U.S. B2 136
Grayback Mountain, mtn., Or., U.S. E3 130
Gray Court, S.C., U.S. B3 133
Grayland, Wa., U.S. C1 140
Grayling, Mi., U.S. D6 115
Graylyn Crest, De., U.S. A3 101
Grays Harbor, co., Wa., U.S. B2 140
Grays Harbor, b., Wa., U.S. C1 140
Grayslake, Il., U.S. A5 106
Grays Lake, sw., Id., U.S. F7 105
Grayson, Ky., U.S. B7 110
Grayson, co., Ky., U.S. C3 110
Grayson, co., Tx., U.S. C4 136
Grayson, co., Va., U.S. D1 139
Grayson Lake, res., Ky., U.S. B7 110
Grays Peak, mtn., Co., U.S. B5 99
Gray Summit, Mo., U.S. g12 118
Graysville, Al., U.S. f7 94
Graysville, Tn., U.S. D8 135
Grayville, Il., U.S. E5 106
Graz, Aus. G14 12
Great Alfold see Alföld, pl., Hung. F6 20
Great Artesian Basin, Austl. F3 62
Great Australian Bight, b., Austl. G4 60
Great Averill Pond, l., Vt., U.S. B5 138
Great Barrier Island, i., N.Z. o14 63c
Great Barrier Reef, rf., Austl. D4 62
Great Barrington, Ma., U.S. B1 114
Great Basin, U.S. C4 92
Great Basin National Park, Nv., U.S. E7 121
Great Bay, b., N.H., U.S. D5 122
Great Bay, b., N.J., U.S. D4 123
Great Bear Lake, l., N.T., Can. E15 82
Great Belt see Storebælt, strt., Den. I4 10
Great Bend, Ks., U.S. D5 109
Great Britain see United Kingdom, ctry., Eur. C6 12
Great Captain Island, i., Ct., U.S. F1 100
Great Channel, strt., Asia E2 34
Great Dismal Swamp, sw., U.S. D6 139
Great Divide Basin, Wy., U.S. E4 143
Great Dividing Range, mts., Austl. H4 62
Great East Lake, l., U.S. C5 122
Great Egg Harbor, stm., N.J., U.S. D3 123
Greater Antilles, is., N.A. E9 76
Greater Khingan Range see Da Hinggan Ling, mts., China B12 28
Greater Sunda Islands, is., Asia D3 36
Great Exuma, i., Bah. D9 76
Great Falls, Mt., U.S. C5 119
Great Falls, S.C., U.S. B6 133
Great Falls, wtfl, Md., U.S. B3 113
Great Falls Dam, Tn., U.S. D6 135
Greathouse Peak, mtn., Mt., U.S. D7 119
Great Inagua, i., Bah. D10 76
Great Indian Desert (Thar Desert), des., Asia D2 40
Great Island, spit, Ma., U.S. C7 114
Great Island, i., N.C., U.S. B6 126
Great Karroo, plat., S. Afr. E3 56
Great Lakes Naval Training Center, mil., Il., U.S. h9 106
Great Miami, stm., U.S. C1 128
Great Misery Island, i., Ma., U.S. f12 114
Great Moose Lake, l., Me., U.S. D3 112
Great Namaqualand, hist. reg., Nmb. D2 56
Great Neck, N.Y., U.S. h13 125
Great Nicobar, i., India H6 40
Great Ouse, stm., Eng., U.K. D7 12
Great Pee Dee, stm., U.S. D9 133
Great Plains, pl., N.A. E9 75
Great Point, c., Ma., U.S. D7 114
Great Ruaha, stm., Tan. E7 54
Great Sacandaga Lake, l., N.Y., U.S. C6 125
Great Salt Lake, l., Ut., U.S. B3 137
Great Salt Lake Desert, des., Ut., U.S. C2 137
Great Salt Plains Lake, res., Ok., U.S. A3 129
Great Salt Pond, b., R.I., U.S. h7 132
Great Sand Dunes National Monument, Co., U.S. D5 99
Great Sandy Desert, des., Austl. E3 60
Great Slave Lake, l., N.T., Can. F17 82
Great Smoky Mountains, mts., U.S. B8 135
Great Smoky Mountains National Park, U.S. B8 135
Great Swamp, sw., R.I., U.S. F3 132
Great Victoria Desert, des., Austl. F4 60
Great Village, N.S., Can. D6 87
Great Wall see Chang Cheng, hist., China B2 30
Great Wass Island, i., Me., U.S. D5 112
Great Yarmouth, Eng., U.K. D7 12
Great Zab, stm., Asia D10 44
Gréboun, mtn., Niger C6 50
Greece, N.Y., U.S. B3 125
Greece, ctry., Eur. E8 18
Greeley, Co., U.S. A6 99
Greeley, Pa., U.S. D12 131
Greeley, co., Ks., U.S. D2 109
Greeley, co., Ne., U.S. C7 120
Green, Or., U.S. D3 130
Green, co., Ky., U.S. C4 110
Green, co., Wi., U.S. F4 142
Green, stm., Il., U.S. B4 106
Green, stm., Ky., U.S. C2 110
Green, stm., Wa., U.S. B3 140
Green, stm., U.S. D6 92
Green, stm., U.S. F3 138
Green Acres, De., U.S. h8 101
Greenacres, Wa., U.S. B8 140
Greenacres City, Fl., U.S. F6 102
Greenback, Tn., U.S. D9 135
Green Bay, Wi., U.S. D6 142
Green Bay, b., U.S. B10 92
Green Bay, b., U.S. D3 115
Greenbelt, Md., U.S. C4 113
Greenbriar, Va., U.S. g12 139
Greenbrier, Ar., U.S. B3 97
Green Brier, Tn., U.S. A5 135
Greenbrier, co., W.V., U.S. D4 141
Greenbrier, stm., W.V., U.S. D4 141
Greenbush, Mn., U.S. B2 116
Greencastle, In., U.S. E4 107
Greencastle, Pa., U.S. G6 131
Green City, Mo., U.S. A5 118
Green Cove Springs, Fl., U.S. C5 102
Greendale, In., U.S. F8 107
Greendale, Wi., U.S. F6 142
Greene, Ia., U.S. B5 108
Greene, N.Y., U.S. C5 125
Greene, co., Al., U.S. C1 94
Greene, co., Ar., U.S. A5 97
Greene, co., Ga., U.S. C3 103
Greene, co., Ia., U.S. B3 108
Greene, co., Il., U.S. D3 106
Greene, co., In., U.S. F4 107
Greene, co., Mo., U.S. D4 118
Greene, co., Ms., U.S. D5 117
Greene, co., N.C., U.S. B5 126
Greene, co., N.Y., U.S. C6 125
Greene, co., Oh., U.S. C2 128
Greene, co., Pa., U.S. G1 131
Greene, co., Tn., U.S. C11 135
Greene, co., Va., U.S. B4 139
Greeneville, Tn., U.S. C11 135
Green Fall, stm., U.S. F1 132
Greenfield, Ca., U.S. D3 98
Greenfield, Ia., U.S. C3 108
Greenfield, Il., U.S. D3 106
Greenfield, In., U.S. E6 107
Greenfield, Ma., U.S. A2 114
Greenfield, Mo., U.S. D4 118
Greenfield, N.H., U.S. E3 122
Greenfield, Oh., U.S. C2 128
Greenfield, Tn., U.S. A3 135
Greenfield, Wi., U.S. n12 142
Greenfield Plaza, Ia., U.S. e8 108
Green Forest, Ar., U.S. A2 97
Green Harbor, Ma., U.S. B6 114
Green Hill Pond, l., R.I., U.S. G3 132
Greenhills, Oh., U.S. n12 128
Green Lake, Wi., U.S. E5 142
Green Lake, co., Wi., U.S. E4 142
Green Lake, l., Me., U.S. D4 112
Green Lake, l., Wi., U.S. E5 142
Greenland, Ar., U.S. B1 97
Greenland, N.H., U.S. D5 122
Greenland, dep., N.A. D30 82
Greenland Basin D23 144
Greenland Sea B9 46
Greenlee, co., Az., U.S. D6 96
Green Lookout Mountain, mtn., Wa., U.S. D3 140
Green Mountain, mtn., Wy., U.S. D5 143
Green Mountain Reservoir, res., Co., U.S. B4 99
Green Mountains, mts., Vt., U.S. F2 138
Greenock, Scot., U.K. C4 12
Greenock, Pa., U.S. F2 131
Green Peter Lake, res., Or., U.S. C4 130
Green Pond, Al., U.S. B2 94
Green Pond, l., N.J., U.S. A4 123
Greenport, N.Y., U.S. m16 125
Green River, Ut., U.S. E5 137
Green River, Wy., U.S. E3 143
Green River Lake, res., Ky., U.S. C4 110
Green River Lock and Dam, U.S. I2 107
Green River Reservoir, res., Vt., U.S. B3 138
Green Rock, Il., U.S. B3 106
Greensboro, Al., U.S. C2 94
Greensboro, Ga., U.S. C3 103
Greensboro, Md., U.S. C6 113
Greensboro, N.C., U.S. A3 126
Greensburg, In., U.S. F7 107
Greensburg, Ks., U.S. E4 109
Greensburg, Ky., U.S. C4 110
Greensburg, Pa., U.S. F2 131
Greens Peak, mtn., Az., U.S. C6 96
Green Springs, Oh., U.S. A2 128
Greensville, co., Va., U.S. D5 139
Green Swamp, sw., N.C., U.S. C4 126
Greentown, In., U.S. D6 107
Greenup, Il., U.S. D5 106
Greenup, Ky., U.S. B7 110
Greenup, co., Ky., U.S. B7 110
Green Valley, Az., U.S. F5 96
Greenview, Il., U.S. C4 106
Greenville, Lib. E3 50
Greenville, Al., U.S. D3 94
Greenville, Ca., U.S. B3 98
Greenville, De., U.S. A3 101
Greenville, Ga., U.S. C2 103
Greenville, Il., U.S. E4 106
Greenville, Ky., U.S. C2 110
Greenville, Me., U.S. C3 112
Greenville, Mi., U.S. E5 115
Greenville, Ms., U.S. B2 117
Greenville, N.C., U.S. B5 126
Greenville, N.H., U.S. E3 122
Greenville, Oh., U.S. B1 128
Greenville, Pa., U.S. D1 131
Greenville, R.I., U.S. C3 132
Greenville, S.C., U.S. B3 133
Greenville, Tx., U.S. C4 136
Greenville, co., S.C., U.S. B3 133
Greenville Creek, stm., Oh., U.S. B1 128
Greenville Junction, Me., U.S. C3 112
Greenwich, Ct., U.S. E1 100
Greenwich, N.Y., U.S. B7 125
Greenwich, Oh., U.S. A3 128
Greenwich Bay, b., R.I., U.S. D4 132
Greenwich Point, c., Ct., U.S. E1 100
Greenwood, B.C., Can. E8 85
Greenwood, Ar., U.S. B1 97
Greenwood, De., U.S. E3 101
Greenwood, In., U.S. E5 107
Greenwood, La., U.S. B2 111
Greenwood, Mo., U.S. k11 118
Greenwood, Ms., U.S. B3 117
Greenwood, Pa., U.S. E5 131
Greenwood, S.C., U.S. C3 133
Greenwood, Wi., U.S. D3 142
Greenwood, co., Ks., U.S. E7 109
Greenwood, co., S.C., U.S. C3 133
Greenwood, Lake, res., In., U.S. G4 107
Greenwood, Lake, res., S.C., U.S. C4 133
Greenwood Lake, N.Y., U.S. D6 125
Greenwood Lake, l., Mn., U.S. C7 116
Greenwood Lake, l., U.S. A4 123
Greer, S.C., U.S. B3 133
Greer, co., Ok., U.S. C2 129
Greers Ferry Lake, res., Ar., U.S. B3 97
Greeson, Lake, res., Ar., U.S. C2 97
Gregg, co., Tx., U.S. C5 136

Name	Map Ref.	Page
Gregory, S.D., U.S.	D6	134
Gregory, co., S.D., U.S.	D6	134
Gregory Range, mts., Austl.	D3	62
Greifswald, Ger.	C13	12
Greilickville, Mi., U.S.	D5	115
Gremiha, Russia	C5	26
Grenada, Ms., U.S.	B4	117
Grenada, co., Ms., U.S.	B4	117
Grenada, ctry., N.A.	F12	76
Grenada Lake, res., Ms., U.S.	B4	117
Grenadines, is., N.A.	F12	76
Grenen, c., Den.	H4	10
Grenoble, Fr.	E9	16
Grenville, P.Q., Can.	D3	90
Grenville, Cape, c., Austl.	C3	62
Grenville, Point, c., Wa., U.S.	B1	140
Gresham, Or., U.S.	B4	130
Gresik, Indon.	E4	36
Gresik, Indon.	D2	36
Gretna, Mb., Can.	E3	86
Gretna, Fl., U.S.	B2	102
Gretna, La., U.S.	E5	111
Gretna, Ne., U.S.	C9	120
Gretna, Va., U.S.	D3	139
Grevená, Grc.	D8	18
Grey, stm., Nf., Can.	E3	88
Greybull, Wy., U.S.	B4	143
Greybull, stm., Wy., U.S.	B4	143
Greylock, Mount, mtn., Ma., U.S.	A1	114
Greymouth, N.Z.	p13	63c
Grey Range, mts., Austl.	F3	62
Greys, stm., Wy., U.S.	C2	143
Greytown, S. Afr.	D5	56
Gridley, Ca., U.S.	C3	98
Gridley, Il., U.S.	C5	106
Griffin, Ga., U.S.	C2	103
Griffiss Air Force Base, mil., N.Y., U.S.	B5	125
Griffith, Austl.	G4	62
Griffith, In., U.S.	A3	107
Grifton, N.C., U.S.	B5	126
Griggs, co., N.D., U.S.	B7	127
Griggsville, Il., U.S.	D3	106
Grim, Cape, c., Austl.	I3	62
Grimes, Ia., U.S.	C4	108
Grimes, co., Tx., U.S.	D4	136
Grimsby, On., Can.	D5	89
Grimsby, Eng., U.K.	D7	12
Grímsey, i., Ice.	k20	10a
Grimshaw, Ab., Can.	A2	84
Grimsley, Tn., U.S.	C9	135
Grímsstaðir, Ice.	l20	10a
Grindall Creek, Va., U.S.	n18	139
Grinnell, Ia., U.S.	C5	108
Griswold, Ia., U.S.	C2	108
Grizzly Mountain, mtn., Id., U.S.	B2	105
Grizzly Mountain, mtn., Or., U.S.	C6	130
Grizzly Mountain, mtn., Wa., U.S.	A7	140
Grjazi, Russia	C15	20
Grjazovec, Russia	C7	22
Groais Island, i., Nf., Can.	C4	88
Groblersdal, S. Afr.	D4	56
Grodno see Hrodnoo, Bela.	C7	20
Groesbeck, Tx., U.S.	D4	136
Groningen, Neth.	D10	12
Groom Lake, l., Nv., U.S.	F6	121
Groom Range, mts., Nv., U.S.	F6	121
Groote Eylandt, i., Austl.	C6	60
Grootfontein, Nmb.	B2	56
Gros Morne National Park, Nf., Can.	D3	88
Grosse Isle Naval Air Station, mil., Mi., U.S.	p15	115
Grosse Pointe Park, Mi., U.S.	p16	115
Grosse Pointe Woods, Mi., U.S.	p16	115
Grosseto, Italy	C3	18
Grossglockner, mtn., Aus.	G13	12
Grossmont, Ca., U.S.	o16	98
Gros Ventre, stm., Wy., U.S.	C2	143
Gros Ventre Range, mts., Wy., U.S.	C2	143
Groswater Bay, b., Nf., Can.	H28	82
Groton, Ct., U.S.	D7	100
Groton, N.Y., U.S.	C4	125
Groton, S.D., U.S.	B7	134
Groton Long Point, Ct., U.S.	D7	100
Grottoes, Va., U.S.	B4	139
Grouse Creek, stm., Ut., U.S.	B2	137
Grouse Creek Mountain, mtn., Id., U.S.	E5	105
Grove, Ok., U.S.	A7	129
Grove City, Fl., U.S.	F4	102
Grove City, Oh., U.S.	C2	128
Grove City, Pa., U.S.	D1	131
Grove Hill, Al., U.S.	D2	94
Groveland, Fl., U.S.	D5	102
Groveland, Ma., U.S.	A5	114
Grove Mountains, mts., Ant.	D12	67
Grove Point, c., Md., U.S.	B5	113
Groveport, Oh., U.S.	C3	128
Grover City, Ca., U.S.	E3	98
Groves, Tx., U.S.	E6	136
Groveton, N.H., U.S.	A3	122
Groveton, Tx., U.S.	D5	136
Groveton, Va., U.S.	g12	139
Grovetown, Ga., U.S.	C4	103
Groveville, N.J., U.S.	C3	123
Growa Point, c., Lib.	F3	50
Growler Peak, mtn., Az., U.S.	E2	96
Groznyj, Russia	E6	26
Grudziądz, Pol.	C5	20
Gruetli-Laager, Tn., U.S.	D8	135
Grulla, Tx., U.S.	F3	136
Grünau, Nmb.	D2	56
Grundy, Va., U.S.	e9	139
Grundy, co., Ia., U.S.	B5	108
Grundy, co., Il., U.S.	B5	106
Grundy, co., Mo., U.S.	A4	118
Grundy, co., Tn., U.S.	D8	135
Grundy Center, Ia., U.S.	B5	108
Grunthal, Mb., Can.	E3	86
Gruver, Tx., U.S.	A2	136
Guacanayabo, Golfo de, b., Cuba	A4	80
Guadalajara, Mex.	C4	78
Guadalajara, Spain	G5	16
Guadalcanal, i., Sol. Is.	B6	62
Guadalquivir, stm., Spain	I4	16
Guadalquivir, Marismas del, sw., Spain	I3	16
Guadalupe, Mex.	C4	78
Guadalupe, Mex.	B4	78
Guadalupe, Az., U.S.	m9	96
Guadalupe, Ca., U.S.	E3	98
Guadalupe, co., N.M., U.S.	C5	124
Guadalupe, co., Tx., U.S.	E4	136
Guadalupe, Isla, i., Mex.	B1	78
Guadalupe Mountains, mts., U.S.	E5	124
Guadalupe Mountains National Park, Tx., U.S.	o12	136
Guadalupe Peak, mtn., Tx., U.S.	o12	136
Guadeloupe, dep., N.A.	E12	76
Guadeloupe Passage, strt., N.A.	B7	80
Guadiana, stm., Eur.	I3	16
Guadix, Spain	I5	16
Guaíra, Braz.	C7	72
Guajará-Mirim, Braz.	F6	70
Guaje, Laguna del, l., Mex.	B4	78
Gualeguay, Arg.	E6	72
Gualeguaychú, Arg.	E6	72
Guam, dep., Oc.	D12	32
Guaminí, Arg.	F5	72
Guamúchil, Mex.	B3	78
Guanaja, Isla de, i., Hond.	B2	80
Guanajuato, Mex.	C4	78
Guanajuato, state, Mex.	C4	78
Guanambi, Braz.	D8	74
Guanare, Ven.	B6	70
Guane, Cuba	A3	80
Guang'an, China	E9	28
Guangde, China	C4	30
Guangdong, state, China	G10	28
Guangji, China	D4	30
Guangling, China	B3	30
Guangnan, China	G8	28
Guangxi Zhuangzu Zizhiqu, state, China	G9	28
Guangyuan, China	E9	28
Guangzhou (Canton), China	E3	30
Guano Lake, l., Or., U.S.	E7	130
Guantánamo, Cuba	A4	80
Guantao, China	B4	30
Guanxian, China	E8	28
Guanyun, China	C4	30
Guapí, Col.	C4	70
Guápiles, C.R.	C3	80
Guaporé, stm., S.A.	F7	70
Guarabira, Braz.	C4	74
Guarapari, Braz.	F3	74
Guarapuava, Braz.	D7	72
Guaratuba, Braz.	D8	72
Guarda, Port.	G3	16
Guardafui, Cape see Gwardafuy, Gees, c., Som.	H15	48
Guardo, Spain	F4	16
Guarenas, Ven.	C6	80
Guárico, stm., Ven.	D6	80
Guasave, Mex.	B3	78
Guasdualito, Ven.	B5	70
Guasipati, Ven.	B7	70
Guatemala, Guat.	C1	80
Guatemala, ctry., N.A.	D6	78
Guatemala Basin	G29	64
Guaviare, stm., Col.	C6	70
Guaxupé, Braz.	F2	74
Guayana see Ciudad Guayana, Ven.	B7	70
Guayana see Guyana, ctry., S.A.	B8	70
Guayape, stm., Hond.	C2	80
Guayaquil, Ec.	D3	70
Guayaquil, Golfo de, b., S.A.	D3	70
Guaymallén, Arg.	E4	72
Guaymas, Mex.	B2	78
Gubaha, Russia	C10	22
Gubbio, Italy	C4	18
Guben, Ger.	E14	12
Guben (Gubin), Pol.	D3	20
Gubin (Guben), Pol.	D3	20
Gubkin, Russia	D14	20
Gudauta, Geor.	A9	44
Gudermes, Russia	B5	42
Gudivāda, India	F4	40
Gudiyāttam, India	G3	40
Gūdūr, India	G3	40
Guékédou, Gui.	E2	50
Guélengdeng, Chad	D8	50
Guelma, Alg.	D5	14
Guelph, On., Can.	D4	89
Guercif, Mor.	E3	14
Güere, stm., Ven.	D7	80
Guéret, Fr.	D7	16
Guernsey, Wy., U.S.	D8	143
Guernsey, co., Oh., U.S.	B4	128
Guernsey, dep., Eur.	F5	12
Guerrero, Mex.	B3	78
Guerrero, state, Mex.	D4	78
Guerrero Negro, Mex.	B2	78
Gueydan, La., U.S.	D3	111
Guga, Russia	D15	26
Gugē, mtn., Eth.	B7	54
Guguan, i., N. Mar. Is.	C12	32
Guiana Basin	G9	66
Guide, China	D8	28
Guiding, China	D2	30
Guildford, Eng., U.K.	E6	12
Guilford, Ct., U.S.	D5	100
Guilford, Me., U.S.	C3	112
Guilford, co., N.C., U.S.	A3	126
Guilin, China	F10	28
Guimarães, Port.	G2	16
Guimaras Island, i., Phil.	D8	34
Guin, Al., U.S.	B2	94
Guinea, ctry., Afr.	D2	50
Guinea, Gulf of, b., Afr.	I10	46
Guinea Basin	H13	66
Guinea-Bissau, ctry., Afr.	D1	50
Güines, Cuba	A3	80
Guingamp, Fr.	C5	16
Guiping, China	E3	30
Güira de Melena, Cuba	A3	80
Guiratinga, Braz.	B7	72
Güiria, Ven.	A7	70
Guitry, C. Iv.	E3	50
Guiuan, Phil.	D9	34
Guixi, China	D4	30
Guixian, China	G9	28
Guiyang, China	F9	28
Guizhou, state, China	F9	28
Gujarāt, prov., India	E2	40
Gujrānwāla, Pak.	D10	42
Gujrāt, Pak.	D10	42
Gulbarga, India	F3	40
Gulbene, Lat.	H12	10
Gulf, co., Fl., U.S.	C1	102
Gulf, The see Persian Gulf, b., Asia	E6	42
Gulf Gate Estates, Fl., U.S.	E4	102
Gulf Islands National Seashore, U.S.	E5	117
Gulf of Alaska Seamount Province	B1	144
Gulfport, Fl., U.S.	E4	102
Gulfport, Ms., U.S.	E4	117
Gulf Shores, Al., U.S.	E2	94
Gulgong, Austl.	G4	62
Gulian, China	A12	28
Gulistan, Uzb.	B9	42
Gullfoss, wtfl, Ice.	l19	10a
Gull Island, i., N.C., U.S.	B7	126
Gullivan Bay, b., Fl., U.S.	G5	102
Gull Lake, l., Ab., Can.	C4	84
Gull Lake, l., Mn., U.S.	D4	116
Güllük Körfezi, b., Tur.	D2	44
Gulu, Ug.	C6	54
Gumboro, De., U.S.	G4	101
Gumdag, Turk.	C6	42
Gumel, Nig.	D6	50
Gümüşhane, Tur.	B8	44
Guna, India	E3	40
Gundagai, Austl.	H4	62
Gundji, D.R.C.	C4	54
Gungu, D.R.C.	E3	54
Gunisao, stm., Mb., Can.	C3	86
Gunmi, Nig.	D6	50
Gunnbjørn Fjeld, mtn., Grnld.	E34	82
Gunnedah, Austl.	G5	62
Gunnison, Co., U.S.	C4	99
Gunnison, Ms., U.S.	B3	117
Gunnison, Ut., U.S.	D4	137
Gunnison, co., Co., U.S.	C3	99
Gunnison, stm., Co., U.S.	C2	99
Gunnison, Mount, mtn., Co., U.S.	C3	99
Gunpowder Neck, c., Md., U.S.	B5	113
Gunpowder River, b., Md., U.S.	B5	113
Guntakal, India	F3	40
Gunter Air Force Base, mil., Al., U.S.	C3	94
Guntersville, Al., U.S.	A3	94
Guntersville Lake, res., Al., U.S.	A3	94
Guntown, Ms., U.S.	A5	117
Guntūr, India	F4	40
Gunungsitoli, Indon.	C1	36
Guoyang, China	C4	30
Gupis, Pak.	C10	42
Gurdon, Ar., U.S.	D2	97
Gurdžaani, Geor.	B11	44
Guri, Embalse de, res., Ven.	B7	70
Gurley, Al., U.S.	A3	94
Gurnee, Il., U.S.	h9	106
Gurnet Point, c., Ma., U.S.	B6	114
Gurskøya, i., Nor.	E1	10
Gürün, Tur.	C7	44
Gurupi, Braz.	D2	74
Gurupi, stm., Braz.	B2	74
Gusau, Nig.	D6	50
Gusev, Russia	B7	20
Gušgy, Turk.	F8	26
Gushi, China	C4	30
Gusinoozersk, Russia	A9	28
Guspini, Italy	E2	18
Gustav Holm, Kap, c., Grnld.	E33	82
Gustine, Ca., U.S.	D3	98
Güstrow, Ger.	D13	12
Guthrie, Ky., U.S.	D2	110
Guthrie, Ok., U.S.	B4	129
Guthrie, W.V., U.S.	m12	141
Guthrie, co., Ia., U.S.	C3	108
Guthrie Center, Ia., U.S.	C3	108
Guttenberg, Ia., U.S.	B6	108
Guttenberg, N.J., U.S.	h8	123
Guwāhāti, India	D6	40
Guyana, ctry., S.A.	B8	70
Guyandotte, stm., W.V., U.S.	C2	141
Guyang, China	A3	30
Guymon, Ok., U.S.	e9	129
Guysborough, N.S., Can.	D8	87
Guyton, Ga., U.S.	D5	103
Guyuan, China	D9	28
Guzar, Uzb.	C9	42
Güzelyurt Körfezi, b., N. Cyp.	E5	44
Guzmán, Mex.	D4	78
Gwaai, Zimb.	B4	56
Gwādar, Pak.	E8	42
Gwalia, Austl.	F3	60
Gwalior, India	D3	40
Gwanda, Zimb.	C4	56
Gwardafuy, Gees, c., Som.	H15	48
Gwayi, stm., Zimb.	B4	56
Gweru, Zimb.	B4	56
Gweta, Bots.	C4	56
Gwinhurst, De., U.S.	h8	101
Gwinn, Mi., U.S.	B3	115
Gwinner, N.D., U.S.	C8	127
Gwinnett, co., Ga., U.S.	C2	103
Gwydyr Bay, b., Ak., U.S.	A10	95
Gwynns Falls, stm., Md., U.S.	g10	113
Gyangzê, China	F5	28
Gyaring Co, l., China	E5	28
Gyaring Hu, l., China	E7	28
Gyda, Russia	B9	26
Gydanskij poluostrov, pen., Russia	B9	26
Gyldenløves Fjord, b., Grnld.	F31	82
Gympie, Austl.	F5	62
Gyöngyös, Hung.	F5	20
Győr, Hung.	F4	20
Gypsum, Co., U.S.	B4	99
Gyzylarbat, Turk.	F7	26

H

Name	Map Ref.	Page
Haakon, co., S.D., U.S.	C4	134
Haapsalu, Est.	G10	10
Haarlem, Neth.	D9	12
Haast, N.Z.	p12	63c
Habarovo, Russia	A11	22
Habarovsk, Russia	E15	26
Ḩabbānīyah, Buḩayrat al-, res., Iraq	F10	44
Habersham, co., Ga., U.S.	B3	103
Hachijō-jima, i., Japan	E15	28
Hachinohe, Japan	C16	28
Hachiōji, Japan	C3	31
Hackberry, La., U.S.	E2	111
Hackensack, N.J., U.S.	B4	123
Hackensack, stm., N.J., U.S.	h8	123
Hackettstown, N.J., U.S.	B3	123
Hackleburg, Al., U.S.	A2	94
Haddam, Ct., U.S.	D5	100
Haddock, Ga., U.S.	C3	103
Haddonfield, N.J., U.S.	D2	123
Haddon Heights, N.J., U.S.	D2	123
Hadejia, Nig.	D7	50
Hadejia, stm., Nig.	D6	50
Ḩadera, Isr.	F6	44
Haderslev, Den.	I3	10
Hadībū, Yemen	H6	38
Ḩadīthah, Iraq	D4	42
Hadjout, Alg.	I8	16
Hadley Lake, l., Me., U.S.	D5	112
Hadrian's Wall, Eng., U.K.	C5	12
Haeju, N. Kor.	D13	28
Hafik, Tur.	C7	44
Hafnarfjörður, Ice.	l17	10a
Haft Gel, Iran	D5	42
Hagan, Ga., U.S.	D5	103
Hagemeister Island, i., Ak., U.S.	D7	95
Hagerman, Id., U.S.	G4	105
Hagerman, N.M., U.S.	D5	124
Hagerstown, In., U.S.	E7	107
Hagerstown, Md., U.S.	A2	113
Hagfors, Swe.	F5	10
Haggin, Mount, mtn., Mt., U.S.	D3	119
Hagi, Japan	D2	31
Ha Giang, Viet.	B5	34
Hague, Sk., Can.	E2	91
Haguenau, Fr.	C10	16
Hagues Peak, mtn., Co., U.S.	A5	99
Ha! Ha!, Baie des, b., P.Q., Can.	C2	88
Hahira, Ga., U.S.	F3	103
Hahnville, La., U.S.	E5	111
Haicheng, China	A5	30
Hai Duong, Viet.	B5	34
Haifa see Ḩefa, Isr.	D2	42
Haig, Austl.	G4	60
Haikang, China	E3	30
Haikou, China	G10	28
Haiku, Hi., U.S.	C5	104
Ḩā'il, Sau. Ar.	E4	38
Hailar, China	B11	28
Hailey, Id., U.S.	F4	105
Haileybury, On., Can.	p20	89
Haileyville, Ok., U.S.	C6	129
Hailin, China	B1	31
Hailun, China	B13	28
Haimen, China	F12	28
Haimen, China	E4	30
Hainan, prov., China	H9	28
Hainan Dao, i., China	H9	28
Hainan Island see Hainan Dao, i., China	H9	28
Haines, Ak., U.S.	D12	95
Haines City, Fl., U.S.	D5	102
Haining, China	C5	30
Hai Ninh, Viet.	B5	34
Hai Phong, Viet.	B5	34
Haisyn, Ukr.	E10	20
Haiti, ctry., N.A.	H12	75
Haitun, China	B7	40
Haiyuan, China	B2	30
Haizhou, China	E11	28
Haizhou Wan, b., China	B4	30
Hajdúböszörmény, Hung.	F6	20
Hajnówka, Pol.	C7	20
Hakkâri, Tur.	D10	44
Hakodate, Japan	C16	28
Ḩalab (Aleppo), Syria	D7	44
Halachó, Mex.	C6	78
Ḩalā'ib, Sudan	F12	48
Halawa, Cape, c., Hi., U.S.	B5	104
Halawa Heights, Hi., U.S.	g10	104
Halberstadt, Ger.	E12	12
Halden, Nor.	G4	10
Haldimand, On., Can.	E5	89
Haldwāni, India	D3	40
Hale, co., Al., U.S.	C2	94
Hale, co., Tx., U.S.	B2	136
Haleakala Crater, crat., Hi., U.S.	C5	104
Haleakala National Park, Hi., U.S.	C6	104
Hale Center, Tx., U.S.	B2	136
Haleiwa, Hi., U.S.	B3	104
Hales Corners, Wi., U.S.	n11	142
Halethorpe, Md., U.S.	B4	113
Haleyville, Al., U.S.	A2	94
Half Moon Bay, Ca., U.S.	k8	98
Halfway, Md., U.S.	A2	113
Haliburton, On., Can.	B6	89
Halibut Point, c., Ma., U.S.	A6	114
Halicarnassus, hist., Tur.	D2	44
Halifax, N.S., Can.	E6	87
Halifax, Va., U.S.	D4	139
Halifax, co., N.C., U.S.	A5	126
Halifax, co., Va., U.S.	D4	139
Haliimaile, Hi., U.S.	C5	104
Hall, co., Ga., U.S.	B3	103
Hall, co., Ne., U.S.	D7	120
Hall, co., Tx., U.S.	B2	136
Halla, Mount see Halla-san, mtn., S. Kor.	E13	28
Hallam Peak, mtn., B.C., Can.	C8	85
Hallandale, Fl., U.S.	G6	102
Ḩallānīyah, Juzur al-, is., Oman	G7	38
Halla-san, mtn., S. Kor.	E13	28
Halle, Ger.	E12	12
Hällefors, Swe.	G6	10
Hallein, Aus.	G13	12
Hallettsville, Tx., U.S.	E4	136
Hallie, Wi., U.S.	D2	142
Hall Island, i., Ak., U.S.	C5	95
Hall Meadow Brook Reservoir, res., Ct., U.S.	B3	100
Hall Mountain, mtn., Wa., U.S.	A8	140
Hallock, Mn., U.S.	B2	116
Hallowell, Me., U.S.	D3	112
Halls, Tn., U.S.	B2	135
Hallsberg, Swe.	G6	10
Halls Creek, Austl.	D4	60
Halls Creek, stm., Ut., U.S.	F5	137
Halls Crossroads, Tn., U.S.	m14	135
Halls Stream, stm., N.H., U.S.	f7	122
Hallstahammar, Swe.	G7	10
Hallstead, Pa., U.S.	C10	131
Hallsville, Mo., U.S.	B5	118
Hallsville, Tx., U.S.	C5	136
Halmahera, i., Indon.	C7	36
Halmahera, Laut (Halmahera Sea), Indon.	D7	36
Halmahera Sea see Halmahera, Laut, Indon.	D7	36
Hal'mer-Ju, Russia	A11	22
Halmstad, Swe.	H5	10
Halsey, Or., U.S.	C3	130
Hälsingland, hist. reg., Swe.	F7	10
Halstad, Mn., U.S.	C2	116
Halstead, Ks., U.S.	E6	109

Name — Map Ref. — Page

Haltiatunturi, mtn., Eur. **B9** 10
Halton Hills, On., Can. **D5** 89
Hamada, Japan **D2** 31
Hamadān, Iran **D5** 42
Ḥamāh, Syria **E7** 44
Ḥamāh, state, Syria **E7** 44
Hamamatsu, Japan **E15** 28
Hamar, Nor. **F4** 10
Hamarøya, Nor. **B6** 10
Hambantota, Sri L. **H4** 40
Hamblen, co., Tn., U.S. **C10** 135
Hamburg, Ger. **D12** 12
Hamburg, Ar., U.S. **D4** 97
Hamburg, Ia., U.S. **D2** 108
Hamburg, N.Y., U.S. **C2** 125
Hamburg, Pa., U.S. **E10** 131
Hamden, Ct., U.S. **D4** 100
Hamden, Oh., U.S. **C3** 128
Hämeenlinna, Fin. **F11** 10
Hamel, Mn., U.S. **m11** 116
Hameln, Ger. **D11** 12
Hamersley Range, mts., Austl. **E2** 60
Hami, China **C6** 28
Hamilton, Austl. **H3** 62
Hamilton, Ber. **B12** 76
Hamilton, On., Can. **D5** 89
Hamilton, N.Z. **o14** 63c
Hamilton, Al., U.S. **A2** 94
Hamilton, Il., U.S. **C2** 106
Hamilton, In., U.S. **A8** 107
Hamilton, Mi., U.S. **F4** 115
Hamilton, Mo., U.S. **B3** 118
Hamilton, Ms., U.S. **B5** 117
Hamilton, Mt., U.S. **D2** 119
Hamilton, N.Y., U.S. **C5** 125
Hamilton, Oh., U.S. **C1** 128
Hamilton, Tx., U.S. **D3** 136
Hamilton, Va., U.S. **A5** 139
Hamilton, co., Fl., U.S. **B3** 102
Hamilton, co., Ia., U.S. **B4** 108
Hamilton, co., Il., U.S. **E5** 106
Hamilton, co., In., U.S. **D5** 107
Hamilton, co., Ks., U.S. **E2** 109
Hamilton, co., Ne., U.S. **D7** 120
Hamilton, co., N.Y., U.S. **B6** 125
Hamilton, co., Oh., U.S. **C1** 128
Hamilton, co., Tn., U.S. **D8** 135
Hamilton, co., Tx., U.S. **D3** 136
Hamilton, Lake, res., Ar., U.S. **C2** 97
Hamilton, Mount, mtn., Ak., U.S. **C8** 95
Hamilton, Mount, mtn., Ca., U.S. **k9** 98
Hamilton, Mount, mtn., Nv., U.S. **D6** 121
Hamilton Inlet, b., Nf., Can. **A2** 88
Hamilton Reservoir, res., Ma., U.S. **B3** 114
Hamilton Sound, strt., Nf., Can. **D4** 88
Hamilton Square, N.J., U.S. **C3** 123
Hamina, Fin. **F12** 10
Hamiota, Mb., Can. **D1** 86
Hamīrpur, India **D4** 40
Hamlet, In., U.S. **B4** 107
Hamlet, N.C., U.S. **C3** 126
Hamlet, Mount, mtn., Ak., U.S. **B6** 95
Hamlin, Pa., U.S. **D11** 131
Hamlin, Tx., U.S. **C2** 136
Hamlin, W.V., U.S. **C2** 141
Hamlin, co., S.D., U.S. **C8** 134
Hamlin Lake, l., Mi., U.S. **D4** 115
Hamm, Ger. **E10** 12
Hammamet, Tun. **F3** 18
Hammamet, Golfe de, b., Tun. **F3** 18
Hammam Lif, Tun. **F3** 18
Ḥammār, Hawr al-, l., Iraq **G12** 44
Hammerfest, Nor. **A10** 10
Hammon, Ok., U.S. **B2** 129
Hammonasset, stm., Ct., U.S. **D5** 100
Hammonasset Point, c., Ct., U.S. **E5** 100
Hammond, In., U.S. **A2** 107
Hammond, La., U.S. **D5** 111
Hammond, Wi., U.S. **D1** 142
Hammond Bay, b., Mi., U.S. **C6** 115
Hammonton, N.J., U.S. **D3** 123
Hamningberg, Nor. **A14** 10
Hampden, Nf., Can. **D3** 88
Hampden, Me., U.S. **D4** 112
Hampden, co., Ma., U.S. **B2** 114
Hampden Highlands, Me., U.S. **D4** 112
Hampshire, Il., U.S. **A5** 106
Hampshire, co., Ma., U.S. **B2** 114
Hampshire, co., W.V., U.S. **B6** 141
Hampstead, Md., U.S. **A4** 113
Hampstead, N.C., U.S. **C5** 126
Hampton, N.B., Can. **D4** 87
Hampton, Ar., U.S. **D3** 97
Hampton, Ga., U.S. **C2** 103
Hampton, Ia., U.S. **B4** 108
Hampton, N.H., U.S. **E5** 122
Hampton, S.C., U.S. **F5** 133
Hampton, Tn., U.S. **C11** 135
Hampton, Va., U.S. **C6** 139
Hampton, co., S.C., U.S. **F5** 133
Hampton Bays, N.Y., U.S. **n16** 125
Hampton Beach, N.H., U.S. **E5** 122
Hampton Butte, mtn., Or., U.S. **D6** 130
Hampton Roads, Va., U.S. **k15** 139
Hampton Roads Bridge-Tunnel, Va., U.S. **k15** 139
Ḥamrā', Al-Ḥamādah al-, des., Libya **F6** 14
Hamra, As Saquia al, stm., W. Sah. **A2** 50
Hams Fork, stm., Wy., U.S. **E2** 143
Hamtramck, Mi., U.S. **p15** 115
Hāmūn, Daryācheh-ye, l., Iran **D8** 42
Han, stm., China **E9** 28
Hana, Hi., U.S. **C6** 104
Hanahan, S.C., U.S. **F7** 133
Hanalei Bay, b., Hi., U.S. **A2** 104
Hanamaki, Japan **D16** 28
Hanamaulu, Hi., U.S. **B2** 104
Hanapepe, Hi., U.S. **B2** 104
Hânceşti, Mol. **F10** 20
Hanceville, Al., U.S. **A3** 94
Hancheng, China **D10** 28
Hancock, Md., U.S. **A1** 113
Hancock, Mi., U.S. **A2** 115
Hancock, Mn., U.S. **E3** 116
Hancock, co., Ga., U.S. **C3** 103
Hancock, co., Ia., U.S. **A4** 108
Hancock, co., Il., U.S. **C2** 106
Hancock, co., In., U.S. **E6** 107
Hancock, co., Ky., U.S. **C3** 110
Hancock, co., Me., U.S. **D4** 112
Hancock, co., Ms., U.S. **E4** 117
Hancock, co., Oh., U.S. **A2** 128
Hancock, co., Tn., U.S. **C10** 135
Hancock, co., W.V., U.S. **A4** 141
Hand, co., S.D., U.S. **C6** 134
Handan, China **D10** 28
Handyga, Russia **C15** 26
Hanford, Ca., U.S. **D4** 98
Hangayn nuruu, mts., Mong. **B7** 28
Hangchow see Hangzhou, China **E12** 28
Hanggin Houqi, China **C9** 28
Hanggin Qi, China **D9** 28
Hangman Creek, stm., Wa., U.S. **B8** 140
Hangokurt, Russia **B11** 22
Hangu, China **B4** 30
Hangzhou, China **E12** 28
Hangzhou Wan, b., China **C5** 30
Hanjiang, China **F11** 28
Hankinson, N.D., U.S. **C9** 127
Hanko, Fin. **G10** 10
Hanna, Ab., Can. **D5** 84
Hanna, Wy., U.S. **E6** 143
Hanna City, Il., U.S. **C4** 106
Hannahville Indian Reservation, Mi., U.S. **C3** 115
Hannibal, Mo., U.S. **B6** 118
Hannover, Ger. **D11** 12
Hanöbukten, b., Swe. **I6** 10
Ha Noi, Viet. **B5** 34
Hanover, On., Can. **C3** 89
Hanover see Hannover, Ger. **D11** 12
Hanover, Il., U.S. **A3** 106
Hanover, In., U.S. **G7** 107
Hanover, Ks., U.S. **C7** 109
Hanover, Ma., U.S. **B6** 114
Hanover, Mn., U.S. **m11** 116
Hanover, N.H., U.S. **C2** 122
Hanover, Pa., U.S. **G8** 131
Hanover, co., Va., U.S. **C5** 139
Hanover Park, Il., U.S. **k8** 106
Hansen, Id., U.S. **G4** 105
Hansford, co., Tx., U.S. **A2** 136
Hanson, Ma., U.S. **B6** 114
Hanson, co., S.D., U.S. **D8** 134
Hanstholm, Den. **H3** 10
Hantsport, N.S., Can. **D5** 87
Hanty-Mansijsk, Russia **C8** 26
Hanyin, China **C2** 30
Hanzhong, China **E9** 28
Hāora, India **E5** 40
Haparanda, Swe. **D11** 10
Hapčeranga, Russia **E13** 26
Hapeville, Ga., U.S. **C2** 103
Happy Valley, N.M., U.S. **E5** 124
Happy Valley-Goose Bay, Nf., Can. **B1** 88
Hāpur, India **D3** 40
Ḥaraḍ, Sau. Ar. **F5** 38
Harahan, La., U.S. **k11** 111
Haralson, co., Ga., U.S. **C1** 103
Harare, Zimb. **B5** 56
Harazé Mangueigne, Chad **B4** 54
Harbala, Russia **C14** 26
Harbeson, De., U.S. **F4** 101
Harbin, China **B13** 28
Harbor, Or., U.S. **E2** 130
Harbor Beach, Mi., U.S. **E8** 115
Harborcreek, Pa., U.S. **B2** 131
Harbor Springs, Mi., U.S. **C6** 115
Harbour Breton, Nf., Can. **E4** 88
Harbour Grace, Nf., Can. **E5** 88
Harcuvar Mountains, mts., Az., U.S. **D2** 96
Hardangerfjorden, b., Nor. **F2** 10
Hardee, co., Fl., U.S. **E5** 102
Hardeeville, S.C., U.S. **G5** 133
Hardeman, co., Tn., U.S. **B2** 135
Hardeman, co., Tx., U.S. **B3** 136
Hardin, Il., U.S. **D3** 106
Hardin, Mt., U.S. **E9** 119
Hardin, co., Ia., U.S. **B4** 108
Hardin, co., Il., U.S. **F5** 106
Hardin, co., Ky., U.S. **C4** 110
Hardin, co., Oh., U.S. **B2** 128
Hardin, co., Tn., U.S. **B3** 135
Hardin, co., Tx., U.S. **D5** 136
Harding, S. Afr. **E4** 56
Harding, co., N.M., U.S. **B5** 124
Harding, co., S.D., U.S. **B2** 134
Harding, Lake, res., U.S. **C4** 94
Hardinsburg, Ky., U.S. **C3** 110
Hardisty, Ab., Can. **C5** 84
Hardoi, India **D4** 40
Hardwick, Ga., U.S. **C3** 103
Hardwick, Vt., U.S. **B4** 138
Hardwood Ridge, mtn., Pa., U.S. **D11** 131
Hardy, co., W.V., U.S. **B6** 141
Hardy Lake, res., In., U.S. **G6** 107
Hare Bay, Nf., Can. **D4** 88
Hare Bay, b., Nf., Can. **C4** 88
Hārer, Eth. **B8** 54
Harford, co., Md., U.S. **A5** 113
Hargeysa, Som. **I13** 48
Har Hu, l., China **D7** 28
Hari, stm., Indon. **D2** 36
Haridwār, India **D3** 40
Harīrūd, stm., Asia **D8** 42
Harkers Island, N.C., U.S. **C6** 126
Harlan, Ia., U.S. **C2** 108
Harlan, In., U.S. **B8** 107
Harlan, Ky., U.S. **D6** 110
Harlan, co., Ky., U.S. **D6** 110
Harlan, co., Ne., U.S. **D6** 120
Harlan County Lake, res., Ne., U.S. **E6** 120
Harlem, Fl., U.S. **F6** 102
Harlem, Ga., U.S. **C4** 103
Harlem, Mt., U.S. **B8** 119
Harleyville, S.C., U.S. **E7** 133
Harlingen, Tx., U.S. **F4** 136
Harlow, Eng., U.K. **E7** 12
Harlowton, Mt., U.S. **D7** 119
Harmånger, Swe. **F7** 10
Harmanli, Bul. **D10** 18
Harmon, co., Ok., U.S. **C2** 129
Harmon Creek, stm., W.V., U.S. **f8** 141
Harmony, In., U.S. **E3** 107
Harmony, Mn., U.S. **G6** 116
Harmony, Pa., U.S. **E1** 131
Harmony, R.I., U.S. **B3** 132
Harnett, co., N.C., U.S. **B4** 126
Harney, co., Or., U.S. **D7** 130
Harney, Lake, l., Fl., U.S. **D5** 102
Harney Lake, l., Or., U.S. **D7** 130
Harney Peak, mtn., S.D., U.S. **D2** 134
Härnösand, Swe. **E7** 10
Haro Strait, strt., Wa., U.S. **A2** 140
Harper, Lib. **F3** 50
Harper, Ks., U.S. **E5** 109
Harper, co., Ks., U.S. **E5** 109
Harper, co., Ok., U.S. **A2** 129
Harper, Mount, mtn., Ak., U.S. **C11** 95
Harpers Ferry, W.V., U.S. **B7** 141
Harpers Ferry National Historical Park, W.V., U.S. **B7** 141
Harpersville, Al., U.S. **B3** 94
Harpeth, stm., Tn., U.S. **A5** 135
Harqin Qi, China **A4** 30
Harquahala Mountain, mtn., Az., U.S. **D2** 96
Harquahala Mountains, mts., Az., U.S. **D2** 96
Harrah, Ok., U.S. **B4** 129
Harricana, stm., Can. **H24** 82
Harriman, Tn., U.S. **D9** 135
Harriman Reservoir, res., Vt., U.S. **F3** 138
Harrington, De., U.S. **E3** 101
Harrington Park, N.J., U.S. **h9** 123
Harris, Mn., U.S. **E6** 116
Harris, R.I., U.S. **D3** 132
Harris, co., Ga., U.S. **D2** 103
Harris, co., Tx., U.S. **E5** 136
Harris, Lake, l., Fl., U.S. **D5** 102
Harrisburg, Ar., U.S. **B5** 97
Harrisburg, Il., U.S. **F5** 106
Harrisburg, Or., U.S. **C3** 130
Harrisburg, Pa., U.S. **F8** 131
Harrisburg, S.D., U.S. **D9** 134
Harrismith, S. Afr. **D4** 56
Harrison, Ar., U.S. **A2** 97
Harrison, Mi., U.S. **D6** 115
Harrison, N.J., U.S. **k8** 123
Harrison, N.Y., U.S. **h13** 125
Harrison, Oh., U.S. **C1** 128
Harrison, Tn., U.S. **h11** 135
Harrison, co., Ia., U.S. **C2** 108
Harrison, co., In., U.S. **H5** 107
Harrison, co., Ky., U.S. **B5** 110
Harrison, co., Mo., U.S. **A3** 118
Harrison, co., Ms., U.S. **E4** 117
Harrison, co., Oh., U.S. **B4** 128
Harrison, co., Tx., U.S. **C5** 136
Harrison, co., W.V., U.S. **B4** 141
Harrison, Cape, c., Nf., Can. **g10** 88
Harrison Bay, b., Ak., U.S. **A9** 95
Harrisonburg, Va., U.S. **B4** 139
Harrison Hot Springs, B.C., Can. **f14** 85
Harrison Lake, l., B.C., Can. **E7** 85
Harrisonville, Mo., U.S. **C3** 118
Harriston, On., Can. **D4** 89
Harristown, Il., U.S. **D4** 106
Harrisville, R.I., U.S. **B2** 132
Harrisville, Ut., U.S. **B4** 137
Harrisville, W.V., U.S. **B3** 141
Harrodsburg, Ky., U.S. **C5** 110
Harrow, On., Can. **E2** 89
Harry S. Truman Reservoir, res., Mo., U.S. **C4** 118
Harry Strunk Lake, res., Ne., U.S. **D5** 120
Harsīn, Iran **E12** 44
Harstad, Nor. **B7** 10
Hart, Mi., U.S. **E4** 115
Hart, Tx., U.S. **B1** 136
Hart, co., Ga., U.S. **B4** 103
Hart, co., Ky., U.S. **C4** 110
Hart, Lake, l., Fl., U.S. **D5** 102
Hartford, Al., U.S. **D4** 94
Hartford, Ar., U.S. **B1** 97
Hartford, Ct., U.S. **B5** 100
Hartford, Ia., U.S. **C4** 108
Hartford, Il., U.S. **E3** 106
Hartford, Ky., U.S. **C3** 110
Hartford, Mi., U.S. **F4** 115
Hartford, S.D., U.S. **D9** 134
Hartford, Vt., U.S. **D4** 138
Hartford, Wi., U.S. **E5** 142
Hartford, co., Ct., U.S. **B4** 100
Hartford City, In., U.S. **D7** 107
Hartington, Ne., U.S. **B8** 120
Hart Lake, l., Or., U.S. **E7** 130
Hartland, N.B., Can. **C2** 87
Hartland, Me., U.S. **D3** 112
Hartland, Wi., U.S. **E5** 142
Hartlepool, Eng., U.K. **C6** 12
Hartley, Ia., U.S. **A2** 108
Hartley, co., Tx., U.S. **B1** 136
Hartney, Mb., Can. **E1** 86
Hartselle, Al., U.S. **A3** 94
Hartshorne, Ok., U.S. **C6** 129
Hartsville, S.C., U.S. **C7** 133
Hartsville, Tn., U.S. **A5** 135
Hartville, Oh., U.S. **B4** 128
Hartwell, Ga., U.S. **B4** 103
Hartwell Lake, res., U.S. **B1** 133
Harvard, Il., U.S. **A5** 106
Harvard, Ne., U.S. **D7** 120
Harvard, Mount, mtn., Co., U.S. **C4** 99
Harvey, Il., U.S. **B6** 106
Harvey, La., U.S. **E5** 111
Harvey, Mi., U.S. **B3** 115
Harvey, N.D., U.S. **B6** 127
Harvey, co., Ks., U.S. **D6** 109
Harvey Lake, res., Pa., U.S. **m16** 131
Harveys Creek, stm., Pa., U.S. **n16** 131
Harwich, Eng., U.K. **E7** 12
Harwich Port, Ma., U.S. **C7** 114
Harwinton, Ct., U.S. **B3** 100
Haryāna, prov., India **D3** 40
Hasalbag, China **B3** 40
Hasbrouck Heights, N.J., U.S. **h8** 123
Haskell, Ar., U.S. **C3** 97
Haskell, Ok., U.S. **B6** 129
Haskell, Tx., U.S. **C3** 136
Haskell, co., Ks., U.S. **E3** 109
Haskell, co., Ok., U.S. **B6** 129
Haskell, co., Tx., U.S. **C3** 136
Haskovo, Bul. **D10** 18
Hassan, India **G3** 40
Hassayampa, stm., Az., U.S. **D3** 96
Hasselt, Bel. **E9** 12
Hassi Messaoud, Alg. **D6** 48
Hässleholm, Swe. **H5** 10
Hastings, On., Can. **C7** 89
Hastings, N.Z. **o14** 63c
Hastings, Eng., U.K. **E7** 12
Hastings, Mi., U.S. **F5** 115
Hastings, Mn., U.S. **F6** 116
Hastings, Ne., U.S. **D7** 120
Hastings, Pa., U.S. **E4** 131
Hastings-on-Hudson, N.Y., U.S. **h13** 125
Hašuri, Geor. **B10** 44
Hatanga, Russia **B12** 26
Hatanga, stm., Russia **B12** 26
Hatangskij zaliv, b., Russia **B12** 26
Hatay (Antioch), Tur. **D7** 44
Hatch, N.M., U.S. **E2** 124
Hatchet Lake, N.S., Can. **E6** 87
Hatchie, stm., Tn., U.S. **B2** 135
Hatchineha, Lake, l., Fl., U.S. **D5** 102
Hat Creek, stm., S.D., U.S. **E2** 134
Hatfield, In., U.S. **I3** 107
Hatfield, Pa., U.S. **F11** 131
Hatgal, Mong. **A8** 28
Hāthras, India **D3** 40
Ha Tinh, Viet. **C5** 34
Hat Mountain, mtn., Az., U.S. **E3** 96
Hatteras, N.C., U.S. **B7** 126
Hatteras, Cape, c., N.C., U.S. **B7** 126
Hatteras Inlet, b., N.C., U.S. **B7** 126
Hattiesburg, Ms., U.S. **D4** 117
Hatton, N.D., U.S. **B8** 127
Hat Yai, Thai. **E4** 34
Hatyrka, Russia **C19** 26
Haubstadt, In., U.S. **H2** 107
Haugesund, Nor. **G1** 10
Haughton, La., U.S. **B2** 111
Haukeligrend, Nor. **G2** 10
Haukivesi, l., Fin. **E13** 10
Hauraki Gulf, b., N.Z. **o13** 63c
Hauser, Or., U.S. **D2** 130
Haut, Isle au, i., Me., U.S. **D4** 112
Haut Atlas, mts., Mor. **E2** 14
Hauula, Hi., U.S. **B4** 104
Havana see La Habana, Cuba **A3** 80
Havana, Fl., U.S. **B2** 102
Havana, Il., U.S. **C3** 106
Havasu, Lake, res., U.S. **C1** 96
Havasupai Indian Reservation, Az., U.S. **A3** 96
Havelock, On., Can. **C7** 89
Havelock, N.C., U.S. **C6** 126
Havelock Island, i., India **G6** 40
Haven, Ks., U.S. **E6** 109
Haverford [Township], Pa., U.S. **o20** 131
Haverhill, Ma., U.S. **A5** 114
Haverstraw, N.Y., U.S. **D7** 125
Haviland, Ks., U.S. **E4** 109
Havre see Le Havre, Fr. **C7** 16
Havre, Mt., U.S. **B7** 119
Havre de Grace, Md., U.S. **A5** 113
Havre North, Mt., U.S. **B7** 119
Havza, Tur. **B6** 44
Haw, stm., N.C., U.S. **B3** 126
Hawaii, co., Hi., U.S. **D6** 104
Hawaii, state, U.S. **C5** 104
Hawaii, i., Hi., U.S. **D6** 104
Hawaii, is., Hi., U.S. **i17** 92a
Hawaiian Islands, is., Hi., U.S. **m14** 104
Hawaiian Ridge **F22** 64
Hawaii Volcanoes National Park, Hi., U.S. **D6** 104
Hawarden, Ia., U.S. **A1** 108
Hawera, N.Z. **o13** 63c
Hawesville, Ky., U.S. **C3** 110
Hawi, Hi., U.S. **C6** 104
Hawke Bay, b., N.Z. **o14** 63c
Hawker, Austl. **G2** 62
Hawkes, Mount, mtn., Ant. **E34** 67
Hawkesbury, On., Can. **B10** 89
Hawkesbury Island, i., B.C., Can. **C3** 85
Hawkins, co., Tn., U.S. **C11** 135
Hawkinsville, Ga., U.S. **D3** 103
Hawley, Mn., U.S. **D2** 116
Hawley, Pa., U.S. **D11** 131
Haworth, N.J., U.S. **h9** 123
Haw River, N.C., U.S. **A3** 126
Hawthorne, Ca., U.S. **n12** 98
Hawthorne, Fl., U.S. **C4** 102
Hawthorne, N.J., U.S. **B4** 123
Hawthorne, Nv., U.S. **E3** 121
Hawthorne, N.Y., U.S. **g13** 125
Hawza, W. Sah. **A2** 50
Haxtun, Co., U.S. **A8** 99
Hay, Austl. **G3** 62
Hayden, Az., U.S. **E5** 96
Hayden, Co., U.S. **A3** 99
Hayden Lake, l., Id., U.S. **B2** 105
Hayes, La., U.S. **D3** 111
Hayes, co., Ne., U.S. **D4** 120
Hayes, stm., Mb., Can. **B5** 86
Hayes, Mount, mtn., Ak., U.S. **C10** 95
Hayfield, Mn., U.S. **G6** 116
Hayford Peak, mtn., Nv., U.S. **G6** 121
Haymock Lake, l., Me., U.S. **B3** 112
Haynesville, La., U.S. **B2** 111
Hayneville, Al., U.S. **C3** 94
Hayrabolu, Tur. **B2** 44
Hays, Ks., U.S. **D4** 109
Hays, N.C., U.S. **A1** 126
Hays, co., Tx., U.S. **D3** 136
Hays Canyon Peak, mtn., Nv., U.S. **B2** 121
Hay Springs, Ne., U.S. **B3** 120
Haystack Mountain, mtn., Nv., U.S. **B6** 121
Haysville, Ks., U.S. **g12** 109
Hayti, Mo., U.S. **E8** 118
Hayti Heights, Mo., U.S. **E8** 118
Hayward, Ca., U.S. **h8** 98
Hayward, Wi., U.S. **B2** 142
Haywood, co., N.C., U.S. **f9** 126
Haywood, co., Tn., U.S. **B2** 135
Hazard, Ky., U.S. **C6** 110
Hazardville, Ct., U.S. **B5** 100
Hazārībāg, India **E5** 40
Hazel Crest, Il., U.S. **k9** 106
Hazel Dell, Wa., U.S. **D3** 140
Hazel Green, Al., U.S. **A3** 94
Hazel Green, Wi., U.S. **F3** 142
Hazel Park, Mi., U.S. **p15** 115
Hazelton Pyramid, mtn., Wy., U.S. **B5** 143
Hazelwood, N.C., U.S. **f10** 126
Hazen, Ar., U.S. **C4** 97
Hazen, N.D., U.S. **B4** 127
Hazen Bay, b., Ak., U.S. **C6** 95
Hazlehurst, Ga., U.S. **E4** 103
Hazlehurst, Ms., U.S. **D3** 117
Hazlet, N.J., U.S. **C4** 123
Hazleton, Ia., U.S. **B6** 108
Hazleton, Pa., U.S. **E10** 131
Head Harbor Island, i., Me., U.S. **D5** 112

Name — Map Ref. — Page

Headland, Al., U.S. **D4** 94
Headley, Mount, mtn., Mt., U.S. **C1** 119
Healdsburg, Ca., U.S. **C2** 98
Healdton, Ok., U.S. **C4** 129
Healesville, Austl. **H4** 62
Healy, Ak., U.S. **C10** 95
Heard, co., Ga., U.S. **C1** 103
Hearne, Tx., U.S. **D4** 136
Hearst, On., Can. **o19** 89
Heart, stm., N.D., U.S. **C3** 127
Heart Butte Dam, N.D., U.S. **C4** 127
Heart Lake, l., Wy., U.S. **B2** 143
Heart's Content, Nf., Can. **E5** 88
Heath, Oh., U.S. **B3** 128
Heath Springs, S.C., U.S. **B6** 133
Heavener, Ok., U.S. **C7** 129
Hebbronville, Tx., U.S. **F3** 136
Hebei, state, China **D11** 28
Heber, Az., U.S. **C5** 96
Heber City, Ut., U.S. **C4** 137
Heber Springs, Ar., U.S. **B3** 97
Hébertville, P.Q., Can. **A6** 90
Hebgen Lake, res., Mt., U.S. **F5** 119
Hebi, China **D10** 28
Hebrides, is., Scot., U.K. **D4** 6
Hebrides, Sea of the, Scot., U.K. **B3** 12
Hebron, N.S., Can. **F3** 87
Hebron, Il., U.S. **A5** 106
Hebron, In., U.S. **B3** 107
Hebron, Ky., U.S. **h13** 110
Hebron, Md., U.S. **D6** 113
Hebron, N.D., U.S. **C3** 127
Hebron, Ne., U.S. **D8** 120
Hebron, Oh., U.S. **C3** 128
Hebron see Al-Khalīl, W.B. **G6** 44
Hecate Strait, strt., B.C., Can. **C2** 85
Hecelchakán, Mex. **C6** 78
Heceta Island, i., Ak., U.S. **n23** 95
Hechi, China **G9** 28
Hechuan, China **D2** 30
Hecla Island, i., Mb., Can. **D3** 86
Hector, Mn., U.S. **F4** 116
Hedemora, Swe. **F6** 10
He Devil, mtn., Id., U.S. **D2** 105
Hedrick, Ia., U.S. **C5** 108
Ḥefa (Haifa), Isr. **D2** 42
Hefei, China **E11** 28
Heflin, Al., U.S. **B4** 94
Hefner, Lake, res., Ok., U.S. **B4** 129
Hegang, China **B14** 28
Hegins, Pa., U.S. **E9** 131
Heide, Ger. **C11** 12
Heidelberg, Ger. **F11** 12
Heidelberg, Ms., U.S. **D5** 117
Heidrick, Ky., U.S. **D6** 110
Heilbron, S. Afr. **D4** 56
Heilbronn, Ger. **F11** 12
Heilong (Amur), stm., Asia **D14** 26
Heilongjiang, state, China **B13** 28
Heilongjiang see Heilong, stm., Asia **D16** 26
Heilongjiang see Amur, stm., Asia **D16** 26
Heinävesi, Fin. **E13** 10
Hejaz see Al-Ḥijāz, reg., Sau. Ar. **E3** 38
Hejian, China **B4** 30
Hejiang, China **D2** 30
Hekimhan, Tur. **C7** 44
Hekla, vol., Ice. **l19** 10a
Hekou, China **G8** 28
Helagsfjället, mtn., Swe. **E5** 10
Helena, Al., U.S. **B3** 94
Helena, Ar., U.S. **C5** 97
Helena, Ga., U.S. **D4** 103
Helena, Mt., U.S. **D4** 119
Helena, Ok., U.S. **A3** 129
Helensville, N.Z. **o13** 63c
Helgoländer Bucht, b., Ger. **C11** 12
Heli, China **A2** 31
Hellam, Pa., U.S. **G8** 131
Hellertown, Pa., U.S. **E11** 131
Hellín, Spain **H6** 16
Hells Canyon, val., U.S. **B10** 130
Hells Canyon National Recreation Area, U.S. **B10** 130
Hell-Ville see Andoany, Madag. **A8** 56
Helmand, stm., Asia **D8** 42
Helmeringhausen, Nmb. **D2** 56
Helmstedt, Ger. **D12** 12
Helotes, Tx., U.S. **h7** 136
Helper, Ut., U.S. **D5** 137
Helsingborg, Swe. **H5** 10
Helsingfors see Helsinki, Fin. **F11** 10
Helsingør, Den. **H5** 10
Helsinki (Helsingfors), Fin. **F11** 10
Hematite, Mo., U.S. **C7** 118
Hemet, Ca., U.S. **F5** 98
Hemingford, Ne., U.S. **B2** 120
Hemingway, S.C., U.S. **D9** 133
Hemlock, Mi., U.S. **E6** 115
Hemlock Reservoir, res., Ct., U.S. **E2** 100
Hemmingford, P.Q., Can. **D4** 90
Hemphill, Tx., U.S. **D6** 136
Hemphill, co., Tx., U.S. **B2** 136
Hempstead, N.Y., U.S. **n15** 125
Hempstead, Tx., U.S. **D4** 136
Hempstead, co., Ar., U.S. **D2** 97
Hemsön, i., Swe. **E8** 10
Henagar, Al., U.S. **A4** 94
Henan, state, China **E10** 28
Hendek, Tur. **B4** 44
Henderson, Ky., U.S. **C2** 110
Henderson, La., U.S. **D4** 111
Henderson, Mn., U.S. **F5** 116
Henderson, N.C., U.S. **A4** 126
Henderson, Ne., U.S. **D8** 120
Henderson, Nv., U.S. **G7** 121
Henderson, Tn., U.S. **B3** 135
Henderson, Tx., U.S. **C5** 136
Henderson, co., Il., U.S. **C3** 106
Henderson, co., Ky., U.S. **C2** 110
Henderson, co., N.C., U.S. **f10** 126
Henderson, co., Tn., U.S. **B3** 135
Henderson, co., Tx., U.S. **C5** 136
Henderson Island, i., Pit. **G17** 58
Henderson's Point, Ms., U.S. **g7** 117
Hendersonville, N.C., U.S. **f10** 126
Hendersonville, Tn., U.S. **A5** 135
Hendricks, Mn., U.S. **F2** 116
Hendricks, co., In., U.S. **E4** 107
Hendry, co., Fl., U.S. **F5** 102
Hengshan, China **D9** 28
Hengshan, China **D3** 30
Hengxian, China **E2** 30
Hengyang, China **F10** 28
Heniches'k, Ukr. **F13** 20
Henlawson, W.V., U.S. **n12** 141
Henlopen, Cape, c., De., U.S. **E5** 101
Hennebont, Fr. **D5** 16
Hennepin, co., Mn., U.S. **E5** 116
Hennessey, Ok., U.S. **A4** 129
Henniker, N.H., U.S. **D3** 122
Henning, Mn., U.S. **D3** 116
Henning, Tn., U.S. **B2** 135
Henrico, co., Va., U.S. **C5** 139
Henrietta, N.C., U.S. **B1** 126
Henrietta, Tx., U.S. **C3** 136
Henrietta Maria, Cape, c., On., Can. **n19** 89
Henry, Il., U.S. **B4** 106
Henry, co., Al., U.S. **D4** 94
Henry, co., Ga., U.S. **C2** 103
Henry, co., Ia., U.S. **C6** 108
Henry, co., Il., U.S. **B3** 106
Henry, co., In., U.S. **E7** 107
Henry, co., Ky., U.S. **B4** 110
Henry, co., Mo., U.S. **C4** 118
Henry, co., Oh., U.S. **A1** 128
Henry, co., Tn., U.S. **A3** 135
Henry, co., Va., U.S. **D3** 139
Henry, Mount, mtn., Mt., U.S. **B1** 119
Henryetta, Ok., U.S. **B6** 129
Henrys Fork, stm., U.S. **E2** 143
Henryville, P.Q., Can. **D4** 90
Henryville, In., U.S. **G6** 107
Hensall, On., Can. **D3** 89
Hentiesbaai, Nmb. **C1** 56
Henzada, Myan. **C3** 34
Hephzibah, Ga., U.S. **C4** 103
Heppner, Or., U.S. **B7** 130
Hepu, China **G9** 28
Hequ, China **B3** 30
Herāt, Afg. **D8** 42
Herbert G. West, Lake, res., Wa., U.S. **C7** 140
Herbes, Isle aux, i., Al., U.S. **E1** 94
Herculaneum, Mo., U.S. **C7** 118
Hereford, Eng., U.K. **D5** 12
Hereford, Md., U.S. **A4** 113
Hereford, Tx., U.S. **B1** 136
Hereford Inlet, b., N.J., U.S. **E3** 123
Herford, Ger. **D11** 12
Herington, Ks., U.S. **D7** 109
Herkimer, N.Y., U.S. **B6** 125
Herkimer, co., N.Y., U.S. **B5** 125
Hermann, Mo., U.S. **C6** 118
Hermano Peak, mtn., Co., U.S. **D2** 99
Hermantown, Mn., U.S. **D6** 116
Hermanus, S. Afr. **E2** 56
Herminie, Pa., U.S. **F2** 131
Hermiston, Or., U.S. **B7** 130
Hermitage, Nf., Can. **E4** 88
Hermitage, Ar., U.S. **D3** 97
Hermitage Bay, b., Nf., Can. **E3** 88
Hermit Islands, is., Pap. N. Gui. **G12** 32
Hermon. Mount, mtn., Asia **F6** 44
Hermosillo, Mex. **B2** 78
Hernando, Fl., U.S. **D4** 102
Hernando, Ms., U.S. **A4** 117
Hernando, co., Fl., U.S. **D4** 102
Herndon, Va., U.S. **B5** 139
Herning, Den. **H3** 10
Heron Lake, Mn., U.S. **G3** 116
Herrera, Arg. **D5** 72
Herrin, Il., U.S. **F4** 106
Herring Bay, b., Md., U.S. **C4** 113
Herring Cove, N.S., Can. **E6** 87
Herrington Lake, res., Ky., U.S. **C5** 110
Herscher, Il., U.S. **B5** 106
Hershey, Pa., U.S. **F8** 131
Hertford, N.C., U.S. **A6** 126
Hertford, co., N.C., U.S. **A5** 126
Hervey Bay, b., Austl. **E5** 62
Heshan, China **E2** 30
Heshun, China **B3** 30
Hesperia, Ca., U.S. **E5** 98
Hesperia, Mi., U.S. **E4** 115
Hesperus Mountain, mtn., Co., U.S. **D2** 99
Hesston, Ks., U.S. **D6** 109
Heta, stm., Russia **B11** 26
Hettinger, N.D., U.S. **D3** 127
Hettinger, co., N.D., U.S. **C3** 127
Hexian, China **G10** 28
Heyburn, Id., U.S. **G5** 105
Heyuan, China **E3** 30
Heyworth, Il., U.S. **C5** 106
Heze, China **B4** 30
Hialeah, Fl., U.S. **G6** 102
Hiawatha, Ia., U.S. **B6** 108
Hiawatha, Ks., U.S. **C8** 109
Hibbing, Mn., U.S. **C6** 116
Hickam Air Force Base, mil., Hi., U.S. **g10** 104
Hickman, Ky., U.S. **f8** 110
Hickman, Ne., U.S. **D9** 120
Hickman, co., Ky., U.S. **f8** 110
Hickman, co., Tn., U.S. **B4** 135
Hickory, N.C., U.S. **B1** 126
Hickory, co., Mo., U.S. **D4** 118
Hicksville, N.Y., U.S. **E7** 125
Hicksville, Oh., U.S. **A1** 128
Hico, Tx., U.S. **D3** 136
Hico, W.V., U.S. **C3** 141
Hidalgo, Mex. **C5** 78
Hidalgo, Tx., U.S. **F3** 136
Hidalgo, state, Mex. **C5** 78
Hidalgo, co., N.M., U.S. **F1** 124
Hidalgo, co., Tx., U.S. **F3** 136
Hidalgo del Parral, Mex. **B3** 78
Hiddenite, N.C., U.S. **B1** 126
Hieroglyphic Mountains, mts., Az., U.S. **k8** 96
Higbee, Mo., U.S. **B5** 118
Higganum, Ct., U.S. **D5** 100
Higgins Lake, l., Mi., U.S. **D6** 115
Higgins Millpond, res., Md., U.S. **C6** 113
Higginsville, Mo., U.S. **B4** 118
High Bridge, N.J., U.S. **B3** 123
High Falls Reservoir, res., Wi., U.S. **C5** 142
High Island, i., Mi., U.S. **C5** 115
Highland, Il., U.S. **E4** 106
Highland, In., U.S. **A3** 107
Highland, Ks., U.S. **C8** 109
Highland, Mi., U.S. **o14** 115
Highland, N.Y., U.S. **D7** 125
Highland, Wi., U.S. **E3** 142
Highland, co., Oh., U.S. **C2** 128
Highland, co., Va., U.S. **B3** 139
Highland Lake, l., Me., U.S. **g7** 112
Highland Lakes, N.J., U.S. **A4** 123
Highland Park, Il., U.S. **A6** 106
Highland Park, Mi., U.S. **p15** 115
Highland Park, Tx., U.S. **n10** 136
Highland Peak, mtn., Ca., U.S. **C4** 98
Highland Point, c., Fl., U.S. **G5** 102
Highlands, N.C., U.S. **f9** 126
Highlands, N.J., U.S. **C5** 123
Highlands, Tx., U.S. **r14** 136
Highlands, co., Fl., U.S. **E5** 102
Highland Springs, Va., U.S. **C5** 139
High Level, Ab., Can. **F7** 84
Highmore, S.D., U.S. **C6** 134
High Point, N.C., U.S. **B2** 126
High Prairie, Ab., Can. **B2** 84
High Ridge, Mo., U.S. **g12** 118
High River, Ab., Can. **D4** 84
Highrock Lake, l., Mb., Can. **B1** 86
High Rock Lake, res., N.C., U.S. **B2** 126
High Spire, Pa., U.S. **F8** 131
High Springs, Fl., U.S. **C4** 102
Hightstown, N.J., U.S. **C3** 123
Highwood, Il., U.S. **A6** 106
Highwood Baldy, mtn., Mt., U.S. **C6** 119
Highwood Mountains, mts., Mt., U.S. **C6** 119
Higuera de Abuya, Mex. **C3** 78
Higüey, Dom. Rep. **B6** 80
Hiiumaa, i., Est. **G10** 10
Hiko Range, mts., Nv., U.S. **F6** 121
Hilbert, Wi., U.S. **D5** 142
Hildale, Ut., U.S. **F3** 137
Hilden, N.S., Can. **D6** 87
Hildesheim, Ger. **D11** 12
Hill, co., Mt., U.S. **B6** 119
Hill, co., Tx., U.S. **D4** 136
Hillaby, Mount, mtn., Barb. **C8** 80
Hill City, Ks., U.S. **C4** 109
Hill City, S.D., U.S. **D2** 134
Hillcrest, Il., U.S. **B4** 106
Hillcrest Heights, Md., U.S. **C4** 113
Hillerød, Den. **I5** 10
Hilliard, Fl., U.S. **B5** 102
Hilliard, Oh., U.S. **k10** 128
Hill Lake, l., Ar., U.S. **h10** 97
Hills, Ia., U.S. **C6** 108
Hills, Mn., U.S. **G2** 116
Hillsboro, Il., U.S. **D4** 106
Hillsboro, Ks., U.S. **D6** 109
Hillsboro, Mo., U.S. **C7** 118
Hillsboro, N.D., U.S. **B8** 127
Hillsboro, N.H., U.S. **D3** 122
Hillsboro, Oh., U.S. **C2** 128
Hillsboro, Or., U.S. **B4** 130
Hillsboro, Tx., U.S. **C4** 136
Hillsboro, Wi., U.S. **E3** 142
Hillsboro Canal, Fl., U.S. **F6** 102
Hillsborough, N.B., Can. **D5** 87
Hillsborough, N.C., U.S. **A3** 126
Hillsborough, co., Fl., U.S. **E4** 102
Hillsborough, co., N.H., U.S. **E3** 122
Hillsborough Bay, b., P.E., Can. **C6** 87
Hillsburgh, On., Can. **D4** 89
Hills Creek Lake, res., Or., U.S. **D4** 130
Hillsdale, Mi., U.S. **G6** 115
Hillsdale, N.J., U.S. **g8** 123
Hillsdale, co., Mi., U.S. **G6** 115
Hillside, N.J., U.S. **k8** 123
Hillsville, Pa., U.S. **D1** 131
Hillsville, Va., U.S. **D2** 139
Hilo, Hi., U.S. **D6** 104
Hilo Bay, b., Hi., U.S. **D6** 104
Hilok, Russia **D13** 26
Hilton, N.Y., U.S. **B3** 125
Hilton Head Island, S.C., U.S. **G6** 133
Hilton Head Island, i., S.C., U.S. **G6** 133
Hilvan, Tur. **D8** 44
Himāchal Pradesh, prov., India **C3** 40
Himalayas, mts., Asia **C3** 40
Himatnagar, India **E2** 40
Himeji, Japan **D2** 31
Ḥimṣ, Syria **E7** 44
Hinchinbrook Island, i., Austl. **D4** 62
Hinchinbrook Island, i., Ak., U.S. **g18** 95
Hinckley, Il., U.S. **B5** 106
Hinckley, Mn., U.S. **D6** 116
Hinckley, Ut., U.S. **D3** 137
Hinckley Reservoir, res., N.Y., U.S. **B5** 125
Hindman, Ky., U.S. **C7** 110
Hinds, co., Ms., U.S. **C3** 117
Hindu Kush, mts., Asia **C1** 40
Hindupur, India **G3** 40
Hines, Or., U.S. **D7** 130
Hinesville, Ga., U.S. **E5** 103
Hinganghāt, India **E3** 40
Hingham, Ma., U.S. **B6** 114
Hingham Bay, b., Ma., U.S. **g12** 114
Hingol, stm., Pak. **E9** 42
Hingoli, India **F3** 40
Hınıs, Tur. **C9** 44
Hinnøya, i., Nor. **B6** 10
Hinsdale, Il., U.S. **k9** 106
Hinsdale, N.H., U.S. **E2** 122
Hinsdale, co., Co., U.S. **D3** 99
Hinton, Ab., Can. **C2** 84
Hinton, Ia., U.S. **B1** 108
Hinton, Ok., U.S. **B3** 129
Hinton, W.V., U.S. **D4** 141
Hīrākud Reservoir, res., India **E4** 40
Hiram, Ga., U.S. **C2** 103
Hiram, Oh., U.S. **A4** 128
Hirara, Japan **B9** 34
Hirfanlı Barajı, res., Tur. **C5** 44
Hiriyūr, India **G3** 40
Hirosaki, Japan **C16** 28
Hiroshima, Japan **E14** 28
Hirson, Fr. **C9** 16
Hirtshals, Den. **H3** 10
Hisār, India **D3** 40
Hispaniola, i., N.A. **A5** 80
Hita, Japan **D2** 31
Hitachi, Japan **D16** 28
Hitchcock, Tx., U.S. **r14** 136
Hitchcock, co., Ne., U.S. **D4** 120
Hitchcock Lake, Ct., U.S. **C4** 100
Hitoyoshi, Japan **D2** 31
Hitra, i., Nor. **E3** 10
Hiva, Uzb. **B8** 42
Hiwassee, stm., Tn., U.S. **D9** 135
Hiwassee Lake, res., N.C., U.S. **f8** 126
Hjälmaren, l., Swe. **G6** 10
Hjelmelandsvågen, Nor. **G2** 10
Hjørring, Den. **H3** 10
Hkakabo Razi, mtn., Myan. **A3** 34
Hlukhiv, Ukr. **D12** 20
Hlusk, Bela. **C10** 20
Hlybokae, Bela. **B9** 20
Ho, Ghana **E5** 50
Hoa Binh, Viet. **B5** 34
Hoagland, In., U.S. **C8** 107
Hoback, stm., Wy., U.S. **C2** 143
Hobart, Austl. **I4** 62
Hobart, In., U.S. **A3** 107
Hobart, Ok., U.S. **B2** 129
Hobbs, N.M., U.S. **E6** 124
Hobbs Coast, Ant. **D28** 67
Hobe Sound, Fl., U.S. **E6** 102
Hoboken, N.J., U.S. **k8** 123
Hobyo, Som. **I14** 48
Ho Chi Minh City see Thanh Pho Ho Chi Minh, Viet. **D5** 34
Hockessin, De., U.S. **A3** 101
Hocking, co., Oh., U.S. **C3** 128
Hocking, stm., Oh., U.S. **C3** 128
Hockley, co., Tx., U.S. **C1** 136
Ḥōḍ, reg., Maur. **C3** 50
Hodeida see Al-Ḥudaydah, Yemen **H4** 38
Hodgeman, co., Ks., U.S. **D4** 109
Hodgenville, Ky., U.S. **C4** 110
Hodges Village Reservoir, res., Ma., U.S. **B4** 114
Hódmezővásárhely, Hung. **F6** 20
Hodna, Chott el, l., Alg. **C5** 48
Hodonín, Czech Rep. **E4** 20
Hodžejli, Uzb. **B7** 42
Hoeryŏng-ŭp, N. Kor. **B1** 31
Hof, Ger. **E12** 12
Höfðakaupstaður, Ice. **l18** 10a
Hoffman Estates, Il., U.S. **h8** 106
Hofors, Swe. **F7** 10
Hofsjökull, Ice. **l19** 10a
Hōfu, Japan **D2** 31
Höganäs, Swe. **H5** 10
Hogansville, Ga., U.S. **C2** 103
Hogback Mountain, mtn., Mt., U.S. **F4** 119
Hoggar see Ahaggar, mts., Alg. **F6** 48
Hog Island, i., Fl., U.S. **C3** 102
Hog Island, i., Mi., U.S. **C5** 115
Hog Island, i., N.C., U.S. **B6** 126
Hog Island, i., R.I., U.S. **D5** 132
Hog Island, i., Va., U.S. **C7** 139
Hoh, stm., Wa., U.S. **B1** 140
Hohenwald, Tn., U.S. **B4** 135
Hoh Head, c., Wa., U.S. **B1** 140
Hohhot, China **C10** 28
Hohoe, Ghana **E5** 50
Ho-Ho-Kus, N.J., U.S. **h8** 123
Hoh Xil Shan, mts., China **D5** 28
Hoi An, Viet. **C5** 34
Hoima, Ug. **C6** 54
Hoisington, Ks., U.S. **D5** 109
Hojniki, Bela. **D10** 20
Hokah, Mn., U.S. **G7** 116
Hoke, co., N.C., U.S. **B3** 126
Hokes Bluff, Al., U.S. **B4** 94
Hokitika, N.Z. **p13** 63c
Hokkaidō, i., Japan **C16** 28
Hoktemberjan, Arm. **B11** 44
Hola Prystan', Ukr. **F12** 20
Holbrook, Az., U.S. **C5** 96
Holbrook, Ma., U.S. **B5** 114
Holcomb, Ks., U.S. **E3** 109
Holden, Ma., U.S. **B4** 114
Holden, Mo., U.S. **C4** 118
Holden, W.V., U.S. **D2** 141
Holdenville, Ok., U.S. **B5** 129
Holdrege, Ne., U.S. **D6** 120
Hole in the Mountain Peak, mtn., Nv., U.S. **C6** 121
Holgate, Oh., U.S. **A1** 128
Holguín, Cuba **A4** 80
Holladay, Ut., U.S. **C4** 137
Holland, In., U.S. **H3** 107
Holland, Mi., U.S. **F4** 115
Holland, Oh., U.S. **A2** 128
Holland, Tx., U.S. **D4** 136
Hollandale, Ms., U.S. **B3** 117
Hollandia see Jayapura, Indon. **G11** 32
Holland Island, i., Md., U.S. **D5** 113
Holland Point, c., Md., U.S. **C4** 113
Holland Straits, strt., Md., U.S. **D5** 113
Holley, N.Y., U.S. **B2** 125
Holliday, Tx., U.S. **C3** 136
Hollidaysburg, Pa., U.S. **F5** 131
Hollins, Va., U.S. **C3** 139
Hollis, Ok., U.S. **C2** 129
Hollister, Ca., U.S. **D3** 98
Hollister, Mo., U.S. **E4** 118
Holliston, Ma., U.S. **B5** 114
Holloman Air Force Base, mil., N.M., U.S. **E3** 124
Hollow Rock, Tn., U.S. **A3** 135
Hollowtop Mountain, mtn., Mt., U.S. **E4** 119
Holly, Co., U.S. **C8** 99
Holly, Mi., U.S. **F7** 115
Holly Grove, Ar., U.S. **C4** 97
Holly Hill, Fl., U.S. **C5** 102
Holly Hill, S.C., U.S. **E7** 133
Holly Pond, Al., U.S. **A3** 94
Holly Ridge, N.C., U.S. **C5** 126
Holly Shelter Swamp, sw., N.C., U.S. **C5** 126
Holly Springs, Ga., U.S. **B2** 103
Holly Springs, Ms., U.S. **A4** 117
Holly Springs, N.C., U.S. **B4** 126
Hollywood, Al., U.S. **A4** 94
Hollywood, Fl., U.S. **F6** 102
Hollywood, Md., U.S. **D4** 113
Hollywood, S.C., U.S. **k11** 133
Hollywood Indian Reservation, Fl., U.S. **r3** 102
Holmen, Wi., U.S. **E2** 142
Holmes, co., Fl., U.S. **u16** 102
Holmes, co., Ms., U.S. **B3** 117
Holmes, co., Oh., U.S. **B4** 128
Holmes, Mount, mtn., Wy., U.S. **B2** 143
Holmsk, Russia **E16** 26
Holoby, Ukr. **D8** 20
Holstebro, Den. **H3** 10
Holstein, Ia., U.S. **B2** 108
Holsteinsborg, Grnld. **E29** 82
Holston, stm., Tn., U.S. **C11** 135
Holston, Middle Fork, stm., Va., U.S. **f10** 139
Holston High Knob, mtn., Tn., U.S. **C11** 135
Holt, Al., U.S. **B2** 94

Name — Map Ref. — Page

Holt, Mi., U.S. **F6** 115
Holt, co., Mo., U.S. **A2** 118
Holt, co., Ne., U.S. **B7** 120
Holt Lake, res., Al., U.S. **B2** 94
Holton, Ks., U.S. **C8** 109
Holtville, Ca., U.S. **F6** 98
Holualoa, Hi., U.S. **D6** 104
Holy Cross, Mountain of the, mtn., Co., U.S. **B4** 99
Holyhead, Wales, U.K. **D4** 12
Holyoke, Co., U.S. **A8** 99
Holyoke, Ma., U.S. **B2** 114
Holyoke Range, hills, Ma., U.S. **B2** 114
Homalin, Myan. **B2** 34
Hombori Tondo, mtn., Mali **C4** 50
Hombre Muerto, Salar del, pl., Arg. **D4** 72
Homecroft, In., U.S. **m10** 107
Homedale, Id., U.S. **F2** 105
Home Hill, Austl. **D4** 62
Homel', Bela. **C11** 20
Homeland, Ga., U.S. **F4** 103
Home Place, In., U.S. **E5** 107
Homer, Ak., U.S. **D9** 95
Homer, Ga., U.S. **B3** 103
Homer, Il., U.S. **C6** 106
Homer, La., U.S. **B2** 111
Homer, Mi., U.S. **F6** 115
Homer, N.Y., U.S. **C4** 125
Homer City, Pa., U.S. **E3** 131
Homerville, Ga., U.S. **E4** 103
Homer Youngs Peak, mtn., Mt., U.S. **E3** 119
Homestead, Fl., U.S. **G6** 102
Homestead, Pa., U.S. **k14** 131
Homestead National Monument of America, Ne., U.S. **D9** 120
Homewood, Al., U.S. **g7** 94
Homewood, Il., U.S. **B6** 106
Homewood, Oh., U.S. **C1** 128
Hominy, Ok., U.S. **A5** 129
Hominy Creek, stm., Ok., U.S. **A5** 129
Homme Dam, N.D., U.S. **A8** 127
Homochitto, stm., Ms., U.S. **D2** 117
Homosassa, Fl., U.S. **D4** 102
Homs see Al-Khums, Libya **E6** 14
Homs see Ḥimṣ, Syria **E7** 44
Honaker, Va., U.S. **e10** 139
Honan see Henan, state, China **E10** 28
Honaunau, Hi., U.S. **D6** 104
Honda, Col. **B5** 70
Hondo, Tx., U.S. **E3** 136
Hondo, stm., N.A. **B2** 80
Hondo, Rio, stm., N.M., U.S. **D4** 124
Honduras, ctry., N.A. **C2** 80
Honduras, Gulf of, b., N.A. **B2** 80
Honea Path, S.C., U.S. **C3** 133
Hønefoss, Nor. **F4** 10
Honeoye Falls, N.Y., U.S. **C3** 125
Honesdale, Pa., U.S. **C11** 131
Honey Brook, Pa., U.S. **F10** 131
Honey Grove, Tx., U.S. **C5** 136
Honey Lake, l., Ca., U.S. **B3** 98
Honeypot Glen, Ct., U.S. **C4** 100
Honeyville, Ut., U.S. **B3** 137
Hong, Song see Red, stm., Asia **B4** 34
Hon Gai, Viet. **B5** 34
Honga River, b., Md., U.S. **D5** 113
Hongjiang, China **F9** 28
Hong Kong see Xianggang, China **E3** 30
Hongliuyuan, China **C7** 28
Hongshui, stm., China **G9** 28
Hongtong, China **B3** 30
Hongze, China **C4** 30
Hongze Hu, l., China **E11** 28
Honiara, Sol. Is. **B6** 62
Honjō, Japan **C3** 31
Honokaa, Hi., U.S. **C6** 104
Honolulu, Hi., U.S. **B4** 104
Honolulu, co., Hi., U.S. **B3** 104
Honolulu International Airport, Hi., U.S. **g10** 104
Honomu, Hi., U.S. **D6** 104
Honouliuli, Hi., U.S. **g9** 104
Honshū, i., Japan **D16** 28
Honuapo Bay, b., Hi., U.S. **D6** 104
Honuu, Russia **C16** 26
Hood, co., Tx., U.S. **C4** 136
Hood, Mount, mtn., Or., U.S. **B5** 130
Hood Canal, b., Wa., U.S. **B2** 140
Hoodoo Peak, mtn., Wa., U.S. **A5** 140
Hood Point, c., Austl. **G2** 60
Hood River, Or., U.S. **B5** 130
Hood River, co., Or., U.S. **B5** 130
Hoodsport, Wa., U.S. **B2** 140
Hoogeveen, Neth. **D10** 12
Hooker, Ok., U.S. **e9** 129
Hooker, co., Ne., U.S. **C4** 120
Hooker Creek, Austl. **D5** 60
Hooksett, N.H., U.S. **D4** 122
Hoonah, Ak., U.S. **D12** 95
Hoopa Valley Indian Reservation, Ca., U.S. **B2** 98
Hooper, Ne., U.S. **C9** 120
Hooper Bay, Ak., U.S. **C6** 95
Hooper Islands, is., Md., U.S. **D5** 113
Hooper Strait, strt., Md., U.S. **D5** 113
Hoopes Reservoir, res., De., U.S. **A3** 101
Hoopeston, Il., U.S. **C6** 106
Hoorn, Neth. **D9** 12
Hoosac Range, mts., U.S. **A1** 114
Hoosic, stm., U.S. **C7** 125
Hoosick Falls, N.Y., U.S. **C7** 125
Hoover Dam, U.S. **G7** 121
Hoover Reservoir, res., Oh., U.S. **B3** 128
Hooverson Heights, W.V., U.S. **f8** 141
Hopa, Tur. **B9** 44
Hopatcong, N.J., U.S. **B3** 123
Hopatcong, Lake, l., N.J., U.S. **A3** 123
Hope, B.C., Can. **E7** 85
Hope, Ar., U.S. **D2** 97
Hope, In., U.S. **F6** 107
Hope, R.I., U.S. **D3** 132
Hope, Point, c., Ak., U.S. **B6** 95
Hopedale, Il., U.S. **C4** 106
Hopedale, Ma., U.S. **B4** 114
Hope Island, i., R.I., U.S. **E5** 132
Hopelchén, Mex. **D7** 78
Hope Mills, N.C., U.S. **C4** 126
Hopër, stm., Russia **D7** 22
Hopes Advance, Cap, c., P.Q., Can. **f13** 90
Hopetoun, Austl. **G3** 60
Hopetown, S. Afr. **D3** 56
Hope Valley, R.I., U.S. **E2** 132
Hopewell, Va., U.S. **C5** 139
Hopewell Junction, N.Y., U.S. **D7** 125
Hopi Indian Reservation, Az., U.S. **A5** 96
Hopkins, Mn., U.S. **n12** 116
Hopkins, S.C., U.S. **D6** 133
Hopkins, co., Ky., U.S. **C2** 110
Hopkins, co., Tx., U.S. **C5** 136
Hopkinsville, Ky., U.S. **D2** 110
Hopkinton, Ia., U.S. **B6** 108
Hopkinton, Ma., U.S. **B4** 114
Hopkinton, R.I., U.S. **F1** 132
Hopkinton Lake, res., N.H., U.S. **D3** 122
Hopwood, Pa., U.S. **G2** 131
Hoquiam, Wa., U.S. **C2** 140
Hor, Russia **A2** 31
Horace, N.D., U.S. **C9** 127
Horace Mountain, mtn., Ak., U.S. **B10** 95
Horasan, Tur. **B10** 44
Horatio, Ar., U.S. **D1** 97
Horicon, Wi., U.S. **E5** 142
Horine, Mo., U.S. **C7** 118
Horlick Mountains, mts., Ant. **E29** 67
Horlivka, Ukr. **E15** 20
Hormuz, Strait of, strt., Asia **E7** 42
Horn, c., Ice. **k17** 10a
Horn, Cape see Hornos, Cabo de, c., Chile **I3** 69
Hornavan, l., Swe. **C7** 10
Hornell, N.Y., U.S. **C3** 125
Hornersville, Mo., U.S. **E7** 118
Horn Island, i., Ms., U.S. **E5** 117
Horn Island Pass, strt., Ms., U.S. **g8** 117
Horn Lake, Ms., U.S. **A3** 117
Hornos, Cabo de (Horn, Cape), c., Chile **I3** 69
Horodenka, Ukr. **E8** 20
Horodnia, Ukr. **D11** 20
Horodok, Ukr. **E7** 20
Horqin Youyi Qianqi, China **B12** 28
Horry, co., S.C., U.S. **D10** 133
Horse, stm., Ct., U.S. **C6** 100
Horse Cave, Ky., U.S. **C4** 110
Horse Creek, stm., U.S. **E8** 143
Horse Creek Reservoir, res., Co., U.S. **C7** 99
Horsehead Lake, l., N.D., U.S. **B6** 127
Horseheads, N.Y., U.S. **C4** 125
Horse Heaven Hills, hills, Wa., U.S. **C6** 140
Horsens, Den. **I3** 10
Horse Peak, mtn., N.M., U.S. **D1** 124
Horseshoe Bend, Id., U.S. **F2** 105
Horseshoe Bend National Military Park, Al., U.S. **C4** 94
Horseshoe Cove, b., Fl., U.S. **C3** 102
Horseshoe Point, c., Fl., U.S. **C3** 102
Horseshoe Reservoir, res., Az., U.S. **C4** 96
Horsham, Austl. **H3** 62
Horten, Nor. **G4** 10
Horton, Ks., U.S. **C8** 109
Horton, stm., N.T., Can. **E15** 82
Hortonia, Lake, l., Vt., U.S. **D2** 138
Hortonville, Wi., U.S. **D5** 142
Horyn', stm., Eur. **D9** 20
Hosa'ina, Eth. **B7** 54
Hoschton, Ga., U.S. **B3** 103
Hosedahard, Russia **A10** 22
Hoshāb, Pak. **E8** 42
Hoshangābād, India **E3** 40
Hoshiārpur, India **C3** 40
Hospers, Ia., U.S. **A2** 108
Hospet, India **F3** 40
Hosta Butte, mtn., N.M., U.S. **B1** 124
Hotan, China **D3** 28
Hotan, stm., China **A4** 40
Hotazel, S. Afr. **D3** 56
Hotchkiss, Co., U.S. **C3** 99
Hot Creek Range, mts., Nv., U.S. **E5** 121
Hot Creek Valley, val., Nv., U.S. **E5** 121
Hot Spring, co., Ar., U.S. **C2** 97
Hot Springs, S.D., U.S. **D2** 134
Hot Springs, co., Wy., U.S. **C4** 143
Hot Springs National Park, Ar., U.S. **C2** 97
Hot Springs National Park, Ar., U.S. **C2** 97
Hot Springs Peak, mtn., Ca., U.S. **B3** 98
Hot Springs Peak, mtn., Nv., U.S. **B4** 121
Houaïlou, N. Cal. **I9** 62a
Houghton, Mi., U.S. **A2** 115
Houghton, N.Y., U.S. **C2** 125
Houghton, co., Mi., U.S. **B2** 115
Houghton Lake, Mi., U.S. **D6** 115
Houghton Lake, l., Mi., U.S. **D6** 115
Houghton Lake Heights, Mi., U.S. **D6** 115
Houlton, Me., U.S. **B5** 112
Houma, China **D10** 28
Houma, La., U.S. **E5** 111
Housatonic, stm., U.S. **D3** 100
House Springs, Mo., U.S. **g12** 118
Houston, De., U.S. **E3** 101
Houston, Mn., U.S. **G7** 116
Houston, Mo., U.S. **D6** 118
Houston, Ms., U.S. **B4** 117
Houston, Pa., U.S. **F1** 131
Houston, Tx., U.S. **E5** 136
Houston, co., Al., U.S. **D4** 94
Houston, co., Ga., U.S. **D3** 103
Houston, co., Mn., U.S. **G7** 116
Houston, co., Tn., U.S. **A4** 135
Houston, co., Tx., U.S. **D5** 136
Houston, stm., La., U.S. **D2** 111
Houston, Lake, res., Tx., U.S. **r14** 136
Houston Intercontinental Airport, Tx., U.S. **r14** 136
Houtman Abrolhos, is., Austl. **F1** 60
Houtzdale, Pa., U.S. **E5** 131
Hovd, Mong. **B6** 28
Hovd, stm., Mong. **B6** 28
Hovenweep National Monument, Ut., U.S. **F6** 137
Hoverla, hora, mtn., Ukr. **E8** 20
Hovmantorp, Swe. **H6** 10
Hövsgöl nuur, l., Mong. **A8** 28
Howard, Ks., U.S. **E7** 109
Howard, S.D., U.S. **C8** 134
Howard, Wi., U.S. **D5** 142
Howard, co., Ar., U.S. **C2** 97
Howard, co., Ia., U.S. **A5** 108
Howard, co., In., U.S. **C5** 107
Howard, co., Md., U.S. **B4** 113
Howard, co., Mo., U.S. **B5** 118
Howard, co., Ne., U.S. **C7** 120
Howard, co., Tx., U.S. **C2** 136
Howard City, Mi., U.S. **E5** 115
Howard Hanson Reservoir, res., Wa., U.S. **B4** 140
Howard Lake, Mn., U.S. **E4** 116
Howard Prairie Lake, res., Or., U.S. **E4** 130
Howards Grove-Millersville, Wi., U.S. **E6** 142
Howe, Cape, c., Austl. **H5** 62
Howell, Mi., U.S. **F7** 115
Howell, co., Mo., U.S. **E6** 118
Howells, Ne., U.S. **C8** 120
Howe Sound, strt., B.C., Can. **E6** 85
Howick, P.Q., Can. **D4** 90
Howland, Me., U.S. **C4** 112
Howland Island, i., Oc. **H21** 64
Hoxie, Ar., U.S. **A5** 97
Hoxie, Ks., U.S. **C3** 109
Hoyerswerda, Ger. **E14** 12
Hoyt Lakes, Mn., U.S. **C6** 116
Hradec Králové, Czech Rep. **D3** 20
Hrodna, Bela. **C7** 20
Hron, stm., Slvk. **E5** 20
Hsilo, Tai. **E5** 30
Hsinchu, Tai. **E5** 30
Hsipaw, Myan. **B3** 34
Huacho, Peru **F4** 70
Huachuca City, Az., U.S. **F5** 96
Hua Hin, Thai. **D3** 34
Huai'an, China **E11** 28
Huai'an, China **A3** 30
Huaibin, China **C4** 30
Huaiji, China **E3** 30
Huailai, China **A4** 30
Huainan, China **E11** 28
Huairou, China **A4** 30
Huaiyang, China **E11** 28
Huajuapan de León, Mex. **D5** 78
Hualalai, vol., Hi., U.S. **D6** 104
Hualapai Indian Reservation, Az., U.S. **B2** 96
Hualapai Mountains, mts., Az., U.S. **C2** 96
Hualapai Peak, mtn., Az., U.S. **B2** 96
Hualien, Tai. **E5** 30
Huallaga, stm., Peru **E4** 70
Huambo, Ang. **F3** 54
Huanan, China **A2** 31
Huancavelica, Peru **F4** 70
Huancayo, Peru **F4** 70
Huang (Yellow), stm., China **D11** 28
Huangchuan, China **E11** 28
Huangho see Huang, stm., China **D11** 28
Huanghua, China **B4** 30
Huanglong, China **B2** 30
Huangshi, China **E11** 28
Huangxian, China **B5** 30
Huangyan, China **D5** 30
Huangyuan, China **D8** 28
Huanta, Peru **A3** 72
Huánuco, Peru **E4** 70
Huanxian, China **B2** 30
Huaral, Peru **F4** 70
Huarocondo, Peru **A3** 72
Huascarán, Nevado, mtn., Peru **E4** 70
Huasco, Chile **C2** 69
Huatabampo, Mex. **B3** 78
Huauchinango, Mex. **C5** 78
Huaxian, China **E3** 30
Huaxian, China **B3** 30
Huazhou, China **E3** 30
Hubbard, Ia., U.S. **B4** 108
Hubbard, Oh., U.S. **A5** 128
Hubbard, Or., U.S. **B4** 130
Hubbard, Tx., U.S. **D4** 136
Hubbard, co., Mn., U.S. **C4** 116
Hubbard Creek Lake, res., Tx., U.S. **C3** 136
Hubbard Lake, l., Mi., U.S. **D7** 115
Hubbardton, stm., Vt., U.S. **D2** 138
Hubbell, Mi., U.S. **A2** 115
Hubei, state, China **E10** 28
Hubli-Dhārwār, India **F3** 40
Huckleberry Mountain, mtn., Or., U.S. **D4** 130
Huddersfield, Eng., U.K. **D6** 12
Hudiksvall, Swe. **F7** 10
Hudson, P.Q., Can. **D3** 90
Hudson, Co., U.S. **A6** 99
Hudson, Fl., U.S. **D4** 102
Hudson, Ia., U.S. **B5** 108
Hudson, Il., U.S. **C5** 106
Hudson, Ma., U.S. **B4** 114
Hudson, Mi., U.S. **G6** 115
Hudson, N.C., U.S. **B1** 126
Hudson, N.H., U.S. **E4** 122
Hudson, N.Y., U.S. **C7** 125
Hudson, Oh., U.S. **A4** 128
Hudson, Wi., U.S. **D1** 142
Hudson, Wy., U.S. **D4** 143
Hudson, co., N.J., U.S. **B4** 123
Hudson, stm., U.S. **E7** 125
Hudson, Lake, res., Ok., U.S. **A6** 129
Hudson Bay, b., Can. **G24** 82
Hudson Falls, N.Y., U.S. **B7** 125
Hudson Hope, B.C., Can. **A6** 85
Hudson Lake, In., U.S. **A4** 107
Hudson Strait, strt., Can. **F25** 82
Hudsonville, Mi., U.S. **F5** 115
Hudspeth, co., Tx., U.S. **o12** 136
Hudžand, Taj. **E8** 26
Hue, Viet. **C5** 34
Huehuetenango, Guat. **B1** 80
Huelva, Spain **I3** 16
Huércal-Overa, Spain **I6** 16
Huerfano, co., Co., U.S. **D5** 99
Huerfano, stm., Co., U.S. **D6** 99
Huerfano Mountain, mtn., N.M., U.S. **A2** 124
Huesca, Spain **F6** 16
Huéscar, Spain **I5** 16
Huetamo de Núñez, Mex. **D4** 78
Hueytown, Al., U.S. **g6** 94
Huffakers, Nv., U.S. **D2** 121
Ḥufrat an-Naḥās, Sudan **B4** 54
Hugh Butler Lake, res., Ne., U.S. **D5** 120
Hughenden, Austl. **E3** 62
Hughes, Ar., U.S. **C5** 97
Hughes, co., Ok., U.S. **B5** 129
Hughes, co., S.D., U.S. **C5** 134
Hughes, North Fork, stm., W.V., U.S. **B3** 141
Hughes, South Fork, stm., W.V., U.S. **B3** 141
Hughesville, Md., U.S. **C4** 113
Hughesville, Pa., U.S. **D8** 131
Hugli, stm., India **E5** 40
Hugo, Co., U.S. **B7** 99
Hugo, Mn., U.S. **m13** 116
Hugo, Ok., U.S. **C6** 129
Hugo Lake, res., Ok., U.S. **C6** 129
Hugoton, Ks., U.S. **E2** 109
Hŭich'ŏn, N. Kor. **C13** 28
Huilai, China **E4** 30
Huili, China **F8** 28
Huimin, China **B4** 30
Huinca Renancó, Arg. **E5** 72
Huishui, China **D2** 30
Huitong, China **D2** 30
Huixian, China **C2** 30
Huixtla, Mex. **D6** 78
Huize, China **F8** 28
Huizhou, China **E3** 30
Hujirt, Mong. **B8** 28
Hulah Lake, res., Ok., U.S. **A5** 129
Hulett, Wy., U.S. **B8** 143
Hulin, China **B14** 28
Hull, P.Q., Can. **D2** 90
Hull, Ia., U.S. **A1** 108
Hull, Ma., U.S. **B6** 114
Huma, China **A13** 28
Humaitá, Braz. **E7** 70
Humaitá, Para. **D6** 72
Humansdorp, S. Afr. **E3** 56
Humansville, Mo., U.S. **D4** 118
Humbe, Ang. **B1** 56
Humble, Tx., U.S. **E5** 136
Humboldt, Az., U.S. **C3** 96
Humboldt, Ia., U.S. **B3** 108
Humboldt, Ks., U.S. **E8** 109
Humboldt, Ne., U.S. **D10** 120
Humboldt, Tn., U.S. **B3** 135
Humboldt, co., Ca., U.S. **B2** 98
Humboldt, co., Ia., U.S. **B3** 108
Humboldt, co., Nv., U.S. **B3** 121
Humboldt, stm., Nv., U.S. **C3** 121
Humboldt Range, mts., Nv., U.S. **C3** 121
Humenné, Slvk. **E6** 20
Hummels Wharf, Pa., U.S. **E8** 131
Humphrey, Ar., U.S. **C4** 97
Humphrey, Ne., U.S. **C8** 120
Humphreys, co., Ms., U.S. **B3** 117
Humphreys, co., Tn., U.S. **A4** 135
Humphreys, Mount, mtn., Ca., U.S. **D4** 98
Humphreys Peak, mtn., Az., U.S. **B4** 96
Humpty Doo, Austl. **C5** 60
Hūn, Libya **F7** 14
Hun, stm., China **A5** 30
Húnaflói, b., Ice. **k18** 10a
Hunan, state, China **F10** 28
Hunchun, China **B2** 31
Hundred Acre Pond, l., R.I., U.S. **E3** 132
Hunedoara, Rom. **G7** 20
Hungary, ctry., Eur. **F5** 20
Hŭngdŏki-dong, N. Kor. **D13** 28
Hungry Horse, Mt., U.S. **B2** 119
Hungry Horse Reservoir, res., Mt., U.S. **B3** 119
Hunjiang, China **C13** 28
Hunsberge, mts., Nmb. **D2** 56
Hunt, co., Tx., U.S. **C4** 136
Hunt, stm., R.I., U.S. **D4** 132
Hunterdon, co., N.J., U.S. **B3** 123
Hunter Island, i., Austl. **I3** 62
Hunter Island, i., B.C., Can. **D3** 85
Huntertown, In., U.S. **B7** 107
Huntingburg, In., U.S. **H4** 107
Huntingdon, P.Q., Can. **D3** 90
Huntingdon, Pa., U.S. **F6** 131
Huntingdon, Tn., U.S. **A3** 135
Huntingdon, co., Pa., U.S. **F5** 131
Hunting Island, i., S.C., U.S. **G7** 133
Huntington, Ar., U.S. **B1** 97
Huntington, In., U.S. **C7** 107
Huntington, N.Y., U.S. **E7** 125
Huntington, Tx., U.S. **D5** 136
Huntington, Ut., U.S. **D5** 137
Huntington, W.V., U.S. **C2** 141
Huntington, co., In., U.S. **C6** 107
Huntington Beach, Ca., U.S. **F4** 98
Huntington Lake, res., In., U.S. **C7** 107
Huntington Woods, Mi., U.S. **p15** 115
Huntingtown, Md., U.S. **C4** 113
Huntland, Tn., U.S. **B5** 135
Huntley, Il., U.S. **A5** 106
Hunt Mountain, mtn., Wy., U.S. **B5** 143
Huntsville, On., Can. **B5** 89
Huntsville, Al., U.S. **A3** 94
Huntsville, Ar., U.S. **A2** 97
Huntsville, Mo., U.S. **B5** 118
Huntsville, Tn., U.S. **C9** 135
Huntsville, Tx., U.S. **D5** 136
Hunucmá, Mex. **C7** 78
Hunyuan, China **D10** 28
Huon Gulf, b., Pap. N. Gui. **H12** 32
Huoxian, China **B3** 30
Hurd, Cape, c., On., Can. **B3** 89
Hurghada, Egypt **E11** 48
Hurley, Ms., U.S. **E5** 117
Hurley, N.M., U.S. **E1** 124
Hurley, N.Y., U.S. **D6** 125
Hurley, Wi., U.S. **B3** 142
Hurlock, Md., U.S. **C6** 113
Huron, Oh., U.S. **A3** 128
Huron, S.D., U.S. **C7** 134
Huron, co., Mi., U.S. **E7** 115
Huron, co., Oh., U.S. **A3** 128
Huron, stm., Mi., U.S. **p14** 115
Huron, Lake, l., N.A. **C11** 92
Huron Mountains, hills, Mi., U.S. **B3** 115
Hurricane, Ut., U.S. **F2** 137
Hurricane, W.V., U.S. **C2** 141
Hurst, Il., U.S. **F4** 106
Hurt, Va., U.S. **C3** 139
Hurtsboro, Al., U.S. **C4** 94
Húsavík, Ice. **k20** 10a

Name	Map Ref.	Page
Huşi, Rom.	F10	20
Hustisford, Wi., U.S.	E5	142
Husum, Ger.	C11	12
Hutag, Mong.	B8	28
Hutchins, Tx., U.S.	n10	136
Hutchinson, Ks., U.S.	D6	109
Hutchinson, Mn., U.S.	F4	116
Hutchinson, co., S.D., U.S.	D8	134
Hutchinson, co., Tx., U.S.	B2	136
Hutchinson Island, i., Fl., U.S.	E6	102
Hutchinson Island, i., S.C., U.S.	k11	133
Hutch Mountain, mtn., Az., U.S.	C4	96
Huttig, Ar., U.S.	D3	97
Huwei, Tai.	E5	30
Huxian, China	C2	30
Huxley, Ia., U.S.	C4	108
Hūzgān, Iran	G13	44
Huzhou, China	E12	28
Hužir, Russia	A9	28
Hvannadalshnúkur, mtn., Ice.	m20	10a
Hwange, Zimb.	B4	56
Hwang Ho see Huang, stm., China	D11	28
Hyannis, Ma., U.S.	C7	114
Hyannis Port, Ma., U.S.	C7	114
Hyargas nuur, l., Mong.	B6	28
Hyattsville, Md., U.S.	C4	113
Hybla Valley, Va., U.S.	g12	139
Hyco, stm., Va., U.S.	D3	139
Hyco Lake, res., N.C., U.S.	A3	126
Hydaburg, Ak., U.S.	D13	95
Hyde, Pa., U.S.	D5	131
Hyde, co., N.C., U.S.	B6	126
Hyde, co., S.D., U.S.	C6	134
Hyden, Austl.	G2	60
Hyde Park, N.Y., U.S.	D7	125
Hyde Park, Ut., U.S.	B4	137
Hyder, Ak., U.S.	D13	95
Hyderābād, India	F3	40
Hyderābād, Pak.	E9	42
Hydeville, Vt., U.S.	D2	138
Hydra see Ídhra, i., Grc.	F9	18
Hydro, Ok., U.S.	B3	129
Hyères, Fr.	F10	16
Hyesan, N. Kor.	C13	28
Hymera, In., U.S.	F3	107
Hyndman, Pa., U.S.	G4	131
Hyndman Peak, mtn., Id., U.S.	F4	105
Hyrum, Ut., U.S.	B4	137
Hythe, Ab., Can.	B1	84
Hyvinkää, Fin.	F11	10

I

Name	Map Ref.	Page
Iaçu, Braz.	D3	74
Ialomiţa, stm., Rom.	G9	20
Iamonia, Lake, l., Fl., U.S.	B2	102
Iaşi, Rom.	F9	20
Iatt, Lake, res., La., U.S.	C3	111
Iba, Phil.	C7	34
Ibadan, Nig.	E5	50
Ibagué, Col.	C4	70
Ibaiti, Braz.	F1	74
Ibapah Peak, mtn., Ut., U.S.	D2	137
Ibarra, Ec.	C4	70
Ibembo, D.R.C.	C4	54
Iberia, Mo., U.S.	C5	118
Iberia, co., La., U.S.	E4	111
Iberian Mountains see Ibérico, Sistema, mts., Spain	G5	16
Ibérico, Sistema, mts., Spain	G5	16
Iberville, P.Q., Can.	D4	90
Iberville, co., La., U.S.	D4	111
Iberville, Mont d' (Caubvick, Mount), mtn., Can.	g14	90
Ibiá, Braz.	E2	74
Ibicaraí, Braz.	D4	74
Ibiza see Eivissa, i., Spain	H7	16
Ibonma, Indon.	D8	36
Ibotirama, Braz.	D3	74
'Ibrī, Oman	F7	42
Ica, Peru	F4	70
Içá (Putumayo), stm., S.A.	D6	70
Içana, Braz.	C6	70
Içana (Isana), stm., S.A.	C6	70
Ice Harbor Dam, Wa., U.S.	C7	140
İçel, Tur.	D6	44
Iceland, ctry., Eur.	l18	10a
Iceland Basin	B25	144
Ichaikaronji, India	F2	40
Ichchāpuram, India	F4	40
Ichnia, Ukr.	D12	20
Icicle Creek, stm., Wa., U.S.	B5	140
Ičinskaja Sopka, vulkan, vol., Russia	D17	26
Icó, Braz.	C4	74
Icy Cape, c., Ak., U.S.	A7	95
Icy Strait, strt., Ak., U.S.	k22	95
Ida, Mi., U.S.	G7	115
Ida, co., Ia., U.S.	B2	108
Ida, Lake, l., Mn., U.S.	D3	116
Idabel, Ok., U.S.	D7	129
Ida Grove, Ia., U.S.	B2	108
Idah, Nig.	E6	50
Idaho, co., Id., U.S.	D3	105
Idaho, state, U.S.	E3	105
Idaho Falls, Id., U.S.	F6	105
Idaho Springs, Co., U.S.	B5	99
Idalou, Tx., U.S.	C2	136
Idamay, W.V., U.S.	k10	141
Idaville, In., U.S.	C4	107
Ider, Al., U.S.	A4	94
Ídhi Óros, mtn., Grc.	G10	18
Ídhra, i., Grc.	F9	18
İdil, Tur.	D9	44
Idiofa, D.R.C.	D3	54
Idlib, state, Syria	E7	44
Idoûkâl-en-Taghès, mtn., Niger	C6	50
Idutywa, S. Afr.	E4	56
Ifakara, Tan.	E7	54
Ife, Nig.	E5	50
Iferouâne, Niger	C6	50
Ifôghas, Adrar des, mts., Afr.	C5	50
Iganga, Ug.	C6	54
Igarapé-Açu, Braz.	B2	74
Igarka, Russia	C10	26
Igboho, Nig.	E5	50
Iğdır, Tur.	C11	44
Iglesias, Italy	E2	18
Ignacio, Co., U.S.	D3	99
Iguaçu, stm., S.A.	D7	72
Iguala, Mex.	D5	78
Igualada, Spain	G7	16
Iguassu Falls see Iguaçu, Cataratas do, wtfl, Braz.	D7	72
Iguatu, Braz.	C4	74
Iguazú see Iguaçu, stm., S.A.	D7	72
Iguéla, Gabon	D1	54
Iguîdi, 'Erg, dunes, Afr.	A3	50
Iharaña, Madag.	A8	56
Iheya-shima, i., Japan	g6	31a
Ihosy, Madag.	C8	56
Iisalmi, Fin.	E12	10
Iizuka, Japan	D2	31
Ijâfene, des., Maur.	B3	50
Ijebu-Ode, Nig.	E5	50
IJsselmeer, l., Neth.	D9	12
Ijuí, Braz.	D7	72
Ika, Russia	D12	26
Ikaría, i., Grc.	F11	18
Ikeja, Nig.	E5	50
Ikela, D.R.C.	D4	54
Ikerre, Nig.	E6	50
Ikom, Nig.	E6	50
Ikot-Ekpene, Nig.	E6	50
Ila, Nig.	E5	50
Ilagan, Phil.	C8	34
Īlām, Iran	D5	42
Ilan, Tai.	E5	30
Ilaro, Nig.	E5	50
Iława, Pol.	C5	20
Ilbenge, Russia	C14	26
Île-à-la-Crosse, Lac, l., Sk., Can.	B2	91
Ilebo, D.R.C.	D4	54
Île-de-France, hist. reg., Fr.	C8	16
Île-Perrot, P.Q., Can.	q19	90
Ilesha, Nig.	E5	50
Ilha de Moçambique, Moz.	B7	56
Ilhéus, Braz.	D4	74
Iliamna Lake, l., Ak., U.S.	D8	95
Iliamna Volcano, vol., Ak., U.S.	C9	95
Iligan, Phil.	E8	34
Iligan Bay, b., Phil.	E8	34
Ilion, N.Y., U.S.	B5	125
Ilio Point, c., Hi., U.S.	B4	104
Ilizi, Alg.	E6	48
Iljinskij, Russia	E16	26
Illampu, Nevado, mtn., Bol.	G6	70
Illana Bay, b., Phil.	E8	34
Illapel, Chile	D2	69
Illéla, Niger	D6	50
Illichivs'k, Ukr.	F11	20
Illimani, Nevado, mtn., Bol.	B4	72
Illinois, state, U.S.	C4	106
Illinois, stm., Il., U.S.	B5	106
Illinois, stm., Or., U.S.	E3	130
Illinois, stm., U.S.	A7	129
Illinois Peak, mtn., Id., U.S.	B3	105
Illiopolis, Il., U.S.	D4	106
Illmo, Mo., U.S.	D8	118
Il'men', ozero, l., Russia	C5	22
Ilo, Peru	G5	70
Iloilo, Phil.	D8	34
Ilorin, Nig.	E5	50
Ilovlja, Russia	F15	8
Ilwaco, Wa., U.S.	C1	140
Ilwaki, Indon.	E7	36
Imabari, Japan	D2	31
Imandra, ozero, l., Russia	C15	10
Imatra, Fin.	F13	10
Imboden, Ar., U.S.	A4	97
Īmī, Eth.	B8	54
İmişli, Azer.	C13	44
Imlay, Nv., U.S.	C3	121
Imlay City, Mi., U.S.	E7	115
Immokalee, Fl., U.S.	F5	102
Imnaha, stm., Or., U.S.	B10	130
Imola, Italy	B3	18
Imperatriz, Braz.	C2	74
Imperia, Italy	C2	18
Imperial, Ca., U.S.	F6	98
Imperial, Mo., U.S.	C7	118
Imperial, Ne., U.S.	D4	120
Imperial, Pa., U.S.	k13	131
Imperial, co., Ca., U.S.	F6	98
Imperial Beach, Ca., U.S.	o15	98
Imperial Dam, U.S.	E1	96
Imperial Reservoir, res., U.S.	E1	96
Imperial Valley, val., Ca., U.S.	F6	98
Impfondo, Congo	C3	54
Imphāl, India	E6	40
I-n-Amenas, Alg.	E6	48
Inanwatan, Indon.	D8	36
Inari, Fin.	B12	10
Inarijärvi, l., Fin.	B12	10
In Belbel, Alg.	F4	14
Inca, Spain	H8	16
Inca de Oro, Chile	C3	69
İnce Burun, c., Tur.	A6	44
Inch'ŏn, S. Kor.	D13	28
Incline Village, Nv., U.S.	D2	121
Indé, Mex.	B3	78
Independence, Ia., U.S.	B6	108
Independence, Ks., U.S.	E8	109
Independence, Ky., U.S.	B5	110
Independence, La., U.S.	D5	111
Independence, Mo., U.S.	B3	118
Independence, Or., U.S.	C3	130
Independence, Va., U.S.	D1	139
Independence, Wi., U.S.	D2	142
Independence, co., Ar., U.S.	B4	97
Independence, stm., N.Y., U.S.	B5	125
Independence Mountains, mts., Nv., U.S.	C5	121
Independence National Historical Park, Pa., U.S.	p21	131
Independence Rock, mtn., Wy., U.S.	D5	143
Inderborskij, Kaz.	E7	26
India, ctry., Asia	E3	40
Indian, stm., On., Can.	B7	89
Indian, stm., De., U.S.	F4	101
Indian, stm., Mi., U.S.	B4	115
Indian, stm., N.Y., U.S.	A5	125
Indiana, Pa., U.S.	E3	131
Indiana, co., Pa., U.S.	E3	131
Indiana, state, U.S.	E5	107
Indiana Dunes National Lakeshore, In., U.S.	A3	107
Indianapolis, In., U.S.	E5	107
Indian Bay, b., Fl., U.S.	D4	102
Indian Cedar Swamp, sw., R.I., U.S.	F2	132
Indian Creek, stm., Oh., U.S.	C1	128
Indian Creek, stm., S.D., U.S.	B2	134
Indian Creek, stm., Tn., U.S.	B3	135
Indian Creek, stm., W.V., U.S.	D4	141
Indian Creek, stm., W.V., U.S.	k9	141
Indian Head, Md., U.S.	C3	113
Indian Island, i., N.C., U.S.	B6	126
Indian Lake, l., Mi., U.S.	C4	115
Indian Lake, l., N.Y., U.S.	B6	125
Indian Lake, l., Oh., U.S.	B2	128
Indian Lake, l., R.I., U.S.	F4	132
Indian Neck, Ct., U.S.	D4	100
Indian Ocean	J11	64
Indianola, Ia., U.S.	C4	108
Indianola, Ms., U.S.	B3	117
Indianola, Ne., U.S.	D5	120
Indian Peak, mtn., Ut., U.S.	E2	137
Indian Peak, mtn., Wy., U.S.	B3	143
Indian Prairie Canal, Fl., U.S.	E5	102
Indian River, co., Fl., U.S.	E6	102
Indian River, b., Fl., U.S.	D6	102
Indian River Bay, b., De., U.S.	F5	101
Indian Rock, mtn., Wa., U.S.	D5	140
Indian Rocks Beach, Fl., U.S.	p10	102
Indian Springs, Nv., U.S.	G6	121
Indian Stream, stm., N.H., U.S.	f7	122
Indiantown, Fl., U.S.	E6	102
Indian Trail, N.C., U.S.	B2	126
Indiga, Russia	A8	22
Indigirka, stm., Russia	C16	26
Indio, Ca., U.S.	F5	98
Indochina, reg., Asia	C4	34
Indonesia, ctry., Asia	D4	36
Indore, India	E3	40
Indramayu, Indon.	E3	36
Indrāvati, stm., India	F4	40
Indus, stm., Asia	D1	40
İnegöl, Tur.	B3	44
Infiernillo, Presa del, res., Mex.	D4	78
Ingal, Niger	C6	50
Ingalls, In., U.S.	E6	107
Ingalls Park, Il., U.S.	B5	106
Ingende, D.R.C.	D3	54
Ingersoll, On., Can.	D4	89
Ingham, Austl.	D4	62
Ingham, co., Mi., U.S.	F6	115
Ingleside, Tx., U.S.	F4	136
Inglewood, Ca., U.S.	n12	98
Ingolstadt, Ger.	F12	12
Ingraham, Lake, l., Fl., U.S.	G5	102
Ingrāj Bāzār, India	E5	40
Ingram, Pa., U.S.	k13	131
Ingrid Christensen Coast, Ant.	D12	67
In Guezzam, Alg.	G6	48
Ingušetija, state, Russia	E6	26
Ingushetia see Ingušetija, state, Russia	E6	26
Inhaca, Ilha da, i., Moz.	D5	56
Inhambane, Moz.	C6	56
Inhambupe, Braz.	F12	70
Inhaminga, Moz.	B6	56
Inharrime, Moz.	C6	56
Inhassoro, Moz.	C6	56
Inhulets', Ukr.	F12	20
Inhumas, Braz.	E2	74
Inírida, stm., Col.	C6	70
Inkerman, N.B., Can.	B5	87
Inkom, Id., U.S.	G6	105
Inkster, Mi., U.S.	p15	115
Inland Sea see Seto-naikai, Japan	E14	28
Inman, Ks., U.S.	D6	109
Inman, S.C., U.S.	A3	133
Inn, stm., Eur.	G12	12
Inner Channel, strt., Belize	B2	80
Inner Hebrides, is., Scot., U.K.	B3	12
Inner Mongolia see Nei Monggol Zizhiqu, prov., China	C10	28
Innisfail, Austl.	D4	62
Innisfail, Ab., Can.	C4	84
Innsbruck, Aus.	G12	12
Inola, Ok., U.S.	A6	129
Inongo, D.R.C.	D3	54
Inowrocław, Pol.	C5	20
In Salah, Alg.	E5	48
Inscription House Ruin, hist., Az., U.S.	A5	96
Institute, W.V., U.S.	m12	141
Inta, Russia	C8	26
Interlachen, Fl., U.S.	C5	102
International Falls, Mn., U.S.	B5	116
Inthanon, Doi, mtn., Thai.	C3	34
Intracoastal Waterway, U.S.	E4	111
Inukjuak, P.Q., Can.	g11	90
Invercargill, N.Z.	q12	63c
Inverell, Austl.	F5	62
Inver Grove Heights, Mn., U.S.	n12	116
Invermere, B.C., Can.	D9	85
Inverness, Scot., U.K.	B4	12
Inverness, Ca., U.S.	C2	98
Inverness, Fl., U.S.	D4	102
Inverness, Ms., U.S.	B3	117
Inverway, Austl.	D4	60
Investigator Strait, strt., Austl.	H2	62
Invisible Mountain, mtn., Id., U.S.	F5	105
Inwood, Ia., U.S.	A1	108
Inwood, N.Y., U.S.	k13	125
Inwood, W.V., U.S.	B6	141
Inyangani, mtn., Zimb.	B5	56
Inyan Kara Creek, stm., Wy., U.S.	B8	143
Inyan Kara Mountain, mtn., Wy., U.S.	B8	143
Inyo, co., Ca., U.S.	D5	98
Inyo, Mount, mtn., Ca., U.S.	D5	98
Inyo Mountains, mts., Ca., U.S.	D4	98
Ioánnina, Grc.	E8	18
Iola, Ks., U.S.	E8	109
Iola, Wi., U.S.	D4	142
Iona, Id., U.S.	F7	105
Ione, Ca., U.S.	C3	98
Iongo, Ang.	E3	54
Ionia, Mi., U.S.	F5	115
Ionia, co., Mi., U.S.	F5	115
Ionian Islands see Iónioi Nísoi, is., Grc.	E7	18
Ionian Sea, Eur.	E7	18
Iónioi Nísoi (Ionian Islands), is., Grc.	E7	18
Iony, ostrov, i., Russia	D16	26
Íos, i., Grc.	F10	18
Iosco, co., Mi., U.S.	D7	115
Iota, La., U.S.	D3	111
Iowa, La., U.S.	D2	111
Iowa, co., Ia., U.S.	C5	108
Iowa, co., Wi., U.S.	E3	142
Iowa, state, U.S.	C4	108
Iowa, stm., Ia., U.S.	C6	108
Iowa, West Branch, stm., Ia., U.S.	B4	108
Iowa City, Ia., U.S.	C6	108
Iowa Falls, Ia., U.S.	B4	108
Iowa Indian Reservation, U.S.	C8	109
Iowa Lake, l., U.S.	A3	108
Iowa Park, Tx., U.S.	C3	136
Ipameri, Braz.	E2	74
Ipatinga, Braz.	E3	74
Ipatovo, Russia	A4	42
Ipeiros, hist. reg., Grc.	E8	18
Iphigenia Bay, b., Ak., U.S.	n22	95
Ipiales, Col.	C4	70
Ipiaú, Braz.	D4	74
Ipoh, Malay.	C2	36
Iporá, Braz.	E1	74
Ippy, C.A.R.	B4	54
Ipswich, Austl.	F5	62
Ipswich, Eng., U.K.	D7	12
Ipswich, Ma., U.S.	A6	114
Ipswich, S.D., U.S.	B6	134
Ipswich, stm., Ma., U.S.	A5	114
Ipu, Braz.	B3	74
Iqaluit, Nu., Can.	F26	82
Iquique, Chile	B2	69
Iquitos, Peru	D5	70
Iraan, Tx., U.S.	D2	136
Iráklion, Grc.	G10	18
Iran, ctry., Asia	D6	42
Iran Mountains, mts., Asia	C5	36
Īrānshahr, Iran	E8	42
Irapuato, Mex.	C4	78
Iraq, ctry., Asia	D4	42
Irati, Braz.	D7	72
Irazú, Volcán, vol., C.R.	C3	80
Irbid, Jord.	D3	42
Irbīl, Iraq	C4	42
Irbit, Russia	C11	22
Irecê, Braz.	D3	74
Iredell, co., N.C., U.S.	B2	126
Ireland, ctry., Eur.	D2	12
Irgiz, Kaz.	E8	26
Irîgui, reg., Afr.	C3	50
Iriklinskij, Russia	D10	22
Iringa, Tan.	E7	54
Iriomote-jima, i., Japan	B8	34
Irion, co., Tx., U.S.	D2	136
Iriri, stm., Braz.	D9	70
Irish, Mount, mtn., Nv., U.S.	F6	121
Irish Sea, Eur.	D4	12
Irkutsk, Russia	D12	26
Irminger Basin	C26	144
Irmo, S.C., U.S.	C5	133
Iroise, b., Fr.	C4	16
Iron, co., Mi., U.S.	B2	115
Iron, co., Mo., U.S.	D7	118
Iron, co., Ut., U.S.	F2	137
Iron, co., Wi., U.S.	B3	142
Irondale, Al., U.S.	f7	94
Irondequoit, N.Y., U.S.	B3	125
Iron Gate, val., Eur.	G7	20
Iron Gate Reservoir, res., Ca., U.S.	B2	98
Iron Knob, Austl.	G2	62
Iron Mountain, Mi., U.S.	C2	115
Iron Mountain, mtn., Az., U.S.	D4	96
Iron Mountains, mts., U.S.	D1	139
Iron Ridge, Wi., U.S.	E5	142
Iron River, Mi., U.S.	B2	115
Iron River, Wi., U.S.	B2	142
Ironton, Mo., U.S.	D7	118
Ironton, Oh., U.S.	D3	128
Ironwood, Mi., U.S.	n11	115
Iroquois, On., Can.	C9	89
Iroquois, co., Il., U.S.	C6	106
Iroquois, stm., U.S.	C6	106
Iroquois, Lake, l., Vt., U.S.	B2	138
Iroquois Falls, On., Can.	o19	89
Irosin, Phil.	D8	34
Irpin', Ukr.	D11	20
Irrawaddy see Ayeyarwady, stm., Myan.	C3	34
Irricana, Ab., Can.	D4	84
Irrigon, Or., U.S.	B7	130
Irtyš see Irtysh, stm., Asia	D8	26
Irtysh, stm., Asia	D8	26
Irtysj see Irtysh, stm., Asia	D8	26
Irtyšsk, Kaz.	D9	26
Irumu, D.R.C.	C5	54
Irún, Spain	F6	16
Iruña see Pamplona, Spain	F6	16
Irvine, Ca., U.S.	n13	98
Irvine, Ky., U.S.	C6	110
Irving, Tx., U.S.	n10	136
Irvington, Al., U.S.	E1	94
Irvington, Il., U.S.	E4	106
Irvington, Ky., U.S.	C3	110
Irvington, N.J., U.S.	k8	123
Irvington, N.Y., U.S.	g13	125
Irwin, Pa., U.S.	F2	131
Irwin, co., Ga., U.S.	E3	103
Irwinton, Ga., U.S.	D3	103
Isa, Nig.	D6	50
Isabel, Mount, mtn., Wy., U.S.	D2	143
Isabela, Isla, i., Ec.	D1	70
Isabella, co., Mi., U.S.	E6	115
Isabella Indian Reservation, Mi., U.S.	E6	115
Isabella Lake, l., Mn., U.S.	C7	116
Ísafjarðardjúp, Ice.	k17	10a
Ísafjörður, Ice.	k17	10a
Isana (Içana), stm., S.A.	C5	70
Isanga, D.R.C.	D4	54
Isangel, Vanuatu	k9	62a
Isanti, Mn., U.S.	E5	116
Isanti, co., Mn., U.S.	E5	116
Isar, stm., Eur.	F13	12
Ischia, Isola d', i., Italy	D4	18
Ise, Japan	D3	31
Isernia, Italy	D5	18
Iset', stm., Russia	D8	26
Iseyin, Nig.	E5	50
Isfahan see Eşfahān, Iran	D6	42
Ishigaki, Japan	B8	34
Ishikari, stm., Japan	B4	31
Ishikawa, Japan	A9	34
Ishinomaki, Japan	D16	28
Ishpeming, Mi., U.S.	B3	115
Išim, Russia	D8	26
Išim, stm., Asia	D9	26
Isinglass, stm., N.H., U.S.	D4	122
Isiolo, Kenya	C7	54
Isiro, D.R.C.	C5	54
Iskăr, stm., Bul.	C10	18
İskenderun, Tur.	D7	44
İskenderun Körfezi, b., Tur.	D6	44
İskilip, Tur.	B6	44
Islāmābād, Pak.	D10	42

Name / Map Ref. / Page

Islamorada, Fl., U.S. **H6** 102
Island, co., Wa., U.S. **A3** 140
Island Beach, N.J., U.S. **D4** 123
Island City, Or., U.S. **B8** 130
Island Falls, Me., U.S. **B4** 112
Island Lake, l., Mb., Can. **C4** 86
Island Park, R.I., U.S. **E6** 132
Island Park Reservoir, res., Id., U.S. **E7** 105
Island Pond, Vt., U.S. **B5** 138
Island Pond, l., N.H., U.S. **E4** 122
Islands, Bay of, b., Nf., Can. **D2** 88
Isla Vista, Ca., U.S. **E4** 98
Islay, i., Scot., U.K. **C3** 12
Isle-aux-Morts, Nf., Can. **E2** 88
Isle of Man, dep., Eur. **C4** 12
Isle of Palms, S.C., U.S. **k12** 133
Isle of Wight, co., Va., U.S. **D6** 139
Isle of Wight Bay, b., Md., U.S. **D7** 113
Isle Royale National Park, Mi., U.S. **h9** 115
Islesboro Island, i., Me., U.S. **D4** 112
Isleta, N.M., U.S. **C3** 124
Isleta Indian Reservation, N.M., U.S. **C3** 124
Islington, Ma., U.S. **h11** 114
Ismailia, Egypt **D11** 48
İsmayıllı, Azer. **B13** 44
Isoka, Zam. **A5** 56
Isola, Ms., U.S. **B3** 117
Isparta, Tur. **D4** 44
İspir, Tur. **B9** 44
Israel, ctry., Asia **D2** 42
Israel, stm., N.H., U.S. **B3** 122
Issaquah, Wa., U.S. **B3** 140
Issaquena, co., Ms., U.S. **C2** 117
Issia, C. Iv. **E3** 50
Issoire, Fr. **E8** 16
Issoudun, Fr. **D8** 16
Issyk-Kul', Kyrg. **E9** 26
Issyk-Kul', ozero, l., Kyrg. **E9** 26
İstanbul, Tur. **B3** 44
İstanbul Boğazı (Bosporus), strt., Tur. **B3** 44
Isto, Mount, mtn., Ak., U.S. **B11** 95
Istokpoga, Lake, l., Fl., U.S. **E5** 102
Itabaiana, Braz. **D4** 74
Itabaiana, Braz. **C4** 74
Itaberaba, Braz. **D3** 74
Itaberaí, Braz. **E2** 74
Itabira, Braz. **E3** 74
Itabuna, Braz. **D4** 74
Itacoatiara, Braz. **D8** 70
Itagüí, Col. **B4** 70
Itaipu Reservoir, res., S.A. **C7** 72
Itaituba, Braz. **D8** 70
Itajaí, Braz. **D8** 72
Itajubá, Braz. **F2** 74
Itajuípe, Braz. **D4** 74
Italy, Tx., U.S. **C4** 136
Italy, ctry., Eur. **C4** 18
Itamaraju, Braz. **E4** 74
Itambé, Braz. **E3** 74
Itānagar, India **D6** 40
Itaobim, Braz. **E3** 74
Itapecuru-Mirim, Braz. **B3** 74
Itaperuna, Braz. **F3** 74
Itapetinga, Braz. **E3** 74
Itapetininga, Braz. **F2** 74
Itapipoca, Braz. **B4** 74
Itapiranga, Braz. **D7** 72
Itaporanga, Braz. **C4** 74
Itaquari, Braz. **F3** 74
Itaqui, Braz. **D6** 72
Itārsi, India **E3** 40
Itasca, Il., U.S. **k8** 106
Itasca, Tx., U.S. **C4** 136
Itasca, co., Mn., U.S. **C5** 116
Itasca, Lake, l., Mn., U.S. **C3** 116
Itaúna, Braz. **F3** 74
Itawamba, co., Ms., U.S. **A5** 117
Itenes see Guaporé, stm., S.A. **F7** 70
Iténez see Guaporé, stm., S.A. **F7** 70
Ithaca, Mi., U.S. **E6** 115
Ithaca, N.Y., U.S. **C4** 125
Ithaca see Itháki, i., Grc. **E8** 18
Itháki, i., Grc. **E8** 18
Itimbiri, stm., D.R.C. **C4** 54
Itoigawa, Japan **C3** 31
Itoko, D.R.C. **D4** 54
Itta Bena, Ms., U.S. **B3** 117
Ituango, Col. **D4** 80
Ituberá, Braz. **D4** 74
Ituiutaba, Braz. **E2** 74
Itumbiara, Braz. **E2** 74
Iturama, Braz. **E1** 74
Iturup, ostrov, i., Russia **E16** 26
Ituverava, Braz. **F2** 74
Itzehoe, Ger. **D11** 12
Iuka, Ms., U.S. **A5** 117
Iul'tin, Russia **C20** 26
Iva, S.C., U.S. **C2** 133
Ivanava, Bela. **C8** 20
Ivangorod, Russia **G13** 10
Ivanhoe, Mn., U.S. **F2** 116
Ivankov, Ukr. **D10** 20
Ivano-Frankivs'k, Ukr. **E8** 20
Ivanovo, Russia **D6** 26
Ivdel', Russia **C8** 26
Ivigtut, Grnld. **F30** 82
Ivins, Ut., U.S. **F2** 137
Ivohibe, Madag. **C8** 56
Ivory Coast see Cote d'Ivoire, ctry., Afr. **E3** 50
Ivoryton, Ct., U.S. **D6** 100
Ivrea, Italy **B1** 18
Iwaki, Japan **D16** 28
Iwo, Nig. **E5** 50
Ixmiquilpan, Mex. **C5** 78
Ixtapa, Mex. **D4** 78
Ixtepec, Mex. **D5** 78
Izabal, Lago de, l., Guat. **B2** 80
Izamal, Mex. **C7** 78
Izard, co., Ar., U.S. **A4** 97
Izberbaš, Russia **A12** 44
Iževsk, Russia **D7** 26
Iziaslav, Ukr. **D9** 20
Izium, Ukr. **E14** 20
Ižma, stm., Russia **A9** 22
Izmaïl, Ukr. **G10** 20
İzmir, Tur. **C2** 44
İzmir Körfezi, b., Tur. **C2** 44
İzmit, Tur. **B3** 44
İzmit Körfezi, b., Tur. **B3** 44
İznik, Tur. **B3** 44
İznik Gölü, l., Tur. **B3** 44
Izucar de Matamoros, Mex. **D5** 78
Izu-shotō, is., Japan **E15** 28
Izu Trench **F17** 64

J

Jabal, Baḩr al- (Mountain Nile), stm., Sudan **I11** 48
Jabalpur, India **E3** 40
Jabiru, Austl. **C5** 60
Jablah, Syria **E6** 44
Jablonec nad Nisou, Czech Rep. **D3** 20
Jablonovyj hrebet, mts., Russia **D13** 26
Jaboatão, Braz. **C4** 74
Jaboticabal, Braz. **F2** 74
Jacareí, Braz. **F2** 74
Jacarezinho, Braz. **F2** 74
Jaciara, Braz. **B7** 72
Jacinto City, Tx., U.S. **r14** 136
Jack, co., Tx., U.S. **C3** 136
Jackfish Lake, l., Sk., Can. **D1** 91
Jackman, Me., U.S. **C2** 112
Jackman Station, Me., U.S. **C2** 112
Jack Mountain, mtn., Mt., U.S. **D4** 119
Jack Mountain, mtn., Wa., U.S. **A5** 140
Jackpot, Nv., U.S. **B7** 121
Jacksboro, Tn., U.S. **C9** 135
Jacksboro, Tx., U.S. **C3** 136
Jacks Mountain, mtn., Pa., U.S. **E6** 131
Jackson, Al., U.S. **D2** 94
Jackson, Ca., U.S. **C3** 98
Jackson, Ga., U.S. **C3** 103
Jackson, Ky., U.S. **C6** 110
Jackson, La., U.S. **D4** 111
Jackson, Mi., U.S. **F6** 115
Jackson, Mn., U.S. **G4** 116
Jackson, Mo., U.S. **D8** 118
Jackson, Ms., U.S. **C3** 117
Jackson, Oh., U.S. **C3** 128
Jackson, S.C., U.S. **E4** 133
Jackson, Tn., U.S. **B3** 135
Jackson, Wi., U.S. **E5** 142
Jackson, Wy., U.S. **C2** 143
Jackson, co., Al., U.S. **A3** 94
Jackson, co., Ar., U.S. **B4** 97
Jackson, co., Co., U.S. **A4** 99
Jackson, co., Fl., U.S. **B1** 102
Jackson, co., Ga., U.S. **B3** 103
Jackson, co., Ia., U.S. **B7** 108
Jackson, co., Il., U.S. **F4** 106
Jackson, co., In., U.S. **G5** 107
Jackson, co., Ks., U.S. **C8** 109
Jackson, co., Ky., U.S. **C5** 110
Jackson, co., La., U.S. **B3** 111
Jackson, co., Mi., U.S. **F6** 115
Jackson, co., Mn., U.S. **G3** 116
Jackson, co., Mo., U.S. **B3** 118
Jackson, co., Ms., U.S. **E5** 117
Jackson, co., N.C., U.S. **f9** 126
Jackson, co., Oh., U.S. **C3** 128
Jackson, co., Ok., U.S. **C2** 129
Jackson, co., Or., U.S. **E4** 130
Jackson, co., S.D., U.S. **D4** 134
Jackson, co., Tn., U.S. **C8** 135
Jackson, co., Tx., U.S. **E4** 136
Jackson, co., W.V., U.S. **C3** 141
Jackson, co., Wi., U.S. **D3** 142
Jackson, stm., Va., U.S. **C3** 139
Jackson, Lake, l., Fl., U.S. **E5** 102
Jackson, Lake, l., Fl., U.S. **B2** 102
Jackson, Mount, mtn., Ant. **D34** 67
Jackson, Mount, mtn., N.H., U.S. **B4** 122
Jackson Center, Oh., U.S. **B1** 128
Jackson Lake, res., Wy., U.S. **C2** 143
Jackson Mountains, mts., Nv., U.S. **B3** 121
Jackson's Arm, Nf., Can. **D3** 88
Jacksons Gap, Al., U.S. **C4** 94
Jacksonville, Al., U.S. **B4** 94
Jacksonville, Ar., U.S. **C3** 97
Jacksonville, Fl., U.S. **B5** 102
Jacksonville, Il., U.S. **D3** 106
Jacksonville, N.C., U.S. **C5** 126
Jacksonville, Or., U.S. **E4** 130
Jacksonville, Tx., U.S. **D5** 136
Jacksonville Beach, Fl., U.S. **B5** 102
Jacksonville Naval Air Station, mil., Fl., U.S. **B5** 102
Jacks Peak, mtn., Ut., U.S. **E3** 137
Jacmel, Haiti **B5** 80
Jacobābād, Pak. **E9** 42
Jacobina, Braz. **D3** 74
Jacques-Cartier, stm., P.Q., Can. **B6** 90
Jacques-Cartier, Détroit de, strt., P.Q., Can. **I27** 82
Jacquet River, N.B., Can. **B4** 87
Jacundá, Braz. **B2** 74
Jada, Nig. **E7** 50
Jaén, Peru **E4** 70
Jaén, Spain **I5** 16
Jaffa, Cape, c., Austl. **H2** 62
Jaffna, Sri L. **H4** 40
Jaffrey, N.H., U.S. **E2** 122
Jagādhri, India **C3** 40
Jagdalpur, India **F4** 40
Jagersfontein, S. Afr. **D4** 56
Jagodnoe, Russia **C16** 26
Jagtiāl, India **F3** 40
Jaguaquara, Braz. **D4** 74
Jaguarão, Braz. **E7** 72
Jaguaribe, Braz. **C4** 74
Jahrom, Iran **E6** 42
Jailolo, Indon. **C7** 36
Jaipur, India **D3** 40
Jaisalmer, India **D2** 40
Jājapur, India **E5** 40
Jakarta, Indon. **E3** 36
Jakobshavn, Grnld. **E29** 82
Jakša, Russia **B10** 22
Jakutija, state, Russia **C14** 26
Jakutsk, Russia **C14** 26
Jal, N.M., U.S. **E6** 124
Jalālābād, Afg. **D10** 42
Jalandhar, India **C3** 40
Jalapa see Xalapa, Mex. **D5** 78
Jālaun, India **D3** 40
Jalgaon, India **E3** 40
Jalingo, Nig. **E7** 50
Jalisco, state, Mex. **C4** 78
Jālna, India **F3** 40
Jālor, India **D2** 40
Jalostotitlán, Mex. **C4** 78
Jalpāiguri, India **D5** 40
Jalūlā', Iraq **E11** 44
Jamaica, ctry., N.A. **E9** 76
Jamaica Bay, b., N.Y., U.S. **k13** 125
Jamaica Channel, strt., N.A. **B4** 80
Jamal, poluostrov, pen., Russia **B8** 26
Jamantau, gora, mtn., Russia **D7** 26
Jambi, Indon. **D2** 36
Jambol, Bul. **C11** 18
Jambusar, India **E2** 40
James, stm., Mo., U.S. **E4** 118
James, stm., Va., U.S. **C5** 139
James, stm., U.S. **C8** 92
James, Lake, l., In., U.S. **A7** 107
James, Lake, res., N.C., U.S. **B1** 126
James Bay, b., Can. **H23** 82
James Branch, stm., De., U.S. **F3** 101
Jamesburg, N.J., U.S. **C4** 123
James City, N.C., U.S. **B5** 126
James City, co., Va., U.S. **C6** 139
James Island, S.C., U.S. **k12** 133
James Island, i., Md., U.S. **C5** 113
James Island, i., S.C., U.S. **F8** 133
James River Bridge, Va., U.S. **k15** 139
Jamestown, Austl. **G2** 62
Jamestown, In., U.S. **E4** 107
Jamestown, Ky., U.S. **D4** 110
Jamestown, N.C., U.S. **B3** 126
Jamestown, N.D., U.S. **C7** 127
Jamestown, N.Y., U.S. **C1** 125
Jamestown, Oh., U.S. **C2** 128
Jamestown, R.I., U.S. **F5** 132
Jamestown, Tn., U.S. **C9** 135
James Town, Wy., U.S. **E3** 143
Jamestown Dam, N.D., U.S. **C7** 127
Jamestown Reservoir, res., N.D., U.S. **C7** 127
Jamkhandi, India **F3** 40
Jammerbugten, b., Den. **H3** 10
Jammu, India **C2** 40
Jammu and Kashmir, hist. reg., Asia **C10** 38
Jamnagar, India **E2** 40
Jämsä, Fin. **F11** 10
Jamshedpur, India **E5** 40
Jamsk, Russia **D17** 26
Jämtland, hist. reg., Swe. **E6** 10
Jamuna, stm., Bngl. **D5** 40
Jana, stm., Russia **C15** 26
Janaúba, Braz. **E3** 74
Janaucu, Ilha, i., Braz. **C10** 70
Janesville, Ca., U.S. **B3** 98
Janesville, Ia., U.S. **B5** 108
Janesville, Mn., U.S. **F5** 116
Janesville, Wi., U.S. **F4** 142
Jan Mayen, i., Nor. **D23** 144
Jan Mayen Ridge **C24** 144
Jansenville, S. Afr. **E3** 56
Janskij, Russia **C15** 26
Janskij zaliv, b., Russia **B15** 26
Januária, Braz. **E3** 74
Jaora, India **E3** 40
Japan, ctry., Asia **D15** 28
Japan, Sea of (East Sea), Asia **C14** 28
Japan Basin **D16** 64
Japan Trench **E17** 64
Japurá (Caquetá), stm., S.A. **D6** 70
Jaraguá, Braz. **E2** 74
Jaransk, Russia **C8** 22
Jarānwāla, Pak. **D10** 42
Jarcevo, Russia **B12** 20
Jardim, Braz. **C6** 72
Jardín América, Arg. **D6** 72
Jari, stm., Braz. **C9** 70
Jarocin, Pol. **D4** 20
Jaroslavl', Russia **D6** 26
Jarosław, Pol. **D7** 20
Jarrettsville, Md., U.S. **A5** 113
Jar-Sale, Russia **A13** 22
Järva-Jaani, Est. **G11** 10
Järvenpää, Fin. **F11** 10
Jarvis Island, i., Oc. **E13** 58
Jasikan, Ghana **E5** 50
Jāsk, Iran **E7** 42
Jaškul', Russia **A5** 42
Jasło, Pol. **E6** 20
Jasmine Estates, Fl., U.S. **D4** 102
Jasnogorsk, Russia **B14** 20
Jason Islands, is., Falk. Is. **H4** 69
Jasonville, In., U.S. **F3** 107
Jasper, Al., U.S. **B2** 94
Jasper, Fl., U.S. **B4** 102
Jasper, Ga., U.S. **B2** 103
Jasper, In., U.S. **H4** 107
Jasper, Mo., U.S. **D3** 118
Jasper, Tn., U.S. **D8** 135
Jasper, Tx., U.S. **D6** 136
Jasper, co., Ga., U.S. **C3** 103
Jasper, co., Ia., U.S. **C4** 108
Jasper, co., Il., U.S. **D5** 106
Jasper, co., In., U.S. **B3** 107
Jasper, co., Mo., U.S. **D3** 118
Jasper, co., Ms., U.S. **C4** 117
Jasper, co., S.C., U.S. **G5** 133
Jasper, co., Tx., U.S. **D5** 136
Jasper National Park, Ab., Can. **C1** 84
Jataí, Braz. **E1** 74
Jatni, India **E5** 40
Jaú, Braz. **F2** 74
Jaunpur, India **D4** 40
Java see Jawa, i., Indon. **E3** 36
Javari (Yavarí), stm., S.A. **D5** 70
Java Sea see Jawa, Laut, Indon. **D3** 36
Java Trench **I13** 64
Jawa (Java), i., Indon. **E3** 36
Jawa, Laut (Java Sea), Indon. **D3** 36
Jawhar, Som. **J14** 48
Jay, Ok., U.S. **A7** 129
Jay, co., In., U.S. **D7** 107
Jaya, Puncak, mtn., Indon. **G10** 32
Jayapura, Indon. **G11** 32
Jaypur, India **F4** 40
Jaz Mūrīān, Hāmūn-e, l., Iran **E7** 42
J. B. Thomas, Lake, res., Tx., U.S. **C2** 136
Jean, Nv., U.S. **H6** 121
Jeanerette, La., U.S. **E4** 111
Jean Lafitte National Historical Park, La., U.S. **k12** 111
Jeannette, Pa., U.S. **F2** 131
Jebba, Nig. **E5** 50
Jeddore Lake, res., Nf., Can. **D3** 88
Jędrzejów, Pol. **D6** 20
Jeff Davis, co., Ga., U.S. **E4** 103
Jeff Davis, co., Tx., U.S. **o12** 136
Jefferson, Ga., U.S. **B3** 103
Jefferson, Ia., U.S. **B3** 108
Jefferson, La., U.S. **k11** 111
Jefferson, N.C., U.S. **A1** 126
Jefferson, Oh., U.S. **A5** 128
Jefferson, Or., U.S. **C3** 130
Jefferson, S.C., U.S. **B7** 133
Jefferson, Tx., U.S. **C5** 136
Jefferson, Wi., U.S. **E5** 142
Jefferson, co., Al., U.S. **B3** 94
Jefferson, co., Ar., U.S. **C3** 97
Jefferson, co., Co., U.S. **B5** 99
Jefferson, co., Fl., U.S. **B3** 102
Jefferson, co., Ga., U.S. **C4** 103
Jefferson, co., Ia., U.S. **C5** 108
Jefferson, co., Id., U.S. **F6** 105
Jefferson, co., Il., U.S. **E5** 106
Jefferson, co., In., U.S. **G6** 107
Jefferson, co., Ks., U.S. **C8** 109
Jefferson, co., Ky., U.S. **B4** 110
Jefferson, co., La., U.S. **E5** 111
Jefferson, co., Mo., U.S. **C7** 118
Jefferson, co., Ms., U.S. **D2** 117
Jefferson, co., Mt., U.S. **D4** 119
Jefferson, co., Ne., U.S. **D8** 120
Jefferson, co., N.Y., U.S. **A5** 125
Jefferson, co., Oh., U.S. **B5** 128
Jefferson, co., Ok., U.S. **C4** 129
Jefferson, co., Or., U.S. **C5** 130
Jefferson, co., Pa., U.S. **D3** 131
Jefferson, co., Tn., U.S. **C10** 135
Jefferson, co., Tx., U.S. **E5** 136
Jefferson, co., W.V., U.S. **B7** 141
Jefferson, co., Wa., U.S. **B1** 140
Jefferson, co., Wi., U.S. **E5** 142
Jefferson, stm., Mt., U.S. **E5** 119
Jefferson, Mount, mtn., Id., U.S. **E7** 105
Jefferson, Mount, mtn., Nv., U.S. **E5** 121
Jefferson, Mount, mtn., Or., U.S. **C5** 130
Jefferson City, Mo., U.S. **C5** 118
Jefferson City, Tn., U.S. **C10** 135
Jefferson Davis, co., La., U.S. **D3** 111
Jefferson Davis, co., Ms., U.S. **D4** 117
Jefferson Farms, De., U.S. **i7** 101
Jefferson Proving Ground, mil., In., U.S. **G7** 107
Jeffersontown, Ky., U.S. **B4** 110
Jeffersonville, Ga., U.S. **D3** 103
Jeffersonville, In., U.S. **H6** 107
Jeffersonville, Ky., U.S. **C6** 110
Jeffersonville, Oh., U.S. **C2** 128
Jeffrey, W.V., U.S. **D3** 141
Jeffrey City, Wy., U.S. **D5** 143
Jeffries Creek, stm., S.C., U.S. **C8** 133
Jega, Nig. **D5** 50
Jehossee Island, i., S.C., U.S. **k11** 133
Jēkabpils, Lat. **H11** 10
Jekyll Island, i., Ga., U.S. **E5** 103
Jelenia Góra, Pol. **D3** 20
Jelgava, Lat. **H10** 10
Jellico, Tn., U.S. **C9** 135
Jelm Mountain, mtn., Wy., U.S. **E7** 143
Jemaja, Pulau, i., Indon. **C3** 36
Jember, Indon. **E4** 36
Jemez, stm., N.M., U.S. **k7** 124
Jemez Canyon Dam, N.M., U.S. **k7** 124
Jemez Indian Reservation, N.M., U.S. **h7** 124
Jemez Pueblo, N.M., U.S. **B3** 124
Jemison, Al., U.S. **C3** 94
Jena, Ger. **E12** 12
Jena, La., U.S. **C3** 111
Jeneponto, Indon. **E5** 36
Jenkins, Ky., U.S. **C7** 110
Jenkins, co., Ga., U.S. **D5** 103
Jenkintown, Pa., U.S. **o21** 131
Jenks, Ok., U.S. **A6** 129
Jennings, La., U.S. **D3** 111
Jennings, Mo., U.S. **f13** 118
Jennings, co., In., U.S. **G6** 107
Jensen Beach, Fl., U.S. **E6** 102
Jens Munks Ø, i., Grnld. **F32** 82
Jequié, Braz. **D3** 74
Jequitinhonha, Braz. **E3** 74
Jequitinhonha, stm., Braz. **E3** 74
Jerada, Mor. **D4** 48
Jerauld, co., S.D., U.S. **C7** 134
Jérémie, Haiti **B5** 80
Jeremoabo, Braz. **D4** 74
Jerez de García Salinas, Mex. **C4** 78
Jerez de la Frontera, Spain **I3** 16
Jerez de los Caballeros, Spain **H3** 16
Jericho see Arīḩā, Gaza Str. **G6** 44
Jericho, Vt., U.S. **B3** 138
Jerid, Chott, l., Tun. **D6** 48
Jerimoth Hill, hill, R.I., U.S. **C1** 132
Jermyn, Pa., U.S. **C10** 131
Jerome, Id., U.S. **G4** 105
Jerome, Pa., U.S. **F4** 131
Jerome, co., Id., U.S. **G4** 105
Jersey, co., Il., U.S. **D3** 106
Jersey, dep., Eur. **F5** 12
Jersey City, N.J., U.S. **B4** 123
Jersey Mountain, mtn., Id., U.S. **E3** 105
Jersey Shore, Pa., U.S. **D7** 131
Jerseyville, Il., U.S. **D3** 106
Jerusalem see Yerushalayim, Isr. **G6** 42
Jervis Inlet, b., B.C., Can. **D6** 85
Jesi, Italy **C4** 18
Jessamine, co., Ky., U.S. **C5** 110
Jesselton see Kota Kinabalu, Malay. **B5** 36
Jessore, Bngl. **E5** 40
Jessup, Md., U.S. **B4** 113
Jessup, Pa., U.S. **m18** 131
Jesup, Ga., U.S. **E5** 103
Jesup, Ia., U.S. **B5** 108
Jesup, Lake, l., Fl., U.S. **D5** 102
Jésus, Île, i., P.Q., Can. **p19** 90
Jesús Carranza, Mex. **D5** 78
Jesús María, Arg. **E5** 72
Jetmore, Ks., U.S. **D4** 109
Jewel Cave National Monument, S.D., U.S. **D2** 134
Jewell, Ia., U.S. **B4** 108
Jewell, co., Ks., U.S. **C5** 109
Jewett City, Ct., U.S. **C8** 100
Jhālāwār, India **E3** 40
Jhang Sadar, Pak. **D10** 42
Jhānsi, India **D3** 40
Jhelum, Pak. **D10** 42
Jhunjhunūn, India **D3** 40
Jiahe, China **D3** 30
Jiali, China **C6** 40
Jialing, stm., China **E8** 28
Jiamusi, China **B14** 28
Ji'an, China **D3** 30
Jianchang, China **A4** 30
Jianchuan, China **F8** 28
Jiande, China **D4** 30

Name Map Ref. Page

Jiang'an, China D2 30
Jiangcheng, China B4 34
Jiangjin, China F9 28
Jiangle, China D4 30
Jiangling, China C3 30
Jiangmen, China G10 28
Jiangsu, state, China E11 28
Jiangxi, state, China F11 28
Jianli, China D3 30
Jian'ou, China F11 28
Jianping, China A4 30
Jianshui, China G8 28
Jianyang, China D4 30
Jianyang, China C1 30
Jiaocheng, China B3 30
Jiaonan, China B4 30
Jiaoxian, China D12 28
Jiaozuo, China D10 28
Jiashan, China C4 30
Jibiya, Nig. D6 50
Jicarilla Apache Indian Reservation, N.M., U.S. A2 124
Jičín, Czech Rep. D3 20
Jiddah, Sau. Ar. F3 38
Jiexiu, China B3 30
Jieyang, China G11 28
Jihlava, Czech Rep. E3 20
Jijel, Alg. I9 16
Jijiga, Eth. B8 54
Jilib, Som. J13 48
Jilin, China C13 28
Jilin, state, China C13 28
Jill, Kediet ej, mtn., Maur. B2 50
Jīma, Eth. B7 54
Jimbolia, Rom. G6 20
Jiménez (Ciudad Jiménez), Mex. B4 78
Jimeta, Nig. E7 50
Jim Hogg, co., Tx., U.S. F3 136
Jim Lake, res., N.D., U.S. B7 127
Jimo, China B5 30
Jim Thorpe, Pa., U.S. E10 131
Jim Wells, co., Tx., U.S. F3 136
Jinan, China D11 28
Jincheng, China B3 30
Jīnd, India D3 40
Jingdezhen, China F11 28
Jinggangshan, China F10 28
Jinghai, China B4 30
Jinghong, China G8 28
Jingning, China B2 30
Jingxi, China E2 30
Jingxian, China D2 30
Jinhua, China F11 28
Jining, China D11 28
Jining, China C10 28
Jinja, Ug. C6 54
Jinning, China E1 30
Jinsha, China D2 30
Jinshi, China F10 28
Jinzhai, China C4 30
Jinzhou, China C12 28
Jinzhou, China D12 28
Ji-Paraná, Braz. F7 70
Jishou, China D2 30
Jisr ash-Shughūr, Syria E7 44
Jiu, stm., Rom. G7 20
Jiujiang, China F11 28
Jiulong (Kowloon), China E3 30
Jiuquan, China D7 28
Jiutai, China C13 28
Jixi, China B14 28
Jixian, China C11 28
Jīzān, Sau. Ar. G4 38
Joanna, S.C., U.S. C4 133
João Pessoa, Braz. C5 74
João Pinheiro, Braz. E2 74
Job Peak, mtn., Nv., U.S. D3 121
Jocassee, Lake, res., U.S. B1 133
Jódar, Spain I5 16
Jo Daviess, co., Il., U.S. A3 106
Jodhpur, India D2 40
Joe Batt's Arm [-Barr'd Islands-Shoal Bay], Nf., Can. D4 88
Joensuu, Fin. E13 10
Joes Brook, stm., Vt., U.S. C4 138
Joes Creek, stm., W.V., U.S. m12 141
Joetsu, Japan D15 28
Joffre, Mount, mtn., Can. D3 84
Johannesburg, S. Afr. D4 56
John, Cape, c., N.S., Can. D6 87
John Day, Or., U.S. C8 130
John Day, stm., Or., U.S. B6 130
John Day Dam, U.S. D5 140
John Day Fossil Beds National Monument, Or., U.S. C6 130
John F. Kennedy Space Center, sci., Fl., U.S. D6 102
John H. Kerr Dam, Va., U.S. D4 139
John H. Kerr Reservoir, res., U.S. D4 139
John Martin Reservoir, res., Co., U.S. C7 99
John Muir National Historical Site, hist., Ca., U.S. h8 98
John Redmond Reservoir, res., Ks., U.S. D8 109
John Sevier, Tn., U.S. m14 135
Johns Island, i., S.C., U.S. F7 133
Johnson, Ks., U.S. E2 109
Johnson, Vt., U.S. B3 138
Johnson, co., Ar., U.S. B2 97
Johnson, co., Ga., U.S. D4 103
Johnson, co., Ia., U.S. C6 108
Johnson, co., Il., U.S. F5 106
Johnson, co., In., U.S. F5 107
Johnson, co., Ks., U.S. D9 109
Johnson, co., Ky., U.S. C7 110
Johnson, co., Mo., U.S. C4 118
Johnson, co., Ne., U.S. D9 120
Johnson, co., Tn., U.S. C12 135
Johnson, co., Tx., U.S. C4 136
Johnson, co., Wy., U.S. B6 143
Johnsonburg, Pa., U.S. D4 131
Johnson City, N.Y., U.S. C5 125
Johnson City, Tn., U.S. C11 135
Johnson City, Tx., U.S. D3 136
Johnson Creek, Wi., U.S. E5 142
Johnsonville, S.C., U.S. D9 133
Johns Pass, strt., Fl., U.S. p10 102
Johnston, Ia., U.S. e8 108
Johnston, R.I., U.S. C4 132
Johnston, S.C., U.S. D4 133
Johnston, co., N.C., U.S. B4 126
Johnston, co., Ok., U.S. C5 129
Johnston Atoll, atoll, Oc. G22 64
Johnston City, Il., U.S. F5 106
Johnston Key, i., Fl., U.S. H5 102
Johnstown, Co., U.S. A6 99
Johnstown, N.Y., U.S. B6 125
Johnstown, Oh., U.S. B3 128
Johnstown, Pa., U.S. F4 131
John W. Flannagan Reservoir, res., Va., U.S. e9 139
Johor Bahru, Malay. C2 36
Joigny, Fr. C8 16
Joiner, Ar., U.S. B5 97
Joinville, Braz. D8 72
Jokkmokk, Swe. C8 10
Jolfā, Iran C11 44
Joliet, Il., U.S. B5 106
Joliette, P.Q., Can. C4 90
Jolo, Phil. E8 34
Jolo Island, i., Phil. E8 34
Jomda, China E7 28
Jones, Ok., U.S. B4 129
Jones, co., Ga., U.S. C3 103
Jones, co., Ia., U.S. B6 108
Jones, co., Ms., U.S. D4 117
Jones, co., N.C., U.S. B5 126
Jones, co., S.D., U.S. D5 134
Jones, co., Tx., U.S. C3 136
Jonesboro, Ar., U.S. B5 97
Jonesboro, Ga., U.S. C2 103
Jonesboro, Il., U.S. F4 106
Jonesboro, In., U.S. D6 107
Jonesboro, La., U.S. B3 111
Jonesborough, Tn., U.S. C11 135
Jonesburg, Mo., U.S. C6 118
Jones Creek, Tx., U.S. s14 136
Jones Mill, Ar., U.S. C3 97
Jonesport, Me., U.S. D5 112
Jonestown, Ms., U.S. A3 117
Jonesville, La., U.S. C4 111
Jonesville, Mi., U.S. G6 115
Jonesville, N.C., U.S. A2 126
Jonesville, S.C., U.S. B4 133
Jonesville, Va., U.S. f8 139
Joniškis, Lith. H10 10
Jonquière, P.Q., Can. A6 90
Jonuta, Mex. D6 78
Joplin, Mo., U.S. D3 118
Joppatowne, Md., U.S. B5 113
Jordan, Mn., U.S. F5 116
Jordan, ctry., Asia D3 42
Jordan, stm., Asia F6 44
Jordan, stm., Ut., U.S. C4 137
Jordan Creek, stm., U.S. E9 130
Jordan Lake, res., Al., U.S. C3 94
Jorhāt, India D6 40
Jornado del Muerto, des., N.M., U.S. D3 124
Joroinen, Fin. E12 10
Jos, Nig. E6 50
José de San Martín, Arg. F2 69
Joseph, Or., U.S. B9 130
Joseph, Lac, l., Nf., Can. h8 88
Joseph Bonaparte Gulf, b., Austl. C4 60
Joseph City, Az., U.S. C5 96
Josephine, co., Or., U.S. E3 130
Joshua, Tx., U.S. n9 136
Joshua Tree, Ca., U.S. E5 98
Joshua Tree National Monument, Ca., U.S. F6 98
Jostedalsbreen, Nor. F2 10
Jourdanton, Tx., U.S. E3 136
Jovellanos, Cuba A3 80
J. Percy Priest Lake, res., Tn., U.S. A5 135
Juab, co., Ut., U.S. D2 137
Juan Aldama, Mex. C4 78
Juan de Fuca, Strait of, strt., N.A. B3 92
Juan Fernandez, Archipiélago, is., Chile E1 72
Juanjuí, Peru E4 70
Juazeiro, Braz. C3 74
Juazeiro do Norte, Braz. C4 74
Juba, Sudan J11 48
Jubba (Genalē), stm., Afr. C8 54
Juby, Cap, c., Mor. A2 50
Júcar, stm., Spain H6 16
Juchitán de Zaragoza, Mex. D5 78
Judenburg, Aus. G14 12
Judith, stm., Mt., U.S. C7 119
Judith, Point, c., R.I., U.S. G4 101
Judith Basin, co., Mt., U.S. C6 119
Judith Island, i., N.C., U.S. B6 126
Judith Mountains, mts., Mt., U.S. C7 119
Judith Peak, mtn., Mt., U.S. C7 119
Judsonia, Ar., U.S. B4 97
Juhnov, Russia B13 20
Juidongshan, China E4 30
Juiz de Fora, Braz. F3 74
Jukta, Russia C12 26
Julesburg, Co., U.S. A8 99
Juliaca, Peru G5 70
Julia Creek, Austl. E3 62
Julian, Ca., U.S. F5 98
Julian, W.V., U.S. C3 141
Julian Alps, mts., Eur. A4 18
Juliana Top, mtn., Sur. C8 70
Julianehåb, Grnld. F30 82
Jumba, Som. D8 54
Jumbo Peak, mtn., Nv., U.S. G7 121
Jumilla, Spain H6 16
Jump, stm., Wi., U.S. C3 142
Jūnāgadh, India E2 40
Junction, Tx., U.S. D3 136
Junction City, Ar., U.S. D3 97
Junction City, Ks., U.S. C7 109
Junction City, Ky., U.S. C5 110
Junction City, La., U.S. A3 111
Junction City, Or., U.S. C3 130
Jundiaí, Braz. F2 74
Juneau, Ak., U.S. D13 95
Juneau, Wi., U.S. E5 142
Juneau, co., Wi., U.S. E3 142
Junee, Austl. G4 62
June in Winter, Lake, l., Fl., U.S. E5 102
Jungar Qi, China D10 28
Junggar Pendi, China B5 28
Juniata, Ne., U.S. D7 120
Juniata, co., Pa., U.S. F7 131
Juniata, stm., Pa., U.S. F7 131
Junín, Arg. E5 72
Junior Lake, l., Me., U.S. C4 112
Juniper Mountains, mts., Az., U.S. B2 96
Junipero Serra Peak, mtn., Ca., U.S. D3 98
Jūniyah, Leb. F6 44
Junlian, China D1 30
Junxian, China E10 28
Jupiter, Fl., U.S. F6 102
Jupiter Inlet, b., Fl., U.S. F6 102
Jupiter Island, i., Fl., U.S. E6 102
Jur, Russia D15 26
Jura, i., Scot., U.K. C4 12
Jurga, Russia D10 26
Jūrmala, Lat. H10 10
Juruá, stm., S.A. E6 70
Juruena, stm., Braz. F8 70
Jurumirim, Represa, res., Braz. C8 72
Juškozero, Russia B5 22
Jussara, Braz. B7 72
Justin, Tx., U.S. C4 136
Jutaí, stm., Braz. D6 70
Jutiapa, Guat. C1 80
Juticalpa, Hond. C2 80
Jutland see Jylland, reg., Den. I3 10
Juventud, Isla de la, i., Cuba A3 80
Juxian, China B4 30
Južno-Sahalinsk, Russia E16 26
Južno-Ural'sk, Russia D11 22
Jylland, reg., Den. I3 10
Jyväskylä, Fin. E11 10

K

K2 (Qogir Feng), mtn., Asia B3 40
Kaaawa, Hi., U.S. f10 104
Kaahka, Turk. C7 42
Kaala, mtn., Hi., U.S. f9 104
Kaalualu Bay, b., Hi., U.S. E6 104
Kaaumakua, Puu, mtn., Hi., U.S. f10 104
Kabaena, Pulau, i., Indon. E6 36
Kabala, S.L. E2 50
Kabale, Ug. D5 54
Kabalega Falls, wtfl, Ug. C6 54
Kabalo, D.R.C. E5 54
Kabambare, D.R.C. D5 54
Kabardino-Balkarija, state, Russia E6 26
Kabba, Nig. E6 50
Kabetogama Lake, l., Mn., U.S. B5 116
Kabinda, D.R.C. E4 54
Kabīr Kūh, mts., Iran F12 44
Kābol, Afg. D9 42
Kabompo, stm., Zam. A3 56
Kabongo, D.R.C. E5 54
Kabūdarāhang, Iran E13 44
Kābul see Kābol, Afg. D9 42
Kabwe, Zam. A4 56
Kabylie, reg., Alg. I9 16
Kachchh, Gulf of, b., India E1 40
Kachess Lake, res., Wa., U.S. B4 140
Kačkanar, Russia C10 22
Kadan Kyun, i., Myan. D3 34
Kade, Ghana E4 50
Kadınhanı, Tur. C5 44
Kadiolo, Mali D3 50
Kadirli, Tur. D7 44
Kadoka, S.D., U.S. D4 134
Kadoma, Zimb. B4 56
Kaduna, Nig. D6 50
Kaduna, stm., Nig. D6 50
Kāduqlī, Sudan H10 48
Kadykčan, Russia C16 26
Kadžerom, Russia B10 22
Kaédi, Maur. C2 50
Kaélé, Cam. A2 54
Kaena Point, c., Hi., U.S. B3 104
Kafanchan, Nig. E6 50
Kaffrine, Sen. D1 50
Kafia Kingi, Sudan I9 48
Kafue, Zam. B4 56
Kafue, stm., Zam. A4 56
Kaga, Japan C3 31
Kaga Bandoro, C.A.R. B3 54
Kagan, Uzb. C8 42
Kagera, stm., Afr. D6 54
Kağızman, Tur. B10 44
Kagoshima, Japan E14 28
Kagul see Cahul, Mol. G10 20
Kahaluu, Hi., U.S. D6 104
Kahaluu, Hi., U.S. g10 104
Kahama, Tan. D6 54
Kahana Bay, b., Hi., U.S. f10 104
Kahemba, D.R.C. E3 54
Kahoka, Mo., U.S. A6 118
Kahoolawe, i., Hi., U.S. C5 104
Kahramanmaraş, Tur. D7 44
Kahuku, Hi., U.S. B4 104
Kahuku Point, c., Hi., U.S. B4 104
Kahului, Hi., U.S. C5 104
Kahului Bay, b., Hi., U.S. C5 104
Kai, Kepulauan, is., Indon. E8 36
Kaibab Indian Reservation, Az., U.S. A3 96
Kaifeng, China E10 28
Kaikoura, N.Z. p13 63c
Kailahun, S.L. E2 50
Kailas see Kangrinboqê Feng, mtn., China E4 28
Kailas Range see Gangdisê Shan, mts., China E4 28
Kaili, China D2 30
Kailu, China C12 28
Kailua, Hi., U.S. B4 104
Kailua Bay, b., Hi., U.S. g11 104
Kailua Kona, Hi., U.S. D6 104
Kainji Lake, res., Nig. D5 50
Kaiping, China E3 30
Kairouan, Tun. C7 48
Kaiserslautern, Ger. F10 12
Kaitaia, N.Z. o13 63c
Kaithal, India D3 40
Kaiwi Channel, strt., Hi., U.S. h17 92a
Kaiwi Channel, strt., Hi., U.S. B4 104
Kaixian, China C2 30
Kaiyuan, China C12 28
Kaiyuan, China E1 30
Kajaani, Fin. D12 10
Kajakī, Band-e, res., Afg. D9 42
Kajang, Malay. C2 36
Kajiado, Kenya D7 54
Kajnar, Kaz. E9 26
Kaka, Sudan A6 54
Kakamas, S. Afr. D3 56
Kakamega, Kenya C6 54
Kaka Point, c., Hi., U.S. C5 104
Kakata, Lib. E2 50
Kake, Ak., U.S. D13 95
Kakhovka Reservoir see Kakhovs'ke vodoskhovyshche, res., Ukr. F13 20
Kakhovs'ke vodoskhovyshche, res., Ukr. F13 20
Kākināda, India F4 40
Kalaa Kebira, Tun. G3 18
Kalaallit Nunaat see Greenland, dep., N.A. D30 82
Kalabahi, Indon. E6 36
Kalabo, Zam. B3 56
Kalač, Russia D7 22
Kalač-na-Donu, Russia E7 22
Kaladan, stm., Asia B2 34
Ka Lae, c., Hi., U.S. E6 104
Kalahari Desert, des., Afr. C3 56
Kalaheo, Hi., U.S. B2 104
Kalajoki, Fin. D10 10
Kalakan, Russia D13 26
Kalama, Wa., U.S. C3 140
Kalámai, Grc. F8 18
Kalamazoo, Mi., U.S. F5 115
Kalamazoo, co., Mi., U.S. F5 115
Kalamazoo, stm., Mi., U.S. F5 115
Kalamits'ka zatoka, b., Ukr. G12 20
Kalanchak, Ukr. F12 20
Kalao, Pulau, i., Indon. E6 36
Kalaotoa, Pulau, i., Indon. E6 36
Kalasin, Thai. C4 34
Kalāt, Pak. E9 42
Kalaupapa Peninsula, pen., Hi., U.S. B5 104
Kalaw, Myan. B3 34
Kalawao, co., Hi., U.S. B5 104
Kalbarri, Austl. F1 60
Kale, Tur. D3 44
Kalecik, Tur. B5 44
Kaleden, B.C., Can. E8 85
Kalemie, D.R.C. E5 54
Kalemyo, Myan. B2 34
Kalena, Puu, mtn., Hi., U.S. g9 104
Kalene Hill, Zam. A3 56
Kalevala, Russia D14 10
Kalewa, Myan. B2 34
Kalgin Island, i., Ak., U.S. g16 95
Kalgoorlie-Boulder, Austl. G3 60
Kalibo, Phil. D8 34
Kalima, D.R.C. D5 54
Kalimantan see Borneo, i., Asia D4 36
Kálimnos, Grc. F11 18
Kálimnos, i., Grc. F11 18
Kālimpang, India D5 40
Kalinin see Tver', Russia D5 26
Kaliningrad, Russia D4 26
Kalinkavičy, Bela. C10 20
Kalispel Indian Reservation, Wa., U.S. A8 140
Kalispell, Mt., U.S. B2 119
Kalisz, Pol. D5 20
Kalixälven, stm., Swe. C9 10
Kalkaska, Mi., U.S. D5 115
Kalkaska, co., Mi., U.S. D5 115
Kallavesi, l., Fin. E12 10
Kalmar, Swe. H7 10
Kalmarsund, strt., Swe. H7 10
Kalmykija, state, Russia E6 26
Kalohi Channel, strt., Hi., U.S. C4 104
Kaloli Point, c., Hi., U.S. D7 104
Kalomo, Zam. B4 56
Kalona, Ia., U.S. C6 108
Kalone Peak, mtn., B.C., Can. C4 85
Kalpin, China A3 40
Kalsūbai, mtn., India F2 40
Kaluga, Russia D5 26
Kalundborg, Den. I4 10
Kalush, Ukr. E8 20
Kalutara, Sri L. H4 40
Kalyān, India F2 40
Kama, D.R.C. D5 54
Kama, stm., Russia D7 26
Kamaishi, Japan D16 28
Kamakou, mtn., Hi., U.S. B5 104
Kamālia, Pak. D10 42
Kaman, Tur. C5 44
Kamarān, i., Yemen G4 38
Kama Reservoir see Kamskoe vodohranilišče, res., Russia C10 22
Kamas, Ut., U.S. C4 137
Kambalda, Austl. G3 60
Kambove, D.R.C. F5 54
Kamčatka, poluostrov, pen., Russia D17 26
Kamchatka Peninsula see Kamčatka, poluostrov, pen., Russia D17 26
Kamen', gora, mtn., Russia C11 26
Kamenka, Russia D15 20
Kamenka, Russia D7 22
Kamen'-na-Obi, Russia D10 26
Kamenskoe, Russia C18 26
Kamensk-Ural'skij, Russia C11 22
Kāmet, mtn., Asia C3 40
Kamiah, Id., U.S. C2 105
Kamiak Butte, mtn., Wa., U.S. C8 140
Kam'ianets'-Podil's'kyi, Ukr. E9 20
Kamina, D.R.C. E5 54
Kamloops, B.C., Can. D7 85
Kamo, Arm. B11 44
Kampala, Ug. C6 54
Kampar, Malay. C2 36
Kampen, Neth. D9 12
Kampeska, Lake, l., S.D., U.S. C8 134
Kamphaeng Phet, Thai. C3 34
Kâmpóng Cham, Camb. D5 34
Kâmpóng Chhnăng, Camb. D4 34
Kâmpóng Saôm, Camb. D4 34
Kâmpóng Thum, Camb. D4 34
Kâmpôt, Camb. D4 34
Kampti, Burkina D4 50
Kampuchea see Cambodia, ctry., Asia D4 34
Kamskoe vodohranilišče, res., Russia C10 22
Kamuela (Waimea), Hi., U.S. C6 104
Kamyšin, Russia D6 26
Kamyšlov, Russia C11 22
Kanab, Ut., U.S. F3 137
Kanab Creek, stm., U.S. A3 96
Kanabec, co., Mn., U.S. E5 116
Kanaga Island, i., Ak., U.S. E4 95
Kanairiktok, stm., Nf., Can. g9 88
Kananga, D.R.C. E4 54
Kanapou Bay, b., Hi., U.S. C5 104
Kanaš, Russia C8 22
Kanata, On., Can. B9 89
Kanawha, Ia., U.S. B4 108
Kanawha, co., W.V., U.S. C3 141
Kanawha, stm., W.V., U.S. C3 141
Kanazawa, Japan D15 28
Kānchenjunga, mtn., Asia D5 40
Kānchipuram, India G3 40
Kandahar see Qandahār, Afg. D9 42
Kandalakša, Russia C15 10
Kandalaksha Bay see Kandalakšskaja guba, b., Russia A5 22

Name — Map Ref. — Page

Kandalakšskaja guba, b., Russia A5 22
Kandale, D.R.C. E3 54
Kandangan, Indon. D5 36
Kandi, Benin D5 50
Kandıra, Tur. B4 44
Kandiyohi, co., Mn., U.S. E3 116
Kandy, Sri L. H4 40
Kane, Pa., U.S. C4 131
Kane, co., Il., U.S. B5 106
Kane, co., Ut., U.S. F3 137
Kanem, prov., Chad D8 50
Kaneohe, Hi., U.S. B4 104
Kaneohe Bay, b., Hi., U.S. g10 104
Kaneohe Bay Marine Corps Air Station, mil., Hi., U.S. g10 104
Kangaba, Mali D3 50
Kangal, Tur. C7 44
Kangān, Iran E6 42
Kangar, Malay. B2 36
Kangaroo Island, i., Austl. H2 62
Kangāvar, Iran E12 44
Kangbao, China A3 30
Kangean, Pulau, i., Indon. E5 36
Kanggye, N. Kor. C13 28
Kango, Gabon C2 54
Kangpu, China A3 34
Kangrinboqê Feng, mtn., China E4 28
Kangshan, Tai. E5 30
Kangto, mtn., Asia A2 34
Kaniama, D.R.C. E4 54
Kaniet Islands, is., Pap. N. Gui. G12 32
Kanin, poluostrov, pen., Russia C6 26
Kaningo, Kenya D7 54
Kanin Nos, Russia A7 22
Kanin Nos, mys, c., Russia C6 26
Kanjiža, Yugo. A8 18
Kankakee, Il., U.S. B6 106
Kankakee, co., Il., U.S. B6 106
Kankakee, stm., U.S. B5 106
Kankan, Gui. D3 50
Kānker, India E4 40
Kanmaw Kyun, i., Myan. D3 34
Kannapolis, N.C., U.S. B2 126
Kannonkoski, Fin. E11 10
Kano, Nig. D6 50
Kanopolis, Ks., U.S. D5 109
Kanopolis Lake, res., Ks., U.S. D5 109
Kanoya, Japan D2 31
Kānpur, India D4 40
Kansas, Il., U.S. D6 106
Kansas, state, U.S. D5 109
Kansas, stm., Ks., U.S. C7 109
Kansas City, Ks., U.S. C9 109
Kansas City, Mo., U.S. B3 118
Kansk, Russia D11 26
Kantang, Thai. E3 34
Kantchari, Burkina D5 50
Kantemirovka, Russia E15 20
Kanye, Bots. D4 56
Kaohsiung, Tai. E5 30
Kaoko Veld, plat., Nmb. B1 56
Kaolack, Sen. D1 50
Kaoma, Zam. A3 56
Kaouar, reg., Niger C7 50
Kapaa, Hi., U.S. A2 104
Kapaau, Hi., U.S. C6 104
Kapan, Arm. C12 44
Kapanga, D.R.C. E4 54
Kapapa Island, i., Hi., U.S. g10 104
Kapčagaj, Kaz. B11 42
Kapčagajskoe vodohranilišče, res., Kaz. B11 42
Kapchagay Reservoir see Kapčagajskoe vodohranilišče, res., Kaz. B11 42
Kapfenberg, Aus. G14 12
Kapiri Mposhi, Zam. A4 56
Kaplan, La., U.S. D3 111
Kapoeta, Sudan C6 54
Kaposvár, Hung. F4 20
Kaptai Lake see Karnaphuli Reservoir, res., Bngl. E6 40
Kapuas, stm., Indon. D3 36
Kapuas, stm., Indon. D4 36
Kapuas Hulu, Pegunungan (Kapuas Hulu, Pergunungan), mts., Asia C4 36
Kapuas Hulu, Pergunungan (Kapuas Hulu, Pegunungan), mts., Asia C4 36
Kapuskasing, On., Can. o19 89
Kapuvár, Hung. F4 20
Kapyl', Bela. C9 20
Kara, Russia C8 26
Kara-Balta, Kyrg. A2 40
Karabaš, Russia C11 22
Kara-Bogaz-Gol, zaliv, b., Turk. E7 26
Kara-Bogaz-Gol Gulf see Kara-Bogaz-Gol, zaliv, b., Turk. E7 26
Karabük, Tur. B5 44
Karabula, Russia D11 26
Karaburun, Tur. C2 44
Karabutak, Kaz. E11 22
Karacabey, Tur. B3 44
Karačaevo-Čerkesija, state, Russia E6 26
Karačev, Russia C13 20
Karāchi, Pak. F9 42
Karād, India F2 40
Karaganda, Kaz. E9 26
Karaginskij, ostrov, i., Russia D18 26
Karaginskij zaliv, b., Russia D18 26
Kāraikkudi, India G3 40
Karaj, Iran C6 42
Karakaya Barajı, res., Tur. C8 44
Karakelong, Pulau, i., Indon. F8 32
Karakol, Kyrg. E9 26
Karakoram Pass, Asia B3 40
Karakoram Range, mts., Asia B3 40
Karakul', Uzb. C8 42
Kara-Kum Canal see Garagumskij kanal imeni Prezidenta Turkmenistana S.A. Nijazova, Turk. C8 42
Karaman, Tur. D5 44
Karamay, China B4 28
Karamea Bight, b., N.Z. p13 63c
Karapınar, Tur. D5 44
Karasay, China B4 40
Karasburg, Nmb. D2 56
Kara Sea see Karskoe more, Russia B8 26
Karasu, Tur. B4 44
Karasu, stm., Tur. C9 44
Karasuk, Russia D9 26
Karatau, Kaz. B10 42
Karatau, hrebet, mts., Kaz. E8 26
Karatobe, Kaz. E9 22
Karaton, Kaz. A6 42
Karatsu, Japan D1 31
Karaul, Kaz. B3 28
Karaul, Russia B10 26
Karawang, Indon. E3 36
Karažal, Kaz. B2 28
Karbalā', Iraq D4 42
Karbalā', state, Iraq F10 44
Kårböle, Swe. F6 10
Karcag, Hung. F6 20
Kardeljevo, Cro. C6 18
Kardhítsa, Grc. E8 18
Kărdžali, Bul. D10 18
Karelia see Karelija, state, Russia C5 26
Karelia, hist. reg., Eur. C12 6
Karelija, state, Russia C5 26
Karema, Tan. E6 54
Karesuando, Swe. B10 10
Kargopol', Russia C5 26
Kariba, Zimb. B4 56
Kariba, Lake, res., Afr. B4 56
Karibib, Nmb. C2 56
Karigasniemi, Fin. B11 10
Karimata, Selat (Karimata Strait), strt., Indon. D3 36
Karimata Strait see Karimata, Selat, strt., Indon. D3 36
Karīmganj, India E6 40
Karīmnagar, India F3 40
Karimunjawa, Pulau, i., Indon. E4 36
Karisimbi, Volcan, vol., Afr. D5 54
Karkaralinsk, Kaz. B3 28
Karkar Island, i., Pap. N. Gui. G12 32
Karkheh, stm., Iran G12 44
Karkinits'ka zatoka, b., Ukr. G12 20
Karkūk, Iraq C4 42
Karlivka, Ukr. E13 20
Karl-Marx-Stadt see Chemnitz, Ger. E13 12
Karlovac, Cro. B5 18
Karlovy Vary, Czech Rep. D2 20
Karlshamn, Swe. H6 10
Karlskoga, Swe. G6 10
Karlskrona, Swe. H6 10
Karlsruhe, Ger. F11 12
Karlstad, Swe. G5 10
Karlstad, Mn., U.S. B2 116
Karma, Niger D5 50
Karnāl, India D3 40
Karnaphuli Reservoir, res., Bngl. E6 40
Karnātaka, prov., India G3 40
Karnes, co., Tx., U.S. E4 136
Karnes City, Tx., U.S. E4 136
Karns, Tn., U.S. n13 135
Kárpathos, i., Grc. G11 18
Karpogory, Russia B7 22
Karratha, Austl. E2 60
Kars, Tur. B10 44
Karsakpaj, Kaz. B1 28
Karši, Uzb. F8 26
Karskie Vorota, proliv, strt., Russia B7 26
Karskoe more, Russia B8 26
Kartaly, Russia D8 26
Karufa, Indon. D8 36
Kārūn, stm., Iran G13 44
Karūr, India G3 40
Karviná, Czech Rep. E5 20
Kārwār, India G2 40
Karymskoe, Russia A10 28
Kasai (Cassai), stm., Afr. D3 54
Kasaji, D.R.C. F4 54
Kasama, Zam. A5 56
Kasane, Bots. B4 56
Kasanga, Tan. E6 54
Kasangulu, D.R.C. D3 54
Kāsaragod, India G3 40
Kasempa, Zam. A4 56
Kasenga, D.R.C. F5 54
Kasenye, D.R.C. C6 54
Kasese, D.R.C. D5 54
Kasese, Ug. C6 54
Kāshān, Iran D6 42
Kashgar see Kashi, China D3 28
Kashi, China D3 28
Kāshmar, Iran C7 42
Kasimov, Russia B16 20
Kasiruta, Pulau, i., Indon. D7 36
Kaskaskia, stm., Il., U.S. D5 106
Kaslo, B.C., Can. E9 85
Kasongo, D.R.C. D5 54
Kasongo-Lunda, D.R.C. E3 54
Kásos, i., Grc. G11 18
Kasota, Mn., U.S. F5 116
Kaspi, Geor. B11 44
Kaspijsk, Russia A12 44
Kaspijskij, Russia E6 26
Kassalā, Sudan G12 48
Kassandra, Gulf of see Kassándras, Kólpos, b., Grc. D9 18
Kassándras, Kólpos, b., Grc. D9 18
Kassel, Ger. E11 12
Kasserine, Tun. C6 48
Kasson, Mn., U.S. F6 116
Kastamonu, Tur. B5 44
Kastoría, Grc. D8 18
Kasulu, Tan. D6 54
Kasūr, Pak. D10 42
Kataba, Zam. B4 56
Katahdin, Mount, mtn., Me., U.S. C4 112
Katako-Kombe, D.R.C. D4 54
Katanga, hist. reg., D.R.C. E4 54
Katangli, Russia D16 26
Katanning, Austl. G2 60
Katchall Island, i., India H6 40
Kateríni, Grc. D9 18
Kates Needle, mtn., Ak., U.S. m24 95
Katha, Myan. B3 34
Katherîna, Gebel, mtn., Egypt E11 48
Katherine, Austl. C5 60
Kāthiāwār Peninsula, pen., India E2 40
Kathleen, Fl., U.S. D4 102
Kāṭhmāṇḍu, Nepal D5 40
Kati, Mali D3 50
Katihār, India D5 40
Katiola, C. Iv. E3 50
Katmai, Mount, mtn., Ak., U.S. D9 95
Katmai National Park, Ak., U.S. D9 95
Kātmāndu see Kāṭhmāṇḍu, Nepal D5 40
Katompi, D.R.C. E5 54
Katoomba, Austl. G5 62
Katowice, Pol. D5 20
Katrineholm, Swe. G7 10
Katsina, Nig. D6 50
Kattakurgan, Uzb. C9 42
Kattegat, strt., Eur. B12 12
Katy, Tx., U.S. r14 136
Kauai, co., Hi., U.S. B1 104
Kauai, i., Hi., U.S. A2 104
Kauai Channel, strt., Hi., U.S. h17 92a
Kauai Channel, strt., Hi., U.S. B3 104
Kau Desert, des., Hi., U.S. D6 104
Kaufbeuren, Ger. G12 12
Kaufman, Tx., U.S. C4 136
Kaufman, co., Tx., U.S. C4 136
Kauiki Head, c., Hi., U.S. C6 104
Kaukauna, Wi., U.S. D5 142
Kaula Island, i., Hi., U.S. m15 104
Kaulakahi Channel, strt., Hi., U.S. A2 104
Kaumakani, Hi., U.S. B2 104
Kaunakakai, Hi., U.S. B4 104
Kauna Point, c., Hi., U.S. D6 104
Kaura-Namoda, Nig. D6 50
Kavača, Russia C19 26
Kavadarci, Mac. D8 18
Kavála, Grc. D10 18
Kavalerovo, Russia C15 28
Kāvali, India G4 40
Kavaratti, India G2 40
Kāveri, stm., India G3 40
Kavieng, Pap. N. Gui. G13 32
Kavīr, Dasht-e, des., Iran D6 42
Kawaihoa Point, c., Hi., U.S. B1 104
Kawaikini, mtn., Hi., U.S. A2 104
Kawambwa, Zam. E5 54
Kawasaki, Japan D15 28
Kawerau, N.Z. o14 63c
Kawich Peak, mtn., Nv., U.S. F5 121
Kawich Range, mts., Nv., U.S. F5 121
Kaw Lake, res., Ok., U.S. A5 129
Kaxgar, stm., China B3 40
Kay, co., Ok., U.S. A4 129
Kaya, Burkina D4 50
Kaycee, Wy., U.S. C6 143
Kayenta, Az., U.S. A5 96
Kayes, Mali D2 50
Kayseri, Tur. C6 44
Kaysville, Ut., U.S. B4 137
Kayuagung, Indon. D2 36
Kazače, Russia B15 26
Kazahskij melkosopočnik, hills, Kaz. D9 26
Kazakh Hills see Kazahskij melkosopočnik, hills, Kaz. D9 26
Kazakstan, ctry., Asia E8 26
Kazalinsk, Kaz. A8 42
Kazan', Russia D6 26
Kazanka, Ukr. F12 20
Kazanlăk, Bul. C10 18
Kazan-rettō, is., Japan F17 64
Kazbek, gora, vol. A11 44
Kāzerūn, Iran E6 42
Kazincbarcika, Hung. E6 20
Kaztalovka, Kaz. E8 22
Kazym, Russia B12 22
Kéa, i., Grc. F10 18
Keaau, Hi., U.S. D6 104
Keahiakahoe, Puu, mtn., Hi., U.S. g10 104
Keahole Point, c., Hi., U.S. D5 104
Kealaikahiki Channel, strt., Hi., U.S. C5 104
Kealaikahiki Point, c., Hi., U.S. C5 104
Kealakekua, Hi., U.S. D6 104
Kealia, Hi., U.S. A2 104
Keams Canyon, Az., U.S. B5 96
Keanapapa Point, c., Hi., U.S. C4 104
Keansburg, N.J., U.S. C4 123
Kearney, Mo., U.S. B3 118
Kearney, Ne., U.S. D6 120
Kearney, co., Ne., U.S. D7 120
Kearns, Ut., U.S. C4 137
Kearny, Az., U.S. D5 96
Kearny, N.J., U.S. h8 123
Kearny, co., Ks., U.S. D2 109
Keban Barajı, res., Tur. C8 44
Keban Reservoir see Keban Barajı, res., Tur. C8 44
Kébèmer, Sen. C1 50
Kebnekaise, mtn., Swe. C8 10
K'ebrī Dehar, Eth. B8 54
Kecskemét, Hung. F5 20
Kedges Straits, strt., Md., U.S. D5 113
Kedgwick, N.B., Can. B2 87
Kediri, Indon. E4 36
Kedon, Russia C17 26
Kédougou, Sen. D2 50
Keego Harbor, Mi., U.S. o15 115
Keene, N.H., U.S. E2 122
Keene, Tx., U.S. n9 136
Keer-Weer, Cape, c., Austl. C3 62
Keeseville, N.Y., U.S. f11 125
Keesler Air Force Base, mil., Ms., U.S. E5 117
Keetmanshoop, Nmb. D2 56
Keet Seel Ruin, hist., Az., U.S. A5 96
Keewatin, On., Can. E4 86
Keewatin, Mn., U.S. C5 116
Kefallinía, i., Grc. E8 18
Kefamenanu, Indon. E6 36
Keffi, Nig. E6 50
Keflavík, Ice. m17 10a
Kegonsa, Lake, l., Wi., U.S. F4 142
Kehra, Est. G11 10
Ke-hsi Mānsām, Myan. B3 34
Keila, Est. G11 10
Keiser, Ar., U.S. B5 97
Keith, co., Ne., U.S. C4 120
Keizer, Or., U.S. C3 130
Kejimkujik National Park, N.S., Can. E4 87
Kekaha, Hi., U.S. B2 104
Kékes, mtn., Hung. F5 20
K'elafo, Eth. B8 54
Kelan, China B3 30
Kelantan, stm., Malay. B2 36
Kelibia, Tun. F3 18
Kelkit, Tur. B8 44
Kelkit, stm., Tur. B7 44
Keller, Tx., U.S. n9 136
Kellerberrin, Austl. G2 60
Kelleys Island, i., Oh., U.S. A3 128
Kellogg, Ia., U.S. C5 108
Kellogg, Id., U.S. B2 105
Kelloselkä, Fin. C13 10
Kelly Air Force Base, mil., Tx., U.S. k7 136
Kelly Island, i., De., U.S. D4 101
Kellyville, Ok., U.S. B5 129
Kélo, Chad E8 50
Kelowna, B.C., Can. E8 85
Kelso, Wa., U.S. C3 140
Keluang, Malay. C2 36
Kem', Russia C5 26
Kembé, C.A.R. C4 54
Kemerovo, Russia D10 26
Kemi, Fin. D11 10
Kemijärvi, Fin. C12 10
Kemijoki, stm., Fin. C11 10
Kemmerer, Wy., U.S. E2 143
Kemp, Tx., U.S. C4 136
Kemp, Lake, res., Tx., U.S. C3 136
Kemper, co., Ms., U.S. C5 117
Kempsey, Austl. G5 62
Kempten, Ger. G12 12
Kemptville, On., Can. B9 89
Kemul, Kong, mtn., Indon. C5 36
Kenai, Ak., U.S. C9 95
Kenai Fjords National Park, Ak., U.S. D10 95
Kenai Mountains, mts., Ak., U.S. h16 95
Kenai Peninsula, pen., Ak., U.S. h16 95
Kenansville, N.C., U.S. C5 126
Kenbridge, Va., U.S. D4 139
Kendal, Eng., U.K. C5 12
Kendall, Fl., U.S. s13 102
Kendall, co., Il., U.S. B5 106
Kendall, co., Tx., U.S. E3 136
Kendall Park, N.J., U.S. C3 123
Kendallville, In., U.S. B7 107
Kendari, Indon. D6 36
Kendawangan, Indon. D4 36
Kenedy, Tx., U.S. E4 136
Kenedy, co., Tx., U.S. F4 136
Kenema, S.L. E2 50
Kenesaw, Ne., U.S. D7 120
Kenge, D.R.C. D3 54
Kēng Tung, Myan. B3 34
Kenhardt, S. Afr. D3 56
Kenilworth, Il., U.S. h9 106
Kénitra, Mor. D3 48
Kenly, N.C., U.S. B4 126
Kenmare, N.D., U.S. A3 127
Kenmore, N.Y., U.S. C2 125
Kennaday Peak, mtn., Wy., U.S. E6 143
Kennebago Lake, l., Me., U.S. C2 112
Kennebec, co., Me., U.S. D3 112
Kennebec, stm., Me., U.S. D3 112
Kennebunk, Me., U.S. E2 112
Kennebunkport, Me., U.S. E2 112
Kennedy, Cape see Canaveral, Cape, c., Fl., U.S. D6 102
Kennedy Entrance, strt., Ak., U.S. D9 95
Kenner, La., U.S. E5 111
Kennesaw, Ga., U.S. B2 103
Kennesaw Mountain, mtn., Ga., U.S. C2 103
Kennett, Mo., U.S. E7 118
Kennett Square, Pa., U.S. G10 131
Kennewick, Wa., U.S. C6 140
Keno, Or., U.S. E5 130
Kénogami, Lac, l., P.Q., Can. A6 90
Kenora, On., Can. o16 89
Kenosha, Wi., U.S. F6 142
Kenosha, co., Wi., U.S. F5 142
Kenova, W.V., U.S. C2 141
Kensett, Ar., U.S. B4 97
Kensico Reservoir, res., N.Y., U.S. g13 125
Kensington, P.E., Can. C6 87
Kensington, Ct., U.S. C4 100
Kensington, Md., U.S. B3 113
Kent, Oh., U.S. A4 128
Kent, Wa., U.S. B3 140
Kent, co., De., U.S. D3 101
Kent, co., Md., U.S. B5 113
Kent, co., Mi., U.S. E5 115
Kent, co., R.I., U.S. D2 132
Kent, co., Tx., U.S. C2 136
Kentau, Kaz. B9 42
Kent City, Mi., U.S. E5 115
Kent Island, i., De., U.S. D4 101
Kent Island, i., Md., U.S. C5 113
Kentland, In., U.S. C3 107
Kenton, De., U.S. D3 101
Kenton, Oh., U.S. B2 128
Kenton, Tn., U.S. A2 135
Kenton, co., Ky., U.S. B5 110
Kent Point, c., Md., U.S. C5 113
Kentucky, state, U.S. C4 110
Kentucky, stm., Ky., U.S. B5 110
Kentucky Lake, res., U.S. D10 92
Kentwood, La., U.S. D5 111
Kentwood, Mi., U.S. F5 115
Kenvil, N.J., U.S. B3 123
Kenvir, Ky., U.S. D6 110
Kenya, ctry., Afr. C7 54
Kenya, Mount see Kirinyaga, mtn., Kenya D7 54
Kenyon, Mn., U.S. F6 116
Kenyon, R.I., U.S. F2 132
Keokea, Hi., U.S. C5 104
Keokuk, Ia., U.S. D6 108
Keokuk, co., Ia., U.S. C5 108
Keokuk Lock and Dam, U.S. D6 108
Keosauqua, Ia., U.S. D6 108
Keota, Ia., U.S. C6 108
Keota, Ok., U.S. B7 129
Keowee, Lake, res., S.C., U.S. B2 133
Kępno, Pol. D4 20
Kerala, prov., India G3 40
Kerang, Austl. H3 62
Kerava, Fin. F11 10
Kerch, Ukr. G14 20
Kerch Strait, strt., Eur. G14 20
Keremeos, B.C., Can. E8 85
Keren, Erit. G12 48
Kerens, Tx., U.S. C4 136
Kerguélen, Îles, is., Afr. M10 64
Kerguelen Plateau N10 64
Kerhonkson, N.Y., U.S. D6 125
Kericho, Kenya D7 54
Kerinci, Gunung, vol., Indon. D2 36

Name	Map Ref.	Page
Kerkhoven, Mn., U.S.	E3	116
Kerki, Turk.	C9	42
Kerkiči, Turk.	F8	26
Kérkira, Grc.	E7	18
Kérkira (Corfu), i., Grc.	E7	18
Kermadec Islands, is., N.Z.	G12	58
Kermadec Ridge	L20	64
Kermadec Trench	L21	64
Kermān, Iran	D7	42
Kermānshāh (Bākhtarān), Iran	D5	42
Kermit, Tx., U.S.	D1	136
Kermode, Mount, mtn., B.C., Can.	C2	85
Kern, co., Ca., U.S.	E4	98
Kern, stm., Ca., U.S.	E4	98
Kernersville, N.C., U.S.	A2	126
Kernville, Ca., U.S.	E4	98
Kérouané, Gui.	E3	50
Kerr, co., Tx., U.S.	D3	136
Kerr, Lake, l., Fl., U.S.	C5	102
Kerrville, Tx., U.S.	D3	136
Kersey, Co., U.S.	A6	99
Kershaw, S.C., U.S.	B6	133
Kershaw, co., S.C., U.S.	C6	133
Kerulen, stm., Asia	B10	28
Keşan, Tur.	B2	44
Kesennuma, Japan	D16	28
Keshena, Wi., U.S.	D5	142
Keskin, Tur.	C5	44
Kesten'ga, Russia	D14	10
Keszthely, Hung.	F4	20
Ket', stm., Russia	D10	26
Keta, Ghana	E5	50
Ketapang, Indon.	D3	36
Ketchikan, Ak., U.S.	D13	95
Ketchum, Id., U.S.	F4	105
Kete-Krachi, Ghana	E4	50
Kętrzyn, Pol.	B6	20
Kettering, Oh., U.S.	C1	128
Kettle, stm., Mn., U.S.	D6	116
Kettle Creek, stm., Pa., U.S.	D6	131
Kettle Creek Lake, res., Pa., U.S.	D6	131
Kettle Falls, Wa., U.S.	A7	140
Keuka Lake, l., N.Y., U.S.	C3	125
Kewanee, Il., U.S.	B4	106
Kewaskum, Wi., U.S.	E5	142
Kewaunee, Wi., U.S.	D6	142
Kewaunee, co., Wi., U.S.	D6	142
Keweenaw, co., Mi., U.S.	A2	115
Keweenaw Bay, b., Mi., U.S.	B2	115
Keweenaw Peninsula, pen., Mi., U.S.	A3	115
Keweenaw Point, c., Mi., U.S.	A3	115
Keya Paha, co., Ne., U.S.	B6	120
Keya Paha, stm., U.S.	A5	120
Keyhole Reservoir, res., Wy., U.S.	B8	143
Key Largo, Fl., U.S.	G6	102
Keyport, N.J., U.S.	C4	123
Keyser, W.V., U.S.	B6	141
Keystone, W.V., U.S.	D3	141
Keystone Heights, Fl., U.S.	C4	102
Keystone Lake, res., Ok., U.S.	A5	129
Keystone Peak, mtn., Az., U.S.	F4	96
Keysville, Va., U.S.	C4	139
Key West, Fl., U.S.	H5	102
Key West Naval Air Station, mil., Fl., U.S.	H5	102
Kezar Falls, Me., U.S.	E2	112
Kezar Lake, l., Me., U.S.	D2	112
Kezi, Zimb.	C4	56
Kežma, Russia	D12	26
Khābūr, Nahr al-, stm., Asia	E9	44
Khadki, India	F2	40
Khairpur, Pak.	E9	42
Khajrāho, India	E4	40
Khakhea, Bots.	C3	56
Khalkhāl, Iran	D13	44
Khalkidhikí, hist. reg., Grc.	D9	18
Khalkís, Grc.	E9	18
Khambhāt, India	E2	40
Khambhāt, Gulf of, b., India	E2	40
Khāmgaon, India	E3	40
Khammam, India	F4	40
Khānābād, Afg.	C9	42
Khān al-Baghdādī, Iraq	F10	44
Khānaqīn, Iraq	E11	44
Khandwa, India	E3	40
Khānewāl, Pak.	D10	42
Khaniá, Grc.	G9	18
Khaníon, Kólpos, b., Grc.	G9	18
Khanka, Lake, l., Asia	C14	28
Khānpur, Pak.	E10	42
Kharagpur, India	E5	40
Khargon, India	E3	40
Kharkiv, Ukr.	E14	20
Khartoum see Al-Kharṭūm, Sudan	G11	48
Khāsh, Afg.	D8	42
Khāsh, Iran	E8	42
Khashm al-Qirbah, Sudan	H12	48
Khemis Melyana, Alg.	I8	16
Khenchla, Alg.	D5	14
Khenifra, Mor.	E2	14
Kherson, Ukr.	F12	20
Khíos, Grc.	E11	18
Khíos, i., Grc.	E10	18
Khmel'nyts'kyi, Ukr.	E9	20
Khmil'nyk, Ukr.	E9	20
Kholm, Afg.	C9	42
Khomeynīshahr, Iran	D6	42
Khong see Mekong, stm., Asia	C4	34
Khon Kaen, Thai.	C4	34
Khorramābād, Iran	D5	42
Khorramshahr, Iran	D5	42
Khotyn, Ukr.	E9	20
Khouribga, Mor.	D3	48
Khrystynivka, Ukr.	E10	20
Khulna, Bngl.	E5	40
Khust, Ukr.	E7	20
Khuzdār, Pak.	E9	42
Khvoy, Iran	C4	42
Khyber Pass, Asia	C2	40
Kiama, D.R.C.	E3	54
Kiamba, Phil.	E8	34
Kiamichi, stm., Ok., U.S.	C6	129
Kiamika, stm., P.Q., Can.	C2	90
Kiana, Ak., U.S.	B7	95
Kiangarow, Mount, mtn., Austl.	F5	62
Kiawah Island, i., S.C., U.S.	F7	133
Kibangou, Congo	D2	54
Kibombo, D.R.C.	D5	54
Kibondo, Tan.	D6	54
Kibre Mengist, Eth.	B7	54
Kičevo, Mac.	D8	18
Kickamuit, stm., R.I., U.S.	D5	132
Kickapoo, stm., Wi., U.S.	E3	142
Kickapoo, Lake, res., Tx., U.S.	C3	136
Kickapoo Indian Reservation, Ks., U.S.	C8	109
Kicking Horse Pass, Can.	D2	84
Kidal, Mali	C5	50
Kidatu, Tan.	E7	54
Kidder, co., N.D., U.S.	C6	127
Kidira, Sen.	D2	50
Kiefer, Ok., U.S.	B5	129
Kiel, Ger.	C12	12
Kiel, Wi., U.S.	E5	142
Kiel Bay see Kieler Bucht, b., Ger.	C12	12
Kiel Canal see Nord-Ostsee-Kanal, Ger.	C11	12
Kielce, Pol.	D6	20
Kieler Bucht, b., Ger.	C12	12
Kiester, Mn., U.S.	G5	116
Kiev see Kyïv, Ukr.	D11	20
Kiev Reservoir see Kyïvs'ke vodoskhovyshche, res., Ukr.	D11	20
Kiffa, Maur.	C2	50
Kigali, Rw.	D6	54
Kigoma, Tan.	D5	54
Kihčik, Russia	D17	26
Kihei, Hi., U.S.	C5	104
Kiholo Bay, b., Hi., U.S.	D5	104
Kii Strait see Kii-suidō, strt., Japan	E15	28
Kii-suidō, strt., Japan	E15	28
Kikinda, Yugo.	B8	18
Kikládhes, is., Grc.	F10	18
Kikori, Pap. N. Gui.	H11	32
Kikwit, D.R.C.	E3	54
Kil, Swe.	G5	10
Kilauea, Hi., U.S.	A2	104
Kilauea Crater, crat., Hi., U.S.	D6	104
Kilauea Point, c., Hi., U.S.	A2	104
Kilchu-ŭp, N. Kor.	B1	31
Kildurk, Austl.	D4	60
Kilgore, Tx., U.S.	C5	136
Kilibo, Benin	E5	50
Kiliia, Ukr.	G10	20
Kilimanjaro, mtn., Tan.	D7	54
Kilimli, Tur.	B4	44
Kilindoni, Tan.	E7	54
Kilis, Tur.	D7	44
Kilkenny, Ire.	D3	12
Kilkís, Grc.	D9	18
Killaloe Station, On., Can.	B7	89
Killam, Ab., Can.	C5	84
Killarney, Mb., Can.	E2	86
Killarney Provincial Park, On., Can.	A3	89
Killdeer, N.D., U.S.	B3	127
Killeen, Tx., U.S.	D4	136
Killen, Al., U.S.	A2	94
Killian, La., U.S.	h10	111
Killik, stm., Ak., U.S.	B9	95
Killiniq Island, i., Can.	F27	82
Killona, La., U.S.	h11	111
Kilmarnock, Scot., U.K.	C4	12
Kilmarnock, Va., U.S.	C6	139
Kilmichael, Ms., U.S.	B4	117
Kiln, Ms., U.S.	E4	117
Kilomines, D.R.C.	C6	54
Kilosa, Tan.	E7	54
Kilttān Island, i., India	G2	40
Kilwa, D.R.C.	E5	54
Kilwa Kivinje, Tan.	E7	54
Kimba, Austl.	G2	62
Kimball, Mn., U.S.	E4	116
Kimball, Ne., U.S.	C2	120
Kimball, S.D., U.S.	D7	134
Kimball, co., Ne., U.S.	C2	120
Kimball, Mount, mtn., Ak., U.S.	C11	95
Kimberley, B.C., Can.	E9	85
Kimberley, S. Afr.	D3	56
Kimberley Plateau, plat., Austl.	D4	60
Kimberlin Heights, Tn., U.S.	n14	135
Kimberly, Al., U.S.	B3	94
Kimberly, Id., U.S.	G4	105
Kimberly, W.V., U.S.	m13	141
Kimberly, Wi., U.S.	h9	142
Kimble, co., Tx., U.S.	D3	136
Kimch'aek, N. Kor.	C13	28
Kimito, i., Fin.	G10	10
Kimry, Russia	C6	22
Kinabalu, Gunong, mtn., Malay.	B5	36
Kinabatangan, stm., Malay.	B5	36
Kinbasket Lake, res., B.C., Can.	D8	85
Kincaid, Il., U.S.	D4	106
Kincaid, W.V., U.S.	m13	141
Kincaid, Lake, res., Il., U.S.	D4	106
Kincardine, On., Can.	C3	89
Kincheloe Air Force Base, mil., Mi., U.S.	B6	115
Kinda, D.R.C.	E5	54
Kinder, La., U.S.	D3	111
Kindia, Gui.	D2	50
Kindu, D.R.C.	D5	54
Kinešma, Russia	C7	22
King, N.C., U.S.	A2	126
King, Wi., U.S.	D4	142
King, co., Tx., U.S.	C2	136
King, co., Wa., U.S.	B3	140
King and Queen, co., Va., U.S.	C6	139
Kingaroy, Austl.	F5	62
King City, Ca., U.S.	D3	98
King City, Mo., U.S.	A3	118
King Cove, Ak., U.S.	E7	95
Kingfield, Me., U.S.	D2	112
Kingfisher, Ok., U.S.	B4	129
Kingfisher, co., Ok., U.S.	B3	129
King George, co., Va., U.S.	B5	139
Kingisepp, Russia	G13	10
King Island, i., Austl.	H3	62
King Island, i., B.C., Can.	C4	85
King Lear Peak, mtn., Nv., U.S.	B3	121
King Leopold Ranges, mts., Austl.	D3	60
Kingman, Az., U.S.	B1	96
Kingman, Ks., U.S.	E5	109
Kingman, co., Ks., U.S.	E5	109
King Mountain, mtn., Or., U.S.	D8	130
King Mountain, mtn., Or., U.S.	E3	130
Kingombe, D.R.C.	D5	54
King Peak, mtn., Ca., U.S.	B1	98
Kings, Ms., U.S.	C3	117
Kings, co., Ca., U.S.	D4	98
Kings, co., N.Y., U.S.	E7	125
Kings, stm., Ar., U.S.	A2	97
Kings, stm., Ca., U.S.	D4	98
Kings, stm., Nv., U.S.	B3	121
King Salmon, Ak., U.S.	D8	95
Kingsburg, Ca., U.S.	D4	98
Kingsbury, co., S.D., U.S.	C8	134
Kings Canyon National Park, Ca., U.S.	D4	98
Kingsey-Falls, P.Q., Can.	D5	90
Kingsford, Mi., U.S.	C2	115
Kingsland, Ga., U.S.	F5	103
Kingsland, Tx., U.S.	D3	136
Kingsley, Ia., U.S.	B2	108
Kingsley, Mi., U.S.	D5	115
King's Lynn, Eng., U.K.	D7	12
Kings Mountain, N.C., U.S.	B1	126
King Sound, strt., Austl.	D3	60
Kings Peak, mtn., Ut., U.S.	C5	137
King's Point, Nf., Can.	D3	88
Kingsport, Tn., U.S.	C11	135
Kingston, On., Can.	C8	89
Kingston, Jam.	B4	80
Kingston, Ga., U.S.	B2	103
Kingston, Id., U.S.	B2	105
Kingston, Ma., U.S.	C6	114
Kingston, N.H., U.S.	E4	122
Kingston, N.Y., U.S.	D6	125
Kingston, Oh., U.S.	C3	128
Kingston, Ok., U.S.	D5	129
Kingston, Pa., U.S.	D10	131
Kingston, R.I., U.S.	F3	132
Kingston, Tn., U.S.	D9	135
Kingston Springs, Tn., U.S.	A4	135
Kingston upon Hull, Eng., U.K.	D6	12
Kingstown see Dún Laoghaire, Ire.	D3	12
Kingstown, St. Vin.	C7	80
Kingstown, Md., U.S.	B5	113
Kingstree, S.C., U.S.	D8	133
Kingsville, On., Can.	E2	89
Kingsville, Md., U.S.	B5	113
Kingsville (North Kingsville), Oh., U.S.	A5	128
Kingsville, Tx., U.S.	F4	136
Kingsville Naval Air Station, mil., Tx., U.S.	F4	136
King William, co., Va., U.S.	C5	139
King William's Town, S. Afr.	E4	56
Kingwood, W.V., U.S.	B5	141
Kinistino, Sk., Can.	E3	91
Kinkaid Lake, res., Il., U.S.	F4	106
Kinkala, Congo	D2	54
Kinloch, Mo., U.S.	f13	118
Kinmundy, Il., U.S.	E5	106
Kinnaird Head, c., Scot., U.K.	B6	12
Kinnelon, N.J., U.S.	B4	123
Kinney, co., Tx., U.S.	E2	136
Kinsey, Al., U.S.	D4	94
Kinshasa, D.R.C.	D3	54
Kinsley, Ks., U.S.	E4	109
Kinston, N.C., U.S.	B5	126
Kintampo, Ghana	E4	50
Kintyre, pen., Scot., U.K.	C4	12
Kinyeti, mtn., Sudan	J11	48
Kinzia, D.R.C.	D3	54
Kiowa, Ks., U.S.	E5	109
Kiowa, Ok., U.S.	C6	129
Kiowa, co., Co., U.S.	C8	99
Kiowa, co., Ks., U.S.	E4	109
Kiowa, co., Ok., U.S.	C2	129
Kiowa Creek, stm., Ok., U.S.	A1	129
Kiparissiakós Kólpos, b., Grc.	F8	18
Kipembawe, Tan.	E6	54
Kipengere Range, mts., Tan.	E6	54
Kipili, Tan.	E6	54
Kipini, Kenya	D8	54
Kipnuk, Ak., U.S.	C7	95
Kipushi, D.R.C.	F5	54
Kirbyville, Tx., U.S.	D6	136
Kirensk, Russia	D12	26
Kirgiz Range, mts., Asia	A2	40
Kiri, D.R.C.	D3	54
Kiribati, ctry., Oc.	E12	58
Kiribati, is., Kir.	D11	58
Kırıkhan, Tur.	D7	44
Kırıkkale, Tur.	C5	44
Kirinyaga (Kenya, Mount), mtn., Kenya	D7	54
Kiriši, Russia	C5	22
Kiritimati (Christmas Island), atoll, Kir.	D14	58
Kırkağaç, Tur.	C2	44
Kirkcaldy, Scot., U.K.	B5	12
Kirkenes, Nor.	B14	10
Kirkjubæjarklaustur, Ice.	m19	10a
Kirkland, Il., U.S.	A5	106
Kirkland, Wa., U.S.	B3	140
Kirkland Lake, On., Can.	o19	89
Kırklareli, Tur.	B2	44
Kirklin, In., U.S.	D5	107
Kirkpatrick, Mount, mtn., Ant.	E22	67
Kirksville, Mo., U.S.	A5	118
Kirkwall, Scot., U.K.	A5	12
Kirkwood, S. Afr.	E4	56
Kirkwood, De., U.S.	B3	101
Kirkwood, Il., U.S.	C3	106
Kirkwood, Mo., U.S.	f13	118
Kirov, Russia	B13	20
Kirov, Russia	D6	26
Kirovabad see Gäncä, Azer.	B12	44
Kirovakan see Vanadzor, Arm.	B11	44
Kirovohrad, Ukr.	E12	20
Kirovsk, Russia	A5	22
Kirovsk, Turk.	C8	42
Kirovskij, Russia	D17	26
Kirovskij, Russia	A2	31
Kirs, Russia	C9	22
Kirsanov, Russia	D7	22
Kırşehir, Tur.	C6	44
Kīrthar Range, mts., Pak.	E9	42
Kirtland, N.M., U.S.	A1	124
Kirtland Air Force Base, mil., N.M., U.S.	k7	124
Kiruna, Swe.	C9	10
Kirwin Reservoir, res., Ks., U.S.	C4	109
Kisangani, D.R.C.	C5	54
Kisar, Pulau, i., Indon.	E7	36
Kisaran, Indon.	C1	36
Kishangarh Bās, India	D2	40
Kishi, Nig.	E5	50
Kishinev see Chişinău, Mol.	F10	20
Kishiwada, Japan	D3	31
Kishwaukee, stm., Il., U.S.	A5	106
Kisii, Kenya	D6	54
Kisiju, Tan.	E7	54
Kiska Island, i., Ak., U.S.	E3	95
Kiskunfélegyháza, Hung.	F5	20
Kiskunhalas, Hung.	F5	20
Kislovodsk, Russia	B4	42
Kismaayo, Som.	D8	54
Kissidougou, Gui.	E2	50
Kissimmee, Fl., U.S.	D5	102
Kissimmee, stm., Fl., U.S.	E5	102
Kissimmee, Lake, l., Fl., U.S.	E5	102
Kississing Lake, l., Mb., Can.	B1	86
Kistler, W.V., U.S.	D3	141
Kisumu, Kenya	D6	54
Kisvárda, Hung.	E7	20
Kita, Mali	D3	50
Kitaibaraki, Japan	C4	31
Kitakyūshū, Japan	E14	28
Kitale, Kenya	C7	54
Kitami, Japan	B4	31
Kit Carson, co., Co., U.S.	B8	99
Kitchener, On., Can.	D4	89
Kíthira, i., Grc.	F9	18
Kíthnos, i., Grc.	F10	18
Kitimat, B.C., Can.	B3	85
Kitsap, co., Wa., U.S.	B3	140
Kitscoty, Ab., Can.	C5	84
Kittanning, Pa., U.S.	E2	131
Kittatinny Mountain, mtn., U.S.	B2	123
Kittery, Me., U.S.	E2	112
Kittery Point, Me., U.S.	E2	112
Kittitas, Wa., U.S.	C5	140
Kittitas, co., Wa., U.S.	B4	140
Kitts, Ky., U.S.	D6	110
Kittson, co., Mn., U.S.	B2	116
Kitty Hawk, N.C., U.S.	A7	126
Kitty Hawk Bay, b., N.C., U.S.	A7	126
Kitui, Kenya	D7	54
Kitwe, Zam.	A4	56
Kiunga, Kenya	D8	54
Kiviõli, Est.	G12	10
Kivu, Lac, l., Afr.	D5	54
Kizëma, Russia	B7	22
Kızılcahamam, Tur.	B5	44
Kızılırmak, stm., Tur.	B6	44
Kızıltepe, Tur.	D9	44
Kizljar, Russia	B5	42
Kizyl-Atrek, Turk.	C6	42
Kjusjur, Russia	B14	26
Kjustendil, Bul.	C9	18
Klabat, Gunung, vol., Indon.	C7	36
Kladno, Czech Rep.	D3	20
Klagenfurt, Aus.	G14	12
Klaipėda, Lith.	I9	10
Klamath, co., Or., U.S.	E5	130
Klamath, stm., U.S.	B2	98
Klamath Falls, Or., U.S.	E5	130
Klamath Mountains, mts., U.S.	E2	130
Klang, Malay.	C2	36
Klatovy, Czech Rep.	E2	20
Klawer, S. Afr.	E2	56
Klawock, Ak., U.S.	D13	95
Kleberg, co., Tx., U.S.	F4	136
Klerksdorp, S. Afr.	D4	56
Kletna, Russia	C12	20
Klickitat, Wa., U.S.	D4	140
Klickitat, co., Wa., U.S.	D4	140
Klickitat, stm., Wa., U.S.	C4	140
Klimpfjäll, Swe.	D6	10
Klin, Russia	C6	22
Klincy, Russia	C12	20
Klipplaat, S. Afr.	E3	56
Ključevskaja Sopka, vulkan, vol., Russia	D18	26
Kłobuck, Pol.	D5	20
Kłodzko, Pol.	D4	20
Klondike, hist. reg., Yk., Can.	F12	82
Klondike Gold Rush National Historical Park, Ak., U.S.	k22	95
Kluczbork, Pol.	D5	20
Klutina Lake, l., Ak., U.S.	g19	95
Knapp Creek, stm., W.V., U.S.	C5	141
Knee Lake, l., Mb., Can.	B4	86
Kneža, Bul.	C10	18
Knife, stm., N.D., U.S.	B3	127
Knightdale, N.C., U.S.	B4	126
Knight Inlet, b., B.C., Can.	D5	85
Knight Island, i., Ak., U.S.	g18	95
Knightstown, In., U.S.	E6	107
Knightsville, In., U.S.	E3	107
Knightville Reservoir, res., Ma., U.S.	B2	114
Knittelfeld, Aus.	G14	12
Knob Noster, Mo., U.S.	C4	118
Knollwood, W.V., U.S.	m12	141
Knossós, hist., Grc.	G10	18
Knott, co., Ky., U.S.	C6	110
Knox, In., U.S.	B4	107
Knox, Pa., U.S.	D2	131
Knox, co., Il., U.S.	B3	106
Knox, co., In., U.S.	G3	107
Knox, co., Ky., U.S.	D6	110
Knox, co., Me., U.S.	D4	112
Knox, co., Mo., U.S.	A5	118
Knox, co., Ne., U.S.	B8	120
Knox, co., Oh., U.S.	B3	128
Knox, co., Tn., U.S.	C10	135
Knox, co., Tx., U.S.	C3	136
Knox, Cape, c., B.C., Can.	B1	85
Knox City, Tx., U.S.	C3	136
Knox Coast, Ant.	C15	67
Knoxville, Ia., U.S.	C4	108
Knoxville, Il., U.S.	C3	106
Knoxville, Tn., U.S.	D10	135
Knysna, S. Afr.	E3	56
Kōbe, Japan	E15	28
København (Copenhagen), Den.	I5	10
Koblenz, Ger.	E10	12
Kobroor, Pulau, i., Indon.	H9	32
Kobryn, Bela.	C8	20
Kobuk, stm., Ak., U.S.	B8	95
Kobuk Valley National Park, Ak., U.S.	B8	95
Kočani, Mac.	D9	18
Kočevo, Russia	C9	22
Kochi (Cochin), India	H3	40
Kōchi, Japan	E14	28
Koch Peak, mtn., Mt., U.S.	E5	119
Kodaikānal, India	G3	40
Kodiak, Ak., U.S.	D9	95
Kodiak Island, i., Ak., U.S.	D9	95
Kodok, Sudan	B6	54
Koës, Nmb.	D2	56
Kofa Mountains, mts., Az., U.S.	D2	96
Köflach, Aus.	G14	12
Koforidua, Ghana	E4	50
Kōfu, Japan	D15	28
Kogaluk, stm., Nf., Can.	g9	88
Køge, Den.	I5	10

Name | Map Ref. | Page

Kohala Mountains, mts., Hi., U.S. **C6** 104
Kohāt, Pak. **D10** 42
Kohīma, India **D6** 40
Kohler, Wi., U.S. **E6** 142
Kohtla-Järve, Est. **G12** 10
Koihoa, India **H6** 40
Koindu, S.L. **E2** 50
Kojgorodok, Russia **B9** 22
Kojonup, Austl. **G2** 60
Kokand, Uzb. **E9** 26
Kokanee Glacier Provincial Park, B.C., Can. **E9** 85
Kokčetav, Kaz. **D8** 26
Kokemäki, Fin. **F10** 10
Kokenau, Indon. **G10** 32
Kokkola, Fin. **E10** 10
Kokoda, Pap. N. Gui. **H12** 32
Koko Head, c., Hi., U.S. **B4** 104
Kokolik, stm., Ak., U.S. **B7** 95
Kokomo, In., U.S. **D5** 107
Koko Nor see Qinghai Hu, l., China **D8** 28
Kokosing, stm., Oh., U.S. **B3** 128
Kokstad, S. Afr. **E4** 56
Kola, Russia **B15** 10
Kolaka, Indon. **D6** 36
Kola Peninsula see Kol'skij poluostrov, pen., Russia **C5** 26
Kolār Gold Fields, India **G3** 40
Kolbio, Kenya **D8** 54
Kolda, Sen. **D2** 50
Kolding, Den. **I3** 10
Kole, D.R.C. **D4** 54
Kolea, Alg. **I8** 16
Kolguev, ostrov, i., Russia **C6** 26
Kolhāpur, India **F2** 40
Kolka, Lat. **H10** 10
Kolmogorovo, Russia **D11** 26
Köln (Cologne), Ger. **E10** 12
Koło, Pol. **C5** 20
Koloa, Hi., U.S. **B2** 104
Kołobrzeg, Pol. **B3** 20
Kolokani, Mali **D3** 50
Kolomna, Russia **D5** 26
Kolonia, Micron. **D9** 58
Kolonodale, Indon. **D6** 36
Kolpaševo, Russia **D10** 26
Kolpino, Russia **C5** 22
Kol'skij poluostrov, pen., Russia **C5** 26
Kolwezi, D.R.C. **F5** 54
Kolyma, stm., Russia **C17** 26
Kolymskaja, Russia **C17** 26
Komandorskie ostrova, is., Russia **D18** 26
Komandorskii Islands see Komandorskie ostrova, is., Russia **D18** 26
Komárno, Slvk. **F5** 20
Komatipoort, S. Afr. **D5** 56
Kome Island, i., Ug. **D6** 54
Komi, state, Russia **C7** 26
Komló, Hung. **F5** 20
Kommunarsk see Alchevs'k, Ukr. **E15** 20
Kommunizma, pik, mtn., Taj. **F9** 26
Komodo, Pulau, i., Indon. **E5** 36
Komoé, stm., Afr. **E4** 50
Komotiní, Grc. **D10** 18
Komsomolec, Kaz. **D11** 22
Komsomolec, ostrov, i., Russia **A11** 26
Komsomol'sk-na-Amure, Russia **D15** 26
Konahuanui, Puu, mtn., Hi., U.S. **g10** 104
Konārak, hist., India **F5** 40
Konawa, Ok., U.S. **C5** 129
Kondagaon, India **F4** 40
Kondinin, Austl. **G2** 60
Kondoa, Tan. **D7** 54
Kondopoga, Russia **C5** 26
Kondūz, Afg. **C9** 42
Koné, N. Cal. **I8** 62a
Kong, stm., Asia **C5** 34
Kongolo, D.R.C. **E5** 54
Kongor, Sudan **B6** 54
Kongsvinger, Nor. **F5** 10
Kongur Shan, mtn., China **D3** 28
Königsberg see Kaliningrad, Russia **D4** 26
Konin, Pol. **C5** 20
Konna, Mali **D4** 50
Konomoc, Lake, res., Ct., U.S. **D7** 100
Konoša, Russia **C6** 26
Konotop, Ukr. **D12** 20
Konstanz, Ger. **G11** 12
Kontagora, Nig. **D6** 50
Kontcha, Cam. **B2** 54
Kon Tum, Viet. **D5** 34
Konya, Tur. **D5** 44
Konza, Kenya **D7** 54
Konžakovskij Kamen', gora, mtn., Russia **C10** 22
Koochiching, co., Mn., U.S. **B4** 116
Kookynie, Austl. **F3** 60
Koolau Range, mts., Hi., U.S. **f10** 104
Koontz Lake, In., U.S. **B5** 107
Kooskia, Id., U.S. **C3** 105
Kootenai, co., Id., U.S. **B2** 105
Kootenay Lake, l., B.C., Can. **E9** 85
Kootenay National Park, B.C., Can. **D9** 85
Kópasker, Ice. **k20** 10a
Kópavogur, Ice. **l18** 10a
Kopejsk, Russia **C11** 22
Kopet Mountains, mts., Asia **C7** 42
Köping, Swe. **G6** 10
Koppang, Nor. **F4** 10
Koppel, Pa., U.S. **E1** 131
Koprivnica, Cro. **A6** 18
Korab (Korabit, Maja e), mtn., Eur. **D8** 18
Korabit, Maja e (Korab), mtn., Eur. **D8** 18
Korāput, India **F4** 40
Korba, India **E4** 40
Korbol, Chad **D8** 50
Korçë, Alb. **D8** 18
Korea, North, ctry., Asia **C13** 28
Korea, South, ctry., Asia **D10** 28
Korea Bay, b., Asia **D12** 28
Korea Strait, strt., Asia **E13** 28
Korenovsk, Russia **A3** 42
Korf, Russia **C18** 26
Korfovskij, Russia **A3** 31
Korhogo, C. Iv. **E3** 50
Korinthiakós Kólpos, b., Grc. **E9** 18
Kórinthos, Grc. **F9** 18
Kōriyama, Japan **C4** 31
Korjakskaja Sopka, vulkan, vol., Russia **D17** 26
Korjakskoe nagor'e, mts., Russia **C18** 26
Korjažma, Russia **B8** 22
Korkino, Russia **D11** 22
Korkuteli, Tur. **D4** 44
Korla, China **C5** 28
Korliki, Russia **C10** 26
Kornat, Otok, i., Cro. **C5** 18
Korogwe, Tan. **E7** 54
Koronadal, Phil. **E8** 34
Koronis, Lake, l., Mn., U.S. **E4** 116
Koror, Palau **E9** 32
Koro Sea, Fiji **F12** 58
Korosten', Ukr. **D10** 20
Korostyshiv, Ukr. **D10** 20
Korovin Volcano, vol., Ak., U.S. **E5** 95
Korsakov, Russia **E16** 26
Korsnäs, Fin. **E9** 10
Kos, i., Grc. **F11** 18
Koš-Agač, Russia **D10** 26
Koščagyl, Kaz. **A6** 42
Kościan, Pol. **C4** 20
Kościerzyna, Pol. **B4** 20
Kosciusko, Ms., U.S. **B4** 117
Kosciusko, co., In., U.S. **B6** 107
Kosciusko, Mount, mtn., Austl. **H4** 62
Koshkonong, Lake, l., Wi., U.S. **F5** 142
Košice, Slvk. **E6** 20
Kosju, Russia **A10** 22
Koslan, Russia **B8** 22
Kosovska Mitrovica, Yugo. **C8** 18
Kossou, Lac de, res., C. Iv. **E3** 50
Kossuth, co., Ia., U.S. **A3** 108
Kostiantynivka, Ukr. **E14** 20
Kostopil', Ukr. **D9** 20
Kostroma, Russia **C7** 22
Kostrzyn, Pol. **C3** 20
Koszalin, Pol. **B4** 20
Kőszeg, Hung. **F4** 20
Kota, India **D3** 40
Kotaagung, Indon. **E2** 36
Kotabaru see Jayapura, Indon. **G11** 32
Kotabaru, Indon. **G6** 32
Kota Belud, Malay. **B5** 36
Kota Bharu, Malay. **B2** 36
Kotabumi, Indon. **D2** 36
Kota Kinabalu, Malay. **B5** 36
Kotamobagu, Indon. **C6** 36
Kotel'nič, Russia **C8** 22
Kotel'nikovo, Russia **E7** 22
Kotel'nyj, ostrov, i., Russia **B15** 26
Kotido, Ug. **C6** 54
Kotka, Fin. **F12** 10
Kot Kapūra, India **C2** 40
Kotlas, Russia **C6** 26
Kotlik, Ak., U.S. **C7** 95
Kotovs'k, Ukr. **F10** 20
Kotri, Pak. **E9** 42
Kottagūdem, India **F4** 40
Kottayam, India **H3** 40
Kotte see Sri Jayawardenepura, Sri L. **H4** 40
Kotto, stm., C.A.R. **B4** 54
Kotuj, stm., Russia **C12** 26
Kotzebue, Ak., U.S. **B7** 95
Kotzebue Sound, strt., Ak., U.S. **B7** 95
Kouchibouguac National Park, N.B., Can. **C5** 87
Koudougou, Burkina **D4** 50
Kouki, C.A.R. **B3** 54
Koulamoutou, Gabon **D2** 54
Koulikoro, Mali **D3** 50
Koumac, N. Cal. **I8** 62a
Koumbia, Gui. **D2** 50
Koumra, Chad **E8** 50
Koundâra, Gui. **D2** 50
Kounradskij, Kaz. **B2** 28
Kountze, Tx., U.S. **D5** 136
Kourou, Fr. Gu. **B9** 70
Kouroussa, Gui. **D3** 50
Kousséri, Cam. **D8** 50
Koussi, Emi, mtn., Chad **C8** 50
Koutiala, Mali **D3** 50
Kouts, In., U.S. **B3** 107
Kouvola, Fin. **F12** 10
Kovdor, Russia **C14** 10
Kovdozero, ozero, res., Russia **C15** 10
Kovel', Ukr. **D8** 20
Kovrov, Russia **C7** 22
Kowloon see Jiulong, China **E3** 30
Koyukuk, stm., Ak., U.S. **B8** 95
Kozan, Tur. **D6** 44
Kozáni, Grc. **D8** 18
Kozel'sk, Russia **B13** 20
Kozhikode (Calicut), India **G3** 40
Koziatyn, Ukr. **E10** 20
Kozlu, Tur. **B4** 44
Kpalimé, Togo **E5** 50
Kra, Isthmus of, Asia **D3** 34
Krâchéh, Camb. **D5** 34
Kragerø, Nor. **G3** 10
Kragujevac, Yugo. **B8** 18
Kraków, Pol. **D5** 20
Kralendijk, Neth. Ant. **C6** 80
Kraljevo, Yugo. **C8** 18
Kramators'k, Ukr. **E14** 20
Kramfors, Swe. **E7** 10
Kranj, Slvn. **A5** 18
Kraśnik, Pol. **D7** 20
Krasnoarmiis'k, Ukr. **E14** 20
Krasnodar, Russia **E5** 26
Krasnogorsk, Russia **B16** 28
Krasnohrad, Ukr. **E13** 20
Krasnojarsk, Russia **D11** 26
Krasnoperekops'k, Ukr. **G12** 20
Krasnosel'kup, Russia **C10** 26
Krasnoturjinsk, Russia **C11** 22
Krasnoufimsk, Russia **C10** 22
Krasnoural'sk, Russia **D8** 26
Krasnovišersk, Russia **B10** 22
Krasnovodsk see Turkmenbaši, Turk. **E7** 26
Krasnoyarsk see Krasnojarsk, Russia **D11** 26
Krasnoznamenskoje, Kaz. **D8** 26
Krasnyi Luch, Ukr. **E15** 20
Krasnystaw, Pol. **D7** 20
Krasyliv, Ukr. **E9** 20
Krebs, Ok., U.S. **C6** 129
Kremenchug Reservoir see Kremenchuts'ke vodoskhovyshche, res., Ukr. **E12** 20
Kremenchuk, Ukr. **E12** 20
Kremenchuts'ke vodoskhovyshche, res., Ukr. **E12** 20
Kremenets', Ukr. **D8** 20
Kremmling, Co., U.S. **A4** 99
Kretinga, Lith. **I9** 10
Kreuztal, Ger. **E11** 12
Kribi, Cam. **C1** 54
Krishna, stm., India **F3** 40
Krishnanagar, India **E5** 40
Kristiansand, Nor. **G3** 10
Kristianstad, Swe. **I6** 10
Kristiansund, Nor. **E2** 10
Kristiinankaupunki, Fin. **E9** 10
Kristineberg, Swe. **D8** 10
Kristinehamn, Swe. **G6** 10
Kríti (Crete), i., Grc. **G10** 18
Kritikón Pélagos, Grc. **G10** 18
Krjukovo, Russia **C17** 26
Krk, Otok, i., Cro. **B5** 18
Krnov, Czech Rep. **D4** 20
Kroměříž, Czech Rep. **E4** 20
Krŏng Kaôh Kŏng, Camb. **D4** 34
Kronštadt, Russia **B4** 22
Kroonstad, S. Afr. **D4** 56
Kropotkin, Russia **A4** 42
Krosno, Pol. **E6** 20
Krotoszyn, Pol. **D4** 20
Krotz Springs, La., U.S. **D4** 111
Krugersdorp, S. Afr. **D4** 56
Krui, Indon. **E2** 36
Krung Thep (Bangkok), Thai. **D4** 34
Kruševac, Yugo. **C8** 18
Kruzof Island, i., Ak., U.S. **m21** 95
Kryčaŭ, Bela. **C11** 20
Krymsk, Russia **G14** 20
Kryms'ki hory, mts., Ukr. **G13** 20
Kryms'kyi pivostriv (Crimean Peninsula), pen., Ukr. **G12** 20
Kryvyi Rih, Ukr. **F12** 20
Ksar-el-Kebir, Mor. **J4** 16
Ksenevka, Russia **A11** 28
Kšenskij, Russia **D14** 20
Kuala Kangsar, Malay. **C2** 36
Kualakapuas, Indon. **D4** 36
Kuala Krai, Malay. **B2** 36
Kuala Lipis, Malay. **C2** 36
Kuala Lumpur, Malay. **C2** 36
Kuala Pilah, Malay. **C2** 36
Kuala Terengganu, Malay. **B2** 36
Kuantan, Malay. **C2** 36
Kuban', stm., Russia **E6** 26
Kuching, Malay. **C4** 36
Kuçovë, Alb. **D8** 18
Kudat, Malay. **B5** 36
Kudus, Indon. **E4** 36
Kudymkar, Russia **C9** 22
Kuee Ruins, hist., Hi., U.S. **D6** 104
Kufstein, Aus. **G13** 12
Kūhdasht, Iran **F12** 44
Kuito, Ang. **F3** 54
Kuiu Island, i., Ak., U.S. **m23** 95
Kujawy, reg., Pol. **C5** 20
Kujbyšev see Samara, Russia **D7** 26
Kujbyšev, Russia **D9** 26
Kujbyševskoe vodohranilišče, res., Russia **D8** 22
Kujgan, Kaz. **A10** 42
Kujū-san, vol., Japan **D2** 31
Kukawa, Nig. **D7** 50
Kula, Tur. **C3** 44
Kula, Hi., U.S. **C5** 104
Kula Kangri, mtn., Bhu. **D6** 40
Kuldīga, Lat. **H9** 10
Kule, Bots. **C3** 56
Kulebaki, Russia **C7** 22
Kuljab, Taj. **F8** 26
Kulmbach, Ger. **E12** 12
Kuloj, Russia **B7** 22
Kulpmont, Pa., U.S. **E9** 131
Kul'sary, Kaz. **E7** 26
Kulu, Tur. **C5** 44
Kulumadau, Pap. N. Gui. **H13** 32
Kumagaya, Japan **C3** 31
Kumai, Indon. **D4** 36
Kumai, Teluk, b., Indon. **D4** 36
Kumamoto, Japan **E14** 28
Kumanovo, Mac. **C8** 18
Kumasi, Ghana **E4** 50
Kumba, Cam. **C1** 54
Kumbakonam, India **G3** 40
Kume-jima, i., Japan **A9** 34
Kuminskij, Russia **C12** 22
Kumluca, Tur. **D4** 44
Kumo, Nig. **E7** 50
Kumta, India **G2** 40
Kumukahi, Cape, c., Hi., U.S. **D7** 104
Kuna, Id., U.S. **F2** 105
Kunašir, ostrov, i., Russia **E16** 26
Kunda, Est. **G12** 10
Kundāpura, India **G2** 40
Kundur, Pulau, i., Indon. **C2** 36
Kunene (Cunene), stm., Afr. **B1** 56
Kunghit Island, i., B.C., Can. **C2** 85
Kungrad, Uzb. **B7** 42
Kungur, Russia **C10** 22
Kunhing, Myan. **B3** 34
Kunlun Shan, mts., China **D5** 28
Kunming, China **F8** 28
Kununurra, Austl. **D4** 60
Kunya, Nig. **D6** 50
Kuopio, Fin. **E12** 10
Kupang, Indon. **F6** 36
Kup'ians'k, Ukr. **E14** 20
Kupreanof Island, i., Ak., U.S. **m23** 95
Kuqa, China **C4** 28
Kuqa, China **C4** 28
Kür, stm., Asia **C13** 44
Kurashiki, Japan **D2** 31
Kuraymah, Sudan **G11** 48
Kurčatov, Russia **D13** 20
Kürdämir, Azer. **B13** 44
Kurdistan, hist. reg., Asia **D10** 44
Kure, Japan **D2** 31
Kure Island, i., Hi., U.S. **k12** 104
Kurejka, stm., Russia **C10** 26
Kuresaare, Est. **G10** 10
Kurgan, Russia **D8** 26
Kurgan-Tjube, Taj. **C9** 42
Kuril Islands see Kuril'skie ostrova, is., Russia **E16** 26
Kuril'sk, Russia **B17** 28
Kuril'skie ostrova (Kuril Islands), is., Russia **E16** 26
Kuril Trench **A7** 144
Kurmuk, Sudan **H11** 48
Kurnool, India **F3** 40
Kursk, Russia **D5** 26
Kurtalan, Tur. **D9** 44
Kurtamyš, Russia **D11** 22
Kurtistown, Hi., U.S. **D6** 104
Kuruman, S. Afr. **D3** 56
Kuruman, stm., S. Afr. **D3** 56
Kurume, Japan **D2** 31
Kurumkan, Russia **D13** 26
Kurunegala, Sri L. **H4** 40
Kuşadası, Tur. **D2** 44
Kuşadası Körfezi, b., Tur. **D2** 44
Kuščevskaja, Russia **F15** 20
Kuş Gölü, l., Tur. **B2** 44
Kushiro, Japan **C16** 28
Kushui, China **C6** 28
Kuskokwim, stm., Ak., U.S. **C8** 95
Kuskokwim Bay, b., Ak., U.S. **D7** 95
Kuskokwim Mountains, mts., Ak., U.S. **C8** 95
Kustanaj, Kaz. **D8** 26
Kūstī, Sudan **H11** 48
Kut, Ko, i., Thai. **D4** 34
Kütahya, Tur. **C3** 44
Kutaisi, Geor. **A10** 44
Kutch see Kachchh, Gulf of, b., India **E1** 40
Kutch, Gulf of see Kachchh, Gulf of, b., India **E1** 40
Kutch, Rann of, reg., Asia **E1** 40
Kutina, Cro. **B6** 18
Kutno, Pol. **C5** 20
Kutu, D.R.C. **D3** 54
Kutztown, Pa., U.S. **E10** 131
Kuujjuaq, P.Q., Can. **g13** 90
Kuusamo, Fin. **D13** 10
Kuusankoski, Fin. **F12** 10
Kuvango, Ang. **A2** 56
Kuwait see Al-Kuwayt, Kuw. **E5** 42
Kuwait, ctry., Asia **E5** 42
Kuybyshev see Kujbyšev, Russia **D9** 26
Kuybyshev see Samara, Russia **D7** 26
Kuybyshev Reservoir see Kujbyševskoe vodohranilišče, res., Russia **D8** 22
Kuz'movka, Russia **C11** 26
Kuzneck, Russia **D6** 26
Kuzomen', Russia **A6** 22
Kvænangen, b., Nor. **A9** 10
Kvaløya, i., Nor. **B8** 10
Kvareli, Geor. **B11** 44
Kwa, stm., D.R.C. **D3** 54
Kwakoegron, Sur. **B8** 70
Kwamouth, D.R.C. **D3** 54
Kwando (Cuando), stm., Afr. **B3** 56
Kwangju, S. Kor. **D13** 28
Kwango (Cuango), stm., Afr. **D3** 54
Kwangsi Chuang see Guangxi Zhuangzu Zizhiqu, state, China **G9** 28
Kwekwe, Zimb. **B4** 56
Kwenge, stm., Afr. **E3** 54
Kwethluk, Ak., U.S. **C7** 95
Kwidzyn, Pol. **C5** 20
Kwigillingok, Ak., U.S. **D7** 95
Kwilu (Cuilo), stm., Afr. **D3** 54
Kyaikto, Myan. **C3** 34
Kyaukkyi, Myan. **C3** 34
Kyaukme, Myan. **B3** 34
Kyaukpyu, Myan. **C2** 34
Kyaukse, Myan. **B3** 34
Kyauktaw, Myan. **B2** 34
Kyaunggon, Myan. **C3** 34
Kyïv (Kiev), Ukr. **D11** 20
Kyïvs'ke vodoskhovyshche, res., Ukr. **D11** 20
Kyle, Tx., U.S. **E4** 136
Kyoga, Lake, l., Ug. **C6** 54
Kyŏngju, S. Kor. **C1** 31
Kyŏngsŏng-ŭp, N. Kor. **B1** 31
Kyōto, Japan **D15** 28
Kyrgyzstan, ctry., Asia **A2** 40
Kyštovka, Russia **D9** 26
Kyštym, Russia **C11** 22
Kyuquot Sound, strt., B.C., Can. **E4** 85
Kyūshū, i., Japan **E14** 28
Kyushu-Palau Ridge **G16** 64
Kyyiv see Kyïv, Ukr. **D11** 20
Kyyjärvi, Fin. **E11** 10
Kyzyl, Russia **D11** 26
Kyzylkum, des., Asia **B8** 42
Kzyl-Orda, Kaz. **E8** 26
Kzyltu, Kaz. **D9** 26

L

Laascaanood, Som. **I14** 48
La Asunción, Ven. **C7** 80
Laau Point, c., Hi., U.S. **B4** 104
Laayoune see El Aaiún, W. Sah. **A2** 50
Labadieville, La., U.S. **E5** 111
La Bañeza, Spain **F4** 16
La Barca, Mex. **C4** 78
La Barge, Wy., U.S. **D2** 143
La Barge Creek, stm., Wy., U.S. **D2** 143
La Baule-Escoublac, Fr. **D5** 16
Labé, Gui. **D2** 50
Labe, stm., Eur. **E14** 12
La Belle, Fl., U.S. **F5** 102
La Belle, Mo., U.S. **A6** 118
Labette, co., Ks., U.S. **E8** 109
Labinsk, Russia **B4** 42
Labis, Malay. **C2** 36
Laboulaye, Arg. **E5** 72
Labrador, reg., Nf., Can. **g9** 88
Labrador Basin **B28** 144
Labrador City, Nf., Can. **h8** 88
Labrador Sea, N.A. **F29** 82
Lábrea, Braz. **E7** 70
Labuan, Malay. **B5** 36
Labuan, Pulau, i., Malay. **B5** 36
Labuha, Indon. **G8** 32
Labuhanbajo, Indon. **E5** 36
Labytnangi, Russia **A12** 22
Laç, Alb. **D7** 18
La Canada Flintridge, Ca., U.S. **m12** 98
La Carlota, Arg. **E5** 72
La Carlota, Phil. **D8** 34
La Carolina, Spain **H5** 16
Lac-Bouchette, P.Q., Can. **A5** 90
Lac-Brome, P.Q., Can. **D5** 90
Laccadive, Minicoy and Amīndīvi Islands see Lakshadweep, prov., India **G2** 40
Laccadive Islands see Lakshadweep, is., India **G2** 40
Lac-Carré, P.Q., Can. **C3** 90

Name **Map Ref.** **Page**

Lac Courte Oreilles Indian Reservation, Wi., U.S. **C2** 142
Lac du Bonnet, Mb., Can. **D3** 86
Lac du Flambeau, Wi., U.S. **B4** 142
Lac du Flambeau Indian Reservation, Wi., U.S. **C3** 142
La Ceiba, Hond. **B2** 80
La Center, Ky., U.S. **e9** 110
Lac-Etchemin, P.Q., Can. **C7** 90
Lacey, Wa., U.S. **B3** 140
La Chaux-de-Fonds, Switz. **A1** 18
Lachine, P.Q., Can. **D4** 90
La Chorrera, Col. **D5** 70
La Chorrera, Pan. **D3** 80
Lachute, P.Q., Can. **D3** 90
La Citadelle, hist., Haiti **B5** 80
Lackawanna, N.Y., U.S. **C2** 125
Lackawanna, co., Pa., U.S. **D10** 131
Lackland Air Force Base, mil., Tx., U.S. **k7** 136
Lac La Biche, Ab., Can. **B5** 84
Lac la Hache, B.C., Can. **D7** 85
Laclede, co., Mo., U.S. **D5** 118
Lac-Mégantic, P.Q., Can. **D7** 90
Lacolle, P.Q., Can. **D4** 90
La Columna see Bolívar, Pico, mtn., Ven. **B5** 70
Lacombe, Ab., Can. **C4** 84
Lacombe, La., U.S. **D6** 111
Lacon, Il., U.S. **B4** 106
La Concepción, Pan. **D3** 80
La Concepción, Ven. **C5** 80
Laconia, N.H., U.S. **C4** 122
Laconia, Gulf of 20 Lakonikós Kólpos, b., Grc. **F9** 18
La Conner, Wa., U.S. **A3** 140
Lacoochee, Fl., U.S. **D4** 102
La Coruña see A Coruña, Spain **F2** 16
Lac qui Parle, co., Mn., U.S. **F2** 116
Lac qui Parle, stm., Mn., U.S. **F2** 116
La Creek Lake, l., S.D., U.S. **D4** 134
La Crescent, Mn., U.S. **G7** 116
La Crete, Ab., Can. **f7** 84
La Crosse, In., U.S. **B4** 107
La Crosse, Ks., U.S. **D4** 109
La Crosse, Wi., U.S. **E2** 142
La Crosse, co., Wi., U.S. **E2** 142
La Crosse, stm., Wi., U.S. **E3** 142
La Cygne, Ks., U.S. **D9** 109
Ladākh Range, mts., Asia **C3** 40
Ladd, Il., U.S. **B4** 106
Ladies Island, i., S.C., U.S. **G6** 133
La Digue, i., Sey. **h13** 57b
Lādīz, Iran **E8** 42
Ladoga, In., U.S. **E4** 107
Ladoga, Lake see Ladožskoe ozero, l., Russia **C5** 26
La Dorada, Col. **D5** 80
Ladožskoe ozero, l., Russia **C5** 26
Ladson, S.C., U.S. **F7** 133
Ladybrand, S. Afr. **D4** 56
Lady Lake, Fl., U.S. **D5** 102
Lady Laurier, Mount, mtn., B.C., Can. **A6** 85
Ladysmith, B.C., Can. **E6** 85
Ladysmith, S. Afr. **D4** 56
Ladysmith, Wi., U.S. **C2** 142
Lae, Pap. N. Gui. **H12** 32
La Encantada, Mex. **B4** 78
Læsø, i., Den. **H4** 10
La Esperanza, Hond. **C2** 80
La Estrada see A Estrada, Spain **F2** 16
La Farge, Wi., U.S. **E3** 142
Lafayette, Al., U.S. **C4** 94
Lafayette, Co., U.S. **B5** 99
Lafayette, Ga., U.S. **B1** 103
Lafayette, In., U.S. **D4** 107
Lafayette, La., U.S. **D3** 111
Lafayette, N.C., U.S. **B3** 126
Lafayette, Or., U.S. **B3** 130
La Fayette, R.I., U.S. **E4** 132
Lafayette, Tn., U.S. **A5** 135
Lafayette, co., Ar., U.S. **D2** 97
Lafayette, co., Fl., U.S. **C3** 102
Lafayette, co., La., U.S. **D3** 111
Lafayette, co., Mo., U.S. **B4** 118
Lafayette, co., Ms., U.S. **A4** 117
Lafayette, co., Wi., U.S. **F3** 142
Lafayette, Mount, mtn., N.H., U.S. **B3** 122
La Feria, Tx., U.S. **F4** 136
Lafia, Nig. **E6** 50
Lafiagi, Nig. **E6** 50
Lafitte, La., U.S. **k11** 111
La Flèche, Fr. **D6** 16
La Follette, Tn., U.S. **C9** 135
La Fontaine, In., U.S. **C6** 107
Lafourche, La., U.S. **E5** 111
Lafourche, co., La., U.S. **E5** 111
La France, S.C., U.S. **B2** 133
La Galite, i., Tun. **F2** 18
Lagarto, Braz. **D4** 74
Lagawe, Phil. **C8** 34
Lågen, stm., Nor. **F3** 10
Lages, Braz. **D7** 72
Laghouat, Alg. **D5** 48
Lago, Mount, mtn., Wa., U.S. **A5** 140
Lagoa da Prata, Braz. **F2** 74
Lago da Pedra, Braz. **B2** 74
La Gomera, i., Spain **A1** 50
Lagonoy Gulf, b., Phil. **D8** 34
Lagos, Nig. **E5** 50
Lagos, Port. **I2** 16
Lagos de Moreno, Mex. **C4** 78
La Gouèra, W. Sah. **B1** 50
La Grande, Or., U.S. **B8** 130
La Grande, stm., P.Q., Can. **h11** 90
La Grande Deux, Réservoir, res., P.Q., Can. **h11** 90
Lagrange, Austl. **D3** 60
La Grange, Ga., U.S. **C1** 103
La Grange, Il., U.S. **B6** 106
Lagrange, In., U.S. **A7** 107
La Grange, Ky., U.S. **B4** 110
La Grange, Mo., U.S. **A6** 118
La Grange, N.C., U.S. **B5** 126
Lagrange, Oh., U.S. **A3** 128
La Grange, Tx., U.S. **E4** 136
Lagrange, co., In., U.S. **A7** 107
La Grange Park, Il., U.S. **k9** 106
La Gran Sabana, pl., Ven. **B7** 70
La Guadeloupe (Saint-Evariste), P.Q., Can. **D7** 90
La Guajira, Península de, pen., S.A. **A5** 70
La Guardia, Bol. **B5** 72
La Guardia see A Guardia, Spain **G2** 16
Laguna, Braz. **D8** 72
Laguna, N.M., U.S. **B2** 124
Laguna Beach, Ca., U.S. **F5** 98
Laguna Dam, U.S. **E1** 96
Laguna Indian Reservation, N.M., U.S. **C2** 124
La Habana (Havana), Cuba **A3** 80
La Habra, Ca., U.S. **n13** 98
Lahad Datu, Malay. **C5** 36
Lahad Datu, Telukan, b., Malay. **C5** 36
Lahaina, Hi., U.S. **C5** 104
La Harpe, Il., U.S. **C3** 106
La Harpe, Ks., U.S. **E8** 109
Lahat, Indon. **D2** 36
La Have, stm., N.S., Can. **E5** 87
Lahdenpohja, Russia **F14** 10
Lāhījān, Iran **C6** 42
Lahoma, Ok., U.S. **A3** 129
Lahontan Reservoir, res., Nv., U.S. **D2** 121
Lahore, Pak. **D10** 42
Lahti, Fin. **F11** 10
Laï, Chad **E8** 50
Lai Chau, Viet. **B4** 34
Laie, Hi., U.S. **B4** 104
Lai-hka, Myan. **B3** 34
Laingsburg, S. Afr. **E3** 56
Laingsburg, Mi., U.S. **F6** 115
Lainioälven, stm., Swe. **B9** 10
Lais, Indon. **D2** 36
Laisamis, Kenya **C7** 54
Laiwu, China **B4** 30
Laiwui, Indon. **G8** 32
Laiyang, China **B5** 30
Laizhou Wan, b., China **D11** 28
La Jara, Co., U.S. **D5** 99
La Jolla, Point, c., Ca., U.S. **o15** 98
La Junta, Co., U.S. **D7** 99
Lakatoro, Vanuatu **k9** 62a
Lake, co., Ca., U.S. **C2** 98
Lake, co., Co., U.S. **B4** 99
Lake, co., Fl., U.S. **D5** 102
Lake, co., Il., U.S. **A6** 106
Lake, co., In., U.S. **B3** 107
Lake, co., Mi., U.S. **E5** 115
Lake, co., Mn., U.S. **C7** 116
Lake, co., Mt., U.S. **C2** 119
Lake, co., Oh., U.S. **A4** 128
Lake, co., Or., U.S. **E6** 130
Lake, co., S.D., U.S. **C8** 134
Lake, co., Tn., U.S. **A2** 135
Lake Alfred, Fl., U.S. **D5** 102
Lake Andes, S.D., U.S. **D7** 134
Lake Ariel, Pa., U.S. **D11** 131
Lake Arrowhead, Ca., U.S. **E5** 98
Lake Arthur, La., U.S. **D3** 111
Lakeba, i., Fiji **m11** 63b
Lake Benton, Mn., U.S. **F2** 116
Lake Bluff, Il., U.S. **A6** 106
Lake Butler, Fl., U.S. **B4** 102
Lake Cargelligo, Austl. **G4** 62
Lake Charles, La., U.S. **D2** 111
Lake Chelan National Recreation Area, Wa., U.S. **A5** 140
Lake City, Ar., U.S. **B5** 97
Lake City, Fl., U.S. **B4** 102
Lake City, Ia., U.S. **B3** 108
Lake City, Mi., U.S. **D5** 115
Lake City, Mn., U.S. **F6** 116
Lake City, Pa., U.S. **B1** 131
Lake City, S.C., U.S. **D8** 133
Lake City, Tn., U.S. **C9** 135
Lake Clark National Park, Ak., U.S. **C9** 95
Lake Cowichan, B.C., Can. **g11** 85
Lake Creek, stm., Wa., U.S. **B7** 140
Lake Crystal, Mn., U.S. **F4** 116
Lake Delta, N.Y., U.S. **B5** 125
Lake Delton, Wi., U.S. **E4** 142
Lake District, reg., Eng., U.K. **C5** 12
Lake Elsinore, Ca., U.S. **F5** 98
Lake Erie Beach, N.Y., U.S. **C1** 125
Lakefield, On., Can. **C6** 89
Lakefield, Mn., U.S. **G3** 116
Lake Forest, Il., U.S. **A6** 106
Lake Fork, stm., Ut., U.S. **C5** 137
Lake Geneva, Wi., U.S. **F5** 142
Lake Hamilton, Ar., U.S. **g7** 97
Lake Havasu City, Az., U.S. **C1** 96
Lake Helen, Fl., U.S. **D5** 102
Lakehurst, N.J., U.S. **C4** 123
Lakehurst Naval Air Station, mil., N.J., U.S. **C4** 123
Lake in the Hills, Il., U.S. **h8** 106
Lake Jackson, Tx., U.S. **r14** 136
Lake Katrine, N.Y., U.S. **D7** 125
Lake King, Austl. **G2** 60
Lakeland, Fl., U.S. **D5** 102
Lakeland, Ga., U.S. **E3** 103
Lake Linden, Mi., U.S. **A2** 115
Lake Louise, Ab., Can. **D2** 84
Lake Magdalene, Fl., U.S. **o11** 102
Lake Mary, Fl., U.S. **D5** 102
Lake Mead National Recreation Area, U.S. **H7** 121
Lake Meredith National Recreation Area, Tx., U.S. **B2** 136
Lake Mills, Ia., U.S. **A4** 108
Lake Mills, Wi., U.S. **E5** 142
Lakemore, Oh., U.S. **A4** 128
Lake Mountain, mtn., Wy., U.S. **E6** 143
Lake Nebagamon, Wi., U.S. **B2** 142
Lake Odessa, Mi., U.S. **F5** 115
Lake of the Woods, co., Mn., U.S. **B4** 116
Lake Orion, Mi., U.S. **F7** 115
Lake Oswego, Or., U.S. **B4** 130
Lake Ozark, Mo., U.S. **C5** 118
Lake Park, Fl., U.S. **F6** 102
Lake Park, Ia., U.S. **A2** 108
Lake Park, Mn., U.S. **D2** 116
Lake Placid, Fl., U.S. **E5** 102
Lake Placid, N.Y., U.S. **A7** 125
Lake Pontchartrain Causeway, La., U.S. **h11** 111
Lakeport, Ca., U.S. **C2** 98
Lake Preston, S.D., U.S. **C8** 134
Lake Providence, La., U.S. **B4** 111
Lake Range, mts., Nv., U.S. **C2** 121
Lakes Entrance, Austl. **H4** 62
Lake Shore, Md., U.S. **B5** 113
Lakeshore, Ms., U.S. **E4** 117
Lakeside, Az., U.S. **C6** 96
Lakeside, Ca., U.S. **F5** 98
Lakeside, Ct., U.S. **D3** 100
Lakeside, Mt., U.S. **B2** 119
Lakeside, Oh., U.S. **A3** 128
Lakeside, Or., U.S. **D2** 130
Lakeside Park, Ky., U.S. **h13** 110
Lake Station, In., U.S. **A3** 107
Lake Station, Ok., U.S. **A5** 129
Lake Stevens, Wa., U.S. **A3** 140
Lake Superior Provincial Park, On., Can. **p18** 89
Lake Swamp, stm., S.C., U.S. **D8** 133
Lake Tansi Village, Tn., U.S. **D8** 135
Lake Valley, val., Nv., U.S. **E7** 121
Lake View, Ia., U.S. **B2** 108
Lakeview, Mi., U.S. **E5** 115
Lakeview, Oh., U.S. **B2** 128
Lakeview, Or., U.S. **E6** 130
Lake View, S.C., U.S. **C9** 133
Lake Villa, Il., U.S. **h8** 106
Lake Village, Ar., U.S. **D4** 97
Lake Village, In., U.S. **B3** 107
Lakeville, Ct., U.S. **B2** 100
Lakeville, In., U.S. **A5** 107
Lakeville, Ma., U.S. **C6** 114
Lakeville, Mn., U.S. **F5** 116
Lake Waccamaw, N.C., U.S. **C4** 126
Lake Wales, Fl., U.S. **E5** 102
Lakewood, Ca., U.S. **n12** 98
Lakewood, Co., U.S. **B5** 99
Lakewood, Ia., U.S. **f8** 108
Lakewood, Il., U.S. **D5** 106
Lakewood, N.J., U.S. **C4** 123
Lakewood, N.Y., U.S. **C1** 125
Lakewood, Oh., U.S. **A4** 128
Lakewood, Wa., U.S. **B3** 140
Lake Worth, Fl., U.S. **F6** 102
Lake Worth Inlet, b., Fl., U.S. **F7** 102
Lake Zurich, Il., U.S. **h8** 106
Lakhdaria, Alg. **I8** 16
Lakhīmpur, India **D4** 40
Lakin, Ks., U.S. **E2** 109
Lakonikós Kólpos, b., Grc. **F9** 18
Lakota, N.D., U.S. **A7** 127
Laksefjorden, b., Nor. **A12** 10
Lakshadweep, prov., India **G2** 40
Lakshadweep, is., India **G2** 40
Lakshadweep Sea, Asia **G2** 40
Lalara, Gabon **C2** 54
Lalībela, Eth. **H12** 48
La Libertad, Guat. **B1** 80
La Línea de la Concepción, Spain **I4** 16
Lalitpur, India **E3** 40
La Loche see Churchill, stm., Can. **G21** 82
La Luz, N.M., U.S. **E4** 124
La Malbaie, P.Q., Can. **B7** 90
La Mancha, reg., Spain **H5** 16
La Manche see English Channel, strt., Eur. **C5** 16
Lamap, Vanuatu **k9** 62a
Lamar, Ar., U.S. **B2** 97
Lamar, Co., U.S. **C8** 99
Lamar, Mo., U.S. **D3** 118
Lamar, Pa., U.S. **D7** 131
Lamar, S.C., U.S. **C7** 133
Lamar, co., Al., U.S. **B1** 94
Lamar, co., Ga., U.S. **C2** 103
Lamar, co., Ms., U.S. **D4** 117
Lamar, co., Tx., U.S. **C5** 136
Lamar, stm., Wy., U.S. **B2** 143
La Mauricie, Parc National de, P.Q., Can. **C5** 90
Lamb, co., Tx., U.S. **B1** 136
Lambaréné, Gabon **D2** 54
Lambayeque, Peru **E4** 70
Lambert, Ms., U.S. **A3** 117
Lambert Glacier, Ant. **D11** 67
Lamberton, Mn., U.S. **F3** 116
Lambert's Bay, S. Afr. **E2** 56
Lambertville, Mi., U.S. **G7** 115
Lambertville, N.J., U.S. **C3** 123
Lame Deer, Mt., U.S. **E10** 119
Lamèque, N.B., Can. **B5** 87
Lamèque, Île, i., N.B., Can. **B5** 87
La Mesa, Ca., U.S. **F5** 98
La Mesa, N.M., U.S. **E3** 124
Lamesa, Tx., U.S. **C2** 136
Lamía, Grc. **E9** 18
Lamoille, Nv., U.S. **C6** 121
Lamoille, co., Vt., U.S. **B3** 138
Lamoille, stm., Vt., U.S. **B3** 138
La Moine, stm., Il., U.S. **C3** 106
Lamon Bay, b., Phil. **D8** 34
Lamoni, Ia., U.S. **D4** 108
Lamont, Ab., Can. **C4** 84
Lamont, Ca., U.S. **E4** 98
La Monte, Mo., U.S. **C4** 118
La Motte, Isle, i., Vt., U.S. **B2** 138
La Moure, N.D., U.S. **C7** 127
La Moure, co., N.D., U.S. **C7** 127
Lampang, Thai. **C3** 34
Lampasas, Tx., U.S. **D3** 136
Lampasas, co., Tx., U.S. **D3** 136
Lampazos de Naranjo, Mex. **B4** 78
Lamphun, Thai. **C3** 34
Lampman, Sk., Can. **H4** 91
Lamprey, stm., N.H., U.S. **D4** 122
Lamu, Kenya **D8** 54
Lanai, i., Hi., U.S. **C4** 104
Lanai City, Hi., U.S. **C5** 104
Lanaihale, mtn., Hi., U.S. **C5** 104
Lanark, On., Can. **C8** 89
Lanark, Il., U.S. **A4** 106
Lanark, W.V., U.S. **D3** 141
Lanbi Kyun, i., Myan. **D3** 34
Lancang see Mekong, stm., Asia **A3** 34
Lancaster, On., Can. **B10** 89
Lancaster, Eng., U.K. **C5** 12
Lancaster, Ca., U.S. **E4** 98
Lancaster, Ky., U.S. **C5** 110
Lancaster, Mo., U.S. **A5** 118
Lancaster, N.H., U.S. **B3** 122
Lancaster, N.Y., U.S. **C2** 125
Lancaster, Oh., U.S. **C3** 128
Lancaster, Pa., U.S. **F9** 131
Lancaster, S.C., U.S. **B6** 133
Lancaster, Tx., U.S. **n10** 136
Lancaster, Wi., U.S. **F3** 142
Lancaster, co., Ne., U.S. **D9** 120
Lancaster, co., Pa., U.S. **G9** 131
Lancaster, co., S.C., U.S. **B6** 133
Lancaster, co., Va., U.S. **C6** 139
Lance Creek, stm., Wy., U.S. **C8** 143
Lanchow see Lanzhou, China **D8** 28
Lanciano, Italy **C5** 18
Lancun, China **B5** 30
Lândana, Ang. **E2** 54
Land Between the Lakes, U.S. **f9** 110
Landeck, Aus. **G12** 12
Landegode, Nor. **C6** 10
Lander, Wy., U.S. **D4** 143
Lander, co., Nv., U.S. **C4** 121
Landerneau, Fr. **C4** 16
Landes, reg., Fr. **E6** 16
Landess, In., U.S. **C6** 107
Landis, N.C., U.S. **B2** 126
Lando, S.C., U.S. **B5** 133
Landrum, S.C., U.S. **A3** 133
Land's End, c., Eng., U.K. **E4** 12
Lands End, c., R.I., U.S. **F5** 132
Landshut, Ger. **F13** 12
Landskrona, Swe. **I5** 10
Lane, co., Ks., U.S. **D3** 109
Lane, co., Or., U.S. **C4** 130
La Negra, Chile **C3** 72
Lanesboro, Mn., U.S. **G7** 116
Lanett, Al., U.S. **C4** 94
Langdon, N.D., U.S. **A7** 127
Langeland, i., Den. **I4** 10
Langeloth, Pa., U.S. **F1** 131
Langfang, China **B4** 30
Langhorne, Pa., U.S. **F12** 131
Langjökull, Ice. **l20** 10a
Langkawi, Pulau, i., Malay. **B1** 36
Langlade, co., Wi., U.S. **C4** 142
Langley, B.C., Can. **f13** 85
Langley, S.C., U.S. **E4** 133
Langley, Wa., U.S. **A3** 140
Langley Air Force Base, mil., Va., U.S. **h15** 139
Langley Park, Md., U.S. **f9** 113
Langøya, i., Nor. **B6** 10
Langres, Fr. **D9** 16
Langsa, Indon. **C1** 36
Lang Son, Viet. **B5** 34
Langston, Ok., U.S. **B4** 129
Languedoc, hist. reg., Fr. **F8** 16
L'Anguille, stm., Ar., U.S. **B5** 97
Langzhong, China **E9** 28
Lanham, Md., U.S. **C4** 113
Lanier, co., Ga., U.S. **E3** 103
Länkäran, Azer. **C13** 44
Lannion, Fr. **C5** 16
Lannon, Wi., U.S. **m11** 142
L'Annonciation, P.Q., Can. **C3** 90
Lanping, China **A3** 34
Lansdale, Pa., U.S. **F11** 131
Lansdowne, Md., U.S. **B4** 113
L'Anse, Mi., U.S. **B2** 115
L'Anse-au-Loup, Nf., Can. **C3** 88
L'Anse Indian Reservation, Mi., U.S. **B2** 115
Lansford, Pa., U.S. **E10** 131
Lanshan, China **D3** 30
Lansing, Ia., U.S. **A6** 108
Lansing, Il., U.S. **B6** 106
Lansing, Ks., U.S. **C9** 109
Lansing, Mi., U.S. **F6** 115
Lantana, Fl., U.S. **F6** 102
Lanxi, China **F11** 28
Lanzarote, i., Spain **A2** 50
Lanzhou, China **D8** 28
Laoag, Phil. **C8** 34
Laoang, Phil. **D9** 34
Lao Cai, Viet. **B4** 34
Laoha, stm., China **C12** 28
Laohekou, China **E10** 28
Laon, Fr. **C8** 16
La Orchila, Isla, i., Ven. **C6** 80
La Oroya, Peru **F4** 70
Laos, ctry., Asia **B3** 32
La Palma, Pan. **D4** 80
La Palma, i., Spain **A1** 50
La Paragua, Ven. **B7** 70
La Paz, Arg. **E6** 72
La Paz, Bol. **B4** 72
La Paz, Mex. **C2** 78
La Paz, co., Az., U.S. **D2** 96
Lapeer, Mi., U.S. **E7** 115
Lapeer, co., Mi., U.S. **E7** 115
Lapel, In., U.S. **D6** 107
La Perouse Strait, strt., Asia **B16** 28
La Pine, Or., U.S. **D5** 130
Lapinlahti, Fin. **E12** 10
La Place, La., U.S. **h11** 111
Lapland (Lappland), hist. reg., Eur. **B8** 10
La Plata, Arg. **F6** 72
La Plata, Md., U.S. **C4** 113
La Plata, Mo., U.S. **A5** 118
La Plata, co., Co., U.S. **D3** 99
La Plata Mountains, mts., Co., U.S. **D3** 99
La Plata Peak, mtn., Co., U.S. **B4** 99
La Platte, stm., Vt., U.S. **C2** 138
La Pocatière, P.Q., Can. **B7** 90
Laporte, Co., U.S. **A5** 99
La Porte, In., U.S. **A4** 107
La Porte, Tx., U.S. **r14** 136
La Porte, co., In., U.S. **A4** 107
La Porte City, Ia., U.S. **B5** 108
Lappeenranta, Fin. **F13** 10
Lappland (Lapland), hist. reg., Eur. **B8** 10
La Prairie, P.Q., Can. **D4** 90
La Pryor, Tx., U.S. **E3** 136
Laptev Sea see Laptevyh, more, Russia **B14** 26
Laptevyh, more, Russia **B14** 26
La Push, Wa., U.S. **B1** 140
Lapwai, Id., U.S. **C2** 105
La Quiaca, Arg. **C4** 72
L'Áquila, Italy **C4** 18
Lār, Iran **E6** 42
Larache, Mor. **C3** 48
Laramie, Wy., U.S. **E7** 143
Laramie, co., Wy., U.S. **E8** 143
Laramie, stm., U.S. **E7** 143
Laramie Mountains, mts., Wy., U.S. **D7** 143
Laramie Peak, mtn., Wy., U.S. **D7** 143
Larantuka, Indon. **E6** 36
Lärbro, Swe. **H8** 10
Larchmont, N.Y., U.S. **h13** 125
Larchwood, Ia., U.S. **A1** 108
Laredo, Spain **F5** 16
Laredo, Tx., U.S. **F3** 136
Largo, Fl., U.S. **E4** 102
Largo, Cañon, val., N.M., U.S. **A2** 124
Largo, Key, i., Fl., U.S. **G6** 102
Larimer, co., Co., U.S. **A5** 99
Larimore, N.D., U.S. **B8** 127
La Rioja, Arg. **D4** 72
La Rioja, reg., Spain **F5** 16
Lárisa, Grc. **E9** 18
Lārkāna, Pak. **E9** 42
Lark Harbour, Nf., Can. **D2** 88
Larkspur, Ca., U.S. **h7** 98
Larksville, Pa., U.S. **n17** 131
Larnaca see Lárnax, Cyp. **E5** 44
Lárnax, Cyp. **E5** 44
Larne, N. Ire., U.K. **C4** 12
Larned, Ks., U.S. **D4** 109

Name — Map Ref. — Page

La Rochelle, Fr. D6 16
La Roche-sur-Yon, Fr. D6 16
La Roda, Spain H5 16
La Romana, Dom. Rep. B6 80
Larose, La., U.S. E5 111
Larrimah, Austl. D5 60
Larsen Ice Shelf, Ant. C34 67
Larue, co., Ky., U.S. C4 110
Larvik, Nor. G4 10
LaSalle, P.Q., Can. q19 90
La Salle, Co., U.S. A6 99
La Salle, Il., U.S. B4 106
La Salle, co., Il., U.S. B4 106
La Salle, co., La., U.S. C3 111
La Salle, co., Tx., U.S. E3 136
Las Animas, Co., U.S. C7 99
Las Animas, co., Co., U.S. D6 99
La Sarre, P.Q., Can. k11 90
Las Casitas, mtn., Mex. C3 78
Las Choapas, Mex. D6 78
La Scie, Nf., Can. D4 88
Las Cruces, N.M., U.S. E3 124
La Selle, Morne, mtn., Haiti B5 80
La Serena, Chile C2 69
La Serena, reg., Spain H4 16
La Seyne-sur-Mer, Fr. F9 16
Las Flores, Arg. F6 72
Lāsh-e Joveyn, Afg. D8 42
Las Heras, Arg. G3 69
Lashio, Myan. B3 34
Lashkar Gāh, Afg. D8 42
Las Margaritas, Mex. D6 78
Las Minas, Cerro, mtn., Hond. C2 80
La Solana, Spain H5 16
Las Palmas de Gran Canaria, Spain A1 50
La Spezia, Italy B2 18
Las Piedras, Ur. E6 72
Las Plumas, Arg. F3 69
Las Rosas, Mex. D6 78
Lassen, co., Ca., U.S. B3 98
Lassen Peak, vol., Ca., U.S. B3 98
Lassen Volcanic National Park, Ca., U.S. B3 98
L'Assomption, P.Q., Can. D4 90
Las Tablas, Pan. D3 80
Last Mountain Lake, l., Sk., Can. F3 91
Lastoursville, Gabon D2 54
Las Tunas, Cuba A4 80
Las Varas, Mex. B3 78
Las Varas, Mex. C3 78
Las Vegas, N.M., U.S. B4 124
Las Vegas, Nv., U.S. G6 121
Latah, co., Id., U.S. C2 105
Latakia see Al-Lādhiqīyah, Syria E6 44
Lathrop, Mo., U.S. B3 118
Latimer, co., Ok., U.S. C6 129
Latina, Italy D4 18
Laton, Ca., U.S. D4 98
La Tortuga, Isla, i., Ven. C6 80
Latouche Treville, Cape, c., Austl. D3 60
Latour Peak, mtn., Id., U.S. B2 105
Latrobe, Pa., U.S. F3 131
Latta, S.C., U.S. C9 133
La Tuque, P.Q., Can. B5 90
Lātūr, India F3 40
Latvia, ctry., Eur. H11 10
Lauderdale, Ms., U.S. C5 117
Lauderdale, co., Al., U.S. A2 94
Lauderdale, co., Ms., U.S. C5 117
Lauderdale, co., Tn., U.S. B2 135
Lauderdale Lakes, Fl., U.S. r13 102
Laughlin, Nv., U.S. H7 121
Laughlin Air Force Base, mil., Tx., U.S. E2 136
Laughlin Peak, mtn., N.M., U.S. A5 124
Laughlintown, Pa., U.S. F3 131
Launceston, Austl. I4 62
Launching Point, c., P.E., Can. C7 87
La Unión, Chile F2 69
La Unión, El Sal. C2 80
La Unión, Spain I6 16
Laurel, De., U.S. F3 101
Laurel, Fl., U.S. E4 102
Laurel, Md., U.S. B4 113
Laurel, Ms., U.S. D4 117
Laurel, Mt., U.S. E8 119
Laurel, Ne., U.S. B8 120
Laurel, Va., U.S. C5 139
Laurel, co., Ky., U.S. C5 110
Laurel, stm., Ky., U.S. D5 110
Laurel Bay, S.C., U.S. G6 133
Laurel Creek, stm., W.V., U.S. n14 141
Laurel Creek, stm., W.V., U.S. m12 141
Laureldale, Pa., U.S. F10 131
Laurel Fork, stm., W.V., U.S. C5 141
Laurel Hill, N.C., U.S. C3 126
Laurel River Lake, res., Ky., U.S. D5 110
Laurence G. Hanscom Air Force Base, mil., Ma., U.S. g10 114
Laurence Harbor, N.J., U.S. C4 123
Laurens, Ia., U.S. B3 108
Laurens, S.C., U.S. C3 133
Laurens, co., Ga., U.S. D4 103
Laurens, co., S.C., U.S. C4 133
Laurentides, P.Q., Can. D4 90
Laurentides, Parc Provincial des, P.Q., Can. B6 90
Lau Ridge K21 64
Laurier, P.Q., Can. C6 90
Laurierville, P.Q., Can. C6 90
Laurinburg, N.C., U.S. C3 126
Laurium, Mi., U.S. A2 115
Lausanne, Switz. A1 18
Laut, Pulau, i., Indon. C3 36
Laut, Pulau, i., Indon. D5 36
Laut, Selat, strt., Indon. D5 36
Lautaro, Chile E2 69
Lauzon (part of Lévis-Lauzon), P.Q., Can. C6 90
Lava Beds National Monument, Ca., U.S. B3 98
Lavaca, Ar., U.S. B1 97
Lavaca, co., Tx., U.S. E4 136
Laval, P.Q., Can. D4 90
Laval, Fr. C6 16
La Vale, Md., U.S. k13 113
La Vall d'Uixó, Spain H6 16
Lavaltrie, P.Q., Can. D4 90
Laveen, Az., U.S. m8 96
La Vega, Dom. Rep. B5 80
L'Avenir, P.Q., Can. D5 90
La Vergne, Tn., U.S. A5 135
La Verkin, Ut., U.S. F2 137
La Verne, Ca., U.S. m13 98
Laverne, Ok., U.S. A2 129
Laverton, Austl. F3 60
La Veta, Co., U.S. D5 99
La Victoria, Ven. C6 80
La Vila Joiosa, Spain H6 16
La Vista, Ne., U.S. g12 120
Lavonia, Ga., U.S. B3 103
Lavon Lake, res., Tx., U.S. m10 136
Lavras, Braz. F2 74
Lavumisa, Swaz. D5 56
Lawai, Hi., U.S. B2 104
Lawn, Nf., Can. E4 88
Lawra, Ghana D4 50
Lawrence, In., U.S. E5 107
Lawrence, Ks., U.S. D8 109
Lawrence, Ma., U.S. A5 114
Lawrence, Mi., U.S. F4 115
Lawrence, N.Y., U.S. k13 125
Lawrence, co., Al., U.S. A2 94
Lawrence, co., Ar., U.S. A4 97
Lawrence, co., Il., U.S. E6 106
Lawrence, co., In., U.S. G4 107
Lawrence, co., Ky., U.S. B7 110
Lawrence, co., Mo., U.S. D4 118
Lawrence, co., Ms., U.S. D3 117
Lawrence, co., Oh., U.S. D3 128
Lawrence, co., Pa., U.S. E1 131
Lawrence, co., Tn., U.S. B4 135
Lawrenceburg, In., U.S. F8 107
Lawrenceburg, Ky., U.S. B5 110
Lawrenceburg, Tn., U.S. B4 135
Lawrence Park, Pa., U.S. B1 131
Lawrenceville, Ga., U.S. C3 103
Lawrenceville, Il., U.S. E6 106
Lawrenceville, Va., U.S. D5 139
Lawson, Mo., U.S. B3 118
Lawsonia, Md., U.S. E6 113
Lawtell, La., U.S. D3 111
Lawton, Mi., U.S. F5 115
Lawton, Ok., U.S. C3 129
Lawz, Jabal al-, mtn., Sau. Ar. E3 42
Laxå, Swe. G6 10
Lay Lake, res., Al., U.S. B3 94
Laysan Island, i., Hi., U.S. k13 104
Layton, Ut., U.S. B4 137
Lazarev, Russia D16 26
Lázaro Cárdenas, Mex. D4 78
Lazo, Russia B2 31
Leachville, Ar., U.S. B5 97
Lead, S.D., U.S. C2 134
Leadbetter Point, c., Wa., U.S. C1 140
Leadville, Co., U.S. B4 99
Leadwood, Mo., U.S. D7 118
Leaf, stm., Ms., U.S. D5 117
Leaf Rapids, Mb., Can. A1 86
Leake, co., Ms., U.S. C4 117
Leakesville, Ms., U.S. D5 117
Lealman, Fl., U.S. p10 102
Leamington, On., Can. E2 89
Leary, Ga., U.S. E2 103
Leatherman Peak, mtn., Id., U.S. E5 105
Leavenworth, Ks., U.S. C9 109
Leavenworth, Wa., U.S. B5 140
Leavenworth, co., Ks., U.S. C8 109
Leavittsburg, Oh., U.S. A5 128
Leawood, Ks., U.S. D9 109
Lebanon, De., U.S. D4 101
Lebanon, Il., U.S. E4 106
Lebanon, In., U.S. D5 107
Lebanon, Ky., U.S. C4 110
Lebanon, Mo., U.S. D5 118
Lebanon, N.H., U.S. C2 122
Lebanon, Oh., U.S. C1 128
Lebanon, Or., U.S. C4 130
Lebanon, Pa., U.S. F9 131
Lebanon, Tn., U.S. A5 135
Lebanon, Va., U.S. f9 139
Lebanon, co., Pa., U.S. F8 131
Lebanon, ctry., Asia E6 44
Lebanon Junction, Ky., U.S. C4 110
Lebanon Mountains see Lubnān, Jabal, mts., Leb. F6 44
Lebedjan', Russia C15 20
Lebedyn, Ukr. D13 20
Lebesby, Nor. A12 10
Lebjaže, Kaz. D9 26
Lebo, Ks., U.S. D8 109
Lębork, Pol. B4 20
Lebu, Chile E2 69
Lecce, Italy D7 18
Lecco, Italy B2 18
Le Center, Mn., U.S. F5 116
Lechang, China D3 30
Le Claire, Ia., U.S. C7 108
Lecompte, La., U.S. C3 111
Lecompton, Ks., U.S. C8 109
Le Creusot, Fr. D9 16
Łęczyca, Pol. C5 20
Ledjanaja, gora, mtn., Russia C19 26
Ledo, India D7 40
Ledu, China B1 30
Leduc, Ab., Can. C4 84
Lee, Ma., U.S. B1 114
Lee, co., Al., U.S. C4 94
Lee, co., Ar., U.S. C5 97
Lee, co., Fl., U.S. F5 102
Lee, co., Ga., U.S. E2 103
Lee, co., Ia., U.S. D6 108
Lee, co., Il., U.S. B4 106
Lee, co., Ky., U.S. C6 110
Lee, co., Ms., U.S. A5 117
Lee, co., N.C., U.S. B3 126
Lee, co., S.C., U.S. C7 133
Lee, co., Tx., U.S. D4 136
Lee, co., Va., U.S. f8 139
Lee, Lake, l., Ms., U.S. B3 117
Leechburg, Pa., U.S. E2 131
Leech Lake, l., Mn., U.S. C4 116
Leech Lake Indian Reservation, Mn., U.S. C4 116
Lee Creek, stm., U.S. B1 97
Leeds, Eng., U.K. D6 12
Leeds, Al., U.S. B3 94
Leelanau, co., Mi., U.S. D5 115
Leelanau, Lake, l., Mi., U.S. C5 115
Lee Park, Pa., U.S. n17 131
Leer, Ger. D10 12
Leesburg, Fl., U.S. D5 102
Leesburg, Ga., U.S. E2 103
Leesburg, Oh., U.S. C2 128
Leesburg, Va., U.S. A5 139
Lees Summit, Mo., U.S. C3 118
Leesville, La., U.S. C2 111
Leesville, S.C., U.S. D4 133
Leesville Lake, res., Va., U.S. C3 139
Leeton, Austl. G4 62
Leeton, Mo., U.S. C4 118
Leetonia, Oh., U.S. B5 128
Leetsdale, Pa., U.S. h13 131
Leeuwarden, Neth. D9 12
Leeuwin, Cape, c., Austl. G1 60
Leeward Islands, is., N.A. E12 76
Leflore, co., Ms., U.S. B3 117
Le Flore, co., Ok., U.S. C7 129
Lega Hida, Eth. B8 54
Legal, Ab., Can. C4 84
Leganés, Spain G5 16
Legaspi, Phil. D8 34
Leghorn see Livorno, Italy C3 18
Legnica, Pol. D4 20
Le Grand, Ca., U.S. D3 98
Le Grand, Ia., U.S. B5 108
Leh, India C3 40
Le Havre, Fr. C7 16
Lehi, Ut., U.S. C4 137
Lehigh, co., Pa., U.S. E10 131
Lehigh, stm., Pa., U.S. E10 131
Lehigh Acres, Fl., U.S. F5 102
Lehighton, Pa., U.S. E10 131
Lehua Island, i., Hi., U.S. A1 104
Lehututu, Bots. C3 56
Leicester, Eng., U.K. D6 12
Leicester, Ma., U.S. B4 114
Leiden, Neth. D9 12
Leighton, Al., U.S. A2 94
Leinster, hist. reg., Ire. D3 12
Leipsic, De., U.S. D3 101
Leipsic, Oh., U.S. A2 128
Leipsic, stm., De., U.S. C3 101
Leipzig, Ger. E13 12
Leiria, Port. H2 16
Leisler, Mount, mtn., Austl. E4 60
Leisure City, Fl., U.S. s13 102
Leitchfield, Ky., U.S. C3 110
Leiyang, China D3 30
Leizhou Bandao, pen., China E3 30
Leka, Nor. D4 10
Leland, Il., U.S. B5 106
Leland, Ms., U.S. B3 117
Leleiwi Point, c., Hi., U.S. D7 104
Leleque, Arg. F2 69
Leling, China B4 30
Leli Shan, mtn., China E4 28
Le Mans, Fr. C7 16
Le Mars, Ia., U.S. B1 108
Lema Shilindi, Eth. C8 54
Lemesós, Cyp. E5 44
Lemhi, co., Id., U.S. E4 105
Lemhi, stm., Id., U.S. E5 105
Lemhi Pass, Id., U.S. E5 105
Lemhi Range, mts., Id., U.S. E5 105
Lemmon, S.D., U.S. B3 134
Lemmon, Mount, mtn., Az., U.S. E5 96
Lemmon Valley, Nv., U.S. D2 121
Lemnos see Límnos, i., Grc. E10 18
Lemon, Lake, l., In., U.S. F5 107
Lemon Fair, stm., Vt., U.S. C2 138
Lemon Grove, Ca., U.S. o15 98
Lemon Island, i., S.C., U.S. G6 133
Lemont, Il., U.S. B5 106
Lemont, Pa., U.S. E6 131
Lemonweir, stm., Wi., U.S. D3 142
Lemoore, Ca., U.S. D4 98
Lemoore Naval Air Station, mil., Ca., U.S. D4 98
Lempa, stm., N.A. C2 80
Lem Peak, mtn., Id., U.S. E5 105
Lena, Il., U.S. A4 106
Lena, stm., Russia B14 26
Lenawee, co., Mi., U.S. G6 115
Lenexa, Ks., U.S. D9 109
Lenghu, China D6 28
Leninakan see Gjumri, Arm. B10 44
Leningrad see Sankt-Peterburg, Russia D5 26
Leninogorsk, Kaz. A4 28
Lenin Peak, mtn., Asia B2 40
Leninsk, Kaz. E8 26
Leninsk-Kuzneckij, Russia D10 26
Leninskoe, Russia E15 26
Lennonville, Austl. F2 60
Lennox, S.D., U.S. D9 134
Lennoxville, P.Q., Can. D6 90
Lenoir, N.C., U.S. B1 126
Lenoir, co., N.C., U.S. B5 126
Lenoir City, Tn., U.S. D9 135
Lenore Lake, l., Sk., Can. E3 91
Lenore Lake, l., Wa., U.S. B6 140
Lenox, Ga., U.S. E3 103
Lenox, Ia., U.S. D3 108
Lenox, Ma., U.S. B1 114
Lens, Fr. B8 16
Lensk, Russia C13 26
Lentini, Italy F5 18
Léo, Burkina D4 50
Leo, In., U.S. B7 107
Leoben, Aus. G14 12
Leominster, Ma., U.S. A4 114
León, Mex. C4 78
León, Nic. C2 80
León, Spain F4 16
Leon, Ia., U.S. D4 108
Leon, Ks., U.S. E7 109
Leon, co., Fl., U.S. B2 102
Leon, co., Tx., U.S. D4 136
Leonard, Tx., U.S. C4 136
Leonardo, N.J., U.S. C4 123
Leonardtown, Md., U.S. D4 113
Leonia, N.J., U.S. h9 123
Leonora, Austl. F3 60
Leonville, La., U.S. D4 111
Leopold and Astrid Coast, Ant. C13 67
Léopoldville see Kinshasa, D.R.C. D3 54
Leoti, Ks., U.S. D2 109
Lepanto, Ar., U.S. B5 97
Lepar, Pulau, i., Indon. D3 36
Lepe, Spain I3 16
Lepel', Bela. B10 20
Leping, China D4 30
L'Épiphanie, P.Q., Can. D4 90
Lepsy, Kaz. B3 28
Le Puy, Fr. E8 16
Le Roy, Il., U.S. C5 106
Le Roy, Mn., U.S. G6 116
Le Roy, N.Y., U.S. C3 125
Lerwick, Scot., U.K. h19 12a
Léry, P.Q., Can. q19 90
Lery, Lake, l., La., U.S. k12 111
Lesbos see Lésvos, i., Grc. E10 18
Les Cayes, Haiti B5 80
Leskovac, Yugo. C8 18
Leslie, Mi., U.S. F6 115
Leslie, S.C., U.S. B6 133
Leslie, co., Ky., U.S. C6 110
Lesosibirsk, Russia D11 26
Lesotho, ctry., Afr. D4 56
Lesozavodsk, Russia B14 28
Les Sables-d'Olonne, Fr. D6 16
Lesser Antilles, is. F12 76
Lesser Caucasus, mts., Asia B11 44
Lesser Khingan Range see Xiao Hinggan Ling, mts., China A1 31
Lesser Slave Lake, l., Ab., Can. B3 84
Lesser Sunda Islands see Tenggara, Nusa, is., Indon. E5 36
Lester Prairie, Mn., U.S. F4 116
Le Sueur, Mn., U.S. F5 116
Le Sueur, co., Mn., U.S. F5 116
Lešukonskoe, Russia B8 22
Lésvos, i., Grc. E10 18
Leszno, Pol. D4 20
Letcher, co., Ky., U.S. C7 110
Lethbridge, Ab., Can. E4 84
Lethbridge, Nf., Can. D5 88
Lethem, Guy. C8 70
Leti, Kepulauan, is., Indon. E7 36
Leticia, Col. D6 70
Leting, China B4 30
Letlhakeng, Bots. C3 56
Letsôk-aw Kyun, i., Myan. D3 34
Levádhia, Grc. E9 18
Levanger, Nor. E4 10
Levelland, Tx., U.S. C1 136
Leveque, Cape, c., Austl. D3 60
Levice, Slvk. E5 20
Levin, N.Z. p14 63c
Levisa Fork, stm., U.S. C7 110
Lévis [-Lauzon], P.Q., Can. C6 90
Levittown, N.Y., U.S. E7 125
Levittown, Pa., U.S. F12 131
Levkás, i., Grc. E8 18
Levy, co., Fl., U.S. C4 102
Levy Lake, l., Fl., U.S. C4 102
Lewes, De., U.S. E5 101
Lewes and Rehoboth Canal, De., U.S. F5 101
Lewis, co., Id., U.S. C2 105
Lewis, co., Ky., U.S. B6 110
Lewis, co., Mo., U.S. A6 118
Lewis, co., N.Y., U.S. B5 125
Lewis, co., Tn., U.S. B4 135
Lewis, co., W.V., U.S. C4 141
Lewis, co., Wa., U.S. C3 140
Lewis, stm., Wa., U.S. C4 140
Lewis, stm., Wy., U.S. B2 143
Lewis, Isle of, i., Scot., U.K. A3 12
Lewis, Mount, mtn., Nv., U.S. C5 121
Lewis and Clark, co., Mt., U.S. C4 119
Lewis and Clark Cavern, Mt., U.S. D5 119
Lewis and Clark Lake, res., U.S. E8 134
Lewisburg, Ky., U.S. D3 110
Lewisburg, Oh., U.S. C1 128
Lewisburg, Pa., U.S. E8 131
Lewisburg, Tn., U.S. B5 135
Lewisburg, W.V., U.S. D4 141
Lewis Creek, stm., Vt., U.S. C2 138
Lewis Lake, l., Wy., U.S. B2 143
Lewisport, Ky., U.S. C3 110
Lewisporte, Nf., Can. D4 88
Lewis Smith Lake, res., Al., U.S. B2 94
Lewiston, Id., U.S. C1 105
Lewiston, Me., U.S. D2 112
Lewiston, Mn., U.S. G7 116
Lewiston, N.Y., U.S. B1 125
Lewiston, Ut., U.S. B4 137
Lewiston Peak, mtn., Ut., U.S. C3 137
Lewiston Woodville, N.C., U.S. A5 126
Lewistown, Il., U.S. C3 106
Lewistown, Mt., U.S. C7 119
Lewistown, Pa., U.S. E6 131
Lewisville, Ar., U.S. D2 97
Lewisville, Tx., U.S. C4 136
Lewisville Lake, res., Tx., U.S. C4 136
Lexington, Al., U.S. A2 94
Lexington, Il., U.S. C5 106
Lexington, Ky., U.S. B5 110
Lexington, Ma., U.S. B5 114
Lexington, Mi., U.S. E8 115
Lexington, Mo., U.S. B4 118
Lexington, Ms., U.S. B3 117
Lexington, N.C., U.S. B2 126
Lexington, Ne., U.S. D6 120
Lexington, Oh., U.S. B3 128
Lexington, Ok., U.S. B4 129
Lexington, S.C., U.S. D5 133
Lexington, Tn., U.S. B3 135
Lexington, Va., U.S. C3 139
Lexington, co., S.C., U.S. D5 133
Lexington Park, Md., U.S. D5 113
Leye, China E2 30
Leyte, i., Phil. D9 34
Lezhë, Alb. D7 18
L'gov, Russia D13 20
Lhasa, China F6 28
Lhazê, China D5 40
Lhokseumawe, Indon. B1 36
Lhorong, China E7 28
L'Hospitalet de Llobregat, Spain G8 16
Lhünzê, China D6 40
Liancheng, China A7 34
Lianga, Phil. E9 34
Lianjiang, China E3 30
Lianxian, China G10 28
Lianyungang, China E11 28
Liao, stm., China C12 28
Liaocheng, China B4 30
Liaodong Bandao, pen., China D12 28
Liaodong Bay see Liaodong Wan, b., China C12 28
Liaodong Wan, b., China C12 28
Liaoning, state, China C12 28
Liaotung, Gulf of see Liaodong Wan, b., China C12 28
Liaotung Bay see Liaodong Wan, b., China C12 28
Liaoyang, China A5 30
Liaoyuan, China C13 28
Liard, stm., Can. F15 82
Libagon, Phil. D9 34
Libby, Mt., U.S. B1 119
Libenge, D.R.C. C3 54
Liberal, Ks., U.S. E3 109
Liberal, Mo., U.S. D3 118
Liberec, Czech Rep. D3 20
Liberia, C.R. C2 80

Name / Map Ref. / Page

Liberia, ctry., Afr. E3 50
Liberty, In., U.S. E8 107
Liberty, Ky., U.S. C5 110
Liberty, Mo., U.S. B3 118
Liberty, Ms., U.S. D3 117
Liberty, N.C., U.S. B3 126
Liberty, N.Y., U.S. D6 125
Liberty, S.C., U.S. B2 133
Liberty, Tx., U.S. D5 136
Liberty, co., Fl., U.S. B2 102
Liberty, co., Ga., U.S. E5 103
Liberty, co., Mt., U.S. B5 119
Liberty, co., Tx., U.S. D5 136
Liberty Center, Oh., U.S. A1 128
Liberty Lake, Wa., U.S. g14 140
Liberty Lake, res., Md., U.S. B4 113
Libertyville, Il., U.S. A6 106
Lībīyah, Aṣ-Ṣaḥrā' al- (Libyan Desert), des., Afr. E9 48
Libo, China D2 30
Libourne, Fr. E6 16
Libreville, Gabon C1 54
Libuse, La., U.S. C3 111
Libya, ctry., Afr. E8 48
Libyan Desert see Lībīyah, Aṣ-Ṣaḥrā' al-, des., Afr. E9 48
Licancábur, Cerro, vol., S.A. C4 72
Licata, Italy F4 18
Lice, Tur. C9 44
Lichinga, Moz. A6 56
Lichuan, China C2 30
Lichuan, China D4 30
Lick Creek, stm., Tn., U.S. C11 135
Licking, Mo., U.S. D6 118
Licking, co., Oh., U.S. B3 128
Licking, stm., Ky., U.S. B6 110
Lida, Bela. C8 20
Lida, Lake, l., Mn., U.S. D3 116
Liden, Swe. E7 10
Lidgerwood, N.D., U.S. C8 127
Lidköping, Swe. G5 10
Lido di Ostia, Italy D4 18
Lidzbark Warmiński, Pol. B6 20
Liebig, Mount, mtn., Austl. E5 60
Liechtenstein, ctry., Eur. A2 18
Liège, Bel. E9 12
Lienz, Aus. G13 12
Liepāja, Lat. H9 10
Lièvre, Rivière du, stm., P.Q., Can. D2 90
Lifou, i., N. Cal. I9 62a
Lighthouse Inlet, b., S.C., U.S. k12 133
Lighthouse Point, c., Fl., U.S. C2 102
Lighthouse Point, c., La., U.S. E3 111
Lighthouse Point, c., Mi., U.S. C5 115
Lightning Creek, stm., Wy., U.S. C8 143
Ligonier, In., U.S. B6 107
Ligonier, Pa., U.S. F3 131
Ligurian Apennines see Appennino Ligure, mts., Italy B2 18
Ligurian Sea, Eur. C2 18
Lihue, Hi., U.S. B2 104
Lijiang, China F8 28
Likasi, D.R.C. F5 54
Likati, D.R.C. C4 54
Lilbourn, Mo., U.S. E8 118
Lilburn, Ga., U.S. h8 103
Lille, Fr. B8 16
Lillebælt, strt., Den. I3 10
Lillehammer, Nor. F4 10
Lillesand, Nor. G3 10
Lillestrøm, Nor. G4 10
Lillian, Al., U.S. E2 94
Lillington, N.C., U.S. B4 126
Lillinonah, Lake, l., Ct., U.S. C2 100
Lillooet, B.C., Can. D7 85
Lillooet, stm., B.C., Can. D6 85
Lilly, Pa., U.S. F4 131
Lilly Fork, stm., W.V., U.S. m13 141
Lilly Grove, W.V., U.S. D3 141
Lilongwe, Mwi. A5 56
Liloy, Phil. E8 34
Lily, Ky., U.S. C5 110
Lima, Peru F4 70
Lima, N.Y., U.S. C3 125
Lima, Oh., U.S. B1 128
Lima Reservoir, res., Mt., U.S. F4 119
Limay Mahuida, Arg. F4 72
Limbe, Cam. C1 54
Limbé, Haiti B5 80
Limeira, Braz. F2 74
Limerick, Ire. D2 12
Limestone, Me., U.S. B5 112
Limestone, co., Al., U.S. A2 94
Limestone, co., Tx., U.S. D4 136
Limestone Point, pen., Mb., Can. C2 86
Limfjorden, l., Den. H3 10
Limingen, l., Nor. D5 10
Limmen Bight, b., Austl. C6 60
Límnos, i., Grc. E10 18
Limoges, On., Can. B9 89
Limoges, Fr. E7 16
Limón, Hond. B2 80
Limon, Co., U.S. B7 99
Limoux, Fr. F8 16
Limpopo, stm., Afr. C5 56
Lin'an, China C4 30
Linapacan Strait, strt., Phil. D7 34
Linares, Chile E2 69
Linares, Mex. C5 78
Linares, Spain H5 16
Lincoln, Arg. E5 72
Lincoln, On., Can. D5 89
Lincoln, Eng., U.K. D6 12
Lincoln, Al., U.S. B3 94
Lincoln, Ar., U.S. B1 97
Lincoln, Ca., U.S. C3 98
Lincoln, De., U.S. E4 101
Lincoln, Id., U.S. F6 105
Lincoln, Il., U.S. C4 106
Lincoln, Ks., U.S. C5 109
Lincoln, Ma., U.S. g10 114
Lincoln, Me., U.S. C4 112
Lincoln, Mo., U.S. C4 118
Lincoln, Ne., U.S. D9 120
Lincoln, N.H., U.S. B3 122
Lincoln, co., Ar., U.S. D4 97
Lincoln, co., Co., U.S. C7 99
Lincoln, co., Ga., U.S. C4 103
Lincoln, co., Id., U.S. G4 105
Lincoln, co., Ks., U.S. C5 109
Lincoln, co., Ky., U.S. C5 110
Lincoln, co., La., U.S. B3 111
Lincoln, co., Me., U.S. D3 112
Lincoln, co., Mn., U.S. F2 116
Lincoln, co., Mo., U.S. B7 118
Lincoln, co., Ms., U.S. D3 117
Lincoln, co., Mt., U.S. B1 119
Lincoln, co., N.C., U.S. B1 126
Lincoln, co., Ne., U.S. D5 120
Lincoln, co., N.M., U.S. D4 124
Lincoln, co., Nv., U.S. F6 121
Lincoln, co., Ok., U.S. B5 129
Lincoln, co., Or., U.S. C3 130
Lincoln, co., S.D., U.S. D9 134
Lincoln, co., Tn., U.S. B5 135
Lincoln, co., W.V., U.S. C2 141
Lincoln, co., Wa., U.S. B7 140
Lincoln, co., Wi., U.S. C4 142
Lincoln, co., Wy., U.S. D2 143
Lincoln, Mount, mtn., Co., U.S. B4 99
Lincoln Acres, Ca., U.S. o15 98
Lincoln City, Or., U.S. C3 130
Lincoln Hav see Lincoln Sea, N.A. B28 82
Lincoln Heights, Oh., U.S. o13 128
Lincoln Park, Co., U.S. C5 99
Lincoln Park, Ga., U.S. D2 103
Lincoln Park, Mi., U.S. p15 115
Lincoln Park, N.J., U.S. B4 123
Lincoln Sea, N.A. B28 82
Lincolnshire, Il., U.S. h9 106
Lincoln Tomb State Memorial, hist., Il., U.S. D4 106
Lincolnton, Ga., U.S. C4 103
Lincolnton, N.C., U.S. B1 126
Lincolnville, S.C., U.S. h11 133
Lincolnwood, Il., U.S. h9 106
Lincroft, N.J., U.S. C4 123
Lindale, Ga., U.S. B1 103
Lindale, Tx., U.S. C5 136
Linden, Guy. B8 70
Linden, Al., U.S. C2 94
Linden, In., U.S. D4 107
Linden, Mi., U.S. F7 115
Linden, N.J., U.S. k8 123
Linden, Tn., U.S. B4 135
Linden, Tx., U.S. C5 136
Lindenhurst, Il., U.S. h8 106
Lindenhurst, N.Y., U.S. n15 125
Lindenwold, N.J., U.S. D3 123
Lindesberg, Swe. G6 10
Lindesnes, c., Nor. H2 10
Lindi, Tan. E7 54
Lindon, Ut., U.S. C4 137
Lindsay, On., Can. C6 89
Lindsay, Ca., U.S. D4 98
Lindsay, Ok., U.S. C4 129
Lindsborg, Ks., U.S. D6 109
Lindstrom, Mn., U.S. E6 116
Line Islands, is., Oc. E14 58
Linesville, Pa., U.S. C1 131
Lineville, Al., U.S. B4 94
Linfen, China D10 28
Lingao, China F2 30
Lingayen, Phil. C8 34
Lingayen Gulf, b., Phil. C8 34
Lingen, Ger. D10 12
Lingga, Kepulauan, is., Indon. D3 36
Lingga, Pulau, i., Indon. D2 36
Lingle, Wy., U.S. D8 143
Linglestown, Pa., U.S. F8 131
Lingqiu, China B3 30
Lingshan, China E2 30
Lingshui, China F3 30
Linguère, Sen. C1 50
Lingyuan, China A4 30
Linhai, China F12 28
Linhares, Braz. E3 74
Linhe, China C9 28
Linière, P.Q., Can. C7 90
Linköping, Swe. G6 10
Linkou, China B14 28
Linn, Mo., U.S. C6 118
Linn, co., Ia., U.S. B6 108
Linn, co., Ks., U.S. D9 109
Linn, co., Mo., U.S. B4 118
Linn, co., Or., U.S. C4 130
Lino Lakes, Mn., U.S. m12 116
Linqing, China B4 30
Linquan, China C4 30
Linru, China E10 28
Lins, Braz. F2 74
Lintan, China C1 30
Linthicum Heights, Md., U.S. B4 113
Linton, In., U.S. F3 107
Linton, N.D., U.S. C5 127
Linwood, N.J., U.S. E3 123
Linxi, China C11 28
Linxia, China D8 28
Linyi, China D11 28
Linyi, China B4 30
Linz, Aus. F14 12
Lion, Golfe du, b., Fr. F9 16
Lion, Gulf of see Lion, Golfe du, b., Fr. F9 16
Lipa, Phil. D8 34
Lipeck, Russia D5 26
Lipova, Rom. F6 20
Lipscomb, Al., U.S. B3 94
Lipscomb, co., Tx., U.S. A2 136
Lipu, China E3 30
Lira, Ug. C6 54
Lisala, D.R.C. C4 54
Lisboa (Lisbon), Port. H2 16
Lisbon see Lisboa, Port. H2 16
Lisbon, Ia., U.S. C6 108
Lisbon, Md., U.S. B3 113
Lisbon, Me., U.S. D2 112
Lisbon, N.D., U.S. C8 127
Lisbon, N.H., U.S. B3 122
Lisbon, Oh., U.S. B5 128
Lisbon Center, Me., U.S. f7 112
Lisbon Falls, Me., U.S. E2 112
Lisburne, Cape, c., Ak., U.S. B6 95
Lishui, China F11 28
Lisianski Island, i., Hi., U.S. k13 104
Lisieux, Fr. C7 16
Liski, Russia D5 26
Lisle, Il., U.S. k8 106
L'Islet-sur-Mer, P.Q., Can. B7 90
L'Isle-Verte, P.Q., Can. A8 90
Lismore, Austl. F5 62
Listowel, On., Can. D4 89
Litang, China E8 28
Litang, China G9 28
Litchfield, Ct., U.S. C3 100
Litchfield, Il., U.S. D4 106
Litchfield, Mi., U.S. F6 115
Litchfield, Mn., U.S. E4 116
Litchfield, co., Ct., U.S. B2 100
Litchfield Park, Az., U.S. m8 96
Lithgow, Austl. G5 62
Lithia Springs, Ga., U.S. h7 103
Lithonia, Ga., U.S. C2 103
Lithuania, ctry., Eur. B7 20
Lititz, Pa., U.S. F9 131
Litovko, Russia B15 28
Little, stm., Ct., U.S. C7 100
Little, stm., Ky., U.S. D2 110
Little, stm., La., U.S. C3 111
Little, stm., N.C., U.S. B3 126
Little, stm., Ok., U.S. B5 129
Little, stm., S.C., U.S. C2 133
Little, stm., Tn., U.S. n14 135
Little, stm., Va., U.S. D7 129
Little, stm., Va., U.S. D2 139
Little, stm., Vt., U.S. C3 138
Little, stm., U.S. B5 97
Little Acres, Az., U.S. D5 96
Little Andaman, i., India G6 40
Little Arkansas, stm., Ks., U.S. D6 109
Little Belt see Lillebælt, strt., Den. I3 10
Little Belt Mountains, mts., Mt., U.S. D6 119
Little Bighorn, stm., U.S. E9 119
Little Black, stm., Me., U.S. A3 112
Little Blue, stm., In., U.S. H5 107
Little Blue, stm., U.S. C6 109
Little Bow, stm., Ab., Can. D4 84
Little Cacapon, stm., W.V., U.S. B6 141
Little Catalina, Nf., Can. D5 88
Little Cayman, i., Cay. Is. B3 80
Little Cedar, stm., Ia., U.S. A5 108
Little Churchill, stm., Mb., Can. A4 86
Little Chute, Wi., U.S. D5 142
Little Coal, stm., W.V., U.S. C3 141
Little Colorado, stm., Az., U.S. B4 96
Little Compton, R.I., U.S. E6 132
Little Creek, De., U.S. D4 101
Little Creek Naval Amphibious Base, mil., Va., U.S. k15 139
Little Creek Peak, mtn., Ut., U.S. F3 137
Little Current, On., Can. B3 89
Little Diomede Island, i., Ak., U.S. B6 95
Little Egg Harbor, b., N.J., U.S. D4 123
Little Egg Inlet, b., N.J., U.S. E4 123
Little Falls, Mn., U.S. E4 116
Little Falls, N.J., U.S. B4 123
Little Falls, N.Y., U.S. B6 125
Little Ferry, N.J., U.S. h8 123
Littlefield, Tx., U.S. C1 136
Little Fishing Creek, stm., W.V., U.S. h9 141
Littlefork, Mn., U.S. B5 116
Little Fork, stm., Mn., U.S. B5 116
Little Goose Creek, stm., Wy., U.S. B6 143
Little Gunpowder Falls, stm., Md., U.S. A4 113
Little Humboldt, stm., Nv., U.S. B4 121
Little Inagua, i., Bah. D10 76
Little Kanawha, stm., W.V., U.S. C4 141
Little Karroo, plat., S. Afr. E3 56
Little Lake, Mi., U.S. B3 115
Little Lake, l., La., U.S. E5 111
Little Lynches, stm., S.C., U.S. C7 133
Little Manatee, stm., Fl., U.S. p11 102
Little Mecatina, stm., Can. h9 88
Little Miami, stm., Oh., U.S. C1 128
Little Minch, The, strt., Scot., U.K. B3 12
Little Missouri, stm., Ar., U.S. D2 97
Little Missouri, stm., U.S. B7 92
Little Muddy, stm., Il., U.S. E4 106
Little Muddy, stm., N.D., U.S. A2 127
Little Namaqualand, hist. reg., S. Afr. D2 56
Little Nicobar, i., India H6 40
Little Osage, stm., U.S. E9 109
Little Otter Creek, stm., Vt., U.S. C2 138
Little Owyhee, stm., U.S. B5 121
Little Pee Dee, stm., S.C., U.S. C9 133
Little Powder, stm., U.S. F11 119
Little Red, stm., Ar., U.S. B4 97
Little River, co., Ar., U.S. D1 97
Little River Inlet, b., S.C., U.S. D10 133
Little Rock, Ar., U.S. C3 97
Little Rock, stm., U.S. A1 108
Little Rock Air Force Base, mil., Ar., U.S. C3 97
Little Sable Point, c., Mi., U.S. E4 115
Little Salt Lake, l., Ut., U.S. F3 137
Little Sandy, stm., Ky., U.S. B6 110
Little Sandy Creek, stm., Wy., U.S. D3 143
Little Sebago Lake, l., Me., U.S. g7 112
Little Silver, N.J., U.S. C4 123
Little Sioux, stm., U.S. B2 108
Little Sioux, West Fork, stm., Ia., U.S. B2 108
Little Smoky, stm., Ab., Can. B2 84
Little Snake, stm., U.S. A2 99
Little Spokane, stm., Wa., U.S. B8 140
Littlestown, Pa., U.S. G7 131
Little Tallapoosa, stm., U.S. B4 94
Little Tenmile Creek, stm., W.V., U.S. k10 141
Little Tennessee, stm., U.S. D9 135
Littleton, Co., U.S. B6 99
Littleton, Ma., U.S. f10 114
Littleton, Me., U.S. B5 112
Littleton, N.C., U.S. A5 126
Littleton, N.H., U.S. B3 122
Littleville, Al., U.S. A2 94
Little Wabash, stm., Il., U.S. E5 106
Little Walnut, stm., Ks., U.S. g13 109
Little White, stm., S.D., U.S. D5 134
Little Wolf, stm., Wi., U.S. D4 142
Little Wood, stm., Id., U.S. F4 105
Little Zab, stm., Asia E10 44
Liucheng, China G9 28
Liuzhou, China G9 28
Live Oak, Ca., U.S. C3 98
Live Oak, Fl., U.S. B4 102
Live Oak, co., Tx., U.S. E3 136
Livermore, Ca., U.S. h9 98
Livermore, Ky., U.S. C2 110
Livermore, Mount, mtn., Tx., U.S. o12 136
Livermore Falls, Me., U.S. D2 112
Liverpool, Eng., U.K. D5 12
Lívingston, Guat. B2 80
Livingston, Al., U.S. C1 94
Livingston, Ca., U.S. D3 98
Livingston, Il., U.S. E4 106
Livingston, La., U.S. D5 111
Livingston, Mt., U.S. E6 119
Livingston, N.J., U.S. B4 123
Livingston, Tn., U.S. C8 135
Livingston, Tx., U.S. D5 136
Livingston, co., Il., U.S. C5 106
Livingston, co., Ky., U.S. e9 110
Livingston, co., La., U.S. D5 111
Livingston, co., Mi., U.S. F7 115
Livingston, co., Mo., U.S. B4 118
Livingston, co., N.Y., U.S. C3 125
Livingston, Lake, res., Tx., U.S. D5 136
Livingstone, Zam. B4 56
Livingstone Falls, wtfl., Afr. E2 54
Livingstonia, Mwi. A5 56
Livny, Russia C14 20
Livonia, La., U.S. D4 111
Livonia, Mi., U.S. F7 115
Livorno, Italy C3 18
Liwale, Tan. E7 54
Liwonde, Mwi. B6 56
Lixi, China F10 28
Lixian, China D3 30
Lizard Head Pass, Co., U.S. D3 99
Lizard Head Peak, mtn., Wy., U.S. D3 143
Lizella, Ga., U.S. D3 103
Ljahovskie ostrova, is., Russia B15 26
Ljubercy, Russia C6 22
Ljubljana, Slvn. A5 18
Ljudinovo, Russia C13 20
Ljungby, Swe. H5 10
Ljusdal, Swe. F7 10
Ljusnan, stm., Swe. E6 10
Ljusterö, i., Swe. G8 10
Llancanelo, Laguna, l., Arg. F4 72
Llano, Tx., U.S. D3 136
Llano, co., Tx., U.S. D3 136
Llano, stm., Tx., U.S. D3 136
Llano Estacado see Estacado, Llano, pl., U.S. C1 136
Llanos, pl., S.A. B6 70
Lleida, Spain G7 16
Llera de Canales, Mex. C5 78
Lloyd, Ky., U.S. B7 110
Lloydminster, Ab., Can. C5 84
Lloyds, stm., Nf., Can. D3 88
Llucmajor, Spain H8 16
Llullaillaco, Volcán, vol., S.A. C4 72
Loami, Il., U.S. D4 106
Loange, stm., Afr. E3 54
Lobamba, Swaz. D5 56
Lobatse, Bots. D4 56
Lobelville, Tn., U.S. B4 135
Lobería, Arg. F6 72
Lobito, Ang. F2 54
Lobos, Cay, i., Bah. A4 80
Lobster Lake, l., Me., U.S. C3 112
Lobva, Russia C11 22
Locarno, Switz. A2 18
Loch Raven Reservoir, res., Md., U.S. B4 113
Lochsa, stm., Id., U.S. C3 105
Lockeport, N.S., Can. F4 87
Lockesburg, Ar., U.S. D1 97
Lockhart, Tx., U.S. E4 136
Lock Haven, Pa., U.S. D7 131
Lockland, Oh., U.S. o13 128
Lockney, Tx., U.S. B2 136
Lockport, Il., U.S. B5 106
Lockport, La., U.S. E5 111
Lockport, N.Y., U.S. B2 125
Lockwood, Mo., U.S. D4 118
Lockwood, Mt., U.S. E8 119
Loc Ninh, Viet. D5 34
Locust, N.C., U.S. B2 126
Locust Fork, stm., Al., U.S. B3 94
Locust Grove, Ga., U.S. C2 103
Locust Grove, Ok., U.S. A6 129
Lodejnoe Pole, Russia B5 22
Lodgepole Creek, stm., U.S. C3 120
Lodi, Italy B2 18
Lodi, Ca., U.S. C3 98
Lodi, N.J., U.S. h8 123
Lodi, Oh., U.S. A3 128
Lodi, Wi., U.S. E4 142
Lodja, D.R.C. D4 54
Lodore, Canyon of, val., Co., U.S. A2 99
Lodwar, Kenya C7 54
Łódź, Pol. D5 20
Loei, Thai. C4 34
Lofoten, is., Nor. B5 10
Lofoten Basin D21 144
Loga, Niger D5 50
Logan, Ia., U.S. C2 108
Logan, Ks., U.S. C4 109
Logan, N.M., U.S. B6 124
Logan, Oh., U.S. C3 128
Logan, Ut., U.S. B4 137
Logan, W.V., U.S. D3 141
Logan, co., Ar., U.S. B2 97
Logan, co., Co., U.S. A7 99
Logan, co., Il., U.S. C4 106
Logan, co., Ks., U.S. D2 109
Logan, co., Ky., U.S. D3 110
Logan, co., N.D., U.S. C6 127
Logan, co., Ne., U.S. C5 120
Logan, co., Oh., U.S. B2 128
Logan, co., Ok., U.S. B4 129
Logan, co., W.V., U.S. D3 141
Logan, Mount, mtn., Yk., Can. F11 82
Logan, Mount, mtn., Wa., U.S. A5 140
Logandale, Nv., U.S. G7 121
Logan Lake, B.C., Can. D7 85
Logan Martin Lake, res., Al., U.S. B3 94
Logan Pass, Mt., U.S. B2 119
Logansport, In., U.S. C5 107
Logansport, La., U.S. C2 111
Loganville, Ga., U.S. C3 103
Loganville, Pa., U.S. G8 131
Loggieville, N.B., Can. B4 87
Log Lane Village, Co., U.S. A7 99
Logone, stm., Afr. B3 54
Logroño, Spain F5 16
Løgstør, Den. H3 10
Loi-kaw, Myan. C3 34
Loimaa, Fin. F10 10
Loire, stm., Fr. D6 16

Name — Map Ref. — Page

Loja, Ec. **D4** 70
Loja, Spain **I4** 16
Lokandu, D.R.C. **D5** 54
Lokan tekojärvi, res., Fin. **C12** 10
Lokichokio, Kenya **C6** 54
Lokoja, Nig. **E6** 50
Lokolama, D.R.C. **D3** 54
Lola, Gui. **E3** 50
Lola, Mount, mtn., Ca., U.S. **C3** 98
Loliondo, Tan. **D7** 54
Lolland, i., Den. **I4** 10
Lolo, Mt., U.S. **D2** 119
Lolo Pass, U.S. **C4** 105
Lom, Bul. **C9** 18
Lomami, stm., D.R.C. **C4** 54
Lomas de Zamora, Arg. **E6** 72
Lombard, Il., U.S. **k8** 106
Lomblen, Pulau, i., Indon. **E6** 36
Lombok, i., Indon. **E5** 36
Lombok, Selat, strt., Indon. **E5** 36
Lomé, Togo **E5** 50
Lomela, D.R.C. **D4** 54
Lomié, Cam. **C2** 54
Lomira, Wi., U.S. **E5** 142
Lomonosov, Russia **G13** 10
Lomonosov Ridge **E8** 144
Lompoc, Ca., U.S. **E3** 98
Lom Sak, Thai. **C4** 34
Łomża, Pol. **C7** 20
Lonaconing, Md., U.S. **k13** 113
Loncoche, Chile **E2** 69
London, On., Can. **E3** 89
London, Eng., U.K. **E6** 12
London, Ar., U.S. **B2** 97
London, Ky., U.S. **C5** 110
London, Oh., U.S. **C2** 128
Londonderry, N. Ire., U.K. **C3** 12
Londonderry, N.H., U.S. **E4** 122
Londonderry, Cape, c., Austl. **C4** 60
Londonderry, Isla, i., Chile **I2** 69
Londontown, Md., U.S. **C4** 113
Londrina, Braz. **F1** 74
Lone Grove, Ok., U.S. **C4** 129
Lone Mountain, mtn., Nv., U.S. **E4** 121
Lone Pine, Ca., U.S. **D4** 98
Lone Tree, Ia., U.S. **C6** 108
Long, co., Ga., U.S. **E5** 103
Longa, proliv, strt., Russia **B19** 26
Long Bar Harbor, Md., U.S. **B5** 113
Long Beach, Ca., U.S. **F4** 98
Long Beach, In., U.S. **A4** 107
Long Beach, Md., U.S. **D5** 113
Long Beach, Ms., U.S. **g7** 117
Long Beach, N.Y., U.S. **E7** 125
Long Beach, Wa., U.S. **C1** 140
Longboat Key, Fl., U.S. **q10** 102
Longboat Key, i., Fl., U.S. **E4** 102
Longboat Pass, strt., Fl., U.S. **q10** 102
Long Branch, N.J., U.S. **C5** 123
Longbranch, Wa., U.S. **B3** 140
Long Creek Mountain, mtn., Wy., U.S. **D5** 143
Longde, China **B2** 30
Longford, Ire. **D3** 12
Long Grove, Ia., U.S. **C7** 108
Long Harbour [-Mount Arlington Heights], Nf., Can. **E5** 88
Longhua, China **A4** 30
Longiram, Indon. **D5** 36
Long Island, i., Bah. **D10** 76
Long Island, i., N.S., Can. **E3** 87
Long Island, i., Ma., U.S. **g12** 114
Long Island, i., Me., U.S. **g7** 112
Long Island, i., N.Y., U.S. **E7** 125
Long Island Sound, strt., U.S. **E7** 125
Longjiang, China **B12** 28
Long Key, i., Fl., U.S. **H6** 102
Long Lake, Il., U.S. **h8** 106
Long Lake, l., Me., U.S. **A4** 112
Long Lake, l., Me., U.S. **D2** 112
Long Lake, l., Mi., U.S. **D5** 115
Long Lake, l., Mi., U.S. **C7** 115
Long Lake, l., Mn., U.S. **D4** 116
Long Lake, l., N.D., U.S. **C6** 127
Long Lake, l., N.Y., U.S. **B6** 125
Long Lake, l., Wa., U.S. **f10** 140
Long Lake, l., Wi., U.S. **C2** 142
Longli, China **F9** 28
Longling, China **B3** 34
Longmeadow, Ma., U.S. **B2** 114
Longmen, China **B6** 34
Longmont, Co., U.S. **A5** 99
Longnan, China **E3** 30
Long Point, c., Mb., Can. **C2** 86
Long Point, pen., On., Can. **E4** 89
Long Pond, res., Fl., U.S. **C4** 102
Long Prairie, Mn., U.S. **E4** 116
Longquan, China **D4** 30
Long Range Mountains, mts., Nf., Can. **D3** 88
Longreach, Austl. **E3** 62
Longshan, China **D2** 30
Longs Peak, mtn., Co., U.S. **A5** 99
Long Strait see Longa, proliv, strt., Russia **B19** 26
Longueuil, P.Q., Can. **D4** 90
Long View, N.C., U.S. **B1** 126
Longview, Tx., U.S. **C5** 136
Longview, Wa., U.S. **C3** 140
Longxi, China **E8** 28
Longxian, China **C2** 30
Long Xuyen, Viet. **D5** 34
Longyan, China **D4** 30
Longzhou, China **G9** 28
Lonoke, Ar., U.S. **C4** 97
Lonoke, co., Ar., U.S. **C4** 97
Lonsdale, Mn., U.S. **F5** 116
Lonsdale, R.I., U.S. **B4** 132
Lons-le-Saunier, Fr. **D9** 16
Loogootee, In., U.S. **G4** 107
Lookout, Ky., U.S. **C7** 110
Lookout, Cape, c., N.C., U.S. **C6** 126
Lookout, Point, c., Mi., U.S. **d7** 115
Lookout Mountain, Tn., U.S. **h11** 135
Lookout Mountain, mtn., Or., U.S. **C6** 130
Lookout Mountain, mtn., U.S. **D8** 135
Lookout Pass, U.S. **B3** 105
Lookout Point Lake, res., Or., U.S. **D4** 130
Loongana, Austl. **G4** 60
Loon Lake, Wa., U.S. **A8** 140
Loon Lake, l., Me., U.S. **B3** 112
Loop Creek, stm., W.V., U.S. **m13** 141
Loosahatchie, stm., Tn., U.S. **B2** 135
Lop, China **B4** 40
Lopatka, mys, c., Russia **D17** 26
Lop Buri, Thai. **D4** 34
Lopez, Cap, c., Gabon **D1** 54
Lopez Island, i., Wa., U.S. **A3** 140
Lop Nor (Lop Nur), l., China **C6** 28
Lop Nur (Lop Nor), l., China **C6** 28
Lopphavet, Nor. **A9** 10
Lora, Hāmūn-i-, l., Asia **E8** 42
Lorain, Oh., U.S. **A3** 128
Lorain, co., Oh., U.S. **A3** 128
Loramie, Lake, res., Oh., U.S. **B1** 128
Lorca, Spain **I6** 16
Lord Howe Rise **K19** 64
Lordsburg, N.M., U.S. **E1** 124
Loreauville, La., U.S. **D4** 111
Lorenzo, Tx., U.S. **C2** 136
Loreto, Braz. **E10** 70
Loreto, Mex. **B2** 78
Lorette, Mb., Can. **E3** 86
Loretteville, P.Q., Can. **C6** 90
Loretto, Ky., U.S. **C4** 110
Loretto, Pa., U.S. **F4** 131
Loretto, Tn., U.S. **B4** 135
Lorica, Col. **B4** 70
Lorient, Fr. **D5** 16
L'Orignal, On., Can. **B10** 89
Loris, S.C., U.S. **C10** 133
Lorn, Firth of, b., Scot., U.K. **B4** 12
Lorne, Austl. **H3** 62
Lorne, N.B., Can. **B3** 87
Lorraine, hist. reg., Fr. **C9** 16
Los, Îles de, is., Gui. **E2** 50
Los Alamos, N.M., U.S. **B3** 124
Los Alamos, co., N.M., U.S. **B3** 124
Los Altos, Ca., U.S. **k8** 98
Los Angeles, Ca., U.S. **E4** 98
Los Angeles, co., Ca., U.S. **E4** 98
Los Angeles Aqueduct, Ca., U.S. **E4** 98
Los Banos, Ca., U.S. **D3** 98
Los Blancos, Arg. **C5** 72
Los Fresnos, Tx., U.S. **F4** 136
Los Gatos, Ca., U.S. **D2** 98
Lošinj, Otok, i., Cro. **B5** 18
Los Lunas, N.M., U.S. **C3** 124
Los Mochis, Mex. **B3** 78
Los Pinos, stm., Co., U.S. **D3** 99
Los Ranchos de Albuquerque, N.M., U.S. **B3** 124
Los Roques, Islas, is., Ven. **C6** 80
Lost, stm., In., U.S. **G4** 107
Lost, stm., W.V., U.S. **B6** 141
Lost, stm., Wa., U.S. **A5** 140
Lost Creek, stm., Wy., U.S. **D4** 143
Lost Peak, mtn., Ut., U.S. **F2** 137
Lost Ranger Peak, mtn., Co., U.S. **A4** 99
Lost River Glacial Caverns, N.H., U.S. **B3** 122
Lost River Range, mts., Id., U.S. **E5** 105
Lost Trail Pass, U.S. **D5** 105
Losuia, Pap. N. Gui. **H13** 32
Los Vilos, Chile **D2** 69
Lot, stm., Fr. **E7** 16
Lota, Chile **F3** 72
Lotawana, Lake, res., Mo., U.S. **k11** 118
Lotbinière, P.Q., Can. **C6** 90
Loto, D.R.C. **D4** 54
Lotung, Tai. **E5** 30
Louang Namtha, Laos **B4** 34
Louangphrabang, Laos **C4** 34
Loubomo, Congo **D2** 54
Loudon, Tn., U.S. **D9** 135
Loudon, co., Tn., U.S. **D9** 135
Loudonville, Oh., U.S. **B3** 128
Loudoun, co., Va., U.S. **A5** 139
Louga, Sen. **C1** 50
Louhi, Russia **A5** 22
Louisa, Ky., U.S. **B7** 110
Louisa, Va., U.S. **B4** 139
Louisa, co., Ia., U.S. **C6** 108
Louisa, co., Va., U.S. **C5** 139
Louisa, Lake, l., Fl., U.S. **D5** 102
Louisbourg, N.S., Can. **D10** 87
Louisburg, Ks., U.S. **D9** 109
Louisburg, N.C., U.S. **A4** 126
Louisdale, N.S., Can. **D8** 87
Louise, Lake, l., Ak., U.S. **f18** 95
Louise Island, i., B.C., Can. **C2** 85
Louiseville, P.Q., Can. **C5** 90
Louisiana, Mo., U.S. **B6** 118
Louisiana, state, U.S. **C3** 111
Louisiana Point, c., La., U.S. **E2** 111
Louis Trichardt, S. Afr. **C4** 56
Louisville, Al., U.S. **D4** 94
Louisville, Co., U.S. **B5** 99
Louisville, Ga., U.S. **C4** 103
Louisville, Il., U.S. **E5** 106
Louisville, Ky., U.S. **B4** 110
Louisville, Ms., U.S. **B4** 117
Louisville, Ne., U.S. **D9** 120
Louisville, Oh., U.S. **B4** 128
Louisville Ridge **L22** 64
Louis-XIV, Pointe, c., P.Q., Can. **h11** 90
Loum, Cam. **C1** 54
Loup, co., Ne., U.S. **C6** 120
Loup, stm., Ne., U.S. **C8** 120
Loup City, Ne., U.S. **C7** 120
Lourdes, Nf., Can. **D2** 88
Lourdes, Fr. **F6** 16
Lourenço Marques see Maputo, Moz. **D5** 56
Louviers, Co., U.S. **B6** 99
Love, co., Ok., U.S. **D4** 129
Loveč, Bul. **C10** 18
Loveland, Co., U.S. **A5** 99
Loveland, Oh., U.S. **n13** 128
Loveland Park, Oh., U.S. **C1** 128
Loveland Pass, Co., U.S. **B5** 99
Lovell, Wy., U.S. **B4** 143
Lovelock, Nv., U.S. **C3** 121
Lovely, Ky., U.S. **C7** 110
Lovenia, Mount, mtn., Ut., U.S. **C5** 137
Love Point, c., Md., U.S. **B5** 113
Loves Park, Il., U.S. **A4** 106
Lovettsville, Va., U.S. **A5** 139
Loving, N.M., U.S. **E5** 124
Loving, co., Tx., U.S. **D1** 136
Lovington, Ia., U.S. **e8** 108
Lovington, Il., U.S. **D5** 106
Lovington, N.M., U.S. **E6** 124
Lóvua, Ang. **E4** 54
Lowden, Ia., U.S. **C7** 108
Lowell, Ar., U.S. **A1** 97
Lowell, In., U.S. **B3** 107
Lowell, Ma., U.S. **A5** 114
Lowell, Mi., U.S. **F5** 115
Lowell, N.C., U.S. **B1** 126
Lowell, Or., U.S. **D4** 130
Lowell, Lake, res., Id., U.S. **F2** 105
Lowellville, Oh., U.S. **A5** 128
Lower Arrow Lake, res., B.C., Can. **E8** 85
Lower Brule Indian Reservation, S.D., U.S. **C6** 134
Lower California see Baja California, pen., Mex. **B2** 78
Lower Hutt, N.Z. **p14** 63c
Lower Klamath Lake, l., Ca., U.S. **B3** 98
Lower Matecumbe Key, i., Fl., U.S. **H6** 102
Lower New York Bay, b., N.J., U.S. **B4** 123
Lower Otay Lake, res., Ca., U.S. **o16** 98
Lower Paia, Hi., U.S. **C5** 104
Lower Red Lake, l., Mn., U.S. **C3** 116
Lower Rice Lake, l., Mn., U.S. **C3** 116
Lower Salmon Dam, Id., U.S. **G4** 105
Lower Trajan's Wall, hist., Eur. **G10** 20
Lower West Pubnico, N.S., Can. **F4** 87
Lowestoft, Eng., U.K. **D7** 12
Lowndes, co., Al., U.S. **C3** 94
Lowndes, co., Ga., U.S. **F3** 103
Lowndes, co., Ms., U.S. **B5** 117
Lowry City, Mo., U.S. **C4** 118
Lowville, N.Y., U.S. **B5** 125
Loxley, Al., U.S. **E2** 94
Loxton, Austl. **G3** 62
Loyal, Wi., U.S. **D3** 142
Loyall, Ky., U.S. **D6** 110
Loyalsock Creek, stm., Pa., U.S. **D8** 131
Loyalty Islands see Loyauté, Îles, is., N. Cal. **I9** 62a
Loyauté, Îles, is., N. Cal. **I9** 62a
Loznica, Yugo. **B7** 18
Lozova, Ukr. **E14** 20
Lualaba, stm., Afr. **D5** 54
Lua Makika, crat., Hi., U.S. **C5** 104
Lu'an, China **C4** 30
Luan, stm., China **C11** 28
Luanda, Ang. **E2** 54
Luang, Thale, l., Thai. **E4** 34
Luanginga, stm., Afr. **A3** 56
Luangwa, stm., Afr. **A5** 56
Luanping, China **A4** 30
Luanshya, Zam. **A4** 56
Luan Toro, Arg. **F4** 72
Luapula, stm., Afr. **A4** 56
Luau, Ang. **F4** 54
Luba, Eq. Gui. **C1** 54
Lubang Islands, is., Phil. **D8** 34
Lubango, Ang. **A1** 56
Lubbock, Tx., U.S. **C2** 136
Lubbock, co., Tx., U.S. **C2** 136
Lubec, Me., U.S. **D6** 112
Lübeck, Ger. **D12** 12
Lubefu, D.R.C. **D4** 54
Lubin, Pol. **D4** 20
Lublin, Pol. **D7** 20
Lubnān, Jabal, mts., Leb. **F6** 44
Lubny, Ukr. **D12** 20
Lubudi, D.R.C. **F5** 54
Lubuklinggau, Indon. **D2** 36
Lubumbashi, D.R.C. **F5** 54
Lubutu, D.R.C. **D5** 54
Lucama, N.C., U.S. **B4** 126
Lucan, On., Can. **D3** 89
Lucapa, Ang. **E4** 54
Lucas, co., Ia., U.S. **C4** 108
Lucas, co., Oh., U.S. **A2** 128
Lucasville, Oh., U.S. **D3** 128
Lucca, Italy **C3** 18
Luce, co., Mi., U.S. **B5** 115
Lucedale, Ms., U.S. **E5** 117
Lucena, Phil. **D8** 34
Lucena, Spain **I4** 16
Lučenec, Slvk. **E5** 20
Lucera, Italy **D5** 18
Lucerne see Luzern, Switz. **A2** 18
Lucerne, Ca., U.S. **C2** 98
Lucerne, Lake see Vierwaldstätter See, l., Switz. **A2** 18
Lucernemines, Pa., U.S. **E3** 131
Lucerne Valley, Ca., U.S. **E5** 98
Luceville, P.Q., Can. **A9** 90
Lucira, Ang. **A1** 56
Luck, Wi., U.S. **C1** 142
Luckenwalde, Ger. **E13** 12
Lucknow, On., Can. **D3** 89
Lucknow, India **D4** 40
Lucky Peak Lake, res., Id., U.S. **F3** 105
Luçon, Fr. **D6** 16
Lucusse, Ang. **A3** 56
Lüda see Dalian, China **D12** 28
Lüderitz, Nmb. **D2** 56
Ludhiāna, India **C3** 40
Ludington, Mi., U.S. **E4** 115
Ludlow, Ky., U.S. **h13** 110
Ludlow, Ma., U.S. **B3** 114
Ludlow, Vt., U.S. **E3** 138
Ludogorie, reg., Bul. **C11** 18
Ludowici, Ga., U.S. **E5** 103
Ludvika, Swe. **F6** 10
Ludwigsburg, Ger. **F11** 12
Ludwigslust, Ger. **D12** 12
Luebo, D.R.C. **E4** 54
Luena, Ang. **F3** 54
Luena, D.R.C. **E5** 54
Lueyang, China **C2** 30
Lufeng, China **E4** 30
Lufkin, Tx., U.S. **D5** 136
Luga, Russia **C4** 22
Lugano, Switz. **A2** 18
Luganville, Vanuatu **k9** 62a
Lugards Falls, wtfl, Kenya **D7** 54
Lugela, Moz. **B6** 56
Lugo, Italy **B3** 18
Lugo, Spain **F3** 16
Lugoff, S.C., U.S. **C6** 133
Lugoj, Rom. **G6** 20
Lugovoj, Kaz. **B10** 42
Luhans'k, Ukr. **E15** 20
Luishia, D.R.C. **F5** 54
Luiza, D.R.C. **E4** 54
Lukachukai, Az., U.S. **A6** 96
Luke Air Force Base, mil., Az., U.S. **D3** 96
Lukenie, stm., D.R.C. **D3** 54
Lukojanov, Russia **D7** 22
Lukolela, D.R.C. **D3** 54
Lukolela, D.R.C. **E4** 54
Lukula, D.R.C. **E2** 54
Lukulu, Zam. **A3** 56
Lula, Ga., U.S. **B3** 103
Luleå, Swe. **D10** 10
Luleälven, stm., Swe. **C9** 10
Lüleburgaz, Tur. **B2** 44
Luliang, China **D1** 30
Lüliang Shan, mts., China **D10** 28
Luling, La., U.S. **k11** 111
Luling, Tx., U.S. **E4** 136
Lulua, stm., D.R.C. **E4** 54
Lumana, D.R.C. **D5** 54
Lumbala N'guimbo, Ang. **A3** 56
Lumber, stm., U.S. **C9** 133
Lumber City, Ga., U.S. **E4** 103
Lumberport, W.V., U.S. **B4** 141
Lumberton, Ms., U.S. **D4** 117
Lumberton, N.C., U.S. **C3** 126
Lumbo, Moz. **B7** 56
Lumby, B.C., Can. **D8** 85
Lumding, India **D6** 40
Lummi Indian Reservation, Wa., U.S. **A3** 140
Lumpkin, Ga., U.S. **D2** 103
Lumpkin, co., Ga., U.S. **B2** 103
Lumsden, Nf., Can. **D5** 88
Lumut, Tanjung, c., Indon. **D3** 36
Luna, co., N.M., U.S. **E2** 124
Luna Pier, Mi., U.S. **G7** 115
Lund, Swe. **I5** 10
Lund, Nv., U.S. **E6** 121
Lundar, Mb., Can. **D2** 86
Lundazi, Zam. **A5** 56
Lüneburg, Ger. **D12** 12
Lunenburg, Ma., U.S. **A4** 114
Lunenburg, co., Va., U.S. **D4** 139
Lunéville, Fr. **C10** 16
Lungué-Bungo (Lungwebungu), stm., Afr. **A2** 56
Lungwebungu (Lungué-Bungo), stm., Afr. **A3** 56
Luninec, Bela. **C9** 20
Luobei, China **A2** 31
Luochuan, China **B2** 30
Luoding, China **E3** 30
Luohe, China **E10** 28
Luotian, China **C4** 30
Luoyang, China **E10** 28
Luoyuan, China **D4** 30
Luozi, D.R.C. **E2** 54
Lupanshui, China **D1** 30
Lupeni, Rom. **G7** 20
Luputa, D.R.C. **E4** 54
Luqu, China **E8** 28
Luray, Va., U.S. **B4** 139
Lure, Lake, res., N.C., U.S. **f10** 126
Luremo, Ang. **E3** 54
Lúrio, Moz. **A7** 56
Lúrio, stm., Moz. **A6** 56
Lusaka, Zam. **B4** 56
Lusambo, D.R.C. **D4** 54
Lusanga, D.R.C. **D3** 54
Lusangi, D.R.C. **D5** 54
Lusby, Md., U.S. **D5** 113
Luseland, Sk., Can. **E1** 91
Lushnjë, Alb. **D7** 18
Lushoto, Tan. **D7** 54
Lüshun, China **D12** 28
Lusk, Wy., U.S. **D8** 143
Lūt, dasht-e, des., Iran **D7** 42
Lutcher, La., U.S. **D5** 111
Luther, Ok., U.S. **B4** 129
Lutherstadt Eisleben, Ger. **E12** 12
Lutherstsadt Wittenberg, Ger. **E13** 12
Luthersville, Ga., U.S. **C2** 103
Lutherville-Timonium, Md., U.S. **B4** 113
Luton, Eng., U.K. **E6** 12
Łutselk'e, N.T., Can. **F17** 82
Luts'k, Ukr. **D8** 20
Luttrell, Tn., U.S. **C10** 135
Lutz, Fl., U.S. **D4** 102
Lutzow-Holm Bay, b., Ant. **C8** 67
Luuq, Som. **J13** 48
Luverne, Al., U.S. **D3** 94
Luverne, Mn., U.S. **G2** 116
Luwingu, Zam. **A4** 56
Luwuk, Indon. **D6** 36
Luxapallila Creek, stm., U.S. **B5** 117
Luxembourg, Lux. **F9** 12
Luxembourg, ctry., Eur. **C10** 16
Luxemburg, Wi., U.S. **D6** 142
Luxi, China **G7** 28
Luxomni, Ga., U.S. **h8** 103
Luxor see El-Uqsor, Egypt **E11** 48
Luxora, Ar., U.S. **B6** 97
Luza, Russia **B8** 22
Luzern, Switz. **A2** 18
Luzerne, Pa., U.S. **n17** 131
Luzerne, co., Pa., U.S. **D9** 131
Luzhai, China **E2** 30
Luzhou, China **F9** 28
Luziânia, Braz. **E2** 74
Luzilândia, Braz. **B3** 74
Luzon, i., Phil. **C8** 34
Luzon Strait, strt., Asia **B8** 34
L'viv, Ukr. **E8** 20
L'vov see L'viv, Ukr. **E8** 20
Lyallpur see Faisalabad, Pak. **D10** 42
Lycksele, Swe. **D8** 10
Lycoming, co., Pa., U.S. **D7** 131
Lycoming Creek, stm., Pa., U.S. **D7** 131
Lydenburg, S. Afr. **D5** 56
Lyell, Mount, mtn., Can. **D2** 84
Lyford, Tx., U.S. **F4** 136
Lykens, Pa., U.S. **E8** 131
Lyle, Wa., U.S. **D4** 140
Lyman, S.C., U.S. **B3** 133
Lyman, Wy., U.S. **E2** 143
Lyman, co., S.D., U.S. **D6** 134
Lyman Lake, res., Az., U.S. **C6** 96
Lyme Bay, b., Eng., U.K. **E5** 12
Lynch, Ky., U.S. **D7** 110
Lynchburg, Oh., U.S. **C2** 128
Lynchburg, Tn., U.S. **B5** 135
Lynchburg, Va., U.S. **C3** 139
Lynches, stm., S.C., U.S. **D8** 133
Lynden, Wa., U.S. **A3** 140
Lynde Point, c., Ct., U.S. **D6** 100
Lyndhurst, N.J., U.S. **h8** 123
Lyndhurst, Oh., U.S. **g9** 128
Lyndon, Ks., U.S. **D8** 109
Lyndon, Ky., U.S. **g11** 110
Lyndon B. Johnson National Historical Site, hist., Tx., U.S. **D3** 136
Lyndon B. Johnson Space Center, sci., Tx., U.S. **r14** 136
Lyndonville, Vt., U.S. **B4** 138
Lyndora, Pa., U.S. **E2** 131
Lyngen, b., Nor. **B9** 10

Name Map Ref. Page

Lynn, Al., U.S. A2 94
Lynn, In., U.S. D8 107
Lynn, Ma., U.S. B6 114
Lynn, co., Tx., U.S. C2 136
Lynn, Lake, res., W.V., U.S. B5 141
Lynn Canal, b., Ak., U.S. k22 95
Lynnfield, Ma., U.S. f11 114
Lynn Garden, Tn., U.S. C11 135
Lynn Haven, Fl., U.S. u16 102
Lynnhaven Roads, b., Va., U.S. k15 139
Lynnville, In., U.S. H3 107
Lynnwood, Wa., U.S. B3 140
Lynwood, Ca., U.S. n12 98
Lyon, Fr. E9 16
Lyon, co., Ia., U.S. A1 108
Lyon, co., Ks., U.S. D7 109
Lyon, co., Ky., U.S. C1 110
Lyon, co., Mn., U.S. F3 116
Lyon, co., Nv., U.S. D2 121
Lyons, Co., U.S. A5 99
Lyons, Ga., U.S. D4 103
Lyons, Il., U.S. k9 106
Lyons, In., U.S. G3 107
Lyons, Ks., U.S. D5 109
Lyons, Mi., U.S. F6 115
Lyons, Ne., U.S. C9 120
Lyons, N.Y., U.S. B3 125
Lyons, Or., U.S. C4 130
Lysekil, Swe. G4 10
Lyster Station, P.Q., Can. C6 90
Lys'va, Russia D7 26
Lysychans'k, Ukr. E15 20
Lytle, Tx., U.S. E3 136
Lyubotyn, Ukr. E13 20

M

Maalaea Bay, b., Hi., U.S. C5 104
Ma'ān, Jord. D3 42
Ma'anshan, China C4 30
Maarianhamina, Fin. F8 10
Ma'arrat an-Nu'mān, Syria E7 44
Maas (Meuse), stm., Eur. B9 16
Maastricht, Neth. E9 12
Mabank, Tx., U.S. C4 136
Mabel, Mn., U.S. G7 116
Maben, Ms., U.S. B4 117
Mableton, Ga., U.S. h7 103
Mabote, Moz. C5 56
Mabscott, W.V., U.S. D3 141
Mabton, Wa., U.S. C5 140
Mača, Russia D13 26
Macaé, Braz. F3 74
Macaíba, Braz. C4 74
Macapá, Braz. A1 74
Macará, Ec. D4 70
Macau, Braz. C4 74
Macau, Macau B5 34
Macau, dep., Asia E3 30
MacClenny, Fl., U.S. B4 102
MacDill Air Force Base, mil., Fl., U.S. E4 102
MacDonnell Ranges, mts., Austl. E5 60
MacDowell Reservoir, res., N.H., U.S. E2 122
Macedonia, Oh., U.S. A4 128
Macedonia, hist. reg., Eur. D9 18
Macedonia, ctry., Eur. D8 18
Maceió, Braz. C4 74
Macenta, Gui. E3 50
Macerata, Italy C4 18
Maces Bay, b., N.B., Can. D3 87
MacGregor, Mb., Can. E2 86
Machado, stm., Braz. E7 70
Machakos, Kenya D7 54
Machala, Ec. D4 70
Macheke, Zimb. B5 56
Macheng, China C3 30
Machias, Me., U.S. D5 112
Machias, stm., Me., U.S. D5 112
Machias, stm., Me., U.S. B4 112
Machias Bay, b., Me., U.S. D5 112
Machias Lakes, l., Me., U.S. C5 112
Machilīpatnam, India F4 40
Machiques, Ven. A5 70
Macho, Arroyo del, val., N.M., U.S. C4 124
Machupicchu, Peru F5 70
Machupicchu, hist., Peru A3 72
Mackay, Austl. E4 62
Mackay, Lake, l., Austl. E4 60
MacKenzie, B.C., Can. B6 85
Mackenzie, stm., N.T., Can. E13 82
Mackenzie Bay, b., Can. E12 82
Mackenzie Mountains, mts., Can. F14 82
Mackinac, co., Mi., U.S. B5 115
Mackinac, Straits of, strt., Mi., U.S. C6 115
Mackinac Bridge, Mi., U.S. C6 115
Mackinac Island, i., Mi., U.S. C6 115
Mackinaw, Il., U.S. C4 106
Mackinaw, stm., Il., U.S. C4 106
Mackinaw City, Mi., U.S. C6 115
Mackinnon Road, Kenya D7 54
Maclean, Austl. F5 62
Maclear, S. Afr. E4 56
Macleod, Lake, l., Austl. E1 60
Maclovio Herrera, Mex. B3 78
Macomb, Il., U.S. C3 106
Macomb, co., Mi., U.S. F8 115
Macomer, Italy D2 18
Mâcon, Fr. D9 16
Macon, Ga., U.S. D3 103
Macon, Il., U.S. D5 106
Macon, Mo., U.S. B5 118
Macon, Ms., U.S. B5 117
Macon, co., Al., U.S. C4 94
Macon, co., Ga., U.S. D2 103
Macon, co., Il., U.S. D4 106
Macon, co., Mo., U.S. B5 118
Macon, co., N.C., U.S. f9 126
Macon, co., Tn., U.S. A5 135
Macon, Bayou, stm., U.S. B4 111
Macoupin, co., Il., U.S. D4 106
Macquarie Island, i., Austl. J23 4
Macquarie Ridge N18 64
MacTier, On., Can. B5 89
Macungie, Pa., U.S. E10 131
Macuspana, Mex. D6 78
Mad, stm., Ca., U.S. B2 98
Mad, stm., Ct., U.S. B3 100
Mad, stm., N.H., U.S. C3 122
Mad, stm., Oh., U.S. C2 128
Mad, stm., Vt., U.S. C3 138
Madagascar, ctry., Afr. B8 56
Madagascar Basin K8 64
Madagascar Plateau L7 64
Madame, Isle, i., N.S., Can. D9 87
Madang, Pap. N. Gui. H12 32
Madaoua, Niger D6 50
Madawaska, Me., U.S. A4 112
Madawaska, stm., Can. B9 90
Madawaska, stm., On., Can. B7 89
Madawaska Lake, l., Me., U.S. A4 112
Madaya, Myan. B3 34
Madeira, Oh., U.S. o13 128
Madeira, stm., S.A. E7 70
Madeira, Arquipélago da, is., Port. D1 48
Madeira Islands see Madeira, Arquipélago da, is., Port. D1 48
Madeleine, Îles de la, is., P.Q., Can. B8 87
Madelia, Mn., U.S. F4 116
Madeline Island, i., Wi., U.S. B3 142
Maden, Tur. C8 44
Madera, Mex. B3 78
Madera, Ca., U.S. D3 98
Madera, co., Ca., U.S. D4 98
Madera see Madeira, stm., S.A. E7 70
Madhya Pradesh, prov., India E3 40
Madill, Ok., U.S. C5 129
Madimba, D.R.C. D3 54
Madingo-Kayes, Congo D2 54
Madingou, Congo D2 54
Madirovalo, Madag. B8 56
Madison, Al., U.S. A3 94
Madison, Ar., U.S. B5 97
Madison, Ct., U.S. D5 100
Madison, Fl., U.S. B3 102
Madison, Ga., U.S. C3 103
Madison, Il., U.S. E3 106
Madison, In., U.S. G7 107
Madison, Ks., U.S. D7 109
Madison, Me., U.S. D3 112
Madison, Mn., U.S. E2 116
Madison, Ms., U.S. C3 117
Madison, N.C., U.S. A3 126
Madison, Ne., U.S. C8 120
Madison, N.J., U.S. B4 123
Madison, Oh., U.S. A4 128
Madison, S.D., U.S. D8 134
Madison, W.V., U.S. C3 141
Madison, Wi., U.S. E4 142
Madison, co., Al., U.S. A3 94
Madison, co., Ar., U.S. B2 97
Madison, co., Fl., U.S. B3 102
Madison, co., Ga., U.S. B3 103
Madison, co., Ia., U.S. C3 108
Madison, co., Id., U.S. F7 105
Madison, co., Il., U.S. E4 106
Madison, co., In., U.S. D6 107
Madison, co., Ky., U.S. C5 110
Madison, co., La., U.S. B4 111
Madison, co., Mo., U.S. D7 118
Madison, co., Ms., U.S. C4 117
Madison, co., Mt., U.S. E5 119
Madison, co., N.C., U.S. f10 126
Madison, co., Ne., U.S. C8 120
Madison, co., N.Y., U.S. C5 125
Madison, co., Oh., U.S. C2 128
Madison, co., Tn., U.S. B3 135
Madison, co., Tx., U.S. D5 136
Madison, co., Va., U.S. B4 139
Madison, stm., Mt., U.S. E5 119
Madison Heights, Mi., U.S. o15 115
Madison Heights, Va., U.S. C3 139
Madison Lake, Mn., U.S. F5 116
Madison Range, mts., Mt., U.S. E5 119
Madisonville, Ky., U.S. C2 110
Madisonville, La., U.S. D5 111
Madisonville, Tn., U.S. D9 135
Madisonville, Tx., U.S. D5 136
Madoc, On., Can. C7 89
Mado Gashi, Kenya C7 54
Madoi, China E7 28
Madona, Lat. H12 10
Madrakah, Ra's al-, c., Oman G7 38
Madras see Chennai, India G4 40
Madras, Or., U.S. C5 130
Madras see Tamil Nādu, prov., India G3 40
Madre, Laguna, b., Tx., U.S. F4 136
Madre, Laguna, l., Mex. B5 78
Madre, Sierra, mts., Phil. C8 34
Madre de Dios, stm., S.A. F6 70
Madre de Dios, Isla, i., Chile H1 69
Madre del Sur, Sierra, mts., Mex. D5 78
Madre Occidental, Sierra, mts., Mex. B3 78
Madre Oriental, Sierra, mts., Mex. C4 78
Madrid, Spain G5 16
Madrid, Ia., U.S. C4 108
Madura, i., Indon. E4 36
Madura, Selat, strt., Indon. E4 36
Madurai, India H3 40
Maebashi, Japan D15 28
Mae Hong Son, Thai. C3 34
Mae Sariang, Thai. C3 34
Maeser, Ut., U.S. C6 137
Mae Sot, Thai. C3 34
Maestra, Sierra, mts., Cuba B4 80
Maevatanana, Madag. B8 56
Maéwo, i., Vanuatu k9 62a
Mafeteng, Leso. D4 56
Mafia Island, i., Tan. E7 54
Magadan, Russia D17 26
Magadi, Kenya D7 54
Magallanes, Estrecho de (Magellan, Strait of), strt., S.A. H2 69
Magangué, Col. B5 70
Magaria, Niger D6 50
Magazine, Ar., U.S. B2 97
Magazine Mountain, mtn., Ar., U.S. B2 97
Magdagači, Russia D14 26
Magdalena, Bol. F7 70
Magdalena, N.M., U.S. C2 124
Magdalena, stm., Col. D5 80
Magdalena, stm., Mex. A2 78
Magdalena, Isla, i., Chile F2 69
Magdalena de Kino, Mex. A2 78
Magdalena Mountains, mts., N.M., U.S. D2 124
Magdeburg, Ger. D12 12
Magee, Ms., U.S. D4 117
Magelang, Indon. E4 36
Magellan, Strait of see Magallanes, Estrecho de, strt., S.A. H2 69
Maggie Creek, stm., Nv., U.S. C5 121
Maggiore, Lago, l., Eur. B2 18
Maghâgha, Egypt F10 14
Maghama, Maur. C2 50
Magic Reservoir, res., Id., U.S. F4 105
Maglie, Italy D7 18
Magna, Ut., U.S. C3 137
Magnetawan, stm., On., Can. B4 89
Magnitogorsk, Russia D7 26
Magnolia, Ar., U.S. D2 97
Magnolia, Ky., U.S. C4 110
Magnolia, Ms., U.S. D3 117
Magnolia, N.C., U.S. C4 126
Magnolia, Oh., U.S. B4 128
Magoffin, co., Ky., U.S. C6 110
Magog, P.Q., Can. D5 90
Magothy River, b., Md., U.S. B4 113
Magrath, Ab., Can. E4 84
Magruder Mountain, mtn., Nv., U.S. F4 121
Magway, Myan. B2 34
Mahābād, Iran C5 42
Mahābaleshwar, India F2 40
Mahabe, Madag. B8 56
Mahābhārat Lek, mts., Nepal D4 40
Mahabo, Madag. C7 56
Mahačkala, Russia E6 26
Mahagi, D.R.C. C6 54
Mahajanga, Madag. B8 56
Mahakam, stm., Indon. C5 36
Mahalapye, Bots. C4 56
Mahānadi, stm., India E4 40
Mahanoro, Madag. B8 56
Mahanoy City, Pa., U.S. E9 131
Mahārāshtra, prov., India E3 40
Maha Sarakham, Thai. C4 34
Mahaska, co., Ia., U.S. C5 108
Mahbūbnagar, India F3 40
Mahd adh-Dhahab, Sau. Ar. F4 38
Mahdia, Tun. G3 18
Mahe, India G3 40
Mahé, i., Sey. h13 57b
Mahébourg, Mrts. g10 57a
Mahenge, Tan. E7 54
Mahesāna, India E2 40
Mahi, stm., India E2 40
Mahilëu, Bela. C11 20
Mahnomen, Mn., U.S. C3 116
Mahnomen, co., Mn., U.S. C3 116
Mahogany Mountain, mtn., Or., U.S. D9 130
Mahomet, Il., U.S. C5 106
Mahón see Maó, Spain H9 16
Mahone Bay, N.S., Can. E5 87
Mahoning, co., Oh., U.S. B5 128
Mahoning, stm., U.S. A5 128
Mahopac, N.Y., U.S. D7 125
Mahuva, India E2 40
Mahwah, N.J., U.S. A4 123
Maicao, Col. C5 80
Maiden, N.C., U.S. B1 126
Maidstone Lake, l., Vt., U.S. B5 138
Maiduguri, Nig. D7 50
Maili, Hi., U.S. g9 104
Maili Point, c., Hi., U.S. g9 104
Main, stm., Ger. F11 12
Main Channel, strt., On., Can. B3 89
Mai-Ndombe, Lac, l., D.R.C. D3 54
Maine, hist. reg., Fr. C6 16
Maine, state, U.S. C3 112
Maine, Gulf of, b., N.A. C14 92
Mainland, i., Scot., U.K. A12
Mainland, i., Scot., U.K. h19 12a
Main Pass, strt., La., U.S. E6 111
Maintirano, Madag. B7 56
Mainz, Ger. E11 12
Maio, i., C.V. g10 50a
Maipú, Arg. F6 72
Maiquetía, Ven. A6 70
Maisonnette, N.B., Can. B4 87
Maitembge, Bots. C4 56
Maitland, Austl. G5 62
Maitland, On., Can. C9 89
Maíz, Islas del, is., Nic. C3 80
Maize, Ks., U.S. g12 109
Maizuru, Japan C3 31
Maja, stm., Russia C15 26
Majene, Indon. D5 36
Majī, Eth. B7 54
Majkop, Russia E6 26
Major, co., Ok., U.S. A3 129
Majorca see Mallorca, i., Spain H8 16
Majuro, atoll, Marsh. Is. D11 58
Maka, Sen. D2 50
Makabana, Congo D2 54
Makaha, Hi., U.S. g9 104
Makaha Point, c., Hi., U.S. A2 104
Makah Indian Reservation, Wa., U.S. A1 140
Makahuena Point, c., Hi., U.S. B2 104
Makakilo City, Hi., U.S. g9 104
Makapuu Head, c., Hi., U.S. B4 104
Makarakomburu, Mount, mtn., Sol. Is. B6 62
Makarov, Russia B16 28
Makarov Basin E34 144
Makasar see Ujungpandang, Indon. E5 36
Makasar, Selat (Makassar Strait), strt., Indon. D5 36
Makassar Strait see Makasar, Selat, strt., Indon. D5 36
Makat, Kaz. E7 26
Makawao, Hi., U.S. C5 104
Makaweli, Hi., U.S. B2 104
Makeni, S.L. E2 50
Makgadikgadi, pl., Bots. C4 56
Makīïvka, Ukr. E14 20
Makindu, Kenya D7 54
Makkah, Sau. Ar. F3 38
Makó, Hung. F6 20
Makokou, Gabon C2 54
Makoua, Congo D3 54
Makrān Coast, Asia E7 42
Mākū, Iran C11 44
Makumbi, D.R.C. E4 54
Makurdi, Nig. E6 50
Makushin Volcano, vol., Ak., U.S. E6 95
Mala, Peru A2 72
Malabar, Fl., U.S. D6 102
Malabar Coast, India G2 40
Malabo, Eq. Gui. C1 54
Malacca see Melaka, Malay. C2 36
Malacca, Strait of, strt., Asia C1 36
Malad City, Id., U.S. G6 105
Maladzečna, Bela. B9 20
Málaga, Col. D5 80
Málaga, Spain I4 16
Malagarasi, Tan. E6 54
Malaimbandy, Madag. C8 56
Malaja Kuril'skaja Grjada, is., Russia B5 31
Malajaroslavec, Russia B14 20
Malaja Višera, Russia C5 22
Malakāl, Sudan I11 48
Malakoff, Tx., U.S. C4 136
Malakula, i., Vanuatu l9 62a
Malambo, Col. C5 80
Malang, Indon. E4 36
Malanje, Ang. E3 54
Malanville, Benin D5 50
Mälaren, l., Swe. G7 10
Malargüe, Arg. F4 72
Malartic, P.Q., Can. k11 90
Malaspina Glacier, Ak., U.S. D11 95
Malatya, Tur. C8 44
Mala Vyska, Ukr. E11 20
Malawi, ctry., Afr. A5 56
Malaŵi, Lake see Nyasa, Lake, l., Afr. F6 54
Malaya see Semenanjung Malaysia, hist. reg., Malay. C2 36
Malaybalay, Phil. E9 34
Malāyer, Iran D5 42
Malay Peninsula, pen., Asia B2 36
Malaysia, ctry., Asia C4 36
Malazgirt, Tur. C10 44
Malbaie, stm., P.Q., Can. B7 90
Malbork, Pol. C5 20
Malbrán, Arg. D5 72
Malcolm, Austl. F3 60
Malden, Ma., U.S. B5 114
Malden, Mo., U.S. E8 118
Malden, W.V., U.S. m12 141
Malden, i., Kir. E14 58
Maldives, ctry., Asia I10 24
Maldonado, Ur. E7 72
Mālegaon, India E2 40
Malek Kandī, Iran D12 44
Malema, Moz. A6 56
Malha Wells, Sudan G10 48
Malheur, co., Or., U.S. D9 130
Malheur, stm., Or., U.S. D9 130
Malheur Lake, l., Or., U.S. D8 130
Mali, Gui. D2 50
Mali, ctry., Afr. C4 50
Malibu, Ca., U.S. m11 98
Malin, Or., U.S. E5 130
Malindi, Kenya D8 54
Malinga, Congo D2 54
Malka, Russia D17 26
Malkara, Tur. B2 44
Mallawi, Egypt F10 14
Malletts Bay, b., Vt., U.S. B2 138
Mallorca (Majorca), i., Spain H8 16
Malmberget, Swe. C9 10
Malmesbury, S. Afr. E2 56
Malmö, Swe. I5 10
Malmstrom Air Force Base, mil., Mt., U.S. C5 119
Maloelap, atoll, Marsh. Is. D11 58
Malolos, Phil. D8 34
Malone, N.Y., U.S. f10 125
Maloney Reservoir, res., Ne., U.S. C5 120
Malonga, D.R.C. F4 54
Malošujka, Russia B6 22
Måløy, Nor. F1 10
Malpelo, Isla de, i., Col. C3 70
Malpeque Bay, b., P.E., Can. C6 87
Malta, Il., U.S. B5 106
Malta, Mt., U.S. B9 119
Malta, ctry., Eur. G5 18
Maltahöhe, Nmb. C2 56
Maluku (Moluccas), is., Indon. D7 36
Maluku, Laut (Molucca Sea), Indon. C7 36
Malumfashi, Nig. D6 50
Mālvan, India F2 40
Malvern, Ar., U.S. C3 97
Malvern, Ia., U.S. D2 108
Malvern, Oh., U.S. B4 128
Malvern, Pa., U.S. o19 131
Malverne, N.Y., U.S. k13 125
Malyj Enisej, stm., Russia A7 28
Malyn, Ukr. D10 20
Mama, Russia D13 26
Mamala Bay, b., Hi., U.S. g10 104
Mamallapuram, hist., India G4 40
Mamaroneck, N.Y., U.S. h13 125
Mamburao, Phil. D8 34
Mamfe, Cam. B1 54
Mammoth, Az., U.S. E5 96
Mammoth Cave National Park, Ky., U.S. C4 110
Mammoth Lakes, Ca., U.S. D4 98
Mammoth Spring, Ar., U.S. A4 97
Mamoré, stm., S.A. F6 70
Mamou, Gui. D2 50
Mamou, La., U.S. D3 111
Mamoudzou, May. A8 56
Mampikony, Madag. B8 56
Mamuju, Indon. D5 36
Man, C. Iv. E3 50
Man, W.V., U.S. D3 141
Manacapuru, Braz. D7 70
Manacor, Spain H8 16
Manado, Indon. C6 36
Managua, Nic. C2 80
Managua, Lago de, l., Nic. C2 80
Manakara, Madag. C8 56
Manāli, India C3 40
Manama see Al-Manāmah, Bahr. E6 42
Manam Island, i., Pap. N. Gui. G12 32
Manana Island, i., Hi., U.S. g11 104
Mananara Avaratra, Madag. B8 56
Mananjary, Madag. C8 56
Manankoro, Mali D3 50
Manantico Creek, stm., N.J., U.S. E3 123
Mana Point, c., Hi., U.S. A2 104
Manas, China C5 28
Manas Hu, l., China B5 28
Manasquan, N.J., U.S. C4 123
Manasquan, stm., N.J., U.S. C4 123
Manassa, Co., U.S. D5 99
Manassas, Va., U.S. B5 139
Manassas National Battlefield Park, Va., U.S. g11 139
Manassas Park, Va., U.S. B5 139
Manatee, co., Fl., U.S. E4 102
Manatee, stm., Fl., U.S. E4 102
Manatuto, Indon. E7 36
Manaus, Braz. D7 70
Manavgat, Tur. D4 44

Name — Map Ref. — Page

Manawa, Wi., U.S. **D5** 142
Manbij, Syria **D7** 44
Mancelona, Mi., U.S. **D5** 115
Manchester, Eng., U.K. **D5** 12
Manchester, Ct., U.S. **B5** 100
Manchester, Ga., U.S. **D2** 103
Manchester, Ia., U.S. **B6** 108
Manchester, Ky., U.S. **C6** 110
Manchester, Ma., U.S. **A6** 114
Manchester, Md., U.S. **A4** 113
Manchester, Me., U.S. **D3** 112
Manchester, Mi., U.S. **F6** 115
Manchester, Mo., U.S. **f12** 118
Manchester, N.H., U.S. **E4** 122
Manchester, N.Y., U.S. **C3** 125
Manchester, Oh., U.S. **D2** 128
Manchester, Pa., U.S. **F8** 131
Manchester, Tn., U.S. **B5** 135
Manchester, Vt., U.S. **E2** 138
Manchester Center, Vt., U.S. **E2** 138
Manchuria, hist. reg., China **B13** 28
Mancos, Co., U.S. **D2** 99
Mancos, stm., U.S. **D2** 99
Manda, Tan. **F6** 54
Mandabe, Madag. **C7** 56
Manda Island, i., Kenya **D8** 54
Mandal, Nor. **G2** 10
Mandalay, Myan. **B3** 34
Mandalgovĭ, Mong. **B9** 28
Mandalī, Iraq **D5** 42
Mandalya, Gulf of see Güllük Körfezi, b., Tur. **D2** 44
Mandan, N.D., U.S. **C5** 127
Mandar, Teluk, b., Indon. **D5** 36
Mandara Mountains, mts., Afr. **A2** 54
Mandeb, Bab el, strt. **H4** 38
Mandera, Kenya **C8** 54
Mandeville, Jam. **B4** 80
Mandeville, Ar., U.S. **D2** 97
Mandeville, La., U.S. **D5** 111
Mandimba, Moz. **A6** 56
Mandioli, Pulau, i., Indon. **D7** 36
Mandla, India **E4** 40
Mandritsara, Madag. **B8** 56
Mandsaur, India **E3** 40
Manduria, Italy **D6** 18
Māndvi, India **E1** 40
Mandya, India **G3** 40
Manendragarh, India **E4** 40
Manfalût, Egypt **E11** 48
Manfredonia, Italy **D5** 18
Manfredonia, Golfo di, b., Italy **D6** 18
Manga, Braz. **D3** 74
Manga, reg., Niger **D7** 50
Mangabeiras, Chapada das, hills, Braz. **C2** 74
Mangai, D.R.C. **D3** 54
Mangalia, Rom. **H10** 20
Mangalore, India **G2** 40
Mangchang, China **F9** 28
Mange, China **C4** 40
Manggar, Indon. **D3** 36
Mangkalihat, Tanjung, c., Indon. **C5** 36
Mangnai, China **D6** 28
Mangochi, Mwi. **A6** 56
Mangoky, stm., Madag. **C7** 56
Mangole, Pulau, i., Indon. **D7** 36
Mangum, Ok., U.S. **C2** 129
Manhattan, Ks., U.S. **C7** 109
Manhattan, Mt., U.S. **E5** 119
Manhattan Beach, Ca., U.S. **n12** 98
Manhattan Island, i., N.Y., U.S. **h13** 125
Manheim, Pa., U.S. **F9** 131
Manhuaçu, Braz. **F3** 74
Manica, Moz. **B5** 56
Manicoré, Braz. **E7** 70
Manicouagan, Réservoir, res., P.Q., Can. **h13** 90
Manignan, C. Iv. **D3** 50
Manila, Phil. **D8** 34
Manila, Ar., U.S. **B5** 97
Manilla, Ia., U.S. **C2** 108
Manipur, prov., India **D6** 40
Manisa, Tur. **C2** 44
Manistee, Mi., U.S. **D4** 115
Manistee, co., Mi., U.S. **D4** 115
Manistee, stm., Mi., U.S. **D5** 115
Manistique, Mi., U.S. **C4** 115
Manistique, stm., Mi., U.S. **B4** 115
Manistique Lake, l., Mi., U.S. **B5** 115
Manito, Il., U.S. **C4** 106
Manitoba, prov., Can. **C3** 86
Manitoba, Lake, l., Mb., Can. **D2** 86
Manitou, Mb., Can. **E2** 86
Manitou, Lake, l., On., Can. **B3** 89
Manitou Island, i., Mi., U.S. **A3** 115
Manitou Lake, l., Sk., Can. **E1** 91
Manitoulin Island, i., On., Can. **B2** 89
Manitou Springs, Co., U.S. **C6** 99
Manitowoc, Wi., U.S. **D6** 142
Manitowoc, co., Wi., U.S. **D6** 142
Manitowoc, stm., Wi., U.S. **h10** 142
Maniwaki, P.Q., Can. **C2** 90
Manizales, Col. **B4** 70
Manja, Madag. **C7** 56
Manjakandriana, Madag. **B8** 56
Manjimup, Austl. **G2** 60
Mānjra, stm., India **F3** 40
Mankanza, D.R.C. **C3** 54
Mankato, Ks., U.S. **C5** 109
Mankato, Mn., U.S. **F5** 116
Manlius, N.Y., U.S. **C5** 125
Manly, Ia., U.S. **A4** 108
Manmād, India **E2** 40
Manna, Indon. **D2** 36
Mannar, Gulf of, b., Asia **H3** 40
Mannford, Ok., U.S. **A5** 129
Mannheim, Ger. **F11** 12
Manning, Ab., Can. **A2** 84
Manning, Ia., U.S. **C2** 108
Manning, S.C., U.S. **D7** 133
Mannington, W.V., U.S. **B4** 141
Manns Creek, stm., W.V., U.S. **n14** 141
Mannville, Ab., Can. **C5** 84
Manokin, stm., Md., U.S. **D6** 113
Manokotak, Ak., U.S. **D8** 95
Manokwari, Indon. **D8** 36
Manomet, Ma., U.S. **C6** 114
Manomet Point, c., Ma., U.S. **C6** 114
Manono, D.R.C. **E5** 54
Manor, Tx., U.S. **D4** 136
Manouane, Lac, l., P.Q., Can. **h12** 90
Manresa, Spain **G7** 16
Mansa, Zam. **A4** 56
Manseau, P.Q., Can. **C5** 90
Mansfield, Eng., U.K. **D6** 12
Mansfield, Ar., U.S. **B1** 97
Mansfield, Il., U.S. **C5** 106
Mansfield, La., U.S. **B2** 111
Mansfield, Ma., U.S. **B5** 114
Mansfield, Mo., U.S. **D5** 118
Mansfield, Oh., U.S. **B3** 128
Mansfield, Pa., U.S. **C7** 131
Mansfield, Tx., U.S. **n9** 136
Mansfield, Mount, mtn., Vt., U.S. **B3** 138
Mansfield Center, Ct., U.S. **B7** 100
Mansfield Hollow Lake, res., Ct., U.S. **B7** 100
Mansôa, Gui.-B. **D1** 50
Manson, Ia., U.S. **B3** 108
Manson, Wa., U.S. **B5** 140
Mansonville, P.Q., Can. **D5** 90
Mansura, La., U.S. **C3** 111
Manta, Ec. **D3** 70
Mantachie, Ms., U.S. **A5** 117
Manteca, Ca., U.S. **D3** 98
Manteno, Il., U.S. **B6** 106
Manteo, N.C., U.S. **B7** 126
Manti, Ut., U.S. **D4** 137
Mantiqueira, Serra da, mts., Braz. **F2** 74
Manton, Mi., U.S. **D5** 115
Mantorville, Mn., U.S. **F6** 116
Mántova, Italy **B3** 18
Mantua, Oh., U.S. **A4** 128
Mantua, Ut., U.S. **B4** 137
Manturovo, Russia **C7** 22
Mäntyluoto, Fin. **F9** 10
Manuae, atoll, Cook Is. **F14** 58
Manui, Pulau, i., Indon. **D6** 36
Manukau, N.Z. **o13** 63c
Manumuskin, stm., N.J., U.S. **E3** 123
Manus Island, i., Pap. N. Gui. **G12** 32
Manvel, Tx., U.S. **r14** 136
Manville, N.J., U.S. **B3** 123
Manville, R.I., U.S. **B4** 132
Many, La., U.S. **C2** 111
Manyara, Lake, l., Tan. **D7** 54
Many Farms, Az., U.S. **A6** 96
Manyoni, Tan. **E6** 54
Manzanillo, Cuba **A4** 80
Manzanillo, Mex. **D4** 78
Manzanillo Bay, b., N.A. **A5** 80
Manzano Mountains, mts., N.M., U.S. **C3** 124
Manzano Peak, mtn., N.M., U.S. **C3** 124
Manzhouli, China **B11** 28
Manzini, Swaz. **D5** 56
Mao, Chad **D8** 50
Mao, Dom. Rep. **B5** 80
Maó, Spain **H9** 16
Maoke, Pegunungan, mts., Indon. **G10** 32
Maoming, China **G10** 28
Mapastepec, Mex. **D6** 78
Mapi, Indon. **H10** 32
Mapinhane, Moz. **C6** 56
Maple, stm., Ia., U.S. **B2** 108
Maple, stm., N.D., U.S. **C8** 127
Maple, stm., U.S. **A7** 134
Maple Bluff, Wi., U.S. **E4** 142
Maple Grove, Mn., U.S. **m12** 116
Maple Heights, Oh., U.S. **h9** 128
Maple Lake, Mn., U.S. **E5** 116
Maple Plain, Mn., U.S. **m11** 116
Maple Shade, N.J., U.S. **D2** 123
Maplesville, Al., U.S. **C3** 94
Mapleton, Ia., U.S. **B2** 108
Mapleton, Mn., U.S. **G5** 116
Mapleton, N.D., U.S. **C8** 127
Mapleton, Or., U.S. **C3** 130
Mapleton, Ut., U.S. **C4** 137
Maple Valley, Wa., U.S. **f11** 140
Mapleville, R.I., U.S. **B2** 132
Maplewood, Mn., U.S. **n12** 116
Maplewood, Mo., U.S. **f13** 118
Maplewood, N.J., U.S. **B4** 123
Maputo, Moz. **D5** 56
Maqṭeïr, reg., Maur. **B2** 50
Maquela do Zombo, Ang. **E3** 54
Maquinchao, Arg. **F3** 69
Maquoketa, Ia., U.S. **B7** 108
Maquoketa, stm., Ia., U.S. **B6** 108
Maquoketa, North Fork, stm., Ia., U.S. **B7** 108
Marabá, Braz. **C2** 74
Maracá, Ilha de, i., Braz. **C9** 70
Maracaibo, Ven. **A5** 70
Maracaibo, Lago de, l., Ven. **B5** 70
Maracaju, Braz. **C6** 72
Maracás, Braz. **D3** 74
Maracay, Ven. **A6** 70
Marādah, Libya **E8** 48
Maradi, Niger **D6** 50
Marāgheh, Iran **C5** 42
Marahuaca, Cerro, mtn., Ven. **C6** 70
Marais des Cygnes, stm., U.S. **D8** 109
Marajó, Baía de, b., Braz. **B2** 74
Marajó, Ilha de, i., Braz. **B2** 74
Maralal, Kenya **C7** 54
Marampa, S.L. **E2** 50
Marana, Az., U.S. **E4** 96
Marand, Iran **C5** 42
Maranguape, Braz. **B4** 74
Maranhão, state, Braz. **B2** 74
Maranhão, stm., Braz. **A8** 72
Marañón, stm., Peru **D5** 70
Marathon, Fl., U.S. **H5** 102
Marathon, Wi., U.S. **D4** 142
Marathon, co., Wi., U.S. **D4** 142
Marawi, Phil. **E8** 34
Marbella, Spain **I4** 16
Marble, Mn., U.S. **C5** 116
Marble, N.C., U.S. **f9** 126
Marble Bar, Austl. **E2** 60
Marble Canyon, val., Az., U.S. **A4** 96
Marble Falls, Tx., U.S. **D3** 136
Marble Hall, S. Afr. **C4** 56
Marblehead, Ma., U.S. **B6** 114
Marble Hill, Mo., U.S. **D8** 118
Marbleton, Wy., U.S. **D2** 143
Marburg, Ger. **E11** 12
Marbury, Md., U.S. **C3** 113
Marceline, Mo., U.S. **B5** 118
Marcellus, Mi., U.S. **F5** 115
March Air Force Base, mil., Ca., U.S. **F5** 98
Marche, hist. reg., Fr. **D7** 16
Mar Chiquita, Laguna, l., Arg. **E5** 72
Marco, Fl., U.S. **G5** 102
Marcus, Ia., U.S. **B2** 108
Marcus Baker, Mount, mtn., Ak., U.S. **g18** 95
Marcus Hook, Pa., U.S. **G11** 131
Marcus Island see Minami-Tori-shima, i., Japan **F18** 64
Marcy, Mount, mtn., N.Y., U.S. **A7** 125
Mardān, Pak. **D10** 42
Mar del Plata, Arg. **F6** 72
Mardin, Tur. **D9** 44
Maré, i., N. Cal. **I9** 62a
Mareeba, Austl. **D4** 62
Marengo, Ia., U.S. **C5** 108
Marengo, Il., U.S. **A5** 106
Marengo, In., U.S. **H5** 107
Marengo, co., Al., U.S. **C2** 94
Marfa, Tx., U.S. **o12** 136
Margaret, Al., U.S. **B3** 94
Margaret River, Austl. **G1** 60
Margarita, Isla de, i., Ven. **A7** 70
Margate, Fl., U.S. **F6** 102
Margate City, N.J., U.S. **E3** 123
Margherita Peak, mtn., Afr. **C5** 54
Margilan, Uzb. **B10** 42
Margrethe, Lake, l., Mi., U.S. **D6** 115
Marha, Russia **C14** 26
Marhanets', Ukr. **F13** 20
Maria, Îles, is., Fr. Poly. **G14** 58
María Elena, Chile **B3** 69
Maria Island, i., Austl. **C6** 60
Mariakani, Kenya **D7** 54
Marian, Lake, l., Fl., U.S. **E5** 102
Mariana Islands, is., Oc. **C11** 32
Mariana Ridge **G17** 64
Mariana Trench **G17** 64
Marianna, Ar., U.S. **C5** 97
Marianna, Fl., U.S. **B1** 102
Marias, stm., Mt., U.S. **B4** 119
Marias Pass, Mt., U.S. **B3** 119
Mariato, Punta, c., Pan. **D3** 80
Maribor, Slvn. **A5** 18
Marica (Évros) (Meriç), stm., Eur. **C10** 18
Maricopa, Az., U.S. **E3** 96
Maricopa, Ca., U.S. **E4** 98
Maricopa, co., Az., U.S. **D3** 96
Maricopa Mountains, mts., Az., U.S. **m7** 96
Marie Byrd Land, reg., Ant. **D29** 67
Marie-Galante, i., Guad. **B7** 80
Mariemont, Oh., U.S. **o13** 128
Mariental, Nmb. **C2** 56
Marienville, Pa., U.S. **D3** 131
Maries, co., Mo., U.S. **C6** 118
Mariestad, Swe. **G5** 10
Marietta, Ga., U.S. **C2** 103
Marietta, Oh., U.S. **C4** 128
Marietta, Ok., U.S. **D4** 129
Marietta, S.C., U.S. **A2** 133
Marieville, P.Q., Can. **D4** 90
Marijampolė, Lith. **I10** 10
Marij El, state, Russia **D6** 26
Marília, Braz. **F2** 74
Marimba, Ang. **E3** 54
Marin, co., Ca., U.S. **C2** 98
Mar"ina Horka, Bela. **C10** 20
Marinduque, i., Phil. **D8** 34
Marine, Il., U.S. **E4** 106
Marine City, Mi., U.S. **F8** 115
Marine On St. Croix, Mn., U.S. **E6** 116
Marinette, Wi., U.S. **C6** 142
Marinette, co., Wi., U.S. **C5** 142
Maringá, Braz. **F1** 74
Maringouin, La., U.S. **D4** 111
Marion, Al., U.S. **C2** 94
Marion, Ar., U.S. **B5** 97
Marion, Ia., U.S. **B6** 108
Marion, Il., U.S. **F5** 106
Marion, In., U.S. **C6** 107
Marion, Ks., U.S. **D6** 109
Marion, Ky., U.S. **e9** 110
Marion, La., U.S. **B3** 111
Marion, Mi., U.S. **D5** 115
Marion, Ms., U.S. **C5** 117
Marion, N.C., U.S. **B1** 126
Marion, Oh., U.S. **B2** 128
Marion, Pa., U.S. **G6** 131
Marion, S.C., U.S. **C9** 133
Marion, S.D., U.S. **D8** 134
Marion, Va., U.S. **f10** 139
Marion, Wi., U.S. **D5** 142
Marion, co., Al., U.S. **A2** 94
Marion, co., Ar., U.S. **A3** 97
Marion, co., Fl., U.S. **C4** 102
Marion, co., Ga., U.S. **D2** 103
Marion, co., Ia., U.S. **C4** 108
Marion, co., Il., U.S. **E4** 106
Marion, co., In., U.S. **E5** 107
Marion, co., Ks., U.S. **D6** 109
Marion, co., Ky., U.S. **C4** 110
Marion, co., Mo., U.S. **B6** 118
Marion, co., Ms., U.S. **D4** 117
Marion, co., Oh., U.S. **B2** 128
Marion, co., Or., U.S. **C4** 130
Marion, co., S.C., U.S. **C9** 133
Marion, co., Tn., U.S. **D8** 135
Marion, co., Tx., U.S. **C5** 136
Marion, co., W.V., U.S. **B4** 141
Marion, Lake, res., S.C., U.S. **E7** 133
Marion Reef, rf., Austl. **D5** 62
Marion Station, Md., U.S. **D6** 113
Marionville, Mo., U.S. **D4** 118
Mariposa, co., Ca., U.S. **D3** 98
Mariscal Estigarribia, Para. **C5** 72
Marissa, Il., U.S. **E4** 106
Maritime Alps, mts., Eur. **B1** 18
Maritime Atlas see Atlas Tellien, mts., Alg. **D4** 14
Mariupol', Ukr. **F14** 20
Märjamaa, Est. **G11** 10
Marka, Som. **J13** 48
Mārkāpur, India **F3** 40
Markdale, On., Can. **C4** 89
Marked Tree, Ar., U.S. **B5** 97
Markesan, Wi., U.S. **E5** 142
Markham, On., Can. **D5** 89
Markham, Il., U.S. **k9** 106
Markham, Tx., U.S. **E4** 136
Markit, China **B3** 40
Markland Lock and Dam, U.S. **B5** 110
Markle, In., U.S. **C7** 107
Markovo, Russia **C19** 26
Marks, Russia **D8** 22
Marks, Ms., U.S. **A3** 117
Marksville, La., U.S. **C3** 111
Mark Twain Lake, res., Mo., U.S. **B6** 118
Marlboro, N.Y., U.S. **D6** 125
Marlboro, Va., U.S. **n17** 139
Marlboro, co., S.C., U.S. **B8** 133
Marlborough, Ct., U.S. **C6** 100
Marlborough, Ma., U.S. **B4** 114
Marlborough, N.H., U.S. **E2** 122
Marlette, Mi., U.S. **E7** 115
Marley, Md., U.S. **B4** 113
Marlin, Tx., U.S. **D4** 136
Marlinton, W.V., U.S. **C4** 141
Marlow, Ok., U.S. **C4** 129
Marlowe, W.V., U.S. **B7** 141
Marlton, N.J., U.S. **D3** 123
Marmaduke, Ar., U.S. **A5** 97
Marmande, Fr. **E7** 16
Marmara, Sea of see Marmara Denizi, Tur. **B3** 44
Marmara Denizi, Tur. **B3** 44
Marmaris, Tur. **D3** 44
Marmet, W.V., U.S. **C3** 141
Marmora, On., Can. **C7** 89
Marne, stm., Fr. **C8** 16
Maroa, Il., U.S. **C5** 106
Maroa, Ven. **C6** 70
Maroantsetra, Madag. **B8** 56
Maromandia, Madag. **A8** 56
Maromokotro, mtn., Madag. **A8** 56
Marondera, Zimb. **B5** 56
Maroni, stm., S.A. **C9** 70
Maros, Indon. **E5** 36
Maroua, Cam. **A2** 54
Marovoay, Madag. **B8** 56
Marowijne see Maroni, stm., S.A. **C9** 70
Marquesas Islands see Marquises, Îles, is., Fr. Poly. **E16** 58
Marquesas Keys, is., Fl., U.S. **H4** 102
Marquette, Mi., U.S. **B3** 115
Marquette, co., Mi., U.S. **B3** 115
Marquette, co., Wi., U.S. **E4** 142
Marquette Heights, Il., U.S. **C4** 106
Marquises, Îles, is., Fr. Poly. **E16** 58
Marrah, Jabal, hill, Sudan **H9** 48
Marrakech, Mor. **D3** 48
Marrero, La., U.S. **E5** 111
Marromeu, Moz. **B6** 56
Mars, Pa., U.S. **E1** 131
Marsá al-Burayqah, Libya **D8** 48
Marsabit, Kenya **C7** 54
Marsala, Italy **F4** 18
Marseille, Fr. **F9** 16
Marseilles, Il., U.S. **B5** 106
Marshall, Sk., Can. **D1** 91
Marshall, Lib. **E2** 50
Marshall, Ar., U.S. **B3** 97
Marshall, Il., U.S. **D6** 106
Marshall, Mi., U.S. **F6** 115
Marshall, Mn., U.S. **F3** 116
Marshall, Mo., U.S. **B4** 118
Marshall, N.C., U.S. **f10** 126
Marshall, Tx., U.S. **C5** 136
Marshall, Va., U.S. **B5** 139
Marshall, Wi., U.S. **E4** 142
Marshall, co., Al., U.S. **A3** 94
Marshall, co., Ia., U.S. **C4** 108
Marshall, co., Il., U.S. **B4** 106
Marshall, co., In., U.S. **B5** 107
Marshall, co., Ks., U.S. **C7** 109
Marshall, co., Ky., U.S. **f9** 110
Marshall, co., Mn., U.S. **B2** 116
Marshall, co., Ms., U.S. **A4** 117
Marshall, co., Ok., U.S. **C5** 129
Marshall, co., S.D., U.S. **B8** 134
Marshall, co., Tn., U.S. **B5** 135
Marshall, co., W.V., U.S. **B4** 141
Marshall Islands, ctry., Oc. **C10** 58
Marshall Islands, is., Marsh. Is. **F24** 4
Marshallton, De., U.S. **B3** 101
Marshalltown, Ia., U.S. **B5** 108
Marshallville, Ga., U.S. **D3** 103
Marshes Siding, Ky., U.S. **D5** 110
Marshfield, Ma., U.S. **B6** 114
Marshfield, Mo., U.S. **D5** 118
Marshfield, Wi., U.S. **D3** 142
Marshfield Hills, Ma., U.S. **B6** 114
Marsh Fork, stm., W.V., U.S. **n13** 141
Mars Hill, Me., U.S. **B5** 112
Mars Hill, N.C., U.S. **f10** 126
Marsh Island, i., La., U.S. **E4** 111
Marsh Lake, res., Mn., U.S. **E2** 116
Marsh Peak, mtn., Ut., U.S. **C6** 137
Marshville, N.C., U.S. **C2** 126
Marsing, Id., U.S. **F2** 105
Märsta, Swe. **G7** 10
Marston, Mo., U.S. **E8** 118
Mart, Tx., U.S. **D4** 136
Martaban, Gulf of, b., Myan. **C3** 34
Martapura, Indon. **D2** 36
Martapura, Indon. **D4** 36
Marthasville, Mo., U.S. **C6** 118
Martha's Vineyard, i., Ma., U.S. **D6** 114
Martí, Cuba **A4** 80
Martigny, Switz. **A1** 18
Martigues, Fr. **F9** 16
Martin, Slvk. **E5** 20
Martin, Ky., U.S. **C7** 110
Martin, S.D., U.S. **D4** 134
Martin, Tn., U.S. **A3** 135
Martin, co., Fl., U.S. **E6** 102
Martin, co., In., U.S. **G4** 107
Martin, co., Ky., U.S. **C7** 110
Martin, co., Mn., U.S. **G4** 116
Martin, co., N.C., U.S. **B5** 126
Martin, co., Tx., U.S. **C2** 136
Martinez, Ca., U.S. **C2** 98
Martinez, Ga., U.S. **C4** 103
Martínez de la Torre, Mex. **C5** 78
Martinique, dep., N.A. **F12** 76
Martinique Passage, strt., N.A. **B7** 80
Martin Lake, res., Al., U.S. **C4** 94
Martin Point, c., Ak., U.S. **A11** 95
Martinsburg, Pa., U.S. **F5** 131
Martinsburg, W.V., U.S. **B7** 141
Martins Ferry, Oh., U.S. **B5** 128
Martinsville, Il., U.S. **D6** 106
Martinsville, In., U.S. **F5** 107
Martinsville, Va., U.S. **D3** 139
Marton, N.Z. **p14** 63c
Martos, Spain **I5** 16
Martti, Fin. **C13** 10
Martuni, Arm. **B11** 44
Marutea, atoll, Fr. Poly. **F15** 58
Marv Dasht, Iran **D6** 42
Marvell, Ar., U.S. **C5** 97
Marvine, Mount, mtn., Ut., U.S. **E4** 137
Mary, Turk. **F8** 26

Name / Map Ref. / Page

Mary, Lake, l., Mn., U.S. E3 116
Mary, Lake, l., Ms., U.S. D2 117
Maryborough, Austl. F5 62
Maryborough, Austl. H3 62
Maryland, state, U.S. B4 113
Maryland City, Md., U.S. B4 113
Maryland Heights, Mo., U.S. f13 118
Maryland Point, c., Md., U.S. D3 113
Marys, stm., Nv., U.S. B6 121
Marys Peak, mtn., Or., U.S. C3 130
Marystown, Nf., Can. E4 88
Marysville, Ca., U.S. C3 98
Marysville, Ks., U.S. C7 109
Marysville, Mi., U.S. F8 115
Marysville, Oh., U.S. B2 128
Marysville, Pa., U.S. F8 131
Marysville, Wa., U.S. A3 140
Maryville, Mo., U.S. A3 118
Maryville, Tn., U.S. D10 135
Masai Steppe, plat., Tan. D7 54
Masaka, Ug. D6 54
Masalembu Besar, Pulau, i., Indon. E4 36
Masallı, Azer. C13 44
Masan, S. Kor. D13 28
Masasi, Tan. F7 54
Masaya, Nic. C2 80
Masbate, Phil. D8 34
Masbate, i., Phil. D8 34
Mascarene Basin J8 64
Mascarene Islands, is., Afr. g10 57a
Mascarene Plateau I8 64
Mascasín, Arg. E4 72
Mascoma, stm., N.H., U.S. C2 122
Mascoma Lake, l., N.H., U.S. C2 122
Mascot, Tn., U.S. C10 135
Mascouche, P.Q., Can. D4 90
Mascoutah, Il., U.S. E4 106
Maseru, Leso. D4 56
Mashapaug Pond, l., Ct., U.S. A7 100
Mashava, Zimb. B5 56
Mashhad, Iran C7 42
Mashra'ar Raqq, Sudan I10 48
Masi-Manimba, D.R.C. D3 54
Masindi, Ug. C6 54
Maṣīrah, i., Oman F7 38
Maṣīrah, Khalīj, b., Oman G7 38
Masjed-e Soleymān, Iran D5 42
Maskinongé, P.Q., Can. C4 90
Mason, Mi., U.S. F6 115
Mason, Nv., U.S. E2 121
Mason, Oh., U.S. C1 128
Mason, Tx., U.S. D3 136
Mason, W.V., U.S. B2 141
Mason, co., Il., U.S. C4 106
Mason, co., Ky., U.S. B6 110
Mason, co., Mi., U.S. D4 115
Mason, co., Tx., U.S. D3 136
Mason, co., W.V., U.S. C3 141
Mason, co., Wa., U.S. B2 140
Mason City, Ia., U.S. A4 108
Mason City, Il., U.S. C4 106
Masontown, Pa., U.S. G2 131
Masontown, W.V., U.S. B5 141
Masqaṭ, Oman F7 38
Massa, Italy B2 18
Massabesic Lake, l., N.H., U.S. E4 122
Massac, co., Il., U.S. F5 106
Massachusetts, state, U.S. B4 114
Massachusetts Bay, b., Ma., U.S. B6 114
Massacre Lake, l., Nv., U.S. B2 121
Massangena, Moz. C5 56
Massapoag Lake, l., Ma., U.S. h11 114
Massasecum, Lake, l., N.H., U.S. D3 122
Massawa see Mitsiwa, Erit. G12 48
Massena, N.Y., U.S. f10 125
Massenya, Chad D8 50
Masset, B.C., Can. C1 85
Massey, On., Can. A2 89
Massillon, Oh., U.S. B4 128
Massina, reg., Mali D4 50
Massinga, Moz. C6 56
Massive, Mount, mtn., Co., U.S. B4 99
Maştağa, Azer. B14 44
Masterton, N.Z. p14 63c
Mastic Beach, N.Y., U.S. n16 125
Mastung, Pak. E9 42
Masuda, Japan D2 31
Masuria see Mazury, reg., Pol. C6 20
Masury, Oh., U.S. A5 128
Masvingo, Zimb. C5 56
Matadi, D.R.C. E2 54
Matagalpa, Nic. C2 80
Matagorda, co., Tx., U.S. E5 136
Matagorda Bay, b., Tx., U.S. E4 136
Matagorda Island, i., Tx., U.S. E4 136
Matagorda Peninsula, pen., Tx., U.S. E5 136
Matala, Ang. A2 56
Matale, Sri L. H4 40
Matam, Sen. C2 50
Matamoras, Pa., U.S. D12 131
Matamoros, Mex. B4 78
Matamoros, Mex. B5 78
Matane, P.Q., Can. k13 90
Matanuska, stm., Ak., U.S. g18 95
Matanzas, Cuba A3 80
Matanzas Inlet, b., Fl., U.S. C5 102
Matapan, Cape see Taínaron, Ákra, c., Grc. F9 18
Matara, Sri L. H4 40
Mataram, Indon. E5 36
Mataranka, Austl. C5 60
Mataró, Spain G8 16
Mātātīla Dam, India D3 40
Matawan, N.J., U.S. C4 123
Matehuala, Mex. C4 78
Matera, Italy D6 18
Matewan, W.V., U.S. D2 141
Mather, Pa., U.S. G1 131
Mather Peaks, mts., Wy., U.S. B5 143
Mathews, La., U.S. E5 111
Mathews, Va., U.S. C6 139
Mathews, co., Va., U.S. C6 139
Mathews, Lake, l., Ca., U.S. n14 98
Mathis, Tx., U.S. E4 136
Mathiston, Ms., U.S. B4 117
Mathura, India D3 40
Mati, Phil. E9 34
Matinicus Island, i., Me., U.S. E3 112
Mato, Cerro, mtn., Ven. B6 70
Matoaca, Va., U.S. n18 139
Mato Grosso, Braz. E5 68
Mato Grosso, state, Braz. F8 70
Mato Grosso, Planalto do, plat., Braz. F8 70
Mato Grosso do Sul, state, Braz. B6 72
Matosinhos, Port. G2 16
Maṭraḥ, Oman F7 42
Matsqui, B.C., Can. f13 85
Matsue, Japan D14 28
Matsumoto, Japan C3 31
Matsuyama, Japan E14 28
Mattamiscontis Lake, l., Me., U.S. C4 112
Mattamuskeet, Lake, l., N.C., U.S. B6 126
Mattapoisett, Ma., U.S. C6 114
Mattaponi, stm., Va., U.S. C5 139
Mattawa, On., Can. A6 89
Mattawamkeag, Me., U.S. C4 112
Mattawamkeag, stm., Me., U.S. C4 112
Mattawamkeag Lake, l., Me., U.S. C4 112
Matterhorn (Cervino), mtn., Eur. A1 18
Matterhorn, mtn., Nv., U.S. B6 121
Matteson, Il., U.S. k9 106
Matthews, Mo., U.S. E8 118
Matthews, N.C., U.S. B2 126
Matthew Town, Bah. A5 80
Mattituck, N.Y., U.S. n16 125
Mattoon, Il., U.S. D5 106
Mattoon, Lake, res., Il., U.S. D5 106
Mattydale, N.Y., U.S. B4 125
Matunuck, R.I., U.S. G3 132
Maturín, Ven. B7 70
Matveev Kurgan, Russia F15 20
Maúa, Moz. A6 56
Maubeuge, Fr. B8 16
Maud, Ok., U.S. B5 129
Maués, Braz. D8 70
Mauganj, India E4 40
Maugansville, Md., U.S. A2 113
Maug Islands, is., N. Mar. Is. C12 32
Maui, co., Hi., U.S. B5 104
Maui, i., Hi., U.S. C6 104
Mauldin, S.C., U.S. B3 133
Maumee, Oh., U.S. A2 128
Maumee, stm., U.S. A2 128
Maumee Bay, b., U.S. G7 115
Maumelle, Lake, res., Ar., U.S. C3 97
Maumere, Indon. E6 36
Maun, Bots. B3 56
Mauna Kea, vol., Hi., U.S. D6 104
Maunaloa, Hi., U.S. B4 104
Mauna Loa, vol., Hi., U.S. D6 104
Maunalua Bay, b., Hi., U.S. g10 104
Maunawili, Hi., U.S. g10 104
Maupihaa, atoll, Fr. Poly. F14 58
Maurepas, Lake, l., La., U.S. D5 111
Maurice, Ia., U.S. B1 108
Maurice, stm., N.J., U.S. E2 123
Mauritania, ctry., Afr. C2 50
Mauritius, ctry., Afr. f10 57a
Mauritius, i., Mrts. G11 52
Maury, co., Tn., U.S. B4 135
Maury City, Tn., U.S. B2 135
Maury Island, i., Wa., U.S. f11 140
Mauston, Wi., U.S. E3 142
Maverick, co., Tx., U.S. E2 136
Mavinga, Ang. B3 56
Mawlaik, Myan. B2 34
Mawlamyine, Myan. C3 34
Maxinkuckee, Lake, l., In., U.S. B5 107
Maxixe, Moz. C6 56
Max Meadows, Va., U.S. D2 139
Maxton, N.C., U.S. C3 126
Maxville, On., Can. B10 89
Maxwell, Ia., U.S. C4 108
Maxwell Acres, W.V., U.S. g8 141
Maxwell Air Force Base, mil., Al., U.S. C3 94
Mayaguana, i., Bah. D10 76
Mayaguana Passage, strt., Bah. A5 80
Mayagüez, P.R. B6 80
Mayang, China D2 30
Mayenne, Fr. C6 16
Mayer, Az., U.S. C3 96
Mayerthorpe, Ab., Can. C3 84
Mayes, co., Ok., U.S. A6 129
Mayesville, S.C., U.S. D7 133
Mayfield, Ky., U.S. f9 110
Mayfield, Pa., U.S. C10 131
Mayfield Heights, Oh., U.S. A4 128
Mayfield Lake, res., Wa., U.S. C3 140
Mayflower, Ar., U.S. C3 97
Mayking, Ky., U.S. C7 110
Maymyo, Myan. B3 34
Maynard, Ma., U.S. B5 114
Maynardville, Tn., U.S. C10 135
Mayne, B.C., Can. g12 85
Mayo, Md., U.S. C4 113
Mayo, S.C., U.S. A4 133
Mayo, stm., Mex. B3 78
Mayodan, N.C., U.S. A3 126
Mayo Ndaga, Nig. E7 50
Mayon Volcano, vol., Phil. D8 34
Mayotte, dep., Afr. A8 56
May Park, Or., U.S. B8 130
Mayport Naval Station, mil., Fl., U.S. B5 102
Maysville, Ga., U.S. B3 103
Maysville, Ky., U.S. B6 110
Maysville, Mo., U.S. B3 118
Maysville, N.C., U.S. C5 126
Maysville, Ok., U.S. C4 129
Mayumba, Gabon D2 54
Māyūram, India G3 40
Mayville, Mi., U.S. E7 115
Mayville, N.D., U.S. B8 127
Mayville, N.Y., U.S. C1 125
Mayville, Wi., U.S. E5 142
Maywood, Il., U.S. k9 106
Maywood, N.J., U.S. h8 123
Mazabuka, Zam. B4 56
Mazamet, Fr. F8 16
Mazara del Vallo, Italy F4 18
Mazār-e Sharīf, Afg. C9 42
Mazaruni, stm., Guy. D7 80
Mazatlán, Mex. C3 78
Mazatzal Mountains, mts., Az., U.S. C4 96
Mazatzal Peak, mtn., Az., U.S. C4 96
Mažeikiai, Lith. H10 10
Mazeppa, Mn., U.S. F6 116
Mazomanie, Wi., U.S. E4 142
Mazon, Il., U.S. B5 106
Mazury, reg., Pol. C6 20
Mazyr, Bela. C10 20
Mbabane, Swaz. D5 56
M'bahiakro, C. Iv. E4 50
Mbaïki, C.A.R. C3 54
Mbaké, Sen. D1 50
Mbala, Zam. E6 54
Mbale, Ug. C6 54
Mbalmayo, Cam. C2 54
Mbamba Bay, Tan. F6 54
Mbandaka, D.R.C. C3 54
Mbanga, Cam. C1 54
M'banza Congo, Ang. E2 54
Mbanza-Ngungu (Thysville), D.R.C. E2 54
Mbarara, Ug. D6 54
Mbeya, Tan. E6 54
Mbigou, Gabon D2 54
Mbinda, Congo D2 54
Mbini, Eq. Gui. C1 54
Mboi, D.R.C. E4 54
Mboki, C.A.R. B5 54
Mbouda, Cam. B2 54
Mbour, Sen. D1 50
Mbout, Maur. C2 50
Mbuji-Mayi, D.R.C. E4 54
McAdam, N.B., Can. D2 87
McAdoo, Pa., U.S. E9 131
McAfee Peak, mtn., Nv., U.S. B6 121
McAlester, Ok., U.S. C6 129
McAlester, Lake, res., Ok., U.S. B6 129
McAllen, Tx., U.S. F3 136
McAlmont, Ar., U.S. h10 97
McAlpine, Md., U.S. B4 113
McAlpine Lock and Dam, U.S. H6 107
McArthur, Oh., U.S. C3 128
McBee, S.C., U.S. C7 133
McCall, Id., U.S. E2 105
McCalla, Al., U.S. g6 94
McCamey, Tx., U.S. D1 136
McCammon, Id., U.S. G6 105
McCandless, Pa., U.S. h13 131
McCartney Mountain, mtn., Mt., U.S. E4 119
McCaysville, Ga., U.S. B2 103
McChord Air Force Base, mil., Wa., U.S. f11 140
McClain, co., Ok., U.S. C4 129
McCleary, Wa., U.S. B2 140
McClintock, Mount, mtn., Ant. D20 67
McCloud, Ca., U.S. B2 98
McClure, Pa., U.S. E7 131
McColl, S.C., U.S. B8 133
McComas, W.V., U.S. D3 141
McComb, Ms., U.S. D3 117
McComb, Oh., U.S. A2 128
McCone, co., Mt., U.S. C11 119
McConnell Air Force Base, mil., Ks., U.S. g12 109
McConnellsburg, Pa., U.S. G6 131
McConnelsville, Oh., U.S. C4 128
McCook, Ne., U.S. D5 120
McCook, co., S.D., U.S. D8 134
McCordsville, In., U.S. E6 107
McCormick, S.C., U.S. D3 133
McCormick, co., S.C., U.S. D3 133
McCracken, co., Ky., U.S. e9 110
McCreary, Mb., Can. D2 86
McCreary, co., Ky., U.S. D5 110
McCrory, Ar., U.S. B4 97
McCulloch, co., Tx., U.S. D3 136
McCullough Mountain, mtn., Nv., U.S. H6 121
McCurtain, co., Ok., U.S. C7 129
McDermitt, Nv., U.S. B4 121
McDonald, co., Mo., U.S. E3 118
McDonough, Ga., U.S. C2 103
McDonough, co., Il., U.S. C3 106
McDougall, Mount, mtn., Wy., U.S. D2 143
McDowell, Ky., U.S. C7 110
McDowell, co., N.C., U.S. f10 126
McDowell, co., W.V., U.S. D3 141
McDowell Mountains, mts., Az., U.S. k9 96
McDowell Peak, mtn., Az., U.S. k9 96
McDuffie, co., Ga., U.S. C4 103
McElroy Creek, stm., W.V., U.S. k9 141
Mcensk, Russia C14 20
McEwen, Tn., U.S. A4 135
McFarland, Ca., U.S. E4 98
McFarland, Wi., U.S. E4 142
McGehee, Ar., U.S. D4 97
McGill, Nv., U.S. D7 121
McGrath, Ak., U.S. C8 95
McGregor, Ia., U.S. A6 108
McGregor, Tx., U.S. D4 136
McGregor, stm., B.C., Can. B7 85
McGregor Lake, l., Ab., Can. D4 84
McGuire, Mount, mtn., Id., U.S. D4 105
McGuire Air Force Base, mil., N.J., U.S. C3 123
McHenry, Il., U.S. A5 106
McHenry, Md., U.S. k12 113
McHenry, co., Il., U.S. A5 106
McHenry, co., N.D., U.S. A5 127
Mchinji, Mwi. A5 56
McIntosh, Mn., U.S. C3 116
McIntosh, co., Ga., U.S. E5 103
McIntosh, co., N.D., U.S. C6 127
McIntosh, co., Ok., U.S. B6 129
McKean, co., Pa., U.S. C4 131
McKee, Ky., U.S. C6 110
McKeesport, Pa., U.S. F2 131
McKees Rocks, Pa., U.S. F1 131
McKenzie, Tn., U.S. A3 135
McKenzie, co., N.D., U.S. B2 127
McKenzie, stm., Or., U.S. C4 130
McKinley, co., N.M., U.S. B1 124
McKinley, Mount, mtn., Ak., U.S. C9 95
McKinleyville, Ca., U.S. B1 98
McKinney, Tx., U.S. C4 136
McKinney, Lake, l., Ks., U.S. E2 109
McKittrick Summit, mtn., Ca., U.S. E4 98
McLaughlin, S.D., U.S. B5 134
McLean, Il., U.S. C4 106
McLean, Va., U.S. g12 139
McLean, co., Il., U.S. C4 106
McLean, co., Ky., U.S. C2 110
McLean, co., N.D., U.S. B4 127
McLeansboro, Il., U.S. E5 106
McLennan, Ab., Can. B2 84
McLennan, co., Tx., U.S. D4 136
McLeod, co., Mn., U.S. F4 116
M'Clintock Channel, strt., Nu., Can. D19 82
McLoud, Ok., U.S. B4 129
McLoughlin, Mount, mtn., Or., U.S. D4 130
McLouth, Ks., U.S. C8 109
McMechen, W.V., U.S. B4 141
McMillan, Lake, res., N.M., U.S. E5 124
McMinn, co., Tn., U.S. D9 135
McMinnville, Or., U.S. B3 130
McMinnville, Tn., U.S. D8 135
McMullen, co., Tx., U.S. E3 136
McMurdo Sound, strt., Ant. D21 67
McNairy, co., Tn., U.S. B3 135
McNary, Az., U.S. C6 96
McNary Dam, U.S. B7 130
McNeil, Ar., U.S. D2 97
McNeil, Mount, mtn., B.C., Can. B2 85
McNeil Island, i., Wa., U.S. f10 140
McNeill, Ms., U.S. E4 117
McPherson, Ks., U.S. D6 109
McPherson, co., Ks., U.S. D6 109
McPherson, co., Ne., U.S. C4 120
McPherson, co., S.D., U.S. B6 134
McQueeney, Tx., U.S. h7 136
McRae, Ar., U.S. B4 97
McRae, Ga., U.S. D4 103
McRoberts, Ky., U.S. C7 110
McSherrystown, Pa., U.S. G7 131
Mdandu, Tan. E6 54
Mead, Wa., U.S. B8 140
Mead, Lake, res., U.S. A1 96
Meade, Ks., U.S. E3 109
Meade, co., Ks., U.S. E3 109
Meade, co., Ky., U.S. C3 110
Meade, co., S.D., U.S. C3 134
Meade, stm., Ak., U.S. B8 95
Meaden Peak, mtn., Co., U.S. A3 99
Meade Peak, mtn., Id., U.S. G7 105
Meadow, stm., W.V., U.S. C4 141
Meadow Creek, stm., W.V., U.S. n14 141
Meadow Lands, Pa., U.S. F1 131
Meadow Valley Wash, val., Nv., U.S. F7 121
Meadowview, Va., U.S. f10 139
Meadville, Pa., U.S. C1 131
Meaford, On., Can. C4 89
Meagher, co., Mt., U.S. D6 119
Meander Creek Reservoir, res., Oh., U.S. A5 128
Meaux, Fr. C8 16
Mebane, N.C., U.S. A3 126
Mecca see Makkah, Sau. Ar. F3 38
Mecca, Ca., U.S. F5 98
Mechanic Falls, Me., U.S. D2 112
Mechanicsburg, Oh., U.S. B2 128
Mechanicsburg, Pa., U.S. F7 131
Mechanicsville, Ia., U.S. C6 108
Mechanicsville, Md., U.S. D4 113
Mechanicsville, Va., U.S. C5 139
Mechanicville, N.Y., U.S. C7 125
Mechant, Lake, l., La., U.S. E4 111
Mecklenburg, co., N.C., U.S. B2 126
Mecklenburg, co., Va., U.S. D4 139
Mecklenburg, hist. reg., Ger. D12 12
Mecklenburg Bay see Mecklenburger Bucht, b., Ger. C12 12
Mecklenburger Bucht, b., Ger. C12 12
Mecosta, co., Mi., U.S. E5 115
Mecúfi, Moz. A7 56
Medan, Indon. C1 36
Medanosa, Punta, c., Arg. G3 69
Medaryville, In., U.S. B4 107
Meddybumps Lake, l., Me., U.S. C5 112
Medellín, Col. B4 70
Médenine, Tun. D7 48
Mederdra, Maur. C1 50
Medfield, Ma., U.S. h10 114
Medford, Ma., U.S. B5 114
Medford, Mn., U.S. F5 116
Medford, Ok., U.S. A4 129
Medford, Or., U.S. E4 130
Medford, Wi., U.S. C3 142
Medford Lakes, N.J., U.S. D3 123
Medgidia, Rom. G10 20
Media, Pa., U.S. G11 131
Mediapolis, Ia., U.S. C6 108
Mediaş, Rom. F8 20
Medical Lake, Wa., U.S. B8 140
Medicine Bow, Wy., U.S. E6 143
Medicine Bow, stm., Wy., U.S. E6 143
Medicine Bow Mountains, mts., U.S. E6 143
Medicine Bow Peak, mtn., Wy., U.S. E6 143
Medicine Hat, Ab., Can. D5 84
Medicine Lodge, Ks., U.S. E5 109
Medicine Lodge, stm., U.S. E4 109
Medina see Al-Madīnah, Sau. Ar. F3 38
Medina, N.Y., U.S. B2 125
Medina, Oh., U.S. A4 128
Medina, Tn., U.S. B3 135
Medina, Wa., U.S. e11 140
Medina, co., Oh., U.S. A4 128
Medina, co., Tx., U.S. E3 136
Medina, stm., Tx., U.S. k7 136
Medina del Campo, Spain G4 16
Medinīpur, India E5 40
Mediterranean Sea D5 14
Mediterraneo, Mar see Mediterranean Sea D5 14
Mednogorsk, Russia D10 22
Mednyj, ostrov, i., Russia D18 26
Medora, In., U.S. G5 107
Médouneu, Gabon C2 54
Medvežegorsk, Russia B5 22
Medvežji ostrova, is., Russia B18 26
Medway, Ma., U.S. B5 114
Medway, Me., U.S. C4 112
Medway, stm., N.S., Can. E5 87
Meekatharra, Austl. F2 60
Meeker, Co., U.S. A3 99
Meeker, Ok., U.S. B5 129
Meeker, co., Mn., U.S. E4 116
Meelpaeg Lake, res., Nf., Can. D3 88
Meerut, India D3 40
Meeteetse, Wy., U.S. B4 143
Mēga, Eth. C7 54
Mégantic, Lac, l., P.Q., Can. D7 90
Mégantic, Mont, mtn., P.Q., Can. D6 90
Meggett, S.C., U.S. F7 133

Name **Map Ref.** **Page**

Meghālaya, prov., India **D6** 40
Meghri, Arm. **C12** 44
Meharry, Mount, mtn., Austl. **H20** 4
Meherrin, stm., U.S. **A4** 126
Mehlville, Mo., U.S. **f13** 118
Mehtarlām, Afg. **D10** 42
Meia Meia, Tan. **E7** 54
Meiganga, Cam. **B2** 54
Meigs, Ga., U.S. **E2** 103
Meigs, co., Oh., U.S. **C3** 128
Meigs, co., Tn., U.S. **D9** 135
Meiktila, Myan. **B3** 34
Meiningen, Ger. **E12** 12
Meishan, China **C1** 30
Meitan, China **D2** 30
Meizhou, China **G11** 28
Mejillones, Chile **B2** 69
Mékambo, Gabon **C2** 54
Mek'elē, Eth. **H12** 48
Mékhé, Sen. **C1** 50
Meknès, Mor. **D3** 48
Mekong, stm., Asia **D5** 34
Mékôngk see Mekong, stm., Asia **D5** 34
Melaka, Malay. **C2** 36
Melanesia, is., Oc. **E10** 58
Melbourne, Austl. **H4** 62
Melbourne, Ar., U.S. **A4** 97
Melbourne, Fl., U.S. **D6** 102
Melbourne, Ia., U.S. **C4** 108
Melbourne, Ky., U.S. **h14** 110
Melbourne Beach, Fl., U.S. **D6** 102
Melcher, Ia., U.S. **C4** 108
Melchor Múzquiz, Mex. **B4** 78
Melenki, Russia **C7** 22
Meleuz, Russia **D10** 22
Mélèzes, Rivière aux, stm., P.Q., Can. **g12** 90
Melfi, Chad **D8** 50
Melilla, Sp. N. Afr. **J5** 16
Melipilla, Chile **E3** 72
Melita, Mb., Can. **E1** 86
Melitopol', Ukr. **F13** 20
Mellen, Wi., U.S. **B3** 142
Mellette, co., S.D., U.S. **D5** 134
Melo, Ur. **E7** 72
Melocheville, P.Q., Can. **q19** 90
Melos see Mílos, i., Grc. **F10** 18
Melrhir, Chott, l., Alg. **D6** 48
Melrose, Austl. **F3** 60
Melrose, Fl., U.S. **C4** 102
Melrose, Ma., U.S. **B5** 114
Melrose, Mn., U.S. **E4** 116
Melrose, N.M., U.S. **C6** 124
Melton Hill Lake, res., Tn., U.S. **D9** 135
Meluco, Moz. **A6** 56
Melun, Fr. **C8** 16
Melvern Lake, res., Ks., U.S. **D8** 109
Melville, La., U.S. **D4** 111
Melville, Cape, c., Austl. **C3** 62
Melville, Lake, l., Nf., Can. **B2** 88
Melville Island, i., Austl. **C5** 60
Melville Sound, strt., Nu., Can. **E18** 82
Melvin, Ky., U.S. **C7** 110
Memboro, Indon. **E5** 36
Memel see Klaipėda, Lith. **I9** 10
Memmingen, Ger. **G11** 12
Mempawah, Indon. **C3** 36
Memphis, Fl., U.S. **p10** 102
Memphis, Mi., U.S. **F8** 115
Memphis, Mo., U.S. **A5** 118
Memphis, Tn., U.S. **B1** 135
Memphis, Tx., U.S. **B2** 136
Memphis Naval Air Station, mil., Tn., U.S. **B2** 135
Mena, Ukr. **D12** 20
Mena, Ar., U.S. **C1** 97
Menahga, Mn., U.S. **D3** 116
Ménaka, Mali **C5** 50
Menan, Id., U.S. **F7** 105
Menands, N.Y., U.S. **C7** 125
Menard, Tx., U.S. **D3** 136
Menard, co., Il., U.S. **C4** 106
Menard, co., Tx., U.S. **D3** 136
Menasha, Wi., U.S. **D5** 142
Mende, Fr. **E8** 16
Mendeleyev Ridge **E4** 144
Mendenhall, Ms., U.S. **D4** 117
Mendham, N.J., U.S. **B3** 123
Mendī, Eth. **B7** 54
Mendi, Pap. N. Gui. **H11** 32
Mendocino, co., Ca., U.S. **C2** 98
Mendocino Fracture Zone **E23** 64
Mendon, Il., U.S. **C2** 106
Mendon, Mi., U.S. **F5** 115
Mendon, Ut., U.S. **B4** 137
Mendota, Ca., U.S. **D3** 98
Mendota, Il., U.S. **B4** 106
Mendota, Lake, l., Wi., U.S. **E4** 142
Mendoza, Arg. **E4** 72
Mene Grande, Ven. **D5** 80
Menemen, Tur. **C2** 44
Mengcheng, China **C4** 30
Menggala, Indon. **D3** 36
Menghai, China **B4** 34
Mengjiawan, China **B2** 30
Mengzi, China **G8** 28
Menifee, co., Ky., U.S. **C6** 110
Menindee, Austl. **G3** 62
Menlo Park, Ca., U.S. **k8** 98
Menno, S.D., U.S. **D8** 134
Menominee, Mi., U.S. **C3** 115
Menominee, co., Mi., U.S. **C3** 115
Menominee, co., Wi., U.S. **C5** 142
Menominee, stm., U.S. **C6** 142
Menominee Indian Reservation, Wi., U.S. **C5** 142
Menomonee, stm., Wi., U.S. **m11** 142
Menomonee Falls, Wi., U.S. **E5** 142
Menomonie, Wi., U.S. **D2** 142
Menongue, Ang. **A2** 56
Menor, Mar, b., Spain **I6** 16
Menorca (Minorca), i., Spain **G9** 16
Mentawai, Kepulauan, is., Indon. **D1** 36
Mentawai, Selat, strt., Indon. **D1** 36
Mentone, In., U.S. **B5** 107
Mentor, Oh., U.S. **A4** 128
Mentor-on-the-Lake, Oh., U.S. **A4** 128
Menzel Bourguiba, Tun. **F2** 18
Menzies, Austl. **F3** 60
Meoqui, Mex. **B3** 78
Meppen, Ger. **D10** 12
Mequinenza, Embalse de, res., Spain **G6** 16
Mequon, Wi., U.S. **E6** 142
Merambéllou, Kólpos, b., Grc. **G10** 18
Meramec, stm., Mo., U.S. **C7** 118
Merano, Italy **A3** 18
Merasheen Island, i., Nf., Can. **E4** 88
Merauke, Indon. **H11** 32
Meraux, La., U.S. **k12** 111
Mercāra, India **G3** 40
Merced, Ca., U.S. **D3** 98
Merced, co., Ca., U.S. **D3** 98
Merced, stm., Ca., U.S. **D3** 98
Mercedes, Arg. **D6** 72
Mercedes, Tx., U.S. **F4** 136
Mercedes, Ur. **E6** 72
Mercer, Pa., U.S. **D1** 131
Mercer, Wi., U.S. **B3** 142
Mercer, co., Il., U.S. **B3** 106
Mercer, co., Ky., U.S. **C5** 110
Mercer, co., Mo., U.S. **A4** 118
Mercer, co., N.D., U.S. **B4** 127
Mercer, co., N.J., U.S. **C3** 123
Mercer, co., Oh., U.S. **B1** 128
Mercer, co., Pa., U.S. **D1** 131
Mercer, co., W.V., U.S. **D3** 141
Mercer Island, Wa., U.S. **B3** 140
Mercer Island, i., Wa., U.S. **e11** 140
Mercersburg, Pa., U.S. **G6** 131
Mercerville, N.J., U.S. **C3** 123
Mercier, P.Q., Can. **D4** 90
Meredith, N.H., U.S. **C3** 122
Meredith, Lake, l., Co., U.S. **C7** 99
Meredith, Lake, res., Tx., U.S. **B2** 136
Meredosia, Il., U.S. **D3** 106
Meredosia Lake, l., Il., U.S. **D3** 106
Mereeg, Som. **J14** 48
Merefa, Ukr. **E14** 20
Merenkurkku (Norra Kvarken), strt., Eur. **E9** 10
Mergui, Myan. **D3** 34
Mergui Archipelago, is., Myan. **D3** 34
Meriç (Évros) (Marica), stm., Eur. **D11** 18
Mérida, Mex. **C7** 78
Mérida, Spain **H3** 16
Mérida, Ven. **B5** 70
Mérida, Cordillera de, mts., Ven. **B5** 70
Meriden, Ct., U.S. **C4** 100
Meriden, Ks., U.S. **C8** 109
Meridian, Id., U.S. **F2** 105
Meridian, Ms., U.S. **C5** 117
Meridian, Pa., U.S. **E2** 131
Meridian, Tx., U.S. **D4** 136
Meridian Hills, In., U.S. **k10** 107
Meridian Naval Air Station, mil., Ms., U.S. **C5** 117
Meridianville, Al., U.S. **A3** 94
Merikarvia, Fin. **F9** 10
Merín, Laguna see Mirim, Lagoa, b., S.A. **E7** 72
Meriwether, co., Ga., U.S. **C2** 103
Merkel, Tx., U.S. **C2** 136
Merlin, On., Can. **E2** 89
Mermentau, La., U.S. **D3** 111
Mermentau, stm., La., U.S. **E3** 111
Meron, Har, mtn., Isr. **F6** 44
Meron, Mount see Meron, Har, mtn., Isr. **F6** 44
Merredin, Austl. **G2** 60
Merriam, Ks., U.S. **k16** 109
Merrick, co., Ne., U.S. **C7** 120
Merrickville, On., Can. **C9** 89
Merrill, Ia., U.S. **B1** 108
Merrill, Mi., U.S. **E6** 115
Merrill, Or., U.S. **E5** 130
Merrill, Wi., U.S. **C4** 142
Merrillville, In., U.S. **B3** 107
Merrimac, Ma., U.S. **A5** 114
Merrimack, N.H., U.S. **E4** 122
Merrimack, co., N.H., U.S. **D3** 122
Merrimack, stm., U.S. **A5** 114
Merritt, B.C., Can. **D7** 85
Merritt Island, Fl., U.S. **D6** 102
Merritt Reservoir, res., Ne., U.S. **B5** 120
Merrymeeting Lake, l., N.H., U.S. **D4** 122
Merryville, La., U.S. **D2** 111
Mersa Matruh, Egypt **D10** 48
Mersing, Malay. **C2** 36
Merthyr Tydfil, Wales, U.K. **E5** 12
Merton, Wi., U.S. **m11** 142
Meru, Kenya **C7** 54
Merwin, Lake, res., Wa., U.S. **C3** 140
Merzifon, Tur. **B6** 44
Mesa, Az., U.S. **D4** 96
Mesa, co., Co., U.S. **C2** 99
Mesabi Range, hills, Mn., U.S. **C6** 116
Mesa Mountain, mtn., Co., U.S. **D4** 99
Mesa Verde National Park, Co., U.S. **D2** 99
Mescalero, N.M., U.S. **D4** 124
Mescalero Indian Reservation, N.M., U.S. **D4** 124
Meschede, Ger. **E11** 12
Meshgīn Shahr, Iran **C12** 44
Mesilla, N.M., U.S. **E3** 124
Mesolóngion, Grc. **E8** 18
Mesopotamia, hist. reg., Asia **D4** 42
Mesquite, N.M., U.S. **E3** 124
Mesquite, Nv., U.S. **G7** 121
Mesquite, Tx., U.S. **n10** 136
Messalonskee Lake, l., Me., U.S. **D3** 112
Messina, Italy **E5** 18
Messina, S. Afr. **C5** 56
Messina, Stretto di, strt., Italy **E5** 18
Messiniakós Kólpos, b., Grc. **F9** 18
Mestghanem, Alg. **C4** 48
Mestre, Italy **B4** 18
Meta, stm., S.A. **B5** 70
Métabetchouan, P.Q., Can. **A6** 90
Métabetchouane, stm., P.Q., Can. **A5** 90
Metairie, La., U.S. **k11** 111
Metamora, Il., U.S. **C4** 106
Metán, Arg. **D5** 72
Metapán, El Sal. **C2** 80
Metapontum, hist., Italy **D6** 18
Metcalfe, On., Can. **B9** 89
Metcalfe, Ms., U.S. **B2** 117
Metcalfe, co., Ky., U.S. **C4** 110
Metedeconk, North Branch, stm., N.J., U.S. **C4** 123
Metedeconk, South Branch, stm., N.J., U.S. **C3** 123
Meteghan, N.S., Can. **E3** 87
Meteghan River, N.S., Can. **E3** 87
Metéora, Grc. **E8** 18
Meteor Crater, crat., Az., U.S. **C4** 96
Methow, stm., Wa., U.S. **A5** 140
Methuen, Ma., U.S. **A5** 114
Metlakatla, Ak., U.S. **D13** 95
Metonga, Lake, l., Wi., U.S. **C5** 142
Metro, Indon. **E3** 36
Metropolis, Il., U.S. **F5** 106
Mettawee, stm., U.S. **E2** 138
Metter, Ga., U.S. **D4** 103
Metuchen, N.J., U.S. **B4** 123
Metz, Fr. **C10** 16
Metzger, Or., U.S. **h12** 130
Meulaboh, Indon. **C1** 36
Meuse (Maas), stm., Eur. **C9** 16
Mexia, Tx., U.S. **D4** 136
Mexia, Lake, res., Tx., U.S. **D4** 136
Mexiana, Ilha, i., Braz. **A2** 74
Mexicali, Mex. **A1** 78
Mexican Basin **F4** 66
Mexico, In., U.S. **C5** 107
Mexico, Me., U.S. **D2** 112
Mexico, Mo., U.S. **B6** 118
México, state, Mex. **D4** 78
Mexico, ctry., N.A. **C4** 78
Mexico, Gulf of, b., N.A. **F10** 92
Mexico City see Ciudad de México, Mex. **D5** 78
Meyersdale, Pa., U.S. **G3** 131
Meyísti, i., Grc. **F12** 18
Meymaneh, Afg. **C8** 42
Mezcala, Mex. **D5** 78
Meždurečenskij, Russia **C12** 22
Mezen', Russia **C6** 26
Mezen', stm., Russia **C6** 26
Mezenskaja guba, b., Russia **A7** 22
Mezőtúr, Hung. **F6** 20
Mfangano Island, i., Kenya **D6** 54
Mgeta, Tan. **E7** 54
M'Goun, Irhil, mtn., Mor. **E2** 14
Mhow, India **E3** 40
Miahuatlán de Porfirio Díaz, Mex. **D5** 78
Miajadas, Spain **H4** 16
Miaméré, C.A.R. **B3** 54
Miami, Az., U.S. **D5** 96
Miami, Fl., U.S. **G6** 102
Miami, Ok., U.S. **A7** 129
Miami, co., In., U.S. **C5** 107
Miami, co., Ks., U.S. **D9** 109
Miami, co., Oh., U.S. **B1** 128
Miami Beach, Fl., U.S. **G6** 102
Miami Canal, Fl., U.S. **F6** 102
Miami International Airport, Fl., U.S. **G6** 102
Miamisburg, Oh., U.S. **C1** 128
Miami Shores, Fl., U.S. **G6** 102
Miami Springs, Fl., U.S. **G6** 102
Mianchi, China **C3** 30
Mīāndoāb, Iran **D12** 44
Miandrivazo, Madag. **B8** 56
Mīāneh, Iran **C5** 42
Mianning, China **A4** 34
Mianus Reservoir, res., U.S. **E1** 100
Miānwāli, Pak. **D10** 42
Mianyang, China **E8** 28
Mianzhu, China **C1** 30
Miass, Russia **D8** 26
Mica Mountain, mtn., Az., U.S. **E5** 96
Micco, Fl., U.S. **E6** 102
Miccosukee, Lake, res., Fl., U.S. **B2** 102
Michalovce, Slvk. **E6** 20
Michelson, Mount, mtn., Ak., U.S. **B11** 95
Michie, Tn., U.S. **B3** 135
Michigamme, Lake, l., Mi., U.S. **B2** 115
Michigamme Reservoir, res., Mi., U.S. **B2** 115
Michigan, state, U.S. **E6** 115
Michigan, stm., Co., U.S. **A4** 99
Michigan, Lake, l., U.S. **C10** 92
Michigan Center, Mi., U.S. **F6** 115
Michigan City, In., U.S. **A4** 107
Michigan Island, i., Wi., U.S. **B3** 142
Michoacán, state, Mex. **D4** 78
Micronesia, is., Oc. **C9** 58
Micronesia, Federated States of, ctry., Oc. **D8** 58
Mičurinsk, Russia **C16** 20
Mid-Atlantic Ridge **F9** 66
Middelburg, S. Afr. **E3** 56
Middelburg, S. Afr. **D4** 56
Middelfart, Den. **I3** 10
Middle, stm., Ia., U.S. **C3** 108
Middle, stm., Mn., U.S. **B2** 116
Middle America Trench **G28** 64
Middle Andaman, i., India **G6** 40
Middleboro (Middleborough Center), Ma., U.S. **C6** 114
Middlebourne, W.V., U.S. **B4** 141
Middleburg, Fl., U.S. **B5** 102
Middleburg, Pa., U.S. **E7** 131
Middleburg Heights, Oh., U.S. **h9** 128
Middlebury, Ct., U.S. **C3** 100
Middlebury, In., U.S. **A6** 107
Middlebury, Vt., U.S. **C2** 138
Middle Caicos, i., T./C. Is. **A5** 80
Middlefield, Ct., U.S. **C5** 100
Middlefield, Oh., U.S. **A4** 128
Middle Island Creek, stm., W.V., U.S. **B3** 141
Middle Nodaway, stm., Ia., U.S. **C3** 108
Middle Park, val., Co., U.S. **A4** 99
Middle Patuxent, stm., Md., U.S. **B4** 113
Middleport, N.Y., U.S. **B2** 125
Middleport, Oh., U.S. **C3** 128
Middle Raccoon, stm., Ia., U.S. **C3** 108
Middle River, Md., U.S. **B5** 113
Middlesboro, Ky., U.S. **D6** 110
Middlesbrough, Eng., U.K. **C6** 12
Middlesex, N.C., U.S. **B4** 126
Middlesex, N.J., U.S. **B4** 123
Middlesex, co., Ct., U.S. **D5** 100
Middlesex, co., Ma., U.S. **A5** 114
Middlesex, co., N.J., U.S. **C4** 123
Middlesex, co., Va., U.S. **C6** 139
Middlesex Fells Reservation, Ma., U.S. **g11** 114
Middleton, N.S., Can. **E4** 87
Middleton, Id., U.S. **F2** 105
Middleton, Ma., U.S. **A5** 114
Middleton, Wi., U.S. **E4** 142
Middletown, Ca., U.S. **C2** 98
Middletown, Ct., U.S. **C5** 100
Middletown, De., U.S. **C3** 101
Middletown, In., U.S. **D6** 107
Middletown, Ky., U.S. **g11** 110
Middletown, Md., U.S. **B2** 113
Middletown, N.J., U.S. **C4** 123
Middletown, N.Y., U.S. **D6** 125
Middletown, Oh., U.S. **C1** 128
Middletown, Pa., U.S. **F8** 131
Middletown, R.I., U.S. **E5** 132
Middletown, Va., U.S. **A4** 139
Middleville, Mi., U.S. **F5** 115
Midfield, Al., U.S. **g7** 94
Mid-Indian Basin **I10** 64
Mid-Indian Ridge **I9** 64
Midland, On., Can. **C5** 89
Midland, Mi., U.S. **E6** 115
Midland, N.C., U.S. **B2** 126
Midland, Pa., U.S. **E1** 131
Midland, Tx., U.S. **D1** 136
Midland, co., Mi., U.S. **E6** 115
Midland, co., Tx., U.S. **D1** 136
Midland City, Al., U.S. **D4** 94
Midland Park, Ks., U.S. **g12** 109
Midland Park, N.J., U.S. **B4** 123
Midland Park, S.C., U.S. **k11** 133
Midlothian, Il., U.S. **k9** 106
Midlothian, Tx., U.S. **C4** 136
Midongy Atsimo, Madag. **C8** 56
Mid-Pacific Mountains **F18** 64
Midvale, Ut., U.S. **C4** 137
Midville, Ga., U.S. **D4** 103
Midway, B.C., Can. **E8** 85
Midway, De., U.S. **F5** 101
Midway, Ky., U.S. **B5** 110
Midway, Pa., U.S. **G7** 131
Midway, Ut., U.S. **C4** 137
Midway Islands, dep., Oc. **B12** 58
Midwest, Wy., U.S. **C6** 143
Midwest City, Ok., U.S. **B4** 129
Midyat, Tur. **D9** 44
Międzyrzecz, Pol. **C3** 20
Miekojärvi, l., Fin. **C11** 10
Mielec, Pol. **D6** 20
Mieres, Spain **F4** 16
Mifflin, co., Pa., U.S. **E6** 131
Mifflinburg, Pa., U.S. **E7** 131
Mifflinville, Pa., U.S. **D9** 131
Miguel Alemán, Presa, res., Mex. **D5** 78
Miguel Auza, Mex. **C4** 78
Mihajlov, Russia **B15** 20
Mihajlovka, Russia **D6** 26
Mikasa, Japan **C16** 28
Mikínai, hist., Grc. **F9** 18
Mikindani, Tan. **F8** 54
Mikkeli, Fin. **F12** 10
Míkonos, i., Grc. **F10** 18
Mikumi, Tan. **E7** 54
Mikun', Russia **B9** 22
Milaca, Mn., U.S. **E5** 116
Milagro, Ec. **D4** 70
Milam, co., Tx., U.S. **D4** 136
Milan see Milano, Italy **B2** 18
Milan, Ga., U.S. **D3** 103
Milan, Il., U.S. **B3** 106
Milan, In., U.S. **F7** 107
Milan, Mi., U.S. **F7** 115
Milan, Mo., U.S. **A4** 118
Milan, N.M., U.S. **B2** 124
Milan, Oh., U.S. **A3** 128
Milan, Tn., U.S. **B3** 135
Milange, Moz. **B6** 56
Milano (Milan), Italy **B2** 18
Milâs, Tur. **D2** 44
Milazzo, Italy **E5** 18
Milbank, S.D., U.S. **B9** 134
Mildmay, On., Can. **C3** 89
Mildura, Austl. **G3** 62
Mile, China **G8** 28
Milesburg, Pa., U.S. **E6** 131
Miles City, Mt., U.S. **D11** 119
Milestone, Sk., Can. **G3** 91
Milet (Miletus), hist., Tur. **D2** 44
Miletus see Milet, hist., Tur. **D2** 44
Milford, Ct., U.S. **E3** 100
Milford, De., U.S. **E4** 101
Milford, Ia., U.S. **A2** 108
Milford, Il., U.S. **C6** 106
Milford, In., U.S. **B6** 107
Milford, Ma., U.S. **B4** 114
Milford, Me., U.S. **D4** 112
Milford, Mi., U.S. **F7** 115
Milford, Ne., U.S. **D8** 120
Milford, N.H., U.S. **E3** 122
Milford, Oh., U.S. **C1** 128
Milford, Pa., U.S. **D12** 131
Milford, Ut., U.S. **E2** 137
Milford Haven, Wales, U.K. **E4** 12
Milford Lake, res., Ks., U.S. **C6** 109
Milford Station, N.S., Can. **D6** 87
Milh, Baḥr al-, res., Iraq **F10** 44
Mililani Town, Hi., U.S. **g9** 104
Milk, stm., N.A. **B6** 92
Mil'kovo, Russia **D17** 26
Milk River, Ab., Can. **E4** 84
Mill, stm., Ma., U.S. **h9** 114
Millard, co., Ut., U.S. **D2** 137
Millau, Fr. **E8** 16
Millbrae, Ca., U.S. **h8** 98
Millbrook, On., Can. **C6** 89
Millbrook, Al., U.S. **C3** 94
Mill Brook, stm., Vt., U.S. **B5** 138
Millburn, N.J., U.S. **B4** 123
Millbury, Ma., U.S. **B4** 114
Millbury, Oh., U.S. **e7** 128
Mill City, Or., U.S. **C4** 130
Millcreek, Ut., U.S. **C4** 137
Mill Creek, W.V., U.S. **C5** 141
Mill Creek, stm., N.J., U.S. **D4** 123
Mill Creek, stm., Oh., U.S. **B2** 128
Mill Creek, stm., Tn., U.S. **g10** 135
Mill Creek, stm., W.V., U.S. **m13** 141
Mill Creek, stm., W.V., U.S. **C3** 141
Millcreek Township, Pa., U.S. **B1** 131
Milledgeville, Ga., U.S. **C3** 103
Milledgeville, Il., U.S. **B4** 106
Mille Îles, Rivière des, stm., P.Q., Can. **p19** 90
Mille Lacs, co., Mn., U.S. **E5** 116
Mille Lacs Indian Reservation, Mn., U.S. **D5** 116
Mille Lacs Lake, l., Mn., U.S. **D5** 116
Millen, Ga., U.S. **D5** 103
Miller, S.D., U.S. **C7** 134
Miller, co., Ar., U.S. **D2** 97
Miller, co., Ga., U.S. **E2** 103
Miller, co., Mo., U.S. **C5** 118
Miller, Mount, mtn., Ak., U.S. **C11** 95
Millerovo, Russia **E7** 22
Miller Peak, mtn., Az., U.S. **F5** 96
Miller Run, stm., Vt., U.S. **B4** 138

Name Map Ref. Page

Millers, stm., Ma., U.S. A3 114
Millersburg, In., U.S. A6 107
Millersburg, Ky., U.S. B5 110
Millersburg, Oh., U.S. B4 128
Millersburg, Pa., U.S. E8 131
Millersport, Oh., U.S. C3 128
Millersville, Pa., U.S. F9 131
Millet, Ab., Can. C4 84
Mill Hall, Pa., U.S. D7 131
Millicent, Austl. H3 62
Milliken, Co., U.S. A6 99
Millington, Mi., U.S. E7 115
Millington, Tn., U.S. B2 135
Millinocket, Me., U.S. C4 112
Millinocket Lake, l., Me., U.S. C4 112
Millinocket Lake, l., Me., U.S. B4 112
Millis, Ma., U.S. B5 114
Millport, Al., U.S. B1 94
Millry, Al., U.S. D1 94
Mills, Wy., U.S. D6 143
Mills, co., Ia., U.S. C2 108
Mills, co., Tx., U.S. D3 136
Millsboro, De., U.S. F4 101
Millsboro, Pa., U.S. G1 131
Millstadt, Il., U.S. E3 106
Millstone, stm., N.J., U.S. C4 123
Milltown, In., U.S. H5 107
Milltown, N.J., U.S. C4 123
Milltown, Wi., U.S. C1 142
Milltown [-Head of Bay d'Espoir], Nf., Can. E4 88
Millvale, Pa., U.S. k14 131
Mill Valley, Ca., U.S. D2 98
Millville, Ma., U.S. B4 114
Millville, N.J., U.S. E2 123
Millville, Pa., U.S. D9 131
Millville, Ut., U.S. B4 137
Millville Lake, N.H., U.S. E4 122
Millwood, Wa., U.S. g14 140
Millwood Lake, res., Ar., U.S. D1 97
Milner Dam, Id., U.S. G5 105
Milnor, N.D., U.S. C8 127
Milo, Ia., U.S. C4 108
Milo, Me., U.S. C4 112
Mílos, Grc. F10 18
Mílos, i., Grc. F10 18
Milparinka, Austl. F3 62
Milroy, In., U.S. F7 107
Milroy, Pa., U.S. E6 131
Milstead, Ga., U.S. C3 103
Milton, On., Can. D5 89
Milton, De., U.S. E4 101
Milton, Fl., U.S. u14 102
Milton, In., U.S. E7 107
Milton, Ma., U.S. B5 114
Milton, N.H., U.S. D5 122
Milton, Pa., U.S. D8 131
Milton, Vt., U.S. B2 138
Milton, W.V., U.S. C2 141
Milton, Wa., U.S. f11 140
Milton, Wi., U.S. F5 142
Milton, Lake, l., Oh., U.S. A4 128
Miltona, Lake, l., Mn., U.S. D3 116
Milton-Freewater, Or., U.S. B8 130
Milton Keynes, Eng., U.K. D6 12
Milton Reservoir, res., Co., U.S. A6 99
Milverton, On., Can. D4 89
Milwaukee, Wi., U.S. E6 142
Milwaukee, co., Wi., U.S. E6 142
Milwaukee, stm., Wi., U.S. m12 142
Milwaukie, Or., U.S. B4 130
Mims, Fl., U.S. D6 102
Min, stm., China F8 28
Min, stm., China D4 30
Mina, Nv., U.S. E3 121
Mīnā' al-Aḥmadī, Kuw. E5 42
Mīnāb, Iran E7 42
Minahasa, pen., Indon. C6 36
Minami-Tori-shima, i., Japan F18 64
Minas, Ur. E6 72
Minas Basin, b., N.S., Can. D5 87
Minas Channel, strt., N.S., Can. D5 87
Minas Gerais, state, Braz. E2 74
Minatare, Ne., U.S. C2 120
Minatitlán, Mex. D6 78
Minbya, Myan. B2 34
Minco, Ok., U.S. B4 129
Mindanao, i., Phil. E8 34
Mindanao Sea see Bohol Sea, Phil. E8 34
Mindelo, C.V. g10 50a
Minden, Ger. D11 12
Minden, La., U.S. B2 111
Minden, Ne., U.S. D7 120
Minden, Nv., U.S. E2 121
Minden, W.V., U.S. D3 141
Mindoro, i., Phil. D8 34
Mindoro Strait, strt., Phil. D8 34
Mine Hill, N.J., U.S. B3 123
Mineiros, Braz. B7 72
Mineola, N.Y., U.S. E7 125
Mineola, Tx., U.S. C5 136
Miner, Mo., U.S. E8 118
Miner, co., S.D., U.S. D8 134
Mineral, co., Co., U.S. D4 99
Mineral, co., Mt., U.S. C1 119
Mineral, co., Nv., U.S. E3 121
Mineral, co., W.V., U.S. B6 141
Mineral Point, Wi., U.S. F3 142
Mineral Springs, Ar., U.S. D2 97
Mineral Wells, Tx., U.S. C3 136
Minersville, Pa., U.S. E9 131
Minersville, Ut., U.S. E3 137
Minerva, Oh., U.S. B4 128
Minetto, N.Y., U.S. B4 125
Minfeng, China D4 28
Mingäçevir, Azer. B12 44
Mingäçevir su anbarı, res., Azer. B12 44
Mingechaur Reservoir see Mingäçevir su anbarı, res., Azer. B12 44
Mingenew, Austl. F2 60
Mingo, co., W.V., U.S. D2 141
Mingo Junction, Oh., U.S. B5 128
Minho (Miño), stm., Eur. G2 16
Minicoy Island, i., India H2 40
Minidoka, co., Id., U.S. G5 105
Minidoka Dam, Id., U.S. G5 105
Minier, Il., U.S. C4 106
Minisink Island, i., N.J., U.S. A3 123
Minitonas, Mb., Can. C1 86
Minle, China D8 28
Minna, Nig. E6 50
Minneapolis, Ks., U.S. C6 109
Minneapolis, Mn., U.S. F5 116
Minnedosa, Mb., Can. D2 86
Minnedosa, stm., Mb., Can. D1 86
Minnehaha, co., S.D., U.S. D9 134
Minneola, Ks., U.S. E3 109
Minneota, Mn., U.S. F3 116
Minnesota, state, U.S. E4 116
Minnesota, stm., Mn., U.S. F2 116
Minnesota Lake, Mn., U.S. G5 116
Minnetonka, Mn., U.S. n12 116
Minnetonka, Lake, l., Mn., U.S. n11 116
Minnewaska, Lake, l., Mn., U.S. E3 116
Miño (Minho), stm., Eur. F3 16
Minocqua, Wi., U.S. C4 142
Minonk, Il., U.S. C4 106
Minooka, Il., U.S. B5 106
Minot, N.D., U.S. A4 127
Minot Air Force Base, mil., N.D., U.S. A4 127
Minqin, China B1 30
Minqing, China D4 30
Minquadale, De., U.S. i7 101
Minsk, Bela. B9 20
Minster, Oh., U.S. B1 128
Mint Hill, N.C., U.S. B2 126
Minto, N.B., Can. C3 87
Minturn, Co., U.S. B4 99
Minusinsk, Russia D11 26
Minute Man National Historical Park, Ma., U.S. g10 114
Minvoul, Gabon C2 54
Minxian, China E8 28
Minya see El-Minya, Egypt E11 48
Mio, Mi., U.S. D6 115
Mīrābād, Afg. D8 42
Mirabel, P.Q., Can. D3 90
Mirabella, Gulf of see Merambéllou, Kólpos, b., Grc. G10 18
Mirador, Braz. E11 70
Miraflores, Col. B5 70
Miraj, India F2 40
Miramar, Fl., U.S. s13 102
Miramar Naval Air Station, mil., Ca., U.S. F5 98
Miramichi Bay, b., N.B., Can. B5 87
Miranda, stm., Braz. B6 72
Miranda de Ebro, Spain F5 16
Mirbāṭ, Oman G6 38
Miri, Malay. C4 36
Miria, Niger D6 50
Mirim, Lagoa (Merín, Laguna), b., S.A. E7 72
Mirnyj, Russia C13 26
Mīrpur, Pak. D10 42
Mīrpur Khās, Pak. E9 42
Mirror Lake, l., N.H., U.S. C4 122
Mirtóön Pélagos, Grc. F9 18
Mirzāpur, India D4 40
Miscouche, P.E., Can. C6 87
Miscou Island, i., N.B., Can. B5 87
Miscou Point, c., N.B., Can. A5 87
Misenheimer, N.C., U.S. B2 126
Mishan, China B14 28
Mishawaka, In., U.S. A5 107
Misheguk Mountain, mtn., Ak., U.S. B7 95
Mishicot, Wi., U.S. D6 142
Miskitos, Cayos, is., Nic. C3 80
Miskolc, Hung. E6 20
Misool, Pulau, i., Indon. D8 36
Mispillion, stm., De., U.S. E4 101
Miṣrātah, Libya D8 48
Missaukee, co., Mi., U.S. D5 115
Missaukee, Lake, l., Mi., U.S. D5 115
Mission, Ks., U.S. m16 109
Mission, S.D., U.S. D5 134
Mission, Tx., U.S. F3 136
Mission Range, mts., Mt., U.S. C3 119
Mission Viejo, Ca., U.S. n13 98
Missisquoi, stm., Vt., U.S. B3 138
Missisquoi Bay, b., Vt., U.S. A2 138
Mississauga, On., Can. D5 89
Mississinewa, stm., U.S. D7 107
Mississinewa Lake, res., In., U.S. C6 107
Mississippi, co., Ar., U.S. B5 97
Mississippi, co., Mo., U.S. E8 118
Mississippi, state, U.S. C4 117
Mississippi, stm., U.S. E9 92
Mississippi Delta, La., U.S. E6 111
Mississippi Sound, strt., U.S. E5 117
Mississippi State, Ms., U.S. B5 117
Missoula, Mt., U.S. D2 119
Missoula, co., Mt., U.S. D2 119
Missouri, state, U.S. C5 118
Missouri, stm., U.S. D9 92
Missouri City, Tx., U.S. r14 136
Missouri Valley, Ia., U.S. C2 108
Mistassini, P.Q., Can. h12 90
Mistassini, Lac, l., P.Q., Can. h12 90
Misti, Volcán, vol., Peru G5 70
Mita, Punta de, c., Mex. C3 78
Mitchell, Austl. F4 62
Mitchell, On., Can. D3 89
Mitchell, Il., U.S. E3 106
Mitchell, In., U.S. G5 107
Mitchell, Ne., U.S. C2 120
Mitchell, S.D., U.S. D7 134
Mitchell, co., Ga., U.S. E2 103
Mitchell, co., Ia., U.S. A5 108
Mitchell, co., Ks., U.S. C5 109
Mitchell, co., N.C., U.S. e10 126
Mitchell, co., Tx., U.S. C2 136
Mitchell, stm., Austl. D3 62
Mitchell, Lake, l., Mi., U.S. D5 115
Mitchell, Lake, res., Al., U.S. C3 94
Mitchell, Mount, mtn., N.C., U.S. f10 126
Mitchell Island, i., La., U.S. E6 111
Mitchellville, Ia., U.S. C4 108
Mitilíni, Grc. E11 18
Mitkof Island, i., Ak., U.S. m23 95
Mito, Japan C4 31
Mitsiwa, Erit. G12 48
Mitú, Col. C5 70
Mitumba, Monts, mts., D.R.C. E5 54
Mitwaba, D.R.C. E5 54
Mitzic, Gabon C2 54
Miyake-jima, i., Japan E15 28
Miyako, Japan D16 28
Miyako-jima, i., Japan B9 34
Miyakonojō, Japan E14 28
Miyazaki, Japan E14 28
Miyazu, Japan D15 28
Miyoshi, Japan D2 31
Miyun, China A4 30
Mīzan Teferī, Eth. B7 54
Mizdah, Libya D7 48
Mizen Head, c., Ire. E2 12
Mizhi, China B3 30
Mizoram, prov., India E6 40
Mizusawa, Japan C4 31
Mjakit, Russia C17 26
Mjölby, Swe. G6 10
Mjøsa, l., Nor. F4 10
Mkalama, Tan. D6 54
Mkokotoni, Tan. D7 54
Mladá Boleslav, Czech Rep. D3 20
Mlanje Peak see Sapitwa, mtn., Mwi. B6 56
Mława, Pol. C6 20
Mmabatho, S. Afr. D4 56
Moab, Ut., U.S. E6 137
Moala, i., Fiji m10 63b
Moamba, Moz. D5 56
Moanda, Gabon D2 54
Moapa River Indian Reservation, Nv., U.S. G7 121
Moba, D.R.C. E5 54
Mobaye, C.A.R. C4 54
Moberly, Mo., U.S. B5 118
Mobile, Al., U.S. E1 94
Mobile, co., Al., U.S. E1 94
Mobile, stm., Al., U.S. E1 94
Mobile Bay, b., Al., U.S. E1 99
Mobridge, S.D., U.S. B5 134
Mobutu Sese Seko, Lac see Albert, Lake, l., Afr. C6 54
Moca, Dom. Rep. B5 80
Mocanaqua, Pa., U.S. D9 131
Moc Chau, Viet. B4 34
Mocha see Al-Mukhā, Yemen H4 38
Mochudi, Bots. C4 56
Mocímboa da Praia, Moz. A7 56
Mocksville, N.C., U.S. B2 126
Moclips, Wa., U.S. B1 140
Môco, Morro de, mtn., Ang. F3 54
Mococa, Braz. F2 74
Moctezuma, Mex. B3 78
Mocuba, Moz. B6 56
Model Reservoir, res., Co., U.S. D6 99
Módena, Italy B3 18
Modesto, Ca., U.S. D3 98
Modoc, co., Ca., U.S. B3 98
Modowi, Indon. G9 32
Moe, Austl. H4 62
Moen-jo-Daro, hist., Pak. E9 42
Moenkopi, Az., U.S. A4 96
Moffat, co., Co., U.S. A2 99
Moffat Tunnel, Co., U.S. B5 99
Mogadishu see Muqdisho, Som. J14 48
Mogadore, Oh., U.S. A4 128
Mogaung, Myan. A3 34
Mogincual, Moz. B7 56
Mogoča, Russia D13 26
Mogogh, Sudan B6 54
Mogok, Myan. B3 34
Mogollon Mountains, mts., N.M., U.S. D1 124
Mogollon Rim, clf, Az., U.S. C5 96
Mogotón, mtn., N.A. F7 76
Mogzon, Russia A10 28
Mohall, N.D., U.S. A4 127
Mohammed, Râs, c., Egypt F10 14
Mohave, co., Az., U.S. B1 96
Mohave, Lake, res., U.S. H7 121
Mohave Mountains, mts., Az., U.S. C1 96
Mohave Valley, Az., U.S. C1 96
Mohawk, N.Y., U.S. C5 125
Mohawk, stm., N.H., U.S. g7 122
Mohawk, stm., N.Y., U.S. C6 125
Mohawk Lake, l., N.J., U.S. A3 123
Mohawk Mountains, mts., Az., U.S. E2 96
Mohe, China A12 28
Mohican, stm., Oh., U.S. B3 128
Mohns Ridge D23 144
Mohnton, Pa., U.S. F10 131
Mohnyin, Myan. B3 34
Mohyliv-Podil's'kyi, Ukr. E9 20
Mo i Rana, Nor. C6 10
Moisie, P.Q., Can. h8 88
Mojave, Ca., U.S. E4 98
Mojave, stm., Ca., U.S. E5 98
Mojave Desert, des., Ca., U.S. E5 98
Mojo, Eth. B7 54
Mojynty, Kaz. E9 26
Mokapu Peninsula, pen., Hi., U.S. g10 104
Mokapu Point, c., Hi., U.S. g11 104
Mokelumne, stm., Ca., U.S. C3 98
Mokena, Il., U.S. k9 106
Mokhotlong, Leso. D4 56
Moknine, Tun. G3 18
Mokolo, Cam. A2 54
Mokp'o, S. Kor. E13 28
Moku Manu, i., Hi., U.S. g11 104
Mola di Bari, Italy D6 18
Molalla, Or., U.S. B4 130
Moldavia, hist. reg., Rom. F9 20
Moldavia see Moldova, ctry., Eur. F10 20
Molde, Nor. E2 10
Moldova, ctry., Eur. F10 20
Moldoveanu, Vârful, mtn., Rom. G8 20
Molepolole, Bots. C4 56
Molfetta, Italy D6 18
Moline, Il., U.S. B3 106
Moline, Mi., U.S. F5 115
Molino, Fl., U.S. u14 102
Mollendo, Peru G5 70
Molokai, i., Hi., U.S. B5 104
Molokai Fracture Zone F24 64
Molokini, i., Hi., U.S. C5 104
Molopo, stm., Afr. D3 56
Molotov see Perm', Russia D7 26
Moloundou, Cam. C3 54
Molson Lake, l., Mb., Can. B3 86
Moluccas see Maluku, is., Indon. D7 36
Molucca Sea see Maluku, Laut, Indon. C7 36
Moma, Moz. B6 56
Mombasa, Kenya D7 54
Mombetsu, Japan C16 28
Momence, Il., U.S. B6 106
Mompós, Col. D5 80
Momskij hrebet, mts., Russia C16 26
Møn, i., Den. I5 10
Mona, Isla de, i., P.R. B6 80
Monaca, Pa., U.S. E1 131
Monaco, ctry., Eur. C1 18
Monadnock, Mount, mtn., N.H., U.S. E2 122
Monadnock Mountain, mtn., Vt., U.S. B5 138
Monahans, Tx., U.S. D1 136
Mona Passage, strt., N.A. B6 80
Mona Quimbundo, Ang. E3 54
Monarch Mills, S.C., U.S. B4 133
Monarch Pass, Co., U.S. C4 99
Monashee Mountains, mts., B.C., Can. D8 85
Monastir, Tun. G3 18
Monção, Braz. D10 70
Mončegorsk, Russia C15 10
Mönchengladbach, Ger. E10 12
Moncks Corner, S.C., U.S. E7 133
Monclova, Mex. B4 78
Moncton, N.B., Can. C5 87
Mondjamboli, D.R.C. C4 54
Mondovi, Wi., U.S. D2 142
Monee, Il., U.S. B6 106
Monessen, Pa., U.S. F2 131
Monett, Mo., U.S. E4 118
Monette, Ar., U.S. B5 97
Monfalcone, Italy B4 18
Monforte de Lemos, Spain F3 16
Mongalla, Sudan B6 54
Möng Hpāyak, Myan. B3 34
Möng Hsat, Myan. B3 34
Mongo, Chad D8 50
Mongol Altayn nuruu, mts., Asia B6 28
Mongolia, ctry., Asia B8 28
Mongonu, Nig. D7 50
Mongu, Zam. B3 56
Monhegan Island, i., Me., U.S. E3 112
Monida Pass, U.S. E6 105
Moniteau, co., Mo., U.S. C5 118
Monitor Range, mts., Nv., U.S. E5 121
Monitor Valley, val., Nv., U.S. D5 121
Monmouth, Il., U.S. C3 106
Monmouth, Or., U.S. C3 130
Monmouth, co., N.J., U.S. C4 123
Monmouth Beach, N.J., U.S. C5 123
Monmouth Mountain, mtn., B.C., Can. D6 85
Mono, co., Ca., U.S. D4 98
Monocacy, stm., Md., U.S. B3 113
Mono Lake, l., Ca., U.S. D4 98
Monomonac, Lake, l., U.S. E3 122
Monomoy Island, i., Ma., U.S. C7 114
Monomoy Point, c., Ma., U.S. C7 114
Monon, In., U.S. C4 107
Monona, Ia., U.S. A6 108
Monona, Wi., U.S. E4 142
Monona, co., Ia., U.S. B1 108
Monona, Lake, l., Wi., U.S. E4 142
Monongah, W.V., U.S. B4 141
Monongahela, Pa., U.S. F2 131
Monongahela, stm., U.S. G2 131
Monongalia, co., W.V., U.S. B4 141
Monopoli, Italy D6 18
Monor, Hung. F5 20
Monroe, Ga., U.S. C3 103
Monroe, Ia., U.S. C4 108
Monroe, In., U.S. C8 107
Monroe, La., U.S. B3 111
Monroe, Mi., U.S. G7 115
Monroe, N.C., U.S. C2 126
Monroe, N.Y., U.S. D6 125
Monroe, Oh., U.S. C1 128
Monroe, Ut., U.S. E3 137
Monroe, Wa., U.S. B4 140
Monroe, Wi., U.S. F4 142
Monroe, co., Al., U.S. D2 94
Monroe, co., Ar., U.S. C4 97
Monroe, co., Fl., U.S. G5 102
Monroe, co., Ga., U.S. D3 103
Monroe, co., Ia., U.S. D5 108
Monroe, co., Il., U.S. E3 106
Monroe, co., In., U.S. F4 107
Monroe, co., Ky., U.S. D4 110
Monroe, co., Mi., U.S. G7 115
Monroe, co., Mo., U.S. B5 118
Monroe, co., Ms., U.S. B5 117
Monroe, co., N.Y., U.S. B3 125
Monroe, co., Oh., U.S. C4 128
Monroe, co., Pa., U.S. D11 131
Monroe, co., Tn., U.S. D9 135
Monroe, co., W.V., U.S. D4 141
Monroe, co., Wi., U.S. E3 142
Monroe Center, Ct., U.S. D3 100
Monroe City, Mo., U.S. B6 118
Monroe Lake, res., In., U.S. F5 107
Monroe Park, De., U.S. h7 101
Monroeville, Al., U.S. D2 94
Monroeville, In., U.S. C8 107
Monroeville, Oh., U.S. A3 128
Monroeville, Pa., U.S. k14 131
Monrovia, Lib. E2 50
Monrovia, Ca., U.S. m13 98
Monrovia, In., U.S. E5 107
Monson, Ma., U.S. B3 114
Mönsterås, Swe. H7 10
Montague, P.E., Can. C7 87
Montague, Ca., U.S. B2 98
Montague, Mi., U.S. E4 115
Montague, co., Tx., U.S. C4 136
Montague Island, i., Ak., U.S. D10 95
Montague Peak, mtn., Ak., U.S. g18 95
Montague Strait, strt., Ak., U.S. h18 95
Mont Alto, Pa., U.S. G6 131
Montana, Bul. C9 18
Montana, state, U.S. D7 119
Montargis, Fr. C8 16
Montauban, Fr. E7 16
Montauk, N.Y., U.S. m17 125
Montbard, Fr. D9 16
Montbéliard, Fr. D10 16
Mont Belvieu, Tx., U.S. E5 136
Montblanc, Spain G7 16
Montcalm, co., Mi., U.S. E5 115
Montceau-les-Mines, Fr. D9 16
Montchanin, De., U.S. h7 101
Montclair, Ca., U.S. m13 98
Montclair, N.J., U.S. B4 123
Mont Clare, Pa., U.S. o19 131
Mont-de-Marsan, Fr. F6 16
Monteagle, Tn., U.S. D8 135
Monte Alegre, Braz. D9 70
Monte Azul, Braz. E3 74
Montebello, P.Q., Can. D3 90
Montebello, Ca., U.S. m12 98
Montecarlo, Arg. D7 72
Monte Caseros, Arg. E6 72
Monte Comán, Arg. E4 72
Montecristo, Isola di, i., Italy C3 18
Montego Bay, Jam. B4 80
Montegut, La., U.S. E5 111

Name — **Map Ref.** — **Page**

Montélimar, Fr. **E9** 16
Montello, Nv., U.S. **B7** 121
Montello, Wi., U.S. **E4** 142
Montemorelos, Mex. **B5** 78
Montenegro see Crna Gora, state, Yugo. **C7** 18
Monte Patria, Chile **E3** 72
Montepuez, Moz. **A6** 56
Montepulciano, Italy **C3** 18
Monte Quemado, Arg. **D5** 72
Monterey, Ca., U.S. **D3** 98
Monterey, Tn., U.S. **C8** 135
Monterey, co., Ca., U.S. **D3** 98
Monterey Bay, b., Ca., U.S. **D2** 98
Monterey Park, Ca., U.S. **m12** 98
Montería, Col. **B4** 70
Montero, Bol. **B5** 72
Monterrey, Mex. **B4** 78
Montesano, Wa., U.S. **C2** 140
Montes Claros, Braz. **E3** 74
Montevallo, Al., U.S. **B3** 94
Montevideo, Mn., U.S. **F3** 116
Montevideo, Ur. **E6** 72
Monte Vista, Co., U.S. **D4** 99
Montezuma, Ga., U.S. **D2** 103
Montezuma, Ia., U.S. **C5** 108
Montezuma, In., U.S. **E3** 107
Montezuma, Ks., U.S. **E3** 109
Montezuma, co., Co., U.S. **D2** 99
Montezuma Castle National Monument, Az., U.S. **C4** 96
Montezuma Peak, mtn., Az., U.S. **D3** 96
Montgomery see Sāhīwāl, Pak. **D10** 42
Montgomery, Al., U.S. **C3** 94
Montgomery, Il., U.S. **B5** 106
Montgomery, La., U.S. **C3** 111
Montgomery, Mn., U.S. **F5** 116
Montgomery, N.Y., U.S. **D6** 125
Montgomery, Oh., U.S. **o13** 128
Montgomery, Pa., U.S. **D8** 131
Montgomery, W.V., U.S. **C3** 141
Montgomery, co., Al., U.S. **C3** 94
Montgomery, co., Ar., U.S. **C2** 97
Montgomery, co., Ga., U.S. **D4** 103
Montgomery, co., Ia., U.S. **C2** 108
Montgomery, co., Il., U.S. **D4** 106
Montgomery, co., In., U.S. **D4** 107
Montgomery, co., Ks., U.S. **E8** 109
Montgomery, co., Ky., U.S. **B6** 110
Montgomery, co., Md., U.S. **B3** 113
Montgomery, co., Mo., U.S. **C6** 118
Montgomery, co., Ms., U.S. **B4** 117
Montgomery, co., N.C., U.S. **B3** 126
Montgomery, co., N.Y., U.S. **C6** 125
Montgomery, co., Oh., U.S. **C1** 128
Montgomery, co., Pa., U.S. **F11** 131
Montgomery, co., Tn., U.S. **A4** 135
Montgomery, co., Tx., U.S. **D5** 136
Montgomery, co., Va., U.S. **C2** 139
Montgomery City, Mo., U.S. **C6** 118
Monticello, Ar., U.S. **D4** 97
Monticello, Fl., U.S. **B3** 102
Monticello, Ga., U.S. **C3** 103
Monticello, Ia., U.S. **B6** 108
Monticello, Il., U.S. **C5** 106
Monticello, In., U.S. **C4** 107
Monticello, Ky., U.S. **D5** 110
Monticello, Mn., U.S. **E5** 116
Monticello, Ms., U.S. **D3** 117
Monticello, N.Y., U.S. **D6** 125
Monticello, Ut., U.S. **F6** 137
Monticello, Wi., U.S. **F4** 142
Mont-Joli, P.Q., Can. **A9** 90
Mont-Laurier, P.Q., Can. **C2** 90
Montluçon, Fr. **D8** 16
Montmagny, P.Q., Can. **C7** 90
Montmorenci, S.C., U.S. **D4** 133
Montmorency, co., Mi., U.S. **C6** 115
Monto, Austl. **E5** 62
Montoro, Spain **H4** 16
Montour, co., Pa., U.S. **D8** 131
Montour Falls, N.Y., U.S. **C4** 125
Montoursville, Pa., U.S. **D8** 131
Montpelier, Id., U.S. **G7** 105
Montpelier, In., U.S. **C7** 107
Montpelier, Oh., U.S. **A1** 128
Montpelier, Vt., U.S. **C3** 138
Montpellier, Fr. **F8** 16
Montréal, P.Q., Can. **D4** 90
Montreal, Wi., U.S. **B3** 142
Montréal, Île de, i., P.Q., Can. **q19** 90
Montreal Lake, l., Sk., Can. **C3** 91
Montréal-Nord, P.Q., Can. **p19** 90
Montreat, N.C., U.S. **f10** 126
Montreux, Switz. **A1** 18
Mont-Rolland, P.Q., Can. **D3** 90
Montrose, B.C., Can. **E9** 85
Montrose, Scot., U.K. **B5** 12
Montrose, Al., U.S. **E2** 94
Montrose, Co., U.S. **C3** 99
Montrose, Ia., U.S. **D6** 108
Montrose, Mi., U.S. **E7** 115
Montrose, Pa., U.S. **C10** 131
Montrose, Va., U.S. **m18** 139
Montrose, co., Co., U.S. **C2** 99
Mont-Royal, P.Q., Can. **p19** 90
Mont-Saint-Michel, Le, Fr. **C6** 16
Montserrat, dep., N.A. **E12** 76
Montserrat, Monasterio de, Spain **G7** 16
Mont-Tremblant, Parc Provincial du, P.Q., Can. **C3** 90
Montvale, N.J., U.S. **A4** 123
Montville, Ct., U.S. **D7** 100
Monument, Co., U.S. **B6** 99
Monument Beach, Ma., U.S. **C6** 114
Monument Peak, mtn., Co., U.S. **B3** 99
Monument Peak, mtn., Id., U.S. **G4** 105
Monument Valley, val., Az., U.S. **A5** 96
Monywa, Myan. **B2** 34
Monza, Italy **B2** 18
Monze, Zam. **B4** 56
Monzón, Spain **G7** 16
Moodus, Ct., U.S. **D6** 100
Moodus Reservoir, res., Ct., U.S. **C6** 100
Moody, Tx., U.S. **D4** 136
Moody, co., S.D., U.S. **C9** 134
Moon Lake, l., Ms., U.S. **A3** 117
Moora, Austl. **G2** 60
Moorcroft, Wy., U.S. **B8** 143
Moore, Ok., U.S. **B4** 129
Moore, co., N.C., U.S. **B3** 126
Moore, co., Tn., U.S. **B5** 135
Moore, co., Tx., U.S. **B2** 136
Moore, Lake, l., Austl. **F2** 60
Moore Dam, U.S. **B3** 122
Moorefield, W.V., U.S. **B6** 141
Moore Haven, Fl., U.S. **F5** 102
Mooreland, Ok., U.S. **A2** 129
Moore Reservoir, res., U.S. **B3** 122
Moores Creek National Military Park, N.C., U.S. **C4** 126
Moores Hill, In., U.S. **F7** 107
Moorestown, N.J., U.S. **D3** 123
Mooresville, In., U.S. **E5** 107
Mooresville, N.C., U.S. **B2** 126
Moorhead, Mn., U.S. **D2** 116
Moorhead, Ms., U.S. **B3** 117
Mooringsport, La., U.S. **B2** 111
Moorreesburg, S. Afr. **E2** 56
Moose, stm., N.H., U.S. **B4** 122
Moose, stm., N.Y., U.S. **B5** 125
Moose, stm., Vt., U.S. **B5** 138
Moosehead Lake, l., Me., U.S. **C3** 112
Moose Jaw, stm., Sk., Can. **G3** 91
Moose Lake, Mb., Can. **C1** 86
Moose Lake, Mn., U.S. **D6** 116
Moose Lake, l., Wi., U.S. **B2** 142
Mooseleuk Stream, stm., Me., U.S. **B4** 112
Mooselookmeguntic Lake, l., Me., U.S. **D2** 112
Moose Mountain Creek, stm., Sk., Can. **H4** 91
Moose Mountain Provincial Park, Sk., Can. **H4** 91
Moosic, Pa., U.S. **m18** 131
Moosup, Ct., U.S. **C8** 100
Moosup, stm., U.S. **C1** 132
Mopang Lake, l., Me., U.S. **D5** 112
Mopti, Mali **D4** 50
Moquegua, Peru **G5** 70
Mora, Cam. **D7** 50
Mora, Spain **H5** 16
Mora, Swe. **F6** 10
Mora, Mn., U.S. **E5** 116
Mora, N.M., U.S. **B4** 124
Mora, co., N.M., U.S. **A5** 124
Mora, stm., N.M., U.S. **B5** 124
Morādābād, India **D3** 40
Morafenobe, Madag. **B7** 56
Moramanga, Madag. **B8** 56
Morant Cays, is., Jam. **B4** 80
Moratuwa, Sri L. **H3** 40
Morava, hist. reg., Czech Rep. **E4** 20
Moravia, Ia., U.S. **D5** 108
Morawa, Austl. **F2** 60
Morawhanna, Guy. **B8** 70
Moray Firth, b., Scot., U.K. **B5** 12
Morbi, India **E2** 40
Morden, Mb., Can. **E2** 86
Mordovia see Mordovija, state, Russia **D6** 26
Mordovija, state, Russia **D6** 26
Mordvinia see Mordovija, state, Russia **D6** 26
Moreau, stm., S.D., U.S. **B3** 134
Moreauville, La., U.S. **C4** 111
Morecambe Bay, b., Eng., U.K. **D5** 12
Moree, Austl. **F4** 62
Morehead, Ky., U.S. **B6** 110
Morehead City, N.C., U.S. **C6** 126
Morehouse, Mo., U.S. **E8** 118
Morehouse, co., La., U.S. **B4** 111
Morelia, Mex. **D4** 78
Morelos, state, Mex. **D5** 78
Morena, Sierra, mts., Spain **H4** 16
Morenci, Az., U.S. **D6** 96
Morenci, Mi., U.S. **G6** 115
Moresby Island, i., B.C., Can. **C2** 85
Moreton Island, i., Austl. **F5** 62
Morey, Lake, l., Vt., U.S. **D4** 138
Morey Peak, mtn., Nv., U.S. **E5** 121
Morgan, Mn., U.S. **F4** 116
Morgan, Ut., U.S. **B4** 137
Morgan, co., Al., U.S. **A3** 94
Morgan, co., Co., U.S. **A7** 99
Morgan, co., Ga., U.S. **C3** 103
Morgan, co., Il., U.S. **D3** 106
Morgan, co., In., U.S. **F5** 107
Morgan, co., Ky., U.S. **C6** 110
Morgan, co., Mo., U.S. **C5** 118
Morgan, co., Oh., U.S. **C4** 128
Morgan, co., Tn., U.S. **C9** 135
Morgan, co., Ut., U.S. **B4** 137
Morgan, co., W.V., U.S. **B6** 141
Morgan City, La., U.S. **E4** 111
Morganfield, Ky., U.S. **C2** 110
Morgan Hill, Ca., U.S. **D3** 98
Morgan Island, i., S.C., U.S. **G6** 133
Morgan Point, c., Ct., U.S. **E4** 100
Morganton, N.C., U.S. **B1** 126
Morgantown, In., U.S. **F5** 107
Morgantown, Ky., U.S. **C3** 110
Morgantown, Ms., U.S. **D2** 117
Morgantown, Tn., U.S. **D8** 135
Morgantown, W.V., U.S. **B5** 141
Morganza, La., U.S. **D4** 111
Morghāb (Murgab), stm., Asia **C8** 42
Moriah, Mount, mtn., Nv., U.S. **D7** 121
Moriarty, N.M., U.S. **C3** 124
Moriki, Nig. **D6** 50
Morinville, Ab., Can. **C4** 84
Morioka, Japan **D16** 28
Morlaix, Fr. **C5** 16
Morley, Mo., U.S. **D8** 118
Mormon Peak, mtn., Nv., U.S. **G7** 121
Morning Sun, Ia., U.S. **C6** 108
Mornington Island, i., Austl. **D2** 62
Morobe, Pap. N. Gui. **H12** 32
Morocco, In., U.S. **C3** 107
Morocco, ctry., Afr. **D3** 48
Morogoro, Tan. **E7** 54
Moro Gulf, b., Phil. **E8** 34
Morombe, Madag. **C7** 56
Morón, Arg. **E6** 72
Morón, Cuba **A4** 80
Mörön, Mong. **B8** 28
Morondava, Madag. **C7** 56
Morón de la Frontera, Spain **I4** 16
Moroni, Com. **A7** 56
Moroni, Ut., U.S. **D4** 137
Morotai, i., Indon. **C7** 36
Moroto, Ug. **C6** 54
Morozovsk, Russia **E7** 22
Morrill, Ne., U.S. **C2** 120
Morrill, co., Ne., U.S. **C2** 120
Morrilton, Ar., U.S. **B3** 97
Morrinhos, Braz. **E2** 74
Morris, Mb., Can. **E3** 86
Morris, Al., U.S. **B3** 94
Morris, Il., U.S. **B5** 106
Morris, Mn., U.S. **E3** 116
Morris, Ok., U.S. **B6** 129
Morris, co., Ks., U.S. **D7** 109
Morris, co., N.J., U.S. **B3** 123
Morris, co., Tx., U.S. **C5** 136
Morrisburg, On., Can. **C9** 89
Morris Island, i., S.C., U.S. **F8** 133
Morris Jesup, Kap, c., Grnld. **B33** 82
Morrison, Il., U.S. **B4** 106
Morrison, Ok., U.S. **A4** 129
Morrison, co., Mn., U.S. **D4** 116
Morrison City, Tn., U.S. **C11** 135
Morrisonville, Il., U.S. **D4** 106
Morrisonville, N.Y., U.S. **f11** 125
Morris Plains, N.J., U.S. **B4** 123
Morristown, In., U.S. **E6** 107
Morristown, Mn., U.S. **F5** 116
Morristown, N.J., U.S. **B4** 123
Morristown, Tn., U.S. **C10** 135
Morristown National Historical Park, N.J., U.S. **B3** 123
Morrisville, N.Y., U.S. **C5** 125
Morrisville, Pa., U.S. **F12** 131
Morrisville, Vt., U.S. **B3** 138
Morro Bay, Ca., U.S. **E3** 98
Morro do Chapéu, Braz. **D3** 74
Morrow, Ga., U.S. **C2** 103
Morrow, Oh., U.S. **C1** 128
Morrow, co., Oh., U.S. **B3** 128
Morrow, co., Or., U.S. **B7** 130
Morrumbala, Moz. **B6** 56
Morrumbene, Moz. **C6** 56
Moršansk, Russia **D7** 22
Morse, La., U.S. **D3** 111
Morse Reservoir, res., In., U.S. **D5** 107
Morses Creek, stm., N.J., U.S. **k8** 123
Mortes, stm., Braz. **F9** 70
Morton, Il., U.S. **C4** 106
Morton, Ms., U.S. **C4** 117
Morton, Tx., U.S. **C1** 136
Morton, Wa., U.S. **C3** 140
Morton, co., Ks., U.S. **E2** 109
Morton, co., N.D., U.S. **C4** 127
Morton Grove, Il., U.S. **h9** 106
Morton Pass, Wy., U.S. **E7** 143
Mortons Gap, Ky., U.S. **C2** 110
Morwell, Austl. **H4** 62
Moscow see Moskva, Russia **D5** 26
Moscow, Id., U.S. **C2** 105
Moscow, Pa., U.S. **m18** 131
Moscow Mills, Mo., U.S. **C7** 118
Mosel (Moselle), stm., Eur. **B10** 16
Moselle, Ms., U.S. **D4** 117
Moselle (Mosel), stm., Eur. **C10** 16
Moses Coulee, val., Wa., U.S. **B6** 140
Moses Lake, Wa., U.S. **B6** 140
Moses Lake, l., Wa., U.S. **B6** 140
Mosheim, Tn., U.S. **C11** 135
Moshi, Tan. **D7** 54
Mosinee, Wi., U.S. **D4** 142
Mosjøen, Nor. **D5** 10
Moskva (Moscow), Russia **D5** 26
Mosqueiro, Braz. **B2** 74
Mosquera, Col. **C4** 70
Mosquito Creek Lake, res., Oh., U.S. **A5** 128
Mosquito Lagoon, b., Fl., U.S. **D6** 102
Mosquitos, Golfo de los, b., Pan. **D3** 80
Moss, Nor. **G4** 10
Mossaka, Congo **D3** 54
Moss Bluff, La., U.S. **D2** 111
Mosselbaai, S. Afr. **E3** 56
Mossman, Austl. **D4** 62
Mossoró, Braz. **C4** 74
Moss Point, Ms., U.S. **E5** 117
Most, Czech Rep. **D2** 20
Mostar, Bos. **C6** 18
Møsting, Kap, c., Grnld. **F32** 82
Mosul see Al-Mawṣil, Iraq **C4** 42
Møsvatnet, l., Nor. **G3** 10
Moswansicut Pond, l., R.I., U.S. **C3** 132
Mot'a, Eth. **A7** 54
Motagua, stm., N.A. **B2** 80
Motala, Swe. **G6** 10
Motherwell, Scot., U.K. **C5** 12
Motley, co., Tx., U.S. **B2** 136
Motril, Spain **I5** 16
Mott, N.D., U.S. **C3** 127
Motueka, N.Z. **p13** 63c
Motyklejka, Russia **D16** 26
Mouaskar, Alg. **D4** 14
Moudjéria, Maur. **C2** 50
Mouila, Gabon **D2** 54
Moulins, Fr. **D8** 16
Moulouya, Oued, stm., Mor. **D4** 48
Moulton, Al., U.S. **A2** 94
Moulton, Ia., U.S. **D5** 108
Moultrie, Ga., U.S. **E3** 103
Moultrie, co., Il., U.S. **D5** 106
Moultrie, Lake, res., S.C., U.S. **E7** 133
Mounana, Gabon **D2** 54
Mound, Mn., U.S. **n11** 116
Mound Bayou, Ms., U.S. **B3** 117
Mound City, Il., U.S. **F4** 106
Mound City, Ks., U.S. **D9** 109
Mound City, Mo., U.S. **A2** 118
Mound City Group National Monument, Oh., U.S. **C2** 128
Moundou, Chad **E8** 50
Moundridge, Ks., U.S. **D6** 109
Mounds, Il., U.S. **F4** 106
Mounds, Ok., U.S. **B5** 129
Mounds View, Mn., U.S. **m12** 116
Moundsville, W.V., U.S. **B4** 141
Moundville, Al., U.S. **C2** 94
Mountainair, N.M., U.S. **C3** 124
Mountainaire, Az., U.S. **B4** 96
Mountain Brook, Al., U.S. **g7** 94
Mountain City, Ga., U.S. **B3** 103
Mountain City, Nv., U.S. **B6** 121
Mountain City, Tn., U.S. **C12** 135
Mountain Fork, stm., U.S. **C7** 129
Mountain Grove, Mo., U.S. **D5** 118
Mountain Home, Ar., U.S. **A3** 97
Mountain Home, Id., U.S. **F3** 105
Mountain Home Air Force Base, mil., Id., U.S. **F3** 105
Mountain Iron, Mn., U.S. **C6** 116
Mountain Lake, Mn., U.S. **G4** 116
Mountain Lake Park, Md., U.S. **m12** 113
Mountain Nile see Jabal, Baḥr al-, stm., Sudan **I11** 48
Mountain Pine, Ar., U.S. **C2** 97
Mountainside, N.J., U.S. **B4** 123
Mountain View, Ar., U.S. **B3** 97
Mountain View, Ca., U.S. **k8** 98
Mountain View, Mo., U.S. **D6** 118
Mountain View, N.M., U.S. **C3** 124
Mountain View, Ok., U.S. **B3** 129
Mountain View, Wy., U.S. **E2** 143
Mountain Village, Ak., U.S. **C7** 95
Mount Airy, Md., U.S. **B3** 113
Mount Airy, N.C., U.S. **A2** 126
Mount Albert, On., Can. **C5** 89
Mount Angel, Or., U.S. **B4** 130
Mount Arlington, N.J., U.S. **B3** 123
Mount Augustus, Austl. **E2** 60
Mount Ayr, Ia., U.S. **D3** 108
Mount Barker, Austl. **G2** 60
Mount Carmel, Il., U.S. **E6** 106
Mount Carmel, Oh., U.S. **o13** 128
Mount Carmel, Pa., U.S. **E9** 131
Mount Carmel [-Mitchell's Brook-Saint Catherine's], Nf., Can. **E5** 88
Mount Carroll, Il., U.S. **A4** 106
Mount Clare, W.V., U.S. **B4** 141
Mount Clemens, Mi., U.S. **F8** 115
Mount Desert Island, i., Me., U.S. **D4** 112
Mount Dora, Fl., U.S. **D5** 102
Mount Forest, On., Can. **D4** 89
Mount Gambier, Austl. **H3** 62
Mount Gay, W.V., U.S. **D2** 141
Mount Gilead, N.C., U.S. **B3** 126
Mount Gilead, Oh., U.S. **B3** 128
Mount Hagen, Pap. N. Gui. **H11** 32
Mount Healthy, Oh., U.S. **o12** 128
Mount Holly, N.C., U.S. **B1** 126
Mount Holly, N.J., U.S. **D3** 123
Mount Holly Springs, Pa., U.S. **F7** 131
Mount Hope, Ks., U.S. **E6** 109
Mount Hope, W.V., U.S. **D3** 141
Mount Hope, stm., Ct., U.S. **B7** 100
Mount Hope Bay, b., U.S. **D6** 132
Mount Horeb, Wi., U.S. **E4** 142
Mount Ida, Ar., U.S. **C2** 97
Mount Isa, Austl. **E2** 62
Mount Jackson, Va., U.S. **B4** 139
Mount Jewett, Pa., U.S. **C4** 131
Mount Joy, Pa., U.S. **F9** 131
Mount Juliet, Tn., U.S. **A5** 135
Mount Kisco, N.Y., U.S. **D7** 125
Mount Lebanon, Pa., U.S. **F1** 131
Mount Magnet, Austl. **F2** 60
Mount Morris, Il., U.S. **A4** 106
Mount Morris, Mi., U.S. **E7** 115
Mount Morris, N.Y., U.S. **C3** 125
Mount Olive, Al., U.S. **B3** 94
Mount Olive, Il., U.S. **D4** 106
Mount Olive, Ms., U.S. **D4** 117
Mount Olive, N.C., U.S. **B4** 126
Mount Olive, Tn., U.S. **n14** 135
Mount Orab, Oh., U.S. **C2** 128
Mount Pearl, Nf., Can. **E5** 88
Mount Penn, Pa., U.S. **F10** 131
Mount Pleasant, Ia., U.S. **D6** 108
Mount Pleasant, Mi., U.S. **E6** 115
Mount Pleasant, N.C., U.S. **B2** 126
Mount Pleasant, Pa., U.S. **F2** 131
Mount Pleasant, S.C., U.S. **F8** 133
Mount Pleasant, Tn., U.S. **B4** 135
Mount Pleasant, Tx., U.S. **C5** 136
Mount Pleasant, Ut., U.S. **D4** 137
Mount Pocono, Pa., U.S. **D11** 131
Mount Prospect, Il., U.S. **A6** 106
Mount Pulaski, Il., U.S. **C4** 106
Mountrail, co., N.D., U.S. **A3** 127
Mount Rainier, Md., U.S. **f9** 113
Mount Rainier National Park, Wa., U.S. **C4** 140
Mount Revelstoke National Park, B.C., Can. **D8** 85
Mount Riddock, Austl. **E5** 60
Mount Rogers National Recreation Area, Va., U.S. **D1** 139
Mount Roskill, N.Z. **o13** 63c
Mount Rushmore National Memorial, hist., S.D., U.S. **D2** 134
Mount Savage, Md., U.S. **k13** 113
Mount Shasta, Ca., U.S. **B2** 98
Mount Sterling, Il., U.S. **D3** 106
Mount Sterling, Ky., U.S. **B6** 110
Mount Sterling, Oh., U.S. **C2** 128
Mount Uniacke, N.S., Can. **E6** 87
Mount Union, Pa., U.S. **F6** 131
Mount Vernon, Austl. **E2** 60
Mount Vernon, Al., U.S. **D1** 94
Mount Vernon, Ga., U.S. **D4** 103
Mount Vernon, Ia., U.S. **C6** 108
Mount Vernon, Il., U.S. **E5** 106
Mount Vernon, In., U.S. **I2** 107
Mount Vernon, Ky., U.S. **C5** 110
Mount Vernon, Mo., U.S. **D4** 118
Mount Vernon, N.Y., U.S. **h13** 125
Mount Vernon, Oh., U.S. **B3** 128
Mount Vernon, Tx., U.S. **C5** 136
Mount Vernon, Wa., U.S. **A3** 140
Mount View, R.I., U.S. **D4** 132
Mount Washington, Ky., U.S. **B4** 110
Mount Wolf, Pa., U.S. **F8** 131
Mount Zion, Il., U.S. **D5** 106
Moura, Braz. **D7** 70
Moussa 'Ali, mtn., Afr. **H4** 38
Moussoro, Chad **D8** 50
Moutong, Indon. **C6** 36
Moville, Ia., U.S. **B1** 108
Moweaqua, Il., U.S. **D4** 106
Mower, co., Mn., U.S. **G6** 116
Moxee City, Wa., U.S. **C5** 140
Moyale, Kenya **C7** 54
Moyamba, S.L. **E2** 50
Moyen Atlas, mts., Mor. **E3** 14
Moyo, Pulau, i., Indon. **E5** 36
Moyobamba, Peru **E4** 70
Moyock, N.C., U.S. **A6** 126
Moyu, China **B3** 40
Mozambique, ctry., Afr. **B5** 56
Mozambique Channel, strt., Afr. **B7** 56
Mozambique Plateau **L6** 64
Mozdok, Russia **B4** 42
Mpala, D.R.C. **E5** 54
Mpanda, Tan. **E6** 54
Mpika, Zam. **A5** 56
Mporokoso, Zam. **E6** 54
Mpulungu, Zam. **E6** 54
Mpwapwa, Tan. **E7** 54
Mscislaŭ, Bela. **C11** 20
M'Sila, Alg. **J9** 16
Mtubatuba, S. Afr. **D5** 56
Mtwara, Tan. **F8** 54

Name / Map Ref. / Page

Muanda, D.R.C. **E2** 54
Muang Hôngsa, Laos **C4** 34
Muang Khammouan, Laos **C4** 34
Muang Không, Laos **D5** 34
Muang Khôngxédôn, Laos **C5** 34
Muang Ngoy, Laos **B4** 34
Muang Pak-Lay, Laos **C4** 34
Muang Pakxan, Laos **C4** 34
Muang Phalan, Laos **C5** 34
Muang Sing, Laos **B4** 34
Muang Thadua, Laos **C4** 34
Muang Vangviang, Laos **C4** 34
Muang Xaignabouri, Laos **C4** 34
Muar, Malay. **C2** 36
Muaraenim, Indon. **D2** 36
Muarasiberut, Indon. **G2** 32
Mubende, Ug. **C6** 54
Mubi, Nig. **D7** 50
Muchinga Mountains, mts., Zam. **A5** 56
Muckleshoot Indian Reservation, Wa., U.S. **f11** 140
Mucojo, Moz. **A7** 56
Muconda, Ang. **F4** 54
Mucujê, Braz. **F11** 70
Mud, stm., Ky., U.S. **C3** 110
Mud, stm., Mn., U.S. **B3** 116
Mud, stm., W.V., U.S. **C2** 141
Mudanjiang, China **C13** 28
Mud Creek, stm., Ok., U.S. **C4** 129
Muddy Boggy Creek, stm., Ok., U.S. **C6** 129
Muddy Creek, stm., Ut., U.S. **E4** 137
Muddy Creek, stm., Wy., U.S. **C4** 143
Muddy Creek, stm., Wy., U.S. **E5** 143
Muddy Creek, stm., Wy., U.S. **E2** 143
Muddy Creek, stm., Wy., U.S. **D6** 143
Muddy Mountains, mts., Nv., U.S. **G7** 121
Muddy Peak, mtn., Nv., U.S. **G7** 121
Mudgee, Austl. **G4** 62
Mud Lake, l., Me., U.S. **A4** 112
Mud Lake, l., Nv., U.S. **F4** 121
Mueda, Moz. **A6** 56
Muenster, Tx., U.S. **C4** 136
Mufulira, Zam. **A4** 56
Muğla, Tur. **D3** 44
Muhlenberg, co., Ky., U.S. **C2** 110
Mühlhausen, Ger. **E12** 12
Muhu, i., Est. **G10** 10
Muié, Ang. **A3** 56
Muirkirk, Md., U.S. **B4** 113
Muir Woods National Monument, Ca., U.S. **h7** 98
Muja, Russia **D13** 26
Mujnak, Uzb. **B7** 42
Mukacheve, Ukr. **E7** 20
Mukah, Malay. **C4** 36
Mukden see Shenyang, China **C12** 28
Mukilteo, Wa., U.S. **B3** 140
Mukinbudin, Austl. **G2** 60
Mukomuk, Indon. **D2** 36
Mukry, Turk. **C9** 42
Mukwonago, Wi., U.S. **F5** 142
Mula, Spain **H6** 16
Mulberry, Ar., U.S. **B1** 97
Mulberry, Fl., U.S. **E4** 102
Mulberry, In., U.S. **D4** 107
Mulberry, N.C., U.S. **A1** 126
Mulberry, stm., Ar., U.S. **B1** 97
Mulberry Fork, stm., Al., U.S. **B3** 94
Muldraugh, Ky., U.S. **C4** 110
Muldrow, Ok., U.S. **B7** 129
Muleshoe, Tx., U.S. **B1** 136
Mulgrave, N.S., Can. **D8** 87
Mulhacén, mtn., Spain **I5** 16
Mulhouse, Fr. **D10** 16
Mull, Island of, i., Scot., U.K. **B3** 12
Mullan, Id., U.S. **B3** 105
Mullan Pass, Mt., U.S. **D4** 119
Mullens, W.V., U.S. **D3** 141
Muller, Pegunungan, mts., Indon. **C4** 36
Mullet Key, i., Fl., U.S. **p10** 102
Mullett Lake, l., Mi., U.S. **C6** 115
Mullewa, Austl. **F2** 60
Mullica, stm., N.J., U.S. **D3** 123
Mullins, S.C., U.S. **C9** 133
Mulongo, D.R.C. **E5** 54
Multān, Pak. **D10** 42
Multnomah, co., Or., U.S. **B4** 130
Mulvane, Ks., U.S. **E6** 109
Mumbai (Bombay), India **F2** 40
Mumbwa, Zam. **A4** 56
Mummy Range, mts., Co., U.S. **A5** 99
Mun, stm., Thai. **C4** 34
Muna, Mex. **C7** 78
Muna, Pulau, i., Indon. **D6** 36
München (Munich), Ger. **F12** 12
Muncie, In., U.S. **D7** 107
Muncy, Pa., U.S. **D8** 131
Munday, Tx., U.S. **C3** 136
Mundelein, Il., U.S. **A5** 106
Münden, Ger. **E11** 12
Mundrabilla, Austl. **G4** 60
Munford, Al., U.S. **B4** 94
Munford, Tn., U.S. **B2** 135
Munfordville, Ky., U.S. **C4** 110
Mungbere, D.R.C. **C5** 54
Munger, India **D5** 40
Munhall, Pa., U.S. **k14** 131
Munhango, Ang. **F3** 54
Munich see München, Ger. **F12** 12
Munising, Mi., U.S. **B4** 115
Münster, Ger. **E10** 12
Munster, In., U.S. **A2** 107
Munster, hist. reg., Ire. **D2** 12
Munsungan Lake, l., Me., U.S. **B3** 112
Muntok, Indon. **D3** 36
Munuscong Lake, l., Mi., U.S. **B6** 115
Muojärvi, l., Fin. **D13** 10
Muonio, Fin. **C10** 10
Muqdisho, Som. **J14** 48
Mur (Mura), stm., Eur. **F3** 20
Mura (Mur), stm., Eur. **F4** 20
Muradiye, Tur. **C10** 44
Murakami, Japan **C3** 31
Murana, Indon. **D8** 36
Muraši, Russia **C8** 22
Murat, stm., Tur. **C9** 44
Murchison, stm., Austl. **F1** 60
Murchison Falls see Kabalega Falls, wtfl, Ug. **C6** 54
Murcia, Spain **I6** 16
Murderkill, stm., De., U.S. **D4** 101
Murdo, S.D., U.S. **D5** 134
Mureş, stm., Eur. **G7** 20
Muret, Fr. **F7** 16
Murewa, Zimb. **B5** 56
Murfreesboro, Ar., U.S. **C2** 97
Murfreesboro, N.C., U.S. **A5** 126
Murfreesboro, Tn., U.S. **B5** 135
Murgab, Taj. **F9** 26
Murgab (Morghāb), stm., Asia **C8** 42
Muriaé, Braz. **F3** 74
Müritz, l., Ger. **D13** 12
Murmansk, Russia **C5** 26
Murom, Russia **D6** 26
Muroran, Japan **C16** 28
Muroto, Japan **D2** 31
Murphy, Mo., U.S. **g13** 118
Murphy, N.C., U.S. **f8** 126
Murphy Island, i., S.C., U.S. **E9** 133
Murphysboro, Il., U.S. **F4** 106
Murray, Ia., U.S. **C4** 108
Murray, Ky., U.S. **f9** 110
Murray, Ut., U.S. **C4** 137
Murray, co., Ga., U.S. **B2** 103
Murray, co., Mn., U.S. **F3** 116
Murray, co., Ok., U.S. **C4** 129
Murray, stm., Austl. **H3** 62
Murray, Lake, l., Pap. N. Gui. **H11** 32
Murray, Lake, res., Ok., U.S. **C4** 129
Murray, Lake, res., S.C., U.S. **C5** 133
Murray Bridge, Austl. **H2** 62
Murray Fracture Zone **E24** 64
Murray Head, c., P.E., Can. **C7** 87
Murraysburg, S. Afr. **E3** 56
Murrayville, Ga., U.S. **B3** 103
Murree, Pak. **C2** 40
Murrells Inlet, S.C., U.S. **D9** 133
Murrells Inlet, b., S.C., U.S. **D10** 133
Murrumbidgee, stm., Austl. **G4** 62
Murrupula, Moz. **B6** 56
Mursala, Pulau, i., Indon. **C1** 36
Murua Island, i., Pap. N. Gui. **H13** 32
Murud, Gunong, mtn., Malay. **C5** 36
Murukta, Russia **C12** 26
Murwāra, India **E4** 40
Murwillumbah, Austl. **F5** 62
Murzuq, Libya **E7** 48
Murzūq, Idhān, des., Libya **B7** 50
Muş, Tur. **C9** 44
Musa Ālī Terara see Moussa 'Ali, mtn., Afr. **H4** 38
Musā'id, Libya **E9** 14
Musala, mtn., Bul. **C9** 18
Musan-ŭp, N. Kor. **B1** 31
Musay'īd, Qatar **F6** 42
Muscat see Masqaṭ, Oman **F7** 38
Muscat and Oman see Oman, ctry., Asia **G7** 38
Muscatatuck, stm., In., U.S. **G5** 107
Muscatine, Ia., U.S. **C6** 108
Muscatine, co., Ia., U.S. **C6** 108
Muscle Shoals, Al., U.S. **A2** 94
Musclow, Mount, mtn., B.C., Can. **C4** 85
Muscoda, Wi., U.S. **E3** 142
Muscogee, co., Ga., U.S. **D2** 103
Musconetcong, stm., N.J., U.S. **B4** 123
Muscooten Bay, l., Il., U.S. **C3** 106
Muse, Pa., U.S. **F1** 131
Musgrave Harbour, Nf., Can. **D5** 88
Musgravetown, Nf., Can. **D5** 88
Mushie, D.R.C. **D3** 54
Mushin, Nig. **E5** 50
Musi, stm., Indon. **D2** 36
Musicians Seamounts **E22** 64
Muskeg Bay, b., Mn., U.S. **B3** 116
Muskeget Island, i., Ma., U.S. **D7** 114
Muskego, Wi., U.S. **F5** 142
Muskego Lake, l., Wi., U.S. **n11** 142
Muskegon, Mi., U.S. **E4** 115
Muskegon, co., Mi., U.S. **E4** 115
Muskegon, stm., Mi., U.S. **E4** 115
Muskegon Heights, Mi., U.S. **E4** 115
Muskegon Lake, l., Mi., U.S. **E4** 115
Muskingum, co., Oh., U.S. **B4** 128
Muskingum, stm., Oh., U.S. **C4** 128
Muskogee, Ok., U.S. **B6** 129
Muskogee, co., Ok., U.S. **B6** 129
Musoma, Tan. **D6** 54
Musquacook Lakes, l., Me., U.S. **B3** 112
Musquodoboit Harbour, N.S., Can. **E6** 87
Mussau Island, i., Pap. N. Gui. **G12** 32
Musselshell, co., Mt., U.S. **D8** 119
Musselshell, stm., Mt., U.S. **D9** 119
Mussende, Ang. **F3** 54
Mussuma, Ang. **A3** 56
Mustafakemalpaşa, Tur. **C3** 44
Mustahīl, Eth. **B8** 54
Mustang, Ok., U.S. **B4** 129
Mustinka, stm., Mn., U.S. **E2** 116
Muswellbrook, Austl. **G5** 62
Mut, Tur. **D5** 44
Mutare, Zimb. **B5** 56
Mutoraj, Russia **C12** 26
Mutsamudu, Com. **A7** 56
Mutshatsha, D.R.C. **F4** 54
Mutsu, Japan **C16** 28
Mutsu-wan, b., Japan **B4** 31
Mutton Mountains, mts., Or., U.S. **C5** 130
Muxima, Ang. **E2** 54
Muyinga, Bdi. **D6** 54
Muyumba, D.R.C. **E5** 54
Muzaffarābād, Pak. **D10** 42
Muzaffargarh, Pak. **D10** 42
Muzaffarnagar, India **D3** 40
Muzaffarpur, India **D5** 40
Muži, Russia **C8** 26
Muzon, Cape, c., Ak., U.S. **n23** 95
Muztag, mtn., China **D5** 28
Mvuma, Zimb. **B5** 56
Mwadui, Tan. **D6** 54
Mwali, i., Com. **A7** 56
Mwanza, Tan. **D6** 54
Mweka, D.R.C. **D4** 54
Mwene-Ditu, D.R.C. **E4** 54
Mwenezi, Zimb. **C5** 56
Mweru, Lake, l., Afr. **E5** 54
Mwinilunga, Zam. **A3** 56
Myakka, stm., Fl., U.S. **E4** 102
Myanaung, Myan. **C3** 34
Myanmar (Burma), ctry., Asia **B3** 34
Myaungmya, Myan. **C2** 34
Myerstown, Pa., U.S. **F9** 131
Myingyan, Myan. **B3** 34
Myitkyinā, Myan. **A3** 34
Myittha, Myan. **B3** 34
Mykolaïv, Ukr. **F11** 20
Mymensingh, Bngl. **E6** 40
Mynaral, Kaz. **A10** 42
Mýrdalsjökull, Ice. **m19** 10a
Myrhorod, Ukr. **E12** 20
Myrtle Beach, S.C., U.S. **D10** 133
Myrtle Grove, Fl., U.S. **u14** 102
Myrtle Point, Or., U.S. **D2** 130
Mysore, India **G3** 40
Mysore see Karnātaka, prov., India **G3** 40
Mystic, Ct., U.S. **D8** 100
Mystic Lakes, l., Ma., U.S. **g11** 114
Mys Vhodnoj, Russia **B10** 26
Mys Želanija, Russia **B8** 26
Myszków, Pol. **D5** 20
My Tho, Viet. **D5** 34
Mzimba, Mwi. **A5** 56
Mzuzu, Mwi. **A5** 56

N

Naalehu, Hi., U.S. **D6** 104
Naberežnye Čelny, Russia **D7** 26
Nabeul, Tun. **C7** 48
Nabire, Indon. **G10** 32
Nabī Shu'ayb, Jabal an-, mtn., Yemen **G4** 38
Nabnasset, Ma., U.S. **A5** 114
Nābulus, W.B. **F6** 44
Nacala-a-Velha, Moz. **A7** 56
Naches, stm., Wa., U.S. **C5** 140
Nachingwea, Tan. **F7** 54
Náchod, Czech Rep. **D4** 20
Nachuge, India **G6** 40
Nacimiento, Lake, res., Ca., U.S. **E3** 98
Naco, Az., U.S. **F6** 96
Nacogdoches, Tx., U.S. **D5** 136
Nacogdoches, co., Tx., U.S. **D5** 136
Nacozari de García, Mex. **A3** 78
Nadiād, India **E2** 40
Nador, Mor. **J5** 16
Nadvirna, Ukr. **E8** 20
Nadym, Russia **C9** 26
Næstved, Den. **I4** 10
Nafada, Nig. **D7** 50
Nafī, Sau. Ar. **E4** 42
Naga, Phil. **D8** 34
Nāgāland, prov., India **D6** 40
Nagano, Japan **D15** 28
Nagaoka, Japan **D15** 28
Nagaon, India **D6** 40
Nāgappattinam, India **G3** 40
Nagasaki, Japan **E13** 28
Nāgaur, India **D2** 40
Nagda, India **E3** 40
Nāgercoil, India **H3** 40
Nago, Japan **A9** 34
Nagoya, Japan **D15** 28
Nāgpur, India **E3** 40
Nagqu, China **E6** 28
Nags Head, N.C., U.S. **B7** 126
Nagykanizsa, Hung. **F4** 20
Naha, Japan **A9** 34
Nahant, Ma., U.S. **g12** 114
Nahāvand, Iran **E13** 44
Nahe, China **B12** 28
Nahmakanta Lake, l., Me., U.S. **C3** 112
Nahodka, Russia **E15** 26
Nahunta, Ga., U.S. **E5** 103
Nain, Nf., Can. **g9** 88
Nairobi, Kenya **D7** 54
Naivasha, Kenya **D7** 54
Najafābād, Iran **D6** 42
Najd, hist. reg., Sau. Ar. **E4** 38
Nájera, Spain **F5** 16
Najin, N. Kor. **C14** 28
Nakano-shima, i., Japan **E1** 31
Nakhichevan see Naxçıvan, Azer. **C11** 44
Nakhon Pathom, Thai. **D4** 34
Nakhon Phanom, Thai. **C4** 34
Nakhon Ratchasima, Thai. **D4** 34
Nakhon Sawan, Thai. **C4** 34
Nakhon Si Thammarat, Thai. **E3** 34
Nakina, On., Can. **o18** 89
Nakło nad Notecią, Pol. **C4** 20
Naknek, Ak., U.S. **D8** 95
Naknek Lake, l., Ak., U.S. **D8** 95
Nakonde, Zam. **E6** 54
Nakskov, Den. **I4** 10
Nakuru, Kenya **D7** 54
Nakusp, B.C., Can. **D9** 85
Nal'čik, Russia **E6** 26
Nalgonda, India **F3** 40
Nallıhan, Tur. **B4** 44
Nālūt, Libya **D7** 48
Namak, daryācheh-ye, l., Iran **D6** 42
Namanga, Kenya **D7** 54
Namangan, Uzb. **E9** 26
Namanock Island, i., N.J., U.S. **A3** 123
Namapa, Moz. **A6** 56
Namarrói, Moz. **B6** 56
Namatanai, Pap. N. Gui. **E9** 58
Nambour, Austl. **F5** 62
Nam Co, l., China **E6** 28
Nam Dinh, Viet. **B5** 34
Namekagon, stm., Wi., U.S. **B2** 142
Namekagon Lake, l., Wi., U.S. **B2** 142
Namen see Namur, Bel. **E9** 12
Nametil, Moz. **B6** 56
Namhkam, Myan. **B3** 34
Namib Desert, des., Nmb. **B1** 56
Namibe, Ang. **B1** 56
Namibia, ctry., Afr. **C2** 56
Namīn, Iran **C13** 44
Namjagbarwa Feng, mtn., China **F7** 28
Namlea, Indon. **D7** 36
Nam Ngum Reservoir, res., Laos **C4** 34
Nampa, Id., U.S. **F2** 105
Nampula, Moz. **B6** 56
Namsang, Myan. **B3** 34
Namsos, Nor. **D4** 10
Namtu, Myan. **B3** 34
Namur, Bel. **E9** 12
Namutoni, Nmb. **B2** 56
Namwala, Zam. **B4** 56
Nan, Thai. **C4** 34
Nanaimo, B.C., Can. **E5** 85
Nanakuli, Hi., U.S. **B3** 104
Nanao, Japan **D15** 28
Nance, co., Ne., U.S. **C7** 120
Nancha, China **A1** 31
Nanchang, China **F11** 28
Nancheng, China **D4** 30
Nanchong, China **E9** 28
Nancy, Fr. **C10** 16
Nanda Devi, mtn., India **C3** 40
Nānded, India **F3** 40
Nandurbār, India **E2** 40
Nandyāl, India **F3** 40
Nanfeng, China **D4** 30
Nanga-Eboko, Cam. **C2** 54
Nanga Parbat, mtn., Pak. **C10** 42
Nangatayap, Indon. **D4** 36
Nangong, China **B4** 30
Nanjing, China **E11** 28
Nankang, China **D3** 30
Nanking see Nanjing, China **E11** 28
Nanle, China **B4** 30
Nannine, Austl. **F2** 60
Nanning, China **G9** 28
Nannup, Austl. **G2** 60
Nanping, China **F11** 28
Nansei-shotō (Ryukyu Islands), is., Japan **A9** 34
Nansemond, stm., Va., U.S. **k14** 139
Nansen Basin **E21** 144
Nansen Cordillera **E22** 144
Nan Shan see Qilian Shan, mts., China **D7** 28
Nantes, Fr. **D6** 16
Nanticoke, On., Can. **E4** 89
Nanticoke, Pa., U.S. **D10** 131
Nanticoke, stm., U.S. **D6** 113
Nanton, Ab., Can. **D4** 84
Nantong, China **E12** 28
Nantucket, Ma., U.S. **D7** 114
Nantucket, co., Ma., U.S. **D7** 114
Nantucket Island, i., Ma., U.S. **D7** 114
Nantucket Sound, strt., Ma., U.S. **C7** 114
Nantulo, Moz. **A6** 56
Nantuxent Point, c., N.J., U.S. **E2** 123
Nanty Glo, Pa., U.S. **F4** 131
Nanuet, N.Y., U.S. **g12** 125
Nanuque, Braz. **E3** 74
Nanusa, Kepulauan, is., Indon. **C7** 36
Nanxiong, China **F10** 28
Nanyang, China **E10** 28
Nanyuki, Kenya **C7** 54
Nanzhao, China **C3** 30
Naoma, W.V., U.S. **n13** 141
Naomi Peak, mtn., Ut., U.S. **B4** 137
Napa, Ca., U.S. **C2** 98
Napa, co., Ca., U.S. **C2** 98
Napanee, On., Can. **C8** 89
Napatree Point, c., R.I., U.S. **G1** 132
Napavine, Wa., U.S. **C3** 140
Napè, Laos **C5** 34
Naperville, Il., U.S. **B5** 106
Napier, N.Z. **o14** 63c
Napier Mountains, mts., Ant. **C10** 67
Napierville, P.Q., Can. **D4** 90
Naples see Napoli, Italy **D5** 18
Naples, Fl., U.S. **F5** 102
Naples, Tx., U.S. **C5** 136
Naples, Ut., U.S. **C6** 137
Napo, stm., S.A. **D5** 70
Napoleon, N.D., U.S. **C6** 127
Napoleon, Oh., U.S. **A1** 128
Napoleonville, La., U.S. **E4** 111
Napoli (Naples), Italy **D5** 18
Napoli, Golfo di, b., Italy **D5** 18
Nappanee, In., U.S. **B5** 107
Naqadeh, Iran **D11** 44
Nara, Japan **E15** 28
Nara, Mali **C3** 50
Naracoorte, Austl. **H3** 62
Naramata, B.C., Can. **E8** 85
Naranja, Fl., U.S. **G6** 102
Narasapur, India **F4** 40
Narathiwat, Thai. **E4** 34
Nārāyanganj, Bngl. **E6** 40
Narberth, Pa., U.S. **p20** 131
Narbonne, Fr. **F8** 16
Nar'jan-Mar, Russia **C7** 26
Narmada, stm., India **E2** 40
Nārnaul, India **D3** 40
Narodnaja, gora, hills, Russia **C8** 26
Naro-Fominsk, Russia **B14** 20
Narooma, Austl. **H5** 62
Narrabri, Austl. **G4** 62
Narragansett, R.I., U.S. **F4** 132
Narragansett Bay, b., R.I., U.S. **E5** 132
Narraguagus, stm., Me., U.S. **D5** 112
Narrandera, Austl. **G4** 62
Narrogin, Austl. **G2** 60
Narromine, Austl. **G4** 62
Narrows, Va., U.S. **C2** 139
Narsaq, Grnld. **F30** 82
Narva, Est. **G13** 10
Narvik, Nor. **B7** 10
Naryn, Kyrg. **E9** 26
Naryn, stm., Asia **A3** 40
Narynkol, Kaz. **C4** 28
Näsåker, Swe. **E7** 10
Nasca, Peru **F5** 70
Naselle, Wa., U.S. **C2** 140
Nash, Tx., U.S. **C5** 136
Nash, co., N.C., U.S. **A4** 126
Nashawena Island, i., Ma., U.S. **D6** 114
Nāshik, India **E2** 40
Nash Stream, stm., N.H., U.S. **A4** 122
Nashua, Ia., U.S. **B5** 108
Nashua, N.H., U.S. **E4** 122
Nashua, stm., U.S. **E3** 122
Nashville, Ar., U.S. **D2** 97
Nashville, Ga., U.S. **E3** 103
Nashville, Il., U.S. **E4** 106
Nashville, In., U.S. **F5** 107
Nashville, Mi., U.S. **F5** 115
Nashville, N.C., U.S. **B5** 126
Nashville, Tn., U.S. **A5** 135
Nashwauk, Mn., U.S. **C5** 116
Nāṣir, Sudan **I11** 48
Nasīrābād, India **D2** 40
Nasīrābād, Pak. **E9** 42
Naskaupi, stm., Nf., Can. **g9** 88
Nassau, Bah. **D9** 76
Nassau, co., Fl., U.S. **B5** 102
Nassau, co., N.Y., U.S. **E7** 125
Nassau, stm., Fl., U.S. **k8** 102

Name | Map Ref. | Page

Nassau Island, i., Cook Is. F13 58
Nassau Sound, b., Fl., U.S. B5 102
Nasser, Lake, res., Afr. F11 48
Nässjö, Swe. H6 10
Nasukoin Mountain, mtn., Mt., U.S. B2 119
Nata, Bots. C4 56
Natal, Braz. C4 74
Natalbany, La., U.S. D5 111
Natalia, Tx., U.S. E3 136
Natashquan, stm., Can. h9 88
Natchaug, stm., Ct., U.S. B7 100
Natchez, Ms., U.S. D2 117
Natchitoches, La., U.S. C2 111
Natchitoches, co., La., U.S. C2 111
Natick, Ma., U.S. B5 114
National City, Ca., U.S. F5 98
Natitingou, Benin D5 50
Natividade, Braz. F10 70
Natron, Lake, l., Afr. D7 54
Natrona, co., Wy., U.S. D5 143
Natrona Heights, Pa., U.S. E2 131
Natuna Besar, i., Indon. C3 36
Natuna Besar, Kepulauan, is., Indon. C3 36
Natuna Selatan, Kepulauan, is., Indon. C3 36
Natural Bridge, Ut., U.S. F3 137
Natural Bridge, Va., U.S. C3 139
Natural Bridges National Monument, Ut., U.S. F6 137
Naturaliste, Cape, c., Austl. G1 60
Nau, Cap de la, c., Spain H7 16
Naugatuck, Ct., U.S. D3 100
Naugatuck, stm., Ct., U.S. D3 100
Nauru, ctry., Oc. E10 58
Naushon Island, i., Ma., U.S. D6 114
Nautilus Park, Ct., U.S. D7 100
Nautla, Mex. C5 78
Nauvoo, Il., U.S. C2 106
Navadwip, India E5 40
Navahrudak, Bela. C8 20
Navajo, co., Az., U.S. B5 96
Navajo Dam, N.M., U.S. A2 124
Navajo Indian Reservation, U.S. A4 96
Navajo Mountain, mtn., Ut., U.S. F5 137
Navajo National Monument, Az., U.S. A5 96
Navajo Reservoir, res., U.S. A2 124
Navan, On., Can. B9 89
Navapolack, Bela. B10 20
Navarin, mys, c., Russia C19 26
Navarino, Isla, i., Chile I3 69
Navarra, hist. reg., Spain F6 16
Navarre, Oh., U.S. B4 128
Navarro, co., Tx., U.S. D4 136
Navasota, Tx., U.S. D4 136
Navassa Island, i., N.A. B4 80
Navlja, Russia C13 20
Navoi, Uzb. E8 26
Navojoa, Mex. B3 78
Navsāri, India E2 40
Nawābshāh, Pak. E9 42
Nawiliwili Bay, b., Hi., U.S. B2 104
Naxçıvan, Azer. C11 44
Naxi, China D2 30
Náxos, Grc. F10 18
Náxos, i., Grc. F10 18
Nayarit, state, Mex. C4 78
Naylor, Mo., U.S. E7 118
Nayoro, Japan C16 28
Nazaré, Braz. D4 74
Nazaré, Port. H2 16
Nazareth see Nazerat, Isr. D3 42
Nazareth, Pa., U.S. E11 131
Nazas, Mex. B4 78
Nazas, stm., Mex. B4 78
Nazca Ridge K5 66
Naze, Japan F13 28
Naze, The see Lindesnes, c., Nor. H2 10
Nazerat, Isr. D3 42
Nazilli, Tur. D3 44
Nazko, stm., B.C., Can. C6 85
Nazran', Russia A11 44
Nazrēt, Eth. B7 54
Nazwá, Oman F7 42
N'dalatando, Ang. E2 54
Ndélé, C.A.R. B4 54
Ndendé, Gabon D2 54
N'Djamena, Chad D8 50
Ndjolé, Gabon D2 54
Ndola, Zam. A4 56
Neagh, Lough, l., N. Ire., U.K. C3 12
Neah Bay, Wa., U.S. A1 140
Néa Páfos, Cyp. E5 44
Neápolis, Grc. F9 18
Near Islands, is., Ak., U.S. E2 95
Nebitdag, Turk. F7 26
Neblina, Pico da, mtn., S.A. C6 70
Nebo, Mount, mtn., Ut., U.S. D4 137
Nebraska, state, U.S. C6 120
Nebraska City, Ne., U.S. D10 120
Nechako, stm., B.C., Can. C5 85
Neches, stm., Tx., U.S. D5 136
Necker Island, i., Hi., U.S. m15 104
Necochea, Arg. F6 72
Nederland, Co., U.S. B5 99
Nederland, Tx., U.S. E6 136
Nêdong, China F6 28
Nédroma, Alg. J6 16
Nedrow, N.Y., U.S. C4 125
Needham, Ma., U.S. g11 114
Needle Mountain, mtn., Wy., U.S. B3 143
Needles, Ca., U.S. E6 98
Needville, Tx., U.S. r14 136
Neenah, Wi., U.S. D5 142
Neepawa, Mb., Can. D2 86
Neffs, Oh., U.S. B5 128
Neffsville, Pa., U.S. F9 131
Neftçala, Azer. C13 44
Negage, Ang. E3 54
Negaunee, Mi., U.S. B3 115
Negēlē, Eth. B7 54
Negley, Oh., U.S. B5 128
Negombo, Sri L. H3 40
Negritos, Peru D3 70
Negro, stm., Arg. F4 69
Negro, stm., S.A. D7 70
Negros, i., Phil. E8 34
Neguac, N.B., Can. B4 87
Nehalem, stm., Or., U.S. A3 130
Nehbandān, Iran D7 42
Neiges, Piton des, mtn., Reu. g10 57a
Neijiang, China D2 30
Neill Point, c., Wa., U.S. f11 140
Neillsville, Wi., U.S. D3 142
Nei Monggol Zizhiqu (Inner Mongolia), prov., China C10 28
Neisse see Nysa, Pol. D4 20
Neiva, Col. C4 70
Nejd see Najd, hist. reg., Sau. Ar. E4 38
Nek'emtē, Eth. B7 54
Nekoosa, Wi., U.S. D4 142
Nelidovo, Russia C5 22
Neligh, Ne., U.S. B7 120
Nel'kan, Russia D15 26
Nellis Air Force Base, mil., Nv., U.S. G6 121
Nellore, India G4 40
Nel'ma, Russia E15 26
Nelson, B.C., Can. E9 85
Nelson, N.Z. p13 63c
Nelson, Ne., U.S. D7 120
Nelson, co., Ky., U.S. C4 110
Nelson, co., N.D., U.S. B7 127
Nelson, co., Va., U.S. C4 139
Nelson, stm., Mb., Can. A4 86
Nelson, Cape, c., Austl. H3 62
Nelsonville, Oh., U.S. C3 128
Nelspruit, S. Afr. D5 56
Néma, Maur. C3 50
Nemacolin, Pa., U.S. G2 131
Nemadji, stm., U.S. B1 142
Nemaha, co., Ks., U.S. C7 109
Nemaha, co., Ne., U.S. D10 120
Neman (Nemunas), stm., Eur. B7 20
Nembe, Nig. F6 50
Nemunas (Neman), stm., Eur. B7 20
Nemuro, Japan C17 28
Nenana, Ak., U.S. C10 95
Nendo, i., Sol. Is. F10 58
Neodesha, Ks., U.S. E8 109
Neoga, Il., U.S. D5 106
Neola, Ia., U.S. C2 108
Neola, Ut., U.S. C5 137
Neopit, Wi., U.S. D5 142
Neosho, Mo., U.S. E3 118
Neosho, co., Ks., U.S. E8 109
Neosho, stm., Ok., U.S. A6 129
Nepal, ctry., Asia D4 40
Nepālgañj, Nepal D4 40
Nepaug Reservoir, res., Ct., U.S. B3 100
Nepean, On., Can. h12 89
Nepewassi Lake, l., On., Can. A4 89
Nephi, Ut., U.S. D4 137
Nepisiguit, stm., N.B., Can. B3 87
Nepisiguit Bay, b., N.B., Can. B4 87
Neponset, stm., Ma., U.S. h11 114
Neptune, N.J., U.S. C4 123
Neptune Beach, Fl., U.S. B5 102
Neptune City, N.J., U.S. C4 123
Nerčinsk, Russia A11 28
Nerčinskij Zavod, Russia D13 26
Nerehta, Russia C7 22
Neriquinha, Ang. B3 56
Nescopeck, Pa., U.S. D9 131
Neshanic, stm., N.J., U.S. C3 123
Neshoba, co., Ms., U.S. C4 117
Neskaupstaður, Ice. l22 10a
Nesna, Nor. C5 10
Nesowadnehunk, l., Me., U.S. B3 112
Nesquehoning, Pa., U.S. E10 131
Ness, co., Ks., U.S. D4 109
Ness, Loch, l., Scot., U.K. B4 12
Ness City, Ks., U.S. D4 109
Néstos, stm., Eur. D10 18
Netanya, Isr. D2 42
Netcong, N.J., U.S. B3 123
Netherlands, ctry., Eur. D9 12
Netherlands Antilles, dep., N.A. F11 76
Netherlands Guiana see Suriname, ctry., S.A. C8 70
Nettie, W.V., U.S. C4 141
Nett Lake, l., Mn., U.S. B5 116
Nett Lake Indian Reservation, Mn., U.S. B6 116
Nettleton, Ms., U.S. A5 117
Neubrandenburg, Ger. D13 12
Neuchâtel, Switz. A1 18
Neuchâtel, Lac de, l., Switz. A1 18
Neufchâtel-en-Bray, Fr. C7 16
Neumarkt in der Oberpfalz, Ger. F12 12
Neumünster, Ger. C12 12
Neuquén, Arg. E3 69
Neuruppin, Ger. D13 12
Neuse, stm., N.C., U.S. B6 126
Neustrelitz, Ger. D13 12
Neuville, P.Q., Can. C6 90
Nevada, Ia., U.S. B4 108
Nevada, Mo., U.S. D3 118
Nevada, co., Ar., U.S. D2 97
Nevada, co., Ca., U.S. C3 98
Nevada, state, U.S. D5 121
Nevada, Sierra, mts., Ca., U.S. D4 98
Nevada City, Ca., U.S. C3 98
Nevado, Cerro, mtn., Arg. F4 72
Nevado, Cerro, mtn., Col. C5 70
Nevel', Russia A10 20
Nevel'sk, Russia E16 26
Never, Russia D14 26
Nevers, Fr. D8 16
Neversink, stm., N.Y., U.S. D6 125
Nevinnomyssk, Russia B4 42
Nevis, i., St. K./N. B7 80
Nevis, Ben, mtn., Scot., U.K. B4 12
Nevjansk, Russia C11 22
Nevşehir, Tur. C6 44
New, stm., Az., U.S. k8 96
New, stm., N.C., U.S. C5 126
New, stm., U.S. C3 141
Newala, Tan. F7 54
New Albany, In., U.S. H6 107
New Albany, Ms., U.S. A4 117
New Albany, Oh., U.S. k11 128
New Amsterdam, Guy. B8 70
Newark, Ar., U.S. B4 97
Newark, Ca., U.S. h8 98
Newark, De., U.S. B3 101
Newark, Il., U.S. B5 106
Newark, N.J., U.S. B4 123
Newark, N.Y., U.S. B3 125
Newark, Oh., U.S. B3 128
Newark Bay, b., N.J., U.S. k8 123
Newark Lake, l., Nv., U.S. D6 121
New Athens, Il., U.S. E4 106
New Augusta, Ms., U.S. D4 117
Newaygo, Mi., U.S. E5 115
Newaygo, co., Mi., U.S. E5 115
New Baden, Il., U.S. E4 106
New Baltimore, Mi., U.S. F8 115
New Bedford, Ma., U.S. C6 114
New Bedford, Pa., U.S. D1 131
Newberg, Or., U.S. B4 130
New Berlin, Il., U.S. D4 106
New Berlin, Wi., U.S. n11 142
New Bern, N.C., U.S. B5 126
Newbern, Tn., U.S. A2 135
Newberry, Fl., U.S. C4 102
Newberry, Mi., U.S. B5 115
Newberry, S.C., U.S. C4 133
Newberry, co., S.C., U.S. C4 133
New Bethlehem, Pa., U.S. D3 131
New Bloomfield, Pa., U.S. F7 131
New Boston, Mi., U.S. p15 115
New Boston, Oh., U.S. D3 128
New Boston, Tx., U.S. C5 136
New Braunfels, Tx., U.S. E3 136
New Bremen, Oh., U.S. B1 128
New Brighton, Mn., U.S. m12 116
New Brighton, Pa., U.S. E1 131
New Britain, Ct., U.S. C4 100
New Britain, i., Pap. N. Gui. H13 32
New Brockton, Al., U.S. D4 94
New Brunswick, N.J., U.S. C4 123
New Brunswick, prov., Can. C3 87
New Buffalo, Mi., U.S. G4 115
Newburg, Wi., U.S. E5 142
Newburgh, On., Can. C8 89
Newburgh, In., U.S. I3 107
Newburgh, N.Y., U.S. D6 125
Newburgh Heights, Oh., U.S. h9 128
Newburyport, Ma., U.S. A6 114
New Caledonia, dep., Oc. I9 62a
New Caledonia Basin K19 64
New Canaan, Ct., U.S. E2 100
New Carlisle, In., U.S. A4 107
New Carlisle, Oh., U.S. C1 128
Newcastle, Austl. G5 62
Newcastle, N.B., Can. C4 87
Newcastle, On., Can. D6 89
Newcastle, S. Afr. D4 56
New Castle, Al., U.S. B3 94
New Castle, Co., U.S. B3 99
New Castle, De., U.S. B3 101
New Castle, In., U.S. E7 107
New Castle, Ky., U.S. B4 110
Newcastle, Ok., U.S. B4 129
New Castle, Pa., U.S. D1 131
Newcastle, Wy., U.S. C8 143
New Castle, co., De., U.S. B3 101
Newcastle upon Tyne, Eng., U.K. C6 12
Newcastle Waters, Austl. D5 60
New City, N.Y., U.S. D6 125
Newcomerstown, Oh., U.S. B4 128
New Concord, Oh., U.S. C4 128
New Cumberland, Pa., U.S. F8 131
New Cumberland, W.V., U.S. A4 141
Newdegate, Austl. G2 60
New Delhi, India D3 40
Newell, Ia., U.S. B2 108
Newell, S.D., U.S. C2 134
Newell, W.V., U.S. A4 141
New Ellenton, S.C., U.S. E4 133
Newellton, La., U.S. B4 111
New England, N.D., U.S. C3 127
Newenham, Cape, c., Ak., U.S. D7 95
New Fairfield, Ct., U.S. D2 100
Newfane, N.Y., U.S. B2 125
Newfields, N.H., U.S. D5 122
New Florence, Mo., U.S. C6 118
Newfound Gap, U.S. f9 126
Newfound Lake, l., N.H., U.S. C3 122
Newfoundland, prov., Can. D4 88
Newfoundland, i., Nf., Can. D3 88
Newfoundland Basin D9 66
New Franklin, Mo., U.S. B5 118
New Freedom, Pa., U.S. G8 131
New Georgia Sound, strt., Sol. Is. B6 62
New Germany, N.S., Can. E5 87
New Glarus, Wi., U.S. F4 142
New Guinea, i. G11 32
Newhall, Ia., U.S. C6 108
New Hampshire, state, U.S. C3 122
New Hampton, Ia., U.S. A5 108
New Hanover, co., N.C., U.S. C5 126
New Hanover, i., Pap. N. Gui. G13 32
New Harbour, Nf., Can. E5 88
New Harmony, In., U.S. H2 107
New Hartford, Ct., U.S. B4 100
New Hartford, Ia., U.S. B5 108
New Haven, Ct., U.S. D4 100
New Haven, In., U.S. B7 107
New Haven, Ky., U.S. C4 110
New Haven, Mi., U.S. F8 115
New Haven, Mo., U.S. C6 118
New Haven, W.V., U.S. C3 141
New Haven, co., Ct., U.S. D4 100
New Haven, stm., Vt., U.S. C2 138
New Haven Harbor, b., Ct., U.S. E4 100
New Hazelton, B.C., Can. B4 85
New Hebrides see Vanuatu, ctry., Oc. F10 58
New Hebrides, is., Vanuatu F10 58
New Hebrides Trench K19 64
New Holland, Ga., U.S. B3 103
New Holland, Pa., U.S. F9 131
New Holstein, Wi., U.S. E5 142
New Hope, Al., U.S. A3 94
New Hope, Ky., U.S. C4 110
New Hope, Mn., U.S. m12 116
New Hope, Pa., U.S. F12 131
New Hudson, Mi., U.S. o14 115
New Iberia, La., U.S. D4 111
Newington, Ct., U.S. C5 100
New Inlet, b., N.C., U.S. D5 126
New Ireland, i., Pap. N. Gui. G13 32
New Jersey, state, U.S. C4 123
New Johnsonville, Tn., U.S. A4 135
New Kensington, Pa., U.S. E2 131
New Kent, co., Va., U.S. C5 139
Newkirk, Ok., U.S. A4 129
New Kowloon see Xinjiulong, China E3 30
New Laguna, N.M., U.S. B2 124
New Lake, l., N.C., U.S. B6 126
New Lenox, Il., U.S. B6 106
New Lexington, Oh., U.S. C3 128
New Lisbon, Wi., U.S. E3 142
New Liskeard, On., Can. p20 89
Newllano, La., U.S. C2 111
New London, Ct., U.S. D7 100
New London, Ia., U.S. D6 108
New London, Mn., U.S. E4 116
New London, Mo., U.S. B6 118
New London, N.H., U.S. D3 122
New London, Oh., U.S. A3 128
New London, Wi., U.S. D5 142
New London, co., Ct., U.S. C7 100
New London Submarine Base, mil., Ct., U.S. D7 100
New Madison, Oh., U.S. C1 128
New Madrid, Mo., U.S. E8 118
New Madrid, co., Mo., U.S. E8 118
Newman, Austl. E2 60
Newman, Ca., U.S. D3 98
Newman, Il., U.S. D6 106
New Manchester, W.V., U.S. e8 141
Newman Grove, Ne., U.S. C8 120
Newman Lake, l., Wa., U.S. B8 140
Newmanstown, Pa., U.S. F9 131
Newmarket, On., Can. C5 89
New Market, Al., U.S. A3 94
New Market, In., U.S. E4 107
Newmarket, N.H., U.S. D5 122
New Market, Tn., U.S. C10 135
New Market, Va., U.S. B4 139
New Martinsville, W.V., U.S. B4 141
New Matamoras, Oh., U.S. C4 128
New Mexico, state, U.S. C3 124
New Miami, Oh., U.S. C1 128
New Milford, Ct., U.S. C2 100
New Milford, N.J., U.S. h8 123
New Milford, Pa., U.S. C10 131
Newnan, Ga., U.S. C2 103
Newnans Lake, l., Fl., U.S. C4 102
New Norfolk, Austl. I4 62
New Orleans, La., U.S. E5 111
New Orleans Naval Air Station, mil., La., U.S. k11 111
New Oxford, Pa., U.S. G7 131
New Palestine, In., U.S. E6 107
New Paltz, N.Y., U.S. D6 125
New Paris, In., U.S. B6 107
New Paris, Oh., U.S. C1 128
New Philadelphia, Oh., U.S. B4 128
New Philadelphia, Pa., U.S. E9 131
New Plymouth, N.Z. o13 63c
New Plymouth, Id., U.S. F2 105
New Point Comfort, c., Va., U.S. C6 139
Newport, Wales, U.K. E5 12
Newport, Ar., U.S. B4 97
Newport, De., U.S. B3 101
Newport, In., U.S. E3 107
Newport, Ky., U.S. A5 110
Newport, Me., U.S. D3 112
Newport, Mi., U.S. G7 115
Newport, Mn., U.S. n13 116
Newport, N.C., U.S. C6 126
Newport, N.H., U.S. D2 122
Newport, Oh., U.S. C4 128
Newport, Or., U.S. C2 130
Newport, Pa., U.S. F7 131
Newport, R.I., U.S. F5 132
Newport, Tn., U.S. D10 135
Newport, Vt., U.S. B4 138
Newport, Wa., U.S. A8 140
Newport, co., R.I., U.S. E5 132
Newport Beach, Ca., U.S. n13 98
Newport News, Va., U.S. D6 139
New Port Richey, Fl., U.S. D4 102
New Prague, Mn., U.S. F5 116
New Preston, Ct., U.S. C2 100
New Providence, N.J., U.S. B4 123
New Providence, i., Bah. C9 76
Newquay, Eng., U.K. E4 12
New Richland, Mn., U.S. G5 116
New Richmond, P.Q., Can. A4 87
New Richmond, Oh., U.S. D1 128
New Richmond, Wi., U.S. C1 142
New River Inlet, b., N.C., U.S. C5 126
New Roads, La., U.S. D4 111
New Rochelle, N.Y., U.S. E7 125
New Rockford, N.D., U.S. B6 127
Newry, N. Ire., U.K. C3 12
New Salem, N.D., U.S. C4 127
New Sarpy, La., U.S. k11 111
New Schwabenland, reg., Ant. D5 67
New Sharon, Ia., U.S. C5 108
New Siberian Islands see Novosibirskie ostrova, is., Russia B16 26
New Site, Al., U.S. B4 94
New Smyrna Beach, Fl., U.S. C6 102
New South Wales, state, Austl. G4 62
New Straitsville, Oh., U.S. C3 128
New Tazewell, Tn., U.S. C10 135
Newton, Al., U.S. D4 94
Newton, Ga., U.S. E2 103
Newton, Ia., U.S. C4 108
Newton, Il., U.S. E5 106
Newton, Ks., U.S. D6 109
Newton, Ma., U.S. B5 114
Newton, Ms., U.S. C4 117
Newton, N.C., U.S. B1 126
Newton, N.J., U.S. A3 123
Newton, Tx., U.S. D6 136
Newton, Ut., U.S. B4 137
Newton, co., Ar., U.S. B2 97
Newton, co., Ga., U.S. C3 103
Newton, co., In., U.S. B3 107
Newton, co., Mo., U.S. E3 118
Newton, co., Ms., U.S. C4 117
Newton, co., Tx., U.S. D6 136
Newton Falls, Oh., U.S. A5 128
Newton Lake, res., Il., U.S. E5 106
Newtown, Ct., U.S. D2 100
New Town, N.D., U.S. B3 127
Newtown, Oh., U.S. C1 128
Newtown Square, Pa., U.S. p20 131
New Ulm, Mn., U.S. F4 116
New Vienna, Oh., U.S. C2 128
Newville, Pa., U.S. F7 131
New Washington, In., U.S. G6 107
New Washington, Oh., U.S. B3 128
New Waterford, Oh., U.S. B5 128
New Westminster, B.C., Can. E6 85
New Whiteland, In., U.S. E5 107
New Wilmington, Pa., U.S. D1 131
New Windsor, Il., U.S. B3 106
New Windsor, Md., U.S. A3 113
New Windsor, N.Y., U.S. D6 125
New World Island, i., Nf., Can. D4 88
New York, N.Y., U.S. E7 125
New York, co., N.Y., U.S. k13 125
New York, state, U.S. C6 125
New York Mills, Mn., U.S. D3 116
New Zealand, ctry., Oc. H10 58

Name — Map Ref. — Page

Neyrīz, Iran E6 42
Neyshābūr, Iran C7 42
Nezahualcóyotl, Presa, res., Mex. D6 78
Nez Perce, co., Id., U.S. C2 105
Nez Perce Indian Reservation, Id., U.S. C2 105
Ngabé, Congo D3 54
Ngangala, Sudan C6 54
Ngangla Ringco, l., China E4 28
Ngaoundéré, Cam. B2 54
Ngeaur, i., Palau E9 32
Ngidinga, D.R.C. E3 54
Ngoring Hu, l., China E7 28
Ngouri, Chad D8 50
Nguigmi, Niger D7 50
Nguru, Nig. D7 50
Nha Trang, Viet. D5 34
Nhill, Austl. H3 62
Nhoma, stm., Afr. B2 56
Niafounké, Mali C4 50
Niagara, Wi., U.S. C6 142
Niagara, co., N.Y., U.S. B2 125
Niagara Falls, On., Can. D5 89
Niagara Falls, N.Y., U.S. B1 125
Niagara-on-the-Lake, On., Can. D5 89
Niah, Malay. C4 36
Niakaramandougou, C. Iv. E3 50
Niamey, Niger D5 50
Niangara, D.R.C. C5 54
Niangua, stm., Mo., U.S. D5 118
Nia-Nia, D.R.C. C5 54
Niantic, Ct., U.S. D7 100
Nias, Pulau, i., Indon. C1 36
Niatupo, Pan. D4 80
Nibley, Ut., U.S. B4 137
Nicaragua, ctry., N.A. F7 76
Nicaragua, Lago de, l., Nic. C2 80
Nicatous Lake, l., Me., U.S. C4 112
Nice, Fr. F10 16
Niceville, Fl., U.S. u15 102
Nichinan, Japan E14 28
Nicholas, co., Ky., U.S. B6 110
Nicholas, co., W.V., U.S. C4 141
Nicholas Channel, strt., N.A. A3 80
Nicholasville, Ky., U.S. C5 110
Nicholls, Ga., U.S. E4 103
Nichols Hills, Ok., U.S. B4 129
Nicholson, Ms., U.S. E4 117
Nickajack Lake, res., Tn., U.S. D8 135
Nickel Centre, On., Can. p19 89
Nickerson, Ks., U.S. D5 109
Nicobar Islands, is., India H6 40
Nicolet, P.Q., Can. C5 90
Nicolet, stm., P.Q., Can. C5 90
Nicolet, Lake, l., Mi., U.S. B6 115
Nicollet, Mn., U.S. F4 116
Nicollet, co., Mn., U.S. F4 116
Nicoma Park, Ok., U.S. B4 129
Nicosia, Cyp. E5 44
Nicoya, Golfo de, b., C.R. D2 80
Nicoya, Península de, pen., C.R. D2 80
Nidzica, Pol. C6 20
Niellé, C. Iv. D3 50
Nienburg, Ger. D11 12
Nieuw Amsterdam, Sur. B8 70
Nieuw Nickerie, Sur. B8 70
Nigadoo, N.B., Can. B4 87
Niğde, Tur. D6 44
Niger, ctry., Afr. C6 50
Niger, stm., Afr. E6 50
Nigeria, ctry., Afr. E6 50
Nihoa, i., Hi., U.S. m15 104
Niigata, Japan D15 28
Niihama, Japan D2 31
Niihau, i., Hi., U.S. B1 104
Nijmegen, Neth. E10 12
Nikel', Russia B14 10
Nikishka, Ak., U.S. g16 95
Nikkō, Japan D15 28
Nikol'sk, Russia D8 22
Nikol'sk, Russia D6 26
Nikopol', Ukr. F13 20
Niksar, Tur. B7 44
Nīkshahr, Iran E8 42
Nikšić, Yugo. C7 18
Nila, Pulau, i., Indon. E7 36
Niland, Ca., U.S. F6 98
Nile, stm., Afr. E11 48
Niles, Il., U.S. h9 106
Niles, Mi., U.S. G4 115
Niles, Oh., U.S. A5 128
Nīmach, India E2 40
Nimba, Mount, mtn., Afr. E3 50
Nîmes, Fr. F9 16
Nimrod Lake, res., Ar., U.S. C2 97
Nimule, Sudan J11 48
Nīnawá, hist., Iraq C4 42
Ninda, Ang. A3 56
Nine Degree Channel, strt., India H2 40
Nine Mile Creek, stm., Ut., U.S. D5 137
Ninemile Point, c., Mi., U.S. C6 115
Ninetyeast Ridge J11 64
Ninety Mile Beach, Austl. H4 62
Ninety Six, S.C., U.S. C3 133
Nineveh see Nīnawá, hist., Iraq C4 42
Ning'an, China B1 31
Ningbo, China F12 28
Ningcheng, China C11 28
Ningde, China D4 30
Ningdu, China F11 28
Ninghai, China D5 30
Ninghua, China D4 30
Ningi, Nig. D6 50
Ningming, China E2 30
Ningnan, China A4 34
Ningshan, China C2 30
Ningsia Hui Autonomous Region see Ningxia Huiza Zizhiqu, prov., China D9 28
Ningxia Huiza Zizhiqu, prov., China D9 28
Ningxiang, China D3 30
Ninh Binh, Viet. B5 34
Ninigo Group, is., Pap. N. Gui. G11 32
Ninigret Pond, l., R.I., U.S. G2 132
Ninilchik, Ak., U.S. C9 95
Ninnescah, stm., Ks., U.S. E6 109
Ninohe, Japan B4 31
Niobrara, co., Wy., U.S. C8 143
Niobrara, stm., U.S. B7 120
Nioki, D.R.C. D3 54
Niono, Mali D3 50
Nioro du Sahel, Mali C3 50
Niort, Fr. D6 16
Niota, Tn., U.S. D9 135
Nipigon, Lake, l., On., Can. o17 89
Nipissing, Lake, l., On., Can. A5 89
Nipomo, Ca., U.S. E3 98
Nipple Mountain, mtn., Co., U.S. D2 99
Niquero, Cuba A4 80
Nirmal, India F3 40
Niš, Yugo. C8 18
Niscemi, Italy F5 18
Niskayuna, N.Y., U.S. C7 125
Nisqually, stm., Wa., U.S. C3 140
Nisswa, Mn., U.S. D4 116
Nistru (Dniester) (Dnister), stm., Eur. F10 20
Niterói, Braz. F3 74
Nitra, Slvk. E5 20
Nitro, W.V., U.S. C3 141
Niue, dep., Oc. F13 58
Niuke, China C4 40
Niulakita, i., Tuvalu E11 58
Niverville, Mb., Can. E3 86
Niwot, Co., U.S. A5 99
Nixa, Mo., U.S. D4 118
Nixon, Nv., U.S. D2 121
Nixon, Tx., U.S. E4 136
Nizāmābād, India F3 40
Nizhyn, Ukr. D11 20
Nizip, Tur. D7 44
Nižneangarsk, Russia D12 26
Nižnee Kujto, ozero, l., Russia D14 10
Nižnekamsk, Russia C9 22
Nižneudinsk, Russia D11 26
Nižnevartovsk, Russia C9 26
Nižnij Novgorod (Gor'kij), Russia D6 26
Nižnij Tagil, Russia D8 26
Nižnjaja Peša, Russia A8 22
Nižnjaja Tunguska, stm., Russia C11 26
Njandoma, Russia C6 26
Njazidja, i., Com. A7 56
Njinjo, Tan. E7 54
Njombe, Tan. E6 54
Njuhča, Russia B8 22
Njurba, Russia C13 26
Njuvčim, Russia B9 22
Nkambe, Cam. B2 54
Nkawkaw, Ghana E4 50
Nkhata Bay, Mwi. A5 56
Nkhotakota, Mwi. A5 56
Nkongsamba, Cam. C1 54
Noākhāli, Bngl. E6 40
Noank, Ct., U.S. D8 100
Noatak, Ak., U.S. B7 95
Noatak, stm., Ak., U.S. B7 95
Nobel, On., Can. B4 89
Nobeoka, Japan D2 31
Noble, Ok., U.S. B4 129
Noble, co., In., U.S. B7 107
Noble, co., Oh., U.S. C4 128
Noble, co., Ok., U.S. A4 129
Nobles, co., Mn., U.S. G3 116
Noblesville, In., U.S. D6 107
Nocatee, Fl., U.S. E5 102
Nocona, Tx., U.S. C4 136
Nodaway, co., Mo., U.S. A3 118
Nodaway, stm., U.S. A2 118
Noel, Mo., U.S. E3 118
Nogales, Mex. A2 78
Nogales, Az., U.S. F5 96
Nogent-le-Rotrou, Fr. C7 16
Noginsk, Russia C6 22
Nohar, India D2 40
Noirmoutier, Île de, i., Fr. D5 16
Nokaneng, Bots. B3 56
Nokia, Fin. F10 10
Nokomis, Fl., U.S. E4 102
Nokomis, Il., U.S. D4 106
Nokomis, Lake, res., Wi., U.S. C4 142
Nokuku, Vanuatu j9 62a
Nola, C.A.R. C3 54
Nolan, co., Tx., U.S. C2 136
Nolichucky, stm., Tn., U.S. C10 135
Nolin, stm., Ky., U.S. C3 110
Nolin Lake, res., Ky., U.S. C3 110
Nolinsk, Russia C9 22
Nomans Land, i., Ma., U.S. D6 114
Nome, Ak., U.S. C6 95
Nominingue, P.Q., Can. C2 90
Nonesuch, stm., Me., U.S. g7 112
Nong'an, China C13 28
Nong Khai, Thai. C4 34
Nonquit Pond, l., R.I., U.S. E6 132
Nooksack, North Fork, stm., Wa., U.S. A4 140
Nooksack, South Fork, stm., Wa., U.S. A3 140
Noonkanbah, Austl. D3 60
Noorvik, Ak., U.S. B7 95
Nootka Sound, strt., B.C., Can. E4 85
No Point, Point, c., Md., U.S. D5 113
Noquebay, Lake, l., Wi., U.S. C6 142
Nóqui, Ang. E2 54
Noranda (part of Rouyn [-Noranda]), P.Q., Can. k11 90
Nora Springs, Ia., U.S. A5 108
Norborne, Mo., U.S. B4 118
Norco, La., U.S. E5 111
Norcross, Ga., U.S. C2 103
Nordaustlandet, i., Nor. A4 26
Norden, Ger. D10 12
Nordenham, Ger. D11 12
Nordenšel'da, arhipelag, is., Russia B11 26
Nordfjordeid, Nor. F2 10
Nordhausen, Ger. E12 12
Nordkapp, c., Nor. A11 10
Nord-Ostsee-Kanal, Ger. C11 12
Nordre Strømfjord, b., Grnld. E29 82
Nordvik, Russia B13 26
Norfolk, Ct., U.S. B3 100
Norfolk, Ne., U.S. B8 120
Norfolk, N.Y., U.S. f9 125
Norfolk, Va., U.S. D6 139
Norfolk, co., Ma., U.S. B5 114
Norfolk Island, dep., Oc. G10 58
Norfolk Naval Base, mil., Va., U.S. k15 139
Norfolk Naval Shipyard, mil., Va., U.S. k15 139
Norfolk Ridge K19 64
Norfork Dam, Ar., U.S. A3 97
Norfork Lake, res., U.S. A3 97
Noril'sk, Russia C10 26
Norland, Fl., U.S. s13 102
Norlina, N.C., U.S. A4 126
Normal, Il., U.S. C5 106
Norman, Ok., U.S. B4 129
Norman, co., Mn., U.S. C2 116
Norman, Lake, res., N.C., U.S. B2 126
Normandie, hist. reg., Fr. C6 16
Normandie, Collines de, hills, Fr. C6 16
Normandy, Mo., U.S. f13 118
Normandy see Normandie, hist. reg., Fr. C6 16
Normandy, Hills of see Normandie, Collines de, hills, Fr. C6 16
Norman Park, Ga., U.S. E3 103
Normanton, Austl. D3 62
Norphlet, Ar., U.S. D3 97
Ñorquinco, Arg. F2 69
Norra Kvarken (Merenkurkku), strt., Eur. E9 10
Norrbotten, hist. reg., Swe. C10 10
Nørresundby, Den. H3 10
Norridge, Il., U.S. k9 106
Norridgewock, Me., U.S. D3 112
Norris, S.C., U.S. B2 133
Norris, Tn., U.S. C9 135
Norris Arm, Nf., Can. D4 88
Norris City, Il., U.S. F5 106
Norris Dam, Tn., U.S. C9 135
Norris Lake, res., Tn., U.S. C10 135
Norris Point, Nf., Can. D3 88
Norristown, Pa., U.S. F11 131
Norrköping, Swe. G7 10
Norrtälje, Swe. G8 10
Norseman, Austl. G3 60
Norsjö, Swe. D8 10
Norsk, Russia D15 26
North, S.C., U.S. D5 133
North, stm., Al., U.S. B2 94
North, stm., Ia., U.S. f8 108
North, stm., Ma., U.S. h12 114
North, stm., W.V., U.S. B6 141
North, Cape, c., N.S., Can. B9 87
North Adams, Ma., U.S. A1 114
North Albany, Or., U.S. k11 130
Northam, Austl. G2 60
North America C5 4
North American Basin E7 66
North Amherst, Ma., U.S. B2 114
Northampton, Austl. F1 60
Northampton, Eng., U.K. D6 12
Northampton, Ma., U.S. B2 114
Northampton, Pa., U.S. E11 131
Northampton, co., N.C., U.S. A5 126
Northampton, co., Pa., U.S. E11 131
Northampton, co., Va., U.S. C7 139
North Andaman, i., India G6 40
North Andover, Ma., U.S. A5 114
North Anna, stm., Va., U.S. B5 139
North Anson, Me., U.S. D3 112
North Apollo, Pa., U.S. E2 131
North Arapaho Peak, mtn., Co., U.S. A5 99
North Arlington, N.J., U.S. h8 123
North Atlanta, Ga., U.S. h8 103
North Attleboro, Ma., U.S. C5 114
North Augusta, S.C., U.S. D4 133
North Aurora, Il., U.S. k8 106
North Australian Basin J14 64
North Baltimore, Oh., U.S. A2 128
North Bay, On., Can. A5 89
North Beach, Md., U.S. C4 113
North Belmont, N.C., U.S. B1 126
North Bend, Ne., U.S. C9 120
North Bend, Or., U.S. D2 130
North Bend, Wa., U.S. B4 140
North Bennington, Vt., U.S. F2 138
North Bergen, N.J., U.S. h8 123
North Berwick, Me., U.S. E2 112
North Billerica, Ma., U.S. A5 114
Northborough, Ma., U.S. B4 114
North Branch, Mi., U.S. E7 115
North Branch, Mn., U.S. E6 116
North Branch, N.H., U.S. D3 122
North Branch, N.J., U.S. B3 123
North Branford, Ct., U.S. D4 100
Northbridge, Ma., U.S. B4 114
Northbrook, Il., U.S. h9 106
North Brookfield, Ma., U.S. B3 114
North Brunswick, N.J., U.S. C4 123
North Caicos, i., T./C. Is. A5 80
North Caldwell, N.J., U.S. B4 123
North Canadian, stm., Ok., U.S. A5 129
North Canton, Ga., U.S. B2 103
North Canton, Oh., U.S. B4 128
North Cape, c., P.E., Can. B6 87
North Cape, c., N.Z. n13 63c
North Cape see Nordkapp, c., Nor. A11 10
North Cape May, N.J., U.S. F3 123
North Carolina, state, U.S. B3 126
North Cascades National Park, Wa., U.S. A4 140
North Channel, strt., On., Can. A2 89
North Channel, strt., U.K. C4 12
North Charleston, S.C., U.S. F8 133
North Chicago, Il., U.S. A6 106
North Clarendon, Vt., U.S. D3 138
Northcliffe, Austl. G2 60
North College Hill, Oh., U.S. o12 128
North Conway, N.H., U.S. B4 122
North Corbin, Ky., U.S. D5 110
North Crossett, Ar., U.S. D4 97
North Cyprus, ctry., Asia E5 44
North Dakota, state, U.S. B5 127
North Dartmouth, Ma., U.S. C6 114
North Eagle Butte, S.D., U.S. B4 134
North East, Md., U.S. A6 113
North East, Pa., U.S. B2 131
Northeast, stm., Md., U.S. A6 113
Northeast Cape, c., Ak., U.S. C6 95
Northeast Cape Fear, stm., N.C., U.S. C5 126
Northeast Harbor, Me., U.S. D4 112
North Easton, Ma., U.S. B5 114
Northeast Pond, l., N.H., U.S. D5 122
North Edisto, stm., S.C., U.S. k11 133
North English, Ia., U.S. C5 108
North English, stm., Ia., U.S. C5 108
North Enid, Ok., U.S. A4 129
Northern Cheyenne Indian Reservation, Mt., U.S. E10 119
Northern Cook Islands, is., Cook Is. F13 58
Northern Donets, stm., Eur. E15 20
Northern Dvina see Severnaja Dvina, stm., Russia C6 26
Northern Indian Lake, l., Mb., Can. A3 86
Northern Ireland, prov., N. Ire., U.K. C3 12
Northern Mariana Islands, dep., Oc. C9 58
Northern Sporades see Vórioi Sporádhes, is., Grc. E10 18
Northern Territory, ter., Austl. D5 60
North Falmouth, Ma., U.S. C6 114
Northfield, Mn., U.S. F5 116
Northfield, N.H., U.S. D3 122
Northfield, N.J., U.S. E3 123
Northfield, Oh., U.S. h9 128
Northfield, Vt., U.S. C3 138
Northfield Falls, Vt., U.S. C3 138
North Fiji Basin J20 64
North Flinders Range, mts., Austl. G2 62
North Fond du Lac, Wi., U.S. E5 142
Northford, Ct., U.S. D4 100
North Fork Reservoir, res., Or., U.S. B4 130
North Fort Myers, Fl., U.S. F5 102
North Fox Island, i., Mi., U.S. C5 115
Northglenn, Co., U.S. B6 99
North Gower, On., Can. B9 89
North Grafton, Ma., U.S. B4 114
North Grosvenordale, Ct., U.S. B8 100
North Gulfport, Ms., U.S. E4 117
North Haledon, N.J., U.S. B4 123
North Hampton, N.H., U.S. E5 122
North Hartland Reservoir, res., Vt., U.S. D4 138
North Hatley, P.Q., Can. D6 90
North Haven, Ct., U.S. D4 100
North Head, N.B., Can. E3 87
North Hero Island, i., Vt., U.S. B2 138
North Horn Lake, l., Tn., U.S. e8 135
North Industry, Oh., U.S. B4 128
North Inlet, b., S.C., U.S. E9 133
North Island, i., N.Z. o14 63c
North Island, i., S.C., U.S. E9 133
North Island Naval Air Station, mil., Ca., U.S. o15 98
North Islands, is., La., U.S. E7 111
North Judson, In., U.S. B4 107
North Kansas City, Mo., U.S. h10 118
North Kingstown, R.I., U.S. E4 132
North Kingsville, Oh., U.S. A5 128
North La Junta, Co., U.S. C7 99
Northlake, Il., U.S. k9 106
North Lakhimpur, India D6 40
North Laramie, stm., Wy., U.S. D7 143
North Las Vegas, Nv., U.S. G6 121
North La Veta Pass, Co., U.S. D5 99
North Lewisburg, Oh., U.S. B2 128
North Liberty, Ia., U.S. C6 108
North Liberty, In., U.S. A5 107
North Lima, Oh., U.S. B5 128
North Little Rock, Ar., U.S. C3 97
North Logan, Ut., U.S. B4 137
North Loon Mountain, mtn., Id., U.S. D3 105
North Magnetic Pole D33 144
North Mamm Peak, mtn., Co., U.S. B3 99
North Manchester, In., U.S. C6 107
North Manitou Island, i., Mi., U.S. C4 115
North Mankato, Mn., U.S. F4 116
North Miami, Fl., U.S. G6 102
North Miami Beach, Fl., U.S. s13 102
North Middletown, Ky., U.S. B5 110
North Moose Lake, l., Mb., Can. B1 86
North Mountain, mtn., Pa., U.S. D9 131
North Muskegon, Mi., U.S. E4 115
North Myrtle Beach, S.C., U.S. D10 133
North Naples, Fl., U.S. F5 102
North New River Canal, Fl., U.S. F6 102
North Ogden, Ut., U.S. B4 137
North Olmsted, Oh., U.S. h9 128
North Ossetia see Severnaja Osetija, state, Russia E6 26
North Palisade, mtn., Ca., U.S. D4 98
North Park, Il., U.S. A4 106
North Park, val., Co., U.S. A4 99
North Pass, strt., La., U.S. E7 111
North Pembroke, Ma., U.S. B6 114
North Plainfield, N.J., U.S. B4 123
North Plains, Or., U.S. B4 130
North Plains, pl., N.M., U.S. C1 124
North Platte, Ne., U.S. C5 120
North Platte, stm., U.S. C7 92
North Point, c., Md., U.S. B5 113
North Point, c., Mi., U.S. C7 115
North Pole E12 144
Northport, Al., U.S. B2 94
North Prairie, Wi., U.S. F5 142
North Providence, R.I., U.S. C4 132
North Raccoon, stm., Ia., U.S. C3 108
North Reading, Ma., U.S. f11 114
North Richland Hills, Tx., U.S. n9 136
Northridge, Oh., U.S. C2 128
North Ridgeville, Oh., U.S. A3 128
North Royalton, Oh., U.S. h9 128
North Rustico, P.E., Can. C6 87
North Salem, N.H., U.S. E4 122
North Salt Lake, Ut., U.S. C4 137
North Santee, stm., S.C., U.S. E9 133
North Saskatchewan, stm., Can. H18 82
North Schell Peak, mtn., Nv., U.S. D7 121
North Scituate, Ma., U.S. h12 114
North Sea, Eur. D6 6
North Shore City, N.Z. o13 63c
North Shoshone Peak, mtn., Nv., U.S. D4 121

Name — Map Ref. — Page

North Siberian Lowland see Severo-Sibirskaja nizmennost', pl., Russia B11 26
North Sioux City, S.D., U.S. E9 134
North Skunk, stm., Ia., U.S. C5 108
North Springfield, Vt., U.S. E3 138
North Springfield Reservoir, res., Vt., U.S. E4 138
North Star, De., U.S. A3 101
North St. Paul, Mn., U.S. m13 116
North Stradbroke Island, i., Austl. F5 62
North Stratford, N.H., U.S. A3 122
North Sudbury, Ma., U.S. g10 114
North Swanzey, N.H., U.S. E2 122
North Syracuse, N.Y., U.S. B4 125
North Taranaki Bight, b., N.Z. o13 63c
North Tarrytown, N.Y., U.S. D7 125
North Terre Haute, In., U.S. E3 107
North Thompson, stm., B.C., Can. D8 85
North Tonawanda, N.Y., U.S. B2 125
North Troy, Vt., U.S. B4 138
North Tunica, Ms., U.S. A3 117
North Twin Lake, l., Wi., U.S. B4 142
Northumberland, Pa., U.S. E8 131
Northumberland, co., Pa., U.S. D8 131
Northumberland, co., Va., U.S. C6 139
Northumberland Strait, strt., Can. C6 87
North Umpqua, stm., Or., U.S. D3 130
North Uxbridge, Ma., U.S. B4 114
Northvale, N.J., U.S. g9 123
North Vancouver, B.C., Can. E6 85
North Vassalboro, Me., U.S. D3 112
North Vernon, In., U.S. F6 107
Northville, Mi., U.S. p15 115
North Wales, Pa., U.S. F11 131
North Walpole, N.H., U.S. D2 122
North Warren, Pa., U.S. C3 131
North Webster, In., U.S. B6 107
North West Cape, c., Austl. E1 60
Northwest Miramichi, stm., N.B., Can. B3 87
Northwest Pacific Basin E18 64
Northwest Territories, ter., Can. E13 82
North Wildwood, N.J., U.S. E3 123
North Wilkesboro, N.C., U.S. A1 126
North Windham, Ct., U.S. C7 100
North Windham, Me., U.S. E2 112
Northwood, Ia., U.S. A4 108
Northwood, N.D., U.S. B8 127
North Woodstock, N.H., U.S. B3 122
North York, On., Can. D5 89
North York, Pa., U.S. G8 131
Norton, N.B., Can. D4 87
Norton, Ks., U.S. C4 109
Norton, Ma., U.S. C5 114
Norton, Oh., U.S. A4 128
Norton, Va., U.S. f9 139
Norton, co., Ks., U.S. C4 109
Norton Bay, b., Ak., U.S. C7 95
Norton Pond, l., Vt., U.S. B5 138
Norton Reservoir, res., Ks., U.S. C3 109
Norton Shores, Mi., U.S. E4 115
Norton Sound, strt., Ak., U.S. C6 95
Nortonville, Ks., U.S. C8 109
Nortonville, Ky., U.S. C2 110
Norvegia, Cape, c., Ant. D3 67
Norwalk, Ca., U.S. n12 98
Norwalk, Ct., U.S. E2 100
Norwalk, Ia., U.S. C4 108
Norwalk, Oh., U.S. A3 128
Norwalk, stm., Ct., U.S. E2 100
Norwalk Islands, is., Ct., U.S. E2 100
Norway, Me., U.S. D2 112
Norway, Mi., U.S. C3 115
Norway, ctry., Eur. B9 8
Norway House, Mb., Can. C3 86
Norway Lake, l., Mn., U.S. E3 116
Norwegian Basin C23 144
Norwegian Sea, Eur. I22 10a
Norwich, Eng., U.K. D7 12
Norwich, Ct., U.S. C7 100
Norwich, N.Y., U.S. C5 125
Norwich, Vt., U.S. D4 138
Norwood, On., Can. C7 89
Norwood, Ma., U.S. B5 114
Norwood, Mn., U.S. F5 116
Norwood, N.C., U.S. B2 126
Norwood, N.J., U.S. h9 123
Norwood, N.Y., U.S. f10 125
Norwood, Oh., U.S. o13 128
Norwood, Pa., U.S. p20 131
Norwoodville, Ia., U.S. e8 108
Noshiro, Japan C16 28
Nosivka, Ukr. D11 20
Nossob, stm., Afr. C2 56
Nosy-Varika, Madag. C8 56
Notasulga, Al., U.S. C4 94
Notch Peak, mtn., Ut., U.S. D2 137
Noteć, stm., Pol. C4 20
Notodden, Nor. G3 10
Noto-hantō, pen., Japan C3 31
Notre Dame, Monts, mts., P.Q., Can. k13 90
Notre Dame Bay, b., Nf., Can. D4 88
Notre Dame de Lourdes, Mb., Can. E2 86
Notre-Dame-du-Lac, P.Q., Can. B9 90
Nottawasaga Bay, b., On., Can. C4 89
Nottaway, stm., P.Q., Can. h11 90
Nottingham, Eng., U.K. D6 12
Nottoway, co., Va., U.S. C4 139
Nottoway, stm., Va., U.S. D5 139
Nouâdhibou, Maur. B1 50
Nouâdhibou, Râs, c., Afr. B1 50
Nouakchott, Maur. C1 50
Nouâmghâr, Maur. C1 50
Nouméa, N. Cal. I9 62a
Noupoort, S. Afr. E3 56
Nouveau-Brunswick see New Brunswick, prov., Can. C3 87
Nouvelle-Calédonie, i., N. Cal. I9 62a
Nova Caipemba, Ang. E2 54
Nova Friburgo, Braz. F3 74
Nova Iguaçu, Braz. F3 74
Novaja Kazanka, Kaz. E8 22
Novaja Sibir', ostrov, i., Russia B17 26
Novaja Zemlja, is., Russia B7 26
Nova Kakhovka, Ukr. F12 20
Nova Lima, Braz. F3 74
Nova Lisboa see Huambo, Ang. F3 54
Nova Mambone, Moz. C6 56
Novara, Italy B2 18
Nova Scotia, prov., Can. D6 87
Novato, Ca., U.S. C2 98
Nova Venécia, Braz. E3 74
Novaya Zemlya see Novaja Zemlja, is., Russia B7 26
Nova Zagora, Bul. C11 18
Nové Zámky, Slvk. E5 20
Novgorod, Russia D5 26
Novhorod-Sivers'kyi, Ukr. D12 20
Novi, Mi., U.S. p15 115
Novikovo, Russia A4 31
Novi Ligure, Italy B2 18
Novi Pazar, Bul. C11 18
Novi Pazar, Yugo. C8 18
Novi Sad, Yugo. B7 18
Novo Aripuanã, Braz. E7 70
Novoazovs'k, Ukr. F15 20
Novočerkassk, Russia E7 22
Novodvinsk, Russia B7 22
Novo Hamburgo, Braz. D7 72
Novohrad-Volyns'kyi, Ukr. D9 20
Novokazalinsk, Kaz. E8 26
Novokujbyševsk, Russia D8 22
Novokuzneck, Russia D10 26
Novomihajlovskij, Russia G15 20
Novomoskovsk, Russia D5 26
Novomoskovs'k, Ukr. E13 20
Novomyrhorod, Ukr. E11 20
Novorossijsk, Russia E5 26
Novošahtinsk, Russia F15 20
Novosergievka, Russia D9 22
Novosibirsk, Russia D10 26
Novosibirskie ostrova, is., Russia B16 26
Novotroick, Russia D10 22
Novotroickoe, Kaz. B10 42
Novotroïts'ke, Ukr. F13 20
Novoukraïnka, Ukr. E11 20
Novouzensk, Russia D8 22
Novovjatsk, Russia C8 22
Novovolyns'k, Ukr. D8 20
Novozybkov, Russia C11 20
Novyi Buh, Ukr. F12 20
Novyj Oskol, Russia D14 20
Novyj Port, Russia C9 26
Novyj Uzen', Kaz. E7 26
Nowa Ruda, Pol. D4 20
Nowata, Ok., U.S. A6 129
Nowata, co., Ok., U.S. A6 129
Nowood, stm., Wy., U.S. B5 143
Nowra, Austl. G5 62
Nowshāk, mtn., Asia B2 40
Nowy Dwór Mazowiecki, Pol. C6 20
Nowy Sącz, Pol. E6 20
Noxon Reservoir, res., Mt., U.S. C1 119
Noxontown Lake, res., De., U.S. C3 101
Noxubee, co., Ms., U.S. B5 117
Noxubee, stm., U.S. B5 117
Noyes Island, i., Ak., U.S. n22 95
Nsanje, Mwi. B6 56
Nsawam, Ghana E4 50
Nsukka, Nig. E6 50
Nsuta, Ghana E4 50
Ntomba, Lac, l., D.R.C. D3 54
Nūbah, Jibāl an-, mts., Sudan A6 54
Nubanusit Lake, l., N.H., U.S. E2 122
Nubian Desert, des., Sudan F11 48
Nuckolls, co., Ne., U.S. D7 120
Nucla, Co., U.S. C2 99
Nueces, co., Tx., U.S. F4 136
Nueces, stm., Tx., U.S. E3 136
Nueltin Lake, l., Can. F20 82
Nueva Antioquia, Col. D6 80
Nueva Gerona, Cuba A3 80
Nueva Imperial, Chile E2 69
Nueva Italia de Ruiz, Mex. D4 78
Nueva Rosita, Mex. B4 78
Nueve de Julio, Arg. F5 72
Nuevitas, Cuba A4 80
Nuevo, Cayo, i., Mex. C6 78
Nuevo, Golfo, b., Arg. F4 69
Nuevo Casas Grandes, Mex. A3 78
Nuevo Laredo, Mex. B5 78
Nuevo León, state, Mex. B5 78
Nui, atoll, Tuvalu E11 58
Nuku'alofa, Tonga G12 58
Nukus, Uzb. E7 26
Nulato, Ak., U.S. C8 95
Nulhegan, stm., Vt., U.S. B5 138
Nullagine, Austl. E3 60
Nullarbor, Austl. G5 60
Nullarbor Plain, pl., Austl. G4 60
Numan, Nig. E7 50
Numancia, hist., Spain G5 16
Numazu, Japan D3 31
Nunavut, ter., Can. E18 82
Nunivak Island, i., Ak., U.S. D6 95
Nunjiang, China B13 28
Nuoro, Italy D2 18
Nuremberg, Pa., U.S. E9 131
Nurmes, Fin. E13 10
Nürnberg, Ger. F12 12
Nusaybin, Tur. D9 44
Nu Shan, mts., China F7 28
Nushki, Pak. E9 42
Nutley, N.J., U.S. B4 123
Nutter Fort, W.V., U.S. k10 141
Nutting Lake, Ma., U.S. f10 114
Nuuanu Pali, Hi., U.S. g10 104
Nuuk see Godthåb, Grnld. F29 82
Nyabing, Austl. G2 60
Nyack, N.Y., U.S. D7 125
Nyainqêntanglha Shan, mts., China E6 28
Nyakanazi, Tan. D6 54
Nyala, Sudan H10 48
Nyamlell, Sudan B5 54
Nyanza-Lac, Bdi. D5 54
Nyasa, Lake (Malaŵi, Lake), l., Afr. F6 54
Nyasaland see Malawi, ctry., Afr. A5 56
Nyaunglebin, Myan. C3 34
Nyborg, Den. I4 10
Nybro, Swe. H6 10
Nyda, Russia C9 26
Nye, co., Nv., U.S. E5 121
Nyeri, Kenya D7 54
Nyimba, Zam. A5 56
Nyingchi, China D6 40
Nyíregyháza, Hung. F6 20
Nykøbing, Den. I4 10
Nyköping, Swe. G7 10
Nylstroom, S. Afr. C4 56
Nynäshamn, Swe. G7 10
Nyngan, Austl. G4 62
Nyš, Russia D16 26
Nysa, Pol. D4 20
Nyssa, Or., U.S. D9 130
Nyunzu, D.R.C. E5 54
Nzébéla, Gui. E3 50
Nzérékoré, Gui. E3 50
N'zeto, Ang. E2 54
Nzwani, i., Com. A7 56

O

Oahe, Lake, res., U.S. B7 92
Oahe Dam, S.D., U.S. C5 134
Oahu, i., Hi., U.S. B4 104
Oak Bay, B.C., Can. h12 85
Oak Bluffs, Ma., U.S. D6 114
Oak Creek, Co., U.S. A4 99
Oak Creek, Wi., U.S. n12 142
Oakdale, Ca., U.S. D3 98
Oakdale, Ga., U.S. h8 103
Oakdale, La., U.S. D3 111
Oakdale, Pa., U.S. k13 131
Oakes, N.D., U.S. C7 127
Oakfield, N.Y., U.S. B2 125
Oakfield, Wi., U.S. E5 142
Oak Forest, Il., U.S. k9 106
Oak Grove, Ky., U.S. D2 110
Oak Grove, La., U.S. B4 111
Oak Grove, Or., U.S. B4 130
Oak Harbor, Oh., U.S. A2 128
Oak Harbor, Wa., U.S. A3 140
Oak Hill, Mi., U.S. D4 115
Oak Hill, Oh., U.S. D3 128
Oak Hill, W.V., U.S. D3 141
Oak Hill, mtn., Ma., U.S. f9 114
Oakhurst, Ok., U.S. A5 129
Oak Island, i., Wi., U.S. B3 142
Oak Lake, l., Mb., Can. E1 86
Oakland, Ca., U.S. D2 98
Oakland, Ia., U.S. C2 108
Oakland, Il., U.S. D5 106
Oakland, Md., U.S. m12 113
Oakland, Me., U.S. D3 112
Oakland, Ne., U.S. C9 120
Oakland, N.J., U.S. A4 123
Oakland, Ok., U.S. C5 129
Oakland, Or., U.S. D3 130
Oakland, R.I., U.S. B2 132
Oakland, co., Mi., U.S. F7 115
Oakland City, In., U.S. H3 107
Oakland Park, Fl., U.S. r13 102
Oak Lawn, Il., U.S. B6 106
Oaklawn, Ks., U.S. g12 109
Oakley, Id., U.S. G5 105
Oakley, Ks., U.S. C3 109
Oakman, Al., U.S. B2 94
Oakmont, Pa., U.S. E2 131
Oak Mountain, mtn., Ga., U.S. D2 103
Oak Orchard, De., U.S. F5 101
Oak Park, Il., U.S. B6 106
Oak Park, Mi., U.S. p15 115
Oak Ridge, N.C., U.S. A3 126
Oakridge, Or., U.S. D4 130
Oak Ridge, Tn., U.S. C9 135
Oak Ridge Reservoir, res., N.J., U.S. A3 123
Oakton, Va., U.S. g12 139
Oaktown, In., U.S. G3 107
Oak Valley, N.J., U.S. D2 123
Oakville, On., Can. D5 89
Oakville, Ct., U.S. C3 100
Oakville, Mo., U.S. g13 118
Oakwood, Ga., U.S. B3 103
Oakwood, Il., U.S. C6 106
Oakwood, Oh., U.S. C1 128
Oamaru, N.Z. q13 63c
Oaxaca, state, Mex. D5 78
Oaxaca de Juárez, Mex. D5 78
Ob', stm., Russia B9 26
Oban, Scot., U.K. B4 12
Ob Bay see Obskaja guba, b., Russia C9 26
Obed, stm., Tn., U.S. C9 135
Oberlin, Ks., U.S. C3 109
Oberlin, La., U.S. D3 111
Oberlin, Oh., U.S. A3 128
Obetz, Oh., U.S. C3 128
Obi, Kepulauan, is., Indon. D7 36
Obi, Pulau, i., Indon. D7 36
Obi, Selat, strt., Indon. D7 36
Óbidos, Braz. D8 70
Obihiro, Japan C16 28
Obion, Tn., U.S. A2 135
Obion, co., Tn., U.S. A2 135
Obion, stm., Tn., U.S. A2 135
Oblong, Il., U.S. D6 106
Obluče, Russia B14 28
Obninsk, Russia B14 20
Obo, C.A.R. B5 54
Obojan', Russia D14 20
O'Brien, co., Ia., U.S. A2 108
Obščij syrt, mts., Eur. D9 22
Observation Peak, mtn., Ca., U.S. B3 98
Obskaja guba, b., Russia C9 26
Obuasi, Ghana E4 50
Obudu, Nig. E6 50
Ocala, Fl., U.S. C4 102
Očamčira, Geor. A9 44
Ocaña, Col. B5 70
Ocaña, Spain H5 16
Occidental, Cordillera, mts., Col. E4 80
Occidental, Cordillera, mts., Peru E4 70
Ocean, co., N.J., U.S. D4 123
Oceana, W.V., U.S. D3 141
Oceana, co., Mi., U.S. E4 115
Oceana Naval Air Station, mil., Va., U.S. k15 139
Ocean Bluff, Ma., U.S. B6 114
Ocean City, Fl., U.S. u15 102
Ocean City, Md., U.S. D7 113
Ocean City, N.J., U.S. E3 123
Ocean Grove, Ma., U.S. C5 114
Ocean Island see Banaba, i., Kir. E10 58
Ocean Park, Wa., U.S. C1 140
Oceanport, N.J., U.S. C4 123
Oceanside, Ca., U.S. F5 98
Ocean Springs, Ms., U.S. E5 117
Ocean [Township], N.J., U.S. C4 123
Ocean View, De., U.S. F5 101
Ocheda Lake, l., Mn., U.S. G3 116
Ocheyedan, stm., Ia., U.S. A2 108
Ochiltree, co., Tx., U.S. A2 136
Ochlockonee, stm., Fl., U.S. B2 102
Ochoco Lake, res., Or., U.S. C6 130
Ocilla, Ga., U.S. E3 103
Ockelbo, Swe. F7 10
Ocmulgee, stm., Ga., U.S. D3 103
Ocoa, Bahía de, b., Dom. Rep. B5 80
Ocoee, Fl., U.S. D5 102
Ocoee, Lake, res., Tn., U.S. D9 135
Oconee, co., Ga., U.S. C3 103
Oconee, co., S.C., U.S. B1 133
Oconee, stm., Ga., U.S. C3 103
Oconee, Lake, res., Ga., U.S. C3 103
Oconomowoc, Wi., U.S. E5 142
Oconto, Wi., U.S. D6 142
Oconto, co., Wi., U.S. D5 142
Oconto, stm., Wi., U.S. D5 142
Oconto Falls, Wi., U.S. D5 142
Ocosingo, Mex. D6 78
Ocotal, Nic. C2 80
Ocotlán, Mex. C4 78
Ocracoke Inlet, b., N.C., U.S. B6 126
Ocracoke Island, i., N.C., U.S. B7 126
October Revolution Island see Oktjabr'skoj Revoljucii, ostrov, i., Russia B11 26
Octoraro Creek, stm., U.S. A5 113
Ocumare del Tuy, Ven. C6 80
Oda, Ghana E4 50
Oda, Jabal, mtn., Sudan F12 48
Odebolt, Ia., U.S. B2 108
Odell, Il., U.S. B5 106
Odell, Or., U.S. B5 130
Odell Lake, l., Or., U.S. E5 130
Odem, Tx., U.S. F4 136
Odemira, Port. I2 16
Ödemiş, Tur. C2 44
Odendaalsrus, S. Afr. D4 56
Odense, Den. I4 10
Odenton, Md., U.S. B4 113
Odenville, Al., U.S. B3 94
Oder, stm., Eur. C3 20
Odesa, Ukr. F11 20
Odessa, On., Can. C8 89
Odessa see Odesa, Ukr. F11 20
Odessa, De., U.S. C3 101
Odessa, Mo., U.S. C4 118
Odessa, Tx., U.S. D1 136
Odessa, Wa., U.S. B7 140
Odienné, C. Iv. E3 50
Odin, Il., U.S. E4 106
Odon, In., U.S. G4 107
O'Donnell, Tx., U.S. C2 136
Odorheiu Secuiesc, Rom. F8 20
Oeiras, Braz. C3 74
Oelwein, Ia., U.S. B6 108
Oenpelli, Austl. C5 60
Of, Tur. B9 44
O'Fallon, Il., U.S. E4 106
O'Fallon, Mo., U.S. f12 118
Ofanto, stm., Italy D5 18
Offa, Nig. E5 50
Offenburg, Ger. F10 12
Offutt Air Force Base, mil., Ne., U.S. g3 120
Ofotfjorden, b., Nor. B7 10
Ogaden, reg., Afr. I14 48
Ogallala, Ne., U.S. C4 120
Ogasawara-guntō, is., Japan F16 64
Ogbomosho, Nig. E5 50
Ogden, Ia., U.S. B3 108
Ogden, Ks., U.S. C7 109
Ogden, Ut., U.S. B4 137
Ogden, Mount, mtn., N.A. k23 95
Ogdensburg, N.J., U.S. A3 123
Ogdensburg, N.Y., U.S. f9 125
Ogeechee, stm., Ga., U.S. D5 103
Ogemaw, co., Mi., U.S. D6 115
Ogle, co., Il., U.S. A4 106
Oglesby, Il., U.S. B4 106
Oglethorpe, Ga., U.S. D2 103
Oglethorpe, co., Ga., U.S. C3 103
Oglethorpe, Mount, mtn., Ga., U.S. B2 103
Ogoja, Nig. E6 50
Ogooué, stm., Afr. D2 54
Ogre, Lat. H11 10
Ogunquit, Me., U.S. E2 112
Ogurdžaly, ostrov, i., Turk. C6 42
Oha, Russia D16 26
Ohanet, Alg. E6 48
Ohatchee, Al., U.S. B3 94
Ohio, co., In., U.S. G7 107
Ohio, co., Ky., U.S. C3 110
Ohio, co., W.V., U.S. A4 141
Ohio, state, U.S. B3 128
Ohio, stm., U.S. D10 92
Ohio Brush Creek, stm., Oh., U.S. D2 128
Ohio City, Oh., U.S. B1 128
Ohio Peak, mtn., Co., U.S. C3 99
Ohioville, Pa., U.S. E1 131
Ohoopee, stm., Ga., U.S. D4 103
Ohotsk, Russia D16 26
Ohrid, Mac. D8 18
Ohrid, Lake, l., Eur. C8 14
Oiapoque, Braz. C9 70
Oiapoque (Oyapok), stm., S.A. C9 70
Oil City, La., U.S. B2 111
Oil City, Pa., U.S. D2 131
Oil Creek, stm., Pa., U.S. C2 131
Oildale, Ca., U.S. E4 98
Oil Springs, On., Can. E2 89
Oilton, Ok., U.S. A5 129
Oise, stm., Eur. C8 16
Ōita, Japan E14 28
Ojai, Ca., U.S. E4 98
Ojinaga, Mex. B4 78
Ojmjakon, Russia C16 26
Ojocaliente, Mex. C4 78
Ojos del Salado, Cerro see Ojos del Salado, Nevado, mtn., S.A. D4 72
Ojos del Salado, Nevado, mtn., S.A. D4 72
Oka, stm., Russia D6 26
Okaba, Indon. H10 32
Okahandja, Nmb. C2 56
Okaloosa, co., Fl., U.S. u15 102
Okamanpeedan Lake, l., U.S. A3 108
Okanagan Falls, B.C., Can. E8 85
Okanagan Lake, l., B.C., Can. D8 85
Okanagan Landing, B.C., Can. D8 85

Name	Map Ref.	Page
Okanogan, Wa., U.S.	**A6**	140
Okanogan, co., Wa., U.S.	**A5**	140
Okāra, Pak.	**D10**	42
Okarche, Ok., U.S.	**B4**	129
Okatibee Reservoir, res., Ms., U.S.	**C5**	117
Okaukuejo, Nmb.	**B2**	56
Okavango (Cubango), stm., Afr.	**B3**	56
Okavango Delta, Bots.	**B3**	56
Okawville, Il., U.S.	**E4**	106
Okaya, Japan	**C3**	31
Okayama, Japan	**E14**	28
Okazaki, Japan	**D3**	31
Okeechobee, Fl., U.S.	**E6**	102
Okeechobee, co., Fl., U.S.	**E6**	102
Okeechobee, Lake, l., Fl., U.S.	**F6**	102
Okeene, Ok., U.S.	**A3**	129
Okefenokee Swamp, sw., U.S.	**F4**	103
Okemah, Ok., U.S.	**B5**	129
Okene, Nig.	**E6**	50
Okfuskee, co., Ok., U.S.	**B5**	129
Okhotsk see Ohotsk, Russia	**D16**	26
Okhotsk, Sea of, Asia	**D16**	26
Okhotsk Basin	**B7**	144
Okhtyrka, Ukr.	**D13**	20
Okinawa, Japan	**g6**	31a
Okinawa-jima, i., Japan	**A9**	34
Okinawa-shotō, is., Japan	**g6**	31a
Okino-Erabu-shima, i., Japan	**A9**	34
Okino-Tori-shima, i., Japan	**G15**	28
Oki-shotō, is., Japan	**D14**	28
Okitipupa, Nig.	**E5**	50
Oklahoma, co., Ok., U.S.	**B4**	129
Oklahoma, state, U.S.	**B4**	129
Oklahoma City, Ok., U.S.	**B4**	129
Oklawaha, Fl., U.S.	**C5**	102
Oklawaha, stm., Fl., U.S.	**C5**	102
Oklawaha, Lake, res., Fl., U.S.	**C5**	102
Okmulgee, Ok., U.S.	**B6**	129
Okmulgee, co., Ok., U.S.	**B5**	129
Okoboji, Ia., U.S.	**A2**	108
Okobojo Creek, stm., S.D., U.S.	**C5**	134
Okolona, Ky., U.S.	**g11**	110
Okolona, Ms., U.S.	**B5**	117
Okondja, Gabon	**D2**	54
Okotoks, Ab., Can.	**D4**	84
Oktibbeha, co., Ms., U.S.	**B5**	117
Oktjabr'sk, Kaz.	**E7**	26
Oktjabr'skij, Russia	**D9**	22
Oktjabr'skoe, Russia	**B12**	22
Oktjabr'skoj Revoljucii, ostrov, i., Russia	**B11**	26
Oktwin, Myan.	**C3**	34
Okushiri-tō, i., Japan	**C15**	28
Ola, Ar., U.S.	**B2**	97
Ólafsfjörður, Ice.	**k19**	10a
Olancha Peak, mtn., Ca., U.S.	**D4**	98
Olanchito, Hond.	**B2**	80
Öland, i., Swe.	**H7**	10
Olanta, S.C., U.S.	**D8**	133
Olathe, Co., U.S.	**C3**	99
Olathe, Ks., U.S.	**D9**	109
Olavarría, Arg.	**F5**	72
Olbia, Italy	**D2**	18
Olcott, N.Y., U.S.	**B2**	125
Old Bahama Channel, strt., N.A.	**A4**	80
Old Bridge, N.J., U.S.	**C4**	123
Old Castile see Castilla la Vieja, hist. reg., Spain	**G5**	16
Oldenburg, Ger.	**D11**	12
Oldenburg, In., U.S.	**F7**	107
Oldenburg in Holstein, Ger.	**C12**	12
Old Faithful Geyser, Wy., U.S.	**B2**	143
Old Forge, Pa., U.S.	**D10**	131
Old Fort, N.C., U.S.	**f10**	126
Oldham, co., Ky., U.S.	**B4**	110
Oldham, co., Tx., U.S.	**B1**	136
Old Harbor, Ak., U.S.	**D9**	95
Old Hickory Lake, res., Tn., U.S.	**A5**	135
Oldman, stm., Ab., Can.	**E4**	84
Old Man of the Mountain, N.H., U.S.	**B3**	122
Oldmans Creek, stm., N.J., U.S.	**D2**	123
Old Orchard Beach, Me., U.S.	**E2**	112
Old Perlican, Nf., Can.	**D5**	88
Old Point Comfort, c., Va., U.S.	**h15**	139
Old Rhodes Key, i., Fl., U.S.	**G6**	102
Old River Lake, l., Ar., U.S.	**k10**	97
Olds, Ab., Can.	**D3**	84
Old Saybrook, Ct., U.S.	**D6**	100
Oldsmar, Fl., U.S.	**o10**	102
Old Tampa Bay, b., Fl., U.S.	**p10**	102
Old Tappan, N.J., U.S.	**g9**	123
Old Tate, Bots.	**C4**	56
Old Topsail Inlet, b., N.C., U.S.	**C5**	126
Old Town, Me., U.S.	**D4**	112
Old Wives Lake, l., Sk., Can.	**G2**	91
Olean, N.Y., U.S.	**C2**	125
O'Leary, P.E., Can.	**C5**	87
Olëkma, stm., Russia	**C14**	26
Olekminsk, Russia	**C14**	26
Oleksandriia, Ukr.	**E12**	20
Olenegorsk, Russia	**B15**	10
Olenëk, Russia	**C13**	26
Olenëk, stm., Russia	**B13**	26
Olenëkskij zaliv, b., Russia	**B14**	26
Olentangy, stm., Oh., U.S.	**B3**	128
Oléron, Île d', i., Fr.	**E6**	16
Olevsk, Ukr.	**D9**	20
Ol'ga, Russia	**E15**	26
Olga, Mount, mtn., Austl.	**F5**	60
Ölgiy, Mong.	**B6**	28
Olhão, Port.	**I3**	16
Olifants (Elefantes), stm., Afr.	**C4**	56
Olifants, stm., Nmb.	**C2**	56
Olifantshoek, S. Afr.	**D3**	56
Ólimbos, mtn., Cyp.	**E5**	44
Ólimbos, Óros, mtn., Grc.	**D9**	18
Olin, Ia., U.S.	**B6**	108
Olinda, Braz.	**C5**	74
Olive Branch, Ms., U.S.	**A4**	117
Olive Hill, Ky., U.S.	**B6**	110
Olivehurst, Ca., U.S.	**C3**	98
Oliveira, Braz.	**F3**	74
Oliver, B.C., Can.	**E8**	85
Oliver, Pa., U.S.	**G2**	131
Oliver, co., N.D., U.S.	**B4**	127
Oliver Dam, U.S.	**C5**	94
Oliver Springs, Tn., U.S.	**C9**	135
Olivet, Mi., U.S.	**F6**	115
Olivia, Mn., U.S.	**F4**	116
Oljutorskij, mys, c., Russia	**D19**	26
Olla, La., U.S.	**C3**	111
Ollagüe, Chile	**B3**	69
Olmito, Tx., U.S.	**F4**	136
Olmos, Peru	**E4**	70
Olmos Park, Tx., U.S.	**k7**	136
Olmsted, co., Mn., U.S.	**G6**	116
Olmsted Falls, Oh., U.S.	**h9**	128
Olney, Il., U.S.	**E5**	106
Olney, Md., U.S.	**B3**	113
Olney, Tx., U.S.	**C3**	136
Olomouc, Czech Rep.	**E4**	20
Olonec, Russia	**B5**	22
Olongapo, Phil.	**D8**	34
Oloron-Sainte-Marie, Fr.	**F6**	16
Olot, Spain	**F8**	16
Olovjannaja, Russia	**A11**	28
Olsztyn, Pol.	**C6**	20
Olteniţa, Rom.	**G9**	20
Olton, Tx., U.S.	**B1**	136
Oltu, Tur.	**B10**	44
Olustee, Ok., U.S.	**C2**	129
Olympia, Wa., U.S.	**B3**	140
Olympic Mountains, mts., Wa., U.S.	**B2**	140
Olympic National Park, Wa., U.S.	**B2**	140
Olympus see Ólimbos, mtn., Cyp.	**E5**	44
Olympus, Mount see Ólimbos, Óros, mtn., Grc.	**D9**	18
Olympus, Mount, mtn., Wa., U.S.	**B2**	140
Olyphant, Pa., U.S.	**D10**	131
Omagh, N. Ire., U.K.	**C3**	12
Omaha, Ne., U.S.	**C10**	120
Omaha Indian Reservation, Ne., U.S.	**B9**	120
Omak, Wa., U.S.	**A6**	140
Omak Lake, l., Wa., U.S.	**A6**	140
Oman, ctry., Asia	**G7**	38
Oman, Gulf of, b., Asia	**F7**	42
Omar, W.V., U.S.	**D3**	141
Omarama, N.Z.	**p12**	63c
Omaruru, Nmb.	**C2**	56
Omatako, stm., Nmb.	**B2**	56
Ombai, Selat, strt., Indon.	**E7**	36
Omboué, Gabon	**D1**	54
Omčak, Russia	**C16**	26
Omdurman see Umm Durmān, Sudan	**G11**	48
Omega, Ga., U.S.	**E3**	103
Omemee, On., Can.	**C6**	89
Omerville, P.Q., Can.	**D5**	90
Ometepe, Isla de, i., Nic.	**C2**	80
Ometepec, Mex.	**D5**	78
Omineca, stm., B.C., Can.	**B5**	85
Omineca Mountains, mts., B.C., Can.	**A4**	85
Ōmiya, Japan	**C3**	31
Ommaney, Cape, c., Ak., U.S.	**D12**	95
Omolon, stm., Russia	**C17**	26
Ompompanoosuc, stm., Vt., U.S.	**D4**	138
Omro, Wi., U.S.	**D5**	142
Omsk, Russia	**D9**	26
Omsukčan, Russia	**C17**	26
Ōmuda (Ōmuta), Japan	**E14**	28
Ōmura, Japan	**D1**	31
Ōmuta (Ōmuda), Japan	**E14**	28
Omutninsk, Russia	**C9**	22
Onaga, Ks., U.S.	**C7**	109
Onalaska, Wa., U.S.	**C3**	140
Onalaska, Wi., U.S.	**E2**	142
Onamia, Mn., U.S.	**D5**	116
Onancock, Va., U.S.	**C7**	139
Onarga, Il., U.S.	**C6**	106
Onawa, Ia., U.S.	**B1**	108
Onawa, Lake, l., Me., U.S.	**C3**	112
Onaway, Mi., U.S.	**C6**	115
Ondangwa, Nmb.	**B2**	56
Ondjiva, Ang.	**B2**	56
Ondo, Nig.	**E5**	50
Öndörhaan, Mong.	**B10**	28
Oneco, Fl., U.S.	**E4**	102
Onega, Russia	**C5**	26
Onega, stm., Russia	**B6**	22
Onega, Lake see Onežskoe ozero, l., Russia	**C5**	26
Onega Bay see Onežskaja guba, b., Russia	**B6**	22
One Hundred Fifty Mile House, B.C., Can.	**C7**	85
One Hundred Mile House, B.C., Can.	**D7**	85
Oneida, Ky., U.S.	**C6**	110
Oneida, N.Y., U.S.	**B5**	125
Oneida, Oh., U.S.	**C1**	128
Oneida, Tn., U.S.	**C9**	135
Oneida, co., Id., U.S.	**G6**	105
Oneida, co., N.Y., U.S.	**B5**	125
Oneida, co., Wi., U.S.	**C4**	142
Oneida Lake, l., N.Y., U.S.	**B5**	125
O'Neill, Ne., U.S.	**B7**	120
Onekotan, ostrov, i., Russia	**E17**	26
Oneonta, Al., U.S.	**B3**	94
Oneonta, N.Y., U.S.	**C5**	125
Oneşti, Rom.	**F9**	20
Onežskaja guba, b., Russia	**B6**	22
Onežskoe ozero, l., Russia	**C5**	26
Ongole, India	**F4**	40
Onida, S.D., U.S.	**C5**	134
Onitsha, Nig.	**E6**	50
Onondaga, co., N.Y., U.S.	**C4**	125
Onondaga Indian Reservation, N.Y., U.S.	**C4**	125
Onota Lake, l., Ma., U.S.	**B1**	114
Onoway, Ab., Can.	**C3**	84
Onseepkans, S. Afr.	**D2**	56
Onset, Ma., U.S.	**C6**	114
Onslow, Austl.	**E1**	60
Onslow, co., N.C., U.S.	**C5**	126
Onslow Bay, b., N.C., U.S.	**C5**	126
Onsted, Mi., U.S.	**F6**	115
Ontario, Ca., U.S.	**E5**	98
Ontario, Oh., U.S.	**B3**	128
Ontario, Or., U.S.	**C10**	130
Ontario, co., N.Y., U.S.	**C3**	125
Ontario, prov., Can.	**C6**	89
Ontario, Lake, l., N.A.	**C12**	92
Ontinyent, Spain	**H6**	16
Ontonagon, Mi., U.S.	**m12**	115
Ontonagon, co., Mi., U.S.	**m12**	115
Ontonagon Indian Reservation, Mi., U.S.	**B1**	115
Oodnadatta, Austl.	**F2**	62
Ooldea, Austl.	**G5**	60
Oolitic, In., U.S.	**G4**	107
Oologah, Ok., U.S.	**A6**	129
Oologah Lake, res., Ok., U.S.	**A6**	129
Ooltewah, Tn., U.S.	**D8**	135
Oostburg, Wi., U.S.	**E6**	142
Oostende, Bel.	**E8**	12
Ootsa Lake, l., B.C., Can.	**C4**	85
Opala, D.R.C.	**D4**	54
Opa-Locka, Fl., U.S.	**s13**	102
Opava, Czech Rep.	**E4**	20
Opelika, Al., U.S.	**C4**	94
Opelousas, La., U.S.	**D3**	111
Opequon Creek, stm., W.V., U.S.	**B6**	141
Opobo, Nig.	**F6**	50
Opočka, Russia	**H13**	10
Opole, Pol.	**D4**	20
Opotiki, N.Z.	**o14**	63c
Opp, Al., U.S.	**D3**	94
Oppdal, Nor.	**E3**	10
Oppelo, Ar., U.S.	**B3**	97
Opportunity, Wa., U.S.	**B8**	140
Optima Reservoir, res., Ok., U.S.	**e9**	129
Opuwo, Nmb.	**B1**	56
Oquawka, Il., U.S.	**C3**	106
Oracle, Az., U.S.	**E5**	96
Oradea, Rom.	**F6**	20
Oradell, N.J., U.S.	**h8**	123
Oradell Reservoir, res., N.J., U.S.	**h9**	123
Öræfajökull, Ice.	**l20**	10a
Orai, India	**D3**	40
Oraibi, Az., U.S.	**B5**	96
Oran see Wahran, Alg.	**C4**	48
Oran, Mo., U.S.	**D8**	118
Oran, Sebkha d', l., Alg.	**J6**	16
Orange, Austl.	**G4**	62
Orange, Fr.	**E9**	16
Orange, Ca., U.S.	**n13**	98
Orange, Ct., U.S.	**D3**	100
Orange, Ma., U.S.	**A3**	114
Orange, N.J., U.S.	**B4**	123
Orange, Tx., U.S.	**D6**	136
Orange, Va., U.S.	**B4**	139
Orange, co., Ca., U.S.	**F5**	98
Orange, co., Fl., U.S.	**D5**	102
Orange, co., In., U.S.	**G4**	107
Orange, co., N.C., U.S.	**A3**	126
Orange, co., N.Y., U.S.	**D6**	125
Orange, co., Tx., U.S.	**D6**	136
Orange, co., Va., U.S.	**B4**	139
Orange, co., Vt., U.S.	**D3**	138
Orange (Oranje), stm., Afr.	**D2**	56
Orange, Cabo, c., Braz.	**C9**	70
Orange Beach, Al., U.S.	**E2**	94
Orangeburg, S.C., U.S.	**E6**	133
Orangeburg, co., S.C., U.S.	**E6**	133
Orange City, Fl., U.S.	**D5**	102
Orange City, Ia., U.S.	**B1**	108
Orange Grove, Ms., U.S.	**E5**	117
Orange Grove, Tx., U.S.	**F4**	136
Orange Lake, l., Fl., U.S.	**C4**	102
Orange Park, Fl., U.S.	**B5**	102
Orangeville, On., Can.	**D4**	89
Orangeville, Ut., U.S.	**D4**	137
Orange Walk, Belize	**B2**	80
Oranienburg, Ger.	**D13**	12
Oranje see Orange, stm., Afr.	**D2**	56
Oranjemund, Nmb.	**D2**	56
Oranjestad, Aruba	**C6**	80
Orbetello, Italy	**C3**	18
Orbost, Austl.	**H4**	62
Orcas Island, i., Wa., U.S.	**A3**	140
Orchard City, Co., U.S.	**C3**	99
Orchard Homes, Mt., U.S.	**D2**	119
Orchard Park, N.Y., U.S.	**C2**	125
Orchards, Wa., U.S.	**D3**	140
Orchard Valley, Wy., U.S.	**E8**	143
Orcutt, Ca., U.S.	**E3**	98
Ord, Ne., U.S.	**C7**	120
Ord, Mount, mtn., Austl.	**D4**	60
Ordu, Tur.	**B7**	44
Ordway, Co., U.S.	**C7**	99
Ordzhonikidze see Vladikavkaz, Russia	**E6**	26
Ordzhonikidze see Yenakiieve, Ukr.	**E15**	20
Ordzhonikidze, Ukr.	**F13**	20
Ordžonikidzeabad, Taj.	**C9**	42
Oreana, Il., U.S.	**D5**	106
Örebro, Swe.	**G6**	10
Oregon, Il., U.S.	**A4**	106
Oregon, Mo., U.S.	**B2**	118
Oregon, Oh., U.S.	**A2**	128
Oregon, Wi., U.S.	**F4**	142
Oregon, co., Mo., U.S.	**E6**	118
Oregon, state, U.S.	**C6**	130
Oregon Caves National Monument, Or., U.S.	**E2**	130
Oregon City, Or., U.S.	**B4**	130
Oregon Inlet, b., N.C., U.S.	**B7**	126
Orehovo-Zuevo, Russia	**C6**	22
Orel, Russia	**D5**	26
Orem, Ut., U.S.	**C4**	137
Ore Mountains see Erzgebirge, mts., Eur.	**E9**	8
Orenburg, Russia	**D7**	26
Orense, Arg.	**F6**	72
Orestiás, Grc.	**D11**	18
Orfanoú, Kólpos, b., Grc.	**D9**	18
Orfordville, Wi., U.S.	**F4**	142
Organ Mountains, mts., N.M., U.S.	**E3**	124
Organ Pipe Cactus National Monument, Az., U.S.	**E3**	96
Orgūn, Afg.	**D9**	42
Orhei, Mol.	**F10**	20
Orhon, stm., Mong.	**A9**	28
Oriental, N.C., U.S.	**B6**	126
Oriental, Cordillera, mts., Col.	**D5**	80
Oriental, Cordillera, mts., Peru	**F5**	70
Orikhiv, Ukr.	**F13**	20
Orillia, On., Can.	**C5**	89
Orinoco, stm., S.A.	**B6**	70
Oriola, Spain	**H6**	16
Orion, Il., U.S.	**B3**	106
Orissa, prov., India	**E4**	40
Oristano, Italy	**E2**	18
Oristano, Golfo di, b., Italy	**E2**	18
Orivesi, Fin.	**F11**	10
Oriximiná, Braz.	**D8**	70
Orizaba, Mex.	**D5**	78
Orkney, S. Afr.	**D4**	56
Orkney Islands, is., U.K.	**A5**	12
Orland, Ca., U.S.	**C2**	98
Orlando, Fl., U.S.	**D5**	102
Orland Park, Il., U.S.	**k9**	106
Orléanais, hist. reg., Fr.	**C7**	16
Orléans, Fr.	**D7**	16
Orleans, Ma., U.S.	**C7**	114
Orleans, Vt., U.S.	**B4**	138
Orleans, co., La., U.S.	**E6**	111
Orleans, co., N.Y., U.S.	**B2**	125
Orleans, co., Vt., U.S.	**B4**	138
Orléans, Île d', i., P.Q., Can.	**C6**	90
Orlik, Russia	**A7**	28
Orman Dam, S.D., U.S.	**C2**	134
Ormāra, Pak.	**E8**	42
Ormoc, Phil.	**D8**	34
Ormond Beach, Fl., U.S.	**C5**	102
Ormstown, P.Q., Can.	**D3**	90
Örnsköldsvik, Swe.	**E8**	10
Orocué, Col.	**C5**	70
Orofino, Id., U.S.	**C2**	105
Oroluk, atoll, Micron.	**D9**	58
Oromocto, N.B., Can.	**D3**	87
Oromocto Lake, l., N.B., Can.	**D2**	87
Oron, Nig.	**F6**	50
Orono, Me., U.S.	**D4**	112
Oronoco, Mn., U.S.	**F6**	116
Oroquieta, Phil.	**E8**	34
Orosei, Golfo di, b., Italy	**D2**	18
Oroville, Ca., U.S.	**C3**	98
Oroville, Wa., U.S.	**A6**	140
Oroville, Lake, res., Ca., U.S.	**C3**	98
Orrick, Mo., U.S.	**B3**	118
Orrville, Oh., U.S.	**B4**	128
Orša, Bela.	**B11**	20
Orsk, Russia	**D7**	26
Ortaca, Tur.	**D3**	44
Ortegal, Cabo, c., Spain	**F3**	16
Orting, Wa., U.S.	**B3**	140
Ortiz, Mex.	**B2**	78
Ortonville, Mi., U.S.	**F7**	115
Ortonville, Mn., U.S.	**E2**	116
Orto-Tokoj, Kyrg.	**A3**	40
Orūmīyeh, Iran	**C5**	42
Orūmīyeh, Daryācheh-ye, l., Iran	**C5**	42
Oruro, Bol.	**B4**	72
Orwell, Oh., U.S.	**A5**	128
Orwigsburg, Pa., U.S.	**E9**	131
Oš, Kyrg.	**E9**	26
Osa, Península de, pen., C.R.	**D3**	80
Osage, Ia., U.S.	**A5**	108
Osage, Wy., U.S.	**C8**	143
Osage, co., Ks., U.S.	**D8**	109
Osage, co., Mo., U.S.	**C6**	118
Osage, co., Ok., U.S.	**A5**	129
Osage, stm., Mo., U.S.	**C3**	118
Osage Beach, Mo., U.S.	**C5**	118
Osage City, Ks., U.S.	**D8**	109
Ōsaka, Japan	**E15**	28
Osakis, Mn., U.S.	**E3**	116
Osakis, Lake, l., Mn., U.S.	**E3**	116
Osawatomie, Ks., U.S.	**D9**	109
Osborne, Ks., U.S.	**C5**	109
Osborne, co., Ks., U.S.	**C5**	109
Osburn, Id., U.S.	**B3**	105
Osceola, Ar., U.S.	**B6**	97
Osceola, Ia., U.S.	**C4**	108
Osceola, In., U.S.	**A5**	107
Osceola, Mo., U.S.	**C4**	118
Osceola, Ne., U.S.	**C8**	120
Osceola, Wi., U.S.	**C1**	142
Osceola, co., Fl., U.S.	**E5**	102
Osceola, co., Ia., U.S.	**A2**	108
Osceola, co., Mi., U.S.	**E5**	115
Osceola Mills, Pa., U.S.	**E5**	131
Oscoda, Mi., U.S.	**D7**	115
Oscoda, co., Mi., U.S.	**D6**	115
Oscura Mountains, mts., N.M., U.S.	**D3**	124
Osgood, In., U.S.	**F7**	107
Oshawa, On., Can.	**D6**	89
Ō-shima, i., Japan	**D3**	31
Oshkosh, Ne., U.S.	**C3**	120
Oshkosh, Wi., U.S.	**D5**	142
Oshnovīyeh, Iran	**D11**	44
Oshogbo, Nig.	**E5**	50
Oshtorīnān, Iran	**E13**	44
Oshwe, D.R.C.	**D3**	54
Osijek, Cro.	**B7**	18
Oskaloosa, Ia., U.S.	**C5**	108
Oskaloosa, Ks., U.S.	**C8**	109
Oskarshamn, Swe.	**H7**	10
Oskū, Iran	**D12**	44
Oslo, Nor.	**G4**	10
Oslofjorden, b., Nor.	**G4**	10
Osmānābād, India	**F3**	40
Osmancık, Tur.	**B6**	44
Osmaniye, Tur.	**D7**	44
Osmond, Ne., U.S.	**B8**	120
Osnabrück, Ger.	**D11**	12
Osorno, Chile	**F2**	69
Osoyoos, B.C., Can.	**E8**	85
Osoyoos Lake, l., Wa., U.S.	**A6**	140
Osprey, Fl., U.S.	**E4**	102
Ossa, Mount, mtn., Austl.	**I4**	62
Ossabaw Island, i., Ga., U.S.	**E5**	103
Osseo, Mn., U.S.	**m12**	116
Osseo, Wi., U.S.	**D2**	142
Ossian, Ia., U.S.	**A6**	108
Ossian, In., U.S.	**C7**	107
Ossining, N.Y., U.S.	**D7**	125
Ossipee, stm., U.S.	**C5**	122
Ossipee Lake, l., N.H., U.S.	**C4**	122
Ossora, Russia	**D18**	26
Ostaškov, Russia	**C5**	22
Östersund, Swe.	**E6**	10
Osterville, Ma., U.S.	**C7**	114
Ostfriesische Inseln, is., Ger.	**D10**	12
Ostrava, Czech Rep.	**E5**	20
Ostróda, Pol.	**C5**	20
Ostrogožsk, Russia	**D15**	20
Ostroh, Ukr.	**D9**	20
Ostrołęka, Pol.	**C6**	20
Ostrov, Russia	**H13**	10
Ostrowiec Świętokrzyski, Pol.	**D6**	20
Ostrów Mazowiecka, Pol.	**C6**	20
Ostrów Wielkopolski, Pol.	**D4**	20
Ostuni, Italy	**D6**	18
Ōsumi-shotō, is., Japan	**E14**	28
Osuna, Spain	**I4**	16
Oswegatchie, stm., N.Y., U.S.	**f9**	125
Oswego, Il., U.S.	**B5**	106
Oswego, Ks., U.S.	**E8**	109
Oswego, N.Y., U.S.	**B4**	125
Oswego, co., N.Y., U.S.	**B4**	125
Oswego, stm., N.J., U.S.	**D4**	123
Oswego, stm., N.Y., U.S.	**B4**	125
Otanmäki, Fin.	**D12**	10
Otaru, Japan	**C16**	28
Otava, Fin.	**F12**	10
Otavi, Nmb.	**B2**	56
Oteen, N.C., U.S.	**f10**	126
Otero, co., Co., U.S.	**D7**	99

Name	Map Ref.	Page
Otero, co., N.M., U.S.	E3	124
Othello, Wa., U.S.	C6	140
Otis Orchards, Wa., U.S.	g14	140
Otis Reservoir, res., Ma., U.S.	B1	114
Otisville, Mi., U.S.	E7	115
Otjikondo, Nmb.	B2	56
Otjiwarongo, Nmb.	C2	56
Otoe, co., Ne., U.S.	D9	120
Otra, stm., Nor.	G2	10
Otradnyj, Russia	D9	22
Ótranto, Italy	D7	18
Otranto, Strait of, strt., Eur.	C7	14
Otsego, Mi., U.S.	F5	115
Otsego, co., Mi., U.S.	C6	115
Otsego, co., N.Y., U.S.	C5	125
Otsego Lake, l., N.Y., U.S.	C6	125
Ōtsu, Japan	C3	31
Ottauquechee, stm., Vt., U.S.	D4	138
Ottawa, On., Can.	B9	89
Ottawa, Il., U.S.	B5	106
Ottawa, Ks., U.S.	D8	109
Ottawa, Oh., U.S.	A1	128
Ottawa, co., Ks., U.S.	C6	109
Ottawa, co., Mi., U.S.	F4	115
Ottawa, co., Oh., U.S.	A2	128
Ottawa, co., Ok., U.S.	A7	129
Ottawa, stm., Can.	I24	82
Ottawa, stm., Oh., U.S.	e6	128
Ottawa Hills, Oh., U.S.	e6	128
Ottenby, Swe.	H7	10
Otterbein, In., U.S.	D3	107
Otter Brook, stm., N.H., U.S.	E2	122
Otter Brook Lake, res., N.H., U.S.	E2	122
Otter Creek, stm., Ut., U.S.	E4	137
Otter Creek, stm., Vt., U.S.	C2	138
Otter Creek Reservoir, res., Ut., U.S.	E4	137
Otter Islands, is., S.C., U.S.	m11	133
Otter Tail, co., Mn., U.S.	D3	116
Otter Tail, stm., Mn., U.S.	D2	116
Otter Tail Lake, l., Mn., U.S.	D3	116
Otterville, On., Can.	E4	89
Ottumwa, Ia., U.S.	C5	108
Otway, Cape, c., Austl.	H3	62
Otwock, Pol.	C6	20
Ouachita, co., Ar., U.S.	D3	97
Ouachita, co., La., U.S.	B3	111
Ouachita, Lake, res., Ar., U.S.	C2	97
Ouachita Mountains, mts., U.S.	E9	92
Ouadda, C.A.R.	B4	54
Ouagadougou, Burkina	D4	50
Ouahigouya, Burkina	D4	50
Ouahran see Wahran, Alg.	C4	48
Oualâta, Maur.	C3	50
Ouallam, Niger	D5	50
Ouallene, Alg.	F5	48
Ouanda Djallé, C.A.R.	B4	54
Ouangolodougou, C. Iv.	E3	50
Ouarâne, reg., Maur.	B2	50
Ouarzazate, Mor.	D3	48
Oubangui (Ubangi), stm., Afr.	D3	54
Oudtshoorn, S. Afr.	E3	56
Oued Rhiou, Alg.	J7	16
Oued-Zem, Mor.	E2	14
Ouellé, C. Iv.	E4	50
Ouémé, stm., Benin	E5	50
Ouessant, Île d', i., Fr.	C4	16
Ouesso, Congo	C3	54
Ouezzane, Mor.	D3	48
Ouham, stm., Afr.	B3	54
Ouidah, Benin	E5	50
Oujda, Mor.	D4	48
Oulu, Fin.	D11	10
Oulujärvi, l., Fin.	D12	10
Oulujoki, stm., Fin.	D12	10
Oum-Chalouba, Chad	G9	48
Oumé, C. Iv.	E3	50
Ounianga Kébir, Chad	G9	48
Ouray, Co., U.S.	C3	99
Ouray, co., Co., U.S.	C3	99
Ouray, Mount, mtn., Co., U.S.	C4	99
Ourense, Spain	F3	16
Ouricuri, Braz.	C3	74
Ourinhos, Braz.	F2	74
Ouro Preto, Braz.	F3	74
Outagamie, co., Wi., U.S.	D5	142
Outardes Quatre, Réservoir, res., P.Q., Can.	h13	90
Outer Hebrides, is., Scot., U.K.	B3	12
Outer Island, i., Wi., U.S.	A3	142
Outer Santa Barbara Passage, strt., Ca., U.S.	F4	98
Outjo, Nmb.	C2	56
Outpost Mountain, mtn., Ak., U.S.	B9	95
Outremont, P.Q., Can.	p19	90
Ouvéa, i., N. Cal.	I9	62a
Ouyen, Austl.	H3	62
Ovalle, Chile	D2	69
Overbrook, Ks., U.S.	D8	109
Overgaard, Az., U.S.	C5	96
Overland, Mo., U.S.	f13	118
Overland Park, Ks., U.S.	m16	109
Overlea, Md., U.S.	B4	113
Overton, Nv., U.S.	G7	121
Overton, Tx., U.S.	C5	136
Overton, co., Tn., U.S.	C8	135
Ovett, Ms., U.S.	D4	117
Ovid, Mi., U.S.	E6	115
Oviedo, Spain	F4	16
Ovoot, Mong.	B10	28
Ovruch, Ukr.	D10	20
Owando, Congo	D3	54
Owasco Lake, l., N.Y., U.S.	C4	125
Owasso, Ok., U.S.	A6	129
Owatonna, Mn., U.S.	F5	116
Owego, N.Y., U.S.	C4	125
Owen, Wi., U.S.	D3	142
Owen, co., In., U.S.	F4	107
Owen, co., Ky., U.S.	B5	110
Owen, Lake, l., Wi., U.S.	B2	142
Owen, Mount, mtn., Co., U.S.	C3	99
Owendo, Gabon	C1	54
Owens, stm., Ca., U.S.	D4	98
Owensboro, Ky., U.S.	C2	110
Owens Cross Roads, Al., U.S.	A3	94
Owens Lake, l., Ca., U.S.	D5	98
Owen Sound, On., Can.	C4	89
Owen Sound, b., On., Can.	C4	89
Owen Stanley Range, mts., Pap. N. Gui.	H12	32
Owensville, In., U.S.	H2	107
Owensville, Mo., U.S.	C6	118
Owensville, Oh., U.S.	C1	128
Owenton, Ky., U.S.	B5	110
Owerri, Nig.	E6	50
Owings Mills, Md., U.S.	B4	113
Owingsville, Ky., U.S.	B6	110
Owl Creek, stm., Wy., U.S.	C4	143
Owl Creek Mountains, mts., Wy., U.S.	C4	143
Owo, Nig.	E6	50
Owosso, Mi., U.S.	E6	115
Owsley, co., Ky., U.S.	C6	110
Owyhee, Nv., U.S.	B5	121
Owyhee, co., Id., U.S.	G2	105
Owyhee, stm., U.S.	E9	130
Owyhee, Lake, res., Or., U.S.	D9	130
Owyhee Dam, Or., U.S.	D9	130
Owyhee Mountains, mts., U.S.	G2	105
Oxbow Dam, U.S.	E2	105
Oxelösund, Swe.	G7	10
Oxford, N.S., Can.	D6	87
Oxford, Eng., U.K.	E6	12
Oxford, Al., U.S.	B4	94
Oxford, Ct., U.S.	D3	100
Oxford, Ga., U.S.	C3	103
Oxford, Ia., U.S.	C6	108
Oxford, In., U.S.	C3	107
Oxford, Ks., U.S.	E6	109
Oxford, Ma., U.S.	B4	114
Oxford, Md., U.S.	C5	113
Oxford, Me., U.S.	D2	112
Oxford, Mi., U.S.	F7	115
Oxford, Ms., U.S.	A4	117
Oxford, N.C., U.S.	A4	126
Oxford, Ne., U.S.	D6	120
Oxford, N.Y., U.S.	C5	125
Oxford, Oh., U.S.	C1	128
Oxford, Pa., U.S.	G10	131
Oxford, co., Me., U.S.	D2	112
Oxford Lake, l., Mb., Can.	B4	86
Oxford Peak, mtn., Id., U.S.	G6	105
Oxnard, Ca., U.S.	E4	98
Oxon Hill, Md., U.S.	f9	113
Oxus see Amu Darya, stm., Asia	B8	42
Oyama, B.C., Can.	D8	85
Oyapok (Oiapoque), stm., S.A.	C9	70
Oyem, Gabon	C2	54
Oyen, Ab., Can.	D5	84
Oyo, Nig.	E5	50
Oyster Bay, N.Y., U.S.	E7	125
Oyster Keys, is., Fl., U.S.	G6	102
Ozamis, Phil.	E8	34
Ozark, Al., U.S.	D4	94
Ozark, Ar., U.S.	B2	97
Ozark, Mo., U.S.	D4	118
Ozark, co., Mo., U.S.	E5	118
Ozark Plateau, plat., U.S.	D9	92
Ozark Reservoir, res., Ar., U.S.	B1	97
Ozarks, Lake of the, res., Mo., U.S.	C5	118
Ozaukee, co., Wi., U.S.	E6	142
Ózd, Hung.	E6	20
Ozernovskij, Russia	D17	26
Ozërnyj, Russia	D11	22
Ozette Lake, l., Wa., U.S.	A1	140
Ozieri, Italy	D2	18
Ozinki, Russia	D8	22
Ozona, Fl., U.S.	o10	102
Ozona, Tx., U.S.	D2	136
Ozurgeti, Geor.	B10	44
P		
Paarl, S. Afr.	E2	56
Paauilo, Hi., U.S.	C6	104
Pabianice, Pol.	D5	20
Pābna, Bngl.	E5	40
Pacajus, Braz.	B4	74
Pacasmayo, Peru	E4	70
Pace, Fl., U.S.	u14	102
Pachacamac, hist., Peru	A2	72
Pachaug Pond, l., Ct., U.S.	C8	100
Pachino, Italy	F5	18
Pachuca de Soto, Mex.	C5	78
Pacific, Mo., U.S.	C7	118
Pacific, Wa., U.S.	f11	140
Pacific, co., Wa., U.S.	C2	140
Pacifica, Ca., U.S.	h8	98
Pacific-Antarctic Ridge	O22	64
Pacific Beach, Wa., U.S.	B1	140
Pacific City, Or., U.S.	B3	130
Pacific Creek, stm., Wy., U.S.	D3	143
Pacific Grove, Ca., U.S.	D3	98
Pacific Ocean	E20	64
Pacific Palisades, Hi., U.S.	g10	104
Pacific Ranges, mts., B.C., Can.	D4	85
Pacific Rim National Park, B.C., Can.	E5	85
Pack Monadnock Mountain, mtn., N.H., U.S.	E3	122
Packwood, Wa., U.S.	C4	140
Pacolet, S.C., U.S.	B4	133
Pacolet, stm., S.C., U.S.	A4	133
Pacolet Mills, S.C., U.S.	B4	133
Pactola Reservoir, res., S.D., U.S.	C2	134
Padang, Indon.	D2	36
Padangpanjang, Indon.	D2	36
Padangsidempuan, Indon.	C1	36
Paddock Lake, Wi., U.S.	n11	142
Paden City, W.V., U.S.	B4	141
Paderborn, Ger.	E11	12
Padma see Ganges, stm., Asia	D5	40
Pádova, Italy	B3	18
Padrauna, India	D4	40
Padre Island, i., Tx., U.S.	F4	136
Padre Island National Seashore, Tx., U.S.	F4	136
Padua see Pádova, Italy	B3	18
Paducah, Ky., U.S.	e9	110
Paducah, Tx., U.S.	B2	136
Paektu, Mount, mtn., Asia	C13	28
Paektu-san see Paektu, Mount, mtn., Asia	C13	28
Paestum, hist., Italy	D5	18
Pafúri, Moz.	C5	56
Pag, Otok, i., Cro.	B5	18
Pagadian, Phil.	E8	34
Pagai Selatan, Pulau, i., Indon.	D2	36
Pagai Utara, Pulau, i., Indon.	D2	36
Pagalu see Annobón, i., Eq. Gui.	C1	52
Pagan, i., N. Mar. Is.	C12	32
Pagasitikós Kólpos, b., Grc.	E9	18
Page, Az., U.S.	A4	96
Page, W.V., U.S.	C3	141
Page, co., Ia., U.S.	D2	108
Page, co., Va., U.S.	B4	139
Pageland, S.C., U.S.	B7	133
Pagoda Peak, mtn., Co., U.S.	A3	99
Pago Pago, Am. Sam.	F12	58
Pagosa Springs, Co., U.S.	D3	99
Paguate, N.M., U.S.	B2	124
Pahala, Hi., U.S.	D6	104
Pahang, stm., Malay.	C2	36
Pahoa, Hi., U.S.	D7	104
Pahokee, Fl., U.S.	F6	102
Pahrump, Nv., U.S.	G6	121
Pahute Mesa, mtn., Nv., U.S.	F5	121
Paia, Hi., U.S.	C5	104
Paide, Est.	G11	10
Päijänne, l., Fin.	F11	10
Pailolo Channel, strt., Hi., U.S.	B5	104
Painan, Indon.	D2	36
Paincourtville, La., U.S.	k9	111
Painesville, Oh., U.S.	A4	128
Paint, stm., Mi., U.S.	B2	115
Paint Creek, stm., Oh., U.S.	C2	128
Paint Creek, stm., W.V., U.S.	m13	141
Paint Creek, North Fork, stm., Oh., U.S.	C2	128
Paint Creek Lake, res., Oh., U.S.	C2	128
Painted Desert, des., Az., U.S.	B4	96
Painted Post, N.Y., U.S.	C3	125
Painted Rock Reservoir, res., Az., U.S.	D3	96
Paintsville, Ky., U.S.	C7	110
Paisley, On., Can.	C3	89
Pajala, Swe.	C10	10
Pakaraima Mountains, mts., S.A.	E7	80
Pakistan, ctry., Asia	E9	42
Pakistan, East see Bangladesh, ctry., Asia	B2	34
Pakokku, Myan.	B3	34
Pakowki Lake, l., Ab., Can.	E5	84
Pak Phanang, Thai.	E4	34
Paks, Hung.	F5	20
Pakxé, Laos	C5	34
Pala, Chad	E7	50
Palacios, Tx., U.S.	E4	136
Palana, Russia	D17	26
Palangkaraya, Indon.	D4	36
Palani, India	G3	40
Pālanpur, India	E2	40
Palaoa Point, c., Hi., U.S.	C4	104
Palapye, Bots.	C4	56
Palatine, Il., U.S.	A5	106
Palatka, Fl., U.S.	C5	102
Palau, ctry., Oc.	F10	32
Palau Islands, is., Palau	E9	32
Palaw, Myan.	D3	34
Palawan, i., Phil.	E7	34
Palawan Passage, strt., Phil.	E7	34
Pālayankottai, India	H3	40
Paldiski, Est.	G11	10
Palembang, Indon.	D2	36
Palencia, Spain	F4	16
Palenque, hist., Mex.	D6	78
Palermo, Italy	E4	18
Palestine, Ar., U.S.	C5	97
Palestine, Il., U.S.	D6	106
Palestine, Tx., U.S.	D5	136
Palestine, hist. reg., Asia	G6	44
Palestine, Lake, res., Tx., U.S.	C5	136
Paletwa, Myan.	B2	34
Pālghāt, India	G3	40
Pāli, India	D2	40
Palikea, mtn., Hi., U.S.	g9	104
Palisade, Co., U.S.	B2	99
Palisades Park, N.J., U.S.	h8	123
Palisades Reservoir, res., U.S.	F7	105
Pālitāna, India	E2	40
Palk Strait, strt., Asia	H3	40
Palliser, Cape, c., N.Z.	p14	63c
Palma, Moz.	A7	56
Palma del Río, Spain	I4	16
Palma de Mallorca, Spain	H8	16
Palmares, Braz.	C4	74
Palmas, Braz.	F10	70
Palma Soriano, Cuba	A4	80
Palm Bay, Fl., U.S.	D6	102
Palm Beach, Fl., U.S.	F6	102
Palm Beach, co., Fl., U.S.	F6	102
Palmdale, Ca., U.S.	E4	98
Palmeira das Missões, Braz.	D7	72
Palmeira dos Índios, Braz.	C4	74
Palmer, Ak., U.S.	C10	95
Palmer, Ma., U.S.	B3	114
Palmer, Mi., U.S.	B3	115
Palmer, Ms., U.S.	D4	117
Palmer, Ne., U.S.	C7	120
Palmer, Tn., U.S.	D8	135
Palmer, Tx., U.S.	n10	136
Palmer Lake, Co., U.S.	B6	99
Palmer Land, reg., Ant.	D34	67
Palmerston, On., Can.	D4	89
Palmerston, atoll, Cook Is.	F13	58
Palmerston North, N.Z.	p14	63c
Palmerton, Pa., U.S.	E10	131
Palmetto, Fl., U.S.	E4	102
Palmetto, Ga., U.S.	C2	103
Palm Harbor, Fl., U.S.	o10	102
Palmi, Italy	E5	18
Palmira, Col.	C4	70
Palms, Isle of, i., S.C., U.S.	F8	133
Palm Springs, Ca., U.S.	F5	98
Palmyra see Tudmur, Syria	E8	44
Palmyra, In., U.S.	H5	107
Palmyra, Mo., U.S.	B6	118
Palmyra, N.J., U.S.	C2	123
Palmyra, N.Y., U.S.	B3	125
Palmyra, Pa., U.S.	F8	131
Palmyra, Wi., U.S.	F5	142
Palmyra, hist., Syria	E8	44
Palo Alto, Ca., U.S.	D2	98
Palo Alto, co., Ia., U.S.	A3	108
Paloich, Sudan	H11	48
Palomar Mountain, mtn., Ca., U.S.	F5	98
Palomas Mountains, mts., Az., U.S.	D2	96
Palo Pinto, co., Tx., U.S.	C3	136
Palopo, Indon.	D6	36
Palo Santo, Arg.	D6	72
Palos Park, Il., U.S.	k9	106
Palos Verdes Estates, Ca., U.S.	n12	98
Palourde, Lake, l., La., U.S.	k9	111
Palouse, Wa., U.S.	C8	140
Palouse, stm., Wa., U.S.	C7	140
Palu, Indon.	D5	36
Palu, Tur.	C8	44
Pamekasan, Indon.	E4	36
Pamiers, Fr.	F7	16
Pamir, mts., Asia	B2	40
Pamlico, co., N.C., U.S.	B6	126
Pamlico, stm., N.C., U.S.	B6	126
Pamlico Sound, strt., N.C., U.S.	B6	126
Pampa, Tx., U.S.	B2	136
Pampa, reg., Arg.	F5	72
Pampa del Infierno, Arg.	D5	72
Pampas, Peru	A3	72
Pamplico, S.C., U.S.	D8	133
Pamplona, Col.	B5	70
Pamplona, Spain	F6	16
Pamunkey, stm., Va., U.S.	C5	139
Pana, Il., U.S.	D4	106
Panaca, Nv., U.S.	F7	121
Panache, Lake, l., On., Can.	A3	89
Panaji, India	F2	40
Panamá, Pan.	D4	80
Panama, Ok., U.S.	B7	129
Panama, ctry., N.A.	I11	75
Panamá, Bahía de, b., Pan.	D4	80
Panamá, Canal de, Pan.	D4	80
Panamá, Golfo de, b., Pan.	D4	80
Panama, Gulf of see Panamá, Golfo de, b., Pan.	D4	80
Panamá, Istmo de, Pan.	D4	80
Panama Basin	H30	64
Panama Canal see Panamá, Canal de, Pan.	D4	80
Panama City see Panamá, Pan.	D4	80
Panama City, Fl., U.S.	u16	102
Panama City Beach, Fl., U.S.	u16	102
Panamint Range, mts., Ca., U.S.	D5	98
Panay, i., Phil.	D8	34
Pancake Range, mts., Nv., U.S.	E6	121
Pančevo, Yugo.	B8	18
Pandharpur, India	F3	40
Pandora, Oh., U.S.	B2	128
Panfilov, Kaz.	E9	26
Pangala, Congo	D2	54
Pangani, Tan.	E7	54
Pangburn, Ar., U.S.	B4	97
Pangi, D.R.C.	D5	54
Pangkajene, Indon.	D5	36
Pangkalanbuun, Indon.	D4	36
Pangkalpinang, Indon.	D3	36
Pango Aluquem, Ang.	E2	54
Panguitch, Ut., U.S.	F3	137
Pangutaran Group, is., Phil.	E7	34
Panhandle, Tx., U.S.	B2	136
Paniau, mtn., Hi., U.S.	B1	104
Panié, Mont, mtn., N. Cal.	I8	62a
Pānīpat, India	D3	40
Panj see Amu Darya, stm., Asia	B8	42
Panjang, Indon.	E3	36
Panjgūr, Pak.	E8	42
Pankshin, Nig.	E6	50
Panna, India	E4	40
Pannawonica, Austl.	E2	60
Panola, co., Ms., U.S.	A3	117
Panola, co., Tx., U.S.	C5	136
Panora, Ia., U.S.	C3	108
Pantar, Pulau, i., Indon.	E6	36
Pantelleria, Isola di, i., Italy	F3	18
Pánuco, Mex.	C5	78
Pánuco, stm., Mex.	C5	78
Panxian, China	F8	28
Panyam, Nig.	E6	50
Panyu, China	B6	34
Paola, Italy	E5	18
Paola, Ks., U.S.	D9	109
Paoli, In., U.S.	G5	107
Paoli, Pa., U.S.	o20	131
Paonia, Co., U.S.	C3	99
Pápa, Hung.	F4	20
Papagayo, Golfo de, b., C.R.	C2	80
Papago Indian Reservation, Az., U.S.	E3	96
Papaikou, Hi., U.S.	D6	104
Papantla de Olarte, Mex.	C5	78
Papawai Point, c., Hi., U.S.	C5	104
Papeete, Fr. Poly.	F15	58
Papenburg, Ger.	D10	12
Paphos see Néa Páfos, Cyp.	E5	44
Papigochic, stm., Mex.	B3	78
Papillion, Ne., U.S.	C9	120
Papineauville, P.Q., Can.	D2	90
Paposo, Chile	C3	72
Papua, Gulf of, b., Pap. N. Gui.	H11	32
Papua New Guinea, ctry., Oc.	H11	32
Papun, Myan.	C3	34
Pará see Belém, Braz.	B2	74
Pará, state, Braz.	E9	70
Parabel', Russia	D10	26
Paraburdoo, Austl.	E2	60
Paracatu, Braz.	E2	74
Paracel Islands (Xisha Qundao), is., China	C6	34
Parachute, Co., U.S.	B2	99
Paraćin, Yugo.	C8	18
Paracuru, Braz.	B4	74
Paradis, La., U.S.	k11	111
Paradise, Ca., U.S.	C3	98
Paradise, Nv., U.S.	G6	121
Paradise, stm., Nf., Can.	B3	88
Paradise Hills, N.M., U.S.	B3	124
Paradise Valley, Az., U.S.	k9	96
Paradise Valley, Nv., U.S.	B4	121
Pāradwīp, India	E5	40
Paragould, Ar., U.S.	A5	97
Paraguai (Paraguay), stm., S.A.	B6	72
Paraguaná, Península de, pen., Ven.	C6	80
Paraguay, ctry., S.A.	C6	72
Paraguay (Paraguai), stm., S.A.	C6	72
Paraíba, state, Braz.	C4	74
Paraíba do Sul, stm., Braz.	F3	74
Parakou, Benin	E5	50
Paramaribo, Sur.	B8	70
Paramirim, Braz.	F11	70
Paramount, Md., U.S.	A2	113
Paramus, N.J., U.S.	h8	123
Paramušir, ostrov, i., Russia	D17	26
Paraná, Arg.	E5	72
Paranã, Braz.	F10	70
Paraná, state, Braz.	C7	72
Paraná, stm., Braz.	F5	68
Paraná, stm., S.A.	E6	72

Name — Map Ref. — Page

Paranaguá, Braz. D8 72
Paranaíba, Braz. E2 74
Paranapanema, stm., Braz. C7 72
Paranavaí, Braz. C7 72
Parang, Phil. E8 34
Parangaba, Braz. B4 74
Paranhos, Braz. C6 72
Paray-le-Monial, Fr. D9 16
Pārbati, stm., India D3 40
Parbhani, India F3 40
Parchment, Mi., U.S. F5 115
Pardeeville, Wi., U.S. E4 142
Pardo, stm., Braz. F2 74
Pardubice, Czech Rep. E3 20
Parecis, Braz. A6 72
Parecis, Chapada dos, mts., Braz. A6 72
Paren', Russia C18 26
Parepare, Indon. D5 36
Paria, stm., U.S. A4 96
Paria, Gulf of, b. C7 80
Pariaman, Indon. D2 36
Parigi, Indon. D6 36
Parika, Guy. B8 70
Paris, On., Can. D4 89
Paris, Fr. C8 16
Paris, Ar., U.S. B2 97
Paris, Il., U.S. D6 106
Paris, Ky., U.S. B5 110
Paris, Mo., U.S. B5 118
Paris, Tn., U.S. A3 135
Paris, Tx., U.S. C5 136
Paris Peak, mtn., Id., U.S. G7 105
Parita, Bahía de, b., Pan. D3 80
Park, co., Co., U.S. B5 99
Park, co., Mt., U.S. E6 119
Park, co., Wy., U.S. B3 143
Park, stm., N.D., U.S. A8 127
Park City, Ks., U.S. g12 109
Park City, Ut., U.S. C4 137
Parkdale, P.E., Can. C6 87
Parke, co., In., U.S. E3 107
Parker, Az., U.S. C1 96
Parker, Co., U.S. B6 99
Parker, Fl., U.S. u16 102
Parker, S.D., U.S. D8 134
Parker, co., Tx., U.S. C4 136
Parker City, In., U.S. D7 107
Parker Dam, U.S. C1 96
Parkersburg, Ia., U.S. B5 108
Parkersburg, W.V., U.S. B3 141
Parkers Prairie, Mn., U.S. D3 116
Parkes, Austl. G4 62
Parkesburg, Pa., U.S. G10 131
Park Falls, Wi., U.S. C3 142
Park Forest, Il., U.S. B6 106
Park Hall, Md., U.S. D5 113
Parkhill, On., Can. D3 89
Park Hills, Ky., U.S. h13 110
Parkin, Ar., U.S. B5 97
Parkland, Wa., U.S. f11 140
Park Layne, Oh., U.S. C1 128
Park Range, mts., Co., U.S. A4 99
Park Rapids, Mn., U.S. D3 116
Park Ridge, Il., U.S. B6 106
Park Ridge, N.J., U.S. g8 123
Park River, N.D., U.S. A8 127
Parkrose, Or., U.S. B4 130
Parksley, Va., U.S. C7 139
Parkston, S.D., U.S. D8 134
Parksville, B.C., Can. E5 85
Parkville, Md., U.S. B4 113
Parkville, Mo., U.S. B3 118
Parkwater, Wa., U.S. g14 140
Parkwood, N.C., U.S. B4 126
Parlākimidi, India F4 40
Parle, Lac qui, l., Mn., U.S. E3 116
Parlier, Ca., U.S. D4 98
Parma, Italy B3 18
Parma, Id., U.S. F2 105
Parma, Mi., U.S. F6 115
Parma, Mo., U.S. E8 118
Parma, Oh., U.S. A4 128
Parmachenee Lake, l., Me., U.S. C2 112
Parma Heights, Oh., U.S. h9 128
Parmer, co., Tx., U.S. B1 136
Parnaguá, Braz. F11 70
Parnaíba, Braz. B3 74
Parnaíba, stm., Braz. B3 74
Parnassós, mtn., Grc. E9 18
Pärnu, Est. G11 10
Paro, Bhu. D5 40
Paromaj, Russia D16 26
Parowan, Ut., U.S. F3 137
Par Pond, res., S.C., U.S. D5 133
Parral, Chile F3 72
Parramatta, Austl. G5 62
Parramore Island, i., Va., U.S. C7 139
Parras de la Fuente, Mex. B4 78
Parrish, Al., U.S. B2 94
Parrsboro, N.S., Can. D5 87
Parry, Mount, mtn., B.C., Can. C3 85
Parry Sound, On., Can. B4 89
Parshall, N.D., U.S. B3 127
Parsons, Ks., U.S. E8 109
Parsons, Tn., U.S. B3 135
Parsons, W.V., U.S. B5 141
Parsonsburg, Md., U.S. D7 113
Parthenay, Fr. D6 16
Partille, Swe. H5 10
Partizansk, Russia B2 31
Partridge Point, c., Nf., Can. C3 88
Paru, stm., Braz. D9 70
Paru de Oeste, stm., Braz. C8 70
Pārvatīpuram, India F4 40
Paryang, China C4 40
Parys, S. Afr. D4 56
Pasadena, Nf., Can. D3 88
Pasadena, Ca., U.S. E4 98
Pasadena, Md., U.S. B4 113
Pasadena, Tx., U.S. r14 136
Pascagoula, Ms., U.S. E5 117
Pascagoula, stm., Ms., U.S. E5 117
Pascagoula Bay, b., Ms., U.S. f8 117
Paşcani, Rom. F9 20
Pasco, Wa., U.S. C6 140
Pasco, co., Fl., U.S. D4 102
Pascoag, R.I., U.S. B2 132
Pascoag Reservoir, res., R.I., U.S. B2 132
Pascua, Isla de (Easter Island), i., Chile K28 64
Pasinler, Tur. B9 44
Pasir Mas, Malay. B2 36
Pasni, Pak. E8 42
Paso de los Libres, Arg. D6 72
Paso de los Toros, Ur. E6 72
Paso Robles, Ca., U.S. E3 98
Pasque Island, i., Ma., U.S. D6 114
Pasquotank, co., N.C., U.S. A6 126
Passaic, N.J., U.S. B4 123
Passaic, co., N.J., U.S. A4 123
Passaic, stm., N.J., U.S. h8 123
Passamaquoddy Bay, b., Me., U.S. C6 112
Passau, Ger. F13 12
Pass Christian, Ms., U.S. E4 117
Passero, Capo, c., Italy F5 18
Passo Fundo, Braz. D7 72
Passos, Braz. F2 74
Passumpsic, stm., Vt., U.S. C4 138
Pastavy, Bela. B9 20
Pastaza, stm., S.A. D4 70
Pasto, Col. C4 70
Pastora Peak, mtn., Az., U.S. A6 96
Pasuruan, Indon. E4 36
Pasvalys, Lith. H11 10
Patadkal, hist., India F3 40
Patagonia, Az., U.S. F5 96
Patagonia, reg., Arg. F3 69
Pātan, India E2 40
Patapsco, stm., Md., U.S. B4 113
Pataskala, Oh., U.S. C3 128
Patchet Brook Reservoir, res., R.I., U.S. E6 132
Patchogue, N.Y., U.S. n15 125
Pategi, Nig. E6 50
Pate Island, i., Kenya D8 54
Paterna, Spain H6 16
Paternò, Italy F5 18
Paterson, N.J., U.S. B4 123
Pathānkot, India C3 40
Pathein, Myan. C2 34
Pathfinder Reservoir, res., Wy., U.S. D6 143
Patiāla, India C3 40
Patience Island, i., R.I., U.S. D5 132
Patman, Lake, res., Tx., U.S. C5 136
Patna, India D5 40
Patnos, Tur. C10 44
Pato Branco, Braz. D7 72
Patoka, In., U.S. H2 107
Patoka, stm., In., U.S. H2 107
Patoka Lake, res., In., U.S. H4 107
Patos, Braz. C4 74
Patos, Lagoa dos, b., Braz. E7 72
Patos de Minas, Braz. E2 74
Patquía, Arg. D4 72
Pátrai, Grc. E8 18
Patraïkós Kólpos, b., Grc. E8 18
Patrick, co., Va., U.S. D2 139
Patrick Air Force Base, mil., Fl., U.S. D6 102
Patrocínio, Braz. E2 74
Pattani, Thai. E4 34
Patten, Me., U.S. C4 112
Patterson, Ga., U.S. E4 103
Patterson, La., U.S. E4 111
Patterson Creek, stm., W.V., U.S. B5 141
Patton, Pa., U.S. E4 131
Patuākhāli, Bngl. E6 40
Patuca, stm., Hond. B3 80
Patuxent, stm., Md., U.S. D4 113
Patuxent Naval Air Test Center, mil., Md., U.S. D5 113
Pátzcuaro, Mex. D4 78
Pau, Fr. F6 16
Paul, Id., U.S. G5 105
Paulding, Oh., U.S. A1 128
Paulding, co., Ga., U.S. C2 103
Paulding, co., Oh., U.S. A1 128
Paulina, La., U.S. h10 111
Paulina Mountains, mts., Or., U.S. D5 130
Paulina Peak, mtn., Or., U.S. E5 130
Paulins Kill, stm., N.J., U.S. A3 123
Paulistana, Braz. E11 70
Paullina, Ia., U.S. B2 108
Paulo Afonso, Braz. C4 74
Paulsboro, N.J., U.S. D2 123
Paul Stream, stm., Vt., U.S. B5 138
Pauls Valley, Ok., U.S. C4 129
Paungde, Myan. C3 34
Pāveh, Iran E12 44
Pavia, Italy B2 18
Pavilion Key, i., Fl., U.S. G5 102
Pāvilosta, Lat. H9 10
Pavlodar, Kaz. D9 26
Pavlof Volcano, vol., Ak., U.S. D7 95
Pavlohrad, Ukr. E13 20
Pavlovo, Russia C7 22
Pavo, Ga., U.S. F3 103
Pawcatuck, Ct., U.S. D8 100
Pawcatuck, stm., R.I., U.S. G1 132
Paw Creek, N.C., U.S. B2 126
Pawhuska, Ok., U.S. A5 129
Pawling, N.Y., U.S. D7 125
Pawnee, Il., U.S. D4 106
Pawnee, Ok., U.S. A5 129
Pawnee, co., Ks., U.S. D4 109
Pawnee, co., Ne., U.S. D9 120
Pawnee, co., Ok., U.S. A5 129
Pawnee, stm., Ks., U.S. D3 109
Pawnee City, Ne., U.S. D9 120
Pawpaw, Il., U.S. B5 106
Paw Paw, Mi., U.S. F5 115
Paw Paw, stm., Mi., U.S. F4 115
Pawpaw Creek, stm., W.V., U.S. h10 141
Pawtuckaway Pond, l., N.H., U.S. D4 122
Pawtucket, R.I., U.S. C4 132
Pawtuxet, stm., R.I., U.S. C4 132
Paxton, Il., U.S. C5 106
Paxton, Ma., U.S. B4 114
Payakumbuh, Indon. D2 36
Payeti, Indon. E6 36
Payette, Id., U.S. E2 105
Payette, co., Id., U.S. E2 105
Payette, North Fork, stm., Id., U.S. E2 105
Payette, South Fork, stm., Id., U.S. E3 105
Payette Lake, res., Id., U.S. E3 105
Payne, Oh., U.S. A1 128
Payne, co., Ok., U.S. A4 129
Payne, Lac, l., Can. G25 82
Paynes Find, Austl. F2 60
Paynesville, Mn., U.S. E4 116
Paysandú, Ur. E6 72
Payson, Az., U.S. C4 96
Payson, Il., U.S. D2 106
Payson, Ut., U.S. C4 137
Pazar, Tur. B9 44
Pazarcık, Tur. D7 44
Pazardžik, Bul. C10 18
Paz de Río, Col. D5 80
Pea, stm., Al., U.S. D3 94
Peabody, Ks., U.S. D6 109
Peabody, Ma., U.S. A6 114
Peabody, stm., N.H., U.S. B4 122
Peace, stm., Can. D8 75
Peace, stm., Fl., U.S. E5 102
Peace Dale, R.I., U.S. F3 132
Peace River, Ab., Can. A2 84
Peach, co., Ga., U.S. D3 103
Peacham Pond, res., Vt., U.S. C4 138
Peach Point, c., Ma., U.S. f12 114
Peach Springs, Az., U.S. B2 96
Peak Hill, Austl. F2 60
Peaks Island, i., Me., U.S. g7 112
Peale, Mount, mtn., Ut., U.S. E6 137
Pea Patch Island, i., De., U.S. B3 101
Pea Ridge, Ar., U.S. A1 97
Pea Ridge National Military Park, Ar., U.S. A1 97
Pearisburg, Va., U.S. C2 139
Pearl, Ms., U.S. C3 117
Pearl, stm., U.S. D3 117
Pearland, Tx., U.S. r14 136
Pearl and Hermes Reef, rf., Hi., U.S. k12 104
Pearl City, Hi., U.S. B4 104
Pearl Harbor, b., Hi., U.S. B3 104
Pearl Harbor Naval Station, mil., Hi., U.S. g10 104
Pearlington, Ms., U.S. E4 117
Pearl River, La., U.S. D6 111
Pearl River, N.Y., U.S. g12 125
Pearl River, co., Ms., U.S. E4 117
Pearsall, Tx., U.S. E3 136
Pearsoll Peak, mtn., Or., U.S. E3 130
Pearson, Ga., U.S. E4 103
Peary Land, reg., Grnld. B32 82
Pease, stm., Tx., U.S. B3 136
Pebane, Moz. B6 56
Peć, Yugo. C8 18
Pecatonica, Il., U.S. A4 106
Pecatonica, stm., U.S. A4 106
Pecatonica, East Branch, stm., Wi., U.S. F4 142
Pečenga, Russia C5 26
Pechora see Pečora, Russia C7 26
Pechora see Pečora, stm., Russia C7 26
Pechora Bay see Pečorskaja guba, b., Russia A9 22
Peckerwood Lake, res., Ar., U.S. C4 97
Pečora, Russia C7 26
Pečora, stm., Russia C7 26
Pečorskaja guba, b., Russia A9 22
Pečorskoe more, Russia C7 26
Pecos, N.M., U.S. B4 124
Pecos, Tx., U.S. D1 136
Pecos, co., Tx., U.S. D1 136
Pecos, stm., U.S. E7 92
Pecos National Monument, N.M., U.S. B4 124
Pécs, Hung. F5 20
Peculiar, Mo., U.S. C3 118
Peddocks Island, i., Ma., U.S. g12 114
Pedernales, Ven. D7 80
Pedra Azul, Braz. E3 74
Pedreiras, Braz. B3 74
Pedro Afonso, Braz. E10 70
Pedro II, Braz. B3 74
Pedro Juan Caballero, Para. C6 72
Peebles, Oh., U.S. D2 128
Peekskill, N.Y., U.S. D7 125
Peel, stm., Can. E13 82
Pegasus Bay, b., N.Z. p13 63c
Pegram, Tn., U.S. A4 135
Pehuajó, Arg. F5 72
Peikang, Tai. E5 30
Peipus, Lake, l., Eur. G12 10
Peixian, China C4 30
Pekalongan, Indon. E3 36
Pekanbaru, Indon. C2 36
Pekin, Il., U.S. C4 106
Pekin, In., U.S. G5 107
Peking see Beijing, China D11 28
Pelagie, Isole, is., Italy G4 18
Pelahatchie, Ms., U.S. C4 117
Pelee Island, i., On., Can. F2 89
Peleng, Pulau, i., Indon. D6 36
Pelham, On., Can. D5 89
Pelham, Al., U.S. B3 94
Pelham, Ga., U.S. E2 103
Pelham, N.H., U.S. E4 122
Pelham Manor, N.Y., U.S. h13 125
Pelican Bay, b., Mb., Can. C1 86
Pelican Lake, l., Mb., Can. C1 86
Pelican Lake, l., Mn., U.S. E5 116
Pelican Lake, l., Mn., U.S. B6 116
Pelican Lake, l., Mn., U.S. D3 116
Pelican Lake, l., Mn., U.S. D4 116
Pelican Lake, l., Wi., U.S. C4 142
Pelican Mountain, mtn., Ab., Can. B4 84
Pelican Rapids, Mn., U.S. D2 116
Pella, Ia., U.S. C5 108
Pell City, Al., U.S. B3 94
Pell Lake, Wi., U.S. n11 142
Pello, Fin. C11 10
Peloponnesus see Pelopónnisos, pen., Grc. F8 18
Pelopónnisos, pen., Grc. F8 18
Pelotas, Braz. E7 72
Pelton, Lake, l., La., U.S. E5 111
Pemadumcook Lake, l., Me., U.S. C3 112
Pematangsiantar, Indon. C1 36
Pemba, Moz. A7 56
Pemba, i., Tan. E7 54
Pemberton, Austl. G2 60
Pemberville, Oh., U.S. A2 128
Pembina, N.D., U.S. A8 127
Pembina, co., N.D., U.S. A8 127
Pembina, stm., Ab., Can. C3 84
Pembroke, On., Can. B7 89
Pembroke, Wales, U.K. E4 12
Pembroke, Ga., U.S. D5 103
Pembroke, Ky., U.S. D2 110
Pembroke, Ma., U.S. B6 114
Pembroke, N.C., U.S. C3 126
Pembroke, Va., U.S. C2 139
Pembroke Pines, Fl., U.S. r13 102
Pemigewasset, stm., N.H., U.S. C3 122
Pemiscot, co., Mo., U.S. E8 118
Penang see George Town, Malay. B2 36
Peñaranda de Bracamonte, Spain G4 16
Pen Argyl, Pa., U.S. E11 131
Peñarroya-Pueblonuevo, Spain H4 16
Penas, Golfo de, b., Chile G1 69
Penasco, N.M., U.S. A4 124
Peñasco, Rio, stm., N.M., U.S. E4 124
Penbrook, Pa., U.S. F8 131
Pendembu, S.L. E2 50
Pendembu, S.L. E2 50
Pender, Ne., U.S. B9 120
Pender, co., N.C., U.S. C4 126
Pendleton, In., U.S. E6 107
Pendleton, Or., U.S. B8 130
Pendleton, S.C., U.S. B2 133
Pendleton, co., Ky., U.S. B5 110
Pendleton, co., W.V., U.S. C5 141
Pend Oreille, co., Wa., U.S. A8 140
Pend Oreille, Lake, l., Id., U.S. A2 105
Pend Oreille, Mount, mtn., Id., U.S. A2 105
Penedo, Braz. D4 74
Penetanguishene, On., Can. C5 89
Penglai, China D12 28
Pengshui, China F9 28
Pengxian, China C1 30
Penhold, Ab., Can. C4 84
Peniche, Port. H2 16
Penida, Nusa, i., Indon. E5 36
Pennant Point, c., N.S., Can. E6 87
Pennask Mountain, mtn., B.C., Can. E7 85
Pennell, Mount, mtn., Ut., U.S. F5 137
Penneru, stm., India G3 40
Penn Hills, Pa., U.S. k14 131
Pennington, co., Mn., U.S. B2 116
Pennington, co., S.D., U.S. D2 134
Pennington Gap, Va., U.S. f8 139
Pennsauken, N.J., U.S. D2 123
Pennsboro, W.V., U.S. B4 141
Pennsburg, Pa., U.S. F11 131
Penns Grove, N.J., U.S. D2 123
Pennsville, N.J., U.S. D1 123
Pennsylvania, state, U.S. E7 131
Pennville, In., U.S. D7 107
Penn Yan, N.Y., U.S. C3 125
Penobscot, co., Me., U.S. C4 112
Penobscot, stm., Me., U.S. C4 112
Penobscot Bay, b., Me., U.S. D3 112
Penobscot Lake, l., Me., U.S. C2 112
Penong, Austl. G5 60
Penonomé, Pan. D3 80
Penrhyn, atoll, Cook Is. E14 58
Penrith, Austl. G5 62
Penrith, Eng., U.K. C5 12
Pensacola, Fl., U.S. u14 102
Pensacola Bay, b., Fl., U.S. u14 102
Pensacola Dam, Ok., U.S. A6 129
Pensacola Mountains, mts., Ant. E36 67
Pentagon Mountain, mtn., Mt., U.S. C3 119
Pentecost Island see Pentecôte, i., Vanuatu k9 62a
Pentecôte, i., Vanuatu k9 62a
Penticton, B.C., Can. E8 85
Pentland Firth, strt., Scot., U.K. A5 12
Pentwater, Mi., U.S. E4 115
Penza, Russia D6 26
Penzance, Eng., U.K. E4 12
Penžinskaja guba, b., Russia C18 26
Peonan Point, c., Mb., Can. D2 86
Peoria, Az., U.S. D3 96
Peoria, Il., U.S. C4 106
Peoria, co., Il., U.S. C4 106
Peoria Heights, Il., U.S. C4 106
Peotone, Il., U.S. B6 106
Pepacton Reservoir, res., N.Y., U.S. C6 125
Pepeekeo, Hi., U.S. D6 104
Pepin, Wi., U.S. D1 142
Pepin, co., Wi., U.S. D2 142
Pepin, Lake, l., U.S. D1 142
Pepperell, Ma., U.S. A4 114
Pequannock, N.J., U.S. B4 123
Pequest, stm., N.J., U.S. B2 123
Pequop Mountains, mts., Nv., U.S. C7 121
Pequot Lakes, Mn., U.S. D4 116
Perabumulih, Indon. D2 36
Percival Lakes, l., Austl. E3 60
Percy, Il., U.S. E4 106
Perdido, Al., U.S. D2 94
Perdido, stm., U.S. E2 94
Perdido Bay, b., Al., U.S. E2 94
Pereira, Col. C4 70
Pereislav-Khmel'nyts'kyi, Ukr. D11 20
Pere Marquette, stm., Mi., U.S. E4 115
Pereslavl'-Zalesskij, Russia C6 22
Pergamino, Arg. E5 72
Pergamum, hist., Tur. C2 44
Perham, Mn., U.S. D3 116
Perico, Arg. C4 72
Pericos, Mex. B3 78
Peridot, Az., U.S. D5 96
Périgueux, Fr. E7 16
Perijá, Serranía de, mts., S.A. G10 76
Perkasie, Pa., U.S. F11 131
Perkins, Ok., U.S. B4 129
Perkins, co., Ne., U.S. D4 120
Perkins, co., S.D., U.S. B3 134
Perkinston, Ms., U.S. E4 117
Perlas, Archipiélago de las, is., Pan. D4 80
Perlas, Laguna de, b., Nic. C3 80
Perm', Russia D7 26
Pernambuco, state, Braz. C4 74
Pernik, Bul. C9 18
Perpignan, Fr. F8 16
Perquimans, co., N.C., U.S. A6 126
Perrine, Fl., U.S. G6 102
Perris, Ca., U.S. F5 98
Perro, Laguna del, l., N.M., U.S. C4 124
Perrot, Île, i., P.Q., Can. q19 90
Perry, Fl., U.S. B3 102
Perry, Ga., U.S. D3 103
Perry, Ia., U.S. C3 108
Perry, Ks., U.S. C8 109
Perry, Mi., U.S. F6 115
Perry, Mo., U.S. B6 118
Perry, N.Y., U.S. C2 125
Perry, Oh., U.S. A4 128
Perry, Ok., U.S. A4 129
Perry, Ut., U.S. B3 137
Perry, co., Al., U.S. C2 94
Perry, co., Ar., U.S. C3 97
Perry, co., Il., U.S. E4 106

Name	Map Ref.	Page
Perry, co., In., U.S.	H4	107
Perry, co., Ky., U.S.	C6	110
Perry, co., Mo., U.S.	D8	118
Perry, co., Ms., U.S.	D4	117
Perry, co., Oh., U.S.	C3	128
Perry, co., Pa., U.S.	F7	131
Perry, co., Tn., U.S.	B4	135
Perry Hall, Md., U.S.	B5	113
Perry Lake, res., Ks., U.S.	C8	109
Perryman, Md., U.S.	B5	113
Perrysburg, Oh., U.S.	A2	128
Perry Stream, stm., N.H., U.S.	f7	122
Perry's Victory and International Peace Memorial, hist., Oh., U.S.	A2	128
Perryton, Tx., U.S.	A2	136
Perryville, Ar., U.S.	B3	97
Perryville, Ky., U.S.	C5	110
Perryville, Md., U.S.	A5	113
Perryville, Mo., U.S.	D8	118
Pershing, co., Nv., U.S.	C3	121
Persia see Iran, ctry., Asia	D6	42
Persian Gulf (The Gulf), b., Asia	E6	42
Person, co., N.C., U.S.	A3	126
Perth, Austl.	G2	60
Perth, On., Can.	C8	89
Perth, Scot., U.K.	B5	12
Perth Amboy, N.J., U.S.	B4	123
Perth-Andover, N.B., Can.	D10	87
Perth Basin	K13	64
Peru, Il., U.S.	B4	106
Peru, In., U.S.	C5	107
Peru, Ne., U.S.	D10	120
Peru, N.Y., U.S.	f11	125
Peru, ctry., S.A.	E4	70
Peru Basin	J5	66
Peru-Chile Trench	J6	66
Perugia, Italy	C4	18
Peruíbe, Braz.	C8	72
Pervari, Tur.	D10	44
Pervomais'k, Ukr.	E11	20
Pervoural'sk, Russia	D7	26
Pesaro, Italy	C4	18
Pescara, Italy	C5	18
Peshastin, Wa., U.S.	B5	140
Peshāwar, Pak.	D10	42
Peshtigo, Wi., U.S.	C6	142
Peshtigo, stm., Wi., U.S.	C5	142
Pesqueira, Braz.	C4	74
Pessac, Fr.	E6	16
Pēštraja Dresva, Russia	C17	26
Petah Tiqwa, Isr.	F6	44
Petal, Ms., U.S.	D4	117
Petaluma, Ca., U.S.	C2	98
Petatlán, Mex.	D4	78
Petawawa, On., Can.	B7	89
Petawawa, stm., On., Can.	A6	89
Petenwell Lake, res., Wi., U.S.	D4	142
Peterborough, Austl.	G2	62
Peterborough, On., Can.	C6	89
Peterborough, Eng., U.K.	D6	12
Peterborough, N.H., U.S.	E3	122
Peterhead, Scot., U.K.	B6	12
Peter I Island, i., Ant.	C31	67
Peter Pond Lake, l., Sk., Can.	m7	91
Petersburg, Ak., U.S.	D13	95
Petersburg, Il., U.S.	C4	106
Petersburg, In., U.S.	H3	107
Petersburg, Mi., U.S.	G7	115
Petersburg, Oh., U.S.	B5	128
Petersburg, Tx., U.S.	C2	136
Petersburg, Va., U.S.	C5	139
Petersburg, W.V., U.S.	B5	141
Peters Creek, stm., W.V., U.S.	m14	141
Peterson, Al., U.S.	B2	94
Peterson Field, mil., Co., U.S.	C6	99
Petersville, Al., U.S.	A2	94
Peter the Great Bay see Petra Velikogo, zaliv, b., Russia	C14	28
Pétion-Ville, Haiti	B5	80
Petit Bois Island, i., Ms., U.S.	E5	117
Petitcodiac, N.B., Can.	D4	87
Petitcodiac, stm., N.B., Can.	C5	87
Petite Amite, stm., La., U.S.	h10	111
Petite Rivière Noire, Piton de la, mtn., Mrts.	g10	57a
Petit Jean, stm., Ar., U.S.	B2	97
Petit Lac Des Allemands, l., La., U.S.	k11	111
Petit Lake, l., La., U.S.	k12	111
Petit-Rocher, N.B., Can.	B4	87
Petitsikapau Lake, l., Nf., Can.	g8	88
Peto, Mex.	C7	78
Petoskey, Mi., U.S.	C6	115
Petra see Al-Batrā', hist., Jord.	D3	42
Petra Velikogo, zaliv, b., Russia	C14	28
Petrič, Bul.	D9	18
Petrified Forest National Park, Az., U.S.	B6	96
Petrila, Rom.	G7	20
Petrodvorec, Russia	G13	10
Petrograd see Sankt-Peterburg, Russia	D5	26
Petrolândia, Braz.	C4	74
Petroleum, co., Mt., U.S.	C8	119
Petrolia, On., Can.	E2	89
Petrolina, Braz.	C3	74
Petropavlovsk, Kaz.	D8	26
Petropavlovsk-Kamčatskij, Russia	D17	26
Petrópolis, Braz.	F3	74
Petros, Tn., U.S.	C9	135
Petroşani, Rom.	G7	20
Petrovsk, Russia	D8	22
Petrozavodsk, Russia	C5	26
Pettaquamscutt Lake Shores, R.I., U.S.	F4	132
Pettingell Peak, mtn., Co., U.S.	B5	99
Pettis, co., Mo., U.S.	C4	118
Pevek, Russia	C19	26
Pevely, Mo., U.S.	g13	118
Pewaukee, Wi., U.S.	E5	142
Pewaukee Lake, l., Wi., U.S.	m11	142
Pewee Valley, Ky., U.S.	B4	110
Pha-an, Myan.	C3	34
Phalaborwa, S. Afr.	C5	56
Phalodi, India	D2	40
Phangan, Ko, i., Thai.	E4	34
Phangnga, Thai.	E3	34
Phanom Dongrak Range, mts., Asia	D4	34
Phan Rang, Viet.	D5	34
Phan Si Pan see Fan Si Pan, mtn., Viet.	B4	34
Phan Thiet, Viet.	D5	34
Pharr, Tx., U.S.	F3	136
Phatthalung, Thai.	E4	34
Phayao, Thai.	C3	34
Phelps, Ky., U.S.	C7	110
Phelps, N.Y., U.S.	C3	125
Phelps, Wi., U.S.	B4	142
Phelps, co., Mo., U.S.	D6	118
Phelps, co., Ne., U.S.	D6	120
Phelps Lake, l., N.C., U.S.	B6	126
Phenix City, Al., U.S.	C4	94
Phetchabun, Thai.	C4	34
Phetchaburi, Thai.	D3	34
Phibun Mangsahan, Thai.	C5	34
Phichit, Thai.	C4	34
Philadelphia, Ms., U.S.	C4	117
Philadelphia, Pa., U.S.	G11	131
Philadelphia, co., Pa., U.S.	G12	131
Philadelphia Naval Shipyard, mil., Pa., U.S.	P21	131
Phil Campbell, Al., U.S.	A2	94
Philip, S.D., U.S.	C4	134
Philippeville see Skikda, Alg.	C6	48
Philippi, W.V., U.S.	B4	141
Philippi see Fílippoi, hist., Grc.	D10	18
Philippine Basin	G15	64
Philippines, ctry., Asia	C8	34
Philippine Sea	H16	24
Philippine Trench	H15	64
Philippopolis see Plovdiv, Bul.	C10	18
Philipsburg, Mt., U.S.	D3	119
Philipsburg, Pa., U.S.	E5	131
Philleo Lake, l., Wa., U.S.	h14	140
Phillips, Me., U.S.	D2	112
Phillips, Tx., U.S.	B2	136
Phillips, Wi., U.S.	C3	142
Phillips, co., Ar., U.S.	C5	97
Phillips, co., Co., U.S.	A8	99
Phillips, co., Ks., U.S.	C4	109
Phillips, co., Mt., U.S.	B8	119
Phillips Brook, stm., N.H., U.S.	A4	122
Phillipsburg, Ks., U.S.	C4	109
Phillipsburg, N.J., U.S.	B2	123
Philmont, N.Y., U.S.	C7	125
Philo, Il., U.S.	C5	106
Philomath, Or., U.S.	C3	130
Philpott Reservoir, res., Va., U.S.	D2	139
Phitsanulok, Thai.	C4	34
Phnom Penh see Phnum Pénh, Camb.	D4	34
Phnum Pénh (Phnom Penh), Camb.	D4	34
Phoenix, Az., U.S.	D3	96
Phoenix, Il., U.S.	k9	106
Phoenix, N.Y., U.S.	B4	125
Phoenix, Or., U.S.	E4	130
Phoenix Islands, is., Kir.	E12	58
Phoenixville, Pa., U.S.	F10	131
Phon, Thai.	C4	34
Phôngsali, Laos	B4	34
Phrae, Thai.	C4	34
Phra Nakhon Si Ayutthaya, Thai.	D4	34
Phuket, Thai.	E3	34
Phuket, Ko, i., Thai.	E3	34
Phumĭ Chhuk, Camb.	D4	34
Phumĭ Kâmpóng Srâlau, Camb.	D5	34
Phumĭ Kaôh Kŏng, Camb.	D4	34
Phu Quoc, Dao, i., Viet.	D4	34
Piacenza, Italy	B2	18
Pianosa, Isola, i., Italy	C3	18
Piatra-Neamţ, Rom.	F9	20
Piatt, co., Il., U.S.	D5	106
Piauí, state, Braz.	C3	74
Piave, stm., Italy	A4	18
Pibor Post, Sudan	I11	48
Picacho, Az., U.S.	E4	96
Picardie, hist. reg., Fr.	C8	16
Picardy see Picardie, hist. reg., Fr.	C8	16
Picayune, Ms., U.S.	E4	117
Piccadilly, Nf., Can.	D2	88
Pichanal, Arg.	C5	72
Picher, Ok., U.S.	A7	129
Pichilemu, Chile	E3	72
Pickaway, co., Oh., U.S.	C2	128
Pickens, Ms., U.S.	C4	117
Pickens, S.C., U.S.	B2	133
Pickens, co., Al., U.S.	B1	94
Pickens, co., Ga., U.S.	B2	103
Pickens, co., S.C., U.S.	B2	133
Pickerel Lake, l., Wi., U.S.	C5	142
Pickering, On., Can.	D5	89
Pickerington, Oh., U.S.	C3	128
Pickett, co., Tn., U.S.	C8	135
Pickwick Lake, res., U.S.	A6	117
Pickworth Point, c., Ma., U.S.	f12	114
Pico de Orizaba, Volcán, vol., Mex.	D5	78
Pico Rivera, Ca., U.S.	n12	98
Picos, Braz.	C3	74
Picton, On., Can.	D7	89
Pictou Island, i., N.S., Can.	D7	87
Picture Butte, Ab., Can.	E4	84
Pictured Rocks National Lakeshore, Mi., U.S.	B4	115
Pidurutalagala, mtn., Sri L.	H4	40
Piedecuesta, Col.	D5	80
Piedmont, Al., U.S.	B4	94
Piedmont, Ca., U.S.	h8	98
Piedmont, Mo., U.S.	D7	118
Piedmont, Ok., U.S.	B4	129
Piedmont, S.C., U.S.	B3	133
Piedmont, W.V., U.S.	B5	141
Piedmont Lake, res., Oh., U.S.	B4	128
Piedra, stm., Co., U.S.	D3	99
Piedras Blancas, Point, c., Ca., U.S.	E3	98
Piedras Negras, Guat.	B1	80
Piedras Negras, Mex.	B4	78
Pieksämäki, Fin.	E12	10
Pielinen, l., Fin.	E13	10
Pierce, Co., U.S.	A6	99
Pierce, Id., U.S.	C3	105
Pierce, Ne., U.S.	B8	120
Pierce, co., Ga., U.S.	E4	103
Pierce, co., N.D., U.S.	A5	127
Pierce, co., Ne., U.S.	B8	120
Pierce, co., Wa., U.S.	C3	140
Pierce, co., Wi., U.S.	D1	142
Pierce, Lake, l., Fl., U.S.	E5	102
Pierce City, Mo., U.S.	E3	118
Pierceton, In., U.S.	B6	107
Pierre, S.D., U.S.	C5	134
Pierrefonds, P.Q., Can.	q19	90
Pierre Part, La., U.S.	k9	111
Pierreville, P.Q., Can.	C5	90
Pierson, Fl., U.S.	C5	102
Pierz, Mn., U.S.	E4	116
Pieštany, Slvk.	E4	20
Pietarsaari, Fin.	E10	10
Pietermaritzburg, S. Afr.	D5	56
Pietersburg, S. Afr.	C4	56
Piet Retief, S. Afr.	D5	56
Pigeon, Mi., U.S.	E7	115
Pigeon, stm., In., U.S.	A6	107
Pigeon, stm., Mn., U.S.	h10	116
Pigeon, stm., Wi., U.S.	k10	142
Pigeon, stm., U.S.	f9	126
Pigeon Cove, Ma., U.S.	A6	114
Pigeon Forge, Tn., U.S.	D10	135
Pigeon Point, c., Mn., U.S.	h10	116
Pigg, stm., Va., U.S.	D3	139
Piggott, Ar., U.S.	A5	97
Pigüé, Arg.	F5	72
Pihlajavesi, l., Fin.	F13	10
Pihtipudas, Fin.	E11	10
Pijijiapan, Mex.	D6	78
Pike, co., Al., U.S.	D4	94
Pike, co., Ar., U.S.	C2	97
Pike, co., Ga., U.S.	C2	103
Pike, co., Il., U.S.	D2	106
Pike, co., In., U.S.	H3	107
Pike, co., Ky., U.S.	C7	110
Pike, co., Mo., U.S.	B6	118
Pike, co., Ms., U.S.	D3	117
Pike, co., Oh., U.S.	C2	128
Pike, co., Pa., U.S.	D11	131
Pike, stm., Wi., U.S.	C6	142
Pike Island Dam, U.S.	f8	141
Pike Lake, Mn., U.S.	D6	116
Pikes Peak, mtn., Co., U.S.	C5	99
Pikesville, Md., U.S.	B4	113
Piketberg, S. Afr.	E2	56
Piketon, Oh., U.S.	C2	128
Pikeville, Ky., U.S.	C7	110
Pikeville, Tn., U.S.	D8	135
Piła, Pol.	C4	20
Pilcomayo, stm., S.A.	C5	72
Pīlībhīt, India	D3	40
Pillar Point, c., Ca., U.S.	k7	98
Pílos, Grc.	F8	18
Pilot Grove, Mo., U.S.	C5	118
Pilot Knob, Mo., U.S.	D7	118
Pilot Knob, mtn., Id., U.S.	D3	105
Pilot Mound, Mb., Can.	E2	86
Pilot Mountain, N.C., U.S.	A2	126
Pilot Peak, mtn., Nv., U.S.	B7	121
Pilot Peak, mtn., Nv., U.S.	E4	121
Pilot Peak, mtn., Wy., U.S.	B3	143
Pilot Point, Tx., U.S.	C4	136
Pilot Range, mts., Nv., U.S.	B7	121
Pilot Rock, Or., U.S.	B8	130
Pilot Station, Ak., U.S.	C7	95
Pilsen see Plzeň, Czech Rep.	E2	20
Pima, Az., U.S.	E6	96
Pima, co., Az., U.S.	E3	96
Pimmit Hills, Va., U.S.	g12	139
Pinal, co., Az., U.S.	E4	96
Pinaleno Mountains, mts., Az., U.S.	E5	96
Pinal Mountains, mts., Az., U.S.	D5	96
Pinang see George Town, Malay.	B2	36
Pınarbaşı, Tur.	C7	44
Pinar del Río, Cuba	A3	80
Pinardville, N.H., U.S.	E3	122
Pincher Creek, Ab., Can.	E4	84
Pinckard, Al., U.S.	D4	94
Pinckney, Mi., U.S.	F7	115
Pinckney Island, i., S.C., U.S.	G6	133
Pinckneyville, Il., U.S.	E4	106
Pinconning, Mi., U.S.	E7	115
Pindaré-Mirim, Braz.	B2	74
Píndhos Óros, mts., Grc.	E8	18
Pindus Mountains see Píndhos Óros, mts., Grc.	E8	18
Pine, Az., U.S.	C4	96
Pine, co., Mn., U.S.	D6	116
Pine, stm., Mi., U.S.	D7	115
Pine, stm., Mi., U.S.	D5	115
Pine, stm., N.H., U.S.	C4	122
Pine, stm., Wi., U.S.	C5	142
Pine, stm., Wi., U.S.	C4	142
Pine Barrens, reg., N.J., U.S.	D3	123
Pine Bluff, Ar., U.S.	C3	97
Pinebluff, N.C., U.S.	B3	126
Pine Bluffs, Wy., U.S.	E8	143
Pine Bridge, Ct., U.S.	D3	100
Pine Castle, Fl., U.S.	D5	102
Pine City, Mn., U.S.	E6	116
Pine Creek, Austl.	C5	60
Pine Creek, stm., Nv., U.S.	C5	121
Pine Creek, stm., Pa., U.S.	C6	131
Pine Creek, stm., Wa., U.S.	B8	140
Pine Creek Lake, res., Ok., U.S.	C6	129
Pinedale, Wy., U.S.	D3	143
Pine Falls, Mb., Can.	D3	86
Pine Forest Range, mts., Nv., U.S.	B3	121
Pine Grove, Pa., U.S.	E9	131
Pine Grove Mills, Pa., U.S.	E6	131
Pine Hill, N.J., U.S.	D3	123
Pine Hills, Fl., U.S.	D5	102
Pinehouse Lake, Sk., Can.	B2	91
Pinehouse Lake, l., Sk., Can.	B2	91
Pinehurst, Ma., U.S.	f11	114
Pinehurst, N.C., U.S.	B3	126
Pine Island, Mn., U.S.	F6	116
Pine Island, i., Fl., U.S.	F4	102
Pine Island Sound, strt., Fl., U.S.	F4	102
Pine Key, i., Fl., U.S.	p10	102
Pine Knot, Ky., U.S.	D5	110
Pine Lake, Ga., U.S.	h8	103
Pine Lake, l., In., U.S.	A4	107
Pine Lake, l., Wi., U.S.	C5	142
Pine Lawn, Mo., U.S.	f13	118
Pine Level, N.C., U.S.	B4	126
Pinellas, co., Fl., U.S.	D4	102
Pinellas, Point, c., Fl., U.S.	p10	102
Pinellas Park, Fl., U.S.	E4	102
Pine Mountain, Ga., U.S.	D2	103
Pine Mountain, mtn., Or., U.S.	D6	130
Pine Mountain, mtn., Wy., U.S.	E3	143
Pine Point, Me., U.S.	E2	112
Pine Prairie, La., U.S.	D3	111
Pine Ridge, S.D., U.S.	D3	134
Pine Ridge Indian Reservation, S.D., U.S.	D3	134
Pine River, Mn., U.S.	D4	116
Pines, Isle of see Juventud, Isla de la, i., Cuba	A3	80
Pines, Lake O' the, res., Tx., U.S.	C5	136
Pinesdale, Mt., U.S.	D2	119
Pinetops, N.C., U.S.	B5	126
Pinetown, S. Afr.	D5	56
Pine Valley, val., Ut., U.S.	E2	137
Pineville, Ky., U.S.	D6	110
Pineville, La., U.S.	C3	111
Pineville, N.C., U.S.	B2	126
Pineville, W.V., U.S.	D3	141
Pinewood, S.C., U.S.	D7	133
Piney Creek, stm., W.V., U.S.	n13	141
Piney Fork, stm., W.V., U.S.	h9	141
Piney Point, Md., U.S.	D4	113
Piney View, W.V., U.S.	n13	141
Pingdu, China	B4	30
Pingelly, Austl.	G2	60
Pingjiang, China	F10	28
Pingle, China	E3	30
Pingliang, China	D9	28
Pingluo, China	B2	30
Pingquan, China	C11	28
Pingtan, China	D4	30
P'ingtung, Tai.	E5	30
Pingwu, China	E8	28
Pingxiang, China	G9	28
Pingxiang, China	F10	28
Pingyang, China	D5	30
Pingyao, China	B3	30
Pingyin, China	B4	30
Pinheiro, Braz.	B2	74
Pini, Pulau, i., Indon.	C1	36
Pinjarra, Austl.	G2	60
Pinjug, Russia	B8	22
Pinnacles National Monument, Ca., U.S.	D3	98
Pinole, Ca., U.S.	h8	98
Pinopolis Dam, S.C., U.S.	E8	133
Pinos, Mount, mtn., Ca., U.S.	E4	98
Pinrang, Indon.	D5	36
Pins, Île des, i., N. Cal.	I9	62a
Pins, Pointe aux, c., On., Can.	E3	89
Pinsk, Bela.	C9	20
Pinsk Marshes see Polesye, reg., Eur.	D8	20
Pinson, Al., U.S.	f7	94
Pinta, Isla, i., Ec.	C1	70
Pinta, Sierra, mts., Az., U.S.	E2	96
Pintados, Chile	C4	72
Pintwater Range, mts., Nv., U.S.	G6	121
Pioche, Nv., U.S.	F7	121
Piombino, Italy	C3	18
Pioneer, Oh., U.S.	A1	128
Pioneer Mountains, mts., Id., U.S.	F5	105
Pioneer Mountains, mts., Mt., U.S.	E3	119
Pioner, ostrov, i., Russia	B10	26
Piotrków Trybunalski, Pol.	D5	20
Pīpār, India	D2	40
Pipe Spring National Monument, Az., U.S.	A3	96
Pipestem Creek, stm., N.D., U.S.	B6	127
Pipestone, Mn., U.S.	G2	116
Pipestone, co., Mn., U.S.	F2	116
Pipestone National Monument, Mn., U.S.	G2	116
Pipestone Pass, Mt., U.S.	E4	119
Pipmuacan, Réservoir, res., P.Q., Can.	k12	90
Piqua, Oh., U.S.	B1	128
Piracicaba, Braz.	F2	74
Piracuruca, Braz.	B3	74
Piraeus see Piraiévs, Grc.	E9	18
Piraiévs, Grc.	E9	18
Piranhas, Braz.	E1	74
Pīrān Shahr, Iran	D11	44
Pirapora, Braz.	E3	74
Pires do Rio, Braz.	E2	74
Pírgos, Grc.	F8	18
Piripiri, Braz.	B3	74
Pirot, Yugo.	C9	18
Pīr Panjāl Range, mts., Asia	E2	28
Pirtleville, Az., U.S.	F6	96
Piru, Indon.	D7	36
Pisa, Italy	C3	18
Pisagua, Chile	A2	69
Piscataqua, stm., N.H., U.S.	D5	122
Piscataquis, co., Me., U.S.	C3	112
Piscataquis, stm., Me., U.S.	C3	112
Piscataquog, stm., N.H., U.S.	D3	122
Piscataway, N.J., U.S.	B4	123
Pisco, Peru	F3	70
Piseco Lake, l., N.Y., U.S.	B6	125
Písek, Czech Rep.	E3	20
Pisgah, Al., U.S.	A4	94
Pisgah, Oh., U.S.	n13	128
Pisgah, Mount, mtn., Wy., U.S.	B8	143
Pisgah Forest, N.C., U.S.	f10	126
Pishan, China	D3	28
Pismo Beach, Ca., U.S.	E3	98
Pisticci, Italy	D6	18
Pistoia, Italy	C3	18
Pistolet Bay, b., Nf., Can.	C4	88
Pit, stm., Ca., U.S.	B3	98
Pita, Gui.	D2	50
Pitcairn, Pa., U.S.	k14	131
Pitcairn, dep., Oc.	K26	64
Piteå, Swe.	D9	10
Piteälven, stm., Swe.	C8	10
Piteşti, Rom.	G8	20
Pithara, Austl.	G2	60
Pitkin, co., Co., U.S.	B4	99
Pitkjaranta, Russia	B5	22
Pitman, N.J., U.S.	D2	123
Pitt, co., N.C., U.S.	B5	126
Pitt Island, i., B.C., Can.	C3	85
Pittsboro, In., U.S.	E5	107
Pittsboro, N.C., U.S.	B3	126
Pittsburg, Ca., U.S.	g9	98
Pittsburg, Ks., U.S.	E9	109
Pittsburg, Ky., U.S.	C5	110
Pittsburg, Tx., U.S.	C5	136
Pittsburg, co., Ok., U.S.	C6	129
Pittsburgh, Pa., U.S.	F1	131
Pittsfield, Il., U.S.	D3	106
Pittsfield, Ma., U.S.	B1	114
Pittsfield, Me., U.S.	D3	112
Pittsfield, N.H., U.S.	D4	122
Pittsford, Vt., U.S.	D2	138
Pittston, Pa., U.S.	D10	131
Pittsville, Md., U.S.	D7	113
Pittsville, Wi., U.S.	D3	142
Pittsylvania, co., Va., U.S.	D3	139

Name — Map Ref. — Page

Pium, Braz. F10 70
Piura, Peru E3 70
Piute, co., Ut., U.S. E3 137
Piute Peak, mtn., Ca., U.S. E4 98
Piute Reservoir, res., Ut., U.S. E3 137
Pivdennyi Buh, stm., Ukr. F11 20
Pixley, Ca., U.S. E4 98
Pjandž, stm., Asia B1 40
Pjaozero, ozero, l., Russia D14 10
Pjasina, stm., Russia B10 26
Pjatigorsk, Russia B4 42
Placentia, Nf., Can. E5 88
Placentia Bay, b., Nf., Can. E4 88
Placer, co., Ca., U.S. C3 98
Placer Mountain, mtn., N.M., U.S. k8 124
Placerville, Ca., U.S. C3 98
Placetas, Cuba A4 80
Placid, Lake, l., Fl., U.S. E5 102
Placid, Lake, l., N.Y., U.S. f11 125
Placitas, N.M., U.S. B3 124
Plain City, Oh., U.S. B2 128
Plain City, Ut., U.S. B3 137
Plain Dealing, La., U.S. B2 111
Plainfield, Ct., U.S. C8 100
Plainfield, Il., U.S. B5 106
Plainfield, In., U.S. E5 107
Plainfield, N.J., U.S. B4 123
Plainfield, Vt., U.S. C4 138
Plainfield, Wi., U.S. D4 142
Plains, Ga., U.S. D2 103
Plains, Ks., U.S. E3 109
Plains, Mt., U.S. C2 119
Plains, Pa., U.S. n17 131
Plains, Tx., U.S. C1 136
Plainview, Ar., U.S. C2 97
Plainview, Mn., U.S. F6 116
Plainview, Ne., U.S. B8 120
Plainview, Tx., U.S. B2 136
Plainville, Ct., U.S. C4 100
Plainville, Ks., U.S. C4 109
Plainville, Ma., U.S. B5 114
Plainwell, Mi., U.S. F5 115
Plaistow, N.H., U.S. E4 122
Plampang, Indon. E5 36
Planeta Rica, Col. D4 80
Plankinton, S.D., U.S. D7 134
Plano, Il., U.S. B5 106
Plano, Tx., U.S. C4 136
Plantagenet, On., Can. B9 89
Plantation, Fl., U.S. r13 102
Plant City, Fl., U.S. D4 102
Plantersville, Al., U.S. C3 94
Plantersville, Ms., U.S. A5 117
Plantsite, Az., U.S. D6 96
Plantsville, Ct., U.S. C4 100
Plaquemine, La., U.S. D4 111
Plaquemines, co., La., U.S. E6 111
Plasencia, Spain G3 16
Plaster Rock, N.B., Can. C2 87
Plata, Río de la, est., S.A. E6 72
Plate, Île, i., Sey. i13 57b
Plato, Col. B5 70
Platte, S.D., U.S. D7 134
Platte, co., Mo., U.S. B3 118
Platte, co., Ne., U.S. C8 120
Platte, co., Wy., U.S. D7 143
Platte, stm., Mn., U.S. E4 116
Platte, stm., Ne., U.S. D6 120
Platte, stm., U.S. B3 118
Platte City, Mo., U.S. B3 118
Platteville, Co., U.S. A6 99
Platteville, Wi., U.S. F3 142
Plattsburg, Mo., U.S. B3 118
Plattsburgh, N.Y., U.S. f11 125
Plattsmouth, Ne., U.S. D10 120
Plauen, Ger. E12 12
Plavsk, Russia C14 20
Playas Lake, l., N.M., U.S. F2 124
Playgreen Lake, l., Mb., Can. B2 86
Play Ku, Viet. D5 34
Pleasant, stm., Me., U.S. C3 112
Pleasant, Lake, res., Az., U.S. D3 96
Pleasant Gap, Pa., U.S. E6 131
Pleasant Garden, N.C., U.S. B3 126
Pleasant Grove, Al., U.S. g7 94
Pleasant Grove, Ut., U.S. C4 137
Pleasant Hill, Ca., U.S. h8 98
Pleasant Hill, Ia., U.S. e8 108
Pleasant Hill, Il., U.S. D3 106
Pleasant Hill, La., U.S. C2 111
Pleasant Hill, Mo., U.S. C3 118
Pleasant Hill, Oh., U.S. B1 128
Pleasant Lake, In., U.S. A7 107
Pleasant Lake, l., Me., U.S. C5 112
Pleasant Lake, l., N.H., U.S. D4 122
Pleasanton, Ca., U.S. h9 98
Pleasanton, Ks., U.S. D9 109
Pleasanton, Tx., U.S. E3 136
Pleasant Prairie, Wi., U.S. n12 142
Pleasants, co., W.V., U.S. B3 141
Pleasant Valley, Ia., U.S. g11 108
Pleasant Valley, Mo., U.S. h11 118
Pleasant View, Ut., U.S. B3 137
Pleasantville, Ia., U.S. C4 108
Pleasantville, N.J., U.S. E3 123
Pleasantville, N.Y., U.S. D7 125
Pleasantville, Oh., U.S. C3 128
Pleasure Beach, Ct., U.S. D7 100
Pleasure Ridge Park, Ky., U.S. g11 110
Pleasureville, Ky., U.S. B4 110
Plenty, Bay of, b., N.Z. o14 63c
Plentywood, Mt., U.S. B12 119
Pleseck, Russia C6 26
Plessisville, P.Q., Can. C6 90
Pleszew, Pol. D4 20
Pleven, Bul. C10 18
Pljussa, Russia G13 10
Płock, Pol. C5 20
Ploiești, Rom. G9 20
Plomosa Mountains, mts., Az., U.S. D1 96
Plonge, Lac la, l., Sk., Can. B2 91
Płońsk, Pol. C6 20
Plovdiv, Bul. C10 18
Plover, Wi., U.S. D4 142
Plover, stm., Wi., U.S. D4 142
Plum, Pa., U.S. k14 131
Plumas, co., Ca., U.S. B3 98
Plum Coulee, Mb., Can. E3 86
Plumerville, Ar., U.S. B3 97
Plum Island, i., Ma., U.S. A6 114
Plummer, Id., U.S. B2 105
Plumsteadville, Pa., U.S. F11 131
Plumtree, Zimb. C4 56
Plungė, Lith. I9 10
Plutarco Elías Calles, Presa, res., Mex. B3 78
Plymouth, Monts. B7 80
Plymouth, Eng., U.K. E4 12
Plymouth, Ct., U.S. C3 100
Plymouth, Fl., U.S. D5 102
Plymouth, In., U.S. B5 107
Plymouth, Ma., U.S. C6 114
Plymouth, Mi., U.S. p15 115
Plymouth, Mn., U.S. m12 116
Plymouth, N.C., U.S. B6 126
Plymouth, N.H., U.S. C3 122
Plymouth, Oh., U.S. A3 128
Plymouth, Pa., U.S. D10 131
Plymouth, Wi., U.S. E6 142
Plymouth, co., Ia., U.S. B1 108
Plymouth, co., Ma., U.S. C6 114
Plymouth Bay, b., Ma., U.S. C6 114
Plzeň, Czech Rep. E2 20
Pô, Burkina D4 50
Po, stm., Italy B3 18
Po, stm., Va., U.S. B5 139
Pobè, Benin E5 50
Pobeda, gora, mtn., Russia C16 26
Pobedy, Peak, mtn., Asia B11 42
Pocahontas, Ar., U.S. A5 97
Pocahontas, Ia., U.S. B3 108
Pocahontas, Il., U.S. E4 106
Pocahontas, co., Ia., U.S. B3 108
Pocahontas, co., W.V., U.S. C4 141
Pocasset, Ma., U.S. C6 114
Pocatalico, W.V., U.S. C3 141
Pocatalico, stm., W.V., U.S. C3 141
Pocatello, Id., U.S. G6 105
Počep, Russia C12 20
Počinok, Russia B12 20
Poções, Braz. D3 74
Pocola, Ok., U.S. B7 129
Pocomoke, stm., Md., U.S. D7 113
Pocomoke City, Md., U.S. D6 113
Pocomoke Sound, strt., Md., U.S. E6 113
Poconé, Braz. B6 72
Pocono Mountains, hills, Pa., U.S. E11 131
Pocono Pines, Pa., U.S. D11 131
Poços de Caldas, Braz. F2 74
Pocotopaug Lake, res., Ct., U.S. C6 100
Podgorica, Yugo. C7 18
Podkamennaja Tunguska, Russia C10 26
Podkamennaja Tunguska, stm., Russia C11 26
Podol'sk, Russia C6 22
Podor, Sen. C2 50
Podporože, Russia B5 22
Pofadder, S. Afr. D2 56
Poge, Cape, c., Ma., U.S. D7 114
Pograničnyj, Russia C14 28
P'ohang, S. Kor. D13 28
Pohénégamook, P.Q., Can. B8 90
Pohjanmaa, reg., Fin. D11 10
Pohnpei, i., Micron. D9 58
Pohue Bay, b., Hi., U.S. E6 104
Pohvistnevo, Russia D9 22
Poinsett, co., Ar., U.S. B5 97
Poinsett, Cape, c., Ant. C16 67
Poinsett, Lake, l., Fl., U.S. D6 102
Poinsett, Lake, l., S.D., U.S. C8 134
Point Clear, Al., U.S. E2 94
Pointe a la Hache, La., U.S. E6 111
Pointe-à-Pitre, Guad. B7 80
Pointe-au-Pic, P.Q., Can. B7 90
Pointe-Calumet, P.Q., Can. p19 90
Pointe-Claire, P.Q., Can. D4 90
Pointe Coupee, co., La., U.S. D4 111
Pointe-des-Cascades, P.Q., Can. q19 90
Point Edward, On., Can. D2 89
Pointe-Noire, Congo D2 54
Pointe-Verte, N.B., Can. B4 87
Point Fortin, Trin. C7 80
Point Hope, Ak., U.S. B6 95
Point Imperial, mtn., Az., U.S. A4 96
Point Judith Pond, l., R.I., U.S. F4 132
Point Leamington, Nf., Can. D4 88
Point Marion, Pa., U.S. G2 131
Point Mugu Naval Air Station, mil., Ca., U.S. E4 98
Point of Rocks, Md., U.S. B2 113
Point Pelee National Park, On., Can. F2 89
Point Pleasant, N.J., U.S. C4 123
Point Pleasant, W.V., U.S. C2 141
Point Pleasant Beach, N.J., U.S. C4 123
Point Reyes National Seashore, Ca., U.S. C2 98
Point Roberts, Wa., U.S. A2 140
Poipu, Hi., U.S. B2 104
Poison Creek, stm., Wy., U.S. C5 143
Poisson Blanc, Lac du, res., P.Q., Can. C2 90
Poitiers, Fr. D7 16
Poitou, hist. reg., Fr. D6 16
Poivre Atoll, i., Sey. i12 57b
Pojarkovo, Russia B13 28
Pokaran, India D2 40
Pokegama Lake, l., Mn., U.S. C5 116
Pokegama Lake, l., Wi., U.S. C2 142
Pokharā, Nepal D4 40
Polacca, Az., U.S. B5 96
Polack, Bela. B10 20
Pola de Lena, Spain F4 16
Pola de Siero, Spain F4 16
Poland, ctry., Eur. C5 20
Polar Bear Provincial Park, On., Can. n18 89
Polatlı, Tur. C5 44
Polecat Creek, stm., Ok., U.S. B5 129
Pol-e Khomrī, Afg. C9 42
Polesye, reg., Eur. D8 20
Polewali, Indon. D5 36
Policastro, Golfo di, b., Italy E5 18
Pólis, Cyp. E5 44
Poljarnyj, Russia B15 10
Polk, Pa., U.S. D2 131
Polk, co., Ar., U.S. C1 97
Polk, co., Fl., U.S. E5 102
Polk, co., Ga., U.S. C1 103
Polk, co., Ia., U.S. C4 108
Polk, co., Mn., U.S. C2 116
Polk, co., Mo., U.S. D4 118
Polk, co., N.C., U.S. f10 126
Polk, co., Ne., U.S. C8 120
Polk, co., Or., U.S. C3 130
Polk, co., Tn., U.S. D9 135
Polk, co., Tx., U.S. D5 136
Polk, co., Wi., U.S. C1 142
Polk City, Fl., U.S. D5 102
Polk City, Ia., U.S. C4 108
Pol'kino, Russia B11 26
Pollāchi, India G3 40
Pollença, Spain H8 16
Polo, Il., U.S. B4 106
Polohy, Ukr. F14 20
Polonnaruwa, Sri L. H4 40
Polonne, Ukr. D9 20
Polson, Mt., U.S. C2 119
Poltava, Ukr. E13 20
Põltsamaa, Est. G12 10
Polunočnoe, Russia B11 22
Polynesia, is., Oc. I23 64
Pombal, Braz. C4 74
Pomerania, hist. reg., Eur. C4 20
Pomeroy, Ia., U.S. B3 108
Pomeroy, Oh., U.S. C3 128
Pomeroy, Wa., U.S. C8 140
Pomme de Terre, stm., Mn., U.S. E3 116
Pomme de Terre, stm., Mo., U.S. D4 118
Pomme de Terre Lake, res., Mo., U.S. D4 118
Pomona, Ca., U.S. E5 98
Pomona, Ks., U.S. D8 109
Pomona Lake, res., Ks., U.S. D7 109
Pompano Beach, Fl., U.S. F6 102
Pompei, Italy D5 18
Pompéu, Braz. E2 74
Pompton Lakes, N.J., U.S. A4 123
Ponaganset, stm., R.I., U.S. C2 132
Ponaganset Reservoir, res., R.I., U.S. B2 132
Ponape see Pohnpei, i., Micron. D9 58
Ponca, Ne., U.S. B9 120
Ponca City, Ok., U.S. A4 129
Ponca Creek, stm., U.S. A6 120
Ponca Indian Reservation, Ne., U.S. B7 120
Ponce, P.R. B6 80
Ponce de Leon Bay, b., Fl., U.S. G5 102
Ponce de Leon Inlet, b., Fl., U.S. C6 102
Poncha Pass, Co., U.S. C4 99
Ponchatoula, La., U.S. D5 111
Pond, stm., Ky., U.S. C2 110
Pond Creek, Ok., U.S. A3 129
Pondera, co., Mt., U.S. B4 119
Pond Fork, stm., W.V., U.S. D3 141
Pondicherry, India G3 40
Pone Island, i., Md., U.S. D5 113
Ponferrada, Spain F3 16
Ponoj, Russia C6 26
Ponoka, Ab., Can. C4 84
Ponta Delgada, Port. F7 46
Ponta Grossa, Braz. D8 72
Pontalina, Braz. E2 74
Ponta Porã, Braz. H8 70
Pontarlier, Fr. D10 16
Pontchartrain, Lake, l., La., U.S. D5 111
Ponteix, Sk., Can. H2 91
Ponte Nova, Braz. F3 74
Pontevedra, Spain F2 16
Ponte Vedra Beach, Fl., U.S. B5 102
Pontiac, Il., U.S. C5 106
Pontiac, Mi., U.S. F7 115
Pontianak, Indon. C3 36
Pontine Islands see Ponziane, Isole, is., Italy D4 18
Pontoosuc Lake, l., Ma., U.S. B1 114
Pontotoc, Ms., U.S. A4 117
Pontotoc, co., Ms., U.S. A4 117
Pontotoc, co., Ok., U.S. C5 129
Pont-Rouge, P.Q., Can. C6 90
Pontus Mountains see Doğu Karadeniz Dağları, mts., Tur. B8 44
Pontypool, On., Can. C6 89
Ponziane, Isole, is., Italy D4 18
Poole, Eng., U.K. E5 12
Pooler, Ga., U.S. D5 103
Pooles Island, i., Md., U.S. B5 113
Poolesville, Md., U.S. B3 113
Poopó, Bol. B4 72
Poopó, Lago, l., Bol. B4 72
Popayán, Col. C4 70
Pope, co., Ar., U.S. B2 97
Pope, co., Il., U.S. F5 106
Pope, co., Mn., U.S. E3 116
Pope Air Force Base, mil., N.C., U.S. B3 126
Poplar, Mt., U.S. B11 119
Poplar, stm., Can. C3 86
Poplar, stm., Mn., U.S. C2 116
Poplar Bluff, Mo., U.S. E7 118
Poplar Island, i., Md., U.S. C5 113
Poplarville, Ms., U.S. E4 117
Popocatépetl, Volcán, vol., Mex. D5 78
Popokabaka, D.R.C. E3 54
Popondetta, Pap. N. Gui. H12 32
Popovo, Bul. C11 18
Popple, stm., Wi., U.S. C5 142
Poprad, Slvk. E6 20
Poquonock, Ct., U.S. B5 100
Poquonock Bridge, Ct., U.S. D7 100
Poquoson, Va., U.S. C6 139
Porangatu, Braz. D2 74
Porbandar, India E1 40
Porcher Island, i., B.C., Can. C2 85
Porcupine, stm., N.A. E11 82
Porcupine Mountains, mts., Mi., U.S. m12 115
Pordenone, Italy B4 18
Pori, Fin. F9 10
Porirua, N.Z. p13 63c
Porlamar, Ven. A7 70
Poronajsk, Russia E16 26
Porpoise Bay, b., Ant. C17 67
Porsangen, b., Nor. A11 10
Porsgrunn, Nor. G3 10
Portachuelo, Bol. B5 72
Port Adelaide, Austl. G2 62
Portadown, N. Ire., U.K. C3 12
Portage, In., U.S. A3 107
Portage, Mi., U.S. F5 115
Portage, Pa., U.S. F4 131
Portage, Wi., U.S. E4 142
Portage, co., Oh., U.S. A4 128
Portage, co., Wi., U.S. D4 142
Portage, stm., Oh., U.S. B2 128
Portage Bay, b., Mb., Can. D2 86
Portage Head, c., Wa., U.S. A1 140
Portage Lake, l., Me., U.S. B4 112
Portage Lakes, Oh., U.S. B4 128
Portage la Prairie, Mb., Can. E2 86
Portageville, Mo., U.S. E8 118
Port Alberni, B.C., Can. E5 85
Portalegre, Port. H3 16
Portales, N.M., U.S. C6 124
Port Alfred, S. Afr. E4 56
Port Alice, B.C., Can. D4 85
Port Allegany, Pa., U.S. C5 131
Port Allen, La., U.S. D4 111
Port Angeles, Wa., U.S. A2 140
Port Antonio, Jam. B4 80
Port Aransas, Tx., U.S. F4 136
Port Arthur see Lüshun, China D12 28
Port Arthur, Tx., U.S. E6 136
Port Augusta, Austl. G2 62
Port au Port Bay, b., Nf., Can. D2 88
Port au Port [West-Aguathuna-Felix Cove], Nf., Can. D2 88
Port-au-Prince, Haiti B5 80
Port au Prince Peninsula, pen., Nf., Can. D2 88
Port Austin, Mi., U.S. D7 115
Port Barre, La., U.S. D4 111
Port Blair, India G6 40
Port Blandford, Nf., Can. D4 88
Port Bolivar, Tx., U.S. E5 136
Port Burwell, On., Can. E4 89
Port Byron, Il., U.S. B3 106
Port Carbon, Pa., U.S. E9 131
Port Carling, On., Can. B5 89
Port-Cartier-Ouest, P.Q., Can. k13 90
Port Chalmers, N.Z. q13 63c
Port Charlotte, Fl., U.S. F4 102
Port Chester, N.Y., U.S. E7 125
Port Clinton, Oh., U.S. A3 128
Port Colborne, On., Can. E5 89
Port Coquitlam, B.C., Can. E6 85
Port Deposit, Md., U.S. A5 113
Port Dickinson, N.Y., U.S. C5 125
Port Edward, B.C., Can. B2 85
Port Edward, S. Afr. E5 56
Port Edwards, Wi., U.S. D4 142
Portel, Braz. B1 74
Port Elgin, On., Can. C3 89
Port Elizabeth, S. Afr. E4 56
Porter, In., U.S. A3 107
Porter, Tx., U.S. D5 136
Porter, co., In., U.S. B3 107
Porter Creek, stm., W.V., U.S. m13 141
Porterdale, Ga., U.S. C3 103
Porterville, Ca., U.S. D4 98
Port Ewen, N.Y., U.S. D7 125
Port Fairy, Austl. H3 62
Port Gamble Indian Reservation, Wa., U.S. B3 140
Port-Gentil, Gabon D1 54
Port Gibson, Ms., U.S. D3 117
Port-Harcourt, Nig. F6 50
Port Hedland, Austl. E2 60
Port Hood, N.S., Can. C8 87
Port Hope, On., Can. D6 89
Port Hope Simpson, Nf., Can. B3 88
Port Hueneme, Ca., U.S. E4 98
Port Huron, Mi., U.S. F8 115
Portimão, Port. I2 16
Port Isabel, Tx., U.S. F4 136
Port Jefferson, N.Y., U.S. n15 125
Port Jervis, N.Y., U.S. D6 125
Port Lairge see Waterford, Ire. D3 12
Portland, Austl. H3 62
Portland, Ct., U.S. C5 100
Portland, In., U.S. D8 107
Portland, Me., U.S. E2 112
Portland, Mi., U.S. F6 115
Portland, N.D., U.S. B8 127
Portland, Or., U.S. B4 130
Portland, Tn., U.S. A5 135
Portland, Tx., U.S. F4 136
Portland, Cape, c., Austl. I4 62
Portland Inlet, b., B.C., Can. B2 85
Port Laoise, Ire. D3 12
Port Lavaca, Tx., U.S. E4 136
Port Lincoln, Austl. G2 62
Port Loko, S.L. E2 50
Port Louis, Mrts. f10 57a
Port Ludlow, Wa., U.S. B3 140
Port Macquarie, Austl. G5 62
Port Madison Indian Reservation, Wa., U.S. B3 140
Port McNeil, B.C., Can. D4 85
Port McNicoll, On., Can. C5 89
Port Monmouth, N.J., U.S. C4 123
Port Moresby, Pap. N. Gui. H12 32
Port Morien, N.S., Can. C10 87
Port Neches, Tx., U.S. E6 136
Portneuf, P.Q., Can. C6 90
Port Nolloth, S. Afr. D2 56
Porto, Port. G2 16
Porto Alegre, Braz. E7 72
Porto Amboim, Ang. F2 54
Portobelo, Pan. D4 80
Porto de Moz, Braz. D9 70
Porto Esperança, Braz. G8 70
Porto Esperidião, Braz. G8 70
Portoferraio, Italy C3 18
Port of Spain, Trin. C7 80
Portola, Ca., U.S. C3 98
Porto Murtinho, Braz. H8 70
Porto Nacional, Braz. D2 74
Porto-Novo, Benin E5 50
Port Orange, Fl., U.S. C6 102
Port Orchard, Wa., U.S. B3 140
Port Orford, Or., U.S. E2 130
Porto Santana, Braz. B1 74
Porto Santo, i., Port. D1 48
Porto Seguro, Braz. E4 74
Porto Torres, Italy D2 18
Porto-Vecchio, Fr. D2 18
Porto Velho, Braz. E7 70
Portoviejo, Ec. D3 70
Port Penn, De., U.S. B3 101
Port Phillip Bay, b., Austl. H3 62
Port Richey, Fl., U.S. D4 102
Port Rowan, On., Can. E4 89
Port Royal, S.C., U.S. G6 133
Port Royal Island, i., S.C., U.S. G6 133
Port Royal Sound, strt., S.C., U.S. G6 133
Port Said see Bûr Sa'îd, Egypt E10 48
Port Saint Joe, Fl., U.S. C1 102
Port Saint Johns, S. Afr. E4 56
Port Saint Lucie, Fl., U.S. E6 102
Port Salerno, Fl., U.S. E6 102
Port Saunders, Nf., Can. C3 88
Port Shepstone, S. Afr. E5 56
Portsmouth, Eng., U.K. E6 12
Portsmouth, N.H., U.S. D5 122
Portsmouth, Oh., U.S. D3 128
Portsmouth, R.I., U.S. E6 132

Name	Map Ref.	Page

Portsmouth, Va., U.S. **D6** 139
Portsmouth Naval Shipyard, mil., Me., U.S. **D5** 122
Port Stanley, On., Can. **E3** 89
Port Stanley see Stanley, Falk. Is. **H5** 69
Port Sudan see Būr Sūdān, Sudan **G12** 48
Port Sulphur, La., U.S. **E6** 111
Port Talbot, Wales, U.K. **E5** 12
Porttipahdan tekojärvi, l., Fin. **B12** 10
Port Townsend, Wa., U.S. **A3** 140
Portugal, ctry., Eur. **G3** 16
Port Union, Nf., Can. **D5** 88
Port Vila, Vanuatu **k9** 62a
Port Washington, N.Y., U.S. **h13** 125
Port Washington, Wi., U.S. **E6** 142
Port Wentworth, Ga., U.S. **D5** 103
Porum, Ok., U.S. **B6** 129
Porvenir, Chile **H2** 69
Porvoo, Fin. **F11** 10
Posadas, Arg. **D6** 72
Posen see Poznań, Pol. **C4** 20
Posen, Il., U.S. **k9** 106
Poset, Russia **E15** 26
Posey, co., In., U.S. **H2** 107
Poseyville, In., U.S. **H2** 107
Posio, Fin. **C13** 10
Poso, Indon. **D6** 36
Posse, Braz. **D2** 74
Post, Tx., U.S. **C2** 136
Post Falls, Id., U.S. **B2** 105
Postmasburg, S. Afr. **D3** 56
Postville, Ia., U.S. **A6** 108
Potawatomi Indian Reservation, Ks., U.S. **C8** 109
Potchefstroom, S. Afr. **D4** 56
Poteau, Ok., U.S. **B7** 129
Poteau, stm., U.S. **B7** 129
Poteet, Tx., U.S. **E3** 136
Potenza, Italy **D5** 18
Potgietersrus, S. Afr. **C4** 56
Poth, Tx., U.S. **E3** 136
Potholes Reservoir, res., Wa., U.S. **B6** 140
Poti, Geor. **A9** 44
Potiskum, Nig. **D7** 50
Potlatch, Id., U.S. **C2** 105
Potomac, Md., U.S. **B3** 113
Potomac, stm., U.S. **D4** 113
Potomac Heights, Md., U.S. **C3** 113
Potomac Park, Md., U.S. **k13** 113
Potosí, Bol. **B4** 72
Potosi, Mo., U.S. **D7** 118
Potsdam, Ger. **D13** 12
Potsdam, N.Y., U.S. **f10** 125
Pottawatomie, co., Ks., U.S. **C7** 109
Pottawatomie, co., Ok., U.S. **B4** 129
Pottawattamie, co., Ia., U.S. **C2** 108
Potter, co., Pa., U.S. **C6** 131
Potter, co., S.D., U.S. **B6** 134
Potter, co., Tx., U.S. **B2** 136
Potter Valley, Ca., U.S. **C2** 98
Potts Creek, stm., U.S. **C2** 139
Pottstown, Pa., U.S. **F10** 131
Pottsville, Ar., U.S. **B2** 97
Pottsville, Pa., U.S. **E9** 131
Pouce Coupe, B.C., Can. **B7** 85
Pouch Cove, Nf., Can. **E5** 88
Poughkeepsie, N.Y., U.S. **D7** 125
Poulan, Ga., U.S. **E3** 103
Poulsbo, Wa., U.S. **B3** 140
Poultney, Vt., U.S. **D2** 138
Poultney, stm., Vt., U.S. **D2** 138
Pound, Va., U.S. **e9** 139
Pound Gap, U.S. **C7** 110
Pouso Alegre, Braz. **F2** 74
Poŭthĭsăt, Camb. **D4** 34
Póvoa de Varzim, Port. **G2** 16
Povungnituk, P.Q., Can. **f11** 90
Powassan, On., Can. **A5** 89
Poway, Ca., U.S. **F5** 98
Powder, stm., Or., U.S. **C9** 130
Powder, stm., U.S. **B6** 92
Powder, Middle Fork, stm., Wy., U.S. **C6** 143
Powder, North Fork, stm., Wy., U.S. **C6** 143
Powder, South Fork, stm., Wy., U.S. **C6** 143
Powder River, co., Mt., U.S. **E11** 119
Powder River Pass, Wy., U.S. **B5** 143
Powder Springs, Ga., U.S. **h8** 103
Powell, Oh., U.S. **B2** 128
Powell, Tn., U.S. **m13** 135
Powell, Wy., U.S. **B4** 143
Powell, co., Ky., U.S. **C6** 110
Powell, co., Mt., U.S. **D4** 119
Powell, stm., U.S. **C10** 135
Powell, Lake, res., U.S. **D5** 92
Powell, Lake, res., U.S. **F5** 137
Powell, Mount, mtn., Co., U.S. **B4** 99
Powell, Mount, mtn., N.M., U.S. **B1** 124
Powell Butte, Or., U.S. **C5** 130
Powell Park, reg., Co., U.S. **A2** 99
Powell River, B.C., Can. **E5** 85
Powellton, W.V., U.S. **C3** 141
Power, co., Id., U.S. **G5** 105
Powers, Or., U.S. **E2** 130
Powerview, Mb., Can. **D3** 86
Poweshiek, co., Ia., U.S. **C5** 108
Powhatan, Va., U.S. **C5** 139
Powhatan, co., Va., U.S. **C5** 139
Powhatan Point, Oh., U.S. **C5** 128
Poxoréu, Braz. **G9** 70
Poyang Hu, l., China **F11** 28
Poyang Lake see Poyang Hu, l., China **F11** 28
Poygan, Lake, l., Wi., U.S. **D5** 142
Poynette, Wi., U.S. **E4** 142
Požarevac, Yugo. **B8** 18
Poza Rica, Mex. **C5** 78
Požega, Cro. **B6** 18
Poznań, Pol. **C4** 20
Pozo Redondo Mountains, mts., Az., U.S. **E3** 96
Pozuelos, Ven. **C7** 80
Prachuap Khiri Khan, Thai. **D3** 34
Prado, Braz. **G12** 70
Prague see Praha, Czech Rep. **D3** 20
Prague, Ok., U.S. **B5** 129
Praha (Prague), Czech Rep. **D3** 20
Praia, C.V. **h10** 50a
Prainha Nova, Braz. **E7** 70
Prairie, co., Ar., U.S. **C4** 97
Prairie, co., Mt., U.S. **D11** 119
Prairie, stm., Mn., U.S. **C5** 116
Prairie, stm., Wi., U.S. **C4** 142
Prairie City, Ia., U.S. **C4** 108
Prairie City, Or., U.S. **C8** 130
Prairie Creek Reservoir, res., In., U.S. **D7** 107
Prairie Dog Creek, stm., U.S. **C3** 109
Prairie du Chien, Wi., U.S. **E2** 142
Prairie du Sac, Wi., U.S. **E4** 142
Prairie Grove, Ar., U.S. **B1** 97
Prairies, Rivière des, stm., P.Q., Can. **p19** 90
Prairie View, Tx., U.S. **D5** 136
Prairie Village, Ks., U.S. **m16** 109
Praslin, i., Sey. **h13** 57b
Pratāpgarh, India **E2** 40
Pratas Island see Tungsha Tao, i., Tai. **E4** 30
Prater Mountain, mtn., Wy., U.S. **C2** 143
Prato, Italy **C3** 18
Pratt, Ks., U.S. **E5** 109
Pratt, co., Ks., U.S. **E5** 109
Prattville, Al., U.S. **C3** 94
Praya, Indon. **E5** 36
Preble, co., Oh., U.S. **C1** 128
Prečistoe, Russia **B12** 20
Premont, Tx., U.S. **F3** 136
Prentiss, Ms., U.S. **D4** 117
Prentiss, co., Ms., U.S. **A5** 117
Prenzlau, Ger. **D13** 12
Preparis Island, i., Myan. **D2** 34
Preparis North Channel, strt., Myan. **C2** 34
Preparis South Channel, strt., Myan. **D2** 34
Přerov, Czech Rep. **E4** 20
Prescott, On., Can. **C9** 89
Prescott, Ar., U.S. **D2** 97
Prescott, Az., U.S. **C3** 96
Prescott, Wi., U.S. **D1** 142
Presho, S.D., U.S. **D5** 134
Presidencia Roque Sáenz Peña, Arg. **C4** 69
Presidente Dutra, Braz. **C3** 74
Presidente Epitácio, Braz. **F1** 74
Presidente Prudente, Braz. **F1** 74
Presidential Range, mts., N.H., U.S. **B4** 122
Presidio, Tx., U.S. **p12** 136
Presidio, co., Tx., U.S. **o12** 136
Prešov, Slvk. **E6** 20
Prespa, Lake, l., Eur. **D8** 18
Presque Isle, Me., U.S. **B5** 112
Presque Isle, co., Mi., U.S. **C6** 115
Prestea, Ghana **E4** 50
Preston, Eng., U.K. **D5** 12
Preston, Ia., U.S. **B7** 108
Preston, Id., U.S. **G7** 105
Preston, Mn., U.S. **G6** 116
Preston, co., W.V., U.S. **B5** 141
Preston Peak, mtn., Ca., U.S. **B2** 98
Prestonsburg, Ky., U.S. **C7** 110
Presumpscot, stm., Me., U.S. **g7** 112
Pretoria, S. Afr. **D4** 56
Prettyboy Reservoir, res., Md., U.S. **A4** 113
Pretty Prairie, Ks., U.S. **E5** 109
Préveza, Grc. **E8** 18
Prewitt Reservoir, res., Co., U.S. **A7** 99
Pribilof Islands, is., Ak., U.S. **D5** 95
Příbram, Czech Rep. **E3** 20
Price, Ut., U.S. **D5** 137
Price, co., Wi., U.S. **C3** 142
Price, stm., Ut., U.S. **D5** 137
Price Inlet, b., S.C., U.S. **k12** 133
Prichard, Al., U.S. **E1** 94
Prieska, S. Afr. **D3** 56
Priest Lake, l., Id., U.S. **A2** 105
Priest Rapids Dam, Wa., U.S. **C6** 140
Priest Rapids Lake, res., Wa., U.S. **C6** 140
Priest River, Id., U.S. **A2** 105
Prievidza, Slvk. **E5** 20
Prijedor, Bos. **B6** 18
Prilep, Mac. **D8** 18
Prim, Point, c., P.E., Can. **C6** 87
Primghar, Ia., U.S. **A2** 108
Primorsk, Russia **F13** 10
Primorsko-Ahtarsk, Russia **F15** 20
Primrose, R.I., U.S. **B3** 132
Primrose Lake, l., Can. **H18** 82
Prince, Lake, res., Va., U.S. **k14** 139
Prince Albert National Park, Sk., Can. **C2** 91
Prince Charles Mountains, mts., Ant. **D11** 67
Prince Edward, co., Va., U.S. **C4** 139
Prince Edward Island, prov., Can. **C6** 87
Prince Edward Island National Park, P.E., Can. **C6** 87
Prince Edward Islands, is., S. Afr. **N13** 46
Prince Frederick, Md., U.S. **C4** 113
Prince George, B.C., Can. **C6** 85
Prince George, co., Va., U.S. **C5** 139
Prince Georges, co., Md., U.S. **C4** 113
Prince of Wales, Cape, c., Ak., U.S. **B6** 95
Prince of Wales Island, i., Austl. **C3** 62
Prince of Wales Island, i., Ak., U.S. **n23** 95
Prince Olav Coast, is., Ant. **C9** 67
Prince Rupert, B.C., Can. **B2** 85
Princes Lakes, In., U.S. **F5** 107
Princess Anne, Md., U.S. **D6** 113
Princess Astrid Coast, Ant. **D5** 67
Princess Martha Coast, Ant. **D3** 67
Princess Ragnhild Coast, Ant. **D7** 67
Princess Royal Channel, strt., B.C., Can. **C3** 85
Princess Royal Island, i., B.C., Can. **C3** 85
Princeton, B.C., Can. **E7** 85
Princeton, Fl., U.S. **G6** 102
Princeton, Ia., U.S. **C7** 108
Princeton, Il., U.S. **B4** 106
Princeton, In., U.S. **H2** 107
Princeton, Ky., U.S. **C2** 110
Princeton, Me., U.S. **C5** 112
Princeton, Mn., U.S. **E5** 116
Princeton, Mo., U.S. **A4** 118
Princeton, N.C., U.S. **B4** 126
Princeton, N.J., U.S. **C3** 123
Princeton, W.V., U.S. **D3** 141
Princeton, Wi., U.S. **E4** 142
Princeton, Mount, mtn., Co., U.S. **C4** 99
Princeville, P.Q., Can. **C6** 90
Princeville, Il., U.S. **C4** 106
Princeville, N.C., U.S. **B5** 126
Prince William, co., Va., U.S. **B5** 139
Prince William Sound, strt., Ak., U.S. **g18** 95
Príncipe, i., S. Tom./P. **C1** 54
Principe Channel, strt., B.C., Can. **C3** 85
Príncipe da Beira, Braz. **F7** 70
Prineville, Or., U.S. **C6** 130
Prineville Reservoir, res., Or., U.S. **C6** 130
Prinzapolka, Nic. **C3** 80
Prior Lake, Mn., U.S. **F5** 116
Priozersk, Russia **F14** 10
Pripet (Pryp'yat') (Pripjat'), stm., Eur. **C9** 20
Pripet Marshes, reg., Eur. **C10** 20
Pripyat see Pripet, stm., Eur. **C9** 20
Priština, Yugo. **C8** 18
Pritchards Island, i., S.C., U.S. **G6** 133
Pritzwalk, Ger. **D13** 12
Privas, Fr. **E9** 16
Privolžskaja vozvyšennost', plat., Russia **D6** 26
Prizren, Yugo. **C8** 18
Probolinggo, Indon. **E4** 36
Proctor, Mn., U.S. **D6** 116
Proctor, Vt., U.S. **D2** 138
Proctor Lake, res., Tx., U.S. **C3** 136
Proctorsville, Vt., U.S. **E3** 138
Proddatūr, India **G3** 40
Progreso, Mex. **C7** 78
Prohladnyj, Russia **F7** 22
Prokopevsk, Russia **D10** 26
Prokuplje, Yugo. **C8** 18
Proletarskij, Russia **D13** 20
Prome, Myan. **C3** 34
Promontory Mountains, mts., Ut., U.S. **B3** 137
Prophetstown, Il., U.S. **B4** 106
Propriá, Braz. **D4** 74
Proserpine, Austl. **E4** 62
Prospect, Ct., U.S. **C4** 100
Prospect, Ky., U.S. **g11** 110
Prospect, Oh., U.S. **B2** 128
Prospect, Or., U.S. **E4** 130
Prospect, Pa., U.S. **E1** 131
Prospect Hill, mtn., Or., U.S. **k11** 130
Prospect Park, N.J., U.S. **B4** 123
Prospect Park, Pa., U.S. **p20** 131
Prosperidad, Phil. **E9** 34
Prosperity, S.C., U.S. **C4** 133
Prosperity, W.V., U.S. **n13** 141
Prosser, Wa., U.S. **C6** 140
Protection, Ks., U.S. **E4** 109
Provadija, Bul. **C11** 18
Provence, hist. reg., Fr. **F9** 16
Providence, Ky., U.S. **C2** 110
Providence, R.I., U.S. **C4** 132
Providence, Ut., U.S. **B4** 137
Providence, co., R.I., U.S. **C2** 132
Providence, stm., R.I., U.S. **C5** 132
Providence Point, c., R.I., U.S. **D5** 132
Providencia, Isla de, i., Col. **C3** 80
Providenija, Russia **C20** 26
Province Lake, l., N.H., U.S. **C5** 122
Provincetown, Ma., U.S. **B7** 114
Provins, Fr. **C8** 16
Provo, Ut., U.S. **C4** 137
Provo, stm., Ut., U.S. **C4** 137
Provost, Ab., Can. **C5** 84
Prowers, co., Co., U.S. **D8** 99
Prudence Island, i., R.I., U.S. **E5** 132
Prudentópolis, Braz. **D7** 72
Prudenville, Mi., U.S. **D6** 115
Prudhoe Bay, Ak., U.S. **A10** 95
Prudhoe Bay, b., Ak., U.S. **A10** 95
Prut, stm., Eur. **G10** 20
Pružany, Bela. **C8** 20
Pryluky, Ukr. **D12** 20
Prymors'k, Ukr. **F14** 20
Pryor, Mt., U.S. **E8** 119
Pryor, Ok., U.S. **A6** 129
Pryor Mountains, mts., Mt., U.S. **E8** 119
Pryp'yat' (Pripet) (Pripjat'), stm., Eur. **D8** 20
Przasnysz, Pol. **C6** 20
Przemyśl, Pol. **E7** 20
Psël (Ps'ol), stm., Eur. **D13** 20
Pskov, Russia **D4** 26
Pskov, Lake, l., Eur. **G13** 10
Ps'ol (Psël), stm., Eur. **D13** 20
Ptolemaïs, Grc. **D8** 18
Pucallpa, Peru **E5** 70
Pucheng, China **F11** 28
Puckaway Lake, l., Wi., U.S. **E4** 142
Pudož, Russia **B6** 22
Pudukkottai, India **G3** 40
Puebla, state, Mex. **D5** 78
Puebla de Zaragoza, Mex. **D5** 78
Pueblo, Co., U.S. **C6** 99
Pueblo, co., Co., U.S. **C6** 99
Pueblo Mountain, mtn., Or., U.S. **E8** 130
Pueblo Mountains, mts., Or., U.S. **E8** 130
Pueblo Reservoir, res., Co., U.S. **C6** 99
Puente Genil, Spain **I4** 16
Pueo Point, c., Hi., U.S. **B1** 104
Puerco, stm., U.S. **C6** 96
Puerco, Rio, stm., N.M., U.S. **B2** 124
Puerto Acosta, Bol. **B4** 72
Puerto Ángel, Mex. **D5** 78
Puerto Armuelles, Pan. **D3** 80
Puerto Asís, Col. **C4** 70
Puerto Ayacucho, Ven. **B6** 70
Puerto Baquerizo Moreno, Ec. **D2** 70
Puerto Barrios, Guat. **B2** 80
Puerto Bermúdez, Peru **F5** 70
Puerto Berrío, Col. **B5** 70
Puerto Bolívar, Col. **C5** 80
Puerto Boyacá, Col. **D5** 80
Puerto Cabello, Ven. **A6** 70
Puerto Cabezas, Nic. **C3** 80
Puerto Carreño, Col. **B6** 70
Puerto Chicama, Peru **E4** 70
Puerto Cortés, Hond. **B2** 80
Puerto Cumarebo, Ven. **A6** 70
Puerto de la Cruz, Spain **A1** 50
Puerto del Rosario, Spain **A2** 50
Puerto Deseado, Arg. **G3** 69
Puerto Esperanza, Arg. **D7** 72
Puerto Guaraní, Para. **C6** 72
Puerto Inírida, Col. **E6** 80
Puerto Juárez, Mex. **C7** 78
Puerto la Cruz, Ven. **A7** 70
Puerto Leguízamo, Col. **D5** 70
Puerto Libertad, Mex. **B2** 78
Puerto Limón, C.R. **C3** 80
Puertollano, Spain **H4** 16
Puerto Lobos, Arg. **F3** 69
Puerto Madryn, Arg. **F3** 69
Puerto Maldonado, Peru **F6** 70
Puerto Montt, Chile **F2** 69
Puerto Morazán, Nic. **C2** 80
Puerto Nariño, Col. **D6** 80
Puerto Natales, Chile **H2** 69
Puerto Padre, Cuba **A4** 80
Puerto Páez, Ven. **B6** 70
Puerto Peñasco, Mex. **A2** 78
Puerto Plata, Dom. Rep. **B5** 80
Puerto Princesa, Phil. **E7** 34
Puerto Rico, Bol. **F6** 70
Puerto Rico, dep., N.A. **B6** 80
Puerto Rico Trench **G7** 66
Puerto San José, Guat. **C1** 80
Puerto San Julián, Arg. **G3** 69
Puerto Santa Cruz, Arg. **H3** 69
Puerto Sastre, Para. **C6** 72
Puerto Suárez, Bol. **B6** 72
Puerto Vallarta, Mex. **C3** 78
Puerto Villamil, Ec. **D1** 70
Puerto Wilches, Col. **B5** 70
Puerto Ybapobó, Para. **C6** 72
Pugačov, Russia **D8** 22
Puget Sound, strt., Wa., U.S. **B3** 140
Puget Sound Naval Shipyard, mil., Wa., U.S. **e10** 140
Pugwash, N.S., Can. **D6** 87
Puhi, Hi., U.S. **B2** 104
Pukalani, Hi., U.S. **C5** 104
Pukaskwa National Park, On., Can. **o18** 89
Pukch'ŏng-ŭp, N. Kor. **C13** 28
Pukeashun Mountain, mtn., B.C., Can. **D8** 85
Pukou, China **C4** 30
Pula, Cro. **B4** 18
Pulaski, N.Y., U.S. **B4** 125
Pulaski, Tn., U.S. **B4** 135
Pulaski, Va., U.S. **C2** 139
Pulaski, Wi., U.S. **D5** 142
Pulaski, co., Ar., U.S. **C3** 97
Pulaski, co., Ga., U.S. **D3** 103
Pulaski, co., Il., U.S. **F4** 106
Pulaski, co., In., U.S. **B4** 107
Pulaski, co., Ky., U.S. **C5** 110
Pulaski, co., Mo., U.S. **D5** 118
Pulaski, co., Va., U.S. **C2** 139
Puławy, Pol. **D7** 20
Pulicat Lake, l., India **G4** 40
Pullman, Wa., U.S. **C8** 140
Pumphrey, Md., U.S. **h11** 113
Puná, Isla, i., Ec. **D3** 70
Punakha, Bhu. **D5** 40
Punata, Bol. **B4** 72
Pune, India **F2** 40
Pungo Lake, l., N.C., U.S. **B6** 126
Punia, D.R.C. **D5** 54
Punjab, prov., India **C3** 40
Punjab, prov., Pak. **D11** 42
Puno, Peru **G5** 70
Punta, Cerro de, mtn., P.R. **B6** 80
Punta Alta, Arg. **F5** 72
Punta Arenas, Chile **H2** 69
Punta de Díaz, Chile **D3** 72
Punta del Este, Ur. **F7** 72
Punta Delgada, Arg. **F4** 69
Punta Gorda, Fl., U.S. **F4** 102
Punta Gorda, Bahía de, b., Nic. **C3** 80
Puntarenas, C.R. **C2** 80
Punto Fijo, Ven. **A5** 70
Punxsutawney, Pa., U.S. **E4** 131
Puolanka, Fin. **D12** 10
Puqi, China **F10** 28
Puquio, Peru **F5** 70
Purcell, Ok., U.S. **B4** 129
Purcellville, Va., U.S. **A5** 139
Purdy, Mo., U.S. **E4** 118
Purgatoire, stm., Co., U.S. **D7** 99
Purgatoire Peak, mtn., Co., U.S. **D5** 99
Puri, India **F5** 40
Pūrnia, India **D5** 40
Purus (Purús), stm., S.A. **D7** 70
Purvis, Ms., U.S. **D4** 117
Purwakarta, Indon. **E3** 36
Purwokerto, Indon. **E3** 36
Pusan, S. Kor. **D13** 28
Pushaw Lake, l., Me., U.S. **D4** 112
Pushkar, India **D2** 40
Pushmataha, co., Ok., U.S. **C6** 129
Puškin, Russia **G15** 10
Putao, Myan. **A3** 34
Putaruru, N.Z. **o14** 63c
Putian, China **D4** 30
Puting, Tanjung, c., Indon. **D4** 36
Putnam, Ct., U.S. **B8** 100
Putnam, co., Fl., U.S. **C5** 102
Putnam, co., Ga., U.S. **C3** 103
Putnam, co., Il., U.S. **B4** 106
Putnam, co., In., U.S. **E4** 107
Putnam, co., Mo., U.S. **A4** 118
Putnam, co., N.Y., U.S. **D7** 125
Putnam, co., Oh., U.S. **B1** 128
Putnam, co., Tn., U.S. **C8** 135
Putnam, co., W.V., U.S. **C3** 141
Putney, Ga., U.S. **E2** 103
Putney, Vt., U.S. **F3** 138
Putorana, plato, plat., Russia **C11** 26
Puttalam, Sri L. **H3** 40
Puttgarden, Ger. **C12** 12
Putumayo (Içá), stm., S.A. **D5** 70
Putussibau, Indon. **C4** 36
Puukohola Heiau National Historic Site, hist., Hi., U.S. **D6** 104
Puula, l., Fin. **F12** 10
Puxico, Mo., U.S. **E7** 118
Puyallup, Wa., U.S. **B3** 140
Puyallup, stm., Wa., U.S. **C3** 140
Puyang, China **B3** 30
Pweto, D.R.C. **E5** 54
Pyandzh see Amu Darya, stm., Asia **B8** 42
Pyapon, Myan. **C3** 34
Pyhäjoki, Fin. **D11** 10
Pyhäselkä, l., Fin. **E13** 10
Pyinmana, Myan. **C3** 34

Name	Map Ref.	Page
Pyles Fork, stm., W.V., U.S.	**h10**	141
Pymatuning Reservoir, res., U.S.	**C1**	131
P'yŏngyang, N. Kor.	**D13**	28
Pyramid Lake, l., Nv., U.S.	**C2**	121
Pyramid Lake Indian Reservation, Nv., U.S.	**D2**	121
Pyramid Mountains, mts., N.M., U.S.	**E1**	124
Pyramid Peak, mtn., N.M., U.S.	**E1**	124
Pyramid Peak, mtn., Wy., U.S.	**C2**	143
Pyrenees, mts., Eur.	**F7**	16
Pyriatyn, Ukr.	**D12**	20
Pyu, Myan.	**C3**	34

Q

Name	Map Ref.	Page
Qaanaaq see Thule, Grnld.	**C26**	82
Qacentina, Alg.	**C6**	48
Qā'emshahr, Iran	**C6**	42
Qā'en, Iran	**D7**	42
Qaidam Pendi, China	**D6**	28
Qalāt, Afg.	**D9**	42
Qal'at Bīshah, Sau. Ar.	**G4**	38
Qal'at Sukkar, Iraq	**G12**	44
Qal'eh-ye Now, Afg.	**D8**	42
Qallābāt, Sudan	**H3**	38
Qamar, Ghubbat al-, b., Yemen	**G6**	38
Qamar Bay see Qamar, Ghubbat al-, b., Yemen	**G6**	38
Qamdo, China	**E7**	28
Qandahār, Afg.	**D9**	42
Qandala, Som.	**H5**	38
Qardho, Som.	**I14**	48
Qareh Sū, stm., Iran	**C12**	44
Qasr el-Boukhari, Alg.	**J8**	16
Qasr Farâfra, Egypt	**E10**	48
Qaṭanā, Syria	**F7**	44
Qatar, ctry., Asia	**E6**	42
Qattâra, Munkhafad el-, depr., Egypt	**E10**	48
Qattara Depression see Qattâra, Munkhafad el-, depr., Egypt	**E10**	48
Qausuituq, Nu., Can.	**D20**	82
Qazımämmäd, Azer.	**B13**	44
Qazvīn, Iran	**C5**	42
Qena, Egypt	**E11**	48
Qeydār, Iran	**D13**	44
Qianwei, China	**D1**	30
Qianxi, China	**D2**	30
Qianyang, China	**D3**	30
Qiemo, China	**D5**	28
Qigong, China	**A4**	34
Qijiang, China	**D2**	30
Qilian Shan, mts., China	**D7**	28
Qimen, China	**D4**	30
Qingdao, China	**D12**	28
Qinghai, state, China	**D7**	28
Qinghai Hu, l., China	**D8**	28
Qingjiang, China	**E11**	28
Qinglong, China	**A4**	30
Qinglong, China	**D2**	30
Qingshen, China	**D1**	30
Qingtang, China	**G10**	28
Qingyang, China	**D9**	28
Qingyuan, China	**E3**	30
Qing Zang Gaoyuan (Tibet, Plateau of), plat., China	**E4**	28
Qinhuangdao, China	**D11**	28
Qin Ling, mts., China	**E9**	28
Qinxian, China	**B3**	30
Qinzhou, China	**E2**	30
Qionghai, China	**F3**	30
Qionglai, China	**E8**	28
Qiongzhong, China	**H9**	28
Qiongzhou Haixia, strt., China	**G9**	28
Qiqihar, China	**B12**	28
Qiryat Shemona, Isr.	**F6**	44
Qishn, Yemen	**G6**	38
Qitai, China	**C5**	28
Qiyang, China	**D3**	30
Qobustan, Azer.	**B13**	44
Qogir Feng see K2, mtn., Asia	**B3**	40
Qom, Iran	**D6**	42
Qomolangma Feng see Everest, Mount, mtn., Asia	**D5**	40
Qomsheh, Iran	**D6**	42
Qorveh, Iran	**E12**	44
Quabbin Reservoir, res., Ma., U.S.	**B3**	114
Quaddick Reservoir, res., Ct., U.S.	**B8**	100
Quail Oaks, Va., U.S.	**n18**	139
Quaker Hill, Ct., U.S.	**D7**	100
Quakertown, Pa., U.S.	**F11**	131
Qualicum Beach, B.C., Can.	**E5**	85
Quanah, Tx., U.S.	**B3**	136
Quang Ngai, Viet.	**C5**	34
Quannapowitt, Lake, l., Ma., U.S.	**f11**	114
Quantico, Va., U.S.	**B5**	139
Quantico Marine Corps Air Station, mil., Va., U.S.	**B5**	139
Quanzhou, China	**G11**	28
Quanzhou, China	**D3**	30
Quapaw, Ok., U.S.	**A7**	129
Qu'Appelle, Sk., Can.	**G4**	91
Qu'Appelle, stm., Can.	**G4**	91
Quarryville, Pa., U.S.	**G9**	131
Quartu Sant'Elena, Italy	**E2**	18
Quartz Mountain, mtn., Or., U.S.	**D4**	130
Quartzsite, Az., U.S.	**D1**	96
Quassapaug, Lake, l., Ct., U.S.	**C3**	100
Quatsino Sound, strt., B.C., Can.	**D3**	85
Quay, co., N.M., U.S.	**C6**	124
Quba, Azer.	**B13**	44
Qūchān, Iran	**C7**	42
Queanbeyan, Austl.	**H4**	62
Québec, P.Q., Can.	**C6**	90
Quebec, prov., Can.	**C5**	90
Quechee, Vt., U.S.	**D4**	138
Queen, stm., R.I., U.S.	**E3**	132
Queen Annes, co., Md., U.S.	**B5**	113
Queen Bess, Mount, mtn., B.C., Can.	**D5**	85
Queen Charlotte, B.C., Can.	**C1**	85
Queen Charlotte Islands, is., B.C., Can.	**C1**	85
Queen Charlotte Mountains, mts., B.C., Can.	**C1**	85
Queen Charlotte Sound, strt., B.C., Can.	**H14**	82
Queen Charlotte Strait, strt., B.C., Can.	**D4**	85
Queen City, Mo., U.S.	**A5**	118
Queen City, Tx., U.S.	**C5**	136
Queen Creek, Az., U.S.	**m9**	96
Queen Mary Coast, Ant.	**C14**	67
Queen Maud Land, reg., Ant.	**D4**	67
Queen Maud Mountains, mts., Ant.	**E25**	67
Queens, co., N.Y., U.S.	**E7**	125
Queensland, state, Austl.	**E3**	62
Queenstown, Austl.	**I4**	62
Queenstown, S. Afr.	**E4**	56
Quela, Ang.	**E3**	54
Quelimane, Moz.	**B6**	56
Querétaro, Mex.	**C4**	78
Querétaro, state, Mex.	**C5**	78
Queshan, China	**C3**	30
Quesnel, B.C., Can.	**C6**	85
Quesnel, stm., B.C., Can.	**C6**	85
Quesnel Lake, l., B.C., Can.	**C7**	85
Questa, N.M., U.S.	**A4**	124
Quetico Provincial Park, On., Can.	**o17**	89
Quetta, Pak.	**D9**	42
Quevedo, Ec.	**D4**	70
Quezon City, Phil.	**D8**	34
Quibala, Ang.	**F3**	54
Quibdó, Col.	**B4**	70
Quicksand Pond, l., R.I., U.S.	**E6**	132
Quiculungo, Ang.	**E3**	54
Quidnessett, R.I., U.S.	**E4**	132
Quidnick, R.I., U.S.	**D3**	132
Quidnick Reservoir, res., R.I., U.S.	**D2**	132
Quila, Mex.	**C3**	78
Quilcene, Wa., U.S.	**B3**	140
Quileute Indian Reservation, Wa., U.S.	**B1**	140
Quillota, Chile	**D2**	69
Quilon, India	**H3**	40
Quimaria, Ang.	**E2**	54
Quimilí, Arg.	**D5**	72
Quimper, Fr.	**D4**	16
Quimperlé, Fr.	**D5**	16
Quinault, stm., Wa., U.S.	**B1**	140
Quinault, Lake, l., Wa., U.S.	**B2**	140
Quinault Indian Reservation, Wa., U.S.	**B1**	140
Quince Mil, Peru	**F5**	70
Quincy, Ca., U.S.	**C3**	98
Quincy, Fl., U.S.	**B2**	102
Quincy, Il., U.S.	**D2**	106
Quincy, Ma., U.S.	**B5**	114
Quincy, Mi., U.S.	**G6**	115
Quincy, Wa., U.S.	**B6**	140
Quincy Bay, b., Ma., U.S.	**g12**	114
Quinebaug, Ct., U.S.	**A8**	100
Quinebaug, stm., Ct., U.S.	**C8**	100
Quinhagak, Ak., U.S.	**D7**	95
Quinlan, Tx., U.S.	**C4**	136
Quinn, stm., Nv., U.S.	**B3**	121
Quinn Canyon Range, mts., Nv., U.S.	**F6**	121
Quinnesec, Mi., U.S.	**C3**	115
Quinnipiac, stm., Ct., U.S.	**D4**	100
Quintana Roo, state, Mex.	**D7**	78
Quinter, Ks., U.S.	**C3**	109
Quinton, Ok., U.S.	**B6**	129
Quirinópolis, Braz.	**E1**	74
Quissanga, Moz.	**A7**	56
Quiterajo, Moz.	**A7**	56
Quitman, Ar., U.S.	**B3**	97
Quitman, Ga., U.S.	**F3**	103
Quitman, Ms., U.S.	**C5**	117
Quitman, Tx., U.S.	**C5**	136
Quitman, co., Ga., U.S.	**E1**	103
Quitman, co., Ms., U.S.	**A3**	117
Quito, Ec.	**D4**	70
Quixadá, Braz.	**B4**	74
Quixeramobim, Braz.	**C4**	74
Qujing, China	**F8**	28
Qumarlêb, China	**E7**	28
Qunayyin, Sabkhat al-, l., Libya	**E8**	14
Quonnipaug Lake, l., Ct., U.S.	**D5**	100
Quonochontaug, R.I., U.S.	**G2**	132
Quonochontaug Pond, l., R.I., U.S.	**G2**	132
Quonset Point, c., R.I., U.S.	**E4**	132
Quseir, Egypt	**E11**	48
Qutdligssat, Grnld.	**D29**	82
Quthing, Leso.	**E4**	56
Qüxü, China	**D6**	40
Quy Nhon, Viet.	**D5**	34
Quzhou, China	**F11**	28

R

Name	Map Ref.	Page
Raab see Győr, Hung.	**F4**	20
Raahe, Fin.	**D11**	10
Rab, Otok, i., Cro.	**B5**	18
Raba, Indon.	**E5**	36
Rába, stm., Eur.	**F4**	20
Rabat, Mor.	**D3**	48
Rabaul, Pap. N. Gui.	**G13**	32
Rabbit Creek, stm., S.D., U.S.	**B3**	134
Rabbit Ears Pass, Co., U.S.	**A4**	99
Rabi, i., Fiji	**m11**	63b
Rābigh, Sau. Ar.	**F3**	38
Rîbnița, Mol.	**F10**	20
Rabun, co., Ga., U.S.	**B3**	103
Rabun Bald, mtn., Ga., U.S.	**B3**	103
Rabyānah, Ramlat, des., Libya	**F8**	48
Raccoon Creek, stm., Oh., U.S.	**D3**	128
Raccourci Island, i., La., U.S.	**D4**	111
Race, Cape, c., Nf., Can.	**E5**	88
Raceland, Ky., U.S.	**B7**	110
Raceland, La., U.S.	**E5**	111
Race Point, c., Ma., U.S.	**B7**	114
Rach Gia, Viet.	**E4**	34
Racine, W.V., U.S.	**C3**	141
Racine, Wi., U.S.	**F6**	142
Racine, co., Wi., U.S.	**F5**	142
Racine Dam, U.S.	**C3**	141
Rădăuți, Rom.	**F8**	20
Radcliff, Ky., U.S.	**C4**	110
Radford, Va., U.S.	**C2**	139
Radom, Pol.	**D6**	20
Radomsko, Pol.	**D5**	20
Radomyshl', Ukr.	**D10**	20
Rāe Bareli, India	**D4**	40
Raeford, N.C., U.S.	**C3**	126
Rafaela, Arg.	**E5**	72
Rafaḥ, Gaza Str.	**G6**	44
Rafḥā', Sau. Ar.	**E4**	38
Rafsanjān, Iran	**D7**	42
Raft, stm., Id., U.S.	**G5**	105
Raft River Mountains, mts., Ut., U.S.	**B2**	137
Raga, Sudan	**I10**	48
Ragay Gulf, b., Phil.	**D8**	34
Ragged Island, i., Me., U.S.	**E4**	112
Ragged Island Range, is., Bah.	**D9**	76
Ragged Lake, l., Me., U.S.	**C3**	112
Ragged Top Mountain, mtn., Wy., U.S.	**E7**	143
Ragland, Al., U.S.	**B3**	94
Ragusa, Italy	**F5**	18
Rahīmyār Khān, Pak.	**E10**	42
Rahway, N.J., U.S.	**B4**	123
Rahway, stm., N.J., U.S.	**k7**	123
Rāichūr, India	**F3**	40
Raiganj, India	**D5**	40
Raigarh, India	**E4**	40
Railroad Valley, val., Nv., U.S.	**E6**	121
Rainbow Bridge National Monument, Ut., U.S.	**F5**	137
Rainbow Falls, wtfl, Tn., U.S.	**D10**	135
Rainbow Flowage, res., Wi., U.S.	**C4**	142
Rainbow Lake, l., Me., U.S.	**C3**	112
Rainelle, W.V., U.S.	**D4**	141
Rainier, Or., U.S.	**A4**	130
Rainier, Wa., U.S.	**C3**	140
Rainier, Mount, mtn., Wa., U.S.	**C4**	140
Rains, co., Tx., U.S.	**C5**	136
Rainsville, Al., U.S.	**A4**	94
Rainy Lake, l., Mn., U.S.	**B5**	116
Rainy River, On., Can.	**o16**	89
Raipur, India	**E4**	40
Rājahmundry, India	**F4**	40
Rajang, stm., Malay.	**C4**	36
Rājapālaiyam, India	**H3**	40
Rājasthān, prov., India	**D2**	40
Rajčihinsk, Russia	**E14**	26
Rāj Gangpur, India	**E4**	40
Rājkot, India	**E2**	40
Rāj Nāndgaon, India	**E4**	40
Rājshāhi, Bngl.	**E5**	40
Rakhiv, Ukr.	**E8**	20
Rakvere, Est.	**G12**	10
Raleigh, Ms., U.S.	**C4**	117
Raleigh, N.C., U.S.	**B4**	126
Raleigh, W.V., U.S.	**n13**	141
Raleigh, co., W.V., U.S.	**D3**	141
Raleigh Bay, b., N.C., U.S.	**C6**	126
Ralls, Tx., U.S.	**C2**	136
Ralls, co., Mo., U.S.	**B6**	118
Ralston, Ne., U.S.	**g12**	120
Ralston Valley, val., Nv., U.S.	**E4**	121
Ramah, N.M., U.S.	**B1**	124
Ramah Indian Reservation, N.M., U.S.	**C1**	124
Ramapo, stm., N.J., U.S.	**A4**	123
Ramblewood, N.J., U.S.	**D3**	123
Rambouillet, Fr.	**C7**	16
Ramea, Nf., Can.	**E3**	88
Rāmeswaram, India	**H3**	40
Rāmhormoz, Iran	**D5**	42
Ramm, Jabal, mtn., Jord.	**E3**	42
Râmnicu Sărat, Rom.	**G9**	20
Râmnicu Vâlcea, Rom.	**G8**	20
Ramona, Ca., U.S.	**F5**	98
Rampart Range, mts., Co., U.S.	**B5**	99
Rāmpur, India	**D3**	40
Ramree Island, i., Myan.	**C2**	34
Ramsay, Mi., U.S.	**n12**	115
Ramsele, Swe.	**E7**	10
Ramseur, N.C., U.S.	**B3**	126
Ramsey, Il., U.S.	**D4**	106
Ramsey, N.J., U.S.	**A4**	123
Ramsey, co., Mn., U.S.	**E5**	116
Ramsey, co., N.D., U.S.	**A7**	127
Ramsgate, Eng., U.K.	**E7**	12
Ramshorn Peak, mtn., Mt., U.S.	**E5**	119
Ramshorn Peak, mtn., Wy., U.S.	**C3**	143
Ramu, Kenya	**C8**	54
Rāna Pratāp Sāgar, res., India	**D2**	40
Rancagua, Chile	**D2**	69
Rancharia, Braz.	**F1**	74
Rancheria Rock, mtn., Or., U.S.	**C6**	130
Ranchester, Wy., U.S.	**B5**	143
Rānchi, India	**E5**	40
Ranchos de Taos, N.M., U.S.	**A4**	124
Rancocas Creek, stm., N.J., U.S.	**C3**	123
Rand, W.V., U.S.	**C3**	141
Randall, co., Tx., U.S.	**B2**	136
Randallstown, Md., U.S.	**B4**	113
Randers, Den.	**H4**	10
Randijaure, l., Swe.	**C8**	10
Randle, Wa., U.S.	**C4**	140
Randleman, N.C., U.S.	**B3**	126
Randolph, Ma., U.S.	**B5**	114
Randolph, Me., U.S.	**D3**	112
Randolph, Ne., U.S.	**B8**	120
Randolph, Vt., U.S.	**D3**	138
Randolph, Wi., U.S.	**E5**	142
Randolph, co., Al., U.S.	**B4**	94
Randolph, co., Ar., U.S.	**A4**	97
Randolph, co., Ga., U.S.	**E2**	103
Randolph, co., Il., U.S.	**E4**	106
Randolph, co., In., U.S.	**D7**	107
Randolph, co., Mo., U.S.	**B5**	118
Randolph, co., N.C., U.S.	**B3**	126
Randolph, co., W.V., U.S.	**C5**	141
Randolph Air Force Base, mil., Tx., U.S.	**h7**	136
Randolph Hills, Md., U.S.	**B3**	113
Random Island, i., Nf., Can.	**D5**	88
Random Lake, Wi., U.S.	**E6**	142
Randsfjorden, l., Nor.	**F4**	10
Rāngāmāti, Bngl.	**E6**	40
Rangeley, Me., U.S.	**D2**	112
Rangeley Lake, l., Me., U.S.	**D2**	112
Rangely, Co., U.S.	**A2**	99
Ranger, Tx., U.S.	**C3**	136
Ranger Lake, l., N.M., U.S.	**D6**	124
Rangoon see Yangon, Myan.	**C3**	34
Rangpur, Bngl.	**D5**	40
Rānībennur, India	**G3**	40
Rankin, Pa., U.S.	**k14**	131
Rankin, co., Ms., U.S.	**C4**	117
Rann of Kutch see Kutch, Rann of, reg., Asia	**E1**	40
Ranohira, Madag.	**C8**	56
Ranong, Thai.	**E3**	34
Ransiki, Indon.	**D8**	36
Ransom, co., N.D., U.S.	**C8**	127
Ranson, W.V., U.S.	**B7**	141
Rantauprapat, Indon.	**C1**	36
Rantoul, Il., U.S.	**C5**	106
Raohe, China	**A2**	31
Raoul, Ga., U.S.	**B3**	103
Rapallo, Italy	**B2**	18
Rapid, stm., Mn., U.S.	**B4**	116
Rapid City, S.D., U.S.	**C2**	134
Rapides, co., La., U.S.	**C3**	111
Rapid River, Mi., U.S.	**C4**	115
Rapids City, Il., U.S.	**B3**	106
Rappahannock, co., Va., U.S.	**B4**	139
Rappahannock, stm., Va., U.S.	**B5**	139
Raquette, stm., N.Y., U.S.	**f10**	125
Raquette Lake, l., N.Y., U.S.	**B6**	125
Raraka, atoll, Fr. Poly.	**F15**	58
Raritan, N.J., U.S.	**B3**	123
Raritan, stm., N.J., U.S.	**C4**	123
Raritan Bay, b., N.J., U.S.	**C4**	123
Rarotonga, i., Cook Is.	**G14**	58
Ra's al-Khaymah, U.A.E.	**E7**	42
Ras Dashen Terara, mtn., Eth.	**H12**	48
Rashid, Egypt	**E10**	14
Rasht, Iran	**C5**	42
Rasšua, ostrov, i., Russia	**E17**	26
Ratangarh, India	**D2**	40
Rāth, India	**D3**	40
Rathbun Lake, res., Ia., U.S.	**D5**	108
Rathdrum, Id., U.S.	**B2**	105
Rat Islands, is., Ak., U.S.	**E3**	95
Ratlām, India	**E3**	40
Ratnāgiri, India	**F2**	40
Ratnapura, Sri L.	**H4**	40
Raton, N.M., U.S.	**A5**	124
Raton Pass, N.M., U.S.	**A5**	124
Rattlesnake Creek, stm., Oh., U.S.	**C2**	128
Rattlesnake Creek, stm., Wa., U.S.	**C6**	140
Rättvik, Swe.	**F6**	10
Raub, Malay.	**C2**	36
Rauch, Arg.	**F6**	72
Rauma, Fin.	**F9**	10
Raurkela, India	**E5**	40
Ravalli, co., Mt., U.S.	**D2**	119
Raven, Va., U.S.	**e10**	139
Ravena, N.Y., U.S.	**C7**	125
Ravenel, S.C., U.S.	**k11**	133
Ravenna, Italy	**B4**	18
Ravenna, Ky., U.S.	**C6**	110
Ravenna, Mi., U.S.	**E5**	115
Ravenna, Ne., U.S.	**C7**	120
Ravenna, Oh., U.S.	**A4**	128
Raven Park, reg., Co., U.S.	**A2**	99
Ravensburg, Ger.	**G11**	12
Ravensthorpe, Austl.	**G3**	60
Ravenswood, W.V., U.S.	**C3**	141
Rāvi, stm., Asia	**C2**	40
Ravnina, Turk.	**C8**	42
Rawaki, atoll, Kir.	**E12**	58
Rāwalpindi, Pak.	**D10**	42
Rawdon, P.Q., Can.	**C4**	90
Rawhide Creek, stm., Wy., U.S.	**D8**	143
Rawlings, Md., U.S.	**k13**	113
Rawlinna, Austl.	**G4**	60
Rawlins, Wy., U.S.	**E5**	143
Rawlins, co., Ks., U.S.	**C2**	109
Rawson, Arg.	**F3**	69
Ray, N.D., U.S.	**A2**	127
Ray, co., Mo., U.S.	**B3**	118
Ray, Cape, c., Nf., Can.	**E2**	88
Raya, Bukit, mtn., Indon.	**C4**	36
Rāyachoti, India	**G3**	40
Rāyadurg, India	**G3**	40
Ray City, Ga., U.S.	**E3**	103
Raymond, Ab., Can.	**E4**	84
Raymond, Il., U.S.	**D4**	106
Raymond, Mn., U.S.	**E3**	116
Raymond, Ms., U.S.	**C3**	117
Raymond, N.H., U.S.	**D4**	122
Raymond, Wa., U.S.	**C2**	140
Raymondville, Tx., U.S.	**F4**	136
Raymore, Sk., Can.	**F3**	91
Raymore, Mo., U.S.	**C3**	118
Rayne, La., U.S.	**D3**	111
Raynham, Ma., U.S.	**C5**	114
Raynham Center, Ma., U.S.	**C5**	114
Rayong, Thai.	**D4**	34
Raytown, Mo., U.S.	**h11**	118
Rayville, La., U.S.	**B4**	111
Razdol'noe, Russia	**B2**	31
Razgrad, Bul.	**C11**	18
Ré, Île de, i., Fr.	**D6**	16
Reader, W.V., U.S.	**B4**	141
Reading, Eng., U.K.	**E6**	12
Reading, Ma., U.S.	**A5**	114
Reading, Mi., U.S.	**G6**	115
Reading, Oh., U.S.	**C1**	128
Reading, Pa., U.S.	**F10**	131
Readlyn, Ia., U.S.	**B5**	108
Reagan, co., Tx., U.S.	**D2**	136
Real, co., Tx., U.S.	**E3**	136
Real, Cordillera, mts., S.A.	**G6**	70
Realicó, Arg.	**E5**	72
Reamstown, Pa., U.S.	**F9**	131
Rebiana Sand Sea see Rabyānah, Ramlat, des., Libya	**F8**	48
Rebun-tō, i., Japan	**B16**	28
Recherche, Archipelago of the, is., Austl.	**G3**	60
Recife, Braz.	**C5**	74
Reconquista, Arg.	**D6**	72
Rector, Ar., U.S.	**A5**	97
Rèčyča, Bela.	**C11**	20
Red, stm., Asia	**B4**	34
Red, stm., N.A.	**B8**	92
Red, stm., Ky., U.S.	**C6**	110
Red, stm., Tn., U.S.	**A4**	135
Red, stm., U.S.	**E9**	92
Red Bank, N.J., U.S.	**C4**	123
Red Bank, Tn., U.S.	**D8**	135
Red Bay, Al., U.S.	**A1**	94
Redberry Lake, l., Sk., Can.	**E2**	91
Redbird, Oh., U.S.	**A4**	128
Red Bird, stm., Ky., U.S.	**C6**	110
Red Bluff, Ca., U.S.	**B2**	98
Red Bluff Lake, res., U.S.	**o12**	136
Red Boiling Springs, Tn., U.S.	**C8**	135
Red Bud, Il., U.S.	**E4**	106
Red Butte, mtn., Ut., U.S.	**B2**	137
Red Cedar, stm., Wi., U.S.	**C2**	142
Red Cedar Lake, l., Wi., U.S.	**C2**	142
Redcliff, Ab., Can.	**D5**	84
Redcliffe, Austl.	**F5**	62

Name | Map Ref. | Page

Redcliffe, Mount, mtn., Austl. **F3** 60
Red Cliff Indian Reservation, Wi., U.S. **B2** 142
Red Cloud, Ne., U.S. **D7** 120
Redcloud Peak, mtn., Co., U.S. **D3** 99
Red Deer, Ab., Can. **C4** 84
Red Deer, stm., Can. **D4** 84
Red Deer, stm., Can. **E4** 91
Redding, Ca., U.S. **B2** 98
Redding, Ct., U.S. **D2** 100
Redeye, stm., Mn., U.S. **D3** 116
Redfield, Ar., U.S. **C3** 97
Redfield, Ia., U.S. **C3** 108
Redfield, S.D., U.S. **C7** 134
Redford, Mi., U.S. **F7** 115
Redgranite, Wi., U.S. **D4** 142
Red Hook, N.Y., U.S. **C7** 125
Red Indian Lake, l., Nf., Can. **D3** 88
Red Jacket, W.V., U.S. **D2** 141
Redkey, In., U.S. **D7** 107
Redlake, Mn., U.S. **C3** 116
Red Lake, co., Mn., U.S. **C2** 116
Red Lake, l., Az., U.S. **B1** 96
Red Lake, stm., Mn., U.S. **C2** 116
Red Lake Falls, Mn., U.S. **C2** 116
Red Lake Indian Reservation, Mn., U.S. **B3** 116
Redlands, Ca., U.S. **E5** 98
Red Lion, Pa., U.S. **G8** 131
Red Lodge, Mt., U.S. **E7** 119
Red Mill Pond, l., De., U.S. **E5** 101
Redmond, Or., U.S. **C5** 130
Redmond, Ut., U.S. **E4** 137
Redmond, Wa., U.S. **e11** 140
Red Mountain, mtn., Ca., U.S. **B2** 98
Red Mountain, mtn., Mt., U.S. **C4** 119
Red Mountain Pass, Co., U.S. **D3** 99
Red Oak, Ga., U.S. **h7** 103
Red Oak, Ia., U.S. **D2** 108
Red Oak, Ok., U.S. **C6** 129
Red Oak, Tx., U.S. **n10** 136
Red Oaks, La., U.S. **h9** 111
Redon, Fr. **D5** 16
Redondo, Wa., U.S. **f11** 140
Redondo Beach, Ca., U.S. **n12** 98
Redoubt Volcano, vol., Ak., U.S. **g15** 95
Red Peak, mtn., Co., U.S. **B4** 99
Red River, co., La., U.S. **B2** 111
Red River, co., Tx., U.S. **C5** 136
Red Rock, stm., Mt., U.S. **F4** 119
Red Rock, Lake, res., Ia., U.S. **C4** 108
Redruth, Eng., U.K. **E4** 12
Red Sea **F3** 38
Red Springs, N.C., U.S. **C3** 126
Red Table Mountain, mts., Co., U.S. **B4** 99
Redwater, Ab., Can. **C4** 84
Redwater, stm., Mt., U.S. **C11** 119
Red Willow, co., Ne., U.S. **D5** 120
Redwillow, stm., Can. **B7** 85
Red Wing, Mn., U.S. **F6** 116
Redwood, co., Mn., U.S. **F3** 116
Redwood, stm., Mn., U.S. **F3** 116
Redwood City, Ca., U.S. **D2** 98
Redwood Falls, Mn., U.S. **F3** 116
Redwood National Park, Ca., U.S. **B2** 98
Redwood Valley, Ca., U.S. **C2** 98
Ree, Lough, l., Ire. **D2** 12
Reed City, Mi., U.S. **E5** 115
Reedley, Ca., U.S. **D4** 98
Reedsburg, Wi., U.S. **E3** 142
Reeds Peak, mtn., N.M., U.S. **D2** 124
Reedsport, Or., U.S. **D2** 130
Reedsville, Pa., U.S. **E6** 131
Reedsville, Wi., U.S. **D6** 142
Reedy, stm., S.C., U.S. **C3** 133
Reedy Lake, l., Fl., U.S. **E5** 102
Reefton, N.Z. **p13** 63c
Reelfoot Lake, l., Tn., U.S. **A2** 135
Reese, Mi., U.S. **E7** 115
Reese, stm., Nv., U.S. **C4** 121
Reese Air Force Base, mil., Tx., U.S. **C1** 136
Reeves, co., Tx., U.S. **o13** 136
Reform, Al., U.S. **B1** 94
Refugio, Tx., U.S. **E4** 136
Refugio, co., Tx., U.S. **E4** 136
Regensburg, Ger. **F12** 12
Reggâne, Alg. **E4** 48
Reggio di Calabria, Italy **E5** 18
Reggio nell'Emilia, Italy **B3** 18
Reghin, Rom. **F8** 20
Regina, Sk., Can. **G3** 91
Régina, Fr. Gu. **C9** 70
Regina Beach, Sk., Can. **G3** 91
Registro, Braz. **C8** 72
Regozero, Russia **D14** 10
Rehoboth, Nmb. **C2** 56
Rehoboth Bay, b., De., U.S. **F5** 101
Rehoboth Beach, De., U.S. **F5** 101
Reid, Mount, mtn., Ak., U.S. **n24** 95
Reidland, Ky., U.S. **e9** 110
Reidsville, Ga., U.S. **D4** 103
Reidsville, N.C., U.S. **A3** 126
Reigate, Eng., U.K. **E6** 12
Reims, Fr. **C9** 16
Reinbeck, Ia., U.S. **B5** 108
Reindeer Island, i., Mb., Can. **C3** 86
Reindeer Lake, l., Can. **G19** 82
Reisterstown, Md., U.S. **B4** 113
Reliance, Wy., U.S. **E3** 143
Remada, Tun. **D7** 48
Remanso, Braz. **C3** 74
Rembang, Indon. **E4** 36
Remington, In., U.S. **C3** 107
Remiremont, Fr. **C10** 16
Remmel Dam, Ar., U.S. **g8** 97
Remsen, Ia., U.S. **B2** 108
Rena, Nor. **F4** 10
Rend Lake, res., Il., U.S. **E5** 106
Rendsburg, Ger. **C11** 12
Renforth, N.B., Can. **D4** 87
Renfrew, On., Can. **B8** 89
Rengat, Indon. **D2** 36
Rengo, Chile **E3** 72
Reng Tlāng, mtn., Asia **B2** 34
Rennes, Fr. **C6** 16
Reno, Nv., U.S. **D2** 121
Reno, co., Ks., U.S. **E5** 109
Reno, Lake, l., Mn., U.S. **E3** 116
Reno Hill, mtn., Wy., U.S. **D6** 143
Renovo, Pa., U.S. **D6** 131
Renqiu, China **B4** 30
Rensselaer, In., U.S. **C3** 107
Rensselaer, N.Y., U.S. **C7** 125
Rensselaer, co., N.Y., U.S. **C7** 125
Renton, Wa., U.S. **B3** 140
Renville, Mn., U.S. **F3** 116
Renville, co., Mn., U.S. **F4** 116
Renville, co., N.D., U.S. **A4** 127
Reo, Indon. **E6** 36
Repentigny, P.Q., Can. **D4** 90
Repetek, Turk. **C8** 42
Republic, Mi., U.S. **B3** 115
Republic, Mo., U.S. **D4** 118
Republic, Pa., U.S. **G2** 131
Republic, Wa., U.S. **A7** 140
Republic, co., Ks., U.S. **C6** 109
Republican, stm., U.S. **C8** 92
Republican, stm., U.S. **C6** 109
Republic of Korea see Korea, South, ctry., Asia **D10** 28
Reşadiye, Tur. **B7** 44
Reserve, La., U.S. **h10** 111
Resistencia, Arg. **D6** 72
Reşiţa, Rom. **G6** 20
Resolute see Qausuituq, Nu., Can. **D20** 82
Resolution Island, i., N.Z. **q12** 63c
Reston, Mb., Can. **E1** 86
Reston, Va., U.S. **B5** 139
Réthimnon, Grc. **G10** 18
Réunion, dep., Afr. **g10** 57a
Reus, Spain **G7** 16
Reutlingen, Ger. **F11** 12
Revelo, Ky., U.S. **D5** 110
Revelstoke, B.C., Can. **D8** 85
Revelstoke, Lake, res., B.C., Can. **D8** 85
Reventazón, Peru **E3** 70
Revere, Ma., U.S. **g11** 114
Revillagigedo, Islas, is., Mex. **D2** 78
Revillagigedo Island, i., Ak., U.S. **n24** 95
Revin, Fr. **C9** 16
Rewa, India **E4** 40
Rex, Ga., U.S. **h8** 103
Rexburg, Id., U.S. **F7** 105
Rexton, N.B., Can. **C5** 87
Rey, Isla del, i., Pan. **D4** 80
Reyes, Point, c., Ca., U.S. **C2** 98
Reyhanlı, Tur. **D7** 44
Reykjanes Ridge **B26** 144
Reykjavík, Ice. **I18** 10a
Reynolds, Ga., U.S. **D2** 103
Reynolds, co., Mo., U.S. **D6** 118
Reynoldsburg, Oh., U.S. **C3** 128
Reynoldsville, Pa., U.S. **D4** 131
Reynosa, Mex. **B5** 78
Rezé, Fr. **D6** 16
Rēzekne, Lat. **H12** 10
Rhaetian Alps, mts., Eur. **A2** 18
Rhea, co., Tn., U.S. **D9** 135
Rheims see Reims, Fr. **C9** 16
Rheine, Ger. **D10** 12
Rhine (Rhein), stm., Eur. **A5** 14
Rhinebeck, N.Y., U.S. **D7** 125
Rhinelander, Wi., U.S. **C4** 142
Rhir, Cap, c., Mor. **D2** 48
Rho, Italy **B2** 18
Rhode Island, state, U.S. **D3** 132
Rhode Island, i., R.I., U.S. **E5** 132
Rhode Island Sound, strt., U.S. **F5** 132
Rhodes see Ródhos, i., Grc. **G12** 18
Rhodesia see Zimbabwe, ctry., Afr. **B4** 56
Rhodes Peak, mtn., Id., U.S. **C4** 105
Rhodes' Tomb, hist., Zimb. **C4** 56
Rhodope Mountains, mts., Eur. **D10** 18
Rhône, stm., Eur. **E9** 16
Riachão do Jacuípe, Braz. **D4** 74
Rialto, Ca., U.S. **m14** 98
Riau, Kepulauan, is., Indon. **C2** 36
Riaza, Spain **G5** 16
Ribáuè, Moz. **A6** 56
Ribe, Den. **I3** 10
Ribeira do Pombal, Braz. **D4** 74
Ribeira Grande, C.V. **g9** 50a
Ribeirão, Braz. **C4** 74
Ribeirão Preto, Braz. **F2** 74
Riberalta, Bol. **F6** 70
Rib Lake, Wi., U.S. **C3** 142
Riccione, Italy **B4** 18
Rice, Mn., U.S. **E4** 116
Rice, co., Ks., U.S. **D5** 109
Rice, co., Mn., U.S. **F5** 116
Riceboro, Ga., U.S. **E5** 103
Rice Lake, Wi., U.S. **C2** 142
Rice Lake, l., On., Can. **C6** 89
Rice Lake, l., Mn., U.S. **D5** 116
Riceville, Ia., U.S. **A5** 108
Rich, co., Ut., U.S. **B4** 137
Rich, Cape, c., On., Can. **C4** 89
Richards Bay, S. Afr. **D5** 56
Richardson, Tx., U.S. **n10** 136
Richardson, co., Ne., U.S. **D10** 120
Richardson Lakes, l., Me., U.S. **D2** 112
Richard Toll, Sen. **C1** 50
Richardton, N.D., U.S. **C3** 127
Rich Creek, Va., U.S. **C2** 139
Riche, Pointe, c., Nf., Can. **C3** 88
Richfield, Mn., U.S. **F5** 116
Richfield, Ut., U.S. **E3** 137
Richford, Vt., U.S. **B3** 138
Rich Hill, Mo., U.S. **C3** 118
Richibucto, N.B., Can. **C5** 87
Richland, Ga., U.S. **D2** 103
Richland, Mo., U.S. **D5** 118
Richland, Wa., U.S. **C6** 140
Richland, co., Il., U.S. **E5** 106
Richland, co., La., U.S. **B4** 111
Richland, co., Mt., U.S. **C12** 119
Richland, co., N.D., U.S. **C8** 127
Richland, co., Oh., U.S. **B3** 128
Richland, co., S.C., U.S. **D6** 133
Richland, co., Wi., U.S. **E3** 142
Richland Balsam, mtn., N.C., U.S. **f10** 126
Richland Center, Wi., U.S. **E3** 142
Richland Creek, stm., Tn., U.S. **B5** 135
Richlands, N.C., U.S. **C5** 126
Richlands, Va., U.S. **e10** 139
Richlandtown, Pa., U.S. **F11** 131
Richmond, Austl. **E3** 62
Richmond, B.C., Can. **E6** 85
Richmond, P.Q., Can. **D5** 90
Richmond, N.Z. **p13** 63c
Richmond, Ca., U.S. **D2** 98
Richmond, Il., U.S. **A5** 106
Richmond, In., U.S. **E8** 107
Richmond, Ky., U.S. **C5** 110
Richmond, Me., U.S. **D3** 112
Richmond, Mi., U.S. **F8** 115
Richmond, Mn., U.S. **E4** 116
Richmond, Mo., U.S. **B4** 118
Richmond, Tx., U.S. **E5** 136
Richmond, Ut., U.S. **B4** 137
Richmond, Va., U.S. **C5** 139
Richmond, Vt., U.S. **C3** 138
Richmond, co., Ga., U.S. **C4** 103
Richmond, co., N.C., U.S. **B3** 126
Richmond, co., N.Y., U.S. **E6** 125
Richmond, co., Va., U.S. **C6** 139
Richmond Heights, Fl., U.S. **s13** 102
Richmond Heights, Mo., U.S. **f13** 118
Richmond Hill, On., Can. **D5** 89
Richmond Hill, Ga., U.S. **E5** 103
Richmond National Battlefield Park, Va., U.S. **n18** 139
Rich Square, N.C., U.S. **A5** 126
Richthofen, Mount, mtn., Co., U.S. **A5** 99
Richton, Ms., U.S. **D5** 117
Richwood, Oh., U.S. **B2** 128
Richwood, W.V., U.S. **C4** 141
Rickman, Tn., U.S. **C8** 135
Riddle, Or., U.S. **E3** 130
Riddle Mountain, mtn., Or., U.S. **D8** 130
Rideau, stm., On., Can. **B9** 89
Ridgecrest, Ca., U.S. **E5** 98
Ridge Farm, Il., U.S. **D6** 106
Ridgefield, Ct., U.S. **D2** 100
Ridgefield, N.J., U.S. **h8** 123
Ridgefield, Wa., U.S. **D3** 140
Ridgefield Park, N.J., U.S. **B4** 123
Ridgeland, Ms., U.S. **C3** 117
Ridgeland, S.C., U.S. **G6** 133
Ridgeley, W.V., U.S. **B6** 141
Ridgely, Md., U.S. **C6** 113
Ridgely, Tn., U.S. **A2** 135
Ridge Spring, S.C., U.S. **D4** 133
Ridgetop, Tn., U.S. **A5** 135
Ridgetown, On., Can. **E3** 89
Ridgeview, W.V., U.S. **C3** 141
Ridgeville, In., U.S. **D7** 107
Ridgeville, S.C., U.S. **E7** 133
Ridgeway, Va., U.S. **D3** 139
Ridgewood, N.J., U.S. **B4** 123
Ridgway, Il., U.S. **F5** 106
Ridgway, Pa., U.S. **D4** 131
Riding Mountain National Park, Mb., Can. **D1** 86
Ridley Park, Pa., U.S. **p20** 131
Riesa, Ger. **E13** 12
Rieti, Italy **C4** 18
Rif, mts., Mor. **E3** 14
Riffe Lake, res., Wa., U.S. **C3** 140
Rifle, Co., U.S. **B3** 99
Rifle, stm., Mi., U.S. **D6** 115
Rift Valley, val., Afr. **C6** 54
Rīga, Lat. **H11** 10
Riga, Gulf of, b., Eur. **G10** 10
Rigaud, P.Q., Can. **D3** 90
Rigby, Id., U.S. **F7** 105
Rīgestān, reg., Afg. **D9** 42
Rigo, Pap. N. Gui. **H12** 32
Riihimäki, Fin. **F11** 10
Riiser-Larsen Peninsula, pen., Ant. **C8** 67
Rijeka, Cro. **B5** 18
Riley, Ks., U.S. **C7** 109
Riley, co., Ks., U.S. **C7** 109
Riley, Mount, mtn., N.M., U.S. **F2** 124
Rimbey, Ab., Can. **C3** 84
Rimersburg, Pa., U.S. **D3** 131
Rimini, Italy **B4** 18
Rimouski, P.Q., Can. **A9** 90
Rimouski, stm., P.Q., Can. **A9** 90
Rimouski-Est, P.Q., Can. **A9** 90
Rimrock Lake, res., Wa., U.S. **C4** 140
Rinca, Pulau, i., Indon. **E5** 36
Rincon, Ga., U.S. **D5** 103
Rincón del Bonete, Lago Artificial de, res., Ur. **E6** 72
Rincón de Romos, Mex. **C4** 78
Rincon Mountains, mts., Az., U.S. **E5** 96
Ringdove, Vanuatu **k9** 62a
Ringgold, Ga., U.S. **B1** 103
Ringgold, La., U.S. **B2** 111
Ringgold, co., Ia., U.S. **D3** 108
Ringim, Nig. **D6** 50
Ringkøbing, Den. **H3** 10
Ringkøbing Fjord, b., Den. **I3** 10
Ringling, Ok., U.S. **C4** 129
Ringvassøya, i., Nor. **B8** 10
Ringwood, N.J., U.S. **A4** 123
Rinjani, Gunung, vol., Indon. **E5** 36
Rio, Fl., U.S. **E6** 102
Rio, Wi., U.S. **E4** 142
Rio Arriba, co., N.M., U.S. **A2** 124
Riobamba, Ec. **D4** 70
Rio Blanco, co., Co., U.S. **B2** 99
Rio Branco, Braz. **E6** 70
Río Bravo, Mex. **B5** 78
Rio Claro, Braz. **F2** 74
Río Colorado, Arg. **E4** 69
Río Cuarto, Arg. **E5** 72
Rio de Janeiro, Braz. **F3** 74
Rio de Janeiro, state, Braz. **F3** 74
Rio Dell, Ca., U.S. **B1** 98
Río Gallegos, Arg. **H3** 69
Río Grande, Arg. **H3** 69
Rio Grande, Braz. **E7** 72
Río Grande, Mex. **C4** 78
Rio Grande, Oh., U.S. **D3** 128
Rio Grande, co., Co., U.S. **D4** 99
Rio Grande (Bravo), stm., N.A. **F7** 92
Rio Grande City, Tx., U.S. **F3** 136
Rio Grande do Norte, state, Braz. **E12** 70
Rio Grande do Sul, state, Braz. **D7** 72
Rio Grande Reservoir, res., Co., U.S. **D3** 99
Ríohacha, Col. **A5** 70
Río Hato, Pan. **D3** 80
Rio Hondo, Tx., U.S. **F4** 136
Rio Largo, Braz. **C4** 74
Riom, Fr. **E8** 16
Río Mayo, Arg. **G2** 69
Ríonegro, Col. **D5** 80
Rio Negro, Pantanal do, sw., Braz. **G8** 70
Rio Rancho, N.M., U.S. **B3** 124
Rio Real, Braz. **D4** 74
Ríosucio, Col. **D4** 80
Río Tercero, Arg. **E5** 72
Rio Tinto, Braz. **C4** 74
Rio Verde, Braz. **E1** 74
Ríoverde, Mex. **C5** 78
Rio Verde de Mato Grosso, Braz. **B7** 72
Rio Vista, Ca., U.S. **C3** 98
Ripley, Ms., U.S. **A5** 117
Ripley, Oh., U.S. **D2** 128
Ripley, Tn., U.S. **B2** 135
Ripley, W.V., U.S. **C3** 141
Ripley, co., In., U.S. **F7** 107
Ripley, co., Mo., U.S. **E7** 118
Ripon, Eng., U.K. **C6** 12
Ripon, Wi., U.S. **E5** 142
Rippowam, stm., Ct., U.S. **E1** 100
Ririe Lake, res., Id., U.S. **F7** 105
Rishiri-tō, i., Japan **B16** 28
Rishon LeZiyyon, Isr. **G6** 44
Rising Sun, De., U.S. **D3** 101
Rising Sun, In., U.S. **G8** 107
Rising Sun, Md., U.S. **A5** 113
Rison, Ar., U.S. **D3** 97
Ristijärvi, Fin. **D13** 10
Ritchie, co., W.V., U.S. **B3** 141
Ritter, Mount, mtn., Ca., U.S. **D4** 98
Rittman, Oh., U.S. **B4** 128
Ritzville, Wa., U.S. **B7** 140
Riva del Garda, Italy **B3** 18
Rivanna, stm., Va., U.S. **C4** 139
Rivas, Nic. **C2** 80
Rivera, Ur. **E6** 72
Riverbank, Ca., U.S. **D3** 98
River Bourgeois, N.S., Can. **D9** 87
River Cess, Lib. **E3** 50
Riverdale, Ca., U.S. **D4** 98
Riverdale, Il., U.S. **k9** 106
Riverdale, Md., U.S. **C4** 113
River Edge, N.J., U.S. **h8** 123
River Falls, Al., U.S. **D3** 94
River Falls, Wi., U.S. **D1** 142
River Forest, Il., U.S. **k9** 106
River Grove, Il., U.S. **k9** 106
Riverhead, N.Y., U.S. **n16** 125
River Hebert, N.S., Can. **D5** 87
River Heights, Ut., U.S. **B4** 137
River Hills, Wi., U.S. **m12** 142
River Pines, Ma., U.S. **f10** 114
River Ridge, La., U.S. **k11** 111
River Road, Or., U.S. **C3** 130
River Rouge, Mi., U.S. **p15** 115
Rivers, Mb., Can. **D1** 86
Riversdale, S. Afr. **E3** 56
Riverside, Al., U.S. **B3** 94
Riverside, Ca., U.S. **F5** 98
Riverside, Ia., U.S. **C6** 108
Riverside, Il., U.S. **k9** 106
Riverside, N.J., U.S. **C3** 123
Riverside, Pa., U.S. **E8** 131
Riverside, co., Ca., U.S. **F5** 98
Riverside Reservoir, res., Co., U.S. **A6** 99
Riverton, Mb., Can. **D3** 86
Riverton, N.Z. **q12** 63c
Riverton, Il., U.S. **D4** 106
Riverton, Ks., U.S. **E9** 109
Riverton, N.J., U.S. **C3** 123
Riverton, Ut., U.S. **C4** 137
Riverton, Vt., U.S. **C3** 138
Riverton, Wy., U.S. **C4** 143
Riverton Heights, Wa., U.S. **f11** 140
River Vale, N.J., U.S. **h8** 123
Riverview, Fl., U.S. **p11** 102
Riverview, Mi., U.S. **p15** 115
Rivesville, W.V., U.S. **B4** 141
Riviera Beach, Fl., U.S. **F6** 102
Riviera Beach, Md., U.S. **B4** 113
Rivière-du-Loup, P.Q., Can. **B8** 90
Rivière-Verte, N.B., Can. **B1** 87
Rivne, Ukr. **D9** 20
Rivoli, Italy **B1** 18
Riyadh see Ar-Riyāḍ, Sau. Ar. **F5** 38
Rizhao, China **D11** 28
Rjazan', Russia **D6** 26
Rjažsk, Russia **C16** 20
Rjukan, Nor. **G3** 10
Roachdale, In., U.S. **E4** 107
Road Town, Br. Vir. Is. **B7** 80
Roane, co., Tn., U.S. **D9** 135
Roane, co., W.V., U.S. **C3** 141
Roan Mountain, Tn., U.S. **C11** 135
Roanne, Fr. **D8** 16
Roanoke, Al., U.S. **B4** 94
Roanoke, Il., U.S. **C4** 106
Roanoke, In., U.S. **C7** 107
Roanoke, La., U.S. **D3** 111
Roanoke, Tx., U.S. **m9** 136
Roanoke, Va., U.S. **C3** 139
Roanoke, co., Va., U.S. **C2** 139
Roanoke see Staunton, stm., U.S. **D12** 92
Roanoke, stm., U.S. **A5** 126
Roanoke Island, i., N.C., U.S. **B7** 126
Roanoke Rapids, N.C., U.S. **A5** 126
Roanoke Rapids Lake, res., U.S. **A5** 126
Roaring Fork, stm., Co., U.S. **C4** 99
Roaring Spring, Pa., U.S. **F5** 131
Roatán, Isla de, i., Hond. **B2** 80
Robbins, Il., U.S. **k9** 106
Robbins, N.C., U.S. **B3** 126
Robbinsdale, Mn., U.S. **m12** 116
Robbinsville, N.C., U.S. **f9** 126
Robe, Austl. **H2** 62
Robersonville, N.C., U.S. **B5** 126
Roberta, Ga., U.S. **D2** 103
Robert Lee, Tx., U.S. **D2** 136
Roberts, Wi., U.S. **C1** 142
Roberts, co., S.D., U.S. **B8** 134
Roberts, co., Tx., U.S. **B2** 136
Roberts, Point, c., Wa., U.S. **A2** 140
Robert's Arm, Nf., Can. **D4** 88
Roberts Creek Mountain, mtn., Nv., U.S. **D5** 121
Robertsdale, Al., U.S. **E2** 94
Robert S. Kerr Reservoir, res., Ok., U.S. **B6** 129
Roberts Mountain, mtn., Ak., U.S. **C6** 95
Roberts Mountain, mtn., Wy., U.S. **D3** 143
Robertson, co., Ky., U.S. **B5** 110
Robertson, co., Tn., U.S. **A5** 135
Robertson, co., Tx., U.S. **D4** 136
Robertsonville, P.Q., Can. **C6** 90
Roberts Port, Lib. **E2** 50
Robertville, N.B., Can. **B4** 87
Roberval, P.Q., Can. **A5** 90
Robeson, co., N.C., U.S. **C3** 126
Robins, Ia., U.S. **B6** 108
Robinson, Il., U.S. **D6** 106
Róbinson Crusoe, Isla, i., Chile **E2** 72

Name | Map Ref. | Page

Robinson Fork, stm., W.V., U.S. **k9** 141
Robinson Fork, stm., W.V., U.S. **m14** 141
Robinvale, Austl. **G3** 62
Roblin, Mb., Can. **D1** 86
Roboré, Bol. **B6** 72
Robson, Mount, mtn., B.C., Can. **C8** 85
Robstown, Tx., U.S. **F4** 136
Roca Partida, Isla, i., Mex. **D2** 78
Rocha, Ur. **E7** 72
Rochefort, Fr. **E6** 16
Rochelle, Ga., U.S. **E3** 103
Rochelle, Il., U.S. **B4** 106
Rochelle Park, N.J., U.S. **h8** 123
Rochester, Il., U.S. **D4** 106
Rochester, In., U.S. **B5** 107
Rochester, Mi., U.S. **F7** 115
Rochester, Mn., U.S. **F6** 116
Rochester, N.H., U.S. **D5** 122
Rochester, N.Y., U.S. **B3** 125
Rochester, Pa., U.S. **E1** 131
Rochester, Vt., U.S. **D3** 138
Rochester, Wa., U.S. **C2** 140
Rochester, Wi., U.S. **n11** 142
Rock, co., Mn., U.S. **G2** 116
Rock, co., Ne., U.S. **B6** 120
Rock, co., Wi., U.S. **F4** 142
Rock, stm., U.S. **B3** 106
Rock, stm., U.S. **A1** 108
Rockall, i., Scot., U.K. **D3** 6
Rockall Rise **B24** 144
Rockaway, N.J., U.S. **B3** 123
Rockaway, Or., U.S. **B3** 130
Rockbridge, co., Va., U.S. **C3** 139
Rockcastle, co., Ky., U.S. **C5** 110
Rockcastle, stm., Ky., U.S. **C5** 110
Rockcliffe Park, On., Can. **h12** 89
Rock Creek, Mn., U.S. **E6** 116
Rock Creek, stm., Nv., U.S. **C5** 121
Rock Creek, stm., Or., U.S. **B6** 130
Rock Creek, stm., Wa., U.S. **B8** 140
Rock Creek, stm., Wa., U.S. **D5** 140
Rock Creek, stm., Wy., U.S. **E6** 143
Rock Creek, stm., U.S. **B3** 113
Rock Creek, stm., U.S. **h14** 140
Rock Creek Butte, mtn., Or., U.S. **C8** 130
Rockdale, Il., U.S. **B5** 106
Rockdale, Md., U.S. **B4** 113
Rockdale, Tx., U.S. **D4** 136
Rockdale, co., Ga., U.S. **C3** 103
Rockefeller Plateau, plat., Ant. **E27** 67
Rockfall, Ct., U.S. **C5** 100
Rock Falls, Il., U.S. **B4** 106
Rockford, Ia., U.S. **A5** 108
Rockford, Il., U.S. **A4** 106
Rockford, Mi., U.S. **E5** 115
Rockford, Mn., U.S. **E5** 116
Rockford, Oh., U.S. **B1** 128
Rockford, Tn., U.S. **D10** 135
Rock Hall, Md., U.S. **B5** 113
Rockhampton, Austl. **E5** 62
Rockhampton Downs, Austl. **D6** 60
Rock Hill, S.C., U.S. **B5** 133
Rockingham, Austl. **G2** 60
Rockingham, N.C., U.S. **C3** 126
Rockingham, co., N.C., U.S. **A3** 126
Rockingham, co., N.H., U.S. **D4** 122
Rockingham, co., Va., U.S. **B4** 139
Rock Island, P.Q., Can. **D5** 90
Rock Island, Il., U.S. **B3** 106
Rock Island, co., Il., U.S. **B3** 106
Rock Island, i., Fl., U.S. **C3** 102
Rock Island, i., Wi., U.S. **C7** 142
Rock Lake, l., Wa., U.S. **B8** 140
Rockland, On., Can. **B9** 89
Rockland, Ma., U.S. **B6** 114
Rockland, Me., U.S. **D3** 112
Rockland, co., N.Y., U.S. **D6** 125
Rockledge, Fl., U.S. **D6** 102
Rockledge, Pa., U.S. **o20** 131
Rocklin, Ca., U.S. **C3** 98
Rockmart, Ga., U.S. **B1** 103
Rock Mountain, mtn., Co., U.S. **D3** 99
Rockport, In., U.S. **I3** 107
Rockport, Ma., U.S. **A6** 114
Rockport, Me., U.S. **D3** 112
Rock Port, Mo., U.S. **A2** 118
Rockport, Tx., U.S. **F4** 136
Rock Rapids, Ia., U.S. **A1** 108
Rock River, Wy., U.S. **E7** 143
Rocksprings, Tx., U.S. **D2** 136
Rock Springs, Wy., U.S. **E3** 143
Rockstone, Guy. **B8** 70
Rockton, Il., U.S. **A4** 106
Rock Valley, Ia., U.S. **A1** 108
Rockville, In., U.S. **E3** 107
Rockville, Md., U.S. **B3** 113
Rockville Centre, N.Y., U.S. **n15** 125
Rockwall, Tx., U.S. **C4** 136
Rockwall, co., Tx., U.S. **C4** 136
Rockwell, Ia., U.S. **B4** 108
Rockwell, N.C., U.S. **B2** 126
Rockwell City, Ia., U.S. **B3** 108
Rockwell Park, N.C., U.S. **B2** 126
Rockwood, Mi., U.S. **F7** 115
Rockwood, Pa., U.S. **G3** 131
Rockwood, Tn., U.S. **D9** 135
Rocky, stm., N.C., U.S. **B2** 126
Rocky, stm., S.C., U.S. **C2** 133
Rocky, East Branch, stm., Oh., U.S. **h9** 128
Rocky, West Branch, stm., Oh., U.S. **h9** 128
Rocky Boys Indian Reservation, Mt., U.S. **B7** 119
Rocky Ford, Co., U.S. **C7** 99
Rocky Fork Lake, l., Oh., U.S. **C2** 128
Rocky Harbour, Nf., Can. **D3** 88
Rocky Hill, Ct., U.S. **C5** 100
Rocky Lake, l., Me., U.S. **D5** 112
Rocky Mount, N.C., U.S. **B5** 126
Rocky Mount, Va., U.S. **D3** 139
Rocky Mountain, mtn., Mt., U.S. **C4** 119
Rocky Mountain House, Ab., Can. **C3** 84
Rocky Mountain National Park, Co., U.S. **A5** 99
Rocky Mountains, mts., N.A. **B5** 92
Rocky Ripple, In., U.S. **k10** 107
Rocky River, Oh., U.S. **A4** 128
Rocky Top, mtn., Or., U.S. **C4** 130
Roddickton, Nf., Can. **C3** 88
Rodeo, Arg. **E4** 72
Roderfield, W.V., U.S. **D3** 141
Rodez, Fr. **E8** 16
Ródhos, Grc. **F12** 18
Ródhos (Rhodes), i., Grc. **G12** 18
Rodney, On., Can. **E3** 89
Rodney, Cape, c., Ak., U.S. **C6** 95
Rodney Village, De., U.S. **D3** 101
Rodrigues, i., Mrts. **F12** 52
Roebourne, Austl. **E2** 60
Roebuck, S.C., U.S. **B4** 133
Roeland Park, Ks., U.S. **k16** 109
Roeselare, Bel. **E8** 12
Roff, Ok., U.S. **C5** 129
Roger Mills, co., Ok., U.S. **B2** 129
Rogers, Ar., U.S. **A1** 97
Rogers, Mn., U.S. **E5** 116
Rogers, Tx., U.S. **D4** 136
Rogers, co., Ok., U.S. **A6** 129
Rogers, Mount, mtn., Va., U.S. **f10** 139
Rogers City, Mi., U.S. **C7** 115
Rogers Lake, res., Ct., U.S. **D6** 100
Rogers Pass, Mt., U.S. **C4** 119
Rogersville, N.B., Can. **C4** 87
Rogersville, Al., U.S. **A2** 94
Rogersville, Mo., U.S. **D4** 118
Rogersville, Tn., U.S. **C10** 135
Rogue, stm., Or., U.S. **E2** 130
Rogue River, Or., U.S. **E3** 130
Rohri, Pak. **E9** 42
Rohtak, India **D3** 40
Roi Et, Thai. **C4** 34
Rokan, stm., Indon. **C2** 36
Roland, Ia., U.S. **B4** 108
Roland, Ok., U.S. **B7** 129
Roland, Lake, res., Md., U.S. **g11** 113
Rolette, N.D., U.S. **A6** 127
Rolette, co., N.D., U.S. **A6** 127
Rolfe, Ia., U.S. **B3** 108
Rolla, Mo., U.S. **D6** 118
Rolla, N.D., U.S. **A6** 127
Rollingbay, Wa., U.S. **e10** 140
Rolling Fork, Ms., U.S. **C3** 117
Rolling Fork, stm., Ar., U.S. **C1** 97
Rolling Fork, stm., Ky., U.S. **C4** 110
Rolling Meadows, Il., U.S. **h8** 106
Rollingstone, Mn., U.S. **F7** 116
Rollinsford, N.H., U.S. **D5** 122
Rolvsøya, i., Nor. **A10** 10
Roma, Austl. **F4** 62
Roma (Rome), Italy **D4** 18
Roma, Tx., U.S. **F3** 136
Romain, Cape, c., S.C., U.S. **F9** 133
Roman, Rom. **F9** 20
Romanche Gap **I12** 66
Romang, Pulau, i., Indon. **E7** 36
Romania, ctry., Eur. **F8** 20
Roman Nose Mountain, mtn., Or., U.S. **D3** 130
Romano, Cape, c., Fl., U.S. **G5** 102
Romano, Cayo, i., Cuba **A4** 80
Romans-sur-Isère, Fr. **E9** 16
Romanzof, Cape, c., Ak., U.S. **C6** 95
Romanzof Mountains, mts., Ak., U.S. **B11** 95
Rome see Roma, Italy **D4** 18
Rome, Ga., U.S. **B1** 103
Rome, Il., U.S. **C4** 106
Rome, N.Y., U.S. **B5** 125
Rome City, In., U.S. **B7** 107
Romeo, Mi., U.S. **F7** 115
Romeoville, Il., U.S. **k8** 106
Romney, W.V., U.S. **B6** 141
Romny, Ukr. **D12** 20
Romorantin-Lanthenay, Fr. **D7** 16
Romulus, Mi., U.S. **p15** 115
Ronan, Mt., U.S. **C2** 119
Roncador, Serra do, plat., Braz. **D1** 74
Ronceverte, W.V., U.S. **D4** 141
Ronda, Spain **I4** 16
Rondônia, state, Braz. **F7** 70
Rondonópolis, Braz. **G9** 70
Rong'an, China **D2** 30
Rongcheng, China **B5** 30
Ronge, Lac la, l., Sk., Can. **B3** 91
Rongelap, atoll, Marsh. Is. **C10** 58
Rongjiang, China **D2** 30
Rongxian, China **E3** 30
Rønne, Den. **I6** 10
Ronneby, Swe. **H6** 10
Ronne Ice Shelf, Ant. **D34** 67
Roodhouse, Il., U.S. **D3** 106
Rooks, co., Ks., U.S. **C4** 109
Roosevelt, Ut., U.S. **C5** 137
Roosevelt, co., Mt., U.S. **B11** 119
Roosevelt, co., N.M., U.S. **C6** 124
Roosevelt, stm., Braz. **E7** 70
Roosevelt Island, i., Ant. **D24** 67
Roosevelt Park, Mi., U.S. **E4** 115
Root, stm., Mn., U.S. **G7** 116
Root, stm., Wi., U.S. **n12** 142
Roper, N.C., U.S. **B6** 126
Roper Valley, Austl. **C5** 60
Ropi, Fin. **B9** 10
Roraima, state, Braz. **C7** 70
Roraima, Mount, mtn., S.A. **B7** 70
Røros, Nor. **E4** 10
Rosamond, Ca., U.S. **E4** 98
Rosario, Arg. **E5** 72
Rosário, Braz. **B3** 74
Rosario, Mex. **C3** 78
Rosario, Para. **C6** 72
Rosario de la Frontera, Arg. **D5** 72
Rosário do Sul, Braz. **E6** 72
Rosário Oeste, Braz. **F8** 70
Roscoe, Il., U.S. **A5** 106
Roscoe, Tx., U.S. **C2** 136
Roscommon, Ire. **D2** 12
Roscommon, Mi., U.S. **D6** 115
Roscommon, co., Mi., U.S. **D6** 115
Rose, Mount, mtn., Nv., U.S. **D2** 121
Roseau, Dom. **B7** 80
Roseau, Mn., U.S. **B3** 116
Roseau, co., Mn., U.S. **B3** 116
Roseau, South Fork, stm., Mn., U.S. **B3** 116
Rose-Blanche [-Harbour le Cou], Nf., Can. **E2** 88
Roseboro, N.C., U.S. **C4** 126
Rosebud, S.D., U.S. **D5** 134
Rosebud, Tx., U.S. **D4** 136
Rosebud, co., Mt., U.S. **D10** 119
Rosebud Indian Reservation, S.D., U.S. **D5** 134
Roseburg, Or., U.S. **D3** 130
Rosedale, In., U.S. **E3** 107
Rosedale, Md., U.S. **g11** 113
Rosedale, Ms., U.S. **B2** 117
Rose Hill, Ks., U.S. **E6** 109
Rose Hill, N.C., U.S. **C4** 126
Rose Hill, Va., U.S. **f8** 139
Roseland, Fl., U.S. **E6** 102
Roseland, In., U.S. **A5** 107
Roseland, La., U.S. **D5** 111
Roseland, Oh., U.S. **B3** 128
Roselle, Il., U.S. **k8** 106
Roselle, N.J., U.S. **k7** 123
Roselle Park, N.J., U.S. **k7** 123
Rosemère, P.Q., Can. **p19** 90
Rosemount, Mn., U.S. **F5** 116
Rosenberg, Tx., U.S. **E5** 136
Rosendale, Wi., U.S. **E5** 142
Rosenheim, Ger. **G13** 12
Rose Peak, mtn., Az., U.S. **D6** 96
Rosepine, La., U.S. **D2** 111
Rose Point, c., B.C., Can. **B2** 85
Roseto, Pa., U.S. **E11** 131
Rosetta see Rashid, Egypt **E10** 14
Roseville, Ca., U.S. **C3** 98
Roseville, Il., U.S. **C3** 106
Roseville, Mi., U.S. **o16** 115
Roseville, Mn., U.S. **m12** 116
Roseville, Oh., U.S. **C3** 128
Rosewood Heights, Il., U.S. **E3** 106
Rosiclare, Il., U.S. **F5** 106
Roşiori de Vede, Rom. **G8** 20
Roskilde, Den. **I5** 10
Roslavl', Russia **C12** 20
Roslyn, Wa., U.S. **B4** 140
Roslyn Heights, N.Y., U.S. **h13** 125
Ross, Oh., U.S. **C1** 128
Ross, co., Oh., U.S. **C2** 128
Rossano, Italy **E6** 18
Ross Barnett Reservoir, res., Ms., U.S. **C3** 117
Rossburn, Mb., Can. **D1** 86
Ross Dam, Wa., U.S. **A4** 140
Rossford, Oh., U.S. **A2** 128
Ross Ice Shelf, Ant. **E23** 67
Rossignol, Lake, l., N.S., Can. **E4** 87
Ross Island, i., Ant. **D22** 67
Ross Island, i., Mb., Can. **B3** 86
Ross Lake National Recreation Area, Wa., U.S. **A5** 140
Rossland, B.C., Can. **E9** 85
Rosso, Maur. **C1** 50
Rossoš', Russia **D15** 20
Ross Sea, Ant. **D24** 67
Røssvatnet, l., Nor. **D5** 10
Rossville, Ga., U.S. **B1** 103
Rossville, Il., U.S. **C6** 106
Rossville, In., U.S. **D4** 107
Rossville, Ks., U.S. **C8** 109
Roštkala, Taj. **C10** 42
Rostock, Ger. **D12** 12
Rostov, Russia **C6** 22
Rostov-na-Donu, Russia **E6** 26
Roswell, Ga., U.S. **B2** 103
Roswell, N.M., U.S. **D5** 124
Rota, i., N. Mar. Is. **D12** 32
Rotan, Tx., U.S. **C2** 136
Rothesay, N.B., Can. **D4** 87
Rothschild, Wi., U.S. **D4** 142
Rothsville, Pa., U.S. **F9** 131
Roti, Pulau, i., Indon. **F6** 36
Rotorùa, N.Z. **o14** 63c
Rotterdam, Neth. **E9** 12
Rotterdam, N.Y., U.S. **C6** 125
Roubaix, Fr. **B8** 16
Rouen, Fr. **C7** 16
Rouge, stm., P.Q., Can. **D3** 90
Rough, stm., Ky., U.S. **C3** 110
Rough River Lake, res., Ky., U.S. **C3** 110
Rouiba, Alg. **I8** 16
Roulette, Pa., U.S. **C5** 131
Round Island, i., Ms., U.S. **g8** 117
Round Lake, Il., U.S. **h8** 106
Round Lake Beach, Il., U.S. **h8** 106
Round Mountain, Nv., U.S. **E4** 121
Round Rock, Tx., U.S. **D4** 136
Roundup, Mt., U.S. **D8** 119
Round Valley Indian Reservation, Ca., U.S. **C2** 98
Round Valley Reservoir, res., N.J., U.S. **B3** 123
Rouses Point, N.Y., U.S. **f11** 125
Routt, co., Co., U.S. **A3** 99
Rouyn [-Noranda], P.Q., Can. **k11** 90
Rouzerville, Pa., U.S. **G6** 131
Rovaniemi, Fin. **C11** 10
Rovereto, Italy **B3** 18
Rovigo, Italy **B3** 18
Rovuma (Ruvuma), stm., Afr. **F8** 54
Rowan, co., Ky., U.S. **B6** 110
Rowan, co., N.C., U.S. **B2** 126
Rowland, N.C., U.S. **C3** 126
Rowlesburg, W.V., U.S. **B5** 141
Roxas, Phil. **D8** 34
Roxboro, N.C., U.S. **A4** 126
Roxburgh, N.Z. **q12** 63c
Roxton Falls, P.Q., Can. **D5** 90
Roxton Pond, P.Q., Can. **D5** 90
Roy, Ut., U.S. **B3** 137
Royal, stm., Me., U.S. **g7** 112
Royal Center, In., U.S. **C4** 107
Royale, Isle, i., Mi., U.S. **h9** 115
Royal Gorge, val., Co., U.S. **C5** 99
Royal Oak, Mi., U.S. **F7** 115
Royal Pines, N.C., U.S. **f10** 126
Royalton, Il., U.S. **F4** 106
Royalton, Mn., U.S. **E4** 116
Royan, Fr. **E6** 16
Royersford, Pa., U.S. **F10** 131
Royerton, In., U.S. **D7** 107
Royse City, Tx., U.S. **C4** 136
Royston, B.C., Can. **E5** 85
Royston, Ga., U.S. **B3** 103
Rtiščevo, Russia **D7** 22
Ruacana Falls, wtfl, Afr. **B1** 56
Ruapehu, Mount, vol., N.Z. **o14** 63c
Rubcovsk, Russia **D10** 26
Rubidoux, Ca., U.S. **n14** 98
Rubondo Island, i., Tan. **D6** 54
Ruby Dome, mtn., Nv., U.S. **C6** 121
Ruby Lake, l., Nv., U.S. **C6** 121
Ruby Mountains, mts., Nv., U.S. **C6** 121
Ruby Range, mts., Co., U.S. **C3** 99
Ruby Range, mts., Mt., U.S. **E4** 119
Rūdbār, Afg. **D8** 42
Rudnja, Russia **B11** 20
Rudnyj, Kaz. **D8** 26
Rudolf, Lake (Turkana, Lake), l., Afr. **C7** 54
Rudyard, Mi., U.S. **B6** 115
Rufiji, stm., Tan. **E7** 54
Rufino, Arg. **E5** 72
Rufisque, Sen. **D1** 50
Rufus Woods Lake, res., Wa., U.S. **A6** 140
Rugby, N.D., U.S. **A6** 127
Rügen, i., Ger. **C13** 12
Ruhengeri, Rw. **D5** 54
Rui'an, China **F12** 28
Ruidoso, N.M., U.S. **D4** 124
Ruidoso Downs, N.M., U.S. **D4** 124
Ruijin, China **F11** 28
Ruiz, Mex. **C3** 78
Ruki, stm., D.R.C. **D3** 54
Rukwa, Lake, l., Tan. **E6** 54
Ruleville, Ms., U.S. **B3** 117
Rum, stm., Mn., U.S. **D5** 116
Ruma, Yugo. **B7** 18
Rumbek, Sudan **I10** 48
Rum Cay, i., Bah. **D10** 76
Rum Creek, stm., W.V., U.S. **n12** 141
Rumford, Me., U.S. **D2** 112
Rum Jungle, Austl. **C5** 60
Rumoi, Japan **C16** 28
Rumphi, Mwi. **A5** 56
Rumson, N.J., U.S. **C4** 123
Rumstick Point, c., R.I., U.S. **D5** 132
Runan, China **E10** 28
Rundu, Nmb. **B2** 56
Runge, Tx., U.S. **E4** 136
Rungwa, Tan. **E6** 54
Runnels, co., Tx., U.S. **D3** 136
Runnemede, N.J., U.S. **D2** 123
Ruoqiang, China **D5** 28
Rupat, Pulau, i., Indon. **C2** 36
Rupert, Id., U.S. **G5** 105
Rupert, W.V., U.S. **D4** 141
Rupert, Rivière de, stm., P.Q., Can. **h11** 90
Rural Hall, N.C., U.S. **A2** 126
Rural Retreat, Va., U.S. **D1** 139
Rurrenabaque, Bol. **A4** 72
Rusagonis, N.B., Can. **D3** 87
Rusape, Zimb. **B5** 56
Ruse, Bul. **C11** 18
Rush, co., In., U.S. **E6** 107
Rush, co., Ks., U.S. **D4** 109
Rush, stm., Mn., U.S. **F4** 116
Rush, stm., Wi., U.S. **D1** 142
Rush City, Mn., U.S. **E6** 116
Rush Creek, stm., Oh., U.S. **B2** 128
Rush Creek, stm., Ok., U.S. **C4** 129
Rushford, Mn., U.S. **G7** 116
Rush Lake, l., Mn., U.S. **D3** 116
Rush Lake, l., Mn., U.S. **E5** 116
Rush Lake, l., Wi., U.S. **E5** 142
Rushmere, Va., U.S. **h14** 139
Rush Springs, Ok., U.S. **C4** 129
Rushville, Il., U.S. **C3** 106
Rushville, In., U.S. **E7** 107
Rushville, Ne., U.S. **B3** 120
Rusk, Tx., U.S. **D5** 136
Rusk, co., Tx., U.S. **C5** 136
Rusk, co., Wi., U.S. **C2** 142
Ruskin, Fl., U.S. **E4** 102
Russas, Braz. **B4** 74
Russell, Mb., Can. **D1** 86
Russell, On., Can. **B9** 89
Russell, Ks., U.S. **D5** 109
Russell, Ky., U.S. **B7** 110
Russell, Pa., U.S. **C3** 131
Russell, co., Al., U.S. **C4** 94
Russell, co., Ks., U.S. **D5** 109
Russell, co., Ky., U.S. **D4** 110
Russell, co., Va., U.S. **f9** 139
Russell, Mount, mtn., Ak., U.S. **f16** 95
Russell Cave National Monument, Al., U.S. **A4** 94
Russell Fork, stm., U.S. **C7** 110
Russell Springs, Ky., U.S. **C4** 110
Russellville, Al., U.S. **A2** 94
Russellville, Ar., U.S. **B2** 97
Russellville, Ky., U.S. **D3** 110
Russellville, Mo., U.S. **C5** 118
Russellville, Tn., U.S. **C10** 135
Russia, ctry., Eur. **C11** 26
Russian, stm., Ca., U.S. **C2** 98
Russiaville, In., U.S. **D5** 107
Russkaja Gavan', Russia **B8** 26
Rustavi, Geor. **B11** 44
Rustburg, Va., U.S. **C3** 139
Rustenburg, S. Afr. **D4** 56
Ruston, La., U.S. **B3** 111
Ruston, Wa., U.S. **B3** 140
Rutana, Bdi. **D6** 54
Ruteng, Indon. **E6** 36
Ruth, Nv., U.S. **D6** 121
Rutherford, N.J., U.S. **B4** 123
Rutherford, Tn., U.S. **A3** 135
Rutherford, co., N.C., U.S. **B1** 126
Rutherford, co., Tn., U.S. **B5** 135
Rutherfordton, N.C., U.S. **B1** 126
Ruthven, Ia., U.S. **A3** 108
Rutland, Ma., U.S. **B4** 114
Rutland, Vt., U.S. **D3** 138
Rutland, co., Vt., U.S. **D2** 138
Rutledge, Ga., U.S. **C3** 103
Rutledge, Tn., U.S. **C10** 135
Rutog, China **C3** 40
Rutshuru, D.R.C. **D5** 54
Ruvuma (Rovuma), stm., Afr. **F8** 54
Ruy Barbosa, Braz. **D3** 74
Ruzaevka, Russia **D7** 22
Rwanda, ctry., Afr. **D5** 54
Ryan, Ok., U.S. **C4** 129
Ryan Peak, mtn., Id., U.S. **F4** 105
Rybače, Kaz. **E10** 26
Rybačij, poluostrov, pen., Russia **B15** 10
Rybinsk, Russia **D5** 26
Rybinskoe vodohranilišče, res., Russia **D5** 26
Rybinsk Reservoir see Rybinskoe vodohranilišče, res., Russia **D5** 26
Rybnik, Pol. **D5** 20
Rycroft, Ab., Can. **B1** 84
Rye, N.H., U.S. **D5** 122
Rye, N.Y., U.S. **h13** 125
Rye Beach, N.H., U.S. **E5** 122
Rye Patch Dam, Nv., U.S. **C3** 121
Rye Patch Reservoir, res., Nv., U.S. **C3** 121
Ryl'sk, Russia **D13** 20
Ryukyu Islands see Nansei-shotō, is., Japan **A9** 34
Ryukyu Trench **F15** 64
Rzeszów, Pol. **D7** 20
Ržev, Russia **D5** 26

S

Saarbrücken, Ger. **F10** 12
Saaremaa, i., Est. **G10** 10
Saarijärvi, Fin. **E11** 10

Name	Map Ref.	Page

Saarlouis, Ger. **F10** 12
Saatlı, Azer. **C13** 44
Saba, i., Neth. Ant. **B7** 80
Šabac, Yugo. **B7** 18
Sabadell, Spain **G8** 16
Sabah, hist. reg., Malay. **B5** 36
Sabana, Archipiélago de, is., Cuba **A3** 80
Sabanalarga, Col. **C5** 80
Sabattus, Me., U.S. **D2** 112
Şāberī, Hāmūn-e, l., Asia **D8** 42
Sabetha, Ks., U.S. **C8** 109
Sabhā, Libya **E7** 48
Sabi (Save), stm., Afr. **B5** 56
Sabillasville, Md., U.S. **A3** 113
Sabina, Oh., U.S. **C2** 128
Sabinal, Tx., U.S. **E3** 136
Sabinal, Cayo, i., Cuba **A4** 80
Sabinas, Mex. **B4** 78
Sabinas Hidalgo, Mex. **B4** 78
Sabine, co., La., U.S. **C2** 111
Sabine, co., Tx., U.S. **D6** 136
Sabine, stm., U.S. **E9** 92
Sabine, stm., U.S. **D6** 136
Sabine Lake, l., U.S. **E2** 111
Sabine Pass, strt., U.S. **E2** 111
Sabirabad, Azer. **B13** 44
Sable, Cape, c., Fl., U.S. **G5** 102
Sable Island, i., N.S., Can. **F10** 87
Sabrina Coast, Ant. **C16** 67
Sabula, Ia., U.S. **B7** 108
Şabyā, Sau. Ar. **G4** 38
Sabzevār, Iran **C7** 42
Sac, co., Ia., U.S. **B2** 108
Sac, stm., Mo., U.S. **D4** 118
Sacajawea, Lake, res., Wa., U.S. **C7** 140
Sacajawea Peak, mtn., Or., U.S. **B9** 130
Sacandaga Lake, l., N.Y., U.S. **B6** 125
Sac and Fox Indian Reservation, Ia., U.S. **C5** 108
Sacaton, Az., U.S. **D4** 96
Sac City, Ia., U.S. **B2** 108
Săcele, Rom. **G8** 20
Sachse, Tx., U.S. **n10** 136
Sachsen, hist. reg., Ger. **E13** 12
Sachuest Point, c., R.I., U.S. **F6** 132
Sackville, N.B., Can. **D5** 87
Saco, Me., U.S. **E2** 112
Saco, stm., U.S. **E2** 112
Saco, East Branch, stm., N.H., U.S. **B4** 122
Sacramento, Ca., U.S. **C3** 98
Sacramento, co., Ca., U.S. **C3** 98
Sacramento, stm., Ca., U.S. **C3** 98
Sacramento, stm., N.M., U.S. **E4** 124
Sacramento Mountains, mts., N.M., U.S. **E4** 124
Sacramento Valley, val., Ca., U.S. **C2** 98
Sacré-Coeur-Saguenay, P.Q., Can. **A8** 90
Sacred Heart, Mn., U.S. **F3** 116
Şa'dah, Yemen **G4** 38
Saddle, stm., N.J., U.S. **h8** 123
Saddleback Mountain, mtn., Az., U.S. **k8** 96
Saddle Brook, N.J., U.S. **h8** 123
Saddlebunch Keys, is., Fl., U.S. **H5** 102
Saddle Mountain, mtn., Or., U.S. **B3** 130
Saddle Mountains, mts., Wa., U.S. **C5** 140
Saddle River, N.J., U.S. **A4** 123
Sa Dec, Viet. **D5** 34
Sado, i., Japan **D15** 28
Sado-kaikyō, strt., Japan **C3** 31
Šadrinsk, Russia **D8** 26
Saegertown, Pa., U.S. **C1** 131
Safâga, Egypt **E11** 48
Safety Harbor, Fl., U.S. **E4** 102
Säffle, Swe. **G5** 10
Safford, Az., U.S. **E6** 96
Safi, Mor. **D3** 48
Safonovo, Russia **B12** 20
Safonovo, Russia **A8** 22
Safranbolu, Tur. **B5** 44
Saga, China **F5** 28
Saga, Japan **D2** 31
Sagadahoc, co., Me., U.S. **E3** 112
Sagaing, Myan. **B3** 34
Sagamore Hills, Oh., U.S. **h9** 128
Saganaga Lake, l., Mn., U.S. **B7** 116
Sāgar, India **E3** 40
Sagarmāthā see Everest, Mount, mtn., Asia **D5** 40
Sagay, Phil. **D8** 34
Sag Harbor, N.Y., U.S. **m16** 125
Saginaw, Mi., U.S. **E7** 115
Saginaw, Tx., U.S. **n9** 136
Saginaw, co., Mi., U.S. **E6** 115
Saginaw Bay, b., Mi., U.S. **E7** 115
Sagiz, Kaz. **E10** 22
Saglek Bay, b., Nf., Can. **f9** 88
Šagonar, Russia **A6** 28
Saguache, co., Co., U.S. **C4** 99
Sagua de Tánamo, Cuba **A4** 80
Sagua la Grande, Cuba **A3** 80
Saguaro Lake, res., Az., U.S. **k10** 96
Saguaro National Monument (Tucson Mountain Section), Az., U.S. **E4** 96
Saguaro National Monument, Az., U.S. **E5** 96
Saguenay, stm., P.Q., Can. **A7** 90
Sagunt, Spain **H6** 16
Sahagún, Col. **D4** 80
Sahalin, ostrov, i., Russia **D16** 26
Sahara, des., Afr. **F6** 48
Sahāranpur, India **D3** 40
Sahel see Sudan, reg., Afr. **H8** 48
Sāhīwāl, Pak. **D10** 42
Sāhīwāl, Pak. **D10** 42
Şahneh, Iran **E12** 44
Šahrisabz, Uzb. **F8** 26
Šahty, Russia **E5** 26
Sahuaripa, Mex. **B3** 78
Sahuarita, Az., U.S. **F5** 96
Šahunja, Russia **C8** 22
Sa Huynh, Viet. **D5** 34
Saibai Island, i., Austl. **B3** 62
Saïda, Alg. **E4** 14
Saidpur, Bngl. **D5** 40
Saidu, Pak. **D10** 42
Saigon see Thanh Pho Ho Chi Minh, Viet. **D5** 34
Saiki, Japan **D2** 31
Šaim, Russia **B11** 22
Saimaa, l., Fin. **F13** 10
Şā'īn Dezh, Iran **D12** 44
Saint Adolphe, Mb., Can. **E3** 86
Sainte-Agathe, P.Q., Can. **C6** 90
Sainte-Agathe-des-Monts, P.Q., Can. **C3** 90
Saint-Aimé (Massueville), P.Q., Can. **D5** 90
Saint-Alban, P.Q., Can. **C5** 90
Saint Alban's, Nf., Can. **E4** 88
Saint Albans, Vt., U.S. **B2** 138
Saint Albans, W.V., U.S. **C3** 141
Saint Albans Bay, b., Vt., U.S. **B2** 138
Saint Albert, Ab., Can. **C4** 84
Saint-Amand-Montrond, Fr. **D8** 16
Saint-Ambroise, P.Q., Can. **A6** 90
Saint-André-Avellin, P.Q., Can. **D2** 90
Saint-André-Est, P.Q., Can. **D3** 90
Saint Andrew Bay, b., Fl., U.S. **u16** 102
Saint Andrews, N.B., Can. **D2** 87
Saint Andrews, Scot., U.K. **B5** 12
Saint Andrews, S.C., U.S. **C5** 133
Saint Andrews, S.C., U.S. **F7** 133
Saint Anne, Il., U.S. **B6** 106
Sainte-Anne-de-Beaupré, P.Q., Can. **B7** 90
Sainte-Anne [-de-Bellevue], P.Q., Can. **q19** 90
Sainte Anne-de-Madawaska, N.B., Can. **B1** 87
Sainte Anne-des-Chênes, Mb., Can. **E3** 86
Saint-Anselme, P.Q., Can. **C7** 90
Saint Ansgar, Ia., U.S. **A5** 108
Saint Anthony, Nf., Can. **C4** 88
Saint Anthony, Id., U.S. **F7** 105
Saint Antoine, N.B., Can. **C5** 87
Saint-Apollinaire, P.Q., Can. **C6** 90
Saint Arnaud, Austl. **H3** 62
Saint Arthur, N.B., Can. **B3** 87
Saint-Aubert, P.Q., Can. **B7** 90
Saint Augustin, stm., Can. **C2** 88
Saint Augustine, Fl., U.S. **C5** 102
Saint Austell, Eng., U.K. **E4** 12
Saint-Avold, Fr. **C10** 16
Saint Basile, N.B., Can. **B1** 87
Saint-Basile [-Sud], P.Q., Can. **C6** 90
Saint-Bernard, P.Q., Can. **C6** 90
Saint Bernard, Al., U.S. **A3** 94
Saint Bernard, La., U.S. **E6** 111
Saint Bernard, Oh., U.S. **o13** 128
Saint Bernard, co., La., U.S. **E6** 111
Saint Bernice, In., U.S. **E2** 107
Saint Bride, Mount, mtn., Ab., Can. **D3** 84
Saint Bride's, Nf., Can. **E4** 88
Saint-Brieuc, Fr. **C5** 16
Saint-Bruno, P.Q., Can. **A6** 90
Saint-Casimir, P.Q., Can. **C5** 90
Saint Catharines, On., Can. **D5** 89
Saint Catherine, Lake, l., Vt., U.S. **E2** 138
Saint Catherines Island, i., Ga., U.S. **E5** 103
Saint-Célestin (Annaville), P.Q., Can. **C5** 90
Saint-Césaire, P.Q., Can. **D4** 90
Saint-Chamond, Fr. **E9** 16
Saint-Charles, P.Q., Can. **C7** 90
Saint Charles, Il., U.S. **B5** 106
Saint Charles, Mi., U.S. **E6** 115
Saint Charles, Mn., U.S. **G6** 116
Saint Charles, Mo., U.S. **C7** 118
Saint Charles, co., La., U.S. **E5** 111
Saint Charles, co., Mo., U.S. **C7** 118
Saint Christopher (Saint Kitts), i., St. K./N. **B7** 80
Saint Christopher and Nevis see Saint Kitts and Nevis, ctry., N.A. **E12** 76
Saint-Chrysostome, P.Q., Can. **D4** 90
Saint Clair, Mi., U.S. **F8** 115
Saint Clair, Mn., U.S. **F5** 116
Saint Clair, Mo., U.S. **C6** 118
Saint Clair, Pa., U.S. **E9** 131
Saint Clair, co., Al., U.S. **B3** 94
Saint Clair, co., Il., U.S. **E3** 106
Saint Clair, co., Mi., U.S. **F8** 115
Saint Clair, co., Mo., U.S. **C4** 118
Saint Clair Shores, Mi., U.S. **p16** 115
Saint Clairsville, Oh., U.S. **B5** 128
Saint Claude, Mb., Can. **E2** 86
Saint Cloud, Fl., U.S. **D5** 102
Saint Cloud, Mn., U.S. **E4** 116
Saint-Coeur-de-Marie, P.Q., Can. **A6** 90
Saint-Constant, P.Q., Can. **q19** 90
Sainte-Croix, P.Q., Can. **C6** 90
Saint Croix, co., Wi., U.S. **C1** 142
Saint Croix, i., V.I.U.S. **B7** 80
Saint Croix, stm., U.S. **C1** 142
Saint Croix, Lake, l., U.S. **D1** 142
Saint Croix Falls, Wi., U.S. **C1** 142
Saint Croix Stream, stm., Me., U.S. **B4** 112
Saint-Damase, P.Q., Can. **D4** 90
Saint David, Az., U.S. **F5** 96
Saint-David-de-l'Auberivière, P.Q., Can. **n17** 90
Saint-Denis, P.Q., Can. **D4** 90
Saint-Denis, Reu. **g10** 57a
Saint-Dié, Fr. **C10** 16
Saint-Dizier, Fr. **C9** 16
Saint-Dominique, P.Q., Can. **D5** 90
Saint Edward, Ne., U.S. **C8** 120
Saint Eleanor's, P.E., Can. **C6** 87
Saint Elias, Cape, c., Ak., U.S. **D11** 95
Saint Elias, Mount, mtn., N.A. **F11** 82
Saint-Élie, Fr. Gu. **C9** 70
Saint Elmo, Al., U.S. **E1** 94
Saint Elmo, Il., U.S. **D5** 106
Saint-Éphrem [-de-Tring], P.Q., Can. **C7** 90
Saint-Étienne, Fr. **E9** 16
Saint-Eustache, P.Q., Can. **D4** 90
Saint-Félicien, P.Q., Can. **A5** 90
Saint-Félix-de-Valois, P.Q., Can. **C4** 90
Saint-Ferdinand (Bernierville), P.Q., Can. **C6** 90
Saint-Ferréol [-les-Neiges], P.Q., Can. **B7** 90
Saint-Flavien, P.Q., Can. **C6** 90
Sainte-Foy, P.Q., Can. **n17** 90
Saint Francis, Ks., U.S. **C2** 109
Saint Francis, Mn., U.S. **E5** 116
Saint Francis, S.D., U.S. **D5** 134
Saint Francis, Wi., U.S. **n12** 142
Saint Francis, co., Ar., U.S. **B5** 97
Saint Francis, stm., U.S. **A5** 97
Saint Francis, Cape, c., Nf., Can. **E5** 88
Saint Francis, Cape, c., S. Afr. **E3** 56
Saint Francisville, Il., U.S. **E6** 106
Saint Francisville, La., U.S. **D4** 111
Saint Francois, co., Mo., U.S. **D7** 118
Saint-François, stm., P.Q., Can. **D5** 90
Saint-François, Lac, l., P.Q., Can. **D6** 90
Saint Francois Mountains, hills, Mo., U.S. **D7** 118
Saint Froid Lake, l., Me., U.S. **B4** 112
Saint-Fulgence, P.Q., Can. **A7** 90
Saint-Gabriel, P.Q., Can. **C4** 90
Saint-Gaudens, Fr. **F7** 16
Saint-Gédéon, P.Q., Can. **D7** 90
Sainte Genevieve, Mo., U.S. **D7** 118
Sainte Genevieve, co., Mo., U.S. **D7** 118
Saint George, Austl. **F4** 62
Saint George, N.B., Can. **D3** 87
Saint George, On., Can. **D4** 89
Saint George, S.C., U.S. **E6** 133
Saint George, Ut., U.S. **F2** 137
Saint George, Cape, c., Nf., Can. **D2** 88
Saint George, Cape, c., Fl., U.S. **C1** 102
Saint George Island, i., Ak., U.S. **D6** 95
Saint George Island, i., Fl., U.S. **C2** 102
Saint George's, Nf., Can. **D2** 88
Saint-Georges, P.Q., Can. **C5** 90
Saint-Georges, Fr. Gu. **C9** 70
Saint George's, Gren. **C7** 80
Saint Georges, De., U.S. **B3** 101
Saint George's Bay, b., Nf., Can. **D2** 88
Saint Georges Bay, b., N.S., Can. **D8** 87
Saint George's Channel, strt., Eur. **B3** 16
Saint-Georges-Ouest (part of Ville-Saint-Georges), P.Q., Can. **C7** 90
Saint-Gervais, P.Q., Can. **C7** 90
Saint-Gilles, P.Q., Can. **C6** 90
Saint Gotthard Pass see San Gottardo, Passo del, Switz. **A2** 18
Saint-Grégoire (Larochelle), P.Q., Can. **C5** 90
Saint-Guillaume-d'Upton, P.Q., Can. **D5** 90
Saint Helen, Lake, l., Mi., U.S. **D6** 115
Saint Helena, Ca., U.S. **C2** 98
Saint Helena, co., La., U.S. **D5** 111
Saint Helena, dep., Afr. **K9** 46
Saint Helena Island, i., S.C., U.S. **G6** 133
Saint Helena Sound, strt., S.C., U.S. **G7** 133
Saint Helens, Or., U.S. **B4** 130
Saint Helens, Mount, vol., Wa., U.S. **C3** 140
Saint Helier, Jersey **F5** 12
Saint Henry, Oh., U.S. **B1** 128
Saint-Honoré, P.Q., Can. **D7** 90
Saint-Hubert, P.Q., Can. **q20** 90
Saint-Hubert-de-Témiscouata, P.Q., Can. **B8** 90
Saint-Hyacinthe, P.Q., Can. **D5** 90
Saint Ignace, Mi., U.S. **C6** 115
Saint Ignatius, Mt., U.S. **C2** 119
Saint Isidore de Prescott, On., Can. **B10** 89
Saint Jacobs, On., Can. **D4** 89
Saint Jacques, N.B., Can. **B1** 87
Saint-Jacques, P.Q., Can. **D4** 90
Saint James, Mn., U.S. **G4** 116
Saint James, Mo., U.S. **D6** 118
Saint James, co., La., U.S. **D5** 111
Saint James, Cape, c., B.C., Can. **D2** 85
Saint James City, Fl., U.S. **F4** 102
Saint-Jean, stm., P.Q., Can. **A7** 90
Saint-Jean, Lac, l., P.Q., Can. **A5** 90
Saint Jean Baptiste, Mb., Can. **E3** 86
Saint-Jean-Chrysostome, P.Q., Can. **o17** 90
Saint-Jean-d'Angély, Fr. **E6** 16
Saint-Jean-sur-Richelieu, P.Q., Can. **D4** 90
Saint-Jérôme, P.Q., Can. **D3** 90
Saint Jo, Tx., U.S. **C4** 136
Saint-Joachim, P.Q., Can. **B7** 90
Saint Joe, stm., Id., U.S. **B3** 105
Saint John, N.B., Can. **D3** 87
Saint John, In., U.S. **B3** 107
Saint John, Ks., U.S. **E5** 109
Saint John, i., V.I.U.S. **B7** 80
Saint John, stm., N.A. **B14** 92
Saint John, Cape, c., Nf., Can. **D4** 88
Saint John Bay, b., Nf., Can. **C3** 88
Saint John's, Antig. **B7** 80
Saint John's, Nf., Can. **E5** 88
Saint Johns, Az., U.S. **C6** 96
Saint Johns, Mi., U.S. **F6** 115
Saint Johns, co., Fl., U.S. **C5** 102
Saint Johns, stm., Fl., U.S. **B5** 102
Saint Johnsbury, Vt., U.S. **C4** 138
Saint Johnsville, N.Y., U.S. **B6** 125
Saint John the Baptist, co., La., U.S. **D5** 111
Saint Jones, stm., De., U.S. **D4** 101
Saint Joseph, N.B., Can. **D5** 87
Saint Joseph, Il., U.S. **C5** 106
Saint Joseph, La., U.S. **C4** 111
Saint Joseph, Mi., U.S. **F4** 115
Saint Joseph, Mn., U.S. **E4** 116
Saint Joseph, Mo., U.S. **B3** 118
Saint Joseph, Tn., U.S. **B4** 135
Saint Joseph, co., In., U.S. **A5** 107
Saint Joseph, co., Mi., U.S. **G5** 115
Saint Joseph, stm., U.S. **F5** 115
Saint-Joseph, Lac, l., P.Q., Can. **n16** 90
Saint Joseph, Lake, l., On., Can. **o17** 89
Saint Joseph Bay, b., Fl., U.S. **C1** 102
Saint-Joseph-de-Beauce, P.Q., Can. **C7** 90
Saint Joseph Point, c., Fl., U.S. **v16** 102
Saint Joseph Sound, strt., Fl., U.S. **o10** 102
Saint-Jovite, P.Q., Can. **C3** 90
Saint-Junien, Fr. **E7** 16
Saint Kilda, i., Scot., U.K. **B2** 12
Saint Kitts see Saint Christopher, i., St. K./N. **B7** 80
Saint Kitts and Nevis, ctry., N.A. **E12** 76
Saint-Lambert, P.Q., Can. **p19** 90
Saint Landry, co., La., U.S. **D3** 111
Saint-Laurent, P.Q., Can. **p19** 90
Saint-Laurent du Maroni, Fr. Gu. **B9** 70
Saint Lawrence, Nf., Can. **E4** 88
Saint Lawrence, co., N.Y., U.S. **A5** 125
Saint Lawrence, stm., N.A. **B14** 92
Saint Lawrence, Cape, c., N.S., Can. **B9** 87
Saint Lawrence, Gulf of, b., Can. **I27** 82
Saint Lawrence Island, i., Ak., U.S. **C5** 95
Saint Lawrence Islands National Park, On., Can. **C9** 89
Saint Léonard, N.B., Can. **B2** 87
Saint-Léonard [-d'Aston], P.Q., Can. **C5** 90
Saint-Liboire, P.Q., Can. **D5** 90
Saint-Lô, Fr. **C6** 16
Saint-Louis, Sen. **C1** 50
Saint Louis, Mi., U.S. **E6** 115
Saint Louis, Mo., U.S. **C7** 118
Saint Louis, co., Mn., U.S. **C6** 116
Saint Louis, co., Mo., U.S. **C7** 118
Saint Louis, stm., U.S. **D6** 116
Saint-Louis, Lac, l., P.Q., Can. **q19** 90
Saint Louis Bay, b., Ms., U.S. **f7** 117
Saint-Louis-de-Gonzague, P.Q., Can. **D3** 90
Saint Louis-de-Kent, N.B., Can. **C5** 87
Saint-Louis-du-Ha! Ha!, P.Q., Can. **B8** 90
Saint Louis Park, Mn., U.S. **n12** 116
Saint-Luc, P.Q., Can. **D4** 90
Saint Lucia, ctry., N.A. **F12** 76
Saint Lucia, Lake, l., S. Afr. **D5** 56
Saint Lucia Channel, strt., N.A. **C7** 80
Saint Lucie, co., Fl., U.S. **E6** 102
Saint Lucie Canal, Fl., U.S. **F6** 102
Saint Lucie Inlet, b., Fl., U.S. **E6** 102
Sainte-Madeleine, P.Q., Can. **D4** 90
Saint Magnus Bay, b., Scot., U.K. **h19** 12a
Saint Malo, Mb., Can. **E3** 86
Saint-Malo, Fr. **C6** 16
Saint-Malo, Golfe de, b., Fr. **C5** 16
Saint-Marc, Haiti **B5** 80
Saint-Marc [-des-Carrières], P.Q., Can. **C5** 90
Saint Margaret Bay, b., Nf., Can. **C3** 88
Sainte-Marguerite, stm., P.Q., Can. **A7** 90
Sainte-Marie, P.Q., Can. **C6** 90
Sainte Marie, Nosy, i., Madag. **B8** 56
Saint Maries, Id., U.S. **B2** 105
Sainte-Marthe, P.Q., Can. **D3** 90
Saint Martin, co., La., U.S. **D4** 111
Saint-Martin, i., N.A. **B7** 80
Saint Martin, Lake, l., Mb., Can. **D2** 86
Saint Martin Island, i., Mi., U.S. **C4** 115
Saint Martinville, La., U.S. **D4** 111
Saint Mary, co., La., U.S. **E4** 111
Saint Mary-of-the-Woods, In., U.S. **E3** 107
Saint Mary Peak, mtn., Austl. **G2** 62
Saint Marys, Austl. **I4** 62
Saint Mary's, Nf., Can. **E5** 88
Saint Mary's, On., Can. **D3** 89
Saint Marys, Ak., U.S. **C7** 95
Saint Marys, Ga., U.S. **F5** 103
Saint Marys, In., U.S. **A5** 107
Saint Marys, Ks., U.S. **C7** 109
Saint Marys, Oh., U.S. **B1** 128
Saint Marys, Pa., U.S. **D4** 131
Saint Marys, W.V., U.S. **B3** 141
Saint Marys, co., Md., U.S. **D4** 113
Saint Marys, stm., N.S., Can. **D8** 87
Saint Marys, stm., Md., U.S. **D5** 113
Saint Marys, stm., U.S. **F5** 103
Saint Marys, stm., U.S. **C8** 107
Saint Mary's, Cape, c., Nf., Can. **E4** 88
Saint Mary's Bay, b., Nf., Can. **E5** 88
Saint Marys Bay, b., N.S., Can. **E3** 87
Saint Marys City, Md., U.S. **D5** 113
Saint Matthew Island, i., Ak., U.S. **C5** 95
Saint Matthews, Ky., U.S. **B4** 110
Saint Matthews, S.C., U.S. **D6** 133
Saint-Maurice, stm., P.Q., Can. **C5** 90
Saint Michael, Mn., U.S. **E5** 116
Saint Michaels, Md., U.S. **C5** 113
Saint-Michel [-de-Bellechasse], P.Q., Can. **C7** 90
Saint-Nazaire, Fr. **D5** 16
Saint-Nicolas, P.Q., Can. **o17** 90
Saint-Odilon, P.Q., Can. **C7** 90
Saint-Omer, Fr. **B8** 16
Saint-Ours, P.Q., Can. **D4** 90
Saint-Pacôme, P.Q., Can. **B8** 90
Saint-Pamphile, P.Q., Can. **C8** 90
Saint Paris, Oh., U.S. **B2** 128
Saint-Pascal, P.Q., Can. **B8** 90
Saint Paul, Ab., Can. **B5** 84
Saint-Paul, Reu. **g10** 57a
Saint Paul, Ak., U.S. **D5** 95

Name	Map Ref.	Page
Saint Paul, In., U.S.	**F6**	107
Saint Paul, Ks., U.S.	**E8**	109
Saint Paul, Mn., U.S.	**F5**	116
Saint Paul, Mo., U.S.	**f12**	118
Saint Paul, Ne., U.S.	**C7**	120
Saint Paul, Va., U.S.	**f9**	139
Saint Paul Island, i., Ak., U.S.	**D5**	95
Saint Paul Park, Mn., U.S.	**n12**	116
Saint Pauls, N.C., U.S.	**C4**	126
Sainte-Perpétue-de-L'Islet, P.Q., Can.	**B8**	90
Saint Peter, Mn., U.S.	**F5**	116
Saint Peter Port, Guernsey	**F5**	12
Saint Peters, N.S., Can.	**D9**	87
Saint Peters, Mo., U.S.	**C7**	118
Saint Petersburg see Sankt-Peterburg, Russia	**D5**	26
Saint Petersburg, Fl., U.S.	**E4**	102
Saint Petersburg Beach, Fl., U.S.	**p10**	102
Saint Phillips Island, i., S.C., U.S.	**G6**	133
Saint-Pie, P.Q., Can.	**D5**	90
Saint-Pierre, Reu.	**g10**	57a
Saint-Pierre, St. P./M.	**E3**	88
Saint Pierre, i., Sey.	**i12**	57b
Saint-Pierre, Lac, l., P.Q., Can.	**C5**	90
Saint Pierre and Miquelon, dep., N.A.	**I28**	82
Saint Pierre-Jolys, Mb., Can.	**E3**	86
Saint-Prime, P.Q., Can.	**A5**	90
Saint Quentin, N.B., Can.	**B2**	87
Saint-Quentin, Fr.	**C8**	16
Saint-Raphaël, P.Q., Can.	**C7**	90
Saint-Raphaël, Fr.	**F10**	16
Saint-Raymond, P.Q., Can.	**C6**	90
Saint-Rédempteur, P.Q., Can.	**o17**	90
Saint Regis, Mt., U.S.	**C1**	119
Saint Regis, West Branch, stm., N.Y., U.S.	**f10**	125
Saint-Rémi, P.Q., Can.	**D4**	90
Saint-Romuald, P.Q., Can.	**C6**	90
Saint Rose, La., U.S.	**k11**	111
Sainte Rose du Lac, Mb., Can.	**D2**	86
Saintes, Fr.	**E6**	16
Saint Sauveur, N.B., Can.	**B4**	87
Saint-Sauveur-des-Monts, P.Q., Can.	**D3**	90
Saint-Siméon, P.Q., Can.	**B8**	90
Saint Simons Island, Ga., U.S.	**E5**	103
Saint Simons Island, i., Ga., U.S.	**E5**	103
Saint Stephen, N.B., Can.	**D2**	87
Saint Stephen, S.C., U.S.	**E8**	133
Saint Tammany, co., La., U.S.	**D5**	111
Sainte-Thècle, P.Q., Can.	**C5**	90
Sainte-Thérèse, P.Q., Can.	**D4**	90
Saint Thomas, On., Can.	**E3**	89
Saint Thomas, i., V.I.U.S.	**B6**	80
Saint Timothée, P.Q., Can.	**q18**	90
Saint-Tite, P.Q., Can.	**C5**	90
Saint-Tropez, Fr.	**F10**	16
Sainte-Véronique, P.Q., Can.	**C3**	90
Saint-Victor, P.Q., Can.	**C7**	90
Saint Vincent, i., St. Vin.	**C7**	80
Saint Vincent and the Grenadines, ctry., N.A.	**F12**	76
Saint Vincent Island, i., Fl., U.S.	**C1**	102
Saint Vincent Passage, strt., N.A.	**C7**	80
Saint Vincent's [-Saint Stephens-Peter's River], Nf., Can.	**E5**	88
Saint Walburg, Sk., Can.	**D1**	91
Saint-Zacharie, P.Q., Can.	**C7**	90
Saipan, i., N. Mar. Is.	**C12**	32
Sajama, Nevado, mtn., Bol.	**B4**	72
Sakakawea, Lake, res., N.D., U.S.	**B3**	127
Sakania, D.R.C.	**F5**	54
Sakarya, Tur.	**B4**	44
Sakarya, stm., Tur.	**B4**	44
Sakata, Japan	**D15**	28
Sakété, Benin	**E5**	50
Sakha see Jakutija, state, Russia	**C14**	26
Sakhalin see Sahalin, ostrov, i., Russia	**D16**	26
Sakon Nakhon, Thai.	**C4**	34
Sakonnet, stm., R.I., U.S.	**E6**	132
Sakonnet Point, c., R.I., U.S.	**F6**	132
Sakrivier, S. Afr.	**E3**	56
Saky, Ukr.	**G12**	20
Sal, i., C.V.	**g10**	50a
Sal, Point, c., Ca., U.S.	**E3**	98
Sala, Swe.	**G7**	10
Salaberry-de-Valleyfield, P.Q., Can.	**D3**	90
Salacgrīva, Lat.	**H11**	10
Sala Consilina, Italy	**D5**	18
Salada, Laguna, l., Mex.	**A1**	78
Saladillo, Arg.	**F6**	72
Salado, stm., Arg.	**F4**	72
Salado, stm., Arg.	**F6**	72
Salado, stm., Arg.	**D5**	72
Salado, stm., Mex.	**B5**	78
Salado, Rio, stm., N.M., U.S.	**C2**	124
Salaga, Ghana	**E4**	50
Salal, Chad	**D8**	50
Şalālah, Oman	**G6**	38
Salamanca, Mex.	**C4**	78
Salamanca, Spain	**G4**	16
Salamanca, N.Y., U.S.	**C2**	125
Salamís, i., Grc.	**F9**	18
Salamis, hist., N. Cyp.	**E5**	44
Salamīyah, Syria	**E7**	44
Salamonie, stm., In., U.S.	**C6**	107
Salamonie Lake, res., In., U.S.	**C6**	107
Salavat, Russia	**D7**	26
Salawati, i., Indon.	**D8**	36
Sala y Gómez, Isla, i., Chile	**K28**	64
Sala y Gomez Ridge	**K28**	64
Saldanha, S. Afr.	**E2**	56
Saldus, Lat.	**H10**	10
Sale, Austl.	**H4**	62
Salé, Mor.	**E2**	14
Sale Creek, Tn., U.S.	**D8**	135
Salehard, Russia	**C8**	26
Salem, India	**G3**	40
Salem, Ar., U.S.	**A4**	97
Salem, Il., U.S.	**E5**	106
Salem, In., U.S.	**G5**	107
Salem, Ky., U.S.	**e9**	110
Salem, Ma., U.S.	**A6**	114
Salem, Mo., U.S.	**D6**	118
Salem, N.H., U.S.	**E4**	122
Salem, N.J., U.S.	**D2**	123
Salem, Oh., U.S.	**B5**	128
Salem, Or., U.S.	**C4**	130
Salem, S.D., U.S.	**D8**	134
Salem, Ut., U.S.	**C4**	137
Salem, Va., U.S.	**C2**	139
Salem, W.V., U.S.	**B4**	141
Salem, Wi., U.S.	**n11**	142
Salem, co., N.J., U.S.	**D2**	123
Salem, stm., N.J., U.S.	**D2**	123
Salem, Lake, l., Vt., U.S.	**B4**	138
Salerno, Italy	**D5**	18
Salerno, Golfo di, b., Italy	**D5**	18
Salgótarján, Hung.	**E5**	20
Salgueiro, Braz.	**C4**	74
Salida, Co., U.S.	**C5**	99
Salihli, Tur.	**C3**	44
Salihorsk, Bela.	**C9**	20
Salima, Mwi.	**A5**	56
Salina, Ks., U.S.	**D6**	109
Salina, Ok., U.S.	**A6**	129
Salina, Ut., U.S.	**E4**	137
Salina Cruz, Mex.	**D5**	78
Salinas, Braz.	**E3**	74
Salinas, Ec.	**D3**	70
Salinas, Ca., U.S.	**D3**	98
Salinas, stm., N.A.	**B1**	80
Salinas, stm., Ca., U.S.	**D3**	98
Salinas de Hidalgo, Mex.	**C4**	78
Salinas Peak, mtn., N.M., U.S.	**D3**	124
Salinas Pueblo Missions National Monument, N.M., U.S.	**C3**	124
Saline, Mi., U.S.	**F7**	115
Saline, co., Ar., U.S.	**C3**	97
Saline, co., Il., U.S.	**F5**	106
Saline, co., Ks., U.S.	**D6**	109
Saline, co., Mo., U.S.	**B4**	118
Saline, co., Ne., U.S.	**D8**	120
Saline, stm., Ar., U.S.	**C1**	97
Saline, stm., Ar., U.S.	**D4**	97
Saline, stm., Ks., U.S.	**C3**	109
Saline, North Fork, stm., Il., U.S.	**F5**	106
Saline Lake, res., La., U.S.	**C3**	111
Salineville, Oh., U.S.	**B5**	128
Salinópolis, Braz.	**B2**	74
Salisbury, Austl.	**G2**	62
Salisbury, N.B., Can.	**C4**	87
Salisbury, Ct., U.S.	**B2**	100
Salisbury, Ma., U.S.	**A6**	114
Salisbury, Md., U.S.	**D6**	113
Salisbury, Mo., U.S.	**B5**	118
Salisbury, N.C., U.S.	**B2**	126
Salisbury see Harare, Zimb.	**B5**	56
Salish Mountains, mts., Mt., U.S.	**B2**	119
Salkehatchie, stm., S.C., U.S.	**E5**	133
Salla, Fin.	**C13**	10
Sallisaw, Ok., U.S.	**B7**	129
Salluit, P.Q., Can.	**f11**	90
Salmās, Iran	**C11**	44
Salmo, B.C., Can.	**E9**	85
Salmon, Id., U.S.	**D5**	105
Salmon, stm., N.B., Can.	**C4**	87
Salmon, stm., Id., U.S.	**D3**	105
Salmon Creek, Wa., U.S.	**D3**	140
Salmon Creek Reservoir, res., Id., U.S.	**G4**	105
Salmon Falls, stm., U.S.	**D5**	122
Salmon Falls Creek, stm., U.S.	**G4**	105
Salmon Mountains, mts., Ca., U.S.	**B2**	98
Salmon Point, c., On., Can.	**D7**	89
Salmon River Mountains, mts., Id., U.S.	**E3**	105
Salmon River Reservoir, res., N.Y., U.S.	**B5**	125
Salo, Fin.	**F10**	10
Salò, Italy	**B3**	18
Salome, Az., U.S.	**D2**	96
Salon-de-Provence, Fr.	**F9**	16
Salonika see Thessaloníki, Grc.	**D9**	18
Salonika, Gulf of see Thermaïkós Kólpos, b., Grc.	**D9**	18
Salonta, Rom.	**F6**	20
Sal'sk, Russia	**E7**	22
Salt, stm., Az., U.S.	**D4**	96
Salt, stm., Ky., U.S.	**C4**	110
Salt, stm., Mo., U.S.	**B6**	118
Salta, Arg.	**C4**	72
Salt Creek, stm., N.M., U.S.	**D5**	124
Salt Creek, stm., Oh., U.S.	**C3**	128
Salt Creek, stm., Wy., U.S.	**C6**	143
Salter Path, N.C., U.S.	**C6**	126
Salt Fork Lake, res., Oh., U.S.	**B4**	128
Saltillo, Mex.	**B4**	78
Saltillo, Ms., U.S.	**A5**	117
Salt Lake, co., Ut., U.S.	**C3**	137
Salt Lake, l., Hi., U.S.	**g10**	104
Salt Lake, l., N.M., U.S.	**E6**	124
Salt Lake City, Ut., U.S.	**C4**	137
Salto, Ur.	**E6**	72
Salton Sea, l., Ca., U.S.	**F5**	98
Saltonstall, Lake, l., Ct., U.S.	**D4**	100
Salt Point, c., Ca., U.S.	**C2**	98
Salt River Indian Reservation, Az., U.S.	**k9**	96
Salt River Range, mts., Wy., U.S.	**D2**	143
Saltsburg, Pa., U.S.	**F3**	131
Salt Springs, Fl., U.S.	**C5**	102
Saltville, Va., U.S.	**f10**	139
Salt Wells Creek, stm., Wy., U.S.	**E4**	143
Saluda, S.C., U.S.	**C4**	133
Saluda, co., S.C., U.S.	**C4**	133
Saluda, stm., S.C., U.S.	**C4**	133
Saluda Dam, S.C., U.S.	**C5**	133
Salûm, Egypt	**D10**	48
Sālūr, India	**F4**	40
Salvador, Braz.	**D4**	74
Salvador, El see El Salvador, ctry., N.A.	**C2**	80
Salvador, Lake, l., La., U.S.	**E5**	111
Salween, stm., Asia	**G7**	28
Salyan, Azer.	**C13**	44
Salyān, Nepal	**D4**	40
Salyersville, Ky., U.S.	**C6**	110
Salzburg, Aus.	**G13**	12
Salzgitter, Ger.	**D12**	12
Samah, Libya	**F7**	14
Samālūţ, Egypt	**F10**	14
Samana Cay, i., Bah.	**A5**	80
Samandağı, Tur.	**D6**	44
Samar, i., Phil.	**D9**	34
Samara (Kujbyšev), Russia	**D7**	26
Samarai, Pap. N. Gui.	**I13**	32
Samarinda, Indon.	**D5**	36
Samarkand, Uzb.	**F8**	26
Sāmarrā', Iraq	**D4**	42
Samar Sea, Phil.	**D8**	34
Şamaxi, Azer.	**B13**	44
Samba Caju, Ang.	**E3**	54
Sambalpur, India	**E4**	40
Sambas, Indon.	**C3**	36
Sambava, Madag.	**A9**	56
Sambhal, India	**D3**	40
Sāmbhar, India	**D3**	40
Sambir, Ukr.	**E7**	20
Samboja, Indon.	**D5**	36
Samborombón, Bahía, b., Arg.	**F6**	72
Samch'ŏk, S. Kor.	**D13**	28
Same, Tan.	**D7**	54
Samfya, Zam.	**A4**	56
Şämkir, Azer.	**B11**	44
Sammamish, Lake, l., Wa., U.S.	**e11**	140
Samoa, ctry., Oc.	**F12**	58
Samoa Islands, is., Oc.	**F12**	58
Samoded, Russia	**B7**	22
Sámos, i., Grc.	**F11**	18
Samoset, Fl., U.S.	**q10**	102
Samothrace see Samothráki, i., Grc.	**D10**	18
Samothráki, i., Grc.	**D10**	18
Sampit, Indon.	**D4**	36
Sampit, stm., S.C., U.S.	**E9**	133
Sampit, Teluk, b., Indon.	**D4**	36
Sampson, co., N.C., U.S.	**B4**	126
Sam Rayburn Reservoir, res., Tx., U.S.	**D5**	136
Samsang, China	**C4**	40
Samson, Al., U.S.	**D3**	94
Sam Son, Viet.	**C5**	34
Samsun, Tur.	**B7**	44
Samtredia, Geor.	**A10**	44
Samuels, Id., U.S.	**A2**	105
Samui, Ko, i., Thai.	**E4**	34
Samur, stm.	**B13**	44
Samut Prakan, Thai.	**D4**	34
Samut Songkhram, Thai.	**D4**	34
San, Mali	**D4**	50
Şan'ā', Yemen	**G4**	38
Sanaba, Burkina	**D4**	50
Sanaga, stm., Cam.	**C2**	54
San Agustin, Cape, c., Phil.	**E9**	34
San Agustin, Plains of, pl., N.M., U.S.	**C2**	124
Sanak Islands, is., Ak., U.S.	**E7**	95
San Ambrosio, Isla, i., Chile	**H7**	2
Sanana, Pulau, i., Indon.	**D7**	36
Sanandaj, Iran	**C5**	42
San Andreas, Ca., U.S.	**C3**	98
San Andrés, Col.	**A3**	70
San Andrés, Isla de, i., Col.	**A3**	70
San Andres Mountains, mts., N.M., U.S.	**E3**	124
San Andres Peak, mtn., N.M., U.S.	**E3**	124
San Andrés Tuxtla, Mex.	**D5**	78
San Angelo, Tx., U.S.	**D2**	136
San Anselmo, Ca., U.S.	**h7**	98
San Antonio, Chile	**E3**	72
San Antonio, Tx., U.S.	**E3**	136
San Antonio, Cabo, c., Arg.	**F6**	72
San Antonio, Cabo de, c., Cuba	**A2**	80
San Antonio Bay, b., Tx., U.S.	**E4**	136
San Antonio de los Baños, Cuba	**A3**	80
San Antonio Mountain, mtn., N.M., U.S.	**A3**	124
San Antonio Oeste, Arg.	**F4**	69
San Augustine, Tx., U.S.	**D5**	136
San Augustine, co., Tx., U.S.	**D5**	136
San Benedetto del Tronto, Italy	**C4**	18
San Benedicto, Isla, i., Mex.	**D2**	78
San Benito, Guat.	**B2**	80
San Benito, Tx., U.S.	**F4**	136
San Benito, co., Ca., U.S.	**D3**	98
San Benito Mountain, mtn., Ca., U.S.	**D3**	98
San Bernardino, Ca., U.S.	**E5**	98
San Bernardino, co., Ca., U.S.	**E5**	98
San Blas, Cape, c., Fl., U.S.	**v16**	102
San Borja, Bol.	**A4**	72
Sanborn, Ia., U.S.	**A2**	108
Sanborn, co., S.D., U.S.	**D7**	134
Sanbornville, N.H., U.S.	**C4**	122
San Bruno, Ca., U.S.	**D2**	98
San Carlos, Arg.	**D4**	72
San Carlos, Chile	**E2**	69
San Carlos, Phil.	**D8**	34
San Carlos, Phil.	**C8**	34
San Carlos, Az., U.S.	**D5**	96
San Carlos, Ca., U.S.	**k8**	98
San Carlos, Ven.	**D6**	80
San Carlos de Bariloche, Arg.	**F2**	69
San Carlos de Bolívar, Arg.	**F5**	72
San Carlos del Zulia, Ven.	**B5**	70
San Carlos de Río Negro, Ven.	**C6**	70
San Carlos Indian Reservation, Az., U.S.	**D5**	96
San Carlos Lake, res., Az., U.S.	**D5**	96
Sánchez, Dom. Rep.	**B6**	80
San Clemente, Ca., U.S.	**F5**	98
San Clemente Island, i., Ca., U.S.	**F4**	98
San Cristóbal, Arg.	**E5**	72
San Cristóbal, Dom. Rep.	**B5**	80
San Cristóbal, Ven.	**B5**	70
San Cristóbal, Isla, i., Ec.	**D2**	70
San Cristóbal de las Casas, Mex.	**D6**	78
Sancti Spíritus, Cuba	**A4**	80
Sancy, Puy de, mtn., Fr.	**E8**	16
Sandakan, Malay.	**B5**	36
Sandaré, Mali	**D2**	50
Sand Creek, stm., Wy., U.S.	**C7**	143
Sandefjord, Nor.	**G4**	10
Sanders, Az., U.S.	**B6**	96
Sanders, co., Mt., U.S.	**C1**	119
Sanderson, Tx., U.S.	**D1**	136
Sandersville, Ga., U.S.	**D4**	103
Sandersville, Ms., U.S.	**D4**	117
Sand Hill, Ma., U.S.	**h13**	114
Sand Hill, stm., Mn., U.S.	**C2**	116
Sandia Crest, mtn., N.M., U.S.	**k8**	124
Sandia Indian Reservation, N.M., U.S.	**k7**	124
Sandia Mountains, mts., N.M., U.S.	**k8**	124
San Diego, Ca., U.S.	**F5**	98
San Diego, Tx., U.S.	**F3**	136
San Diego, co., Ca., U.S.	**F5**	98
San Diego, stm., Ca., U.S.	**o15**	98
San Diego, Cabo, c., Arg.	**H3**	69
San Diego Naval Station, mil., Ca., U.S.	**o15**	98
San Diego Naval Training Center, mil., Ca., U.S.	**o15**	98
Sand Island, i., Hi., U.S.	**g10**	104
Sand Island, i., Wi., U.S.	**B3**	142
Sand Key, i., Fl., U.S.	**E4**	102
Sandlick Creek, stm., W.V., U.S.	**n13**	141
Sandnes, Nor.	**G1**	10
Sandoa, D.R.C.	**E4**	54
Sandoval, Il., U.S.	**E4**	106
Sandoval, co., N.M., U.S.	**B2**	124
Sandoway, Myan.	**C2**	34
Sand Point, Ak., U.S.	**D7**	95
Sandpoint, Id., U.S.	**A2**	105
Sands Key, i., Fl., U.S.	**s3**	102
Sand Springs, Ok., U.S.	**A5**	129
Sandston, Va., U.S.	**m18**	139
Sandstone, Austl.	**F2**	60
Sandstone, Mn., U.S.	**D6**	116
Sandusky, Mi., U.S.	**E8**	115
Sandusky, Oh., U.S.	**A3**	128
Sandusky, co., Oh., U.S.	**A2**	128
Sandusky, stm., Oh., U.S.	**B2**	128
Sandvika, Nor.	**G4**	10
Sandviken, Swe.	**F7**	10
Sandwich, Il., U.S.	**B5**	106
Sandwich, Ma., U.S.	**C7**	114
Sandwich Bay, b., Nf., Can.	**B3**	88
Sandy, Or., U.S.	**B4**	130
Sandy, Ut., U.S.	**C4**	137
Sandy, stm., Me., U.S.	**D2**	112
Sandy Cape, c., Austl.	**E5**	62
Sandy Creek, stm., Oh., U.S.	**B4**	128
Sandy Creek, stm., Ok., U.S.	**C2**	129
Sandy Hook, Ct., U.S.	**D2**	100
Sandy Hook, spit, N.J., U.S.	**C5**	123
Sandy Island, i., S.C., U.S.	**D9**	133
Sandykači, Turk.	**F8**	26
Sandy Lake, l., Nf., Can.	**D3**	88
Sandy Lake, l., On., Can.	**n16**	89
Sandy Neck, pen., Ma., U.S.	**C7**	114
Sandy Point, c., R.I., U.S.	**h7**	132
Sandy Springs, Ga., U.S.	**h8**	103
Sandy Springs, S.C., U.S.	**B2**	133
Sandyville, Md., U.S.	**A4**	113
San Felipe, Chile	**E3**	72
San Felipe, Col.	**C6**	70
San Felipe, Mex.	**A2**	78
San Felipe, Ven.	**A6**	70
San Felipe Indian Reservation, N.M., U.S.	**k8**	124
San Felipe Pueblo, N.M., U.S.	**B3**	124
San Fernando, Chile	**D2**	69
San Fernando, Mex.	**C5**	78
San Fernando, Phil.	**C8**	34
San Fernando, Phil.	**C8**	34
San Fernando, Spain	**I3**	16
San Fernando, Trin.	**C7**	80
San Fernando, Ca., U.S.	**m12**	98
San Fernando de Apure, Ven.	**B6**	70
San Fernando de Atabapo, Ven.	**C6**	70
San Fernando del Valle de Catamarca, Arg.	**D4**	72
Sanford, Co., U.S.	**D5**	99
Sanford, Fl., U.S.	**D5**	102
Sanford, Me., U.S.	**E2**	112
Sanford, Mi., U.S.	**E6**	115
Sanford, N.C., U.S.	**B3**	126
Sanford, Mount, mtn., Ak., U.S.	**C11**	95
San Francisco, Arg.	**E5**	72
San Francisco, Ca., U.S.	**D2**	98
San Francisco, co., Ca., U.S.	**D2**	98
San Francisco, stm., U.S.	**D6**	96
San Francisco Bay, b., Ca., U.S.	**h8**	98
San Francisco del Oro, Mex.	**B3**	78
San Francisco del Rincón, Mex.	**C4**	78
San Francisco de Macorís, Dom. Rep.	**B5**	80
San Gabriel Mountains, mts., Ca., U.S.	**m12**	98
Sangamner, India	**F2**	40
Sangamon, co., Il., U.S.	**D4**	106
Sangamon, stm., Il., U.S.	**C3**	106
Sangar, Russia	**C14**	26
Sange, D.R.C.	**E5**	54
Sanger, Ca., U.S.	**D4**	98
Sanger, Tx., U.S.	**C4**	136
Sanggau, Indon.	**C4**	36
Sangha, stm., Afr.	**D3**	54
Sangihe, Kepulauan, is., Indon.	**C7**	36
Sangihe, Pulau, i., Indon.	**C7**	36
San Gil, Col.	**D5**	80
San Giovanni in Fiore, Italy	**E6**	18
Sangiyn Dalay, Mong.	**C9**	28
Sāngli, India	**F2**	40
Sangmélima, Cam.	**C2**	54
San Gorgonio Mountain, mtn., Ca., U.S.	**E5**	98
San Gottardo, Passo del, Switz.	**A2**	18
Sanibel, Fl., U.S.	**F4**	102
Sanibel Island, i., Fl., U.S.	**F4**	102
San Ignacio, Mex.	**B2**	78
San Ignacio, Para.	**D6**	72
San Ignacio de Moxo, Bol.	**A4**	72
San Ignacio de Velasco, Bol.	**G7**	70
Sanilac, co., Mi., U.S.	**E8**	115
San Isidro, Arg.	**E6**	72
San Jacinto, Col.	**D4**	80
San Jacinto, Ca., U.S.	**F5**	98
San Jacinto, co., Tx., U.S.	**D5**	136
San Jacinto, stm., Tx., U.S.	**r14**	136
San Javier, Bol.	**B5**	72
San Joaquín, Bol.	**F7**	70
San Joaquin, co., Ca., U.S.	**D3**	98
San Joaquin, stm., Ca., U.S.	**D3**	98
San Joaquin Valley, val., Ca., U.S.	**D3**	98
San Jorge, Arg.	**E5**	72
San Jorge, Golfo, b., Arg.	**G3**	69
San José, C.R.	**D3**	80
San Jose, Ca., U.S.	**D3**	98
San José, Isla, i., Mex.	**C2**	78
San José de Chiquitos, Bol.	**B5**	72
San José de Guanipa, Ven.	**D7**	80
San José de Jáchal, Arg.	**E4**	72
San José de las Lajas, Cuba	**A3**	80

Name — Map Ref. — Page

San José del Cabo, Mex. **C3** 78
San José del Guaviare, Col. **C5** 70
San Jose Island, i., Tx., U.S. **E4** 136
San Juan, Arg. **E4** 72
San Juan, P.R. **B6** 80
San Juan, Tx., U.S. **F3** 136
San Juan, co., Co., U.S. **D3** 99
San Juan, co., N.M., U.S. **A1** 124
San Juan, co., Ut., U.S. **F5** 137
San Juan, co., Wa., U.S. **A2** 140
San Juan, stm., N.A. **F8** 76
San Juan Bautista, Para. **D6** 72
San Juan Capistrano, Ca., U.S. **F5** 98
San Juan de Colón, Ven. **D5** 80
San Juan de la Maguana, Dom. Rep. **B5** 80
San Juan del Norte, Nic. **C3** 80
San Juan de los Morros, Ven. **D6** 80
San Juan del Sur, Nic. **C2** 80
San Juan Island, i., Wa., U.S. **A2** 140
San Juan Mountains, mts., Co., U.S. **D3** 99
San Justo, Arg. **E5** 72
Sankt Gallen, Switz. **A2** 18
Sankt-Peterburg (Saint Petersburg), Russia **D5** 26
Sankt Pölten, Aus. **F14** 12
Sankuru, stm., D.R.C. **D4** 54
San Lázaro, Cabo, c., Mex. **C2** 78
San Leandro, Ca., U.S. **h8** 98
Şanlıurfa, Tur. **D8** 44
San Lorenzo, Arg. **E5** 72
San Lorenzo, Bol. **C5** 72
San Lorenzo, Ec. **C4** 70
San Lorenzo, Cabo, c., Ec. **D3** 70
Sanlúcar de Barrameda, Spain **I3** 16
San Lucas, Bol. **C4** 72
San Lucas, Mex. **C3** 78
San Lucas, Cabo, c., Mex. **C3** 78
San Luis, Arg. **E4** 72
San Luis, Guat. **B2** 80
San Luis, Az., U.S. **E1** 96
San Luis, Co., U.S. **D5** 99
San Luis, Point, c., Ca., U.S. **E3** 98
San Luis Obispo, Ca., U.S. **E3** 98
San Luis Obispo, co., Ca., U.S. **E3** 98
San Luis Pass, strt., Tx., U.S. **r14** 136
San Luis Peak, mtn., Co., U.S. **D4** 99
San Luis Potosí, Mex. **C4** 78
San Luis Potosí, state, Mex. **C4** 78
San Luis Río Colorado, Mex. **A2** 78
San Luis Valley, val., Co., U.S. **D4** 99
San Manuel, Az., U.S. **E5** 96
San Marcos, Tx., U.S. **E4** 136
San Marcos, stm., Tx., U.S. **h8** 136
San Marino, Ca., U.S. **m12** 98
San Marino, ctry., Eur. **C4** 18
San Martín, Arg. **E4** 72
San Martín, Col. **E5** 80
San Martín, Lago, l., S.A. **G2** 69
San Martín de los Andes, Arg. **F2** 69
San Mateo, Ca., U.S. **D2** 98
San Mateo, co., Ca., U.S. **D2** 98
San Mateo Mountains, mts., N.M., U.S. **B2** 124
San Mateo Mountains, mts., N.M., U.S. **D2** 124
San Matías, Golfo, b., Arg. **F4** 69
Sanmenxia, China **E10** 28
San Miguel, El Sal. **C2** 80
San Miguel, co., Co., U.S. **D2** 99
San Miguel, co., N.M., U.S. **B5** 124
San Miguel, stm., Co., U.S. **C2** 99
San Miguel, Golfo de, b., Pan. **D4** 80
San Miguel de Tucumán, Arg. **D4** 72
San Miguel Island, i., Ca., U.S. **E3** 98
San Miguel Mountains, mts., Co., U.S. **D2** 99
Sanming, China **D4** 30
Sannār, Sudan **H11** 48
San Nicolás, Peru **B2** 72
San Nicolás de los Arroyos, Arg. **E5** 72
San Nicolás de los Garza, Mex. **B4** 78
San Nicolas Island, i., Ca., U.S. **F4** 98
Sânnicolau Mare, Rom. **F6** 20
Sannikova, proliv, strt., Russia **B15** 26
Sanok, Pol. **E7** 20
San Pablo, Phil. **D8** 34
San Pablo Bay, b., Ca., U.S. **g8** 98
San Patricio, co., Tx., U.S. **E4** 136
San Pedro, Arg. **C5** 72
San Pedro, Arg. **E6** 72
San-Pédro, C. Iv. **F3** 50
San Pedro, stm., N.A. **A2** 78
San Pedro, stm., Az., U.S. **E5** 96
San Pedro Bay, b., Ca., U.S. **n12** 98
San Pedro de las Colonias, Mex. **B4** 78
San Pedro de Macorís, Dom. Rep. **B6** 80
San Pedro de Ycuamandiyú, Para. **C6** 72
San Pedro Peaks, mts., N.M., U.S. **A3** 124
San Pedro Sula, Hond. **B2** 80
Sanpete, co., Ut., U.S. **D4** 137
San Pietro, Isola di, i., Italy **E2** 18
Sanpoil, stm., Wa., U.S. **A7** 140
San Quintín, Cabo, c., Mex. **A1** 78
San Rafael, Arg. **E4** 72
San Rafael, Ca., U.S. **D2** 98
San Rafael, N.M., U.S. **B2** 124
San Rafael, Ven. **C5** 80
San Rafael, stm., Ut., U.S. **D5** 137
San Rafael Knob, mtn., Ut., U.S. **E5** 137
San Rafael Mountains, mts., Ca., U.S. **E4** 98
San Ramon, Ca., U.S. **h9** 98
San Ramón de la Nueva Orán, Arg. **C5** 72
San Remo, Italy **C1** 18
San Roque, Punta, c., Mex. **B2** 78
San Saba, Tx., U.S. **D3** 136
San Saba, co., Tx., U.S. **D3** 136
San Salvador, El Sal. **C2** 80
San Salvador, i., Bah. **D10** 76
San Salvador de Jujuy, Arg. **C4** 72
Sansanné-Mango, Togo **D5** 50
San Sebastián see Donostia, Spain **F6** 16
San Severo, Italy **D5** 18
San Simon, stm., Az., U.S. **E6** 96
Santa Ana, Bol. **A4** 72
Santa Ana, El Sal. **C1** 80
Santa Ana, Mex. **A2** 78
Santa Ana, Ca., U.S. **F5** 98
Santa Ana, stm., Ca., U.S. **n13** 98
Santa Ana Indian Reservation, N.M., U.S. **h7** 124
Santa Ana Mountains, mts., Ca., U.S. **n13** 98
Santa Anna, Tx., U.S. **D3** 136
Santa Bárbara, Hond. **B2** 80
Santa Bárbara, Mex. **B3** 78
Santa Barbara, Ca., U.S. **E4** 98
Santa Bárbara, Ven. **D5** 80
Santa Barbara, co., Ca., U.S. **E3** 98
Santa Barbara Channel, strt., Ca., U.S. **E3** 98
Santa Barbara Island, i., Ca., U.S. **F4** 98
Santa Catalina, Gulf of, b., Ca., U.S. **F5** 98
Santa Catalina Island, i., Ca., U.S. **F4** 98
Santa Catalina Mountains, mts., Az., U.S. **E5** 96
Santa Catarina, state, Braz. **D7** 72
Santa Catarina, Ilha de, i., Braz. **D8** 72
Santa Clara, Cuba **A3** 80
Santa Clara, Ca., U.S. **D2** 98
Santa Clara, Ut., U.S. **F2** 137
Santa Clara, co., Ca., U.S. **D3** 98
Santa Clara, stm., Ca., U.S. **E4** 98
Santa Claus, In., U.S. **H4** 107
Santa Cruz, Phil. **D8** 34
Santa Cruz, Ca., U.S. **D2** 98
Santa Cruz, N.M., U.S. **B3** 124
Santa Cruz, co., Az., U.S. **F5** 96
Santa Cruz, co., Ca., U.S. **D2** 98
Santa Cruz, stm., Az., U.S. **E4** 96
Santa Cruz, Isla, i., Ec. **D1** 70
Santa Cruz de la Palma, Spain **A1** 50
Santa Cruz de la Sierra, Bol. **B5** 72
Santa Cruz del Quiché, Guat. **B1** 80
Santa Cruz del Sur, Cuba **A4** 80
Santa Cruz de Tenerife, Spain **A1** 50
Santa Cruz do Sul, Braz. **D7** 72
Santa Cruz Island, i., Ca., U.S. **F4** 98
Santa Cruz Islands, is., Sol. Is. **F10** 58
Santa Elena, Arg. **E6** 72
Santa Fe, Arg. **E5** 72
Santa Fe, N.M., U.S. **B4** 124
Santa Fe, Tx., U.S. **r14** 136
Santa Fe, co., N.M., U.S. **B3** 124
Santa Fe, stm., N.M., U.S. **h8** 124
Santa Fe Baldy, mtn., N.M., U.S. **B4** 124
Santa Fé do Sul, Braz. **F1** 74
Santa Filomena, Braz. **E10** 70
Santa Helena, Braz. **B2** 74
Santa Helena de Goiás, Braz. **E1** 74
Santai, China **E9** 28
Santa Inés, Isla, i., Chile **H2** 69
Santa Isabel, Arg. **F4** 72
Santa Isabel, i., Sol. Is. **B6** 62
Santa Isabel see Malabo, Eq. Gui. **C1** 54
Santa Lucia Range, mts., Ca., U.S. **E3** 98
Santa Magdalena, Isla, i., Mex. **B2** 78
Santa Margarita, Ca., U.S. **E3** 98
Santa Margarita, Isla, i., Mex. **C2** 78
Santa Maria, Braz. **D7** 72
Santa Maria, Ca., U.S. **E3** 98
Santa Maria, i., Vanuatu **j9** 62a
Santa Maria, stm., Az., U.S. **C2** 96
Santa Maria, Cabo de, c., Ang. **A1** 56
Santa María, Isla, i., Ec. **D1** 70
Santa Maria Mountains, mts., Az., U.S. **C3** 96
Santa Marta, Col. **A5** 70
Santa Monica, Ca., U.S. **m12** 98
Santana, Braz. **D3** 74
Santana do Livramento, Braz. **E6** 72
Santander, Phil. **E8** 34
Santander, Spain **F5** 16
Santanilla, Islas, is., Hond. **B3** 80
Sant'Antioco, Italy **E2** 18
Sant'Antioco, Isola di, i., Italy **E2** 18
Sant Antoni de Portmany, Spain **H7** 16
Santa Paula, Ca., U.S. **E4** 98
Santaquin, Ut., U.S. **D4** 137
Santarém, Braz. **D9** 70
Santarém, Port. **H2** 16
Santa Rita, Hond. **B2** 80
Santa Rita, Ven. **C5** 80
Santa Rosa, Arg. **F5** 72
Santa Rosa, Braz. **D7** 72
Santa Rosa, Ec. **D4** 70
Santa Rosa, Ca., U.S. **C2** 98
Santa Rosa, N.M., U.S. **C5** 124
Santa Rosa, Ven. **D6** 80
Santa Rosa, co., Fl., U.S. **u14** 102
Santa Rosa de Copán, Hond. **C2** 80
Santa Rosa Island, i., Ca., U.S. **F3** 98
Santa Rosa Island, i., Fl., U.S. **u14** 102
Santa Rosalía, Mex. **B2** 78
Santa Rosa Range, mts., Nv., U.S. **B4** 121
Šantarskie ostrova, is., Russia **D15** 26
Santa Sylvina, Arg. **D5** 72
Santa Vitória do Palmar, Braz. **E7** 72
Santa Ynez, Ca., U.S. **E3** 98
Santee, Ca., U.S. **o16** 98
Santee, stm., S.C., U.S. **E8** 133
Santee Dam, S.C., U.S. **E7** 133
Santee Indian Reservation, Ne., U.S. **B8** 120
Sant Feliu de Guíxols, Spain **G8** 16
Santiago, Braz. **D7** 72
Santiago, Chile **D2** 69
Santiago, Mex. **C3** 78
Santiago, Pan. **D3** 80
Santiago, i., C.V. **h10** 50a
Santiago, Isla, i., Ec. **D1** 70
Santiago de Compostela, Spain **F2** 16
Santiago de Cuba, Cuba **B4** 80
Santiago del Estero, Arg. **D5** 72
Santiago de los Caballeros, Dom. Rep. **B5** 80
Santiago Ixcuintla, Mex. **C3** 78
Santiago Jamiltepec, Mex. **D5** 78
Santiago Papasquiaro, Mex. **B3** 78
Santiago Peak, mtn., Ca., U.S. **n13** 98
Santiago Reservoir, res., Ca., U.S. **n13** 98
Santiam Pass, Or., U.S. **C4** 130
Sant Jordi, Golf de, b., Spain **G7** 16
Santo Amaro, Braz. **D4** 74
Santo André, Braz. **F2** 74
Santo Ângelo, Braz. **D7** 72
Santo Antão, i., C.V. **g10** 50a
Santo Antônio, S. Tom./P. **C1** 54
Santo Antônio de Jesus, Braz. **D4** 74
Santo Antônio do Içá, Braz. **D6** 70
Santo Domingo, Dom. Rep. **B6** 80
Santo Domingo see Hispaniola, i., N.A. **A5** 80
Santo Domingo Indian Reservation, N.M., U.S. **h8** 124
Santo Domingo Pueblo, N.M., U.S. **B3** 124
Santorini see Thíra, i., Grc. **F10** 18
Santos, Braz. **F2** 74
Santos Dumont, Braz. **F3** 74
Santo Tomé de Guayana see Ciudad Guayana, Ven. **B7** 70
San Valentín, Monte, mtn., Chile **G2** 69
San Vicente, El Sal. **C2** 80
San Vicente de Cañete, Peru **F4** 70
San Vicente del Caguán, Col. **C5** 70
San Vicente Reservoir, res., Ca., U.S. **o16** 98
San Xavier Indian Reservation, Az., U.S. **E4** 96
Sanya, China **H9** 28
Sanyuan, China **E9** 28
Sanza Pombo, Ang. **E3** 54
São Bento, Braz. **B3** 74
São Borja, Braz. **D6** 72
São Carlos, Braz. **F2** 74
São Domingos, Braz. **A8** 72
São Domingos, Gui.-B. **D1** 50
São Francisco, Braz. **E3** 74
São Francisco, stm., Braz. **C4** 74
São Francisco do Sul, Braz. **D8** 72
São Gabriel, Braz. **E7** 72
Sao Hill, Tan. **E7** 54
São João da Barra, Braz. **F3** 74
São João da Boa Vista, Braz. **F2** 74
São João da Madeira, Port. **G2** 16
São João Del Rei, Braz. **F3** 74
São João do Araguaia, Braz. **E10** 70
São Jorge, i., Port. **F7** 46
São José, Braz. **D8** 72
São José do Rio Preto, Braz. **F2** 74
São José dos Campos, Braz. **F2** 74
São Leopoldo, Braz. **D7** 72
São Lourenço, Pantanal de, sw., Braz. **G8** 70
São Lourenço do Sul, Braz. **E7** 72
São Luís, Braz. **B3** 74
São Luís Gonzaga, Braz. **D7** 72
São Manuel, stm., Braz. **E8** 70
São Mateus, Braz. **E4** 74
São Miguel, i., Port. **F7** 46
São Miguel do Araguaia, Braz. **D1** 74
Saona, Isla, i., Dom. Rep. **B6** 80
Saône, stm., Fr. **D9** 16
São Nicolau, i., C.V. **g10** 50a
São Paulo, Braz. **F2** 74
São Paulo, state, Braz. **C7** 72
São Paulo de Olivença, Braz. **D6** 70
São Raimundo Nonato, Braz. **C3** 74
São Roque, Cabo de, c., Braz. **C4** 74
São Sebastião, Braz. **F2** 74
São Sebastião, Ilha de, i., Braz. **F2** 74
São Sebastião do Paraíso, Braz. **F2** 74
São Simão, Represa de, res., Braz. **B7** 72
São Tomé, S. Tom./P. **C1** 54
São Tomé, i., S. Tom./P. **C1** 54
São Tomé, Cabo de, c., Braz. **F3** 74
Sao Tome and Principe, ctry., Afr. **C1** 54
São Vicente, Braz. **F2** 74
São Vicente, i., C.V. **g9** 50a
São Vicente, Cabo de, c., Port. **I2** 16
Sapé, Braz. **C4** 74
Sapele, Nig. **E6** 50
Sapelo Island, i., Ga., U.S. **E5** 103
Sapitwa, mtn., Mwi. **B6** 56
Sappa Creek, stm., U.S. **E5** 120
Sapphire Mountains, mts., Mt., U.S. **D3** 119
Sappington, Mo., U.S. **f13** 118
Sapporo, Japan **C16** 28
Sapulpa, Ok., U.S. **B5** 129
Sapwe, D.R.C. **F5** 54
Saqqez, Iran **C5** 42
Sarāb, Iran **C5** 42
Saraburi, Thai. **D4** 34
Saragossa see Zaragoza, Spain **G6** 16
Sarajevo, Bos. **C7** 18
Sarakhs, Iran **C8** 42
Saraktaš, Russia **D10** 22
Saraland, Al., U.S. **E1** 94
Saranac, Mi., U.S. **F5** 115
Saranac, stm., N.Y., U.S. **F11** 125
Saranac Lake, N.Y., U.S. **f10** 125
Saranac Lakes, l., N.Y., U.S. **f10** 125
Sarandë, Alb. **E8** 18
Sārangarh, India **E4** 40
Saranpaul', Russia **B11** 22
Saransk, Russia **D6** 26
Sarapul, Russia **D7** 26
Sarasota, Fl., U.S. **E4** 102
Sarasota, co., Fl., U.S. **E4** 102
Sarasota Bay, b., Fl., U.S. **E4** 102
Saratoga, Ca., U.S. **k8** 98
Saratoga, Tx., U.S. **D5** 136
Saratoga, Wy., U.S. **E6** 143
Saratoga, co., N.Y., U.S. **B7** 125
Saratoga Lake, l., N.Y., U.S. **C7** 125
Saratoga National Historical Park, N.Y., U.S. **B7** 125
Saratoga Springs, N.Y., U.S. **B7** 125
Saratov, Russia **D6** 26
Saratov Reservoir see Saratovskoe vodohranilišče, res., Russia **D8** 22
Saratovskoe vodohranilišče, res., Russia **D8** 22
Saravan, Laos **C5** 34
Sarawak, hist. reg., Malay. **C4** 36
Saray, Tur. **B2** 44
Saraya, Gui. **D2** 50
Sarayköy, Tur. **D3** 44
Sarcoxie, Mo., U.S. **D3** 118
Sardārshahr, India **D2** 40
Sar Dasht, Iran **D11** 44
Sardegna (Sardinia), i., Italy **D2** 18
Sardinia see Sardegna, i., Italy **D2** 18
Sardis, Ga., U.S. **D5** 103
Sardis, Ms., U.S. **A4** 117
Sardis Lake, res., Ms., U.S. **A4** 117
Sarek, mtn., Swe. **C7** 10
Sar-e Pol, Afg. **C9** 42
Sarepta, La., U.S. **B2** 111
Sargent, Ga., U.S. **C2** 103
Sargent, Ne., U.S. **C6** 120
Sargent, co., N.D., U.S. **C8** 127
Sargodha, Pak. **D10** 42
Sarh, Chad **B3** 54
Sārī, Iran **C6** 42
Sarigan, i., N. Mar. Is. **C12** 32
Sarıkamış, Tur. **B10** 44
Sarıkaya, Tur. **C6** 44
Sarikei, Malay. **C4** 36
Sarīr, Libya **F8** 14
Sariwŏn, N. Kor. **D13** 28
Sarıyar Barajı, res., Tur. **C4** 44
Šarja, Russia **D6** 26
Şarkikaraağaç, Tur. **C4** 44
Şarkışla, Tur. **C7** 44
Şarköy, Tur. **B2** 44
Sarmi, Indon. **G10** 32
Särna, Swe. **F5** 10
Sarnia, On., Can. **E2** 89
Sarny, Ukr. **D9** 20
Saronic Gulf see Saronikós Kólpos, b., Grc. **F9** 18
Saronikós Kólpos, b., Grc. **F9** 18
Saros Körfezi, b., Tur. **B2** 44
Sarpy, co., Ne., U.S. **C9** 120
Sarreguemines, Fr. **C10** 16
Sartell, Mn., U.S. **E4** 116
Sartène, Fr. **D2** 18
Şärur, Azer. **C11** 44
Sarus see Seyhan, stm., Tur. **D6** 44
Saryg-Sep, Russia **D11** 26
Sarykamyšskoe ozero, l., Asia **B7** 42
Saryozek, Kaz. **E9** 26
Sarysu, stm., Kaz. **E8** 26
Sary-Taš, Kyrg. **B2** 40
Sasabeneh, Eth. **B8** 54
Sāsarām, India **E4** 40
Sasebo, Japan **D1** 31
Saskatchewan, prov., Can. **E3** 91
Saskatchewan, stm., Can. **H19** 82
Saskylah, Russia **B13** 26
Sasovo, Russia **B16** 20
Sassafras, stm., Md., U.S. **B5** 113
Sassafras Mountain, mtn., U.S. **A2** 133
Sassandra, C. Iv. **E3** 50
Sassandra, stm., C. Iv. **E3** 50
Sassari, Italy **D2** 18
Sassnitz, Ger. **C13** 12
Satah Mountain, mtn., B.C., Can. **C5** 85
Sata-misaki, c., Japan **D2** 31
Satanta, Ks., U.S. **E3** 109
Sātāra, India **F2** 40
Säter, Swe. **F6** 10
Satilla, stm., Ga., U.S. **E5** 103
Satka, Russia **D10** 22
Satluj see Sutlej, stm., Asia **D2** 40
Satna, India **E4** 40
Sátoraljaújhely, Hung. **E6** 20
Sātpura Range, mts., India **E3** 40
Satsuma, Al., U.S. **E1** 94
Satu Mare, Rom. **F7** 20
Satun, Thai. **E3** 34
Satus Creek, stm., Wa., U.S. **C5** 140
Sauceda Mountains, mts., Az., U.S. **E3** 96
Sauðárkrókur, Ice. **l19** 10a
Saudi Arabia, ctry., Asia **F4** 38
Saufley Field Naval Air Station, mil., Fl., U.S. **u14** 102
Saugatuck, Mi., U.S. **F4** 115
Saugatuck, stm., Ct., U.S. **D2** 100
Saugatucket, stm., R.I., U.S. **F4** 132
Saugatuck Reservoir, res., Ct., U.S. **D2** 100
Saugerties, N.Y., U.S. **C7** 125
Saugus, Ma., U.S. **B5** 114
Saugus, stm., Ma., U.S. **g11** 114
Sauk, co., Wi., U.S. **E4** 142
Sauk, stm., Mn., U.S. **E4** 116
Sauk, stm., Wa., U.S. **A4** 140
Sauk Centre, Mn., U.S. **E4** 116
Sauk City, Wi., U.S. **E4** 142
Sauk Rapids, Mn., U.S. **E4** 116
Saukville, Wi., U.S. **E6** 142
Saül, Fr. Gu. **C9** 70
Saulnierville, N.S., Can. **E3** 87
Sault-au-Mouton, P.Q., Can. **A8** 90
Sault Sainte Marie, On., Can. **p18** 89
Sault Sainte Marie, Mi., U.S. **B6** 115
Saumarez Reef, rf., Austl. **E5** 62
Saumlaki, Indon. **E8** 36
Saumur, Fr. **D6** 16
Saunders, co., Ne., U.S. **C9** 120
Saunderstown, R.I., U.S. **E4** 132
Saurimo, Ang. **E4** 54
Sausalito, Ca., U.S. **D2** 98
Sava, stm., Eur. **G5** 20
Savage, Md., U.S. **B4** 113
Savage, stm., Md., U.S. **k12** 113
Savage River Reservoir, res., Md., U.S. **k12** 113
Savai'i, i., Samoa **F12** 58
Savalou, Benin **E5** 50
Savanna, Il., U.S. **A3** 106
Savanna, Ok., U.S. **C6** 129
Savannah, Ga., U.S. **D5** 103
Savannah, Mo., U.S. **B3** 118

Name / Map Ref. / Page

Savannah, Tn., U.S. B3 135
Savannah, stm., U.S. E11 92
Savannah, stm., U.S. F5 133
Savannah River Plant, sci., S.C., U.S. E4 133
Savannakhét, Laos C4 34
Savanna Lake, l., Md., U.S. D6 113
Savanna-la-Mar, Jam. B4 80
Savaştepe, Tur. C2 44
Savè, Benin E5 50
Save (Sabi), stm., Afr. C5 56
Sāveh, Iran C6 42
Savelugu, Ghana E4 50
Saverne, Fr. C10 16
Saville Dam, Ct., U.S. B4 100
Savitaipale, Fin. F12 10
Savona, Italy B2 18
Savonlinna, Fin. F13 10
Savoonga, Ak., U.S. C5 95
Savoy, Il., U.S. C5 106
Savu Sea see Sawu, Laut, Indon. E6 36
Sawāi Mādhopur, India D3 40
Sawākin, Sudan G12 48
Sawankhalok, Thai. C3 34
Sawatch Range, mts., Co., U.S. B4 99
Sawdā', Jabal as-, hills, Libya F7 14
Sawdā', Qurnat as-, mtn., Leb. E7 44
Sawnee Mountain, mtn., Ga., U.S. B2 103
Sawtooth Mountains, mts., Id., U.S. F4 105
Sawtooth National Recreation Area, Id., U.S. E3 105
Sawu, Laut (Savu Sea), Indon. E6 36
Sawu, Pulau, i., Indon. F6 36
Sawyer, co., Wi., U.S. C2 142
Sawyerville, P.Q., Can. D6 90
Saxonburg, Pa., U.S. E2 131
Saxtons, stm., Vt., U.S. E3 138
Saxtons River, Vt., U.S. E3 138
Sayan Mountains, mts., Asia D11 26
Saybrook, Il., U.S. C5 106
Saybrook Manor, Ct., U.S. D6 100
Şaydā, Leb. F6 44
Saydel, Ia., U.S. e8 108
Sayḩūt, Yemen G6 38
Saylac, Som. H4 38
Saylesville, R.I., U.S. B4 132
Saylorsburg, Pa., U.S. E11 131
Saylorville, Ia., U.S. e8 108
Saylorville Lake, res., Ia., U.S. C4 108
Saynshand, Mong. C10 28
Sayre, Al., U.S. B3 94
Sayre, Ok., U.S. B2 129
Sayre, Pa., U.S. C8 131
Sayreville, N.J., U.S. C4 123
Sayula, Mex. D4 78
Sayville, N.Y., U.S. n15 125
Saywūn, Yemen G5 38
Sba, Alg. F3 14
Scalp Level, Pa., U.S. F4 131
Scanlon, Mn., U.S. D6 116
Scapegoat Mountain, mtn., Mt., U.S. C3 119
Scappoose, Or., U.S. B4 130
Scarborough, On., Can. m15 89
Scarborough, Trin. C7 80
Scarborough, Eng., U.K. C6 12
Scarborough, Me., U.S. E2 112
Scarbro, W.V., U.S. n13 141
Scarsdale, N.Y., U.S. h13 125
Ščekino, Russia C14 20
Ščerbakovo, Russia C18 26
Schaefferstown, Pa., U.S. F9 131
Schaller, Ia., U.S. B2 108
Schaumburg, Il., U.S. h8 106
Schell Creek Range, mts., Nv., U.S. D7 121
Schenectady, N.Y., U.S. C7 125
Schenectady, co., N.Y., U.S. C6 125
Schererville, In., U.S. B3 107
Schertz, Tx., U.S. h7 136
Schiller Park, Il., U.S. k9 106
Schio, Italy B3 18
Schleicher, co., Tx., U.S. D2 136
Schleswig, Ger. C11 12
Schleswig, Ia., U.S. B2 108
Schley, co., Ga., U.S. D2 103
Schofield, Wi., U.S. D4 142
Schofield Barracks, mil., Hi., U.S. g9 104
Schoharie, co., N.Y., U.S. C6 125
Schoharie Creek, stm., N.Y., U.S. C6 125
Schoodic Lake, l., Me., U.S. C4 112
Schoolcraft, Mi., U.S. F5 115
Schoolcraft, co., Mi., U.S. B4 115
Schroon Lake, l., N.Y., U.S. B7 125
Schulenburg, Tx., U.S. E4 136
Schulter, Ok., U.S. B6 129
Schurz, Nv., U.S. E3 121
Schuyler, Ne., U.S. C8 120
Schuyler, co., Il., U.S. C3 106
Schuyler, co., Mo., U.S. A5 118
Schuyler, co., N.Y., U.S. C4 125
Schuylkill, co., Pa., U.S. E9 131
Schuylkill, stm., Pa., U.S. F10 131
Schuylkill Haven, Pa., U.S. E9 131
Schwaben, hist. reg., Ger. F11 12
Schwarzwald (Black Forest), mts., Ger. F11 12
Schwedt, Ger. D14 12
Schwerin, Ger. D12 12
Schwyz, Switz. A2 18
Sciacca, Italy F4 18
Science Hill, Ky., U.S. C5 110
Ščigry, Russia D14 20
Scilly, Isles of, is., Eng., U.K. F3 12
Scio, Or., U.S. C4 130
Scioto, co., Oh., U.S. D3 128
Scioto, stm., Oh., U.S. B2 128
Scituate, Ma., U.S. B6 114
Scituate Reservoir, res., R.I., U.S. C3 132
Scobey, Mt., U.S. B11 119
Scofield Reservoir, res., Ut., U.S. D4 137
Scotch Plains, N.J., U.S. B4 123
Scotia, Ca., U.S. B1 98
Scotia, N.Y., U.S. C7 125
Scotia Ridge N8 66
Scotia Sea B36 67
Scotland, On., Can. D4 89
Scotland, S.D., U.S. D8 134
Scotland, prov., U.K. B5 12
Scotland, co., Mo., U.S. A5 118
Scotland, co., N.C., U.S. C3 126
Scotland Neck, N.C., U.S. A5 126
Scotlandville, La., U.S. D4 111
Scotrun, Pa., U.S. D11 131
Scotstown, P.Q., Can. D6 90
Scott, La., U.S. D3 111
Scott, co., Ar., U.S. C1 97
Scott, co., Ia., U.S. C7 108
Scott, co., Il., U.S. D3 106
Scott, co., In., U.S. G6 107
Scott, co., Ks., U.S. D3 109
Scott, co., Ky., U.S. B5 110
Scott, co., Mn., U.S. F5 116
Scott, co., Mo., U.S. D8 118
Scott, co., Ms., U.S. C4 117
Scott, co., Tn., U.S. C9 135
Scott, co., Va., U.S. f9 139
Scott, Cape, c., B.C., Can. D3 85
Scott, Mount, mtn., Or., U.S. E4 130
Scott Air Force Base, mil., Il., U.S. E4 106
Scott City, Ks., U.S. D3 109
Scott City, Mo., U.S. D8 118
Scottdale, Ga., U.S. h8 103
Scottdale, Pa., U.S. F2 131
Scott Mountain, mtn., Id., U.S. E3 105
Scott Peak, mtn., Id., U.S. E6 105
Scott Reef, rf., Austl. C3 60
Scott Reservoir, res., N.C., U.S. A1 126
Scottsbluff, Ne., U.S. C2 120
Scotts Bluff, co., Ne., U.S. C2 120
Scotts Bluff National Monument, Ne., U.S. C2 120
Scottsboro, Al., U.S. A3 94
Scottsburg, In., U.S. G6 107
Scottsdale, Az., U.S. D4 96
Scottsville, Ky., U.S. D3 110
Scottsville, N.Y., U.S. B3 125
Scottville, Mi., U.S. E4 115
Scraggly Lake, l., Me., U.S. B4 112
Scranton, Ks., U.S. D8 109
Scranton, Pa., U.S. D10 131
Scranton, S.C., U.S. D8 133
Screven, Ga., U.S. E4 103
Screven, co., Ga., U.S. D5 103
Scribner, Ne., U.S. C9 120
Ščučinsk, Kaz. D8 26
Scugog, Lake, l., On., Can. C6 89
Scurry, co., Tx., U.S. C2 136
Scutari see Shkodër, Alb. C7 18
Scutari, Lake, l., Eur. C7 18
Scyros see Skíros, i., Grc. E10 18
Seaboard, N.C., U.S. A5 126
Seabreeze, De., U.S. F5 101
Seabrook, N.H., U.S. E5 122
Seabrook, Tx., U.S. r14 136
Seabrook Island, i., S.C., U.S. F7 133
Seadrift, Tx., U.S. E4 136
Seaford, De., U.S. F3 101
Seaford, Va., U.S. h15 139
Seaforth, On., Can. D3 89
Seagoville, Tx., U.S. n10 136
Seagraves, Tx., U.S. C1 136
Sea Islands, is., U.S. E11 92
Sea Isle City, N.J., U.S. E3 123
Seal Cove, Nf., Can. D3 88
Seal Point, c., P.E., Can. C5 87
Seal Rock, Or., U.S. C2 130
Sealy, Tx., U.S. E4 136
Seaman, Oh., U.S. D2 128
Seaman Range, mts., Nv., U.S. F6 121
Searchlight, Nv., U.S. H7 121
Searcy, Ar., U.S. B4 97
Searcy, co., Ar., U.S. B3 97
Searles Lake, l., Ca., U.S. E5 98
Searsport, Me., U.S. D4 112
Seaside, Or., U.S. B3 130
Seat Pleasant, Md., U.S. C4 113
Seattle, Wa., U.S. B3 140
Seattle-Tacoma International Airport, Wa., U.S. f11 140
Seaview, Wa., U.S. C1 140
Sebago Lake, Me., U.S. E2 112
Šebalino, Russia D10 26
Sebangka, Pulau, i., Indon. C2 36
Sebastian, Fl., U.S. E6 102
Sebastian, co., Ar., U.S. B1 97
Sebastian, Cape, c., Or., U.S. E2 130
Sebastian Inlet, b., Fl., U.S. E6 102
Sebastián Vizcaíno, Bahía, b., Mex. B2 78
Sebasticook Lake, l., Me., U.S. D3 112
Sebec Lake, l., Me., U.S. C3 112
Sebeka, Mn., U.S. D3 116
Šebekino, Russia D14 20
Sebeş, Rom. G7 20
Sebewaing, Mi., U.S. E7 115
Şebinkarahisar, Tur. B8 44
Seboeis, stm., Me., U.S. B4 112
Seboeis Lake, l., Me., U.S. C4 112
Seboomook Lake, l., Me., U.S. C3 112
Sebree, Ky., U.S. C2 110
Sebring, Fl., U.S. E5 102
Sebring, Oh., U.S. B4 128
Secaucus, N.J., U.S. h8 123
Sechelt, B.C., Can. E6 85
Sechura, Bahía de, b., Peru E3 70
Second Lake, l., N.H., U.S. f7 122
Second Mesa, Az., U.S. B5 96
Secret Lake, l., R.I., U.S. E4 132
Section, Al., U.S. A4 94
Security, Co., U.S. C6 99
Seda, China E8 28
Sedalia, Mo., U.S. C4 118
Sedan, Fr. C9 16
Sedan, Ks., U.S. E7 109
Sedgewick, Ab., Can. C5 84
Sedgewick, Mount, mtn., N.M., U.S. B1 124
Sedgwick, Ks., U.S. E6 109
Sedgwick, co., Co., U.S. A8 99
Sedgwick, co., Ks., U.S. E6 109
Sédhiou, Sen. D1 50
Sedley, Va., U.S. D6 139
Sedona, Az., U.S. C4 96
Sedro Woolley, Wa., U.S. A3 140
Seekonk, Ma., U.S. C5 114
Seekonk, stm., R.I., U.S. C4 132
Seeley, Ca., U.S. F6 98
Seeley Lake, Mt., U.S. C3 119
Seelyville, In., U.S. F3 107
Şefaatli, Tur. C6 44
Sefadu, S.L. E2 50
Seferihisar, Tur. C2 44
Segamat, Malay. C2 36
Segesta, hist., Italy F4 18
Segeža, Russia C5 26
Ségou, Mali D3 50
Segovia, Spain G4 16
Seguam Island, i., Ak., U.S. E5 95
Seguam Pass, strt., Ak., U.S. E5 95
Séguédine, Niger B7 50
Séguéla, C. Iv. E3 50
Seguin, Tx., U.S. E4 136
Segura, stm., Spain I6 16
Seiling, Ok., U.S. A3 129
Seinäjoki, Fin. E10 10
Seine, stm., Fr. C7 16
Seine, Baie de la, b., Fr. C6 16
Sejm, stm., Eur. D12 20
Sejmčan, Russia C17 26
Şeki, Azer. B12 44
Sekiu, Wa., U.S. A1 140
Sekondi-Takoradi, Ghana F4 50
Selah, Wa., U.S. C5 140
Selaru, Pulau, i., Indon. E8 36
Selatan, Tanjung, c., Indon. D4 36
Selawik, Ak., U.S. B7 95
Selawik Lake, l., Ak., U.S. B7 95
Selayar, Pulau, i., Indon. E6 36
Selby, S.D., U.S. B5 134
Selbyville, De., U.S. G5 101
Selçuk, Tur. D2 44
Seldovia, Ak., U.S. D9 95
Selebi-Phikwe, Bots. C4 56
Selenge, D.R.C. D3 54
Selenge, stm., Asia E12 26
Sélibabi, Maur. C2 50
Seligman, Az., U.S. B3 96
Šelihova, zaliv, b., Russia C17 26
Selinsgrove, Pa., U.S. E8 131
Seljord, Nor. G3 10
Selkirk, Mb., Can. D3 86
Sellersburg, In., U.S. H6 107
Sellersville, Pa., U.S. F11 131
Sells, Az., U.S. F4 96
Selma, Al., U.S. C2 94
Selma, Ca., U.S. D4 98
Selma, In., U.S. D7 107
Selma, N.C., U.S. B4 126
Selmer, Tn., U.S. B3 135
Selvagens, Ilhas, is., Port. D1 48
Selvas, for., Braz. E6 70
Selway, stm., Id., U.S. C3 105
Selwyn Lake, l., Can. G15 82
Selwyn Mountains, mts., Can. F13 82
Selwyn Range, mts., Austl. E3 62
Semara, W. Sah. A2 50
Semarang, Indon. E4 36
Semenanjung Malaysia, hist. reg., Malay. C2 36
Semenivka, Ukr. C12 20
Semenov, Russia C7 22
Semey see Semipalatinsk, Kaz. D10 26
Semiluki, Russia D15 20
Seminoe Mountains, mts., Wy., U.S. D6 143
Seminoe Reservoir, res., Wy., U.S. D6 143
Seminole, Ok., U.S. B5 129
Seminole, Tx., U.S. C1 136
Seminole, co., Fl., U.S. D5 102
Seminole, co., Ga., U.S. F2 103
Seminole, co., Ok., U.S. B5 129
Seminole, Lake, res., U.S. F2 103
Semipalatinsk, Kaz. D10 26
Semisopochnoi Island, i., Ak., U.S. E3 95
Semitau, Indon. C4 36
Semmes, Al., U.S. E1 94
Semnān, Iran C6 42
Senachwine Lake, l., Il., U.S. B4 106
Senador Pompeu, Braz. C4 74
Senaki, Geor. A10 44
Sena Madureira, Braz. E6 70
Senanga, Zam. B3 56
Senath, Mo., U.S. E7 118
Senatobia, Ms., U.S. A4 117
Sendai, Japan D16 28
Sendelingsdrif, Nmb. D2 56
Seneca, Il., U.S. B5 106
Seneca, Ks., U.S. C7 109
Seneca, Mo., U.S. E3 118
Seneca, Pa., U.S. D2 131
Seneca, S.C., U.S. B2 133
Seneca, co., N.Y., U.S. C4 125
Seneca, co., Oh., U.S. A2 128
Seneca Falls, N.Y., U.S. C4 125
Seneca Lake, l., N.Y., U.S. C4 125
Senecaville Lake, res., Oh., U.S. C4 128
Sénégal, stm., Afr. C2 50
Senegal, ctry., Afr. D1 50
Senekal, S. Afr. D4 56
Senftenberg, Ger. E13 12
Senhor do Bonfim, Braz. D3 74
Senica, Slvk. E4 20
Senigallia, Italy C4 18
Senja, i., Nor. B7 10
Šenkursk, Russia B7 22
Senneterre, P.Q., Can. k11 90
Senoia, Ga., U.S. C2 103
Senqu see Orange, stm., Afr. D2 56
Sens, Fr. C8 16
Senta, Yugo. B8 18
Sentinel, Ok., U.S. B2 129
Seoni, India E3 40
Seoul see Sŏul, S. Kor. D13 28
Sepanjang, Pulau, i., Indon. E5 36
Sepik, stm., Pap. N. Gui. G11 32
Sept-Îles (Seven Islands), P.Q., Can. h13 90
Sepulga, stm., Al., U.S. D3 94
Sequatchie, co., Tn., U.S. D8 135
Sequatchie, stm., Tn., U.S. D8 135
Sequim, Wa., U.S. A2 140
Sequoia National Park, Ca., U.S. D4 98
Sequoyah, co., Ok., U.S. B7 129
Šerabad, Uzb. C9 42
Serafimovič, Russia E7 22
Seram (Ceram), i., Indon. D7 36
Seram, Laut (Ceram Sea), Indon. D7 36
Serang, Indon. E3 36
Serasan, Pulau, i., Indon. C3 36
Serasan, Selat, strt., Indon. C3 36
Serbia see Srbija, prov., Yugo. B8 18
Serdobsk, Russia D7 22
Sered', Slvk. E4 20
Şereflikoçhisar, Tur. C5 44
Seremban, Malay. C2 36
Serengeti Plain, pl., Tan. D6 54
Serenje, Zam. A5 56
Sergač, Russia C8 22
Sergeant Bluff, Ia., U.S. B1 108
Sergeevka, Russia B2 31
Sergeja Kirova, ostrova, is., Russia B10 26
Sergiev Posad, Russia D5 26
Serginskij, Russia C8 26
Sergipe, state, Braz. D4 74
Seria, Bru. C4 36
Serian, Malay. C4 36
Sérifos, i., Grc. F10 18
Şerik, Tur. D4 44
Šerlovaja Gora, Russia A11 28
Serov, Russia D8 26
Serowe, Bots. C4 56
Serpa, Port. I3 16
Serpiente, Boca de la, strt. D7 80
Serpuhov, Russia B14 20
Serra do Navio, Braz. C9 70
Sérrai, Grc. D9 18
Serra Talhada, Braz. C4 74
Serrezuela, Arg. E4 72
Serrinha, Braz. D4 74
Sertânia, Braz. C4 74
Sêrxü, China E7 28
Sese Islands, is., Ug. D6 54
Sesfontein, Nmb. B1 56
Sesheke, Zam. B3 56
Sesser, Il., U.S. E4 106
Sestroreck, Russia F13 10
Sète, Fr. F8 16
Sete Lagoas, Braz. E3 74
Seth, W.V., U.S. C3 141
Sétif, Alg. C6 48
Seto-naikai, Japan E14 28
Setté Cama, Gabon D1 54
Setúbal, Port. H2 16
Setúbal, Baía de, b., Port. H2 16
Seul, Lac, l., On., Can. o16 89
Seul Choix Point, c., Mi., U.S. C5 115
Sevan, Arm. B11 44
Sevana Lich, l., Arm. B11 44
Sevastopol', Ukr. G12 20
Seven Devils Lake, res., Ar., U.S. D4 97
Seven Devils Mountains, mts., Id., U.S. D2 105
Seven Hills, Oh., U.S. h9 128
Seven Mile Beach, N.J., U.S. E3 123
Severn, Md., U.S. B4 113
Severn, stm., On., Can. n17 89
Severn, stm., U.K. D5 12
Severnaja Dvina, stm., Russia C6 26
Severnaja Osetija, state, Russia E6 26
Severnaja Sos'va, stm., Russia B11 22
Severnaja Zemlja, is., Russia B12 26
Severna Park, Md., U.S. B4 113
Severn River, b., Md., U.S. B4 113
Severnye uvaly, hills, Russia D6 26
Severodvinsk, Russia C5 26
Severo-Enisejskij, Russia C11 26
Severomorsk, Russia B15 10
Severo-Sibirskaja nizmennost', pl., Russia B11 26
Severoural'sk, Russia B11 22
Sevier, co., Ar., U.S. D1 97
Sevier, co., Tn., U.S. D10 135
Sevier, co., Ut., U.S. E4 137
Sevier, stm., Ut., U.S. D3 137
Sevier Bridge Reservoir, res., Ut., U.S. D4 137
Sevier Lake, l., Ut., U.S. E2 137
Sevierville, Tn., U.S. D10 135
Sevilla, Col. E4 80
Sevilla (Seville), Spain I4 16
Seville see Sevilla, Spain I4 16
Seville, Oh., U.S. A4 128
Sewanee, Tn., U.S. D8 135
Seward, Ak., U.S. C10 95
Seward, Ne., U.S. D8 120
Seward, co., Ks., U.S. E3 109
Seward, co., Ne., U.S. D8 120
Seward Peninsula, pen., Ak., U.S. B7 95
Sewickley, Pa., U.S. E1 131
Sexsmith, Ab., Can. B1 84
Seychelles, ctry., Afr. i12 57b
Seychelles, is., Afr. h13 57b
Seydişehir, Tur. D4 44
Seyðisfjörður, Ice. l21 10a
Seyhan, stm., Tur. D6 44
Seyhan Barajı, res., Tur. D6 44
Seymour, Austl. H4 62
Seymour, Ct., U.S. D3 100
Seymour, Ia., U.S. D4 108
Seymour, In., U.S. G6 107
Seymour, Mo., U.S. D5 118
Seymour, Tx., U.S. C3 136
Seymour, Wi., U.S. D5 142
Seymour Inlet, b., B.C., Can. D4 85
Seymour Johnson Air Force Base, mil., N.C., U.S. B5 126
Seymour Lake, l., Vt., U.S. B4 138
Seymourville, La., U.S. h9 111
Sfântu Gheorghe, Rom. G8 20
Sfax, Tun. D7 48
's-Gravenhage (The Hague), Neth. D8 12
Shaanxi, state, China D9 28
Shabbona, Il., U.S. B5 106
Shabeelle (Shebelē Wenz, Wabē), stm., Afr. C8 54
Shabunda, D.R.C. D5 54
Shache, China D3 28
Shackelford, co., Tx., U.S. C3 136
Shackleton Ice Shelf, Ant. C14 67
Shackleton Range, mts., Ant. E2 67
Shadehill Dam, S.D., U.S. B3 134
Shadehill Reservoir, res., S.D., U.S. B3 134
Shadow Mountain National Recreation Area, Co., U.S. A4 99
Shady Cove, Or., U.S. E4 130
Shady Side, Md., U.S. C4 113
Shadyside, Oh., U.S. C5 128
Shady Spring, W.V., U.S. D3 141
Shafer, Lake, l., In., U.S. C4 107
Shafer Butte, mtn., Id., U.S. F2 105
Shafter, Ca., U.S. E4 98
Shaftsbury, Vt., U.S. E2 138
Shag Rocks, rock, S. Geor. H8 69
Shah Alam, Malay. C2 36
Shahdol, India E4 40
Shāhjahānpur, India D3 40
Shāhpura, India D2 40
Shahr-e Kord, Iran D6 42
Shahr-e Rey, Iran C6 42
Shājāpur, India E3 40
Shakawe, Bots. B3 56

Name — Map Ref. — Page

Shaker Heights, Oh., U.S. A4 128
Shaki, Nig. E5 50
Shakopee, Mn., U.S. F5 116
Shala Hāyk', l., Eth. B7 54
Shallotte, N.C., U.S. D4 126
Shallotte Inlet, b., N.C., U.S. D4 126
Shallowater, Tx., U.S. C2 136
Shām, Jabal ash-, mtn., Oman F7 38
Shambe, Sudan B6 54
Shambu, Eth. B7 54
Shamokin, Pa., U.S. E8 131
Shamokin Dam, Pa., U.S. E8 131
Shamrock, Tx., U.S. B2 136
Shamva, Zimb. B5 56
Shandī, Sudan G11 48
Shandong, state, China D11 28
Shandong Bandao, pen., China D12 28
Shangcai, China C3 30
Shangcheng, China C4 30
Shangchuan Dao, i., China E3 30
Shangdu, China A3 30
Shanghai, China E12 28
Shanghang, China D4 30
Shangqiu, China E11 28
Shangrao, China F11 28
Shangxian, China E10 28
Shangzhi, China B13 28
Shanhaiguan, China A4 30
Shannock, R.I., U.S. F2 132
Shannon, Ga., U.S. B1 103
Shannon, Il., U.S. A4 106
Shannon, Ms., U.S. A5 117
Shannon, co., Mo., U.S. D6 118
Shannon, co., S.D., U.S. D3 134
Shannon, stm., Ire. D2 12
Shannon, Lake, l., Wa., U.S. A4 140
Shannontown, S.C., U.S. D7 133
Shantou, China G11 28
Shantung Peninsula see Shandong Bandao, pen., China D12 28
Shanxi, state, China D10 28
Shanxian, China C4 30
Shanyin, China B3 30
Shaoguan, China G10 28
Shaowu, China F11 28
Shaoxing, China E12 28
Shaoyang, China F10 28
Shaqrā', Sau. Ar. E5 38
Shaqrā', Yemen H5 38
Šhara, gora, mtn., Asia A10 44
Shark Bay, b., Austl. F1 60
Sharkey, co., Ms., U.S. C3 117
Shark Point, c., Fl., U.S. H5 102
Sharm El Sheikh, Egypt E11 48
Sharon, Ct., U.S. B2 100
Sharon, Ma., U.S. B5 114
Sharon, Pa., U.S. D1 131
Sharon, Tn., U.S. A3 135
Sharon, Wi., U.S. F5 142
Sharon Hill, Pa., U.S. p20 131
Sharon Park, Oh., U.S. n12 128
Sharon Springs, Ks., U.S. D2 109
Sharonville, Oh., U.S. n13 128
Sharp, co., Ar., U.S. A4 97
Sharpe, Lake, res., S.D., U.S. C6 134
Sharpes, Fl., U.S. D6 102
Sharpley, De., U.S. h7 101
Sharpsburg, Md., U.S. B2 113
Sharpsburg, N.C., U.S. B5 126
Sharpsburg, Pa., U.S. k14 131
Sharpsville, In., U.S. D5 107
Sharpsville, Pa., U.S. D1 131
Sharptown, Md., U.S. C6 113
Shashe, stm., Afr. C4 56
Shashemenē, Eth. B7 54
Shashi, China E10 28
Shasta, co., Ca., U.S. B3 98
Shasta, Mount, vol., Ca., U.S. B2 98
Shasta Lake, res., Ca., U.S. B2 98
Shattuck, Ok., U.S. A2 129
Shaw, Ms., U.S. B3 117
Shaw Air Force Base, mil., S.C., U.S. D7 133
Shawano, Wi., U.S. D5 142
Shawano, co., Wi., U.S. D5 142
Shawano Lake, l., Wi., U.S. D5 142
Shawinigan, P.Q., Can. C5 90
Shawinigan-Sud, P.Q., Can. C5 90
Shawnee, Ks., U.S. k16 109
Shawnee, Ok., U.S. B5 129
Shawnee, co., Ks., U.S. D8 109
Shawneetown, Il., U.S. F5 106
Shawsheen, stm., Ma., U.S. f11 114
Shay Gap, Austl. E3 60
Shaykh, Jabal ash- see Hermon, Mount, mtn., Asia F6 44
Shaykh Sa'd, Iraq F12 44
Shaykh 'Uthmān, Yemen H5 38
Shebelē Wenz, Wabē (Shabeelle), stm., Afr. B8 54
Sheberghān, Afg. C9 42
Sheboygan, Wi., U.S. E6 142
Sheboygan, co., Wi., U.S. E6 142
Sheboygan, stm., Wi., U.S. k10 142
Sheboygan Falls, Wi., U.S. E6 142
Shediac, N.B., Can. C5 87
Sheenjek, stm., Ak., U.S. B11 95
Sheep Mountain, mtn., Az., U.S. E1 96
Sheep Mountain, mtn., Wy., U.S. B5 143
Sheep Mountain, mtn., Wy., U.S. C2 143
Sheep Peak, mtn., Nv., U.S. G6 121
Sheep Range, mts., Nv., U.S. G6 121
Sheet Harbour, N.S., Can. E7 87
Sheffield, Eng., U.K. D6 12
Sheffield, Al., U.S. A2 94
Sheffield, Ia., U.S. B4 108
Sheffield, Il., U.S. B4 106
Sheffield, Pa., U.S. C3 131
Sheffield Lake, Oh., U.S. A3 128
Shehong, China C2 30
Sheila, N.B., Can. B5 87
Shekhūpura, Pak. D10 42
Shelagyote Peak, mtn., B.C., Can. B4 85
Shelbiana, Ky., U.S. C7 110
Shelbina, Mo., U.S. B5 118
Shelburn, In., U.S. F3 107
Shelburne, On., Can. C4 89
Shelburne Falls, Ma., U.S. A2 114
Shelburne Pond, l., Vt., U.S. C2 138
Shelby, Al., U.S. B3 94
Shelby, Ia., U.S. C2 108
Shelby, In., U.S. B3 107
Shelby, Mi., U.S. E4 115
Shelby, Ms., U.S. B3 117
Shelby, Mt., U.S. B5 119
Shelby, N.C., U.S. B1 126
Shelby, Ne., U.S. C8 120
Shelby, Oh., U.S. B3 128
Shelby, co., Al., U.S. B3 94
Shelby, co., Ia., U.S. C2 108
Shelby, co., Il., U.S. D5 106
Shelby, co., In., U.S. E6 107
Shelby, co., Ky., U.S. B4 110
Shelby, co., Mo., U.S. B5 118
Shelby, co., Oh., U.S. B1 128
Shelby, co., Tn., U.S. B2 135
Shelby, co., Tx., U.S. D5 136
Shelbyville, Il., U.S. D5 106
Shelbyville, In., U.S. F6 107
Shelbyville, Ky., U.S. B4 110
Shelbyville, Tn., U.S. B5 135
Shelbyville, Lake, res., Il., U.S. D5 106
Sheldon, Ia., U.S. A2 108
Sheldon, Il., U.S. C6 106
Sheldon, Tx., U.S. r14 136
Shelekhov, Gulf of see Šelihova, zaliv, b., Russia C17 26
Shelikof Strait, strt., Ak., U.S. D9 95
Shell Creek, stm., Wy., U.S. B5 143
Shell Creek, stm., U.S. A2 99
Shelley, Id., U.S. F6 105
Shellharbour, Austl. G5 62
Shell Lake, Wi., U.S. C2 142
Shell Lake, l., Mn., U.S. D3 116
Shell Lake, l., Wi., U.S. C2 142
Shellman, Ga., U.S. E2 103
Shell Rock, Ia., U.S. B5 108
Shell Rock, stm., Ia., U.S. B5 108
Shellsburg, Ia., U.S. B6 108
Shelly Mountain, mtn., Id., U.S. F5 105
Shelter Island, N.Y., U.S. m16 125
Shelton, Ct., U.S. D3 100
Shelton, Ne., U.S. D7 120
Shelton, Wa., U.S. B2 140
Shemya Air Force Base, mil., Ak., U.S. E2 95
Shenandoah, Ia., U.S. D2 108
Shenandoah, Pa., U.S. E9 131
Shenandoah, Va., U.S. B4 139
Shenandoah, co., Va., U.S. B4 139
Shenandoah, stm., U.S. A5 139
Shenandoah, North Fork, stm., Va., U.S. B4 139
Shenandoah, South Fork, stm., Va., U.S. B4 139
Shenandoah Mountain, mtn., U.S. B3 139
Shenandoah National Park, Va., U.S. B4 139
Shenango River Lake, res., U.S. D1 131
Shendam, Nig. E6 50
Shenipsit Lake, l., Ct., U.S. B6 100
Shenmu, China B3 30
Shenqiu, China C4 30
Shenxian, China B4 30
Shenyang, China C12 28
Shenzhen, China E3 30
Shepaug, stm., Ct., U.S. C2 100
Shepaug Dam, Ct., U.S. D2 100
Shepaug Reservoir, res., Ct., U.S. C2 100
Shepetivka, Ukr. D9 20
Shepherd, Mi., U.S. E6 115
Shepherd, Tx., U.S. D5 136
Shepherdstown, W.V., U.S. B7 141
Shepherdsville, Ky., U.S. C4 110
Sheppard Air Force Base, mil., Tx., U.S. C3 136
Shepparton, Austl. H4 62
Sherborn, Ma., U.S. h10 114
Sherbro Island, i., S.L. E2 50
Sherbrooke, P.Q., Can. D6 90
Sherburn, Mn., U.S. G4 116
Sherburne, co., Mn., U.S. E5 116
Sheridan, Ar., U.S. C3 97
Sheridan, Il., U.S. B5 106
Sheridan, In., U.S. D5 107
Sheridan, Mi., U.S. E5 115
Sheridan, Mt., U.S. E4 119
Sheridan, Or., U.S. B3 130
Sheridan, Wy., U.S. B6 143
Sheridan, co., Ks., U.S. C3 109
Sheridan, co., Mt., U.S. B12 119
Sheridan, co., N.D., U.S. B5 127
Sheridan, co., Ne., U.S. B3 120
Sheridan, co., Wy., U.S. B5 143
Sheridan, Mount, mtn., Wy., U.S. B2 143
Sherman, Tx., U.S. C4 136
Sherman, co., Ks., U.S. C2 109
Sherman, co., Ne., U.S. C6 120
Sherman, co., Or., U.S. B6 130
Sherman, co., Tx., U.S. A2 136
Sherman Reservoir, res., Ne., U.S. C7 120
Sherpur, Bngl. D6 40
Sherrill, N.Y., U.S. B5 125
Sherwood, P.E., Can. C6 87
Sherwood, Ar., U.S. C3 97
Sherwood, Or., U.S. h12 130
Sherwood, Wi., U.S. h9 142
Sherwood Manor, Ct., U.S. A5 100
Sherwood Park, De., U.S. i7 101
Shetek, Lake, l., Mn., U.S. G3 116
Shetland Islands, is., Scot., U.K. h19 12a
Shetucket, stm., Ct., U.S. C7 100
Sheyenne, stm., N.D., U.S. C8 127
Sheyenne Lake, res., N.D., U.S. B5 127
Shiawassee, co., Mi., U.S. F6 115
Shibām, Yemen G5 38
Shicheng, China A7 34
Shickshinny, Pa., U.S. D9 131
Shidao, China D12 28
Shiguaigou, China A3 30
Shijiazhuang, China D10 28
Shikārpur, Pak. E9 42
Shikoku, i., Japan E14 28
Shilabo, Eth. B8 54
Shiliguri, India D5 40
Shillington, Pa., U.S. F10 131
Shillong, India D6 40
Shiloh National Military Park, Tn., U.S. B3 135
Shimla, India C3 40
Shimoga, India G3 40
Shimonoseki, Japan E14 28
Shīndand, Afg. D8 42
Shiner, Tx., U.S. E4 136
Shinglehouse, Pa., U.S. C5 131
Shingū, Japan E15 28
Shinnston, W.V., U.S. B4 141
Shinyanga, Tan. D6 54
Shiocton, Wi., U.S. D5 142
Shiono-misaki, c., Japan D3 31
Shiping, China B4 34
Ship Island, i., Ms., U.S. E5 117
Ship Island Pass, strt., Ms., U.S. g7 117
Shippegan, N.B., Can. B5 87
Shippensburg, Pa., U.S. F6 131
Shiprock, N.M., U.S. A1 124
Ship Rock, mtn., N.M., U.S. A1 124
Shīrāz, Iran E6 42
Shiretoko-misaki, c., Japan B5 31
Shirley, In., U.S. E6 107
Shirley, Ma., U.S. A4 114
Shirley Mountains, mts., Wy., U.S. D6 143
Shīrvān, Iran C7 42
Shishaldin Volcano, vol., Ak., U.S. E7 95
Shishmaref, Ak., U.S. B6 95
Shithāthah, Iraq F10 44
Shively, Ky., U.S. B4 110
Shivpuri, India D3 40
Shizuoka, Japan C3 31
Shkodër, Alb. C7 18
Shoal Creek, stm., U.S. B4 135
Shoal Harbour, Nf., Can. D4 88
Shoal Lake, Mb., Can. D1 86
Shoals, In., U.S. G4 107
Shoals, Isles of, is., Me., U.S. E2 112
Shoalwater, Cape, c., Wa., U.S. C1 140
Shoemakersville, Pa., U.S. F10 131
Shongopovi, Az., U.S. B5 96
Shonto, Az., U.S. A5 96
Shoreham, Mi., U.S. F4 115
Shores Acres, R.I., U.S. E4 132
Shoreview, Mn., U.S. m12 116
Shorewood, Il., U.S. k8 106
Shorewood, Mn., U.S. n11 116
Shorewood, Wi., U.S. E6 142
Short Beach, Ct., U.S. D4 100
Shoshone, Id., U.S. G4 105
Shoshone, co., Id., U.S. B2 105
Shoshone, stm., Wy., U.S. B4 143
Shoshone Falls, wtfl, Id., U.S. G4 105
Shoshone Lake, l., Wy., U.S. B2 143
Shoshone Mountains, mts., Nv., U.S. E4 121
Shoshone Peak, mtn., Nv., U.S. G5 121
Shoshone Range, mts., Nv., U.S. C5 121
Shoshong, Bots. C4 56
Shoshoni, Wy., U.S. C4 143
Shostka, Ukr. D12 20
Shouchang, China D4 30
Shouguang, China B4 30
Shoup, Id., U.S. D4 105
Shouxian, China C4 30
Show Low, Az., U.S. C5 96
Shreve, Oh., U.S. B3 128
Shreveport, La., U.S. B2 111
Shrewsbury, Eng., U.K. D5 12
Shrewsbury, Ma., U.S. B4 114
Shrewsbury, N.J., U.S. C4 123
Shrewsbury, Pa., U.S. G8 131
Shuangcheng, China B13 28
Shuangjiang, China B3 34
Shuangliao, China C12 28
Shuangyashan, China B14 28
Shubenacadie, N.S., Can. D6 87
Shubrâ El-Kheima, Egypt E10 14
Shuksan, Mount, mtn., Wa., U.S. A4 140
Shule, China B3 40
Shullsburg, Wi., U.S. F3 142
Shumagin Islands, is., Ak., U.S. E7 95
Shunde, China B6 34
Shungnak, Ak., U.S. B8 95
Shurugwi, Zimb. B5 56
Shūsh, Iran F13 44
Shūshtar, Iran D5 42
Shuswap Lake, l., B.C., Can. D8 85
Shuyang, China C4 30
Shwebo, Myan. B3 34
Shwenyaung, Myan. B3 34
Shyok, stm., Asia C3 40
Siālkot, Pak. D10 42
Siam see Thailand, ctry., Asia C4 34
Siam, Gulf of see Thailand, Gulf of, b., Asia D4 34
Sian see Xi'an, China E9 28
Siargao Island, i., Phil. E9 34
Šiaškotan, ostrov, i., Russia E17 26
Siau, Pulau, i., Indon. C7 36
Šibaj, Russia D10 22
Šibenik, Cro. C5 18
Siberia see Sibir', reg., Russia C12 26
Siberut, Pulau, i., Indon. D1 36
Sibi, Pak. E9 42
Sibir' (Siberia), reg., Russia C12 26
Sibircevo, Russia B2 31
Sibirjakova, ostrov, i., Russia B9 26
Sibiti, Congo D2 54
Sibiu, Rom. G8 20
Sibley, Ia., U.S. A2 108
Sibley, La., U.S. B2 111
Sibley, co., Mn., U.S. F4 116
Sibolga, Indon. C1 36
Sibsāgar, India D6 40
Sibu, Malay. C4 36
Sibuguey Bay, b., Phil. E8 34
Sibut, C.A.R. B3 54
Sibutu Island, i., Phil. F7 34
Sibuyan Island, i., Phil. D8 34
Sibuyan Sea, Phil. D8 34
Sicamous, B.C., Can. D8 85
Sichuan, prov., China E8 28
Sicilia (Sicily), i., Italy F4 18
Sicily see Sicilia, i., Italy F4 18
Sicily, Strait of, strt. F3 18
Sico Tinto, stm., Hond. B2 80
Sicuani, Peru F5 70
Siddipet, India F3 40
Sidéradougou, Burkina D4 50
Siderno, Italy E6 18
Sidhi, India E4 40
Sîdi Barrâni, Egypt D10 48
Sidi bel Abbès, Alg. C4 48
Sidi-Ifni, Mor. E2 48
Sidley, Mount, mtn., Ant. D28 67
Sidney, B.C., Can. E6 85
Sidney, Ia., U.S. D2 108
Sidney, Il., U.S. C5 106
Sidney, Mt., U.S. C12 119
Sidney, Ne., U.S. C3 120
Sidney, N.Y., U.S. C5 125
Sidney, Oh., U.S. B1 128
Sidney Lanier, Lake, res., Ga., U.S. B2 103
Sidon see Şaydā, Leb. F6 44
Sidra, Gulf of see Surt, Khalīj, b., Libya D8 48
Sidrolândia, Braz. C6 72
Siedlce, Pol. C7 20
Siegen, Ger. E11 12
Siena, Italy C3 18
Sieradz, Pol. D5 20
Sierpc, Pol. C5 20
Sierra, co., Ca., U.S. C3 98
Sierra, co., N.M., U.S. D2 124
Sierra Blanca Peak, mtn., N.M., U.S. D4 124
Sierra Estrella, mts., Az., U.S. m8 96
Sierra Gorda, Chile C4 72
Sierra Leone, ctry., Afr. E2 50
Sierra Madre, Ca., U.S. m12 98
Sierra Nevada see Nevada, Sierra, mts., Ca., U.S. D4 98
Sierra Vista, Az., U.S. F5 96
Siesta Key, i., Fl., U.S. E4 102
Sieverodonets'k, Ukr. E15 20
Sífnos, i., Grc. F10 18
Sig, Alg. J6 16
Sighetu Marmaţiei, Rom. F7 20
Sighişoara, Rom. F8 20
Siglan, Russia D17 26
Siglufjörður, Ice. k19 10a
Signal Mountain, Tn., U.S. D8 135
Signal Peak, mtn., Az., U.S. D1 96
Signal Peak, mtn., Ut., U.S. F2 137
Sigourney, Ia., U.S. C5 108
Siguatepeque, Hond. C2 80
Siguiri, Gui. D3 50
Sigulda, Lat. H11 10
Siguri Falls, wtfl, Tan. E7 54
Sihanoukville see Kâmpóng Saôm, Camb. D4 34
Sihote-Alin', mts., Russia E15 26
Siirt, Tur. D9 44
Sīkar, India D3 40
Sikasso, Mali D3 50
Sikeston, Mo., U.S. E8 118
Sikiá, Grc. D9 18
Sikiang see Xi, stm., China G10 28
Sikkim, prov., India D5 40
Šikotan, ostrov, i., Russia E16 26
Siktjah, Russia B14 26
Silao, Mex. C4 78
Silchar, India E6 40
Şile, Tur. B3 44
Siler City, N.C., U.S. B3 126
Silesia, hist. reg., Eur. D4 20
Siletz, Or., U.S. C3 130
Silghāt, India D6 40
Silhouette, i., Sey. h13 57b
Silifke, Tur. D5 44
Siling Co, l., China E5 28
Silistra, Bul. B11 18
Şilivri, Tur. B3 44
Siljan, l., Swe. F6 10
Šilka, Russia D13 26
Šilka, stm., Russia D13 26
Silkeborg, Den. H3 10
Sillery, P.Q., Can. n17 90
Sillustani, hist., Peru B3 72
Siloam Springs, Ar., U.S. A1 97
Šilovo, Russia B16 20
Silsbee, Tx., U.S. D5 136
Silt, Co., U.S. B3 99
Šilutė, Lith. I9 10
Silvan, Tur. C9 44
Silvassa, India E2 40
Silver Bay, Mn., U.S. C7 116
Silver Bow, co., Mt., U.S. E4 119
Silver City, N.M., U.S. E1 124
Silver City, Nv., U.S. D2 121
Silver Creek, Ne., U.S. C8 120
Silver Creek, N.Y., U.S. C1 125
Silver Creek, stm., Or., U.S. D7 130
Silverdale, Wa., U.S. B3 140
Silver Grove, Ky., U.S. h14 110
Silver Hill, Md., U.S. f9 113
Silver Lake, Ks., U.S. C8 109
Silver Lake, Ma., U.S. f11 114
Silver Lake, Mn., U.S. F4 116
Silver Lake, Wi., U.S. F5 142
Silver Lake, l., De., U.S. D3 101
Silver Lake, l., Ia., U.S. A3 108
Silver Lake, l., Me., U.S. C3 112
Silver Lake, l., N.H., U.S. C4 122
Silver Lake, l., N.H., U.S. E2 122
Silver Lake, l., Or., U.S. D7 130
Silver Lake, l., Wa., U.S. g13 140
Silverpeak, Nv., U.S. F4 121
Silver Peak Range, mts., Nv., U.S. F4 121
Silver Spring, Md., U.S. C3 113
Silver Springs, Nv., U.S. D2 121
Silver Star Mountain, mtn., Wa., U.S. A5 140
Silverthrone Mountain, mtn., B.C., Can. D4 85
Silvertip Mountain, mtn., Mt., U.S. C3 119
Silverton, Co., U.S. D3 99
Silverton, Id., U.S. B3 105
Silverton, N.J., U.S. C4 123
Silverton, Oh., U.S. o13 128
Silverton, Or., U.S. C4 130
Silvies, stm., Or., U.S. D7 130
Silview, De., U.S. B3 101
Silvis, Il., U.S. B3 106
Šimanovsk, Russia D14 26
Simao, China G8 28
Simav, stm., Tur. C3 44
Simba, D.R.C. C4 54
Simcoe, On., Can. E4 89
Simcoe, Lake, l., On., Can. C5 89
Simeulue, Palau, i., Indon. C1 36
Simferopol', Ukr. G13 20
Simití, Col. B5 70
Simi Valley, Ca., U.S. E4 98
Simmesport, La., U.S. D4 111
Simms Stream, stm., N.H., U.S. g7 122
Simonette, stm., Ab., Can. B1 84
Simon's Town, S. Afr. E2 56
Simpson, Pa., U.S. C11 131
Simpson, co., Ky., U.S. D3 110
Simpson, co., Ms., U.S. D4 117
Simpson Creek, stm., W.V., U.S. k10 141
Simpson Desert, des., Austl. E6 60
Simpsonville, Ky., U.S. B4 110
Simpsonville, S.C., U.S. B3 133

Name — Map Ref. — Page

Simsboro, La., U.S. **B3** 111
Simsbury, Ct., U.S. **B4** 100
Simušir, ostrov, i., Russia **E17** 26
Sinabang, Indon. **C1** 36
Sinai, pen., Egypt **E11** 48
Sinai Peninsula see Sinai, pen., Egypt **E11** 48
Sinaloa, state, Mex. **B3** 78
Sīnāwin, Libya **D7** 48
Sincelejo, Col. **B4** 70
Sinclair, Wy., U.S. **E5** 143
Sindangbarang, Indon. **E3** 36
Sindara, Gabon **D2** 54
Sindor, Russia **B9** 22
Sinfra, C. Iv. **E3** 50
Singalamwe, Nmb. **B3** 56
Singapore, Sing. **C2** 36
Singapore, ctry., Asia **C2** 36
Singaraja, Indon. **H6** 32
Singen, Ger. **G11** 12
Singida, Tan. **D6** 54
Singkaling Hkāmti, Myan. **A3** 34
Singkang, Indon. **D6** 36
Singkawang, Indon. **C3** 36
Singkep, Pulau, i., Indon. **D2** 36
Singleton, Austl. **G5** 62
Sinjai, Indon. **E6** 36
Sinjār, Iraq **D9** 44
Sinkāt, Sudan **G12** 48
Sinkiang see Xinjiang Uygur Zizhiqu, prov., China **C5** 28
Sinnemahoning Creek, stm., Pa., U.S. **D5** 131
Sinop, Tur. **A6** 44
Sinskoe, Russia **C14** 26
Sintang, Indon. **C4** 36
Sint Helenabaai, b., S. Afr. **E2** 56
Sinton, Tx., U.S. **E4** 136
Siocon, Phil. **E8** 34
Siófok, Hung. **F5** 20
Sion, Switz. **A1** 18
Sioux, co., Ia., U.S. **A1** 108
Sioux, co., N.D., U.S. **C4** 127
Sioux, co., Ne., U.S. **B2** 120
Sioux Center, Ia., U.S. **A1** 108
Sioux City, Ia., U.S. **B1** 108
Sioux Falls, S.D., U.S. **D9** 134
Sioux Lookout, On., Can. **o17** 89
Sioux Rapids, Ia., U.S. **B2** 108
Sipalay, Phil. **E8** 34
Siping, China **C12** 28
Sipiwesk Lake, l., Mb., Can. **B3** 86
Siple, Mount, mtn., Ant. **D28** 67
Sipsey, stm., Al., U.S. **B2** 94
Sipsey Fork, stm., Al., U.S. **A2** 94
Sipura, Pulau, i., Indon. **D1** 36
Siquijor Island, i., Phil. **E8** 34
Si Racha, Thai. **D4** 34
Siracusa, Italy **F5** 18
Sirājganj, Bngl. **E5** 40
Sir Douglas, Mount, mtn., Can. **D3** 84
Sir Edward Pellew Group, is., Austl. **D6** 60
Siren, Wi., U.S. **C1** 142
Siret, stm., Eur. **G9** 20
Sīrjān, Iran **E7** 42
Şırnak, Tur. **D10** 44
Sirohi, India **E2** 40
Sironj, India **E3** 40
Síros, i., Grc. **F10** 18
Sirsa, India **D3** 40
Sir Sandford, Mount, mtn., B.C., Can. **D9** 85
Sirte, Gulf of see Surt, Khalīj, b., Libya **D8** 48
Sir Wilfrid Laurier, Mount, mtn., B.C., Can. **C8** 85
Sisaba, mtn., Tan. **E5** 54
Sisak, Cro. **B6** 18
Si Sa Ket, Thai. **C4** 34
Sishen, S. Afr. **D3** 56
Sisian, Arm. **C12** 44
Siskiyou, co., Ca., U.S. **B2** 98
Siskiyou Mountains, mts., U.S. **F3** 130
Siskiyou Pass, Or., U.S. **E4** 130
Sisŏphŏn, Camb. **D4** 34
Sisseton, S.D., U.S. **B8** 134
Sisseton Indian Reservation, U.S. **B8** 134
Sissiboo, stm., N.S., Can. **E4** 87
Sisson Branch Reservoir, res., N.B., Can. **B2** 87
Sissonville, W.V., U.S. **C3** 141
Sisters, Or., U.S. **C5** 130
Sistersville, W.V., U.S. **B4** 141
Sītāpur, India **D4** 40
Sitasjaure, l., Eur. **C7** 10
Sitka, Ak., U.S. **D12** 95
Sitka National Historical Park, Ak., U.S. **m22** 95
Sitka Sound, strt., Ak., U.S. **m22** 95
Sittoung, stm., Myan. **C3** 34
Sittwe, Myan. **B2** 34
Sivas, Tur. **C7** 44
Sivers'kyi Donets' see Northern Donets, stm., Eur. **E14** 20
Sivrihisar, Tur. **C4** 44
Siwa, Egypt **E10** 48
Sixian, China **C4** 30
Sixth Cataract, wtfl, Sudan **G11** 48
Siyäzän, Azer. **B13** 44
Siziwang Qi, China **A3** 30
Sjælland, i., Den. **I4** 10
Skadovs'k, Ukr. **F12** 20
Skærbæk, Den. **I3** 10
Skagen, Den. **H4** 10
Skagerrak, strt., Eur. **B11** 12
Skagit, co., Wa., U.S. **A4** 140
Skagway, Ak., U.S. **D12** 95
Skamania, co., Wa., U.S. **D3** 140
Skanderborg, Den. **H3** 10
Skåne, hist. reg., Swe. **I5** 10
Skaneateles, N.Y., U.S. **C4** 125
Skaneateles Lake, l., N.Y., U.S. **C4** 125
Skārdu, Pak. **C11** 42
Skarżysko-Kamienna, Pol. **D6** 20
Skaudvilė, Lith. **I10** 10
Skaw, The see Grenen, c., Den. **H4** 10
Skegness, Eng., U.K. **D7** 12
Skeleton Lake, l., On., Can. **B5** 89
Skellefteå, Swe. **D9** 10
Skellefteälven, stm., Swe. **D8** 10
Ski, Nor. **G4** 10
Skiatook, Ok., U.S. **A5** 129
Skiatook Reservoir, res., Ok., U.S. **A5** 129
Skien, Nor. **G3** 10
Skierniewice, Pol. **D6** 20
Skihist Mountain, mtn., B.C., Can. **D7** 85
Skikda, Alg. **C6** 48
Skillet Fork, stm., Il., U.S. **E5** 106
Skive, Den. **H3** 10
Sklad, Russia **B14** 26
Skokie, Il., U.S. **A6** 106
Skokomish Indian Reservation, Wa., U.S. **B2** 140
Skópelos, i., Grc. **E9** 18
Skopin, Russia **C15** 20
Skopje, Mac. **C8** 18
Skövde, Swe. **G5** 10
Skowhegan, Me., U.S. **D3** 112
Skull Valley, val., Ut., U.S. **C3** 137
Skull Valley Indian Reservation, Ut., U.S. **C3** 137
Skuna, stm., Ms., U.S. **B4** 117
Skunk, stm., Ia., U.S. **D6** 108
Skvyra, Ukr. **E10** 20
Skwentna, stm., Ak., U.S. **g15** 95
Skye, Island of, i., Scot., U.K. **B3** 12
Skykomish, stm., Wa., U.S. **B4** 140
Skyland, N.C., U.S. **f10** 126
Skyland, Nv., U.S. **D2** 121
Skyline, Al., U.S. **A3** 94
Slagnäs, Swe. **D8** 10
Slamet, Gunung, vol., Indon. **E3** 36
Slancy, Russia **G13** 10
Slater, Ia., U.S. **C4** 108
Slater, Mo., U.S. **B4** 118
Slater, S.C., U.S. **A3** 133
Slatersville, R.I., U.S. **A3** 132
Slatersville Reservoir, res., R.I., U.S. **B3** 132
Slatina, Rom. **G8** 20
Slatington, Pa., U.S. **E10** 131
Slaton, Tx., U.S. **C2** 136
Slaughter, La., U.S. **D4** 111
Slautnoe, Russia **C18** 26
Slave, stm., Can. **F17** 82
Slave Lake, Ab., Can. **B3** 84
Slavgorod, Russia **D9** 26
Slavjanka, Russia **B2** 31
Slavjansk-na-Kubani, Russia **G15** 20
Slavonia see Slavonija, hist. reg., Cro. **B6** 18
Slavonija, hist. reg., Cro. **B6** 18
Slavonski Brod, Cro. **B6** 18
Slavuta, Ukr. **D9** 20
Sławno, Pol. **B4** 20
Slayton, Mn., U.S. **G3** 116
Sleeping Bear Dunes National Lakeshore, Mi., U.S. **D4** 115
Sleeping Bear Point, c., Mi., U.S. **D4** 115
Sleepy Eye, Mn., U.S. **F4** 116
Slickville, Pa., U.S. **F2** 131
Slidell, La., U.S. **D6** 111
Sliderock Mountain, mtn., Mt., U.S. **D3** 119
Sligo, Ire. **C2** 12
Slinger, Wi., U.S. **E5** 142
Slippery Rock, Pa., U.S. **D1** 131
Sliven, Bul. **C11** 18
Sljudjanka, Russia **D12** 26
Sloan, Ia., U.S. **B1** 108
Sloan, N.Y., U.S. **C2** 125
Slobodskoj, Russia **D7** 26
Slobozia, Mol. **F10** 20
Slobozia, Rom. **G9** 20
Slocomb, Al., U.S. **D4** 94
Slonim, Bela. **C8** 20
Slope, co., N.D., U.S. **C2** 127
Slough, Eng., U.K. **E6** 12
Slovakia, ctry., Eur. **E6** 20
Slovenia, ctry., Eur. **A5** 18
Slov'ians'k, Ukr. **E14** 20
Sluch, stm., Ukr. **D9** 20
Sluck, Bela. **C9** 20
Słupsk, Pol. **B4** 20
Smackover, Ar., U.S. **D3** 97
Småland, hist. reg., Swe. **H6** 10
Small Point, c., Me., U.S. **g8** 112
Smallwood Reservoir, res., Nf., Can. **g8** 88
Smarhon', Bela. **B9** 20
Smederevo, Yugo. **B8** 18
Smethport, Pa., U.S. **C5** 131
Smidovič, Russia **B14** 28
Šmidta, ostrov, i., Russia **A9** 26
Smila, Ukr. **E11** 20
Smith, co., Ks., U.S. **C5** 109
Smith, co., Ms., U.S. **C4** 117
Smith, co., Tn., U.S. **A5** 135
Smith, co., Tx., U.S. **C5** 136
Smith, stm., Mt., U.S. **D5** 119
Smith, stm., U.S. **D3** 139
Smith and Sayles Reservoir, res., R.I., U.S. **B2** 132
Smith Bay, b., Ak., U.S. **A9** 95
Smith Canyon, val., Co., U.S. **D7** 99
Smith Center, Ks., U.S. **C5** 109
Smithers, B.C., Can. **B4** 85
Smithers, W.V., U.S. **C3** 141
Smithfield, N.C., U.S. **B4** 126
Smithfield, Pa., U.S. **G2** 131
Smithfield, Ut., U.S. **B4** 137
Smithfield, Va., U.S. **D6** 139
Smith Island, i., Va., U.S. **C7** 139
Smith Island, i., U.S. **D5** 113
Smith Mountain Lake, res., Va., U.S. **C3** 139
Smith Peak, mtn., Id., U.S. **A2** 105
Smith Point, c., Ma., U.S. **D7** 114
Smith Point, c., Va., U.S. **C6** 139
Smiths, Al., U.S. **C4** 94
Smithsburg, Md., U.S. **A2** 113
Smiths Falls, On., Can. **C8** 89
Smiths Grove, Ky., U.S. **C3** 110
Smithton, Austl. **I4** 62
Smithton, Il., U.S. **E4** 106
Smithtown, N.Y., U.S. **n15** 125
Smithville, Ga., U.S. **E2** 103
Smithville, Mo., U.S. **B3** 118
Smithville, Ms., U.S. **A5** 117
Smithville, Oh., U.S. **B4** 128
Smithville, Tn., U.S. **D8** 135
Smithville, Tx., U.S. **D4** 136
Smithville Lake, res., Mo., U.S. **B3** 118
Smoke Creek Desert, des., Nv., U.S. **C2** 121
Smokey, Cape, c., N.S., Can. **C9** 87
Smokey Dome, mtn., Id., U.S. **F4** 105
Smoky, stm., Ab., Can. **B1** 84
Smoky Hill, stm., U.S. **D5** 109
Smoky Lake, Ab., Can. **B4** 84
Smoky Mountains, mts., Id., U.S. **F4** 105
Smøla, i., Nor. **E3** 10
Smolensk, Russia **D5** 26
Smoljan, Bul. **D10** 18
Smooth Rock Falls, On., Can. **o19** 89
Smoothstone Lake, l., Sk., Can. **C2** 91
Smyrna see İzmir, Tur. **C2** 44
Smyrna, De., U.S. **C3** 101
Smyrna, Ga., U.S. **C2** 103
Smyrna, Tn., U.S. **B5** 135
Smyrna, stm., De., U.S. **C3** 101
Smyth, co., Va., U.S. **f10** 139
Snake, stm., Mn., U.S. **B1** 116
Snake, stm., Ne., U.S. **B4** 120
Snake, stm., U.S. **C4** 92
Snake, stm., U.S. **D5** 116
Snake Range, mts., Nv., U.S. **E7** 121
Snake River Plain, pl., Id., U.S. **F2** 105
Snake River Range, mts., U.S. **C2** 143
Sneads, Fl., U.S. **B2** 102
Sneedville, Tn., U.S. **C10** 135
Snihurivka, Ukr. **F12** 20
Snipe Keys, is., Fl., U.S. **H5** 102
Snøhetta, mtn., Nor. **E3** 10
Snohomish, Wa., U.S. **B3** 140
Snohomish, co., Wa., U.S. **A4** 140
Snoqualmie, Wa., U.S. **B4** 140
Snoqualmie, stm., Wa., U.S. **B4** 140
Snoqualmie Pass, Wa., U.S. **B4** 140
Snøtinden, mtn., Nor. **C5** 10
Snowbank Lake, l., Mn., U.S. **B7** 116
Snowdon, mtn., Wales, U.K. **D4** 12
Snowdrift see Łutselk'e, N.T., Can. **F17** 82
Snowflake, Az., U.S. **C5** 96
Snow Hill, Md., U.S. **D7** 113
Snow Hill, N.C., U.S. **B5** 126
Snowking Mountain, mtn., Wa., U.S. **A4** 140
Snow Lake, Mb., Can. **B1** 86
Snowmass Mountain, mtn., Co., U.S. **B3** 99
Snow Peak, mtn., Wa., U.S. **A7** 140
Snowshoe Lake, l., Me., U.S. **B4** 112
Snowshoe Peak, mtn., Mt., U.S. **B1** 119
Snow Water Lake, l., Nv., U.S. **C7** 121
Snowy Mountains, mts., Austl. **H4** 62
Snowyside Peak, mtn., Id., U.S. **F4** 105
Snyder, Ok., U.S. **C3** 129
Snyder, Tx., U.S. **C2** 136
Snyder, co., Pa., U.S. **E7** 131
Soacha, Col. **E5** 80
Soalala, Madag. **B8** 56
Soap Lake, Wa., U.S. **B6** 140
Sobradinho, Represa de, res., Braz. **D3** 74
Sobral, Braz. **B3** 74
Socastee, S.C., U.S. **D9** 133
Soči, Russia **E5** 26
Social Circle, Ga., U.S. **C3** 103
Société, Archipel de la (Society Islands), is., Fr. Poly. **F14** 58
Society Hill, S.C., U.S. **B8** 133
Society Islands see Société, Archipel de la, is., Fr. Poly. **F14** 58
Socorro, Col. **B5** 70
Socorro, N.M., U.S. **C3** 124
Socorro, co., N.M., U.S. **D2** 124
Socorro, Isla, i., Mex. **D2** 78
Socotra see Suquṭrā, i., Yemen **H6** 38
Soc Trang, Viet. **E5** 34
Sodankylä, Fin. **C12** 10
Soda Springs, Id., U.S. **G7** 105
Soddy-Daisy, Tn., U.S. **D8** 135
Söderköping, Swe. **G7** 10
Södertälje, Swe. **G7** 10
Sodo, Eth. **B7** 54
Sodus, N.Y., U.S. **B3** 125
Soe, Indon. **E6** 36
Sofala, Moz. **C5** 56
Sofia see Sofija, Bul. **C9** 18
Sofija, Bul. **C9** 18
Sogamoso, Col. **D5** 80
Sognefjorden, b., Nor. **F1** 10
Sog Xian, China **E6** 28
Sointula, B.C., Can. **D4** 85
Soissons, Fr. **C8** 16
Sojat, India **D2** 40
Šojna, Russia **A7** 22
Söke, Tur. **D2** 44
Sokodé, Togo **E5** 50
Sokol, Russia **C7** 22
Sokol, Russia **B14** 26
Sokółka, Pol. **C7** 20
Sokolo, Mali **D3** 50
Sokoto, Nig. **D6** 50
Sokoto, stm., Nig. **D5** 50
Solai, Kenya **C7** 54
Solana, Fl., U.S. **F5** 102
Solano, Phil. **C8** 34
Solano, co., Ca., U.S. **C3** 98
Solāpur, India **F3** 40
Soldier, stm., Ia., U.S. **C2** 108
Soldier Key, i., Fl., U.S. **s3** 102
Soldotna, Ak., U.S. **g16** 95
Soledad, Col. **A5** 70
Soledad, Ca., U.S. **D3** 98
Soledad Díez Gutiérrez, Mex. **C4** 78
Solikamsk, Russia **D7** 26
Sol'-Ileck, Russia **D10** 22
Solimões see Amazon, stm., S.A. **D6** 70
Sollefteå, Swe. **E7** 10
Sóller, Spain **H8** 16
Šologoncy, Russia **C13** 26
Solomon, Ks., U.S. **D6** 109
Solomon, stm., Ks., U.S. **C6** 109
Solomon Basin **I18** 64
Solomon Islands, ctry., Oc. **B6** 62
Solomons, Md., U.S. **D5** 113
Solomon Sea, Oc. **B5** 62
Solon, China **B12** 28
Solon, Ia., U.S. **C6** 108
Solon, Oh., U.S. **A4** 128
Solothurn, Switz. **A1** 18
Solov'evsk, Russia **A11** 28
Solvay, N.Y., U.S. **B4** 125
Solway Firth, b., U.K. **C5** 12
Solwezi, Zam. **A4** 56
Soma, Tur. **C2** 44
Somabhula, Zimb. **B4** 56
Somalia, ctry., Afr. **I14** 46
Somali Basin **H8** 64
Sombor, Yugo. **B7** 18
Sombrerete, Mex. **C4** 78
Sombrero Channel, strt., India **H6** 40
Somerdale, N.J., U.S. **D2** 123
Somers, Ct., U.S. **B6** 100
Somers, Mt., U.S. **B2** 119
Somerset, Mb., Can. **E2** 86
Somerset, Ky., U.S. **C5** 110
Somerset, Ma., U.S. **C5** 114
Somerset, N.J., U.S. **B3** 123
Somerset, Oh., U.S. **C3** 128
Somerset, Pa., U.S. **F3** 131
Somerset, Tx., U.S. **k7** 136
Somerset, Wi., U.S. **C1** 142
Somerset, co., Md., U.S. **D6** 113
Somerset, co., Me., U.S. **C2** 112
Somerset, co., N.J., U.S. **B3** 123
Somerset, co., Pa., U.S. **G3** 131
Somerset East, S. Afr. **E4** 56
Somerset Reservoir, res., Vt., U.S. **E3** 138
Somers Point, N.J., U.S. **E3** 123
Somersville, Ct., U.S. **B6** 100
Somersworth, N.H., U.S. **D5** 122
Somerton, Az., U.S. **E1** 96
Somervell, co., Tx., U.S. **C4** 136
Somerville, Ma., U.S. **B5** 114
Somerville, N.J., U.S. **B3** 123
Somerville, Tn., U.S. **B2** 135
Somerville, Tx., U.S. **D4** 136
Somerville Lake, res., Tx., U.S. **D4** 136
Somonauk, Il., U.S. **B5** 106
Son, stm., India **E4** 40
Sønderborg, Den. **I3** 10
Søndre Strømfjord, Grnld. **E29** 82
Søndre Strømfjord, b., Grnld. **E29** 82
Sondrio, Italy **A2** 18
Sonepur, India **E4** 40
Song, Nig. **E7** 50
Song Cau, Viet. **D5** 34
Songea, Tan. **F7** 54
Songhua, stm., China **B14** 28
Songhua Hu, res., China **C13** 28
Songkhla, Thai. **E4** 34
Songnim, N. Kor. **D13** 28
Songololo, D.R.C. **E2** 54
Songpan, China **C1** 30
Sonid Youqi, China **C10** 28
Sonīpat, India **D3** 40
Sonkël', ozero, l., Kyrg. **A3** 40
Son La, Viet. **B4** 34
Sonmiāni Bay, b., Pak. **E9** 42
Sonneberg, Ger. **E12** 12
Sonoma, Ca., U.S. **C2** 98
Sonoma, co., Ca., U.S. **C2** 98
Sonoma Peak, mtn., Nv., U.S. **C4** 121
Sonoma Range, mts., Nv., U.S. **C4** 121
Sonora, Ca., U.S. **D3** 98
Sonora, Tx., U.S. **D2** 136
Sonora, state, Mex. **B2** 78
Sonora, stm., Mex. **B2** 78
Sonoran Desert, des., N.A. **E5** 92
Sonoyta, Mex. **A2** 78
Sonqor, Iran **E12** 44
Sonsón, Col. **D4** 80
Sonsonate, El Sal. **C1** 80
Sonsorol Islands, is., Palau **E9** 32
Son Tay, Viet. **B5** 34
Sonthofen, Ger. **G12** 12
Soochow see Suzhou, China **E12** 28
Soperton, Ga., U.S. **D4** 103
Sophia, W.V., U.S. **D3** 141
Sopot, Pol. **B5** 20
Sopron, Hung. **F4** 20
Sopur, India **C2** 40
Sorel, P.Q., Can. **C4** 90
Sorgun, Tur. **C6** 44
Soria, Spain **G5** 16
Soroca, Mol. **E10** 20
Sorocaba, Braz. **F2** 74
Soročinsk, Russia **D9** 22
Sorong, Indon. **D8** 36
Soroti, Ug. **C6** 54
Sørøya, i., Nor. **A10** 10
Sorrento, La., U.S. **D5** 111
Sør Rondane Mountains, mts., Ant. **D7** 67
Sorsele, Swe. **D7** 10
Sorsogon, Phil. **D8** 34
Sort, Spain **F7** 16
Sortavala, Russia **F14** 10
Sosnogorsk, Russia **B9** 22
Sosnovka, Russia **A7** 22
Sosnovo-Ozërskoe, Russia **A10** 28
Sosnowiec, Pol. **D5** 20
Sos'va, Russia **B11** 22
Sotouboua, Togo **E5** 50
Soubré, C. Iv. **E3** 50
Soucook, stm., N.H., U.S. **D4** 122
Soudan, Mn., U.S. **C6** 116
Souderton, Pa., U.S. **F11** 131
Souhegan, stm., N.H., U.S. **E3** 122
Sŏul (Seoul), S. Kor. **D13** 28
Souq Ahras, Alg. **F1** 18
Sources, Mont-aux-, mtn., Afr. **D4** 56
Soure, Braz. **B2** 74
Souris, Mb., Can. **E1** 86
Souris, P.E., Can. **C7** 87
Souris, stm., N.A. **B7** 92
Sousa, Braz. **C4** 74
Sousse, Tun. **C7** 48
South, stm., Ia., U.S. **C4** 108
South, stm., N.C., U.S. **C4** 126
South Acton, Ma., U.S. **g10** 114
South Africa, ctry., Afr. **E3** 56
South Amboy, N.J., U.S. **C4** 123
South America **G9** 4
South Amherst, Ma., U.S. **B2** 114
South Amherst, Oh., U.S. **A3** 128
Southampton, On., Can. **C3** 89
Southampton, Eng., U.K. **E6** 12
Southampton, N.Y., U.S. **n16** 125
Southampton, co., Va., U.S. **D5** 139
South Andaman, i., India **G6** 40
South Anna, stm., Va., U.S. **C5** 139
South Australia, state, Austl. **F5** 60
South Australian Basin **L16** 64
Southaven, Ms., U.S. **A3** 117
South Bald Mountain, mtn., Co., U.S. **A5** 99
South Baldy, mtn., N.M., U.S. **D2** 124

Name | Map Ref. | Page

South Barre, Vt., U.S. C3 138
South Bay, Fl., U.S. F6 102
South Beloit, Il., U.S. A4 106
South Bend, In., U.S. A5 107
South Bend, Wa., U.S. C2 140
South Berwick, Me., U.S. E2 112
South Bloomfield, Oh., U.S. C3 128
South Boston, Va., U.S. D4 139
South Bound Brook, N.J., U.S. B3 123
South Branch Lake, l., Me., U.S. C4 112
Southbridge, Ma., U.S. B3 114
South Bristol, Me., U.S. E3 112
South Britain, Ct., U.S. D3 100
South Broadway, Wa., U.S. C5 140
South Burlington, Vt., U.S. C2 138
Southbury, Ct., U.S. D3 100
South Carolina, state, U.S. D6 133
South Charleston, Oh., U.S. C2 128
South Charleston, W.V., U.S. C3 141
South Chicago Heights, Il., U.S. m9 106
South China Basin G14 64
South China Sea, Asia D5 32
South Coffeyville, Ok., U.S. A6 129
South Congaree, S.C., U.S. D5 133
South Connellsville, Pa., U.S. G2 131
South Dakota, state, U.S. C5 134
South Dartmouth, Ma., U.S. C6 114
South Daytona, Fl., U.S. C5 102
South Deerfield, Ma., U.S. B2 114
South Dennis, Ma., U.S. C7 114
South Duxbury, Ma., U.S. B6 114
South East Cape, c., Austl. I4 62
Southeast Cape, c., Ak., U.S. C6 95
Southeast Indian Ridge M13 64
South Easton, Ma., U.S. B5 114
Southeast Pacific Basin O25 64
Southeast Pass, strt., La., U.S. E7 111
South East Point, c., Austl. H4 62
Southeast Point, c., R.I., U.S. h7 132
South Elgin, Il., U.S. B5 106
Southend-on-Sea, Eng., U.K. E7 12
Southern Alps, mts., N.Z. p13 63c
Southern Cook Islands, is., Cook Is. F13 58
Southern Cross, Austl. G2 60
Southern Indian Lake, l., Mb., Can. f8 86
Southern Ocean J19 4
Southern Pines, N.C., U.S. B3 126
Southern Ute Indian Reservation, Co., U.S. D2 99
South Euclid, Oh., U.S. g9 128
Southey, Sk., Can. G3 91
South Fabius, stm., Mo., U.S. A5 118
South Fallsburg, N.Y., U.S. D6 125
Southfield, Mi., U.S. o15 115
South Fiji Basin K20 64
South Fork, Pa., U.S. F4 131
South Fox Island, i., Mi., U.S. C5 115
South Fulton, Tn., U.S. A3 135
South Gastonia, N.C., U.S. B1 126
South Gate, Ca., U.S. n12 98
Southgate, Ky., U.S. h14 110
Southgate, Mi., U.S. p15 115
South Georgia, i., S. Geor. H9 69
South Glastonbury, Ct., U.S. C5 100
South Glens Falls, N.Y., U.S. B7 125
South Grafton, Ma., U.S. B4 114
South Grand, stm., Mo., U.S. C3 118
South Hadley, Ma., U.S. B2 114
South Hadley Falls, Ma., U.S. B2 114
South Hamilton, Ma., U.S. A6 114
South Haven, In., U.S. A3 107
South Haven, Mi., U.S. F4 115
South Hero Island, i., Vt., U.S. B2 138
South Hill, Va., U.S. D4 139
South Hingham, Ma., U.S. h12 114
South Holland, Il., U.S. k9 106
South Holston Lake, res., U.S. A9 135
South Honshu Ridge E16 64
South Hooksett, N.H., U.S. D4 122
South Hopkinton, R.I., U.S. F1 132
South Houston, Tx., U.S. r14 136
South Hutchinson, Ks., U.S. f11 109
South Indian Basin N12 64
South Indian Lake, Mb., Can. A2 86
Southington, Ct., U.S. C4 100
South International Falls, Mn., U.S. B5 116
South Island, i., N.Z. I10 58
South Island, i., S.C., U.S. E9 133
South Jacksonville, Il., U.S. D3 106
South Jordan, Ut., U.S. C3 137
South Kenosha, Wi., U.S. F6 142
South Korea see Korea, South, ctry., Asia D10 28
South Lake Tahoe, Ca., U.S. C4 98
South Lancaster, Ma., U.S. B4 114
South Lebanon, Oh., U.S. C1 128
South Lyon, Mi., U.S. F7 115
South Magnetic Pole C18 67
South Manitou Island, i., Mi., U.S. C4 115
South Marsh Island, i., Md., U.S. D5 113
South Miami, Fl., U.S. G6 102
South Miami Heights, Fl., U.S. s13 102
South Mills, N.C., U.S. A6 126
South Milwaukee, Wi., U.S. F6 142
Southmont, N.C., U.S. B2 126
South Moose Lake, l., Mb., Can. C1 86
South Mountain, mtn., Id., U.S. G2 105
South Mountain, mtn., N.M., U.S. k8 124
South Mountains, mts., Az., U.S. m8 96
South Mountains, mts., N.C., U.S. B1 126
South New River Canal, Fl., U.S. r3 102
South Ogden, Ut., U.S. B4 137
Southold, N.Y., U.S. m16 125
South Orange, N.J., U.S. B4 123
South Orkney Islands, is., Ant. C36 67
South Paris, Me., U.S. D2 112
South Park, val., Co., U.S. B5 99
South Pass, Wy., U.S. D4 143
South Pass, strt., La., U.S. F6 111
South Patrick Shores, Fl., U.S. D6 102
South Pekin, Il., U.S. C4 106
South Pittsburg, Tn., U.S. D8 135
South Plainfield, N.J., U.S. B4 123
South Platte, stm., U.S. C7 92
South Point, c., Mi., U.S. D7 115
South Pole E35 67
Southport (Gold Coast), Austl. F5 62
Southport, Fl., U.S. u16 102
Southport, In., U.S. E5 107
Southport, N.C., U.S. D4 126
Southport, N.Y., U.S. C4 125
South Portland, Me., U.S. E2 112
South Portsmouth, Ky., U.S. B6 110
South Range, Mi., U.S. A2 115
South River, On., Can. B5 89
South River, N.J., U.S. C4 123
South River, b., Md., U.S. C4 113
South Royalton, Vt., U.S. D3 138
South Saint Paul, Mn., U.S. n12 116
South Sandwich Islands, is., S. Geor. B2 67
South Sandwich Trench N11 66
South San Francisco, Ca., U.S. h8 98
South Shetland Islands, is., Ant. B35 67
Southside, Al., U.S. B3 94
Southside Place, Tx., U.S. r14 136
South Sioux City, Ne., U.S. B9 120
South Skunk, stm., Ia., U.S. C4 108
South Streator, Il., U.S. B5 106
South Taranaki Bight, b., N.Z. o13 63c
South Tasman Rise M17 64
South Toms River, N.J., U.S. D4 123
South Torrington, Wy., U.S. D8 143
South Tucson, Az., U.S. E5 96
South Venice, Fl., U.S. E4 102
South Ventana Cone, vol., Ca., U.S. D3 98
South Waverly, Pa., U.S. C8 131
South Wellfleet, Ma., U.S. C8 114
South Wellington, B.C., Can. f12 85
South Wenatchee, Wa., U.S. B5 140
South West Africa see Namibia, ctry., Afr. C2 56
South West Cape, c., N.Z. q12 63c
Southwest Channel, strt., Fl., U.S. E4 102
South West City, Mo., U.S. E3 118
Southwest Harbor, Me., U.S. D4 112
Southwest Head, c., N.B., Can. E3 87
Southwest Indian Ridge L8 64
Southwest Miramichi, stm., N.B., Can. C3 87
Southwest Pacific Basin L23 64
Southwest Pass, strt., La., U.S. E3 111
Southwest Pass, strt., La., U.S. F6 111
Southwest Point, c., R.I., U.S. h7 132
South Weymouth Naval Air Station, mil., Ma., U.S. h12 114
South Whitley, In., U.S. B6 107
South Williamson, Ky., U.S. C7 110
South Williamsport, Pa., U.S. D7 131
South Windham, Ct., U.S. C7 100
South Windham, Me., U.S. E2 112
South Windsor, Ct., U.S. B5 100
Southwood Acres, Ct., U.S. A5 100
South Woodstock, Ct., U.S. B8 100
South Yarmouth, Ma., U.S. C7 114
South Zanesville, Oh., U.S. C3 128
Sovetsk, Russia I9 10
Sovetsk, Russia C8 22
Sovetskaja Gavan', Russia E16 26
Soviets'kyi, Ukr. G13 20
Soyo, Ang. E2 54
Sozh, stm., Eur. C11 20
Spain, ctry., Eur. H5 16
Spalding, co., Ga., U.S. C2 103
Spanaway, Wa., U.S. B3 140
Spangler, Pa., U.S. E4 131
Spaniard's Bay, Nf., Can. E5 88
Spanish Fork, Ut., U.S. C4 137
Spanish Fort, Al., U.S. E2 94
Spanish Lake, Mo., U.S. f13 118
Spanish Peak, mtn., Or., U.S. C7 130
Spanish Sahara see Western Sahara, dep., Afr. B2 50
Spanish Town, Jam. B4 80
Sparks, Ga., U.S. E3 103
Sparks, Nv., U.S. D2 121
Sparta, Ga., U.S. C4 103
Sparta, Il., U.S. E4 106
Sparta, Mi., U.S. E5 115
Sparta, Mo., U.S. D4 118
Sparta, N.C., U.S. A1 126
Sparta (Lake Mohawk), N.J., U.S. A3 123
Sparta, Tn., U.S. D8 135
Sparta, Wi., U.S. E3 142
Spartanburg, S.C., U.S. B4 133
Spartanburg, co., S.C., U.S. B3 133
Spárti, Grc. F9 18
Spartivento, Capo, c., Italy E2 18
Sparwood, B.C., Can. E10 85
Spassk-Dal'nij, Russia E15 26
Spavinaw Creek, stm., Ok., U.S. A7 129
Spear, Cape, c., Nf., Can. E5 88
Spearfish, S.D., U.S. C2 134
Spearman, Tx., U.S. A2 136
Spearville, Ks., U.S. E4 109
Speed, In., U.S. H6 107
Speedway, In., U.S. E5 107
Speke Gulf, b., Tan. D6 54
Spence Bay see Taloyoak, Nu., Can. E21 82
Spencer, Ia., U.S. A2 108
Spencer, In., U.S. F4 107
Spencer, Ma., U.S. B4 114
Spencer, N.C., U.S. B2 126
Spencer, Tn., U.S. D8 135
Spencer, W.V., U.S. C3 141
Spencer, Wi., U.S. D3 142
Spencer, co., In., U.S. H4 107
Spencer, co., Ky., U.S. B4 110
Spencer, Cape, c., Austl. H2 62
Spencer, Cape, c., Ak., U.S. k21 95
Spencer Gulf, b., Austl. G2 62
Spencer Lake, l., Me., U.S. C2 112
Spencerport, N.Y., U.S. B3 125
Spencerville, Md., U.S. B4 113
Spencerville, Oh., U.S. B1 128
Sperry, Ok., U.S. A6 129
Spesutie Island, i., Md., U.S. B5 113
Speyer, Ger. F11 12
Spezia see La Spezia, Italy B2 18
Spiceland, In., U.S. E7 107
Spicer, Mn., U.S. E4 116
Spider Lake, l., Wi., U.S. B2 142
Spindale, N.C., U.S. B1 126
Spink, co., S.D., U.S. C7 134
Spirit Lake, Ia., U.S. A2 108
Spirit Lake, Id., U.S. B2 105
Spirit Lake, l., Ia., U.S. A2 108
Spirit Lake, l., Wa., U.S. C3 140
Spirit River, Ab., Can. B1 84
Spirit River Flowage, res., Wi., U.S. C4 142
Spiro, Ok., U.S. B7 129
Spišská Nová Ves, Slvk. E6 20
Spitsbergen, i., Nor. B3 26
Spittal an der Drau, Aus. G13 12
Split, Cro. C6 18
Split, Cape, c., N.S., Can. D5 87
Split Lake, l., Mb., Can. A4 86
Split Rock Creek, stm., U.S. G2 116
Spofford Lake, l., N.H., U.S. E2 122
Spokane, Wa., U.S. B8 140
Spokane, co., Wa., U.S. B8 140
Spokane, stm., U.S. B8 140
Spokane, Mount, mtn., Wa., U.S. B8 140
Spokane Indian Reservation, Wa., U.S. B8 140
Spoleto, Italy C4 18
Spoon, stm., Il., U.S. C3 106
Spooner, Wi., U.S. C2 142
Spooner Lake, l., Wi., U.S. C2 142
Spornoe, Russia C17 26
Spotswood, N.J., U.S. C4 123
Spotsylvania, co., Va., U.S. B5 139
Sprague, W.V., U.S. n13 141
Sprague, stm., Or., U.S. E5 130
Sprague Lake, l., Wa., U.S. B7 140
Spratly Islands, is., Asia E6 34
Spring, stm., Ar., U.S. A4 97
Spring Arbor, Mi., U.S. F6 115
Spring Bay, b., Ut., U.S. B3 137
Springbok, S. Afr. D2 56
Springboro, Oh., U.S. C1 128
Spring Brook, stm., Pa., U.S. n18 131
Spring City, Pa., U.S. F10 131
Spring City, Tn., U.S. D9 135
Spring City, Ut., U.S. D4 137
Spring Creek, stm., N.D., U.S. B3 127
Spring Creek, stm., Nv., U.S. C4 121
Spring Creek, stm., U.S. D4 120
Springdale, Nf., Can. D3 88
Springdale, Ar., U.S. A1 97
Springdale, Oh., U.S. n13 128
Springdale, Pa., U.S. E2 131
Springdale, S.C., U.S. D5 133
Springer, N.M., U.S. A5 124
Springerville, Az., U.S. C6 96
Springfield, Co., U.S. D8 99
Springfield, Fl., U.S. u16 102
Springfield, Ga., U.S. D5 103
Springfield, Il., U.S. D4 106
Springfield, Ky., U.S. C4 110
Springfield, Ma., U.S. B2 114
Springfield, Mn., U.S. F4 116
Springfield, Mo., U.S. D4 118
Springfield, Ne., U.S. C9 120
Springfield, N.J., U.S. B4 123
Springfield, Oh., U.S. C2 128
Springfield, Or., U.S. C4 130
Springfield, Pa., U.S. p20 131
Springfield, S.D., U.S. E8 134
Springfield, Tn., U.S. A5 135
Springfield, Va., U.S. g12 139
Springfield, Vt., U.S. E4 138
Springfield, Lake, res., Il., U.S. D4 106
Springfontein, S. Afr. E4 56
Spring Garden, Guy. B8 70
Spring Glen, Ut., U.S. D5 137
Spring Green, Wi., U.S. E3 142
Spring Grove, Il., U.S. h8 106
Spring Grove, Mn., U.S. G7 116
Spring Grove, Pa., U.S. G8 131
Spring Hill, Fl., U.S. D4 102
Spring Hill, Ks., U.S. D9 109
Springhill, La., U.S. A2 111
Spring Hill, Tn., U.S. B5 135
Spring Hope, N.C., U.S. B4 126
Spring Island, i., S.C., U.S. G6 133
Spring Lake, Mi., U.S. E4 115
Spring Lake, N.C., U.S. B4 126
Spring Lake, N.J., U.S. C4 123
Spring Lake, l., Me., U.S. C2 112
Spring Lake, res., U.S. B3 106
Spring Lake Heights, N.J., U.S. C4 123
Spring Mountains, mts., Nv., U.S. G6 121
Springport, Mi., U.S. F6 115
Springs, S. Afr. D4 56
Springside, Sk., Can. F4 91
Springsure, Austl. E4 62
Springvale, Me., U.S. E2 112
Spring Valley, Ca., U.S. o16 98
Spring Valley, Il., U.S. B4 106
Spring Valley, Mn., U.S. G6 116
Spring Valley, N.Y., U.S. g12 125
Spring Valley, Wi., U.S. D1 142
Springville, Al., U.S. B3 94
Springville, Ia., U.S. B6 108
Springville, N.Y., U.S. C2 125
Springville, Ut., U.S. C4 137
Spruce Fork, stm., W.V., U.S. m12 141
Spruce Grove, Ab., Can. C4 84
Spruce Knob, mtn., W.V., U.S. C6 141
Spruce Knob-Seneca Rocks National Recreation Area, W.V., U.S. C5 141
Spruce Mountain, mtn., Az., U.S. C3 96
Spruce Mountain, mtn., Nv., U.S. C7 121
Spruce Pine, N.C., U.S. f10 126
Spruce Run Reservoir, res., N.J., U.S. B3 123
Spur, Tx., U.S. C2 136
Spurr, Mount, mtn., Ak., U.S. g15 95
Squam Lake, l., N.H., U.S. C4 122
Squapan Lake, l., Me., U.S. B4 112
Square Lake, l., Me., U.S. A4 112
Squatec, P.Q., Can. B9 90
Squaw Cap Mountain, mtn., N.B., Can. B3 87
Squaw Hill, mtn., Wy., U.S. E7 143
Squaw Peak, mtn., Mt., U.S. C2 119
Squibnocket Point, c., Ma., U.S. D6 114
Squillace, Golfo di, b., Italy E6 18
Squire, W.V., U.S. D3 141
Srbija (Serbia), prov., Yugo. B8 18
Srbobran, Yugo. B7 18
Sredinnyj hrebet, mts., Russia D17 26
Srednee Kujto, ozero, l., Russia D14 10
Srednekolymsk, Russia C17 26
Srednerusskaja vozvyšennost', plat., Russia D5 26
Srednesibirskoe ploskogor'e, plat., Russia C12 26
Śrem, Pol. C4 20
Sremska Mitrovica, Yugo. B7 18
Sretensk, Russia D13 26
Sri Jayawardenepura, Sri L. H4 40
Srīkākulam, India F4 40
Sri Kālahasti, India G3 40
Sri Lanka, ctry., Asia H4 40
Srīnagar, India C2 40
Stack Reservoir, res., R.I., U.S. C3 132
Stade, Ger. D11 12
Stafford, Eng., U.K. D5 12
Stafford, Ks., U.S. E5 109
Stafford, Va., U.S. B5 139
Stafford, co., Ks., U.S. D5 109
Stafford, co., Va., U.S. B5 139
Stafford Pond, l., R.I., U.S. D6 132
Stafford Springs, Ct., U.S. B6 100
Staked Plain see Estacado, Llano, pl., U.S. E7 92
Stakhanov, Ukr. E15 20
Stalin see Varna, Bul. C11 18
Stalingrad see Volgograd, Russia E6 26
Stalinogorsk see Novomoskovsk, Russia D5 26
Stalinsk see Novokuzneck, Russia D10 26
Stalowa Wola, Pol. D7 20
Stambaugh, Mi., U.S. B2 115
Stamford, Ct., U.S. E1 100
Stamford, Tx., U.S. C3 136
Stamford, Vt., U.S. F2 138
Stamford, Lake, res., Tx., U.S. C3 136
Stamping Ground, Ky., U.S. B5 110
Stampriet, Nmb. C2 56
Stamps, Ar., U.S. D2 97
Stanaford, W.V., U.S. D3 141
Stanberry, Mo., U.S. A3 118
Standerton, S. Afr. D4 56
Standing Rock Indian Reservation, U.S. B4 134
Standish, Mi., U.S. E7 115
Stanfield, Az., U.S. E3 96
Stanfield, Or., U.S. B7 130
Stanford, Ky., U.S. C5 110
Stanhope, N.J., U.S. B3 123
Stanislaus, co., Ca., U.S. D3 98
Stanley, Falk. Is. H5 69
Stanley, N.C., U.S. B1 126
Stanley, N.D., U.S. A3 127
Stanley, Va., U.S. B4 139
Stanley, Wi., U.S. D3 142
Stanley, co., S.D., U.S. C5 134
Stanley Falls, wtfl, D.R.C. C5 54
Stanley Reservoir, res., India G3 40
Stanleytown, Va., U.S. D3 139
Stanleyville, N.C., U.S. A2 126
Stanly, co., N.C., U.S. B2 126
Stanovoe nagor'e, mts., Russia D13 26
Stanovoj hrebet, mts., Russia D14 26
Stanovoy Mountains see Stanovoe nagor'e, mts., Russia D13 26
Stanstead, P.Q., Can. D5 90
Stanthorpe, Austl. F5 62
Stanton, Ia., U.S. D2 108
Stanton, Ky., U.S. C6 110
Stanton, Mi., U.S. E5 115
Stanton, Ne., U.S. C8 120
Stanton, Tx., U.S. C2 136
Stanton, co., Ks., U.S. E2 109
Stanton, co., Ne., U.S. C8 120
Stantonsburg, N.C., U.S. B5 126
Stanwood, Ia., U.S. C6 108
Stanwood, Wa., U.S. A3 140
Staples, Mn., U.S. D4 116
Stapleton, Al., U.S. E2 94
Star, Id., U.S. F2 105
Star, N.C., U.S. B3 126
Staraja Russa, Russia C5 22
Stara Planina (Balkan Mountains), mts., Eur. C9 18
Stara Zagora, Bul. C10 18
Starbuck, Mn., U.S. E3 116
Starbuck, i., Kir. E14 58
Star City, Ar., U.S. D4 97
Star City, W.V., U.S. B5 141
Stargard Szczeciński, Pol. C3 20
Stargo, Az., U.S. D6 96
Stark, co., Il., U.S. B4 106
Stark, co., N.D., U.S. C3 127
Stark, co., Oh., U.S. B4 128
Starke, Fl., U.S. C4 102
Starke, co., In., U.S. B4 107
Starks, La., U.S. D2 111
Starkville, Ms., U.S. B5 117
Star Lake, l., Mn., U.S. D3 116
Starobil's'k, Ukr. E15 20
Starodub, Russia C12 20
Starogard Gdański, Pol. C5 20
Star Peak, mtn., Nv., U.S. C3 121
Starr, co., Tx., U.S. F3 136
Startex, S.C., U.S. B3 133
Staryj Oskol, Russia D5 26
State Center, Ia., U.S. B4 108
State College, Pa., U.S. E6 131
Stateline, Nv., U.S. E2 121
State Line, Pa., U.S. G6 131
Staten Island see Estados, Isla de los, i., Arg. H4 69
Staten Island, i., N.Y., U.S. k12 125
Statenville, Ga., U.S. F4 103
Statesboro, Ga., U.S. D5 103
Statesville, N.C., U.S. B2 126
Statham, Ga., U.S. C3 103
Statue of Liberty National Monument, N.J., U.S. k8 123

Name — Map Ref. — Page

Staunton, Il., U.S. D4 106
Staunton, Va., U.S. B3 139
Staunton, stm., U.S. D12 92
Stavanger, Nor. G1 10
Stavropol see Toljatti, Russia D6 26
Stavropol', Russia E6 26
Stawell, Austl. H3 62
Stayner, On., Can. C4 89
Stayton, Or., U.S. C4 130
Steamboat, Nv., U.S. D2 121
Steamboat Mountain, mtn., Mt., U.S. C4 119
Steamboat Mountain, mtn., Wy., U.S. E4 143
Steamboat Springs, Co., U.S. A4 99
Stearns, Ky., U.S. D5 110
Stearns, co., Mn., U.S. E4 116
Stearns Brook, stm., N.H., U.S. A4 122
Stebbins, Ak., U.S. C7 95
Steele, Al., U.S. B3 94
Steele, Mo., U.S. E8 118
Steele, N.D., U.S. C6 127
Steele, co., Mn., U.S. F5 116
Steele, co., N.D., U.S. B8 127
Steele, Mount, mtn., Wy., U.S. E6 143
Steeleville, Il., U.S. E4 106
Steelton, Pa., U.S. F8 131
Steelville, Mo., U.S. D6 118
Steens Mountain, mts., Or., U.S. E8 130
Stefanie, Lake, l., Afr. C7 54
Steger, Il., U.S. B6 106
Steilacoom, Wa., U.S. f10 140
Steinbach, Mb., Can. E3 86
Steinhatchee, stm., Fl., U.S. C3 102
Steinkjer, Nor. E4 10
Steinkopf, S. Afr. D2 56
Stellenbosch, S. Afr. E2 56
Stendal, Ger. D12 12
Stepanakert see Xankändi, Azer. C12 44
Stephen, Mn., U.S. B2 116
Stephens, Ar., U.S. D2 97
Stephens, co., Ga., U.S. B3 103
Stephens, co., Ok., U.S. C4 129
Stephens, co., Tx., U.S. C3 136
Stephens City, Va., U.S. A4 139
Stephens Lake, res., Mb., Can. A4 86
Stephenson, Mi., U.S. C3 115
Stephenson, co., Il., U.S. A4 106
Stephens Passage, strt., Ak., U.S. m23 95
Stephenville, Nf., Can. D2 88
Stephenville, Tx., U.S. C3 136
Stephenville Crossing, Nf., Can. D2 88
Sterkstroom, S. Afr. E4 56
Sterling, Ak., U.S. g16 95
Sterling, Co., U.S. A7 99
Sterling, Il., U.S. B4 106
Sterling, Ks., U.S. D5 109
Sterling, Ok., U.S. C3 129
Sterling, Va., U.S. A5 139
Sterling, co., Tx., U.S. D2 136
Sterling City, Tx., U.S. D2 136
Sterling Heights, Mi., U.S. o15 115
Sterling Reservoir, res., Co., U.S. A7 99
Sterlington, La., U.S. B3 111
Sterlitamak, Russia D7 26
Stettler, Ab., Can. C4 84
Steuben, co., In., U.S. A7 107
Steuben, co., N.Y., U.S. C3 125
Steubenville, Oh., U.S. B5 128
Stevens, co., Ks., U.S. E2 109
Stevens, co., Mn., U.S. E3 116
Stevens, co., Wa., U.S. A7 140
Stevens Creek Dam, U.S. C4 103
Stevenson, Al., U.S. A4 94
Stevenson, Ct., U.S. D3 100
Stevenson, Wa., U.S. D4 140
Stevenson Lake, l., Mb., Can. C4 86
Stevens Pass, Wa., U.S. B4 140
Stevens Peak, mtn., Id., U.S. B3 105
Stevens Point, Wi., U.S. D4 142
Stevensville, Md., U.S. C5 113
Stevensville, Mi., U.S. F4 115
Stevensville, Mt., U.S. D2 119
Stewart, co., Ga., U.S. D2 103
Stewart, co., Tn., U.S. A4 135
Stewart Island, i., N.Z. q12 63c
Stewart Mountain, mtn., Az., U.S. k9 96
Stewartstown, Pa., U.S. G8 131
Stewartsville, Mo., U.S. B3 118
Stewartville, Mn., U.S. G6 116
Stewiacke, N.S., Can. D6 87
Steyr, Aus. F14 12
Stigler, Ok., U.S. B6 129
Stikine, stm., Ak., U.S. D13 95
Still, stm., Ct., U.S. B3 100
Stillaguamish, North Fork, stm., Wa., U.S. A4 140
Stillaguamish, South Fork, stm., Wa., U.S. A4 140
Stillhouse Hollow Lake, res., Tx., U.S. D4 136
Stillman Valley, Il., U.S. A4 106
Stillmore, Ga., U.S. D4 103
Stillwater, Mn., U.S. E6 116
Stillwater, Ok., U.S. A4 129
Stillwater, co., Mt., U.S. E7 119
Stillwater Range, mts., Nv., U.S. D3 121
Stillwater Reservoir, res., N.Y., U.S. B5 125
Stillwater Reservoir, res., R.I., U.S. B3 132
Stilwell, Ok., U.S. B7 129
Stimson, Mount, mtn., Mt., U.S. B3 119
Stine Mountain, mtn., Mt., U.S. E3 119
Stinking Lake, l., N.M., U.S. A3 124
Stinnett, Tx., U.S. B2 136
Štip, Mac. D9 18
Stirling, Austl. G2 60
Stirling, Austl. E5 60
Stirling, Ab., Can. E4 84
Stirling, On., Can. C7 89
Stockbridge, Ga., U.S. C2 103
Stockbridge, Mi., U.S. F6 115
Stockbridge-Munsee Indian Reservation, Wi., U.S. D5 142
Stockdale, Tx., U.S. E4 136
Stockholm, Swe. G8 10
Stockton, Ca., U.S. D3 98
Stockton, Il., U.S. A3 106
Stockton, Ks., U.S. C4 109
Stockton, Md., U.S. D7 113
Stockton, Mo., U.S. D4 118
Stockton Island, i., Wi., U.S. B3 142
Stockton Lake, res., Mo., U.S. D4 118
Stoddard, Wi., U.S. E2 142
Stoddard, co., Mo., U.S. E8 118
Stœng Trêng, Camb. D5 34
Stoke-on-Trent, Eng., U.K. D5 12
Stokes, co., N.C., U.S. A2 126
Stokesdale, N.C., U.S. A3 126
Stolbovoj, ostrov, i., Russia B15 26
Stolin, Bela. D9 20
Stollings, W.V., U.S. n12 141
Stone, co., Ar., U.S. B3 97
Stone, co., Mo., U.S. E4 118
Stone, co., Ms., U.S. E4 117
Stoneboro, Pa., U.S. D1 131
Stone Corral Lake, l., Or., U.S. E7 130
Stoneham, Ma., U.S. g11 114
Stonehaven, Scot., U.K. B5 12
Stonehenge, hist., Eng., U.K. E6 12
Stone Mountain, Ga., U.S. C2 103
Stone Mountain, mtn., Ga., U.S. C2 103
Stones River National Battlefield, hist., Tn., U.S. B4 135
Stoneville, N.C., U.S. A3 126
Stonewall, Mb., Can. D3 86
Stonewall, La., U.S. B2 111
Stonewall, Ms., U.S. C5 117
Stonewall, co., Tx., U.S. C2 136
Stonewood, W.V., U.S. k10 141
Stoney Creek, On., Can. D5 89
Stonington, Ct., U.S. D8 100
Stonington, Il., U.S. D4 106
Stonington, Me., U.S. D4 112
Stono, stm., S.C., U.S. k11 133
Stono Inlet, b., S.C., U.S. F8 133
Stony Brook, N.Y., U.S. n15 125
Stony Brook, stm., N.J., U.S. C3 123
Stony Creek, stm., Va., U.S. C5 139
Stony Island, i., N.Y., U.S. B4 125
Stony Plain, Ab., Can. C3 84
Stony Point, N.C., U.S. B1 126
Storavan, l., Swe. D8 10
Storebælt, strt., Den. I4 10
Storey, co., Nv., U.S. D2 121
Storlien, Swe. E5 10
Storm Bay, b., Austl. I4 62
Storm Lake, Ia., U.S. B2 108
Storm Lake, l., Ia., U.S. B2 108
Storm Mountain, mtn., Ak., U.S. h16 95
Stornoway, Scot., U.K. A3 12
Storrs, Ct., U.S. B7 100
Storsjön, l., Swe. E6 10
Storslett, Nor. B9 10
Storuman, Swe. D7 10
Storuman, l., Swe. D7 10
Story, Wy., U.S. B6 143
Story, co., Ia., U.S. B4 108
Story City, Ia., U.S. B4 108
Stoubcy, Bela. C9 20
Stoughton, Sk., Can. H4 91
Stoughton, Ma., U.S. B5 114
Stoughton, Wi., U.S. F4 142
Stover, Mo., U.S. C5 118
Stow, Oh., U.S. A4 128
Stow Creek, stm., N.J., U.S. E2 123
Stowe, Pa., U.S. F10 131
Stowe, Vt., U.S. C3 138
Stoyoma Mountain, mtn., B.C., Can. E7 85
Strabane, Pa., U.S. F1 131
Strafford, Mo., U.S. D4 118
Strafford, co., N.H., U.S. D4 122
Straffordville, On., Can. E4 89
Strakonice, Czech Rep. E2 20
Stralsund, Ger. C13 12
Strand, S. Afr. E2 56
Stranraer, Scot., U.K. C4 12
Strasbourg, Fr. C10 16
Strasburg, Co., U.S. B6 99
Strasburg, Oh., U.S. B4 128
Strasburg, Pa., U.S. G9 131
Strasburg, Va., U.S. B4 139
Stratford, On., Can. D3 89
Stratford, N.Z. o13 63c
Stratford, Ct., U.S. E3 100
Stratford, Ia., U.S. B4 108
Stratford, N.J., U.S. D2 123
Stratford, Ok., U.S. C5 129
Stratford, Tx., U.S. A1 136
Stratford, Wi., U.S. D3 142
Stratford Point, c., Ct., U.S. E3 100
Stratham, N.H., U.S. D5 122
Strathmore, Ab., Can. D4 84
Strathmore, Ca., U.S. D4 98
Strathroy, On., Can. E3 89
Stratton, Co., U.S. B8 99
Straubing, Ger. F13 12
Strawberry, stm., Ar., U.S. A4 97
Strawberry, stm., Ut., U.S. C5 137
Strawberry Mountain, mtn., Or., U.S. C8 130
Strawberry Point, Ia., U.S. B6 108
Strawberry Point, c., Ma., U.S. B6 114
Strawberry Range, mts., Or., U.S. C8 130
Strawberry Reservoir, res., Ut., U.S. C4 137
Streaky Bay, b., Austl. G5 60
Streator, Il., U.S. B5 106
Strelka-Čunja, Russia C12 26
Strimón (Struma), stm., Eur. D9 18
Strimon, Gulf of see Orfanoú, Kólpos, b., Grc. D9 18
Stromsburg, Ne., U.S. C8 120
Strömsund, Swe. E6 10
Strong, Ar., U.S. D3 97
Strong, Me., U.S. D2 112
Strong, stm., Ms., U.S. C4 117
Strong City, Ks., U.S. D7 109
Stronghurst, Il., U.S. C3 106
Strongsville, Oh., U.S. A4 128
Stroud, Ok., U.S. B5 129
Stroudsburg, Pa., U.S. E11 131
Stroudwater, stm., Me., U.S. g7 112
Strum, Wi., U.S. D2 142
Struma (Strimón), stm., Eur. D9 18
Strumica, Mac. D9 18
Struthers, Oh., U.S. A5 128
Strydenburg, S. Afr. D3 56
Stryi, Ukr. E7 20
Stryker, Oh., U.S. A1 128
Stuart, Fl., U.S. E6 102
Stuart, Ia., U.S. C3 108
Stuart, Ne., U.S. B6 120
Stuart, Va., U.S. D2 139
Stuart, Mount, mtn., Wa., U.S. B5 140
Stuart Lake, l., B.C., Can. B5 85
Stuarts Draft, Va., U.S. B3 139
Stull, stm., Can. B5 86
Stump Lake, l., N.D., U.S. B7 127
Stump Pond, res., R.I., U.S. D2 132
Stupino, Russia B15 20
Sturbridge, Ma., U.S. B3 114
Sturgeon, Mo., U.S. B5 118
Sturgeon, stm., Mi., U.S. B4 115
Sturgeon Bay, Wi., U.S. D6 142
Sturgeon Bay, b., Mb., Can. C3 86
Sturgeon Falls, On., Can. A5 89
Sturgeon Lake, l., On., Can. C6 89
Sturgis, Sk., Can. F4 91
Sturgis, Ky., U.S. e10 110
Sturgis, Mi., U.S. G5 115
Sturgis, S.D., U.S. C2 134
Sturtevant, Wi., U.S. F6 142
Sturt Stony Desert, des., Austl. F3 62
Stutsman, co., N.D., U.S. B6 127
Stutterheim, S. Afr. E4 56
Stuttgart, Ger. F11 12
Stuttgart, Ar., U.S. C4 97
Styr, stm., Eur. D8 20
Su, Kaz. E9 26
Suaita, Col. D5 80
Subarkuduk, Kaz. E10 22
Sūbāṭ, stm., Sudan I11 48
Subei, China B7 40
Sublette, Ks., U.S. E3 109
Sublette, co., Wy., U.S. D2 143
Sublett Range, mts., Id., U.S. G6 105
Sublimity, Or., U.S. C4 130
Subotica, Yugo. A7 18
Sucarnoochee, stm., Al., U.S. C1 94
Succasunna, N.J., U.S. B3 123
Suceava, Rom. F9 20
Sucre, Bol. B4 72
Sud, Canal du, strt., Haiti B5 80
Sudan, ctry., Afr. H10 48
Sudan, reg., Afr. H8 48
Sudbury, On., Can. A4 89
Sudbury, Ma., U.S. B5 114
Sudbury, stm., Ma., U.S. B5 114
Sudbury Center, Ma., U.S. g10 114
Sudbury Reservoir, res., Ma., U.S. g10 114
Suez see El-Suweis, Egypt E11 48
Suez, Gulf of see Suweis, Khalîg el-, b., Egypt F10 14
Suez Canal see Suweis, Qanâ el-, Egypt E10 14
Suffern, N.Y., U.S. D6 125
Suffield, Ct., U.S. B5 100
Suffolk, Va., U.S. D6 139
Suffolk, co., Ma., U.S. B5 114
Suffolk, co., N.Y., U.S. n15 125
Sugar, stm., N.H., U.S. D2 122
Sugar, stm., U.S. F4 142
Sugar City, Id., U.S. F7 105
Sugar Creek, Mo., U.S. h11 118
Sugarcreek, Pa., U.S. D2 131
Sugar Creek, stm., Oh., U.S. C2 128
Sugar Creek, stm., Pa., U.S. C8 131
Sugar Grove, Va., U.S. D1 139
Sugar Hill, Ga., U.S. B2 103
Sugar Island, i., Mi., U.S. B6 115
Sugar Land, Tx., U.S. E5 136
Sugar Loaf, Va., U.S. C3 139
Sugarloaf Mountain, mtn., Mt., U.S. C4 119
Sugar Notch, Pa., U.S. n17 131
Suggi Lake, l., Sk., Can. C4 91
Suğla Gölü, l., Tur. D5 44
Suhag, Egypt E11 48
Suhana, Russia C13 26
Şuḥār, Oman F7 38
Sühbaatar, Mong. A9 28
Suhl, Ger. E12 12
Suhona, stm., Russia C6 26
Suhumi, Geor. A9 44
Suiattle, stm., Wa., U.S. A4 140
Suichang, China D4 30
Suichuan, China D3 30
Suide, China D10 28
Suijiang, China D1 30
Suining, China E9 28
Suining, China C4 30
Suitland, Md., U.S. C4 113
Suixi, China C4 30
Suiyang, China B2 31
Suizhong, China C12 28
Suizhou, China E10 28
Sukabumi, Indon. E3 36
Sukadana, Indon. D3 36
Sukaraja, Indon. D4 36
Sukarnapura see Jayapura, Indon. G11 32
Sukhothai, Thai. C3 34
Sukkertoppen, Grnld. E29 82
Sukkozero, Russia B5 22
Sukkur, Pak. E9 42
Sukses, Nmb. C2 56
Sukumo, Japan D2 31
Sula, Kepulauan, is., Indon. D7 36
Sulaimān Range, mts., Pak. E9 42
Sulawesi (Celebes), i., Indon. D6 36
Sulawesi, Laut see Celebes Sea, Asia C6 36
Sulechów, Pol. C3 20
Sullana, Peru D3 70
Sulligent, Al., U.S. B1 94
Sullivan, Il., U.S. D5 106
Sullivan, In., U.S. F3 107
Sullivan, Mo., U.S. C6 118
Sullivan, co., In., U.S. F3 107
Sullivan, co., Mo., U.S. A4 118
Sullivan, co., N.H., U.S. D2 122
Sullivan, co., N.Y., U.S. D6 125
Sullivan, co., Pa., U.S. D9 131
Sullivan, co., Tn., U.S. C11 135
Sullivan Lake, l., Ab., Can. D5 84
Sullivans Island, S.C., U.S. k12 133
Sully, Ia., U.S. C5 108
Sully, co., S.D., U.S. C5 134
Sulmona, Italy C4 18
Sulphur, La., U.S. D2 111
Sulphur, Ok., U.S. C5 129
Sulphur, stm., U.S. D2 97
Sulphur Spring Range, mts., Nv., U.S. C5 121
Sulphur Springs, Tx., U.S. C5 136
Sultan, Wa., U.S. B4 140
Sultānpur, India D4 40
Sulu Archipelago, is., Phil. F7 34
Sulūq, Libya D9 48
Sulu Sea, Asia E7 34
Sumas, Wa., U.S. A3 140
Sumatera (Sumatra), i., Indon. C2 36
Sumatra see Sumatera, i., Indon. C2 36
Sumba, i., Indon. F5 36
Sumba, Selat, strt., Indon. E6 36
Sumbawa, i., Indon. E5 36
Sumbawa Besar, Indon. E5 36
Sumbawanga, Tan. E6 54
Sumbe, Ang. F2 54
Sumedang, Indon. E3 36
Šumen, Bul. C11 18
Sumenep, Indon. E4 36
Šumerlja, Russia C8 22
Šumiha, Russia C11 22
Sumisu-jima, i., Japan E16 28
Sumiton, Al., U.S. B2 94
Summerfield, N.C., U.S. A3 126
Summerford, Nf., Can. D4 88
Summer Island, i., Mi., U.S. C4 115
Summer Lake, l., Or., U.S. E6 130
Summerland, B.C., Can. E8 85
Summers, co., W.V., U.S. D4 141
Summerside, P.E., Can. C6 87
Summersville, W.V., U.S. C4 141
Summersville Lake, res., W.V., U.S. C4 141
Summerton, S.C., U.S. D7 133
Summertown, Tn., U.S. B4 135
Summerville, Ga., U.S. B1 103
Summerville, S.C., U.S. E7 133
Summit, Il., U.S. k9 106
Summit, Ms., U.S. D3 117
Summit, N.J., U.S. B4 123
Summit, Tn., U.S. h11 135
Summit, co., Co., U.S. B4 99
Summit, co., Oh., U.S. A4 128
Summit, co., Ut., U.S. C5 137
Summit Hill, Pa., U.S. E10 131
Summit Lake, l., Ia., U.S. C3 108
Summit Lake Indian Reservation, Nv., U.S. B2 121
Summit Mountain, mtn., Nv., U.S. D5 121
Summit Peak, mtn., Co., U.S. D4 99
Summitville, In., U.S. D6 107
Sumner, Ia., U.S. B5 108
Sumner, Il., U.S. E6 106
Sumner, Wa., U.S. B3 140
Sumner, co., Ks., U.S. E6 109
Sumner, co., Tn., U.S. A5 135
Sumner, Lake, res., N.M., U.S. C5 124
Sumner Dam, N.M., U.S. C5 124
Sumner Strait, strt., Ak., U.S. m23 95
Šumperk, Czech Rep. E4 20
Sumqayıt, Azer. B13 44
Sumrall, Ms., U.S. D4 117
Šumšu, ostrov, i., Russia D17 26
Sumter, S.C., U.S. D7 133
Sumter, co., Al., U.S. C1 94
Sumter, co., Fl., U.S. D4 102
Sumter, co., Ga., U.S. D2 103
Sumter, co., S.C., U.S. D7 133
Sumy, Ukr. D13 20
Sumzom, China D7 40
Sun, stm., Mt., U.S. C4 119
Sunapee, N.H., U.S. D2 122
Sunapee Lake, l., N.H., U.S. D2 122
Sunbright, Tn., U.S. C9 135
Sunbury, Oh., U.S. B3 128
Sunbury, Pa., U.S. E8 131
Sunchales, Arg. E5 72
Suncho Corral, Arg. D5 72
Sun City, Az., U.S. k8 96
Suncook, N.H., U.S. D4 122
Suncook, stm., N.H., U.S. D4 122
Suncook Lakes, l., N.H., U.S. D4 122
Sunda, Selat, strt., Indon. E3 36
Sundance, Wy., U.S. B8 143
Sundance Mountain, mtn., Wy., U.S. B8 143
Sundarbans, reg., Asia B1 34
Sunda Shelf H13 64
Sunda Strait see Sunda, Selat, strt., Indon. E3 36
Sunderland, On., Can. C5 89
Sunderland, Eng., U.K. C6 12
Sundown, Austl. F5 60
Sundown, Tx., U.S. C1 136
Sundre, Ab., Can. D3 84
Sundridge, On., Can. B5 89
Sundsvall, Swe. E7 10
Sunflower, Ms., U.S. B3 117
Sunflower, co., Ms., U.S. B3 117
Sunflower, Mount, mtn., Ks., U.S. C2 109
Sungaidareh, Indon. D2 36
Sungai Kolok, Thai. E4 34
Sungai Petani, Malay. B2 36
Sungari see Songhua, stm., China B14 28
Sungari Reservoir see Songhua Hu, res., China C13 28
Sungurlu, Tur. B6 44
Sunland Park, N.M., U.S. F3 124
Sunlight Creek, stm., Wy., U.S. B3 143
Sunman, In., U.S. F7 107
Sunne, Swe. G5 10
Sunnyside, Nf., Can. E5 88
Sunnyside, Wa., U.S. C5 140
Sunnyvale, Ca., U.S. k8 98
Sun Prairie, Wi., U.S. E4 142
Sunray, Tx., U.S. A2 136
Sunset, La., U.S. D3 111
Sunset, Ut., U.S. B4 137
Sunset Beach, Hi., U.S. f9 104
Sunset Crater National Monument, Az., U.S. B4 96
Sunset Lake, l., Vt., U.S. D2 138
Sunshine, Austl. H3 62
Suntar, Russia C13 26
Suntar-Hajata, hrebet, mts., Russia C16 26
Suntaug Lake, l., Ma., U.S. f11 114
Sun Valley, Id., U.S. F4 105
Sun Valley, Nv., U.S. D2 121
Sunyani, Ghana E4 50
Suojarvi, Russia B5 22
Suomussalmi, Fin. D13 10
Superior, Az., U.S. D4 96
Superior, Mt., U.S. C2 119
Superior, Ne., U.S. D7 120
Superior, Wi., U.S. B1 142
Superior, Wy., U.S. E4 143
Superior, Lake, l., N.A. B10 92
Superstition Mountains, mts., Az., U.S. m10 96
Suphan Buri, Thai. D4 34

Name — Map Ref. — Page

Suquamish, Wa., U.S. **B3** 140
Suquṭrā, i., Yemen **H6** 38
Ṣūr, Leb. **F6** 44
Ṣūr, Oman **F7** 38
Sur, Point, c., Ca., U.S. **D3** 98
Sura, stm., Russia **E15** 6
Surabaya, Indon. **E4** 36
Surakarta, Indon. **E4** 36
Sūrat, India **E2** 40
Sūratgarh, India **D2** 40
Surat Thani, Thai. **E3** 34
Surendranagar, India **E2** 40
Surfside, Fl., U.S. **s13** 102
Surfside Beach, S.C., U.S. **D10** 133
Surgoinsville, Tn., U.S. **C11** 135
Surgut, Russia **C9** 26
Surigao, Phil. **E9** 34
Surigao Strait, strt., Phil. **E9** 34
Surin, Thai. **D4** 34
Suriname, ctry., S.A. **C8** 70
Surprise, Az., U.S. **k8** 96
Surrey, N.D., U.S. **A4** 127
Surry, co., N.C., U.S. **A2** 126
Surry, co., Va., U.S. **C6** 139
Surry Mountain Lake, res., N.H., U.S. **D2** 122
Surt, Libya **B8** 48
Surt, Khalīj, b., Libya **B8** 48
Sürüç, Tur. **D8** 44
Surulangun, Indon. **D2** 36
Šuryškary, Russia **A12** 22
Sūsangerd, Iran **G13** 44
Susanville, Ca., U.S. **B3** 98
Suşehri, Tur. **B8** 44
Susitna, stm., Ak., U.S. **C10** 95
Susquehanna, Pa., U.S. **C10** 131
Susquehanna, co., Pa., U.S. **C10** 131
Susquehanna, stm., U.S. **A5** 113
Susquehanna, West Branch, stm., Pa., U.S. **D5** 131
Sussex, N.B., Can. **D4** 87
Sussex, N.J., U.S. **A3** 123
Sussex, Wi., U.S. **m11** 142
Sussex, co., De., U.S. **F4** 101
Sussex, co., N.J., U.S. **A3** 123
Sussex, co., Va., U.S. **D5** 139
Susuman, Russia **C16** 26
Susurluk, Tur. **C3** 44
Sutherland, S. Afr. **E3** 56
Sutherland, Ia., U.S. **B2** 108
Sutherland, Ne., U.S. **C4** 120
Sutherlin, Or., U.S. **D3** 130
Sutlej (Satluj), stm., Asia **D2** 40
Sutter, co., Ca., U.S. **C3** 98
Sutter Creek, Ca., U.S. **C3** 98
Sutton, P.Q., Can. **D5** 90
Sutton, Ne., U.S. **D8** 120
Sutton, W.V., U.S. **C4** 141
Sutton, co., Tx., U.S. **D2** 136
Sutton Lake, res., W.V., U.S. **C4** 141
Sutwik Island, i., Ak., U.S. **D8** 95
Süüj, Mong. **B8** 28
Suur Munamägi, hill, Est. **H12** 10
Suva, Fiji **F11** 58
Suwałki, Pol. **B7** 20
Suwanee, Ga., U.S. **B2** 103
Suwannee, co., Fl., U.S. **B3** 102
Suwannee, stm., U.S. **C4** 102
Suwannee Sound, strt., Fl., U.S. **C3** 102
Suwanose-jima, i., Japan **F14** 28
Suwarrow, atoll, Cook Is. **F13** 58
Suweis, Khalîg el- (Suez, Gulf of), b., Egypt **F10** 14
Suweis, Qanâ el- (Suez Canal), Egypt **E10** 14
Suwŏn, S. Kor. **D13** 28
Suzak, Kaz. **B9** 42
Suzhou, China **E12** 28
Suzhou, China **E11** 28
Svalbard, dep., Nor. **D20** 144
Svaliava, Ukr. **E7** 20
Svappavaara, Swe. **C9** 10
Svatove, Ukr. **E15** 20
Svay Riĕng, Camb. **D5** 34
Sveg, Swe. **E6** 10
Švenčionėliai, Lith. **I11** 10
Svendborg, Den. **I4** 10
Svensen, Or., U.S. **A3** 130
Sverdlovsk see Ekaterinburg, Russia **D8** 26
Sverdrup, ostrov, i., Russia **B9** 26
Svetlahorsk, Bela. **C10** 20
Svetlaja, Russia **E15** 26
Svetlograd, Russia **A4** 42
Svetlyj, Russia **D11** 22
Svetlyj, Russia **D13** 26
Svetogorsk, Russia **F13** 10
Svetozarevo, Yugo. **C8** 18
Svirsk, Russia **A8** 28
Svištov, Bul. **C10** 18
Svitavy, Czech Rep. **E4** 20
Svjatoj Nos, mys, c., Russia **A7** 22
Svjatoj Nos, mys, c., Russia **B15** 26
Svobodnyj, Russia **D14** 26
Svolvær, Nor. **B6** 10
Swabia see Schwaben, hist. reg., Ger. **F11** 12
Swain, co., N.C., U.S. **f9** 126
Swain Reefs, rf., Austl. **E5** 62
Swainsboro, Ga., U.S. **D4** 103
Swakopmund, Nmb. **C1** 56
Swampscott, Ma., U.S. **B6** 114
Swan, stm., Can. **C1** 86
Swan Creek, stm., Oh., U.S. **e6** 128
Swan Falls, wtfl, Id., U.S. **F2** 105
Swan Hill, Austl. **H3** 62
Swan Hills, Ab., Can. **B3** 84
Swan Islands see Santanilla, Islas, is., Hond. **B3** 80
Swan Lake, l., Mb., Can. **C1** 86
Swan Lake, l., Me., U.S. **D4** 112
Swan Lake, l., Ne., U.S. **C3** 120
Swannanoa, N.C., U.S. **f10** 126
Swan Peak, mtn., Mt., U.S. **C3** 119
Swan Range, mts., Mt., U.S. **C3** 119
Swan River, Mb., Can. **C1** 86
Swansboro, N.C., U.S. **C5** 126
Swansea, Wales, U.K. **E4** 12
Swansea, Il., U.S. **E4** 106
Swanson Lake, res., Ne., U.S. **D4** 120
Swanton, Oh., U.S. **A2** 128
Swanton, Vt., U.S. **B2** 138
Swanzey Center, N.H., U.S. **E2** 122
Swarthmore, Pa., U.S. **p20** 131
Swartswood Lake, l., N.J., U.S. **A3** 123
Swartz Creek, Mi., U.S. **F7** 115
Swayzee, In., U.S. **C6** 107
Swaziland, ctry., Afr. **D5** 56
Swea City, Ia., U.S. **A3** 108
Sweden, ctry., Eur. **E7** 10
Swedru, Ghana **E4** 50
Sweeny, Tx., U.S. **r14** 136
Sweet Grass, co., Mt., U.S. **E7** 119
Sweet Home, Or., U.S. **C4** 130
Sweetser, In., U.S. **C6** 107
Sweet Springs, Mo., U.S. **C4** 118
Sweetwater, Tn., U.S. **D9** 135
Sweetwater, Tx., U.S. **C2** 136
Sweetwater, co., Wy., U.S. **E3** 143
Sweetwater, stm., Wy., U.S. **D4** 143
Sweetwater Creek, Fl., U.S. **p10** 102
Sweetwater Creek, stm., Ok., U.S. **B1** 129
Swellendam, S. Afr. **E3** 56
Swepsonville, N.C., U.S. **A3** 126
Świdwin, Pol. **C3** 20
Świebodzin, Pol. **C3** 20
Świecie, Pol. **C5** 20
Swift, co., Mn., U.S. **E3** 116
Swift, stm., N.H., U.S. **B4** 122
Swift Creek, stm., N.C., U.S. **B5** 126
Swift Creek, stm., Va., U.S. **n17** 139
Swift Diamond, stm., N.H., U.S. **g7** 122
Swifton, Ar., U.S. **B4** 97
Swift Reservoir, res., Wa., U.S. **C3** 140
Swindon, Eng., U.K. **E6** 12
Swinomish Indian Reservation, Wa., U.S. **A3** 140
Świnoujście, Pol. **C3** 20
Swisher, Ia., U.S. **C6** 108
Swisher, co., Tx., U.S. **B2** 136
Swissvale, Pa., U.S. **k14** 131
Switzer, W.V., U.S. **D3** 141
Switzerland, Fl., U.S. **m8** 102
Switzerland, co., In., U.S. **G7** 107
Switzerland, ctry., Eur. **A2** 18
Swoyerville, Pa., U.S. **D10** 131
Syalah, Russia **C14** 26
Sycamore, Al., U.S. **B3** 94
Sycamore, Il., U.S. **B5** 106
Sycamore, Oh., U.S. **B2** 128
Sycamore Creek, stm., W.V., U.S. **m13** 141
Sydenham, On., Can. **C8** 89
Sydney, Austl. **G5** 62
Sykesville, Md., U.S. **B4** 113
Sykesville, Pa., U.S. **D4** 131
Syktyvkar, Russia **C7** 26
Sylacauga, Al., U.S. **B3** 94
Sylhet, Bngl. **E6** 40
Sylt, i., Ger. **C11** 12
Sylva, N.C., U.S. **f9** 126
Sylvania, Al., U.S. **A4** 94
Sylvania, Ga., U.S. **D5** 103
Sylvania, Oh., U.S. **A2** 128
Sylvan Lake, Ab., Can. **C3** 84
Sylvan Lake, Mi., U.S. **o15** 115
Sylvan Lake, l., In., U.S. **B7** 107
Sylvan Pass, Wy., U.S. **B2** 143
Sylvester, Ga., U.S. **E3** 103
Sym, Russia **C10** 26
Šymkent, Kaz. **E8** 26
Symmes Creek, stm., Oh., U.S. **D3** 128
Symsonia, Ky., U.S. **f9** 110
Syracuse, In., U.S. **B6** 107
Syracuse, Ks., U.S. **E2** 109
Syracuse, Ne., U.S. **D9** 120
Syracuse, N.Y., U.S. **B4** 125
Syracuse, Ut., U.S. **B3** 137
Syrdarja, Uzb. **B9** 42
Syr Darya (Syrdar'ja), stm., Asia **B9** 42
Syria, ctry., Asia **E8** 44
Syriam, Myan. **C3** 34
Syrian Desert, des., Asia **F8** 44
Syros see Ermoúpolis, Grc. **F10** 18
Sysladobsis Lake, l., Me., U.S. **C4** 112
Syvash, zatoka, strt., Ukr. **F13** 20
Syzran', Russia **D6** 26
Szamotuły, Pol. **C4** 20
Szczecin, Pol. **C3** 20
Szczecinek, Pol. **C4** 20
Szczytno, Pol. **C6** 20
Szechwan see Sichuan, prov., China **E8** 28
Szeged, Hung. **F6** 20
Székesfehérvár, Hung. **F5** 20
Szekszárd, Hung. **F5** 20
Szentes, Hung. **F6** 20
Szolnok, Hung. **F6** 20
Szombathely, Hung. **F4** 20

T

Tabar Islands, is., Pap. N. Gui. **G13** 32
Tabarka, Tun. **F2** 18
Tabasco, state, Mex. **D6** 78
Tabayin, Myan. **B3** 34
Tabbys Peak, mtn., Ut., U.S. **C3** 137
Tabelbala, Alg. **E4** 48
Taber, Ab., Can. **E4** 84
Tablas Island, i., Phil. **D8** 34
Table Head, c., Nf., Can. **B4** 88
Table Mountain, mtn., Az., U.S. **E5** 96
Table Rock Lake, res., U.S. **E4** 118
Table Top, mtn., Az., U.S. **E3** 96
Tábor, Czech Rep. **E3** 20
Tabor, Russia **B17** 26
Tabor, Ia., U.S. **D2** 108
Tabora, Tan. **D6** 54
Tabor City, N.C., U.S. **C4** 126
Tabou, C. Iv. **F3** 50
Tabrīz, Iran **C5** 42
Tabūk, Sau. Ar. **E3** 38
Tabuleiro do Norte, Braz. **C4** 74
Täby, Swe. **G8** 10
Tacloban, Phil. **D9** 34
Tacna, Peru **G5** 70
Tacoma, Wa., U.S. **B3** 140
Taconic Range, mts., U.S. **A1** 114
Tacuarembó, Ur. **E6** 72
Tacurong, Phil. **E8** 34
Tademaït, Plateau du, plat., Alg. **E5** 48
Tadjemout, Alg. **A5** 50
Tadoussac, P.Q., Can. **A8** 90
T'aebaek-sanmaek, mts., Asia **D13** 28
Taegu, S. Kor. **D13** 28
Taejŏn, S. Kor. **D13** 28
Tafalla, Spain **F6** 16
Tafo, Ghana **E4** 50
Taft, Ca., U.S. **E4** 98
Taft, Tx., U.S. **F4** 136
Taganrog, Russia **F15** 20
Tagânt, reg., Maur. **C2** 50
Tagaytay, Phil. **D8** 34
Tagbilaran, Phil. **E8** 34
Taguke, China **E4** 28
Tagum, Phil. **E9** 34
Tagus, stm., Eur. **H2** 16
Tahan, Gunong, mtn., Malay. **C2** 36
Tahat, mtn., Alg. **F6** 48
Tahiataš, Uzb. **B7** 42
Tahifet, Alg. **B6** 50
Tahiti, i., Fr. Poly. **F15** 58
Tahlequah, Ok., U.S. **B7** 129
Tahoe, Lake, l., U.S. **D3** 92
Tahoe, Lake, l., U.S. **E1** 121
Tahoe City, Ca., U.S. **C3** 98
Tahoka, Tx., U.S. **C2** 136
Taholah, Wa., U.S. **B1** 140
Tahoua, Niger **D6** 50
Tahquamenon, stm., Mi., U.S. **B5** 115
Tahsis, B.C., Can. **E4** 85
Ṭahṭā, Egypt **F10** 14
Tahta-Bazar, Turk. **C8** 42
Tahtakupyr, Uzb. **B8** 42
Tahtsa Peak, mtn., B.C., Can. **C4** 85
Tahulandang, Pulau, i., Indon. **C7** 36
Tahuna, Indon. **C7** 36
Tai'an, China **D11** 28
Taibai Shan, mtn., China **C2** 30
Taibus Qi, China **A4** 30
T'aichung, Tai. **E5** 30
Taigu, China **B3** 30
Taihang Shan, mts., China **B3** 30
Taihape, N.Z. **o14** 63c
Taihe, China **D3** 30
Taihu, China **C4** 30
Tai Hu, l., China **E11** 28
Taikang, China **C4** 30
Tailai, China **B12** 28
Tai Lake see Tai Hu, l., China **E11** 28
Taimba, Russia **C11** 26
T'ainan, Tai. **E5** 30
Taínaron, Ákra, c., Grc. **F9** 18
Tainaron, Cape see Taínaron, Ákra, c., Grc. **F9** 18
T'aipei, Tai. **D5** 30
Taiping, Malay. **C2** 36
Taisha, Japan **C2** 31
Taishan, China **E3** 30
Taishun, China **F11** 28
Taitao, Península de, pen., Chile **G1** 69
T'aitung, Tai. **E5** 30
Taivalkoski, Fin. **D13** 10
Taiwan, ctry., Asia **B8** 34
Taiwan Strait, strt., Asia **E4** 30
Taiyuan, China **D10** 28
Taizhou, China **C4** 30
Ta'izz, Yemen **H4** 38
Tajikistan, ctry., Asia **B2** 40
Tāj Mahal, hist., India **D3** 40
Tajmyr, ozero, l., Russia **B12** 26
Tajmyr, poluostrov, pen., Russia **B12** 26
Tajo see Tagus, stm., Eur. **H5** 16
Tajšet, Russia **D11** 26
Tak, Thai. **C3** 34
Takāb, Iran **D12** 44
Takalar, Indon. **E5** 36
Takamatsu, Japan **E14** 28
Takaoka, Japan **C3** 31
Takasaki, Japan **C3** 31
Takatsuki, Japan **D3** 31
Takêv, Camb. **D4** 34
Takhli, Thai. **C4** 34
Takikawa, Japan **B4** 31
Takla Lake, l., B.C., Can. **B5** 85
Taklimakan Shamo, des., China **D4** 28
Takoma Park, Md., U.S. **f8** 113
Taku Glacier, Ak., U.S. **k22** 95
Takum, Nig. **E7** 50
Takutea, i., Cook Is. **F14** 58
Talak, reg., Niger **C6** 50
Talara, Peru **D3** 70
Talas, Kyrg. **E9** 26
Talasea, Pap. N. Gui. **H13** 32
Talata Mafara, Nig. **D6** 50
Talaud, Kepulauan, is., Indon. **C7** 36
Talavera de la Reina, Spain **H4** 16
Talawdī, Sudan **A6** 54
Talbot, co., Ga., U.S. **D2** 103
Talbot, co., Md., U.S. **C5** 113
Talbot Island, i., Fl., U.S. **B5** 102
Talbot Lake, l., Mb., Can. **B2** 86
Talbotton, Ga., U.S. **D2** 103
Talca, Chile **E2** 69
Talcahuano, Chile **E2** 69
Taldykorgan, Kaz. **E9** 26
Talent, Or., U.S. **E4** 130
Talgar, Kaz. **B11** 42
Taliabu, Pulau, i., Indon. **D6** 36
Taliaferro, co., Ga., U.S. **C4** 103
Talihina, Ok., U.S. **C6** 129
Talish Mountains see Ṭavālesh, Kūhhā-ye, mts., Asia **D13** 44
Taliwang, Indon. **E5** 36
Talkeetna, Ak., U.S. **C10** 95
Talkeetna Mountains, mts., Ak., U.S. **f17** 95
Talladega, Al., U.S. **B3** 94
Talladega, co., Al., U.S. **B3** 94
Tall 'Afar, Iraq **D10** 44
Tallahassee, Fl., U.S. **B2** 102
Tallahatchie, co., Ms., U.S. **B3** 117
Tallahatchie, stm., Ms., U.S. **B3** 117
Tallangatta, Austl. **H4** 62
Tallapoosa, Ga., U.S. **C1** 103
Tallapoosa, co., Al., U.S. **C4** 94
Tallapoosa, stm., Al., U.S. **C3** 94
Tallassee, Al., U.S. **C4** 94
Talleyville, De., U.S. **A3** 101
Tallinn, Est. **G11** 10
Tall Kūjik, Syria **D9** 44
Tallmadge, Oh., U.S. **A4** 128
Tallulah, La., U.S. **B4** 111
Tal'ne, Ukr. **E11** 20
Talok, Indon. **C5** 36
Tāloqān, Afg. **C9** 42
Talquin, Lake, res., Fl., U.S. **B2** 102
Talsi, Lat. **H10** 10
Taltal, Chile **C2** 69
Talu, Indon. **C1** 36
Taluk, Indon. **D2** 36
Talurqjuak, Nu., Can. **E21** 82
Tama, Ia., U.S. **C5** 108
Tama, co., Ia., U.S. **B5** 108
Tamale, Ghana **E4** 50
Tamalpais, Mount, mtn., Ca., U.S. **h7** 98
Tamaqua, Pa., U.S. **E10** 131
Tamaroa, Il., U.S. **E4** 106
Tamaulipas, state, Mex. **C5** 78
Tamazulapan del Progreso, Mex. **D5** 78
Tamazunchale, Mex. **C5** 78
Tambacounda, Sen. **D2** 50
Tambej, Russia **B9** 26
Tambelan, Kepulauan, is., Indon. **C3** 36
Tamberías, Arg. **E4** 72
Tambohorano, Madag. **B7** 56
Tambora, Gunung, vol., Indon. **E5** 36
Tambov, Russia **D6** 26
Tambura, Sudan **I10** 48
Tâmchekkeṭ, Maur. **C2** 50
Tame, Col. **B5** 70
Tamel Aike, Arg. **G2** 69
Tamenghest, Alg. **F6** 48
Tamiahua, Mex. **C5** 78
Tamiahua, Laguna de, l., Mex. **C5** 78
Tamiami Canal, Fl., U.S. **G6** 102
Tamil Nādu, prov., India **G3** 40
Tam Ky, Viet. **C5** 34
Tampa, Fl., U.S. **E4** 102
Tampa Bay, b., Fl., U.S. **E4** 102
Tampere, Fin. **F10** 10
Tampico, Mex. **C5** 78
Tampico, Il., U.S. **B4** 106
Tam Quan, Viet. **D5** 34
Tamsagbulag, Mong. **B11** 28
Tamu, Myan. **B2** 34
Tamworth, Austl. **G5** 62
Tana (Teno), stm., Eur. **B12** 10
Tana, stm., Kenya **D7** 54
Tanabe, Japan **D3** 31
Tanafjorden, Nor. **A13** 10
Tanaga Island, i., Ak., U.S. **E4** 95
Tanahbala, Pulau, i., Indon. **D1** 36
Tanahjampea, Pulau, i., Indon. **E5** 36
Tanahmasa, Pulau, i., Indon. **D1** 36
Tanahmerah, Indon. **H11** 32
Tanami Desert, des., Austl. **D4** 60
Tanana, Ak., U.S. **B9** 95
Tanana, stm., Ak., U.S. **C10** 95
Tananarive see Antananarivo, Madag. **B8** 56
Tanch'ŏn-ŭp, N. Kor. **C13** 28
Tandag, Phil. **E9** 34
Ţăndărei, Rom. **G9** 20
Tandil, Arg. **F6** 72
Tanega-shima, i., Japan **E14** 28
Taney, co., Mo., U.S. **E4** 118
Taneycomo, Lake, res., Mo., U.S. **E4** 118
Taneytown, Md., U.S. **A3** 113
Tanezrouft, des., Afr. **B4** 50
Tanga, Tan. **E7** 54
Tanganyika see Tanzania, ctry., Afr. **E6** 54
Tanganyika, Lake, l., Afr. **E5** 54
Tanger, Mor. **C3** 48
Tanggula Shan, mts., China **E5** 28
Tanghe, China **C3** 30
Tangier, Va., U.S. **C7** 139
Tangier Island, i., Va., U.S. **C6** 139
Tangier Sound, strt., Md., U.S. **D6** 113
Tangipahoa, co., La., U.S. **D5** 111
Tangipahoa, stm., La., U.S. **D5** 111
Tangmai, China **C7** 40
Tangra Yumco, l., China **C5** 40
Tangshan, China **D11** 28
Tangyin, China **B3** 30
Tangyuan, China **A1** 31
Tanhoj, Russia **A9** 28
Tanimbar, Kepulauan, is., Indon. **E8** 36
Tanjungbalai, Indon. **C1** 36
Tanjungkarang-Telukbetung, Indon. **E3** 36
Tanjungpandan, Indon. **D3** 36
Tanjungpinang, Indon. **C2** 36
Tanjungredep, Indon. **C5** 36
Tānk, Pak. **D10** 42
Tanna, i., Vanuatu **k9** 62a
Tännäs, Swe. **E5** 10
Tanner, Al., U.S. **A3** 94
Tannu-Ola Mountains, mts., Asia **A6** 28
Tanout, Niger **C6** 50
Tanta, Egypt **D11** 48
Tan-Tan, Mor. **A2** 50
Tantoyuca, Mex. **C5** 78
Tanzania, ctry., Afr. **E6** 54
Taormina, Italy **F5** 18
Taos, Mo., U.S. **C5** 118
Taos, N.M., U.S. **A4** 124
Taos, co., N.M., U.S. **A4** 124
Taos Pueblo, N.M., U.S. **A4** 124
Taoudenni, Mali **B4** 50
Taounate, Mor. **E3** 14
Taourirt, Mor. **E3** 14
Tapa, Est. **G11** 10
Tapachula, Mex. **E6** 78
Tapajós, stm., Braz. **D8** 70
Tapaktuan, Indon. **C1** 36
Taphan Hin, Thai. **C4** 34
Tāpi, stm., India **E2** 40
Tappahannock, Va., U.S. **C6** 139
Tappan, N.Y., U.S. **g13** 125
Tappan, Lake, res., N.J., U.S. **g9** 123
Tappan Lake, res., Oh., U.S. **B4** 128
Tapul Group, is., Phil. **E8** 34
Tapuruquara, Braz. **D6** 70
Taqāṭu' Hayyā, Sudan **G12** 48
Taquari Novo, stm., Braz. **G8** 70
Tar, stm., N.C., U.S. **B5** 126
Tara, On., Can. **C3** 89
Tara, Russia **D9** 26
Tarabuco, Bol. **B5** 72
Ṭarābulus (Tripoli), Leb. **E6** 44
Ṭarābulus (Tripoli), Libya **D7** 48
Ṭarābulus (Tripolitania), hist. reg., Libya **E7** 14
Tarakan, Indon. **C5** 36
Taranaki, Mount (Egmont, Mount), vol., N.Z. **o13** 63c
Tarancón, Spain **G5** 16
Taranto, Italy **D6** 18
Taranto, Golfo di, b., Italy **D6** 18
Taranto, Gulf of see Taranto, Golfo di, b., Italy **D6** 18
Tarapoto, Peru **E4** 70
Taraquá, Braz. **C6** 70
Tarat, Alg. **A6** 50
Tarata, Bol. **B4** 72
Tarauacá, Braz. **E5** 70
Tarawa, atoll, Kir. **D11** 58
Tarazona, Spain **G6** 16

Name **Map Ref.** **Page**

Tarbagatay Range, mts., Asia **B4** 28
Tarbes, Fr. **F7** 16
Tarboro, N.C., U.S. **B5** 126
Tarbū, Libya **E8** 48
Tarcoola, Austl. **G5** 60
Tardoki-Jani, gora, mtn., Russia **B15** 28
Taree, Austl. **G5** 62
Tareja, Russia **B11** 26
Tarentum, Pa., U.S. **E2** 131
Tarfaya, Mor. **E2** 48
Targhee Pass, U.S. **E7** 105
Târgovište, Bul. **C11** 18
Târgovişte, Rom. **G8** 20
Târgu Jiu, Rom. **G7** 20
Târgu Mureş, Rom. **F8** 20
Târgu-Neamţ, Rom. **F9** 20
Târgu Ocna, Rom. **F9** 20
Tarifa, Spain **I4** 16
Tariffville, Ct., U.S. **B4** 100
Tarija, Bol. **C5** 72
Tarim, stm., China **C4** 28
Tarim Pendi, China **D4** 28
Tarīn Kowt, Afg. **D9** 42
Tarkastad, S. Afr. **E4** 56
Tarkio, Mo., U.S. **A2** 118
Tarko-Sale, Russia **C9** 26
Tarkwa, Ghana **E4** 50
Tarma, Peru **F4** 70
Tarn, stm., Fr. **F7** 16
Tärnaby, Swe. **D6** 10
Târnăveni, Rom. **F8** 20
Tarnobrzeg, Pol. **D6** 20
Tarnów, Pol. **E6** 20
Tarpey, Ca., U.S. **D4** 98
Tarpon, Lake, l., Fl., U.S. **o10** 102
Tarpon Springs, Fl., U.S. **D4** 102
Tarquinia, Italy **C3** 18
Tarragona, Spain **G7** 16
Tarrant, Al., U.S. **B3** 94
Tarrant, co., Tx., U.S. **C4** 136
Tarryall Mountains, mts., Co., U.S. **B5** 99
Tarrytown, N.Y., U.S. **D7** 125
Tarsus, Tur. **D6** 44
Tartagal, Arg. **C5** 72
Tärtär, Azer. **B12** 44
Tartu, Est. **G12** 10
Ţarţūs, Syria **E6** 44
Tarutung, Indon. **C1** 36
Tasāwah, Libya **A7** 50
Tasbuget, Kaz. **B9** 42
Taseko Mountain, mtn., B.C., Can. **D6** 85
Ţashk, Daryācheh-ye, l., Iran **E6** 42
Tashkent see Taškent, Uzb. **E8** 26
Taškent, Uzb. **E8** 26
Taškepri, Turk. **C8** 42
Taşköprü, Tur. **B6** 44
Tasman Basin **M18** 64
Tasman Bay, b., N.Z. **p13** 63c
Tasmania, state, Austl. **I4** 62
Tasmania, i., Austl. **I3** 62
Tasman Sea, Oc. **L18** 64
Taşova, Tur. **B7** 44
Tasso, Tn., U.S. **D9** 135
Taštagol, Russia **D10** 26
Tata, Hung. **F5** 20
Tatarbunary, Ukr. **G10** 20
Tatarija, state, Russia **D6** 26
Tatarsk, Russia **D9** 26
Tatarskij proliv, strt., Russia **E16** 26
Tatarstan see Tatarija, state, Russia **D6** 26
Tatar Strait see Tatarskij proliv, strt., Russia **E16** 26
Tate, Ga., U.S. **B2** 103
Tate, co., Ms., U.S. **A4** 117
Tateville, Ky., U.S. **D5** 110
Tatnam, Cape, c., Mb., Can. **f9** 86
Tatta, Pak. **F9** 42
Tattnall, co., Ga., U.S. **D4** 103
Tatum, N.M., U.S. **D6** 124
Tatvan, Tur. **C10** 44
Tauá, Braz. **C3** 74
Taučik, Kaz. **B6** 42
Taujskaja guba, b., Russia **D17** 26
Taum Sauk Mountain, mtn., Mo., U.S. **D6** 118
Taunggyi, Myan. **B3** 34
Taungup, Myan. **C2** 34
Taunton, Eng., U.K. **E5** 12
Taunton, Ma., U.S. **C5** 114
Taunton, stm., Ma., U.S. **C5** 114
Taupo, N.Z. **o14** 63c
Taupo, Lake, l., N.Z. **o14** 63c
Tauranga, N.Z. **o14** 63c
Taureau, Réservoir, res., P.Q., Can. **C4** 90
Taurus Mountains see Toros Dağları, mts., Tur. **D5** 44
Ţavālesh, Kūhhā-ye, mts., Asia **D13** 44
Tavares, Fl., U.S. **D5** 102
Tavas, Tur. **D3** 44
Tavda, Russia **D8** 26
Tavda, stm., Russia **D8** 26
Tavernier, Fl., U.S. **G6** 102
Taveuni, i., Fiji **m11** 63b
Tavşanlı, Tur. **C3** 44
Tawakoni, Lake, res., Tx., U.S. **C4** 136
Tawas City, Mi., U.S. **D7** 115
Tawas Lake, l., Mi., U.S. **D7** 115
Tawau, Malay. **C5** 36
Tawitawi Group, is., Phil. **E8** 34
Ţawkar, Sudan **G12** 48
Ţāwūq, Iraq **E11** 44
Taxco de Alarcón, Mex. **D5** 78
Taxkorgan Tajik Zizhixian, China **B3** 40
Taylor, B.C., Can. **A7** 85
Taylor, Ar., U.S. **D2** 97
Taylor, Az., U.S. **C5** 96
Taylor, Mi., U.S. **p15** 115
Taylor, Pa., U.S. **D10** 131
Taylor, Tx., U.S. **D4** 136
Taylor, co., Fl., U.S. **B3** 102
Taylor, co., Ga., U.S. **D2** 103
Taylor, co., Ia., U.S. **D3** 108
Taylor, co., Ky., U.S. **C4** 110
Taylor, co., Tx., U.S. **C3** 136
Taylor, co., W.V., U.S. **B4** 141
Taylor, co., Wi., U.S. **C3** 142
Taylor, stm., Co., U.S. **C4** 99
Taylor, Mount, mtn., N.M., U.S. **B2** 124
Taylor Mill, Ky., U.S. **k14** 110
Taylor Mountain, mtn., Id., U.S. **E4** 105
Taylor Park Reservoir, res., Co., U.S. **C4** 99
Taylors, S.C., U.S. **B3** 133
Taylors Falls, Mn., U.S. **E6** 116
Taylors Island, i., Md., U.S. **D5** 113
Taylorsville, In., U.S. **F6** 107
Taylorsville, Ky., U.S. **B4** 110
Taylorsville, Ms., U.S. **D4** 117
Taylorsville, N.C., U.S. **B1** 126
Taylorville, Il., U.S. **D4** 106
Taymā', Sau. Ar. **E3** 38
Taymyr Peninsula see Tajmyr, poluostrov, pen., Russia **B12** 26
Tay Ninh, Viet. **D5** 34
Taytay, Phil. **D7** 34
Taz, stm., Russia **D9** 26
Taza, Mor. **E3** 14
Tazewell, Tn., U.S. **C10** 135
Tazewell, Va., U.S. **e10** 139
Tazewell, co., Il., U.S. **C4** 106
Tazewell, co., Va., U.S. **e10** 139
Tazovskij, Russia **C9** 26
Tbessa, Alg. **C6** 48
Tbilisi, Geor. **B11** 44
Tchaourou, Benin **E5** 50
Tchefuncta, stm., La., U.S. **D5** 111
Tchibanga, Gabon **D2** 54
Tchula, Ms., U.S. **B3** 117
Tczew, Pol. **B5** 20
Tea, S.D., U.S. **D9** 134
Teague, Tx., U.S. **D4** 136
Teakean Butte, mtn., Id., U.S. **C2** 105
Teaneck, N.J., U.S. **h8** 123
Teapa, Mex. **D6** 78
Teaticket, Ma., U.S. **C6** 114
Te Awamutu, N.Z. **o14** 63c
Tebingtinggi, Indon. **C1** 36
Tebingtinggi, Pulau, i., Indon. **C2** 36
Téboursouk, Tun. **F2** 18
Techlé, W. Sah. **B2** 50
Tecka, Arg. **F2** 69
Tecomán, Mex. **D4** 78
Tecpan de Galeana, Mex. **D4** 78
Tecuala, Mex. **C3** 78
Tecuci, Rom. **G9** 20
Tecumseh, On., Can. **E2** 89
Tecumseh, Ks., U.S. **k14** 109
Tecumseh, Mi., U.S. **G7** 115
Tecumseh, Ne., U.S. **D9** 120
Tecumseh, Ok., U.S. **B5** 129
Tedžen, Turk. **F8** 26
Teeli, Russia **D10** 26
Teeswater, On., Can. **C3** 89
Tefé, Braz. **D7** 70
Tegal, Indon. **E3** 36
Tégama, reg., Niger **C6** 50
Tegucigalpa, Hond. **C2** 80
Tehachapi, Ca., U.S. **E4** 98
Tehachapi Mountains, mts., Ca., U.S. **E4** 98
Tehama, co., Ca., U.S. **B2** 98
Tehrān, Iran **C6** 42
Tehuacán, Mex. **D5** 78
Tehuantepec, Golfo de, b., Mex. **D6** 78
Tehuantepec, Istmo de, Mex. **D6** 78
Teide, Pico del, mtn., Spain **A1** 50
Teixeira Pinto, Gui.-B. **D1** 50
Tejo see Tagus, stm., Eur. **H3** 16
Tekamah, Ne., U.S. **C9** 120
Tekax, Mex. **C7** 78
Tekeli, Kaz. **E9** 26
Tekes, China **A4** 40
Tekirdağ, Tur. **B2** 44
Tekoa, Wa., U.S. **B8** 140
Tekonsha, Mi., U.S. **F5** 115
Telavi, Geor. **B11** 44
Tel Aviv-Yafo, Isr. **D2** 42
Teleckoe, ozero, l., Russia **A5** 28
Telêmaco Borba, Braz. **C7** 72
Telemark, prov., Nor. **G3** 10
Telén, Arg. **F4** 72
Telescope Peak, mtn., Ca., U.S. **D5** 98
Telfair, co., Ga., U.S. **E4** 103
Telford, Eng., U.K. **D5** 12
Telford, Pa., U.S. **F11** 131
Télimélé, Gui. **D2** 50
Telkwa, B.C., Can. **B4** 85
Tell City, In., U.S. **I4** 107
Teller, co., Co., U.S. **C5** 99
Tellicherry, India **G3** 40
Tellico Plains, Tn., U.S. **D9** 135
Telluride, Co., U.S. **D3** 99
Telos Lake, l., Me., U.S. **B3** 112
Telsen, Arg. **F3** 69
Telukbatang, Indon. **D3** 36
Teluk Intan, Malay. **C2** 36
Tema, Ghana **E5** 50
Temax, Mex. **C7** 78
Tembilahan, Indon. **D2** 36
Temecula, Ca., U.S. **F5** 98
Teminaabuan, Indon. **D8** 36
Temir, Kaz. **E10** 22
Temirtau, Kaz. **E9** 26
Témiscouata, Lac, l., P.Q., Can. **B9** 90
Te-Moak Indian Reservation, Nv., U.S. **C6** 121
Temora, Austl. **G4** 62
Temosachic, Mex. **B3** 78
Tempe, Az., U.S. **D4** 96
Temperance, Mi., U.S. **G7** 115
Temperance, stm., Mn., U.S. **C8** 116
Temple, Ga., U.S. **C1** 103
Temple, Ok., U.S. **C3** 129
Temple, Pa., U.S. **F10** 131
Temple, Tx., U.S. **D4** 136
Temple Terrace, Fl., U.S. **o11** 102
Temrjuk, Russia **G14** 20
Temuco, Chile **E2** 69
Tenafly, N.J., U.S. **B5** 123
Tenaha, Tx., U.S. **D5** 136
Tena Kourou, mtn., Burkina **D3** 50
Tenāli, India **F4** 40
Tenasserim, Myan. **D3** 34
Tendaho, Eth. **H13** 48
Ten Degree Channel, strt., India **H6** 40
Ténéré, des., Niger **C6** 50
Tenerife, i., Spain **A1** 50
Tengchong, China **G7** 28
Tenggara, Nusa (Lesser Sunda Islands), is., Indon. **E5** 36
Tengiz, ozero, l., Kaz. **D8** 26
Tengréla, C. Iv. **D3** 50
Tengxian, China **B4** 30
Tengxian, China **E3** 30
Tenino, Wa., U.S. **C3** 140
Tenke, D.R.C. **F5** 54
Tenkeli, Russia **C16** 26
Tenkiller Ferry Lake, res., Ok., U.S. **B6** 129
Tenkodogo, Burkina **D4** 50
Tenmile, stm., U.S. **B5** 132
Tenmile Creek, stm., W.V., U.S. **k10** 141
Tenmile Lake, l., Mn., U.S. **D4** 116
Tennant Creek, Austl. **D5** 60
Tennessee, state, U.S. **B5** 135
Tennessee, stm., U.S. **B3** 135
Tennessee Pass, Co., U.S. **B4** 99
Tennessee Ridge, Tn., U.S. **A4** 135
Tennille, Ga., U.S. **D4** 103
Teno (Tana), stm., Eur. **B12** 10
Tenosique, Mex. **D6** 78
Tensas, co., La., U.S. **B4** 111
Tensas, stm., La., U.S. **B4** 111
Tensaw, stm., Al., U.S. **E2** 94
Ten Sleep, Wy., U.S. **B5** 143
Tenterfield, Austl. **F5** 62
Ten Thousand Islands, is., Fl., U.S. **G5** 102
Teófilo Otoni, Braz. **E3** 74
Tepa, Indon. **E7** 36
Tepehuanes, Mex. **B3** 78
Tepic, Mex. **C4** 78
Téra, Niger **D5** 50
Teramo, Italy **C4** 18
Terceira, i., Port. **F7** 46
Terek, Russia **A11** 44
Terek, stm., Russia **B5** 42
Teresina, Braz. **C3** 74
Tergüün Bodg uul, mtn., Mong. **C8** 28
Termas de Río Hondo, Arg. **D5** 72
Terme, Tur. **B7** 44
Termez, Uzb. **C9** 42
Términos, Laguna de, b., Mex. **D6** 78
Ternej, Russia **A3** 31
Terneuzen, Neth. **E8** 12
Terni, Italy **C4** 18
Ternopil', Ukr. **E8** 20
Terpenija, mys, c., Russia **E16** 26
Terra Alta, W.V., U.S. **B5** 141
Terrace, B.C., Can. **B3** 85
Terracina, Italy **D4** 18
Terra Nova National Park, Nf., Can. **D4** 88
Terrassa, Spain **G8** 16
Terrebonne, P.Q., Can. **D4** 90
Terrebonne, Or., U.S. **C5** 130
Terrebonne, co., La., U.S. **E5** 111
Terrebonne Bay, b., La., U.S. **E5** 111
Terre Haute, In., U.S. **F3** 107
Terre Hill, Pa., U.S. **F9** 131
Terrell, Tx., U.S. **C4** 136
Terrell, co., Ga., U.S. **E2** 103
Terrell, co., Tx., U.S. **D1** 136
Terrell Hills, Tx., U.S. **k7** 136
Terrenceville, Nf., Can. **E4** 88
Terry, Ms., U.S. **C3** 117
Terry, Mt., U.S. **D11** 119
Terry, co., Tx., U.S. **C1** 136
Terrytown, Ne., U.S. **C2** 120
Terryville, Ct., U.S. **C3** 100
Teruel, Spain **G6** 16
Teseney, Erit. **G12** 48
Teshekpuk Lake, l., Ak., U.S. **A9** 95
Teshio, Japan **B4** 31
Tessalit, Mali **B5** 50
Tessaoua, Niger **D6** 50
Tesuque, N.M., U.S. **B4** 124
Tete, Moz. **B5** 56
Teteriv, stm., Ukr. **D10** 20
Teton, co., Id., U.S. **F7** 105
Teton, co., Mt., U.S. **C4** 119
Teton, co., Wy., U.S. **C2** 143
Teton, stm., Mt., U.S. **C5** 119
Teton Pass, Wy., U.S. **C2** 143
Teton Range, mts., Wy., U.S. **C2** 143
Teton Village, Wy., U.S. **C2** 143
Tetouan, Mor. **C3** 48
Tetovo, Mac. **C8** 18
Teulon, Mb., Can. **D3** 86
Teutopolis, Il., U.S. **D5** 106
Tevere, stm., Italy **C4** 18
Teverya, Isr. **D3** 42
Tewksbury, Ma., U.S. **A5** 114
Texada Island, i., B.C., Can. **E5** 85
Texarkana, Ar., U.S. **D1** 97
Texarkana, Tx., U.S. **C5** 136
Texas, co., Mo., U.S. **D5** 118
Texas, co., Ok., U.S. **e9** 129
Texas, state, U.S. **D3** 136
Texas City, Tx., U.S. **E5** 136
Texel, i., Neth. **D9** 12
Texhoma, Ok., U.S. **e9** 129
Texico, N.M., U.S. **C6** 124
Texoma, Lake, res., U.S. **D5** 129
Teziutlán, Mex. **D5** 78
Tezpur, India **D6** 40
Thabana-Ntlenyana, mtn., Leso. **D4** 56
Thabazimbi, S. Afr. **C4** 56
Thai Binh, Viet. **B5** 34
Thailand, ctry., Asia **C4** 34
Thailand, Gulf of, b., Asia **D4** 34
Thai Nguyen, Viet. **B5** 34
Thames, N.Z. **o14** 63c
Thames, stm., On., Can. **E3** 89
Thames, stm., Eng., U.K. **E7** 12
Thames, stm., Ct., U.S. **D7** 100
Thamesville, On., Can. **E3** 89
Thāna, India **F2** 40
Thanh Hoa, Viet. **C5** 34
Thanh Pho Ho Chi Minh (Saigon), Viet. **D5** 34
Thanjāvūr, India **G3** 40
Tharād, India **E2** 40
Thar Desert (Great Indian Desert), des., Asia **D2** 40
Tharrawaddy, Myan. **C3** 34
Tharros, hist., Italy **E2** 18
Tharthār, Buḥayrat ath-, res., Iraq **E10** 44
Thásos, Grc. **D10** 18
Thásos, i., Grc. **D10** 18
Thatcher, Az., U.S. **E6** 96
Thaton, Myan. **C3** 34
Thayer, Mo., U.S. **E6** 118
Thayer, co., Ne., U.S. **D8** 120
Thayetmyo, Myan. **C3** 34
Thayne, Wy., U.S. **D1** 143
Thazi, Myan. **B3** 34
Thealka, Ky., U.S. **C7** 110
The Barrens, plat., Tn., U.S. **B5** 135
Thebes see Thívai, Grc. **E9** 18
The Dalles, Or., U.S. **B5** 130
The Dells, val., Wi., U.S. **E4** 142
Thedford, On., Can. **D3** 89
The Everglades, sw., Fl., U.S. **G6** 102
The Flat Tops, mts., Co., U.S. **B3** 99
The Flume, wtfl, N.H., U.S. **B3** 122
The Graves, is., Ma., U.S. **g12** 114
The Hague see 's-Gravenhage, Neth. **D8** 12
The Heads, c., Or., U.S. **E2** 130
The Little Minch see Little Minch, The, strt., Scot., U.K. **B3** 12
The Minch, strt., Scot., U.K. **A4** 12
The Narrows, strt., Wa., U.S. **f10** 140
Theodore, Al., U.S. **E1** 94
Theodore Roosevelt Lake, res., Az., U.S. **D4** 96
Theodore Roosevelt National Park (North Unit), N.D., U.S. **B2** 127
Theodore Roosevelt National Park (South Unit), N.D., U.S. **C2** 127
The Pas, Mb., Can. **C1** 86
The Plains, Oh., U.S. **C3** 128
Theresa, Wi., U.S. **E5** 142
Thermaïkós Kólpos, b., Grc. **D9** 18
Thermopílai, hist., Grc. **E9** 18
Thermopolis, Wy., U.S. **C4** 143
Thermopylae see Thermopílai, hist., Grc. **E9** 18
The Rockies, mts., Wa., U.S. **C3** 140
Thessalía, hist. reg., Grc. **E9** 18
Thessalon, On., Can. **p19** 89
Thessaloníki (Salonika), Grc. **D9** 18
Thessaly see Thessalía, hist. reg., Grc. **E9** 18
Thetford Mines, P.Q., Can. **C6** 90
The Thimbles, is., Ct., U.S. **E5** 100
The Valley, Anguilla **B7** 80
The Village, Ok., U.S. **B4** 129
The Wash, b., Eng., U.K. **D7** 12
Thibodaux, La., U.S. **E5** 111
Thief, stm., Mn., U.S. **B2** 116
Thief Lake, l., Mn., U.S. **B3** 116
Thief River Falls, Mn., U.S. **B2** 116
Thielsen, Mount, mtn., Or., U.S. **D4** 130
Thiensville, Wi., U.S. **E6** 142
Thiès, Sen. **D1** 50
Thika, Kenya **D7** 54
Thimphu, Bhu. **D5** 40
Thingvellir, Ice. **l18** 10a
Thio, N. Cal. **I9** 62a
Thionville, Fr. **C10** 16
Thíra, i., Grc. **F10** 18
Third Cataract, wtfl, Sudan **G11** 48
Third Lake, l., N.H., U.S. **f7** 122
Thisted, Den. **H3** 10
Thistilfjörður, b., Ice. **k21** 10a
Thívai, Grc. **E9** 18
Thjórsá, stm., Ice. **m18** 10a
Thomas, Ok., U.S. **B3** 129
Thomas, co., Ga., U.S. **F3** 103
Thomas, co., Ks., U.S. **C2** 109
Thomas, co., Ne., U.S. **C5** 120
Thomasboro, Il., U.S. **C5** 106
Thomaston, Ct., U.S. **C3** 100
Thomaston, Ga., U.S. **D2** 103
Thomaston, Me., U.S. **D3** 112
Thomaston Reservoir, res., Ct., U.S. **C3** 100
Thomasville, Al., U.S. **D2** 94
Thomasville, Ga., U.S. **F3** 103
Thomasville, N.C., U.S. **B2** 126
Thompson, Mb., Can. **B3** 86
Thompson, Ct., U.S. **B8** 100
Thompson, N.D., U.S. **B8** 127
Thompson, stm., U.S. **A4** 118
Thompson Falls, Mt., U.S. **C1** 119
Thompson Island, i., Ma., U.S. **g11** 114
Thompson Lake, l., U.S. **D2** 112
Thompson Peak, mtn., Ca., U.S. **B2** 98
Thompson Peak, mtn., N.M., U.S. **h9** 124
Thompson Reservoir, res., Or., U.S. **E5** 130
Thomson, Ga., U.S. **C4** 103
Thongwa, Myan. **C3** 34
Thonon-les-Bains, Fr. **D10** 16
Thonotosassa, Fl., U.S. **D4** 102
Thonze, Myan. **C3** 34
Thorburn, N.S., Can. **D7** 87
Thoreau, N.M., U.S. **B1** 124
Thornbury, On., Can. **C4** 89
Thorndale, Tx., U.S. **D4** 136
Thornton, On., Can. **C5** 89
Thorntown, In., U.S. **D4** 107
Thorold, On., Can. **D5** 89
Thorp, Wi., U.S. **D3** 142
Thorsby, Al., U.S. **C3** 94
Thorshavn see Tórshavn, Far. Is. **n23** 10b
Thórshöfn, Ice. **k21** 10a
Thouars, Fr. **D6** 16
Thousand Islands, is., N.Y., U.S. **A4** 125
Thousand Lake Mountain, mtn., Ut., U.S. **E4** 137
Thousand Springs Creek, stm., U.S. **B7** 121
Thrace, hist. reg., Eur. **D11** 18
Thrakikón Pélagos, Grc. **D10** 18
Three Fingered Jack, mtn., Or., U.S. **C5** 130
Three Forks, Mt., U.S. **E5** 119
Three Hills, Ab., Can. **D4** 84
Three Hummock Island, i., Austl. **I4** 62
Three Kings Islands, is., N.Z. **n13** 63c
Three Lakes, Wi., U.S. **C4** 142
Three Mile Plains, N.S., Can. **E5** 87
Three Oaks, Mi., U.S. **G4** 115
Three Pagodas Pass, Asia **C3** 34
Three Points, Cape, c., Ghana **F4** 50
Three Rivers, Ma., U.S. **B3** 114
Three Rivers, Mi., U.S. **G5** 115
Three Rivers, Tx., U.S. **E3** 136
Three Sisters, mtn., Or., U.S. **C5** 130
Three Springs, Austl. **F2** 60
Throckmorton, co., Tx., U.S. **C3** 136
Throop, Pa., U.S. **m18** 131
Thule (Qaanaaq), Grnld. **C26** 82
Thun, Switz. **A1** 18
Thunder Bay, On., Can. **o17** 89

Name	Map Ref.	Page
Thunder Bay, b., Mi., U.S.	D7	115
Thunder Bay, stm., Mi., U.S.	D6	115
Thunderbird, Lake, res., Ok., U.S.	B4	129
Thunderbolt, Ga., U.S.	D5	103
Thunder Butte Creek, stm., S.D., U.S.	B3	134
Thurmont, Md., U.S.	A3	113
Thurso, P.Q., Can.	D2	90
Thurso, Scot., U.K.	A5	12
Thurston, co., Ne., U.S.	B9	120
Thurston, co., Wa., U.S.	C2	140
Thy, reg., Den.	H3	10
Thyolo, Mwi.	B6	56
Tianchang, China	C4	30
Tiandong, China	E2	30
Tianguá, Braz.	B3	74
Tianjin, China	D11	28
Tianjun, China	D7	28
Tianlin, China	E2	30
Tianmen, China	E10	28
Tianshui, China	E9	28
Tiantai, China	F12	28
Tianyang, China	E2	30
Tianzhu, China	D8	28
Tiassalé, C. Iv.	E4	50
Tibasti, Sarīr, des., Libya	B8	50
Tibati, Cam.	B2	54
Tiber see Tevere, stm., Italy	C4	18
Tiberias see Teverya, Isr.	D3	42
Tibesti, mts., Afr.	B8	50
Tibet see Xizang Zizhiqu, prov., China	E5	28
Tibet, Plateau of see Qing Zang Gaoyuan, plat., China	E4	28
Tiburón, Isla, i., Mex.	B2	78
Tice, Fl., U.S.	F5	102
Tîchît, Maur.	C3	50
Tickfaw, stm., La., U.S.	C5	111
Ticonderoga, N.Y., U.S.	B7	125
Ticul, Mex.	C7	78
Tidaholm, Swe.	G5	10
Tide Head, N.B., Can.	B3	87
Tidjikja, Maur.	C2	50
Tiébissou, C. Iv.	E3	50
Tieli, China	A1	31
Tieling, China	C12	28
Tien Shan, mts., Asia	C3	28
Tientsin see Tianjin, China	D11	28
Tierp, Swe.	F7	10
Tierra Amarilla, N.M., U.S.	A3	124
Tierra Blanca, Mex.	D5	78
Tierra de Campos, reg., Spain	F4	16
Tierra del Fuego, i., S.A.	H3	69
Tietê, stm., Braz.	F1	74
Tieton, Wa., U.S.	C5	140
Tieton, stm., Wa., U.S.	C4	140
Tieton Dam, Wa., U.S.	C4	140
Tiffany Mountain, mtn., Wa., U.S.	A6	140
Tiffin, Oh., U.S.	A2	128
Tiffin, stm., Oh., U.S.	A1	128
Tift, co., Ga., U.S.	E3	103
Tifton, Ga., U.S.	E3	103
Tigard, Or., U.S.	h12	130
Tigerton, Wi., U.S.	D4	142
Tighina, Mol.	F10	20
Tigil', Russia	D17	26
Tignall, Ga., U.S.	C4	103
Tignish, P.E., Can.	C5	87
Tigris (Dicle) (Dijlah), stm., Asia	D5	42
Tiguentourine, Alg.	F5	14
Tihert, Alg.	D4	14
Tihoreck, Russia	E6	26
Tihvin, Russia	C5	22
Tijuana, Mex.	A1	78
Tikal, hist., Guat.	B2	80
Tīkamgarh, India	E3	40
Tikrīt, Iraq	D4	42
Tikšeozero, ozero, l., Russia	C15	10
Tiksi, Russia	B14	26
Tilburg, Neth.	E9	12
Tilbury, On., Can.	E2	89
Tilden, Il., U.S.	E4	106
Tilden, Ne., U.S.	B8	120
Tilghman, Md., U.S.	C5	113
Tilghman Island, i., Md., U.S.	C5	113
Tilimsen, Alg.	D4	48
Tillabéri, Niger	D5	50
Tillamook, Or., U.S.	B3	130
Tillamook, co., Or., U.S.	B3	130
Tillanchāng Dwīp, i., India	H6	40
Tillery, Lake, res., N.C., U.S.	B2	126
Tillman, co., Ok., U.S.	C2	129
Tillmans Corner, Al., U.S.	E1	94
Tillsonburg, On., Can.	E4	89
Tílos, i., Grc.	F11	18
Tilton, Il., U.S.	C6	106
Tilton, N.H., U.S.	D3	122
Tiltonsville, Oh., U.S.	B5	128
Timanskij krjaž, hills, Russia	C7	26
Timaru, N.Z.	p13	63c
Timaševsk, Russia	G15	20
Timbalier Island, i., La., U.S.	E5	111
Timbaúba, Braz.	C4	74
Timbedgha, Maur.	C3	50
Timberlake, Va., U.S.	C3	139
Timberville, Va., U.S.	B4	139
Timbuktu see Tombouctou, Mali	C4	50
Timimoun, Alg.	E5	48
Timirist, Râs, c., Maur.	C1	50
Timişoara, Rom.	G6	20
Timmins, On., Can.	o19	89
Timmonsville, S.C., U.S.	C8	133
Timms Hill, hill, Wi., U.S.	C3	142
Timon, Braz.	C3	74
Timor, i., Indon.	E7	36
Timor Sea	F6	58
Timošino, Russia	B6	22
Timpanogos Cave National Monument, Ut., U.S.	C4	137
Timšer, Russia	B9	22
Tims Ford Lake, res., Tn., U.S.	B5	135
Tinaca Point, c., Phil.	E9	34
Tinaquillo, Ven.	C6	80
Tindouf, Alg.	E3	48
Tinghert, Ḥamādat, plat., Afr.	E7	48
Tingmerkpuk Mountain, mtn., Ak., U.S.	B7	95
Tingo María, Peru	E4	70
Tingsryd, Swe.	H6	10
Tinian, i., N. Mar. Is.	D12	32
Tinker Air Force Base, mil., Ok., U.S.	B4	129
Tinley Park, Il., U.S.	k9	106
Tinniswood, Mount, mtn., B.C., Can.	D6	85
Tinogasta, Arg.	D4	72
Tínos, i., Grc.	F10	18
Tinsukia, India	D7	40
Tintina, Arg.	D5	72
Tinton Falls, N.J., U.S.	C4	123
Tioga, La., U.S.	C3	111
Tioga, N.D., U.S.	A3	127
Tioga, co., N.Y., U.S.	C4	125
Tioga, co., Pa., U.S.	C7	131
Tioga, stm., Pa., U.S.	B7	131
Tiogue Lake, res., R.I., U.S.	D3	132
Tioman, Pulau, i., Malay.	C2	36
Tionesta Creek, stm., Pa., U.S.	C3	131
Tionesta Lake, res., Pa., U.S.	D3	131
Tioughnioga, stm., N.Y., U.S.	C4	125
Tipitapa, Nic.	C2	80
Tippah, co., Ms., U.S.	A5	117
Tippah, stm., Ms., U.S.	A4	117
Tipp City, Oh., U.S.	C1	128
Tippecanoe, co., In., U.S.	D4	107
Tippecanoe, stm., In., U.S.	C4	107
Tipperary, Austl.	C5	60
Tipton, Ca., U.S.	D4	98
Tipton, Ia., U.S.	C6	108
Tipton, In., U.S.	D5	107
Tipton, Mo., U.S.	C5	118
Tipton, Ok., U.S.	C2	129
Tipton, co., In., U.S.	D5	107
Tipton, co., Tn., U.S.	B2	135
Tipton, Mount, mtn., Az., U.S.	B1	96
Tiptonville, Tn., U.S.	A2	135
Tirana see Tiranë, Alb.	D7	18
Tiranë, Alb.	D7	18
Tiraspol, Mol.	F10	20
Tire, Tur.	C2	44
Tirebolu, Tur.	B8	44
Tiree, i., Scot., U.K.	B3	12
Tírnavos, Grc.	E9	18
Tiruchchirāppalli, India	G3	40
Tirunelveli, India	H3	40
Tirupati, India	G3	40
Tiruppur, India	G3	40
Tiruvannāmalai, India	G3	40
Tirūvottiyūr, India	G4	40
Tisa (Tisza) (Tysa), stm., Eur.	G6	20
Tishomingo, Ok., U.S.	C5	129
Tishomingo, co., Ms., U.S.	A5	117
Tiskilwa, Il., U.S.	B4	106
Tissemsilt, Alg.	J7	16
Tīsta, stm., Asia	A1	34
Tisza (Tisa) (Tysa), stm., Eur.	F6	20
Titicaca, Lake, l., S.A.	E4	68
Titilāgarh, India	E4	40
Titograd see Podgorica, Yugo.	C7	18
Titonka, Ia., U.S.	A3	108
Titov Veles, Mac.	D8	18
Titran, Nor.	E3	10
Titule, D.R.C.	C5	54
Titus, co., Tx., U.S.	C5	136
Titusville, Fl., U.S.	D6	102
Titusville, Pa., U.S.	C2	131
Tivaouane, Sen.	C1	50
Tiverton, On., Can.	C3	89
Tiverton, R.I., U.S.	D6	132
Tizimín, Mex.	C7	78
Tizi-Ouzou, Alg.	C5	48
Tjeggelvas, l., Swe.	C7	10
Tjukalinsk, Russia	D9	26
Tjul'gan, Russia	D10	22
Tjumen', Russia	D8	26
Tkibuli, Geor.	A10	44
Tkvarčeli, Geor.	A9	44
Tlahualilo de Zaragoza, Mex.	B4	78
Tlalnepantla, Mex.	D5	78
Tlaquepaque, Mex.	C4	78
Tlaxcala, state, Mex.	D5	78
Tlaxcala de Xicohténcatl, Mex.	D5	78
Tmassah, Libya	A8	50
Toamasina, Madag.	B8	56
Toano, Va., U.S.	C6	139
Toano Range, mts., Nv., U.S.	C7	121
Toast, N.C., U.S.	A2	126
Toba, Danau, l., Indon.	C1	36
Tobacco Root Mountains, mts., Mt., U.S.	E5	119
Tobago, i., Trin.	C7	80
Toba Inlet, b., B.C., Can.	D5	85
Toba Kākar Range, mts., Pak.	D9	42
Tobejuba, Isla, i., Ven.	D7	80
Tobin, Mount, mtn., Nv., U.S.	C4	121
Tobin Lake, l., Sk., Can.	D4	91
Tobin Range, mts., Nv., U.S.	C4	121
Tobique, stm., N.B., Can.	B2	87
Tobol, Kaz.	D11	22
Tobol, stm., Asia	D8	26
Tobol'sk, Russia	D8	26
Tobyhanna, Pa., U.S.	D11	131
Tocantínia, Braz.	E10	70
Tocantinópolis, Braz.	C2	74
Tocantins, state, Braz.	D2	74
Tocantins, stm., Braz.	B2	74
Toccoa, Ga., U.S.	B3	103
Toccoa, stm., Ga., U.S.	B2	103
Toccoa Falls, Ga., U.S.	B3	103
Tocopilla, Chile	B2	69
Todd, co., Ky., U.S.	D2	110
Todd, co., Mn., U.S.	D4	116
Todd, co., S.D., U.S.	D5	134
Tofield, Ab., Can.	C4	84
Tofino, B.C., Can.	E5	85
Togiak, Ak., U.S.	D7	95
Togian, Kepulauan, is., Indon.	D6	36
Togo, ctry., Afr.	E5	50
Togtoh, China	A3	30
Togwotee Pass, Wy., U.S.	C2	143
Tohakum Peak, mtn., Nv., U.S.	C2	121
Tohatchi, N.M., U.S.	B1	124
Tohopekaliga, Lake, l., Fl., U.S.	D5	102
Toiyabe Range, mts., Nv., U.S.	D4	121
Tok, Ak., U.S.	C11	95
Tōkamachi, Japan	C3	31
Tokat, Tur.	B7	44
Tokelau, dep., Oc.	E12	58
Tokmak, Kyrg.	A3	40
Tokmak, Ukr.	F13	20
Tokoroa, N.Z.	o14	63c
Toktogul, Kyrg.	A2	40
Tokuno-shima, i., Japan	A9	34
Tokushima, Japan	D2	31
Tōkyō, Japan	D16	28
Tôlañaro, Madag.	D8	56
Toledo, Braz.	C7	72
Toledo, Spain	H4	16
Toledo, Ia., U.S.	B5	108
Toledo, Il., U.S.	D5	106
Toledo, Oh., U.S.	A2	128
Toledo, Or., U.S.	C3	130
Toledo Bend Reservoir, res., U.S.	E9	92
Toledo Bend Reservoir, res., U.S.	C2	111
Toler, Ky., U.S.	C7	110
Toliara, Madag.	C7	56
Tolima, Nevado del, vol., Col.	C4	70
Tolitoli, Indon.	C6	36
Toljatti, Russia	D6	26
Tol'ka, Russia	C10	26
Tolland, Ct., U.S.	B6	100
Tolland, co., Ct., U.S.	B6	100
Tollesboro, Ky., U.S.	B6	110
Tolleson, Az., U.S.	m8	96
Tolmezzo, Italy	A4	18
Tolo, D.R.C.	D3	54
Tolo, Gulf of see Tolo, Teluk, b., Indon.	D6	36
Tolo, Teluk, b., Indon.	D6	36
Tolono, Il., U.S.	D5	106
Tolstoj, mys, c., Russia	D17	26
Tolt Reservoir, res., Wa., U.S.	B4	140
Tolú, Col.	D4	80
Toluca, Il., U.S.	C4	106
Toluca de Lerdo, Mex.	D5	78
Tomah, Wi., U.S.	E3	142
Tomahawk, Wi., U.S.	C4	142
Tomahawk Lake, l., Wi., U.S.	C4	142
Tomakomai, Japan	C16	28
Tomaszów Lubelski, Pol.	D7	20
Tomaszów Mazowiecki, Pol.	D6	20
Tomball, Tx., U.S.	D5	136
Tombe, Sudan	B6	54
Tombigbee, stm., U.S.	D1	94
Tombouctou, Mali	C4	50
Tombstone, Az., U.S.	F5	96
Tombua, Ang.	B1	56
Tomé, Chile	F3	72
Tomé-Açu, Braz.	B2	74
Tomelloso, Spain	H5	16
Tom Green, co., Tx., U.S.	D2	136
Tomini, Indon.	C6	36
Tomini, Gulf of see Tomini, Teluk, b., Indon.	D6	36
Tomini, Teluk, b., Indon.	D6	36
Tom Nevers Head, c., Ma., U.S.	D8	114
Tomo, stm., Col.	B6	70
Tompkins, co., N.Y., U.S.	C4	125
Tompkinsville, Ky., U.S.	D4	110
Tom Price, Austl.	E2	60
Tomptokan, Russia	D15	26
Toms, stm., N.J., U.S.	C4	123
Tomsk, Russia	D10	26
Toms River, N.J., U.S.	D4	123
Tonalá, Mex.	D6	78
Tonasket, Wa., U.S.	A6	140
Tonawanda Indian Reservation, N.Y., U.S.	B2	125
Tondano, Indon.	C6	36
Tonekābon, Iran	C6	42
Tonga, ctry., Oc.	F12	58
Tonganoxie, Ks., U.S.	C8	109
Tonga Ridge	J21	64
Tongatapu, i., Tonga	G12	58
Tonga Trench	K21	64
Tongcheng, China	E11	28
Tongchuan, China	D9	28
Tongguan, China	E10	28
Tonghai, China	G8	28
Tonghua, China	C13	28
Tongjiang, China	C2	30
Tongjiang, China	A2	31
Tongjosŏn-man, b., N. Kor.	D13	28
Tongliao, China	C12	28
Tongoy, Chile	D2	69
Tongren, China	F9	28
Tongren, China	B1	30
Tongsa Dzong, Bhu.	D6	40
Tongtian, stm., China	E7	28
Tongue, stm., Mt., U.S.	E10	119
Tongue, stm., Tx., U.S.	p13	136
Tongxian, China	D11	28
Tongyu, China	C12	28
Tongzi, China	F9	28
Tonk, India	D3	40
Tonkawa, Ok., U.S.	A4	129
Tonkin, Gulf of, b., Asia	B5	34
Tônlé Sab, Bœng, l., Camb.	D4	34
Tonle Sap see Tônlé Sab, Bœng, l., Camb.	D4	34
Tonopah, Nv., U.S.	E4	121
Tønsberg, Nor.	G4	10
Tonstad, Nor.	G2	10
Tonto National Monument, Az., U.S.	D4	96
Tonto Natural Bridge, Az., U.S.	C4	96
Tooele, Ut., U.S.	C3	137
Tooele, co., Ut., U.S.	C2	137
Toole, co., Mt., U.S.	B5	119
Toombs, co., Ga., U.S.	D4	103
Toomsboro, Ga., U.S.	D3	103
Toora-Hem, Russia	D11	26
Toowoomba, Austl.	F5	62
Topeka, In., U.S.	A6	107
Topeka, Ks., U.S.	C8	109
Topock, Az., U.S.	C1	96
Topol'čany, Slvk.	E5	20
Topolobampo, Mex.	B3	78
Topozero, ozero, l., Russia	D14	10
Toppenish, Wa., U.S.	C5	140
Topsfield, Ma., U.S.	A6	114
Topsham, Me., U.S.	E3	112
Top Springs, Austl.	D5	60
Topton, Pa., U.S.	F10	131
Toquima Range, mts., Nv., U.S.	E5	121
Tor, Eth.	B6	54
Torbalı, Tur.	C2	44
Torbat-e Ḥeydarīyeh, Iran	C7	42
Torbat-e Jām, Iran	C8	42
Torbay, Nf., Can.	E5	88
Torbay see Torquay, Eng., U.K.	E5	12
Torbert, Mount, mtn., Ak., U.S.	g15	95
Torch Lake, l., Mi., U.S.	D5	115
Tordesillas, Spain	G4	16
Töre, Swe.	D10	10
Torez, Ukr.	E15	20
Torino (Turin), Italy	B1	18
Torit, Sudan	J11	48
Torneälven (Tornionjoki), stm., Eur.	C9	10
Torneträsk, l., Swe.	B8	10
Torngat Mountains, mts., Can.	f8	88
Tornio, Fin.	D11	10
Tornionjoki (Torneälven), stm., Eur.	C10	10
Tornquist, Arg.	F5	72
Toro, Spain	G4	16
Toronto, On., Can.	D5	89
Toronto, Oh., U.S.	B5	128
Toronto Lake, res., Ks., U.S.	E7	109
Toro Peak, mtn., Ca., U.S.	F5	98
Tororo, Ug.	C6	54
Toros Dağları, mts., Tur.	D5	44
Torquay, Eng., U.K.	E5	12
Torrance, Ca., U.S.	n12	98
Torrance, co., N.M., U.S.	C3	124
Torrelavega, Spain	F4	16
Torremolinos, Spain	I4	16
Torrens, Lake, l., Austl.	G2	62
Torrent, Spain	H6	16
Torreón, Mex.	B4	78
Torres, Îles, is., Vanuatu	j9	62a
Torres Strait, strt., Oc.	B3	62
Torres Vedras, Port.	H2	16
Torrington, Ct., U.S.	B3	100
Torrington, Wy., U.S.	D8	143
Tórshavn, Far. Is.	n23	10b
Tórtolas, Cerro las, mtn., S.A.	D4	72
Tortosa, Spain	G7	16
Tortue, Île de la, i., Haiti	A5	80
Toruń, Pol.	C5	20
Toržok, Russia	C5	22
Tostado, Arg.	D5	72
Tõstamaa, Est.	G10	10
Tosya, Tur.	B5	44
Totagatic, stm., Wi., U.S.	B2	142
Totana, Spain	I6	16
Toteng, Bots.	C3	56
Tot'ma, Russia	B7	22
Totowa, N.J., U.S.	B4	123
Totson Mountain, mtn., Ak., U.S.	C8	95
Tottenham (part of Alliston Beeton Tecumseth and Tottenham), On., Can.	C5	89
Tottori, Japan	C2	31
Touba, C. Iv.	E3	50
Toubkal, Jebel, mtn., Mor.	D3	48
Touchet, stm., Wa., U.S.	C7	140
Toudao see Songhua, stm., China	B14	28
Touggourt, Alg.	D6	48
Touisset, Ma., U.S.	C5	114
Toul, Fr.	C9	16
Touliu, Tai.	E5	30
Toulon, Fr.	F9	16
Toulon, Il., U.S.	B4	106
Toulouse, Fr.	F7	16
Toumodi, C. Iv.	E3	50
Toungoo, Myan.	C3	34
Touraine, hist. reg., Fr.	D7	16
Tournai, Bel.	E8	12
Tours, Fr.	D7	16
Toussaint Creek, stm., Oh., U.S.	f7	128
Toussidé, Pic, vol., Chad	B8	50
Toutle, North Fork, stm., Wa., U.S.	C3	140
Touwsrivier, S. Afr.	E3	56
Tovarkovskij, Russia	C15	20
Tovuz, Azer.	B11	44
Towanda, Il., U.S.	C5	106
Towanda, Ks., U.S.	E7	109
Towanda, Pa., U.S.	C9	131
Towanda Creek, stm., Pa., U.S.	C8	131
Tower City, Pa., U.S.	E8	131
Town Creek, Al., U.S.	A2	94
Towner, N.D., U.S.	A5	127
Towner, co., N.D., U.S.	A6	127
Towns, co., Ga., U.S.	B3	103
Townsend, De., U.S.	C3	101
Townsend, Mt., U.S.	D5	119
Townshend Reservoir, res., Vt., U.S.	E3	138
Townsville, Austl.	D4	62
Towson, Md., U.S.	B4	113
Towuti, Danau, l., Indon.	D6	36
Toyama, Japan	D15	28
Toyohashi, Japan	D3	31
Toyota, Japan	C3	31
Tozeur, Tun.	D6	48
Trabzon, Tur.	B8	44
Tracadie, N.B., Can.	B5	87
Tracy, N.B., Can.	D3	87
Tracy, P.Q., Can.	C4	90
Tracy, Ca., U.S.	D3	98
Tracy, Mn., U.S.	F3	116
Tracy City, Tn., U.S.	D8	135
Tracyton, Wa., U.S.	e10	140
Tradewater, stm., Ky., U.S.	C2	110
Traer, Ia., U.S.	B5	108
Trafford, Pa., U.S.	k14	131
Trafford, Lake, l., Fl., U.S.	F5	102
Trail, B.C., Can.	E9	85
Trail Creek, In., U.S.	A4	107
Traill, co., N.D., U.S.	B8	127
Trail Ridge, mtn., U.S.	F4	103
Tralee, Ire.	D2	12
Tranås, Swe.	G6	10
Trancas, Arg.	D4	72
Trang, Thai.	E3	34
Trangan, Pulau, i., Indon.	E8	36
Trani, Italy	D6	18
Transantarctic Mountains, mts., Ant.	E32	67
Transkei, hist. reg., S. Afr.	E4	56
Transylvania, co., N.C., U.S.	f10	126
Transylvania, hist. reg., Rom.	F7	20
Transylvanian Alps see Carpații Meridionali, mts., Rom.	G7	20
Trapani, Italy	E4	18
Trappe, Md., U.S.	C5	113
Trapper Peak, mtn., Mt., U.S.	E2	119
Traralgon, Austl.	H4	62
Trârza, reg., Maur.	C1	50
Trasimeno, Lago, l., Italy	C3	18
Travelers Rest, S.C., U.S.	B3	133
Traverse, co., Mn., U.S.	E2	116
Traverse, Lake, l., U.S.	B9	134
Traverse City, Mi., U.S.	D5	115
Tra Vinh, Viet.	E5	34
Travis, co., Tx., U.S.	D4	136
Travis Air Force Base, mil., Ca., U.S.	C2	98
Travnik, Bos.	B6	18
Tray Mountain, mtn., Ga., U.S.	B3	103

Name	Map Ref.	Page
Trayning, Austl.	G2	60
Treasure, co., Mt., U.S.	D9	119
Treasure Island Naval Station, mil., Ca., U.S.	h8	98
Třebíč, Czech Rep.	E3	20
Trebišov, Slvk.	E6	20
Trego, co., Ks., U.S.	D4	109
Treherne, Mb., Can.	E2	86
Treinta y Tres, Ur.	E7	72
Trelew, Arg.	F3	69
Trelleborg, Swe.	I5	10
Tremblant, Mont, mtn., P.Q., Can.	C3	90
Tremont, Il., U.S.	C4	106
Tremont, Pa., U.S.	E9	131
Tremonton, Ut., U.S.	B3	137
Tremp, Spain	F7	16
Trempealeau, Wi., U.S.	D2	142
Trempealeau, co., Wi., U.S.	D2	142
Trempealeau, stm., Wi., U.S.	D2	142
Trenche, stm., P.Q., Can.	B5	90
Trenčín, Slvk.	E5	20
Trenque Lauquen, Arg.	F5	72
Trent, stm., Eng., U.K.	D6	12
Trent, stm., N.C., U.S.	B5	126
Trente et un Milles, Lac des, l., P.Q., Can.	C2	90
Trento, Italy	A3	18
Trenton, On., Can.	C7	89
Trenton, Fl., U.S.	C4	102
Trenton, Ga., U.S.	B1	103
Trenton, Il., U.S.	E4	106
Trenton, Mi., U.S.	F7	115
Trenton, Mo., U.S.	A4	118
Trenton, Ne., U.S.	D4	120
Trenton, N.J., U.S.	C3	123
Trenton, Oh., U.S.	C1	128
Trenton, Tn., U.S.	B3	135
Trepassey, Nf., Can.	E5	88
Trepassey Bay, b., Nf., Can.	E5	88
Tres Arroyos, Arg.	F5	72
Tresckow, Pa., U.S.	E10	131
Três Corações, Braz.	F2	74
Tres Esquinas, Col.	C4	70
Três Lagoas, Braz.	F1	74
Tres Marías, Islas, is., Mex.	C3	78
Três Marias, Represa de, res., Braz.	E2	74
Tres Puntas, Cabo, c., Arg.	G3	69
Três Rios, Braz.	F3	74
Tres Zapotes, hist., Mex.	D5	78
Treutlen, co., Ga., U.S.	D4	103
Treviso, Italy	B4	18
Trevor, Wi., U.S.	n11	142
Trevorton, Pa., U.S.	E8	131
Treynor, Ia., U.S.	C2	108
Trezevant, Tn., U.S.	A3	135
Triadelphia, W.V., U.S.	A4	141
Triadelphia Reservoir, res., Md., U.S.	B3	113
Triangle, Va., U.S.	B5	139
Tribune, Ks., U.S.	D2	109
Tricase, Italy	E7	18
Trichinopoly see Tiruchchirāppalli, India	G3	40
Trichūr, India	G3	40
Tri City, Or., U.S.	E3	130
Trident Peak, mtn., Nv., U.S.	B3	121
Trier, Ger.	F10	12
Trieste, Italy	B4	18
Trigg, co., Ky., U.S.	D2	110
Triglav, mtn., Slvn.	A4	18
Trigo Mountains, mts., Az., U.S.	D1	96
Tríkala, Grc.	E8	18
Trikora, Puncak, mtn., Indon.	G10	32
Tri Lakes, In., U.S.	B7	107
Trimble, Tn., U.S.	A2	135
Trimble, co., Ky., U.S.	B4	110
Trimont, Mn., U.S.	G4	116
Trincomalee, Sri L.	H4	40
Tring Jonction, P.Q., Can.	C6	90
Trinidad, Bol.	A5	72
Trinidad, Col.	B5	70
Trinidad, Cuba	A3	80
Trinidad, Co., U.S.	D6	99
Trinidad, Tx., U.S.	C4	136
Trinidad, Ur.	E6	72
Trinidad, i., Trin.	C7	80
Trinidad and Tobago, ctry., N.A.	F12	76
Trinidad Head, c., Ca., U.S.	B1	98
Trinity, Al., U.S.	A2	94
Trinity, Tx., U.S.	D5	136
Trinity, co., Ca., U.S.	B2	98
Trinity, co., Tx., U.S.	D5	136
Trinity, stm., Ca., U.S.	B2	98
Trinity, stm., Tx., U.S.	D5	136
Trinity Bay, b., Nf., Can.	D5	88
Trinity Islands, is., Ak., U.S.	D9	95
Trinity Mountain, mtn., Id., U.S.	F3	105
Trinity Mountains, mts., Ca., U.S.	B2	98
Trinity Peak, mtn., Nv., U.S.	C3	121
Trinity Range, mts., Nv., U.S.	C3	121
Trion, Ga., U.S.	B1	103
Tripoli see Ṭarābulus, Leb.	E6	44
Tripoli see Ṭarābulus, Libya	D7	48
Tripoli, Ia., U.S.	B5	108
Trípolis, Grc.	F9	18
Tripolitania see Ṭarābulus, hist. reg., Libya	E7	14
Tripp, S.D., U.S.	D8	134
Tripp, co., S.D., U.S.	D6	134
Tripura, prov., India	E6	40
Tristan da Cunha Group, is., St. Hel.	M8	46
Triumph, La., U.S.	E6	111
Trivandrum, India	H3	40
Trnava, Slvk.	E4	20
Trochu, Ab., Can.	D4	84
Troick, Russia	D8	26
Troicko-Pečorsk, Russia	B10	22
Trois-Pistoles, P.Q., Can.	A8	90
Trois-Rivières, P.Q., Can.	C5	90
Trois-Rivières-Ouest, P.Q., Can.	C5	90
Troïts'ke, Ukr.	F11	20
Trollhättan, Swe.	G5	10
Tromsø, Nor.	B8	10
Trona, Ca., U.S.	E5	98
Tronador, Monte, mtn., S.A.	F2	69
Trondheim, Nor.	E4	10
Trondheimsfjorden, b., Nor.	E4	10
Trophy Mountain, mtn., B.C., Can.	D8	85
Trotwood, Oh., U.S.	C1	128
Troup, co., Ga., U.S.	C1	103
Trousdale, co., Tn., U.S.	A5	135
Trout, stm., Fl., U.S.	m8	102
Trout, stm., Vt., U.S.	B3	138
Trout Creek, On., Can.	B5	89
Trout Creek Pass, Co., U.S.	C5	99
Trout Lake, Wa., U.S.	D4	140
Trout Lake, l., On., Can.	o16	89
Trout Lake, l., Mn., U.S.	B6	116
Trout Lake, l., Wi., U.S.	B4	142
Troutman, N.C., U.S.	B2	126
Trout Peak, mtn., Wy., U.S.	B3	143
Trout River, Nf., Can.	D2	88
Troy, Al., U.S.	D4	94
Troy, Id., U.S.	C2	105
Troy, Il., U.S.	E4	106
Troy, Ks., U.S.	C8	109
Troy, Mi., U.S.	o15	115
Troy, Mo., U.S.	C7	118
Troy, Mt., U.S.	B1	119
Troy, N.C., U.S.	B3	126
Troy, N.H., U.S.	E2	122
Troy, N.Y., U.S.	C7	125
Troy, Oh., U.S.	B1	128
Troy, Pa., U.S.	C8	131
Troy, Tn., U.S.	A2	135
Troy see Truva, hist., Tur.	C2	44
Troyes, Fr.	C8	16
Troy Peak, mtn., Nv., U.S.	E6	121
Trubčevsk, Russia	C12	20
Truchas Peak, mtn., N.M., U.S.	B4	124
Trucial States see United Arab Emirates, ctry., Asia	F6	42
Truckee, Ca., U.S.	C3	98
Truckee, stm., U.S.	D2	121
Trujillo, Hond.	B2	80
Trujillo, Peru	E4	70
Trujillo, Spain	H4	16
Trujillo, Ven.	B5	70
Truk Islands see Chuuk Islands, is., Micron.	D9	58
Truman, Mn., U.S.	G4	116
Trumann, Ar., U.S.	B5	97
Trumansburg, N.Y., U.S.	C4	125
Trumbull, Ct., U.S.	E3	100
Trumbull, co., Oh., U.S.	A5	128
Trumbull, Mount, mtn., Az., U.S.	A2	96
Trussville, Al., U.S.	B3	94
Trustom Pond, l., R.I., U.S.	G3	132
Truth or Consequences (Hot Springs), N.M., U.S.	D2	124
Truva (Troy), hist., Tur.	C2	44
Tryon, N.C., U.S.	f10	126
Trzcianka, Pol.	C4	20
Tsaidam Basin see Qaidam Pendi, China	D6	28
Tsala Apopka Lake, l., Fl., U.S.	D4	102
Tsaratanana, Madag.	B8	56
Tsaratanana, mts., Madag.	A8	56
Tsau, Bots.	C3	56
Tsavo, Kenya	D7	54
Tschida, Lake, res., N.D., U.S.	C4	127
Tselinograd see Akmola, Kaz.	D9	26
Tses, Nmb.	D2	56
Tsévié, Togo	E5	50
Tshabong, Bots.	D3	56
Tshane, Bots.	C3	56
Tshela, D.R.C.	E2	54
Tshikapa, D.R.C.	E4	54
Tshofa, D.R.C.	E5	54
Tshumbe (Chiumbe), stm., Afr.	E4	54
Tsimlyansk Reservoir see Cimljanskoe vodohranilišče, res., Russia	E7	22
Tsintsabis, Nmb.	B2	56
Tsiombe, Madag.	D8	56
Tsiroanomandidy, Madag.	B8	56
Tsu, Japan	D3	31
Tsugaru-kaikyō, strt., Japan	C16	28
Tsumeb, Nmb.	B2	56
Tsuruoka, Japan	D15	28
Tsushima, is., Japan	D1	31
Tsuyama, Japan	C2	31
Tswaane, Bots.	C3	56
Tual, Indon.	E8	36
Tualatin, stm., Or., U.S.	h11	130
Tuamotu, Îles, is., Fr. Poly.	F15	58
Tuamotu Ridge	J24	64
Tuangku, Pulau, i., Indon.	C1	36
Tuapse, Russia	E5	26
Tuba City, Az., U.S.	A4	96
Tuban, Indon.	E4	36
Tubarão, Braz.	D8	72
Tübingen, Ger.	F11	12
Ṭubruq, Libya	D9	48
Tubuai, i., Fr. Poly.	G15	58
Tucacas, Ven.	A6	70
Tucannon, stm., Wa., U.S.	C8	140
Tucano, Braz.	D4	74
Tuckahoe, N.Y., U.S.	h13	125
Tuckahoe, stm., N.J., U.S.	E3	123
Tuckanarra, Austl.	F2	60
Tucker, Ga., U.S.	h8	103
Tucker, co., W.V., U.S.	B5	141
Tucker Island, i., N.J., U.S.	E4	123
Tuckerman, Ar., U.S.	B4	97
Tuckernuck Island, i., Ma., U.S.	D7	114
Tuckerton, N.J., U.S.	D4	123
Tucson, Az., U.S.	E5	96
Tucumcari, N.M., U.S.	B6	124
Tucumcari Mountain, mtn., N.M., U.S.	B6	124
Tucupita, Ven.	B7	70
Tucuruí, Braz.	B2	74
Tucuruí, Represa de, res., Braz.	B2	74
Tudela, Spain	F6	16
Tudmur, Syria	E8	44
Tugaloo Lake, res., U.S.	B1	133
Tugela, stm., S. Afr.	D5	56
Tug Fork, stm., U.S.	C2	141
Tuguegarao City, Phil.	C8	34
Tugur, Russia	D15	26
Tujmazy, Russia	D9	22
Tukangbesi, Kepulauan, is., Indon.	E6	36
Ṭūkrah, Libya	E8	14
Tukums, Lat.	H10	10
Tukuyu, Tan.	E6	54
Tukwila, Wa., U.S.	f11	140
Tula, Mex.	C5	78
Tula, Russia	D5	26
Tulalip Indian Reservation, Wa., U.S.	A3	140
Tulancingo, Mex.	C5	78
Tulare, Ca., U.S.	D4	98
Tulare, co., Ca., U.S.	D4	98
Tulare Lake, l., Ca., U.S.	D4	98
Tularosa, N.M., U.S.	D3	124
Tularosa Mountains, mts., N.M., U.S.	D1	124
Tularosa Valley, val., N.M., U.S.	E3	124
Tulbagh, S. Afr.	E2	56
Tulcán, Ec.	C4	70
Tulcea, Rom.	G10	20
Tul'chyn, Ukr.	E10	20
Tule Lake, sw., Ca., U.S.	B3	98
Tule River Indian Reservation, Ca., U.S.	E4	98
Tule Valley, val., Ut., U.S.	D2	137
Tuli, Zimb.	C4	56
Tulia, Tx., U.S.	B2	136
Tullahoma, Tn., U.S.	B5	135
Tulle, Fr.	E7	16
Tully, Austl.	D4	62
Tulsa, Ok., U.S.	A6	129
Tulsa, co., Ok., U.S.	B6	129
Tuluá, Col.	E4	80
Tulun, Russia	D12	26
Tulungagung, Indon.	E4	36
Tumacacori National Monument, Az., U.S.	F4	96
Tumaco, Col.	C4	70
Tuman-gang (Tumen), stm., Asia	B1	31
Tumanovo, Russia	B13	20
Tumbarumba, Austl.	H4	62
Tumbes, Peru	D3	70
Tumble Mountain, mtn., Mt., U.S.	E7	119
Tumbler Ridge, B.C., Can.	B7	85
Tumen, China	C13	28
Tumen (Tuman-gang), stm., Asia	B1	31
Tumeremo, Ven.	B7	70
Tumkūr, India	G3	40
Tumuc-Humac Mountains, mts., S.A.	C8	70
Tumut, Austl.	H4	62
Tumwater, Wa., U.S.	B3	140
Tunceli, Tur.	C8	44
Tunduru, Tan.	F7	54
Tunga, Nig.	E6	50
Tungabhadra, stm., India	F3	40
Tungabhadra Reservoir, res., India	F3	40
Tungkang, Tai.	E5	30
Tungsha Tao (Pratas Island), i., Tai.	E4	30
Tuni, India	F4	40
Tunica, Ms., U.S.	A3	117
Tunica, co., Ms., U.S.	A3	117
Tunis, Tun.	C7	48
Tunis, Golfe de, b., Tun.	F3	18
Tunis, Gulf of see Tunis, Golfe de, b., Tun.	F3	18
Tunisia, ctry., Afr.	D7	48
Tunja, Col.	B5	70
Tunkhannock, Pa., U.S.	C10	131
Tunk Lake, l., Me., U.S.	D4	112
Tunnel Hill, Ga., U.S.	B1	103
Tunp Range, mts., Wy., U.S.	D2	143
Tununak, Ak., U.S.	C6	95
Tunuyán, Arg.	E4	72
Tunxi, China	D4	30
Tuolumne, Ca., U.S.	D3	98
Tuolumne, co., Ca., U.S.	C4	98
Tuolumne, stm., Ca., U.S.	D3	98
Tupã, Braz.	F1	74
Tupaciguara, Braz.	E2	74
Tupelo, Ms., U.S.	A5	117
Tupiza, Bol.	C4	72
Tupper Lake, N.Y., U.S.	A6	125
Tupper Lake, l., N.Y., U.S.	A6	125
Tura, India	D6	40
Tura, Russia	C11	26
Tura, stm., Russia	D18	6
Turan, Russia	A6	28
Turan Lowland, pl., Asia	B7	42
Ṭurayf, Sau. Ar.	G8	44
Turbat, Pak.	E8	42
Turbeville, S.C., U.S.	D7	133
Turbo, Col.	B4	70
Turda, Rom.	F7	20
Turgaj, Kaz.	E8	26
Turgaj, stm., Kaz.	E8	26
Turgajskaja ložbina, reg., Kaz.	D8	26
Turgutlu, Tur.	C2	44
Turhal, Tur.	B7	44
Turia, stm., Spain	H6	16
Turin see Torino, Italy	B1	18
Turinsk, Russia	C11	22
Turkana, Lake see Rudolf, Lake, l., Afr.	C7	54
Turkestan, Kaz.	E8	26
Turkey, ctry., Asia	C3	38
Turkey, stm., Ia., U.S.	B6	108
Turkey Creek, stm., Ok., U.S.	A3	129
Turkey Point, c., Md., U.S.	B5	113
Turkish Republic of Northern Cyprus see North Cyprus, ctry., Asia	C2	44
Turkmenbaši, Turk.	E7	26
Turkmenistan, ctry., Asia	C7	42
Türkoğlu, Tur.	D7	44
Turks and Caicos Islands, dep., N.A.	D10	76
Turks Islands, is., T./C. Is.	A5	80
Turku (Åbo), Fin.	F10	10
Turley, Ok., U.S.	A6	129
Turlock, Ca., U.S.	D3	98
Turnbull, Mount, mtn., Az., U.S.	D5	96
Turneffe Islands, is., Belize	B2	80
Turner, Or., U.S.	C4	130
Turner, co., Ga., U.S.	E3	103
Turner, co., S.D., U.S.	D8	134
Turners Falls, Ma., U.S.	A2	114
Turner Valley, Ab., Can.	D3	84
Turnor Lake, l., Sk., Can.	m7	91
Turnu Măgurele, Rom.	H8	20
Turpan, China	C5	28
Turpan Pendi, depr., China	C5	28
Turquino, Pico, mtn., Cuba	B4	80
Turrell, Ar., U.S.	B5	97
Turret Peak, mtn., Az., U.S.	C4	96
Turtle Creek, Pa., U.S.	k14	131
Turtle Flambeau Flowage, res., Wi., U.S.	B3	142
Turtle Lake, N.D., U.S.	B5	127
Turtle Lake, Wi., U.S.	C1	142
Turtle Lake, l., Sk., Can.	D1	91
Turtle Mountain Indian Reservation, N.D., U.S.	A6	127
Turuhansk, Russia	C10	26
Tuscaloosa, Al., U.S.	B2	94
Tuscaloosa, co., Al., U.S.	B2	94
Tuscarawas, co., Oh., U.S.	B4	128
Tuscarawas, stm., Oh., U.S.	B4	128
Tuscarora Indian Reservation, N.Y., U.S.	B2	125
Tuscarora Mountain, mtn., Pa., U.S.	F6	131
Tuscarora Mountains, mts., Nv., U.S.	B5	121
Tuscola, Il., U.S.	D5	106
Tuscola, co., Mi., U.S.	E7	115
Tuscumbia, Al., U.S.	A2	94
Tuskegee, Al., U.S.	C4	94
Tusket, stm., N.S., Can.	E4	87
Tustumena Lake, l., Ak., U.S.	g16	95
Tutak, Tur.	C10	44
Tuticorin, India	H3	40
Tutrakan, Bul.	B11	18
Tuttle, Ok., U.S.	B4	129
Tuttle Creek Lake, res., Ks., U.S.	C7	109
Tuttlingen, Ger.	F11	12
Tutuila, i., Am. Sam.	F12	58
Tutupaca, Volcán, vol., Peru	G5	70
Tututalak Mountain, mtn., Ak., U.S.	B7	95
Tutwiler, Ms., U.S.	A3	117
Tuva, state, Russia	D11	26
Tuvalu, ctry., Oc.	E11	58
Ṭuwayq, Jabal, mts., Sau. Ar.	F5	38
Tuxedo, N.C., U.S.	f10	126
Tuxedo Park, De., U.S.	i7	101
Tuxpan, Mex.	C3	78
Tuxpan de Rodríguez Cano, Mex.	C5	78
Tuxtepec, Mex.	D5	78
Tuxtla Gutiérrez, Mex.	D6	78
Tuyen Quang, Viet.	B5	34
Tuy Ḥoa, Viet.	D5	34
Tūysarkān, Iran	E13	44
Tuz, Iraq	E11	44
Tuz Gölü, l., Tur.	C5	44
Tuzigoot National Monument, Az., U.S.	C4	96
Tuzla, Bos.	B7	18
Tver', Russia	D5	26
Tweed, On., Can.	C7	89
Tweedsmuir Provincial Park, B.C., Can.	C4	85
Tweedy Mountain, mtn., Mt., U.S.	E4	119
Twelvepole Creek, stm., W.V., U.S.	C2	141
Twentymile Creek, stm., W.V., U.S.	C3	141
Twentynine Palms, Ca., U.S.	E5	98
Twentynine Palms Marine Corps Base, mil., Ca., U.S.	E5	98
Twiggs, co., Ga., U.S.	D3	103
Twillingate, Nf., Can.	D4	88
Twin Buttes, mtn., Or., U.S.	C4	130
Twin Buttes Reservoir, res., Tx., U.S.	D2	136
Twin City, Ga., U.S.	D4	103
Twin Creek, stm., Oh., U.S.	C1	128
Twin Falls, Id., U.S.	G4	105
Twin Falls, co., Id., U.S.	G4	105
Twin Knolls, Az., U.S.	m9	96
Twin Lakes, Ga., U.S.	F3	103
Twin Lakes, Wi., U.S.	F5	142
Twin Lakes, l., Ct., U.S.	A2	100
Twin Lakes, l., Ia., U.S.	B3	108
Twin Lakes, l., Me., U.S.	C4	112
Twin Mountains, mtn., Wy., U.S.	E7	143
Twin Peaks, mts., Id., U.S.	E4	105
Twin Rivers, N.J., U.S.	C4	123
Twinsburg, Oh., U.S.	A4	128
Twin Valley, Mn., U.S.	C2	116
Twisp, Wa., U.S.	A5	140
Two Harbors, Mn., U.S.	C7	116
Two Hills, Ab., Can.	C5	84
Two Mile Beach, N.J., U.S.	F3	123
Two Rivers, Wi., U.S.	D6	142
Two Rivers, North Branch, stm., Mn., U.S.	B2	116
Two Rivers, South Branch, stm., Mn., U.S.	B2	116
Tybee Island, Ga., U.S.	D6	103
Tygart Lake, res., W.V., U.S.	B5	141
Tygart River, Falls of the, wtfl, W.V., U.S.	k10	141
Tygart Valley, stm., W.V., U.S.	B4	141
Tyger, stm., S.C., U.S.	B4	133
Tyler, Mn., U.S.	F2	116
Tyler, Tx., U.S.	C5	136
Tyler, co., Tx., U.S.	D5	136
Tyler, co., W.V., U.S.	B4	141
Tyler, Lake, res., Tx., U.S.	C5	136
Tyler Branch, stm., Vt., U.S.	B3	138
Tyler Heights, W.V., U.S.	C3	141
Tylertown, Ms., U.S.	D3	117
Tymochtee Creek, stm., Oh., U.S.	B2	128
Tynda, Russia	D14	26
Tyndall, S.D., U.S.	E8	134
Tyndall Air Force Base, mil., Fl., U.S.	u16	102
Tyne, stm., Eng., U.K.	C5	12
Tyonek, Ak., U.S.	C9	95
Tyre see Ṣūr, Leb.	F6	44
Tyrifjorden, l., Nor.	F3	10
Tyrma, Russia	A14	28
Tyrone, N.M., U.S.	E1	124
Tyrone, Ok., U.S.	e9	129
Tyrone, Pa., U.S.	E5	131
Tyronza, Ar., U.S.	B5	97
Tyrrell, co., N.C., U.S.	B6	126
Tyrrhenian Sea, Eur.	D3	18
Tysa (Tisa) (Tisza), stm., Eur.	E7	20
Tysnesøya, i., Nor.	G1	10
Tzaneen, S. Afr.	C5	56

U

Name	Map Ref.	Page
Uaupés (Vaupés), stm., S.A.	C6	70
Ubá, Braz.	F3	74
Ubangi (Oubangui), stm., Afr.	D3	54
Ubatã, Braz.	D4	74
Ube, Japan	E14	28
Úbeda, Spain	I5	16
Uberaba, Braz.	E2	74
Uberlândia, Braz.	E2	74
Ubly, Mi., U.S.	E8	115
Ubon Ratchathani, Thai.	C4	34
Ubrique, Spain	I4	16
Ubundu, D.R.C.	D5	54
Učaly, Russia	D10	22

Name — Map Ref. — Page

Učami, Russia . . . **C11** 26
Ucar, Azer. . . . **B12** 44
Ucayali, stm., Peru . . . **E5** 70
Uchiura-wan, b., Japan . . . **C16** 28
Uchiza, Peru . . . **E4** 70
Učkuduk, Uzb. . . . **B8** 42
Ucluelet, B.C., Can. . . . **E5** 85
Ucon, Id., U.S. . . . **F7** 105
Udagamandalam, India . . . **G3** 40
Udaipur, India . . . **E2** 40
Udall, Ks., U.S. . . . **E6** 109
Uddevalla, Swe. . . . **G4** 10
Uddjaure, l., Swe. . . . **D7** 10
Udgīr, India . . . **F3** 40
Udine, Italy . . . **A4** 18
Udmurtia see Udmurtija, state, Russia . . . **D7** 26
Udmurtija, state, Russia . . . **D7** 26
Udon Thani, Thai. . . . **C4** 34
Udupi, India . . . **G2** 40
Ueda, Japan . . . **C3** 31
Uedinenija, ostrov, i., Russia **B10** 26
Uele, stm., D.R.C. . . . **C4** 54
Uel'kal', Russia . . . **C19** 26
Uelzen, Ger. . . . **D12** 12
Ufa, Russia . . . **D7** 26
Uganda, ctry., Afr. . . . **C6** 54
Ugarit, hist., Syria . . . **E6** 44
Ugashik Lakes, l., Ak., U.S. . . **D8** 95
Uglegorsk, Russia . . . **E16** 26
Uglič, Russia . . . **C6** 22
Uherské Hradiště, Czech Rep. . . . **E4** 20
Uhrichsville, Oh., U.S. . . . **B4** 128
Uhta, Russia . . . **C7** 26
Uíge, Ang. . . . **E3** 54
Uil, Kaz. . . . **E9** 22
Uinta, co., Wy., U.S. . . . **E2** 143
Uinta, stm., Ut., U.S. . . . **C5** 137
Uintah, co., Ut., U.S. . . . **D6** 137
Uintah and Ouray Indian Reservation, Ut., U.S. . **C5** 137
Uinta Mountains, mts., Ut., U.S. . . . **C5** 137
Uitenhage, S. Afr. . . . **E4** 56
Uivak, Cape, c., Nf., Can. . **f9** 88
Ujar, Russia . . . **D11** 26
Ujelang, atoll, Marsh. Is. . . . **D10** 58
Ujiji, Tan. . . . **D5** 54
Ujjain, India . . . **E3** 40
Ujungpandang, Indon. . . . **E5** 36
Uka, Russia . . . **D18** 26
Ukara Island, i., Tan. . . . **D6** 54
Ukerewe Island, i., Tan. . . . **D6** 54
Ukiah, Ca., U.S. . . . **C2** 98
Ukyr, Russia . . . **B9** 28
Ulaanbaatar (Ulan Bator), Mong. . . . **B9** 28
Ulaangom, Mong. . . . **B6** 28
Ulaan-Uul, Mong. . . . **C10** 28
Ulak Island, i., Ak., U.S. . . . **E4** 95
Ulan Bator see Ulaanbaatar, Mong. . . . **B9** 28
Ulan-Ude, Russia . . . **D12** 26
Ulan Ul Hu, l., China . . . **C6** 40
Ulchin, S. Kor. . . . **C1** 31
Ulcinj, Yugo. . . . **D7** 18
Ulhāsnagar, India . . . **F2** 40
Uliastay, Mong. . . . **B7** 28
Ulja, Russia . . . **D16** 26
Uljanovsk, Russia . . . **D6** 26
Ullŭng-do, i., S. Kor. . . . **C2** 31
Ulm, Ger. . . . **F11** 12
Ulóngué, Moz. . . . **A5** 56
Ulsan, S. Kor. . . . **C1** 31
Ulster, co., N.Y., U.S. . . . **D6** 125
Ulster, hist. reg., Eur. . . . **C3** 12
Ulu, Indon. . . . **C7** 36
Ulu, Russia . . . **C14** 26
Ulúa, stm., Hond. . . . **B2** 80
Ulubat Gölü, l., Tur. . . . **B3** 44
Ulundi, S. Afr. . . . **D5** 56
Ulungur Hu, l., China . . . **B5** 28
Uluru (Ayers Rock), mtn., Austl. . . . **F5** 60
Ulverstone, Austl. . . . **I4** 62
Ulysses, Ks., U.S. . . . **E2** 109
Umán, Mex. . . . **C7** 78
Uman', Ukr. . . . **E11** 20
Umanak, Grnld. . . . **D29** 82
Umarkot, Pak. . . . **E9** 42
Umatilla, Fl., U.S. . . . **D5** 102
Umatilla, Or., U.S. . . . **B7** 130
Umatilla, co., Or., U.S. . . . **B8** 130
Umatilla, stm., Or., U.S. . . . **B7** 130
Umatilla Indian Reservation, Or., U.S. . . . **B8** 130
Umba, Russia . . . **A5** 22
Umbagog Lake, l., U.S. . . . **A4** 122
Umboi Island, i., Pap. N. Gui. . . . **H12** 32
Umcolcus Lake, l., Me., U.S. **B4** 112
Umeå, Swe. . . . **E9** 10
Umeälven, stm., Swe. . . . **D9** 10
Umm al-'Abīd, Libya . . . **A8** 50
Umm Durmān, Sudan . . . **G11** 48
Umm Lajj, Sau. Ar. . . . **E3** 42
Umnak Island, i., Ak., U.S. . **E6** 95
Umpqua, stm., Or., U.S. . . . **D3** 130
Umsaskis Lake, l., Me., U.S. **B3** 112
Umtata, S. Afr. . . . **E4** 56
Umuarama, Braz. . . . **H9** 70
Umzinto, S. Afr. . . . **E5** 56
Unadilla, Ga., U.S. . . . **D3** 103
Unadilla, stm., N.Y., U.S. . . **C5** 125

Unaí, Braz. . . . **E2** 74
Unalakleet, Ak., U.S. . . . **C7** 95
Unalaska Island, i., Ak., U.S. **E6** 95
'Unayzah, Sau. Ar. . . . **E4** 38
'Unayzah, Jabal, mtn., Asia . **F8** 44
Uncasville, Ct., U.S. . . . **D7** 100
Uncompahgre, stm., Co., U.S. . . . **C3** 99
Uncompahgre Mountains, mts., Co., U.S. . . . **C3** 99
Uncompahgre Peak, mtn., Co., U.S. . . . **C3** 99
Underwood, Al., U.S. . . . **B3** 94
Underwood, N.D., U.S. . . . **B4** 127
Uneča, Russia . . . **C12** 20
Ungava, Péninsule d', pen., P.Q., Can. . . . **g12** 90
Ungava Bay, b., Can. . . . **G26** 82
Ungava Peninsula see Ungava, Péninsule d', pen., P.Q., Can. . . . **F25** 82
União, Braz. . . . **B3** 74
Uniãoda Vitória, Braz. . . . **D7** 72
União dos Palmares, Braz. . **C4** 74
Unicoi, Tn., U.S. . . . **C11** 135
Unicoi, co., Tn., U.S. . . . **C11** 135
Unicoi Mountains, mts., U.S. . . . **D9** 135
Unimak Island, i., Ak., U.S. **D7** 95
Unimak Pass, strt., Ak., U.S. **E6** 95
Unión, Arg. . . . **F4** 72
Union, Ky., U.S. . . . **k13** 110
Union, Mo., U.S. . . . **C6** 118
Union, Ms., U.S. . . . **C4** 117
Union, Or., U.S. . . . **B9** 130
Union, S.C., U.S. . . . **B4** 133
Union, Wa., U.S. . . . **B2** 140
Union, co., Ar., U.S. . . . **D3** 97
Union, co., Fl., U.S. . . . **B4** 102
Union, co., Ga., U.S. . . . **B2** 103
Union, co., Ia., U.S. . . . **C3** 108
Union, co., Il., U.S. . . . **F4** 106
Union, co., In., U.S. . . . **E8** 107
Union, co., Ky., U.S. . . . **C2** 110
Union, co., La., U.S. . . . **B3** 111
Union, co., Ms., U.S. . . . **A4** 117
Union, co., N.C., U.S. . . . **B2** 126
Union, co., N.J., U.S. . . . **B4** 123
Union, co., N.M., U.S. . . . **A6** 124
Union, co., Oh., U.S. . . . **B2** 128
Union, co., Or., U.S. . . . **B8** 130
Union, co., Pa., U.S. . . . **E7** 131
Union, co., S.C., U.S. . . . **B4** 133
Union, co., S.D., U.S. . . . **E9** 134
Union, co., Tn., U.S. . . . **C10** 135
Union, West Branch, stm., Me., U.S. . . . **D4** 112
Union Beach, N.J., U.S. . . . **C4** 123
Union Bridge, Md., U.S. . . . **A3** 113
Union City, Ca., U.S. . . . **h8** 98
Union City, Ga., U.S. . . . **C2** 103
Union City, In., U.S. . . . **D8** 107
Union City, Mi., U.S. . . . **F5** 115
Union City, N.J., U.S. . . . **h8** 123
Union City, Oh., U.S. . . . **B1** 128
Union City, Ok., U.S. . . . **B4** 129
Union City, Pa., U.S. . . . **C2** 131
Union City, Tn., U.S. . . . **A2** 135
Union Flat Creek, stm., Wa., U.S. . . . **C8** 140
Union Gap, Wa., U.S. . . . **C5** 140
Union Grove, Wi., U.S. . . . **F5** 142
Union Lake, l., N.J., U.S. . . **E2** 123
Union Pier, Mi., U.S. . . . **G4** 115
Union Point, Ga., U.S. . . . **C3** 103
Union Springs, Al., U.S. . . . **C4** 94
Uniontown, Al., U.S. . . . **C2** 94
Uniontown, Ky., U.S. . . . **C2** 110
Uniontown, Oh., U.S. . . . **B4** 128
Uniontown, Pa., U.S. . . . **G2** 131
Union Village, R.I., U.S. . . . **B3** 132
Union Village Reservoir, res., Vt., U.S. . . . **D4** 138
Unionville, Ct., U.S. . . . **B4** 100
Unionville, Mo., U.S. . . . **A4** 118
United Arab Emirates, ctry., Asia . . . **F6** 42
United Arab Republic see Egypt, ctry., Afr. . . . **E10** 48
United Kingdom, ctry., Eur. **C6** 12
United Nations Headquarters, N.Y., U.S. . . . **h12** 125
United States, ctry., N.A. . . **D6** 92
United States Air Force Academy, mil., Co., U.S. . . . **B6** 99
United States Military Academy, mil., N.Y., U.S. . . . **C6** 125
United States Naval Academy, mil., Md., U.S. . . . **C4** 113
Unity Reservoir, res., Or., U.S. . . . **C8** 130
University City, Mo., U.S. . . **C7** 118
University Heights, Ia., U.S. **C6** 108
University Heights, Oh., U.S. . . . **h9** 128
University Park, Ia., U.S. . . **C5** 108
University Park, N.M., U.S. . **E3** 124
University Park, Tx., U.S. . . **n10** 136
University Place, Wa., U.S. . **f10** 140
Unnāo, India . . . **D4** 40
Unuli Horog, China . . . **B6** 40

Ünye, Tur. . . . **B7** 44
Unža, stm., Russia . . . **C7** 22
Upata, Ven. . . . **B7** 70
Upernavik, Grnld. . . . **D28** 82
Upington, S. Afr. . . . **D3** 56
Upland, Ca., U.S. . . . **E5** 98
Upland, In., U.S. . . . **D7** 107
Upolu, i., Samoa . . . **F12** 58
Upolu Point, c., Hi., U.S. . . **C6** 104
Upper Ammonoosuc, stm., N.H., U.S. . . . **A4** 122
Upper Arlington, Oh., U.S. . **B2** 128
Upper Arrow Lake, res., B.C., Can. . . . **D9** 85
Upperco, Md., U.S. . . . **A4** 113
Upper Darby, Pa., U.S. . . . **G11** 131
Upper Greenwood Lake, N.J., U.S. . . . **A4** 123
Upper Humber, stm., Nf., Can. . . . **D3** 88
Upper Hutt, N.Z. . . . **p14** 63c
Upper Iowa, stm., Ia., U.S. . **A5** 108
Upper Island Cove, Nf., Can. . . . **E5** 88
Upper Klamath Lake, l., Or., U.S. . . . **E4** 130
Upper Marlboro, Md., U.S. **C4** 113
Upper New York Bay, b., U.S. . . . **k8** 123
Upper Red Lake, l., Mn., U.S. . . . **B4** 116
Upper Saddle River, N.J., U.S. . . . **A4** 123
Upper Sandusky, Oh., U.S. **B2** 128
Upper Sheila [Haut Sheila], N.B., Can. . . . **B5** 87
Upper Volta see Burkina Faso, ctry., Afr. . . . **D4** 50
Uppland, hist. reg., Swe. . . **F7** 10
Uppsala, Swe. . . . **G7** 10
Upright, Cape, c., Ak., U.S. **C5** 95
Upshur, co., Tx., U.S. . . . **C5** 136
Upshur, co., W.V., U.S. . . . **C4** 141
Upson, co., Ga., U.S. . . . **D2** 103
Upton, P.Q., Can. . . . **D5** 90
Upton, Ky., U.S. . . . **C4** 110
Upton, Ma., U.S. . . . **B4** 114
Upton, Wy., U.S. . . . **B8** 143
Upton, co., Tx., U.S. . . . **D2** 136
Uraj, Russia . . . **B12** 22
Urakawa, Japan . . . **B4** 31
Ural, stm. . . . **E9** 22
Ural Mountains see Ural'skie gory, mts., Russia . . . **D7** 26
Ural'sk, Kaz. . . . **D7** 26
Ural'skie gory (Ural Mountains), mts., Russia **D7** 26
Urania, La., U.S. . . . **C3** 111
Ura-Tjube, Taj. . . . **C9** 42
Urbana, Il., U.S. . . . **C5** 106
Urbana, Oh., U.S. . . . **B2** 128
Urbancrest, Oh., U.S. . . . **m10** 128
Urbandale, Ia., U.S. . . . **C4** 108
Urbino, Italy . . . **C4** 18
Ures, Mex. . . . **B2** 78
Urfa see Şanlıurfa, Tur. . . . **D8** 44
Urgenč, Uzb. . . . **E8** 26
Ürgüp, Tur. . . . **C6** 44
Uribia, Col. . . . **A5** 70
Urjung-Haja, Russia . . . **B13** 26
Urjupinsk, Russia . . . **D7** 22
Urla, Tur. . . . **C2** 44
Urmia see Orūmīyeh, Iran . **C5** 42
Urmia, Lake see Orūmīyeh, Daryācheh-ye, l., Iran . **C5** 42
Uromi, Nig. . . . **E6** 50
Uroševac, Yugo. . . . **C8** 18
Urrao, Col. . . . **D4** 80
Uruapan del Progreso, Mex. **D4** 78
Uruguai (Uruguay), stm., S.A. . . . **E6** 72
Uruguaiana, Braz. . . . **D6** 72
Uruguay, ctry., S.A. . . . **E6** 72
Uruguay (Uruguai), stm., S.A. . . . **D6** 72
Ürümqi, China . . . **C5** 28
Urundi see Burundi, ctry., Afr. . . . **D5** 54
Urup, ostrov, i., Russia . . . **E17** 26
Urziceni, Rom. . . . **G9** 20
Uržum, Russia . . . **C8** 22
Usa, Japan . . . **D2** 31
Uşak, Tur. . . . **C3** 44
Usakos, Nmb. . . . **C2** 56
Usborne, Mount, mtn., Falk. Is. . . . **H5** 69
Usedom, i., Eur. . . . **B3** 20
Ushuaia, Arg. . . . **H3** 69
Usinsk, Russia . . . **C7** 26
Usman', Russia . . . **C15** 20
Usoke, Tan. . . . **E6** 54
Usole-Sibirskoe, Russia . . . **D12** 26
Usquepaug, R.I., U.S. . . . **F3** 132
Ussuri (Wusuli), stm., Asia . **E15** 26
Ussurijsk, Russia . . . **E15** 26
Ust'-Barguzin, Russia . . . **D12** 26
Ust'-Belaja, Russia . . . **C19** 26
Ust'-Čaun, Russia . . . **C19** 26
Ust'-Cil'ma, Russia . . . **A9** 22
Ust'-Ilimsk, Russia . . . **D12** 26
Ústí nad Labem, Czech Rep. . . . **D3** 20
Ustinov see Iževsk, Russia . **D7** 26
Ustka, Pol. . . . **B4** 20

Ust'-Kamčatsk, Russia . . . **D18** 26
Ust'-Kamenogorsk, Kaz. . . . **E10** 26
Ust'-Koksa, Russia . . . **A5** 28
Ust'-Kujda, Russia . . . **C15** 26
Ust'-Kut, Russia . . . **D12** 26
Ust'-Lyža, Russia . . . **A10** 22
Ust'-Maja, Russia . . . **C15** 26
Ust'-Man'ja, Russia . . . **B11** 22
Ust'-Nera, Russia . . . **C16** 26
Ust'-Njukža, Russia . . . **D14** 26
Uštobe, Kaz. . . . **B3** 28
Ust'-Tym, Russia . . . **D10** 26
Ust-Urt Plateau, plat., Asia . **B7** 42
Usu, China . . . **C4** 28
Usulután, El Sal. . . . **C2** 80
Usumacinta, stm., N.A. . . . **D6** 78
Ušumun, Russia . . . **A13** 28
Utah, co., Ut., U.S. . . . **C4** 137
Utah, state, U.S. . . . **D4** 137
Utah Lake, l., Ut., U.S. . . . **C4** 137
Ute Creek, stm., N.M., U.S. **A6** 124
Ute Mountain Indian Reservation, U.S. . . . **D2** 99
Utena, Lith. . . . **I11** 10
Ute Reservoir, res., N.M., U.S. . . . **B6** 124
Utete, Tan. . . . **E7** 54
Uthai Thani, Thai. . . . **C4** 34
Utiariti, Braz. . . . **F8** 70
Utica, Il., U.S. . . . **B5** 106
Utica, Mi., U.S. . . . **F7** 115
Utica, Ms., U.S. . . . **C3** 117
Utica, Ne., U.S. . . . **D8** 120
Utica, N.Y., U.S. . . . **B5** 125
Utica, Oh., U.S. . . . **B3** 128
Utiel, Spain . . . **H6** 16
Utikuma Lake, l., Ab., Can. **B3** 84
Utila, Isla de, i., Hond. . . . **B2** 80
Utopia, Austl. . . . **E5** 60
Utrecht, Neth. . . . **D9** 12
Utrecht, S. Afr. . . . **D5** 56
Utrera, Spain . . . **I4** 16
Utsunomiya, Japan . . . **D16** 28
Uttaradit, Thai. . . . **C4** 34
Uttar Pradesh, prov., India . **D3** 40
Uusikaupunki, Fin. . . . **F9** 10
Uvalde, Tx., U.S. . . . **E3** 136
Uvalde, co., Tx., U.S. . . . **E3** 136
Uvarovo, Russia . . . **D7** 22
Uvinza, Tan. . . . **E6** 54
Uvira, D.R.C. . . . **D5** 54
Uvs Lake, l., Asia . . . **A6** 28
Uwajima, Japan . . . **E14** 28
Uwayl, Sudan . . . **B5** 54
Uwharrie, stm., N.C., U.S. . **B3** 126
Uxbridge, Ma., U.S. . . . **B4** 114
Uyo, Nig. . . . **E6** 50
Uyuni, Bol. . . . **C4** 72
Uyuni, Salar de, pl., Bol. . . **C4** 72
Uzbekistan, ctry., Asia . . . **C8** 42
Uzhhorod, Ukr. . . . **E7** 20
Uzlovaja, Russia . . . **C15** 20
Uzunköprü, Tur. . . . **B2** 44
Užur, Russia . . . **D11** 26

V

Vaal, stm., S. Afr. . . . **D4** 56
Vaaldam, res., S. Afr. . . . **D4** 56
Vaasa, Fin. . . . **E9** 10
Vác, Hung. . . . **F5** 20
Vaca Key, i., Fl., U.S. . . . **H5** 102
Vacaria, Braz. . . . **D7** 72
Vacaville, Ca., U.S. . . . **C3** 98
Vache, Île à, i., Haiti . . . **B5** 80
Vacherie, La., U.S. . . . **h10** 111
Vadodara, India . . . **E2** 40
Vadsø, Nor. . . . **A13** 10
Vaduz, Liech. . . . **G11** 12
Vaga, stm., Russia . . . **B7** 22
Vah, stm., Russia . . . **C9** 26
Váh, stm., Slvk. . . . **E4** 20
Vaiden, Ms., U.S. . . . **B4** 117
Vail, Co., U.S. . . . **B4** 99
Vajgač, ostrov, i., Russia . . **B7** 26
Vākhān, hist. reg., Afg. . . . **C10** 42
Val-Bélair, P.Q., Can. . . . **n17** 90
Valcourt, P.Q., Can. . . . **D5** 90
Valdai Hills see Valdajskaja vozvyšennost', hills, Russia . . . **C5** 22
Valdaj, Russia . . . **C5** 22
Valdajskaja vozvyšennost', hills, Russia . . . **C5** 22
Val-David, P.Q., Can. . . . **C3** 90
Valday see Valdaj, Russia . . **C5** 22
Valdemarsvik, Swe. . . . **G7** 10
Valdepeñas, Spain . . . **H5** 16
Valders, Wi., U.S. . . . **D6** 142
Valdés, Península, pen., Arg. **F4** 69
Valdese, N.C., U.S. . . . **B1** 126
Valdez, Ak., U.S. . . . **C10** 95
Valdivia, Chile . . . **E2** 69
Val-d'Or, P.Q., Can. . . . **k11** 90
Valdosta, Ga., U.S. . . . **F3** 103
Vale, Or., U.S. . . . **D9** 130
Valemount, B.C., Can. . . . **C8** 85
Valença, Braz. . . . **D4** 74
Valença do Piauí, Braz. . . . **C3** 74
Valence, Fr. . . . **E9** 16
València, Spain . . . **H6** 16
Valencia, Az., U.S. . . . **m7** 96
Valencia, Ven. . . . **B6** 70
Valencia, co., N.M., U.S. . . **C3** 124
València, Golf de, b., Spain **H7** 16

Valencia de Alcántara, Spain **H3** 16
Valencia Heights, S.C., U.S. **D6** 133
Valenciennes, Fr. . . . **B8** 16
Valentine, Ne., U.S. . . . **B5** 120
Valera, Ven. . . . **B5** 70
Valga, Est. . . . **H12** 10
Valhalla, N.Y., U.S. . . . **D7** 125
Valhermoso Springs, Al., U.S. . . . **A3** 94
Valjevo, Yugo. . . . **B7** 18
Valkeakoski, Fin. . . . **F11** 10
Valladolid, Mex. . . . **C7** 78
Valladolid, Spain . . . **G4** 16
Vallecito Reservoir, res., Co., U.S. . . . **D3** 99
Valle de la Pascua, Ven. . . . **B6** 70
Valledupar, Col. . . . **A5** 70
Vallée-Jonction, P.Q., Can. . **C7** 90
Vallegrande, Bol. . . . **B5** 72
Valle Hermoso, Mex. . . . **B5** 78
Vallejo, Ca., U.S. . . . **C2** 98
Vallenar, Chile . . . **C2** 69
Valletta, Malta . . . **G5** 18
Valley, Ne., U.S. . . . **C9** 120
Valley, co., Id., U.S. . . . **E3** 105
Valley, co., Mt., U.S. . . . **B10** 119
Valley, co., Ne., U.S. . . . **C6** 120
Valley, stm., Mb., Can. . . . **D1** 86
Valley Center, Ks., U.S. . . . **E6** 109
Valley City, N.D., U.S. . . . **C8** 127
Valley Cottage, N.Y., U.S. . **g13** 125
Valley East, On., Can. . . . **p19** 89
Valley Falls, Ks., U.S. . . . **C8** 109
Valley Falls, R.I., U.S. . . . **B4** 132
Valley Forge, Pa., U.S. . . . **o20** 131
Valley Mills, Tx., U.S. . . . **D4** 136
Valley Park, Mo., U.S. . . . **f12** 118
Valley Springs, S.D., U.S. . . **D9** 134
Valley Station, Ky., U.S. . . **g11** 110
Valley Stream, N.Y., U.S. . . **n15** 125
Valleyview, Ab., Can. . . . **B2** 84
Valley View, Pa., U.S. . . . **E8** 131
Valliant, Ok., U.S. . . . **D6** 129
Valls, Spain . . . **G7** 16
Vallscreek, W.V., U.S. . . . **D3** 141
Valmeyer, Il., U.S. . . . **E3** 106
Valmiera, Lat. . . . **H11** 10
Valona see Vlorë, Alb. . . . **D7** 18
Vālpārai, India . . . **G3** 40
Valparaíso, Chile . . . **D2** 69
Valparaiso, Fl., U.S. . . . **u15** 102
Valparaiso, In., U.S. . . . **B3** 107
Vals, Tanjung, c., Indon. . . . **H10** 32
Valsbaai, b., S. Afr. . . . **E2** 56
Valtimo, Fin. . . . **E13** 10
Valujki, Russia . . . **D15** 20
Val Verda, Ut., U.S. . . . **C4** 137
Val Verde, co., Tx., U.S. . . . **E2** 136
Valverde del Camino, Spain **I3** 16
Van, Tur. . . . **C10** 44
Van, Tx., U.S. . . . **C5** 136
Van, W.V., U.S. . . . **n12** 141
Vanadzor, Arm. . . . **B11** 44
Van Alstyne, Tx., U.S. . . . **C4** 136
Vanavara, Russia . . . **C12** 26
Van Buren, Ar., U.S. . . . **B1** 97
Van Buren, In., U.S. . . . **C6** 107
Van Buren, Me., U.S. . . . **A5** 112
Van Buren, Mo., U.S. . . . **E6** 118
Van Buren, co., Ar., U.S. . . **B3** 97
Van Buren, co., Ia., U.S. . . **D6** 108
Van Buren, co., Mi., U.S. . . **F4** 115
Van Buren, co., Tn., U.S. . . **D8** 135
Vanč, Taj. . . . **C10** 42
Vance, co., N.C., U.S. . . . **A4** 126
Vance Air Force Base, mil., Ok., U.S. . . . **A3** 129
Vanceboro, N.C., U.S. . . . **B5** 126
Vanceburg, Ky., U.S. . . . **B6** 110
Vancleave, Ms., U.S. . . . **E5** 117
Vancouver, B.C., Can. . . . **E6** 85
Vancouver, Wa., U.S. . . . **D3** 140
Vancouver Island, i., B.C., Can. . . . **E4** 85
Vancouver Island Ranges, mts., B.C., Can. . . . **D4** 85
Vandalia, Il., U.S. . . . **E4** 106
Vandalia, Mo., U.S. . . . **B6** 118
Vandenberg Air Force Base, mil., Ca., U.S. . . . **E3** 98
Vander, N.C., U.S. . . . **B4** 126
Vanderbilt Peak, mtn., N.M., U.S. . . . **E1** 124
Vanderburgh, co., In., U.S. . **H2** 107
Vandergrift, Pa., U.S. . . . **E2** 131
Vanderhoof, B.C., Can. . . . **C5** 85
Vanderlin Island, i., Austl. . . **D2** 62
Van Diemen Gulf, b., Austl. **C5** 60
Vänern, l., Swe. . . . **G5** 10
Vänersborg, Swe. . . . **G5** 10
Vangaindrano, Madag. . . . **C8** 56
Van Gölü, l., Tur. . . . **C10** 44
Van Horn, Tx., U.S. . . . **o12** 136
Van Horne, Ia., U.S. . . . **B5** 108
Vanier, On., Can. . . . **h12** 89
Vanimo, Pap. N. Gui. . . . **G11** 32
Vanino, Russia . . . **B16** 28
Vankarem, Russia . . . **C20** 26
Vankleek Hill, On., Can. . . . **B10** 89
Van Kull, Kill, stm., N.J., U.S. . . . **k8** 123
Van Lear, Ky., U.S. . . . **C7** 110
Van Meter, Ia., U.S. . . . **C4** 108
Vännäs, Swe. . . . **E8** 10
Vannes, Fr. . . . **D5** 16

Name Map Ref. Page

Van Rees, Pegunungan, mts., Indon. **G10** 32
Vanrhynsdorp, S. Afr. **E2** 56
Vansant, Va., U.S. **e9** 139
Vanua Lava, i., Vanuatu **j9** 62a
Vanua Levu, i., Fiji **F11** 58
Vanuatu, ctry., Oc. **F10** 58
Van Vleck, Tx., U.S. **r14** 136
Van Wert, Oh., U.S. **B1** 128
Van Wert, co., Oh., U.S. **B1** 128
Vanwyksvlei, S. Afr. **E3** 56
Van Zandt, co., Tx., U.S. **C5** 136
Vārānasi (Benares), India **D4** 40
Varangerfjorden, b., Nor. **A13** 10
Varaždin, Cro. **A6** 18
Varberg, Swe. **H5** 10
Vardaman, Ms., U.S. **B4** 117
Vardar (Axiós), stm., Eur. **D9** 18
Varde, Den. **I3** 10
Vardø, Nor. **A14** 10
Varennes, P.Q., Can. **D4** 90
Varese, Italy **B2** 18
Varginha, Braz. **F2** 74
Varina, Va., U.S. **C5** 139
Varkaus, Fin. **E12** 10
Värmland, hist. reg., Swe. **G5** 10
Varna, Bul. **C11** 18
Varna, Russia **D11** 22
Värnamo, Swe. **H6** 10
Varnville, S.C., U.S. **F5** 133
Varto, Tur. **C9** 44
Várzea Grande, Braz. **B6** 72
Vashon, Point, c., Wa., U.S. **e11** 140
Vashon Island, i., Wa., U.S. **f11** 140
Vaslui, Rom. **F9** 20
Vass, N.C., U.S. **B3** 126
Vassar, Mi., U.S. **E7** 115
Vastenjaure, l., Swe. **C7** 10
Västerås, Swe. **G7** 10
Västerbotten, hist. reg., Swe. **D8** 10
Västerdalälven, stm., Swe. **F5** 10
Västervik, Swe. **H7** 10
Vasto, Italy **C5** 18
Vasylivka, Ukr. **F13** 20
Vasyl'kiv, Ukr. **D11** 20
Vatican City, ctry., Eur. **D4** 18
Vatnajökull, Ice. **I20** 10a
Vatomandry, Madag. **B8** 56
Vatra Dornei, Rom. **F8** 20
Vättern, l., Swe. **G6** 10
Vaudreuil, P.Q., Can. **D3** 90
Vaughan, On., Can. **D5** 89
Vaughn, Mt., U.S. **C5** 119
Vaughn, N.M., U.S. **C4** 124
Vaukavysk, Bela. **C8** 20
Vaupés (Uaupés), stm., S.A. **C5** 70
Vauxhall, Ab., Can. **D4** 84
Vava'u, i., Tonga **F12** 58
Vavoua, C. Iv. **E3** 50
Vavuniya, Sri L. **H4** 40
Växjö, Swe. **H6** 10
Vaygach Island see Vajgač, ostrov, i., Russia **B7** 26
Važgort, Russia **B8** 22
Veazie, Me., U.S. **D4** 112
Veedersburg, In., U.S. **D3** 107
Veendam, Neth. **D10** 12
Vega, i., Nor. **D4** 10
Vegreville, Ab., Can. **C4** 84
Veinticinco de Mayo, Arg. **F5** 72
Vejle, Den. **I3** 10
Vélez-Málaga, Spain **I4** 16
Velika Morava, stm., Yugo. **B8** 18
Velikie Luki, Russia **D5** 26
Velikij Ustjug, Russia **C6** 26
Velingara, Sen. **D2** 50
Velletri, Italy **D4** 18
Vellore, India **G3** 40
Velma, Ok., U.S. **C4** 129
Vel'sk, Russia **C6** 26
Velva, N.D., U.S. **A5** 127
Venado Tuerto, Arg. **E5** 72
Venango, co., Pa., U.S. **D2** 131
Vendôme, Fr. **D7** 16
Veneta, Or., U.S. **C3** 130
Venézia (Venice), Italy **B4** 18
Venezuela, ctry., S.A. **B6** 70
Venezuela, Golfo de, b., S.A. **A5** 70
Venezuela, Gulf of see Venezuela, Golfo de, b., S.A. **A5** 70
Venezuelan Basin **G7** 66
Veniaminof, Mount, mtn., Ak., U.S. **D8** 95
Venice see Venézia, Italy **B4** 18
Venice, Fl., U.S. **E4** 102
Venice, Il., U.S. **E3** 106
Venice, Gulf of, b., Eur. **B4** 18
Venta, stm., Eur. **H10** 10
Ventimiglia, Italy **C1** 18
Ventnor City, N.J., U.S. **E4** 123
Ventspils, Lat. **H9** 10
Ventura (San Buenaventura), Ca., U.S. **E4** 98
Ventura, co., Ca., U.S. **E4** 98
Vera, Arg. **D5** 72
Vera, Spain **I6** 16
Veracruz, Mex. **D5** 78
Veracruz, state, Mex. **D5** 78
Verāval, India **E2** 40
Verbania, Italy **B2** 18
Vercelli, Italy **B2** 18
Verchères, P.Q., Can. **D4** 90
Verda, Ky., U.S. **D6** 110
Verde, stm., Az., U.S. **C4** 96
Verden, Ger. **D11** 12
Verdi, Nv., U.S. **D2** 121
Verdigre, Ne., U.S. **B7** 120
Verdigris, Ok., U.S. **A6** 129
Verdigris, stm., U.S. **A6** 129
Verdi Peak, mtn., Nv., U.S. **C6** 121
Verdun, P.Q., Can. **q19** 90
Verdun-sur-Meuse, Fr. **C9** 16
Vereeniging, S. Afr. **D4** 56
Vereščagino, Russia **C10** 26
Vergennes, Vt., U.S. **C2** 138
Verhneimbatsk, Russia **C10** 26
Verhnemulomskoe vodohranilišče, res., Russia **B14** 10
Verhnetulomskij, Russia **B14** 10
Verhneural'sk, Russia **D10** 22
Verhnij Baskunčak, Russia **E8** 22
Verhnij Ufalej, Russia **C11** 22
Verhnjaja Amga, Russia **D14** 26
Verhnjaja Inta, Russia **A11** 22
Verhnjaja Salda, Russia **C11** 22
Verhojansk, Russia **C15** 26
Verhojanskij hrebet, mts., Russia **C14** 26
Verhoture, Russia **C11** 22
Verkhoyansk see Verhojansk, Russia **C15** 26
Vermilion, Ab., Can. **C5** 84
Vermilion, Oh., U.S. **A3** 128
Vermilion, co., Il., U.S. **C6** 106
Vermilion, co., La., U.S. **E3** 111
Vermilion, stm., Ab., Can. **C5** 84
Vermilion, stm., Il., U.S. **C5** 106
Vermilion, stm., La., U.S. **E3** 111
Vermilion, stm., Mn., U.S. **B6** 116
Vermilion, stm., Oh., U.S. **A3** 128
Vermilion Bay, b., La., U.S. **E3** 111
Vermilion Lake, l., Mn., U.S. **C6** 116
Vermilion Pass, Can. **D2** 84
Vermillion, S.D., U.S. **E9** 134
Vermillion, co., In., U.S. **E2** 107
Vermillion, East Fork, stm., S.D., U.S. **D8** 134
Vermillon, stm., P.Q., Can. **B4** 90
Vermont, Il., U.S. **C3** 106
Vermont, state, U.S. **D3** 138
Vermontville, Mi., U.S. **F5** 115
Vernal, Ut., U.S. **C6** 137
Vernon, B.C., Can. **D8** 85
Vernon, Al., U.S. **B1** 94
Vernon, Tx., U.S. **B3** 136
Vernon, co., La., U.S. **C2** 111
Vernon, co., Mo., U.S. **D3** 118
Vernon, co., Wi., U.S. **E3** 142
Vernon Hills, Il., U.S. **h9** 106
Vernonia, Or., U.S. **B3** 130
Vero Beach, Fl., U.S. **E6** 102
Véroia, Grc. **D9** 18
Verona, On., Can. **C8** 89
Verona, Italy **B3** 18
Verona, Ms., U.S. **A5** 117
Verona, N.J., U.S. **B4** 123
Verona, Pa., U.S. **k14** 131
Verona, Wi., U.S. **E4** 142
Verret, Lake, l., La., U.S. **E4** 111
Versailles, Fr. **C8** 16
Versailles, In., U.S. **F7** 107
Versailles, Ky., U.S. **B5** 110
Versailles, Mo., U.S. **C5** 118
Versailles, Oh., U.S. **B1** 128
Vert, Cap, c., Sen. **D1** 50
Vertientes, Cuba **A4** 80
Vesele, Ukr. **F13** 20
Vešenskaja, Russia **F15** 8
Vesoul, Fr. **D10** 16
Vestal, N.Y., U.S. **C4** 125
Vestavia Hills, Al., U.S. **g7** 94
Vesterålen, is., Nor. **B6** 10
Vestfjorden, b., Nor. **C5** 10
Vestmannaeyjar, Ice. **m18** 10a
Vesuvio, vol., Italy **D5** 18
Vesuvius see Vesuvio, vol., Italy **D5** 18
Veszprém, Hung. **F4** 20
Vetlanda, Swe. **H6** 10
Vetluga, Russia **C8** 22
Vetluga, stm., Russia **C8** 22
Vevay, In., U.S. **G7** 107
Vezirköprü, Tur. **B6** 44
Viacha, Bol. **B4** 72
Vian, Ok., U.S. **B7** 129
Viana, Braz. **B2** 74
Viana do Castelo, Port. **G2** 16
Viangchan (Vientiane), Laos **C4** 34
Viangphoukha, Laos **B4** 34
Viareggio, Italy **C3** 18
Viborg, Den. **H3** 10
Viborg, S.D., U.S. **D8** 134
Vibo Valentia, Italy **E5** 18
Viburnum, Mo., U.S. **D6** 118
Vic, Spain **G8** 16
Vicebsk, Bela. **B11** 20
Vicente, Point, c., Ca., U.S. **n12** 98
Vicente Guerrero, Presa, res., Mex. **C5** 78
Vicenza, Italy **B3** 18
Vichada, stm., Col. **C5** 70
Vichy, Fr. **D8** 16
Vici, Ok., U.S. **A2** 129
Vicksburg, Mi., U.S. **F5** 115
Vicksburg, Ms., U.S. **C3** 117
Vicksburg National Military Park, Ms., U.S. **C3** 117
Victor, Ia., U.S. **C5** 108
Victor, N.Y., U.S. **C3** 125
Victoria see Limbe, Cam. **C1** 54
Victoria, B.C., Can. **E6** 85
Victoria, Nf., Can. **E5** 88
Victoria, Chile **E2** 69
Victoria see Xianggang, China **E3** 30
Victoria, Gui. **D2** 50
Victoria, Sey. **h13** 57b
Victoria, Ks., U.S. **D4** 109
Victoria, Tx., U.S. **E4** 136
Victoria, state, Austl. **H3** 62
Victoria, co., Tx., U.S. **E4** 136
Victoria, stm., Austl. **D5** 60
Victoria, Lake, l., Afr. **D6** 54
Victoria, Mount, mtn., Pap. N. Gui. **H12** 32
Victoria Falls, wtfl, Afr. **B4** 56
Victoria Harbour, On., Can. **C5** 89
Victoria Island, i., Can. **D17** 82
Victoria Lake, res., Nf., Can. **D3** 88
Victoria Land, reg., Ant. **D21** 67
Victoria Nile, stm., Ug. **C6** 54
Victoria Peak, mtn., Belize **B2** 80
Victoria River Downs, Austl. **D5** 60
Victorias, Phil. **D8** 34
Victoriaville, P.Q., Can. **C6** 90
Victoria West, S. Afr. **E3** 56
Victorville, Ca., U.S. **E5** 98
Vicuña Mackenna, Arg. **E5** 72
Vidalia, Ga., U.S. **D4** 103
Vidalia, La., U.S. **C4** 111
Vidin, Bul. **C9** 18
Vidisha, India **E3** 40
Vidor, Tx., U.S. **D5** 136
Viedma, Arg. **F4** 69
Viedma, Lago, l., Arg. **G2** 69
Vienna see Wien, Aus. **F15** 12
Vienna, Ga., U.S. **D3** 103
Vienna, Il., U.S. **F5** 106
Vienna, Mo., U.S. **C6** 118
Vienna, Va., U.S. **B5** 139
Vienna, W.V., U.S. **B3** 141
Vienne, Fr. **E9** 16
Vienne, stm., Fr. **D7** 16
Vientiane see Viangchan, Laos **C4** 34
Vieques, Isla de, i., P.R. **B6** 80
Vierwaldstätter See, l., Switz. **A2** 18
Vierzon, Fr. **D8** 16
Vieste, Italy **D6** 18
Vietnam, ctry., Asia **C5** 34
Viet Tri, Viet. **B5** 34
Vieux Desert, Lac, l., Wi., U.S. **B4** 142
Vigan, Phil. **C8** 34
Vigo, Spain **F2** 16
Vigo, co., In., U.S. **F3** 107
Vijayawāda, India **F4** 40
Vike, Arm. **C11** 44
Viking, Ab., Can. **C5** 84
Vikna, Nor. **D4** 10
Vikna, i., Nor. **D4** 10
Vikramasingapuram, India **H3** 40
Vila de Sena, Moz. **B6** 56
Vila do Ibo, Moz. **A7** 56
Vila Fontes, Moz. **B6** 56
Vila Gamito, Moz. **A5** 56
Vilagarcía de Arousa, Spain **F2** 16
Vilandro, Tanjona, c., Madag. **B7** 56
Vilankulo, Moz. **C6** 56
Vilanova i la Geltrú, Spain **G7** 16
Vila Real, Port. **G3** 16
Vilas, co., Wi., U.S. **B4** 142
Vila Velha, Braz. **F3** 74
Vilejka, Bela. **B9** 20
Vilhelmina, Swe. **D7** 10
Vilhena, Braz. **F7** 70
Viljandi, Est. **G11** 10
Viljuj, stm., Russia **C14** 26
Viljujsk, Russia **C14** 26
Vil'kickogo, proliv, strt., Russia **B11** 26
Villa Ángela, Arg. **D5** 72
Villa Bella, Bol. **F6** 70
Villacañas, Spain **H5** 16
Villacarrillo, Spain **H5** 16
Villach, Aus. **G13** 12
Villa Dolores, Arg. **E4** 72
Villa Grove, Il., U.S. **D5** 106
Villaguay, Arg. **E6** 72
Villahermosa, Mex. **D6** 78
Villaldama, Mex. **D4** 78
Villalonga, Arg. **F4** 69
Villa María, Arg. **E5** 72
Villa Mercedes, Arg. **E4** 72
Villa Montes, Bol. **C5** 72
Villanueva de la Serena, Spain **H4** 16
Villa Ocampo, Arg. **D6** 72
Villa Ojo de Agua, Arg. **D5** 72
Villa Park, Il., U.S. **k8** 106
Villa Rica, Ga., U.S. **C2** 103
Villarrica, Chile **E2** 69
Villarrica, Para. **D6** 72
Villarrobledo, Spain **H5** 16
Villas, N.J., U.S. **E3** 123
Villa Unión, Mex. **C3** 78
Villa Valeria, Arg. **E4** 72
Villavicencio, Col. **C5** 70
Villefranche-sur-Saône, Fr. **E9** 16
Villena, Spain **H6** 16
Villeneuve-sur-Lot, Fr. **E7** 16
Ville Platte, La., U.S. **D3** 111
Ville Saint-Georges, P.Q., Can. **C7** 90
Villeurbanne, Fr. **E9** 16
Villisca, Ia., U.S. **D3** 108
Vilnius, Lith. **I11** 10
Vilonia, Ar., U.S. **B3** 97
Vimmerby, Swe. **H6** 10
Viña del Mar, Chile **D2** 69
Vinalhaven, Me., U.S. **D4** 112
Vinalhaven Island, i., Me., U.S. **D4** 112
Vinaròs, Spain **G7** 16
Vincennes, In., U.S. **G2** 107
Vincennes Bay, b., Ant. **C15** 67
Vincent, Al., U.S. **B3** 94
Vindhya Range, mts., India **E3** 40
Vine Brook, stm., Ma., U.S. **g11** 114
Vinegar Hill, mtn., Or., U.S. **C8** 130
Vine Grove, Ky., U.S. **C4** 110
Vineland, N.J., U.S. **E2** 123
Vineyard Haven, Ma., U.S. **D6** 114
Vineyard Sound, strt., Ma., U.S. **D6** 114
Vinh, Viet. **C5** 34
Vinh Long, Viet. **D5** 34
Vinita, Ok., U.S. **A6** 129
Vinkovci, Cro. **B7** 18
Vinson Massif, mtn., Ant. **D32** 67
Vinton, Ia., U.S. **B5** 108
Vinton, La., U.S. **D2** 111
Vinton, Va., U.S. **C3** 139
Vinton, co., Oh., U.S. **C3** 128
Viola, Il., U.S. **B3** 106
Violet, La., U.S. **k12** 111
Virac, Phil. **D8** 34
Viramgām, India **E2** 40
Virandozero, Russia **C14** 8
Viranşehir, Tur. **D8** 44
Virden, Mb., Can. **E1** 86
Virden, Il., U.S. **D4** 106
Vire, Fr. **C6** 16
Virgin, stm., U.S. **G8** 121
Virgin Gorda, i., Br. Vir. Is. **B7** 80
Virginia, S. Afr. **D4** 56
Virginia, Al., U.S. **g6** 94
Virginia, Il., U.S. **D3** 106
Virginia, Mn., U.S. **C6** 116
Virginia, state, U.S. **C4** 139
Virginia Beach, Va., U.S. **D7** 139
Virginia City, Nv., U.S. **D2** 121
Virginia Peak, mtn., Nv., U.S. **D2** 121
Virgin Islands, dep., N.A. **B7** 80
Virgin Islands, is., N.A. **E11** 76
Viroqua, Wi., U.S. **E3** 142
Virovitica, Cro. **B6** 18
Virrat, Fin. **E10** 10
Virtsu, Est. **G10** 10
Virudunagar, India **H3** 40
Vis, Otok, i., Cro. **C6** 18
Visalia, Ca., U.S. **D4** 98
Visayan Sea, Phil. **D8** 34
Visby, Swe. **H8** 10
Viscount Melville Sound, strt., Can. **D17** 82
Viseu, Port. **G3** 16
Vishākhapatnam, India **F4** 40
Vista, Ca., U.S. **F5** 98
Vistula see Wisła, stm., Pol. **C5** 20
Vitarte, Peru **F4** 70
Viterbo, Italy **C3** 18
Viti Levu, i., Fiji **F11** 58
Vitim, Russia **D13** 26
Vitim, stm., Russia **D13** 26
Vitória, Braz. **F3** 74
Vitoria see Gasteiz, Spain **F5** 16
Vitória da Conquista, Braz. **D3** 74
Vitré, Fr. **C6** 16
Vitry-le-François, Fr. **C9** 16
Vittoria, Italy **F5** 18
Vittorio Veneto, Italy **B4** 18
Vivian, La., U.S. **B2** 111
Vize, ostrov, i., Russia **B9** 26
Vizianagaram, India **F4** 40
Vizinga, Russia **B9** 22
Vjatka, stm., Russia **D7** 26
Vjatskie Poljany, Russia **C9** 22
Vjazemskij, Russia **B14** 28
Vjaz'ma, Russia **B13** 20
Vladikavkaz, Russia **E6** 26
Vladikavkaz see Ordzhonikidze, Ukr. **F13** 20
Vladimir, Russia **D6** 26
Vladivostok, Russia **E15** 26
Vlissingen, Neth. **E8** 12
Vlorë, Alb. **D7** 18
Vogel Peak see Dimlang, mtn., Nig. **E7** 50
Vohimena, Tanjona, c., Madag. **D8** 56
Voi, Kenya **D7** 54
Voinjama, Lib. **E3** 50
Voj-Vož, Russia **B9** 22
Volcano, Hi., U.S. **D6** 104
Volcano Islands see Kazan-rettō, is., Japan **F17** 64
Volga, S.D., U.S. **C9** 134
Volga, stm., Russia **E6** 26
Volga-Baltic Canal see Volgo-Baltijskij kanal, Russia **B6** 22
Volga Plateau see Privolžskaja vozvyšennost', plat., Russia **D6** 26
Volgo-Baltijskij kanal, Russia **B6** 22
Volgodonsk, Russia **E6** 26
Volgograd, Russia **E6** 26
Volgograd Reservoir see Volgogradskoe vodohranilišče, res., Russia **D8** 22
Volgogradskoe vodohranilišče, res., Russia **D8** 22
Volhov, Russia **D12** 6
Volksrust, S. Afr. **D4** 56
Volnovakha, Ukr. **F14** 20
Voločanka, Russia **B11** 26
Volodarskoe, Kaz. **D8** 26
Volodymyr-Volyns'kyi, Ukr. **D8** 20
Vologda, Russia **D6** 26
Vólos, Grc. **E9** 18
Volos, Gulf of see Pagasitikós Kólpos, b., Grc. **E9** 18
Volosovo, Russia **G13** 10
Vol'sk, Russia **D6** 26
Volta, stm., Ghana **E5** 50
Volta Lake, res., Ghana **E5** 50
Volta Redonda, Braz. **F3** 74
Volterra, Italy **C3** 18
Volusia, co., Fl., U.S. **C5** 102
Volžsk, Russia **C8** 22
Volžskij, Russia **E6** 26
Vondrozo, Madag. **C8** 56
Von Frank Mountain, mtn., Ak., U.S. **C9** 95
Vonore, Tn., U.S. **D9** 135
Vordingborg, Den. **I4** 10
Vórioi Sporádhes, is., Grc. **E10** 18
Vórios Evvoïkós Kólpos, b., Grc. **E9** 18
Vorkuta, Russia **C8** 26
Vormsi, i., Est. **G10** 10
Voronež, Russia **D5** 26
Voroshilovsk see Alchevs'k, Ukr. **E15** 20
Vorpommern, hist. reg., Ger. **D13** 12
Võrtsjärv, l., Est. **G12** 10
Võru, Est. **H12** 10
Vosges, mts., Fr. **C10** 16
Voss, Nor. **F2** 10
Vostočno-Sibirskoe more, Russia **B17** 26
Vostočnyj Sajan, mts., Russia **D11** 26
Vostok, i., Kir. **F14** 58
Votkinsk, Russia **D7** 26
Votuporanga, Braz. **F2** 74
Voyageurs National Park, Mn., U.S. **B5** 116
Vožega, Russia **B7** 22
Voznesens'k, Ukr. **F11** 20
Vraca, Bul. **C9** 18
Vrangelja, ostrov, i., Russia **B20** 26
Vranje, Yugo. **C8** 18
Vrede, S. Afr. **D4** 56
Vršac, Yugo. **B8** 18
Vryburg, S. Afr. **D3** 56
Vryheid, S. Afr. **D5** 56
Vsevidof, Mount, mtn., Ak., U.S. **E6** 95
Vukovar, Cro. **B7** 18
Vulcan, Ab., Can. **D4** 84
Vyborg, Russia **C4** 26
Vyčegda, stm., Russia **C6** 26
Vym', stm., Russia **B9** 22
Vyšnij Voloček, Russia **C5** 22
Vytegra, Russia **B6** 22

W

Wa, Ghana **D4** 50
Waajid, Som. **C8** 54
Waal, stm., Eur. **E9** 12
Waawaa, Puu, mtn., Hi., U.S. **D6** 104
Wabag, Pap. N. Gui. **H11** 32
Wabana (Bell Island), Nf., Can. **E5** 88
Wabasca, Ab., Can. **B4** 84
Wabasca, stm., Ab., Can. **f1** 84
Wabash, In., U.S. **C6** 107
Wabash, co., Il., U.S. **E6** 106
Wabash, co., In., U.S. **C6** 107
Wabash, stm., U.S. **D10** 92
Wabash, stm., U.S. **H2** 107
Wabasha, Mn., U.S. **F6** 116
Wabasha, co., Mn., U.S. **F6** 116
Wabasso, Fl., U.S. **E6** 102
Wabasso, Mn., U.S. **F3** 116
Wabaunsee, co., Ks., U.S. **D7** 109
Wabeno, Wi., U.S. **C5** 142
Wabowden, Mb., Can. **B2** 86
Wabush, Nf., Can. **h8** 88
Waccamaw, stm., U.S. **D9** 133
Waccamaw, Lake, l., N.C., U.S. **C4** 126
Waccasassa Bay, b., Fl., U.S. **C4** 102
Wachusett Mountain, mtn., Ma., U.S. **B4** 114
Wachusett Reservoir, res., Ma., U.S. **B4** 114
Waco, Tx., U.S. **D4** 136

Name — Map Ref. — Page

Waco Lake, res., Tx., U.S. **D4** 136
Waconda Lake, res., Ks., U.S. **C5** 109
Waconia, Mn., U.S. **F5** 116
Waddān, Libya **E8** 48
Waddenzee, strt., Neth. **D9** 12
Waddi Chappal, Afr. **B2** 54
Waddington, Mount, mtn., B.C., Can. **D5** 85
Wadena, Mn., U.S. **D3** 116
Wadena, co., Mn., U.S. **D4** 116
Wadesboro, N.C., U.S. **C2** 126
Wādī Ḥalfā', Sudan **F11** 48
Wading, stm., N.J., U.S. **D3** 123
Wadley, Ga., U.S. **D4** 103
Wad Madanī, Sudan **H11** 48
Wadmalaw Island, i., S.C., U.S. **F7** 133
Wadsworth, Il., U.S. **h9** 106
Wadsworth, Nv., U.S. **D2** 121
Wadsworth, Oh., U.S. **A4** 128
Wafangdian, China **B5** 30
Wagadugu see Ouagadougou, Burkina **D4** 50
Wagener, S.C., U.S. **D5** 133
Wagga Wagga, Austl. **H4** 62
Wagin, Austl. **G2** 60
Wagner, S.D., U.S. **D7** 134
Wagoner, Ok., U.S. **B6** 129
Wagoner, co., Ok., U.S. **B6** 129
Wagontire Mountain, mtn., Or., U.S. **D7** 130
Waha, Libya **E9** 48
Wahai, Indon. **D7** 36
Wāh Cantonment, Pak. **D10** 42
Wahiawa, Hi., U.S. **B3** 104
Wahiawa Reservoir, res., Hi., U.S. **g9** 104
Wahkiakum, co., Wa., U.S. **C2** 140
Wahoo, Ne., U.S. **C9** 120
Wahpeton, N.D., U.S. **C9** 127
Wahran, Alg. **C4** 48
Wahweap Creek, stm., Ut., U.S. **F4** 137
Waialua, Hi., U.S. **B3** 104
Waialua Bay, b., Hi., U.S. **B3** 104
Waianae, Hi., U.S. **B3** 104
Waianae Range, mts., Hi., U.S. **f9** 104
Waidhofen an der Ybbs, Aus. **G14** 12
Waigeo, Pulau, i., Indon. **C8** 36
Waikabubak, Indon. **E5** 36
Waikapu, Hi., U.S. **C5** 104
Waikato, stm., N.Z. **o14** 63c
Waikiki Beach, Hi., U.S. **g10** 104
Wailua, Hi., U.S. **A2** 104
Wailuku, Hi., U.S. **C5** 104
Waimanalo, Hi., U.S. **B4** 104
Waimanalo Bay, b., Hi., U.S. **g11** 104
Waimate, N.Z. **p13** 63c
Waimea, Hi., U.S. **B2** 104
Waimea, Hi., U.S. **f9** 104
Wainganga, stm., India **E3** 40
Waingapu, Indon. **E6** 36
Wainwright, Ab., Can. **C5** 84
Wainwright, Ak., U.S. **A8** 95
Waipahu, Hi., U.S. **B3** 104
Waipara, N.Z. **p13** 63c
Waipio Acres, Hi., U.S. **g9** 104
Waipio Peninsula, pen., Hi., U.S. **g10** 104
Wairoa, N.Z. **o14** 63c
Waitara, N.Z. **o13** 63c
Waitemata, N.Z. **o13** 63c
Waite Park, Mn., U.S. **E4** 116
Waits, stm., Vt., U.S. **C4** 138
Waitsburg, Wa., U.S. **C7** 140
Wajir, Kenya **C8** 54
Waka, D.R.C. **C4** 54
Waka, Eth. **B7** 54
Wakarusa, In., U.S. **A5** 107
Wakarusa, stm., Ks., U.S. **D8** 109
Wakasa-wan, b., Japan **C3** 31
Wakatomika Creek, stm., Oh., U.S. **B3** 128
Wakayama, Japan **E15** 28
Wake, co., N.C., U.S. **B4** 126
WaKeeney, Ks., U.S. **C4** 109
Wakefield, P.Q., Can. **D2** 90
Wakefield, Ks., U.S. **C6** 109
Wakefield, Ma., U.S. **B5** 114
Wakefield, Mi., U.S. **n12** 115
Wakefield, Ne., U.S. **B9** 120
Wakefield, R.I., U.S. **F3** 132
Wakefield, Va., U.S. **D6** 139
Wake Forest, N.C., U.S. **B4** 126
Wake Island, dep., Oc. **C10** 58
Wakema, Myan. **C3** 34
Wakeman, Oh., U.S. **A3** 128
Wakkanai, Japan **B16** 28
Waku Kungo, Ang. **F3** 54
Wakulla, co., Fl., U.S. **B2** 102
Walachia, hist. reg., Rom. **G8** 20
Walbridge, Oh., U.S. **e6** 128
Wałbrzych, Pol. **D4** 20
Walcott, Ia., U.S. **C7** 108
Walcott, Lake, res., Id., U.S. **G5** 105
Wałcz, Pol. **C4** 20
Walden, On., Can. **A3** 89
Walden, Co., U.S. **A4** 99
Walden, N.Y., U.S. **D6** 125
Waldenburg see Wałbrzych, Pol. **D4** 20
Walden Ridge, mtn., Tn., U.S. **D8** 135
Waldheim, Sk., Can. **E2** 91
Waldo, Ar., U.S. **D2** 97
Waldo, co., Me., U.S. **D3** 112
Waldoboro, Me., U.S. **D3** 112
Waldo Lake, l., Ma., U.S. **h11** 114
Waldo Lake, l., Or., U.S. **D4** 130
Waldport, Or., U.S. **C2** 130
Waldron, Ar., U.S. **C1** 97
Waldron, In., U.S. **F6** 107
Waldwick, N.J., U.S. **A4** 123
Wales, prov., U.K. **E4** 12
Waleska, Ga., U.S. **B2** 103
Walgett, Austl. **G4** 62
Walgreen Coast, Ant. **D30** 67
Walhalla, N.D., U.S. **A8** 127
Walhalla, S.C., U.S. **B1** 133
Walhonding, stm., Oh., U.S. **B3** 128
Walikale, D.R.C. **D5** 54
Walker, Ia., U.S. **B6** 108
Walker, La., U.S. **g10** 111
Walker, Mi., U.S. **E5** 115
Walker, Mn., U.S. **C4** 116
Walker, co., Al., U.S. **B2** 94
Walker, co., Ga., U.S. **B1** 103
Walker, co., Tx., U.S. **D5** 136
Walker, stm., Nv., U.S. **D3** 121
Walker Lake, l., Nv., U.S. **E3** 121
Walker River Indian Reservation, Nv., U.S. **D3** 121
Walkersville, Md., U.S. **B3** 113
Walkerton, On., Can. **C3** 89
Walkerton, In., U.S. **B5** 107
Walkertown, N.C., U.S. **A2** 126
Walkerville, Mt., U.S. **D4** 119
Wall, S.D., U.S. **D3** 134
Wallace, Id., U.S. **B3** 105
Wallace, N.C., U.S. **B4** 126
Wallace, co., Ks., U.S. **D2** 109
Wallaceburg, On., Can. **E2** 89
Wallace Lake, res., La., U.S. **B2** 111
Walla Walla, Wa., U.S. **C7** 140
Walla Walla, co., Wa., U.S. **C7** 140
Walla Walla, stm., U.S. **C7** 140
Walled Lake, Mi., U.S. **o15** 115
Wallen, In., U.S. **B7** 107
Wallenpaupack, Lake, l., Pa., U.S. **D11** 131
Waller, Tx., U.S. **q14** 136
Waller, co., Tx., U.S. **E4** 136
Wallingford, Ct., U.S. **D4** 100
Wallingford, Vt., U.S. **E3** 138
Wallington, N.J., U.S. **h8** 123
Wallis, Îles, is., Wal./F. **F12** 58
Wallis and Futuna, dep., Oc. **F12** 58
Wallkill, N.Y., U.S. **D6** 125
Wallkill, stm., N.Y., U.S. **D6** 125
Wall Lake, Ia., U.S. **B2** 108
Wall Lake, l., Ia., U.S. **B4** 108
Walloomsac, stm., U.S. **F2** 138
Walloon Lake, l., Mi., U.S. **C6** 115
Wallowa, Or., U.S. **B9** 130
Wallowa, co., Or., U.S. **B9** 130
Wallowa Mountains, mts., Or., U.S. **B9** 130
Wallula, Lake, res., U.S. **C7** 140
Wallum Lake, l., U.S. **A1** 132
Walnut, Ia., U.S. **C2** 108
Walnut, Il., U.S. **B4** 106
Walnut, stm., Ks., U.S. **E6** 109
Walnut Canyon National Monument, Az., U.S. **B4** 96
Walnut Cove, N.C., U.S. **A2** 126
Walnut Creek, Ca., U.S. **h8** 98
Walnut Creek, stm., Ks., U.S. **D4** 109
Walnut Grove, Al., U.S. **A3** 94
Walnut Grove, Mn., U.S. **F3** 116
Walnutport, Pa., U.S. **E10** 131
Walnut Ridge, Ar., U.S. **A5** 97
Walpole, Austl. **H2** 60
Walpole, Ma., U.S. **B5** 114
Walpole, N.H., U.S. **D2** 122
Walsall, Eng., U.K. **D6** 12
Walsenburg, Co., U.S. **D6** 99
Walsh, Co., U.S. **D8** 99
Walsh, co., N.D., U.S. **A8** 127
Walterboro, S.C., U.S. **F6** 133
Walter F. George Dam, U.S. **D4** 94
Walter F. George Lake, res., U.S. **D4** 94
Walters, Ok., U.S. **C3** 129
Walthall, co., Ms., U.S. **D3** 117
Waltham, Ma., U.S. **B5** 114
Walthill, Ne., U.S. **B9** 120
Walthourville, Ga., U.S. **E5** 103
Walton, In., U.S. **C5** 107
Walton, Ky., U.S. **B5** 110
Walton, N.Y., U.S. **C5** 125
Walton, co., Fl., U.S. **u15** 102
Walton, co., Ga., U.S. **C3** 103
Walvis Bay, Nmb. **C1** 56
Walvis Bay, b., Nmb. **C1** 56
Walvis Ridge **K14** 66
Walworth, Wi., U.S. **F5** 142
Walworth, co., S.D., U.S. **B5** 134
Walworth, co., Wi., U.S. **F5** 142
Wamac, Il., U.S. **E4** 106
Wamba, D.R.C. **C5** 54
Wamba, Nig. **E6** 50
Wamba, stm., Afr. **E3** 54
Wamego, Ks., U.S. **C7** 109
Wamesit, Ma., U.S. **A5** 114
Wamsutter, Wy., U.S. **E5** 143
Wanaka, N.Z. **p12** 63c
Wanamingo, Mn., U.S. **F6** 116
Wanapum Dam, Wa., U.S. **C6** 140
Wanapum Lake, res., Wa., U.S. **B6** 140
Wanaque, N.J., U.S. **A4** 123
Wanaque Reservoir, res., N.J., U.S. **A4** 123
Wanatah, In., U.S. **B4** 107
Wanchese, N.C., U.S. **B7** 126
Wando, stm., S.C., U.S. **F8** 133
Wando Woods, S.C., U.S. **k11** 133
Wanfoxia, China **A7** 40
Wanganui, N.Z. **p13** 63c
Wangaratta, Austl. **H4** 62
Wangiwangi, Pulau, i., Indon. **E6** 36
Wangqing, China **B1** 31
Wanigela, Pap. N. Gui. **H12** 32
Wanneroo, Austl. **G2** 60
Wanning, China **F3** 30
Wanxian, China **E9** 28
Wanyuan, China **C2** 30
Wanzai, China **D3** 30
Wapakoneta, Oh., U.S. **B1** 128
Wapato, Wa., U.S. **C5** 140
Wapawekka Lake, l., Sk., Can. **C3** 91
Wapello, Ia., U.S. **C6** 108
Wapello, co., Ia., U.S. **C5** 108
Wapiti, stm., Can. **B1** 84
Wappapello, Lake, res., Mo., U.S. **D7** 118
Wappingers Falls, N.Y., U.S. **D7** 125
Wapsipinicon, stm., Ia., U.S. **B6** 108
War, W.V., U.S. **D3** 141
Waramaug, Lake, l., Ct., U.S. **C2** 100
Warangal, India **F3** 40
Ward, Ar., U.S. **B4** 97
Ward, co., N.D., U.S. **A4** 127
Ward, co., Tx., U.S. **D1** 136
Warden, Wa., U.S. **C6** 140
Wardha, India **E3** 40
Ward Mountain, mtn., Mt., U.S. **D2** 119
Ware, Ma., U.S. **B3** 114
Ware, co., Ga., U.S. **E4** 103
Ware, stm., Ma., U.S. **B3** 114
War Eagle Mountain, mtn., Id., U.S. **G2** 105
Wareham, Ma., U.S. **C6** 114
Warehouse Point, Ct., U.S. **B5** 100
Waren, Indon. **G10** 32
Ware Shoals, S.C., U.S. **C3** 133
Warfield, B.C., Can. **E9** 85
Wargla, Alg. **D6** 48
Warialda, Austl. **F5** 62
Warin Chamrap, Thai. **C4** 34
Warmbad, Nmb. **D2** 56
Warmbad, S. Afr. **C4** 56
Warminster, Pa., U.S. **F11** 131
Warm Springs Indian Reservation, Or., U.S. **C5** 130
Warm Springs Reservoir, res., Or., U.S. **D8** 130
Warner, N.H., U.S. **D3** 122
Warner, Ok., U.S. **B6** 129
Warner, stm., N.H., U.S. **D3** 122
Warner Mountains, mts., Ca., U.S. **B3** 98
Warner Peak, mtn., Or., U.S. **E7** 130
Warner Robins, Ga., U.S. **D3** 103
Warracknabeal, Austl. **H3** 62
Warr Acres, Ok., U.S. **B4** 129
Warragul, Austl. **H4** 62
Warren, Ar., U.S. **D3** 97
Warren, Il., U.S. **A4** 106
Warren, In., U.S. **C7** 107
Warren, Ma., U.S. **B3** 114
Warren, Mi., U.S. **F7** 115
Warren, Mn., U.S. **B2** 116
Warren, Oh., U.S. **A5** 128
Warren, Or., U.S. **B4** 130
Warren, Pa., U.S. **C3** 131
Warren, R.I., U.S. **D5** 132
Warren, Vt., U.S. **C3** 138
Warren, co., Ga., U.S. **C4** 103
Warren, co., Ia., U.S. **C4** 108
Warren, co., Il., U.S. **C3** 106
Warren, co., In., U.S. **D3** 107
Warren, co., Ky., U.S. **C3** 110
Warren, co., Mo., U.S. **C6** 118
Warren, co., Ms., U.S. **C3** 117
Warren, co., N.C., U.S. **A4** 126
Warren, co., N.J., U.S. **B3** 123
Warren, co., N.Y., U.S. **B7** 125
Warren, co., Oh., U.S. **C1** 128
Warren, co., Pa., U.S. **C3** 131
Warren, co., Tn., U.S. **D8** 135
Warren, co., Va., U.S. **B4** 139
Warren, stm., U.S. **D5** 132
Warren Park, In., U.S. **k10** 107
Warren Peaks, mts., Wy., U.S. **B8** 143
Warrensburg, Il., U.S. **D4** 106
Warrensburg, Mo., U.S. **C4** 118
Warrensburg, N.Y., U.S. **B7** 125
Warrensville Heights, Oh., U.S. **h9** 128
Warrenton, S. Afr. **D3** 56
Warrenton, Ga., U.S. **C4** 103
Warrenton, Mo., U.S. **C6** 118
Warrenton, N.C., U.S. **A4** 126
Warrenton, Or., U.S. **A3** 130
Warrenton, Va., U.S. **B5** 139
Warrenville, Il., U.S. **k8** 106
Warrenville, S.C., U.S. **D4** 133
Warri, Nig. **E6** 50
Warrick, co., In., U.S. **H3** 107
Warrington, Fl., U.S. **u14** 102
Warrior, Al., U.S. **B3** 94
Warrior Lake, res., Al., U.S. **C2** 94
Warrnambool, Austl. **H3** 62
Warroad, Mn., U.S. **B3** 116
Warsaw see Warszawa, Pol. **C6** 20
Warsaw, Il., U.S. **C2** 106
Warsaw, In., U.S. **B6** 107
Warsaw, Ky., U.S. **B5** 110
Warsaw, Mo., U.S. **C4** 118
Warsaw, N.C., U.S. **B4** 126
Warsaw, N.Y., U.S. **C2** 125
Warsaw, Va., U.S. **C6** 139
Warszawa (Warsaw), Pol. **C6** 20
Wartburg, Tn., U.S. **C9** 135
Warwick, Austl. **F5** 62
Warwick, P.Q., Can. **D6** 90
Warwick, Md., U.S. **B6** 113
Warwick, N.Y., U.S. **D6** 125
Warwick, R.I., U.S. **D4** 132
Wasaga Beach, On., Can. **C4** 89
Wasatch, co., Ut., U.S. **C4** 137
Wasco, Ca., U.S. **E4** 98
Wasco, co., Or., U.S. **B5** 130
Waseca, Mn., U.S. **F5** 116
Waseca, co., Mn., U.S. **F5** 116
Washakie, co., Wy., U.S. **C5** 143
Washakie Needles, mts., Wy., U.S. **C3** 143
Washburn, Ia., U.S. **B5** 108
Washburn, Il., U.S. **C4** 106
Washburn, Me., U.S. **B4** 112
Washburn, N.D., U.S. **B5** 127
Washburn, Wi., U.S. **B3** 142
Washburn, co., Wi., U.S. **C2** 142
Washburn, Mount, mtn., Wy., U.S. **B2** 143
Wāshīm, India **E3** 40
Washington, D.C., U.S. **C3** 113
Washington, Ga., U.S. **C4** 103
Washington, Ia., U.S. **C6** 108
Washington, Il., U.S. **C4** 106
Washington, In., U.S. **G3** 107
Washington, Ks., U.S. **C6** 109
Washington, Ky., U.S. **B6** 110
Washington, La., U.S. **D3** 111
Washington, Mo., U.S. **C6** 118
Washington, Ms., U.S. **D2** 117
Washington, N.C., U.S. **B5** 126
Washington, N.J., U.S. **B3** 123
Washington, Pa., U.S. **F1** 131
Washington, Ut., U.S. **F2** 137
Washington, co., Al., U.S. **D1** 94
Washington, co., Ar., U.S. **A1** 97
Washington, co., Co., U.S. **B7** 99
Washington, co., Fl., U.S. **u16** 102
Washington, co., Ga., U.S. **C4** 103
Washington, co., Ia., U.S. **C6** 108
Washington, co., Id., U.S. **E2** 105
Washington, co., Il., U.S. **E4** 106
Washington, co., In., U.S. **G5** 107
Washington, co., Ks., U.S. **C6** 109
Washington, co., Ky., U.S. **C4** 110
Washington, co., La., U.S. **D5** 111
Washington, co., Md., U.S. **A2** 113
Washington, co., Me., U.S. **D5** 112
Washington, co., Mn., U.S. **E6** 116
Washington, co., Mo., U.S. **D7** 118
Washington, co., Ms., U.S. **B3** 117
Washington, co., N.C., U.S. **B6** 126
Washington, co., Ne., U.S. **C9** 120
Washington, co., N.Y., U.S. **B7** 125
Washington, co., Oh., U.S. **C4** 128
Washington, co., Ok., U.S. **A6** 129
Washington, co., Or., U.S. **B3** 130
Washington, co., Pa., U.S. **F1** 131
Washington, co., R.I., U.S. **E2** 132
Washington, co., Tn., U.S. **C11** 135
Washington, co., Tx., U.S. **D4** 136
Washington, co., Ut., U.S. **F2** 137
Washington, co., Va., U.S. **f9** 139
Washington, co., Vt., U.S. **C3** 138
Washington, co., Wi., U.S. **E5** 142
Washington, state, U.S. **B5** 140
Washington, Lake, l., Fl., U.S. **D6** 102
Washington, Lake, l., Mn., U.S. **E4** 116
Washington, Lake, l., Ms., U.S. **B3** 117
Washington, Lake, l., Wa., U.S. **e11** 140
Washington, Mount, mtn., N.H., U.S. **B4** 122
Washington Court House, Oh., U.S. **C2** 128
Washington Island, i., Wi., U.S. **C7** 142
Washington Park, Il., U.S. **E3** 106
Washington Terrace, Ut., U.S. **B4** 137
Washita, co., Ok., U.S. **B2** 129
Washita, stm., Ok., U.S. **C4** 129
Washoe, co., Nv., U.S. **C2** 121
Washoe City, Nv., U.S. **D2** 121
Washougal, Wa., U.S. **D3** 140
Washow Bay, b., Mb., Can. **D3** 86
Washtenaw, co., Mi., U.S. **F7** 115
Wasilla, Ak., U.S. **C10** 95
Wasior, Indon. **D8** 36
Waskom, Tx., U.S. **C5** 136
Waspam, Nic. **C3** 80
Wasque Point, c., Ma., U.S. **D7** 114
Wassookeag, Lake, l., Me., U.S. **C3** 112
Wassuk Range, mts., Nv., U.S. **E3** 121
Wataga, Il., U.S. **B3** 106
Watampone, Indon. **D6** 36
Watansopeng, Indon. **D5** 36
Watauga, co., N.C., U.S. **A1** 126
Watauga, stm., Tn., U.S. **C12** 135
Watauga Lake, res., Tn., U.S. **C12** 135
Watchaug Pond, l., R.I., U.S. **F2** 132
Watch Hill Point, c., R.I., U.S. **G1** 132
Watchung, N.J., U.S. **B4** 123
Waterbury, Ct., U.S. **C3** 100
Waterbury, Vt., U.S. **C3** 138
Waterbury Center, Vt., U.S. **C3** 138
Waterbury Reservoir, res., Vt., U.S. **C3** 138
Wateree, stm., S.C., U.S. **D6** 133
Wateree Lake, res., S.C., U.S. **C6** 133
Waterford, Ire. **D3** 12
Waterford, Ct., U.S. **D7** 100
Waterford, N.Y., U.S. **C7** 125
Waterford, Pa., U.S. **C2** 131
Waterford, Wi., U.S. **F5** 142
Waterhen Lake, l., Mb., Can. **C2** 86
Waterloo, Bel. **E9** 12
Waterloo, On., Can. **D4** 89
Waterloo, P.Q., Can. **D5** 90
Waterloo, Ia., U.S. **B5** 108
Waterloo, Il., U.S. **E3** 106
Waterloo, In., U.S. **B7** 107
Waterloo, N.Y., U.S. **C4** 125
Waterloo, Wi., U.S. **E5** 142
Waterman, Il., U.S. **B5** 106
Waterman Reservoir, res., R.I., U.S. **B3** 132
Waterproof, La., U.S. **C4** 111
Watersmeet, Mi., U.S. **n12** 115
Waterton Lakes National Park, Ab., Can. **E3** 84
Watertown, Ct., U.S. **C3** 100
Watertown, Ma., U.S. **g11** 114
Watertown, N.Y., U.S. **B5** 125
Watertown, S.D., U.S. **C8** 134
Watertown, Tn., U.S. **A5** 135
Watertown, Wi., U.S. **E5** 142
Water Valley, Ms., U.S. **A4** 117
Waterville, Ks., U.S. **C7** 109
Waterville, Me., U.S. **D3** 112
Waterville, Mn., U.S. **F5** 116
Waterville, N.Y., U.S. **C5** 125
Waterville, Oh., U.S. **A2** 128
Waterville, Wa., U.S. **B5** 140
Watervliet, Mi., U.S. **F4** 115
Watervliet, N.Y., U.S. **C7** 125
Watford, On., Can. **E3** 89
Watford City, N.D., U.S. **B2** 127
Wathena, Ks., U.S. **C9** 109
Watheroo, Austl. **G2** 60
Watkins, Mn., U.S. **E4** 116
Watkins Glen, N.Y., U.S. **C4** 125
Watkinsville, Ga., U.S. **C3** 103
Watling Island see San Salvador, i., Bah. **D10** 76
Watonga, Ok., U.S. **B3** 129
Watonwan, co., Mn., U.S. **F4** 116
Watonwan, stm., Mn., U.S. **G4** 116
Watsa, D.R.C. **C5** 54
Watseka, Il., U.S. **C6** 106
Watsontown, Pa., U.S. **D8** 131
Watsonville, Ca., U.S. **D3** 98
Watts Bar Dam, Tn., U.S. **D9** 135
Watts Bar Lake, res., Tn., U.S. **D9** 135
Wattsville, S.C., U.S. **B4** 133
Watubela, Kepulauan, is., Indon. **D8** 36
Waubaushene, On., Can. **C5** 89
Waubay, S.D., U.S. **B8** 134
Waubay Lake, l., S.D., U.S. **B8** 134
Wauchope, Austl. **E5** 60
Wauchula, Fl., U.S. **E5** 102
Wauconda, Il., U.S. **h8** 106
Waugh Mountain, mtn., Id., U.S. **D4** 105
Waukee, Ia., U.S. **C4** 108
Waukegan, Il., U.S. **A6** 106
Waukesha, Wi., U.S. **F5** 142
Waukesha, co., Wi., U.S. **E5** 142
Waukewan, Lake, l., N.H., U.S. **C3** 122
Waukomis, Ok., U.S. **A4** 129
Waukon, Ia., U.S. **A6** 108
Waunakee, Wi., U.S. **E4** 142
Wauneta, Ne., U.S. **D4** 120
Waungumbaug Lake, l., Ct., U.S. **B6** 100
Waupaca, Wi., U.S. **D4** 142
Waupaca, co., Wi., U.S. **D5** 142
Waupun, Wi., U.S. **E5** 142
Wauregan, Ct., U.S. **C8** 100
Waurika, Ok., U.S. **C4** 129
Waurika Lake, res., Ok., U.S. **C3** 129

Name	Map Ref.	Page
Wausau, Wi., U.S.	**D4**	142
Wausau, Lake, res., Wi., U.S.	**D4**	142
Wauseon, Oh., U.S.	**A1**	128
Waushara, co., Wi., U.S.	**D4**	142
Wautoma, Wi., U.S.	**D4**	142
Wauwatosa, Wi., U.S.	**m12**	142
Wave Hill, Austl.	**D5**	60
Waveland, Ms., U.S.	**E4**	117
Waverley, N.S., Can.	**E6**	87
Waverly, Ia., U.S.	**B5**	108
Waverly, Il., U.S.	**D4**	106
Waverly, Ks., U.S.	**D8**	109
Waverly, Mn., U.S.	**E5**	116
Waverly, Mo., U.S.	**B4**	118
Waverly, Ne., U.S.	**D9**	120
Waverly, N.Y., U.S.	**C4**	125
Waverly, Oh., U.S.	**C3**	128
Waverly, Tn., U.S.	**A4**	135
Waverly, Va., U.S.	**C5**	139
Waverly, W.V., U.S.	**B3**	141
Waverly Hall, Ga., U.S.	**D2**	103
Wāw, Sudan	**I10**	48
Wāw al-Kabīr, Libya	**E8**	48
Wawanesa, Mb., Can.	**E2**	86
Wawasee, Lake, l., In., U.S.	**B6**	107
Wawayanda Lake, l., N.J., U.S.	**A4**	123
Wawota, Sk., Can.	**H4**	91
Waxahachie, Tx., U.S.	**C4**	136
Waxhaw, N.C., U.S.	**C2**	126
Waycross, Ga., U.S.	**E4**	103
Wayland, Ia., U.S.	**C6**	108
Wayland, Ma., U.S.	**g10**	114
Wayland, Mi., U.S.	**F5**	115
Wayland, N.Y., U.S.	**C3**	125
Waylyn, S.C., U.S.	**k12**	133
Waymart, Pa., U.S.	**C11**	131
Wayne, Mi., U.S.	**p15**	115
Wayne, Ne., U.S.	**B8**	120
Wayne, N.J., U.S.	**B4**	123
Wayne, W.V., U.S.	**C2**	141
Wayne, co., Ga., U.S.	**E5**	103
Wayne, co., Ia., U.S.	**D4**	108
Wayne, co., Il., U.S.	**E5**	106
Wayne, co., In., U.S.	**E7**	107
Wayne, co., Ky., U.S.	**D5**	110
Wayne, co., Mi., U.S.	**F7**	115
Wayne, co., Mo., U.S.	**D7**	118
Wayne, co., Ms., U.S.	**D5**	117
Wayne, co., N.C., U.S.	**B4**	126
Wayne, co., Ne., U.S.	**B8**	120
Wayne, co., N.Y., U.S.	**B3**	125
Wayne, co., Oh., U.S.	**B4**	128
Wayne, co., Pa., U.S.	**C11**	131
Wayne, co., Tn., U.S.	**B4**	135
Wayne, co., Ut., U.S.	**E4**	137
Wayne, co., W.V., U.S.	**C2**	141
Wayne City, Il., U.S.	**E5**	106
Waynesboro, Ga., U.S.	**C4**	103
Waynesboro, Ms., U.S.	**D5**	117
Waynesboro, Pa., U.S.	**G6**	131
Waynesboro, Tn., U.S.	**B4**	135
Waynesboro, Va., U.S.	**B4**	139
Waynesburg, Oh., U.S.	**B4**	128
Waynesburg, Pa., U.S.	**G1**	131
Waynesville, Mo., U.S.	**D5**	118
Waynesville, N.C., U.S.	**f10**	126
Waynesville, Oh., U.S.	**C1**	128
Waynetown, In., U.S.	**D3**	107
Waynewood, Va., U.S.	**g12**	139
Waynoka, Ok., U.S.	**A3**	129
Wayzata, Mn., U.S.	**n11**	116
Waza, Cam.	**D7**	50
We, Pulau, i., Indon.	**B1**	36
Weakley, co., Tn., U.S.	**A3**	135
Weatherford, Ok., U.S.	**B3**	129
Weatherford, Tx., U.S.	**C4**	136
Weatherly, Pa., U.S.	**E10**	131
Weatogue, Ct., U.S.	**B4**	100
Weaver, Al., U.S.	**B4**	94
Weaver Mountains, mts., Az., U.S.	**C3**	96
Weaverville, Ca., U.S.	**B2**	98
Weaverville, N.C., U.S.	**f10**	126
Webb, Al., U.S.	**D4**	94
Webb, Ms., U.S.	**B3**	117
Webb, co., Tx., U.S.	**F3**	136
Webb City, Mo., U.S.	**D3**	118
Webbers Falls, Ok., U.S.	**B6**	129
Webberville, Mi., U.S.	**F6**	115
Webb Lake, l., Me., U.S.	**D2**	112
Weber, co., Ut., U.S.	**B4**	137
Weber City, Va., U.S.	**f9**	139
Webster, Ma., U.S.	**B4**	114
Webster, N.Y., U.S.	**B3**	125
Webster, Pa., U.S.	**F2**	131
Webster, S.D., U.S.	**B8**	134
Webster, co., Ga., U.S.	**D2**	103
Webster, co., Ia., U.S.	**B3**	108
Webster, co., Ky., U.S.	**C2**	110
Webster, co., La., U.S.	**B2**	111
Webster, co., Mo., U.S.	**D5**	118
Webster, co., Ms., U.S.	**B4**	117
Webster, co., Ne., U.S.	**D7**	120
Webster, co., W.V., U.S.	**C4**	141
Webster City, Ia., U.S.	**B4**	108
Webster Groves, Mo., U.S.	**f13**	118
Webster Reservoir, res., Ks., U.S.	**C4**	109
Webster Springs, W.V., U.S.	**C4**	141
Websterville, Vt., U.S.	**C4**	138
Weda, Indon.	**C7**	36
Weddell Sea, Ant.	**C1**	67
Wedgeport, N.S., Can.	**F4**	87
Wedgewood, Mo., U.S.	**f13**	118
Wedowee, Al., U.S.	**B4**	94
Weed, Ca., U.S.	**B2**	98
Weed Heights, Nv., U.S.	**E2**	121
Weedon, P.Q., Can.	**D6**	90
Weedsport, N.Y., U.S.	**B4**	125
Weedville, Pa., U.S.	**D5**	131
Weehawken, N.J., U.S.	**h8**	123
Weeksbury, Ky., U.S.	**C7**	110
Weeping Water, Ne., U.S.	**D9**	120
Weichang, China	**A4**	30
Weiden in der Oberpfalz, Ger.	**F12**	12
Weifang, China	**D11**	28
Weihai, China	**D12**	28
Weimar, Ger.	**E12**	12
Weimar, Tx., U.S.	**E4**	136
Weinan, China	**E9**	28
Weiner, Ar., U.S.	**B5**	97
Weippe, Id., U.S.	**C3**	105
Weir, Ks., U.S.	**E9**	109
Weir, Lake, l., Fl., U.S.	**C5**	102
Weirsdale, Fl., U.S.	**D5**	102
Weirton, W.V., U.S.	**A4**	141
Weiser, Id., U.S.	**E2**	105
Weiser, stm., Id., U.S.	**E2**	105
Weishan Hu, l., China	**B4**	30
Weissenburg in Bayern, Ger.	**F12**	12
Weissenfels, Ger.	**E12**	12
Weiss Lake, res., U.S.	**A4**	94
Weixi, China	**A3**	34
Weixian, China	**B4**	30
Wejherowo, Pol.	**B5**	20
Welbourn Hill, Austl.	**F5**	60
Welch, W.V., U.S.	**D3**	141
Welcome, Mn., U.S.	**G4**	116
Welcome, S.C., U.S.	**B3**	133
Weld, co., Co., U.S.	**A6**	99
Weldon, N.C., U.S.	**A5**	126
Weldon Spring, Mo., U.S.	**f12**	118
Weleetka, Ok., U.S.	**B5**	129
Welk'ītē, Eth.	**B7**	54
Welkom, S. Afr.	**D4**	56
Welland, On., Can.	**E5**	89
Wellesley, On., Can.	**D4**	89
Wellesley, Ma., U.S.	**B5**	114
Wellesley Islands, is., Austl.	**D2**	62
Wellford, S.C., U.S.	**B3**	133
Wellington, Austl.	**G4**	62
Wellington, On., Can.	**D7**	89
Wellington, N.Z.	**I11**	58
Wellington, Co., U.S.	**A5**	99
Wellington, Ks., U.S.	**E6**	109
Wellington, Mo., U.S.	**B4**	118
Wellington, Nv., U.S.	**E2**	121
Wellington, Oh., U.S.	**A3**	128
Wellington, Tx., U.S.	**B2**	136
Wellington, Ut., U.S.	**D5**	137
Wellington, Isla, i., Chile	**G2**	69
Wellman, Ia., U.S.	**C6**	108
Wells, Me., U.S.	**E2**	112
Wells, Mi., U.S.	**C3**	115
Wells, Mn., U.S.	**G5**	116
Wells, Nv., U.S.	**B7**	121
Wells, co., In., U.S.	**C7**	107
Wells, co., N.D., U.S.	**B6**	127
Wells, stm., Vt., U.S.	**C4**	138
Wellsboro, Pa., U.S.	**C7**	131
Wellsburg, Ia., U.S.	**B5**	108
Wellsburg, W.V., U.S.	**A4**	141
Wellston, Oh., U.S.	**C3**	128
Wellston, Ok., U.S.	**B4**	129
Wellsville, Ks., U.S.	**D8**	109
Wellsville, Mo., U.S.	**B6**	118
Wellsville, N.Y., U.S.	**C3**	125
Wellsville, Oh., U.S.	**B5**	128
Wellsville, Ut., U.S.	**B4**	137
Wellton, Az., U.S.	**E1**	96
Wels, Aus.	**F13**	12
Welsh, La., U.S.	**D3**	111
Wembley, Ab., Can.	**B1**	84
Wenatchee, Wa., U.S.	**B5**	140
Wenatchee, stm., Wa., U.S.	**B5**	140
Wenatchee Lake, l., Wa., U.S.	**B5**	140
Wenatchee Mountains, mts., Wa., U.S.	**B5**	140
Wenchang, China	**F3**	30
Wenchi, Ghana	**E4**	50
Wendell, Id., U.S.	**G4**	105
Wendell, N.C., U.S.	**B4**	126
Wendeng, China	**B5**	30
Wendover, Ut., U.S.	**C1**	137
Wengyuan, China	**E3**	30
Wenham, Ma., U.S.	**A6**	114
Wenham Lake, l., Ma., U.S.	**f12**	114
Wenling, China	**D5**	30
Wenshan, China	**G8**	28
Wenshang, China	**B4**	30
Wensu, China	**A4**	40
Wentworth, Austl.	**G3**	62
Wentworth, Lake, l., N.H., U.S.	**C4**	122
Wentzville, Mo., U.S.	**C7**	118
Wenzhou, China	**F12**	28
Weohyakapka, Lake, l., Fl., U.S.	**E5**	102
Werda, Bots.	**D3**	56
Weri, Indon.	**D8**	36
Werribee, Austl.	**H3**	62
Wesel, Ger.	**E10**	12
Weser, stm., Ger.	**D11**	12
Weslaco, Tx., U.S.	**F4**	136
Wesleyville, Nf., Can.	**D5**	88
Wesleyville, Pa., U.S.	**B2**	131
Wessel, Cape, c., Austl.	**C6**	60
Wessel Islands, is., Austl.	**C6**	60
Wesserunsett Lake, l., Me., U.S.	**D3**	112
Wessington Springs, S.D., U.S.	**C7**	134
Wesson, Ms., U.S.	**D3**	117
West, Tx., U.S.	**D4**	136
West, stm., Ct., U.S.	**D5**	100
West, stm., Ma., U.S.	**h9**	114
West, stm., Vt., U.S.	**E3**	138
West Acton, Ma., U.S.	**g10**	114
West Alexandria, Oh., U.S.	**C1**	128
West Allis, Wi., U.S.	**m11**	142
West Alton, Mo., U.S.	**f13**	118
West Andover, Ma., U.S.	**A5**	114
West Antarctica, reg., Ant.	**E29**	67
West Baden Springs, In., U.S.	**G4**	107
West Baton Rouge, co., La., U.S.	**D4**	111
West Bay, b., Fl., U.S.	**u16**	102
West Bay, b., N.C., U.S.	**B6**	126
West Bay, b., Tx., U.S.	**r15**	136
West Bend, Ia., U.S.	**B3**	108
West Bend, Wi., U.S.	**E5**	142
West Bengal, prov., India	**E5**	40
West Berlin, N.J., U.S.	**D3**	123
West Billerica, Ma., U.S.	**f10**	114
West Blocton, Al., U.S.	**B2**	94
Westborough, Ma., U.S.	**B4**	114
West Bountiful, Ut., U.S.	**C4**	137
West Boylston, Ma., U.S.	**B4**	114
West Branch, Ia., U.S.	**C6**	108
West Branch, Mi., U.S.	**D6**	115
West Branch Reservoir, res., Ct., U.S.	**B3**	100
West Bridgewater, Ma., U.S.	**B5**	114
Westbrook, Ct., U.S.	**D6**	100
Westbrook, Me., U.S.	**E2**	112
Westbrook, Mn., U.S.	**F3**	116
West Burlington, Ia., U.S.	**D6**	108
West Butte, mtn., Mt., U.S.	**B5**	119
Westby, Wi., U.S.	**E3**	142
West Cache Creek, stm., Ok., U.S.	**C3**	129
West Caldwell, N.J., U.S.	**B4**	123
West Canada Creek, stm., N.Y., U.S.	**B6**	125
West Cape Howe, c., Austl.	**H2**	60
West Caroline Basin	**H16**	64
West Carroll, co., La., U.S.	**B4**	111
West Carrollton, Oh., U.S.	**C1**	128
West Carthage, N.Y., U.S.	**B5**	125
Westchester, Il., U.S.	**k9**	106
West Chester, Pa., U.S.	**G10**	131
Westchester, co., N.Y., U.S.	**D7**	125
West Chicago, Il., U.S.	**k8**	106
West Chop, c., Ma., U.S.	**D6**	114
West College Corner, In., U.S.	**E8**	107
West Columbia, S.C., U.S.	**D5**	133
West Columbia, Tx., U.S.	**E5**	136
West Concord, Ma., U.S.	**B5**	114
West Concord, Mn., U.S.	**F6**	116
West Concord, N.C., U.S.	**B2**	126
Westconnaug Reservoir, res., R.I., U.S.	**C2**	132
West Cote Blanche Bay, b., La., U.S.	**E4**	111
West Covina, Ca., U.S.	**m13**	98
West Crossett, Ar., U.S.	**D4**	97
West Cumberland, Me., U.S.	**E2**	112
West Dennis, Ma., U.S.	**C7**	114
West Des Moines, Ia., U.S.	**C4**	108
West Elk Mountains, mts., Co., U.S.	**C3**	99
West Elk Peak, mtn., Co., U.S.	**C3**	99
Westerly, R.I., U.S.	**F1**	132
Western Australia, state, Austl.	**E2**	60
Western Desert, des., Egypt	**F9**	14
Western Dvina (Zapadnaja Dvina), stm., Eur.	**C4**	22
Western Ghāts, mts., India	**F2**	40
Westernport, Md., U.S.	**m12**	113
Western Sahara, dep., Afr.	**B2**	50
Western Samoa see Samoa, ctry., Oc.	**F12**	58
Western Sayans see Zapadnyj Sajan, mts., Russia	**D11**	26
Western Springs, Il., U.S.	**k9**	106
Westerville, Oh., U.S.	**B3**	128
West European Basin	**D11**	66
West Falkland, i., Falk. Is.	**H4**	69
West Falmouth, Ma., U.S.	**C6**	114
West Fargo, N.D., U.S.	**C9**	127
West Feliciana, co., La., U.S.	**D4**	111
Westfield, N.B., Can.	**D3**	87
Westfield, In., U.S.	**D5**	107
Westfield, Ma., U.S.	**B2**	114
Westfield, N.J., U.S.	**B4**	123
Westfield, N.Y., U.S.	**C1**	125
Westfield, Pa., U.S.	**C6**	131
Westfield, Wi., U.S.	**E4**	142
Westfield, stm., Ma., U.S.	**B2**	114
West Fork, Ar., U.S.	**B1**	97
West Fork, stm., W.V., U.S.	**B4**	141
West Frankfort, Il., U.S.	**F5**	106
West Freehold, N.J., U.S.	**C4**	123
West Friendship, Md., U.S.	**B4**	113
Westgate, Fl., U.S.	**F6**	102
West Grand Lake, l., Me., U.S.	**C5**	112
West Grove, Pa., U.S.	**G10**	131
West Hanover, Ma., U.S.	**h12**	114
West Hartford, Ct., U.S.	**B4**	100
West Haven, Ct., U.S.	**D4**	100
West Hazleton, Pa., U.S.	**E9**	131
West Helena, Ar., U.S.	**C5**	97
West Hill Reservoir, res., Ma., U.S.	**B4**	114
Westhope, N.D., U.S.	**A4**	127
West Ice Shelf, Ant.	**C13**	67
West Indies, is.	**D11**	76
West Island, i., Ma., U.S.	**C6**	114
West Jefferson, N.C., U.S.	**A1**	126
West Jefferson, Oh., U.S.	**C2**	128
West Jordan, Ut., U.S.	**C3**	137
West Kingston, R.I., U.S.	**F3**	132
West Lafayette, In., U.S.	**D4**	107
West Lafayette, Oh., U.S.	**B4**	128
Westlake, La., U.S.	**D2**	111
Westlake, Oh., U.S.	**h9**	128
West Lake, l., Me., U.S.	**C4**	112
Westland, Mi., U.S.	**F7**	115
West Laramie, Wy., U.S.	**E7**	143
West Lawn, Pa., U.S.	**F10**	131
West Lebanon, In., U.S.	**D3**	107
West Liberty, Ia., U.S.	**C6**	108
West Liberty, Ky., U.S.	**C6**	110
West Liberty, Oh., U.S.	**B2**	128
West Liberty, W.V., U.S.	**f8**	141
West Linn, Or., U.S.	**B4**	130
Westlock, Ab., Can.	**B4**	84
West Long Branch, N.J., U.S.	**C4**	123
West Lorne, On., Can.	**E3**	89
West Marion, N.C., U.S.	**f10**	126
West Medway, Ma., U.S.	**B5**	114
West Memphis, Ar., U.S.	**B5**	97
West Miami, Fl., U.S.	**s13**	102
West Middlesex, Pa., U.S.	**D1**	131
West Mifflin, Pa., U.S.	**F2**	131
West Milton, Oh., U.S.	**C1**	128
West Milwaukee, Wi., U.S.	**m12**	142
Westminster, Ca., U.S.	**n12**	98
Westminster, Co., U.S.	**B5**	99
Westminster, Md., U.S.	**A4**	113
Westminster, S.C., U.S.	**B1**	133
West Monroe, La., U.S.	**B3**	111
Westmont, Il., U.S.	**k9**	106
Westmont, N.J., U.S.	**D2**	123
Westmont, Pa., U.S.	**F4**	131
Westmoreland, Tn., U.S.	**A5**	135
Westmoreland, co., Pa., U.S.	**F2**	131
Westmoreland, co., Va., U.S.	**B6**	139
Westmorland, Ca., U.S.	**F6**	98
West Musquash Lake, l., Me., U.S.	**C5**	112
West Mystic, Ct., U.S.	**D8**	100
West Newton, Pa., U.S.	**F2**	131
West New York, N.J., U.S.	**h8**	123
West Nicholson, Zimb.	**C4**	56
West Nishnabotna, stm., Ia., U.S.	**C2**	108
West Norriton, Pa., U.S.	**o20**	131
Weston, Ct., U.S.	**E2**	100
Weston, Ma., U.S.	**g10**	114
Weston, Mo., U.S.	**B3**	118
Weston, Oh., U.S.	**A2**	128
Weston, Or., U.S.	**B8**	130
Weston, W.V., U.S.	**B4**	141
Weston, co., Wy., U.S.	**C8**	143
Weston-super-Mare, Eng., U.K.	**E5**	12
West Orange, N.J., U.S.	**B4**	123
Westover, Md., U.S.	**D6**	113
Westover, W.V., U.S.	**B5**	141
Westover Air Force Base, mil., Ma., U.S.	**B2**	114
West Palm Beach, Fl., U.S.	**F6**	102
West Pawlet, Vt., U.S.	**E2**	138
West Pearl, stm., La., U.S.	**D6**	111
West Pelzer, S.C., U.S.	**B3**	133
West Pensacola, Fl., U.S.	**u14**	102
West Peoria, Il., U.S.	**C4**	106
Westphalia, Mi., U.S.	**F6**	115
West Pittsburg, Pa., U.S.	**E1**	131
West Pittston, Pa., U.S.	**m17**	131
West Plains, Mo., U.S.	**E6**	118
West Point, Ca., U.S.	**C3**	98
West Point, Ga., U.S.	**D1**	103
West Point, Ia., U.S.	**D6**	108
West Point, Ky., U.S.	**C4**	110
West Point, Ms., U.S.	**B5**	117
West Point, Ne., U.S.	**C9**	120
West Point, N.Y., U.S.	**D7**	125
West Point, Va., U.S.	**C6**	139
West Point, mtn., Ak., U.S.	**C11**	95
West Point Lake, res., U.S.	**C1**	103
Westport, On., Can.	**C8**	89
Westport, Ct., U.S.	**E2**	100
Westport, In., U.S.	**F6**	107
Westport, Wa., U.S.	**C1**	140
West Portsmouth, Oh., U.S.	**D2**	128
West Quoddy Head, c., Me., U.S.	**D6**	112
West Reading, Pa., U.S.	**F10**	131
West Rutland, Vt., U.S.	**D2**	138
West Saint Paul, Mn., U.S.	**n12**	116
West Salem, Il., U.S.	**E5**	106
West Salem, Oh., U.S.	**B3**	128
West Salem, Wi., U.S.	**E2**	142
West Scarborough, Me., U.S.	**E2**	112
West Seneca, N.Y., U.S.	**C2**	125
West Siberian Lowland see Zapadno-Sibirskaja ravnina, pl., Russia	**C9**	26
West Simsbury, Ct., U.S.	**B4**	100
West Slope, Or., U.S.	**g12**	130
West Spanish Peak, mtn., Co., U.S.	**D6**	99
West Springfield, Ma., U.S.	**B2**	114
West Springfield, Va., U.S.	**g12**	139
West Swanzey, N.H., U.S.	**E2**	122
West Terre Haute, In., U.S.	**F3**	107
West Thompson Lake, res., Ct., U.S.	**B8**	100
West Union, Ia., U.S.	**B6**	108
West Union, Oh., U.S.	**D2**	128
West Union, W.V., U.S.	**B4**	141
West Unity, Oh., U.S.	**A1**	128
West University Place, Tx., U.S.	**r14**	136
West Valley City, Ut., U.S.	**C4**	137
West Vancouver, B.C., Can.	**f12**	85
West Van Lear, Ky., U.S.	**C7**	110
West View, Pa., U.S.	**h13**	131
Westville, Il., U.S.	**C6**	106
Westville, In., U.S.	**A4**	107
Westville, N.H., U.S.	**E4**	122
Westville, N.J., U.S.	**D2**	123
Westville, Ok., U.S.	**A7**	129
Westville Lake, res., Ma., U.S.	**B3**	114
West Virginia, state, U.S.	**C4**	141
West Walker, stm., U.S.	**E2**	121
West Wareham, Ma., U.S.	**C6**	114
West Warwick, R.I., U.S.	**D3**	132
Westwego, La., U.S.	**k11**	111
Westwood, Ca., U.S.	**B3**	98
Westwood, Ks., U.S.	**k16**	109
Westwood, Ky., U.S.	**B7**	110
Westwood, Ma., U.S.	**B5**	114
Westwood, N.J., U.S.	**B4**	123
Westwood Lakes, Fl., U.S.	**s13**	102
West Wyalong, Austl.	**G4**	62
West Wyoming, Pa., U.S.	**n17**	131
West Yarmouth, Ma., U.S.	**C7**	114
West Yellowstone, Mt., U.S.	**F5**	119
West York, Pa., U.S.	**G8**	131
Wetar, Pulau, i., Indon.	**E7**	36
Wetar, Selat, strt., Indon.	**E7**	36
Wetaskiwin, Ab., Can.	**C4**	84
Wete, Tan.	**D7**	54
Wethersfield, Ct., U.S.	**C5**	100
Wet Mountains, mts., Co., U.S.	**C5**	99
Wetumka, Ok., U.S.	**B5**	129
Wetumpka, Al., U.S.	**C3**	94
Wetzel, co., W.V., U.S.	**B4**	141
Wetzlar, Ger.	**E11**	12
Wewahitchka, Fl., U.S.	**B1**	102
Wewak, Pap. N. Gui.	**G11**	32
Wewoka, Ok., U.S.	**B5**	129
Wexford, Ire.	**D3**	12
Wexford, co., Mi., U.S.	**D5**	115
Weyauwega, Wi., U.S.	**D5**	142
Weymouth, Eng., U.K.	**E5**	12
Weymouth, Ma., U.S.	**B6**	114
Whakatane, N.Z.	**o14**	63c
Whaleysville, Md., U.S.	**D7**	113
Whangarei, N.Z.	**o13**	63c
Wharton, N.J., U.S.	**B3**	123
Wharton, Tx., U.S.	**E4**	136
Wharton, co., Tx., U.S.	**E4**	136
Wharton Basin	**J13**	64
What Cheer, Ia., U.S.	**C5**	108
Whatcom, co., Wa., U.S.	**A4**	140
Whatcom, Lake, l., Wa., U.S.	**A3**	140
Wheatfield, In., U.S.	**B3**	107
Wheatland, Ca., U.S.	**C3**	98
Wheatland, Ia., U.S.	**C7**	108
Wheatland, Wy., U.S.	**D8**	143
Wheatland, co., Mt., U.S.	**D7**	119
Wheatland Reservoir, res., Wy., U.S.	**E7**	143
Wheatley, On., Can.	**E2**	89
Wheaton, Il., U.S.	**B5**	106
Wheaton, Md., U.S.	**B3**	113
Wheaton, Mn., U.S.	**E2**	116
Wheaton, Mo., U.S.	**E3**	118
Wheat Ridge, Co., U.S.	**B5**	99
Wheelbarrow Peak, mtn., Nv., U.S.	**F5**	121
Wheeler, Ms., U.S.	**A5**	117
Wheeler, Tx., U.S.	**B2**	136
Wheeler, co., Ga., U.S.	**D4**	103
Wheeler, co., Ne., U.S.	**C7**	120
Wheeler, co., Or., U.S.	**C6**	130
Wheeler, co., Tx., U.S.	**B2**	136
Wheeler Air Force Base, mil., Hi., U.S.	**g9**	104
Wheeler Lake, res., Al., U.S.	**A2**	94
Wheeler Peak, mtn., Ca., U.S.	**C4**	98
Wheeler Peak, mtn., N.M., U.S.	**A4**	124
Wheeler Peak, mtn., Nv., U.S.	**E7**	121
Wheelersburg, Oh., U.S.	**D3**	128
Wheeling, Il., U.S.	**h9**	106
Wheeling, W.V., U.S.	**A4**	141
Wheeling Creek, stm., W.V., U.S.	**f8**	141

Name Map Ref. Page

Wheelwright, Ky., U.S. **C7** 110
Whetstone, stm., U.S. **E2** 116
Whidbey Island, i., Wa., U.S. **A3** 140
Whidbey Island Naval Air Station, mil., Wa., U.S. **A3** 140
Whigham, Ga., U.S. **F2** 103
Whiskey Peak, mtn., Wy., U.S. **D5** 143
Whiskeytown-Shasta-Trinity National Recreation Area, Ca., U.S. **B2** 98
Whistler, B.C., Can. **D6** 85
Whitacres, Ct., U.S. **A5** 100
Whitakers, N.C., U.S. **A5** 126
Whitbourne, Nf., Can. **E5** 88
Whitby, On., Can. **D6** 89
Whitchurch-Stouffville, On., Can. **D5** 89
White, co., Ar., U.S. **B4** 97
White, co., Ga., U.S. **B3** 103
White, co., Il., U.S. **E5** 106
White, co., In., U.S. **C4** 107
White, co., Tn., U.S. **D8** 135
White, stm., Az., U.S. **D5** 96
White, stm., In., U.S. **H2** 107
White, stm., Mi., U.S. **E4** 115
White, stm., Nv., U.S. **E6** 121
White, stm., Tx., U.S. **C2** 136
White, stm., Vt., U.S. **D4** 138
White, stm., Wa., U.S. **B5** 140
White, stm., Wa., U.S. **B4** 140
White, stm., U.S. **C4** 97
White, stm., U.S. **D5** 134
White, stm., U.S. **C7** 137
White Bay, b., Nf., Can. **D3** 88
White Bear, stm., Nf., Can. **E3** 88
White Bear Lake, Mn., U.S. **E5** 116
White Bluff, Tn., U.S. **A4** 135
White Butte, mtn., N.D., U.S. **C2** 127
White Castle, La., U.S. **D4** 111
White Center, Wa., U.S. **e11** 140
White City, Or., U.S. **E4** 130
White Clay Creek, stm., U.S. **A3** 120
White Cliffs, Austl. **F3** 60
White Cliffs, Austl. **G3** 62
White Cloud, Mi., U.S. **E5** 115
Whitecourt, Ab., Can. **B3** 84
White Creek, stm., U.S. **E2** 138
Whiteday, stm., W.V., U.S. **h10** 141
White Deer, Tx., U.S. **B2** 136
White Earth Indian Reservation, Mn., U.S. **C3** 116
White Earth Lake, l., Mn., U.S. **C3** 116
Whiteface, stm., Mn., U.S. **C6** 116
Whiteface Mountain, mtn., N.Y., U.S. **f11** 125
Whitefield, N.H., U.S. **B3** 122
Whitefish, Mt., U.S. **B2** 119
Whitefish Bay, Wi., U.S. **m12** 142
Whitefish Bay, b., Mi., U.S. **B6** 115
Whitefish Lake, l., Mn., U.S. **D4** 116
Whitefish Range, mts., Mt., U.S. **B2** 119
Whiteford, Md., U.S. **A5** 113
White Hall, Al., U.S. **C3** 94
White Hall, Ar., U.S. **C3** 97
White Hall, Il., U.S. **D3** 106
Whitehall, Mi., U.S. **E4** 115
Whitehall, Mt., U.S. **E4** 119
Whitehall, N.Y., U.S. **B7** 125
Whitehall, Oh., U.S. **m11** 128
Whitehall, Wi., U.S. **D2** 142
Whitehall Reservoir, res., Ma., U.S. **h9** 114
Whitehaven, Eng., U.K. **C5** 12
White Haven, Pa., U.S. **D10** 131
Whitehorn, Point, c., Wa., U.S. **A3** 140
Whitehorse, Yk., Can. **F13** 82
White Horse, N.J., U.S. **C3** 123
Whitehouse, Oh., U.S. **A2** 128
White House, Tn., U.S. **A5** 135
White Island Shores, Ma., U.S. **C6** 114
White Knob Mountains, mts., Id., U.S. **F5** 105
White Lake, l., La., U.S. **E3** 111
Whiteman Air Force Base, mil., Mo., U.S. **C4** 118
White Mesa Natural Bridge, Az., U.S. **A4** 96
White Mountain Peak, mtn., Ca., U.S. **D4** 98
White Mountains, mts., N.H., U.S. **B3** 122
White Mountains, mts., U.S. **D4** 98
Whitemouth, stm., Mb., Can. **E4** 86
Whitemouth Lake, l., Mb., Can. **E4** 86
White Nile see Abyad, Al-Bahr al-, stm., Sudan **H11** 48
White Oak, Oh., U.S. **o12** 128
White Oak Creek, stm., Oh., U.S. **D2** 128
Whiteoak Creek, stm., Tn., U.S. **A4** 135
White Oak Lake, res., Ar., U.S. **D2** 97
White Pigeon, Mi., U.S. **G5** 115
White Pine, Mi., U.S. **m12** 115
White Pine, Tn., U.S. **C10** 135
White Pine, co., Nv., U.S. **D6** 121
White Plains, Md., U.S. **C4** 113
White Plains, N.Y., U.S. **D7** 125
Whiteriver, Az., U.S. **D6** 96
White River Junction, Vt., U.S. **D4** 138
White Rock, B.C., Can. **E6** 85
White Russia see Belarus, ctry., Eur. **C9** 20
White Salmon, Wa., U.S. **D4** 140
White Salmon, stm., Wa., U.S. **D4** 140
White Sands Missile Range, mil., N.M., U.S. **E3** 124
White Sands National Monument, N.M., U.S. **E3** 124
Whitesboro, N.Y., U.S. **B5** 125
Whitesboro, Tx., U.S. **C4** 136
Whitesburg, Ga., U.S. **C2** 103
Whitesburg, Ky., U.S. **C7** 110
Whites Creek, stm., Tn., U.S. **g10** 135
White Sea see Beloe more, Russia **C5** 26
Whiteside, co., Il., U.S. **B3** 106
White Sulphur Springs, Mt., U.S. **D6** 119
White Sulphur Springs, W.V., U.S. **D4** 141
Whitesville, Ky., U.S. **C3** 110
White Swan, Wa., U.S. **C5** 140
White Tank Mountains, mts., Az., U.S. **k7** 96
Whiteville, N.C., U.S. **C4** 126
Whiteville, Tn., U.S. **B2** 135
White Volta, stm., Afr. **E4** 50
Whitewater, Ks., U.S. **E6** 109
Whitewater, Wi., U.S. **F5** 142
Whitewater, stm., Ks., U.S. **E6** 109
Whitewater, stm., U.S. **F7** 107
Whitewater Baldy, mtn., N.M., U.S. **D1** 124
Whitewater Bay, b., Fl., U.S. **G6** 102
Whitewood, S.D., U.S. **C2** 134
Whitewright, Tx., U.S. **C4** 136
Whitfield, co., Ga., U.S. **B2** 103
Whitfield Estates, Fl., U.S. **q10** 102
Whiting, Ia., U.S. **B1** 108
Whiting, In., U.S. **A3** 107
Whiting, Wi., U.S. **D4** 142
Whiting Field Naval Air Station, mil., Fl., U.S. **u14** 102
Whitinsville, Ma., U.S. **B4** 114
Whitley, co., In., U.S. **B6** 107
Whitley, co., Ky., U.S. **D5** 110
Whitley City, Ky., U.S. **D5** 110
Whitman, Ma., U.S. **B6** 114
Whitman, W.V., U.S. **D2** 141
Whitman, co., Wa., U.S. **B8** 140
Whitman Square, N.J., U.S. **D2** 123
Whitmire, S.C., U.S. **B4** 133
Whitmore Lake, Mi., U.S. **p14** 115
Whitmore Mountains, mts., Ant. **E31** 67
Whitmore Village, Hi., U.S. **f9** 104
Whitney, S.C., U.S. **B4** 133
Whitney, Tx., U.S. **D4** 136
Whitney, Lake, res., Tx., U.S. **D4** 136
Whitney, Mount, mtn., Ca., U.S. **D4** 98
Whitney Point Lake, res., N.Y., U.S. **C5** 125
Whitsunday Island, i., Austl. **E4** 62
Whittier, Ak., U.S. **C10** 95
Whittier, Ca., U.S. **F4** 98
Whitwell, Tn., U.S. **D8** 135
Whyalla, Austl. **G2** 62
Wiarton, On., Can. **C3** 89
Wibaux, Mt., U.S. **D12** 119
Wibaux, co., Mt., U.S. **D12** 119
Wichita, Ks., U.S. **E6** 109
Wichita, co., Ks., U.S. **D2** 109
Wichita, co., Tx., U.S. **B3** 136
Wichita Falls, Tx., U.S. **C3** 136
Wichita Mountains, mts., Ok., U.S. **C3** 129
Wick, Scot., U.K. **A5** 12
Wickenburg, Az., U.S. **D3** 96
Wickham, Austl. **E2** 60
Wickham, Cape, c., Austl. **H3** 62
Wickiup Reservoir, res., Or., U.S. **E5** 130
Wickliffe, Ky., U.S. **f8** 110
Wickliffe, Oh., U.S. **A4** 128
Wicklow, Ire. **D3** 12
Wicomico, co., Md., U.S. **D6** 113
Wicomico, stm., Md., U.S. **D6** 113
Wiconisco, Pa., U.S. **E8** 131
Widefield, Co., U.S. **C6** 99
Widgiemooltha, Austl. **G3** 60
Wieluń, Pol. **D5** 20
Wien, Aus. **F15** 12
Wiener Neustadt, Aus. **G15** 12
Wieprz, stm., Pol. **D7** 20
Wiesbaden, Ger. **E11** 12
Wiggins, Ms., U.S. **E4** 117
Wiggins Peak, mtn., Wy., U.S. **C3** 143
Wight, Isle of, i., Eng., U.K. **E6** 12
Wikwemikong, On., Can. **B3** 89
Wilbarger, co., Tx., U.S. **B3** 136
Wilber, Ne., U.S. **D9** 120
Wilberforce, Oh., U.S. **C2** 128
Wilbraham, Ma., U.S. **B3** 114
Wilbur, Wa., U.S. **B7** 140
Wilburton, Ok., U.S. **C6** 129
Wilcannia, Austl. **G3** 62
Wilcox, Pa., U.S. **C4** 131
Wilcox, co., Al., U.S. **D2** 94
Wilcox, co., Ga., U.S. **E3** 103
Wild, stm., U.S. **B4** 122
Wild Ammonoosuc, stm., N.H., U.S. **B3** 122
Wild Branch, stm., Vt., U.S. **B4** 138
Wilder, Id., U.S. **F2** 105
Wilder, Vt., U.S. **D4** 138
Wilder Dam, U.S. **C2** 122
Wildhorse Creek, stm., Ok., U.S. **C4** 129
Wild Horse Reservoir, res., Nv., U.S. **B6** 121
Wildorado, Tx., U.S. **B1** 136
Wild Rice, stm., Mn., U.S. **C2** 116
Wild Rice, stm., N.D., U.S. **C8** 127
Wildwood, Fl., U.S. **D4** 102
Wildwood, N.J., U.S. **F3** 123
Wildwood Crest, N.J., U.S. **F3** 123
Wilhelm, Mount, mtn., Pap. N. Gui. **H12** 32
Wilhelmina Peak see Trikora, Puncak, mtn., Indon. **G10** 32
Wilhelmshaven, Ger. **D10** 12
Wilkes, co., Ga., U.S. **C4** 103
Wilkes, co., N.C., U.S. **A1** 126
Wilkes-Barre, Pa., U.S. **D10** 131
Wilkesboro, N.C., U.S. **A1** 126
Wilkes Land, reg., Ant. **D16** 67
Wilkin, co., Mn., U.S. **D2** 116
Wilkinsburg, Pa., U.S. **F2** 131
Wilkinson, W.V., U.S. **D3** 141
Wilkinson, co., Ga., U.S. **D3** 103
Wilkinson, co., Ms., U.S. **D2** 117
Will, co., Il., U.S. **B6** 106
Willacoochee, Ga., U.S. **E3** 103
Willacy, co., Tx., U.S. **F4** 136
Willamette, stm., Or., U.S. **C3** 130
Willamette Pass, Or., U.S. **D4** 130
Willamina, Or., U.S. **B3** 130
Willapa Bay, b., Wa., U.S. **C1** 140
Willard, Mo., U.S. **D4** 118
Willard, Oh., U.S. **A3** 128
Willard, Ut., U.S. **B3** 137
Willard Bay, b., Ut., U.S. **B3** 137
Willards, Md., U.S. **D7** 113
Willard Stream, stm., Vt., U.S. **B5** 138
Willcox, Az., U.S. **E6** 96
Willcox Playa, l., Az., U.S. **E5** 96
Willemstad, Neth. Ant. **C6** 80
William Bill Dannelly Reservoir, res., Al., U.S. **C2** 94
Williams, Az., U.S. **B3** 96
Williams, Ca., U.S. **C2** 98
Williams, co., N.D., U.S. **A2** 127
Williams, co., Oh., U.S. **A1** 128
Williams, stm., Vt., U.S. **E3** 138
Williams, stm., W.V., U.S. **C4** 141
Williams Bay, Wi., U.S. **F5** 142
Williamsburg, Ia., U.S. **C5** 108
Williamsburg, In., U.S. **E8** 107
Williamsburg, Ky., U.S. **D5** 110
Williamsburg, Oh., U.S. **C1** 128
Williamsburg, Pa., U.S. **F5** 131
Williamsburg, Va., U.S. **C6** 139
Williamsburg, co., S.C., U.S. **D8** 133
Williams Fork, stm., Co., U.S. **A3** 99
Williams Lake, B.C., Can. **C6** 85
Williamson, N.Y., U.S. **B3** 125
Williamson, W.V., U.S. **D2** 141
Williamson, co., Il., U.S. **F4** 106
Williamson, co., Tn., U.S. **B5** 135
Williamson, co., Tx., U.S. **D4** 136
Williamsport, In., U.S. **D3** 107
Williamsport, Md., U.S. **A2** 113
Williamsport, Pa., U.S. **D7** 131
Williamston, Mi., U.S. **F6** 115
Williamston, N.C., U.S. **B5** 126
Williamston, S.C., U.S. **B3** 133
Williamstown, Ky., U.S. **B5** 110
Williamstown, Ma., U.S. **A1** 114
Williamstown, N.J., U.S. **D3** 123
Williamstown, Pa., U.S. **E8** 131
Williamstown, Vt., U.S. **C3** 138
Williamstown, W.V., U.S. **B3** 141
Williamsville, Il., U.S. **D4** 106
Williamsville, N.Y., U.S. **C2** 125
Willimantic, Ct., U.S. **C7** 100
Willimantic, stm., Ct., U.S. **B6** 100
Willimantic Reservoir, res., Ct., U.S. **C7** 100
Willingboro, N.J., U.S. **C3** 123
Willis, Tx., U.S. **D5** 136
Willis Group, is., Austl. **D5** 62
Williston, S. Afr. **E3** 56
Williston, Fl., U.S. **C4** 102
Williston, N.D., U.S. **A2** 127
Williston, S.C., U.S. **E5** 133
Williston Lake, res., B.C., Can. **B6** 85
Willits, Ca., U.S. **C2** 98
Willmar, Mn., U.S. **E3** 116
Willoughby, Oh., U.S. **A4** 128
Willoughby, Lake, l., Vt., U.S. **B4** 138
Willoughby Hills, Oh., U.S. **A4** 128
Willow, Ak., U.S. **g17** 95
Willow Creek, stm., Nv., U.S. **E5** 121
Willow Creek, stm., Ut., U.S. **D6** 137
Willow Creek, stm., Wy., U.S. **C6** 143
Willow Grove Naval Air Station, mil., Pa., U.S. **F11** 131
Willowick, Oh., U.S. **A4** 128
Willowmore, S. Afr. **E3** 56
Willow Reservoir, res., Wi., U.S. **C3** 142
Willow Run, De., U.S. **i7** 101
Willow Run, Mi., U.S. **p14** 115
Willows, Ca., U.S. **C2** 98
Willow Springs, Il., U.S. **k9** 106
Willow Springs, Mo., U.S. **E6** 118
Wilmar, Ar., U.S. **D4** 97
Wilmerding, Pa., U.S. **k14** 131
Wilmette, Il., U.S. **A6** 106
Wilmington, De., U.S. **B3** 101
Wilmington, Il., U.S. **B5** 106
Wilmington, Ma., U.S. **A5** 114
Wilmington, N.C., U.S. **C5** 126
Wilmington, Oh., U.S. **C2** 128
Wilmington, Vt., U.S. **F3** 138
Wilmington Manor, De., U.S. **i7** 101
Wilmore, Ky., U.S. **C5** 110
Wilmot, Ar., U.S. **D4** 97
Wilson, Ar., U.S. **B5** 97
Wilson, Ks., U.S. **D5** 109
Wilson, La., U.S. **D4** 111
Wilson, N.C., U.S. **B5** 126
Wilson, Ok., U.S. **C4** 129
Wilson, Pa., U.S. **E11** 131
Wilson, Wy., U.S. **C2** 143
Wilson, co., Ks., U.S. **E8** 109
Wilson, co., N.C., U.S. **B5** 126
Wilson, co., Tn., U.S. **A5** 135
Wilson, co., Tx., U.S. **E3** 136
Wilson, Mount, mtn., Az., U.S. **B1** 96
Wilson, Mount, mtn., Ca., U.S. **m12** 98
Wilson, Mount, mtn., Co., U.S. **D2** 99
Wilson, Mount, mtn., Nv., U.S. **E7** 121
Wilson, Mount, mtn., Or., U.S. **B5** 130
Wilson Creek, stm., Wa., U.S. **B5** 140
Wilson Creek, stm., Wa., U.S. **B6** 140
Wilson Lake, res., Al., U.S. **A2** 94
Wilson Lake, res., Ks., U.S. **D4** 109
Wilsons Beach, N.B., Can. **E3** 87
Wilsons Promontory, pen., Austl. **H4** 62
Wilsonville, Al., U.S. **B3** 94
Wilsonville, Or., U.S. **h12** 130
Wilton, Al., U.S. **B3** 94
Wilton, Ct., U.S. **E2** 100
Wilton, Ia., U.S. **C6** 108
Wilton, Me., U.S. **D2** 112
Wilton, N.D., U.S. **B5** 127
Wilton, N.H., U.S. **E3** 122
Wiluna, Austl. **F3** 60
Wimauma, Fl., U.S. **E4** 102
Wimico, Lake, l., Fl., U.S. **C1** 102
Winamac, In., U.S. **B4** 107
Winburg, S. Afr. **D4** 56
Wincheck Pond, l., R.I., U.S. **E1** 132
Winchendon, Ma., U.S. **A3** 114
Winchester, On., Can. **B9** 89
Winchester, Eng., U.K. **E6** 12
Winchester, Il., U.S. **D3** 106
Winchester, In., U.S. **D8** 107
Winchester, Ks., U.S. **k15** 109
Winchester, Ky., U.S. **C5** 110
Winchester, Ma., U.S. **g11** 114
Winchester, N.H., U.S. **E2** 122
Winchester, Nv., U.S. **G6** 121
Winchester, Oh., U.S. **D2** 128
Winchester, Tn., U.S. **B5** 135
Winchester, Va., U.S. **A4** 139
Winchester Bay, Or., U.S. **D2** 130
Wind, stm., Wa., U.S. **D4** 140
Wind, stm., Wy., U.S. **C4** 143
Windber, Pa., U.S. **F4** 131
Wind Cave National Park, S.D., U.S. **D2** 134
Winder, Ga., U.S. **C3** 103
Windfall, In., U.S. **D6** 107
Windgap, Pa., U.S. **E11** 131
Windham, Ct., U.S. **C7** 100
Windham, Oh., U.S. **A4** 128
Windham, co., Ct., U.S. **B7** 100
Windham, co., Vt., U.S. **F3** 138
Windhoek, Nmb. **C2** 56
Wind Lake, Wi., U.S. **F5** 142
Wind Lake, l., Wi., U.S. **n11** 142
Windmill Point, c., Va., U.S. **C6** 139
Windom, Mn., U.S. **G3** 116
Windom Peak, mtn., Co., U.S. **D3** 99
Window Rock, Az., U.S. **B6** 96
Wind Point, Wi., U.S. **n12** 142
Wind River Indian Reservation, Wy., U.S. **C4** 143
Wind River Peak, mtn., Wy., U.S. **D3** 143
Wind River Range, mts., Wy., U.S. **C3** 143
Windsor (part of Grand Falls-Windsor), Nf., Can. **D4** 88
Windsor, On., Can. **E1** 89
Windsor, P.Q., Can. **D5** 90
Windsor, Co., U.S. **A6** 99
Windsor, Ct., U.S. **B5** 100
Windsor, Il., U.S. **D5** 106
Windsor, Mo., U.S. **C4** 118
Windsor, N.C., U.S. **A6** 126
Windsor, Pa., U.S. **G8** 131
Windsor, Va., U.S. **D6** 139
Windsor, Vt., U.S. **E4** 138
Windsor, co., Vt., U.S. **D3** 138
Windsor Heights, Ia., U.S. **e8** 108
Windsor Locks, Ct., U.S. **B5** 100
Windward Islands, is., N.A. **F12** 76
Windward Passage, strt., N.A. **E10** 76
Windy Hill, S.C., U.S. **C8** 133
Windy Peak, mtn., Wa., U.S. **A6** 140
Winefred Lake, l., Ab., Can. **B5** 84
Winfield, Al., U.S. **B2** 94
Winfield, Ia., U.S. **C6** 108
Winfield, Ks., U.S. **E7** 109
Winfield, Mo., U.S. **C7** 118
Winfield, W.V., U.S. **C3** 141
Wing, stm., Mn., U.S. **D3** 116
Wingate, N.C., U.S. **C2** 126
Wingham, On., Can. **D3** 89
Winifrede, W.V., U.S. **m12** 141
Winisk, stm., On., Can. **n18** 89
Wink, Tx., U.S. **D1** 136
Winkelman, Az., U.S. **E5** 96
Winkler, Mb., Can. **E3** 86
Winkler, co., Tx., U.S. **D1** 136
Winlock, Wa., U.S. **C3** 140
Winn, co., La., U.S. **C3** 111
Winneba, Ghana **E4** 50
Winnebago, Il., U.S. **A4** 106
Winnebago, Mn., U.S. **G4** 116
Winnebago, Ne., U.S. **B9** 120
Winnebago, Wi., U.S. **h8** 142
Winnebago, co., Ia., U.S. **A4** 108
Winnebago, co., Il., U.S. **A4** 106
Winnebago, co., Wi., U.S. **D5** 142
Winnebago, stm., Ia., U.S. **A4** 108
Winnebago, Lake, l., Wi., U.S. **E5** 142
Winnebago Indian Reservation, Ne., U.S. **B9** 120
Winneconne, Wi., U.S. **D5** 142
Winnemucca, Nv., U.S. **C4** 121
Winnemucca Lake, l., Nv., U.S. **C2** 121
Winner, S.D., U.S. **D6** 134
Winneshiek, co., Ia., U.S. **A6** 108
Winnetka, Il., U.S. **A6** 106
Winnfield, La., U.S. **C3** 111
Winnibigoshish, Lake, l., Mn., U.S. **C4** 116
Winnipeg, Mb., Can. **E3** 86
Winnipeg, stm., Can. **D4** 86
Winnipeg, Lake, l., Mb., Can. **C3** 86
Winnipeg Beach, Mb., Can. **D3** 86
Winnipegosis, Mb., Can. **D2** 86
Winnipegosis, Lake, l., Mb., Can. **C2** 86
Winnipesaukee, Lake, l., N.H., U.S. **C4** 122
Winnisquam, N.H., U.S. **C3** 122
Winnisquam Lake, l., N.H., U.S. **C3** 122
Winnsboro, La., U.S. **B4** 111
Winnsboro, S.C., U.S. **C5** 133
Winnsboro, Tx., U.S. **C5** 136
Winnsboro Mills, S.C., U.S. **C5** 133
Winona, Mn., U.S. **F7** 116
Winona, Mo., U.S. **D6** 118
Winona, Ms., U.S. **B4** 117
Winona, co., Mn., U.S. **F7** 116
Winona Lake, In., U.S. **B6** 107
Winona Lake, l., Vt., U.S. **C2** 138
Winooski, Vt., U.S. **C2** 138
Winooski, stm., Vt., U.S. **C3** 138
Winslow, Az., U.S. **C5** 96
Winslow, In., U.S. **H3** 107
Winslow, Me., U.S. **D3** 112
Winsted, Ct., U.S. **B3** 100
Winsted, Mn., U.S. **F4** 116
Winston, Fl., U.S. **D4** 102
Winston, Or., U.S. **D3** 130
Winston, co., Al., U.S. **A2** 94
Winston, co., Ms., U.S. **B4** 117
Winston-Salem, N.C., U.S. **A2** 126
Winter Garden, Fl., U.S. **D5** 102
Winter Harbor, Me., U.S. **D4** 112
Winter Haven, Fl., U.S. **D5** 102
Winter Park, Fl., U.S. **D5** 102
Winter Park, N.C., U.S. **C5** 126
Winterport, Me., U.S. **D4** 112
Winter Ridge, mtn., Or., U.S. **E6** 130
Winters, Ca., U.S. **C2** 98
Winters, Tx., U.S. **D3** 136
Winterset, Ia., U.S. **C4** 108
Wintersville, Oh., U.S. **B5** 128
Winterthur, Switz. **G11** 12
Winterton, Nf., Can. **E5** 88
Winterville, Ga., U.S. **C3** 103
Winterville, N.C., U.S. **B5** 126

Name	Map Ref.	Page
Winthrop, Ia., U.S.	B6	108
Winthrop, Ma., U.S.	B6	114
Winthrop, Me., U.S.	D3	112
Winthrop, Mn., U.S.	F4	116
Winthrop, Lake, l., Ma., U.S.	h10	114
Winthrop Harbor, Il., U.S.	A6	106
Wintinna, Austl.	F5	60
Winton, Austl.	E3	62
Winton, N.Z.	q12	63c
Winton, N.C., U.S.	A6	126
Winton Lake, res., Oh., U.S.	o12	129
Winyah Bay, b., S.C., U.S.	E9	133
Wirt, co., W.V., U.S.	B3	141
Wiscasset, Me., U.S.	D3	112
Wisconsin, state, U.S.	D4	142
Wisconsin, stm., Wi., U.S.	E3	142
Wisconsin, Lake, res., Wi., U.S.	E4	142
Wisconsin Dells, Wi., U.S.	E4	142
Wisconsin Rapids, Wi., U.S.	D4	142
Wise, Va., U.S.	f9	139
Wise, co., Tx., U.S.	C4	136
Wise, co., Va., U.S.	e9	139
Wishek, N.D., U.S.	C6	127
Wishram, Wa., U.S.	D4	140
Wisła, stm., Pol.	C5	20
Wismar, Ger.	D12	12
Wisner, La., U.S.	C4	111
Wisner, Ne., U.S.	C9	120
Wissota, Lake, res., Wi., U.S.	D2	142
Wister, Ok., U.S.	C7	129
Wister Lake, res., Ok., U.S.	C7	129
Witbank, S. Afr.	D4	56
Withamsville, Oh., U.S.	C1	128
Witherspoon, Mount, mtn., Ak., U.S.	g18	95
Withlacoochee, stm., Fl., U.S.	C4	102
Withlacoochee, stm., U.S.	B3	102
Witless Bay, Nf., Can.	E5	88
Witt, Il., U.S.	D4	106
Wittenberg, Wi., U.S.	D4	142
Wittenberge, Ger.	D12	12
Wittenoom, Austl.	E2	60
Wittlich, Ger.	E10	12
Wittman, Md., U.S.	C5	113
Wittmann, Az., U.S.	D3	96
Witu Islands, is., Pap. N. Gui.	G12	32
Wixom, Mi., U.S.	o14	115
Wixom Lake, res., Mi., U.S.	E6	115
Włocławek, Pol.	C5	20
Woburn, Ma., U.S.	B5	114
Wodonga, Austl.	H4	62
Wokam, Pulau, i., Indon.	H9	32
Wolcott, Ct., U.S.	C4	100
Wolcott, In., U.S.	C3	107
Wolcottville, In., U.S.	A7	107
Woleai, atoll, Micron.	D8	58
Wolf, stm., Ms., U.S.	E4	117
Wolf, stm., Tn., U.S.	e9	135
Wolf, stm., Wi., U.S.	C5	142
Wolf, Volcán, vol., Ec.	C1	70
Wolf Creek, Or., U.S.	E3	130
Wolf Creek, stm., W.V., U.S.	m13	141
Wolf Creek, stm., U.S.	A2	129
Wolf Creek Pass, Co., U.S.	D3	99
Wolfe, co., Ky., U.S.	C6	110
Wolfeboro, N.H., U.S.	C4	122
Wolfeboro Falls, N.H., U.S.	C4	122
Wolfe City, Tx., U.S.	C4	136
Wolfen, Ger.	E13	12
Wolf Lake, Mi., U.S.	E4	115
Wolf Lake, l., Il., U.S.	k9	106
Wolf Mountain, mtn., Ak., U.S.	B9	95
Wolf Point, Mt., U.S.	B11	119
Wolfsberg, Aus.	G14	12
Wolfsburg, Ger.	D12	12
Wolf Swamp, sw., N.C., U.S.	C5	126
Wollaston, Islas, is., Chile	I3	69
Wollaston Lake, l., Sk., Can.	m8	91
Wollongong, Austl.	G5	62
Wolmaransstad, S. Afr.	D4	56
Wolverhampton, Eng., U.K.	D5	12
Woman Lake, l., Mn., U.S.	D4	116
Womelsdorf, Pa., U.S.	F9	131
Wonder Lake, Il., U.S.	A5	106
Wondinong, Austl.	F2	60
Wonewoc, Wi., U.S.	E3	142
Wŏnsan, N. Kor.	D13	28
Wonthaggi, Austl.	H4	62
Wood, co., Oh., U.S.	A2	128
Wood, co., Tx., U.S.	C5	136
Wood, co., W.V., U.S.	B3	141
Wood, co., Wi., U.S.	D3	142
Wood, stm., Sk., Can.	H2	91
Wood, stm., R.I., U.S.	F2	132
Wood, stm., Wy., U.S.	C3	143
Wood, Mount, mtn., Mt., U.S.	E7	119
Woodall Mountain, mtn., Ms., U.S.	A5	117
Woodbine, Ga., U.S.	F5	103
Woodbine, Ia., U.S.	C2	108
Woodbine, Ky., U.S.	D5	110
Woodbine, N.J., U.S.	E3	123
Woodbridge, Ct., U.S.	D3	100
Woodbridge, Va., U.S.	B5	139
Woodbridge [Township], N.J., U.S.	B4	123
Woodburn, In., U.S.	B8	107
Woodburn, Or., U.S.	B4	130
Woodbury, Ct., U.S.	C3	100
Woodbury, Ga., U.S.	D2	103
Woodbury, Mn., U.S.	F6	116
Woodbury, N.J., U.S.	D2	123
Woodbury, Tn., U.S.	B5	135
Woodbury, co., Ia., U.S.	B1	108
Woodcliff Lake, N.J., U.S.	g8	123
Woodcliff Lake, l., N.J., U.S.	g8	123
Wood Dale, Il., U.S.	k9	106
Wood End, spit, Ma., U.S.	B7	114
Woodfield, S.C., U.S.	C6	133
Woodford, co., Il., U.S.	C4	106
Woodford, co., Ky., U.S.	B5	110
Woodhull, Il., U.S.	B3	106
Woodlake, Ca., U.S.	D4	98
Woodland, Ca., U.S.	C3	98
Woodland, Me., U.S.	C5	112
Woodland, N.C., U.S.	A5	126
Woodland, Wa., U.S.	D3	140
Woodland Acres, Co., U.S.	D6	99
Woodland Park, Co., U.S.	C5	99
Woodlawn, Ky., U.S.	e9	110
Woodlawn, Md., U.S.	g10	113
Woodlawn, Oh., U.S.	n13	128
Woodlawn, Va., U.S.	D2	139
Woodmont, Ct., U.S.	E4	100
Woodmoor, Md., U.S.	B4	113
Woodridge, Il., U.S.	k8	106
Wood-Ridge, N.J., U.S.	h8	123
Wood River, Il., U.S.	E3	106
Wood River, Ne., U.S.	D7	120
Woodroffe, Mount, mtn., Austl.	F5	60
Woodruff, S.C., U.S.	B3	133
Woodruff, Wi., U.S.	C4	142
Woodruff, co., Ar., U.S.	B4	97
Woods, co., Ok., U.S.	A3	129
Woods, Lake, res., Tn., U.S.	B5	135
Woods, Lake of the, l., N.A.	B9	92
Woodsboro, Tx., U.S.	E4	136
Woods Cross, Ut., U.S.	C4	137
Woodsfield, Oh., U.S.	C4	128
Woods Hole, Ma., U.S.	C6	114
Woodson, Ar., U.S.	C3	97
Woodson, co., Ks., U.S.	E8	109
Woodstock, N.B., Can.	C2	87
Woodstock, On., Can.	D4	89
Woodstock, Ga., U.S.	B2	103
Woodstock, Il., U.S.	A5	106
Woodstock, Md., U.S.	B4	113
Woodstock, N.Y., U.S.	C6	125
Woodstock, Va., U.S.	B4	139
Woodstock, Vt., U.S.	D3	138
Woodstown, N.J., U.S.	D2	123
Woodsville, N.H., U.S.	B2	122
Woodville, Fl., U.S.	B2	102
Woodville, Ms., U.S.	D2	117
Woodville, Oh., U.S.	A2	128
Woodville, Tx., U.S.	D5	136
Woodville, Wi., U.S.	D1	142
Woodward, Ia., U.S.	C4	108
Woodward, Ok., U.S.	A2	129
Woodward, co., Ok., U.S.	A2	129
Woodworth, La., U.S.	C3	111
Woolmarket, Ms., U.S.	E5	117
Woolrich, Pa., U.S.	D7	131
Woolsey Peak, mtn., Az., U.S.	D3	96
Woomera, Austl.	G2	62
Woonsocket, R.I., U.S.	A3	132
Woonsocket, S.D., U.S.	C7	134
Woonsocket Reservoir Number Three, res., R.I., U.S.	B3	132
Wooster, Oh., U.S.	B4	128
Worcester, S. Afr.	E2	56
Worcester, Eng., U.K.	D5	12
Worcester, Ma., U.S.	B4	114
Worcester, co., Ma., U.S.	A3	114
Worcester, co., Md., U.S.	D7	113
Worden, Il., U.S.	E4	106
Worden Pond, l., R.I., U.S.	F3	132
Worland, Wy., U.S.	B5	143
Worms, Ger.	F11	12
Worth, Il., U.S.	k9	106
Worth, co., Ga., U.S.	E3	103
Worth, co., Ia., U.S.	A4	108
Worth, co., Mo., U.S.	A3	118
Worthing, Eng., U.K.	E6	12
Worthington, In., U.S.	F4	107
Worthington, Ky., U.S.	B7	110
Worthington, Mn., U.S.	G3	116
Worthington, Oh., U.S.	B2	128
Worthington Peak, mtn., Nv., U.S.	F6	121
Wosu, Indon.	D6	36
Wour, Chad	B8	50
Wowoni, Pulau, i., Indon.	D6	36
Woy Woy, Austl.	G5	62
Wrangel Island see Vrangelja, ostrov, i., Russia	B20	26
Wrangell, Ak., U.S.	D13	95
Wrangell, Cape, c., Ak., U.S.	E2	95
Wrangell, Mount, mtn., Ak., U.S.	f19	95
Wrangell Island, i., Ak., U.S.	m24	95
Wrangell Mountains, mts., Ak., U.S.	C11	95
Wrangell-Saint Elias National Park, Ak., U.S.	C11	95
Wrath, Cape, c., Scot., U.K.	A4	12
Wray, Co., U.S.	A8	99
Wrens, Ga., U.S.	C4	103
Wrentham, Ma., U.S.	B5	114
Wrexham, Wales, U.K.	D5	12
Wright, co., Ia., U.S.	B4	108
Wright, co., Mn., U.S.	E4	116
Wright, co., Mo., U.S.	D5	118
Wright, Mount, mtn., Mt., U.S.	C4	119
Wright Brothers National Memorial, hist., N.C., U.S.	A7	126
Wright City, Mo., U.S.	C6	118
Wright City, Ok., U.S.	C6	129
Wright Patman Lake, res., Tx., U.S.	A6	78
Wright-Patterson Air Force Base, mil., Oh., U.S.	C1	128
Wrightson, Mount, mtn., Az., U.S.	F5	96
Wrightstown, N.J., U.S.	C3	123
Wrightstown, Wi., U.S.	D5	142
Wrightsville, Ar., U.S.	C3	97
Wrightsville, Ga., U.S.	D4	103
Wrightsville, Pa., U.S.	F8	131
Wrightsville Beach, N.C., U.S.	C5	126
Wrightsville Reservoir, res., Vt., U.S.	C3	138
Wrocław, Pol.	D4	20
Wu, stm., China	F9	28
Wuchuan, China	E3	30
Wuchuan, China	A3	30
Wuda, China	B2	30
Wudaoliang, China	D6	28
Wudi, China	B4	30
Wuding, China	A4	34
Wudu, China	E8	28
Wugang, China	F10	28
Wuhai, China	D9	28
Wuhan, China	E10	28
Wuhe, China	C4	30
Wuhu, China	E11	28
Wŭjang, China	E3	28
Wukari, Nig.	E6	50
Wuliang Shan, mts., China	G8	28
Wuming, China	B5	34
Wupatki National Monument, Az., U.S.	B4	96
Wuppertal, Ger.	E10	12
Wuqi, China	B2	30
Wuqing, China	B4	30
Wurno, Nig.	D6	50
Würzburg, Ger.	F12	12
Wushan, China	C2	30
Wushenqi, China	D9	28
Wusuli (Ussuri), stm., Asia	E15	26
Wutai Shan, mtn., China	D10	28
Wutongqiao, China	F8	28
Wuvulu Island, i., Pap. N. Gui.	G11	32
Wuwei, China	D8	28
Wuwei, China	C4	30
Wuxi, China	E12	28
Wuyi Shan, mts., China	F11	28
Wuyuan, China	C9	28
Wuzhi Shan, mtn., China	H9	28
Wuzhong, China	D9	28
Wuzhou, China	G10	28
Wyaconda, stm., Mo., U.S.	A6	118
Wyandot, co., Oh., U.S.	B2	128
Wyandotte, Mi., U.S.	F7	115
Wyandotte, co., Ks., U.S.	C9	109
Wyanet, Il., U.S.	B4	106
Wye, stm., U.K.	D5	12
Wylie, Lake, res., U.S.	A5	133
Wyman Lake, res., Me., U.S.	C3	112
Wymore, Ne., U.S.	D9	120
Wyndham, Austl.	D4	60
Wynndel, B.C., Can.	E9	85
Wynne, Ar., U.S.	B5	97
Wynnewood, Ok., U.S.	C4	129
Wynoochee, stm., Wa., U.S.	B2	140
Wyoming, On., Can.	E2	89
Wyoming, De., U.S.	D3	101
Wyoming, Ia., U.S.	B6	108
Wyoming, Il., U.S.	B4	106
Wyoming, Mi., U.S.	F5	115
Wyoming, Mn., U.S.	E6	116
Wyoming, Oh., U.S.	o13	128
Wyoming, Pa., U.S.	n17	131
Wyoming, R.I., U.S.	E2	132
Wyoming, co., N.Y., U.S.	C2	125
Wyoming, co., Pa., U.S.	D9	131
Wyoming, co., W.V., U.S.	D3	141
Wyoming, state, U.S.	C5	143
Wyoming Peak, mtn., Wy., U.S.	D2	143
Wyoming Range, mts., Wy., U.S.	D2	143
Wyomissing, Pa., U.S.	F10	131
Wyong, Austl.	G5	62
Wysocking Bay, b., N.C., U.S.	B7	126
Wythe, co., Va., U.S.	D1	139
Wytheville, Va., U.S.	D1	139

X

Name	Map Ref.	Page
Xaafuun, Raas, c., Som.	H15	48
Xaçmaz, Azer.	B13	44
Xaidulla, China	D3	28
Xainza, China	E5	28
Xai-Xai, Moz.	D5	56
Xalapa, Mex.	D5	78
Xam Nua, Laos	B4	34
Xá-Muteba, Ang.	E3	54
Xangongo, Ang.	B2	56
Xankändi, Azer.	C12	44
Xánthi, Grc.	D10	18
Xanxerê, Braz.	D7	72
Xapuri, Braz.	F6	70
Xàtiva, Spain	H6	16
Xau, Lake, pl., Bots.	C3	56
Xenia, Oh., U.S.	C2	128
Xi, stm., China	G10	28
Xiachuan Dao, i., China	E3	30
Xiamen, China	G11	28
Xi'an, China	E9	28
Xianfeng, China	D2	30
Xiang, stm., China	D3	30
Xiangfan, China	E10	28
Xianggang (Hong Kong), China	E3	30
Xiangkhoang, Laos	C4	34
Xiangride, China	D7	28
Xiangtan, China	F10	28
Xianju, China	D5	30
Xianning, China	D3	30
Xianyang, China	C2	30
Xianyou, China	F11	28
Xiaogan, China	E10	28
Xiao Hinggan Ling, mts., China	A1	31
Xiaojin, China	C1	30
Xiapu, China	F12	28
Xiayi, China	C4	30
Xichang, China	F8	28
Xigazê, China	F5	28
Ximiao, China	C8	28
Xin'anjiang Shuiku, res., China	D4	30
Xinavane, Moz.	C5	56
Xincai, China	C4	30
Xing'an, China	F10	28
Xingcheng, China	A5	30
Xinghe, China	A3	30
Xingren, China	D2	30
Xingtai, China	D10	28
Xingu, stm., Braz.	D9	70
Xingxian, China	B3	30
Xingyi, China	F8	28
Xinhua, China	D3	30
Xining, China	D8	28
Xinji, China	B4	30
Xinjiang Uygur Zizhiqu (Sinkiang), prov., China	C5	28
Xinjin, China	C1	30
Xinjin, China	B5	30
Xinjiulong (New Kowloon), China	E3	30
Xinning, China	D3	30
Xinwen, China	B4	30
Xinxian, China	B3	30
Xinxiang, China	D10	28
Xinyang, China	E10	28
Xique-Xique, Braz.	D3	74
Xisha Qundao (Paracel Islands), is., China	C6	34
Xiushan, China	D2	30
Xiushui, China	D3	30
Xixiang, China	C2	30
Xizang Zizhiqu (Tibet), prov., China	E5	28
Xuancheng, China	E11	28
Xuanhan, China	C2	30
Xuanhua, China	A4	30
Xuanwei, China	D1	30
Xuchang, China	E10	28
Xupu, China	D3	30
Xuwen, China	G10	28
Xuyong, China	F9	28
Xuzhou, China	E11	28

Y

Name	Map Ref.	Page
Yaan, China	E8	28
Yablonovy Range see Jablonovyj hrebet, mts., Russia	D13	26
Yabrīn, Sau. Ar.	F5	42
Yacolt, Wa., U.S.	D3	140
Yacuiba, Bol.	C5	72
Yādgīr, India	F3	40
Yadkin, co., N.C., U.S.	A2	126
Yadkin, stm., N.C., U.S.	B2	126
Yadkinville, N.C., U.S.	A2	126
Yadong, China	A1	34
Yafran, Libya	E6	14
Yagoua, Cam.	A3	54
Yagradagzê Shan, mtn., China	D7	28
Yahyalı, Tur.	C6	44
Yainax Butte, mtn., Or., U.S.	E5	130
Yakima, Wa., U.S.	C5	140
Yakima, co., Wa., U.S.	C4	140
Yakima, stm., Wa., U.S.	C6	140
Yakima Indian Reservation, Wa., U.S.	C5	140
Yako, Burkina	D4	50
Yakobi Island, i., Ak., U.S.	m21	95
Yakoma, D.R.C.	C4	54
Yakumo, Japan	B3	31
Yaku-shima, i., Japan	E14	28
Yakutat, Ak., U.S.	D12	95
Yakutat Bay, b., Ak., U.S.	D11	95
Yakutia see Jakutija, state, Russia	C14	26
Yakutsk see Jakutsk, Russia	C14	26
Yakymivka, Ukr.	F13	20
Yala, Thai.	E4	34
Yale, Mi., U.S.	E8	115
Yale, Ok., U.S.	A5	129
Yale, Mount, mtn., Co., U.S.	C5	99
Yale Lake, res., Wa., U.S.	D3	140
Yalgoo, Austl.	F2	60
Yalinga, C.A.R.	B4	54
Yalobusha, co., Ms., U.S.	A4	117
Yalobusha, stm., Ms., U.S.	B4	117
Yalong, stm., China	E7	28
Yalova, Tur.	B3	44
Yalta, Ukr.	G13	20
Yalu, stm., Asia	C13	28
Yalvaç, Tur.	C4	44
Yamachiche, P.Q., Can.	C5	90
Yamagata, Japan	D16	28
Yamaguchi, Japan	D2	31
Yamal Peninsula see Jamal, poluostrov, pen., Russia	B8	26
Yambio, Sudan	J10	48
Yamdena, Pulau, i., Indon.	E8	36
Yamethin, Myan.	B3	34
Yamhill, Or., U.S.	h11	130
Yamhill, co., Or., U.S.	B3	130
Yamoussoukro, C. Iv.	E3	50
Yampa, stm., Co., U.S.	A2	99
Yampil', Ukr.	E10	20
Yamsay Mountain, mtn., Or., U.S.	E5	130
Yamuna, stm., India	D4	40
Yamunānagar, India	C3	40
Yamzho Yumco, l., China	F6	28
Yana see Jana, stm., Russia	C15	26
Yanam, India	F4	40
Yan'an, China	D9	28
Yanbu' al-Baḥr, Sau. Ar.	F3	38
Yancey, co., N.C., U.S.	f10	126
Yanceyville, N.C., U.S.	A3	126
Yancheng, China	E12	28
Yanchi, China	D9	28
Yanfolila, Mali	D3	50
Yangambi, D.R.C.	C4	54
Yangchun, China	E3	30
Yanggao, China	A3	30
Yangjiang, China	G10	28
Yangliuqing, China	B4	30
Yangon (Rangoon), Myan.	C3	34
Yangquan, China	D10	28
Yangshan, China	E3	30
Yangshuo, China	E3	30
Yangtze see Chang, stm., China	E9	28
Yangxian, China	C2	30
Yangxin, China	D4	30
Yangzhou, China	E11	28
Yanji, China	C13	28
Yankton, S.D., U.S.	E8	134
Yankton, co., S.D., U.S.	D8	134
Yanqi, China	C5	28
Yantai, China	D12	28
Yantic, stm., Ct., U.S.	C7	100
Yanting, China	C2	30
Yanyuan, China	A4	34
Yanzhou, China	B4	30
Yaoundé, Cam.	C2	54
Yap, i., Micron.	E10	32
Yapen, Pulau, i., Indon.	G10	32
Yaqui, stm., Mex.	B3	78
Yardley, Pa., U.S.	F12	131
Yardville, N.J., U.S.	C3	123
Yarīm, Yemen	H4	38
Yarkand see Shache, China	D3	28
Yarkand see Yarkant, stm., China	B3	40
Yarkant, stm., China	B3	40
Yarloop, Austl.	G2	60
Yarmouth, Me., U.S.	E2	112
Yarnell, Az., U.S.	C3	96
Yaroslavl' see Jaroslavl', Russia	D6	26
Yarumal, Col.	B4	70
Yass, Austl.	G4	62
Yatağan, Tur.	D3	44
Yaté, N. Cal.	I9	62a
Yates, co., N.Y., U.S.	C3	125
Yates Center, Ks., U.S.	E8	109
Yates City, Il., U.S.	C3	106
Yatsushiro, Japan	E14	28
Yatta Plateau, plat., Kenya	D7	54
Yavapai, co., Az., U.S.	C3	96
Yavarí (Javari), stm., S.A.	D5	70
Yavatmāl, India	E3	40
Yaví, Cerro, mtn., Ven.	B6	70
Yawgoog Pond, l., R.I., U.S.	E1	132
Yazd, Iran	D6	42
Yazoo, co., Ms., U.S.	C3	117
Yazoo, stm., Ms., U.S.	C3	117
Yazoo City, Ms., U.S.	C3	117
Ye, Myan.	C3	34
Yeadon, Pa., U.S.	p21	131
Yeagertown, Pa., U.S.	E6	131
Yecheng, China	D3	28
Yecla, Spain	H6	16
Yeeda, Austl.	D3	60
Yei, Sudan	C6	54
Yélimané, Mali	C2	50
Yell, co., Ar., U.S.	B2	97
Yellow see Huang, stm., China	D11	28
Yellow, stm., In., U.S.	B4	107
Yellow, stm., Wi., U.S.	C3	142

Name — Map Ref. — Page

Yellow, stm., Wi., U.S. **D3** 142
Yellow, stm., U.S. **u15** 102
Yellow Creek, stm., Tn., U.S. **A4** 135
Yellowhead Pass, Can. **C1** 84
Yellowjacket Mountains, mts., Id., U.S. **D4** 105
Yellowknife, N.T., Can. **F17** 82
Yellow Lake, l., Wi., U.S. **C1** 142
Yellow Medicine, co., Mn., U.S. **F2** 116
Yellow Sea, Asia **D12** 28
Yellow Springs, Oh., U.S. **C2** 128
Yellowstone, co., Mt., U.S. **D8** 119
Yellowstone, stm., U.S. **D10** 119
Yellowstone Lake, l., Wy., U.S. **B2** 143
Yellowstone National Park, co., Mt., U.S. **E6** 119
Yellowstone National Park, U.S. **B2** 143
Yellville, Ar., U.S. **A3** 97
Yelm, Wa., U.S. **C3** 140
Yemassee, S.C., U.S. **F6** 133
Yemen, ctry., Asia **G5** 38
Yenagoa, Nig. **F6** 50
Yenakiieve, Ukr. **E15** 20
Yenangyaung, Myan. **B2** 34
Yen Bai, Viet. **B4** 34
Yendéré, Burkina **D4** 50
Yendi, Ghana **E4** 50
Yengisar, China **D3** 28
Yenice, stm., Tur. **B5** 44
Yenişehir, Tur. **B3** 44
Yenisey see Enisej, stm., Russia **C10** 26
Yentna, stm., Ak., U.S. **f16** 95
Yerevan, Arm. **B11** 44
Yerington, Nv., U.S. **E2** 121
Yerington Indian Reservation, Nv., U.S. **D2** 121
Yerköy, Tur. **C6** 44
Yermo, Ca., U.S. **E5** 98
Yerupaja, Nevado, mtn., Peru **F4** 70
Yerushalayim, Isr. **D3** 42
Yeşilhisar, Tur. **C6** 44
Yetti, reg., Afr. **A3** 50
Yeu, Île d', i., Fr. **D5** 16
Yevpatoriia, Ukr. **G12** 20
Ygatimí, Para. **C6** 72
Yi'an, China **B13** 28
Yibin, China **F8** 28
Yichang, China **E10** 28
Yichuan, China **B3** 30
Yichun, China **B13** 28
Yichun, China **D3** 30
Yidu, China **B4** 30
Yidu, China **C3** 30
Yilan, China **B13** 28
Yıldızeli, Tur. **C7** 44
Yiliang, China **G8** 28
Yinchuan, China **D9** 28
Yingde, China **E3** 30
Yingkou, China **C12** 28
Yingtan, China **F11** 28
Yining, China **C4** 28
Yinmabin, Myan. **B2** 34
Yirga 'Alem, Eth. **B7** 54
Yirol, Sudan **B6** 54
Yishan, China **E2** 30
Yitulihe, China **A12** 28
Yiyang, China **F10** 28
Yiyang, China **D4** 30
Yizhang, China **D3** 30
Yli-Kitka, l., Fin. **C13** 10
Yoakum, Tx., U.S. **E4** 136
Yoakum, co., Tx., U.S. **C1** 136
Yockanookany, stm., Ms., U.S. **C4** 117
Yocona, stm., Ms., U.S. **A4** 117
Yogyakarta, Indon. **E4** 36
Yoho National Park, B.C., Can. **D9** 85
Yokadouma, Cam. **C2** 54
Yoko, Cam. **B2** 54
Yokohama, Japan **D15** 28
Yokosuka, Japan **C3** 31
Yokote, Japan **C4** 31
Yola, Nig. **E7** 50
Yolo, co., Ca., U.S. **C2** 98
Yom, stm., Thai. **C3** 34
Yomba Indian Reservation, Nv., U.S. **D4** 121
Yonago, Japan **D14** 28
Yoncalla, Or., U.S. **D3** 130
Yonezawa, Japan **C3** 31
Yong'an, China **F11** 28
Yongchang, China **B1** 30
Yongchuan, China **D2** 30
Yongding, China **E4** 30
Yongfeng, China **A7** 34
Yongkang, China **D5** 30
Yongping, China **A3** 34
Yongren, China **F8** 28
Yongshan, China **F8** 28
Yongxiu, China **D4** 30
Yongzhou, China **F10** 28
Yonkers, N.Y., U.S. **E7** 125
Yonne, stm., Fr. **C8** 16
Yopal, Col. **D5** 80
Yopurga, China **B3** 40
York, Austl. **G2** 60
York, On., Can. **D5** 89
York, Eng., U.K. **C6** 12
York, Al., U.S. **C1** 94
York, Me., U.S. **E2** 112
York, Ne., U.S. **D8** 120
York, Pa., U.S. **G8** 131
York, S.C., U.S. **B5** 133
York, co., Me., U.S. **E2** 112
York, co., Ne., U.S. **D8** 120
York, co., Pa., U.S. **G8** 131
York, co., S.C., U.S. **A5** 133
York, co., Va., U.S. **C6** 139
York, stm., On., Can. **B7** 89
York, stm., Va., U.S. **C6** 139
Yreka, Cape, c., Austl. **C3** 62
York, Kap, c., Grnld. **C26** 82
York Beach, Me., U.S. **E2** 112
Yorke Peninsula, pen., Austl. **G2** 62
York Harbor, Me., U.S. **E2** 112
Yorklyn, De., U.S. **A3** 101
Yorktown, In., U.S. **D7** 107
Yorktown, Tx., U.S. **E4** 136
Yorktown, Va., U.S. **C6** 139
Yorktown Manor, R.I., U.S. **E4** 132
Yorkville, Il., U.S. **B5** 106
Yorkville, N.Y., U.S. **B5** 125
Yorkville, Oh., U.S. **B5** 128
Yoro, Hond. **B2** 80
Yoron-jima, i., Japan **g6** 31a
Yosemite National Park, Ca., U.S. **D4** 98
Yos Sudarso, Pulau, i., Indon. **H10** 32
Yotaú, Bol. **B5** 72
You, stm., China **G9** 28
Youbou, B.C., Can. **g11** 85
Youghiogheny, stm., U.S. **F2** 131
Youghiogheny River Lake, res., U.S. **G3** 131
Young, Austl. **G4** 62
Young, Az., U.S. **C5** 96
Young, co., Tx., U.S. **C3** 136
Young Harris, Ga., U.S. **B3** 103
Youngs, Lake, l., Wa., U.S. **f11** 140
Youngstown, N.Y., U.S. **B1** 125
Youngstown, Oh., U.S. **A5** 128
Youngsville, La., U.S. **D3** 111
Youngsville, Pa., U.S. **C3** 131
Youngtown, Az., U.S. **k8** 96
Youngwood, Pa., U.S. **F2** 131
Youxian, China **D3** 30
Youyang, China **F9** 28
Yozgat, Tur. **C6** 44
Ypacarai, Para. **D6** 72
Ypsilanti, Mi., U.S. **F7** 115
Yreka, Ca., U.S. **B2** 98
Ystad, Swe. **I5** 10
Yuanling, China **F10** 28
Yuanmou, China **F8** 28
Yuba, co., Ca., U.S. **C3** 98
Yuba, stm., Ca., U.S. **C3** 98
Yuba City, Ca., U.S. **C3** 98
Yūbari, Japan **C16** 28
Yucatán, state, Mex. **C7** 78
Yucatan Channel, strt., N.A. **A2** 80
Yucatan Peninsula, pen., N.A. **B2** 80
Yucca Lake, l., Nv., U.S. **F5** 121
Yucca Mountain, mtn., Nv., U.S. **G5** 121
Yucheng, China **B4** 30
Yudu, China **D4** 30
Yueqing, China **D5** 30
Yuexi, China **A4** 34
Yueyang, China **F10** 28
Yugoslavia, ctry., Eur. **C8** 18
Yukon, Ok., U.S. **B4** 129
Yukon, ter., Can. **F12** 82
Yukon, stm., N.A. **F7** 82
Yulee, Fl., U.S. **B5** 102
Yulin, China **D9** 28
Yulin, China **G10** 28
Yuma, Az., U.S. **E1** 96
Yuma, Co., U.S. **A8** 99
Yuma, co., Az., U.S. **E1** 96
Yuma, co., Co., U.S. **A8** 99
Yuma Marine Corps Air Station, mil., Az., U.S. **E1** 96
Yumbi, D.R.C. **D3** 54
Yumbo, Col. **E4** 80
Yumen, China **D7** 28
Yuncheng, China **D10** 28
Yunnan, state, China **G8** 28
Yunxian, China **E10** 28
Yunxiao, China **E4** 30
Yunyang, China **C2** 30
Yurimaguas, Peru **E4** 70
Yuruá see Juruá, stm., S.A. **E6** 70
Yushan, China **D4** 30
Yü Shan, mtn., Tai. **E5** 30
Yushu, China **E7** 28
Yutan, Ne., U.S. **C9** 120
Yutian, China **D4** 28
Yuyao, China **C5** 30
Yvetot, Fr. **C7** 16

Z

Žabasak, Kaz. **D11** 22
Zabīd, Yemen **H4** 38
Zābol, Iran **D8** 42
Zacapa, Guat. **B2** 80
Zacapu, Mex. **D4** 78
Zacatecas, Mex. **C4** 78
Zacatecas, state, Mex. **C4** 78
Zachary, La., U.S. **D4** 111
Zadar, Cro. **B5** 18
Zadoi, China **C7** 40
Zadonsk, Russia **C15** 20
Zafer Burnu, c., N. Cyp. **E6** 44
Zafra, Spain **H3** 16
Zagazig, Egypt **E10** 14
Zagora, Mor. **E2** 14
Zagreb, Cro. **B5** 18
Zāgros, Kūhhā-ye (Zagros Mountains), mts., Iran **D6** 42
Zagros Mountains see Zāgros, Kūhhā-ye, mts., Iran **D6** 42
Zāhedān, Iran **E8** 42
Zahīrābād, India **F3** 40
Zaḥlah, Leb. **F6** 44
Zaire see Congo, Democratic Republic of the, ctry., Afr. **D4** 54
Zaïre see Congo, stm., Afr. **D2** 54
Zaječar, Yugo. **C9** 18
Zajsan, Kaz. **E10** 26
Zajsan, ozero, l., Kaz. **E10** 26
Zakamensk, Russia **D12** 26
Zakho, Iraq **D10** 44
Zákinthos, Grc. **F8** 18
Zákinthos, i., Grc. **F8** 18
Zakopane, Pol. **E6** 20
Zakouma, Chad **A3** 54
Zalaegerszeg, Hung. **F4** 20
Zalău, Rom. **F7** 20
Zalishchyky, Ukr. **E8** 20
Zamantı, stm., Tur. **D6** 44
Zambeze (Zambezi), stm., Afr. **A3** 56
Zambezi, Zam. **A3** 56
Zambezi (Zambeze), stm., Afr. **B5** 56
Zambia, ctry., Afr. **E5** 52
Zamboanga, Phil. **E8** 34
Zamboanga Peninsula, pen., Phil. **E8** 34
Zambrów, Pol. **C7** 20
Zâmbuè, Moz. **B5** 56
Žambyl, Kaz. **E9** 26
Zamora, Spain **G4** 16
Zamora de Hidalgo, Mex. **D4** 78
Zamość, Pol. **D7** 20
Zanaga, Congo **D2** 54
Žanatas, Kaz. **B9** 42
Zanesville, Oh., U.S. **C4** 128
Zanjān, Iran **C5** 42
Zante see Zákinthos, i., Grc. **F8** 18
Zanthus, Austl. **G3** 60
Zanzibar, Tan. **E7** 54
Zanzibar, i., Tan. **E7** 54
Zanzibar Channel, strt., Tan. **E7** 54
Zaozhuang, China **C4** 30
Zapadno-Sibirskaja ravnina, pl., Russia **C9** 26
Zapadnyj Sajan, mts., Russia **D11** 26
Zapala, Arg. **E2** 69
Zapata, Tx., U.S. **F3** 136
Zapata, co., Tx., U.S. **F3** 136
Zapopan, Mex. **C4** 78
Zaporizhzhia, Ukr. **F13** 20
Zaqatala, Azer. **B12** 44
Zara, Tur. **C7** 44
Zaragoza, Spain **G6** 16
Zarajsk, Russia **B15** 20
Zaranj, Afg. **D8** 42
Zarasai, Lith. **I12** 10
Zárate, Arg. **E6** 72
Zarembo Island, i., Ak., U.S. **m23** 95
Zarghūn Shahr, Afg. **D9** 42
Zaria, Nig. **D6** 50
Žarkamys, Kaz. **E10** 22
Žarma, Kaz. **B4** 28
Żary, Pol. **D3** 20
Zāskār Mountains, mts., Asia **C3** 40
Zavala, co., Tx., U.S. **E3** 136
Zave, Zimb. **B5** 56
Zavitinsk, Russia **A13** 28
Zawiercie, Pol. **D5** 20
Zāwiyat Masūs, Libya **E8** 14
Zaysan, Lake see Zajsan, ozero, l., Kaz. **E10** 26
Zdolbuniv, Ukr. **D9** 20
Zduńska Wola, Pol. **D5** 20
Zearing, Ia., U.S. **B4** 108
Zebulon, Ga., U.S. **C2** 103
Zebulon, N.C., U.S. **B4** 126
Zeehan, Austl. **I4** 62
Zeeland, Mi., U.S. **F5** 115
Zeerust, S. Afr. **D4** 56
Zeigler, Il., U.S. **F4** 106
Zeja, Russia **D14** 26
Zeja, stm., Russia **D14** 26
Zejskoe vodohranilišče, res., Russia **D14** 26
Zelenogorsk, Russia **F13** 10
Zelenokumsk, Russia **B4** 42
Železnodorožnyj, Russia **B9** 22
Železnogorsk, Russia **C13** 20
Železnogorsk-Ilimskij, Russia **D12** 26
Zelienople, Pa., U.S. **E1** 131
Zell am See, Aus. **G13** 12
Zémio, C.A.R. **B5** 54
Zenica, Bos. **B6** 18
Zenith, Wa., U.S. **f11** 140
Zenobia Peak, mtn., Co., U.S. **A2** 99
Zenza do Itombe, Ang. **E2** 54
Zephyr Cove, Nv., U.S. **E2** 121
Zephyrhills, Fl., U.S. **D4** 102
Žerdevka, Russia **D7** 22
Zestafoni, Geor. **A10** 44
Zeya see Zeja, stm., Russia **D14** 26
Zeya Reservoir see Zejskoe vodohranilišče, res., Russia **D14** 26
Žezkazgan, Kaz. **E8** 26
Zgierz, Pol. **D5** 20
Zhalun, China **C4** 40
Zhangjiakou, China **C10** 28
Zhangping, China **F11** 28
Zhangpu, China **E4** 30
Zhangye, China **D8** 28
Zhangzhou, China **G11** 28
Zhanhua, China **B4** 30
Zhanjiang, China **G10** 28
Zhao'an, China **G11** 28
Zhaojue, China **D1** 30
Zhaoqing, China **G10** 28
Zhaotong, China **F8** 28
Zhashkiv, Ukr. **E11** 20
Zhaxigang, China **E3** 28
Zhdanov see Mariupol', Ukr. **F14** 20
Zhejiang, state, China **F11** 28
Zhenghe, China **D4** 30
Zhenglan Qi, China **A4** 30
Zhengzhou, China **D10** 28
Zhenjiang, China **C4** 30
Zhenning, China **D2** 30
Zhenping, China **E10** 28
Zhenxiong, China **D1** 30
Zhenyuan, China **F9** 28
Zhidoi, China **C6** 40
Zhijiang, China **D2** 30
Zhmerynka, Ukr. **E10** 20
Zhob, Pak. **D9** 42
Zhob, stm., Pak. **D9** 42
Zhongba, China **E4** 28
Zhongdian, China **F7** 28
Zhongning, China **D9** 28
Zhongshan, China **B6** 34
Zhongwei, China **B2** 30
Zhongxian, China **C2** 30
Zhongxiang, China **E10** 28
Zhoushan Qundao, is., China **E12** 28
Zhovtneve, Ukr. **F12** 20
Zhuanghe, China **B5** 30
Zhucheng, China **B4** 30
Zhumadian, China **C3** 30
Zhuolu, China **A4** 30
Zhuozhou, China **D11** 28
Zhushan, China **E10** 28
Zhuzhou, China **F10** 28
Zhytomyr, Ukr. **D10** 20
Zia Indian Reservation, N.M., U.S. **h7** 124
Zibo, China **D11** 28
Ziebach, co., S.D., U.S. **C4** 134
Zielona Góra, Pol. **D3** 20
Žigalovo, Russia **D12** 26
Žigansk, Russia **C14** 26
Zigong, China **F8** 28
Ziguinchor, Sen. **D1** 50
Zihuatanejo, Mex. **D4** 78
Zile, Tur. **B6** 44
Žilina, Slvk. **E5** 20
Zillah, Libya **E8** 48
Zillah, Wa., U.S. **C5** 140
Zilwaukee, Mi., U.S. **E7** 115
Zima, Russia **D12** 26
Zimbabwe, ctry., Afr. **B4** 56
Zimi, S.L. **E2** 50
Zimmerman, Mn., U.S. **E5** 116
Zinder, Niger **D6** 50
Zion, Il., U.S. **A6** 106
Zion National Park, Ut., U.S. **F3** 137
Zion Reservoir, res., Az., U.S. **C6** 96
Zionsville, In., U.S. **E5** 107
Zipaquirá, Col. **D5** 80
Zirkel, Mount, mtn., Co., U.S. **A4** 99
Zitong, China **C2** 30
Zittau, Ger. **E14** 12
Zitundo, Moz. **D5** 56
Ziway Hāyk', l., Eth. **B7** 54
Ziyun, China **D2** 30
Zlatoust, Russia **D7** 26
Zlīṭan, Libya **D7** 48
Žlobin, Bela. **C11** 20
Złotów, Pol. **C4** 20
Zmeinogorsk, Russia **A4** 28
Znam'ianka, Ukr. **E12** 20
Znojmo, Czech Rep. **E4** 20
Žodzina, Bela. **B10** 20
Zolfo Springs, Fl., U.S. **E5** 102
Zomba, Mwi. **B6** 56
Zonguldak, Tur. **B4** 44
Zouar, Chad **B8** 50
Zouérat, Maur. **B2** 50
Zrenjanin, Yugo. **B8** 18
Žuantobe, Kaz. **B9** 42
Zug, Switz. **A2** 18
Zugdidi, Geor. **A9** 44
Zugspitze, mtn., Eur. **G12** 12
Žukovka, Russia **C12** 20
Zumbo, Moz. **B5** 56
Zumbro, stm., Mn., U.S. **F6** 116
Zumbrota, Mn., U.S. **F6** 116
Zuni (Zuni Pueblo), N.M., U.S. **B1** 124
Zuni, stm., U.S. **C6** 96
Zuni Indian Reservation, N.M., U.S. **B1** 124
Zuni Mountains, mts., N.M., U.S. **B1** 124
Zunyi, China **F9** 28
Zūrābād, Iran **C11** 44
Zurich, On., Can. **D3** 89
Zürich, Switz. **A2** 18
Zurich, Lake see Zürichsee, l., Switz. **A2** 18
Zürichsee, l., Switz. **A2** 18
Zuru, Nig. **D6** 50
Zuwārah, Libya **E6** 14
Zvishavane, Zimb. **C4** 56
Zvolen, Slvk. **E5** 20
Zwedru, Lib. **E3** 50
Zwickau, Ger. **E13** 12
Zwolle, Neth. **D10** 12
Zwolle, La., U.S. **C2** 111
Żyrardów, Pol. **C6** 20
Zyrjanka, Russia **C17** 26
Zyrjanovsk, Kaz. **E10** 26
Żywiec, Pol. **E5** 20